7th International Workshop on Semantic Evaluation

(SemEval 2013)

Held with SEM 2013

Atlanta, Georgia, USA
14 – 15 June 2013

ISBN: 978-1-63439-627-1

Printed from e-media with permission by:

Curran Associates, Inc.
57 Morehouse Lane
Red Hook, NY 12571

Some format issues inherent in the e-media version may also appear in this print version.

Printed by Curran Associates, Inc. (2015)

Association for Computational Linguistics
209 N. Eighth Street
Stroudsburg, Pennsylvania 18360

Phone: 1-570-476-8006
Fax: 1-570-476-0860

acl@aclweb.org

Additional copies of this publication are available from:

Curran Associates, Inc.
57 Morehouse Lane
Red Hook, NY 12571 USA
Phone: 845-758-0400
Fax: 845-758-2634
Email: curran@proceedings.com
Web: www.proceedings.com

Volume 2:

*SEM 2013: The Second Joint Conference on Lexical and Computational Semantics

Proceedings of the Seventh International Workshop on Semantic Evaluation (SemEval 2013)

June 14-15, 2013
Atlanta, Georgia, USA

Production and Manufacturing by
Omnipress, Inc.
2600 Anderson Street
Madison, WI 53707
USA

Sponsored in part by:
The US Defense Advanced Research Projects Agency (DARPA)

Organized and sponsored in part by:
The ACL Special Interest Group on the Lexicon (SIGLEX)
The ACL Special Interest Group on Computational Semantics (SIGSEM)

Introduction to *SEM 2013

Building on the momentum generated by the spectacular success of the Joint Conference on Lexical and Computational Semantics (*SEM) in 2012, bringing together the ACL SIGLEX and ACL SIGSEM communities, we are delighted to bring to you the second edition of the conference, as a top-tier showcase of the latest research in computational semantics. We accepted 14 papers (11 long and 3 short) for publication at the conference, out of a possible 45 submissions (a 31% acceptance rate). This is on par with some of the most competitive conferences in computational linguistics, and we are confident will set the stage for a scintillating conference.

This year, we started a tradition that we intend to maintain in all future iterations of the conference in integrating a shared task into the conference. The shared task was selected by an independent committee comprising members from SIGLEX and SIGSEM, based on an open call for proposals, and revolved around Semantic Textual Similarity (STS). The task turned out to be a huge success with 34 teams participating, submitting a total of 103 system runs.

*SEM 2013 features a number of highlight events:

Day One, June 13th:

- A timely and impressive panel on *Towards Deep Natural Language Understanding*, featuring the following panelists:
  - Kevin Knight (USC/Information Sciences Institute)
  - Chris Manning (Stanford University)
  - Martha Palmer (University of Colorado at Boulder)
  - Owen Rambow (Columbia University)
  - Dan Roth (University of Illinois at Urbana-Champaign)
- A Reception and Shared Task Poster Session in the evening, thanks to the generous sponsorship of the DARPA Deft program.

Day Two, June 14th:

- In the morning, a keynote address by David Forsyth from the Computer Science Department at the University of Illinois at Urbana Champagne on issues of Vision and Language. It promises to be an extremely stimulating speech, and is not to be missed.
- In the early afternoon, a panel on the relation between and future of *SEM, the *SEM Shared Task, SemEval and other events on computational semantics. In this panel, we will attempt to clarify and explain as well as devise plans for these different entities.
- Finally, at the end of the day, an award ceremony for the Best Long Paper and Best Short Paper.

As always, *SEM 2013 would not have been possible without the considerable efforts of our area chairs and an impressive assortment of reviewers, drawn from the ranks of SIGLEX and SIGSEM, and the computational semantics community at large. We would also like to acknowledge the generous support for the STS Task from the DARPA Deft Program.

We hope you enjoy *SEM 2013, and look forward to engaging with all of you,

Mona Diab (The George Washington University, General Chair)
Timothy Baldwin (The University of Mebourne, Program Committee Co-Chair)
Marco Baroni (University of Trento, Program Committee Co-Chair)

Introduction to SemEval

The Semantic Evaluation (SemEval) series of workshops focus on the evaluation and comparison of systems that can analyse diverse semantic phenomena in text with the aim of extending the current state-of-the-art in semantic analysis and creating high quality annotated datasets in a range of increasingly challenging problems in natural language semantics. SemEval provides an exciting forum for researchers to propose challenging research problems in semantics and to build systems/techniques to address such research problems.

SemEval-2013 is the seventh workshop in the series. The first three workshops, SensEval-1 (1998), SensEval-2 (2001), and SensEval-3 (2004), were focused on word sense disambiguation, each time growing in the number of languages offered in the tasks and in the number of participating teams. In 2007 the workshop was renamed SemEval and in the next three workshops SemEval-2007, SemEval-2010 and SemEval-2012 the nature of the tasks evolved to include semantic analysis tasks outside of word sense disambiguation. Starting in 2012 SemEval turned into a yearly event associated with *SEM.

This volume contains papers accepted for presentation at the SemEval-2013 International Workshop on Semantic Evaluation Exercises. SemEval-2013 is co-organized with the *SEM-2013 The Second Joint Conference on Lexical and Computational Semantics and co-located with The 2013 Conference of the North American Chapter of the Association for Computational Linguistics: Human Language Technologies (NAACL HLT).

SemEval-2013 included the following 12 tasks for evaluation:

- TempEval-3 Temporal Annotation
- Sentiment Analysis in Twitter
- Spatial Role Labeling
- Free Paraphrases of Noun Compounds
- Evaluating Phrasal Semantics
- The Joint Student Response Analysis and 8th Recognizing Textual Entailment Challenge
- Cross-lingual Textual Entailment for Content Synchronization
- Extraction of Drug-Drug Interactions from BioMedical Texts
- Cross-lingual Word Sense Disambiguation
- Evaluating Word Sense Induction & Disambiguation within An End-User Application
- Multilingual Word Sense Disambiguation
- Word Sense Induction for Graded and Non-Graded Senses

About 100 teams submitted more than 300 systems for the 12 tasks of SemEval-2013. This volume contains both Task Description papers that describe each of the above tasks and System Description papers that describe the systems that participated in the above tasks. A total of 12 task description papers and 101 system description papers are included in this volume.

We are indebted to all program committee members for their high quality, elaborate and thoughtful reviews. The papers in this proceedings have surely benefited from this feedback. We are grateful to *SEM 2013 and NAACL-HLT 2013 conference organizers for local organization and the forum. We most gratefully acknowledge the support of our sponsors, the ACL Special Interest Group on the Lexicon (SIGLEX) and the ACL Special Interest Group on Computational Semantics (SIGSEM).

Welcome to SemEval-2013!

Suresh Manandhar and Deniz Yuret

Organizers:

General Chair:

Mona Diab (George Washington University)

Program Committee Chairs:

Tim Baldwin (University of Melbourne)

Marco Baroni (University of Trento)

STS Shared Task Committee Chairs:

Anna Korhonen (University of Cambridge)

Malvina Nissim (University of Bologna)

SemEval Chairs:

Suresh Manandhar (University of York, UK)

Deniz Yuret (Koc University, Turkey)

Publications Chair:

Yuval Marton (Microsoft)

Sponsorship Chair:

Bernardo Magnini (Fondazione Bruno Kessler)

Panel organizer:

Martha Palmer (University of Colorado, Boulder)

Area Chairs:

Shane Bergsma (Johns Hopkins University)
Chris Biemann (TU Darmstadt)
Eduardo Blanco (Lymba Corporation)
Gemma Boleda (University of Texas, Austin)
Francis Bond (Nanyang Technological University)
Paul Cook (University of Melbourne)
Amaç Herdagdelen (Facebook)
Lauri Karttunen (Stanford University)
Diana McCarthy (University of Cambridge)
Roser Morante (University of Antwerp)
Smara Muresan (Rutgers University)
Preslav Nakov (Qatar Computing Research Institute)
Roberto Navigli (Sapienza University of Rome)
Hwee Tou Ng (National University of Singapore)
Becky Passonneau (Columbia University)
Laura Rimell (University of Cambridge)
Caroline Sporleder (University of Trier)
Fabio Massimo Zanzotto (University of Rome Tor Vergata)

Program Committee for Volume 1:

Nabil Abdullah (University of Windsor), Eneko Agirre (University of the Basque Country), Nicholas Asher (CNRS Institut de Recherche en Informatique de Toulouse), Eser Aygün, Timothy Baldwin (The University of Melbourne), Eva Banik (Computational Linguistics Ltd), Marco Baroni (University of Trento), Alberto Barrón-Cedeño (Universitat Politècnica de Catalunya), Roberto Basili (University of Roma, Tor Vergata), Miroslav Batchkarov (University of Sussex), Cosmin Bejan, Sabine Bergler (Concordia University), Shane Bergsma (Johns Hopkins University), Steven Bethard (University of Colorado Boulder), Ergun Bicici (Centre for Next Generation Localisation), Chris Biemann (TU Darmstadt), Eduardo Blanco (Lymba Corporation), Gemma Boleda (The University of Texas at Austin), Francis Bond (Nanyang Technological University), Paul Buitelaar (DERI, National University of Ireland, Galway), Razvan Bunescu (Ohio University), Harry Bunt (Tilburg University), Aljoscha Burchardt (DFKI), Davide Buscaldi (LIPN, Université Paris 13), Olivia Buzek (Johns Hopkins University), Nicoletta Calzolari (ILC-CNR), Annalina Caputo (Dept. Computer Science - Univ. of Bari Aldo Moro), Sandra Carberry (University of Delaware), Marine Carpuat (National Research Council), Irene Castellon (University of Barcelona), Julio Castillo (National University of Cordoba), Daniel Cer (Stanford University), Yee Seng Chan (Raytheon BBN Technologies), David Chen (Google), Colin Cherry (NRC), Jackie Chi Kit Cheung (University of Toronto), Christian Chiarcos, Sung-Pil Choi, Grzegorz Chrupała (Tilburg University), Philipp Cimiano (Univ. Bielefeld), Daoud Clarke, Bob Coecke (Oxford University), Paul Cook (The University of Melbourne), Bonaventura Coppola (IBM Research), Danilo Croce (University of Roma, Tor Vergata), Montse Cuadros (Vicomtech-IK4), Walter Daelemans (University of Antwerp, CLiPS), Ido Dagan (Bar-Ilan University), Avishek Dan (Indian Institute of Technology Bombay), Kareem Darwish (Qatar Computing Research Institute, Qatar Foundation), Dipanjan Das (Google Inc.), Marie-Catherine de Marneffe (The Ohio State University), Gerard de Melo (ICSI Berkeley), Pascal Denis, Mona Diab (GWU), Georgiana Dinu (University of Trento), Bill Dolan (Microsoft Research), Rebecca Dridan (University of Oslo), Kevin Duh (Nara Institute of Science and Technology), Micha Elsner (The Ohio State University), David Elson (Google), Stefan Evert (FAU Erlangen-Nürnberg), Dan Flickinger (Stanford), Anette Frank (Heidelberg Universiy), Andre Freitas (DERI, National University of Ireland, Galway), Claire Gardent (CNRS/LORIA, Nancy), Spandana Gella (University of Melbourne), Matthew Gerber (University of Virginia), Eugenie Giesbrecht (Karlsruhe Institute of Technology), Kevin Gimpel (Toyota Technological Institute at Chicago), Claudio Giuliano (FBK), Dan Goldwasser (University of Maryland), Edward Grefenstette (University of Oxford Department of Computer Science), Weiwei Guo (Columbia University), Iryna Gurevych (Ubiquitous Knowledge Processing (UKP) Lab), Yoan Gutiérrez (University of Matanzas), Nizar Habash (Columbia University), Bo Han (University of Melbourne), Lushan Han (University of Maryland, Baltimore County), Chikara Hashimoto (NICT), Mike Heilman (Educational Testing Service), Iris Hendrickx (Center for Language Studies, Radboud University Nijmegen), Verena Henrich (University of Tübingen), Aurelie Herbelot (Universität Potsdam), Amac Herdagdelen (Facebook), Veronique Hoste (Ghent University), Dirk Hovy (USC's Information Sciences Institute), Nancy Ide (Vassar College), Adrian Iftene (Al. I. Cuza University of Iasi), Diana Inkpen (University of Ottawa), Sambhav Jain (LTRC, IIIT Hyderabad), Sneha Jha, Sergio Jimenez (National University of Colombia), Richard Johansson (University of Gothenburg), David Jurgens (University of California, Los Angeles), Dimitri Kartsaklis (University of Oxford), Lauri Karttunen (Stanford University), Sophia Katrenko (Utrecht University), Bill Keller (The University of Sussex), Douwe Kiela (University of Cambridge Computer Laboratory), Su Nam Kim, Alexandre Klementiev (Saarland University), Valia Kordoni (Humboldt University Berlin), Ioannis Korkontzelos (National Centre for Text Mining, The University of Manchester), Zornitsa Kozareva (USC Information Sciences Institute), Ivana Kruijff-Korbayova, Man Lan (ECNU), Jey Han Lau (University of Melbourne), Yoong Keok Lee (MIT), Alessandro Lenci (University of Pisa), Maria Liakata (University of

Warwick), Ting Liu, Nitin Madnani (Educational Testing Service), Nikolaos Malandrakis (Signal Analysis and Interpretation Laboratory (SAIL), USC, Los Angeles, CA 90089, USA), Suresh Manandhar (University of York), Daniel Marcu (SDL), Erwin Marsi (Norwegian University of Science and Technology (NTNU)), Toni Marti (University of Barcelona), Diana McCarthy (University of Cambridge (DTAL)), John McCrae (University Bielefeld), Rada Mihalcea (University of North Texas), Shachar Mirkin (Xerox Research Centre Europe), Ray Mooney (University of Texas at Austin), Roser Morante (University of Antwerp), Paul Morarescu (Syracuse University), Mathieu Morey (Aix-Marseille Université), Alessandro Moschitti (DIS, University of Trento), Rutu Mulkar, Smaranda Muresan (Rutgers University), Preslav Nakov (Qatar Computing Research Institute, Qatar Foundation), Vivi Nastase (FBK), Roberto Navigli (Sapienza University of Rome), Ani Nenkova (University of Pennsylvania), Hwee Tou Ng (National University of Singapore), Shengjian Ni (College of Chinese Language and Literature,Wuhan University), John Niekrasz, malvina nissim (University of Bologna), Diarmuid Ó Séaghdha (University of Cambridge), Brendan O'Connor (Carnegie Mellon University), Kemal Oflazer (Carnegie Mellon University - Qatar), Akira Ohtani (Osaka Gakuin University), Manabu Okumura (Tokyo Institute of Technology), Lubomir Otrusina (Faculty of Information Technology, Brno University of Technology), Sebastian Pado (Heidelberg University), Alexis Palmer (Saarland University), Martha Palmer (University of Colorado), Rebecca J. Passonneau (Columbia University), Michael J. Paul (Johns Hopkins University), Anselmo Peñas (NLP & IR Group, UNED), Sasa Petrovic, Mohammad Taher Pilehvar (Sapienza University of Rome), Manfred Pinkal (Saarland University), Emily Pitler (University of Pennsylvania), Laura Plaza, Massimo Poesio (University of Essex), Tamara Polajnar (University of Cambridge), Simone Paolo Ponzetto (University of Mannheim), Hoifung Poon (Microsoft Research), octavian popescu (FBK-irst), Matt Post (Johns Hopkins University), Alexandros Potamianos (Technical University of Crete), Richard Power, Vinodkumar Prabhakaran (Columbia University), Stephen Pulman (Oxford University), Uwe Quasthoff, Carlos Ramisch (Université Joseph Fourier), Delip Rao (Johns Hopkins University), Reinhard Rapp (Aix-Marseille Université), Jonathon Read (University of Oslo), Marta Recasens (Stanford University), Siva Reddy (University of Edinburgh), Ines Rehbein (Potsdam University), Joseph Reisinger, Antonio Reyes (Laboratorio de Tecnologías Lingüísticas, Instituto Superior de Intérpretes y Traductores), Hannes Rieser, German Rigau (UPV/EHU), Ellen Riloff (University of Utah), Laura Rimell (University of Cambridge), Alan Ritter (University of Washington), Horacio Rodriguez (UPC), Carolyn Rose (Carnegie Mellon University), Andrew Rosenberg (CUNY Queens College), Paolo Rosso (Universitat Politècnica de València), Josef Ruppenhofer, patrick saint-dizier (IRIT-CNRS), Mark Sammons (University of Illinois at Urbana-Champaign), Fernando Sánchez-Vega (Laboratorio de Tecnologías del Lenguaje, Instituto Nacional de Astrofísica, Óptica y Electrónica, Puebla, Estado de México), Marina Santini, Christina Sauper, Roser Saurí (Barcelona Media), Hansen Andrew Schwartz (University of Pennsylvania), Aliaksei Severyn (University of Trento), Ehsan Shareghi (Concordia University - Master's Student), Eyal Shnarch (Bar Ilan University), Niraj Shrestha (KUL), Ekaterina Shutova (University of California at Berkeley), Ravi Sinha, Gabriel Skantze (KTH Speech Music and Hearing), Aitor Soroa (assistant lecturer), Caroline Sporleder (Trier University), Manfred Stede (University of Potsdam), Herman Stehouwer (Max Planck for Psycholinguistics), Benno Stein, Matthew Stone (Rutgers University), Veselin Stoyanov (Facebook), Michael Strube (HITS gGmbH), L V Subramaniam (IBM Research India), Md. Sultan (University of Colorado - Boulder), György Szarvas (Nuance Communications AG), Stefan Thater (Universität des Saarlandes), Kristina Toutanova (Microsoft Research), Yulia Tsvetkov (CMU), Tim Van de Cruys (IRIT & CNRS), Antal van den Bosch (Radboud University Nijmegen), Eva Vecchi (CIMeC - University of Trento), Paola Velardi, Erik Velldal, Noortje Venhuizen, Sriram Venkatapathy (Xerox Research Centre Europel), Yannick Versley (University of Tuebingen), Darnes Vilariño (Benemérita Universidad Autónoma de Puebla), Aline Villavicencio (Institute of Informatics, Federal University of Rio Grande do SUl), Veronika Vincze (University of Szeged), Vinod Vydiswaran (University of Illinois),

Ruibo WANG (Shanxi Univ. Wucheng Road 92, Taiyuan, Shanxi), Sai Wang (Shanxi University), Xinglong Wang, Yi-Chia Wang (Carnegie Mellon University), Bonnie Webber (University of Edinburgh), Julie Weeds (University of Sussex), Ben Wellner (The MITRE Corporation), Jan Wiebe (University of Pittsburgh), Michael Wiegand (Saarland University), Theresa Wilson (JHU HLTCOE), Kristian Woodsend (University of Edinburgh), Dekai Wu (HKUST), Stephen Wu (Mayo Clinic), Feiyu Xu (DFKI LT Lab), Jian Xu (The Hong Kong Polytechnic University), Eric Yeh (SRI International), Michael Yip (The Hong Kong Institute of Education), Deniz Yuret (Koc University), Roberto Zamparelli (Università di Trento), Fabio Massimo Zanzotto (University of Rome "Tor Vergata"), Luke Zettlemoyer (University of Washington), and Hermann Ziak (Know-Center GmbH).

Program Committee for Volume 2:

Ameeta Agrawal (York University), Itziar Aldabe (University of the Basque Country (UPV/EHU)), Marianna Apidianaki (LIMSI-CNRS), Pedro Balage Filho (University of São Paulo), Alexandra Balahur (European Commission Joint Research Centre), Timothy Baldwin (The University of Melbourne), Marco Baroni (University of Trento), Osman Baskaya (Koc University), Emanuele Bastianelli (University of Roma, Tor Vergata), Wesley Baugh (University of North Texas), Lee Becker (Avaya Labs), Satyabrata Behera (IIT Bombay), Luisa Bentivogli (Fondazione Bruno Kessler), Steven Bethard (University of Colorado Boulder), Ergun Bicici (Centre for Next Generation Localisation), Jari Björne (University of Turku), Tamara Bobic (Fraunhofer SCAI), Lorna Byrne (University College Dublin), Marine Carpuat (National Research Council), Giuseppe Castellucci (University of Roma, Tor Vergata), Tawunrat Chalothorn (University of Northumbria at Newcastle), Nate Chambers (US Naval Academy), Angel Chang (Stanford University), Karan Chawla (Indian Institute of Technology Bombay), Colin Cherry (NRC), Md. Faisal Mahbub Chowdhury (University of Trento, Italy and FBK-irst, Italy), Sam Clark (Swarthmore College), Kevin Cohen (Computational Bioscience Program, U. Colorado School of Medicine), Paul Cook (The University of Melbourne), Francisco M Couto (University of Lisbon), Leon Derczynski (University of Sheffield), Mohamed Dermouche (AMI Software R&D / Université de Lyon, ERIC (Lyon 2)), ALBERTO DIAZ (Universidad Complutense de Madrid), Myroslava Dzikovska (University of Edinburgh), Michele Filannino (University of Manchester), João Filgueiras (INESC-ID), Björn Gambäck (Norwegian University of Science and Technology), Martin Gleize (LIMSI-CNRS), Yvette Graham (The University of Melbourne, Centre for Next Generation Localisation), Tobias Günther (University of Gothenburg), Yoan Gutiérrez (University of Matanzas), Hussam Hamdan (AMU), Qi Han (IMS, University of Stuttgart), Viktor Hangya (University of Szeged), Mike Heilman (Educational Testing Service), David Hope (University of Sussex), Diana Inkpen (University of Ottawa), Harshit Jain (International Institute of Information Technology, Hyderabad), Sergio Jimenez (National University of Colombia), David Jurgens (University of California, Los Angeles), Ioannis Klapaftis, Nadin Kökciyan (Bogazici University), Oleksandr Kolomiyets (KU Leuven), Ioannis Korkontzelos (National Centre for Text Mining, The University of Manchester), Milen Kouylekov (CELI S.R.L.), Amitava Kundu (Jadavpur University), Man Lan (ECNU), Natsuda Laokulrat (The University of Tokyo), Alberto Lavelli (FBK-irst), Els Lefever (LT3, Hogeschool Gent), Clement Levallois (Erasmus University Rotterdam), Omer Levy (Bar-Ilan University), Nikolaos Malandrakis (Signal Analysis and Interpretation Laboratory (SAIL), USC, Los Angeles, CA 90089, USA), Suresh Manandhar (University of York), Morgane Marchand (CEA-LIST / CNRS-LIMSI), Eugenio Martínez-Cámara (University of Jaén), Saif Mohammad (National Research Council Canada), Preslav Nakov (Qatar Computing Research Institute, Qatar Foundation), Roberto Navigli (Sapienza University of Rome), Sapna Negi (University of Malta), Matteo Negri (Fondazione Bruno Kessler), Diarmuid Ó Séaghdha (University of Cambridge), IFEYINWA OKOYE (University of Colorado at Boulder), Reynier Ortega Bueno (CERPAMID, Cuba), Niels Ott (Eberhard Karls Universität Tübingen), Prabu palanisamy (Serendio), John Pavlopoulos (Athens

University of Economics and Business), Ted Pedersen (University of Minnesota, Duluth), David Pinto (Benemérita Universidad Autónoma de Puebla), Matt Post (Johns Hopkins University), Thomas Proisl (FAU Erlangen-Nürnberg), Majid Rastegar-Mojarad (University of Wisconsin-Milwaukee), Hilke Reckman (SAS Institute), Robert Remus (University of Leipzig), Tim Rocktäschel (Humboldt-Universität zu Berlin, Knowledge Management in Bioinformatics, Unter den Linden 6, Berlin, 10099), Carlos Rodriguez-Penagos (Barcelona Media Innovació), Sara Rosenthal (Columbia University), Alex Rudnick (Indiana University), Jose Saias (Departamento de Informatica - Universidade de Evora), Daniel Sanchez-Cisneros (Universidad Carlos III de Madrid), Didier Schwab (Univ. Grenoble Alpes), Isabel Segura-Bedmar (Carlos III University of Madrid), Reda Siblini (Concordia University), Amanda Stent (AT&T Labs - Research), Jannik Strötgen (Heidelberg University), Nitesh Surtani (IIIT-H), Liling Tan (Nanyang Technological University), Philippe Thomas (Humboldt-Universität zu Berlin, Knowledge Management in Bioinformatics, Unter den Linden 6, 10099 Berlin), Tim Van de Cruys (IRIT & CNRS), Maarten van Gompel (Radboud University Nijmegen), Daniele Vannella (Sapienza University of Rome), Yannick Versley (University of Tuebingen), Christian Wartena (Hochschule Hannover - University of Applied Sciences and Arts), Deniz Yuret (Koc University), Vanni Zavarella (Joint Research Center - European Commission), Zhemin Zhu (CTIT Database Group, EEMCS, University of Twente), and Hans-Peter Zorn (UKP Lab, Technische Universität Darmstadt).

Invited Speaker:

David Forsyth (University of Illinois, Urbana-Champaign)

Panelists for *SEM panel:

Kevin Knight (USC Information Sciences Institute)

Chris Manning (Stanford University)

Martha Palmer (University of Colorado at Boulder)

Owen Rambow (Columbia University)

Dan Roth (University of Illinois at Urbana-Champaign)

Panelists for Shared *SEM/SemEval panel:

*SEM and SemEval organizers

Table of Contents

This page intentionally left blank.

Conference Program Summary

	*SEM Main Conference and STS Shared Task (International D)	SemEval (starting on Day 2 below)
Day 1: Thursday June 13th 2013		
08:00--08:45	Registration	
08:45--10:30	Opening Remarks and *SEM Long Papers 1	*SEM1
10:30--11:00	Coffee Break	
11:00--12:30	STS Shared Task 1	ST1
12:30--2:00	Lunch	
2:00--3:30	STS Shared Task 2 and STS Poster boosters	ST2
3:30--4:00	Coffee Break	
4:00-4:25	*SEM Short Papers 1	*SEM2
4:30--6:00	*SEM Panel: Toward Deep Natural Language Understanding: Kevin Knight, Christopher Manning, Martha Palmer, Owen Rambow, and Dan Roth	*SEM2
6:30--8:30	*SEM Reception and STS Poster Session (PLN1)	

<table>
<tr><th></th><th colspan="2">*SEM Main Conference and STS Shared Task (International D)</th><th colspan="2">SemEval (International E)</th></tr>
<tr><td colspan="5">Day 2: Friday June 14th 2013</td></tr>
<tr><td>08:00--08:30</td><td colspan="4">Registration</td></tr>
<tr><td>08:30--09:30</td><td>*SEM Short Papers 2</td><td>*SEM3</td><td>SemEval Session 1</td><td>SE1</td></tr>
<tr><td>09:30--10:30</td><td colspan="4">Keynote Address: David Forsyth (PLN2)</td></tr>
<tr><td>10:30--11:00</td><td colspan="4">Coffee Break</td></tr>
<tr><td>11:00--12:30</td><td>*SEM Long Papers 2</td><td>*SEM4</td><td>SemEval Session 2</td><td>SE2</td></tr>
<tr><td>12:30--1:30</td><td colspan="2">Lunch (ends earlier!)</td><td>Lunch + Poster Session 1 for Tasks 1, 5, 8</td><td>SP1</td></tr>
<tr><td>1:30--2:30</td><td colspan="4">Joint Panel: Future of *SEM / STS Shared Task / SemEval (PLN3)</td></tr>
<tr><td>2:30--3:30</td><td>*SEM Long Papers 3</td><td>*SEM5</td><td>SemEval Session 3</td><td>SE3</td></tr>
<tr><td>3:30--4:00</td><td colspan="2">Coffee Break</td><td rowspan="2">Coffee + Poster Session 2 for Tasks 4, 10, 11, 12</td><td rowspan="2">SP2</td></tr>
<tr><td>4:00--4:30</td><td rowspan="2">*SEM Long Papers 4</td><td rowspan="2">*SEM6</td></tr>
<tr><td>4:30--5:30</td><td rowspan="3">4:30--6:30 SemEval Session 4</td><td rowspan="3">SE4</td></tr>
<tr><td>5:30--6:00</td><td rowspan="2">Best Papers Awards & Closing remarks</td><td rowspan="2">*SEM7</td></tr>
<tr><td>6:00--6:30</td></tr>
</table>

<table>
<tr><th></th><th colspan="2"></th><th colspan="2">SemEval (International E)</th></tr>
<tr><td colspan="5">Day 3: Saturday June 15th 2013</td></tr>
<tr><td>08:40--10:30</td><td></td><td></td><td>SemEval Session 5</td><td>SE5</td></tr>
<tr><td>10:30--11:00</td><td></td><td></td><td colspan="2">Coffee Break</td></tr>
<tr><td>11:00--1:10</td><td></td><td></td><td>SemEval Session 6</td><td>SE6</td></tr>
<tr><td>1:10-3:30</td><td></td><td></td><td>Lunch + Poster Session 3 for Tasks 2, 3, 7, 9, 13</td><td>SP3</td></tr>
</table>

Conference Program

Day 1: Thursday June 13, 2013

***SEM Main Conference and Shared Task Sessions (no SemEval on Day 1)**

Session PLN1: (6:30–8:30) *SEM Opening Reception and STS Poster Session (All SemEval attendees are invited)

Day 2: Friday June 14, 2013

(08:00–08:30) Registration

Session SE1: (08:30–09:30) Session 1

08:30–08:40 Opening remarks

08:40–09:00 *SemEval-2013 Task 1: TempEval-3: Evaluating Time Expressions, Events, and Temporal Relations*
Naushad UzZaman, Hector Llorens, Leon Derczynski, James Allen, Marc Verhagen and James Pustejovsky

09:00–09:20 *ClearTK-TimeML: A minimalist approach to TempEval 2013*
Steven Bethard

09:20–09:30 *HeidelTime: Tuning English and Developing Spanish Resources for TempEval-3*
Jannik Strötgen, Julian Zell and Michael Gertz

Session PLN2: (09:30–10:30) Keynote address: David Forsyth

(10:30–11:00) Coffee Break

Session SE2: (11:00–12:30) Session 2

11:00–11:10 *ATT1: Temporal Annotation Using Big Windows and Rich Syntactic and Semantic Features*
Hyuckchul Jung and Amanda Stent

11:10–11:30 *Semeval-2013 Task 8: Cross-lingual Textual Entailment for Content Synchronization*
Matteo Negri, Alessandro Marchetti, Yashar Mehdad, Luisa Bentivogli and Danilo Giampiccolo

11:30–11:50 *SOFTCARDINALITY: Learning to Identify Directional Cross-Lingual Entailment from Cardinalities and SMT*
Sergio Jimenez, Claudia Becerra and Alexander Gelbukh

11:50–12:10 *SemEval-2013 Task 5: Evaluating Phrasal Semantics*
Ioannis Korkontzelos, Torsten Zesch, Fabio Massimo Zanzotto and Chris Biemann

Day 2: Friday June 14, 2013 (continued)

12:10–12:30 *HsH: Estimating Semantic Similarity of Words and Short Phrases with Frequency Normalized Distance Measures*
Christian Wartena

Session SP1: (12:30–13:30) Lunch Break + Poster Session 1 for Tasks 1, 5, 8

SemEval-2013 Task 1: TempEval-3: Evaluating Time Expressions, Events, and Temporal Relations
Naushad UzZaman, Hector Llorens, Leon Derczynski, James Allen, Marc Verhagen and James Pustejovsky

ClearTK-TimeML: A minimalist approach to TempEval 2013
Steven Bethard

ManTIME: Temporal expression identification and normalization in the TempEval-3 challenge
Michele Filannino, Gavin Brown and Goran Nenadic

HeidelTime: Tuning English and Developing Spanish Resources for TempEval-3
Jannik Strötgen, Julian Zell and Michael Gertz

FSS-TimEx for TempEval-3: Extracting Temporal Information from Text
Vanni Zavarella and Hristo Tanev

ATT1: Temporal Annotation Using Big Windows and Rich Syntactic and Semantic Features
Hyuckchul Jung and Amanda Stent

JU_CSE: A CRF Based Approach to Annotation of Temporal Expression, Event and Temporal Relations
Anup Kumar Kolya, Amitava Kundu, Rajdeep Gupta, Asif Ekbal, Sivaji Bandyopadhyay

NavyTime: Event and Time Ordering from Raw Text
Nate Chambers

SUTime: Evaluation in TempEval-3
Angel Chang and Christopher D. Manning

KUL: Data-driven Approach to Temporal Parsing of Newswire Articles
Oleksandr Kolomiyets and Marie-Francine Moens

UTTime: Temporal Relation Classification using Deep Syntactic Features
Natsuda Laokulrat, Makoto Miwa, Yoshimasa Tsuruoka and Takashi Chikayama

SemEval-2013 Task 5: Evaluating Phrasal Semantics
Ioannis Korkontzelos, Torsten Zesch, Fabio Massimo Zanzotto and Chris Biemann

Day 2: Friday June 14, 2013 (continued)

Day 2: Friday June 14, 2013 (continued)

Session PLN3: (13:30–14:30) Joint Panel: Future of *SEM / STS Shared Task / SemEval

Session SE3: (14:30–15:30) Session 3

14:30–14:50 *UNAL: Discriminating between Literal and Figurative Phrasal Usage Using Distributional Statistics and POS tags*
Sergio Jimenez, Claudia Becerra and Alexander Gelbukh

14:50–15:10 *SemEval-2013 Task 4: Free Paraphrases of Noun Compounds*
Iris Hendrickx, Zornitsa Kozareva, Preslav Nakov, Diarmuid Ó Séaghdha, Stan Szpakowicz and Tony Veale

15:10–15:30 *MELODI: A Supervised Distributional Approach for Free Paraphrasing of Noun Compounds*
Tim Van de Cruys, Stergos Afantenos and Philippe Muller

Session SP2: (15:30–16:30) Coffee Break + Poster Session 2 for Tasks 4, 10, 11, 12

SemEval-2013 Task 4: Free Paraphrases of Noun Compounds
Iris Hendrickx, Zornitsa Kozareva, Preslav Nakov, Diarmuid Ó Séaghdha, Stan Szpakowicz and Tony Veale

SFS-TUE: Compound Paraphrasing with a Language Model and Discriminative Reranking
Yannick Versley

IIIT-H: A Corpus-Driven Co-occurrence Based Probabilistic Model for Noun Compound Paraphrasing
Nitesh Surtani, Arpita Batra, Urmi Ghosh and Soma Paul

MELODI: A Supervised Distributional Approach for Free Paraphrasing of Noun Compounds
Tim Van de Cruys, Stergos Afantenos and Philippe Muller

SemEval-2013 Task 10: Cross-lingual Word Sense Disambiguation
Els Lefever and Véronique Hoste

XLING: Matching Query Sentences to a Parallel Corpus using Topic Models for WSD
Liling Tan and Francis Bond

HLTDI: CL-WSD Using Markov Random Fields for SemEval-2013 Task 10
Alex Rudnick, Can Liu and Michael Gasser

Day 2: Friday June 14, 2013 (continued)

LIMSI : Cross-lingual Word Sense Disambiguation using Translation Sense Clustering
Marianna Apidianaki

WSD2: Parameter optimisation for Memory-based Cross-Lingual Word-Sense Disambiguation
Maarten van Gompel and Antal van den Bosch

NRC: A Machine Translation Approach to Cross-Lingual Word Sense Disambiguation (SemEval-2013 Task 10)
Marine Carpuat

SemEval-2013 Task 11: Word Sense Induction and Disambiguation within an End-User Application
Roberto Navigli and Daniele Vannella

Duluth : Word Sense Induction Applied to Web Page Clustering
Ted Pedersen

SATTY : Word Sense Induction Application in Web Search Clustering
Satyabrata Behera, Upasana Gaikwad, Ramakrishna Bairi and Ganesh Ramakrishnan

UKP-WSI: UKP Lab Semeval-2013 Task 11 System Description
Hans-Peter Zorn and Iryna Gurevych

unimelb: Topic Modelling-based Word Sense Induction for Web Snippet Clustering
Jey Han Lau, Paul Cook and Timothy Baldwin

SemEval-2013 Task 12: Multilingual Word Sense Disambiguation
Roberto Navigli, David Jurgens and Daniele Vannella

GETALP System : Propagation of a Lesk Measure through an Ant Colony Algorithm
Didier Schwab, Andon Tchechmedjiev, Jérôme Goulian, Mohammad Nasiruddin, Gilles Sérasset and Hervé Blanchon

UMCC_DLSI: Reinforcing a Ranking Algorithm with Sense Frequencies and Multidimensional Semantic Resources to solve Multilingual Word Sense Disambiguation
Yoan Gutiérrez, Yenier Castañeda, Andy González, Rainel Estrada, Dennys D. Piug, Jose I. Abreu, Roger Pérez, Antonio Fernández Orquín, Andrés Montoyo, Rafael Muñoz and Franc Camara

DAEBAK!: Peripheral Diversity for Multilingual Word Sense Disambiguation
Steve L. Manion, and Raazesh Sainudiin

Day 2: Friday June 14, 2013 (continued)

Session SE4: (16:30–18:30) Session 4

Day 3: Saturday June 15, 2013

Session SE5: (08:40–10:30) Session 5

Day 3: Saturday June 15, 2013 (continued)

09:35–09:50 *SOFTCARDINALITY: Hierarchical Text Overlap for Student Response Analysis*
Sergio Jimenez, Claudia Becerra and Alexander Gelbukh

09:50–10:00 *UKP-BIU: Similarity and Entailment Metrics for Student Response Analysis*
Omer Levy, Torsten Zesch, Ido Dagan and Iryna Gurevych

10:00–10:20 *SemEval-2013 Task 13: Word Sense Induction for Graded and Non-Graded Senses*
David Jurgens and Ioannis Klapaftis

10:20–10:30 *AI-KU: Using Substitute Vectors and Co-Occurrence Modeling For Word Sense Induction and Disambiguation*
Osman Baskaya, Enis Sert, Volkan Cirik and Deniz Yuret

(10:30–11:00) Coffee Break

Session SE6: (11:00–13:10) Session 6

11:00–11:10 *unimelb: Topic Modelling-based Word Sense Induction*
Jey Han Lau, Paul Cook and Timothy Baldwin

11:10–11:30 *SemEval-2013 Task 2: Sentiment Analysis in Twitter*
Preslav Nakov, Sara Rosenthal, Zornitsa Kozareva, Veselin Stoyanov, Alan Ritter and Theresa Wilson

11:30–11:50 *NRC-Canada: Building the State-of-the-Art in Sentiment Analysis of Tweets*
Saif Mohammad, Svetlana Kiritchenko and Xiaodan Zhu

11:50–12:00 *GU-MLT-LT: Sentiment Analysis of Short Messages using Linguistic Features and Stochastic Gradient Descent*
Tobias Günther and Lenz Furrer

12:00–12:10 *AVAYA: Sentiment Analysis on Twitter with Self-Training and Polarity Lexicon Expansion*
Lee Becker, George Erhart, David Skiba and Valentine Matula

12:10–12:30 *SemEval-2013 Task 9 : Extraction of Drug-Drug Interactions from Biomedical Texts (DDIExtraction 2013)*
Isabel Segura-Bedmar, Paloma Martínez and María Herrero Zazo

12:30–12:50 *FBK-irst : A Multi-Phase Kernel Based Approach for Drug-Drug Interaction Detection and Classification that Exploits Linguistic Information*
Md. Faisal Mahbub Chowdhury and Alberto Lavelli

12:50–13:10 *WBI-NER: The impact of domain-specific features on the performance of identifying and classifying mentions of drugs*
Tim Rocktäschel, Torsten Huber, Michael Weidlich and Ulf Leser

Day 3: Saturday June 15, 2013 (continued)

Session SP3: (13:10–15:30) Lunch Break + Poster Session 3 for Tasks 2, 3, 7, 9, 13

Day 3: Saturday June 15, 2013 (continued)

Day 3: Saturday June 15, 2013 (continued)

Day 3: Saturday June 15, 2013 (continued)

Day 3: Saturday June 15, 2013 (continued)

CoMeT: Integrating different levels of linguistic modeling for meaning assessment
Niels Ott, Ramon Ziai, Michael Hahn and Detmar Meurers

SemEval-2013 Task 9 : Extraction of Drug-Drug Interactions from Biomedical Texts (DDIExtraction 2013)
Isabel Segura-Bedmar, Paloma Martínez and María Herrero Zazo

UC3M: A kernel-based approach to identify and classify DDIs in bio-medical texts.
Daniel Sanchez-Cisneros

UEM-UC3M: An Ontology-based named entity recognition system for biomedical texts.
Daniel Sanchez-Cisneros and Fernando Aparicio Gali

FBK-irst : A Multi-Phase Kernel Based Approach for Drug-Drug Interaction Detection and Classification that Exploits Linguistic Information
Md. Faisal Mahbub Chowdhury and Alberto Lavelli

WBI-DDI: Drug-Drug Interaction Extraction using Majority Voting
Philippe Thomas, Mariana Neves, Tim Rocktäschel and Ulf Leser

WBI-NER: The impact of domain-specific features on the performance of identifying and classifying mentions of drugs
Tim Rocktäschel, Torsten Huber, Michael Weidlich and Ulf Leser

UMCC_DLSI: Semantic and Lexical features for detection and classification Drugs in biomedical texts
Armando Collazo, Alberto Ceballo, Dennys D. Puig, Yoan Gutiérrez, José I. Abreu, Roger Pérez, Antonio Fernández Orquín, Andrés Montoyo, Rafael Muñoz and Franc Camara

NIL_UCM: Extracting Drug-Drug interactions from text through combination of sequence and tree kernels
Behrouz Bokharaeian and ALBERTO DIAZ

UTurku: Drug Named Entity Recognition and Drug-Drug Interaction Extraction Using SVM Classification and Domain Knowledge
Jari Björne, Suwisa Kaewphan and Tapio Salakoski

LASIGE: using Conditional Random Fields and ChEBI ontology
Tiago Grego, Francisco Pinto and Francisco M Couto

UWM-TRIADS: Classifying Drug-Drug Interactions with Two-Stage SVM and Post-Processing
Majid Rastegar-Mojarad, Richard D. Boyce and Rashmi Prasad

Day 3: Saturday June 15, 2013 (continued)

SemEval-2013 Task 1: TempEval-3: Evaluating Time Expressions, Events, and Temporal Relations

Naushad UzZaman[♣⋈], **Hector Llorens**[◇⋈], **Leon Derczynski**[♡],
Marc Verhagen[♠], **James Allen**[♣] and **James Pustejovsky**[♠]
♣: University of Rochester, USA; ◇: University of Alicante, Spain
♡: Department of Computer Science, University of Sheffield, UK
♠: Computer Science Department, Brandeis University, USA
⋈: Nuance Communications
naushad@cs.rochester.edu, hllorens@dlsi.ua.es, leon@dcs.shef.ac.uk

Abstract

Within the SemEval-2013 evaluation exercise, the TempEval-3 shared task aims to advance research on temporal information processing. It follows on from TempEval-1 and -2, with: a three-part structure covering temporal expression, event, and temporal relation extraction; a larger dataset; and new single measures to rank systems – in each task and in general. In this paper, we describe the participants' approaches, results, and the observations from the results, which may guide future research in this area.

1 Introduction

The TempEval task (Verhagen et al., 2009) was added as a new task in SemEval-2007. The ultimate aim of research in this area is the automatic identification of temporal expressions (timexes), events, and temporal relations within a text as specified in TimeML annotation (Pustejovsky et al., 2005). However, since addressing this aim in a first evaluation challenge was deemed too difficult a staged approach was suggested.

TempEval (henceforth TempEval-1) was an initial evaluation exercise focusing only on the categorization of temporal relations and only in English. It included three relation types: event-timex, event-dct,[1] and relations between main events in consecutive sentences.

TempEval-2 (Verhagen et al., 2010) extended TempEval-1, growing into a multilingual task, and consisting of six subtasks rather than three. This included event and timex extraction, as well as the three relation tasks from TempEval-1, with the addition of a relation task where one event subordinates another.

TempEval-3 (UzZaman et al., 2012b) is a follow-up to TempEval 1 and 2, covering English and Spanish. TempEval-3 is different from its predecessors in a few respects:

Size of the corpus: the dataset used has about 600K word silver standard data and about 100K word gold standard data for training, compared to around 50K word corpus used in TempEval 1 and 2. Temporal annotation is a time-consuming task for humans, which has limited the size of annotated data in previous TempEval exercises. Current systems, however, are performing close to the inter-annotator reliability, which suggests that larger corpora could be built from automatically annotated data with minor human reviews. We want to explore whether there is value in adding a large automatically created silver standard to a hand-crafted gold standard.

End-to-end temporal relation processing task: the temporal relation classification tasks are performed from raw text, i.e. participants need to extract their own events and temporal expressions first, determine which ones to link and then obtain the relation types. In previous TempEvals, gold timexes, events, and relations (without category) were given to participants.

Temporal relation types: the full set of temporal relations in TimeML are used, rather than the reduced set used in earlier TempEvals.

Platinum test set: A new test dataset has been developed for this edition. It is based on manual annotations by experts over new text (unseen in previous editions).

Evaluation: we report a temporal awareness score for evaluating temporal relations, which helps to rank systems with a single score.

2 Data

In TempEval-3, we reviewed and corrected existing corpora, and also released new corpora.

2.1 Reviewing Existing Corpora

We considered the existing TimeBank (Pustejovsky et al., 2003) and AQUAINT[2] data for TempEval-3. TempEval-

[1] DCT stands for document creation time

[2] See http://timeml.org/site/timebank/timebank.html

*Second Joint Conference on Lexical and Computational Semantics (*SEM), Volume 2: Seventh International Workshop on Semantic Evaluation (SemEval 2013)*, pages 1–9, Atlanta, Georgia, June 14-15, 2013.

Entity	Agreement
Event	0.87
Event class	0.92
Timex	0.87
Timex value	0.88

Table 1: Platinum corpus entity inter-annotator agreement.

Corpus	# of words	Standard
TimeBank	61,418	Gold
AQUAINT	33,973	Gold
TempEval-3 Silver	666,309	Silver
TempEval-3 Eval	6,375	Platinum
TimeBank-ES Train	57,977	Gold
TimeBank-ES Eval	9,833	Gold

Table 2: Corpora used in TempEval-3.

1 and TempEval-2 had the same documents as TimeBank but different relation types and events.

For both TimeBank and AQUAINT, we, (i) cleaned up the formatting for all files making it easy to review and read, (ii) made all files XML and TimeML schema compatible, (iii) added some missing events and temporal expressions. In TimeBank, we, (i) borrowed the events from the TempEval-2 corpus and (ii) borrowed the temporal relations from TimeBank corpus, which contains a full set of temporal relations. In AQUAINT, we added the temporal relations between event and DCT (document creation time), which was missing for many documents in that corpus. These existing corpora comprised the high-quality component of our training set.

2.2 New Corpora

We created two new datasets: a small, manually-annotated set over new text (platinum); and a machine-annotated, automatically-merged dataset based on outputs of multiple systems (silver).

The TempEval-3 *platinum* evaluation corpus was annotated/reviewed by the organizers, who are experts in the area. This process used the TimeML Annotation Guidelines v1.2.1 (Saurí et al., 2006). Every file was annotated independently by at least two expert annotators, and a third was dedicated to adjudicating between annotations and merging the final result. Some annotators based their work on TIPSem annotation suggestions (Llorens et al., 2012b). The GATE Annotation Diff tool was used for merging (Cunningham et al., 2013), a custom TimeML validator ensured integrity,[3] and CAVaT (Derczynski and Gaizauskas, 2010) was used to determine various modes of TimeML mis-annotation and inconsistency that are inexpressable via XML schema. Post-exercise, that corpus (TempEval-3 Platinum with around 6K tokens, on completely new text) is released for the community to review and improve.[4] Inter-annotator agreement (measured with F1, as per Hripcsak and Rothschild (2005)) and the number of annotation passes per document were higher than in existing TimeML corpora, hence the name. Details are given in Table 1. Attribute value scores are given based on the agreed entity set. These are for exact matches.

The TempEval-3 *silver* evaluation corpus is a 600K word corpus collected from Gigaword (Parker et al., 2011). We automatically annotated this corpus by TIPSem, TIPSem-B (Llorens et al., 2013) and TRIOS (UzZaman and Allen, 2010). These systems were retrained on the corrected TimeBank and AQUAINT corpus to generate the original TimeML temporal relation set. We then merged these three state-of-the-art system outputs using our merging algorithm (Llorens et al., 2012a). In our selected merged configuration all entities and relations suggested by the best system (TIPSem) are added in the merged output. Suggestions from other systems (TRIOS and TIPSem-B) are added in the merged output, only if they are also supported by another system. The weights considered in our configuration are: TIPSem 0.36, TIPSemB 0.32, TRIOS 0.32.

For Spanish, Spanish TimeBank 1.0 corpus (Saurí and Badia, 2012) wads used. It is the same corpus that was used in TempEval-2, with a major review of entity annotation and an important improvement regarding temporal relation annotation. For TempEval-3, we converted ES-TimeBank link types to the TimeML standard types based on Allen's temporal relations (Allen, 1983).

Table 2 summarizes our released corpora, measured with PTB-scheme tokens as words. All data produced was annotated using a well-defined subset of TimeML, designed for easy processing, and for reduced ambiguity compared to standard TimeML. Participants were encouraged to validate their submissions using a purpose-built tool to ensure that submitted runs were legible. We called this standard TimeML-strict, and release it separately (Derczynski et al., 2013).

3 Tasks

The three main tasks proposed for TempEval-3 focus on TimeML entities and relations:

3.1 Task A (Timex extraction and normalization)

Determine the extent of the timexes in a text as defined by the TimeML TIMEX3 tag. In addition, determine the value of the features TYPE and VALUE. The possible values of TYPE are time, date, duration, and set; VALUE is a normalized value as defined by the TIMEX3 standard.

[3] See https://github.com/hllorens/TimeML-validator

[4] In the ACL data and code repository, reference ADCR2013T001. See also https://bitbucket.org/leondz/te3-platinum

3.2 Task B (Event extraction and classification)

Determine the extent of the events in a text as defined by the TimeML EVENT tag and the appropriate CLASS.

3.3 Task ABC (Annotating temporal relations)

This is the ultimate task for evaluating an end-to-end system that goes from raw text to TimeML annotation of entities and links. It entails performing tasks A and B. From raw text extract the temporal entities (events and timexes), identify the pairs of temporal entities that have a temporal link (TLINK) and classify the temporal relation between them. Possible pair of entities that can have a temporal link are: (i) main events of consecutive sentences, (ii) pairs of events in the same sentence, (iii) event and timex in the same sentence and (iv) event and document creation time. In TempEval-3, TimeML relation are used, i.e.: BEFORE, AFTER, INCLUDES, IS-INCLUDED, DURING, SIMULTANEOUS, IMMEDIATELY AFTER, IMMEDIATELY BEFORE, IDENTITY, BEGINS, ENDS, BEGUN-BY and ENDED-BY.

In addition to this main tasks, we also include two extra temporal relation tasks:

Task C (Annotating relations given gold entities) Given the gold entities, identify the pairs of entities that have a temporal link (TLINK) and classify the temporal relations between them.

Task C relation only (Annotating relations given gold entities and related pairs) Given the temporal entities and the pair of entities that have a temporal link, classify the temporal relation between them.

4 Evaluation Metrics

The metrics used to evaluate the participants are:

4.1 Temporal Entity Extraction

To evaluate temporal entities (*events* and *temporal expressions*), we need to evaluate, (i) How many entities are correctly identified, (ii) If the extents for the entities are correctly identified, and (iii) How many entity attributes are correctly identified. We use classical precision and recall for recognition.

How many entities are correctly identified: We evaluate our entities using the entity-based evaluation with the equations below.

$$Precision = \frac{|Sys_{entity} \cap Ref_{entity}|}{|Sys_{entity}|}$$

$$Recall = \frac{|Sys_{entity} \cap Ref_{entity}|}{|Ref_{entity}|}$$

where, Sys_{entity} contains the entities extracted by the system that we want to evaluate, and Ref_{entity} contains the entities from the reference annotation that are being compared.

If the extents for the entities are correctly identified: We compare our entities with both strict match and relaxed match. When there is a exact match between the system entity and gold entity then we call it strict match, e.g. "sunday morning" vs "sunday morning". When there is a overlap between the system entity and gold entity then we call it relaxed match, e.g. "sunday" vs "sunday morning". When there is a relaxed match, we compare the attribute values.

How many entity attributes are correctly identified: We evaluate our entity attributes using the attribute F1-score, which captures how well the system identified both the entity and attribute (attr) together.

$$\textit{Attribute Recall} = \frac{|\{\forall x \mid x \in (Sys_{entity} \cap Ref_{entity}) \land Sys_{attr}(x) == Ref_{attr}(x)\}|}{|Ref_{entity}|}$$

$$\textit{Attribute Precision} = \frac{|\{\forall x \mid x \in (Sys_{entity} \cap Ref_{entity}) \land Sys_{attr}(x) == Ref_{attr}(x)\}|}{|Sys_{entity}|}$$

$$\textit{Attribute F1-score} = \frac{2*p*r}{p+r}$$

Attribute (Attr) accuracy, precision and recall can be calculated as well from the above information.

Attr Accuracy = Attr F1 / Entity Extraction F1

*Attr R = Attr Accuracy * Entity R*

*Attr P = Attr Accuracy * Entity P*

4.2 Temporal Relation Processing

To evaluate relations, we use the evaluation metric presented by UzZaman and Allen (2011).[5] This metric captures the temporal awareness of an annotation in terms of precision, recall and F1 score. Temporal awareness is defined as the performance of an annotation as identifying and categorizing temporal relations, which implies the correct recognition and classification of the temporal entities involved in the relations. Unlike TempEval-2 relation score, where only categorization is evaluated for relations, this metric evaluates how well pairs of entities are identified, how well the relations are categorized, and how well the events and temporal expressions are extracted.

$$Precision = \frac{|Sys^{-}_{relation} \cap Ref^{+}_{relation}|}{|Sys^{-}_{relation}|}$$

$$Recall = \frac{|Ref^{-}_{relation} \cap Sys^{+}_{relation}|}{|Ref^{-}_{relation}|}$$

where, G^{+} is the closure of graph G and G^{-} is the reduced of graph G, where redundant relations are removed.[6]

We calculate the $Precision$ by checking the number of reduced system relations ($Sys^{-}_{relation}$) that can be verified from the reference annotation temporal closure graph ($Ref^{+}_{relation}$), out of number of temporal relations in the

[5] We used a minor variation of the formula, where we consider the reduced graph instead of all system or reference relations. Details can be found in Chapter 6 of UzZaman (2012).

[6] A relation is redundant if it can be inferred through other relations.

	F1	P	R	strict F1	value F1
HeidelTime-t	90.30	93.08	87.68	81.34	**77.61**
HeidelTime-bf	87.31	90.00	84.78	78.36	72.39
HeidelTime-1.2	86.99	89.31	84.78	78.07	72.12
NavyTime-1,2	**90.32**	89.36	**91.30**	79.57	70.97
ManTIME-4	89.66	95.12	84.78	74.33	68.97
ManTIME-6	87.55	98.20	78.99	73.09	68.27
ManTIME-3	87.06	94.87	80.43	69.80	67.45
SUTime	**90.32**	89.36	**91.30**	79.57	67.38
ManTIME-1	87.20	97.32	78.99	70.40	67.20
ManTIME-5	87.20	97.32	78.99	69.60	67.20
ManTIME-2	88.10	97.37	80.43	72.22	66.67
ATT-2	85.25	98.11	75.36	78.69	65.57
ATT-1	85.60	**99.05**	75.36	79.01	65.02
ClearTK-1,2	90.23	93.75	86.96	**82.71**	64.66
JU-CSE	86.38	93.28	80.43	75.49	63.81
KUL	83.67	92.92	76.09	69.32	62.95
KUL-TE3RunABC	82.87	92.04	75.36	73.31	62.15
ClearTK-3,4	87.94	94.96	81.88	77.04	61.48
ATT-3	80.85	97.94	68.84	72.34	60.43
FSS-TimEx	85.06	90.24	80.43	49.04	58.24
TIPSem (TE2)	84.90	97.20	75.36	81.63	65.31

Table 3: Task A - Temporal Expression Performance.

reduced system relations ($Sys^{-}_{relation}$). Similarly, we calculate the $Recall$ by checking the number of reduced reference annotation relations ($Ref^{-}_{relation}$) that can be verified from the system output's temporal closure graph ($Sys^{+}_{relation}$), out of number of temporal relations in the reduced reference annotation ($Ref^{-}_{relation}$).

This metric evaluates Task ABC together. For Task C and Task C - relation only, all the gold annotation entities were provided and then evaluated using the above metric.

Our evaluation toolkit that evaluated TempEval-3 participants is available online.[7]

5 Evaluation Results

The aim of this evaluation is to provide a meaningful report of the performance obtained by the participants in the tasks defined in Section 3.

Furthermore, the results include TIPSem as reference for comparison. This was used as a pre-annotation system in some cases. TIPSem obtained the best results in event processing task in TempEval-2 and offered very competitive results in timex and relation processing. The best timex processing system in TempEval-2 (HeidelTime) is participating in this edition as well, therefore we included TIPSem as a reference in all tasks.

We only report results in main measures. Results are divided by language and shown per task. Detailed scores can be found on the task website.[8]

[7] See http://www.cs.rochester.edu/u/naushad/temporal

[8] See http://www.cs.york.ac.uk/semeval-2013/task1/

5.1 Results for English

5.1.1 Task A: Timexes

We had nine participants and 21 unique runs for temporal expression extraction task, Task A. Table 3 shows the results. Details about participants' approaches can be found in Table 4.

We rank the participants for Task A on the F1 score of most important timex attribute – *Value*. To get the attribute *Value* correct, a system needs to correctly normalise the temporal expression. This score (*Value* F1) captures the performance of extracting the timex and identifying the attribute *Value* together (*Value F1* = *Timex F1* * *Value Accuracy*).

Participants approached the temporal expression extraction task with rule-engineered methods, machine learning methods and also hybrid methods. For temporal expression normalization (identifying the timex attribute value), all participants used rule-engineered approaches.

Observations: We collected the following observations from the results and from participants' experiments.

Strategy: Competition was close for timex recognition and the best systems all performed within 1% of each other. On our newswire corpus, statistical systems (ClearTK) performed best at strict matching, and rule-engineered system best at relaxed matching (NavyTime, SUTime, HeidelTime).

Strategy: post-processing, on top of machine learning-base temporal expression extraction, provided a statistically significant improvement in both precision and recall (ManTIME).

Data: using the large silver dataset, alone or together with human annotated data, did not give improvements in performance for Task A. Human-annotated gold standard data alone provided the best performance (ManTIME).

Data: TimeBank alone was better than TimeBank and AQUAINT together for Task A (ClearTK).

Features: syntactic and gazetteers did not provide any statistically significant increment of performance with respect to the morphological features alone (ManTIME).

Regarding the two sub-tasks of timex annotation, recognition and interpretation/normalisation, we noticed a shift in the state of the art. While normalisation is currently (and perhaps inherently) done best by rule-engineered systems, recognition is now done well by a variety of methods. Where formerly, rule-engineered timex recognition always outperformed other classes of approach, now it is clear that rule-engineering and machine learning are equally good at timex recognition.

5.1.2 Task B: Events

For event extraction (Task B) we had seven participants and 10 unique runs. The results for this task can be found in Table 6. We rank the participants for TaskB on the F1 score of most important event attribute – *Class*. *Class*

Strategy	System	Training data	Classifier used
Data-driven	ATT-1, 2, 3	TBAQ + TE3Silver	MaxEnt
	ClearTK-1, 2	TimeBank	SVM, Logit
	ClearTK-3, 4	TBAQ	SVM, Logit
	JU-CSE	TBAQ	CRF
	ManTIME-1	TBAQ + TE3Silver	CRF
	ManTIME-3	TBAQ	CRF
	ManTIME-5	TE3Silver	CRF
	Temp : ESAfeature	TBAQ	MaxEnt
	Temp : WordNetfeature	TBAQ	MaxEnt
	TIPSem (TE2)	TBAQ	CRF
Rule-based	FSS-TimEx (EN)	None	None
	FSS-TimEx (ES)	None	None
	HeidelTime-1.2, bf (EN)	None	None
	HeidelTime-t (EN)	TBAQ	None
	HeidelTime (ES)	Gold	None
	NavyTime-1, 2	None	None
	SUTime	None	None
Hybrid	KUL	TBAQ + TE3Silver	Logit + post-processing
	KUL-TE3RunABC	TBAQ +TE3Silver	Logit + post-processing
	ManTIME-2	TBAQ + TE3Silver	CRF + post-processing
	ManTIME-4	TBAQ	CRF + post-processing
	ManTIME-6	TE3Silver	CRF + post-processing

Table 4: Automated approaches for TE3 Timex Extraction

Strategy	System	Training data	Classifier used	Linguistic Knowledge
Data-driven	ATT-1, 2, 3	TBAQ + TE3Silver	MaxEnt	*ms, ss*
	ClearTK-1, 2	TimeBank	SVM, Logit	*ms*
	ClearTK-3, 4	TBAQ	SVM, Logit	*ms*
	JU-CSE	TBAQ	CRF	
	KUL	TBAQ +TE3Silver	Logit	*ms, ls*
	KUL-TE3RunABC	TBAQ +TE3Silver	Logit	*ms, ls*
	NavyTime-1	TBAQ	MaxEnt	*ms, ls*
	NavyTime-2	TimeBank	MaxEnt	*ms, ls*
	Temp : ESAfeature	TBAQ	MaxEnt	*ms, ls, ss*
	Temp : WordNetfeature	TBAQ	MaxEnt	*ms, ls*
	TIPSem (TE2)	TBAQ	CRF/SVM	*ms, ls, ss*
Rule-based	FSS-TimEx (EN)	None	None	*ls, ms*
	FSS-TimEx (ES)	None	None	*ls, ms*

Table 5: Automated approaches for Event Extraction

	F1	P	R	class F1
ATT-1	**81.05**	81.44	80.67	**71.88**
ATT-2	80.91	81.02	**80.81**	71.10
KUL	79.32	80.69	77.99	70.17
ATT-3	78.63	**81.95**	75.57	69.55
KUL-TE3RunABC	77.11	77.58	76.64	68.74
ClearTK-3,4	78.81	81.40	76.38	67.87
NavyTime-1	80.30	80.73	79.87	67.48
ClearTK-1,2	77.34	81.86	73.29	65.44
NavyTime-2	79.37	80.52	78.26	64.81
Temp:ESAfeature	68.97	78.33	61.61	54.55
JU-CSE	78.62	80.85	76.51	52.69
Temp:WordNetfeature	63.90	78.90	53.69	50.00
FSS-TimEx	65.06	63.13	67.11	42.94
TIPSem (TE2)	82.89	83.51	82.28	75.59

Table 6: Task B - Event Extraction Performance.

	F1	P	R
ClearTK-2	**30.98**	34.08	**28.40**
ClearTK-1	29.77	**34.49**	26.19
ClearTK-3	28.62	30.94	26.63
ClearTK-4	28.46	29.73	27.29
NavyTime-1	27.28	31.25	24.20
JU-CSE	24.61	19.17	34.36
NavyTime-2	21.99	26.52	18.78
KUL-TE3RunABC	19.01	17.94	20.22
TIPSem (TE2)	42.39	38.79	46.74

Table 7: Task ABC - Temporal Awareness Evaluation (Task C evaluation from raw text).

F1 captures the performance of extracting the event and identifying the attribute *Class* together (*Class F1 = Event F1 * Class Accuracy*).

All the participants except one used machine learning approaches. Details about the participants' approaches and the linguistic knowledge[9] used to solve this problem, and training data, are in Table 5.

Observations: We collected the following observations from the results and from participants' experiments.

Strategy: All the high performing systems for event extraction (Task B) are machine learning-based.

Data: Systems using silver data, along with the human annotated gold standard data, performed very well (top three participants in the task – ATT, KUL, KUL-TE3RunABC). Additionally, TimeBank and AQUAINT together performed better than just TimeBank alone (NavyTime-1, ClearTK-3,4).

Linguistic Features: Semantic features (*ls* and *ss*) have played an important role, since the best systems (TIPSem, ATT1 and KUL) include them. However, these three are not the only systems using semantic features.

[9] Abbreviations used in the table: TBAQ – *TimeBank + AQUAINT corpus* ms – *morphosyntactic information*, e.g. POS, lexical information, morphological information and syntactic parsing related features; ls –*lexical semantic information*, e.g. WordNet synsets; ss – *sentence-level semantic information*, e.g. Semantic Role labels.

	F1	P	R
ClearTK-2	**36.26**	37.32	35.25
ClearTK-4	35.86	35.17	36.57
ClearTK-1	35.19	**37.64**	33.04
UTTime-5	34.90	35.94	33.92
ClearTK-3	34.13	33.27	35.03
NavyTime-1	31.06	35.48	27.62
UTTime-4	28.81	37.41	23.43
JU-CSE	26.41	21.04	35.47
NavyTime-2	25.84	31.10	22.10
KUL-TE3RunABC	24.83	23.35	26.52
UTTime-1	24.65	15.18	**65.64**
UTTime-3	24.28	15.10	61.99
UTTime-2	24.05	14.80	64.20
TIPSem (TE2)	44.25	39.71	49.94

Table 8: Task C - TLINK Identification and Classification.

	F1	P	R
UTTime-1, 4	**56.45**	**55.58**	**57.35**
UTTime-3, 5	54.70	53.85	55.58
UTTime-2	54.26	53.20	55.36
NavyTime-1	46.83	46.59	47.07
NavyTime-2	43.92	43.65	44.20
JU-CSE	34.77	35.07	34.48

Table 9: Task C - relation only: Relation Classification.

5.1.3 Task C: Relation Evaluation

For complete temporal annotation from raw text (Task ABC - Task C from raw text) and for temporal relation only tasks (Task C, Task C relation only), we had five participants in total.

For relation evaluation, we primarily evaluate on Task ABC (Task C from raw text), which requires joint entity extraction, link identification and relation classification. The results for this task can be found in Table 7.

While TIPSem obtained the best results in task ABC, especially in recall, it was used by some annotators to pre-label data. In the interest of rigour and fairness, we separate out this system.

For task C, for provided participants with entities and participants identified: between which entity pairs a relation exists (link identification); and the class of that relation. Results are given in Table 8. We also evaluate the participants on the relation by providing the entities and the links (performance in Table 9) – TIPSem could not be evaluated in this setting since the system is not prepared to do categorization only unless the relations are divided as in TempEval-2. For these Task C related tasks, we had only one new participant, who didn't participate in Task A and B: UTTime.

Identifying which pair of entities to consider for temporal relations is a new task in this TempEval challenge. The participants approached the problems in data-driven, rule-based and also in hybrid ways (Table 10[10]). On

[10] New abbreviation in the table, e-attr – *entity attributes, e.g. event class, tense, aspect, polarity, modality; timex type, value.*

Strategy	System	Training data	Classifier used	Linguistic Knowledge
Data-driven	ClearTK-1	TimeBank	SVM, Logit	*e-attr, ms*
	ClearTK-2	TimeBank + Bethard et al. (2007)	SVM, Logit	*e-attr, ms*
	ClearTK-3	TBAQ	SVM, Logit	*e-attr, ms*
	ClearTK-4	TBAQ + Muller's inferences	SVM, Logit	*e-attr, ms*
	KULRunABC	TBAQ	SVM, Logit	*ms*
Rule-based	JU-CSE	None	None	
	UTTime-1, 2 ,3	None	None	
	TIPSem (TE2)	None	None	*e-attr, ms, ls, ss*
Hybrid	NavyTime-1	TBAQ	MaxEnt	*ms*
	NavyTime-2	TimeBank	MaxEnt	*ms*
	UTTime-4	TBAQ	Logit	*ms, ls, ss*
	UTTime-5	TBAQ + inverse relations	Logit	*ms, ls, ss*

Table 10: Automated approaches for TE3 TLINK Identification

Strategy	System	Training data	Classifier used	Linguistic Knowledge
Data-driven	ClearTK-1	TimeBank	SVM, Logit	*ms, ls*
	ClearTK-2	TimeBank + Bethard et al. (2007)	SVM, Logit	*ms, ls*
	ClearTK-3	TBAQ	SVM, Logit	*ms, ls*
	ClearTK-4	TBAQ + Muller's inferences	SVM, Logit	*ms, ls*
	JU-CSE	TBAQ	CRF	
	KULRunABC	TBAQ	SVM, Logit	*ms*
	NavyTime-1	TBAQ	MaxEnt	*ms, ls*
	NavyTime-2	TimeBank	MaxEnt	*ms, ls*
	UTTime-1,4, 2	TBAQ	Logit	*ms, ls, ss*
	UTTime-3,5	TBAQ + inverse relations	Logit	*ms, ls, ss*
	TIPSem (TE-2)	TBAQ	CRF/SVM	*ms, ls, ss*

Table 11: Automated approaches for Relation Classification

the other hand, all the participants used data-driven approaches for temporal relations (Table 11).

Observations: We collected the following observations from the results and from participants' experiments.

Strategy: For relation classification, all participants used partially or fully machine learning-based systems.

Data: None of the participants implemented their systems training on the silver data. Most of the systems use the combined TimeBank and AQUAINT (TBAQ) corpus.

Data: Adding additional high-quality relations, either Philippe Muller's closure-based inferences or the verb clause relations from Bethard et al. (2007), typically increased recall and the overall performance (ClearTK runs two and four).

Features: Participants mostly used the morphosyntactic and lexical semantic information. The best performing systems from TempEval-2 (TIPSem and TRIOS) additionally used sentence level semantic information. One participant in TempEval-3 (UTTime) also did deep parsing for the sentence level semantic features.

Features: Using more Linguistic knowledge is important for the task, but it is more important to execute it properly. Many systems performed better using less linguistic knowledge. Hence a system (e.g. ClearTK) with basic morphosyntactic features is hard to beat with more semantic features, if not used properly.

	entity extraction				
	strict	relaxed			
	F1	F1	P	R	value
HeidelTime	**85.3**	**90.1**	96.0	84.9	**87.5**
TIPSemB-F	82.6	87.4	93.7	81.9	82.0
FSS-TimEx	49.5	65.2	86.6	52.3	62.7

Table 12: Task A: Temporal Expression (Spanish).

				class	tense	aspect
	F1	P	R	F1	F1	F1
FSS-TimEx	57.6	89.8	42.4	24.9	-	-
TIPSemB-F	**88.8**	91.7	86.0	**57.6**	41.0	36.3

Table 13: Task B: Event Extraction (Spanish).

Classifier: Across the various tasks, ClearTK tried Mallet CRF, Mallet MaxEnt, OpenNLP MaxEnt, and LIBLINEAR (SVMs and logistic regression). They picked the final classifiers by running a grid search over models and parameters on the training data, and for all tasks, a LIBLINEAR model was at least as good as all the other models. As an added bonus, it was way faster to train than most of the other models.

6 Evaluation Results (Spanish)

There were two participants for Spanish. Both participated in task A and only one of them in task B. In this

	F1	P	R
TIPSemB-F	**41.6**	37.8	46.2

Table 14: Task ABC: Temporal Awareness (Spanish).

	entity extraction				attributes	
	strict	relaxed			val	type
	F1	F1	P	R	F1	F1
HeidelTime	86.4	89.8	94.0	85.9	**87.5**	**89.8**
FSS-TimEx	42.1	68.4	86.7	56.5	48.7	65.8
TIPSem	**86.9**	**93.7**	98.8	89.1	75.4	88.0
TIPSemB-F	84.3	89.9	93.0	87.0	82.0	86.5

Table 15: Task A: TempEval-2 test set (Spanish).

case, TIPSemB-Freeling is provided as a state-of-the-art reference covering all the tasks. TIPSemB-Freeling is the Spanish version of TIPSem with the main difference that it does not include semantic roles. Furthermore, it uses Freeling (Padró and Stanilovsky, 2012) to obtain the linguistic features automatically.

Table 12 shows the results obtained for task A. As it can be observed HeidelTime obtains the best results. It improves the previous state-of-the-art results (TIPSemB-F), especially in normalization (value F1).

Table 13 shows the results from event extraction. In this case, the previous state-of-the-art is not improved.

Table 14 only shows the results obtained in temporal awareness by the state-of-the-art system since there were not participants on this task. We observe that TIPSemB-F approach offers competitive results, which is comparable to results obtained in TE3 English test set.

6.1 Comparison with TempEval-2

TempEval-2 Spanish test set is included as a subset of this TempEval-3 test set. We can therefore compare the performance across editions. Furthermore, we can include the full-featured TIPSem (Llorens et al., 2010), which unlike TIPSemB-F used the AnCora (Taulé et al., 2008) corpus annotations as features including semantic roles.

For timexes, as can be seen in Table 15, the original TIPSem obtains better results for timex extraction, which favours the hypothesis that machine learning systems are very well suited for this task (if the training data is sufficiently representative). However, for normalization (value F1), HeidelTime – a rule-engineered system – obtains better results. This indicates that rule-based approaches have the upper hand in this task. TIPSem uses a partly data-driven normalization approach which, given the small amount of training data available, seemed less suited to the task.

	F1	P	R	class F1	tense F1	aspect F1
FSS-TimEx	59.0	90.3	43.9	24.6	-	-
TIPSemB-F	**90.2**	92.5	88.0	58.6	39.7	38.1
TIPSem	88.2	90.6	85.8	**58.7**	84.9	78.7

Table 16: Task B: TempEval-2 test set (Spanish).

Table 16 shows event extraction performance in TE2 test set. TIPSemB-F and TIPSem obtained a similar performance. TIPSemB-F performed better in extraction and TIPSem better in attribute classification.

7 Conclusion

In this paper, we described the TempEval-3 task within the SemEval 2013 exercise. This task involves identifying temporal expressions (timexes), events and their temporal relations in text. In particular participating systems were required to automatically annotate raw text using TimeML annotation scheme

This is the first time end-to-end systems are evaluated with a new single score (temporal awareness). In TempEval-3 participants had to obtain temporal relations from their own extracted timexes and events which is a very challenging task and was the ultimate evaluation aim of TempEval. It was proposed at TempEval-1 but has not been carried out until this edition.

The newly-introduced silver data proved not so useful for timex extraction or relation classification, but did help with event extraction. The new single-measure helped to rank systems easily.

Future work could investigate temporal annotation in specific applications. Current annotations metrics evaluate relations for entities in the same consecutive sentence. For document-level understanding we need to understand discourse and pragmatic information. Temporal question answering-based evaluation (UzZaman et al., 2012a) can help us to evaluate participants on document level temporal information understanding without creating any additional training data. Also, summarisation, machine translation, and information retrieval need temporal annotation. Application-oriented challenges could further research in these areas.

From a TimeML point of view, we still haven't tackled subordinate relations (TimeML SLINKs), aspectual relations (TimeML ALINKs), or temporal signal annotation (Derczynski and Gaizauskas, 2011). The critical questions of which links to annotate, and whether the current set of temporal relation types are appropriate for linguistic annotation, are still unanswered.

Acknowledgments

We thank the participants – especially Steven Bethard, Jannik Strötgen, Nate Chambers, Oleksandr Kolomiyets, Michele Filannino, Philippe Muller and others – who helped us to improve TempEval-3 with their valuable feedback. The third author also thanks Aarhus University, Denmark who kindly provided facilities.

References

J. F. Allen. 1983. Maintaining knowledge about temporal intervals. *Communications of the ACM*, 26(11):832–843.

S. Bethard, J. H. Martin, and S. Klingenstein. 2007. Timelines from text: Identication of syntactic temporal relations. In *Proceedings of IEEE International Conference on Semantic Computing*.

H. Cunningham, V. Tablan, A. Roberts, and K. Bontcheva. 2013. Getting More Out of Biomedical Documents with GATE's Full Lifecycle Open Source Text Analytics. *PLoS computational biology*, 9(2):e1002854.

L. Derczynski and R. Gaizauskas. 2010. Analysing Temporally Annotated Corpora with CAVaT. In *Proceedings of the 7th International Conference on Language Resources and Evaluation*, pages 398–404.

L. Derczynski and R. Gaizauskas. 2011. A Corpus-based Study of Temporal Signals. In *Proceedings of the 6th Corpus Linguistics Conference*.

L. Derczynski, H. Llorens, and N. UzZaman. 2013. TimeML-strict: clarifying temporal annotation. *CoRR*, abs/1304.

G. Hripcsak and A. S. Rothschild. 2005. Agreement, the f-measure, and reliability in information retrieval. *Journal of the American Medical Informatics Association*, 12(3):296–298.

H. Llorens, E. Saquete, and B. Navarro. 2010. TIPSem (English and Spanish): Evaluating CRFs and Semantic Roles in TempEval-2. In *Proceedings of the 5th International Workshop on Semantic Evaluation*, pages 284–291. Association for Computational Linguistics.

H. Llorens, N. UzZaman, and J. Allen. 2012a. Merging Temporal Annotations. In *Proceedings of the TIME Conference*.

H. Llorens, E. Saquete, and B. Navarro-Colorado. 2012b. Automatic system for identifying and categorizing temporal relations in natural language. *International Journal of Intelligent Systems*, 27(7):680–703.

H. Llorens, E. Saquete, and B. Navarro-Colorado. 2013. Applying Semantic Knowledge to the Automatic Processing of Temporal Expressions and Events in Natural Language. *Information Processing & Management*, 49(1):179–197.

L. Padró and E. Stanilovsky. 2012. Freeling 3.0: Towards wider multilinguality. In *Proceedings of the Language Resources and Evaluation Conference (LREC 2012)*, Istanbul, Turkey, May. ELRA.

R. Parker, D. Graff, J. Kong, K. Chen, and K. Maeda. 2011. English Gigaword Fifth Edition. LDC catalog ref. LDC2011T07.

J. Pustejovsky, P. Hanks, R. Saurí, A. See, R. Gaizauskas, A. Setzer, D. Radev, B. Sundheim, D. Day, L. Ferro, et al. 2003. The TimeBank corpus. In *Corpus Linguistics*.

J. Pustejovsky, B. Ingria, R. Saurí, J. Castano, J. Littman, R. Gaizauskas, A. Setzer, G. Katz, and I. Mani. 2005. The specification language TimeML. *The Language of Time: A reader*, pages 545–557.

R. Saurí and T. Badia. 2012. Spanish TimeBank 1.0. LDC catalog ref. LDC2012T12.

R. Saurí, J. Littman, B. Knippen, R. Gaizauskas, A. Setzer, and J. Pustejovsky. 2006. TimeML Annotation Guidelines Version 1.2.1.

M. Taulé, M. A. Martı, and M. Recasens. 2008. Ancora: Multilevel annotated corpora for catalan and spanish. In *Proceedings of the 6th International Conference on Language Resources and Evaluation (LREC-2008)*.

N. UzZaman and J. Allen. 2010. TRIPS and TRIOS system for TempEval-2: Extracting temporal information from text. In *Proceedings of the 5th International Workshop on Semantic Evaluation*, pages 276–283. Association for Computational Linguistics.

N. UzZaman and J. Allen. 2011. Temporal Evaluation. In *Proceedings of The 49th Annual Meeting of the Association for Computational Linguistics: Human Language Technologies*.

N. UzZaman, H. Llorens, and J. Allen. 2012a. Evaluating temporal information understanding with temporal question answering. In *Proceedings of IEEE International Conference on Semantic Computing*.

N. UzZaman, H. Llorens, J. F. Allen, L. Derczynski, M. Verhagen, and J. Pustejovsky. 2012b. TempEval-3: Evaluating Events, Time Expressions, and Temporal Relations. *CoRR*, abs/1206.5333.

N. UzZaman. 2012. *Interpreting the Temporal Aspects of Language*. Ph.D. thesis, University of Rochester, Rochester, NY.

M. Verhagen, R. Gaizauskas, F. Schilder, M. Hepple, J. Moszkowicz, and J. Pustejovsky. 2009. The TempEval challenge: identifying temporal relations in text. *Language Resources and Evaluation*, 43(2):161–179.

M. Verhagen, R. Saurí, T. Caselli, and J. Pustejovsky. 2010. SemEval-2010 task 13: TempEval-2. In *Proceedings of the 5th International Workshop on Semantic Evaluation*, pages 57–62. Association for Computational Linguistics.

ClearTK-TimeML: A minimalist approach to TempEval 2013

Steven Bethard
Center for Computational Language and Education Research
University of Colorado Boulder
Boulder, Colorado 80309-0594, USA
steven.bethard@colorado.edu

Abstract

The ClearTK-TimeML submission to TempEval 2013 competed in all English tasks: identifying events, identifying times, and identifying temporal relations. The system is a pipeline of machine-learning models, each with a small set of features from a simple morpho-syntactic annotation pipeline, and where temporal relations are only predicted for a small set of syntactic constructions and relation types. ClearTK-TimeML ranked 1st for temporal relation F1, time extent strict F1 and event tense accuracy.

1 Introduction

The TempEval shared tasks (Verhagen et al., 2007; Verhagen et al., 2010; UzZaman et al., 2013) have been one of the key venues for researchers to compare methods for temporal information extraction. In TempEval 2013, systems are asked to identify events, times and temporal relations in unstructured text.

This paper describes the ClearTK-TimeML system submitted to TempEval 2013. This system is based off of the ClearTK framework for machine learning (Ogren et al., 2008)[1], and decomposes TempEval 2013 into a series of sub-tasks, each of which is formulated as a machine-learning classification problem. The goals of the ClearTK-TimeML approach were:

- To use a small set of simple features that can be derived from either tokens, part-of-speech tags or syntactic constituency parses.
- To restrict temporal relation classification to a subset of constructions and relation types for which the models are most confident.

Thus, each classifier in the ClearTK-TimeML pipeline uses only the features shared by successful models in previous work (Bethard and Martin, 2006; Bethard and Martin, 2007; Llorens et al., 2010; UzZaman and Allen, 2010) that can be derived from a simple morpho-syntactic annotation pipeline[2]. And each of the temporal relation classifiers is restricted to a particular syntactic construction and to a particular set of temporal relation labels. The following sections describe the models, classifiers and datasets behind the ClearTK-TimeML approach.

2 Time models

Time extent identification was modeled as a BIO token-chunking task, where each token in the text is classified as being at the B(eginning) of, I(nside) of, or O(utside) of a time expression. The following features were used to characterize tokens:

- The token's text
- The token's stem
- The token's part-of-speech
- The unicode character categories for each character of the token, with repeats merged (e.g. *Dec28* would be 'LuLlNd')
- The temporal type of each alphanumeric sub-token, derived from a 58-word gazetteer of time words
- All of the above features for the preceding 3 and following 3 tokens

Time type identification was modeled as a multi-class classification task, where each time is classified

[1] http://cleartk.googlecode.com/

[2] OpenNLP sentence segmenter, ClearTK PennTreebankTokenizer, Apache Lucene Snowball stemmer, OpenNLP part-of-speech tagger, and OpenNLP constituency parser

*Second Joint Conference on Lexical and Computational Semantics (*SEM), Volume 2: Seventh International Workshop on Semantic Evaluation (SemEval 2013)*, pages 10–14, Atlanta, Georgia, June 14-15, 2013.

as DATE, TIME, DURATION or SET. The following features were used to characterize times:

- The text of all tokens in the time expression
- The text of the last token in the time expression
- The unicode character categories for each character of the token, with repeats merged
- The temporal type of each alphanumeric sub-token, derived from a 58-word gazetteer of time words

Time value identification was not modeled by the system. Instead, the TimeN time normalization system (Llorens et al., 2012) was used.

3 Event models

Event extent identification, like time extent identification, was modeled as BIO token chunking. The following features were used to characterize tokens:

- The token's text
- The token's stem
- The token's part-of-speech
- The syntactic category of the token's parent in the constituency tree
- The text of the first sibling of the token in the constituency tree
- The text of the preceding 3 and following 3 tokens

Event aspect identification was modeled as a multi-class classification task, where each event is classified as PROGRESSIVE, PERFECTIVE, PERFECTIVE-PROGRESSIVE or NONE. The following features were used to characterize events:

- The part-of-speech tags of all tokens in the event
- The text of any verbs in the preceding 3 tokens

Event class identification was modeled as a multi-class classification task, where each event is classified as OCCURRENCE, PERCEPTION, REPORTING, ASPECTUAL, STATE, I-STATE or I-ACTION. The following features were used to characterize events:

- The stems of all tokens in the event
- The part-of-speech tags of all tokens in the event

Event modality identification was modeled as a multi-class classification task, where each event is classified as one of WOULD, COULD, CAN, etc. The following features were used to characterize events:

- The text of any prepositions, adverbs or modal verbs in the preceding 3 tokens

Event polarity identification was modeled as a binary classification task, where each event is classified as POS or NEG. The following features were used to characterize events:

- The text of any adverbs in the preceding 3 tokens

Event tense identification was modeled as a multi-class classification task, where each event is classified as FUTURE, INFINITIVE, PAST, PASTPART, PRESENT, PRESPART or NONE. The following features were used to characterize events:

- The last two characters of the event
- The part-of-speech tags of all tokens in the event
- The text of any prepositions, verbs or modal verbs in the preceding 3 tokens

4 Temporal relation models

Three different models, described below, were trained for temporal relation identification. All models followed a multi-class classification approach, pairing an event and a time or an event and an event, and trying to predict a temporal relation type (BEFORE, AFTER, INCLUDES, etc.) or NORELATION if there was no temporal relation between the pair.

While the training and evaluation data allowed for 14 possible relation types, each of the temporal relation models was restricted to a subset of relations, with all other relations mapped to the NORELATION type. The subset of relations for each model was selected by inspecting the confusion matrix of the model's errors on the training data, and removing relations that were frequently confused and whose removal improved performance on the training data.

Event to document creation time relations were classified by considering (event, time) pairs where each event in the text was paired with the document creation time. The classifier was restricted to the relations BEFORE, AFTER and INCLUDES. The following features were used to characterize such relations:

- The event's aspect (as classified above)
- The event's class (as classified above)
- The event's modality (as classified above)
- The event's polarity (as classified above)
- The event's tense (as classified above)
- The text of the event, only if the event was identified as having class ASPECTUAL

Event to same sentence time relations were classified by considering (event, time) pairs where the syntactic path from event to time matched a regular expression of syntactic categories and up/down movements through the tree: ^((NP|PP|ADVP)↑)* ((VP|SBAR|S)↑)* (S|SBAR|VP|NP) (↓(VP|SBAR|S))* (↓(NP|PP|ADVP))*$. The classifier relations were restricted to INCLUDES and IS-INCLUDED. The following features were used to characterize such relations:

- The event's class (as classified above)
- The event's tense (as classified above)
- The text of any prepositions or verbs in the 5 tokens following the event
- The time's type (as classified above)
- The text of all tokens in the time expression
- The text of any prepositions or verbs in the 5 tokens preceding the time expression

Event to same sentence event relations were classified by considering (event, event) pairs where the syntactic path from one event to the other matched ^((VP↑|ADJP↑|NP↑)? (VP|ADJP|S|SBAR) (↓(S|SBAR|PP))* ((↓VP|↓ADJP)*|(↓NP)*)$. The classifier relations were restricted to BEFORE and AFTER. The following features were used to characterize such relations:

- The aspect (as classified above) for each event
- The class (as classified above) for each event
- The tense (as classified above) for each event
- The text of the first child of the grandparent of the event in the constituency tree, for each event
- The path through the syntactic constituency tree from one event to the other
- The tokens appearing between the two events

5 Classifiers

The above models described the translation from TempEval tasks to classification problems and classifier features. For BIO token-chunking problems, Mallet[3] conditional random fields and LIBLINEAR[4] support vector machines and logistic regression were applied. For the other problems, LIBLINEAR, Mallet MaxEnt and OpenNLP MaxEnt[5] were applied. All classifiers have hyper-parameters that must be tuned during training – LIBLINEAR has the classifier type and the cost parameter, Mallet CRF has the iteration count and the Gaussian prior variance, etc.[6]

The best classifier for each training data set was selected via a grid search over classifiers and parameter settings. The grid of parameters was manually selected to provide several reasonable values for each classifier parameter. Each (classifier, parameters) point on the grid was evaluated with a 2-fold cross validation on the training data, and the best performing (classifier, parameters) was selected as the final model to run on the TempEval 2013 test set.

6 Data sets

The classifiers were trained using the following sources of training data:

TB The TimeBank event, time and relation annotations, as provided by the TempEval organizers.

AQ The AQUAINT event, time and relation annotations, as provided by the TempEval organizers.

SLV The "Silver" event, time and relation annotations, from the TempEval organizers' system.

BMK The verb-clause temporal relation annotations of (Bethard et al., 2007). These relations are added on top of the original relations.

PM The temporal relations inferred via closure on the TimeBank and AQUAINT data by Philippe Muller[7]. These relations replace the original ones, except in files where no relations were inferred (because of temporal inconsistencies).

7 Results

Table 1 shows the performance of the ClearTK-TimeML models across the different tasks when trained on different sets of training data. The "Data" column of each row indicates both the training data sources (as in Section 6), and whether the events and times were predicted by the models ("system") or taken from the annotators ("human"). Performance is reported in terms of strict precision (P), Recall (R) and F1 for event extents, time extents and temporal relations, and in terms of Accuracy (A) on the correctly identified extents for event and time attributes.

[3]http://mallet.cs.umass.edu/

[4]http://www.csie.ntu.edu.tw/~cjlin/liblinear/

[5]http://opennlp.apache.org/

[6]For BIO token-chunking tasks, LIBLINEAR also had a parameter for how many previous classifications to use as features.

[7]https://groups.google.com/d/topic/tempeval/LJNQKwYHgL8

Data		Event						Time					Relation		
annotation	events	extent			class	tense	aspect	extent			value	type	type		
sources	& times	F1	P	R	A	A	A	F1	P	R	A	A	F1	P	R
TB+BMK	system	77.3	81.9	73.3	84.6	**80.4**	91.0	**82.7**	85.9	79.7	71.7	93.3	**31.0**	34.1	28.4
TB	system	77.3	81.9	73.3	84.6	**80.4**	91.0	**82.7**	85.9	79.7	71.7	93.3	29.8	**34.5**	26.2
TB+AQ	system	78.8	81.4	76.4	86.1	78.2	90.9	77.0	83.2	71.7	69.9	92.9	28.6	30.9	26.6
TB+AQ+PM	system	78.8	81.4	76.4	86.1	78.2	90.9	77.0	83.2	71.7	69.9	92.9	28.5	29.7	27.3
*TB+AQ+SLV	system	80.5	**82.1**	78.9	88.4	71.6	91.2	80.0	**91.6**	71.0	73.6	91.5	27.8	26.5	29.3
Highest in TempEval		81.1	82.0	80.8	89.2	80.4	91.8	82.7	91.4	80.4	86.0	93.7	31.0	34.5	34.4
TB+BMK	human	-	-	-	-	-	-	-	-	-	-	-	**36.3**	37.3	35.2
TB	human	-	-	-	-	-	-	-	-	-	-	-	35.2	**37.6**	33.0
TB+AQ	human	-	-	-	-	-	-	-	-	-	-	-	34.1	33.3	35.0
TB+AQ+PM	human	-	-	-	-	-	-	-	-	-	-	-	35.9	35.2	36.6
*TB+AQ+SLV	human	-	-	-	-	-	-	-	-	-	-	-	**37.7**	34.9	41.0
Highest in TempEval		-	-	-	-	-	-	-	-	-	-	-	36.3	37.6	65.6

Table 1: Performance across different training data. Systems marked with * were tested after the official evaluation. Scores in bold are at least as high as the highest in TempEval.

Training on the AQUAINT (AQ) data in addition to the TimeBank (TB) hurt times and relations. Adding the AQUAINT data caused a -2.7 drop in extent precision, a -8.0 drop in extent recall, a -1.8 drop in value accuracy and a -0.4 drop in type accuracy, and a -3.6 to -4.3 drop in relation recall.

Training on the "Silver" (SLV) data in addition to TB+AQ data gave mixed results. There were big gains for time extent precision (+8.4), time value accuracy (+3.7), event extent recall (+2.5) and event class accuracy (+2.3), but a big drop for event tense accuracy (-6.6). Relation recall improved (+2.7 with system events and times, +6.0 with manual) but precision varied (-4.4 with system, +1.6 with manual).

Adding verb-clause relations (BMK) and closure-inferred relations (PM) increased recall but lowered precision. With system-annotated events and times, the change was +2.2/-0.4 (recall/precision) for verb-clause relations, and +0.7/-1.2 for closure-inferred relations. With manually-annotated events and times, the change was +2.2/-0.3 for verb-clause relations, and (the one exception where recall improved) +1.5/+1.9 for closure-inferred relations.

8 Discussion

Overall, the ClearTK-TimeML ranked 1st in relation F1, time extent strict F1 and event tense accuracy.

Analysis across the different ClearTK-TimeML runs showed that including annotations from the AQUAINT corpus hurt model performance across a variety of tasks. A manual inspection of the AQUAINT corpus revealed many annotation errors, suggesting that the drop may be the result of attempting to learn from inconsistent training data. The AQUAINT corpus may thus have to be partially re-annotated to be useful as a training corpus.

Analysis also showed that adding more relation annotations increased recall, typically at the cost of precision, even though the added annotations were highly accurate: (Bethard et al., 2007) reported agreement of 90%, and temporal closure relations were 100% deterministic from the already-annotated relations. One would expect that adding such high-quality relations would only improve performance. But not all temporal relations were annotated by the TempEval 2013 annotators, so the system could be marked wrong for a finding a true temporal relation that was not noticed by the annotators. Further analysis is necessary to investigate this hypothesis.

Acknowledgements

Thanks to Philippe Muller for providing the closure-inferred relations. The project described was supported in part by Grant Number R01LM010090 from the National Library Of Medicine. The content is solely the responsibility of the authors and does not necessarily represent the official views of the National Library Of Medicine or the National Institutes of Health.

References

[Bethard and Martin2006] Steven Bethard and James H. Martin. 2006. Identification of event mentions and their semantic class. In *Empirical Methods in Natural Language Processing (EMNLP)*, page 146154. (Acceptance rate 31%).

[Bethard and Martin2007] Steven Bethard and James H. Martin. 2007. CU-TMP: temporal relation classification using syntactic and semantic features. In *Proceedings of the 4th International Workshop on Semantic Evaluations*, pages 129–132, Prague, Czech Republic. Association for Computational Linguistics.

[Bethard et al.2007] Steven Bethard, James H. Martin, and Sara Klingenstein. 2007. Finding temporal structure in text: Machine learning of syntactic temporal relations. *International Journal of Semantic Computing*, 01(04):441.

[Llorens et al.2010] Hector Llorens, Estela Saquete, and Borja Navarro. 2010. TIPSem (English and Spanish): Evaluating CRFs and semantic roles in TempEval-2. In *Proceedings of the 5th International Workshop on Semantic Evaluation*, page 284291, Uppsala, Sweden, July. Association for Computational Linguistics.

[Llorens et al.2012] Hector Llorens, Leon Derczynski, Robert Gaizauskas, and Estela Saquete. 2012. TIMEN: an open temporal expression normalisation resource. In *Proceedings of the Eight International Conference on Language Resources and Evaluation (LREC'12)*, Istanbul, Turkey, May. European Language Resources Association (ELRA).

[Ogren et al.2008] Philip V. Ogren, Philipp G. Wetzler, and Steven Bethard. 2008. ClearTK: A UIMA toolkit for statistical natural language processing. In *Towards Enhanced Interoperability for Large HLT Systems: UIMA for NLP workshop at Language Resources and Evaluation Conference (LREC)*, 5.

[UzZaman and Allen2010] Naushad UzZaman and James Allen. 2010. TRIPS and TRIOS system for TempEval-2: extracting temporal information from text. In *Proceedings of the 5th International Workshop on Semantic Evaluation*, page 276283, Uppsala, Sweden, July. Association for Computational Linguistics.

[UzZaman et al.2013] Naushad UzZaman, Hector Llorens, James F. Allen, Leon Derczynski, Marc Verhagen, and James Pustejovsky. 2013. SemEval-2013 task 1: TempEval-3 evaluating time expressions, events, and temporal relations. In *Proceedings of the 7th International Workshop on Semantic Evaluation (SemEval 2013), in conjunction with the Second Joint Conference on Lexical and Computational Semantcis (*SEM 2013)*. Association for Computational Linguistics, June.

[Verhagen et al.2007] Marc Verhagen, Robert Gaizauskas, Frank Schilder, Mark Hepple, Graham Katz, and James Pustejovsky. 2007. SemEval-2007 task 15: TempEval temporal relation identification. In *Proceedings of the 4th International Workshop on Semantic Evaluations*, pages 75–80, Prague, Czech Republic. Association for Computational Linguistics.

[Verhagen et al.2010] Marc Verhagen, Roser Sauri, Tommaso Caselli, and James Pustejovsky. 2010. SemEval-2010 task 13: TempEval-2. In *Proceedings of the 5th International Workshop on Semantic Evaluation*, page 5762, Uppsala, Sweden, July. Association for Computational Linguistics.

HeidelTime: Tuning English and Developing Spanish Resources for TempEval-3

Jannik Strötgen Julian Zell Michael Gertz
Institute of Computer Science, Heidelberg University
Im Neuenheimer Feld 348, 69120 Heidelberg, Germany
{stroetgen,gertz}@uni-hd.de, j.zell@stud.uni-heidelberg.de

Abstract

In this paper, we describe our participation in the TempEval-3 challenge. With our multilingual temporal tagger HeidelTime, we addressed task A, the extraction and normalization of temporal expressions for English and Spanish. Exploiting HeidelTime's strict separation between source code and language-dependent parts, we tuned HeidelTime's existing English resources and developed new Spanish resources. For both languages, we achieved the best results among all participants for task A, the combination of extraction and normalization. Both the improved English and the new Spanish resources are publicly available with HeidelTime.

1 Introduction

The task of temporal annotation, which is addressed in the TempEval-3 challenge, consists of three subtasks: (A) the extraction and normalization of temporal expressions, (B) event extraction, and (C) the annotation of temporal relations (UzZaman et al., 2012). This makes sub-task A, i.e., temporal tagging, a prerequisite for the full task of temporal annotating documents. In addition, temporal tagging is important for many further natural language processing and understanding tasks, and can also be exploited for search and exploration scenarios in information retrieval (Alonso et al., 2011).

In the context of the TempEval-2 challenge (Verhagen et al., 2010), we developed our temporal tagger HeidelTime (Strötgen and Gertz, 2010), which achieved the best results for the extraction and normalization of temporal expressions for English documents. For our work on multilingual information retrieval (e.g., Strötgen et al. (2011)), we extended HeidelTime with a focus on supporting the simple integration of further languages (Strötgen and Gertz, 2012a). For TempEval-3, we now tuned HeidelTime's English resources and developed new Spanish resources to address both languages that are part of TempEval-3. As the evaluation results demonstrate, HeidelTime outperforms the systems of all other participants for the full task of temporal tagging by achieving high quality results for the extraction and normalization for English and Spanish.

The remainder of the paper is structured as follows: We explain HeidelTime's system architecture in Section 2. Section 3 covers the tuning of HeidelTime's English and the development of the Spanish resources. Finally, we discuss the evaluation results in Section 4, and conclude the paper in Section 5.

2 HeidelTime

HeidelTime is a multilingual, cross-domain temporal tagger. So far, it can process English, German, and Dutch text. In previous work, we analyzed domain-dependent challenges and demonstrated that domain-sensitive strategies for normalizing temporal expressions result in significant normalization improvements when switching between news- and narrative-style documents (Strötgen and Gertz, 2012b). Although TempEval-3 only addresses news documents, the tuned English and new Spanish resources can be used to process news and also narrative-style documents such as Wikipedia articles with high extraction and normalization quality.

*Second Joint Conference on Lexical and Computational Semantics (*SEM), Volume 2: Seventh International Workshop on Semantic Evaluation (SemEval 2013)*, pages 15–19, Atlanta, Georgia, June 14-15, 2013. ©2013 Association for Computational Linguistics

Architecture of HeidelTime. HeidelTime is a rule-based system with a strict separation between source code and language-dependent resources. While the strategies for processing different domains are part of the source code, resources consist of files for (i) patterns, (ii) normalizations, and (iii) rules. They are read by HeidelTime's resource interpreter and thus have to be developed based on HeidelTime's well-defined rule syntax.

The pattern files contain words and phrases, which are typically used to express temporal expressions, e.g., names of months. The normalization files contain normalization information about the patterns, e.g., the value of a specific month's name. Finally, the rule files contain rules for date, time, duration, and set expressions.

All rules have an extraction part and a normalization part. The extraction part, in which the pattern resources can be used for generalization, defines the expressions that have to be matched in a document. The normalization part normalizes the context-independent content of the expression using the normalization resources. While explicit temporal expressions (e.g., *May 1st, 2013*) can directly be fully normalized, underspecified (*November*) and relative (*today, two weeks ago*) expressions can only be normalized in an underspecified manner. The full normalization depends on the domain of the document that is to be processed and the context of the expression. For this, HeidelTime applies domain-sensitive strategies to normalize such expressions during its disambiguation phase, which is called after the extraction and the normalization phases.

The TempEval-3 data is from the news domain. Here, HeidelTime usually uses the document creation time as reference time. The temporal relation to it is identified based on the tense in the sentence.[1]

Preprocessing. HeidelTime requires sentence, token, and part-of-speech information. For this, the TreeTagger (Schmid, 1994) is used. Since there is a Spanish model for the TreeTagger, adding Spanish preprocessing capabilities to HeidelTime was fairly easy. A wrapper for the TreeTagger is also part of the UIMA HeidelTime kit described next.

[1]For further details on HeidelTime's rule syntax, its domain-dependent normalization strategies, and its architecture in general, we refer to Strötgen and Gertz (2012a).

UIMA HeidelTime kit. For processing TempEval-3 data, we used the UIMA version of HeidelTime, developed a collection reader and a CAS consumer to read and write TempEval-3 input and output data, and added both components to our UIMA HeidelTime kit. This makes HeidelTime's evaluation results reproducible on the training and test sets.

3 HeidelTime for TempEval-3

In TempEval-3, we participated with one Spanish and three English runs: For Spanish, we used our newly developed resources. For English, we used (i) HeidelTime 1.2, which was released in May 2012, (ii) a version containing several bug fixes and improvements, which were implemented independently from TempEval-3, and (iii) HeidelTime with its new English resources tuned for TempEval-3.

In general, our goal when developing HeidelTime resources is to achieve high quality normalization results. Thus, we only want to extract temporal expressions which can be normalized correctly with high probability – an issue, which will be further looked at in the discussion in the evaluation section. Before that, we next describe language-independent adaptations to HeidelTime. Then, we present the tuning of the English resources (Section 3.2) and the development of the Spanish resources (Section 3.3).

3.1 General HeidelTime Adaptations

We performed the following language-independent changes to HeidelTime:

(i) Weekday normalization: In news-style documents, extracted weekdays that are equal to the weekday of the document creation time (dct) are now normalized to the date of the dct independent of the tense in the sentence.

(ii) Century/decade normalization: So far, decade and century expressions were not correctly normalized by HeidelTime according to TimeML, e.g., "199X" instead of "199" for "the 1990s".

The first change is based on the intuitive assumption that information in news-style documents is temporally focused around the dct. In addition, this assumption is supported by the English and the Spanish training data. The second change is related to the annotation standard. Both changes can thus be generalized in a language-independent manner.

3.2 Tuning HeidelTime's English Resources

Three training corpora were provided by the organizers: the Aquaint and TimeBank gold standard corpora, and a large corpus referred to as silver standard, which was created by merging results of three tools (Llorens et al., 2012). After a brief analysis, we decided not to use the silver standard due to the rather low annotation quality. Motivated by observations in the gold standard corpora, we performed the following English-specific modifications in addition to the general adaptations described above:

(i) REF-value expressions: expressions normalized to past, present, or future are not consistently annotated in the training data. Since such expressions are rather less valuable for further tasks and to avoid false positives, we removed some of those patterns from the resources.

(ii) Ambiguous expressions: We added negative rules for expressions such as *may*, *march*, and *fall* to filter them out if they do not refer to a date.

(iii) Article/modifier: We allowed some more combinations of articles and modifiers.

Note that HeidelTime was already a state-of-the-art tool for English temporal tagging so that the changes are rather minor.

3.3 Developing Spanish Resources

In this section, we explain the resource development process for Spanish. Then, we detail language-specific challenges we faced during this process.

Resource Development Process. So far, there were no HeidelTime resources for Spanish, and we thus started the development from scratch.

(i) Preprocessing: As mentioned in Section 2, we use the TreeTagger with its Spanish module for sentence, token, and part-of-speech annotation.

(ii) Translation of pattern files: Starting with HeidelTime's English pattern resources, we developed the Spanish pattern resources. The goal was that all patterns that are frequently used to express temporal expressions are included in the resources. Note that it is not important that the patterns are context independent. The context in which a pattern should occur can be defined within the rules.

(iii) Translation of normalization files: Similar to the patterns, we translated the English normalization files and adapted them to the new Spanish patterns.

(iv) Rule Development: Based on the English rules for dates, times, durations, and sets, we developed similar Spanish rules. Using the Spanish training corpus to check for partially matching patterns, false positives, false negatives, and incorrect normalizations, we then iteratively adapted the rules, but also the pattern and normalization resources.

Challenges. Spanish as a Romance language is rich in inflection. Nouns, adjectives, and determiners are inflected with respect to number and gender. During the development of the pattern and normalization resources, this had to be taken into account.

As for nouns, there are many inflection forms of verbs in Spanish, e.g., to represent tense. While verbs are usually not part of temporal expressions, the inflection of verbs has to be considered for the normalization of ambiguous expressions such as *el lunes* (Monday) or *junio* (June). As mentioned above, in news-style documents, HeidelTime uses the tense of the sentence to determine the relation to the reference time, i.e., to decide whether the expression refers to a previous or upcoming date.

The tense is determined using part-of-speech information, and, if necessary, pattern information of words with specific part-of-speech tags. For each language, this information is defined in the pattern resources. Unfortunately, the Spanish tag-set of the TreeTagger module does not contain tags covering tense information, e.g., all finite lexical verbs are tagged as VLfin. Thus, we created regular expression patterns to match typical inflection patterns representing tense information and check words tagged as verbs by the tagger for these patterns.

However, due to the ambiguity of the Spanish inflection, we can only add patterns to detect future tense. If no tense is identified, the year is set to the year of the reference time. As detailed in the discussion of the evaluation results described in Section 4, identifying the correct relation to the reference time is a frequent source of normalization errors.

4 Evaluation Results

Measures. For the extraction task, precision (P), recall (R), and f_1-score (F1) are used for strict and relaxed matching. The value F1 and type F1 measures combine relaxed matching with correct normalization. Systems are ranked by value F1 (value).

	strict match			relaxed match			normalization	
a) Aquaint	P	R	F1	P	R	F1	**value**	type
tuned	80.17	81.69	80.92	90.85	92.57	91.7	72.37	83.32
bug-fixed	77.56	81.17	79.32	88.28	92.40	90.30	70.21	82.03
1.2	73.32	81.17	77.05	83.46	92.40	87.70	67.87	79.67
b) TimeBank	P	R	F1	P	R	F1	**value**	type
tuned	85.39	84.15	84.76	92.16	90.83	91.49	79.01	88.74
bug-fixed	83.17	82.70	82.94	90.86	90.35	90.60	76.24	87.78
1.2	82.89	82.62	82.76	90.72	90.43	90.57	76.39	87.75
c) Spanish	P	R	F1	P	R	F1	**value**	type
new	90.53	81.26	85.65	96.23	86.38	91.04	84.10	89.40

Table 1: Results on training data ranked by *value F1*.

	strict match			relaxed match			normalization	
a) English	P	R	F1	P	R	F1	**value**	type
tuned	83.85	78.99	81.34	93.08	87.68	90.30	**77.61**	82.09
bug-fixed	80.77	76.09	78.36	90.00	84.78	87.31	72.39	79.10
1.2	80.15	76.09	78.07	89.31	84.78	86.99	72.12	78.81
next best*	78.72	80.43	79.57	89.36	91.30	90.32	70.97	80.29
b) Spanish	P	R	F1	P	R	F1	**value**	type
HeidelTime	90.91	80.40	85.33	96.02	84.92	90.13	**85.33**	87.47
TipSemB	88.51	77.39	82.57	93.68	81.91	87.40	71.85	82.04
jrc-1/2	65.83	39.70	49.53	86.67	52.26	65.20	50.78	62.70

Table 2: TempEval-3 task A evaluation results ranked by *value F1* (* next best: NavyTime).

Results on Training Data. Table 1 shows the results on the Aquaint (a), TimeBank (b), and Spanish training corpora (c). On both English corpora, HeidelTime's TempEval-3 tuned version outperforms the other two versions. The big differences between the two English corpora are rather due to the better annotation quality of TimeBank than due to different challenges in the documents of the two corpora.

TempEval-3 Evaluation. The evaluation results on the test data are presented in Table 2. For English, HeidelTime's TempEval-3 tuned version achieves the best results, and all three HeidelTime versions outperform the systems of the eight other participating teams with a total number of 21 submissions (task A ranking measure *value F1*). For comparison, the results of the next best system (NavyTime) is listed in Table 2(a). For Spanish, we highly outperform the other two systems, as shown in Table 2(b).

Discussion. In order to be able to interpret HeidelTime's results on the training and test data, we performed an error analysis (TimeBank and Spanish training corpus). The most important findings are:

(i) For a rule-based system, HeidelTime's recall is relatively low (many false negatives; FN). However, note that several FN are intentional. 55% and 29% of 117 and 149 FN in the English and Spanish training corpora are due to imprecise expressions (*some time*; *the latest period*). These are difficult to normalize correctly, e.g., *some time* can refer to seconds or years. To guarantee high quality normalization, we do not extract expressions that cannot be normalized correctly with high probability.

(ii) There is a trade-off between precision and recall due to expressions referring to past, present, or future (X_REF). These are annotated either only in some contexts or inconsistently throughout the training data, and thus result in FN (21%/en; 34%/es) and false positives (43% of 98 FP in English training and 43%/es of 35 FP in Spanish training corpora).

(iii) The main sources for incorrect value normalization of underspecified expressions (*Feb. 1*; *Monday*) are wrongly detected reference times or relations to them (e.g., due to wrong tense identification), annotation errors in the corpora (e.g., *last week* annotated as WXX instead of the week it is referring to), granularity errors (e.g., *a year ago* can refer to a day, month, quarter, or year), and ambiguities (e.g., *the year* can be a duration or a specific year).

(iv) Some expressions in the Spanish test set were extracted and normalized correctly although no similar expressions exist in the Spanish training data. Here, the Spanish resources highly benefited from the high quality English resources as starting point of the development process, and from HeidelTime's language-independent normalization strategies.

(v) A reoccurring error in the English test set is that HeidelTime matches and normalizes expressions such as *two days earlier* while only *two days* should be annotated according to TimeML. This results in a relaxed match with false type and value.

5 Conclusions & Ongoing Work

In this paper, we presented HeidelTime's results in the TempEval-3 temporal tagging task. For both languages, English and Spanish, we achieved the best results of all participants (value F1). We showed that adding a new language to HeidelTime can result in high quality temporal tagging of the new language.

Currently, we are working on improving the Spanish tense detection to better normalize underspecified temporal expressions. Furthermore, we will make available HeidelTime resources for Arabic, Italian, and Vietnamese (HeidelTime, 2013).

References

Omar Alonso, Jannik Strötgen, Ricardo Baeza-Yates, and Michael Gertz. 2011. Temporal Information Retrieval: Challenges and Opportunities. In *Proceedings of the 1st International Temporal Web Analytics Workshop (TWAW 2011)*, pages 1–8.

HeidelTime. 2013. http://code.google.com/p/heideltime/.

Hector Llorens, Naushad UzZaman, and James F. Allen. 2012. Merging Temporal Annotations. In *19th International Symposium on Temporal Representation and Reasoning, TIME 2012*, pages 107–113.

Helmut Schmid. 1994. Probabilistic Part-of-Speech Tagging Using Decision Trees. In *Proceedings of the International Conference on New Methods in Language Processing*.

Jannik Strötgen and Michael Gertz. 2010. HeidelTime: High Quality Rule-Based Extraction and Normalization of Temporal Expressions. In *Proceedings of the 5th International Workshop on Semantic Evaluation (SemEval'10)*, pages 321–324.

Jannik Strötgen and Michael Gertz. 2012a. Multilingual and Cross-domain Temporal Tagging. *Language Resources and Evaluation*, Online first.

Jannik Strötgen and Michael Gertz. 2012b. Temporal Tagging on Different Domains: Challenges, Strategies, and Gold Standards. In *Proceedings of the 8th International Conference on Language Resources and Evaluation*, pages 3746–3753.

Jannik Strötgen, Michael Gertz, and Conny Junghans. 2011. An Event-centric Model for Multilingual Document Similarity. In *Proceeding of the 34rd International ACM SIGIR Conference on Research and Development in Information Retrieval (SIGIR'11)*, pages 953–962.

Naushad UzZaman, Hector Llorens, James F. Allen, Leon Derczynski, Marc Verhagen, and James Pustejovsky. 2012. TempEval-3: Evaluating Events, Time Expressions, and Temporal Relations. *CoRR*, abs/1206.5333.

Marc Verhagen, Roser Sauri, Tommaso Caselli, and James Pustejovsky. 2010. SemEval-2010 Task 13: TempEval-2. In *Proceedings of the 5th International Workshop on Semantic Evaluation (SemEval'10)*, pages 57–62.

ATT1: Temporal Annotation Using Big Windows and Rich Syntactic and Semantic Features

Hyuckchul Jung and **Amanda Stent**
AT&T Labs - Research
180 Park Ave
Florham Park, NJ 07932, USA
hjung, stent@research.att.com

Abstract

In this paper we present the results of experiments comparing (a) rich syntactic and semantic feature sets and (b) big context windows, for the TempEval time expression and event segmentation and classification tasks. We show that it is possible for models using only lexical features to approach the performance of models using rich syntactic and semantic feature sets.

1 Introduction

TempEval-3 Temporal Annotation Task (UzZaman et al., 2012) has three subtasks:

A *Time expression extraction and classification* - extract time expressions from input text, and determine the type and normalised value for each extracted time expression.

B *Event extraction and classification* - extract event mentions from input text, and determine the class, tense and aspect features for each extracted event.

C *Temporal link identification* - identify and categorise temporal links between events in the same or consecutive sentences, events and time expressions in the same sentence, and events and the document creation time of the input text.

Here we report results for the first two tasks.

Previous TempEval competitions have shown that rich syntactic and semantic feature sets can lead to good performance on event and time expression extraction and classification tasks (*e.g.* (Llorens et al., 2010; UzZaman and Allen, 2010)). In this work, we show that with large windows of context, it is possible for models using only lexical features to approach the performance of models using rich syntactic and semantic feature sets.

	Type	Files	EVENT	TIMEX
AQUAINT	gold	73	4431	579
TimeBank	gold	183	6698	1243
TE3-Silver	silver	2452	81329	12739

Table 1: Frequency of event and time expressions in the text portions of the TempEval-3 data sets

2 Data

Using the gold and silver data distributed by the TempEval-3 task organizers (see Table 1), we processed each input file with the Stanford CoreNLP (Stanford Natural Language Processing Group, 2012) and SENNA (Collobert et al., 2011) open-source NLP tools. From the Stanford CoreNLP tools we obtained a tokenization of the input text, the lemma and part of speech (POS) tag for each token, and dependency and constituency parses for each sentence. From SENNA, we obtained a semantic role labelling for each sentence.

3 Approach

We were curious to explore the tradeoff between additional context on the one hand, and additional layers of representation on the other, for the event and time expression extraction tasks. Researchers have investigated the impacts of different sets of features (Adafre and de Rijke, 2005; Angeli et al., 2012;

*Second Joint Conference on Lexical and Computational Semantics (*SEM), Volume 2: Seventh International Workshop on Semantic Evaluation (SemEval 2013)*, pages 20–24, Atlanta, Georgia, June 14-15, 2013.

Feature type	Features	Used in
Lexical 1	token	ATT1, ATT2, ATT3
Lexical 2	lemma	ATT1, ATT2
Part of speech	POS tag	ATT1, ATT2
Dependency	governing verb, governing verb POS, governing preposition, phrase tag, path to root of parse tree, head word, head word lemma, head word POS	ATT1, ATT2
Constituency parse	governing verb, governing verb POS, governing preposition, phrase tag, path to root of parse tree	ATT1, ATT2
Semantic role	semantic role label, semantic role labels along path to root of parse tree	ATT1

Table 2: Features used in our models

Tag type	Tags
time expression extraction tags	B_DATE, B_DURATION, B_SET, B_TIME, I_DATE, I_DURATION, I_SET, I_TIME, O
Event expression extraction tags	B_ACTION, B_ASPECTUAL, B_ACTION, B_OCCURRENCE, B_PERCEPTION, B_REPORTING, B_STATE, O
Event tense	FUTURE, INFINITIVE, PAST, PASTPART, PRESENT, PRESPART, NONE, O
Event aspect	PROGRESSIVE, PREFECTIVE_PROGRESSIVE, PERFECTIVE, NONE, O
Event polarity	NEG, POS
Event modality	'D, CAN, CLOSE, COULD, DELETE, HAVE TO, HAVE_TO, LIKELIHOOD, MAY, MIGHT, MUST, NONE, O, POSSIBLE, POTENTIAL, SHOULD, SHOULD HAVE TO, TO, UNLIKELY, UNTIL, WOULD, WOULD HAVE TO

Table 3: Tags assigned by our classifiers for TempEval-3 tasks A and B

Rigo and Lavelli, 2011). In particular, (Rigo and Lavelli, 2011) also examined performance based on different sizes of n-grams in a small scale (n=1,3).

In this work, we intended to systematically investigate the performance of various models with different layers of representation (based on much larger sets of rich syntactic/semantic features) as well as additional context. For each time expression/event segmentation/classification task, we trained twelve models exploring these two dimensions, three of which we submitted for TempEval-3.

Additional layers of representation We trained three types of model: (ATT1) STANFORD+SENNA, (ATT2) STANFORD and (ATT3) WORDS ONLY. The basic features used in each type of model are given in Table 2: ATT1 models include lexical, syntactic and semantic features, ATT2 models include only lexical and syntactic features, and ATT3 models include only lexical features. For the ATT1 models we had 18 basic features per token, for the ATT2 models we had 16 basic features per token, and for the ATT3 models we had one basic feature per token.

Additional context We experimented with context windows of 0, 1, 3, and 7 words preceding and following the token to be labeled (*i.e.* window sizes of 1, 3, 7, and 15). For each window size, we trained ATT1, ATT2 and ATT3 models. The ATT1 models had 18 basic features per token in the context window, for up to 15 tokens, so up to 270 basic features for each token to be labeled. The ATT2 models had 16 basic features per token in the context window, so up to 240 basic features for each token to be labeled. The ATT3 models had 1 basic feature per token in the context window, so up to 15 basic features for each token to be labeled.

Model training For event extraction and classification, time expression extraction and classification, and event feature classification, we used the machine learning toolkit LLAMA (Haffner, 2006). LLAMA encodes multiclass classification problems using binary MaxEnt classifiers to increase the speed of training and to scale the method to large data sets. We also used a front-end to LLAMA that builds unigram, bigram and trigram extended features from basic features; for example, from the basic feature "go there today", it would build the features "go", "there", "today", "go there", "there today", and "go there today". We grouped our basic features (see Table 2) by type rather than by token, and the LLAMA front-end then produced ngram features. We chose LLAMA primarily because of the proven power of the ngram feature-extraction front-end for NLP tasks.

4 Event and Time Expression Extraction

For event and time expression extraction, we trained BIO classifiers. A BIO classifier tags each input token as either Beginning, In, or Out of an event/time expression. Our classifier for events simultaneously assigns a B, I or O to each token, and classifies the class of the event for tokens that Begin or are In an event. Our time expression classifier simultaneously assigns a B, I, or O to each token, and classifies the type of the time expression for tokens that Begin or are In a time expression (see Table 3).

A BIO model may sometimes be inconsistent; for example, a token may be labeled as Inside a segment of a particular type, while the previous token may be labeled as Out of any segment. We considered the two most likely labels for each token (as long as each had likelihood at least 0.9), choosing the one most consistent with the context.

5 Event Feature Classification

We determined the event features for each extracted event using four additional classifiers, one each for tense, aspect, polarity and modality. These classifiers were trained only on tokens identified as part of event expressions. Since the event expressions were single words for all but a few (erroneous) cases in the silver data, for determining the event features, we used the same features as before, with the single addition of the event class (during testing, we used the dynamically assigned event class from the event segmentation classifier). As before, we experimented with ATT1, ATT2, and ATT3 models. TempEval-3 only includes evaluation of tense and aspect features, so we only report for those. The tags assigned by each classifier are listed in Table 3.

6 Time Normalization

To compute TIMEX3 standard based values for extracted time expressions, we used the TIMEN (Llorens et al., 2012) and TRIOS (UzZaman and Allen, 2010) time normalizers. Values from the normalizers were validated in post-processing (*e.g.* "T2445" is invalid) and, when the normalizers returned different non-nil values, TIMEN's values were selected without further reasoning. Time normalization was out of scope in our research for this evaluation, but it remains as part of our future work.

7 Results and Discussion

Our results for event segmentation/classification on the TempEval-3 test data are provided in Table 4. The absence of semantic features causes only small changes in F1. The absence of syntactic features causes F1 to drop slightly (less than 2.5% for all but the smallest window size), with recall decreasing while precision improves somewhat. Attribute F1 is also impacted minimally by the absence of semantic features, and about 2-5% by the absence of syntactic features for all but the smallest window size.[1]

Our results for time expression extraction and classification on the TempEval-3 test data are provided in Table 5. Here, the performance drops more in the absence of semantic and syntactic features; however, there is an interaction between length of time expression and performance drop which we may be able to ameliorate in future work by handling consistency issues in the BIO time expression extraction model better.

[1] In Tables 4 and 5, we present results that are slightly different from our submission due to a minor fix in our models by removing some redundant feature values used twice.

Features	Window size	F1	P	R	Class	Tense	Aspect
STANFORD+SENNA	15 (ATT1)	81.16	81.49	80.83	71.60	59.62	73.76
	7	81.08	81.74	80.43	71.49	59.05	73.78
	3	80.35	81.23	79.49	71.41	58.67	73.17
	1	80.94	80.77	81.10	72.37	58.06	73.71
STANFORD	15 (ATT2)	80.86	81.02	80.70	71.05	59.10	73.34
	7	81.30	81.90	80.70	71.57	59.01	74.14
	3	80.87	81.58	80.16	71.94	58.96	73.70
	1	80.78	80.72	80.83	71.80	57.47	73.41
WORDS ONLY	15 (ATT3)	78.58	81.95	75.47	69.5	55.27	70.76
	7	78.40	82.21	74.93	69.14	55.54	70.27
	3	78.14	82.44	74.26	69.39	52.75	70.38
	1	73.55	79.78	68.23	66.33	44.94	63.15

Table 4: Event extraction results (F1, P and R, strict match); feature classification results (attribute F1)

Features	Window size	F1	P	R	Type	Value
STANFORD+SENNA	15 (ATT1)	80.17 (85.95)	93.27 (100)	70.29 (75.36)	77.69	65.29
	7	76.99 (83.68)	91.09 (99.01)	66.67 (72.46)	75.31	64.44
	3	75.52 (83.82)	88.35 (98.06)	65.94 (73.19)	75.52	63.07
	1	66.12 (83.27)	75.70 (95.33)	58.70 (73.91)	72.65	59.59
STANFORD	15 (ATT2)	78.69 (85.25)	90.57 (98.11)	69.57 (75.36)	76.23	65.57
	7	78.51 (84.30)	91.35 (98.08)	68.84 (73.91)	76.03	63.64
	3	78.19 (84.77)	90.48 (98.10)	68.84 (74.64)	75.72	64.20
	1	67.48 (83.74)	76.85 (95.37)	60.14 (74.64)	73.17	59.35
WORDS ONLY	15 (ATT3)	72.34 (80.85)	87.63 (97.94)	61.59 (68.84)	74.04	60.43
	7	72.34 (80.85)	87.63 (97.94)	61.59 (67.84)	74.04	59.57
	3	74.48 (82.85)	88.12 (98.02)	64.49 (71.74)	75.31	61.09
	1	44.62 (82.87)	49.56 (92.04)	40.58 (75.36)	70.92	39.84

Table 5: Time expression extraction results (F1, P and R, strict match with relaxed match in parentheses); attribute F1 for type and value features

A somewhat surprising finding is that both event and time expression extraction are subject to relatively tight constraints from the lexical context. We were surprised by how well the ATT3 (WORDS ONLY) models performed, especially in terms of precision. We were also surprised that the words only models with window sizes of 3 and 7 performed as well as the models with a window size of 15. We think these results are promising for "big data" text analytics, where there may not be time to do heavy preprocessing of input text or to train large models.

8 Future Work

For us, participation in TempEval-3 is a first step in developing a temporal understanding component for text analytics and virtual agents. We now intend to appy our best performing models to this task. In future work, we plan to evaluate our initial results with larger data sets (e.g., cross validation on the tempeval training data) and experiment with hybrid/ensemble methods for performing time expression and temporal link extraction.

Acknowledgments

We thank Srinivas Bangalore, Patrick Haffner, and Sumit Chopra for helpful discussions and for supplying LLAMA and its front-end for our use.

References

S. F. Adafre and M. de Rijke. 2005. Feature engineering and post-processing for temporal expression recognition using conditional random fields. In *Proceedings of the ACL Workshop on Feature Engineering for Machine Learning in Natural Language Processing*.

G. Angeli, C. D. Manning, and D. Jurafsky. 2012. Parsing time: Learning to interpret time expressions. In *Proceedings of the Conference of the North American Chapter of the Association for Computational Linguistics: Human Language Technologies (HLT-NAACL)*.

R. Collobert, J. Weston, L. Bottou, M. Karlen, K. Kavukcuoglu, and P. Kuksa. 2011. Natural language processing (almost) from scratch. *Journal of Machine Learning Research*, 12.

P. Haffner. 2006. Scaling large margin classifiers for spoken language understanding. *Speech Communication*, 48(3–4).

H. Llorens, E. Saquete, and B. Navarro. 2010. TIPSem (English and Spanish): Evaluating CRFs and semantic roles in TempEval-2. In *Proceedings of the International Workshop on Semantic Evaluation (SemEval)*.

H. Llorens, L. Derczynski, R. Gaizauskas, and E. Saquete. 2012. Timen: An open temporal expression normalisation resource. In *Proceedings of the International Conference on Language Resources and Evaluation (LREC)*.

S. Rigo and A. Lavelli. 2011. Multisex - a multi-language timex sequential extractor. In *Proceedings of Temporal Representation and Reasoning (TIME)*.

Stanford Natural Language Processing Group. 2012. Stanford CoreNLP. `http://nlp.stanford.edu/software/corenlp.shtml`.

N. UzZaman and J. F. Allen. 2010. TRIPS and TRIOS system for TempEval-2: Extracting temporal information from text. In *Proceedings of the International Workshop on Semantic Evaluation (SemEval)*.

N. UzZaman, H. Llorens, J. Allen, L. Derczynski, M. Verhagen, and J. Pustejovsky. 2012. Tempeval-3: Evaluating events, time expressions, and temporal relations. `http://arxiv.org/abs/1206.5333v1`.

Semeval-2013 Task 8: Cross-lingual Textual Entailment for Content Synchronization

Matteo Negri
FBK-irst
Trento, Italy
negri@fbk.eu

Alessandro Marchetti
CELCT
Trento, Italy
amarchetti@celct.it

Yashar Mehdad
UBC
Vancouver, Canada
mehdad@cs.ubc.ca

Luisa Bentivogli
FBK-irst
Trento, Italy
bentivo@fbk.eu

Danilo Giampiccolo
CELCT
Trento, Italy
giampiccolo@celct.it

Abstract

This paper presents the second round of the task on *Cross-lingual Textual Entailment for Content Synchronization*, organized within SemEval-2013. The task was designed to promote research on semantic inference over texts written in different languages, targeting at the same time a real application scenario. Participants were presented with datasets for different language pairs, where multi-directional entailment relations ("forward", "backward", "bidirectional", "no_entailment") had to be identified. We report on the training and test data used for evaluation, the process of their creation, the participating systems (six teams, 61 runs), the approaches adopted and the results achieved.

1 Introduction

The cross-lingual textual entailment task (Mehdad et al., 2010) addresses textual entailment (TE) recognition (Dagan and Glickman, 2004) under the new dimension of cross-linguality, and within the new challenging application scenario of content synchronization. Given two texts in different languages, the cross-lingual textual entailment (CLTE) task consists of deciding if the meaning of one text can be inferred from the meaning of the other text. Cross-linguality represents an interesting direction for research on recognizing textual entailment (RTE), especially due to its possible application in a variety of tasks. Among others (*e.g.* question answering, information retrieval, information extraction, and document summarization), multilingual content synchronization represents a challenging application scenario to evaluate CLTE recognition components geared to the identification of sentence-level semantic relations.

Given two documents about the same topic written in different languages (*e.g.* Wikipedia pages), the content synchronization task consists of automatically detecting and resolving differences in the information they provide, in order to produce aligned, mutually enriched versions of the two documents (Monz et al., 2011; Bronner et al., 2012). Towards this objective, a crucial requirement is to identify the information in one page that is either equivalent or novel (more informative) with respect to the content of the other. The task can be naturally cast as an entailment recognition problem, where bidirectional and unidirectional entailment judgements for two text fragments are respectively mapped into judgements about semantic equivalence and novelty. The task can also be seen as a machine translation evaluation problem, where judgements about semantic equivalence and novelty depend on the possibility to fully or partially translate a text fragment into the other.

The recent advances on monolingual TE on the one hand, and the methodologies used in Statistical Machine Translation (SMT) on the other, offer promising solutions to approach the CLTE task. In line with a number of systems that model the RTE task as a similarity problem (*i.e.* handling similarity scores between T and H as features contributing to the entailment decision), the standard sentence and word alignment programs used in SMT offer a strong baseline for CLTE (Mehdad et al., 2011;

*Second Joint Conference on Lexical and Computational Semantics (*SEM), Volume 2: Seventh International Workshop on Semantic Evaluation (SemEval 2013)*, pages 25–33, Atlanta, Georgia, June 14-15, 2013.

```
<entailment-corpus languages="spa-eng">
  <pair id="1" entailment="bidirectional">
    <t1>Mozart nació en la ciudad de Salzburgo</t1>
    <t2>Mozart was born in Salzburg</t2>
  </pair>
   <pair id="2" entailment="forward">
    <t1>Mozart nació el 27 de enero de 1756 en Salzburgo</t1>
    <t2> Mozart was born in 1756 in the city of Salzburg</t2>
  </pair>
<pair id="3" entailment="backward">
    <t1>Mozart nació en la ciudad de Salzburgo</t1>
    <t2>Mozart was born on the 27th January 1756 in Salzburg</t2>
  </pair>  <pair id="4" entailment="no_entailment">
    <t1>Mozart nació el 27 de enero de 1756 en Salzburgo</t1>
    <t2>Mozart was born to Leopold and Anna Maria Pertl Mozart</t2>
  </pair>
</entailment-corpus>
```

Figure 1: Example of SP-EN CLTE pairs.

Mehdad et al., 2012). However, although representing a solid starting point to approach the problem, similarity-based techniques are just approximations, open to significant improvements coming from semantic inference at the multilingual level (*e.g.* cross-lingual entailment rules such as "perro"→"animal"). Taken in isolation, similarity-based techniques clearly fall short of providing an effective solution to the problem of assigning directions to the entailment relations (especially in the complex CLTE scenario, where entailment relations are multi-directional). Thanks to the contiguity between CLTE, TE and SMT, the proposed task provides an interesting scenario to approach the issues outlined above from different perspectives, and offers large room for mutual improvement.

Building on the success of the first CLTE evaluation organized within SemEval-2012 (Negri et al., 2012a), the remainder of this paper describes the second evaluation round organized within SemEval-2013. The following sections provide an overview of the datasets used, the participating systems, the approaches adopted, the achieved results, and the lessons learned.

2 The task

Given a pair of topically related text fragments (*T1* and *T2*) in different languages, the CLTE task consists of automatically annotating it with one of the following entailment judgements (see Figure 1 for Spanish/English examples of each judgement):

- **bidirectional** ($T1 \rightarrow T2$ & $T1 \leftarrow T2$): the two fragments entail each other (semantic equivalence);
- **forward** ($T1 \rightarrow T2$ & $T1 \not\leftarrow T2$): unidirectional entailment from *T1* to *T2*;
- **backward** ($T1 \not\rightarrow T2$ & $T1 \leftarrow T2$): unidirectional entailment from *T2* to *T1*;
- **no_entailment** ($T1 \not\rightarrow T2$ & $T1 \not\leftarrow T2$): there is no entailment between *T1* and *T2* in either direction;

In this task, both *T1* and *T2* are assumed to be true statements. Although contradiction is relevant from an application-oriented perspective, contradictory pairs are not present in the dataset.

3 Dataset description

The CLTE-2013 dataset is composed of four CLTE corpora created for the following language combinations: Spanish/English (SP-EN), Italian/English (IT-EN), French/English (FR-EN), German/English (DE-EN). Each corpus consists of 1,500 sentence pairs (1,000 for training and 500 for test), balanced across the four entailment judgements.

In this year's evaluation, as training set we used the CLTE-2012 corpus[1] that was created for the SemEval-2012 evaluation exercise[2] (including both training and test sets). The CLTE-2013 test set was created from scratch, following the methodology described in the next section.

3.1 Data collection and annotation

To collect the entailment pairs for the 2013 test set we adopted a slightly modified version of the crowdsourcing methodology followed to create the CLTE-2012 corpus (Negri et al., 2011). The main difference with last year's procedure is that we did not take advantage of crowdsourcing for the whole data collection process, but only for part of it.

As for CLTE-2012, the collection and annotation process consists of the following steps:

1. First, English sentences were manually extracted from Wikipedia and Wikinews. The selected sentences represent one of the elements (*T1*) of each entailment pair;

[1]http://www.celct.it/resources.php?id_page=CLTE
[2]http://www.cs.york.ac.uk/semeval-2012/task8/

2. Next, each *T1* was modified in various ways in order to obtain a corresponding *T2*. While in the CLTE-2012 dataset the whole *T2* creation process was carried out through crowdsourcing, for the CLTE-2013 test set we crowdsourced only the first phase of *T1* modification, namely the creation of paraphrases. Focusing on the creation of high quality paraphrases, we followed the crowdsourcing methodology experimented in Negri et al. (2012b), in which a paraphrase is obtained through an iterative modification process of an original sentence, by asking workers to introduce meaning-preserving lexical and syntactic changes. At each round of the iteration, new workers are presented with the output of the previous iteration in order to increase divergence from the original sentence. At the end of the process, only the more divergent paraphrases according to the Lesk score (Lesk, 1986) are selected. As for the second phase of *T2* creation process, this year it was carried out by expert annotators, who followed the same criteria used last year for the crowdsourced tasks, i.e. *i)* remove information from the input (paraphrased) sentence and *ii)* add information from sentences surrounding *T1* in the source article;

3. Each *T2* was then paired to the original *T1*, and the resulting pairs were annotated with one of the four entailment judgements. In order to reduce the correlation between the difference in sentences' length and entailment judgements, only the pairs where the difference between the number of words in *T1* and *T2* (*length_diff*) was below a fixed threshold (10 words) were retained.[3] The final result is a monolingual English dataset annotated with multi-directional entailment judgements, which are well distributed over *length_diff* values ranging from 0 to 9;

4. In order to create the cross-lingual datasets, each English *T1* was manually translated into four different languages (*i.e.* Spanish, German, Italian and French) by expert translators;

5. By pairing the translated *T1* with the corresponding *T2* in English, four cross-lingual datasets were obtained.

To ensure the good quality of the datasets, all the collected pairs were cross-annotated and filtered to retain only those pairs with full agreement in the entailment judgement between two expert annotators. The final result is a multilingual parallel entailment corpus, where *T1*s are in 5 different languages (*i.e.* English, Spanish, German, Italian, and French), and *T2*s are in English. It is worth mentioning that the monolingual English corpus, a by-product of our data collection methodology, will be publicly released as a further contribution to the research community.

3.2 Dataset statistics

As described in section 3.1, the methodology followed to create the training and test sets was the same except for the crowdsourced tasks. This allowed us to obtain two datasets with the same balance across the entailment judgements, and to keep under control the distribution of the pairs for different *length_diff* values in each language combination.

Training Set. The training set is composed of 1,000 CLTE pairs for each language combination, balanced across the four entailment judgements (bidirectional, forward, backward, and no_entailment). As shown in Table 1, our data collection procedure led to a dataset where the majority of the pairs falls in the +5 -5 *length_diff* range for each language pair (67.2% on average across the four language pairs). This characteristic is particularly relevant as our assumption is that such data distribution makes entailment judgements based on mere surface features such as sentence length ineffective, thus encouraging the development of alternative, deeper processing strategies.

Test Set. The test set is composed of 500 entailment pairs for each language combination, balanced across the four entailment judgements. As shown in Table 2, also in this dataset the majority of the collected entailment pairs is uniformly distributed

[3] Such constraint has been applied in order to focus as much as possible on semantic aspects of the problem, by reducing the applicability of simple association rules such as *IF length(T1)>length(T2) THEN T1→T2*.

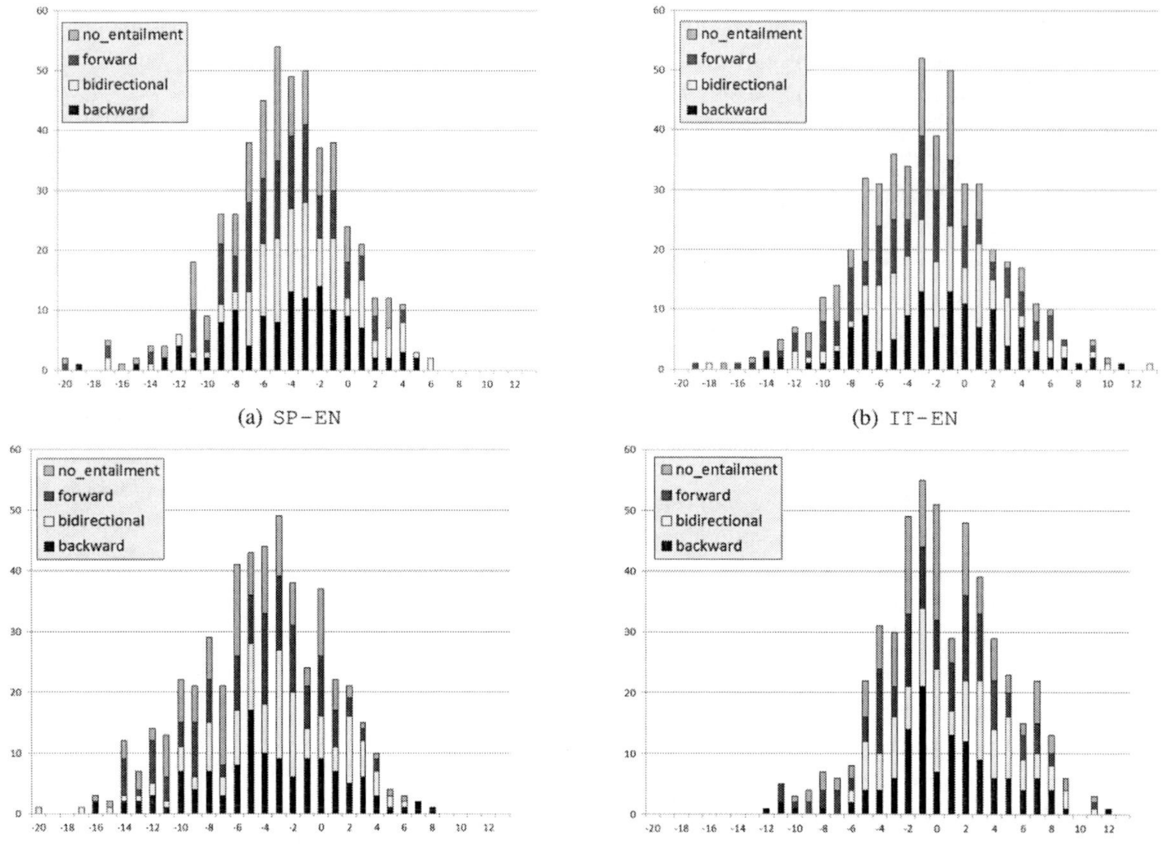

(a) SP-EN (b) IT-EN (c) FR-EN (d) DE-EN

Figure 2: Pair distribution in the 2013 test set: total number of pairs (y-axis) for different *length_diff* values (x-axis).

	SP-EN	IT-EN	FR-EN	DE-EN
Forward	104	132	121	179
Backward	202	182	191	123
No entailment	163	173	169	174
Bidirectional	175	199	193	209
ALL	644	686	674	685
% (out of 1,000)	64.4	68.6	67.4	68.5

Table 1: Training set pair distribution within the -5/+5 *length_diff* range.

	SP-EN	IT-EN	FR-EN	DE-EN
backward	82	89	82	102
bidirectional	89	92	90	106
forward	69	78	76	98
no_entailment	71	80	59	100
ALL	311	339	307	406
% (out of 500)	62.2	67.8	61.4	81.2

Table 2: Test set pair distribution within the -5/+5 *length_diff* range.

in the [-5,+5] *length_diff* range (68.1% on average across the four language pairs).

However, comparing training and test set for each language pair, it can be seen that while the Spanish-English and Italian-English datasets are homogeneous with respect to the *length_diff* feature, the French-English and German-English datasets present noticeable differences between training and test set. These figures show that, despite the considerable effort spent to produce comparable training and test sets, the ideal objective of a full homogeneity between the datasets for these two languages was difficult to reach.

Complete details about the distribution of the pairs in terms of *length_diff* for the four cross-lingual corpora in the test set are provided in Figure 2. Vertical bars represent, for each *length_diff* value, the proportion of pairs belonging to the four entailment classes.

4 Evaluation metrics and baselines

Evaluation results have been automatically computed by comparing the entailment judgements returned by each system with those manually assigned by human annotators in the gold standard. The metrics used for systems' ranking is accuracy over the whole test set, *i.e.* the number of correct judgements out of the total number of judgements in the test set. Additionally, we calculated precision, recall, and F1 measures for each of the four entailment judgement categories taken separately. These scores aim at giving participants the possibility to gain clearer insights into their system's behaviour on the entailment phenomena relevant to the task.

To allow comparison with the CLTE-2012 results, the same three baselines were calculated on the CLTE-2013 test set for each language combination. The first one is the 0.25 accuracy score obtained by assigning each test pair in the balanced dataset to one of the four classes. The other two baselines consider the length difference between *T1* and *T2*:

- **Composition of binary judgements (Binary).** To calculate this baseline an SVM classifier is trained to take binary entailment decisions ("YES", "NO"). The classifier uses *length(T1)/length(T2)* and *length(T2)/length(T1)* as features respectively to check for entailment from *T1* to *T2* and vice-versa. For each test pair, the unidirectional judgements returned by the two classifiers are composed into a single multi-directional judgement ("YES-YES"="bidirectional", "YES-NO"="forward", "NO-YES"="backward", "NO-NO"="no_entailment");

- **Multi-class classification (Multi-class).** A single SVM classifier is trained with the same features to directly assign to each pair one of the four entailment judgements.

Both the baselines have been calculated with the LIBSVM package (Chang and Lin, 2011), using default parameters. Baseline results are reported in Table 3.

Although the four CLTE datasets are derived from the same monolingual EN-EN corpus, baseline results present slight differences due to the effect of translation into different languages. With respect to last year's evaluation, we can observe a slight drop in the binary classification baseline results. This might be due to the fact that the length distribution of examples is slightly different this year. However, there are no significant differences between the multi-class baseline results of this year in comparison with the previous round results. This might suggest that multi-class classification is a more robust approach for recognizing multi-directional entailment relations. Moreover, both baselines failed in capturing the *"no-entailment"* examples in all datasets ($F1_{no-entailment} = 0$).

	SP-EN	IT-EN	FR-EN	DE-EN
1-class	0.25	0.25	0.25	0.25
Binary	0.35	0.39	0.37	0.39
Multi-class	**0.43**	**0.44**	**0.42**	**0.42**

Table 3: Baseline accuracy results.

5 Submitted runs and results

Like in the 2012 round of the CLTE task, participants were allowed to submit up to five runs for each language combination. A total of twelve teams registered for participation and downloaded the training set. Out of them, six[4] submitted valid runs. Five teams produced submissions for all the four language combinations, while one team participated only in the DE-EN task. In total, 61 runs have been submitted and evaluated (16 for DE-EN, and 15 for each of the other language pairs).

Accuracy results are reported in Table 4. As can be seen from the table, the performance of the best systems is quite similar across the four language combinations, with the best submissions achieving results in the 43.4-45.8% accuracy interval. Similarly, also average and median results are close to each other, with a small drop on DE-EN. This drop might be explained by the difference between the training and test set with respect to the *length_diff* feature. Moreover, the performance of DE-EN automatic translation might affect approaches based on "pivoting", (*i.e.* addressing CLTE by automatically translating *T1* in the same language of *T2*, as described in Section 6).

[4]Including the task organizers.

System_name	SP-EN	IT-EN	FR-EN	DE-EN
altn_run1*	**0.428**	**0.432**	**0.420**	**0.388**
BUAP_run1	0.364	0.358	0.368	0.322
BUAP_run2	0.374	0.358	0.364	0.318
BUAP_run3	0.380	0.358	0.362	0.316
BUAP_run4	0.364	**0.388**	**0.392**	**0.350**
BUAP_run5	**0.386**	0.360	0.372	0.318
celi_run1	0.340	**0.324**	0.334	**0.342**
celi_run2	**0.342**	**0.324**	**0.340**	**0.342**
ECNUCS_run1	**0.428**	**0.426**	0.438	0.422
ECNUCS_run2	0.404	0.420	0.450	0.436
ECNUCS_run3	0.408	**0.426**	**0.458**	0.432
ECNUCS_run4	0.422	0.416	0.436	**0.452**
ECNUCS_run5	0.392	0.402	0.442	0.426
SoftCard_run1	**0.434**	**0.454**	0.416	**0.414**
SoftCard_run2	0.432	0.448	**0.426**	0.402
umelb_run1	–	–	–	**0.324**
Highest	0.434	0.454	0.458	0.452
Average	0.404	0.404	0.401	0.378
Median	0.428	0.426	0.420	0.369
Lowest	0.342	0.324	0.340	0.324

Table 4: CLTE-2013 accuracy results (61 runs) over the 4 language combinations. Highest, average, median and lowest scores are calculated considering only the best run for each team (*task organizers' system).

Compared to the results achieved last year, shown in Table 5, a sensible decrease in the highest scores can be observed. While in CLTE-2012 the top systems achieved an accuracy well above 0.5 (with a maximum of 0.632 in SP-EN), the results for this year are far below such level (the peak is now at 45,8% for FR-EN). A slight decrease with respect to 2012 can also be noted for average performances. However, it's worth remarking the general increase of the lowest and median scores, which are less sensitive to isolate outstanding results achieved by single teams. This indicates that a progress in CLTE research has been made building on the lessons learned after the first round of the initiative.

To better understand the behaviour of each system, Table 6 provides separate precision, recall, and F1 scores for each entailment judgement, calculated over the best runs of each participating team. In contrast to CLTE-2012, where the "bidirectional" and "no entailment" categories consistently proved to be more problematic than "forward" and "backward" judgements, this year's results are more homogeneous across the different classes. Nevertheless, on average, the classification of "bidirectional" pairs is still worse for three language pairs (SP-EN, IT-EN and FR-EN), and results for "no entailment" are lower for two of them (SP-EN and DE-EN).

	SP-EN	IT-EN	FR-EN	DE-EN
Highest	0.632	0.566	0.570	0.558
Average	0.440	0.411	0.408	0.408
Median	0.407	0.350	0.365	0.363
Lowest	0.274	0.326	0.296	0.296

Table 5: CLTE-2012 accuracy results. Highest, average, median and lowest scores are calculated considering only the best run for each team.

As regards the comparison with the baselines, this year's results confirm that the *length_diff*-based baselines are hard to beat. More specifically, most of the systems are slightly above the binary classification baseline (with the exception of the DE-EN dataset where only two systems out of six outperformed it), whereas for all the language combinations the multi-class baseline was beaten only by the best participating system.

This shows that, despite the effort in keeping the distribution of the entailment classes uniform across different *length_diff* values, eliminating the correlation between sentence length and correct entailment decisions is difficult. As a consequence, although disregarding semantic aspects of the problem, features considering length information are quite effective in terms of overall accuracy. Such features, however, perform rather poorly when dealing with challenging cases (*e.g. "no-entailment"*), which are better handled by participating systems.

6 Approaches

A rough classification of the approaches adopted by participants can be made along two orthogonal dimensions, namely:

- **Pivoting vs. Cross-lingual.** Pivoting methods rely on the automatic translation of one of the two texts (either single words or the entire sentence) into the language of the other (typically English) in order perform monolingual TE recognition. Cross-lingual methods assign entailment judgements without preliminary translation.

- **Composition of binary judgements vs. Multi-class classification.** Compositional approaches map unidirectional ("YES"/"NO")

	SP-EN											
	Forward			Backward			No entailment			Bidirectional		
System name	*P*	*R*	*F1*	*P*	*R*	*F1*	*P*	*R*	*F1*	*P*	*R*	F1
altn_full_spa-eng	**0.509**	**0.464**	**0.485**	0.440	0.264	0.330	**0.464**	0.416	0.439	0.357	**0.568**	0.438
BUAP_spa-eng_run5	0.446	0.360	0.398	0.521	0.296	0.378	0.385	0.456	0.418	0.300	0.432	0.354
celi_spa-eng_run2	0.396	0.352	0.373	0.431	0.400	0.415	0.325	0.328	0.327	0.245	0.288	0.265
ECNUCS_spa-eng_run1	0.458	0.432	0.444	0.533	0.320	0.400	0.406	0.416	0.411	**0.380**	0.544	**0.447**
SoftCard_spa-eng_run1	0.462	0.344	0.394	**0.619**	**0.480**	**0.541**	0.418	**0.472**	**0.444**	0.325	0.440	0.374
AVG.	0.454	0.390	0.419	0.509	0.352	0.413	0.400	0.418	0.408	0.321	0.454	0.376
	IT-EN											
	Forward			Backward			No entailment			Bidirectional		
System name	*P*	*R*	*F1*	*P*	*R*	*F1*	*P*	*R*	*F1*	*P*	*R*	F1
altn_full_ita-eng	0.448	0.376	0.409	0.417	0.344	0.377	**0.512**	**0.496**	**0.504**	**0.374**	**0.512**	**0.432**
BUAP_ita-eng_run4	0.418	0.328	0.368	0.462	0.384	0.419	0.379	0.440	0.407	0.327	0.400	0.360
celi_ita-eng_run1	0.288	0.256	0.271	0.395	0.408	0.402	0.336	0.304	0.319	0.279	0.328	0.301
ECNUCS_ita-eng_run1	0.422	**0.456**	0.438	0.592	0.336	0.429	0.440	0.440	0.440	0.349	0.472	0.401
SoftCard_ita-eng_run1	**0.514**	**0.456**	**0.483**	**0.612**	**0.480**	**0.538**	0.392	0.464	0.425	0.364	0.416	0.388
AVG.	0.418	0.374	0.394	0.496	0.390	0.433	0.412	0.429	0.419	0.339	0.426	0.376
	FR-EN											
	Forward			Backward			No entailment			Bidirectional		
System name	*P*	*R*	*F1*	*P*	*R*	*F1*	*P*	*R*	*F1*	*P*	*R*	F1
altn_full_fra-eng	0.405	0.392	0.398	0.420	0.296	0.347	0.500	0.440	0.468	0.381	0.552	0.451
BUAP_fra-eng_run4	0.407	**0.472**	0.437	0.431	0.376	0.402	0.379	0.376	0.378	0.352	0.344	0.348
celi_fra-eng_run2	0.394	0.344	0.368	0.364	0.376	0.370	0.352	0.352	0.352	0.263	0.288	0.275
ECNUCS_fra-eng_run3	0.422	0.432	0.427	**0.667**	0.352	0.461	**0.514**	**0.432**	**0.470**	**0.383**	**0.616**	**0.472**
SoftCard_fra-eng_run2	**0.477**	0.416	**0.444**	0.556	**0.400**	**0.465**	0.412	**0.432**	0.422	0.335	0.456	0.386
AVG.	0.421	0.411	0.415	0.488	0.360	0.409	0.431	0.406	0.418	0.343	0.451	0.386
	DE-EN											
	Forward			Backward			No entailment			Bidirectional		
System name	*P*	*R*	*F1*	*P*	*R*	*F1*	*P*	*R*	*F1*	*P*	*R*	F1
altn_full_deu-eng	0.432	0.408	0.420	0.378	0.272	0.316	**0.445**	0.392	**0.417**	0.330	0.480	0.391
BUAP_deu-eng_run4	0.364	0.344	0.354	0.389	0.280	0.326	0.352	0.352	0.352	0.317	0.424	0.363
celi_deu-eng_run1	0.346	0.352	0.349	0.414	**0.424**	0.419	0.351	0.264	0.301	0.272	0.328	0.297
ECNUCS_deu-eng_run4	0.429	**0.432**	**0.430**	**0.611**	0.352	**0.447**	0.415	0.392	0.403	**0.429**	**0.632**	**0.511**
SoftCard_deu-eng_run1	**0.511**	0.368	0.428	0.527	0.384	0.444	0.417	**0.400**	0.408	0.317	0.504	0.389
umelb_deu-eng_run1	0.323	0.320	0.321	0.240	0.184	0.208	0.362	0.376	0.369	0.347	0.416	0.378
AVG.	0.401	0.371	0.384	0.426	0.316	0.360	0.390	0.363	0.375	0.335	0.464	0.389

Table 6: Precision, recall and F1 scores, calculated for each team's best run for all the language combinations.

entailment decisions taken separately into single judgements (similar to the *Binary* baseline in Section 4). Methods based on multi-class classification directly assign one of the four entailment judgements to each test pair (similar to our *Multi-class* baseline).

In contrast with CLTE-2012, where the combination of pivoting and compositional methods was the option adopted by the majority of the approaches, this year's solutions do not show a clear trend. Concerning the former dimension, participating systems are equally distributed in cross-lingual and pivoting methods relying on external automatic translation tools. Regarding the latter dimension, in addition to compositional and multi-class strategies, also alternative solutions that leverage more sophisticated meta-classification strategies have been proposed. Besides the recourse to MT tools (*e.g.* Google Translate), other tools and resources used by participants include: WordNet, word alignment tools (*e.g.* Giza++), part-of-speech taggers (*e.g.* Stanford POS Tagger), stemmers (*e.g.* Snowball), machine learning libraries (*e.g.* Weka, SVMlight), parallel corpora (*e.g.* Europarl), and stopword lists. More in detail:

ALTN [cross-lingual, compositional] (Turchi and Negri, 2013) adopts a supervised learning method based on features that consider word alignments between the two sentences obtained with GIZA++ (Och et al., 2003). Binary entailment judgements are taken separately, and combined into final CLTE decisions.

BUAP [pivoting, multi-class and meta-classifier] (Vilariño et al., 2013) adopts a pivoting method based on translating *T1* into the language of

T2 and vice versa (using Google Translate[5]). Similarity measures (*e.g.* Jaccard index) and features based on n-gram overlap, computed at the level of words and part of speech categories, are used (either alone or in combination) by different classification strategies including: multi-class, a meta-classifier (*i.e.* combining the output of 2/3/4-class classifiers), and majority voting.

CELI [cross-lingual, meta-classifier] (Kouylekov, 2013) uses dictionaries for word matching, and a multilingual corpus extracted from Wikipedia for term weighting. A variety of distance measures implemented in the RTE system EDITS (Kouylekov and Negri, 2010; Negri et al., 2009) are used to extract features to train a meta-classifier. Such classifier combines binary decisions ("YES"/"NO") taken separately for each of the four CLTE judgements.

ECNUCS [pivoting, multi-class] (Jiang and Man, 2013) uses Google Translate to obtain the English translation of each T1. After a pre-processing step aimed at maximizing the commonalities between the two sentences (*e.g.* abbreviation replacement), a number of features is extracted to train a multi-class SVM classifier. Such features consider information about sentence length, text similarity/difference measures, and syntactic information.

SoftCard [pivoting, multi-class] (Jimenez et al., 2013) after automatic translation with Google Translate, uses SVMs to learn entailment decisions based on information about the cardinality of: *T1*, *T2*, their intersection and their union. Cardinalities are computed in different ways, considering tokens in *T1* and *T2*, their IDF, and their similarity.

Umelb [cross-lingual, pivoting, compositional] (Graham et al., 2013) adopts both pivoting and cross-lingual approaches. For the latter, GIZA++ was used to compute word alignments between the input sentences. Word alignment features are used to train binary SVM classifiers whose decisions are eventually composed into CLTE judgements.

7 Conclusion

Following the success of the first round of the *Cross-lingual Textual Entailment for Content Synchronization* task organized within SemEval-2012, a second evaluation task has been organized within SemEval-2013. Despite the decrease in the number of participants (six teams - four less than in the first round - submitted a total of 61 runs) the new experience is still positive. In terms of data, a new test set has been released, extending the old one with 500 new CLTE pairs. The resulting 1,500 cross-lingual pairs, aligned over four language combinations (in addition to the monolingual English version), and annotated with multiple entailment relations, represent a significant contribution to the research community and a solid starting point for further developments.[6] In terms of results, in spite of a significant decrease of the top scores, the increase of both median and lower results demonstrates some encouraging progress in CLTE research. Such progress is also demonstrated by the variety of the approaches proposed. While in the first round most of the teams adopted more intuitive and "simpler" solutions based on pivoting (*i.e.* translation of *T1* and *T2* in the same language) and compositional entailment decision strategies, this year new ideas and more complex solutions have emerged. Pivoting and cross-lingual approaches are equally distributed, and new classification methods have been proposed. Our hope is that the large room for improvement, the increase of available data, and the potential of CLTE as a way to address complex NLP tasks and applications will motivate further research on the proposed problem.

Acknowledgments

This work has been partially supported by the EC-funded project CoSyne (FP7-ICT-4-248531). The authors would also like to acknowledge Pamela Forner and Giovanni Moretti from CELCT, and the volunteer translators that contributed to the creation of the dataset: Giusi Calo, Victoria Díaz, Bianca Jeremias, Anne Kauffman, Laura López Ortiz, Julie Mailfait, Laura Morán Iglesias, Andreas Schwab.

[5] `http://translate.google.com/`

[6] Together with the datasets derived from translation of the RTE data (Negri and Mehdad, 2010), this is the only material currently available to train and evaluate CLTE systems.

References

Amit Bronner, Matteo Negri, Yashar Mehdad, Angela Fahrni, and Christof Monz. 2012. Cosyne: Synchronizing multilingual wiki content. In *Proceedings of WikiSym 2012*.

Chih-Chung Chang and Chih-Jen Lin. 2011. Libsvm: a library for support vector machines. *ACM Transactions on Intelligent Systems and Technology (TIST)*, 2(3):27.

Ido Dagan and Oren Glickman. 2004. Probabilistic Textual Entailment: Generic Applied Modeling of Language Variability. In *Proceedings of the PASCAL Workshop of Learning Methods for Text Understanding and Mining*.

Yvette Graham, Bahar Salehi, and Tim Baldwin. 2013. Unimelb: Cross-lingual Textual Entailment with Word Alignment and String Similarity Features. In *Proceedings of the 7th International Workshop on Semantic Evaluation (SemEval 2013)*.

Zhao Jiang and Lan Man. 2013. ECNUCS: Recognizing Cross-lingual Textual Entailment Using Multiple Feature Types. . In *Proceedings of the 7th International Workshop on Semantic Evaluation (SemEval 2013)*.

Sergio Jimenez, Claudia Becerra, and Alexander Gelbukh. 2013. Soft Cardinality-CLTE: Learning to Identify Directional Cross-Lingual Entailmens from Cardinalities and SMT. In *Proceedings of the 7th International Workshop on Semantic Evaluation (SemEval 2013)*.

Milen Kouylekov and Matteo Negri. 2010. An open-source package for recognizing textual entailment. In *Proceedings of the ACL 2010 System Demonstrations*.

Milen Kouylekov. 2013. Celi: EDITS and Generic Text Pair Classification. In *Proceedings of the 7th International Workshop on Semantic Evaluation (SemEval 2013)*.

Michael Lesk. 1986. Automated Sense Disambiguation Using Machine-readable Dictionaries: How to Tell a Pine Cone from an Ice Cream Cone. In *Proceedings of the 5th annual international conference on Systems documentation (SIGDOC86)*.

Yashar Mehdad, Matteo Negri, and Marcello Federico. 2010. Towards Cross-Lingual Textual Entailment. In *Proceedings of the 11th Annual Conference of the North American Chapter of the Association for Computational Linguistics (NAACL HLT 2010)*.

Yashar Mehdad, Matteo Negri, and Marcello Federico. 2011. Using Bilingual Parallel Corpora for Cross-Lingual Textual Entailment. In *Proceedings of the 49th Annual Meeting of the Association for Computational Linguistics: Human Language Technologies (ACL HLT 2011)*.

Yashar Mehdad, Matteo Negri, and Marcello Federico. 2012. Detecting Semantic Equivalence and Information Disparity in Cross-lingual Documents. In *Proceedings of the 50th Annual Meeting of the Association for Computational Linguistics (ACL 2012)*.

Christof Monz, Vivi Nastase, Matteo Negri, Angela Fahrni, Yashar Mehdad, and Michael Strube. 2011. Cosyne: a framework for multilingual content synchronization of wikis. In *Proceedings of WikiSym 2011*.

Matteo Negri and Yashar Mehdad. 2010. Creating a Bilingual Entailment Corpus through Translations with Mechanical Turk: $100 for a 10-day Rush. In *Proceedings of the NAACL HLT 2010 Workshop on Creating Speech and Language Data with Amazonś Mechanical Turk*.

Matteo Negri, Milen Kouylekov, Bernardo Magnini, Yashar Mehdad, and Elena Cabrio. 2009. Towards extensible textual entailment engines: the edits package. In *AI* IA 2009: Emergent Perspectives in Artificial Intelligence*, pages 314–323. Springer.

Matto Negri, Luisa Bentivogli, Yashar Mehdad, Danilo Giampiccolo, and Alessandro Marchetti. 2011. Divide and Conquer: Crowdsourcing the Creation of Cross-Lingual Textual Entailment Corpora. *Proceedings of the 2011 Conference on Empirical Methods in Natural Language Processing (EMNLP 2011)*.

Matteo Negri, Alessandro Marchetti, Yashar Mehdad, Luisa Bentivogli, and Danilo Giampiccolo. 2012a. Semeval-2012 Task 8: Cross-lingual Textual Entailment for Content Synchronization. In *Proceedings of the 6th International Workshop on Semantic Evaluation (SemEval 2012)*.

Matteo Negri, Yashar Mehdad, Alessandro Marchetti, Danilo Giampiccolo, and Luisa Bentivogli. 2012b. Chinese Whispers: Cooperative Paraphrase Acquisition. In *Proceedings of the Eight International Conference on Language Resources and Evaluation (LREC12)*, volume 2, pages 2659–2665.

F. Och, H. Ney, F. Josef, and O. H. Ney. 2003. A systematic comparison of various statistical alignment models. *Computational Linguistics*.

Marco Turchi and Matteo Negri. 2013. ALTN: Word Alignment Features for Cross-Lingual Textual Entailment. In *Proceedings of the 7th International Workshop on Semantic Evaluation (SemEval 2013)*.

Darnes Vilariño, David Pinto, Saul León, Yuridiana Alemán, and Helena Gómez-Adorno. 2013. BUAP: N-gram based Feature Evaluation for the Cross-Lingual Textual Entailment Task. In *Proceedings of the 7th International Workshop on Semantic Evaluation (SemEval 2013)*.

SOFTCARDINALITY: Learning to Identify Directional Cross-Lingual Entailment from Cardinalities and SMT

Sergio Jimenez, Claudia Becerra
Universidad Nacional de Colombia
Ciudad Universitaria,
edificio 453, oficina 114
Bogotá, Colombia
sgjimenezv@unal.edu.co
cjbecerrac@unal.edu.co

Alexander Gelbukh
CIC-IPN
Av. Juan Dios Bátiz, Av. Mendizábal,
Col. Nueva Industrial Vallejo
CP 07738, DF, México
gelbukh@gelbukh.com

Abstract

In this paper we describe our system submitted for evaluation in the CLTE-SemEval-2013 task, which achieved the best results in two of the four data sets, and finished third in average. This system consists of a SVM classifier with features extracted from texts (and their translations SMT) based on a cardinality function. Such function was the soft cardinality. Furthermore, this system was simplified by providing a single model for the 4 pairs of languages obtaining better (unofficial) results than separate models for each language pair. We also evaluated the use of additional circular-pivoting translations achieving results 6.14% above the best official results.

1 Introduction

The Cross-Lingual Textual Entailment (CLTE) task consists in determining the type of directional entailment (i.e. *forward*, *backward*, *bidirectional* or *no-entailment*) between a pair of texts T_1 and T_2, each one written in different languages (Negri et al., 2013). The texts and reference annotations for this task were obtained through crowdsourcing applied to simpler sub-tasks (Negri et al., 2011). CLTE has as main applications content synchronization and aggregation in different languages (Mehdad et al., 2012; Duh et al., 2013). We participated in the first evaluation of this task in 2012 (Negri et al., 2012), achieving third place on average among 29 participating systems (Jimenez et al., 2012).

Since in the CLTE task text pairs are in different languages, in our system, all comparisons made between two texts imply that one of them was written by a human and the other is a translation provided by statistical machine translation (SMT). Our approach is based on an SVM classifier (Cortes and Vapnik, 1995) whose features were cardinalities combined with similarity scores. That system was motivated by the fact that most text similarity functions are symmetric, e.g. Edit Distance (Levenshtein, 1966), longest common sub-sequence (Hirschberg, 1977), Jaro-Winkler similarity (Winkler, 1990), cosine similarity (Salton et al., 1975). Thus, the use of these functions as only resource seems counter-intuitive since CLTE task is asymmetric for the *forward* and *backward* entailment classes.

Moreover, cardinality is the central component of the resemblance coefficients such as Jaccard, Dice, overlap, etc. For instance, if T_1 and T_2 are texts represented as bag of words, it is only necessary to know the cardinalities $|T_1|$, $|T_2|$ and $|T_1 \cap T_2|$ to obtain a similarity score using a resemblance coefficient such as the Dice's coefficient (i.e. $2 \cdot |T_1 \cap T_2|/(|T_1| + |T_2|)$). Therefore, the idea is to use the individual cardinalities to enrich a set of features extracted from texts.

Cardinality gives a rough idea of the amount of information in a collection of elements (i.e. words) providing the number of different elements therein. That is, in a collection of elements whose majority are repetitions contains less information than a collection whose elements are mostly different. However, the classical sets cardinality is a rigid measure as do not take account the degree of similarity among the elements. Unlike the sets cardinality, soft cardinality (Jimenez et al., 2010) uses the similarities among the elements providing a more flexible

*Second Joint Conference on Lexical and Computational Semantics (*SEM), Volume 2: Seventh International Workshop on Semantic Evaluation (SemEval 2013)*, pages 34–38, Atlanta, Georgia, June 14-15, 2013.

measurement of the amount of information in a collection. In the 2012 CLTE evaluation campaign, it was noted that the soft cardinality overcame classical cardinality in the task at hand. All the models used in our participation and proposed in this paper are based on the soft cardinality. A brief description of the soft cardinality is presented in Section 2, along with a description of the functions used to provide the similarities between words. Besides, the set of features that are derived from all pairs of texts and their cardinalities are presented in Section 3.

Section 4 provides a detailed description for each of the 4 models (one for each language pair) used to get the predictions submitted for evaluation. In Section 5 a simplified-multilingual model is tested with several word-similarity functions and circular-pivoting translations.

In sections 6 and 7 a brief discussion of the results and conclusions of our participation in this evaluation campaign are presented.

2 Soft Cardinality

The soft cardinality (Jimenez et al., 2010) of a collection of words T is calculated with the following expression:

$$|T|' = \sum_{i=1}^{n} w_i \left(\sum_{j=1}^{n} \mathbf{sim}(t_i, t_j)^p \right)^{-1} \quad (1)$$

Having $T = \{t_1, t_2, \ldots, t_n\}$; $w_i \geq 0$; $p \geq 0$; $1 > \mathbf{sim}(x, y) \geq 0$, $x \neq y$; and $\mathbf{sim}(x, x) = 1$. The parameter p controls the degree of "softness" of the cardinality (the larger the "harder"). The coefficients w_i are weights associated with each word (or term) t, which can represent the importance or informative character of each word (e.g. *idf* weights). The function **sim** is a word-similarity function. Three such functions are considered in this paper:

***Q*-grams**: each word a_i is represented as a collection of character q-grams (Kukich, 1992). Instead of single length q-grams, a combination of a range of lengths q_1 to q_2 was used. Next, a couple of words are compared with the following resemblance coefficient: $\mathbf{sim}(t_i, t_j) = \frac{|t_i \cap t_j| + bias}{\alpha \cdot \max(|t_i|, |t_j|) + (1-\alpha) \cdot \min(|t_i|, |t_j|)}$. The parameters of this word-similarity function are q_1, q_2, α and $bias$.

Group 1: basic cardinalities			
#1	$\|T_1\|'$	#4	$\|T_1 \cup T_2\|'$
#2	$\|T_2\|'$	#5	$\|T_1 - T_2\|'$
#3	$\|T_1 \cap T_2\|'$	#6	$\|T_2 - T_1\|'$
Group 2: asymmetrical ratios			
#7	$\|T_1 \cap T_2\|' / \|T_1\|'$	#8	$\|T_1 \cap T_2\|' / \|T_2\|'$
Group 3: similarity and arithmetical* scores			
#9	$\|T_1 \cap T_2\|' / \|T_1 \cup T_2\|'$	#10	$\frac{2 \cdot \|T_1 \cap T_2\|'}{\|T_1\|' + \|T_2\|'}$
#11	$\|T_1 \cap T_2\|' / \sqrt{\|T_1\|' \cdot \|T_2\|'}$	#12	$\frac{\|T_1 \cap T_2\|'}{\min[\|T_1\|', \|T_2\|']}$
#13	$\frac{\|T_1 \cap T_2\|' + \|T_1\|' + \|T_2\|'}{2 \cdot \|T_1\|' \cdot \|T_2\|'}$	#14*	$\|T_1\|' \cdot \|T_2\|'$

Table 1: Set of features derived from texts T_1 and T_2

Edit-Distance: a similarity score for a pair of words can be obtained from their Edit Distance (Levenshtein, 1966) by normalizing and converting distance to similarity with the following expression: $\mathbf{sim}(t_i, t_j) = 1 - \frac{\text{EditDistance}(t_i, t_j)}{\max[\text{len}(t_i), \text{len}(t_j)]}$.

Jaro-Winkler: this measure is based on the Jaro (1989) similarity, which is given by this expression $\text{Jaro}(t_i, t_j) = \frac{1}{3}\left(\frac{c}{\text{len}(t_i)} + \frac{c}{\text{len}(t_j)} + \frac{c-m}{c}\right)$, where c is the number of characters in common within a sliding window of length $\frac{\max[\text{len}(t_i), \text{len}(t_j)]}{2} - 1$. To avoid division by 0, when $c = 0$ then $\text{Jaro}(t_i, t_j) = 0$. The number of transpositions m is obtained sorting the common characters according to their occurrence in each of the words and counting the number of non-matching characters. Winkler (1990) proposed an extension to this measure taking into account the common prefix length l through this expression: $\mathbf{sim}(t_i, t_j) = \text{Jaro}(t_i, t_j) + \frac{l}{10}(1 - \text{Jaro}(t_i, t_j))$.

3 Features from Cardinalities

For a pair of texts T_1 and T_2 represented as bags of words three basic soft cardinalities can be calculated: $|T_1|'$, $|T_2|'$ and $|T_1 \cup T_2|'$. The soft cardinality of their union is calculated using the concatenation of T_1 and T_2. More additional features can be derived from these three basic features, e.g. $|T_1 \cap T_2|' = |T_1|' + |T_2|' - |T_1 \cup T_2|'$ and $|T_1 - T_2|' = |T_1|' - |T_1 \cap T_2|'$. The complete set of features classified into three groups are shown in Table 1.

4 Submitted Runs Description

The data for the 2013 CLTE task consists of 4 data sets (*spa-eng*, *ita-eng*, *fra-eng* and *deu-eng*) each

Data set	q_1	q_2	α	$bias$
deu-eng	2	2	0.5	0.0
fra-eng	2	3	0.5	0.0
ita-eng	2	4	0.6	0.0
spa-eng	1	3	0.5	0.1

Table 2: Parameters of the q-grams word-similarity function for each language pair

with 1,000 pairs of texts for training and 500 for testing. For each pair of texts T_1 and T_2 written in two different languages, two translations are provided using the Google's translator[1]. Thus, T_1^t is a translation of T_1 into the language of T_2 and T_2^t is a translation of T_2 into the language of T_1. Using these pivoting translations, two pairs of texts can be compared: T_1 with T_2^t and T_1^t with T_2.

Then all training and testing texts and their translations were pre-processed with the following sequence of actions: *i)* text strings were tokenized, *ii)* uppercase characters are converted into lowercase equivalents, *iii)* stop words were removed, *iv)* punctuation marks were removed, and *v)* words were stemmed using the Snowball[2] multilingual stemmers provided by the NLTK Toolkit (Loper and Bird, 2002). Then every stemmed word is tagged with its *idf* weight (Jones, 2004) calculated with the complete collection of texts and translations in the same language.

Five instances of the soft cardinality are provided using 1, 2, 3, 4 and 5 as values of the parameter p. Therefore, the total number of features for each pair of texts is the multiplication of the number of features in the feature set (i.e. 14, see Table 1) by the number of soft cardinality functions (5) and by 2, corresponding to the two pairs of comparable texts. That is, $14 \times 5 \times 2 = 140$ features.

The **sim** function used was q-grams, whose parameters were adjusted for each language pair. These parameters, which are shown in Table 2, were obtained by manual exploration using the training data.

Four vector data sets for training (one for each language pair) were built by extracting the 140 features from the 1,000 training instances and using

[1]https://translate.google.com
[2]http://snowball.tartarus.org

	ECNUCS-team's system				
	spa-eng	*ita-eng*	*fra-eng*	*deu-eng*	average
run4	0.422	0.416	0.436	**0.452**	**0.432**
run3	0.408	0.426	**0.458**	0.432	0.431
	SOFTCARDINALITY-team's system				
	spa-eng	*ita-eng*	*fra-eng*	*deu-eng*	average
run1	**0.434**	**0.454**	0.416	0.414	0.430
run2	0.432	0.448	0.426	0.402	0.427

Table 3: Official results for our system and the top performing system ECNUCS (accuracies)

their gold-standard annotations as class attribute. Predictions for the 500 test cases were obtained through a SVM classifier trained with each data set. For the submitted *run1*, this SVM classifier used a linear kernel with its complexity parameter set to its default value $C = 1$. For the *run2*, this parameter was adjusted for each pair of languages with the following values: $C_{spa-eng} = 2.0$, $C_{ita-eng} = 1.5$, $C_{fra-eng} = 2.3$ and $C_{deu-eng} = 2.0$. The implementation of the SVM used is that which is available in WEKA v.3.6.9 (SMO) (Hall et al., 2009). Official results for *run1*, *run2* and best accuracies obtained among all participant systems are shown in Table 3.

5 A Single Multilingual Model

This section presents the results of our additional experiments in search for a simplified model and in turn to respond to the following questions: i) Can one simplified-multilingual model overcome the approach presented in Section 4? ii) Does using additional circular-pivoting translations improve performance? and iii) Do other word-similarity functions work better than the q-grams measure?

First, it is important to note that the approach described in Section 4 used only patterns discovered in cardinalities. This means, that no language-dependent features was used, with the exception of the stemmers. Therefore, we wonder whether the patterns discovered in a pair of languages can be useful in other language pairs. To answer this question, a single prediction model was built by aggregating instances from each of the vector data sets into one data set with 4,000 training instances. Afterward, this model was used to provide predictions for the 2,000 test cases.

Moreover, customization for each pair of languages in the word-similarity function, which is show in Table 2, was set on the following unique set of parameters: $q_1 = 1, q_2 = 3, \alpha = 0.5, bias = 0.0$. Thus, the words are compared using q-grams and the Dice coefficient. In addition to the measure of q-grams, two "off-the-shelf" measures were used as nonparametric alternatives, namely: Edit Distance (Levenshtein, 1966) and the Jaro-Winkler similarity (Winkler, 1990).

In another attempt to simplify this model, we evaluated the predictive ability of each of the three groups of features shown in Table 1. The combination of groups 2 and 3, consistently obtained better results when the evaluation with 10 fold cross-validation was used in the training data. This result was consistent with the simple training versus test data evaluation. The sum of all previous simplifications significantly reduced the number of parameters and features in comparison with the model described in Section 4. That is, only one SVM and 4 parameters, namely: α, $bias$, q_1 and q_2.

Besides, the additional use of circular-pivoting translations was tested. In the original model, for every pair of texts (T_1, T_2) their pivot translations (T_1^t, T_2^t) were provided allowing the calculation of $|T_1 \cup T_2^t|$ and $|T_1^t \cup T_2|$. Translations T_1^t and T_2^t can also be translated back to their original languages obtaining T_1^{tt} and T_2^{tt}. These additional translations in turn allows the calculation of $|T_1^{tt} \cup T_2^t|$ and $|T_1^t \cup T_2^{tt}|$. This procedure can be repeated again to obtain T_1^{ttt} and T_2^{ttt}, which in turn provides $|T_1 \cup T_2^{ttt}|$, $|T_1^{ttt} \cup T_2|$, $|T_1^{tt} \cup T_2^{ttt}|$ and $|T_1^{ttt} \cup T_2^{tt}|$. The original feature set is denoted as *t*. The extended feature sets using double-pivoting translations and triple-pivot translations are denoted respectively as *tt* and *ttt*.

The results obtained with this simplified model using single, double and triple pivot translations are shown in Table 4. The first column indicates the word-similarity function used by the soft cardinality and the second column indicates the number of pivoting translations.

6 Discussion

In spite of the customization of the parameter C in the *run2*, the *run1* obtained better results than *run2* (see Table 3). This result indicates that the simpler model produced better predictions in unseen data.

Soft C.	#*t*	*spa-e*	*ita-e*	*fra-e*	*deu-e*	avg.
Ed.Dist.	*t*	0.444	0.450	0.440	0.410	0.436
Ed.Dist.	*tt*	0.452	0.464	0.434	0.432	0.446
Ed.Dist.	*ttt*	**0.464**	0.468	0.440	0.424	0.449
Jaro-W.	*t*	0.422	0.450	0.426	0.406	0.426
Jaro-W.	*tt*	0.430	0.456	0.444	0.400	0.433
Jaro-W.	*ttt*	0.426	0.458	0.430	0.430	0.436
q-grams	*t*	0.428	0.456	0.456	**0.432**	0.443
q-grams	*tt*	0.436	**0.478**	0.444	0.430	0.447
q-grams	*ttt*	0.452	0.474	**0.464**	0.442	**0.458**

Table 4: Single-multilingual model results (accuracies)

It is also important to note that two of the three multilingual systems proposed in Section 5 achieved higher scores than the best official results (see rows containing "*t*" in Table 4). This indicates that the proposed simplified model is able to discover patterns in the cardinalities of a pair of languages and project them into the other language pairs.

Regarding the use of additional circular-pivoting translations, Table 4 shows that *t* was overcome on average by *tt* and *tt* by *ttt* in all cases of the three sets of results. The relative improvement obtained by comparing *t* versus *ttt* for each group was 3.0% in Edit Distance, 2.3% for Jaro-Winkler and 3.4% for the q-gram measure. This same trend holds roughly for each language pair.

7 Conclusions

We described the SOFTCARDINALITY system that participated in the SemEval CLTE evaluation campaign in 2013, obtaining the best results in data sets *spa-eng* and *ita-eng,* and achieving the third place on average. This result was obtained using separate models for each language pair. It was also concluded that a single-multilingual model outperforms that approach. Besides, we found that the use of additional pivoting translations provide better results. Finally, the measure based on q-grams of characters, used within the soft cardinality, resulted to be the best option among other measures of word similarity. In conclusion, the soft cardinality method used in combination with SMT and SVM classifiers is a competitive method for the CLTE task.

Acknowledgments

This research was funded in part by the Systems and Industrial Engineering Department, the Office of Student Welfare of the National University of Colombia, Bogotá, and through a grant from the Colombian Department for Science, Technology and Innovation, Colciencias, proj. 1101-521-28465 with funding from "El Patrimonio Autónomo Fondo Nacional de Financiamiento para la Ciencia, la Tecnología y la Innovación, Francisco José de Caldas." The third author recognizes the support from Mexican Government (SNI, COFAA-IPN, SIP 20131702, CONACYT 50206-H) and CONACYT–DST India (proj. 122030 "Answer Validation through Textual Entailment").

References

Corinna Cortes and Vladimir N. Vapnik. 1995. Support-vector networks. *Machine Learning*, 20(3):273–297.

Kevin Duh, Ching-Man Au Yeung, Tomoharu Iwata, and Masaaki Nagata. 2013. Managing information disparity in multilingual document collections. *ACM Trans. Speech Lang. Process.*, 10(1):1:1–1:28, March.

Mark Hall, Frank Eibe, Geoffrey Holmes, and Bernhard Pfahringer. 2009. The WEKA data mining software: An update. *SIGKDD Explorations*, 11(1):10–18.

Daniel S. Hirschberg. 1977. Algorithms for the longest common subsequence problem. *J. ACM*, 24(4):664–675, October.

M.A. Jaro. 1989. Advances in record-linkage methodology as applied to matching the 1985 census of tampa, florida. *Journal of the American Statistical Association*, pages 414–420, June.

Sergio Jimenez, Fabio Gonzalez, and Alexander Gelbukh. 2010. Text comparison using soft cardinality. In Edgar Chavez and Stefano Lonardi, editors, *String Processing and Information Retrieval*, volume 6393 of *LNCS*, pages 297–302. Springer, Berlin, Heidelberg.

Sergio Jimenez, Claudia Becerra, and Alexander Gelbukh. 2012. Soft cardinality+ ML: learning adaptive similarity functions for cross-lingual textual entailment. In *Proceedings of the 6th International Workshop on Semantic Evaluation (SemEval, *SEM 2012)*, Montreal, Canada. ACL.

Karen Spärck Jones. 2004. A statistical interpretation of term specificity and its application in retrieval. *Journal of Documentation*, 60(5):493–502, October.

Karen Kukich. 1992. Techniques for automatically correcting words in text. *ACM Computing Surveys*, 24:377–439, December.

Vladimir I. Levenshtein. 1966. Binary codes capable of correcting deletions, insertions, and reversals. *Soviet Physics Doklady*, 10(8):707–710.

Edward Loper and Steven Bird. 2002. NLTK: the natural language toolkit. In *Proceedings of the ACL Workshop on Effective Tools and Methodologies for Teaching Natural Language Processing and Computational Linguistics. Philadelphia*. Association for Computational Linguistics.

Yashar Mehdad, Matteo Negri, and Marcello Federico. 2012. Detecting semantic equivalence and information disparity in cross-lingual documents. In *Proceedings of the 50th Annual Meeting of the Association for Computational Linguistics: Short Papers - Volume 2*, ACL '12, page 120–124, Stroudsburg, PA, USA. Association for Computational Linguistics.

Matteo Negri, Luisa Bentivogli, Yashar Mehdad, Danilo Giampiccolo, and Alessandro Marchetti. 2011. Divide and conquer: crowdsourcing the creation of cross-lingual textual entailment corpora. In *Proceedings of the Conference on Empirical Methods in Natural Language Processing*, EMNLP '11, page 670–679, Stroudsburg, PA, USA. Association for Computational Linguistics.

Matteo Negri, Alessandro Marchetti, Yashar Mehdad, Luisa Bentivogli, and Danilo Giampiccolo. 2012. 2012. semeval-2012 task 8: Cross-lingual textual entailment for content synchronization. In *Proceedings of the 6th International Workshop on Semantic Evaluation (SemEval 2012)*, Montreal, Canada.

Matteo Negri, Alessandro Marchetti, Yashar Mehdad, and Luisa Bentivogli. 2013. Semeval-2013 task 8: Cross-lingual textual entailment for content synchronization. In *Proceedings of the 7th International Workshop on Semantic Evaluation (SemEval 2013)*.

Gerard Salton, Andrew K. C. Wong, and Chung-Shu Yang. 1975. A vector space model for automatic indexing. *Commun. ACM*, 18(11):613–620.

William E. Winkler. 1990. String comparator metrics and enhanced decision rules in the fellegi-sunter model of record linkage. In *Proceedings of the Section on Survey Research Methods*, pages 354–359. American Statistical Association.

SemEval-2013 Task 5: Evaluating Phrasal Semantics

Ioannis Korkontzelos
National Centre for Text Mining
School of Computer Science
University of Manchester, UK
ioannis.korkontzelos@man.ac.uk

Torsten Zesch
UKP Lab, CompSci Dept.
Technische Universität Darmstadt
Germany
zesch@ukp.informatik.tu-darmstadt.de

Fabio Massimo Zanzotto
Department of Enterprise Engineering
University of Rome "Tor Vergata"
Italy
zanzotto@info.uniroma2.it

Chris Biemann
FG Language Technology, CompSci Dept.
Technische Universität Darmstadt
Germany
biem@cs.tu-darmstadt.de

Abstract

This paper describes the SemEval-2013 Task 5: "Evaluating Phrasal Semantics". Its first subtask is about computing the semantic similarity of words and compositional phrases of minimal length. The second one addresses deciding the compositionality of phrases in a given context. The paper discusses the importance and background of these subtasks and their structure. In succession, it introduces the systems that participated and discusses evaluation results.

1 Introduction

Numerous past tasks have focused on leveraging the meaning of word types or words in context. Examples of the former are noun categorization and the TOEFL test, examples of the latter are word sense disambiguation, metonymy resolution, and lexical substitution. As these tasks have enjoyed a lot success, a natural progression is the pursuit of models that can perform similar tasks taking into account multiword expressions and complex compositional structure. In this paper, we present two subtasks designed to evaluate such phrasal models:

a. Semantic similarity of words and compositional phrases

b. Evaluating the compositionality of phrases in context

For example, the first subtask addresses computing how similar the word "valuation" is to the compositional sequence "price assessment", while the second subtask addresses deciding whether the phrase "piece of cake" is used literally or figuratively in the sentence "Labour was a piece of cake!".

The aim of these subtasks is two-fold. Firstly, considering that there is a spread interest lately in phrasal semantics in its various guises, they provide an opportunity to draw together approaches to numerous related problems under a common evaluation set. It is intended that after the competition, the evaluation setting and the datasets will comprise an on-going benchmark for the evaluation of these phrasal models.

Secondly, the subtasks attempt to bridge the gap between established lexical semantics and full-blown linguistic inference. Thus, we anticipate that they will stimulate an increased interest around the general issue of phrasal semantics. We use the notion of phrasal semantics here as opposed to lexical compounds or compositional semantics. Bridging the gap between lexical semantics and linguistic inference could provoke novel approaches to certain established tasks, such as lexical entailment and paraphrase identification. In addition, it could ul-

*Second Joint Conference on Lexical and Computational Semantics (*SEM), Volume 2: Seventh International Workshop on Semantic Evaluation (SemEval 2013)*, pages 39–47, Atlanta, Georgia, June 14-15, 2013.

timately lead to improvements in a wide range of applications in natural language processing, such as document retrieval, clustering and classification, question answering, query expansion, synonym extraction, relation extraction, automatic translation, or textual advertisement matching in search engines, all of which depend on phrasal semantics.

The remainder of this paper is structured as follows: Section 2 presents details about the data sources and the variety of sources applicable to the task. Section 3 discusses the first subtask, which is about semantic similarity of words and compositional phrases. In subsection 3.1 the subtask is described in detail together with some information about its background. Subsection 3.2 discusses the data creation process and subsection 3.3 discusses the participating systems and their results. Section 4 introduces the second subtask, which is about evaluating the compositionality of phrases in context. Subsection 4.1 explains the data creation process for this subtask. In subsection 4.2 the evaluation statistics of participating systems are presented. Section 5 is a discussion about the conclusions of the entire task. Finally, in section 6 we summarize this presentation and discuss briefly our vision about challenges in distributional semantics.

2 Data Sources & Methodology

Data instances of both subtasks are drawn from the large-scale, freely available WaCky corpora (Baroni et al., 2009). The resource contains corpora in 4 languages: English, French, German and Italian. The English corpus, *ukWaC*, consists of 2 billion words and was constructed by crawling to the .uk domain of the web and using medium-frequency words from the *BNC* as seeds. The corpus is part-of-speech (PoS) tagged and lemmatized using the TreeTagger (Schmid, 1994). The French corpus, *frWaC*, contains 1.6 billion word corpus and was constructed by web-crawling the .fr domain and using medium-frequency words from the *Le Monde Diplomatique* corpus and basic French vocabulary lists as seeds. The corpus was PoS tagged and lemmatized with the TreeTagger. The French corpus, *deWaC*, consists of 1.7 billion word corpus and was constructed by crawling the .de domain and using medium-frequency words from the *SudDeutsche Zeitung corpus* and basic German vocabulary lists as seeds. The corpus was PoS tagged and lemmatized with the TreeTagger. The Italian corpus, *itWaC*, is a 2 billion word corpus constructed from the .it domain of the web using medium-frequency words from the *Repubblica corpus* and basic Italian vocabulary lists as seeds. The corpus was PoS tagged with the TreeTagger, and lemmatized using the *Morph-it!* lexicon (Zanchetta and Baroni, 2005). Several versions of the WaCky corpora, with various extra annotations or modifications are also available[1].

We ensured that data instances occur frequently enough in the WaCky corpora, so that participating systems could gather statistics for building distributional vectors or other uses. As the evaluation data only contains very small annotated samples from freely available web documents, and the original source is provided, we could provide them without violating copyrights.

The size of the WaCky corpora is suitable for training reliable distributional models. Sentences are already lemmatized and part-of-speech tagged. Participating approaches making use of distributional methods, part-of-speech tags or lemmas, were strongly encouraged to use these corpora and their shared preprocessing, to ensure the highest possible comparability of results. Additionally, this had the potential to considerably reduce the workload of participants. For the first subtask, data were provided in English, German and Italian and for the second subtask in English and German.

The range of methods applicable to both subtasks was deliberately not limited to any specific branch of methods, such as distributional or vector models of semantic compositionality. We believe that the subtasks can be tackled from different directions and we expect a great deal of the scientific benefit to lie in the comparison of very different approaches, as well as how these approaches can be combined. An exception to this rule is the fact that participants in the first subtask were not allowed to use directly definitions extracted from dictionaries or lexicons. Since the subtask is considered fundamental and its data were created from online knowledge resources, systems using the same tools to address it would be of limited use. However, participants were allowed to

[1] WaCky website: wacky.sslmit.unibo.it

use other information residing in dictionaries, such as Wordnet synsets or synset relations.

Participating systems were allowed to attempt one or both subtasks, in one or all of the languages supported. However, it was expected that systems performing well at the first basic subtask would provide a good starting point for dealing with the second subtask, which is considered harder. Moreover, language-independent models were of special interest.

3 Subtask 5a: Semantic Similarity of Words and Compositional Phrases

The aim of this subtask is to evaluate the component of a semantic model that computes the similarity between word sequences of different length. Participating systems are asked to estimate the semantic similarity of a word and a short sequence of two words. For example, they should be able to figure out that *contact* and *close interaction* are similar whereas *megalomania* and *great madness* are not.

This subtask addresses a core problem, since satisfactory performance in computing the similarity of full sentences depends on similarity computations on shorter sequences.

3.1 Background and Description

This subtask is based on the assumption that we first need a basic set of functions to compose the meaning of two words, in order to construct more complex models that compositionally determine the meaning of sentences, as a second step. For compositional distributional semantics, the need for these basic functions is discussed in Mitchell and Lapata (2008). Since then, many models have been proposed for addressing the task (Mitchell and Lapata, 2010; Baroni and Zamparelli, 2010; Guevara, 2010), but still comparative analysis is in general based on comparing sequences that consist of two words.

As in Zanzotto et al. (2010), this subtask proposes to compare the similarity of a 2-word sequence and a single word. This is important as it is the basic step to analyse models that can compare any word sequences of different length.

The development and testing set for this subtask were built based on the idea described in Zanzotto et al. (2010). Dictionaries were used as sources of

contact/[kon-takt]

1. the act or state of touching; a touching or meeting, as of two things or people.
2. close interaction
3. an acquaintance, colleague, or relative through whom a person can gain access to information, favors, influential people, and the like.

Figure 1: The definition of *contact* in a sample dictionary

positive training examples. Dictionaries are natural repositories of equivalences between words under definition and sequences of words used for defining them. Figure 1 presents the definition of the word *contact*, from which the pair *(contact, close interaction)* can be extracted. Such equivalences extracted from dictionaries can be seen as natural and unbiased data instances. This idea opens numerous opportunities:

- Since definitions in dictionaries are syntactically rich, we are able to create examples for different syntactic relations.
- We have the opportunity to extract positive examples for languages for which dictionaries with sufficient entries are available.

Negative examples were generated by matching words under definition with randomly chosen defining sequences. In the following subsection, we provide details about the application of this idea to build the development and testing set for subtask 5a.

3.2 Data Creation

Data for this subtask were provided in English, German and Italian. Pairs of words under definitions and defining sequences were extracted from the English, German and Italian part of Wiktionary, respectively. In particular, for each language, all Wiktionary entries were downloaded and part-of-speech tagged using the Genia tagger (Tsuruoka et al., 2005). In succession, definitions that start with noun phrases

Language	Train set	Test set	Total
English	5,861	3,907	9,768
German	1,516	1,010	2,526
Italian	1,275	850	2,125
German - no names	1,101	733	1,834

Table 1: Quantitative characteristics of the datasets

were kept, only. For the purpose of extracting word and sequence pairs for this subtask, we consider as noun phrases, sequences that consist of adjectives or noun and end with a noun. In cases where the extracted noun phrase was longer than two words, the right-most two sequences were kept, since in most cases noun phrases are governed by their right-most component. Subsequently, we discarded instances whose words occur too infrequently in the WaCky corpora (Baroni et al., 2009) of each language. WaCky corpora are available freely and are large enough for participating systems to extract distributional statistics. Taking the numbers of extracted instances into account, we set the frequency thresholds at 10 occurrences for English and 5 for German and Italian.

Data instances extracted following this process were then checked by a computational linguist. Candidate pairs in which the definition sequence was not judged to be a precise and adequate definition of the word under definition were discarded. These cases were very limited and mostly account for shortcomings of the very simple pattern used for extraction. For example, the pair *(standard, transmission vehicle)* coming from the definition of "standard" as "A manual transmission vehicle" was discarded. Similarly in German, the pair *(Fremde (Eng. stranger), weibliche Person (Eng. female person))* was discarded. "Fremde", which is of female grammatical genre, was defined as "weibliche Person, die man nicht kennt *(Eng. female person, one does not know)*". In Italian, the pair *(paese (Eng. land, country, region), grande estensione (Eng. large tract))* was discarded, since the original definition was "grande estensione di terreno abitato e generalmente coltivato *(Eng. large tract of land inhabited and cultivated in general)*".

The final data sets were divided into training and held-out testing sets, according to a 60% and 40% ratio, respectively. The first three rows of table 1 present the numbers of the train and test sets for the three languages chosen. It was identified that a fair percentage of the German instances (approximately 27%) refer to the definitions of first names or family names. This is probably a flaw of the German part of Wiktionary. In addition, the pattern used for extraction happens to apply to the definitions of names. Name instances were discarded from the German data set to produce the data set described in the last row of table 1.

The training set was released approximately 3 months earlier than the test data. Instances in both set ware annotated as positive or negative. Test set annotations were not released to the participants, but were used for evaluation, only.

3.3 Results

Participating systems were evaluated on their ability to predict correctly whether the components of each test instance, i.e. word-sequence pair, are semantically similar or distinct. Participants were allowed to use or ignore the training data, i.e. the systems could be supervised or unsupervised. Unsupervised systems were allowed to use the training data for development and parameter tuning. Since this is a core task, participating systems were not be able to use dictionaries or other prefabricated lists. Instead, they were allowed to use distributional similarity models, selectional preferences, measures of semantic similarity etc.

Participating system responses were scored in terms of standard information retrieval measures: accuracy (A), precision (P), recall (R) and F_1 score (Radev et al., 2003). Systems were encouraged to submit at most 3 solutions for each language, but submissions for fewer languages were accepted.

Five research teams participated. Ten system runs were submitted for English, one for German (on data set: German - no names) and one for Italian. Table 2 illustrates the results of the evaluation process. The teams of *(HsH)* (Wartena, 2013), *CLaC* (Siblini and Kosseim, 2013), *UMCC_DLSI-(EPS)* (Dávila et al., 2013), and *ITNLP*, the Harbin Institute of Technology, approached the task in a supervised way, while *MELODI* (Van de Cruys et al., 2013) participated with two unsupervised approaches. Interestingly,

Language	Rank	Participant Id	run Id	A	R	P	rej. R	rej. P	F_1
English	1	HsH	1	.803	.752	.837	.854	.775	.792
	3	CLaC	3	.794	.707	.856	.881	.750	.774
	2	CLaC	2	.794	.695	.867	.893	.745	.771
	4	CLaC	1	.788	.638	.910	.937	.721	.750
	5	MELODI	lvw	.748	.614	.838	.882	.695	.709
	6	UMCC_DLSI-(EPS)	1	.724	.613	.787	.834	.683	.689
	7	ITNLP	3	.703	.501	.840	.904	.645	.628
	8	MELODI	dm	.689	.481	.825	.898	.634	.608
	9	ITNLP	1	.663	.392	.857	.934	.606	.538
	10	ITNLP	2	.659	.427	.797	.891	.609	.556
German	1	HsH	1	.825	.765	.870	.885	.790	.814
Italian	1	UMCC_DLSI-(EPS)	1	.675	.576	.718	.774	.646	.640

Table 2: Task 5a: Evaluation results. A, P, R, rej. and F_1 stand for accuracy, precision, recall, rejection and F_1 score, respectively.

these approaches performed better than some supervised ones for this experiment. Below, we summarise the properties of participating systems.

(HsH) (Wartena, 2013) used distributed similarity and especially random indexing to compute similarities between words and possible definitions, under the hypothesis that a word and its definition are distributionally more similar than a word and an arbitrary definition. Considering all open-class words, context vectors over the entire WaCky corpus were computed for the word under definition, the defining sequence, its component words separately, the addition and multiplication of the vectors of the component words and a general context vector. Then, various similarity measures were computed on the vectors, including an innovative length-normalised version of Jensen-Shannon divergence. The similarity values are used to train a Support Vector Machine (SVM) classifier (Cortes and Vapnik, 1995).

The first approach (run 1) of *CLaC* (Siblini and Kosseim, 2013) is based on a weighted semantic network to measure semantic relatedness between the word and the components of the phrase. A PART classifier is used to generate a partial decision trained on the semantic relatedness information of the labelled training set. The second approach uses a supervised distributional method based on words frequently occurring in the Web1TB corpus to calculate relatedness. A JRip classifier is used to generate rules trained on the semantic relatedness information of the training set. This approach was used in conjunction with the first one as a backup method (run 2). In addition, features generated by both approaches were used to train the JRIP classifier collectively (run 3).

The first approach of *MELODI* (Van de Cruys et al., 2013), called *lvw*, uses a dependency-based vector space model computed over the ukWaC corpus, in combination with Latent Vector Weighting (Van de Cruys et al., 2011). The system computes the similarity between the first noun and the head noun of the second phrase, which was weighted according to the semantics of the modifier. The second approach, called *dm*, used a dependency-based vector space model, but, unlike the first approach, disregarded the modifier in the defining sequence. Since both systems are unsupervised, the training data was used to train a similarity threshold parameter, only.

UMCC_DLSI-(EPS) (Dávila et al., 2013) locates the synsets of words in data instances and computes the semantic distances between each synset of the word under definition and each synsets of the defining sequence words. In succession, a classifier is trained using features based on distance and WordNet relations.

The first attempt of *ITNLP* (run 1) consisted of an SVM classifier trained on semantic similarity computations between the word under definition and the defining sequence in each instance. Their second attempt also uses an SVM, however trained on WordNet-based similarities. The third attempt of *ITNLP* is a combination of the previous two; it combines their features to train an SVM classifier.

4 Subtask 5b: Semantic Compositionality in Context

An interesting sub-problem of semantic compositionality is to decide whether a target phrase is used in its literal or figurative meaning in a given context. For example "big picture" might be used literally as in *Click here for a bigger picture* or figuratively as in *To solve this problem, you have to look at the bigger picture.* Another example is "old school" which can also be used literally or figuratively: *He will go down in history as one of the old school, a true gentlemen.* vs. *During the 1970's the hall of the old school was converted into the library.*

Being able to detect whether a phrase is used literally or figuratively is e.g. especially important for information retrieval, where figuratively used words should be treated separately to avoid false positives. For example, the example sentence *He will go down in history as one of the old school, a true gentlemen.* should probably not be retrieved for the query "school". Rather, the insights generated from subtask 5a could be utilized to retrieve sentences using a similar phrase such as "gentleman-like behavior". The task may also be of interest to the related research fields of metaphor detection and idiom identification.

There were no restrictions regarding the array of methods, and the kind of resources that could be employed for this task. In particular, participants were allowed to make use of pre-fabricated lists of phrases annotated with their probability of being used figuratively from publicly available sources, or to produce these lists from corpora. Assessing how well the phrase suits its context might be tackled using e.g. measures of semantic relatedness as well as distributional models learned from the underlying corpus.

Participants of this subtask were provided with real usage examples of target phrases. For each usage example, the task is to make a binary decision whether the target phrase is used literally or figuratively in this context. Systems were tested in two different disciplines: a *known phrases* task where all target phrases in the test set were contained in the training, and an *unknown phrases* setting, where all target phrases in the test set were unseen.

4.1 Data Creation

The first step in creating the corpus was to compile a list of phrases that can be used either literally or metaphorically. Thus, we created an initial list of several thousand English idioms from Wiktionary by listing all entries under the category ENGLISH IDIOMS using the JWKTL Wiktionary API (Zesch et al., 2008). We manually filtered the list removing most idioms that are very unlikely to be ever used literally (anymore), e.g. *to knock on heaven's door.* For each of the resulting list of phrases, we extracted usage contexts from the ukWaC corpus (Baroni et al., 2009). Each usage context contains 5 sentences, where the sentence with the target phrase appears in a randomized position. Due to segmentation errors, some usage contexts actually might contain less than 5 sentences, but we manually filtered all usage contexts where the remaining context was insufficient. This was done in the final cleaning step where we also manually removed (near) duplicates, obvious spam, encoding problems etc.

The target phrases in context were annotated for *figurative, literal, both* or *impossible to tell* usage, using the CrowdFlower[2] crowdsourcing annotation platform. We used about 8% of items as "gold" items for quality assurance, and had each example annotated by three crowdworkers. The task was comparably easy for crowdworkers, who reached 90%-94% pairwise agreement, and 95% success on the gold items. About 5% of items with low agreement and marked as impossible were removed. Table 3 summarizes the quantitative characteristics of all datasets resulting from this process. We took care in sampling the data as to keep similar distributions across the training, development and testing parts.

4.2 Results

Training and development datasets were made available in advance, test data was provided during the evaluation period without labels. System perfor-

[2] www.crowdflower.com

Task	Dataset	# Phrases	# Items	Items per phrase	# Liter.	# Figur.	# Both
	train	10	1,424	68–188	702	719	3
known	dev	10	358	17–47	176	181	1
	test	10	594	28–78	294	299	1
	train	31	1,114	4–75	458	653	3
unseen	dev	9	342	4–74	141	200	1
	test	15	518	8–73	198	319	1

Table 3: Quantitative characteristics of the datasets

Rank	System	Run	Accuracy
1	IIRG	3	.779
2	UNAL	2	.754
3	UNAL	1	.722
5	IIRG	1	.530
4	*Baseline MFC*	-	.503
6	IIRG	2	.502

Table 4: Task 5b: Evaluation results for the known phrases setting

Rank	System	Run	Accuracy
1	UNAL	1	.668
2	UNAL	2	.645
3	*Baseline MFC*	-	.616
4	CLaC	1	.550

Table 5: Task 5b: Evaluation results for the unseen phrases setting

mance was measured in accuracy. Since all participants provided classifications for all test items, the accuracy score is equivalent to precision/recall/F1. Participants were allowed to enter up to three different runs for evaluation. We also provide baseline accuracy scores, which are obtained by always assigning the most frequent class (figurative).

Table 4 provides the evaluation results for the known phrases task, while Table 5 ranks participants for the unseen phrases task. As expected, the *unseen phrases* setting is much harder than the *known phrases* setting, as for unseen phrases it is not possible to learn lexicalised contextual clues. In both settings, the winning entries were able to beat the MFC baseline. While performance in the *known phrases* setting is close to 80% and thus acceptable, the general task of recognizing the literal or figurative use of unseen phrases remains very challenging, with only a small improvement over the baseline. We refer to the system descriptions for more details on the techniques used for this subtask: *UNAL* (Jimenez et al., 2013), *IIRG* (Byrne et al., 2013) and *CLaC* (Siblini and Kosseim, 2013).

5 Task Conclusions

In this section, we further discuss the findings and conclusion of the evaluation challenge in the task of "Phrasal Semantics".

Looking at the results of both subtasks, one observes that the maximum performance achieved is higher for the first than the second subtask. For this comparison to be fair, trivial baselines should be taken into account. A system randomly assigning an output value would be on average 50% correct in the first subtask, since the numbers of positive and negative instances in the testing set are equal. Similarly, a system assigning the most frequent class, i.e. the figurative use of any phrase, would be 50.3% and 61.6% accurate in the second subtask for seen and unseen test instances, respectively. It should also be noted that the testing instances in the first subtask are unseen in the respective training set. As a result, in terms of baselines, the second subtask on unseen data (Table 5) should be considered easier than the first subtask (Table 2). However, the best performing systems achieved much higher accuracy in the first than in the second subtask. This contradiction confirms our conception that the first subtask is less complex than the second.

In the first subtask, it is evident that no method performs much better or much worse than the others.

Although the participating systems have employed a wide variety of approaches and tools, the difference between the best and worst accuracy achieved is relatively limited, in particular approximately 14%. Even more interestingly, unsupervised approaches performed better than some supervised ones. This observation suggests that no "golden recipe" has been identified so far for this task. Thus, probably different processing tools take advantage of different sources of information. It is a matter of future research to identify these sources and the corresponding tools, and then develop hybrid methods of improved performance.

In the second subtask, the results of evaluation on known phrases are much higher than on unseen phrases. This was expected, as for unseen phrases it is not possible to learn lexicalised contextual clues. Thus, the second subtask has succeeded in identifying the complexity threshold up to which the current state-of-the-art can address the computational problem. Further than this threshold, i.e. for unseen phrases, current systems have not yet succeeded in addressing it. In conclusion, the difficulty in evaluating the compositionality of previously unseen phrases in context highlights the overall complexity of the second subtask.

6 Summary and Future Work

In this paper we have presented the 5th task of SemEval 2013, "Evaluating Phrasal Semantics", which consists of two subtasks: (1) semantic similarity of words and compositional phrases, and (2) compositionality of phrases in context. The former subtask, which focussed on the first step of composing the meaning of phrases of any length, is less complex than the latter subtask, which considers the effect of context to the semantics of a phrase. The paper presents details about the background and importance of these subtasks, the data creation process, the systems that took part in the evaluation and their results.

In the future, we expect evaluation challenges on phrasal semantics to progress towards two directions: (a) the synthesis of semantics of sequences longer than two words, and (b) aiming to improve the performance of systems that determine the compositionality of previously unseen phrases in context. The evaluation results of the first task suggest that state-of-the-art systems can compose the semantics of two word sequences with a promising level of success. However, this task should be seen as the first step towards composing the semantics of sentence-long sequences. As far as subtask 5b is concerned, the accuracy achieved by the participating systems on unseen testing data was low, only slightly better than the most frequent class baseline, which assigns the figurative use to all test phrases. Thus, the subtask cannot be considered well addressed by the state-of-the-art and further progress should be sought.

Acknowledgements

The work relevant to subtask 5a described in this paper is funded by the European Community's Seventh Framework Program (FP7/2007-2013) under grant agreement no. 318736 (OSSMETER).

We would like to thank Tristan Miller for helping with the subtleties of English idiomatic expressions, and Eugenie Giesbrecht for support in the organization of subtask 5b. This work has been supported by the Volkswagen Foundation as part of the Lichtenberg-Professorship Program under grant No. I/82806, and by the Hessian research excellence program Landes-Offensive zur Entwicklung Wissenschaftlich-ökonomischer Exzellenz (LOEWE) as part of the research center *Digital Humanities*.

References

Marco Baroni and Roberto Zamparelli. 2010. Nouns are vectors, adjectives are matrices: Representing adjective-noun constructions in semantic space. In *Proceedings of the 2010 Conference on Empirical Methods in Natural Language Processing*, pages 1183–1193, Cambridge, MA. Association for Computational Linguistics.

Marco Baroni, Silvia Bernardini, Adriano Ferraresi, and Eros Zanchetta. 2009. The WaCky wide web: a collection of very large linguistically processed web-crawled corpora. *Language Resources and Evaluation*, 43(3):209–226.

Lorna Byrne, Caroline Fenlon, and John Dunnion. 2013. IIRG: A naive approach to evaluating phrasal semantics. In *Proceedings of the 6th International Workshop on Semantic Evaluation (SemEval 2012)*, Atlanta, Georgia, USA.

Corinna Cortes and Vladimir Vapnik. 1995. Support-vector networks. *Machine Learning*, 20(3):273–297.

Héctor Dávila, Antonio Fernández Orquín, Alexander Chávez, Yoan Gutiérrez, Armando Collazo, José I. Abreu, Andrés Montoyo, and Rafael Muñoz. 2013. UMCC_DLSI-(EPS): Paraphrases detection based on semantic distance. In *Proceedings of the 6th International Workshop on Semantic Evaluation (SemEval 2012)*, Atlanta, Georgia, USA.

Emiliano Guevara. 2010. A regression model of adjective-noun compositionality in distributional semantics. In *Proceedings of the 2010 Workshop on GEometrical Models of Natural Language Semantics*, pages 33–37, Uppsala, Sweden. Association for Computational Linguistics.

Sergio Jimenez, Claudia Becerra, and Alexander Gelbukh. 2013. UNAL: Discriminating between literal and figurative phrasal usage using distributional statistics and POS tags. In *Proceedings of the 6th International Workshop on Semantic Evaluation (SemEval 2012)*, Atlanta, Georgia, USA.

Jeff Mitchell and Mirella Lapata. 2008. Vector-based models of semantic composition. In *Proceedings of ACL-08: HLT*, pages 236–244, Columbus, Ohio. Association for Computational Linguistics.

Jeff Mitchell and Mirella Lapata. 2010. Composition in distributional models of semantics. *Cognitive Science*, 34(8):1388–1429.

Dragomir R. Radev, Simone Teufel, Horacio Saggion, Wai Lam, John Blitzer, Hong Qi, Arda Çelebi, Danyu Liu, and Elliott Drabek. 2003. Evaluation challenges in large-scale document summarization. In *Proceedings of the 41st Annual Meeting on Association for Computational Linguistics - Volume 1*, ACL '03, pages 375–382, Morristown, NJ, USA. Association for Computational Linguistics.

Helmut Schmid. 1994. Probabilistic Part-of-Speech tagging using decision trees. In *Proceedings of the International Conference on New Methods in Language Processing*, Manchester, UK.

Reda Siblini and Leila Kosseim. 2013. CLaC: Semantic relatedness of words and phrases. In *Proceedings of the 6th International Workshop on Semantic Evaluation (SemEval 2012)*, Atlanta, Georgia, USA.

Yoshimasa Tsuruoka, Yuka Tateishi, Jin-Dong Kim, Tomoko Ohta, John McNaught, Sophia Ananiadou, and Jun'ichi Tsujii. 2005. Developing a robust Part-of-Speech tagger for biomedical text. In Panayiotis Bozanis and Elias N. Houstis, editors, *Advances in Informatics*, volume 3746, chapter 36, pages 382–392. Springer Berlin Heidelberg, Berlin, Heidelberg.

Tim Van de Cruys, Thierry Poibeau, and Anna Korhonen. 2011. Latent vector weighting for word meaning in context. In *Proceedings of the Conference on Empirical Methods in Natural Language Processing*, EMNLP '11, pages 1012–1022, Stroudsburg, PA, USA. Association for Computational Linguistics.

Tim Van de Cruys, Stergos Afantenos, and Philippe Muller. 2013. MELODI: Semantic similarity of words and compositional phrases using latent vector weighting. In *Proceedings of the 6th International Workshop on Semantic Evaluation (SemEval 2012)*, Atlanta, Georgia, USA.

Christian Wartena. 2013. HsH: Estimating semantic similarity of words and short phrases with frequency normalized distance measures. In *Proceedings of the 6th International Workshop on Semantic Evaluation (SemEval 2012)*, Atlanta, Georgia, USA.

Eros Zanchetta and Marco Baroni. 2005. Morph-it!: A free corpus-based morphological resource for the italian language. *Corpus Linguistics 2005*, 1(1).

Fabio Massimo Zanzotto, Ioannis Korkontzelos, Francesca Fallucchi, and Suresh Manandhar. 2010. Estimating linear models for compositional distributional semantics. In *Proceedings of the 23rd International Conference on Computational Linguistics (COLING)*.

Torsten Zesch, Christof Müller, and Iryna Gurevych. 2008. Extracting lexical semantic knowledge from Wikipedia and Wiktionary. *Proceedings of the Conference on Language Resources and Evaluation (LREC)*, 15:60.

HsH: Estimating Semantic Similarity of Words and Short Phrases with Frequency Normalized Distance Measures

Christian Wartena
Hochschule Hannover – University of Applied Sciences and Arts
Department of Information and Communication
Expo Plaza 12, 30539 Hannover, Germany
Christian.Wartena@hs-hannover.de

Abstract

This paper describes the approach of the Hochschule Hannover to the SemEval 2013 Task *Evaluating Phrasal Semantics*. In order to compare a single word with a two word phrase we compute various distributional similarities, among which a new similarity measure, based on Jensen-Shannon Divergence with a correction for frequency effects. The classification is done by a support vector machine that uses all similarities as features. The approach turned out to be the most successful one in the task.

1 Introduction

The task *Evaluating Phrasal Semantics* of the 2013 International Workshop on Semantic Evaluation (Manandhar and Yuret, 2013) consists of two subtasks. For the first subtask a list of pairs consisting of a single word and a two word phrase are given. For the English task a labeled list of 11,722 pairs was provided for training and a test set with 3,906 unlabeled examples. For German the training set contains 2,202 and the test set 732 pairs. The system should be able to tell whether the two word phrase is a definition of the single word or not. This task is somewhat different from the usual perspective of finding synonyms, since definitions are usually more general than the words they define.

In distributional semantics words are represented by context vectors and similarities of these context vectors are assumed to reflect similarities of the words they represent. We compute context vectors for all words using the lemmatized version of the Wacky Corpora for English (UKWaC, approximately 2,2 billion words) and German (DeWaC, 1,7 billion words) (Baroni et al., 2009). For the phrases we compute the context vectors as well directly on the base of occurrences of that phrase, as well as by construction from the context vectors of the two components. For the similarities between the vectors we use Jensen-Shannon divergence (JSD) and cosine similarity. Since the JSD is extremely dependent on the number of occurrences of the words, we define a new similarity measure that corrects for this dependency. Since none of the measures gives satisfactory results, we use all measures to train a support vector machine that classifies the pairs.

The remainder of this paper is organized as follows. We start with an overview of related work. In section 3 we discuss the dependence of JSD on word frequency and introduce a new similarity measure. Section 4 then describes the system. The results are given in section 5 and are discussed in section 6.

2 Related Work

Though distributional similarity has widely been studied and has become an established method to find similar words, there is no consensus on the way the context of a word has to be defined and on the best way to compute the similarity between two contexts. In the most general definitions the context of a word consists of a number of words and their relation to the given word (Grefenstette, 1992; Curran and Moens, 2002). In the following we will only consider the simplest case in which there is only one relation: the relation of being in the same sentence. Each word can be represented by a so called *con-*

*Second Joint Conference on Lexical and Computational Semantics (*SEM), Volume 2: Seventh International Workshop on Semantic Evaluation (SemEval 2013)*, pages 48–52, Atlanta, Georgia, June 14-15, 2013.

text vector in a high dimensional word space. Since these vectors will be sparse, often dimensionality reduction techniques are applied. In the present paper we use random indexing, introduced by Karlgren and Sahlgren (2001) and Sahlgren (2005) to reduce the size of the context vectors.

The way in which the context vectors are constructed also determines what similarity measures are suited. For random indexing Görnerup and Karlgren (2010) found that best results are obtained using L1-norm or Jensen-Shannon divergence (JSD). they also report that these measures highly correlate. We could confirm this in a preliminary experiment and therefore only use JSD in the following.

Recently, the question whether and how an appropriate context vector for a phrase can be derived from the context vectors of its components has become a central issue in distributional semantics (Clark and Pulman, 2007; Mitchell and Lapata, 2008; Widdows, 2008; Clarke et al., 2008). It is not yet clear which way of combining the vectors of the components is best suited for what goals. Giesbrecht (2010) and Mitchell and Lapata (2008) e.g. find that for noun-noun compounds the product of context vectors (corresponding to the intersection of contexts) and more complex tensor products give best results, while Guevara (2011) obtains best results for adjective-noun phrases with addition of vectors (corresponding to union of contexts). Since we do not (yet) have a single best similarity measure to distinguish definitions from non-definitions, we use a combination of similarity measures to train a model as e.g. also was done by Bär et al. (2012).

3 Frequency Dependency Correction of Jensen-Shannon Divergence

Weeds et al. (2004) observed that in tasks in which related words have to be found, some measures prefer words with a frequency similar to that of the target word while others prefer high frequent words, regardless of the frequency of the target word. Since Görnerup and Karlgren (2010) found that L1-norm and JSD give best results for similarity of random index vectors, we are especially interested in JSD. The JSD of two distributions p and q is given by

$$\text{JSD}(p,q) = \tfrac{1}{2}D(p||\tfrac{1}{2}p+\tfrac{1}{2}q)+\tfrac{1}{2}D(q||\tfrac{1}{2}p+\tfrac{1}{2}q) \quad (1)$$

where $D(p||q) = \Sigma_i p(i)\frac{\log p(i)}{\log q(i)}$ is the Kullback-Leibler divergence. We will follow the usual terminology of context *vectors*. However, we will always normalize the vectors, such that they can be interpreted as probability mass distributions. According to Weeds et al. (2004) the JSD belongs to the category of distance measures that tends to give small distances for highly frequent words. In Wartena et al. (2010) we also made this observation and therefore we added an additional constraint on the selection of keywords that should avoid the selection of too general words. In the present paper we try to explicitly model the dependency between the JSD and the number of occurrences of the involved words. We then use the difference between the JSD of the co-occurrence vectors of two words and the JSD expected on the base of the frequency of these words as a similarity measure. In the following we will use the dependency between the JSD and the frequency of the words directly. In (Wartena, 2013) we model the JSD instead as a function of the number of non zero values in the context vectors. The latter dependency can be modeled by a simpler function, but did not work as well with the SemEval data set.

Given two words w_1 and w_2 the JSD of their context vectors can be modeled as a function of the minimum of the number of occurrences of w_1 and w_2. Figure 3 shows the JSD of the context vectors of the words of the training set and the context vector of the definition phrase. In this figure the JSD of the positive and the negative examples is marked with different marks. The lower bound of the negative examples is roughly marked by a (red) curve, that is defined for context vectors c_1 and c_2 for words w_1 and w_2, respectively, by

$$\text{JSD}^{\text{exp}}(c_1, c_2) = a + \frac{1}{\hat{n}^b + c} \quad (2)$$

where $\hat{n} = \min(n(w_1), n(w_2))$ with $n(w)$ the number of occurrences of w in the corpus and with a, b and c constants that are estimated for each set of word pairs. For the pairs from the English training and test set the values are: $a = 0.15$, $b = 0.3$ and $c = 0.5$. Experiments on the training data showed that the final results are not very dependent on the exact values of these constants.

Finally, our new measure is simply defined by

$$\text{JSD}^{\text{norm}}(p,q) = \text{JSD}(p,q) - \text{JSD}^{\text{exp}}(p,q). \quad (3)$$

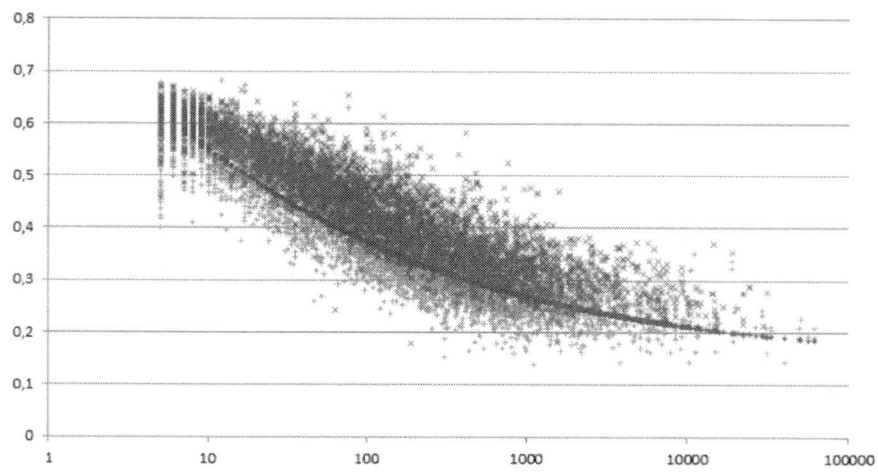

Figure 1: JSD (y-axis) of all pairs in the English training set versus the number of occurrences of the definition phrase (x-axis) in the UkWaC-Corpus. The positives examples are marked by a $+$, the negative examples by a $\times$. Most positive examples are hidden behind the negative ones. The solid (red) line gives the expected JSD.

4 System Description

The main assumption for our approach is, that a word and its definition are distributionally more similar than a word and an arbitrary definition. We use random indexing to capture distributional properties of words and phrases. Since similarity measures for random index vectors have biases for frequent or infrequent pairs, we use a combination of different measures. For the two-word definition phrases we can either estimate the context vector on the base of the two words that make up the phrase, or compute it directly from occurrences of the whole phrase in the corpus. The latter method has the advantage of being independent of assumptions about semantic composition, but might have the problem that it is based on a few examples only. Thus we use both distributions, and also include the similarities between the single word and each of the words of the definition.

4.1 Distributions

Consider a pair (w, d) with w a word and d a definition consisting of two words: $d = (d_1, d_2)$. Now for each of the words w, d_1, d_2 and the multiword d we compute context vectors using the random indexing technique. The context vectors are computed over the complete Wacky corpus. The context used for a word are all open-class words (i.e. Noun, Verb, Adjective, Adverb, etc. but not Auxiliary, Pronoun, etc.) in a sentence. Each word is represented by a random index vector of $10\,000$ dimensions in which 8 random positions have a non-zero value. The random vectors of all words in all contexts are summed up to construct context vectors (with length $10\,000$), denoted v_w, v_d, v_{d_1}, v_{d_2}. In many cases there are only very few occurrences of d, making the context vector v_d very unreliable. Thus we also compute the vectors $v_d^{\text{add}} = v_{d_1} + v_{d_2}$ and $v_d^{\text{mult}} = v_{d_1} \cdot v_{d_2}$. Finally, we also compute the general context vector (or background distribution) v_{gen} which is the context vector obtained by aggregating all used contexts.

4.2 Similarities

Table 1 gives an overview of the similarities computed for the context vector v_w. In addition we also compute $D(v_w||v_{\text{gen}})$, $D(v_d||v_{\text{gen}})$, $D(v_{d_1}||v_{\text{gen}})$, $D(v_{d_2}||v_{\text{gen}})$. The original intuition was that the definition of a word is usual given as a more general term or hypernym. It turned out that this is not the case. However, in combination with other features these divergences proved to be useful for the machine learning algorithm. Finally, we also use the direct (first-order) co-occurrence between w and d by computing the ratio between the probability with which we expect w and d to co-occur in one sentence if they would be independent, and the real probability of co-occurrence found in the corpus:

$$\text{co-occurrence-ratio}(w, d) = \frac{p(w, d)}{p(w) \cdot p(d)} \quad (4)$$

Table 1: Similarity measures used to compute the similarity of a context vector of some word to various context vectors for a phrase $d = (d_1, d_2)$.

	v_d	v_{d_1}	v_{d_2}	v_d^{add}	v_d^{mult}
jsd	✓	✓	✓	✓	
jsd-norm	✓	✓	✓	✓	
cossim				✓	✓

Table 2: Results for English and German (no names dataset). Results on train sets are averaged results from 10-fold cross validation. Results on the test set are the official task results.

	AUC	Accuracy	F-Measure
Train English	0.88	0.80	0.79
Test English	-	0.80	0.79
Train German	0.90	0.83	0.82
Test German	-	0.83	0.81

where $p(w, d)$ is the probability that w and d are found in the same sentence, and $p(w)$, with w a word or phrase, the probability that a sentence contains w.

For the computation of $\text{JSD}^{\text{norm}}(v_w, v_d^{\text{add}})$ we need the number of occurrences on which v_d^{add} is based. As an estimate for this number we use $\max(n(d_1), n(d_2))$. The constants a, b and c in equation 2 are set to the following values: for all cases $a = 0.15$; for $\text{JSD}^{\text{norm}}(v_w, v_d)$ we let $b = 0.3$ and $c = 0.5$; for $\text{JSD}^{\text{norm}}(v_w, v_{d_1})$ and $\text{JSD}^{\text{norm}}(v_w, v_{d_2})$ we let $b = 0.35$ and $c = -0.1$; for $\text{JSD}^{\text{norm}}(v_w, v_d^{\text{add}})$ we let $b = 0.4$ and $c = -0.1$. For the German subtask $a = 0.28$ and slightly different values for b and c were used to account for slightly different frequency dependencies.

4.3 Combining Similarities

The 15 attributes for each pair obtained in this way are used to train a support vector machine (SVM) using LibSVM (Chang and Lin, 2011). Optimal parameters for the SVM were found by grid-search and 10-fold cross validation on the training data.

5 Results

In Table 2 the results are summarized. Since the task can also be seen as a ranking task, we include the Area Under the ROC-Curve (AUC) as a classical measure for ranking quality. We can observe that the results are highly stable between training set and test set and across languages. Table 3 gives the results that are obtained on the training set using one feature. We can observe that the normalized versions of the JSD always perform better than the JSD itself. Furthermore, we see that for the composed vectors the cosine performs better than the normalized JSD, while it performs worse than JSD for the other vectors (not displayed in the table). This eventually can be explained by the fact that we have to estimate the number of contexts for the calculation of jsd^{exp}.

Table 3: Results for English train set (average from 10-fold cross validation) using one feature

feature	Accuracy	AUC
$\text{jsd}(v_w, v_d)$	0.50	0.57
$\text{jsd}^{\text{norm}}(v_w, v_d)$	0.59	0.70
$\text{jsd}(v_w, v_{d_1})$	0.54	0.63
$\text{jsd}^{\text{norm}}(v_w, v_{d_1})$	0.61	0.69
$\text{jsd}(v_w, v_{d_2})$	0.57	0.65
$\text{jsd}^{\text{norm}}(v_w, v_{d_2})$	0.63	0.71
$\text{jsd}(v_w, v_d^{add})$	0.59	0.67
$\text{jsd}^{\text{norm}}(v_w, v_d^{add})$	0.66	0.74
$\text{cossim}(v_w, v_d^{add})$	0.69	0.76
$\text{cossim}(v_w, v_d^{mult})$	0.62	0.71
$\text{co-occ-ratio}(w, d)$	0.61	0.71

6 Conclusion

Though there are a number of ad-hoc decisions in the system the approach was very successful and performed best in the SemEval task on phrasal semantics. The main insight from the development of the system is, that there is not yet a single best similarity measure to compare random index vectors. The normalized JSD turns out to be a useful improvement of the JSD but is problematic for constructed context vectors, the formula in equation (2) is rather ad hoc and the constants are just rough estimates. The formulation in (Wartena, 2013) might be a step in the right direction, but also there we are still far away from a unbiased similarity measure with a well founded theoretical basis.

Finally, it is unclear, what is the best way to represent a phrase in distributional similarity. Here we use three different vectors in parallel. It would be more elegant if we had a way to merge context vectors based on direct observations of the phrase with a constructed context vector.

References

Daniel Bär, Chris Biemann, Iryna Gurevych, and Torsten Zesch. 2012. Ukp: Computing semantic textual similarity by combining multiple content similarity measures. In *Proceedings of the Sixth International Workshop on Semantic Evaluation (SemEval-2012)*, pages 435–440.

M. Baroni, S. Bernardini, A. Ferraresi, and E. Zanchetta. 2009. The wacky wide web: A collection of very large linguistically processed web-crawled corpora. *Language Resources and Evaluation 43 (3): 209-226*, 43(3):209–226.

C.-C. Chang and C.-J. Lin. 2011. Libsvm : a library for support vector machines. *ACM Transactions on Intelligent Systems and Technology*, 2(3):1–27.

Stephen Clark and Stephen Pulman. 2007. Combining symbolic and distributional models of meaning. In *Proceedings of the AAAI Spring Symposium on Quantum Interaction*, pages 52–55.

Daoud Clarke, Rudi Lutz, and David Weir. 2008. Semantic composition with quotient algebras. In *Proceedings of the 9th International Conference on Computational Semantics (IWCS 2011)*.

James R. Curran and Marc Moens. 2002. Improvements in automatic thesaurus extraction. In *Unsupervised Lexical Acquisition: Proceedings of the Workshop of the ACL Special Interest Group on the Lexicon (SIGLAX).*, pages 59–66. Association of Computational Linguistics.

Eugenie Giesbrecht. 2010. Towards a matrix-based distributional model of meaning. In *Proceedings of the NAACL HLT 2010 Student Research Workshop*, pages 23–28, Los Angeles, California. ACL.

Olaf Görnerup and Jussi Karlgren. 2010. Cross-lingual comparison between distributionally determined word similarity networks. In *Proceedings of the 2010 Workshop on Graph-based Methods for Natural Language Processing*, pages 48–54. ACL.

Gregory Grefenstette. 1992. Use of syntactic context to produce term association lists for text retrieval. In *SIGIR '92: Proceedings of the 15th annual international ACM SIGIR conference on Research and development in information retrieval*, pages 89–97. ACM.

Emiliano Guevara. 2011. Computing semantic compositionality in distributional semantics. In *Proceedings of the 9th International Conference on Computational Semantics (IWCS 2011)*, pages 135–144.

Jussi Karlgren and Magnus Sahlgren. 2001. From words to understanding. In *Foundations of Real-World Intelligence*, pages 294–308. CSLI Publications, Stanford, California.

Suresh Manandhar and Deniz Yuret, editors. 2013. *Proceedings of the 7th International Workshop on Semantic Evaluation (SemEval 2013), in conjunction with the Second Joint Conference on Lexical and Computational Semantcis (*SEM 2013)*, Atlanta.

Jeff Mitchell and Mirella Lapata. 2008. Vector-based models of semantic composition. In *ACL 2008, Proceedings of the 46th Annual Meeting of the Association for Computational Linguistics*, pages 236–244.

Magnus Sahlgren. 2005. An introduction to random indexing. In *Methods and Applications of Semantic Indexing Workshop at the 7th International Conference on Terminology and Knowledge Engineering, TKE*, volume 5.

Christian Wartena, Rogier Brussee, and Wouter Slakhorst. 2010. Keyword extraction using word co-occurrence. In *Database and Expert Systems Applications (DEXA), 2010 Workshop on*, pages 54–58. IEEE.

Christian Wartena. 2013. Distributional similarity of words with different frequencies. In *Proceedings of the Dutch-Belgian Information Retrieval Workshop*, Delft. To Appear.

Julie Weeds, David J. Weir, and Diana McCarthy. 2004. Characterising measures of lexical distributional similarity. In *COLING 2004, Proceedings of the 20th International Conference on Computational Linguistics*.

Dominic Widdows. 2008. Semantic vector products: Some initial investigations. In *Second Conference on Quantum Interaction, Oxford, 26th 28th March 2008*.

ManTIME: Temporal expression identification and normalization in the TempEval-3 challenge

Michele Filannino, Gavin Brown, Goran Nenadic
The University of Manchester
School of Computer Science
Manchester, M13 9PL, UK
{m.filannino, g.brown, g.nenadic}@cs.man.ac.uk

Abstract

This paper describes a temporal expression identification and normalization system, ManTIME, developed for the TempEval-3 challenge. The identification phase combines the use of conditional random fields along with a post-processing identification pipeline, whereas the normalization phase is carried out using NorMA, an open-source rule-based temporal normalizer. We investigate the performance variation with respect to different feature types. Specifically, we show that the use of WordNet-based features in the identification task negatively affects the overall performance, and that there is no statistically significant difference in using gazetteers, shallow parsing and propositional noun phrases labels on top of the morphological features. On the test data, the best run achieved 0.95 (P), 0.85 (R) and 0.90 (F1) in the identification phase. Normalization accuracies are 0.84 (type attribute) and 0.77 (value attribute). Surprisingly, the use of the silver data (alone or in addition to the gold annotated ones) does not improve the performance.

1 Introduction

Temporal information extraction (Verhagen et al., 2007; Verhagen et al., 2010) is pivotal for many Natural Language Processing (NLP) applications such as question answering, text summarization and machine translation. Recently the topic aroused increasing interest also in the medical domain (Sun et al., 2013; Kovaćević et al., 2013).

Following the work of Ahn et al. (2005), the temporal expression extraction task is now conventionally divided into two main steps: identification and normalization. In the former step, the effort is concentrated on how to detect the right boundary of temporal expressions in the text. In the normalization step, the aim is to interpret and represent the temporal meaning of the expressions using TimeML (Pustejovsky et al., 2003) format. In the TempEval-3 challenge (UzZaman et al., 2012) the normalization task is focused only on two temporal attributes: *type* and *value*.

2 System architecture

ManTIME mainly consists of two components, one for the identification and one for the normalization.

2.1 Identification

We tackled the problem of identification as a sequencing labeling task leading to the choice of Linear Conditional Random Fields (CRF) (Lafferty et al., 2001). We trained the system using both human-annotated data (TimeBank and AQUAINT corpora) and silver data (TE3Silver corpus) provided by the organizers of the challenge in order to investigate the importance of the silver data.

Because the silver data are far more numerous (660K tokens vs. 95K), our main goal was to reinforce the human-annotated data, under the assumption that they are more informative with respect to the training phase. Similarly to the approach proposed by Adafre and de Rijke (2005), we developed a post-processing pipeline on top of the CRF sequence labeler to boost the results. Below we describe each component in detail.

*Second Joint Conference on Lexical and Computational Semantics (*SEM), Volume 2: Seventh International Workshop on Semantic Evaluation (SemEval 2013)*, pages 53–57, Atlanta, Georgia, June 14-15, 2013.

2.1.1 Conditional Random Fields

The success of applying CRFs mainly depends on three factors: the labeling scheme (*BI*, *BIO*, *BIOE* or *BIOEU*), the topology of the factor graph and the quality of the features used. We used the *BIO* format in all the experiments performed during this research. The factor graph has been generated using the following topology: (w_0), (w_{-1}), (w_{-2}), (w_{+1}), (w_{+2}), $(w_{-2} \wedge w_{-1})$, $(w_{-1} \wedge w_0)$, $(w_0 \wedge w_{+1})$, $(w_{-1} \wedge w_0 \wedge w_{+1})$, $(w_0 \wedge w_{+1} \wedge w_{+2})$, $(w_{+1} \wedge w_{+2})$, $(w_{-2} \wedge w_{-1} \wedge w_0)$, $(w_{-1} \wedge w_{+1})$ and $(w_{-2} \wedge w_{+2})$.

The system tokenizes each document in the corpus and extracts 94 features. These belong to the following four disjoint categories:

- **Morphological**: This set includes a comprehensive list of features typical of Named Entity Recognition (NER) tasks, such as the word as it is, lemma, stem, pattern (e.g. *'Jan-2003': 'Xxx-dddd'*), collapsed pattern (e.g. *'Jan-2003': 'Xx-d'*), first 3 characters, last 3 characters, upper first character, presence of 's' as last character, word without letters, word without letters or numbers, and verb tense. For lemma and POS tags we use TreeTagger (Schmid, 1994). Boolean values are included, indicating if the word is lower-case, alphabetic, digit, alphanumeric, titled, capitalized, acronym (capitalized with dots), number, decimal number, number with dots or stop-word. Additionally, there are features specifically crafted to handle temporal expressions in the form of regular expression matching: cardinal and ordinal numbers, times, dates, temporal periods (e.g. *morning, noon, nightfall*), day of the week, seasons, past references (e.g. *ago, recent, before*), present references (e.g. *current, now*), future references (e.g. *tomorrow, later, ahead*), temporal signals (e.g. *since, during*), fuzzy quantifiers (e.g. *about, few, some*), modifiers, temporal adverbs (e.g. *daily, earlier*), adjectives, conjunctions and prepositions.

- **Syntactic**: Chunks and propositional noun phrases belong to this category. Both are extracted using the shallow parsing software MBSP[1].

- **Gazetteers**: These features are expressed using the BIO format because they can include expressions longer than one word. The integrated gazetteers are: male and female names, U.S. cities, nationalities, world festival names and ISO countries.

- **WordNet**: For each word we use the number of senses associated to the word, the first and the second sense name, the first 4 lemmas, the first 4 entailments for verbs, the first 4 antonyms, the first 4 hypernyms and the first 4 hyponyms. Each of them is defined as a separate feature.

The features mentioned above have been combined in 4 different models:

- **Model 1**: Morphological only
- **Model 2**: Morphological + syntactic
- **Model 3**: Morphological + gazetteers
- **Model 4**: Morphological + gazetteers + WordNet

All the experiments have been carried out using CRF++ 0.57[2] with parameters $C = 1$, $\eta = 0.0001$ and L2-regularization function.

2.1.2 Model selection

The model selection was performed over the entire training corpus. Silver data and human-annotated data were merged, shuffled at sentence-level (seed = 490) and split into two sets: 80% as cross-validation set and 20% as real-world test set. The cross-validation set was shuffled 5 times, and for each of these, the 10-fold cross validation technique was applied.

The analysis is statistically significant ($p = 0.0054$ with ANOVA test) and provides two important outcomes: (i) the set of WordNet features negatively affects the overall classification performance, as suggested by Rigo et al. (2011). We believe this is due to the sparseness of the labels: many tokens did not have any associated WordNet sense. (ii) There is no statistically significant difference among the first three models, despite the presence of apparently important information such as chunks, propositional

[1] http://www.clips.ua.ac.be/software/mbsp-for-python

[2] https://code.google.com/p/crfpp/

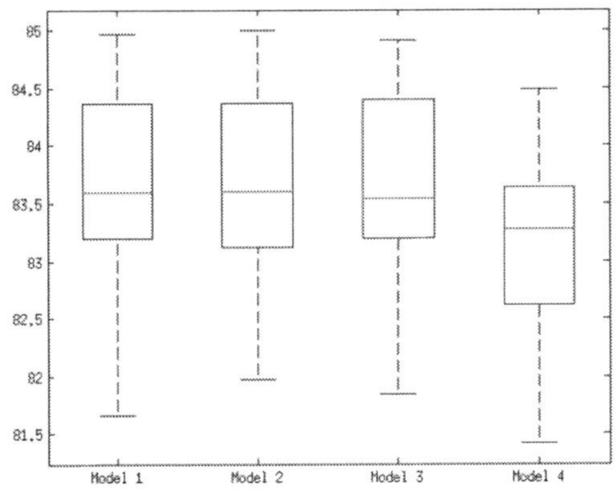

Figure 1: Differences among models using 5x10-fold cross-validation

noun phrases and gazetteers. The Figure 1 shows the box plots for each model.

In virtue of this analysis, we opted for the smallest feature set (Model 1) to prevent overfitting.

In order to get a reliable estimation of the performance of the selected model on the real world data, we trained it on the entire cross-validation set and tested it against the real-word test set. The results for all the models are shown in the following table:

System	Pre.	Rec.	$F_{\beta=1}$
Model 1	83.20	**85.22**	**84.50**
Model 2	**83.57**	85.12	84.33
Model 3	83.51	85.12	84.31
Model 4	83.15	84.44	83.79

Precision, Recall and $F_{\beta=1}$ score are computed using strict matching.

The models used for the challenge have been trained using the entire training set.

2.1.3 Post-processing identification pipeline

Although CRFs already provide reasonable performance, equally balanced in terms of precision and recall, we focused on boosting the baseline performance through a post-processing pipeline. For this purpose, we introduced 3 different modules.

Probabilistic correction module averages the probabilities from the trained CRFs model with the ones extracted from human-annotated data only. For each token, we extracted: (i) the conditional probability for each label to be assigned (*B*, *I* or *O*), and (ii) the prior probability of the labels in the human-annotated data only. The two probabilities are averaged for every label of each token. The list of tokens extracted in the human-annotated data was restricted to those that appeared within the span of temporal expressions at least twice. The application of this module in some cases has the effect of changing the most likely label leading to an improvement of recall, although its major advantage is making CRFs predictions less strict.

BIO fixer fixes wrong label sequences. For the BIO labeling scheme, the sequence *O-I* is necessarily wrong. We identified *B-I* as the appropriate substitution. This is the case in which the first token has been incorrectly annotated (e.g. *"Three/O days/I ago/I ./O"* is converted into *"Three/B days/I ago/I ./O"*). We also merged close expressions such as *B-B* or *I-B*, because different temporal expressions are generally divided at least by a symbol or a punctuation character (e.g. *"Wednesday/B morning/B"* is converted into *"Wednesday/B morning/I"*).

Threshold-based label switcher uses the probabilities extracted from the human-annotated data. When the most likely label (in the human-annotated data) has a prior probability greater than a certain threshold, the module changes the CRFs predicted label to the most likely one. This leads to force the probabilities learned from the human-annotated data.

Through repeated empirical experiments on a small sub-set of the training data, we found an optimal threshold value (0.87) and an optimal sequence of pipeline components (Probabilistic correction module, BIO fixer, Threshold-based label switcher, BIO fixer).

We analyzed the effectiveness of the post-processing identification pipeline using a 10-fold cross-validation over the 4 models. The difference between CRFs and CRFs + post-processing pipeline is statistically significant ($p = 3.51 \times 10^{-23}$ with paired T-test) and the expected average increment is 2.27% with respect to the strict $F_{\beta=1}$ scores.

2.2 Normalization

The normalization component is an updated version of NorMA (Filannino, 2012), an open-source rule-based system.

#	Training data	Identification						Normalization		Overall
		Strict matching			Lenient matching			Accuracy		
run	(post-processing)	Pre.	Rec.	$F_{\beta=1}$	Pre.	Rec.	$F_{\beta=1}$	Type	Value	score
1	Human&Silver (no)	78.57	63.77	70.40	97.32	78.99	87.20	88.99	77.06	67.20
2	Human&Silver (yes)	79.82	65.94	72.22	97.37	80.43	88.10	87.38	75.68	66.67
3	Human (no)	76.07	64.49	69.80	94.87	80.43	87.06	87.39	77.48	67.45
4	Human (yes)	78.86	**70.29**	**74.33**	95.12	**84.78**	**89.66**	86.31	76.92	**68.97**
5	Silver (no)	77.68	63.04	69.60	97.32	78.99	87.20	88.99	77.06	67.20
6	Silver (yes)	**81.98**	65.94	73.09	**98.20**	78.99	87.55	**90.83**	**77.98**	68.27

Table 1: Performance on the TempEval-3 test set.

3 Results and Discussion

We submitted six runs as combinations of different training sets and the use of the post-processing identification pipeline. The results are shown in Table 1 where the *overall score* is computed as multiplication between lenient $F_{\beta=1}$ score and the *value* accuracy.

In all the runs, recall is lower than precision. This is an indication of a moderate lexical difference between training data and test data. The relatively low *type* accuracy testifies the normalizer's inability to recognize new lexical patterns. Among the correctly typed temporal expressions, there is still about 10% of them for which an incorrect *value* is provided. The normalization task is proved to be challenging.

The training of the system by using human-annotated data only, in addition to the post-processing pipeline, provided the best results, although not the highest normalization accuracy. Surprisingly, the silver data do not improve the performance, both when used alone or in addition to human-annotated data (regardless of the post-processing pipeline usage).

The post-processing pipeline produces the highest precision when applied to the silver data only. In this case, the pipeline acts as a reinforcement of the human-annotated data. As expected, the post-processing pipeline boosts the performance of both precision and recall. We registered the best improvement with the human-annotated data.

Due to the small number of temporal expressions in the test set (138), further analysis is required to draw more general conclusions.

4 Conclusions

We described the overall architecture of ManTIME, a temporal expression extraction pipeline, in the context of TempEval-3 challenge.

This research shows, in the limits of its generality, the primary and exhaustive importance of morphological features to the detriment of syntactic features, as well as gazetteer and WordNet-related ones. In particular, while syntactic and gazetteer-related features do not affect the performance, WordNet-related features affect it negatively.

The research also proves the use of a post-processing identification pipeline to be promising for both precision and recall enhancement.

Finally, we found out that the silver data do not improve the performance, although we consider the test set too small for this result to be generalizable.

To aid replicability of this work, the system code, machine learning pre-trained models, statistical validation details and an online DEMO are available at: `http://www.cs.man.ac.uk/~filannim/projects/tempeval-3/`

Acknowledgments

We would like to thank the organizers of the TempEval-3 challenge. The first author would like also to acknowledge Marilena Di Bari, Joseph Mellor and Daniel Jamieson for their support and the UK Engineering and Physical Science Research Council for its support in the form of a doctoral training grant.

References

Sisay Fissaha Adafre and Maarten de Rijke. 2005. Feature engineering and post-processing for temporal expression recognition using conditional random fields. In *Proceedings of the ACL Workshop on Feature Engineering for Machine Learning in Natural Language Processing*, FeatureEng '05, pages 9–16, Stroudsburg, PA, USA. Association for Computational Linguistics.

David Ahn, Sisay Fissaha Adafre, and Maarten de Rijke. 2005. Towards task-based temporal extraction and recognition. In Graham Katz, James Pustejovsky, and Frank Schilder, editors, *Annotating, Extracting and Reasoning about Time and Events*, number 05151 in Dagstuhl Seminar Proceedings, Dagstuhl, Germany. Internationales Begegnungs- und Forschungszentrum für Informatik (IBFI), Schloss Dagstuhl, Germany.

Michele Filannino. 2012. Temporal expression normalisation in natural language texts. *CoRR*, abs/1206.2010.

Aleksandar Kovačević, Azad Dehghan, Michele Filannino, John A Keane, and Goran Nenadic. 2013. Combining rules and machine learning for extraction of temporal expressions and events from clinical narratives. *Journal of American Medical Informatics*.

John D. Lafferty, Andrew McCallum, and Fernando C. N. Pereira. 2001. Conditional random fields: Probabilistic models for segmenting and labeling sequence data. In *ICML*, pages 282–289.

James Pustejovsky, José Castaño, Robert Ingria, Roser Saurí, Robert Gaizauskas, Andrea Setzer, and Graham Katz. 2003. Timeml: Robust specification of event and temporal expressions in text. In *in Fifth International Workshop on Computational Semantics (IWCS-5*.

Stefan Rigo and Alberto Lavelli. 2011. Multisex - a multi-language timex sequential extractor. In *Temporal Representation and Reasoning (TIME), 2011 Eighteenth International Symposium on*, pages 163–170.

Helmut Schmid. 1994. Probabilistic part-of-speech tagging using decision trees. In *Proceedings of the International Conference on New Methods in Language Processing*, Manchester, UK.

Weiyi Sun, Anna Rumshisky, and Ozlem Uzuner. 2013. Evaluating temporal relations in clinical text: 2012 i2b2 challenge. *Journal of the American Medical Informatics Association*.

Naushad UzZaman, Hector Llorens, James F. Allen, Leon Derczynski, Marc Verhagen, and James Pustejovsky. 2012. Tempeval-3: Evaluating events, time expressions, and temporal relations. *CoRR*, abs/1206.5333.

Marc Verhagen, Robert Gaizauskas, Frank Schilder, Mark Hepple, Graham Katz, and James Pustejovsky. 2007. Semeval-2007 task 15: Tempeval temporal relation identification. In *Proceedings of the 4th International Workshop on Semantic Evaluations*, pages 75–80, Prague.

Marc Verhagen, Roser Saurí, Tommaso Caselli, and James Pustejovsky. 2010. Semeval-2010 task 13: Tempeval-2. In *Proceedings of the 5th International Workshop on Semantic Evaluation*, SemEval '10, pages 57–62, Stroudsburg, PA, USA. Association for Computational Linguistics.

FSS-TimEx for TempEval-3: Extracting Temporal Information from Text

Vanni Zavarella
Joint Research Centre
European Commission
21027 Ispra, Italy
vanni.zavarella
@jrc.ec.europa.eu

Hristo Tanev
Joint Research Centre
European Commission
21027 Ispra, Italy
hristo.tanev
@jrc.ec.europa.eu

Abstract

We describe FSS-TimEx, a module for the recognition and normalization of temporal expressions we submitted to Task A and B of the TempEval-3 challenge. FSS-TimEx was developed as part of a multilingual event extraction system, Nexus, which runs on top of the EMM news processing engine. It consists of finite-state rule cascades, using minimalistic text processing stages and simple heuristics to model the relations between events and temporal expressions. Although FSS-TimEx is already deployed within an IE application in the medical domain, we found it useful to customize its output to the TimeML standard in order to have an independent performance measure and guide further developments.

1 Introduction

The FSS-TimEx (Finite State-based Shallow Time Extractor) system participating in TempEval-3 is integrated in the event extraction engine Nexus (Tanev et al., 2008), developed at the EC's Joint Research Center for extracting event information from on-line news articles gathered by the Europe Media Monitor (EMM) news aggregation and analysis family of applications(Steinberger et al., 2009). Nexus is highly multilingual[1] and easily portable across domains through semi-automatic learning of lexical resources. In the domain of epidemiological surveillance, the event extraction task required a particularly deep temporal information analysis, in order to detect temporal relations among event reports and mitigate the classical event duplication problem. As an example, from a report like:

> The overall death toll has risen to 160 **since the beginning of the year**, after 2 patients in Gulu and 2 in Masindi died **on Tue 5 Dec 2000**.

a system might be prevented to wrongly sum up the two victim counts (160+4) only if it is made aware of the inclusion relation between the first time interval and the date, which in turn implies normalizing the two temporal expressions.

Currently, FSS-TimEx is deployed for French, English and Italian and extensions are foreseen for further languages. Given such requirements for multilinguality, we developed FSS-TimEx using a linguistically light-weight approach, applying shallow processing modules only. On the other hand, as we need to extract highly structured information out of the detected temporal expressions, to be used in the subsequent normalization phase, we mostly opted for a rule-based approach, using finite-state grammar cascades, rather than machine learning methods. Nonetheless, some of the required lexicons were semi-automatically learned.

In our participation in Tasks A and B of the TempEval-3, we experimented with adapting an existing timex recognition module for the English language, to Spanish.

We first describe our system in 2,3 and 4, then in 5 we show and shortly discuss the results for Task A and Task B, and conclude with some thoughts on prospective developments.

[1] Currently, it covers English, French, Italian, Spanish, Portuguese, Turkish, Russian, Arabic.

*Second Joint Conference on Lexical and Computational Semantics (*SEM), Volume 2: Seventh International Workshop on Semantic Evaluation (SemEval 2013)*, pages 58–63, Atlanta, Georgia, June 14-15, 2013.

2 System Modules

The system makes use of cascades of finite-state grammar rules applied to the output of a set of shallow text processing modules.

Text Processing Modules. These include tokenization, sentence splitting, domain-specific dictionary look-up and morphological analysis, which are all part of the CORLEONE (Core Linguistic Entity Online Extraction) engine (Piskorski, 2008). Morphological analysis purely consists of matching text tokens over full-form entries of a dictionary from the MULTEXT project (Erjavec, 2004), which encodes rich morphological features in a cross-lingual standard. Consequently, no PoS-tagging or parsing is performed upstream of the extraction grammars.

Finite-State Grammar Engine. We use the ExPRESS finite-state grammar engine (Piskorski, 2007). Grammars in the ExPRESS formalism consist of cascades of pattern-action rules, whose left-hand side (LHS) are regular expressions over flat feature structures (FFS) and the right-hand side (RHS) consists of a list of FFS (see Figure 1 below for an example). Variable binding from LHS to RHS, as well as string processing and Boolean operators on the RHS, allow to impose relatively complex constraints in the form of Boolean-valued predicates.

Weakly-supervised Learning of Lexical Resources. In order to determine the Class feature for the event extraction task, we experimented with using a language-independent method for weakly-supervised lexical acquisition. The algorithm takes as input a small set of seed terms, an unannotated text corpus and a parameter for the number of bootstrapping iterations: it then learns a ranked list of further terms, which are likely to belong to the same class, based on distributional n-gram features and term clustering (Tanev et al., in press). Although manual post-filtering is required, output term accuracy is reasonably high, and very high for top ranked terms.

3 Event and Event Feature Detection (Task B)

Although Nexus is a high precision event extraction system, we have not deployed it to model the event detection task. The reason is that Nexus is customized to recognize a number of highly domain-specific event types (e.g. `Armed_Conflict`, `Earthquake`,`Terrorist_Attack`) and will necessarily perform low in recall given the general, domain-independent definition of events in Task B. Instead, we tentatively used a small set of language-dependent finite-state rules to model verb phrase structure. Rules take as input MULTEXT morphological tokens and detect verb phrases along with a number of VP features, including Tense, which is used by the temporal normalizer to ground event modifying temporal expressions (see 4.2).

Class attribute was encoded in the morphological dictionary by using the output of the machine learning method sketched above: for each TimeML Event Class (Pustejovsky et al., 2003), we provided seed verb forms for all of its sub-classes, performed multi-class learning, and used the main Class label to annotate the union of output forms in the lexicon, after some manual cleaning.

The `OCCURRENCE` class was used as the default Class value for event verb forms, and it was overridden whenever a more specific event Class value was present[2].

We do not cover event nominal forms, as after some tests event referring and non-event referring noun classes appeared too difficult to tell apart by machine learning methods. Consequently, we expect system recall in Task B to be heavily limited.

4 Temporal Expressions (Task A)

FSS-TimEx's temporal expression processing consists of two stages.

In the Recognition phase, temporal expressions are detected and segmented in text and a more abstract representation of them is filled for further processing. Local parsing of timexes is performed by a cascade of hand-coded, partially language-dependent finite-state grammar rules using the ExPRESS engine, resulting in an intermediate fea-

[2] Otherwise, we chose randomly among alternative values of Class-ambiguous event expressions.

```
rule :> ( (lex & [TYPE:"temp_signal", SURFACE:#signal, NORMALIZED:"INCLUDED"]
              | lex & [TYPE:"temp_signal", NORMALIZED:"DURING"])
  lex & [TYPE:"quantifier", NORMALIZED:#mod]? determiner?
  lex & [TYPE:"temp_mod", OP:#op, REF_TYPE:#ref_type]
  ( (lex & [TYPE: "numeral", NORMALIZED:#amount1]
 lex & [TYPE: "numeral", NORMALIZED:#amount2]?)
      | token & [TYPE: "any_natural_number", SURFACE:#amount1]
 lex & [TYPE:"time_unit", NUM:"p", GRAN:#gran]):x
-> x: period & [DIR:#op,REF_TYPE:#ref_type,MOD:#mod,GRAN:#gran,QUANT:#amount,SIGNAL:#signal]
& #amount := ConcForSum(#amount1,#amount2).
```

Figure 1: Sample recognition rule

ture structure-like representation, which is subsequently used by a language-independent Normalization stage to compute exact values of the time expressions, according to the TimeML standard.

We judge that such a strict coupling of recognition and normalization is better achieved through feature extraction rules than by deploying two separate processes[3].

4.1 Recognizing Temporal Expressions

A cascade of around 90 rules is deployed for the English language. These comprise lower-level rules, in charge of modelling language constructions in the target language, and typization rules that check the attribute configuration of lower-level rule output and return a corresponding structure, typed according to an intermediate annotation type set, exporting all attribute values relevant for normalization.

As an example, the rule shown in Figure1 detects single-boundary period expressions (e.g. *in the previous four weeks* or *during the next five days*).

Notice that the rule output type is the non TimeML-compliant `period` (i.e. an anchored time duration). This is an intermediate annotation type which is subsequently converted into a TimeML type (`Duration`) during the Normalization phase.

The temporal lexicon referenced by the grammar contains around 300 entries for the English language, classified into as many as 24 types, each described by a small attribute list. Sample entries from the English lexicon are listed in Figure 2.

```
monday | TYPE:day_name | NORMALIZED:Monday
weeks | TYPE:time_unit | GRAN:week | NUM:p
night | TYPE:day_period_name | NORMALIZED:NI
ago | TYPE:temp_adv | OP:- | REF_TYPE:speaker
last | TYPE:temp_mod | OP:- | REF_TYPE:speaker
since | TYPE:temp_signal | NORMALIZED:BEGIN
early | TYPE:mod | NORMALIZED:START
```

Figure 2: Sample lexicon entries

This lexicon structure (types and attributes) was applied as such to the Spanish language; lexicon population was manually done in one day of work, by first translating lexical triggers (e.g. day, month names, numerals) and then gathering more functional entries (temporal adverbs, modifiers, etc.) by running test rules on large corpora. It turned out that, by using a parallel lexicon structure, we could reduce the cross-lingual re-arrangement of extraction rules for the Spanish grammar, minimizing the work cost to only 2 days, excluding fine tuning.

4.2 Normalization

Normalization is a fully language-independent process, working with calendar representations of temporal expressions[4] built out of the output feature structures from the Recognition phase. It comprises two sub-processes:

Anchor selection. First, anchor selection determines and maintains a reference time for relative timex resolution, starting by using the Article Creation Date and updating it along the resolution process according to a simple search heuristic: select the closest preceding resolved timex with a compatible level of granularity. We experimented with two alternative settings for this, one restricting the search to timexes within the same sentence, the other spanning over the whole article text: we noticed a systematic gain in normalization accuracy with the former setting and we used it for Task A.

[3]This architecture is very close to the one proposed by the ITA-Chronos system (Negri, 2007).

[4]The normalization is entirely implemented in Java code.

Timex-Event mapping. For certain timex classes[5] we need to resort to Tense information from event-referring verb phrases in order to disambiguate between future and past interpretation. For this purpose, a simple, syntax-free heuristic is implemented to compute a mapping from each time expression onto the event it modifies, which just uses a weighted token distance metric, promoting events preceding the timex over those following it.

Finally, calendar arithmetic is used to resolve and normalize the value of relative timexes.

5 Results[6]

5.1 Temporal Expression Extraction

For English, our system scored in the middle range over all participant systems on relaxed match F1 measure. Strict match figures are not indicative: indeed, temporal signals (like *on* in *on Friday*) were systematically included in the extracted extent, contrary to the TIMEX3 tag specification, because this is required by finite-state parsing of the IE system with which FSS-TimEx was integrated.

Compared to the best performing system (BestEN in Table1), our approach mainly suffered from relatively low recall. Although such a rate of false negatives can be expected from a rule-based approach, in our case it was mostly due to two main "bugs" in the normalization code: first, in the process of tuning system output types to TimeML, we erroneously discarded date expressions introduced by temporal signals, like in *from now*; secondly, we do not normalize single adverbial expressions (*currently*), although they are detected by grammar rules.

We outperformed in Precision the best F1 system. Many false positives were all coming from a single article, where the word season in *flu season* was systematically annotated as an event in the gold standard. This kind of context-based inference seems to be out of reach for our rule-based, local parsing approach.

The major flaw in porting the system to Spanish language was a 28% Recall drop. Main types of false negatives included fuzzy expressions (e.g. *hace tiempo*), and compositional expressions.

Performance in timex classification and normalization still falls behind top scoring systems. Finite-state techniques can only parse local constructions, greedily consuming as long text spans as possible: therefore we systematically miss clausal relations like in: ***The day** before Raymond Roth was **pulled*** where we wrongly parsed a fully specified, relative timex *The day before*. Similar cases resulted at the same time in incorrect `Type` assignment, like in ***Two years** after his brain-cancer **diagnosis*** where we wrongly detect a `Date` type expression (*Two years after*).

Inaccurate event `Tense` attribute extraction sometimes caused wrong timex `Value` normalization. One noticeable source of such an error is reported speech, which temporarily changes the discourse utterance time and that we do not attempt to model in our anchor selection procedure. Interestingly, we noticed that even in cases when both timex-event mapping, and event `Tense` were correct,`Value` normalization was not. For example, in: *Northern Ireland's World Cup qualifier with Russia has been postponed until 15:00 GMT Saturday*, one can see that a shallow approach like ours, with no access to lexico-semantic knowledge, cannot pick up the implicit future tense interpretation of the event verb.

5.2 Event and Event Attribute Extraction

Results for Spanish (Table 2) show that a small set of rules were sufficient to detect event verbal expressions with high precision. The task was much harder for English, where morphological derivation is less often marked and given that we were not performing any PoS disambiguation.

Our main aim for Task B exercise was evaluating the performance of semi-automatic methods for verb classification, and to see how much verb tense information could help normalizing time expressions. `Class` attribute performance is rather poor, even considering that 7% of false hits in English were due to a bug in the MULTEXT lexicon causing the frequent form *said* not to be annotated as `REPORTING` event. A high rate of overlapping occurs among verb classes, causing our attempt to "lexicalize" the `Class` attribute, rather than trying to compute it

[5]E.g. what we refer to as `relativeTime` or `relativeOffset`, like *on Thursday* and *this weekend*, respectively.

[6]Results were obtained in 1.89 and 1.97 seconds of computation time respectively for English and Spanish data, on an Intel Core i3 M380 2.53GHz processor.

	Recognition						*Normalization*			
	Relaxed			*Strict*			*Value*		*Type*	
System	F1	P	R	F1	P	R	F1	A	F1	A
EN	0.85	0.90	0.80	0.49	0.52	0.46	0.58	0.68	0.69	0.81
BestEN	0.90	0.89	0.91	0.79	0.78	0.80	0.78	0.86	0.80	0.88
ES	0.65	0.86	0.52	0.49	0.65	0.39	0.50	0.77	0.62	0.95
BestES	0.90	0.96	0.84	0.85	0.90	0.80	0.85	0.94	0.87	0.97

Table 1: Performance of Temporal Expression Extraction and Normalization.

	Recognition			*Class*		*Tense*	
System	F1	P	R	F1	A	F1	A
EN	0.65	0.63	0.67	0.43	0.66	0.39	0.60
BestEN	0.81	0.81	0.81	0.72	0.89	0.60	0.73
ES	0.58	0.90	0.42	0.26	0.45	0.49	0.84
BestES	0.89	0.92	0.86	0.85	0.96	0.87	0.98

Table 2: Performance of Event and Event Attribute Extraction.

from context features of verb instances, to be unfeasible. `Tense` attribute performance[7] was too low to draw any conclusion on its impact on the Normalization task. However, for Spanish its accuracy (A in Figure 2) was higher and yet this did not result in increased timex `Value` scores[8].

6 Conclusion

The main positive outcome of our participation in TempEval-3 was that we were able to build a system with acceptable performance on Task A for Spanish, after a relatively quick adaptation from an existing English system. Recall was the bottleneck of such an experiment, while precision figures did not drop significantly, and Normalization accuracy even increased for Spanish[9], suggesting that a developer may be able to iteratively add language-specific rules so as to reduce false negatives, without endangering overall system precision.

A major flaw of our finite-state, local parsing approach is in recognizing event-anchored time expressions. In order to address this, our timex recognition rules must be further tuned to the TimeML standard in order to fully isolate temporal signals, and event detection recall must be significantly increased so as to cover event nominalizations. The detection of event referring expressions according to the general, context-independent definition in TimeML is not our main research target, however we plan to use statistical classification methods to increase the performance on this task as this is a prerequisite to achieve a reliable evaluation of our event-timex mapping heuristic. Event *Tense* extraction should be increased with the same purpose.

Acknowledgments

Many thanks to Maud Ehrmann for several useful discussions on the ontology of temporal entities and the TimeML standard.

References

Tomaz Erjavec. 2004. MULTEXT - East Morphosyntactic Specifications. *URL:http://nl.ijs.si/ME/V3/msd/html/.*

Silja Huttunen, Roman Yangarber, and Ralph Grishman. 2002. Diversity of Scenarios in Information Extraction. *Proceedings of the Third International Conference On Language Resources And Evaluation*, Las Palmas.

Matteo Negri. 2007. Dealing with Italian Temporal Expressions: The ITA-Chronos System. *Proceedings of EVALITA 2007*, Workshop held in conjunction with AI*IA 2007.

[7] `Tense` figures are unofficial, as we did not manage to export this attribute value because of a bug in the submitted system. However, we were able to reproduce the evaluation on a fixed system.

[8] We do not have independent performance figures of the timex-event mapping, although this mechanism was invariable across the two languages.

[9] Due to low F1 for timex entity extraction.

Piskorski, Jakub. 2007. ExPRESS Extraction Pattern Recognition Engine and Specification Suite. In *In Proceedings of the International Workshop Finite-State Methods and Natural language Processing 2007 (FSMNLP2007)*, Postdam, Germany.

Piskorski, Jakub. 2008. CORLEONE Core Linguistic Entity Online Extraction. Technical Report, EN 23393, Joint Research Center of the European Commission, Ispra, Italy.

James Pustejovsky, Jos M. Castao, Robert Ingria, Roser Sauri, Robert J. Gaizauskas, Andrea Setzer, Graham Katz, and Dragomir R. Radev. 2003. TimeML: Robust Specification of Event and Temporal Expressions in Text. In Mark T. Maybury, editor *New Directions in Question Answering*, pages 2834. AAAI Press, 2003.

Pustejovsky, J., P. Hanks, R. Sauri, A. See, R. Gaizauskas, A. Setzer, D. Radev, B. Sundheim, D. Day, L. Ferro, et al. 2003. The TimeBank corpus. In *Corpus Linguistics*volume 2003, 40.

Steinberger Ralf, Bruno Pouliquen & Erik van der Goot. 2009. An introduction to the Europe Media Monitor Family of Applications. In Fredric Gey, Noriko Kando & Jussi Karlgren (eds.): *Information Access in a Multilingual World - Proceedings of the SIGIR 2009 Workshop (SIGIR-CLIR'2009)*, pp.1-8.

Tanev Hristo, Piskorski Jakub, Atkinson Martin. 2008. Real-Time News Event Extraction for Global Crisis Monitoring. In *Proceedings of NLDB 2008*,2008:207218.

Hristo Tanev and Vanni Zavarella. in press. Multilingual Learning and Population of Event Ontologies. A Case Study for Social Media. In Paul Buitelaar and Philipp Cimiano editors *Towards the Multilingual Semantic Web*, Springer.

Naushad UzZaman, Hector Llorens, James F. Allen, Leon Derczynski, Marc Verhagen, James Pustejovsky. 2012. TempEval-3: Evaluating Events, Time Expressions, and Temporal Relations. *arXiv:1206.5333v1*.

Verhagen, M., R. Sauri, T. Caselli, and J. Pustejovsky 2010. SemEval-2010 task 13: TempEval-2. In *Proceedings of the 5th International Workshop on Semantic Evaluation*, 5762, Association for Computational Linguistics.

JU_CSE: A CRF Based Approach to Annotation of Temporal Expression, Event and Temporal Relations

Anup Kumar Kolya[1], Amitava Kundu[1], Rajdeep Gupta[1]
[1]Dept. of Computer Science & Engineering
Jadavpur Univeristy
Kolkata-700 032, India
{anup.kolya,amitava.jucse,
rajdeepgupta20}@gmail.com

Asif Ekbal[2], Sivaji Bandyopadhyay[1]
[2]Dept. of Computer Science & Engineering
IIT Patna
Patna-800 013, India
asif@iitp.ac.in,
sivaji_ju_cse@yahoo.com

Abstract

In this paper, we present the JUCSE system, designed for the TempEval-3 shared task. The system extracts events and temporal information from natural text in English. We have participated in all the tasks of TempEval-3, namely Task A, Task B & Task C. We have primarily utilized the Conditional Random Field (CRF) based machine learning technique, for all the above tasks. Our system seems to perform quite competitively in Task A and Task B. In Task C, the system's performance is comparatively modest at the initial stages of system development. We have incorporated various features based on different lexical, syntactic and semantic information, using Stanford CoreNLP and Wordnet based tools.

1 Introduction

Temporal information extraction has been a popular and interesting research area of Natural Language Processing (NLP) for quite some time. Generally, a lot of events are described in a variety of newspaper texts, stories and other important documents where the different events described happen at different time instants. The temporal location and ordering of these events are either specified or implied. Automatic identification of time expressions and events and annotation of temporal relations constitute an important task in text analysis. These are also important in a wide range of NLP applications that include temporal question answering, machine translation and document summarization.

A lot of research in the area of temporal information extraction has been conducted on multiple languages, including English and several European languages. The TimeML was first developed in 2002 in an extended workshop called TERQAS (Time and Event Recognition for Question Answering Systems) and, in 2003, it was further developed in the context of the TANGO workshop (TimeML Annotation Graphical Organizer). Since then most of the works in this research arena have been conducted in English. The variety of works include TimeML (Pustejovsky et al., 2003), the development of a temporally annotated corpus Time-Bank (Pustejovsky et al., 2003), the temporal evaluation challenges TempEval-1 (Verhagen et al., 2007), TempEval-2 (Pustejovsky and Verhagen, 2010). In the series of Message Understanding Conferences (MUCs) that started from 1987 and the Sheffield Temporal Annotation scheme (STAG) (Setzer &Gaizauskas, 2000) the aim was to identify events in news text and determine their relationship with points on a temporal line.

In the series of TempEval evaluation exercises, TempEval-1 was the first one where the focus was on identification of three types of temporal relation: relation between an event and a time expression in the same sentence, relation between an

*Second Joint Conference on Lexical and Computational Semantics (*SEM), Volume 2: Seventh International Workshop on Semantic Evaluation (SemEval 2013)*, pages 64–72, Atlanta, Georgia, June 14-15, 2013.

event and the document creation time, and relation between two main events in consecutive sentences.

TempEval-2 was a follow up to TempEval-1 and consisted of six subtasks rather than three. It added (i) identification of time expressions and determination of values of the attributes TYPE and VAL (ii) identification of event expressions and determination of its attribute values. It included the previous three relation tasks from TempEval-1 and an additional task of annotating temporal relation between a pair of events where one subordinates the other.

We have participated in all three tasks of TempEval-3- Task A, Task B and Task C. A combination of CRF based machine learning and rule based techniques has been adopted for temporal expression extraction and determination of attribute values of the same (Task A). We have used a CRF based technique for event extraction (Task B), with the aid of lexical, semantic and syntactic features. For determination of event attribute values we have used simple rule based techniques. Automatic annotation of temporal relation between event-time in the same sentence, event-DCT relations, mainevent-mainevent relations in consecutive sentences and subevent-subevent relations in the same sentences has been introduced as a new task (Task-C) in the TempEval-3 exercise. We have adopted a CRF based technique for the same as well.

2 The JU_CSE System Approach

The JU_CSE system for the TempEval-3 shared task uses mainly a Conditional Random Field (CRF) machine learning approach to achieve Task A, Task B & Task C. The workflow of our system is illustrated in Figure 1.

2.1 Task A: Temporal Expression Identification and Normalization

Temporal Expression Identification:

We have used CRF++ 0.57[1], an open source implementation of the Conditional Random Field (CRF) machine learning classifier for our experiments. CRF++ templates have been used to capture the relation between the different features in a sequence to identify temporal expressions. Temporal expressions mostly appear as multi-word entities such as "the next three days". Therefore the use of CRF classifier that uses context information of a token seemed most appropriate.

Initially, all the sentences have been changed to a vertical token-by-token level sequential structure for temporal expressions representation by a B-I-O encoding, using a set of mostly lexical features. In this encoding of temporal expression, "B" indicates the 'beginning of sequence', "I" indicates a token inside a sequence and "O" indicates an outside word. We have carefully chosen the features list based on the several entities that denote month names, year, weekdays, various digit expressions (*day, time, AM, PM* etc.) In certain temporal expression patterns (*several months, last evening*) some words (*several, last*) act as modifiers to the following words that represent the time expression. Temporal expressions include time expression modifiers, relative days, periodic temporal set, year-eve day, month name with their short pattern forms, season of year, time of day, decade list and so on. We have used the POS information of each token as a feature. We have carefully accounted for a simple intuition revelation that most temporal expressions contain some tokens conveying the *"time"* information while others possibly conveying the "quantity" of time. For example, in the expression *"next three days"*, *"three"* quantifies *"days"*. Following are the different temporal expressions lists that have been utilized:

- A list of time expression modifiers: *this, mid, recent, earlier, beginning, late* etc.
- A list of relative days: *yesterday, tomorrow* etc.
- A list of periodic temporal set: *hourly, nightly* etc.
- A list of year eve day: *Christmas Day, Valentine Day* etc.
- A list of month names with their short pattern forms: *April, Apr.* etc.
- A list of season of year: *spring, winter* etc.
- A list of time of day: *morning, afternoon,* evening etc.
- A list of decades list: *twenties, thirties* etc.

[1] http://crfpp.googlecode.com/svn/trunk/doc/index.html

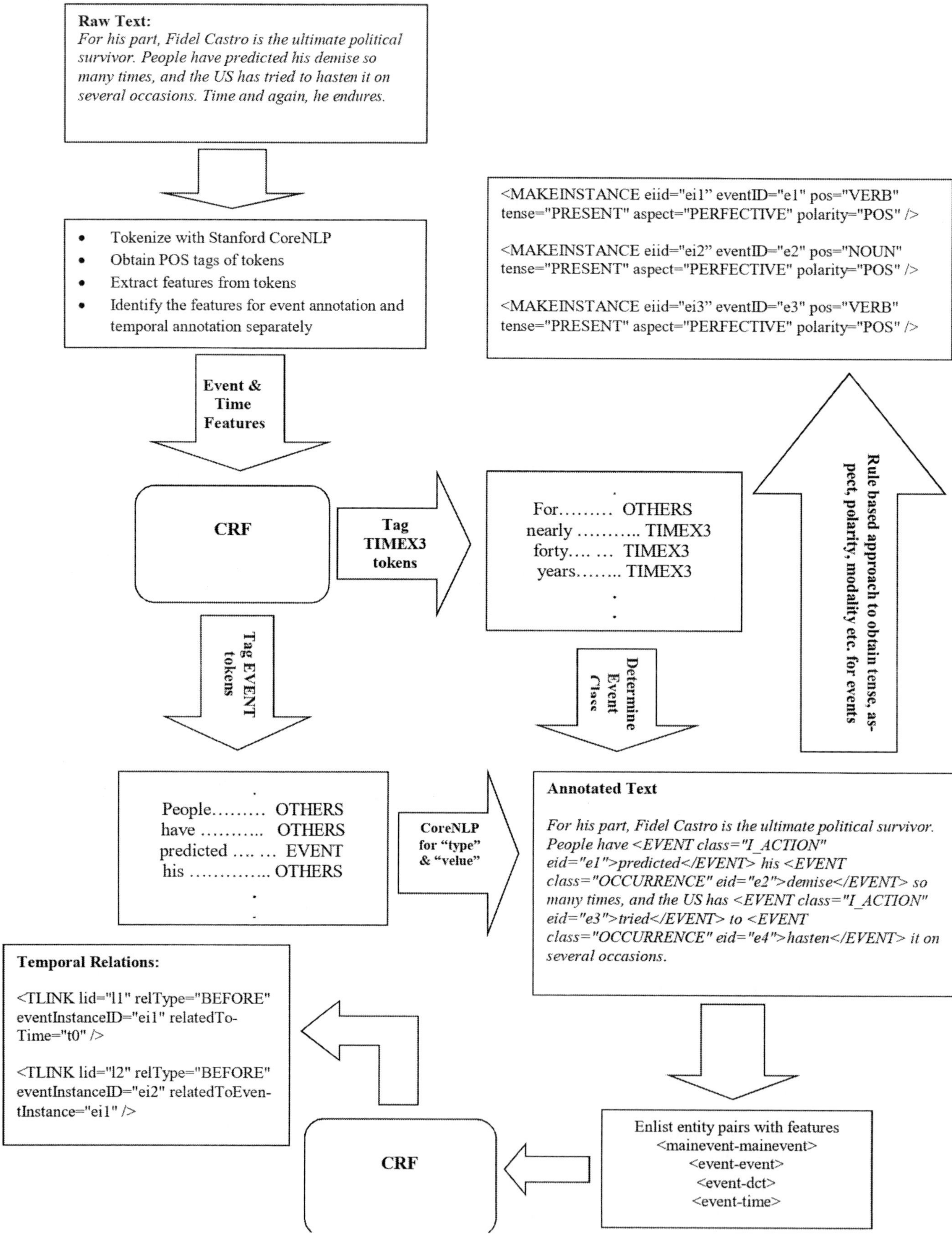

Figure 1.The JU_CSE System Architecture

Determination of Normalized *value* and *type* of Temporal Expressions:

Temporal expressions in documents are generally defined with the *type* and *value* attributes. All the temporal expressions can be differentiated into three types (i) explicit (ii) relative and (iii) implicit temporal expressions. For example, the expression *"October 1998"* refers to a specific month of the year which can be normalized without any additional information. On the other hand, the relative expression *"yesterday"* can't be normalized without the knowledge of a corresponding reference time. The reference time can either be a temporal expression or the Document Creation Time marked in the document. Consider the following piece of text: *"Yesterday was the 50th independence of India". The First Independence Day of India is 15th august 1947."* Here *"Yesterday"* can be normalized as *"15-08-1997"*. It may be noted that information such as *"First Independence Day of India"* can be directly accessed from the timestamp calendar, through the metadata of a document. The third type of temporal expressions includes implicit expressions such as names of festival days, birthdays and holidays or events. These expressions are mapped to available calendar timeline to find out their normalized values.

Temporal Expression	Type	Value
A couple of years	DURATION	P2Y
October	DATE	"1997-10"
Every day	SET	P1D
2 P.M.	TIME	2013-02-01T14:00
Now	DATE	PRESENT_REF"

Table 1: TimeML normalized type and value attributes for temporal expressions

We have implemented a combined technique using our handcrafted rules and annotations given by the Stanford CoreNLP tool to determine the 'type'-s and 'value'-s. Four types TIME, DATE, DURATION and SET of temporal expressions are defined in the TimeML framework. Next, we have evaluated the normalized value of temporal expressions using Document Creation Time (DCT) from the documents. In this way, values of different dates have been inferred e.g. *last year*, *Monday*, and *today*.

2.2 Task B: Extraction of Event Words and Determination of Event Attribute Values

Event Extraction

In our evaluation framework, we have used the Stanford CoreNLP tool extensively to tokenize, lemmatize, named-entity annotate and part-of-speech tag the text portions of the input files. For event extraction, the features have been considered at word level, where each word has its own set of features. The general features used to train our CRF model are:

Morphological Features: Event words are represented mostly as verbs and nouns. The major problem is detecting the events having non-verbal PoS labels. Linguistically, non-verbal wordforms are derived from verbal wordforms. Various inflectional and derivational morphological rules are involved in the process of evolving from verbal to non-verbal wordforms. We have used a set of handcrafted rules to identify the suffixes such as (*'-ción', '-tion' or '-ion')*, i.e., the morphological markers of word token, where Person, Location and Organization words are not considered. The POS and lemma, in a 5-window (-2, +2), has been used for event extraction.

Syntactic Feature: Different event words notions are contained in the sentences such as: verb-noun combinations structure, the complements of aspectual prepositional phrases (PPs) headed by prepositions and a particular type of complex prepositions. These notions are captured to be used as syntactic features for event extraction.

WordNet Feature: The RiTa Wordnet[2] package has been effectively used to extract different properties of words, such as Synonyms, Antonyms, Hypernyms, & Hyponyms, Holonyms, Meronyms, Coordinates, & Similars, Nominalizations, Verb-Groups, & Derived-terms. We have used these Wordnet properties in the training file for the CRF in the form of binary features for verbs and nouns indicating if the words like "act", "activity", "phenomenon" etc. occur in different relations of the Wordnet ontology.

[2] http://www.rednoise.org/rita/wordnet/documentation/

Features using Semantic Roles: We use Semantic Role Label (SRL) (Gildea et el, 2002; Pradhan et al, 2004; Gurevich et al, 2006) to identify different useful features for event extraction. For each predicate in a sentence acting as event word, semantic roles extract all constituents; determine their arguments (agent, patient, etc.) and adjuncts (locative, temporal, etc.). Some of the other features like predicate, voice and verb subcategorization are shared by all the nodes in the tree. In the present work, we use predicate as an event. Semantic roles can be used to detect the events that are nominalizations of verbs such as *agreement* for *agree* or *construction* for *construct*. Event nominalizations often share the same semantic roles as verbs, and often replace them in written language. Noun words, morphologically derived from verbs, are commonly defined as deverbal nouns. Event and result nominalizations constitute the bulk of deverbal nouns. The first class refers to an event/activity/process, with the nominal expressing this action (e.g., killing, destruction etc.). Nouns in the second class describe the result or goal of an action (e.g., agreement, consensus etc.). Many nominals denote both the event and result (e.g., selection). A smaller class is agent/patient nominalizations that are usually identified by suffixes such as -er, -or etc., while patient nominalizations end with -ee, -ed (e.g. employee).

Object information of Dependency Relations (DR): We have developed handcrafted rules to identify features for CRF training, based on the object information present in the dependency relations of parsed sentences. Stanford Parser (de Marneffe et al., 2006), a probabilistic lexicalized parser containing 45 different Part-of-Speech (PoS) tags of Penn Treebank is used to get the parsed sentences with dependency relations. The dependency relations are found out for the predicates "dobj" so that the direct object related components in the "dobj" predicate is considered as the feature for the event expression. Initially the input sentences are passed to the dependency parser[3]. From the parsed output verb noun combination direct object (dobj) dependency relations are extracted. These dobj relations basically inform us that direct object of a VP is the noun phrase which is the (accusative) object of the verb; the direct object of a clause is the direct object of the VP which is the predicate of that clause. Within the dobj relation governing verb word and dependent noun words are acting as important features for event identification when dependent word is not playing any role in other dependency relation (nsubj, prep_of, nn ,etc.) of the sentence.

In this way, we have set list of word tokens and its features to train the recognition model. Then the model will give to each word one of the valid labels.

Determination of various Event Attribute Values:

Values of different event attributes have been computed as follows:

Class: Identification of the class of an event has been done using a simple, intuitive, rule based approach. Here too, the hypernym list of an event token from RitaWordnet has been deployed to determine the class of the respective event. In this case, OCCURRENCE has been considered the default class.

Tense, Aspect, POS: These three attributes are the obligatory attributes of MAKEINSTANCE tags. To determine the tense, aspect and polarity of an event, we have used the "parse" annotator in CoreNLP. We annotated each sentence with the Stanford dependency relations using the above annotator. Thereafter various specific relations were used to determine the tense, aspect and POS of an event token, with another rule based approach. For example, in the phrase "*has been abducted*", the token "*been*" appears as the dependent in an "aux" relation with the event token "*abducted*"; and hence the aspect "PERFECTIVE" is inferred. The value "NONE" has been used as the default value for both tense and aspect.

Polarity and Modality: Polarity of event tokens are determined using Stanford dependency relations too; here the "neg" relation. To determine the modality we search for modal words in "aux" relations with the event token.

2.3 Task C: Temporal Relation Annotation

We have used the gold-standard TimeBank features for events and times for training the CRF. In the present work, we mainly use the various combinations of the following features:

[3] http://nlp.stanford.edu:8080/parser/

(i) Part of Speech (POS)
(ii) Event Tense
(iii) Event Aspect
(iv) Event Polarity
(v) Event Modality
(vi) Event Class
(vii) Type of temporal expression
(vii) Event Stem
(viii) Document Creation Time (DCT).

The following subsections describe how various temporal relations are computed.

Event-DCT

We take the combined features of every event present in the text and the DCT for this purpose.

Derived Features: We have identified different types of context based syntactic features which are derived from text to distinguish the different types of temporal relations. In this task, following features help us to identify the event-DCT relations, specially "AFTER" temporal relations:
(i)Modal Context: Whether or not the event word has one of the modal context words like- *will, shall, can, may,* or any of their variants (*might, could, would,* etc.).In the sentence: *"The entire world **will** [EVENT **see**] images of the Pope in Cuba".* Here *"will"* context word helps us to determine event-DCT relation 'AFTER'.
(ii)Preposition Context: Any prepositions preceding an event or time expression. We consider an example:*"Children and invalids would be permitted **to** [EVENT leave] **Iraq**".* Here the preposition *to* helps us to determine event-DCT relation 'AFTER'. The same principle goes for time too: in the expressions *on Friday* and *for nearly forty years*, the prepositions *on* and *for* governs the time.
(iii)Context word before or after temporal expression: context words like *before, after, less than, greater than* etc. help us to determine event-time temporal relation identification. Consider an example: *"**After** ten years of [EVENT boom] ...."*

Event-Time

Derived Features: We extract all events from every sentence. For every temporal expression in a sentence, we pair an event in the sentence with the former so that the temporal relation can be determined.

Similar to annotation of event-DCT relations, here too, we have identified different types of context based temporal expression features which are derived from text to distinguish the different types of temporal relations. In this task, the following features help us to distinguish between event and time relations, specially "AFTER" and "BEFORE" temporal relations. The following features are derived from text.
(i)Type of temporal expression: Represents the temporal relationship holding between events, times, or between an event and a time of the event.
(ii)Temporal signal: Represents temporal prepositions *"on"* (*on this coming Sunday*) and slightly contribute to the overall score of classifiers
(iii)Temporal Expression in the target sentence: Takes the values *greater than, less than, equal* or *none*. These values contribute to the overall score of classifiers.

Mainevent-Mainevent and Subevent-Subevent

The task demands that the main event of every sentence be determined. As a heuristic decision, we have assumed that the first event that appears in a sentence is its main event. We pair up main events (if present) from consecutive sentences and use their combined features to determine their temporal relation. For the events belonging to a single sentence, we take into account the combined features of all possible pairs of sentential events.

Derived Features: We have identified different types of context based syntactic features which are derived from text to distinguish the different types of temporal relations.
(i)Relational context: If a relation holding between the previous event and the current event is "AFTER", the current one is in the past. This information helps us to identify the temporal relation between the current event and successive event.
(ii)Modal Context: Whether or not the event word has one of the context words like, *will, shall, can, may,* or any of their variants (*might, could, would,* etc.). The verb and auxiliaries governing the next event play as an important feature in event-event temporal relation identification.

(iii)Ordered based context: In event-event relation identification, when EVENT-1, EVENT-2, and EVENT-3 are linearly ordered, then we have assigned true/false as feature value from tense and aspect shifts in this ordered pair.

(iv) Co-reference based feature: We have used co-referential features as derived feature using our in-house system based on Standford CoreNLP tool, where two event words within or outside one sentence are referring to the same event, i.e. two event words co-refer in a discourse.

(v)Event-DCT relation based feature: We have included event-document creation times (DCT) temporal relation types as feature of event-event relation identification.

(ii) Preposition Context: Any prepositions before the event or time, we consider an example: *"Children and invalids would be permitted* ***to*** *[EVENT leave]* ***Iraq"***. Here the preposition *to* helps us determine the event-DCT relation 'AFTER'.

(vi) Context word before or after temporal expression: Context words like *before, after, less than, greater than* help us determine event- event temporal relations .We consider an example: ***"After*** *ten years of [EVENT boom] ...."*

(vii)Stanford parser based clause boundaries features: The two consecutive sentences are first parsed using Stanford dependency parser and then clause boundaries are identified. Then, considering the prepositional context and tense verb of the clause, temporal relations are identified where all temporal expressions are situated in the same clause.

3 Results and Evaluation

For the extraction of time expressions and events (tasks A and B), precision, recall and F1-score have been used as evaluation metrics, using the following formulae:

precision (P) = tp/(tp + fp)
recall (R) = tp/(tp + fn)
F-measure = 2 *(P * R) / (P + R).

Where, tp is the number of tokens that are part of an extent in keys and response, fp is the number of tokens that are part of an extent in the response but not in the key, and fn is the number of tokens that are part of an extent in the key but not in the response. Additionally attribute accuracies computed according to the following formulae have also been reported.

Attr. Accuracy = Attr. F1 / Entity Extraction F1
Attr. R = Attr. Accuracy * Entity R
Attr. P = Attr. Accuracy * Entity P

Performance in task C is judged with the aid of the Temporal Awareness score proposed by UzZaman and Allen (2011)

The JU_CSE system was evaluated on the TE-3 platinum data. Table 2 reports JU_CSE's performance in timex extraction Task A. Under the relaxed match scheme, the F1-score stands at 86.38% while the strict match scheme yields a F1-score of 75.41%. As far as TIMEX attributes are concerned, the F1-scores are 63.81% and 73.15% for *value* and *type* respectively.

Timex Extraction						Timex Attribute			
F1	**P**	**R**	**Strict F1**	**Strict P**	**Strict R**	**Value F1**	**Type F1**	**Value Accuracy**	**Type Accuracy**
86.38	93.28	80.43	75.49	81.51	70.29	63.81	73.15	73.87	84.68

Table 2:JU_CSE system's TE-3 Results on Timex Task A

Event Extraction			Event Attribute					
F1	**P**	**R**	**Class F1**	**Tense F1**	**Aspect F1**	**Class Accuracy**	**Tense Accuracy**	**Aspect Accuracy**
78.57	80.85	76.41	52.65	58.58	72.09	67.01	74.56	91.75

Table 3:JU_CSE system's TE-3 Results on Event Task B

Table 3 reports the system's performance in event extraction (Task B) on TE-3 platinum data. F1-score for event extraction is 78.57%. Attribute F1-scores are 52.65%, 58.58% and 72.09% for *class*, *tense* and *aspect* respectively.

In both entities extraction tasks recall is notably lower than precision. The F1-scores for event attributes are modest given that the attributes were computed using handcrafted rules. However, the handcrafted approach can be treated as a good baseline to start with. Normalization is proved to be a challenging task.

Task	F1	P	R
Task-ABC	24.61	19.17	34.36
Task-C	26.41	21.04	35.47
Task-C-relation-only	34.77	35.07	34.48

Table 4: JU_CSE system's TE-3 Temporal Awareness results on Task ABC, TaskC-only & TaskC-relation-only

Table 4 presents the Temporal Awareness F1-score for TaskABC, TaskC and TaskC-relation-only. For TaskC-only evaluation, the event and timex annotated data was provided and one had to identify the TLINKs and classify the temporal relations. In the TaskC-relation-only version the timex and event annotations including their attributes as well as TLINKs were provided save the relation classes. Only the relation classes had to be determined. The system yielded a temporal awareness F1-score of 24.6% for TaskABC, 26.41% for TaskC-only and 34.77% for TaskC-relation-only version.

4 Conclusions and Future Directions

In this paper, we have presented the JU_CSE system for the TempEval-3 shared task. Our system in TempEval-3 may be seen upon as an improvement over our earlier endeavor in TempEval-2. We have participated in all tasks of the TempEval-3 exercise. We have incorporated a CRF based approach in our system for all tasks. The JU_CSE system for temporal information extraction is currently undergoing a lot of extensive experimentation. The one reported in this article seemingly has a significant scope of improvement. Preliminarily, the results yielded are quite competitive and encouraging. Event extraction and Timex extraction F1-scores at 78.58% and 86.38% encourage us to further develop our CRF based scheme. We expect better results with additional features and like to continue our experimentations with other semantic features for the CRF classifier. Our rule-based approach for event attribute determination however yields modest F1-scores- 52.65% & 58.58% for class and tense. We intend to explore other machine learning techniques for event attribute classification. We also intend to use parse tree based approaches for temporal relation annotation.

Acknowledgments

This work has been partially supported by a grant from the English to Indian language Machine Translation (EILMT) project funded by the Department of Information and Technology (DIT), Government of India. We would also like to thank to Mr. Jiabul Sk. for his technical contribution.

References

A. Setzer, and R. Gaizauskas. 2000. Annotating Events and Temporal Information in Newswire Texts. In LREC 2000, pages 1287–1294, Athens.

D. Gildea, and D. Jurafsky. 2002. Automatic Labeling of Semantic Roles. Computational Linguistics, 28(3):245–288.

James Pustejovsky, José Castano, Robert Ingria, Roser Sauri, Robert Gaizauskas, Andrea Setzer, Graham Katz, and Dragomir Radev. 2003. TimeML: Robust specification of event and temporal expressions in text. New directions in question answering, 3: 28-34.

Marc Verhagen, Robert Gaizauskas, Frank Schilder, Mark Hepple, Graham Katz, and James Pustejovsky. 2007. Semeval-2007 task 15: Tempeval temporal relation identification. In Proceedings of the 4th International Workshop on Semantic Evaluations, pages 75-80, ACL.

Marc Verhagen, Roser Sauri, Tommaso Caselli, and James Pustejovsky. 2010. Semeval-2010 task 13: Tempeval-2. In Proceedings of the 5th International Workshop on Semantic Evaluation, pages 57- 62. ACL.

Olga Gurevich, Richard Crouch, Tracy H. King, and V. de Paiva. 2006. Deverbal Nouns in Knowledge Representation. Proceedings of FLAIRS, pages 670–675, Melbourne Beach, FL.

Sameer Pradhan, Wayne Ward, Kadri Hacioglu, James H. Martin, and Daniel Jurafsky. 2004. Shallow Semantic Parsing using Support Vector Machine. Proceedings of HLT/NAACL-2004, Boston, MA.

UzZaman, N. and J.F. Allen (2011), "Temporal Evaluation." In Proceedings of The 49th Annual Meeting of the Association for Computational Linguistics: Human Language Technologies (Short Paper), Portland, Oregon, USA.

NavyTime: Event and Time Ordering from Raw Text

Nathanael Chambers
United States Naval Academy
Annapolis, MD 21401, USA
nchamber@usna.edu

Abstract

This paper describes a complete event/time ordering system that annotates raw text with events, times, and the ordering relations between them at the SemEval-2013 Task 1. Task 1 is a unique challenge because it starts from raw text, rather than pre-annotated text with known events and times. A working system first identifies events and times, then identifies which events and times should be ordered, and finally labels the ordering relation between them. We present a *split classifier* approach that breaks the ordering tasks into smaller decision points. Experiments show that more specialized classifiers perform better than few joint classifiers. The NavyTime system ranked second both overall and in most subtasks like event extraction and relation labeling.

1 Introduction

The SemEval-2013 Task 1 (TempEval-3) contest is the third instantiation of an event ordering challenge. However, it is the first to start from raw text with the challenge to create an end-to-end algorithm for event ordering. Previous challenges included the individual aspects of such a system, including event extraction, timex extraction, and event/time ordering (Verhagen et al., 2007; Verhagen et al., 2010). However, neither task was dependent on the other. This paper presents NavyTime, a system inspired partly by this previous breakup of the tasks. We focus on breaking up the event/time ordering task further, and show that 5 classifiers yield better performance than the traditional 3 (or even 1).

The first required steps to annotate a document are to extract its events and time expressions. This paper describes a new event extractor with a rich set of contextual features that is a top performer for event attributes at Tempeval-3. We then explore additions to SUTime, a top rule-based extractor for time expressions (Chang and Manning, 2012). However, the core challenge is to link these extracted events and times together. We describe new models for these difficult tasks: (1) identifying ordered pairs, and (2) labeling the ordering relations.

Relation identification is rarely addressed in the literature. Given a set of events, which pairs of events are temporally related? Almost all previous work assumes we are given the pairs, and the task is to label the relation (before, after, etc.). Raw text presents a new challenge: extract the relevant pairs before labeling them. We present some of the first results that compare rule-based approaches to trained probabilistic classifiers. These are the first such comparisons to our knowledge.

Finally, after relation identification, we label relations between the pairs. This is the traditional event ordering task, although we now start from noisy pairs. Our main contribution is to build independent classifiers for intra-sentence event/time pairs. We show improved performance when training these *split* classifiers. NavyTime's approach is highly competitive, achieving 2nd place in relation labeling (and overall).

2 Dataset

All models are developed on the TimeBank (Pustejovsky et al., 2003) and AQUAINT corpora (Mani

*Second Joint Conference on Lexical and Computational Semantics (*SEM), Volume 2: Seventh International Workshop on Semantic Evaluation (SemEval 2013)*, pages 73–77, Atlanta, Georgia, June 14-15, 2013. ©2013 Association for Computational Linguistics

et al., 2007). These labeled newspaper articles have fueled many years of event ordering research. TimeBank includes 183 documents and AQUAINT includes 73. The annotators of each were given different guidance, so they provide unique distributions of relations. Development of the algorithms in this paper were solely on 10-fold cross validation on the union of the two corpora.

The SemEval-2013 Task 1 (TempEval-3) provides unseen raw text to then evaluate the final systems. Final results are from this set of unseen newspaper articles. They were annotated by a different set of people who annotated TimeBank and AQUAINT.

3 Event Extraction

The first stage to processing raw text is to extract the event mentions. We treat this as a binary classification task, classifying each token as either *event* or *not-event*. Events are always single tokens in the TimeBank/AQUAINT corpora, so a document with n tokens requires n classifications. Further, each event is marked up with its *tense*, *aspect*, and *class*.

We used a maximum entropy classification framework based on the lexical and syntactic context of the target word. The same features are used to first identify events (binary decision), and then three classifiers are trained for the tense, aspect, and class. The following features were used:

Token N-grams: Standard n-gram context that includes the target token (1,2,3grams), as well as the unigrams and bigrams that occur directly before and after the target token.
Part of Speech n-grams: The POS tag of the target, and the bigram and trigram ending with the target.
Lemma: The lemmatized token in WordNet.
WordNet-Event: A binary feature, true if the token is a descendent of the Event synset in WordNet.
Parse Path: The tree path from the token's leaf node to the root of the syntactic parse tree.
Typed Dependencies: The typed dependency triple of any edge that begins or ends with the target.

We used 10-fold cross validation on the combined corpora of TimeBank and AQUAINT to develop the above features, and then trained one classifier on the entire dataset. Our approach was the 2nd best event extraction system out of 8 submission sites on the unseen test set from TempEval-3. Detailed results are given in Figure 1.

Results on event *attribute* extraction were also good (Figure 1). We again ranked 2nd best in both Tense and Aspect. Only with the Class attribute did we fare worse (4th of 8). We look forward to comparing approaches to see why this particular attribute was not as successful.

4 Temporal Expression Extraction

As with event extraction, time expressions need to be identified from the raw text. Recent work on time extraction has suggested that rule-based approaches outperform others (Chang and Manning, 2012), so we adopted the proven SUTime system for this task. SUTime is a rule-based system that extracts phrases and normalizes them to a TimeML time. However, we improved it with some TimeBank specific rules.

We observed that the phrases *'a year ago'* and *'the latest quarter'* were often inconsistent with standard TimeBank annotations. These tend to involve fiscal quarters, largely due to TimeBank's heavy weight on the financial genre. For these phrases, we first determine the current fiscal quarter, and adjust the normalized time to include the quarter, not just the year (e.g., 2nd quarter of 2012, rather than just 2012). Further, the generic phrase *'last year'* should normalize to just a year, and not include a more specific month or quarter. We added rules to strip off months.

SUTime was the best system for *time extraction*, and our usage matched its performance as one would hope. Full credit goes to SUTime, and its extraction is not a contribution of this paper. However, NavyTime outperformed SUTime by over 3.5 F1 points on *time normalization*. Our additional rulebank appears to have helped significantly, allowing NavyTime to be the 2nd best in this category behind HeidelTime. We recommend users to use either HeidelTime or SUTime with the NavyTime rulebank.

5 Temporal Relation Extraction

After events and time expressions are identified, it remains to create *temporal links* between them. A temporal link is an ordering relation that occurs in four possible entity pairings: event-event, event-time, time-time, and event-DCT (DCT is the document creation time).

Event Extraction F1

ATT-1	81.05
NavyTime	**80.30**
KUL	79.32
cleartk-4 & cleartk-3	78.81
ATT-3	78.63
JU-CSE	78.62
KUL-TE3RunABC	77.11
Temp:ESAfeature	68.97
FSS-TimEx	65.06
Temp:WordNetfeature	63.90

Class Attribute

System	Class F1
ATT	71.88
KUL	70.17
cleartk	67.87
NavyTime	67.48
Temp:ESA	54.55
JU-CSE	52.69
Temp:WNet	50.00
FSS-TimEx	42.94

Tense and Aspect Attributes

System	Tense F1	Aspect F1
cleartk	62.18	70.40
NavyTime	61.67	72.43
ATT	59.47	73.50
JU-CSE	58.62	72.14
KUL	49.70	63.20
not all systems participated		

Figure 1: Complete event rankings on all subtasks scored by F1. Extraction is token span matching.

It is unrealistic to label all possible pairs in a document. Many event/time pairs have ambiguous orderings, and others are simply not labeled by the annotators. We propose a two-stage approach where we first identify likely pairs (*relation identification*), and then independently decide what specific ordering relation holds between them (*relation labeling*).

5.1 Relation Identification

TempEval-3 defined the set of possible relations to exist in particular configurations: (1) any pairs in the same sentence, (2) event-event pairs of main events in adjacent sentences, and (3) event-DCT pairs. However, the training and test corpora do not follow these rules. Many pairs are skipped to save human effort. This task is thus a difficult balance between labeling all true relations, but also matching the human annotators. We tried two approaches to identifying pairs: rule-based, and data-driven learning.

Rule-Based: We extract all event-event and event-time pairs in the same sentence if they are adjacent to each other (no intervening events or times). We also extract main event pairs of adjacent sentences. We identify main events by finding the highest VP in the parse tree.

Data-Driven: This approach treats it as a binary classification task. Given a pair of entities, determine if they are *ordered* or *not-ordered*. We condense the training corpora's TLINK relations into *ordered*, and label all non-labeled pairs as *not-ordered*. We tried a variety of classifiers for each event/time pair type: (1) intra-sentence event-event, (2) intra-sentence event-time, (3) inter-sentence event-event, and (4) event-DCT.

Event-Event Features

- Token, lemma, wordnet synset
- POS tag n-grams surrounding events
- Syntactic tree dominance
- Linear order in text
- Does another event appear in between?
- Parse path from e1 to e2
- Typed dependency path from e1 to e2

Event-Time Features

- Event POS, token, lemma, wordnet synset
- Event tense, aspect, and class
- Is time a day of the week?
- Entire time phrase
- Last token in time phrase
- Does time end the sentence?
- Bigram of event token and time token
- Syntactic tree dominance
- Parse path from event to time
- Typed dependency path from event to time

Event-DCT Feature

- Event POS, token, lemma, wordnet synset
- Event tense, aspect, and class
- Bag-of-words unigrams surrounding the event

Figure 2: Features in the 3 types of classifiers.

The data-driven features are shown in Figure 2. After labeling pairs of entities, the *ordered* pairs are then labeled with specific relations, described next.

5.2 Relation Labeling

This is the traditional ordering task. Given a set of entity pairs, label each with a temporal relation. TempEval-3 uses the full set of 12 relations.

Traditionally, ordering research trains a single classifier for all event-event links, and a second for all event-time links. We experimented with more

UTTime Best	56.45
NavyTime (TimeBank+AQUAINT)	46.83
NavyTime (TimeBank)	43.92
JU-CSE Best	34.77

Table 1: Task Crel, F1 scores of relation labeling.

specific classifiers, observing that two events in the same sentence share a syntactic context that does not exist between two events in different sentences. We must instead rely on discourse cues and word semantics for the latter. We thus propose using different classifiers to learn better feature weights for these unique contexts. Splitting into separate classifiers is largely unexplored on TimeBank, and just recently applied to a medical domain (Xu et al., 2013).

We train two MaxEnt classifiers for event-event links (inter and intra-sentence), and two for event-time links. The event-DCT links also have their own classifier for a total of 5 classifiers. We use the same features (Figure 2) as in relation identification.

5.3 Experiments and Results

All models were created by using 10-fold cross validation on TimeBank+AQUAINT. The best model was then trained on the entire set. Features seen only once were trimmed from training. The relation labeling confidence threshold was set to 0.3. Final results are reported on the held out test set provided by SemEval-2013 Task 1 (TempEval-3).

Our first experiments focus on *relation labeling*. This is a simpler task than identification in that we start with known pairs of entities, and the task is to assign a label to them (Task C-relation at SemEval-2013 Task 1). Table 1 gives the results. Our system initially ranked second with 46.83.

The next task is both *relation identification* and *relation labeling* combined (Task C). This is unfortunately a task that is difficult to define. Without a completely labeled graph of events and times, it is not about true extraction, but matching human labeling decisions that were constrained by time and effort. We experimented with rule-based vs data-driven extractors. We held our relation labeling model constant, and swapped different identification models in and out. Our best configuration was evaluated on test. Results are shown in Table 2. NavyTime is the third best performer.

Finally, the full task from raw text requires all

cleartk Best	36.26
UTTime-5	34.90
NavyTime (TimeBank+AQUAINT)	31.06
JU-CSE Best	26.41
NavyTime (TimeBank)	25.84
KUL	24.83

Table 2: Task C, F1 scores of relation ID and labeling.

cleartk Best	30.98
NavyTime (TimeBank+AQUAINT)	27.28
JU-CSE	24.61
NavyTime (TimeBank)	21.99
KUL	19.01

Table 3: Task ABC, Extraction and labeling raw text.

stages of this paper, starting from event and temporal extraction, then applying relation ID and labeling. Results are shown in Table 3. Our system ranked 2nd of 4 systems.

Our best performing setup uses trained classifiers for relation identification of event-event and event-DCT links, but deterministic rules for event-time links (Sec 5.1). It then uses trained classifiers for relation labeling of all pair types. Training with TimeBank+AQUAINT outperformed just TimeBank. The *split classifier* approach for intra and inter-sentence event-event relations also outperformed a single event-event classifier. We cannot give more specific results due to space constraints.

6 Discussion

Our system was 2nd in most of the subtasks and overall (Task ABC). Split-classifiers for inter and intra-sentence pairs are beneficial. Syntactic features help event extraction. Compared to *cleartk*, NavyTime was better in event and time extraction individually, but worse overall. Our approach to *relation identification* is likely the culprit.

We urge future work to focus on relation identification. Event and time performance is high, and relation labeling is covered in the literature. For identification, it is not clear that TimeBank-style corpora are appropriate for evaluation. Human annotators do not create connected graphs. How can we evaluate systems that do? Do we want systems that mimic imperfect, but testable human effort? Accurate evaluation on raw text requires fully labeled test sets.

References

Angel Chang and Christopher D. Manning. 2012. Sutime: a library for recognizing and normalizing time expressions. In *Proceedings of the Language Resources and Evaluation Conference*.

Inderjeet Mani, Ben Wellner, Marc Verhagen, and James Pustejovsky. 2007. Three approaches to learning tlinks in timeml. Technical Report CS-07-268, Brandeis University.

James Pustejovsky, Patrick Hanks, Roser Sauri, Andrew See, Robert Gaizauskas, Andrea Setzer, Dragomir Radev, Beth Sundheim, David Day, Lisa Ferro, et al. 2003. The timebank corpus. In *Corpus linguistics*, volume 2003, page 40.

Marc Verhagen, Robert Gaizauskas, Frank Schilder, Mark Hepple, Graham Katz, and James Pustejovsky. 2007. Semeval-2007 task 15: Tempeval temporal relation identification. In *Proceedings of the 4th International Workshop on Semantic Evaluations*, pages 75–80. Association for Computational Linguistics.

Marc Verhagen, Roser Sauri, Tommaso Caselli, and James Pustejovsky. 2010. Semeval-2010 task 13: Tempeval-2. In *Proceedings of the 5th International Workshop on Semantic Evaluation*, pages 57–62. Association for Computational Linguistics.

Yan Xu, Yining Wang, Tianren Liu, Junichi Tsujii, and Eric I-Chao Chang. 2013. An end-to-end system to identify temporal relation in discharge summaries: 2012 i2b2 challenge. *Journal of the American Medical Informatics Association*.

SUTIME: Evaluation in TempEval-3

Angel X. Chang
Stanford University
angelx@cs.stanford.edu

Christopher D. Manning
Stanford University
manning@cs.stanford.edu

Abstract

We analyze the performance of SUTIME, a temporal tagger for recognizing and normalizing temporal expressions, on TempEval-3 Task A for English. SUTIME is available as part of the Stanford CoreNLP pipeline and can be used to annotate documents with temporal information. Testing on the TempEval-3 evaluation corpus showed that this system is competitive with state-of-the-art techniques.

1 Introduction

The importance of modeling temporal information is increasingly apparent in natural language applications, such as information extraction and question answering. Extracting temporal information requires the ability to recognize temporal expressions, and to convert them from text to a normalized form that is easy to process. Temporal tagging systems are designed to address this problem. In this paper, we evaluate the performance of the SUTIME (Chang and Manning, 2012) rule-based temporal tagging system.

We evaluate the performance of SUTIME on extracting temporal information in TempEval-3 (UzZaman et al., 2013), which requires systems to automatically annotate documents with temporal information using TimeML (Pustejovsky et al., 2003). The TempEval-3 training data contains gold human annotated data from TimeBank, AQUAINT, and a new dataset of silver data automatically annotated using a combination of TipSem (Llorens et al., 2010) and TRIOS (UzZaman and Allen, 2010), two of the best performing systems from TempEval-2 (Verhagen et al., 2010).

2 System Description

We use the Stanford CoreNLP[1] pipeline with SUTIME to identify and normalize TIMEX3[2] expressions. SUTIME is incorporated into Stanford CoreNLP as part of the Named Entity Recognition annotator. For TempEval-3, we use the standard set of rules provided with SUTIME. Since SUTIME can also recognize temporal expressions whose values are not specified by TIMEX3, we ran SUTIME in a TIMEX3 compatible mode.[3]

2.1 SUTime

SUTIME is a rule-based temporal tagger built on regular expression patterns over tokens. Temporal expressions are bounded in their complexity, so many of them can be captured using finite automata. As shown by systems such as FASTUS (Hobbs et al., 1997), a cascade of finite automata can be very effective at extracting information from text. With SUTIME, we follow a similar staged strategy of (i) building up patterns over individual words to find numerical expressions; then (ii) using patterns over words and numerical expressions to find simple temporal expressions; and finally (iii) forming composite patterns over the discovered temporal expressions.

SUTIME recognizes **Time**, **Duration**, **Interval**, and **Set** according to the TIMEX3 specification. In

[1] nlp.stanford.edu/software/corenlp.shtml
[2] www.timeml.org
[3] sutime.restrictToTimex3 = true

*Second Joint Conference on Lexical and Computational Semantics (*SEM), Volume 2: Seventh International Workshop on Semantic Evaluation (SemEval 2013)*, pages 78–82, Atlanta, Georgia, June 14-15, 2013.

addition, it recognizes nested time expressions and duration ranges. To achieve this it uses a temporal pattern language defined over tokens (a regular expression language for expressing how tokenized text should be mapped to temporal objects). SUTIME is built on top of TOKENSREGEX,[4] a generic framework included in Stanford CoreNLP for definining patterns over text and mapping to semantic objects. With TOKENSREGEX we have access to any annotations provided by the Stanford CoreNLP system, such as the part-of-speech tag or the lemma. The full specification of the pattern language is available at `nlp.stanford.edu/software/sutime.shtml`.

To recognize temporal expressions, SUTIME applies three types of rules, in the following order: 1) text regex rules: mappings from simple regular expressions over characters or tokens to temporal representations; 2) compositional rules: mappings from regular expressions over chunks (both tokens and temporal objects) to temporal representations and 3) filtering rules: in which ambiguous expressions that are likely to not be temporal expressions are removed from the list of candidates (such as *fall* and *spring* by themselves). The compositional rules are applied repeatedly until the final list of time expressions stablizes.

After all the temporal expressions have been recognized, each temporal expression is associated with a temporal object. Each temporal object is resolved with respect to the reference date using heuristic rules. In this step, relative times are converted to an absolute time, and composite time objects are simplified as much as possible. The final resolution of relative temporal expressions is currently limited due to the usage of simple hard-coded rules (e.g. relative to document date with local context informing before and after heuristics). Finally, SUTIME will take the internal time representation and produce a TIMEX3 annotation for each temporal expression. SUTIME currently only handles English. It can however, be extended to other languages by creating sets of rules for additional languages.

3 Evaluation

We evaluated SUTIME's performance on the TempEval-3 Task A for English. Task A consists of determining the extent of time expressions as defined by the TimeML TIMEX3 tag, as well as providing normalized attributes for *type* and *value*. Extracted temporal expressions from the system and the gold are matched, and precision, recall, and F_1 are computed. For the evaluation of extents, there are two metrics: a relaxed match score for identifying a matching temporal expression, and a strict match that requires the text to be matched exactly. For example, identifying *the twentieth century* when the gold is *twentieth centry* will give a relaxed match but not a strict match. For the type and value attributes, an accuracy and a measure of the F_1 with respect to the relaxed match is given.

We compare SUTIME's performance with several other top systems on the English TempEval-3 Task A. We also include TIPSem which was used to create the silver data for TempEval-3 as a baseline. Of the systems that prepared multiple runs, we selected the best performing run to report. Table 1 gives the results for these systems on the TempEval-3 evaluation set. Interestingly, NavyTime which uses SUTIME for Task A, actually did better than SUTIME in the value normalization and is effectively the 2nd best system in Task A. The performance of NavyTime is otherwise identical to SUTIME. In NavyTime the normalization was tuned to the TimeBank annotation whereas the SUTIME submission was untuned. SUTIME has the highest recall in discovering temporal expressions. It also has the highest overall relaxed F_1, slightly higher than HeidelTime (Strötgen and Gertz, 2010) (cleartk had the highest strict F_1 of 82.71). Not surprisingly, the system used to generate the silver data, TIPSem, had the highest precision when extracting temporal expressions. For normalization, HeidelTime had the overall best performance on value and type. Both SUTIME and HeidelTime are rule-based, indicating the effectiveness of using rules for this domain. Another top performing system, ManTime used conditional random fields, a machine learning approach, for identifying temporal expressions and rules for normalization.

[4]`nlp.stanford.edu/software/tokensregex.shtml`

	Identification						*Normalization*			
	Relaxed			*Strict*			*Value*		*Type*	
System	F_1	P	R	F_1	P	R	F_1	Accuracy	F_1	Accuracy
SUTime	**90.32**	89.36	**91.30**	79.57	78.72	**80.43**	67.38	74.60	80.29	88.90
NavyTime	**90.32**	89.36	**91.30**	79.57	78.72	**80.43**	70.97	78.58	80.29	88.90
HeidelTime	90.30	93.08	87.68	81.34	83.85	78.99	**77.61**	**85.95**	**82.09**	**90.91**
ManTime	89.66	95.12	84.78	74.33	78.86	70.29	68.97	76.92	77.39	86.31
TIPSem	84.90	**97.20**	75.36	81.63	**93.46**	72.46	65.31	76.93	75.92	89.42

Table 1: TempEval-3; English Platinum Test set.

4 Error Analysis

Given the small size of the platinum data set, we were able to perform thorough error analysis of the errors made by SUTIME on the data set.

Table 2 shows the number of temporal expressions marked by the evaluation script as being incorrect. The errors can be grouped into three broad categories: i) those proposed by the system but not in the gold (relaxed precision errors), ii) those in the gold but not identified by the system (relaxed recall errors), and iii) temporal expressions with the wrong value (and sometimes type) normalization.

Of the 14 precision errors, many of the temporal expressions suggested by the system are reasonable. For instance, *current* is identified by the system. A few of the errors are not actual temporal expressions. For example, in the phrase *British Summer Time*, *Summer* was identified as a temporal expression which is not correct.

Given SUTime's high recall, only a few temporal expressions in the gold are not found by the system. In most cases, the temporal expressions missed by SUTIME do not have a well defined value associated with them (e.g. "digital age", "each season").

Performance using the strict match metric is not as good as some other systems. SUTIME was derived from GUTime (Mani, 2004) and focuses on matching longer time expressions as per earlier guidelines. Thus it is less conformant to the more current TimeML guidelines of having minimal blocks. For instance, SUTIME treats 2009-2010 as a range, whereas the gold standard treats it as two separate dates. This results in an incorrect value normalization and a recall error.

We now examine the cases where the SUTIME normalization differed from the gold. Table 3 shows a further breakdown of these errors.

Error type	Count
System not in gold (precision)	14
Gold not in system (recall)	12
Wrong value	32

Table 2: Summary of errors made by SUTIME on the platinum data set

Error type	Count
Value incorrectly resolved wrt to DCT	7
Value should not be resolved wrt to DCT	5
DURATION resolved to DATE	6
DATE misidentified as DURATION	3
Wrong granularity	4
Wrong normalization for set	2
Different normalization	3
Other	2

Table 3: Break down of value errors made by SUTime on the platinum data set

One weakness of SUTIME is that temporal expressions are always resolved with respect to the document creation time (DCT). While this heuristic works fairly well in most cases, and SUTime can achieve reasonable performance, there are obvious limitations with this approach. For instance, sometimes it is more appropriate to resolve the temporal expression with respect to nearby dates or events in the text. As an example, in the test document CNN_20130322_1003 there is the sentence *Call me Sunday night at 8 PM at the resort* that is part of an email of an unknown date. In this case, SUTIME still attempts to resolve the temporal expression *Sunday night at 8 PM* using the document creation time which is incorrect.

There can be inherent ambiguity as to which time point a time expression refers to. For instance, given a reference date of **2011-09-19**, a Monday, it is unclear whether *Friday* refers to **2011-09-16** or **2011-09-23**. SUTIME will normally resolve to the closest date/time with respect to the reference date. SUTIME also has some rules that will use the verb tense of the surrounding words to attempt to resolve the ambiguity. For instance, if a verb close to the temporal expression has a POS tag of VBD (past tense verb) then the expression will be resolved so that it occurs before the document date.

Most of the type errors are due to confusions between DATE and DURATION. Often SUTIME will attempt to resolve a DURATION as a DATE. For instance, given the phrase "the following decade", SUTIME will attempt to resolve that as a DATE with value **202X** (using a DCT of 2013-03-22). While this can be desirable in some cases, this is not what the gold annotation contains: type of DURATION and value of **P1DE**. In some other cases, SUTIME misidentifies DURATION as a DATE. For instance, it lacks rules to parse the *3:07:35* in *finishing in 3:07:35* as a duration.

Another problem faced by SUTIME is in figuring out the correct granularity to use. Given a document date of **2013-03-22**, it will identify *two years ago* as being **2011-03-22**. However, since these expressions indicate a less precise date, the gold annotation is a simple **2011**.

SUTIME also provided the wrong normalization for SET in several cases. For the expression *every morning*, SUTIME reported a value of **TMO** when the gold annotation was **XXXX-XX-XXTMO**. In other cases, SUTIME offered an alternative normalization, for instance, a value of **19XX** for *the 20th century* instead of just **19**. And **PTXM** instead of **PXM** for *minutes*. In this case, the **PTXM** is more correct as the **T** is required by ISO-8601 to differentiate between **M** for month, and **M** for minutes. The remaining errors are due to lacking rules such as SUTIME's inability to handle time zones in certain cases.

5 Discussion

As a rule-based system, SUTIME is limited by the coverage of its rule set for the different types of temporal expressions it can recognize. Many of the errors in SUTIME can be resolved by adding more rules to the system.

One key to improving the normalization of the value is to have better resolution of ambiguous temporal expressions. Identifying when temporal expressions should not be resolved using the document creation time, and how the temporal expression relates to other temporal expressions or events within the document is also critical. This suggests that normalization can benefit from being able to perform TempEval-3 Task C well.

Another approach to improving the system would be to provide different modes of use: a mode for end users that would like complex temporal expressions to be identified, or a mode for more basic temporal expressions that can be used as input for other temporal systems. Allowing for nested TIMEXes would also benefit the system's performance. For example, *2009-2010* should be a range, with a nested timex for *2009* and *2010*.

Another interesting direction to explore would be to evaluate the performance of SUTIME on domains other than current news. Since SUTIME also supports temporal expressions such as holidays and more distant dates such as *400 B.C.*, it would be interesting to see how well SUTIME can extract these different types of temporal expressions.

6 Conclusion

We have evaluated SUTIME by participating in TempEval-3 Task A and have shown that it is a competitive system for extracting time expressions. By providing it as part of the Stanford CoreNLP pipeline, we hope that it can be easily used as a basic component for building temporally aware systems.

Acknowledgements

We would like to acknowledge Justin Heermann, Jonathan Potter, Garrett Schlesinger and John Bauer for helping to implement parts of the system for TempEval-3.

References

Angel X. Chang and Christopher D. Manning. 2012. SUTIME: A library for recognizing and normalizing time expressions. In *8th International Conference on Language Resources and Evaluation (LREC 2012)*.

Jerry R. Hobbs, Douglas E. Appelt, John Bear, David Israel, Megumi Kameyama, Mark Stickel, and Mabry

Tyson. 1997. FASTUS: A cascaded finite-state transducer for extracting information from natural-language text. *Finite State Devices for Natural Language Processing*, pages 383–406.

Hector Llorens, Estela Saquete, and Borja Navarro. 2010. TIPSem (English and Spanish): Evaluating CRFs and semantic roles in TempEval-2. In *Proceedings of the 5th International Workshop on Semantic Evaluation*, pages 284–291. Association for Computational Linguistics.

Inderjeet Mani. 2004. Recent developments in temporal information extraction. In *Proceedings of RANLP03*, pages 45–60.

James Pustejovsky, Jos Castao, Robert Ingria, Roser Saur, Robert Gaizauskas, Andrea Setzer, and Graham Katz. 2003. TimeML: Robust specification of event and temporal expressions in text. In *in Fifth International Workshop on Computational Semantics (IWCS-5*.

Jannik Strötgen and Michael Gertz. 2010. HeidelTime: High quality rule-based extraction and normalization of temporal expressions. In *Proceedings of the 5th International Workshop on Semantic Evaluation*, pages 321–324.

Naushad UzZaman and James F Allen. 2010. TRIPS and TRIOS system for TempEval-2: Extracting temporal information from text. In *Proceedings of the 5th International Workshop on Semantic Evaluation*, pages 276–283. Association for Computational Linguistics.

Naushad UzZaman, Hector Llorens, Leon Derczynski, Marc Verhagen, James Allen, and James Pustejovsky. 2013. SemEval-2013 Task 1: TempEval-3: Evaluating time expressions, events, and temporal relations. In *Proceedings of the 7th International Workshop on Semantic Evaluation*, SemEval '13.

Marc Verhagen, Roser Saurí, Tommaso Caselli, and James Pustejovsky. 2010. SemEval-2010 task 13: TempEval-2. In *Proceedings of the 5th International Workshop on Semantic Evaluation*, SemEval '10, pages 57–62. Association for Computational Linguistics.

KUL: A Data-driven Approach to Temporal Parsing of Documents

Oleksandr Kolomiyets
KU Leuven
Celestijnenlaan 200A
Heverlee 3001, Belgium
Department of Computer Science
`oleksandr.kolomiyets@cs.kuleuven.be`

Marie-Francine Moens
KU Leuven
Celestijnenlaan 200A
Heverlee 3001, Belgium
Department of Computer Science
`sien.moens@cs.kuleuven.be`

Abstract

This paper describes a system for temporal processing of text, which participated in the Temporal Evaluations 2013 campaign. The system employs a number of machine learning classifiers to perform the core tasks of: identification of time expressions and events, recognition of their attributes, and estimation of temporal links between recognized events and times. The central feature of the proposed system is temporal parsing – an approach which identifies temporal relation arguments (event-event and event-timex pairs) and *the semantic label* of the relation as a single decision.

1 Introduction

Temporal Evaluations 2013 (TempEval-3) is the third iteration of temporal evaluations (after TempEval-1 (Verhagen et al., 2007) and TempEval-2 (Verhagen et al., 2010)) which addresses the task of temporal information processing of text. In contrast to the previous evaluation campaigns where the temporal relation recognition task was simplified by restricting grammatical context (events in adjacent sentences, events and times in the same sentences) and proposed relation pairs, TempEval-3 does not set any context in which temporal relations have to be identified. Thus, for temporal relation recognition the challenges consist of: first, detecting a pair of events, or an event and a time that constitutes a temporal relation; and, second, determining what semantic label to assign to the proposed pair. Moreover, TempEval-3 proposes the task of **end-to-end** temporal processing in which events and times, their attributes and relations have to be identified from a raw text input.

In this paper we present a data-driven approach to all-around temporal processing of text. A number of machine-learning detectors were designed to recognize temporal "markables" (events and times) and their attributes. The key feature of our approach is that argument pairs, as well as relations between them, are jointly estimated without specifying in advance the context in which these pairs have to occur.

2 Our Approach

2.1 Timex Processing

2.1.1 Timex Recognition and Normalization

The proposed method for timex recognition implements a supervised machine learning approach that processes each chunk-phrase derived from the parse tree. Time expressions are detected by the model as phrasal chunks in the parse with their corresponding spans. In addition, the model is bootstrapped by substitutions of temporal triggers with their synonyms learned by the Latent Words Language Model (Deschacht et al., 2012) as described in (Kolomiyets et al., 2011). We implemented a logistic regression model that makes use of the following features:

- the head word of the phrase and its POS tag;
- all tokens and POS tags in the phrase as a bag of words;
- the word-shape representation of the head word and the entire phrase, e.g. `Xxxxx 99` for the expression *April 30*;

*Second Joint Conference on Lexical and Computational Semantics (*SEM), Volume 2: Seventh International Workshop on Semantic Evaluation (SemEval 2013)*, pages 83–87, Atlanta, Georgia, June 14-15, 2013. ©2013 Association for Computational Linguistics

- the condensed word-shape representation for the head word and the entire phrase, e.g. `X(x) (9)` for the expression *April 30*;
- the concatenated string of the syntactic types of the children of the phrase in the parse tree;
- the depth in the parse tree.

In addition, we considered a special label for single tokens of time expressions. In this way, we detect parts of temporal expressions if they cannot be found in the chunk-based fashion. In detail, if a token is recognized as part of a timex and satisfies the pre-condition on its POS tag, we employ a "look-behind" rule for the phrasal chunk to match the begin token of the temporal expression. The legitimate start POS tags are determiners, adjectives, and cardinals. Another set of rules specifies unsuitable timexes, such as single cardinals with values outside predefined ranges of *day-of-month*, *month-of-year* and *year* numbers.

Normalization of temporal expressions is a process of estimating standard temporal values and types for temporal expressions. Due to a large variance of expressions denoting the same date and vagueness in language, rule-based approaches are usually employed for the normalization task, and our implementation is a rule-based system. The normalization procedure is the same as described in (Kolomiyets and Moens, 2010), which participated in TempEval-2.

2.2 Event Processing

The proposed method to event recognition implements a supervised machine learning approach that classifies every single token in the input sentence as an event instance of a specific semantic type. We implemented a logistic regression model with features largely derived from the work of Bethard and Martin (2006):

- the token, its lemma, coarse and fine-grained POS tags, token's suffixes and affixes;
- token's hypernyms and derivations in WordNet;
- the grammatical class of the chunk, in which the token occurs;
- the lemma of the governing verb of the token;
- phrasal chunks in the contextual window;
- the *light* verb feature for the governing verb;
- the polarity of the token's context;
- the determiner of the token and the sentence's subject;

In addition, we classify the tense attribute for the detected event by applying a set of thirteen handcrafted rules.

2.3 Temporal Relation Processing

Temporal relation recognition is the most difficult task of temporal information processing, as it requires recognitions of argument pairs, and subsequent classifications of relation types. Our approach employs a shift-reduce parsing technique, which treats each document as a dependency structure of annotations labeled with temporal relations (Kolomiyets et al., 2012). On the one hand, the advantage of the model is that the relation arguments and the relation between them are extracted as a single decision of a statistical classification model. On the other hand, such a decision is local and might not lead to the optimal global solution[1]. The following features for deterministic shift-reduce temporal parsing are employed:

- the token, its lemma, suffixes, coarse and fine-grained POS tags;
- the governing verb, its POS tag and suffixes;
- the sentence's root verb, its lemma and POS tag;
- features for a prepositional phrase occurrence, and domination by an auxiliary or modal verb;
- features for the presence of a temporal signal in the chunk and co-occurrence in the same sentence;
- a feature indicating if the sentence root verb lemmas of the arguments are the same;
- the temporal relation between the argument and the document creation time (DCT) (see below);
- a feature indicating if one argument is labeled as a semantic role of the other;
- timex value generation pattern (e.g. `YYYY-MM` for `2013-02`, or `PXY` for `P5Y`) and timex granularity (e.g. `DAY-OF-MONTH` for *Friday*, `MONTH-OF-YEAR` for *February* etc.);

[1]For further details on the deterministic temporal parsing model we refer the reader to (Kolomiyets et al., 2012).

Training	Test	P	R	F_1
TimeBank	TimeBank 10-fold	0.907	0.99	0.947
	AQUAINT	0.755	0.972	0.850
	Silver	0.736	0.963	0.834
AQUAINT	TimeBank	0.918	0.986	0.951
	AQUAINT 10-fold	0.795	0.970	0.874
	Silver	0.746	0.959	0.851
Silver	TimeBank	0.941	0.976	0.958
	AQUAINT	0.822	0.955	0.883
	Silver 10-fold	0.798	0.944	0.865

Table 1: Results for timex detection in different corpora.

As one of the features above provides information about the temporal relation between the argument and the DCT, we employ an interval-based algebra to classify relations between timexes and the DCT. In case the argument is an event, we use a simple logistic regression classifier with the following features:

- the event token, its lemma, coarse and fine-grained POS tags;
- tense, polarity, modality and aspect attributes;
- the token's suffixes;
- the governing verb, its POS tag, tense and the grammatical class of the chunk, in which the event occurs;
- preceding tokens of the chunk;

3 Results

3.1 Pre-Evaluation Results

The following results are obtained by 10-fold cross-validations and corpus cross-validations with respect to the evaluation criteria and metrics used in TempEval-2. Tables 1 and 2 present the results for the timex recognition and normalization tasks (Task A), and, Tables 3 and 4 present the results for the event recognition task (Task B).

As can be seen from the pre-evaluation results, the most accurate classification of timexes on all corpora in terms of F_1 score is achieved for the model trained on the Silver corpus. As for timex normalization, the performances on TimeBank and the Silver corpus are not very different for type and value accuracies. Similarly, we observe the tendency for a better performance on larger datasets with an exception for 10-fold cross-validation using the AQUAINT corpus.

Test Corpus	Type Acc.	Value Acc.
TimeBank	0.847	0.742
AQUAINT	0.852	0.714
Silver	0.853	0.739

Table 2: Results for normalization in different corpora.

Training	Test	P	R	F_1
TimeBank	TimeBank 10-fold	0.82	0.641	0.72
	AQUAINT	0.864	0.649	0.741
	Silver	0.888	0.734	0.804
AQUAINT	TimeBank	0.766	0.575	0.657
	AQUAINT 10-fold	0.900	0.776	0.836
	Silver	0.869	0.755	0.808
Silver	TimeBank	0.827	0.717	0.768
	AQUAINT	0.906	0.807	0.854
	Silver 10-fold	0.916	0.888	0.902

Table 3: Results for event detection in different corpora.

Training	Test	Class Acc.
TimeBank	TimeBank 10-fold	0.691
	AQUAINT	0.717
	Silver	0.804
AQUAINT	TimeBank	0.620
	AQUAINT 10-fold	0.830
	Silver	0.794
Silver	TimeBank	0.724
	AQUAINT	0.829
	Silver 10-fold	0.900

Table 4: Results for event classification in different corpora.

3.2 Evaluation Results

For the official evaluations we submitted three runs of the system, one of which addresses Tasks A and B (timex and event recognition)[2], one (KUL-

[2]During the official evaluation period, this run was re-submitted with no changes in the output together with KUL-TE3RunABC, which led to duplicate evaluation results known

Run	Relaxed Evaluation			
	P	R	F_1	Rank
KULRun-1	0.929	0.769	0.836	21/23
KUL-TE3RunABC	0.921	0.754	0.829	22/23
Run	Strict Evaluation			
	P	R	F_1	Rank
KULRun-1	0.77	0.63	0.693	22/23
KUL-TE3RunABC	0.814	0.667	0.733	15/23

Table 5: Results for the timex detection task.

TE3RunABC) provides a full temporal information processing pipeline (Task ABC), and the one for Task C only (KUL-TaskC). For KULRun-1 we employed the recognition models described above, all trained on the aggregated corpus comprising all three available training corpora in the evaluations. For KUL-TE3RunABC we also trained the markable recognition models on the aggregated corpus, but the event recognition output was slightly changed in order to merge multiple consequent events of the same semantic class into a single multi-token event. The temporal dependency parsing model was trained on the TimeBank and AQUAINT corpora only, with a reduced set of relation labels. This decision was motivated by the time constraints and the training time needed. The final relation label set contains the following temporal relation labels: `BEFORE`, `AFTER`, `DURING`, `DURING_INV`, `INCLUDES` and `IS_INCLUDED`. Below we present the obtained results for each task separately. The results for Task A are presented in Tables 5 and 6, for Task B in Tables 7 and 8, and, for Task ABC and Task-C-only in Table 9. It is worth mentioning that for Task B the aspect value was provided as `NONE`, thus this evaluation criterion is not representative for our system.

4 Conclusion

For TempEval-3 we proposed a number of statistical and rule-based approaches. For Task A we employed a logistic regression classifier whose output

as KULRun-1 and KULRun-2. Further in the paper, we refer to this run as simply to KULRun-1.

Run			Rank
KULRun-1	F_1		18/23
	Value	Type	
	0.629	0.741	
	Accuracy		14/23
	Value	Type	
	0.752	0.886	
KUL-TE3RunABC	F_1		19/23
	Value	Type	
	0.621	0.733	
	Accuracy		15/23
	Value	Type	
	0.750	0.885	

Table 6: Results for the timex normalization task.

Run	P	R	F_1	Rank
KULRun-1	0.807	0.779	0.792	5/15
KUL-TE3RunABC	0.776	0.765	0.77	12/15

Table 7: Results for the event detection task.

Run				Rank
KULRun-1	F_1			3/15
	Class	Tense	Aspect	
	0.701	n.a.	n.a.	
	Accuracy			3/15
	Class	Tense	Aspect	
	0.884	n.a.	n.a.	
KUL-TE3RunABC	F_1			5/15
	Class	Tense	Aspect	
	0.687	0.497	0.632	
	Accuracy			1/15
	Class	Tense	Aspect	
	0.891	0.644	0.82	

Table 8: Results for the event attribute recognition task.

Run	P	R	F_1	Rank
KUL-TE3RunABC	0.18	0.202	0.191	8/8
KUL-TaskC	0.234	0.265	0.248	10/13

Table 9: Results for Tasks ABC (end-to-end processing) and C (gold entities are given).

was augmented by a small number of hand-crafted rules to increase the recall. For the temporal expression normalization subtask we employed a rule-based system which estimates the attribute values for the recognized timexes. For Task B we proposed a logistic regression classifier which processes input tokens and classifies them as event instances of particular semantic classes. The optional tense attribute was estimated by a number of manually designed rules. For the most difficult tasks, Task ABC and Task C, we proposed a dependency parsing technique that jointly learns from data what arguments constitute a temporal relation and what the temporal relation label is. Due to evaluation time constraints and the time needed to model training, we reduced the set of relation labels and trained the model on two small annotated corpora.

The evaluations evidenced that the use of larger annotated data sets did not improve the timex recognition performance as it was expected from the pre-evaluations. Interestingly, we did not observe the expected improvement in terms of recall, as it was the case in the pre-evaluations. Yet, the timex normalization performance levels in the official evaluations were slightly higher than in the pre-evaluations. In contrast to timex recognition, the use of a large annotated corpus improved the results for event recognition. The pilot implementation of a temporal parser for newswire articles showed the lowest performance in the evaluations for Task ABC, but still provided decent results for Task C. One of the advantages of the proposed temporal parser is that the parser selects arguments for a temporal relation and classifies it at the same time. The decision is drawn by a statistical model trained on the annotated data, that is, the parser does not consider any particular predefined grammatical context in which the relation arguments have to be found. Another weak point of the parser is that it requires a large volume of high-quality annotations and long training times. The last two facts made it impossible to fully evaluate the proposed temporal parsing model, and we will further investigate the effectiveness of the model.

Acknowledgments

The presented research was supporter by the TERENCE (EU FP7-257410) and MUSE (EU FP7-296703) projects.

References

Steven Bethard and James H Martin. 2006. Identification of Event Mentions and their Semantic Class. In *Proceedings of the 2006 Conference on Empirical Methods in Natural Language Processing*, pages 146–154. Association for Computational Linguistics.

Koen Deschacht, Jan De Belder, and Marie-Francine Moens. 2012. The Latent Words Language Model. *Computer Speech & Language*.

Oleksandr Kolomiyets and Marie-Francine Moens. 2010. Kul: Recognition and Normalization of Temporal Expressions. In *Proceedings of the 5th International Workshop on Semantic Evaluation*, pages 325–328. Association for Computational Linguistics.

Oleksandr Kolomiyets, Steven Bethard, and Marie-Francine Moens. 2011. Model-Portability Experiments for Textual Temporal Analysis. In *Proceedings of the 49th Annual Meeting of the Association for Computational Linguistics: Human Language Technologies*, pages 271–276.

Oleksandr Kolomiyets, Steven Bethard, and Marie-Francine Moens. 2012. Extracting Narrative Timelines as Temporal Dependency Structures. In *Proceedings of the 50th Annual Meeting of the Association for Computational Linguistics*, pages 88–97. Association for Computational Linguistics.

Marc Verhagen, Robert Gaizauskas, Frank Schilder, Mark Hepple, Graham Katz, and James Pustejovsky. 2007. Semeval-2007 Task 15: TempEval Temporal Relation Identification. In *Proceedings of the 4th International Workshop on Semantic Evaluations*, pages 75–80. Association for Computational Linguistics.

Marc Verhagen, Roser Sauri, Tommaso Caselli, and James Pustejovsky. 2010. Semeval-2010 Task 13: TempEval-2. In *Proceedings of the 5th International Workshop on Semantic Evaluation*, pages 57–62. Association for Computational Linguistics.

UTTime: Temporal Relation Classification using Deep Syntactic Features

Natsuda Laokulrat
The University of Tokyo
3-7-1 Hongo, Bunkyo-ku,
Tokyo, Japan
natsuda@logos.t.u-tokyo.ac.jp

Makoto Miwa
The University of Manchester
131 Princess Street,
Manchester, M1 7DN, UK
makoto.miwa@manchester.ac.uk

Yoshimasa Tsuruoka
The University of Tokyo
3-7-1 Hongo, Bunkyo-ku,
Tokyo, Japan
tsuruoka@logos.t.u-tokyo.ac.jp

Takashi Chikayama
The University of Tokyo
3-7-1 Hongo, Bunkyo-ku,
Tokyo, Japan
chikayama@logos.t.u-tokyo.ac.jp

Abstract

In this paper, we present a system, UTTime, which we submitted to TempEval-3 for Task C: Annotating temporal relations. The system uses logistic regression classifiers and exploits features extracted from a deep syntactic parser, including paths between event words in phrase structure trees and their path lengths, and paths between event words in predicate-argument structures and their subgraphs. UTTime achieved an F1 score of 34.9 based on the graphed-based evaluation for Task C (ranked 2nd) and 56.45 for Task C-relation-only (ranked 1st) in the TempEval-3 evaluation.

1 Introduction

Temporal annotation is the task of identifying temporal relationships between pairs of temporal entities, namely temporal expressions and events, within a piece of text. The temporal relationships are important to support other NLP applications such as textual entailment, document summarization, and question answering. The temporal annotation task consists of several subtasks, including temporal expression extraction, event extraction, and temporal link identification and relation classification.

In TempEval-3, there are three subtasks of the temporal annotation process offered, i.e., Task A: Temporal expression extraction and normalization, Task B: Event extraction, and Task C: Annotating temporal relations. This paper presents a system to handle Task C. Based on the annotated data provided, this subtask requires identifying pairs of temporal entities and classifying the pairs into one of the 14 relation types according to TimeML (Pustejovsky et al., 2005), i.e., *BEFORE, AFTER, IMMEDIATELY BEFORE, IMMEDIATELY AFTER, INCLUDES, IS INCLUDED, DURING, DURING INVERSE, SIMULTANEOUS, IDENTITY, BEGINS, BEGUN BY, END, and ENDED BY.*

The motivation behind our work is to utilize syntactic and semantic relationships between a pair of temporal entities in the temporal relation classification task, since we believe that these relationships convey the temporal relation. In addition to general features, which are easily extracted from sentences (e.g., part of speech tags, lemmas, synnonyms), we use features extracted using a deep syntactic parser. The features from the deep parser can be divided into two groups: features from phrase structure trees and features from predicate-argument structures. These features are only applicable in the case that the temporal entities appear in the same sentence, so we use only the general features for inter-sentence relations.

Predicate-argument structure expresses semantic relations between words. This information can be extracted from a deep syntactic parser. Features from predicate-argument structures can capture important temporal information (e.g., prepositions of time) from sentences effectively.

The remaining part of this paper is organized as follows. We explain our approach in detail in Section 2 and then show the evaluation and results in Section 3. Finally, we conclude with directions for future work in Section 4.

2 Approach

Our system, UTTime, is based on a supervised machine learning approach. UTTime performs two tasks; TLINK identification and classification. In

*Second Joint Conference on Lexical and Computational Semantics (*SEM), Volume 2: Seventh International Workshop on Semantic Evaluation (SemEval 2013)*, pages 88–92, Atlanta, Georgia, June 14-15, 2013.

other words, UTTime identifies pairs of temporal entities and classifies these pairs into temporal relation types.

2.1 TLINK identification

A pair of temporal entities that have a temporal relation is called a TLINK. The system first determines which pairs of temporal entities are linked by using a ruled-based approach as a baseline approach.

All the TempEval-3's possible pairs of temporal entities are extracted by a set of simple rules; pairs of temporal entities that satisfy one of the following rules are considered as TLINKs.

- Event and document creation time
- Events in the same sentence
- Event and temporal expression in the same sentence
- Events in consecutive sentences

2.2 TLINK classification

Each TLINK is classified into a temporal relation type. We use a machine learning approach for the temporal relation classification. Two L2-regularized logistic regression classifiers, LIBLINEAR (Fan et al., 2008), are used; one for event-event TLINKs, and another one for event-time TLINKs. In addition to general features at different linguistic levels, features extracted by a deep syntactic parser are used.

The general features we employed are:

- Event and timex attributes

  All attributes associated with events (class, tense, aspect, modality, and polarity) and temporal expressions (type, value, functionInDocument, and temporalFunction) are used. For event-event TLINKs, we also use tense/class/aspect match, tense/class/aspect bigrams as features (Chambers et al., 2007).

- Morphosyntactic information

  Words, part of speech tags, lemmas within a window before/after event words are extracted using Stanford coreNLP (Stanford NLP Group, 2012).

- Lexical semantic information

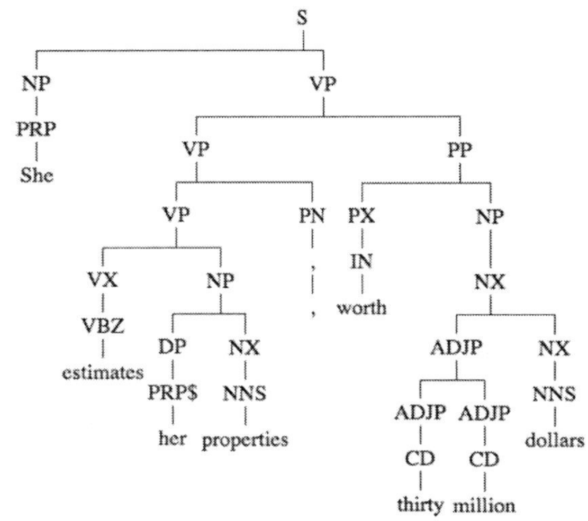

Figure 1: Phrase structure tree

  Synonyms of event word tokens from WordNet lexical database (Fellbaum, 1998) are used as features.

- Event-Event information

  For event-event TLINKs, we use *same_sentence* feature to differentiate pairs of events in the same sentence from pairs of events from different sentences (Chambers et al., 2007).

In the case that temporal entities of a particular TLINK are in the same sentence, we extract two new types of sentence-level semantic information from a deep syntactic parser. We use the Enju parser (Miyao and Tsujii, 2008). It analyzes syntactic/semantic structures of sentences and provides phrase structures and predicate-argument structures. The features we extract from the deep parser are

- Paths between event words in the phrase structure tree, and up(↑)/down(↓) lengths of paths.

  We use 3-grams of paths as features instead of full paths since these are too sparse. An example is shown in Figure 1. In this case, the path between the event words, *estimates* and *worth*, is *VBZ↑, VX↑, VP↑, VP↑, VP, PP↓, PX↓, IN↓*. The 3-grams of the path are, therefore, {*VBZ↑-VX↑-VP↑, VX↑-VP↑-VP↑, VP↑-VP↑-VP, VP↑-VP-PP↓, VP-PP↓-PX↓, PP↓-PX-↓-IN↓*}. The up/down path

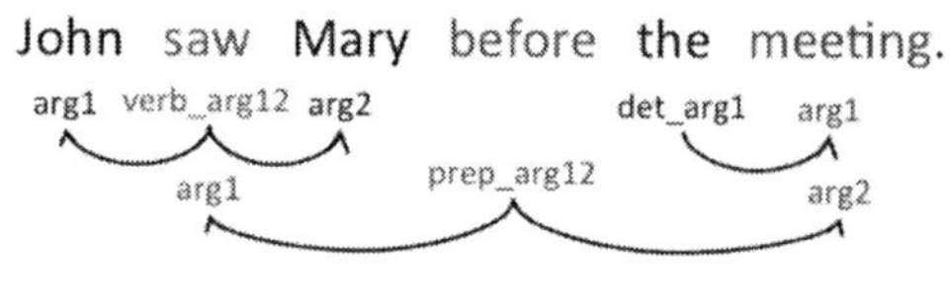

Figure 2: Predicate argument structure

lengths are 4 *(VBZ↑, VX↑, VP↑, VP↑)* and 3 *(PP↓, PX↓, IN↓)* respectively.

- Paths between event words in predicate-argument structure, and their subgraphs.

  For the previous example, we can express the relations in predicate-argument structure representation as

  - verb_arg12: estimate (she, properties)
  - prep_arg12: worth (estimate, dollars)

  In this case, the path between the event words, *estimates* and *worth*, is *←prep_arg12:arg1*. That is, the type of the predicate *worth* is *prep_arg12* and it has *estimate* as the first argument (arg1). The path from *estimate* to *worth* is in reverse direction (←).

  The next example sentence, *John saw mary before the meeting*, gives an idea of a more complex predicate-argument structure as shown in Figure 2. The path between the event words, *saw* and *meeting* is *←prep_arg12:arg1, prep_arg12:arg2*.

  We use (v, e, v) and (e, v, e) tuples of the edges and vertices on the path as features. For example, in Figure 2, the (v,e,v) tuples are *(see, ←prep_arg12:arg1, before)* and *(before, prep_arg12:arg2, meeting)*. In the same way, the (e,v,e) tuple is *(←prep_arg12:arg1, before, prep_arg12:arg2)*. The subgraphs of (v, e, v) and (e, v, e) tuples are also used, including *(see, ←prep_arg12:arg1, *), (*, ←prep_arg12:arg1, before), (*, ←prep_arg12:arg1, *), (*, prep_arg12:arg2, meeting), (before, prep_arg12:arg2, *), (*, prep_arg12:arg2, *), (*, before, prep_arg12:arg2), (←prep_arg12:arg1, before, *), (*, before, *)*.

From the above example, the features from predicate argument structure can properly capture the preposition *before*. It can also capture a preposition from a compound sentence such as *John met Mary before he went back home*. The path between the event words *met* and *went* are *(←conj_arg12:arg1, conj_arg12:arg2)* and the (v, e, v) and (e, v, e) tuples are *(met, ←conj_arg12:arg1, before), (before, conj_arg12:arg2, went)*, and *(←prep_arg12:arg1, before, prep_arg12:arg2)*.

2.3 Hybrid approach

The rule-based approach described in Section 2.1 produces many unreasonable and excessive links. We thus use a machine learning approach to filter out those unreasonable links by training the model in Section 2.2 with an additional relation type, *UNKNOWN*, for links that satisfy the rules in Section 2.1 but do not appear in the training data.

In this way, for Task C, we first extract all the links that satisfy the rules and classify the relation types of those links. After classifying temporal relations, we remove the links that are classified as *UNKNOWN*.

3 Evaluation

The scores are calculated by the graph-based evaluation metric proposed by UzZaman and Allen (2011). We trained the models with TimeBank and AQUAINT corpora. We also trained our models on the training set with inverse relations. The performance analysis is based on 10-fold cross validation on the development data.

3.1 Task C

In Task C, a system has to identify appropriate temporal links and to classify each link into one temporal relation type. For Task C evaluation, we compare the results of the models trained with and without the features from the deep parser. The results are shown in Table 1. The rule-based approach gives a very low precision.

3.2 Task C-relation-only

Task C-relation-only provides a system with all the appropriate temporal links and only needs the system to classify the relation types. Since our goal is to exploit the features from the deep parser, in Task C-relation-only, we measured the contribution of those features to temporal relation classification in Table 2.

Features	F1	P	R
gen. (rule)	22.51	14.32	52.58
gen. + ph. + pas. (rule)	22.61	14.30	54.01
gen. + ph. + pas. (hyb.)	33.52	36.23	31.19
gen. + ph. + pas. (hyb. + inv.)	39.53	37.56	41.70

Table 1: Result of Task C. (rule: rule-based approach, hyb.: hybrid approach, gen.: general features, ph.:phrase structure tree features, pas.:predicate-argument structure features, and inv.: Inverse relations are used for training.)

Features	F1	P	R
gen.	64.42	64.59	64.25
gen. + ph.	65.24	65.42	65.06
gen. + pas.	66.40	66.55	66.25
gen. + ph. + pas.	66.39	66.55	66.23
gen. + ph. + pas. (inv.)	65.30	65.39	65.20

Table 2: Result of Task C-relation-only. (gen.: general features, ph.:phrase structure tree features, pas.:predicate-argument structure features, and inv.: Inverse relations are used for training.)

The predicate-argument-structure features contributed to the improvement more than those of phrase structures in both precision and recall. The reason is probably that the features from phrase structures that we used did not imply a temporal relation of events in the sentence. For instance, the sentence "*John* ***saw*** *Mary before the* ***meeting***" gives exactly the same path as of the sentence "*John* ***saw*** *Mary after the* ***meeting***".

3.3 Results on test data

Tables 3 and 4 show the results on the test data, which were manually annotated and provided by the TempEval-3 organizer. We also show the scores of the other systems in the tables. For the evaluation on the test data, we used the models trained with general features, phrase structure tree features, and predicate-argument structure features.

UTTime-5 ranked 2nd best in Task C. Interestingly, training the models with inverse relations improved the system only when using the hybrid approach. This means that the inverse relations did not improve the temporal classification but helped the system filter out unreasonable links (UNKNOWN) in the hybrid approach. As expected, the ruled-based approach got a very high recall score at the expense of precision. UTTime-1, although it achieved the F1 score of only 24.65, got the highest recall among all the systems.

Approach	F1	P	R
rule (UTTime-1)	24.65	15.18	65.64
rule + inv (UTTime-3)	24.28	15.1	61.99
hyb. (UTTime-4)	28.81	37.41	23.43
hyb. + inv. (UTTime-5)	34.9	35.94	33.92
cleartk	**36.26**	**37.32**	**35.25**
NavyTime	31.06	35.48	27.62
JU-CSE	26.41	21.04	35.47
KUL-KULTaskC	24.83	23.35	26.52

Table 3: Result of Tack C on test data. (rule: rule-based approach, hyb.: hybrid approach, and inv.: Inverse relations are used for training.)

Approach	F1	P	R
gen. + ph. + pas. (UTTime-1)	**56.45**	**55.58**	**57.35**
gen. + ph. + pas. (UTTime-2)	54.26	53.2	55.36
gen. + ph. + pas. (inv.) (UTTime-3)	54.7	53.85	55.58
NavyTime	46.83	46.59	47.07
JU-CSE	34.77	35.07	34.48

Table 4: Result of Task C-relation-only on test data. (gen.: general features, ph.:phrase structure tree features, pas.:predicate-argument structure features, and inv.: Inverse relations are used for training.)

For Task C-relation-only, we achieved the highest F1 score, precision, and recall. UTTime-2 basically had the same models as that of UTTime-1, but we put different weights for each relation type. The results show that using the weights did not improve the score in graph-based evaluation.

4 Conclusion

The system, UTTime, identifying temporal links and classifying temporal relation, is proposed. The links were identified based on the rule-based approach and then some links were filtered out by a classifier. The filtering helped improve the system considerably. For the relation classification task, the features extracted from phrase structures and predicate-argument structures were proposed, and the features improved the classification in precision, recall, and F-score.

In future work, we hope to improve the classification performance by constructing timegraphs (Miller and Schubert, 1999), so that the system can use information from neighbor TLINKs as features.

References

James Pustejovsky, Robert Ingria, Roser Saurí, José Castaño, Jessica Littman, Rob Gaizauskas, Andrea Setzer, Graham Katz, Inderjeet Mani 2005. The specification language TimeML. *The Language of Time: A reader*, pages 545–557

Stanford Natural Language Processing Group. 2012. Stanford CoreNLP.

Christiane Fellbaum. 1998. WordNet: An Electronic Lexical Database. Cambridge, MA: MIT Press.

Rong-En Fan, Kai-Wei Chang, Cho-Jui Hsieh, Xiang-Rui Wang, and Chih-Jen Lin. 2008. LIBLINEAR: A Library for Large Linear Classification.

Nathanael Chambers, Shan Wang and Dan Jurafsky. 2007. Classifying Temporal Relations between Events. In *ACL 2007*, pages 173–176.

Yusuke Miyao and Jun'ichi Tsujii. 2008. Feature Forest Models for Probabilistic HPSG Parsing. In *Computational Linguistics*. 34(1). pages 35–80, MIT Press.

Naushad UzZaman and James F. Allen. 2011. Temporal Evaluation. In *ACL 2011*, pages 351–356.

Stephanie A. Miller and Lenhart K. Schubert. 1999. Time Revisited. In *Computational Intelligence 6*, pages 108–118.

UMCC_DLSI-(EPS): Paraphrases Detection Based on Semantic Distance

Héctor Dávila, Antonio Fernández Orquín, Alexander Chávez, Yoan Gutiérrez, Armando Collazo, José I. Abreu
DI, University of Matanzas
Autopista a Varadero km 3 ½
Matanzas, Cuba.
{hector.davila, tony, alexander.chavez, yoan.gutierrez, armando.collazo, jose.abreu}@umcc.cu

Andrés Montoyo, Rafael Muñoz
DLSI, University of Alicante Carretera de San Vicente S/N Alicante, Spain.
{montoyo, rafael}@dlsi.ua.es

Abstract

This paper describes the specifications and results of UMCC_DLSI-(EPS) system, which participated in the first Evaluating Phrasal Semantics of SemEval-2013. Our supervised system uses different kinds of semantic features to train a bagging classifier used to select the correct similarity option. Related to the different features we can highlight the resource WordNet used to extract semantic relations among words and the use of different algorithms to establish semantic similarities. Our system obtains promising results with a precision value around 78% for the English corpus and 71.84% for the Italian corpus.

1 Introduction

It is well known finding words similarity, even when it is lexical or semantic can improve entailment recognition and paraphrase identification; and ultimately lead to improvements in a wide range of applications in Natural Language Processing (NLP). Several areas like question answering, query expansion, information retrieval, and many others, depend on phrasal semantics (PS). PS, is concerned with how the meaning of a sentence is composed both from the meaning of the constituent words, and from extra meaning contained within the structural organization of the sentence itself (Dominey, 2005).

The aim of SemEval 2013 competition is also discovering similarity, specifically in Evaluating Phrasal Semantics (EPS). The goal of this task is to evaluate how well systems can judge the semantic similarity of a word and a short sequence of words. That is, given a set of pairs of this type; classify it on negative (if the meaning of the word is semantically different to the meaning of the sequence) or positive (if the meaning of the sequence, as a whole, is semantically close to the meaning of the word).

Based on this, we developed a system capable to detect if two phrases are semantically close.

The rest of this paper, specifically section 2 is a brief Related Work. Section 3 describes the system architecture and our run. Continuing with section 4 we describe the training phase. Following that, section 5 presents the results and discussion for our Machine Learning System. Finally we conclude and propose our future works (Section 6).

2 Related Work

There have been many WordNet-based similarity measures, among other highlights the work of researchers like (Budanitsky and Hirst, 2006; Leacock and Chodorow, 1998; Mihalcea *et al.*, 2006; Richardson *et al.*, 1994).

On the other hand, WordNet::Similarity[1] (Pedersen *et al.*, 2004) has been used by other researchers in an interesting array of domains. WordNet::Similarity implements measures of similarity and relatedness between a pair of concepts (or synsets[2]) based on the structure and content of WordNet. According to (Pedersen *et al.*, 2004), three of the six measures of similarity are based on the information content of the least

[1]http://sourceforge.net/projects/wn-similarity/
[2] A group of English words into sets of synonyms.

*Second Joint Conference on Lexical and Computational Semantics (*SEM), Volume 2: Seventh International Workshop on Semantic Evaluation (SemEval 2013)*, pages 93–97, Atlanta, Georgia, June 14-15, 2013.

common subsumer (LCS). These measures include res (Resnik, 1995), lin (Lin, 1998), and jcn (Jiang and Conrath, 1997).

Pursuant to Pedersen, there are three other similarity measures based on path lengths between a pair of concepts: lch (Leacock and Chodorow, 1998), wup (Wu and Palmer, 1994), and path.
Our proposal differs from those of WordNet::Similarity and other measures of similarity in the way we selected the relevant WordNet relations (see section 3.2 for detail). Unlike others, our measure assign weight to WordNet relations (any we consider relevant) depending to the place they occupy in the minimum path and the previously visited relations.

Besides these, the novelty of our approach is using the weights as a function of semantic relations in a minimal distance path and also the method we used to arrive to those weight functions or rules.

3 System Architecture and description of the run

As we can see in Figure 1 our run begin with the pre-processing of SemEval 2013's training set. Every sentence pair is tokenized, lemmatized and POS-tagged using Freeling 2.2 tool (Atserias *et al.*, 2006). Afterwards, several methods and algorithms are applied in order to extract all features for our Machine Learning System (MLS). The system trains the classifier using a model based on bagging (using JRip[3]). The training corpus has been provided by SemEval-2013 competition, in concrete by the EPS task. As a result, we obtain a trained model capable to detect if one phrase implies other. Finally, we test our system with the SemEval 2013 test set (see Table 2 with the results of our run). The following section describes the features extraction process.

3.1 Description of the features used in the Machine Learning System

In order to detect entailment between a pair of phrases, we developed an algorithm that searches a semantic distance, according to WordNet (Miller *et al.*, 1990), between each word in the first phrase with each one in the second phrase.

We used four features which intend to measure the level of proximity between both sentences:

- The minimum distance to align the first phrase with the second (MinDist). See section 3.2 for details.
- The maximal distance to align the first phrase with the second (MaxDist).
- The average of all distances results to align the first phrase with the second one. (AverageDistance).
- The absolute relative error of all distances results to align the first phrase with the second respect to the average of them.

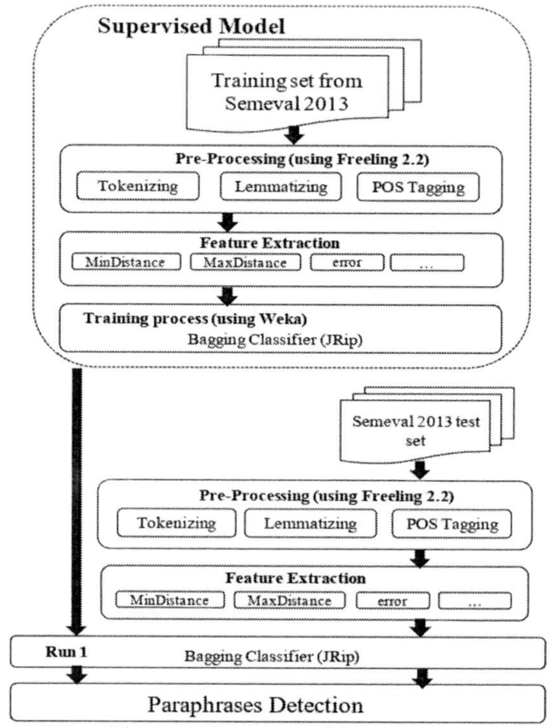

Figure 1. System Architecture.

Other features included are the most frequent relations contained in the shorted path of the minimum distance; result to align the first phrase with the second one. Following table shows the relations selected as most frequent.

A weight was added to each of them, according to the place it occupy in the shortest path between two synsets. The shortest path was calculated using Breadth -First-Search algorithm (BFS) (Cormen *et al.*, 2001).

In addition, there is one feature that takes into account any other relationship that is not previously considered.

Finally, as a result we obtain 22 features from this alignment method.

[3] JRip is an inference and rules-based learner.

Relation	Weight (W function)
Antonym	1000
Synonym	0
Hyponym/ Hypernym	100 if exist an antonym before, 30 if exist other relation before (except synonym, hyponym, hypernym), 5 otherwise.
Meber_Holonym/ PartHolonym	100 if exist an antonym before, 20 if exist a hyponym or a hypernym,10 otherwise.
Cause/ Entailment	100 if exist an antonym before, 2 otherwise.
Similar_To	100 if exist an antonym before, 3 otherwise.
Attribute	100 if exist an antonym before, 8 otherwise.
Also_See	100 if exist an antonym before, 10 otherwise.
Derivationaly_Related_Form	100 if exist an antonym before, 5 otherwise.
Domain_Of_Synset_Topic	100 if exist an antonym before, 13 otherwise.
Domain_Of_Synset_Usage	100 if exist an antonym before, 60 otherwise.
Member_Of_Domain_Topic	100 if exist an antonym before, 13 otherwise.
Member_Of_Domain_Usage	100 if exist an antonym before, 60 otherwise.
Other	100

Table 1. Most frequents relations with their weight.

3.2 Semantic Distance

As aforementioned, our distance depends on calculating the similarity between sentences, based on the analysis of WordNet relations, and we only took into account the most frequent ones. When searching the shortest path between two WordNet synsets, frequents relations were considered the ones extracted according to the analysis made in the training corpus, provided by SemEval-2013.

The distance between two synsets is calculated with the relations found; and simply it is the sum of the weights assigned to each connection.

$$MinDistP(P,Q) = MinDistS(P_X, Q_Y), \forall\, (X,Y) \quad (1)$$

$$MinDistS(X,Y) = Min(X_i, Y_j), \forall (i,j) \quad (2)$$

$$Min(X_i; Y_j) = \sum_{k=0}^{k=m} W(Rel(L[k], L[k+1])) \quad (3)$$

$$L = BFS(X_i; Y_j) \quad (4)$$

Where i and j represents the i-th and j-th sense of the word; P and Q represents words collections; P_X is the X-th word of P; Q_Y is the Y-th word of Q; $MinDistP$ obtains a value that represents a minimal semantic distance across WordNet (Miller *et al.*, 2006) resource (this resource is involved into the integrator resource, ISR-WN (Gutiérrez *et al.*, 2011a; 2010a); $MinDistS$ the minimal semantic distance between two words; Min represents the minimal semantic distance between two senses collections; L is a collection of synsets that represents the minimal path between two synsets using BFS; Rel obtains semantic relation types between two synsets; W is a functions that apply the rules described in Table 1. The maximum and average distance is calculated in a similar fashion but using the maximum and average instead of the minimum.

3.3 Semantic Alignment

First, the two sentences are pre-processed with Freeling 2.2 and the words are classified according to their parts-of-speech. Then, all senses of every word are taken and treated as a group. Distance between two groups will be the minimal distance (described in 3.1) between senses of any pair of words belonging to the group.

In the example of Figure 2, Dist=280 is selected for the pair "Balance-Culture" (minimal cost).

Following the explanation on section 3.1 we extract the features guided to measure the level of proximity between both sentences.

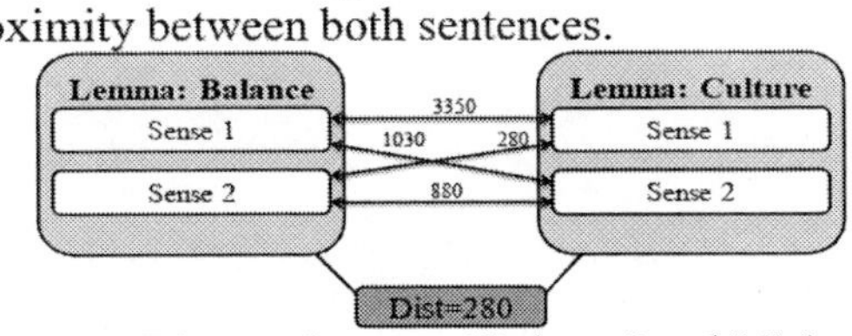

Figure 2. Distance between "Balance" and "Culture".

A maximum and average distance is calculated in a similar fashion, but using the maximum and average instead of the minimum.

4 Description of the training phase

For the training process, we used a supervised learning framework (based on Weka[4]), including all the training set (positive and negative instances) as a training corpus. We conduct several experiments in order to select the correct classifier, the best result being obtained with a model based on bagging (using JRip algorithm). Finally, we used 10-fold cross validation technique with the selected classifier, obtaining a classification value of 73.21%.

[4] http://prdownloads.sourceforge.net/weka/

5 Results and discussion

EPS task of SemEval-2013 offered many official measures to rank the systems. Some of them are the following:

- F-Measure (FM): Correct Response (CR), Instances correctly classified, True positives (TP), Instances correctly classified as positive. False Positives (FP), Instances incorrectly classified as positive, True Negatives (TN), Instances correctly classified as negative, False Negatives (FN), Instances incorrectly classified as negative.

Corpus	FM	CR	TP	FP	TN	FN
English	0.6892	2826	1198	325	1628	755
Italian	0.6396	574	245	96	329	180

Table 2. Official SemEval 2013 results.

The behavior of our system, for English and Italian corpus is shown in Table 2.

The only thing that changes to process the Italian corpus is that Freeling is used as input to identify Italian words and it returns the English WN synsets. The process continues in the same way as English.

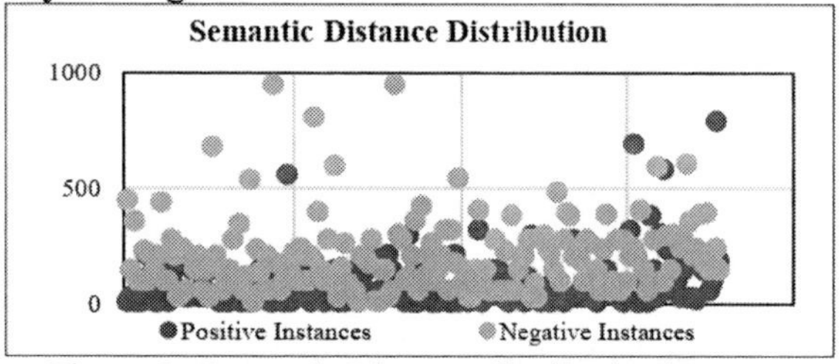

Figure 3: Semantic Distance distribution between negative and positive instances.

As shown in Table 2, our main drawback is to classify positive instances. Sometimes, the distance between positive phrases is very far. This is due to the relations found in the minimum path are very similar to the one found in other pairs of negatives instances; this can be the cause of our MLS classifies them as negatives (see Figure 3).

Figure 3 shows a distributional graphics that take a sample of 200 negative and positive instances. The graphics illustrate how close to zero value the positive instances are, while the negatives are far away from this value. However, in the approximate range between 80 and 200, we can see values of positive and negative instances positioning together. This can be the cause that our MLS misclassified some positive instances as negative.

6 Conclusion and future work

This paper introduced a new framework for EPS, which depends on the extraction of several features from WordNet relations. We have conducted the semantic features extraction in a multidimensional context using the resource ISR-WN(Gutiérrez *et al.*, 2010a).

Our semantic distance provides an appealing approach for dealing with phrasal detection based on WordNet relation. Our team reached the sixth position of ten runs for English corpus, with a small difference of 0.07 points compared to the best results with respect to accuracy parameter.

Despite the problems caused by poorly selected positive instances, our distance (labeled as Our) obtained very similar results to those obtained by the best team (labeled as First[5]), which indicates that our work is well underway (see Table 3 for details).

Team	accuracy	recall	precision
First	0.802611	0.751664	0.836944128
Our	0.723502	0.613415	0.786605384

Table 3. Comparative results (English corpus).

It is important to remark that our system has been the only competitor to evaluate Italian texts. It has been possible due to our system include Freeling in the preprocessing stage.

Our future work will aim to resolve instances misclassified by our algorithm. In addition, we will introduce lexical substitutions (synonyms) to expand the corpus, we will also apply conceptual semantic similarity using relevant semantic trees (Gutiérrez *et al.*, 2010b; Gutiérrez *et al.*, 2011b).

Acknowledgments

This research work has been partially funded by the Spanish Government through the project TEXT-MESS 2.0 (TIN2009-13391-C04), "Análisis de Tendencias Mediante Técnicas de Opinión Semántica" (TIN2012-38536-C03-03) and "Técnicas de Deconstrucción en la Tecnologías del Lenguaje Humano" (TIN2012-31224); and by the Valencian Government through the project PROMETEO (PROMETEO/2009/199).

References

Atserias, J.; B. Casas; E. Comelles; M. González; L. Padró and M. Padró. FreeLing 1.3: Syntactic and

[5] christian_wartena. Team HsH.

semantic services in an open-source NLP library. Proceedings of the 5th International Conference on Language Resources and Evaluation (LREC'06), 2006. 48-55 p.

Budanitsky, A. and G. Hirst Evaluating wordnet-based measures of lexical semantic relatedness Computational Linguistics, 2006, 32(1): 13-47.

Cormen, T. H.; C. E. Leiserson; R. L. Rivest and C. Stein. Introduction to algorithms. MIT press, 2001. 0262032937.

Dominey, P. F. Aspects of descriptive, referential, and information structure in phrasal semantics: A construction-based model Interaction Studies, 2005, 6(2): 287-310.

Gutiérrez, Y.; A. Fernández; A. Montoyo and S. Vázquez. Integration of semantic resources based on WordNet. XXVI Congreso de la Sociedad Española para el Procesamiento del Lenguaje Natural, Universidad Politécnica de Valencia, Valencia, SEPLN 2010, 2010a. 161-168 p. 1135-5948.

Gutiérrez, Y.; A. Fernández; A. Montoyo and S. Vázquez. UMCC-DLSI: Integrative resource for disambiguation task. Proceedings of the 5th International Workshop on Semantic Evaluation, Uppsala, Sweden, Association for Computational Linguistics, 2010b. 427-432 p.

Gutiérrez, Y.; A. Fernández; A. Montoyo and S. Vázquez Enriching the Integration of Semantic Resources based on WordNet Procesamiento del Lenguaje Natural, 2011a, 47: 249-257.

Gutiérrez, Y.; S. Vázquez and A. Montoyo. Improving WSD using ISR-WN with Relevant Semantic Trees and SemCor Senses Frequency. Proceedings of the International Conference Recent Advances in Natural Language Processing 2011, Hissar, Bulgaria, RANLP 2011 Organising Committee, 2011b. 233--239 p.

Jiang, J. J. and D. W. Conrath Semantic similarity based on corpus statistics and lexical taxonomy arXiv preprint cmp-lg/9709008, 1997.

Leacock, C. and M. Chodorow Combining local context and WordNet similarity for word sense identification WordNet: An electronic lexical database, 1998, 49(2): 265-283.

Lin, D. An information-theoretic definition of similarity. Proceedings of the 15th international conference on Machine Learning, San Francisco, 1998. 296-304 p.

Mihalcea, R.; C. Corley and C. Strapparava. Corpus-based and knowledge-based measures of text semantic similarity. Proceedings of the national conference on artificial intelligence, Menlo Park, CA; Cambridge, MA; London; AAAI Press; MIT Press; 1999, 2006. 775 p.

Miller, G. A.; R. Beckwith; C. Fellbaum; D. Gross and K. Miller Introduction to WordNet: An On-line Lexical Database International Journal of Lexicography, 3(4):235-244., 1990.

Miller, G. A.; C. Fellbaum; R. Tengi; P. Wakefield; H. Langone and B. R. Haskell. WordNet a lexical database for the English language. Cognitive Science Laboratory Princeton University 2006.

Pedersen, T.; S. Patwardhan and J. Michelizzi. WordNet:: Similarity: measuring the relatedness of concepts. Demonstration Papers at HLT-NAACL 2004, Association for Computational Linguistics, 2004. 38-41 p.

Resnik, P. Using information content to evaluate semantic similarity in a taxonomy arXiv preprint cmp-lg/9511007, 1995.

Richardson, R.; A. F. Smeaton and J. Murphy. Using WordNet as a knowledge base for measuring semantic similarity between words, Technical Report Working Paper CA-1294, School of Computer Applications, Dublin City University, 1994.

Wu, Z. and M. Palmer. Verbs semantics and lexical selection. Proceedings of the 32nd annual meeting on Association for Computational Linguistics, Association for Computational Linguistics, 1994. 133-138 p.

MELODI: Semantic Similarity of Words and Compositional Phrases using Latent Vector Weighting

Tim Van de Cruys
IRIT, CNRS
tim.vandecruys@irit.fr

Stergos Afantenos
IRIT, Toulouse University
stergos.afantenos@irit.fr

Philippe Muller
IRIT, Toulouse University
philippe.muller@irit.fr

Abstract

In this paper we present our system for the SemEval 2013 Task 5a on semantic similarity of words and compositional phrases. Our system uses a dependency-based vector space model, in combination with a technique called latent vector weighting. The system computes the similarity between a particular noun instance and the head noun of a particular noun phrase, which was weighted according to the semantics of the modifier. The system is entirely unsupervised; one single parameter, the similarity threshold, was tuned using the training data.

1 Introduction

In the course of the last two decades, vector space models have gained considerable momentum for semantic processing. Initially, these models only dealt with individual words, ignoring the context in which these words appear. More recently, two different but related approaches emerged that take into account the interaction between different words within a particular context. The first approach aims at building a joint, compositional representation for larger units beyond the individual word level (e.g., the composed, semantic representation of the noun phrase *crispy chips*). The second approach, different but related to the first one, computes the specific meaning of a word within a particular context (e.g. the meaning of the noun *bank* in the context of the adjective *bankrupt*).

In this paper, we describe our system for the SemEval 2013 Task 5a: semantic similarity of words and compositional phrases – which follows the latter approach. Our system uses a dependency-based vector space model, in combination with a technique called latent vector weighting (Van de Cruys et al., 2011). The system computes the similarity between a particular noun instance and the head noun of a particular noun phrase, which was weighted according to the semantics of the modifier. The system is entirely unsupervised; one single parameter, the similarity threshold, was tuned using the training data.

2 Related work

In recent years, a number of methods have been developed that try to capture the compositional meaning of units beyond the individual word level within a distributional framework. One of the first approaches to tackle compositional phenomena in a systematic way is Mitchell and Lapata's (2008) approach. They explore a number of different models for vector composition, of which vector addition (the sum of each feature) and vector multiplication (the elementwise multiplication of each feature) are the most important. Baroni and Zamparelli (2010) present a method for the composition of adjectives and nouns. In their model, an adjective is a linear function of one vector (the noun vector) to another vector (the vector for the adjective-noun pair). The linear transformation for a particular adjective is represented by a matrix, and is learned automatically from a corpus, using partial least-squares regression. Coecke et al. (2010) present an abstract theoretical framework in which a sentence vector is a function of the Kronecker product of its word vectors, which allows for greater interaction between the different

*Second Joint Conference on Lexical and Computational Semantics (*SEM), Volume 2: Seventh International Workshop on Semantic Evaluation (SemEval 2013)*, pages 98–102, Atlanta, Georgia, June 14-15, 2013.

word features. And Socher et al. (2012) present a model for compositionality based on recursive neural networks.

Closely related to the work on compositionality is research on the computation of word meaning in context. Erk and Padó (2008, 2009) make use of selectional preferences to express the meaning of a word in context. And Dinu and Lapata (2010) propose a probabilistic framework that models the meaning of words as a probability distribution over latent factors. This allows them to model contextualized meaning as a change in the original sense distribution.

Our work takes the latter approach of computing word meaning in context, and is described in detail below.

3 Methodology

Our method uses latent vector weighting (Van de Cruys et al., 2011) in order to compute a semantic representation for the meaning of a word within a particular context. The method relies upon a factorization model in which words, together with their window-based context features and their dependency-based context features, are linked to latent dimensions. The factorization model allows us to determine which dimensions are important for a particular context, and adapt the dependency-based feature vector of the word accordingly. The modified feature vector is then compared to the target noun feature vector with the cosine similarity function.

This following sections describe our model in more detail. In section 3.1, we describe non-negative matrix factorization – the factorization technique that our model uses. Section 3.2 describes our way of combining dependency-based context features and window-based context features within the same factorization model. Section 3.3, then, describes our method of computing the meaning of a word within a particular context.

3.1 Non-negative Matrix Factorization

Our latent model uses a factorization technique called non-negative matrix factorization (Lee and Seung, 2000) in order to find latent dimensions. The key idea is that a non-negative matrix **A** is factorized into two other non-negative matrices, **W** and **H**

$$\mathbf{A}_{i \times j} \approx \mathbf{W}_{i \times k} \mathbf{H}_{k \times j} \quad (1)$$

where k is much smaller than i, j so that both instances and features are expressed in terms of a few components. Non-negative matrix factorization enforces the constraint that all three matrices must be non-negative, so all elements must be greater than or equal to zero.

Using the minimization of the Kullback-Leibler divergence as an objective function, we want to find the matrices **W** and **H** for which the divergence between **A** and **WH** (the multiplication of **W** and **H**) is the smallest. This factorization is carried out through the iterative application of update rules. Matrices **W** and **H** are randomly initialized, and the rules in 2 and 3 are iteratively applied – alternating between them. In each iteration, each vector is adequately normalized, so that all dimension values sum to 1.

$$\mathbf{H}_{a\mu} \leftarrow \mathbf{H}_{a\mu} \frac{\sum_i \mathbf{W}_{ia} \frac{\mathbf{A}_{i\mu}}{(\mathbf{WH})_{i\mu}}}{\sum_k \mathbf{W}_{ka}} \quad (2)$$

$$\mathbf{W}_{ia} \leftarrow \mathbf{W}_{ia} \frac{\sum_\mu \mathbf{H}_{a\mu} \frac{\mathbf{A}_{i\mu}}{(\mathbf{WH})_{i\mu}}}{\sum_v \mathbf{H}_{av}} \quad (3)$$

3.2 Combining syntax and context words

Using an extension of non-negative matrix factorization (Van de Cruys, 2008), it is possible to jointly induce latent factors for three different modes: nouns, their window-based context words, and their dependency-based context features. The intuition is that the window-based context words inform us about broad, topical similarity, whereas the dependency-based features get at a tighter, synonym-like similarity. As input to the algorithm, two matrices are constructed that capture the pairwise co-occurrence frequencies for the different modes. The first matrix contains co-occurrence frequencies of words cross-classified by dependency-based features, and the second matrix contains co-occurrence frequencies of words cross-classified by words that appear in the word's context window. NMF is then applied to the two matrices, and the separate factorizations are interleaved (i.e. matrix **W**, which contains the nouns by latent dimensions, is shared between both factorizations). A graphical representation of the interleaved factorization algorithm is given in figure 1. The numbered arrows indicate the sequence of the updates.

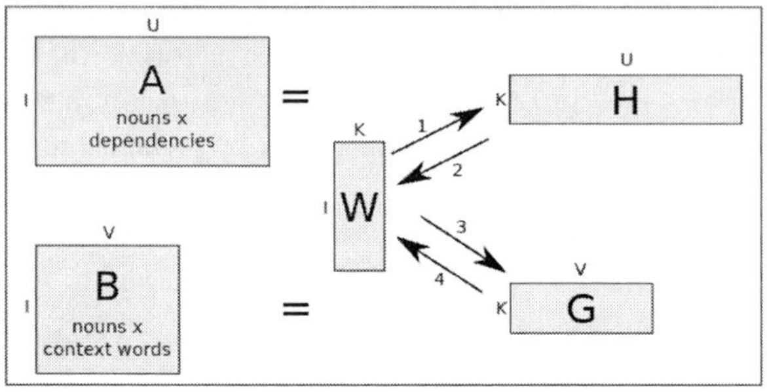

Figure 1: A graphical representation of the interleaved NMF

When the factorization is finished, the three different modes (words, window-based context words and dependency-based context features) are all represented according to a limited number of latent factors.

The factorization that comes out of the NMF model can be interpreted probabilistically (Gaussier and Goutte, 2005; Ding et al., 2008). More specifically, we can transform the factorization into a standard latent variable model of the form

$$p(w_i, d_j) = \sum_{z=1}^{K} p(z)p(w_i|z)p(d_j|z) \tag{4}$$

by introducing two $K \times K$ diagonal scaling matrices $\mathbf{X}$ and $\mathbf{Y}$, such that $\mathbf{X}_{kk} = \sum_i \mathbf{W}_{ik}$ and $\mathbf{Y}_{kk} = \sum_j \mathbf{H}_{kj}$. The factorization $\mathbf{WH}$ can then be rewritten as

$$\begin{aligned} \mathbf{WH} &= (\mathbf{WX}^{-1}\mathbf{X})(\mathbf{YY}^{-1}\mathbf{H}) \\ &= (\mathbf{WX}^{-1})(\mathbf{XY})(\mathbf{Y}^{-1}\mathbf{H}) \end{aligned} \tag{5}$$

such that $\mathbf{WX}^{-1}$ represents $p(w_i|\mathbf{z})$, $(\mathbf{Y}^{-1}\mathbf{H})^T$ represents $p(d_j|\mathbf{z})$, and $\mathbf{XY}$ represents $p(\mathbf{z})$. Using Bayes' theorem, it is now straightforward to determine $p(\mathbf{z}|d_j)$.

$$p(\mathbf{z}|d_j) = \frac{p(d_j|\mathbf{z})p(\mathbf{z})}{p(d_j)} \tag{6}$$

3.3 Meaning in Context

3.3.1 Overview

Using the results of the factorization model described above, we can now adapt a word's feature vector according to the context in which it appears. Intuitively, the context of the word (in our case, the dependency-based context feature that acts as an adjectival modifier to the head noun) pinpoint the important semantic dimensions of the particular instance, creating a probability distribution over latent factors. The required probability vector, $p(\mathbf{z}|d_j)$, is yielded by our factorization model. This probability distribution over latent factors can be interpreted as a semantic fingerprint of the passage in which the target word appears. Using this fingerprint, we can now determine a new probability distribution over dependency features given the context.

$$p(\mathbf{d}|d_j) = p(\mathbf{z}|d_j)p(\mathbf{d}|\mathbf{z}) \tag{7}$$

The last step is to weight the original probability vector of the word according to the probability vector of the dependency features given the word's context, by taking the pointwise multiplication of probability vectors $p(\mathbf{d}|w_i)$ and $p(\mathbf{d}|d_j)$.

$$p(\mathbf{d}|w_i, d_j) = p(\mathbf{d}|w_i) \cdot p(\mathbf{d}|d_j) \tag{8}$$

Note that this final step is a crucial one in our approach. We do not just build a model based on latent factors, but we use the latent factors to determine which of the features in the original word vector are the salient ones given a particular context. This allows us to compute an accurate adaptation of the original word vector in context.

3.3.2 Example

Let us exemplify the procedure with an example. Say we want to compute the distributionally similar words to the noun *instrument* within the phrases (1) and (2), taken from the task's test set:

(1) musical instrument

(2) optical instrument

First, we extract the context feature for both instances, in this case $C_1 = \{musical_{adj}\}$ for phrase (1), and $C_2 = \{optical_{adj}\}$ for phrase (2). Next, we look up $p(\mathbf{z}|C_1)$ and $p(\mathbf{z}|C_2)$ – the probability distributions over latent factors given the context – which are yielded by our factorization model. Using these probability distributions over latent factors, we can now determine the probability of each dependency feature given the different contexts – $p(\mathbf{d}|C_1)$ and $p(\mathbf{d}|C_2)$ (equation 7).

The former step yields a general probability distribution over dependency features that tells us how likely a particular dependency feature is given the context that our target word appears in. Our last step is now to weight the original probability vector of the target word (the aggregate of dependency-based context features over all contexts of the target word) according to the new distribution given the context in which the target word appears (equation 8).

We can now return to our original matrix $\mathbf{A}$ and compute the top similar words for the two adapted vectors of *instrument* given the different contexts, which yields the results presented below.

1. **instrument**$_N$, C_1: *percussion, flute, violin, melody, harp*
2. **instrument**$_N$, C_2: *sensor, detector, amplifier, device, microscope*

3.4 Implementational details

Our model has been trained on the UKWaC corpus (Baroni et al., 2009). The corpus has been part of speech tagged and lemmatized with Stanford Part-Of-Speech Tagger (Toutanova and Manning, 2000; Toutanova et al., 2003), and parsed with MaltParser (Nivre et al., 2006) trained on sections 2-21 of the Wall Street Journal section of the Penn Treebank extended with about 4000 questions from the QuestionBank[1], so that dependency triples could be extracted.

The matrices needed for our interleaved NMF factorization are extracted from the corpus. Our model was built using 5K nouns, 80K dependency relations, and 2K context words[2] (excluding stop words) with highest frequency in the training set, which yields matrices of 5K nouns × 80K dependency relations, and 5K nouns × 2K context words.

[1] http://maltparser.org/mco/english_parser/engmalt.html

[2] We used a fairly large, paragraph-like window of four sentences.

model	accuracy	precision	recall	F1
dist	.69	.83	.48	.61
lvw	**.75**	**.84**	**.61**	**.71**

Table 1: Results of the distributional model (dist) and latent vector weighting model (lvw) on the SemEval task 5a

The interleaved NMF model was carried out using $K = 600$ (the number of factorized dimensions in the model), and applying 100 iterations. The interleaved NMF algorithm was implemented in Matlab; the preprocessing scripts and scripts for vector computation in context were written in Python.

The model is entirely unsupervised. The only parameter to set, the cosine similarity threshold ϕ, is induced from the training set. We set $\phi = .049$.

4 Results

Table 1 shows the evaluation results of the simple distributional model (which only takes into account the head noun) and our model that uses latent vector weighting. The results indicate that our model based on latent vector weighting performs quite a bit better than a standard dependency-based distributional model. The *lvw* model attains an accuracy of .75 – a 6% improvement over the distributional model – and an F-measure of .71 – a 10% improvement over the distributional model.

5 Conclusion

In this paper we presented an entirely unsupervised system for the assessment of the similarity of words and compositional phrases. Our system uses a dependency-based vector space model, in combination with latent vector weighting. The system computes the similarity between a particular noun instance and the head noun of a particular noun phrase, which was weighted according to the semantics of the modifier. Using our system yields a substantial improvement over a simple dependency-based distributional model, which only takes the head noun into account.

References

Marco Baroni and Roberto Zamparelli. 2010. Nouns are vectors, adjectives are matrices: Representing adjective-noun constructions in semantic space. In *Proceedings of the 2010 Conference on Empirical Methods in Natural Language Processing*, pages 1183–1193, Cambridge, MA, October. Association for Computational Linguistics.

Marco Baroni, Silvia Bernardini, Adriano Ferraresi, and Eros Zanchetta. 2009. The wacky wide web: A collection of very large linguistically processed web-crawled corpora. *Language Resources and Evaluation*, 43(3):209–226.

Bob Coecke, Mehrnoosh Sadrzadeh, and Stephen Clark. 2010. Mathematical foundations for a compositional distributed model of meaning. *Lambek Festschrift, Linguistic Analysis, vol. 36*, 36.

Chris Ding, Tao Li, and Wei Peng. 2008. On the equivalence between non-negative matrix factorization and probabilistic latent semantic indexing. *Computational Statistics & Data Analysis*, 52(8):3913–3927.

Georgiana Dinu and Mirella Lapata. 2010. Measuring distributional similarity in context. In *Proceedings of the 2010 Conference on Empirical Methods in Natural Language Processing*, pages 1162–1172, Cambridge, MA, October.

Katrin Erk and Sebastian Padó. 2008. A structured vector space model for word meaning in context. In *Proceedings of the Conference on Empirical Methods in Natural Language Processing*, pages 897–906, Waikiki, Hawaii, USA.

Katrin Erk and Sebastian Padó. 2009. Paraphrase assessment in structured vector space: Exploring parameters and datasets. In *Proceedings of the Workshop on Geometrical Models of Natural Language Semantics*, pages 57–65, Athens, Greece.

Eric Gaussier and Cyril Goutte. 2005. Relation between PLSA and NMF and implications. In *Proceedings of the 28th annual international ACM SIGIR conference on Research and development in information retrieval*, pages 601–602, Salvador, Brazil.

Daniel D. Lee and H. Sebastian Seung. 2000. Algorithms for non-negative matrix factorization. In *Advances in Neural Information Processing Systems 13*, pages 556–562.

Jeff Mitchell and Mirella Lapata. 2008. Vector-based models of semantic composition. *proceedings of ACL-08: HLT*, pages 236–244.

Joakim Nivre, Johan Hall, and Jens Nilsson. 2006. Maltparser: A data-driven parser-generator for dependency parsing. In *Proceedings of LREC-2006*, pages 2216–2219.

Richard Socher, Brody Huval, Christopher D. Manning, and Andrew Y. Ng. 2012. Semantic compositionality through recursive matrix-vector spaces. In *Proceedings of the 2012 Joint Conference on Empirical Methods in Natural Language Processing and Computational Natural Language Learning*, pages 1201–1211, Jeju Island, Korea, July. Association for Computational Linguistics.

Kristina Toutanova and Christopher D. Manning. 2000. Enriching the knowledge sources used in a maximum entropy part-of-speech tagger. In *Proceedings of the Joint SIGDAT Conference on Empirical Methods in Natural Language Processing and Very Large Corpora (EMNLP/VLC-2000)*, pages 63–70.

Kristina Toutanova, Dan Klein, Christopher Manning, and Yoram Singer. 2003. Feature-rich part-of-speech tagging with a cyclic dependency network. In *Proceedings of HLT-NAACL 2003*, pages 252–259.

Tim Van de Cruys, Thierry Poibeau, and Anna Korhonen. 2011. Latent vector weighting for word meaning in context. In *Proceedings of the 2011 Conference on Empirical Methods in Natural Language Processing*, pages 1012–1022, Edinburgh, Scotland, UK., July. Association for Computational Linguistics.

Tim Van de Cruys. 2008. Using three way data for word sense discrimination. In *Proceedings of the 22nd International Conference on Computational Linguistics (Coling 2008)*, pages 929–936, Manchester.

IIRG: A Naïve Approach to Evaluating Phrasal Semantics

Lorna Byrne, Caroline Fenlon, John Dunnion
School of Computer Science and Informatics
University College Dublin
Ireland
{lorna.byrne@ucd.ie, caroline.fenlon@ucdconnect.ie, john.dunnion@ucd.ie}

Abstract

This paper describes the IIRG [1] system entered in SemEval-2013, the 7th International Workshop on Semantic Evaluation. We participated in Task 5 Evaluating Phrasal Semantics. We have adopted a token-based approach to solve this task using 1) Naïve Bayes methods and 2) Word Overlap methods, both of which rely on the extraction of syntactic features. We found that the word overlap method significantly out-performs the Naïve Bayes methods, achieving our highest overall score with an accuracy of approximately 78%.

1 Introduction

The Phrasal Semantics task consists of two related subtasks. Task 5A requires systems to evaluate the semantic similarity of words and compositional phrases. Task 5B requires systems to evaluate the compositionality of phrases in context. We participated in Task 5B and submitted three runs for evaluation, two runs using the Naïve Bayes Machine Learning Algorithm and a Word Overlap run using a simple bag-of-words approach.

Identifying non-literal expressions poses a major challenge in NLP because they occur frequently and often exhibit irregular behavior by not adhering to grammatical constraints. Previous research in the area of identifying literal/non-literal use of expressions includes generating a wide range of different features for use with a machine learning prediction algorithm. (Li and Sporleder, 2010) present a system involving identifying the global and local contexts of a phrase. Global context was determined by looking for occurrences of semantically related words in a given passage, while local context focuses on the words immediately preceding and following the phrase. Windows of five words at each side of the target were taken as features. More syntactic features were also used, including details of nodes from the dependency tree of each example. The system produced approximately 90% accuracy when tested, for both idiom-specific and generic models. It was found that the statistical features (global and local contexts) performed well, even on unseen phrases. (Katz and Giesbrecht, 2006) found that similarities between words in the expression and its context indicate literal usage. This is comparable to (Sporleder and Li, 2009), which used cohesion-based classifiers based on lexical chains and graphs. Unsupervised approaches to classifying idiomatic use include clustering (Fazly et al., 2009), which classified data based on semantic analyzability (whether the meaning of the expression is similar to the meanings of its parts) and lexical and syntactic flexibility (measurements of how much variation exists within the expression).

2 Task 5B

In Task 5B, participants were required to make a binary decision as to whether a target phrase is used figuratively or literally within a given context. The phrase "drop the ball" can be used figuratively, for example in the sentence
We get paid for completing work, so we've designed a detailed workflow process to make sure we don't

[1] Intelligent Information Retrieval Group

*Second Joint Conference on Lexical and Computational Semantics (*SEM), Volume 2: Seventh International Workshop on Semantic Evaluation (SemEval 2013)*, pages 103–107, Atlanta, Georgia, June 14-15, 2013.

drop the ball.
and literally, for example in the sentence
In the end, the Referee drops the ball with the attacking player nearby.

In order to train systems, participants were given training data consisting of approximately 1400 text snippets (one or more sentences) containing 10 target phrases, together with real usage examples sampled from the WaCky (Baroni et al., 2009) corpora. The number of examples and distribution of figurative and literal instances varied for each phrase.

Participants were allowed to submit three runs for evaluation purposes.

2.1 Approach

The main assumption for our approach is that tokens preceding and succeeding the target phrase might indicate the usage of the target phrase, i.e. whether the target phrase is being used in a literal or figurative context. Firstly, each text snippet was processed using the Stanford Suite of Core NLP Tools[2] to tokenise the snippet and produce part-of-speech tags and lemmas for each token.

During the training phase, we identified and extracted a target phrase boundary for each of the target phrases. A target phrase boundary consists of a window of tokens immediately before and after the target phrase. The phrase boundaries identified for the first two runs were restricted to windows of one, i.e. the token immediately before and after the target phrase were extracted, tokens were also restricted to the canonical form.

For example, the target phrase boundary identified for the snippet: *"The returning team will drop the ball and give you a chance to recover ."* is as follows:

```
before:will
after:and
```

and the target phrase boundary identified for the snippet: *"Meanwhile , costs are going through the roof."* is as follows:

```
before:go
after:.
```

[2]http://nlp.stanford.edu/software

IIRG Training Runs	
RunID	Accuracy (%)
Run0	85.29
Run1	81.84
Run2	95.92

Table 1: Results of IIRG Training Runs

We then trained multiple Naïve Bayes classifiers on these extracted phrase boundaries. The first classifier was trained on the set of target phrase boundaries extracted from the entire training set of target phrases and usage examples (Run0); the second classifier was trained on the set of target phrase boundaries extracted from the entire training set of target phrases and usage examples including the phrase itself as a predictor variable (Run1); and a set of target-phrase classifiers, one per target phrase, were trained on the set of target phrase boundaries extracted from each individual target phrase (Run2).

The results of the initial training runs can be seen in Table 1. Although Run0 yielded very high accuracy scores on the training data, outperforming Run1, in practice this approach performed poorly on unseen data and was biased towards a figurative classification. We thus opted not to implement this run in the testing phase and instead concentrated on Run1 and Run2.

For our third submitted run, we adopted a word overlap method which implemented a simple bag-of-words approach. For each target phrase we created a bag-of-words by selecting the canonical form of all of the noun tokens in each corresponding training usage example. The frequency of occurrence of each token within a given context was recorded and each token was labeled as *figurative* or *literal* depending on its frequency of occurrence within a given context. The frequency of occurrence of each token was also recorded in order to adjust the threshold of token occurrences for subsequent runs. For this run, Run3, the token frequency threshold was set to 2, so that a given token must occur two or more times in a given context to be added to the bag-of-words.

3 Results

System performance is measured in terms of accuracy. The results of the submitted runs can be seen in Table 2.

Of the submitted runs, the Word Overlap method (Run3) performed best overall. This approach was also consistently good across all phrases, with scores ranging from 70% to 80%, as seen in Table 3.

The classifiers trained on the canonical phrase boundaries (Run1 and Run2) performed poorly on unseen data. They were also biased towards a figurative prediction. For several phrases they incorrectly classified all literal expressions as figurative. They were not effective at processing all of the phrases: in Run1, some phrases had very high scores relative to the overall score (e.g. "break a leg"), while others scored very poorly (e.g. "through the roof"). In Run2, a similar effect was found. Interestingly, even though separate classifiers were trained for each phrase, the accuracy was lower than that of Run1 in several cases (e.g. "through the roof"). This may be a relic of the small, literally-skewed, training data for some of the phrases, or may suggest that this approach is not suitable for those expressions. The very high accuracy of the classifiers tested on a subset of the training data may be attributed to overfitting. The approach used in Run1 and Run2 is unlikely to yield very accurate results for the classification of general data, due to the potential for many unseen canonical forms of word boundaries.

3.1 Additional Runs

After the submission deadline, we completed some additional runs, the results of which can be seen in Table 4.

These runs were similar to Run1 and Run2, where we used Naïve Bayes Classifiers to train on extracted target phrase boundaries. However, for Run4 and Run5 we restricted the phrase boundaries to the canonical form of the nearest verb (Run4) or nearest noun (Run5) that was present in a bag-of-words.

We used the same bag-of-words created for Run3 for the noun-based bag-of-words, and this same approach was used to create the (canonical form) verb-based bag-of-words. If there were no such verbs or nouns present then the label NULL was applied. If a phrase occurred at the start or end of a text snippet this information was also captured. The Naïve Bayes classifiers were then trained using labels from the following set of input labels: FIGURATIVE, LITERAL, START, END or NULL, which indicate the target phrase boundaries of the target phrases.

For example, the target phrase boundaries identified for the snippet: *"Meanwhile , costs are going through the roof ."* for Run4 and Run5, respectively, are as follows:

```
before:FIGURATIVE
after:END
```

where the FIGURATIVE label is the classification of the token *'going'* as indicated in the verb-based bag-of-words, and

```
before:FIGURATIVE
after:END
```

where the FIGURATIVE label is the classification of the token *'costs'* as indicated in the noun-based bag-of-words.

As in Run1 and Run2, an entire-set classifier and individual target-phrase classifiers were trained for both runs. These additional runs performed well, yielding high accuracy results and significantly outperforming Run1 and Run2.

The Run4 classifiers did not perform comparatively well across all phrases. In particular, the target phrase "break a leg", had very low accuracy scores, possibly because the training data for the phrase was small and contained mostly literal examples. The ranges of phrase scores for the noun classification runs (Run5) were similar to those of the Word Overlap runs. The results across each phrase were also consistent, with no scores significantly lower than the overall accuracy. Using target phrase boundaries based on noun classifications may prove to yield reasonable results when extended to more phrases, as opposed to the erratic results found when using verb classifications.

In both Run4 and Run5, very similar overall results were produced from both the entire-set and target-phrase classifiers. In most cases, the run performed poorly on the same phrases in both instances, indicating that the approach may not be appropriate for the particular phrase. For example, the verb classifications runs scored low accuracy for "drop the ball", while the noun classifications run was approximately 80% accurate for the same phrase using both

IIRG Submitted Runs (%)					
RunID	Overall Accuracy	Precision (Figurative)	Recall (Figurative)	Precision (Literal)	Recall (Literal)
Run1	53.03	52.03	89.97	60.25	15.65
Run2	50.17	50.81	41.81	54.06	58.84
Run3	77.95	79.65	75.92	76.62	80.27

Table 2: Results of Runs Submitted to Sem-Eval 2013

IIRG Submitted Runs - Per Phrase Accuracy (%)										
RunID	At the end of the day	Bread and butter	Break a leg	Drop the ball	In the bag	In the fast lane	Play ball	Rub it in	Through the roof	Under the microscope
Run1	68.92	57.89	40.00	40.82	43.42	67.86	52.63	66.67	64.94	33.33
Run2	45.95	38.16	83.33	57.14	48.68	75.00	46.05	56.67	29.87	62.82
Run3	75.68	82.89	73.33	83.67	72.37	75.00	78.95	60.00	80.52	83.33

Table 3: Results of Runs Submitted to Sem-Eval 2013 (per phrase)

IIRG Additional Runs - Accuracy (%)		
RunID	Entire-Set Classifier	Target-Phrase Classifier
Run4	64.81	65.99
Run5	75.25	76.60

Table 4: Accuracy of Additional Unsubmitted Runs

an entire-set and target-phrase classifier.

4 Conclusion

This is the first year we have taken part in the Semantic Evaluation Exercises, participating in Task 5b, Evaluating Phrasal Semantics. Task 5B requires systems to evaluate the compositionality of phrases in context. We have adopted a token-based approach to solve this task using 1) Naïve Bayes methods whereby target phrase boundaries were identified and extracted in order to train multiple classifiers; and 2) Word Overlap methods, whereby a simple bag-of-words was created for each target phrase. We submitted three runs for evaluation purposes, two runs using Naïve Bayes methods (Run1 and Run2) and one run based on a Word Overlap approach (Run3). The Word Overlap approach, which limited each bag-of-words to using the canonical form of the nouns in the text snippets, yielded the highest accuracy scores of all submitted runs, at approximately 78% accurate. An additional run (Run5), also using the canonical form of the nouns in the usage examples but implementing a Naïve Bayes approach, yielded similar results, almost 77% accuracy. The approaches which were restricted to using the nouns in the text snippets yielded the highest accuracy results, thus indicating that nouns provide important contextual information for distinguishing literal and figurative usage.

In future work, we will explore whether we can improve the performance of the target phrase boundaries by experimenting with the local context window sizes. Another potential improvement might be to examine whether implementing more sophisticated strategies for selecting tokens for the bags-of-words improves the effectiveness of the Word Overlap methods.

References

M. Baroni, S. Bernardini, A. Ferraresi, and E. Zanchetta. 2009. The WaCky Wide Web: A Collection of Very Large Linguistically Processed Web-Crawled Corpora. *Language Resources and Evaluation 43*, 3(3):209–226.

Afsaneh Fazly, Paul Cook, and Suzanne Stevenson. 2009. Unsupervised Type and Token Identification of Idiomatic Expressions. *Computational Linguistics*, 35(1):61–103, March.

Graham Katz and Eugenie Giesbrecht. 2006. Automatic Identification of Non-Compositional Multi-Word Expressions using Latent Semantic Analysis. In *Proceedings of the ACL/COLING-06 Workshop on Multiword Expressions: Identifying and Exploiting Underlying Properties*, pages 12–19.

Linlin Li and Caroline Sporleder. 2010. Linguistic Cues for Distinguishing Literal and Non-Literal Usages. In *Proceedings of the 23rd International Conference on Computational Linguistics (COLING '10)*, pages 683–691.

Caroline Sporleder and Linlin Li. 2009. Unsupervised Recognition of Literal and Non-Literal Use of Idiomatic expressions. In *Proceedings of the 12th Conference of the European Chapter of the ACL (EACL 2009)*.

ClaC: Semantic Relatedness of Words and Phrases

Reda Siblini
Concordia University
1400 de Maisonneuve Blvd. West
Montreal, Quebec, Canada, H3G 1M8
r_sibl@encs.concordia.ca

Leila Kosseim
Concordia University
1400 de Maisonneuve Blvd. West
Montreal, Quebec, Canada, H3G 1M8
kosseim@encs.concordia.ca

Abstract

The measurement of phrasal semantic relatedness is an important metric for many natural language processing applications. In this paper, we present three approaches for measuring phrasal semantics, one based on a semantic network model, another on a distributional similarity model, and a hybrid between the two. Our hybrid approach achieved an F-measure of 77.4% on the task of evaluating the semantic similarity of words and compositional phrases.

1 Introduction

Phrasal semantic relatedness is a measurement of how multiword expressions are related in meaning. Many natural language processing applications such as textual entailment, question answering, or information retrieval require a robust measurement of phrasal semantic relatedness. Current approaches to address this problem can be categorized into three main categories: those that rely on a knowledge base and its structure, those that use the distributional hypothesis on a large corpus, and hybrid approaches. In this paper, we propose supervised approaches for comparing phrasal semantics that are based on a semantic network model, a distributional similarity model, and a hybrid between the two. Those approaches have been evaluated on the task of semantic similarity of words and compositional phrases and on the task of evaluating the compositionality of phrases in context.

2 Semantic Similarity of Words and Compositional Phrases

The semantic similarity of words and compositional phrases is the task of evaluating the similarity of a word and a short phrase of two or more words; for example, the word *Interview* and the phrase *Formal Meeting*. In the next section we present our semantic network model for computing phrasal semantic relatedness between a word and a phrase, followed by a distributional similarity model, that we evaluate on the task of semantic similarity of words and compositional phrases.

2.1 Semantic Network Model

Knowledge-based approaches to semantic relatedness use the features of the knowledge base to measure the relatedness. One of most frequently used semantic network is the Princeton's WordNet (Fellbaum, 1998) which groups words into synonyms sets (called synsets) and includes 26 semantic relations between those synsets, including: hypernymy, hyponymy, meronymy, entailment ...
To measure relatedness, most of those approaches rely on the structure of the semantic network, such as the semantic link path, depth (Leacock and Chodorow, 1998; Wu and Palmer, 1994), direction (Hirst and St-Onge, 1998), or type (Tsatsaronis et al., 2010). Our phrasal semantic relatedness approach is inspired from those methods. However, our approach is based on the idea that the combination of the least costly types of relations that relate one concept to a set of concepts are a suitable indicator of their semantic relatedness. The type of relations considered includes not only the hy-

*Second Joint Conference on Lexical and Computational Semantics (*SEM), Volume 2: Seventh International Workshop on Semantic Evaluation (SemEval 2013)*, pages 108–113, Atlanta, Georgia, June 14-15, 2013. ©2013 Association for Computational Linguistics

Figure 1: Example of the semantic network around the word *car*.

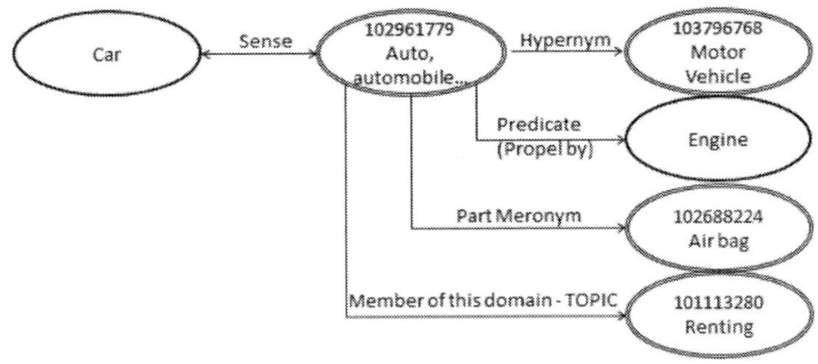

ponym/hypernym relations but also all 26 available semantic relations found in WordNet in addition to relations extracted from each of the eXtended WordNet (Harabagiu et al., 1999) synset's logical form.

To implement our idea, we created a weighted and directed semantic network based on the relations of WordNet and eXtended WordNet. We used WordNet's words and synsets as the nodes of the network. Each word is connected by an edge to its synsets, and each synset is in turn connected to other synsets based on the semantic relations included in WordNet. In addition each synset is connected by a labeled edge to the predicate arguments that are extracted from the eXtended WordNet synset's logical form. Every synset in the eXtended WordNet is related to a logical form, which contains a set of predicate relations that relates the synset to set of words. Each predicate in this representation is added as an edge to the graph connecting the synset to a word. For example, Figure 1 shows part of the semantic network created around the word *car*. In this graph, single-line ovals represent words, while double-line ovals represent synsets.

To compute the semantic relatedness between nodes in the semantic network, it is necessary to take into consideration the semantic relation involved between two nodes. Indeed, WordNet's 26 semantic relations are not equally distributed nor do they contribute equally to the semantic relatedness between concept. In order to indicate the contribution of each relation, we have classified them into seven categories: *Similar*, *Hypernym*, *Sense*, *Predicate*, *Part*, *Instance*, and *Other*. By classifying WordNet's relations into these classes, we are able to weight the contribution of a relation based on the class it belongs to, as opposed to assigning a contributory weight to each relations. The weights were assigned by manually comparing the semantic features of a set of concepts that are related by a specific semantic relations. Table 1 shows the seven semantic categories that we defined, their corresponding weight, and the relations they include. For example the category *Similar* includes WordNet's relations of *entailment*, *cause*, *verb group*, *similar to*, *participle of verb*, *antonym*, and *pertainym*. This class of relations has the most common semantic features when comparing two concepts related with any of those relations and hence was assigned the lowest weight[1] of 1. All the 26 relations in the table are the ones found in WordNet, for the exception of the predicate (and inverse predicate) relations which are the predicate relations extracted from the eXtended WordNet. This can be seen in Figure 1, for example, where the word *car* is related to the word *Engine* with the *Predicate* relation extracted from the eXtended WordNet logical form and more specifically the predicate *propel by*.

The computation of semantic relatedness between a word and a compositional phrase is then the combination of weights of the shortest weighted path[2] in the weighted semantic network between that word and every word in that phrase, normalized by the maximum path cost.

[1]The weight can be seen as the cost of traversing an edge; hence a lower weight is assigned to a highly contributory relation.

[2]The shortest path is based on an implementation of Dijkstras graph search algorithm (Dijkstra, 1959)

Category	Weight	Semantic Relations in WordNet or xWordnet
Similar	1	similar to, pertainym, participle of verb, entailment, cause, antonym, verb group
Hypernym	2	hypernym, instance hypernym, derivationally related
Sense	4	lemma-synset
Predicate	6	predicate (extracted from Extended WordNet)
Part	8	holonym (instance, member, substance), meronym (instance, member, substance), inverse predicate (extracted from Extended WordNet)
Instance	10	hyponym, instance hyponym
Other	12	attribute, also see, domain of synset (topic, region, usage), member of this domain (topic, region, usage)

Table 1: Relations Categories and Corresponding Weights.

Figure 2 shows an extract of the network involving the words *Interview* and the phrase *Formal Meeting*. For the shortest path from *Interview* to *Formal*, the word *Interview* is connected with a *Sense* relation to the synset *#107210735 [Interview]*. As indicated in Table 1, the weight of this relation is defined as 4, This synset is connected to the synset *Examination* through a *Hypernym* relation type with a weight of 2, which is connected to the word *Formal* with a predicate (IS) relation of weight 6. Overall, the sum of the shortest path from *Interview* to *Formal Meeting* is hence equal to the sum of the edges shown in Figure 1 (4+2+6+4+6+4+6 = 32). By normalizing the sum to the maximum, In our approach, 24 is maximum path cost after which we assume that two words are not related (which we assume to be traversing two times maximum weighted path, 2 * maximum path weight of 12) and 8 is the minimum number of edges between 2 words (which is equal to traversing from the word to itself, 2 * sense weight of 4)). Taking into consideration the number of words in the phrase, the semantic relatedness will be (24*2 - (32-8*2))/24*2 = 66.7%. In the next section, we will introduce our distributional similarity model.

2.2 Distributional Similarity Model

Distributional similarity models rely on the distributional hypothesis (Harris, 1954) to represent a word by its context in order to compare word semantics. There are various approach for the selection, representation, and comparison of contextual data. Most use the vector space model to represent the context as dimensions in a vector space, where the feature are frequency of co-occurrence of the context words, and the comparison is usually the cosine similarity. To go beyond lexical semantics and to represent phrases, a compositional model is created, some use the addition or multiplication of vectors such as Mitchell and Lapata (2008), or the use of tensor product to account for word order as in the work of Widdows (2008), or a more complex model as the work of Grefenstette and Sadrzadeh (2011). In our model, we are inspired by those various work, and more specifically by the work of Mitchell and Lapata (2008). The compositional model is based on phrase words vectors addition, where each vector is composed of the collocation pointwise mutual information of the word up to a window of 3 words left and right of the main word. The corpus used to collect the features and their frequencies is the Web 1TB corpus (Brants and Franz, 2006). For the *Interview* to *Formal Meeting* example, the vector of the word *interview* is first created from the corpus of the top 1000 words collocating *interview* between the window of 1 to 3 words with their frequencies. A similar vector is created for the word *Formal* and the word *Meeting*, the vector representing *Formal Meeting* is then the addition of vector *Formal* to vector *Meeting*. The comparison of vector *Interview* to vector *Formal Meeting* is then the cosine of both vectors.

2.3 Evaluation

We evaluated our approaches for word-phrase semantic relatedness on the SemEval task of evaluating phrasal semantics, and more specifically on the sub-task of evaluating the semantic similarity between words and phrases. The task provided an English dataset of 15,628 word-phrases, 60% annotated for training and 40% for testing, with the goal of classifying each word-phrase as either positive or negative. To transform the semantic relatedness measure to a semantic similarity classification one, we first calculated the semantic relatedness of each word-phrase in the training set, and used JRip, WEKA's (Witten et al., 1999) implementation of Cohen's RIPPER rule learning algorithm (Cohen and Singer, 1999), in order to learn a set of rules that can differentiate between a positive semantic similarity and a negative one. The classifier resulted in rules for the semantic network model based relatedness that could be summarized as follows: *If the semantic relatedness of the word-phrase is over 61% then the similarity is positive, otherwise it is negative.* So for the example *Interview - Formal meeting*, which resulted in a semantic relatedness of 66.7% in the semantic network approach, it will be classified positively by the generated rule. This method was our first submitted test run to this task, which resulted in a recall of 63.79%, a precision of 91.01%, and an F-measure of 75.00% on the testing set.

For the second run, we trained the distributional similarity model using the same classifier. This resulted with the following rule that could be summarized as follows: *If the semantic relatedness of the word-phrase is over 40% then the similarity is positive, otherwise it is negative.* It was obvious from the training set that the semantic network model was more accurate than the distributional similarity model, but the distributional model had more coverage. So for our second submitted test run, we used the semantic network approach as the main result, but used the distributional model as a backup approach if one of the words in the phrase was not available in WordNet, thus combining the precision and coverage of both approaches. This method resulted in a recall of 69.48%, a precision of 86.70%, and an F-measure of 77.14% on the testing set.

For the last run, we used the same classifier but this time we training it using two features: the semantic network model relatedness measure (SN), and the distributional similarity model (DS). This training resulted in a set of rules that could be summarized as follows: *if SN > 61% then the similarity is positive, else if DS > 40% then the similarity is also positive, and lastly if SN > 53% and DS > 31% then also in this case the similarity is positive, otherwise the similarity is negative.* This was our third submitted test run, which resulted a recall of 70.66%, a precision of 85.55%, and an F-measure of 77.39% on the testing set.

3 Semantic Compositionality in Context

The semantic compositional in context is the task of evaluating if a phrase is used literally or figuratively in context. For example, the phrase *big picture* is used literally in the sentence *Click here for a bigger picture* and figuratively in *To solve this problem, you have to look at the bigger picture.*

Our approach for this task is a supervised approached based on two main components: first, the availability of the phrases most frequent collocating expressions in a large corpus, and more specifically the top 1000 phrases by frequency in Web 1TB corpus (Brants and Franz, 2006). For example, for the phrase *big picture*, we collect the top 1000 phrases that come before and after the phrase in a corpus, those includes *look at the, see the, understand the* ..... If the context contain any of those phrase, then this component returns 1, indicating that the phrase is most probably used figuratively. The intuition is that, the use of phrases figuratively is more frequent than their use in a literal meaning, and hence the most frequent use will be collocated with phrases that indicate this use.

The second component, is the phrase compositionality. We calculate the semantic relatedness using the semantic network model relatedness measure, that was explained in Section 2.1, between the phrase and the first content word before it and after it. The intuition here is that the semantic relatedness of the figurative use of the phrase to its context should be different than the relatedness to its literal use. So for the example, the phrase *old school* in the context *he is one of the old school* versus *the hall of*

Figure 2: Shortest Path Between the Word *Interview* and the Phrase *Formal Meeting*.

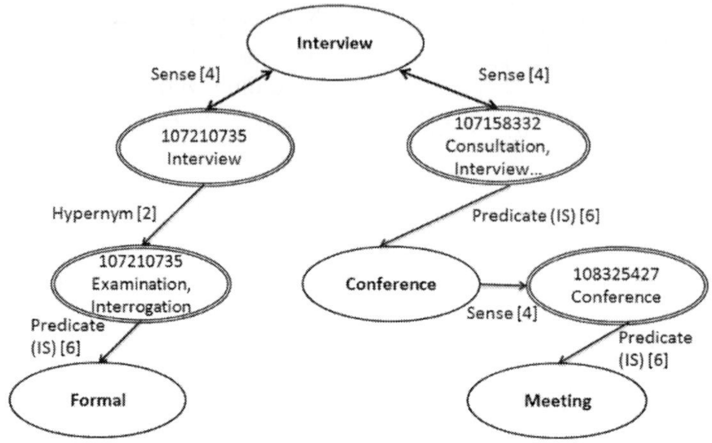

the old school, we can notice that *hall* will be more related to *old school* than the word *one*. This component will result in two features: the relatedness to the word before the phrase (SRB) and the relatedness to word after the phrase in context (SRA).

To combine both componenets, we evaluated our approaches on the data set presented by the SemEval task of evaluating phrasal semantics, and more specifically on the sub task of evaluating semantic compositionality in context. The data set contains a total of 1114 training instances, and 518 test instances. We use the training data and computed the three features (Frequent Collocation (FC), Semantic Relatedness word Before (SRB), and Semantic Relatedness word After (SRA), and used JRip, WEKA's (Witten et al., 1999) implementation of Cohen's RIPPER rule learning algorithm (Cohen and Singer, 1999) to learn a set of rule that differentiate between a figurative and literal phrase use. This method resulted in a set of rules that can be summarized as follows: *if FC is equal to 0 and SRB < 75% then it is used literally in this context, else if FC is equal to 0 and SRA < 75% then it is is also used literally, otherwise it is used figuratively*. This method resulted in an accuracy of 55.01% on the testing set.

4 Conclusion

In this paper we have presented state of the art word-phrase semantic relatedness approaches that are based on a semantic network model, a distributional model, and a combination of the two. The novelty of the semantic network model approach is the use of the sum of the shortest path between a word and a phrase from a weighted semantic network to calculate word-phrase semantic relatedness. We evaluated the approach on the SemEval task of evaluating phrasal semantics, once in a supervised standalone configuration, another with a backup distributional similarity model, and last in a hybrid configuration with the distributional model. The hybrid model achieved the highest f-measure in those three configuration of 77.4% on the task of evaluating the semantic similarity of words and compositional phrases. We also evaluated this approach on the subtask of evaluating the semantic compositionality in context with less success, and an accuracy of of 55.01%.

Acknowledgments

We would like to thank the reviewers for their suggestions and valuable comments.

References

Thorsten Brants and Alex Franz. 2006. Web 1t 5-gram version 1.

William W Cohen and Yoram Singer. 1999. A simple, fast, and effective rule learner. In *Proceedings of the National Conference on Artificial Intelligence*, pages 335–342. John Wiley & Sons Ltd.

Edsger W Dijkstra. 1959. A note on two problems in connexion with graphs. *Numerische mathematik*, 1(1):269–271.

Christiane Fellbaum. 1998. *WordNet: An Electronic Lexical Database*. MIT Press.

Edward Grefenstette and Mehrnoosh Sadrzadeh. 2011. Experimental support for a categorical compositional distributional model of meaning. In *Proceedings of the Conference on Empirical Methods in Natural Language Processing*, pages 1394–1404. Association for Computational Linguistics.

Sanda Harabagiu, George Miller, and Dan Moldovan. 1999. Wordnet 2- a morphologically and semantically enhanced resource. In *Proceedings of SIGLEX*, volume 99, pages 1–8.

Zellig S Harris. 1954. Distributional structure. *Word*.

Graeme Hirst and David St-Onge. 1998. Lexical chains as representations of context for the detection and correction of malapropisms. *WordNet An electronic lexical database*, pages 305–332, April.

Claudia Leacock and Martin Chodorow. 1998. Combining local context and wordnet similarity for word sense identification. *WordNet: An electronic lexical database*, 49(2):265–283.

Jeff Mitchell and Mirella Lapata. 2008. Vector-based models of semantic composition. *proceedings of ACL-08: HLT*, pages 236–244.

George Tsatsaronis, Iraklis Varlamis, and Michalis Vazirgiannis. 2010. Text relatedness based on a word thesaurus. *Journal of Artificial Intelligence Research*, 37(1):1–40.

Dominic Widdows. 2008. Semantic vector products: Some initial investigations. In *To appear in Second AAAI Symposium on Quantum Interaction*, volume 26, page 28th. Citeseer.

Ian H Witten, Eibe Frank, Leonard E Trigg, Mark A Hall, Geoffrey Holmes, and Sally Jo Cunningham. 1999. Weka: Practical machine learning tools and techniques with java implementations.

Zhibiao Wu and Martha Palmer. 1994. Verbs semantics and lexical selection. In *Proceedings of the 32nd annual meeting on Association for Computational Linguistics*, pages 133–138, New Mexico, June.

UNAL: Discriminating between Literal and Figurative Phrasal Usage Using Distributional Statistics and POS tags

Sergio Jimenez, Claudia Becerra
Universidad Nacional de Colombia
Ciudad Universitaria,
edificio 453, oficina 114
Bogotá, Colombia
sgjimenezv@unal.edu.co
cjbecerrac@unal.edu.co

Alexander Gelbukh
CIC-IPN
Av. Juan Dios Bátiz, Av. Mendizábal,
Col. Nueva Industrial Vallejo
CP 07738, DF, México
gelbukh@gelbukh.com

Abstract

In this paper we describe the system used to participate in the sub task 5b in the Phrasal Semantics challenge (task 5) in SemEval 2013. This sub task consists in discriminating literal and figurative usage of phrases with compositional and non-compositional meanings in context. The proposed approach is based on part-of-speech tags, stylistic features and distributional statistics gathered from the same development-training-test text collection. The system obtained a relative improvement in accuracy against the most-frequent-class baseline of 49.8% in the "unseen contexts" (*LexSample*) setting and 8.5% in "unseen phrases" (*AllWords*).

1 Introduction

The Phrasal Semantics task-5b in SemEval 2013 consisted in the discrimination of literal of figurative usage of phrases in context (Korkontzelos et al., 2013). For instance, the occurrence in a text of the phrase "a piece of cake" can be used whether to refer to something that is pretty easy or to an actual piece of cake. The motivation for this task is that such discrimination could improve the quality and performance of other tasks like machine translation and information retrieval.

This problem has been studied in the past. Lin (1999) observed that the distributional characteristics of the literal and figurative usage are different. Katz and Giesbrecht (2006) showed that the similarities among contexts are correlated with their literal or figurative usage. Birke and Sarkar (2006) clustered literal and figurative contexts using a word-sense-disambiguation approach. Fazly et al. (2009) showed that literal and figurative usages are related to particular syntactical forms. Sporleder and Li (2009) showed that for a particular phrase the contexts of its literal usages are more cohesive than those of its figurative usages. Inspired by these works and in a new observation, we proposed a set or features based on cohesiveness, syntax and stylometry (Section 2), which are used to train a machine learning classifier.

The cohesiveness between a phrase an its context can be measured aggregating the relatedness of the context words against the target phrase. This cohesiveness should be high for phrases used literally. Conversely, figurative usages can occur in a large variety of contexts implying low cohesiveness. For instance, the cohesiveness of the phrase "a piece of cake" against context words such as "coffee", "birthday" and "bakery" should be high. The distributional measures used to obtain the needed relatedness scores and the proposed measures of cohesiveness are presented in subsection 2.1.

Moreover, we observed a stylistic trend in the training data set. That is, figurative usage tends to occur later in the document in comparison with the literal usage. Consequently, a small set of features that exploits this particular observation is proposed in subsection 2.2.

Fazly et al. (2009) showed that idiomatic phrases composed of a verb and a noun (e.g. "break a leg") differ from their literal usages in the use of some syntactic structures. For instance, idiomatic phrases are less flexible in the use of determiners, pluraliza-

*Second Joint Conference on Lexical and Computational Semantics (*SEM), Volume 2: Seventh International Workshop on Semantic Evaluation (SemEval 2013)*, pages 114–117, Atlanta, Georgia, June 14-15, 2013. ©2013 Association for Computational Linguistics

tion and passivization. In order to capture that notion in a simple way, a set of features form a part-of-speech tagger was included in the feature set (see subsection 2.3).

In Section, additional details of the proposed system are provided jointly with the obtained official results. Finally, in sections 4 and 5 a brief discussion of the results and some concluding remarks are presented.

2 Features

Each instance of the training and test sets consist of a short document d where one or more occurrences of its target phase p_d are annotated. For each particular phrase p, several instances are provided corresponding to literal or figurative usages. In this section, the set of features that was extracted from each instance to provide a vectorial representation is presented.

2.1 Cohesiveness Features

Let's start with some definitions borrowed from the information retrieval field: D is a collection of documents, $\mathrm{df}(w)$ is the number of documents in D where the word w occurs (document frequency), $\mathrm{df}(w \wedge p_d)$ is the number of documents where w and a target phrase p_d co-occur, $\mathrm{tf}(w,d)$ is the number of occurrences of w in a document $d \in D$ (term frequency), and $\mathrm{idf}(w) = \log_2 \frac{\mathrm{df}(w)}{|D|}$ is the inverse document frequency of w (Jones, 2004).

A simple distributional measure of relatedness between w and p can be obtained with the following ratio:

$$\mathrm{R}(w,p) = \frac{\mathrm{df}(w \wedge p_d)}{\mathrm{df}(w)} \quad (1)$$

Pointwise mutual information (PMI) (Church and Hanks, 1990) is another distributional measure that can be used for measuring the relatedness of w and p. The probabilities needed for its calculation can be obtained by maximum likelihood estimation (MLE): $P(w) \approx \frac{\mathrm{df}(w)}{|D|}$, $P(p_d) \approx \frac{\mathrm{df}(p_d)}{|D|}$ and $P(w \wedge p_d) \approx \frac{\mathrm{df}(w \wedge p_d)}{|D|}$.

Thus, PMI is given by this expression:

$$\mathrm{PMI}(w,p_d) = \log_2 \left(\frac{P(w \wedge p_d)}{P(w) \cdot P(p_d)} \right) \quad (2)$$

F1:	$\sum_{w \in d'} \mathrm{R}(w,p_d)$
F2:	$\sum_{w \in d'} \mathrm{tf}(w,d)$
F3:	$\sum_{w \in d'} \mathrm{idf}(w)$
F4:	$\sum_{w \in d'} \mathrm{PMI}(w,p_d)$
F5:	$\sum_{w \in d'} \mathrm{NPMI}(w,p_d)$
F6:	$\sum_{w \in d'} (\mathrm{tf(w,d)} \cdot \mathrm{R}(w,p_d))$
F7:	$\sum_{w \in d'} (\mathrm{idf}(w) \cdot \mathrm{R}(w,p_d))$
F8	$\sum_{w \in d'} (\mathrm{R}(w,p_d) \cdot \mathrm{PMI}(w,p_d))$
F9:	$\sum_{w \in d'} (\mathrm{R}(w,p_d) \cdot \mathrm{NPMI}(w,p_d))$
F10:	$\sum_{w \in d'} (\mathrm{tf}(w,d) \cdot \mathrm{idf(w)})$
F11:	$\sum_{w \in d'} (\mathrm{tf}(w,p_d) \cdot \mathrm{PMI}(w,p_d))$
F12:	$\sum_{w \in d'} (\mathrm{tf}(w,p_d) \cdot \mathrm{NPMI}(w,p_d))$
F13:	$\sum_{w \in d'} (\mathrm{idf}(w) \cdot \mathrm{PMI}(w,p_d))$
F14:	$\sum_{w \in d'} (\mathrm{idf}(w) \cdot \mathrm{NPMI}(w,p_d))$
F15:	$\sum_{w \in d'} (\mathrm{PMI}(w,p_d) \cdot \mathrm{NPMI}(w,p_d))$
F16:	$\sum_{w \in d'} (\mathrm{tf}(w,d) \cdot \mathrm{idf(w)} \cdot \mathrm{R(w,p_d)})$
F17:	$\sum_{w \in d'} (\mathrm{tf}(w,d) \cdot \mathrm{R}(w,p_d) \cdot \mathrm{PMI}(w,p_d))$
F18:	$\sum_{w \in d'} (\mathrm{tf}(w,d) \cdot \mathrm{R}(w,p_d) \cdot \mathrm{NPMI}(w,p_d))$
F19:	$\sum_{w \in d'} (\mathrm{tf}(w,d) \cdot \mathrm{idf(w)} \cdot \mathrm{PMI(w,p_d)})$
F20:	$\sum_{w \in d'} (\mathrm{tf}(w,d) \cdot \mathrm{idf(w)} \cdot \mathrm{NPMI(w,p_d)})$

Table 1: Cohesiveness features

Furthermore, the scores obtained through eq. 2 can be normalized in the interval [+2,0] with the following expression:

$$\mathrm{NPMI}(w,p_d) = \frac{\mathrm{PMI}(w,p_d)}{-\log_2(P(w \wedge p_d))} + 1 \quad (3)$$

A measure of the cohesiveness between a document d against its target phrase p_d, can be obtained by aggregating the pairwise relatedness scores between all the words in d and p_d. For instance, using eq. 1 that measure is $\sum_{w \in d'} \mathrm{R}(w,p_d)$, where d' is the set of different words in d. The equations 1, 2 and 3 can be used as weights associated to each word, which can also be combined among them and with *tf* and *idf* weights. Such weight combinations produce measures that can be used as cohesiveness features for a document. The set of 20 features obtained using this approach is shown in Table 1.

2.2 Stylistic Features

The set of stylistic features related to the document length, vocabulary size and relative position of the occurrence of the target phrase in a document is shown in Table 2.

F21:	Relative position of p_d in d
F22:	Document length in characters
F23:	Document length in tokens
F24:	Number of different words

Table 2: Stylistic features

2.3 Syntactic Features

The features F25 to F67 correspond to the set of 43 part-of-speech tags of the NLTK English POS tagger (Loper and Bird, 2002). Each feature contains the frequency of occurrence of each POS-tag in a document d.

3 Experimental Setup and Results

The data provided for this task consists of two data sets *LexSample* and *AllWords*, which are divided into development, training and test sets. Nevertheless, we considered a single training set aggregating the development and training parts from both data sets for a total of 3,230 instances. Each training instance has a class label whether "literally" or "figuratively" depending on the usage or the target phrase. Similarly, the aggregated test set contains 1,112 instances, but with unknown values in the class attribute.

Firstly, the syntactic features for each text were obtained using the POS tagger included in the NLTK v.2.0.4 (Loper and Bird, 2002). Secondly, all texts were preprocessed by tokenizing, lowecasing, stop-word removing, punctuation removing and stemming using the Porter's algorithm (1980). This preprocessed version of the texts was used to obtain the remaining cohesiveness and stylistic features. The resulting vectorial data set was used to produce the predictions labeled "UNAL.RUN1" through a Logistic classifier (Cessie and Houwelingen, 1992). The implementation used for this classifier was the included in WEKA v.3.6.9 (Hall et al., 2009). The accuracies obtained by the different feature groups in the training set using 10-fold cross validation are shown in Table 3. The last column shows the percentage of relative improvement of different feature sets combinations from the most frequent class baseline to our best system using all features.

The predictions labeled "UNAL.RUN2" were obtained with the same vectorial data set but adding as a nominal feature the target phrase of each instance. The official results obtained by both submitted runs are shown in Table 4. Note that official results in the test set are reported separately for the data sets *LexSample* and *AllWords*. The *LexSample* test set contains instances whose target phrases were seen in the training set (i.e. unseen contexts). Unlike *LexSample*, *AllWords* contains instances whose target phrases were unseen in the training set (i.e. unseen phrases).

Features	Accuracy	% improv.
All features	**0.7272**	100.0%
Cohesiveness+Syntactic	0.7034	87.1%
Cohesiveness	0.6833	76.2%
Syntactic	0.6229	43.5%
Stylistic	0.5492	3.5%
Baseline MFC	0.5427	0.0%

Table 3: Results by group of features in the training set using 10-fold cross validation

System	*LexSample*	*AllWords*	Both
UNAL.RUN1	0.7222	**0.6680**	0.6970
UNAL.RUN2	**0.7542**	0.6448	**0.7032**
Baseline MFC	0.5034	0.6158	0.5558
Best SemEval'13	0.7795	0.6680	0.7276
# test instances	594	518	1,112

Table 4: Official results in the test set (accuracy)

4 Discussion

As it was expected, the results obtained in the "unseen context" setting were consistently better than in "unseen phrases". This result suggests that the discrimination of literal and figurative usage heavily depends on particular idiomatic phrases. This can also be confirmed by the best accuracy obtained by RUN2 compared with RUN1 in *LexSample*. Clearly, the classifier used in RUN2 exploited the identification of the phrase to leverage a priori information about the phrase such as the most frequent usage.

Another factor that could undermine the results in the "unseen phrases" setting is the low number of instances per phrase in the *AllWords* test set, roughly a third in comparison with *LexSample*. Given that the effectiveness of the cohesiveness features depends on the number of documents where the idiomatic phrase occurs, the predictions for this test set relied mainly on the less effective features, namely syntactic and stylistic features (see Table 3). However, this problem could be alleviated obtaining the distributional statistics from a large corpus with enough occurrences of the unseen phrases.

Besides it is important to note, that in spite of the low individual contribution of the stylistic features to the overall accuracy (3.5%), when these are combined with the remaining features they provide an improvement of 12.9% (see Table 3).

5 Conclusions

We participated in the Phrasal Semantics sub task 5b in SemEval 2013. Our system proved the effectiveness of the use of cohesiveness, stylistic and syntactic features for discriminating literal from figurative usage of idiomatic phrases. The most-frequent-class baseline was overcame by 49.8% in the "unseen contexts" setting (*LexSample*) and 8.5% in "unseen phrases" (*AllWords*).

Acknowledgments

This research was funded in part by the Systems and Industrial Engineering Department, the Office of Student Welfare of the National University of Colombia, Bogotá, and through a grant from the Colombian Department for Science, Technology and Innovation, Colciencias, proj. 1101-521-28465 with funding from "El Patrimonio Autónomo Fondo Nacional de Financiamiento para la Ciencia, la Tecnología y la Innovación, Francisco José de Caldas." The third author recognizes the support from Mexican Government (SNI, COFAA-IPN, SIP 20131702, CONACYT 50206-H) and CONACYT–DST India (proj. 122030 "Answer Validation through Textual Entailment").

References

Julia Birke and Anoop Sarkar. 2006. A clustering approach for nearly unsupervised recognition of nonliteral language. In *Proceedings of the 11th Conference of the European Chapter of the Association for Computational Linguistics*, Trento, Italy.

S. Le Cessie and J. C. Van Houwelingen. 1992. Ridge estimators in logistic regression. *Applied Statistics*, 41(1):191.

Kenneth Ward Church and Patrick Hanks. 1990. Word association norms, mutual information, and lexicography. *Comput. Linguist.*, 16(1):22–29, March.

Afsaneh Fazly, Paul Cook, and Suzanne Stevenson. 2009. Unsupervised type and token identification of idiomatic expressions. *Comput. Linguist.*, 35(1):61–103, March.

Mark Hall, Frank Eibe, Geoffrey Holmes, and Bernhard Pfahringer. 2009. The WEKA data mining software: An update. *SIGKDD Explorations*, 11(1):10–18.

Karen Spärck Jones. 2004. A statistical interpretation of term specificity and its application in retrieval. *Journal of Documentation*, 60(5):493–502, October.

Graham Katz and Eugenie Giesbrecht. 2006. Automatic identification of non-compositional multi-word expressions using latent semantic analysis. In *Proceedings of the Workshop on Multiword Expressions: Identifying and Exploiting Underlying Properties*, MWE '06, pages 12–19, Stroudsburg, PA, USA. Association for Computational Linguistics.

Ioannis Korkontzelos, Torsten Zesch, Fabio Massimo Zanzotto, and Chris Biemann. 2013. SemEval-2013 task 5: Evaluating phrasal semantics. In *Proceedings of the 7th International Workshop on Semantic Evaluation (SemEval 2013)*.

Dekang Lin. 1999. Automatic identification of non-compositional phrases. In *Proceedings of the 37th annual meeting of the Association for Computational Linguistics on Computational Linguistics*, ACL '99, page 317–324, Stroudsburg, PA, USA. Association for Computational Linguistics.

Edward Loper and Steven Bird. 2002. NLTK: the natural language toolkit. In *Proceedings of the ACL Workshop on Effective Tools and Methodologies for Teaching Natural Language Processing and Computational Linguistics. Philadelphia*. Association for Computational Linguistics.

Martin Porter. 1980. An algorithm for suffix stripping. *Program*, 3(14):130–137, October.

Caroline Sporleder and Linlin Li. 2009. Unsupervised recognition of literal and non-literal use of idiomatic expressions. In *Proceedings of the 12th Conference of the European Chapter of the Association for Computational Linguistics*, EACL '09, page 754–762, Stroudsburg, PA, USA. Association for Computational Linguistics.

ECNUCS: Recognizing Cross-lingual Textual Entailment Using Multiple Text Similarity and Text Difference Measures

Jiang ZHAO
Department of Computer Science and Technology
East China Normal University
Shanghai, P.R.China
51121201042@ecnu.cn

Man LAN*
Department of Computer Science and Technology
East China Normal University
Shanghai, P.R.China
mlan@cs.ecnu.edu.cn

Zheng-Yu NIU
Baidu Inc.
Beijing, P.R.China
niuzhengyu@baidu.com

Abstract

This paper presents our approach used for cross-lingual textual entailment task (task 8) organized within SemEval 2013. Cross-lingual textual entailment (CLTE) tries to detect the entailment relationship between two text fragments in different languages. We solved this problem in three steps. Firstly, we use a off-the-shelf machine translation (MT) tool to convert the two input texts into the same language. Then after performing a text preprocessing, we extract multiple feature types with respect to surface text and grammar. We also propose novel feature types regarding to sentence difference and semantic similarity based on our observations in the preliminary experiments. Finally, we adopt a multiclass SVM algorithm for classification. The results on the cross-lingual data collections provided by SemEval 2013 show that (1) we can build portable and effective systems across languages using MT and multiple effective features; (2) our systems achieve the best results among the participants on two test datasets, i.e., FRA-ENG and DEU-ENG.

1 Introduction

The Cross-lingual Textual Entailment (CLTE) task in SemEval 2013 consists in detecting the entailment relationship between two topic-related text fragments (usually called **T**(ext) and **H**(ypothesis)) in different languages, which is a cross-lingual extension of TE task in (Dagan and Glickman, 2004). We say T entails H if the meaning of H can be inferred from the meaning of T. Mehdad et al. (2010b) firstly proposed this problem within a new challenging application scenario, i.e., content synchronization. In consideration of the directionality, the task needs to assign one of the following entailment judgments to a pair of sentences (1) forward: unidirectional entailment from T to H; (2) backward: unidirectional entailment from H to T; (3) bidirectional: the two fragments entail each other (i.e., semantic equivalence); (4) non-entailment: there is no entailment between T and H.

During the last decades, many researchers and communities have paid a lot of attention to resolve the TE detection (e.g., seven times of the Recognizing Textual Entailment Challenge, i.e., from RTE1 to RET7, have been held) since identifying the relationship between two sentences is at the core of many NLP applications, such as text summarization (Lloret et al., 2008) or question answering (Harabagiu and Hickl, 2006). For example, in text summarization, a redundant sentence should be omitted from the summary if this sentence can be entailed from other expressions in the summary. CLTE extends those tasks with lingual dimensionality, where more than one language is involved. Although it is a relatively new task, a basic solution has been provided in (Mehdad et al., 2010b), which brings the problem back to monolingual scenario using MT to translate H into the language of T. The promising performance indicates the potentialities of such a simple approach which integrates MT and monolingual TE algorithms (Castillo, 2011; Jimenez et al., 2012; Mehdad et al., 2010a).

In this work, we regard CLTE as a multiclass classification problem, in which multiple feature types are used in conjunction with a multiclass SVM classifier. Specifically, our approach can be divided into three steps. Firstly, following (Esplà-Gomis et al., 2012; Meng et al., 2012), we use MT to

*Second Joint Conference on Lexical and Computational Semantics (*SEM), Volume 2: Seventh International Workshop on Semantic Evaluation (SemEval 2013)*, pages 118–123, Atlanta, Georgia, June 14-15, 2013. ©2013 Association for Computational Linguistics

bridge the gap of language differences between T and H. Secondly, we perform a preprocessing procedure to maximize the similarity of the two text fragments so as to make a more accurate calculation of surface text similarity measures. Besides several features described in previous work (Malakasiotis, 2009; Esplà-Gomis et al., 2012), we also propose several novel features regarding to sentence difference and semantic similarity. Finally, all these features are combined together and serves as input of a multiclass SVM classifier. After analyzing of the results obtained in preliminary experiments, we also cast this problem as a hierarchical classification problem.

The remainder of the paper is organized as follows. Section 2 describes different features used in our systems. Section 3 presents the system settings including the datasets and preprocessing. Section 4 shows the results of different systems on different language pairs. Finally, we conclude this paper with future work in Section 5.

2 Features

In this section, we will describe a variety of feature types used in our experiments.

2.1 Basic features

The BC feature set consists of length measures on variety sets including $|A|$, $|B|$, $|A-B|$, $|B-A|$, $|A \cup B|$, $|A \cap B|$, $|A|/|B|$ and $|B|/|A|$, where A and B represent two texts, and the length of set is the number of non-repeated elements in this set. Once we view the text as a set of words, $A - B$ means the set of words found in A but not in B, $A \cup B$ means the set of words found in either A or B and $A \cap B$ means the set of shared words found in both A and B.

Given a pair of texts, i.e., <T,H>, which are in different languages, we use MT to translate one of them to make them in the same language. Thus, we can get two pairs of texts, i.e., $<T^t$,H$>$ and $<$T,$H^t>$. We apply the above eight length measures to the two pairs, resulting in a total of 16 features.

2.2 Surface Text Similarity features

Following (Malakasiotis and Androutsopoulos, 2007), the surface text similarity (STS) feature set contains nine similarity measures:

Jaccard coefficient: It is defined as $\frac{|A \cap B|}{|A \cup B|}$, where $|A \cap B|$ and $|A \cup B|$ are as in the BC.
Dice coefficient: Defined as $\frac{2*|A \cap B|}{|A|+|B|}$.
Overlap coefficient: This is the following quantity, $Overlap(A, B) = \frac{|A \cap B|}{|A|}$.
Weighted overlap coefficient: We assign the *tf*idf* value to each word in the sentence to distinguish the importance of different words. The weighted overlap coefficient is defined as follows:

$$WOverlap(A, B) = \frac{\sum_{w_i \in A \cap B} W_{w_i}}{\sum_{w_i \in A} W_{w_i}},$$

where W_{w_i} is the weight of word w_i.
Cosine similarity: $\cos(\overrightarrow{x}, \overrightarrow{y}) = \frac{\overrightarrow{x} \cdot \overrightarrow{y}}{\|\overrightarrow{x}\| \cdot \|\overrightarrow{y}\|}$, where $\overrightarrow{x}$ and $\overrightarrow{y}$ are vectorial representations of texts (i.e. A and B) in $tf * idf$ schema.
Manhattan distance: Defined as $M(\overrightarrow{x}, \overrightarrow{y}) = \sum_{i=1}^{n} |x_i - y_i|$.
Euclidean distance: Defined as $E(\overrightarrow{x}, \overrightarrow{y}) = \sqrt{\sum_{i=1}^{n} (x_i - y_i)^2}$.
Edit distance: This is the minimum number of operations needed to transform A to B. We define an operation as an insertion, deletion or substitution of a word.
Jaro-Winker distance: Following (Winkler and others, 1999), the Jaro-Winkler distance is a measure of similarity between two strings at the word level.

In total, we can get 11 features in this feature set.

2.3 Sematic Similarity features

Almost every previous work used the surface texts or exploited the meanings of words in the dictionary to calculate the similarity of two sentences rather than the actual meaning in the sentence. In this feature set (SS), we introduce a latent model to model the semantic representations of sentences since latent models are capable of capturing the contextual meaning of words in sentences. We used weighted textual matrix factorization (WTMF) (Guo and Diab, 2012) to model the semantics of the sentences. The model factorizes the original term-sentence matrix X into two matrices such that $X_{i,j} \approx P_{*,i}^T Q_{*,j}$, where $P_{*,i}$ is a latent semantics vector profile for word w_i and $Q_{*,j}$ is the vector profile that represents the sentence s_j. The weight matrix W is introduced in the optimization process in order to model the missing words at the right level of emphasis. We propose three similarity measures according to different strategies:

wtw: word-to-word based similarity defined as $sim(A, B) = \lg \frac{\sum_{w_i \in A} W_{w_i} \cdot \max_{w_j \in B}(P_{*,i}, P_{*,j})}{\sum_{w_i \in A} W_{w_i}}$.

wts: word-to-sentence based similarity defined as $sim(A, B) = \lg \frac{\sum_{w_i \in A} W_{w_i} \cdot P_{*,i} \cdot Q_{*,k}}{\sum_{w_i \in A} W_{w_i}}$.

sts: sentence-to-sentence based similarity defined as $sim(A, B) = \lg (Q_{*,i} \cdot Q_{*,j})$.

Also we calculate the cosine similarity, Euclidean and Manhattan distance, weighted overlap coefficient using those semantics vectors, resulting in 10 features.

2.4 Sentence Difference features

Most of those above measures are symmetric and only a few are asymmetric, which means they may not be very suitable for the task that requires dealing with directional problems. We solve this problem by introducing sentence difference measures.

We observed that many entailment relationships between two sentences are determined by only tiny parts of the sentences. As a result, the similarity of such two sentences by using above measures will be close to 1, which may mislead the classifier. Furthermore, almost all similarity measures in STS are symmetric, which means the same similarity has no help to distinguish the different directions. Based on the above considerations, we propose a novel sentence difference (SD) feature set to discover the differences between two sentences and tell the classifier the possibility the entailment should not hold.

The sentence difference features are extracted as follows. Firstly, a word in one sentence is considered as matched if we can find the same word in the other sentence. Then we find all matched words and count the number of unmatched words in each sentence, resulting in 2 features. If one sentence has no unmatched words, we say that this sentence can be entailed by the other sentence. That is, we can infer the entailment class through the number of unmatched words. We regard this label as our third feature type. Secondly, different POS types of unmatched words may have different impacts on the classification, therefore we count the number of unmatched words in each sentence that belong to a small set of POS tags (here consider only NN, JJ, RB, VB and CD tags), which produces 10 features, resulting in a total of 13 sentence difference features.

2.5 Grammatical Relationship features

The grammatical relationship feature type (GR) is designed to capture the grammatical relationship between two sentences. We first replace the words in a sentence with their part-of-speech (POS) tags, then apply the STS measures on this new "sentence".

In addition, we use the Stanford Parser to get the dependency information represented in a form of relation units (e.g. nsubj(example, this)). We calculate the BC measures on those units and the overlap coefficients together with the harmonic mean of them. Finally, we get 22 features.

2.6 Bias features

The bias features (BS) are to check the differences between two sentences in certain special aspects, such as polarity and named entity. We use a method based on subjectivity of lexicons (Loughran and McDonald, 2011) to get the polarity of a sentence by simply comparing the numbers of positive and negative words. If the numbers are the same, then we set the feature to 1, otherwise -1. Also, we check whether one sentence entails the other using only the named entity information. We consider four categories of named entities, i.e., person, organization, location, number, which are recognized by using the Stanford NER toolkit. We set the feature to 1 if the named entities in one sentence are found in the other sentence, otherwise -1. As a result, this feature set contains 9 features.

3 Experimental Setting

We evaluated our approach using the data sets provided in the task 8 of SemEval 2013 (Negri et al., 2013). The data sets consist of a collection of 1500 text fragment pairs (1000 for training consisting of training and test set in SemEval 2012 and 500 for test) in each language pair. Four different language pairs are provided: German-English, French-English, Italian-English and Spanish-English. See (Negri et al., 2013) for more detailed description.

3.1 Preprocess

We performed the following text preprocessing. Firstly, we employed the state-of-the-art Statistical Machine Translator, i.e., Google translator, to translate each pair of texts <T,H> into <T^t,H> and <T,H^t>, thus they were in the same language. Then we extracted all above described feature sets from the pair <T^t,H> (note that <T,H^t> are also used in BC), so the below steps were mainly operated on this pair. After that, all sentences were tokenized and lemmatized using the Stanford Lemmatizer and all stop words were removed, followed by the equivalent replacement procedure. The replacement procedure consists of the following 3 steps:

Abbreviative replacement. Many phrases or organizations can be abbreviated to a set of capitalized letters, e.g. *"New Jersey"* is usually wrote as *"NJ"* for short. In this step, we checked every word whose length is 2 or 3 and if it is the same as the "word" consisting of the first letters of the successive words in another sentence, then we replaced it by them.

Semantic replacement. We observed that although some lemmas in H and T were in the different forms, they actually shared the same meaning, e.g. *"happen"* and *"occur"*. Here, we focused on replacing a lemma in one sentence with another lemma in the other sentence if they were: 1) in the same synonymy set; or 2) gloss-related. Two lemmas were gloss-related if a lemma appeared in the gloss of the other. For example, the gloss of "trip" is *"a journey for some purpose"* (WordNet 2.1 was used for looking up the synonymy and gloss of a lemma), so the lemma "journey" is gloss-related with "trip". No word sense disambiguation was performed and all synsets for a particular lemma were considered.

Context replacement. The context of a lemma is defined as the non-stopword lemmas around it. Given two text fragments, i.e., **T.** *...be erroneously label as a "register sex offender."* and **H.** *...be mistakenly inscribe as a "register sex offender".*, after the semantic replacement, we can recognize the lemma *"erroneously"* was replaceable by *"mistakenly"*. However, WordNet 2.1 cannot recognize the lemmas *"label"* and *"inscribe"* which can also be replaceable. To address this problem, we simply assumed that two lemmas surrounded by the same context can be replaceable as well. In the experiments, we set the window size of context replacement as 3.

This step is the foundation of the extraction of the sentence different features and can also alleviate the imprecise similarity measure problem existing in STS caused by the possibility of the lemmas in totally different forms sharing the same sense.

3.2 System Configuration

We selected 500 samples from the training data as development set (i.e. test set in SemEval 2012) and performed a series of preliminary experiments to evaluate the effectiveness of different feature types in isolation and also in different combinations. According to the results on the development set, we configured five different systems on each language pair as our final submissions with different feature types and classification strategies. Table1 shows the five configurations of those systems.

System	Feature Set	Description
1	all	flat, SVM
2	best feature sets	flat, SVM
3	best feature sets	flat, Majority Voting
4	best feature sets	flat, only 500 instances for train, SVM
5	best feature sets	hierarchical, SVM

Table 1: System configurations using different strategies based on the results of preliminary experiments.

Among them, System 1 serves as a baseline that used all features and was trained using a flat SVM while System 2 used only the best feature combinations. In our preliminary experiments, different language pairs had different best feature combinations (showed in Table 2). In System 3 we performed a majority voting strategy to combine the results of different algorithm (i.e. MaxEnt, SVM, liblinear) to further improve performance. System 4 is a backup system that used only the training set in SemEval 2012 to explore the influence of the different size of train set. Based on the analysis of the preliminary results on development set, we also find that the misclassification mainly occur between the class of backward and others. So in System 5, we adopted hierarchical classification technique to filter out backward class in the first level using a binary classifier and then conducted multi-class classification among the remaining three classes.

We used a linear SVM with the trade-off parameter C=1000 (also in liblinear). The parameters in SS are set as below: the dimension of sematic space is 100, the weight of missing words is 100 and the regularization factor is 0.01. In the hierarchical classification, we use the liblinear (Fan et al., 2008) to train a binary classifier and SVM for a multi-class classifier with the same parameters in other Systems.

4 Results and discussion

Table 2 lists the final results of our five systems on the test samples in terms of four language pairs. The best feature set combinations for different language pairs are also shown. The last two rows list the results of the best and runner-up team among six participants, which is released by the organizers.

From this table, we have some interesting findings.

Firstly, the feature types BC and SD appear in all best feature combinations. This indicates that the length and sentence difference information are good and effective label indicators.

Secondly, based on the comparison between System 1 and System 2, we find that the behavior of the best feature sets of different language pairs on test and development datasets is quite different. Specifically, the best feature set performs better on FRA-ENG and DEU-ENG data sets than the full feature set. However, the full feature set performs the best on SPA-ENG and ITA-ENG data sets. The reason may be the different distribution properties of test and development data sets.

Thirdly, although the only difference between System 2 and System 4 is the size of training samples, System 4 trained on a small number of training instances even makes a 1.6% improvement in accuracy over System 2 on DEU-ENG data set. This is beyond our expectation and it indicates that the CLTE may not be sensitive to the size of data set.

Fourthly, by adopting a majority voting scheme, System 3 achieves the best results on two data sets among five systems and obtains 45.8% accuracy on FRA-ENG which is the best result among all participants. This indicates the majority voting strategy is a effective way to boost the performance.

Fifthly, System 5 which adopts hierarchical classification technique fails to make further improvement. But it still outperforms the runner-up system in this task on FRA-ENG and DEU-ENG. We speculate that the failure of System 5 may be caused by the errors sensitive to hierarchical structure in hierarchical classification.

In general, our approaches obtained very good results on all the language pairs. On FRA-ENG and DEU-ENG, we achieved the best results among the 16 systems with the accuracy 45.8% and 45.3% respectively and largely outperformed the runner-up. The results on SPA-ENG and ITA-ENG were also promising, achieving the second and third place among the 16 systems.

5 Conclusion

We have proposed several effectively features consisting of sentence semantic similarity and sentence difference, which work together with other features presented by the previous work to solve the cross-lingual textual entailment problem. With the aid of machine translation, we can handle the cross-linguality. We submitted five systems on each language pair and obtained the best result on two data sets, i.e., FRA-ENG and DEU-ENG, and ranked the 2nd and the 3rd on other two language pairs respectively. Interestingly, we find some simple feature types like BC and SD are good class indicators and can be easily acquired. In future work, we will investigate the discriminating power of different feature types in the CLTE task on different languages.

Acknowledgements

The authors would like to thank the organizers and reviewers for this interesting task and their helpful suggestions and comments, which improves the final version of this paper. This research is supported by grants from National Natural Science Foundation of China (No.60903093), Shanghai Pujiang Talent Program (No.09PJ1404500), Doctoral Fund of Ministry of Education of China (No. 20090076120029) and Shanghai Knowledge Service Platform Project (No. ZF1213).

References

Julio Javier Castillo. 2011. A wordnet-based semantic approach to textual entailment and cross-lingual

System	SPA-ENG	ITA-ENG	FRA-ENG	DEU-ENG
1	**0.428**	**0.426**	0.438	0.422
2	0.404	0.420	0.450	0.436
3	0.408	**0.426**	**0.458**	0.432
4	0.422	0.416	0.436	**0.452**
5	0.392	0.402	0.442	0.426
Best feature set	BC+STS+SS +GR+SD	BC+SD+SS +GR+BS	SD+BC+STS	BC+STS+SS +BS+SD
Best	0.434	0.454	0.458	0.452
runner-up	0.428	0.432	0.426	0.414

Table 2: The accuracy results of our systems on different language pairs released by the organizer.

textual entailment. *International Journal of Machine Learning and Cybernetics*, 2(3):177–189.

Ido Dagan and Oren Glickman. 2004. Probabilistic textual entailment: Generic applied modeling of language variability. In *Proceedings of the PASCAL Workshop on Learning Methods for Text Understanding and Mining*.

Miquel Esplà-Gomis, Felipe Sánchez-Martínez, and Mikel L. Forcada. 2012. Ualacant: Using online machine translation for cross-lingual textual entailment. In *Proceedings of the Sixth International Workshop on Semantic Evaluation (SemEval 2012)*, pages 472–476, Montréal, Canada, 7-8 June.

Rong-En Fan, Kai-Wei Chang, Cho-Jui Hsieh, Xiang-Rui Wang, and Chih-Jen Lin. 2008. Liblinear: A library for large linear classification. *The Journal of Machine Learning Research*, 9:1871–1874.

Weiwei Guo and Mona Diab. 2012. Modeling sentences in the latent space. In *Proceedings of the 50th Annual Meeting of the Association for Computational Linguistics*.

Sanda Harabagiu and Andrew Hickl. 2006. Methods for using textual entailment in open-domain question answering. In *Proceedings of the 21st International Conference on Computational Linguistics and 44th Annual Meeting of the Association for Computational Linguistics*, pages 905–912, Sydney, Australia, July.

Sergio Jimenez, Claudia Becerra, and Alexander Gelbukh. 2012. Soft cardinality+ ml: Learning adaptive similarity functions for cross-lingual textual entailment. In *Proceedings of the 6th International Workshop on Semantic Evaluation (SemEval 2012)*.

Elena Lloret, Oscar Ferrández, Rafael Munoz, and Manuel Palomar. 2008. A text summarization approach under the influence of textual entailment. In *Proceedings of the 5th International Workshop on Natural Language Processing and Cognitive Science (NLPCS 2008)*, pages 22–31.

Tim Loughran and Bill McDonald. 2011. When is a liability not a liability? textual analysis, dictionaries, and 10-ks. *The Journal of Finance*, 66(1):35–65.

Prodromos Malakasiotis and Ion Androutsopoulos. 2007. Learning textual entailment using svms and string similarity measures. In *Proceedings of the ACL-PASCAL Workshop on Textual Entailment and Paraphrasing*, pages 42–47.

Prodromos Malakasiotis. 2009. Paraphrase recognition using machine learning to combine similarity measures. In *Proceedings of the ACL-IJCNLP 2009 Student Research Workshop*, pages 27–35.

Yashar Mehdad, Alessandro Moschitti, and Fabio Massimo Zanzotto. 2010a. Syntactic/semantic structures for textual entailment recognition. In *Human Language Technologies: The 2010 Annual Conference of the North American Chapter of the Association for Computational Linguistics*, pages 1020–1028.

Yashar Mehdad, Matteo Negri, and Marcello Federico. 2010b. Towards cross-lingual textual entailment. In *Human Language Technologies: The 2010 Annual Conference of the North American Chapter of the Association for Computational Linguistics*, pages 321–324, Los Angeles, California, June.

Fandong Meng, Hao Xiong, and Qun Liu. 2012. Ict: A translation based method for cross-lingual textual entailment. In *Proceedings of the Sixth International Workshop on Semantic Evaluation (SemEval 2012)*, pages 715–720, Montréal, Canada, 7-8 June.

M. Negri, A. Marchetti, Y. Mehdad, L. Bentivogli, and D. Giampiccolo. 2013. Semeval-2013 Task 8: Cross-lingual Textual Entailment for Content Synchronization. In *Proceedings of the 7th International Workshop on Semantic Evaluation (SemEval 2013)*.

William E Winkler et al. 1999. The state of record linkage and current research problems.

BUAP: N-gram based Feature Evaluation for the Cross-Lingual Textual Entailment Task

Darnes Vilariño, David Pinto, Saúl León, Yuridiana Alemán, Helena Gómez-Adorno
Benemérita Universidad Autónoma de Puebla
Faculty of Computer Science
14 Sur y Av. San Claudio, CU
Puebla, Puebla, México
{darnes, dpinto, saul.leon, candy.aleman, helena.gomez}@cs.buap.mx

Abstract

This paper describes the evaluation of different kinds of textual features for the Cross-Lingual Textual Entailment Task of SemEval 2013. We have counted the number of N-grams for three types of textual entities (character, word and PoS tags) that exist in the pair of sentences from which we are interested in determining the judgment of textual entailment. Difference, intersection and distance (Euclidian, Manhattan and Jaccard) of N-grams were considered for constructing a feature vector which is further introduced in a support vector machine classifier which allows to construct a classification model. Five different runs were submitted, one of them considering voting system of the previous four approaches. The results obtained show a performance below the median of six teams that have participated in the competition.

1 Introduction

The cross-lingual textual entailment (CLTE), recently proposed by (Mehdad et al., 2012) and (Mehdad et al., 2011), is an extension of the textual entailment task (Dagan and Glickman, 2004). Formally speaking, given a pair of topically related text fragments ($T1$ and $T2$ which are assumed to be TRUE statements) written in different languages, the CLTE task consists of automatically annotating it with one of the following entailment judgments:

- bidirectional ($T1 \rightarrow T2$ & $T1 \leftarrow T2$): the two fragments entail each other (semantic equivalence);
- forward ($T1 \rightarrow T2$ & $T1 \not\leftarrow T2$): unidirectional entailment from $T1$ to $T2$;
- backward ($T1 \not\rightarrow T2$ & $T1 \leftarrow T2$): unidirectional entailment from $T2$ to $T1$;
- no entailment (T1 $\not\rightarrow$ $T2$ & $T1 \not\leftarrow T2$): there is no entailment between $T1$ and $T2$ in both directions;

The Cross-lingual datasets evaluated were available for the following language combinations ($T1$-$T2$):

- Spanish-English (SPA-ENG)
- German-English (DEU-ENG)
- Italian-English (ITA-ENG)
- French-English (FRA-ENG)

In this paper we describe the evaluation of different features extracted from each pair of topically related sentences. N-grams of characters, words and PoS tags were counted with the aim of constructing a representative vector for each judgment entailment (FORWARD, BACKWARD, BI-DIRECTIONAL or NO-ENTAILMENT). The resulting vectors were fed into a supervised classifier based on Support Vector Machines (SVM)[1] which attempted to construct a classification model. The description of the features and the vectorial representation is given in Section 2. The obtained results are shown and discussed in Section 3. Finally, the findings of this work are given in Section 4.

[1] We have employed the implementation of the Weka tool (Hall et al., 2009).

*Second Joint Conference on Lexical and Computational Semantics (*SEM), Volume 2: Seventh International Workshop on Semantic Evaluation (SemEval 2013)*, pages 124–127, Atlanta, Georgia, June 14-15, 2013. ©2013 Association for Computational Linguistics

2 Experimental Setup

We have considered the task as a classification problem using the pivot approach. Thus, we have translated[2] each pair to their corresponding language in order to have two pairs of sentences written in the same language. Let $Pair(T1, T2)$ be the original pair of topically related sentences. Then, we have obtained the English translation of $T1$, denoted by $T3$, which will be aligned with $T2$. On the other hand, we have translated $T2$ to the other language (Spanish, German, Italian or French), denoted by $T4$, which will be aligned with $T1$. The two pairs of sentences, $Pair(T2, T3)$ (English) and $Pair(T1, T4)$ (other language), are now written in the same language, and we can proceed to calculate the textual features we are interested in.

The features used to represent both sentences are described below:

- N-grams of characters, with $N = 2, \cdots, 5$.
- N-grams of words, with $N = 2, \cdots, 4$.
- N-grams of PoS tags, with $N = 2, \cdots, 4$.
- Euclidean measure between each pair of sentences ($Pair(T1, T4)$ and $Pair(T2, T3)$).
- Manhattan measure between each pair of sentences ($Pair(T1, T4)$ and $Pair(T2, T3)$).
- Jaccard coefficient, expanding English terms in both sentences, $T2$ and $T3$, with their corresponding synonyms (none disambiguation process was considered).

The manner we have used the above mentioned features is described in detail in the following subsections.

2.1 Approach 1: Difference operator

For each pair of sentences written in the same language, this approach counts the number of N-grams that occur in the first sentence (for instance $T1$), and do not occur in the second sentence (for instance $T4$) and viceversa. Formally speaking, the values obtained are $\overrightarrow{Pair}(T1, T2) = \{D_1, D_2, \cdots, D_k\}$, with $D_1 = |T1 - T4|$, $D_2 = |T4 - T1|$, $D_3 = |T2 - T3|$, $D_4 = |T3 - T2|$, $\cdots$. This vector is calculated for all the possible values of N for each type of N-gram, i.e., character, word and PoS tag. The cardinality of $\overrightarrow{Pair}(T1, T2)$ will be 34, that is, 16 values when the N-grams of characters are considered, 12 values with word N-grams, and 6 values when the PoS tag N-grams are used.

[2]For this purpose we have used Google Translate

Table 1: Classes considered in the composition of binary classifiers

Class 1	Class 2
BACKWARD	OTHER
BI-DIRECTIONAL	OTHER
FORWARD	OTHER
NO-ENTAILMENT	OTHER
BACKWARD & BI-DIRECTIONAL	OTHER
BACKWARD & FORWARD	OTHER
BACKWARD & NO-ENTAILMENT	OTHER
BI-DIRECTIONAL & NO-ENTAILMENT	OTHER
FORWARD & BI-DIRECTIONAL	OTHER
FORWARD & NO-ENTAILMENT	OTHER

The vectors obtained are labeled with the corresponding tag in order to construct a training dataset which will be further used to feed a multiclass classifier which constructs the final classification model. In this case, the system will directly return one of the four valid entailment judgments (i.e. forward, backward, bidirectional, no_entailment).

2.2 Approach 2: Difference and Intersection operators

This approach enriches the previous one, by adding the intersection between the two sentences of each pair. In a sense, we have considered all the features appearing in the pair of sentences. In this case, the total number of features extracted, i.e., the cardinality of the $\overrightarrow{Pair}(T1, T2)$ vector is 51.

2.3 Approach 3: Metaclassifier

In this approach, we have constructed a system which is a composition of different binary classification models. The binary judgments were constructed considering the classes shown in Table 1.

The approach 2 was also considered in this composition generating a total of 11 models. 10 of them are based on the features used by Approach 1, and the last one is based on the features used by Approach 2. The result obtained is a vector which tells whether or not a pair is judged to have some kind of textual entailment or not (the OTHER class). This vector is then labeled with the correct class obtained from the gold standard (training corpus) for automatically obtaining a decision tree which allows us to determine the correct class. Thus, the different outputs of multiple classifiers are then introduced to another supervised classifier which constructs the final classification model.

2.4 Approach 4: Distances measures

This approach is constructed by adding five distance values to the Approach 2. These values are calculated as follows :

- The Euclidean distance between $T2$ and $T3$, and between $T1$ and $T4$. We have used the frequency of each word for constructing a representative vector of each sentence.
- The Manhattan distance between $T2$ and $T3$, and between $T1$ and $T4$. We have used the frequency of each word for constructing a representative vector of each sentence.
- A variant of the Jaccard's Coefficient that consider synonyms (Carrillo et al., 2012). Since we have only obtained synonyms for the English language, this measure was only calculated between $T2$ and $T3$.

Therefore, the total number of features of the $\overrightarrow{Pair}(T1, T2)$ vector is 56.

2.5 Approach 5: Voting system

With the results of the previous four models, we prepared a voting system which uses the majority criterion (3 of 4).

3 Experimental results

The results obtained in the competition are presented and discussed in this section. First, we describe the training and test corpus, and thereafter, the results obtained with the different approaches submitted.

3.1 Dataset

In order to train the different approaches already discussed, we have constructed a training corpus made up of two datasets: the training data provided by the task organizers the task 8 of SemEval 2013 (Negri et al., 2013), and the test dataset together with the gold standard of CLTE task of SemEval 2012 (Negri et al., 2011). Thus, the training corpus contains 4000 sentence pairs. The test set provided in the competition contains 2000 sentence pairs. The corpus is balanced, with 1000 pairs for each language in the training dataset, whereas, 500 pairs are given in the test set for each language (see Table 2).

Table 2: Description of the dataset

Languages	Training	Test
SPA-ENG	1000	500
DEU-ENG	1000	500
ITA-ENG	1000	500
FRA-ENG	1000	500
Total	**4000**	**2000**

3.2 Results

In Table 3 we can see the results obtained by each one of the five approaches we submitted to the competition. Each approach has been labeled with the prefix "BUAP-R" for indicating the approach used by each submitted run. For instance, the BUAP-R1 run corresponds to the approach 1 described in the previous section. As can be seen, the behavior of the five approaches is quite similar, which we consider it is expected because the underlying methodology employed is almost the same for all the approaches. With exception of the pair of sentences written in SPA-ENG in which the best approach was obtained by the BUAP-R5 run, the approach 4 outperformed the other appproaches. We believe that this has been a result of introducing measures of similarity between the two sentences and their translations. In this table it is also reported the Highest, Average, Median and Lowest values of the competition. The results we obtained are under the Median but outperformed the results of two teams in the competition.

With the purpose of analyzing the behavior of the approach 4 in each one of the entailment judgments, we have provided the results obtained in Table 4. There we can see that the BACKWARD class is the easiest one for being predicted, independently of the language. The second easiest class is FORWARD, followed by NO-ENTAILMENT. Also we can see that the BI-DIRECTIONAL class is the one that produce more confusion, thus leading to obtain a lower performance than the other ones.

Table 3: Overall statistics obtained in the Task-8 of SemEval 2013

RUN	SPA-ENG	ITA-ENG	FRA-ENG	DEU-ENG
Highest	0.434	0.454	0.458	0.452
Average	0.393	0.393	0.401	0.375
Median	0.392	0.402	0.416	0.369
Lowest	0.340	0.324	0.334	0.316
BUAP-R1	0.364	0.358	0.368	0.322
BUAP-R2	0.374	0.358	0.364	0.318
BUAP-R3	0.380	0.358	0.362	0.316
BUAP-R4	0.364	**0.388**	**0.392**	**0.350**
BUAP-R5	**0.386**	0.360	0.372	0.318

Table 4: Statistics of the approach 4, detailed by entailment judgment

ENTAILMENT JUDGEMENT	SPA-ENG	ITA-ENG	FRA-ENG	DEU-ENG
BACKWARD	0.495	0.462	0.431	0.389
FORWARD	0.374	0.418	0.407	0.364
NO-ENTAILMENT	0.359	0.379	0.379	0.352
BI-DIRECTIONAL	0.277	0.327	0.352	0.317

4 Conclusions

Five different approaches for the Cross-lingual Textual Entailment for the Content Synchronization task of Semeval 2013 are reported in this paper. We used several features for determining the textual entailment judgment between two texts $T1$ and $T2$ (written in two different languages). The approach 4 proposed, which employed lexical similarity and semantic similarity in English language only was the one that performed better. As future work, we would like to include more distance metrics which allow to extract additional features of the pair of sentences topically related.

References

Maya Carrillo, Darnes Vilariño, David Pinto, Mireya Tovar, Saul León, and Esteban Castillo. Fcc: Three approaches for semantic textual similarity. In **SEM 2012: The First Joint Conference on Lexical and Computational Semantics – Volume 1 and 2 (SemEval 2012)*, pages 631–634, Montréal, Canada, 7-8 June 2012. Association for Computational Linguistics.

Ido Dagan and Oren Glickman. Probabilistic textual entailment: Generic applied modeling of language variability. In *PASCAL Workshop on Learning Methods for Text Understanding and Mining*, 2004.

Mark Hall, Eibe Frank, Geoffrey Holmes, Bernhard Pfahringer, Peter Reutemann, and Ian H. Witten. The weka data mining software: an update. *SIGKDD Explor. Newsl.*, 11(1):10–18, November 2009. ISSN 1931-0145.

Yashar Mehdad, Matteo Negri, and Marcello Federico. Using bilingual parallel corpora for cross-lingual textual entailment. In *Proc. of the 49th Annual Meeting of the Association for Computational Linguistics: Human Language Technologies - Volume 1*, HLT '11, pages 1336–1345, Stroudsburg, PA, USA, 2011. Association for Computational Linguistics.

Yashar Mehdad, Matteo Negri, and Marcello Federico. Detecting semantic equivalence and information disparity in cross-lingual documents. In *Proc. of the 50th Annual Meeting of the Association for Computational Linguistics: Short Papers - Volume 2*, ACL '12, pages 120–124, Stroudsburg, PA, USA, 2012. Association for Computational Linguistics.

M. Negri, A. Marchetti, Y. Mehdad, L. Bentivogli, and D. Giampiccolo. Semeval-2013 Task 8: Cross-lingual Textual Entailment for Content Synchronization. In *Proceedings of the 7th International Workshop on Semantic Evaluation (SemEval 2013)*, 2013.

Matteo Negri, Luisa Bentivogli, Yashar Mehdad, Danilo Giampiccolo, and Alessandro Marchetti. Divide and conquer: crowdsourcing the creation of cross-lingual textual entailment corpora. In *Proc. of the Conference on Empirical Methods in Natural Language Processing*, EMNLP '11, pages 670–679, Stroudsburg, PA, USA, 2011. Association for Computational Linguistics. ISBN 978-1-937284-11-4.

ALTN: Word Alignment Features for Cross-lingual Textual Entailment

Marco Turchi and Matteo Negri
Fondazione Bruno Kessler
Trento, Italy
{turchi,negri}@fbk.eu

Abstract

We present a supervised learning approach to cross-lingual textual entailment that explores statistical word alignment models to predict entailment relations between sentences written in different languages. Our approach is language independent, and was used to participate in the CLTE task (Task#8) organized within Semeval 2013 (Negri et al., 2013). The four runs submitted, one for each language combination covered by the test data (*i.e.* Spanish/English, German/English, French/English and Italian/English), achieved encouraging results. In terms of accuracy, performance ranges from 38.8% (for German/English) to 43.2% (for Italian/English). On the Italian/English and Spanish/English test sets our systems ranked second among five participants, close to the top results (respectively 43.4% and 45.4%).

1 Introduction

Cross-lingual textual entailment (CLTE) is an extension of the Textual Entailment task (Dagan and Glickman, 2004) that consists in deciding, given two texts T and H written in different languages (respectively called text and hypothesis), if H can be inferred from T (Mehdad et al., 2010). In the case of SemEval 2013, the task is formulated as a multi-class classification problem in which there are four possible relations between T and H: forward ($T \rightarrow H$), backward ($T \leftarrow H$), bidirectional ($T \leftrightarrow H$) and "no entailment".

Targeting the identification of semantic equivalence and information disparity between topically related sentences, CLTE recognition can be seen as a core task for a number of cross-lingual applications. Among others, multilingual content synchronization has been recently proposed as an ideal framework for the exploitation of CLTE components and the integration of semantics and machine translation (MT) technology (Mehdad et al., 2011; Mehdad et al., 2012b; Bronner et al., 2012; Monz et al., 2011).

In the last few years, several methods have been proposed for CLTE. These can be roughly divided in two main groups (Negri et al., 2012): *i)* those using a *pivoting* strategy by translating H into the language of T and then using monolingual TE components[1], and those directly using cross-lingual strategies. Among this second group, several sources of cross-lingual knowledge have been used, such as dictionaries (Kouylekov et al., 2012; Perini, 2012), phrase and paraphrase tables (Mehdad et al., 2012a), GIZA++ (Och and Ney, 2003) word alignment models (Wäschle and Fendrich, 2012), MT of sub-segments (Esplà-Gomis et al., 2012), or semantic Wordnets (Castillo, 2011).

In this work we propose a CLTE detection method based on a new set of features using word alignment as a source of cross-lingual knowledge. This set, which is richer than the one by (Wäschle and Fendrich, 2012), is aimed not only at grasping information about the proportion of aligned words, but also about the distribution of the alignments in both

[1]In the first CLTE evaluation round at Semeval 2012, for instance, the system described in (Meng et al., 2012) used the open source EDITS system (Kouylekov and Negri, 2010; Negri et al., 2009) to calculate similarity scores between monolingual English pairs.

*Second Joint Conference on Lexical and Computational Semantics (*SEM), Volume 2: Seventh International Workshop on Semantic Evaluation (SemEval 2013)*, pages 128–132, Atlanta, Georgia, June 14-15, 2013.

H and T. This set of features is later used by two support vector machine (SVM) classifiers for detecting CLTE separately in both directions ($T \rightarrow H$ and $T \leftarrow H$). We use the combined output of both classifiers for performing the CLTE detection.

The paper is organized as follows: Section 2 describes the features used and the classification method; Section 3 explains the experimental framework and the results obtained for the different language-pair sets; finally, the conclusions obtained from the results are summarised in Section 4.

2 ALTN System

In our approach we have implemented a system based on supervised learning. It takes an unlabeled sentence pair as input (T and H) and labels it automatically with one of the possible four valid entailment relations. The architecture is depicted in Figure 1.

A key component to our approach is the word alignment model. In a preprocessing step it is trained on a set of parallel texts for the target language pair. Next, different features based on the word alignment are extracted. Taking the features and the target language pair labels as input, a supervised learning algorithm is run to fit a model to the data. The last step is to use the model to automatically label unseen instances with entailment relations.

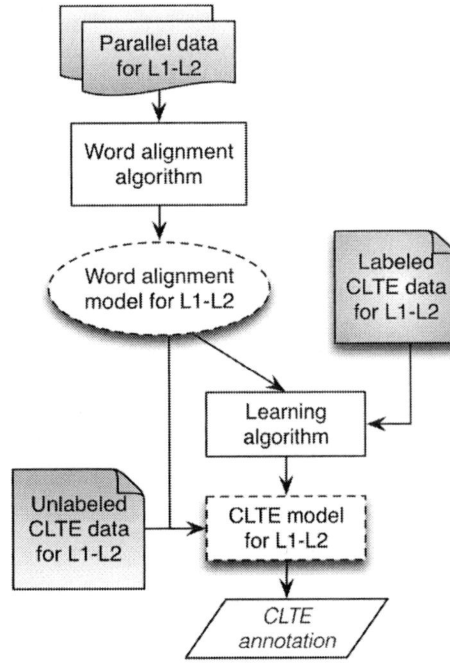

Figure 1: System architecture

2.1 Features

What characterizes our submission is the use of word alignment features to capture entailment relations. We extract the following features from a word alignment model for a given sentence pair (all features are calculated for both T and H):

- proportion of aligned words in the sentence (baseline);
- number of unaligned sequences of words normalized by the length of the sentence;
- length of the longest sequence of aligned words normalized by the length of the sentence;
- length of the longest sequence of unaligned words normalized by the length of the sentence;
- average length of the aligned word sequences;
- average length of the unaligned word sequences;
- position of the first unaligned word normalized by the length of the sentence;
- position of the last unaligned word normalized by the lenght of the sentence;
- proportion of aligned n-grams in the sentence (n varying from 1 to 5).

These features are language independent as they are obtained from statistical models that take as input a parallel corpus. Provided that there exist parallel data for a given language pair, the only constraint in terms of resources, the adoption of these features makes our approach virtually portable across languages with limited effort.

2.2 CLTE Model

Our CLTE model is composed by two supervised binary classifiers that predict whether there is entailment between the T and H. One classifier checks for forward entailment ($T \rightarrow H$) and the other checks for backward entailment ($T \leftarrow H$). The output of both classifiers is combined to form the four valid entailment decisions:

- forward and backward classifier output `true`: "bidirectional" entailment;
- forward is `true` and backward is `false`: "forward" entailment;
- forward is `false` and backward is `true`: "backward" entailment;
- both forward and backward output `false`: "no entailment" relation.

Both binary classifiers were implemented using the SVM implementation of Weka (Hall et al., 2009).

3 Experiments

In our submission we experimented with three standard word alignment algorithms: the *hidden Markov model* (HMM) (Vogel et al., 1996) and *IBM models* 3 and 4 (Brown et al., 1993). They are implemented in the MGIZA++ package (Gao and Vogel, 2008). Building on a probabilistic lexical model to establish mappings between words in two languages, these models compute alignments between the word positions in two input sentences S_1 and S_2. The models are trained incrementally: HMM is the base for IBM model 3, which is the base for IBM model 4. To train our models, we used 5 iterations of HMM, and 3 iterations of IBM models 3 and 4.

Word alignments produced by these models are asymmetric ($S_1 \rightarrow S_2 \neq S_2 \rightarrow S_1$). To cope with this, different heuristics (Koehn et al., 2005) have been proposed to obtain symmetric alignments from two asymmetric sets ($S_1 \leftrightarrow S_2$). We experimented with three symmetrization heuristics, namely: *union*, *intersection*, and *grow-diag-final-and*, a more complex symmetrization method which combines intersection with some alignments from the union.

To train the word alignment models we used the Europarl parallel corpus (Koehn, 2005) concatenated with the News Commentary corpus[2] for three language pairs: English-German (2,079,049 sentences), English-Spanish (2,123,036 sentences), English-French (2,144,820 sentences). For English-Italian we only used the parallel data available in Europarl (1,909,115 sentences) since this language pair is not covered by the News Commentary corpus.

For our submitted run the SVM classifiers were trained using the whole training set. Such dataset consists of 1,000 pairs for each of the four language combinations, resulting from a concatenation of the training and test sets used for the first round of evaluation at SemEval 2012 (Negri et al., 2012; Negri et al., 2011). We have set a polynomial kernel with parameters empirically estimated on the training set: $C = 2.0$, and $d = 1$. After some preliminary experiments we have concluded that the HMM model in conjunction with the *intersection* symmetrization provides the best results.

Our results, calculated over the 500 test pairs provided for each language combination, are presented in Table 3. As can be seen from the table, our system consistently outperforms the best average run of all participants and is the second best system for Spanish/English and Italian/English. For the other two languages, French/English and German/English, it is the 3rd best system with a larger distance from top results. The motivations for such lower results, currently under investigation, might be related to lower performance in terms of word alignment, the core of our approach. The first step of our analysis will hence address, and in case try to cope with, significant differences in word alignment performance affecting results.

Overall, considering the small distance from top results, and the fact that our approach does not require deep linguistic processing to be reasonably effective for any language pair for which parallel corpora are available, our results are encouraging and motivate further research along such direction.

4 Conclusion

In this paper we presented the participation of the Fondazione Bruno Kessler in the Semeval 2013 Task#8 on Cross-lingual Textual Entailment for Content Synchronization. To identify entailment relations between texts in different languages, our system explores the use of word alignment features

[2] `http://www.statmt.org/wmt11/translation-task.html#download`

Features / Language pair	German/English	Spanish/English	French/English	Italian/English
Avg best runs	0.378	0.404	0.407	0.405
ALTN	0.388	0.428	0.420	0.432
Best system	0.452	0.434	0.458	0.454

Table 1: Accuracy results for the language pairs evaluated for the average of the best runs of the participating systems, our submission and the best systems.

within a supervised learning setting. In our approach, word alignment models obtained by statistical methods from parallel corpora leverage information about the number, the proportion, and the distribution of aligned terms in the input sentences. In terms of accuracy results over the SemEval 2013 CLTE test data, performance ranges from 38.8% (for German/English) to 43.2% (for Italian/English). On the Italian/English and Spanish/English test sets our systems ranked second among five participants, close to the top results (respectively 43.4% and 45.4%). Such results suggest that the use of word alignment models to capture sentence-level semantic relations in different language settings represents a promising research direction.

Acknowledgments

This work has been partially supported by the EC-funded project CoSyne (FP7-ICT-4-248531).

References

Amit Bronner, Matteo Negri, Yashar Mehdad, Angela Fahrni, and Christof Monz. 2012. CoSyne: Synchronizing Multilingual Wiki Content. In *Proceedings of the Eighth Annual International Symposium on Wikis and Open Collaboration*, WikiSym '12, pages 33:1–33:4, New York, NY, USA. ACM.

Peter F. Brown, Stephen A. Della Pietra, Vincent J. Della Pietra, and Robert L. Mercer. 1993. The Mathematics of Statistical Machine Translation: Parameter Estimation. *Computational Linguistics*, 19(2):263–311.

Julio J. Castillo. 2011. A WordNet-based Semantic Approach to Textual Entailment and Cross-lingual Textual Entailment. *International Journal of Machine Learning and Cybernetics*, 2(3):177–189.

Ido Dagan and Oren Glickman. 2004. Probabilistic Textual Entailment: Generic Applied Modeling of Language Variability. In *Proceedings of the PASCAL Workshop of Learning Methods for Text Understanding and Mining*, Grenoble, France.

Miquel Esplà-Gomis, Felipe Sánchez-Martínez, and Mikel L. Forcada. 2012. UAlacant: Using Online Machine Translation for Cross-Lingual Textual Entailment. In *Proceedings of the 6th International Workshop on Semantic Evaluation (SemEval 2012)*, pages 472–476, Montréal, Canada.

Qin Gao and Stephan Vogel. 2008. Parallel Implementations of Word Alignment Tool. In *Software Engineering, Testing, and Quality Assurance for Natural Language Processing*, pages 49–57, Columbus, Ohio, USA.

Mark Hall, Eibe Frank, Geoffrey Holmes, Bernhard Pfahringer, Peter Reutemann, and Ian H. Witten. 2009. The WEKA Data Mining Software: an Update. *SIGKDD Explorations*, 11(1):10–18.

Philipp Koehn, Amittai Axelrod, Alexandra Birch Mayne, Chris Callison-Burch, Miles Osborne, and David Talbot. 2005. Edinburgh System Description for the 2005 IWSLT Speech Translation Evaluation. In *Proceedings of the International Workshop on Spoken Language Translation*, Pittsburgh, Pennsylvania, USA.

Philip Koehn. 2005. Europarl: a Parallel Corpus for Statistical Machine Translation. In *Proceedings of Machine Translation Summit X*, pages 79–86, Phuket, Thailand.

Milen Kouylekov and Matteo Negri. 2010. An Open-source Package for Recognizing Textual Entailment. In *Proceedings of the ACL 2010 System Demonstrations*.

Milen Kouylekov, Luca Dini, Alessio Bosca, and Marco Trevisan. 2012. CELI: an Experiment with Cross Language Textual Entailment. In *Proceedings of the 6th International Workshop on Semantic Evaluation (SemEval 2012)*, pages 696–700, Montréal, Canada.

Yashar Mehdad, Matteo Negri, and Marcello Federico. 2010. Towards Cross-Lingual Textual Entailment. In *Proceedings of the 11th Annual Conference of the North American Chapter of the Association for Computational Linguistics (NAACL HLT 2010)*.

Yashar Mehdad, Matteo Negri, and Marcello Federico. 2011. Using Bilingual Parallel Corpora for Cross-Lingual Textual Entailment. In *Proceedings of the 49th Annual Meeting of the Association for Compu-*

tational Linguistics: Human Language Technologies (ACL HLT 2011).

Yashar Mehdad, Matteo Negri, and José Guilherme C. de Souza. 2012a. FBK: cross-lingual textual entailment without translation. In *Proceedings of the 6th International Workshop on Semantic Evaluation (SemEval 2012)*, pages 701–705, Montréal, Canada.

Yashar Mehdad, Matteo Negri, and Marcello Federico. 2012b. Detecting Semantic Equivalence and Information Disparity in Cross-lingual Documents. In *Proceedings of the 50th Annual Meeting of the Association for Computational Linguistics (ACL 2012)*.

Fandong Meng, Hao Xiong, and Qun Liu. 2012. ICT: A Translation based Cross-lingual Textual Entailment. In *Proceedings of the 6th International Workshop on Semantic Evaluation (SemEval 2012)*.

Christoph Monz, Vivi Nastase, Matteo Negri, Angela Fahrni, Yashar Mehdad, and Michael Strube. 2011. CoSyne: a Framework for Multilingual Content Synchronization of Wikis. In *Proceedings of Wikisym 2011, the International Symposium on Wikis and Open Collaboration*, pages 217–218, Mountain View, California, USA.

Matteo Negri, Milen Ognianov Kouylekov, Bernardo Magnini, Yashar Mehdad, and Elena Cabrio. 2009. Towards Extensible Textual Entailment Engines: the EDITS Package. In *AI*IA 2009: XIth International Conference of the Italian Association for Artificial Intelligence*.

Matteo Negri, Luisa Bentivogli, Yashar Mehdad, Danilo Giampiccolo, and Alessandro Marchetti. 2011. Divide and Conquer: Crowdsourcing the Creation of Cross-Lingual Textual Entailment Corpora. *Proceedings of the 2011 Conference on Empirical Methods in Natural Language Processing (EMNLP 2011)*.

Matteo Negri, Alessandro Marchetti, Yashar Mehdad, Luisa Bentivogli, and Danilo Giampiccolo. 2012. Semeval-2012 Task 8: Cross-Lingual Textual Entailment for Content Synchronization. In *Proceedings of the 6th International Workshop on Semantic Evaluation (SemEval 2012)*, pages 399–407, Montréal, Canada.

Matteo Negri, Alessandro Marchetti, Yashar Mehdad, Luisa Bentivogli, and Danilo Giampiccolo. 2013. Semeval-2013 Task 8: Cross-lingual Textual Entailment for Content Synchronization. In *Proceedings of the 7th International Workshop on Semantic Evaluation (SemEval 2013)*.

Franz J. Och and Hermann Ney. 2003. A Systematic Comparison of Various Statistical Alignment Models. *Computational Linguistics*, 29(1):19–51.

Alpár Perini. 2012. DirRelCond3: detecting textual entailment across languages with conditions on directional text relatedness scores. In *Proceedings of the 6th International Workshop on Semantic Evaluation (SemEval 2012)*, pages 710–714, Montréal, Canada.

Stephan Vogel, Hermann Ney, and Christoph Tillmann. 1996. HMM-based word alignment in statistical translation. In *Proceedings of the 16th International Conference on Computational Linguistics (ACL'96)*, pages 836–841, Copenhagen, Denmark.

Katharina Wäschle and Sascha Fendrich. 2012. HDU: Cross-lingual Textual Entailment with SMT Features. In *Proceedings of the 6th International Workshop on Semantic Evaluation (SemEval 2012)*, pages 467–471, Montréal, Canada.

Umelb: Cross-lingual Textual Entailment with Word Alignment and String Similarity Features

Yvette Graham **Bahar Salehi** **Timothy Baldwin**
Department of Computing and Information Systems
The University of Melbourne
{ygraham,bsalehi,tbaldwin}@unimelb.edu.au

Abstract

This paper describes The University of Melbourne NLP group submission to the Cross-lingual Textual Entailment shared task, our first tentative attempt at the task. The approach involves using parallel corpora and automatic word alignment to align text fragment pairs, and statistics based on unaligned words as features to classify items as forward and backward before a compositional combination into the final four classes, as well as experiments with additional string similarity features.

1 Introduction

Cross-lingual Textual Entailment (CLTE) (Negri et al., 2012) proposes the task of automatically identifying the kind of relation that exists between pairs of semantically-related text fragments written in two distinct languages, a variant of the traditional Recognizing Textual Entailment (RTE) task (Bentivogli et al., 2009; Bentivogli et al., 2010). The task targets the cross-lingual content synchronization scenario proposed in Mehdad et al. (2010, 2011). Compositional classification can be used by training two distinct binary classifiers for forward and backward entailment classification, before combining labels into the four final entailment categories that now include bidirectional and no_entailment labels. The most similar previous work to this work is the cross-lingual approach of the FBK system (Mehdad et al., 2012) from Semeval 2012 (Negri et al., 2012), in which the entailment classification is obtained without translating T1 into T2 for the Spanish–English language pair. We apply the cross-lingual approach to German–English and instead of cross-lingual matching features, we use Giza++ (Och et al., 1999) and Moses (Koehn et al., 2007) to automatically word align text fragment pairs to compute statistics of unaligned words. In addition, we include some additional experiments using string similarity features.

2 Compositional Classification

Given a pair of topically related fragments, T1 (German) and T2 (English), we automatically annotate it with one of the following entailment labels: bidirectional, forward, backward, no_entailment. We take the compositional approach and separately train a forward, as well as a backward binary classifier. Each classifier is run separately on the set of text fragment pairs to produce two binary labels for forward and backward entailment. The two sets of labels are logically combined to produce a final classification for each test pair of forward, backward, bidirectional or no_entailment.

3 Word Alignment Features

The test set of topically-related text fragments, T1 (German) and T2 (English) were added to Europarl German–English parallel text (Koehn, 2005) and Giza++ was used for automatic word alignment in both language directions. Moses (Koehn et al., 2007) was then used for symmetrization with the *grow_diag_final_and* algorithm. This produces a many-to-many alignment between the words of the

*Second Joint Conference on Lexical and Computational Semantics (*SEM), Volume 2: Seventh International Workshop on Semantic Evaluation (SemEval 2013)*, pages 133–137, Atlanta, Georgia, June 14-15, 2013.

German, T1, and English, T2, with words also remaining unaligned.

The following features are computed for each test pair feature scores for the *forward* classifier:

- A1: count of unaligned words in T2
- A2: count of words comprised soley of digits in T2 not in T1
- A3: count of unaligned words in T2 with low probability of appearing unaligned in Europarl (with threshold p=0.11)

The number of words in T2 (English) that are not aligned with anything in T1 (German) should provide an indication that, for example, the English text fragment contains information not present in the corresponding German text fragment and subsequently evidence against the presence of forward entailment. We there include the feature, A1, that is simply a count of unaligned words in English T2. In addition, we hypothesize that the absence of a number from T2 may be a more significant missing element of T2 from T1. We therefore include as a feature the count of tokens comprised of digits in T2 that are not also present in T1. The final word alignment feature attempts to refine A1, by distinguishing words that are rarely unaligned in German–English translations. Statistics are computed for every lexical item from German–English Europarl translations to produce a lexical unalignment probability, computed for each lexical item based on its relative frequency in the corpus when it is not aligned to any other word.

The *backward* classifier uses the same features but computed for each test pair on counts of unaligned T1 words.

4 Results

Results for several combinations of features are shown in Table 1 when the system is trained on the 500-pair development set training corpus and tested on the 500-pair held-out development test set (DEV), in addition to results for feature combinations when trained on the entire 1000-pair development data and tested on the held-out 500-pair gold standard (TEST) (Negri et al., 2011), when the system is evaluated as two separate binary *forward* and *backward* classifiers (2-CLASS) as well as the final evaluation including all four entailment classes (4-CLASS). The highest accuracy is achieved by the classifier using the single feature of counts of unaligned words, A1, of 34.6%. As two separate binary classifiers, the alignment features, A1+A2+A3, achieve a relatively high accuracy of 74.0% for forward with somewhat less accurate for backward (65.8%) classification (both over the DEV data). When combined to the final four CLTE classes, however, accuracy drops significantly to an overall accuracy of 50% (also over DEV). A main cause is inaccurate labeling of no_entailment gold standard test pairs, as the most severe decline is for recall of test pairs for this label (38.4%).

Accuracy on the development set for the word alignment features, A1+A2+A3, compared to the test set shows a sever decline, from 50% to 32%. On the test data, however, a main cause of inaccuracy is that backward gold standard test pairs, although achieving close accuracy to forward when evaluated as binary classifiers, are inaccurately labeled in the 4-class evaluation, as recall for backward drops to only 18.4% for this label.

Another insight revealed for the alignment features, A1+A2+A3, in the 4-class evaluation is that when run on the development set, the classes forward and backward achieve significantly higher f-scores compared to no_entailment. However, the contrary is observed for the test data, as no_entailment achieve higher results than both unidirectional classes. This appears at first to be a somewhat counter-intuitive result, but in this case, the system is simply better at predicting forward and backward when no entailment exists for a translation pair compared to when a unidirectional entailment is present.

4.1 String Similarity Features

In addition to the word alignment features, subsequent to submitting results to the shared task, we have carried out additional experiments using string similarity features, based on our recent success in apply string similarity to both the estimation of compositionality of MWEs (Salehi and Cook, to appear) and also the estimation of similarity between short

			2-CLASS				4-CLASS				
			Acc.	Prec	Recall	F1	Acc.		Prec	Recall	F1
DEV	A1 + A2 + A3	bwrd	**65.80**	**63.12**	**76.00**	**68.96**	**50.00**	bwrd	**54.80**	**59.20**	**56.90**
		fwrd	**74.00**	**72.22**	**78.00**	**75.00**		fwrd	**54.80**	**45.60**	**49.80**
								none	**50.50**	38.40	**43.60**
								bidir	**42.80**	**56.80**	**48.80**
	S1 + S2 + S3	bwrd	58.20	57.75	61.20	59.42	27.40	bwrd	14.30	0.80	1.50
		fwrd	47.00	47.17	50.00	59.42		fwrd	0.00	0.00	0.00
								none	30.70	**39.70**	39.70
								bidir	25.60	52.80	34.50
TEST	A1	bwrd	57.00	**58.54**	48.00	52.75	**34.60**	bwrd	25.50	19.20	21.90
		fwrd	58.40	58.75	56.40	57.55		fwrd	**34.90**	**36.00**	**35.40**
								none	36.70	48.80	**41.90**
								bidir	**38.70**	34.40	36.40
	A2	bwrd	50.00	0.00	0.00	0.00	33.60	bwrd	24.70	18.40	21.10
		fwrd	51.60	50.85	**95.20**	**66.29**		fwrd	34.70	34.40	34.50
								none	36.90	38.40	37.60
								bidir	35.30	**43.20**	**38.80**
	A3	bwrd	54.80	55.61	47.60	51.29	34.20	bwrd	**32.70**	**26.40**	29.20
		fwrd	**61.20**	61.57	59.60	60.57		fwrd	33.30	34.40	33.90
								none	36.90	46.40	41.10
								bidir	32.70	29.60	31.10
	A1+A2	bwrd	57.60	57.72	**56.80**	57.26	33.60	bwrd	24.70	18.40	21.10
		fwrd	59.80	58.84	65.20	61.86		fwrd	34.70	34.40	34.50
								none	36.90	38.40	37.60
								bidir	35.30	**43.20**	**38.80**
	A1+A3	bwrd	57.20	57.96	52.40	55.04	33.00	bwrd	26.60	20.00	22.80
		fwrd	58.60	58.05	62.00	59.96		fwrd	31.90	34.40	33.10
								none	36.70	40.80	38.60
								bidir	34.80	36.80	35.80
	A2+A3	bwrd	54.80	55.83	46.00	50.44	33.40	bwrd	32.30	25.60	28.60
		fwrd	61.00	**61.70**	58.00	59.79		fwrd	32.80	33.60	33.20
								none	34.90	46.40	39.90
								bidir	32.70	28.00	30.20
	A1 + A2 + A3	bwrd	57.60	57.72	**56.80**	57.26	32.00	bwrd	24.00	18.40	20.80
		fwrd	59.20	58.39	64.00	61.07		fwrd	32.30	32.00	32.10
								none	36.20	37.60	36.90
								bidir	34.70	41.60	37.80
	S1 + S2 + S3	bwrd	53.20	53.77	45.60	49.35	26.00	bwrd	20.00	1.50	**29.50**
		fwrd	48.60	48.36	41.20	44.49		fwrd	16.70	0.80	31.50
								none	28.00	**63.20**	38.80
								bidir	23.70	39.20	29.50
	A1 + A2 + A3 + S1	bwrd	57.40	58.30	52.00	54.97	33.00	bwrd	27.60	19.20	22.60
		fwrd	59.80	58.84	65.20	61.86		fwrd	29.80	33.60	31.60
								none	**38.20**	41.60	39.80
								bidir	34.60	37.60	36.00
	A1 + A2 + A3 + S2	bwrd	57.80	58.52	53.60	55.95	32.60	bwrd	26.70	19.20	22.30
		fwrd	59.60	58.70	64.80	61.60		fwrd	30.70	33.60	32.10
								none	37.30	40.00	38.60
								bidir	33.80	37.60	35.60
	A1 + A2 + A3 +S3	bwrd	**58.20**	58.51	56.40	**57.44**	32.80	bwrd	24.70	19.20	21.60
		fwrd	59.60	58.82	64.00	61.30		fwrd	32.00	32.80	32.40
								none	37.40	39.20	38.30
								bidir	34.70	40.00	37.20

Table 1: Cross-lingual Textual Entailment Results for Word alignment Features and String Similarity Measures, A1 = count of unaligned words in T2, A2 = count of unaligned numbers in T2, A3 = count of unaligned words in T2 with unaligned probability < 0.11, S1 = Number of matched words in the aligned sequence given by Smith-Waterman algorithm, S2 = Penalty of aligning sentences using Smith-Waterman algorithm, S3 = Levenshtein distance between the sentences

texts in the *SEM 2013 Shared Task (Gella et al., to appear). Using the alignments, we replace each English word with its corresponding word in German. The resulting German sentence is compared with the actual one using string similarity measures. As the structure of both English and German sentences are usually SVO, we hypothesize that when there is no entailment between the two given sentences, the newly-made German sentence and the original German sentence will differ a lot in word order.

In order to compare the two German sentences, we use the Levenshtein (Levenshtein, 1966) and the Smith-Waterman (Smith and Waterman, 1981) algorithm. The Levenshtein algorithm measures the number of world-level edits to change one sentence into another. The edit operators consist of insertion and deletion. We consider substitution as two edits (combination of insertion and deletion) based on the findings of Baldwin (2009).

We also use Smith-Waterman (SW) algorithm, which was originally developed to find the most similar region between two proteins. The algorithm looks for the longest common substring, except that it permits small numbers of penalized editions consisting of insertion, deletion and substitution. We call the best found substring the 'SW aligned sequence'. In this experiment, we consider the number of matched words and the number of penalties in the SW aligned sequence as features.

Results for the string similarity features are shown in Table 1. Since the string similarity feature scores do not take the entailment direction into account, i.e. there is a single set of feature scores for each text fragment pair as there is no distinction between forward and backward entailment, and they are not suited for standalone use in compositional classification. We do, however, include these scores in Table 1 to illustrate how with the compositional approach using the same set of features for forward and backward ultimately results in a classification of test pairs as either bidirectional or no_entailment.

When individual string similarity features are added to the word alignment features, minor gains in accuracy are achieved over the word alignment features alone, +1% for S1, +0.6% for S2 and +0.8% for S3 (= Levenstein).

5 Possible Additions: Dictionary Features

We hypothesize that when there is no entailment between the two sentences, the aligner may not accurately align words. An on-line dictionary containing lemmatized words, such as Panlex (Baldwin and Colowick, 2010), could be used to avoid errors in such cases. Dictionary-based feature scores based on the presence or absence of alignments in the dictionary could then be applied.

6 Conclusions

This paper describes a compositional cross-lingual approach to CLTE with experiments carried out for the German-English language pair. Our results showed that in the first stages of binary classification as *forward* and *backward*, the word alignment features alone achieved good accuracy but when combined suffer severely. Accuracy of the approach using word alignment features could benefit from a more directional multi-class classification as opposed to the compositional approach we used. In addition, results showed minor increases in accuracy can be achieved using string similarity measures.

Acknowledgments

This work was supported by the Australian Research Council.

References

Timothy Baldwin and Jonathan Pool Susan M. Colowick. 2010. Panlex and lextract: Translating all words of all languages of the world. In *Proceedings of the 23rd International Conference on Computational Linguistics: Demonstrations*, pages 37–40.

Timothy Baldwin. 2009. The hare and the tortoise: Speed and reliability in translation retrieval. *Machine Translation*, 23(4):195–240.

L. Bentivogli, I. Dagan, H. T. Dang, D. Giampiccolo, and B. Magnini. 2009. The fifth PASCAL recognizing textual entailment challenge. In *TAC 2009 Workshop Proceedings*, Gaithersburg, MD.

L. Bentivogli, P. Clark, I. Dagan, H. T. Dang, and D. Giampiccolo. 2010. The sixth PASCAL recognizing textual entailment challenge. In *TAC 2010 Workshop Proceedings*, Gaithersburg, MD.

Spandana Gella, Bahar Salehi, Marco Lui, Karl Grieser, Paul Cook, and Timothy Baldwin. to appear. Integrating predictions from multiple domains and feature sets for estimating semantic textual similarity. In *Proceedings of *SEM 2013 Shared Task STS.*

Philipp Koehn, Hieu Hoang, Alexandra Birch, Chris Callison-Burch, Marcello Federico, Nicola Bertoldi, Brooke Cowan, Wade Shen, Christine Moran, Richard Zens, Chris Dyer, Ondrej Bojar, Alexandra Constantin, and Evan HerbstHieu Hoang. 2007. Moses: Open Source Toolkit for Statistical Machine Translation. In *Annual Meeting of the Association for Computational Linguistics (ACL), demonstration session*, Prague, Czech Republic, June.

Philipp Koehn. 2005. Europarl: A parallel corpus for statistical machine translation. In *Proceedings of the 10th Machine Translation Summit*, Phuket, Thailand.

Vladimir I Levenshtein. 1966. Binary codes capable of correcting deletions, insertions and reversals. In *Soviet physics doklady*, volume 10, page 707.

Y. Mehdad, M. Negri, and M. Federico. 2010. Towards cross-lingual textual entailment. In *Proceedings of NAACL-HLT.*

Y. Mehdad, M. Negri, and M. Federico. 2011. Using parallel corpora for cross-lingual textual entailment. In *Proceedings of ACL-HLT 2011.*

Yashar Mehdad, Matteo Negri, and Jose G. C. de Souza. 2012. Fbk: Cross-lingual textual entailment with-out translation. In *Proceedings of the 6th International Workshop on Semantic Evaluation (SemEval2012).*

M. Negri, L. Bentivogli, Y. Mehdad, D. Giampiccolo, and A. Marchetti. 2011. Divide and conquer: Crowdsourcing the creation of cross-lingual textual entailment corpora. In *Proceedings of EMNLP 2011.*

Matteo Negri, Alessandro Marchetti, Yashar Mehdad, Luisa Bentivogli, and Danilo Giampiccolo. 2012. Semeval-2012 task 8: Cross-lingual textual entailment for content synchronization. In *First Joint Conference on Lexical and Computational Semantics*, pages 399–407, Montreal, Canada.

Franz Josef Och, Christoph Tillmann, and Hermann Ney. 1999. Improved alignment models for statistical machine translation. In *Proceedings of the 1999 Joint SIGDAT Conference on Empirical Methods in Natural Language Processing and Very Large Corpora*, pages 20–28, College Park, MD.

Bahar Salehi and Paul Cook. to appear. Predicting the compositionality of multiword expressions using translations in multiple languages. In *Proceedings of the Second Joint Conference on Lexical and Computational Semantics (*SEM 2013).*

Temple F Smith and Michael S Waterman. 1981. The identification of common molecular subsequences. *Journal of Molecular Biology*, 147:195–197.

SemEval-2013 Task 4: Free Paraphrases of Noun Compounds

Iris Hendrickx
Radboud University Nijmegen &
Universidade de Lisboa
iris@clul.ul.pt

Zornitsa Kozareva
University of Southern California
kozareva@isi.edu

Preslav Nakov
QCRI, Qatar Foundation
pnakov@qf.org.qa

Diarmuid Ó Séaghdha
University of Cambridge
do242@cam.ac.uk

Stan Szpakowicz
University of Ottawa &
Polish Academy of Sciences
szpak@eecs.uottawa.ca

Tony Veale
University College Dublin
tony.veale@ucd.ie

Abstract

In this paper, we describe SemEval-2013 Task 4: the definition, the data, the evaluation and the results. The task is to capture some of the meaning of English noun compounds via paraphrasing. Given a two-word noun compound, the participating system is asked to produce an explicitly ranked list of its free-form paraphrases. The list is automatically compared and evaluated against a similarly ranked list of paraphrases proposed by human annotators, recruited and managed through Amazon's Mechanical Turk. The comparison of raw paraphrases is sensitive to syntactic and morphological variation. The "gold" ranking is based on the relative popularity of paraphrases among annotators. To make the ranking more reliable, highly similar paraphrases are grouped, so as to downplay superficial differences in syntax and morphology. Three systems participated in the task. They all beat a simple baseline on one of the two evaluation measures, but not on both measures. This shows that the task is difficult.

1 Introduction

A noun compound (NC) is a sequence of nouns which act as a single noun (Downing, 1977), as in these examples: *colon cancer, suppressor protein, tumor suppressor protein, colon cancer tumor suppressor protein*, etc. This type of compounding is highly productive in English. NCs comprise 3.9% and 2.6% of all tokens in the Reuters corpus and the British National Corpus (BNC), respectively (Baldwin and Tanaka, 2004).

The frequency spectrum of compound types follows a Zipfian distribution (Ó Séaghdha, 2008), so many NC tokens belong to a "long tail" of low-frequency types. More than half of the two-noun types in the BNC occur exactly once (Kim and Baldwin, 2006). Their high frequency and high productivity make robust NC interpretation an important goal for broad-coverage semantic processing of English texts. Systems which ignore NCs may give up on salient information about the semantic relationships implicit in a text. Compositional interpretation is also the only way to achieve broad NC coverage, because it is not feasible to list in a lexicon all compounds which one is likely to encounter. Even for relatively frequent NCs occurring 10 times or more in the BNC, static English dictionaries provide only 27% coverage (Tanaka and Baldwin, 2003).

In many natural language processing applications it is important to understand the syntax and semantics of NCs. NCs often are structurally similar, but have very different meaning. Consider *caffeine headache* and *ice-cream headache*: a lack of caffeine causes the former, an excess of ice-cream – the latter. Different interpretations can lead to different inferences, query expansion, paraphrases, translations, and so on. A question answering system may have to determine whether *protein acting as a tumor suppressor* is an accurate paraphrase for *tumor suppressor protein*. An information extraction system might need to decide whether *neck vein thrombosis* and *neck thrombosis* can co-refer in the same document. A machine translation system might paraphrase the unknown compound *WTO Geneva headquarters* as *WTO headquarters located in Geneva*.

*Second Joint Conference on Lexical and Computational Semantics (*SEM), Volume 2: Seventh International Workshop on Semantic Evaluation (SemEval 2013)*, pages 138–143, Atlanta, Georgia, June 14-15, 2013.

Research on the automatic interpretation of NCs has focused mainly on common two-word NCs. The usual task is to classify the semantic relation underlying a compound with either one of a small number of predefined relation labels or a paraphrase from an open vocabulary. Examples of the former take on classification include (Moldovan et al., 2004; Girju, 2007; Ó Séaghdha and Copestake, 2008; Tratz and Hovy, 2010). Examples of the latter include (Nakov, 2008b; Nakov, 2008a; Nakov and Hearst, 2008; Butnariu and Veale, 2008) and a previous NC paraphrasing task at SemEval-2010 (Butnariu et al., 2010), upon which the task described here builds.

The assumption of a small inventory of predefined relations has some advantages – parsimony and generalization – but at the same time there are limitations on expressivity and coverage. For example, the NCs *headache pills* and *fertility pills* would be assigned the same semantic relation (*PURPOSE*) in most inventories, but their relational semantics are quite different (Downing, 1977). Furthermore, the definitions given by human subjects can involve rich and specific meanings. For example, Downing (1977) reports that a subject defined the NC *oil bowl* as "the bowl into which the oil in the engine is drained during an oil change", compared to which a minimal interpretation *bowl for oil* seems very reductive. In view of such arguments, linguists such as Downing (1977), Ryder (1994) and Coulson (2001) have argued for a fine-grained, essentially open-ended space of interpretations.

The idea of working with fine-grained paraphrases for NC semantics has recently grown in popularity among NLP researchers (Butnariu and Veale, 2008; Nakov and Hearst, 2008; Nakov, 2008a). Task 9 at SemEval-2010 (Butnariu et al., 2010) was devoted to this methodology. In that previous work, the paraphrases provided by human subjects were required to fit a restrictive template admitting only verbs and prepositions occurring between the NC's constituent nouns. Annotators recruited through Amazon Mechanical Turk were asked to provide paraphrases for the dataset of NCs. The gold standard for each NC was the ranked list of paraphrases given by the annotators; this reflects the idea that a compound's meaning can be described in different ways, at different levels of granularity and capturing different interpretations in the case of ambiguity.

For example, a *plastic saw* could be a *saw made of plastic* or a *saw for cutting plastic*. Systems participating in the task were given the set of attested paraphrases for each NC, and evaluated according to how well they could reproduce the humans' ranking.

The design of this task, SemEval-2013 Task 4, is informed by previous work on compound annotation and interpretation. It is also influenced by similar initiatives, such as the English Lexical Substitution task at SemEval-2007 (McCarthy and Navigli, 2007), and by various evaluation exercises in the fields of paraphrasing and machine translation. We build on SemEval-2010 Task 9, extending the task's flexibility in a number of ways. The restrictions on the form of annotators' paraphrases was relaxed, giving us a rich dataset of close-to-freeform paraphrases (Section 3). Rather than ranking a set of attested paraphrases, systems must now both generate and rank their paraphrases; the task they perform is essentially the same as what the annotators were asked to do. This new setup required us to innovate in terms of evaluation measures (Section 4).

We anticipate that the dataset and task will be of broad interest among those who study lexical semantics. We believe that the overall progress in the field will significantly benefit from a public-domain set of free-style NC paraphrases. That is why our primary objective is the challenging endeavour of preparing and releasing such a dataset to the research community. The common evaluation task which we establish will also enable researchers to compare their algorithms and their empirical results.

2 Task description

This is an English NC interpretation task, which explores the idea of interpreting the semantics of NCs via free paraphrases. Given a noun-noun compound such as *air filter*, the participating systems are asked to produce an explicitly ranked list of free paraphrases, as in the following example:

1 filter for air
2 filter of air
3 filter that cleans the air
4 filter which makes air healthier
5 a filter that removes impurities from the air
...

Such a list is then automatically compared and evaluated against a similarly ranked list of paraphrases proposed by human annotators, recruited and managed via Amazon's Mechanical Turk. The comparison of raw paraphrases is sensitive to syntactic and morphological variation. The ranking of paraphrases is based on their relative popularity among different annotators. To make the ranking more reliable, highly similar paraphrases are grouped so as to downplay superficial differences in syntax and morphology.

3 Data collection

We used Amazon's *Mechanical Turk* service to collect diverse paraphrases for a range of "gold-standard" NCs.[1] We paid the workers a small fee ($0.10) per compound, for which they were asked to provide five paraphrases. Each paraphrase should contain the two nouns of the compound (in singular or plural inflectional forms, but not in another derivational form), an intermediate non-empty linking phrase and optional preceding or following terms. The paraphrasing terms could have any part of speech, so long as the resulting paraphrase was a well-formed noun phrase headed by the NC's head.

We gave the workers feedback during data collection if they appeared to have misunderstood the nature of the task. Once raw paraphrases had been collected from all workers, we collated them into a spreadsheet, and we merged identical paraphrases in order to calculate their overall frequencies. Ill-formed paraphrases – those violating the syntactic restrictions described above – were manually removed following a consensus decision-making procedure; every paraphrase was checked by at least two task organizers. We did not require that the paraphrases be semantically felicitous, but we performed minor edits on the remaining paraphrases if they contained obvious typos.

The remaining well-formed paraphrases were sorted by frequency separately for each NC. The most frequent paraphrases for a compound are assigned the highest rank 0, those with the next-highest frequency are given a rank of 1, and so on.

[1]Since the annotation on Mechanical Turk was going slowly, we also recruited four other annotators to do the same work, following exactly the same instructions.

	Total	**Min / Max / Avg**
Trial/Train (174 NCs)		
paraphrases	6,069	1 / 287 / 34.9
unique paraphrases	4,255	1 / 105 / 24.5
Test (181 NCs)		
paraphrases	9,706	24 / 99 / 53.6
unique paraphrases	8,216	21 / 80 / 45.4

Table 1: Statistics of the trial and test datasets: the total number of paraphrases with and without duplicates, and the minimum / maximum / average per noun compound.

Paraphrases with a frequency of 1 – proposed for a given NC by only one annotator – always occupy the lowest rank on the list for that compound.

We used 174+181 noun-noun compounds from the NC dataset of Ó Séaghdha (2007). The trial dataset, which we initially released to the participants, consisted of 4,255 human paraphrases for 174 noun-noun pairs; this dataset was also the training dataset. The test dataset comprised paraphrases for 181 noun-noun pairs. The "gold standard" contained 9,706 paraphrases of which 8,216 were unique for those 181 NCs. Further statistics on the datasets are presented in Table 1.

Compared with the data collected for the SemEval-2010 Task 9 on the interpretation of noun compounds, the data collected for this new task have a far greater range of variety and richness. For example, the following (selected) paraphrases for *work area* vary from parsimonious to expansive:

- area for work
- area of work
- area where work is done
- area where work is performed
- ...
- an area cordoned off for persons responsible for work
- an area where construction work is carried out
- an area where work is accomplished and done
- area where work is conducted
- office area assigned as a work space
- ...

4 Scoring

Noun compounding is a generative aspect of language, but so too is the process of NC interpretation: human speakers typically generate a range of possible interpretations for a given compound, each emphasizing a different aspect of the relationship between the nouns. Our evaluation framework reflects the belief that there is rarely a single right answer for a given noun-noun pairing. Participating systems are thus expected to demonstrate some generativity of their own, and are scored not just on the accuracy of individual interpretations, but on the overall breadth of their output.

For evaluation, we provided a scorer implemented, for good portability, as a Java class. For each noun compound to be evaluated, the scorer compares a list of system-suggested paraphrases against a "gold-standard" reference list, compiled and rank-ordered from the paraphrases suggested by our human annotators. The score assigned to each system is the mean of the system's performance across all test compounds. Note that the scorer removes all determiners from both the reference and the test paraphrases, so a system is neither punished for not reproducing a determiner or rewarded for producing the same determiners.

The scorer can match words identically or non-identically. A match of two identical words W_{gold} and W_{test} earns a score of 1.0. There is a partial score of $(2\ |P|\ /\ (|PW_{gold}|\ +\ |PW_{test}|))^2$ for a match of two words PW_{gold} and PW_{test} that are not identical but share a common prefix P, $|P| > 2$, e.g., $wmatch(cutting, cuts) = (6/11)^2 = 0.297$.

Two n-grams $N_{gold} = [GW_1, \ldots, GW_n]$ and $N_{test} = [TW_1, \ldots, TW_n]$ can be matched if $wmatch(GW_i, TW_i) > 0$ for all i in $1..n$. The score assigned to the match of these two n-grams is then $\sum_i wmatch(GW_i, TW_i)$. For every n-gram $N_{test} = [TW_1, \ldots, TW_n]$ in a system-generated paraphrase, the scorer finds a matching n-gram $N_{gold} = [GW_1, \ldots, GW_n]$ in the reference paraphrase $Para_{gold}$ which maximizes this sum.

The overall n-gram overlap score for a reference paraphrase $Para_{gold}$ and a system-generated paraphrase $Para_{test}$ is the sum of the score calculated for all n-grams in $Para_{test}$, where n ranges from 1 to the size of $Para_{test}$.

This overall score is then normalized by dividing by the maximum value among the n-gram overlap score for $Para_{gold}$ compared with itself and the n-gram overlap score for $Para_{test}$ compared with itself. This normalization step produces a paraphrase match score in the range [0.0 – 1.0]. It punishes a paraphrase $Para_{test}$ for both over-generating (containing more words than are found in $Para_{gold}$) and under-generating (containing fewer words than are found in $Para_{gold}$). In other words, $Para_{test}$ should ideally reproduce everything in $Para_{gold}$, and nothing more or less.

The reference paraphrases in the "gold standard" are ordered by rank; the highest rank is assigned to the paraphrases which human judges suggested most often. The rank of a reference paraphrase matters because a good participating system will aim to reproduce the top-ranked "gold-standard" paraphrases as produced by human judges. The scorer assigns a multiplier of $R/(R+n)$ to reference paraphrases at rank n; this multiplier asymptotically approaches 0 for the higher values of n of ever lower-ranked paraphrases. We choose a default setting of $R = 8$, so that a reference paraphrase at rank 0 (the highest rank) has a multiplier of 1, while a reference paraphrase at rank 5 has a multiplier of $8/13 = 0.615$.

When a system-generated paraphrase $Para_{test}$ is matched with a reference paraphrase $Para_{gold}$, their normalized n-gram overlap score is scaled by the rank multiplier attaching to the rank of $Para_{gold}$ relative to the other reference paraphrases provided by human judges. The scorer automatically chooses the reference paraphrase $Para_{gold}$ for a test paraphrase $Para_{test}$ so as to maximize this product of normalized n-gram overlap score and rank multiplier.

The overall score assigned to each system for a specific compound is calculated in two different ways: using *isomorphic matching* of suggested paraphrases to the "gold-standard's" reference paraphrases (on a *one-to-one* basis); and using *non-isomorphic matching* of system's paraphrases to the "gold-standard's" reference paraphrases (in a potentially *many-to-one* mapping).

Isomorphic matching rewards both precision and recall. It rewards a system for accurately reproducing the paraphrases suggested by human judges, and for reproducing as many of these as it can, and in much the same order.

In isomorphic mode, system's paraphrases are matched 1-to-1 with reference paraphrases on a first-come first-matched basis, so ordering can be crucial.

Non-isomorphic matching rewards only precision. It rewards a system for accurately reproducing the top-ranked human paraphrases in the "gold standard". A system will achieve a higher score in a non-isomorphic match if it reproduces the top-ranked human paraphrases as opposed to lower-ranked human paraphrases. The ordering of system's paraphrases is thus not important in non-isomorphic matching.

Each system is evaluated using the scorer in both modes, *isomorphic* and *non-isomorphic*. Systems which aim only for precision should score highly on non-isomorphic match mode, but poorly in isomorphic match mode. Systems which aim for precision *and* recall will face a more substantial challenge, likely reflected in their scores.

A naïve baseline

We decided to allow preposition-only paraphrases, which are abundant in the paraphrases suggested by human judges in the crowdsourcing Mechanical Turk collection process. This abundance means that the top-ranked paraphrase for a given compound is often a preposition-only phrase, or one of a small number of very popular paraphrases such as *used for* or *used in*. It is thus straightforward to build a naïve baseline generator which we can expect to score reasonably on this task, at least in *non-isomorphic matching* mode. For each test compound *M H*, the baseline system generates the following paraphrases, in this precise order: *H of M*, *H in M*, *H for M*, *H with M*, *H on M*, *H about M*, *H has M*, *H to M*, *H used for M*, *H used in M*.

This naïve baseline is truly unsophisticated. No attempt is made to order paraphrases by their corpus frequencies or by their frequencies in the training data. The same sequence of paraphrases is generated for each and every test compound.

5 Results

Three teams participated in the challenge, and all their systems were supervised. The MELODI system relied on semantic vector space model built from the UKWAC corpus (window-based, 5 words). It used only the features of the right-hand head noun to train a maximum entropy classifier.

Team	isomorphic	non-isomorphic
SFS	23.1	17.9
IIITH	23.1	25.8
MELODI-Primary	13.0	54.8
MELODI-Contrast	13.6	53.6
Naive Baseline	*13.8*	*40.6*

Table 2: Results for the participating systems; the baseline outputs the same paraphrases for all compounds.

The IIITH system used the probabilities of the preposition co-occurring with a relation to identify the class of the noun compound. To collect statistics, it used Google n-grams, BNC and ANC.

The SFS system extracted templates and fillers from the training data, which it then combined with a four-gram language model and a MaxEnt reranker. To find similar compounds, they used Lin's WordNet similarity. They further used statistics from the English Gigaword and the Google n-grams.

Table 2 shows the performance of the participating systems, SFS, IIITH and MELODI, and the naïve baseline. The baseline shows that it is relatively easy to achieve a moderately good score in non-isomorphic match mode by generating a fixed set of paraphrases which are both common and generic: two of the three participating systems, SFS and IIITH, under-perform the naïve baseline in non-isomorphic match mode, but outperform it in isomorphic mode. The only system to surpass this baseline in non-isomorphic match mode is the MELODI system; yet, it under-performs against the same baseline in isomorphic match mode. No participating team submitted a system which would outperform the naïve baseline in both modes.

6 Conclusions

The conclusions we draw from the experience of organizing the task are mixed. Participation was reasonable but not large, suggesting that NC paraphrasing remains a niche interest – though we believe it deserves more attention among the broader lexical semantics community and hope that the availability of our freeform paraphrase dataset will attract a wider audience in the future.

We also observed a varied response from our annotators in terms of embracing their freedom to generate complex and rich paraphrases; there are many possible reasons for this including laziness, time pressure and the fact that short paraphrases are often very appropriate paraphrases. The results obtained by our participants were also modest, demonstrating that compound paraphrasing is both a difficult task and a novel one that has not yet been "solved".

Acknowledgments

This work has partially supported by a small but effective grant from Amazon; the credit allowed us to hire sufficiently many Turkers – thanks! And a thank-you to our additional annotators Dave Carter, Chris Fournier and Colette Joubarne for their complete sets of paraphrases of the noun compounds in the test data.

References

Timothy Baldwin and Takaaki Tanaka. 2004. Translation by machine of complex nominals: Getting it right. *Proc. ACL04 Workshop on Multiword Expressions: Integrating Processing*, Barcelona, Spain, 24-31.

Cristina Butnariu and Tony Veale. 2008. A concept-centered approach to noun-compound interpretation. *Proc. 22nd International Conference on Computational Linguistics (COLING-08)*, Manchester, UK, 81-88.

Cristina Butnariu, Su Nam Kim, Preslav Nakov, Diarmuid Ó Séaghdha, Stan Szpakowicz, and Tony Veale. 2010. SemEval-2010 Task 9: The interpretation of noun compounds using paraphrasing verbs and prepositions. *Proc. 5th International ACL Workshop on Semantic Evaluation*, Uppsala, Sweden, 39-44.

Seana Coulson. 2001. *Semantic Leaps: Frame-Shifting and Conceptual Blending in Meaning Construction*. Cambridge University Press, Cambridge, UK.

Pamela Downing. 1977. On the creation and use of English compound nouns. *Language*, **53**(4): 810-842.

Roxana Girju. 2007. Improving the interpretation of noun phrases with cross-linguistic information. *Proc. 45th Annual Meeting of the Association of Computational Linguistics*, Prague, Czech Republic, 568-575.

Su Nam Kim and Timothy Baldwin. 2006. Interpreting semantic relations in noun compounds via verb semantics. *Proc. ACL-06 Main Conference Poster Session*, Sydney, Australia, 491-498.

Diana McCarthy and Roberto Navigli. 2007. Semeval-2007 task 10: English lexical substitution task. *Proc. Fourth International Workshop on Semantic Evaluations (SemEval-2007)*, Prague, Czech Republic, 48-53.

Dan Moldovan, Adriana Badulescu, Marta Tatu, Daniel Antohe, and Roxana Girju. 2004. Models for the semantic classification of noun phrases. Dan Moldovan and Roxana Girju, eds., *HLT-NAACL 2004: Workshop on Computational Lexical Semantics*, Boston, MA, USA, 60-67.

Preslav Nakov and Marti Hearst. 2008. Solving relational similarity problems using the Web as a corpus. *Proc. 46th Annual Meeting of the Association for Computational Linguistics ACL-08*, Columbus, OH, USA, 452-460.

Preslav Nakov. 2008a. Improved statistical machine translation using monolingual paraphrases. *Proc. 18th European Conference on Artificial Intelligence ECAI-08*, Patras, Greece, 338-342.

Preslav Nakov. 2008b. Noun compound interpretation using paraphrasing verbs: Feasibility study. *Proc. 13th International Conference on Artificial Intelligence: Methodology, Systems, Applications AIMSA-08*, Varna, Bulgaria, *Lecture Notes in Computer Science* **5253**, Springer, 103-117.

Diarmuid Ó Séaghdha. 2007. Designing and Evaluating a Semantic Annotation Scheme for Compound Nouns. In *Proceedings of the 4th Corpus Linguistics Conference*, Birmingham, UK.

Diarmuid Ó Séaghdha. 2008. *Learning compound noun semantics*. Ph.D. thesis, Computer Laboratory, University of Cambridge. Published as University of Cambridge Computer Laboratory Technical Report 735.

Diarmuid Ó Séaghdha and Ann Copestake. 2009. Using lexical and relational similarity to classify semantic relations. *Proc. 12th Conference of the European Chapter of the Association for Computational Linguistics EACL-09*, Athens, Greece, 621-629.

Diarmuid Ó Séaghdha and Ann Copestake. 2008. Semantic classification with distributional kernels. In *Proc. 22nd International Conference on Computational Linguistics (COLING-08)*, Manchester, UK.

Mary Ellen Ryder. 1994. *Ordered Chaos: The Interpretation of English Noun-Noun Compounds*. University of California Press, Berkeley, CA, USA.

Takaaki Tanaka and Tim Baldwin. 2003. Noun-noun compound machine translation: A feasibility study on shallow processing. *Proc. ACL-2003 Workshop on Multiword Expressions: Analysis, Acquisition and Treatment*, Sapporo, Japan, 17-24.

Stephen Tratz and Eduard Hovy. 2010. A taxonomy, dataset, and classifier for automatic noun compound interpretation. *Proc. 48th Annual Meeting of the Association for Computational Linguistics ACL-10*, Uppsala, Sweden, 678-687.

MELODI: A Supervised Distributional Approach for Free Paraphrasing of Noun Compounds

Tim Van de Cruys
IRIT, CNRS
tim.vandecruys@irit.fr

Stergos Afantenos
IRIT, Toulouse University
stergos.afantenos@irit.fr

Philippe Muller
IRIT, Toulouse University
philippe.muller@irit.fr

Abstract

This paper describes the system submitted by the MELODI team for the SemEval-2013 Task 4: Free Paraphrases of Noun Compounds (Hendrickx et al., 2013). Our approach combines the strength of an unsupervised distributional word space model with a supervised maximum-entropy classification model; the distributional model yields a feature representation for a particular compound noun, which is subsequently used by the classifier to induce a number of appropriate paraphrases.

1 Introduction

Interpretation of noun compounds is making explicit the relation between the component nouns, for instance that *running shoes* are shoes used in running activities, while *leather shoes* are made from leather. The relations can have very different meanings, and existing work either postulates a fixed set of relations (Tratz and Hovy, 2010) or relies on appropriate descriptions of the relations, through constrained verbal paraphrases (Butnariu et al., 2010) or unconstrained paraphrases as in the present campaign. The latter is much simpler for annotation purposes, but raises difficult challenges involving not only compound interpretation but also paraphrase evaluation and ranking.

In terms of constrained verbal paraphrases Wubben (2010), for example, uses a supervised memory-based ranker using features from the Google *n*-gram corpus as well as WordNet. Nulty and Costello (2010) rank paraphrases of compounds according to the number of times they co-occurred with other paraphrases for other compounds. They use these co-occurrences to compute conditional probabilities estimating is-a relations between paraphrases. Li et al. (2010) provide a hybrid system which combines a Bayesian algorithm exploiting Google *n*-grams, a score which captures human preferences at the tail distribution of the training data, as well as a metric that captures pairwise paraphrase preferences.

Our methodology consists of two steps. First, an unsupervised distributional word space model is constructed, which yields a feature representation for a particular compound. The feature representation is then used by a maximum entropy classifier to induce a number of appropriate paraphrases.

2 Methodology

2.1 Distributional word space model

In order to induce appropriate feature representations for the various noun compounds, we start by constructing a standard distributional word space model for nouns. We construct a co-occurrence matrix of the 5K most frequent nouns[1] by the 2K most frequent context words[2], which occur in a window of 5 words to the left and right of the target word. The bare frequencies of the word-context matrix are weighted using pointwise mutual information (Church and Hanks, 1990).

Next, we compute a joint, compositional representation of the noun compound, combining the se-

[1] making sure all nouns that appear in the training and test set are included

[2] excluding the 50 most frequent context words as stop words

*Second Joint Conference on Lexical and Computational Semantics (*SEM), Volume 2: Seventh International Workshop on Semantic Evaluation (SemEval 2013)*, pages 144–147, Atlanta, Georgia, June 14-15, 2013.

mantics of the head noun with the modifier noun. To do so, we make use of a simple vector-based multiplicative model of compositionality, as proposed by Mitchell and Lapata (2008). In order to compute the compositional representation of a compound noun, this model takes the elementwise multiplication of the vectors for the head noun and the modifier noun, i.e.

$$p_i = u_i v_i$$

for each feature i. The resulting features are used as input to our next classification step.

We compare the performance of the abovementioned compositional model with a simpler model that only takes into account the semantics of the head noun. This model only uses the context features for the head noun as input to our second classification step. This means that the model only takes into account the semantics of the head noun, and ignores the semantics of the modifier noun.

2.2 Maximum entropy classification

The second step of our paraphrasing system consists of a supervised maximum entropy classification approach. Training vectors for each noun compound from the training set are constructed according to the approach described in the previous section. The (non-zero) context features yielded by the first step are used as input for the maximum entropy classifier, together with the appropriate paraphrase labels and the label counts (used to weight the instances), which are extracted from the training set.

We then deploy the model in order to induce a probability distribution over the various paraphrase labels. Every paraphrase label above a threshold ϕ is considered an appropriate paraphrase. Using a portion of held-out training data (20%), we set $\phi = 0.01$ for our official submission. In this paper, we show a number of results using different thresholds.

2.3 Set of paraphrases labels

For our classification approach to work, we need to extract an appropriate set of paraphrase labels from the training data. In order to create this set, we substitute the nouns that appear in the training set's paraphrases by dummy variables. Table 1 gives an example of three different paraphrases and the resulting paraphrase labels after substitution. Note that we did not apply any NLP techniques to properly deal with inflected words.

We apply a frequency threshold of 2 (counted over all the instances), so we discard paraphrase labels that appear only once in the training set. This gives us a total of 285 possible paraphrase labels.

One possible disadvantage of this supervised approach is a loss of recall on unseen paraphrases. A rough estimation shows that our set of training labels accounts for only 25% of the similarly constructed labels extracted from the test set. However, the most frequently used paraphrase labels are present in both training and test set, so this does not prevent our system to come up with a number of suitable paraphrases for the test set.

2.4 Implementational details

All frequency co-occurrence information has been extracted from the ukWaC corpus (Baroni et al., 2009). The corpus has been part of speech tagged and lemmatized with Stanford Part-Of-Speech Tagger (Toutanova and Manning, 2000; Toutanova et al., 2003). Distributional word space algorithms have been implemented in Python. The maximum entropy classifier was implemented using the Maximum Entropy Modeling Toolkit for Python and C++ (Le, 2004).

3 Results

Table 2 shows the results of the different systems in terms of the isomorphic and non-isomorphic evaluation measures defined by the task organizers (Hendrickx et al., 2013). For comparison, we include a number of baselines. The first baseline assigns the two most frequent paraphrase labels (*Y of X*, *Y for X*) to each test instance; the second baseline assigns the four most frequent paraphrase labels (*Y of X*, *Y for X*, *Y on X*, *Y in X*); and the third baseline assigns all of the possible 285 paraphrase labels as correct answer for each test instance.

For both our primary system (the multiplicative model) and our contrastive system (the head noun model), we vary the threshold used to select the final set of paraphrases. A threshold $\phi = 0.01$ results in a smaller set of paraphrases, whereas a threshold of $\phi = 0.001$ results in a broad set of paraphrases. Our official submission uses the former threshold.

compound	**paraphrase**	**paraphrase label**
textile company	company that makes textiles	Y that makes Xs
textile company	company that produces textiles	Y that produces Xs
textile company	company in textile industry	Y in X industry

Table 1: Example of induced paraphrase labels

model	ϕ	isomorphic	non-isomorphic
baseline (2)	–	.058	.808
baseline (4)	–	.090	.633
baseline (all)	–	.332	.200
multiplicative	.01	.130	.548
	.001	.270	.259
head noun	.01	.136	.536
	.001	.277	.302

Table 2: Results

First of all, we note that the different baseline models are able to obtain substantial scores for the different evaluation measures. The first two baselines, which use a limited number of paraphrase labels, perform very well in terms of the non-isomorphic evaluation measure. The third baseline, which uses a very large number of candidate paraphrase labels, gets more balanced results in terms of both the isomorphic and non-isomorphic measure.

Considering our different thresholds, the results of our models are in line with the baseline results. A larger threshold, which results in a smaller number of paraphrase labels, reaches a higher non-isomorphic score. A smaller threshold, which results in a larger number of paraphrase labels, gives more balanced results for the isomorphic and non-isomorphic measure.

There does not seem to be a significant difference between our primary system (multiplicative) and our contrastive system (head noun). For $\phi = 0.01$, the results of both models are very similar; for $\phi = 0.001$, the head noun model reaches slightly better results, in particular for the non-isomorphic score.

Finally, we note that our models do not seem to improve significantly on the baseline scores. For $\phi = 0.001$, the results of our models seem somewhat more balanced compared to the *all* baseline, but the differences are not very large. In general, our systems (in line with the other systems participating in the task) seem to have a hard time beating a number of simple baselines, in terms of the evaluation measures defined by the task.

4 Conclusion

We have presented a system for producing free paraphrases of noun compounds. Our methodology consists of two steps. First, an unsupervised distributional word space model is constructed, which is used to compute a feature representation for a particular compound. The feature representation is then used by a maximum entropy classifier to induce a number of appropriate paraphrases.

Although our models do seem to yield slightly more balanced scores than the baseline models, the differences are not very large. Moreover, there is no substantial difference between our primary multiplicative model, which takes into account the semantics of both head and modifier noun, and our contrastive model, which only uses the semantics of the head noun.

References

Marco Baroni, Silvia Bernardini, Adriano Ferraresi, and Eros Zanchetta. 2009. The wacky wide web: A collection of very large linguistically processed web-crawled corpora. *Language Resources and Evaluation*, 43(3):209–226.

Cristina Butnariu, Su Nam Kim, Preslav Nakov, Diarmuid Ó Séaghdha, Stan Szpakowicz, and Tony Veale. 2010. Semeval-2 task 9: The interpretation of noun compounds using paraphrasing verbs and prepositions. In *Proceedings of the 5th International Workshop on Semantic Evaluation*, pages 39–44, Uppsala, Sweden, July. Association for Computational Linguistics.

Kenneth W. Church and Patrick Hanks. 1990. Word association norms, mutual information & lexicography. *Computational Linguistics*, 16(1):22–29.

Iris Hendrickx, Zornitsa Kozareva, Preslav Nakov, Diarmuid Ó Séaghdha, Stan Szpakowicz, and Tony Veale. 2013. SemEval-2013 task 4: Free paraphrases of noun compounds. In *Proceedings of the International Workshop on Semantic Evaluation*, SemEval '13, June.

Zhang Le. 2004. Maximum entropy modeling toolkit for python and c++. `http://homepages.inf.ed.ac.uk/lzhang10/maxent_toolkit.html`.

Guofu Li, Alejandra Lopez-Fernandez, and Tony Veale. 2010. Ucd-goggle: A hybrid system for noun compound paraphrasing. In *Proceedings of the 5th International Workshop on Semantic Evaluation*, pages 230–233, Uppsala, Sweden, July. Association for Computational Linguistics.

Jeff Mitchell and Mirella Lapata. 2008. Vector-based models of semantic composition. *proceedings of ACL-08: HLT*, pages 236–244.

Paul Nulty and Fintan Costello. 2010. Ucd-pn: Selecting general paraphrases using conditional probability. In *Proceedings of the 5th International Workshop on Semantic Evaluation*, pages 234–237, Uppsala, Sweden, July. Association for Computational Linguistics.

Kristina Toutanova and Christopher D. Manning. 2000. Enriching the knowledge sources used in a maximum entropy part-of-speech tagger. In *Proceedings of the Joint SIGDAT Conference on Empirical Methods in Natural Language Processing and Very Large Corpora (EMNLP/VLC-2000)*, pages 63–70.

Kristina Toutanova, Dan Klein, Christopher Manning, and Yoram Singer. 2003. Feature-rich part-of-speech tagging with a cyclic dependency network. In *Proceedings of HLT-NAACL 2003*, pages 252–259.

Stephen Tratz and Eduard Hovy. 2010. A taxonomy, dataset, and classifier for automatic noun compound interpretation. In *Proceedings of the 48th Annual Meeting of the Association for Computational Linguistics*, pages 678–687, Uppsala, Sweden, July. Association for Computational Linguistics.

Sander Wubben. 2010. Uvt: Memory-based pairwise ranking of paraphrasing verbs. In *Proceedings of the 5th International Workshop on Semantic Evaluation*, pages 260–263, Uppsala, Sweden, July. Association for Computational Linguistics.

SFS-TUE: Compound Paraphrasing with a Language Model and Discriminative Reranking

Yannick Versley
SfS / SFB 833
University of Tübingen
versley@sfs.uni-tuebingen.de

Abstract

This paper presents an approach for generating free paraphrases of compounds (task 4 at SemEval 2013) by decomposing the training data into a collection of templates and fillers and recombining/scoring these based on a generative language model and discriminative MaxEnt reranking.

The system described in this paper achieved the highest score (with a very small margin) in the (default) *isomorphic* setting of the scorer, for which it was optimized, at a disadvantage to the *non-isomorphic* score.

1 Introduction

Compounds are an interesting phenomenon in natural language semantics as they normally realize a semantic relation (between head and modifier noun) that is both highly ambiguous as to the type of relation and usually nonambiguous as to the concepts it relates (namely, those of the two nouns).

Besides inventory-based approaches, where the relation is classified into a fixed number of relations, many researchers have argued that the full variability of the semantic relations inherent in compounds is best captured with paraphrases: Lauer (1995) proposes to use a preposition as a proxy for the meaning of a compound. Finin (1980) and later Nakov (2008) and others propose less restrictive schemes based on paraphrasing verbs.

A previous SemEval task (task 9 in 2010; Butnariu et al., 2009). The most successsful approaches for this task such as Nulty and Costello (2010), Li et al. (2010), and Wubben (2010), or the subsequent approach of Wijaya and Gianfortoni (2011), all make efficient use of both the training data and general evidence from WordNet or statistics derived from large corpora. The paper of Li et al. mentions that solely inducing a global ranking of paraphrasing verbs from the training data (looking which verb is ranked higher in those cases where both were considered for the same compound) yielded higher scores than an unsupervised approach based on the semantic resources, underlining the need to combine training data and resources efficiently.

SemEval 2013 task 4 The present task on providing free paraphrases for noun compounds (Hendrickx et al., 2013) uses a dataset collected from Mechanical Turk workers asked to paraphrase a given compound (without context). Prepositional, verbal, and other paraphrases all occur in the data:

(1) a. *bar* for *wine*
b. *bar* that serves *wine*
c. *bar* where *wine* is sold
d. sweet *vinegar* made from *wine*

In the examples, the words of the compound (*wine bar* and *wine vinegar*, respectively) are put in italics, and other content words in the paraphrase are underlined.

It is clear that certain paraphrases (*X* for *Y*) will be common across many compounds, whereas the ones containing more lexical material will differ even between relatively similar compounds (consider *wine bar* from the example, and *liquor store*, which allows paraphrase c, but not paraphrase b).

*Second Joint Conference on Lexical and Computational Semantics (*SEM), Volume 2: Seventh International Workshop on Semantic Evaluation (SemEval 2013)*, pages 148–152, Atlanta, Georgia, June 14-15, 2013.

2 General Approach

The approach chosen in the SFS-TUE system is based on first retrieving a number of similar compounds, then extracting a set of building blocks (patterns and fillers) from these compounds, recombining these building blocks, and finally ranking the list of potential paraphrases. The final list is post-processed by keeping only one variant of each set of paraphrases that only differ in a determiner (e.g., '*strike* from *air*' and '*strike* from the *air*') in order to make a 1:1 mapping between system response and gold standard possible.

As a first step, the system retrieves the most similar compounds from the training data.

This is achieved Lin's wordnet similarity measure (Lin, 1998) using the implementation in NLTK (Bird et al., 2009). The similarity of two compounds X_1Y_1 and X_2Y_2 is calculated as

$$s_C = \min(sim(X_1, X_2), sim(Y_1, Y_2)) + 0.1 \cdot (sim(X_1, X_2) + sim(Y_1, Y_2))$$

which represents a compromise between requiring that both modifier and head are approximately similar, and still giving a small boost to pairs that have very high modifier similarity but low head similarity, or vice versa. For training, the target compound is excluded from the most-similar compounds list so that candidate construction is only based on actual neighbours.

The paraphrases for the most similar compound entries (such as 2a) are broken down into templates (2b) and fillers (2c), by replacing modifier and head by X and Y, respectively, and other content words by their part-of-speech tag.

(2) a. *bar* that serves *wine*
b. X that VBZ Y
c. VBZ:serve

Conversely, template fillers consist of all the extracted content words, categorized by their part-of-speech. (Part-of-speech tags were assigned using the Stanford POS tagger: Toutanova et al., 2003).

Both paraphrase templates and template fillers are weighted by the product of the similarity value s_C between the target compound and the neighbour, and the total frequency of occurrence in that neighbour's paraphrases. (For example, if Mechanical Turk participants named "*bar that sells wine*" twice and "*bar that serves wine*" once, the total frequency of "*X* that VBZ *Y*" would be three).

type	examples
Y_of	*Y* of *X* (159) / *Y* of the *X* (59) / *Y* of a *X* (47)
Y_for	*Y* for *X* (114) / *Y* for the *X* (33)
Y_VBZ	*Y* that VBZ *X* (91)/ *Y* which VBZ *X* (45)
Y_VBG	*Y* VBG *X* (90) / *Y* VBG the *X*/ *Y* VBG with *X*
Y_VBN	*Y* VBN for *X* (82) / *Y* VBN by *X* (52)
Y_in	*Y* in *X* (31)
Y_on	*Y* on *X* (38)

Table 1: Most frequent paraphrase pattern types and pattern instances

Paraphrase candidates are then constructed by combining any paraphrase templates from a similarity neighbour with any fillers matching the given part-of-speech tag. The list of all candidates is cut down to a shortlist of 512 paraphrase candidates. These are subsequently ranked by assigning features to each of the candidate paraphrases and scoring them using weights learned in a maximum ranker by optimizing a loss derived from the probability of all candidates that have been mentioned at least two times in the training set in proportion to the probability of all candidates that are not part of the training annotation for that compound at all. (Paraphrases that were named only once are not used for the parameter estimation).

After scoring, determiners are removed from the paraphrase string and duplicates are removed from the list. The generated list is cut off to yield at most 60 items.

2.1 Data Sources

As sources of evidence in the fit (or lack thereof) of a given verb (as a suspected template filler) with the two target words of a compounds, we use data derived from the fifth revision of the English Gigaword[1], tokenized, tagged and parsed with the RASP parsing toolchain (Briscoe et al., 2006), and from Google's web n-gram dataset[2].

[1]Robert Parker, David Graff, Junbo Kong, Ke Chen and Kazuaki Maeda (2011): *English Gigaword Fifth Edition*. LDC2011T07, Linguistic Data Consortium, Philadelphia.

[2]Thorsten Brants, Alex Franz (2006): *Web 1T 5-gram Version 1*. LDC2006T13, Linguistic Data Consortium, Philadel-

To reproduce very general estimates of linguistic plausibility, we built a four-gram language model based on the combined text of the English Gigaword and the British National Corpus (Burnard, 1995), using the KenLM toolkit (Heafield, 2011). On the one hand, free paraphrases are quite unrestricted, which means that the language model helps also in the case of more exotic paraphrases such as (1d) in the first section. On the other hand, many of the more specialized aspects of plausibility such as preposition attachment or selectional preferences for subjects and direct objects can be cast as modeling (smoothed) probabilities for a certain class of short surface strings, for which an n-gram model is a useful first approximation.

Using the grammatical relations extracted by the RASP toolkit, we created a database of plausible verb-subject and verb-object combinations, defined as having a positive pointwise mutual information score.

In a similar fashion, we used a list of verbs and the `morphg` morphological realizer (Minnen et al., 2001) to extract all occurrences of the patterns "N PREP N", "N PREP (DET) N" for noun-preposition-noun combinations, and "N *that* VBZ" as well as "N VBN *by*" for finding typical cases of an active or passive verb that modifies a given noun.

2.2 Ranking features

The following properties used to score each paraphrase candidate (using weights learned by the MaxEnt ranker):

- language model score `lm`
  The score assigned by the 4-gram model learned on the English Gigaword and the BNC.

- pattern type `tp=`*`type`*
  The pattern type (usually the first two 'interesting' tokens from the paraphrase template, i.e., filtering out determiners and auxiliaries). A list of the most frequent pattern types can be found in Table 1.

- pattern weight `pat`
  The pattern weight as the sum of the (neighbour similarity times number of occurrences) contribution from each pattern template.

phia.

- linking preposition `prep_`*`prep`*`=`*`type`*
  This feature correlates occurring prepositions (*prep*) to types of patterns, with the goal of learning high feature weights for preposition/type combinations that fit well together. The obvious example for this would be, e.g., that the *of* preposition pattern fits well with *Y_of_X* paraphrases.

- absent preposition `noprep=`*`type`*
  This feature is set when no *X prep Y* or similar pattern could be found.

- subject preference (VBG, VBZ)
  `subj_subj0`, `subj_n_that_vbz`

  object preference (VBN)
  `obj_dobj0`, `obj_n_vbn_by`
  In cases of verbal paraphrases where the compound head is the subject, we can directly check for corpus evidence for the corresponding subject-verb pattern. A similar check is done for verb-object (or verb-patient) patterns in the paraphrases that involve the head in a passive construction.

- frequent/infrequent subject verb (VBG, VBZ)
  `subj_`*`verb`*, `subj_infrequent`
  Some verbs (*belong, come, concern, consist, contain, deal, give, have, involve, make, provide, regard, run, sell, show, use, work*) occur frequent enough that we want to introduce a (data-induced) bias towards or away from them. Other verbs, which are more rare, are treated as a single class in this regard (which means that their goodness of fit is mostly represented through the language model and the selectional preference models).

- frequent/infrequent object verb (VBN)
  a similar distinction is made for a list of verbs that often occur in passive form (*appointed, associated, based, carried, caused, conducted, designed, found, given, held, kept, meant, needed, performed, placed, prepared, produced, provided, related, taken*)

- co-occurrence of filler with *X* (other patterns)
  `other_`*`POS`*`_cooc`, `other_`*`POS`*`_none`
  For pattern types where we cannot use one of

System	isomorphic	non-isom.
SFS	**0.2313**	0.1795
IIITH	0.2309	0.2584
MELODI I	0.1300	**0.5485**
MELODI II	0.1358	0.5360
of+for baseline	0.0472	0.8294

Table 2: Official evaluation results + simple baseline

the selectional preference models, we use a model akin to Pado&Lapata's (2007) syntax-based model that provides association scores based on syntactic dependency arc distance.

3 Evaluation Results

The official evaluation results for the task are summarized in Table 2. Two evaluation scores were used:

- **Isomorphic scoring** maps system paraphrases to (unmapped) paraphrases from the reference dataset, and requires systems to produce the full set of paraphrases gathered from Mechanical Turk workers in order to get a perfect score.
- **Nonisomorphic scoring** scores each system paraphrase with respect to the best match from the reference dataset, and averages these scores over all system paraphrases. A system that performs well in nonisomorphic scoring does not need to produce all paraphrases, but will get punished for producing non-reliable paraphrases.

As apparent from the table, systems either score well on the isomorphic score (producing a large number of paraphrases in order to get good coverage of the range of expressions in the reference) or on the non-isomorphic score (producing a smaller number of paraphrases that are highly ranked in the reference). The difference is also apparent in the case of a hypothetical system that produces "Y for X" and and "Y of X" as the paraphrase for any compound (e.g. *bar for wine* and *bar of wine* for *wine bar*). Because these paraphrases occur quite often as most frequent responses, this would yield a high *non-isomorphic* score, but an *isomorphic* score that is very low.

During system development, the relative quality of system paraphrases for each compound was estimated using Maximum Average Precision (MAP)

Compound	closest neighbour	MAP	R_{max}
share holding	withdrawal line	1.000	0.800
union power	community life	1.000	0.750
truth value	accounting treatment	1.000	0.750
amateur championship	computer study	1.000	0.750
government authority	unit manager	1.000	0.680
wine bar	computer industry	0.000	0.040
mammoth task	consumer benefit	0.000	0.040
obstacle course	work area	0.000	0.040
operating system	telephone system	0.000	0.000
deadweight burden	divorce rate	0.000	0.000

Table 3: Best and worst compounds in cross-validation on the training data

and the total achievable recall (R_{max}) of the generated paraphrase list. Table 3 shows the MAP score (for paraphrases that were listed at least two times) and achievable recall (for all paraphrases). These measures, unlike the official scores, do not attempt to deal with paraphrase variants (e.g. different prepositions for a verbal paraphrase), but are robust and simple enough to give an impression of the quality of the system response.

As can be seen by looking at the *achievable recall* figures, it is not always the case that all reference paraphrases are in the list that is ranked by the MaxEnt model. In the lower half of table 3, we see that for these cases, the most-similar item selected by the WordNet-based similarity measure is not very close semantically; whether this is the only influencing factor remains to be seen since some of the best-ranked items in the upper half are also abstract concepts with only-somewhat-close neighbours. Future work would therefore have to cover both improvements to the similarity measure itself and to the ranking mechanism used for the reranking of generated paraphrases.

Acknowledgments

The author's work was funded as part of SFB 833 ("*Constitution of Meaning*") by the Deutsche Forschungsgemeinschaft (DFG).

References

Bird, S., Loper, E., and Klein, E. (2009). *Natural Language Processing with Python*. O'Reilly Media Inc.

Briscoe, E., Carroll, J., and Watson, R. (2006). The second release of the RASP system. In *Proceedings of the COLING/ACL 2006 Interactive Presentation Sessions*.

Burnard, L., editor (1995). *Users Reference Guide British National Corpus Version 1.0*. Oxford University Computing Service.

Butnariu, C., Kim, S. N., Nakov, P., Seaghdha, D. O., Spakowicz, S., and Veale, T. (2009). SemEval-2010 task 9: The interpretation of noun compounds using paraphrasing verbs and preposition. In *Proceedings of the NAACL HLT Workshop on Semantic Evaluations: Recent Achievements and Future Directions*.

Finin, T. W. (1980). The semantic interpretation of compound nominals. Report T-96, University of Illinois, Coordinated Science Laboratory.

Heafield, K. (2011). KenLM: Faster and smaller language model queries. In *Proceedings of the EMNLP 2011 Sixth Workshop on Statistical Machine Translation*.

Hendrickx, I., Kozareva, Z., Nakov, P., Séaghdha, D. O., Szpakowicz, S., and Veale, T. (2013). SemEval-2013 task 4: Free paraphrases of noun compounds. In *Proceedings of the International Workshop on Semantic Evaluation*, SemEval '13.

Lauer, M. (1995). Corpus statistics meet the noun compound: some empirical results. In *Proceedings of the 33rd Annual Meeting of the Association for Computational Linguistics (ACL 1995)*.

Li, G., Lopez-Fernandez, A., and Veale, T. (2010). Ucd-goggle: A hybrid system for noun compound paraphrasing. In *Proceedings of the 5th International Workshop on Semantic Evaluation*.

Lin, D. (1998). An information-theoretic definition of similarity. In *Proceedings of International Conference on Machine Learning*.

Minnen, G., Caroll, J., and Pearce, D. (2001). Applied morphological processing of English. *Natural Language Engineering*, 7(3):207–223.

Nakov, P. (2008). Noun compound interpretation using paraphrasing verbs: Feasibility study. In Dochev, D., Pistore, M., and Traverso, P., editors, *Artificial Intelligence: Methodology, Systems, and Applications*, volume 5253 of *Lecture Notes in Computer Science*, pages 103–117. Springer Berlin Heidelberg.

Nulty, P. and Costello, F. (2010). Ucd-pn: Selecting general paraphrases using conditional probability. In *Proceedings of the 5th International Workshop on Semantic Evaluation*.

Padó, S. and Lapata, M. (2007). Dependency-based construction of semantic space models. *Computational Linguistics*, 33(2):161–199.

Toutanova, K., Klein, D., Manning, C. D., and Singer, Y. (2003). Feature-rich part-of-speech tagging with a cyclic dependency network. In *Proc. NAACL 2003*, pages 252–259.

Wijaya, D. T. and Gianfortoni, P. (2011). "nut case: what does it mean?": understanding semantic relationship between nouns in noun compounds through paraphrasing and ranking the paraphrases. In *Proceedings of the 1st international workshop on Search and mining entity-relationship data*, SMER '11, pages 9–14.

Wubben, S. (2010). Uvt: Memory-based pairwise ranking of paraphrasing verbs. In *Proceedings of the 5th International Workshop on Semantic Evaluation*.

IIITH: A Corpus-Driven Co-occurrence Based Probabilistic Model for Noun Compound Paraphrasing

Nitesh Surtani, Arpita Batra, Urmi Ghosh and Soma Paul
Language Technologies Research Centre
IIIT Hyderabad
Hyderabad, Andhra Pradesh-500032
{nitesh.surtaniug08, arpita.batra, urmi.ghosh}@students.iiit.ac.in, soma@iiit.ac.in

Abstract

This paper presents a system for automatically generating a set of plausible paraphrases for a given noun compound and rank them in decreasing order of their usage represented by the confidence value provided by the human annotators. Our system implements a corpus-driven probabilistic co-occurrence based model for predicting the paraphrases, that uses a seed list of paraphrases extracted from corpus to predict other paraphrases based on their co-occurrences. The corpus study reveals that the prepositional paraphrases for the noun compounds are quite frequent and well covered but the verb paraphrases, on the other hand, are scarce, revealing the unsuitability of the model for standalone corpus-driven approach. Therefore, to predict other paraphrases, we adopt a two-fold approach: (i) Prediction based on Verb-Verb co-occurrences, in case the seed paraphrases are greater than threshold; and (ii) Prediction based on Semantic Relation of NC, otherwise. The system achieves a comparabale score of 0.23 for the isomorphic system while maintaining a score of 0.26 for the non-isomorphic system.

1 Introduction

Semeval 2013 Task 4 (Hendrickx et. al., 2013), "Free Paraphrases of Noun Compounds" is a paraphrase generation task that requires the system to generate multiple paraphrases for a given noun compound and rank them to the best approximation of the human rankings, represented by the corresponding confidence value. The task is an extension of Semeval 2010 Task 9 (Butnariu et al., 2010), where the participants were asked to rank the set of given paraphrases for each noun compound. Although the ranking task is quite distinct from the task of generating paraphrases, however, we have taken many insights from the systems developed for the ranking task, and have reported them appropriately in our system description.

This paper describes a system for generating a ranked set of paraphrases for a given NC. A paraphrase can be Prepositional, Verb or Verb + Prepositional. Since the prepositional paraphrases are easily available in the corpus while the occurrences of verb or verb+prep paraphrases is scarce, the task of paraphrasing becomes significant in finding out a method for predicting reliable paraphrases with verbs for a given NC. Our system implements a model that is based on co-occurrences of the paraphrases and selects those paraphrases that have a higher probability of co-occurring with a set of extracted paraphrases which are referred to as *Seed Paraphrases*. Keeping the verb-paraphrase scarcity issue in mind, we develop a two-way model: (i) Model 1 is used when the seed paraphrases are considerable in number i.e., greater than the threshold value. In this case, other verb paraphrases are predicted based on their co-occurrence with the set of extracted verb paraphrases. (ii) Model 2 is used when the size of the seed list falls below the threshold value, in which case, we make use of the prepositional paraphrases to predict the relation of the noun compound and select verbs that mostly co-occur with that relation. Our system achieves an isomorphic score of 0.23 with a non-isomorphic of 0.26 with the human generated paraphrases. The next section discusses the system.

2 System Description

This section of the paper describes each module of the system in detail. The first module of the system

*Second Joint Conference on Lexical and Computational Semantics (*SEM), Volume 2: Seventh International Workshop on Semantic Evaluation (SemEval 2013)*, pages 153–157, Atlanta, Georgia, June 14-15, 2013.

talks about the Seed data extraction using corpus search. The next module uses the seed data for predicting more verbs that would be used in paraphrasing. The third module uses these predicted verbs in template generation for generating NC Paraphrasing and the generated paraphrases are ranked in the last module.

2.1 Seed Data Extraction Module

We have relied mostly on the Google N-gram Corpus for extracting the seed paraphrases. Google has publicly released their web data as n-grams, also known as Web-1T corpus, via the Linguistic Data Consortium (Brants and Franz, 2006). It contains sequences of *n*-terms that occur more than 40 times on the web. Since the corpus consists of raw data from the web, certain pre-processing steps are essential before it can be used. We extract a set of POS templates from the training data, and generalize them enough to accommodate the legitimate paraphrases extracted from the corpus. The following templates are used for extracting n-gram data:

Head-Mod N-gram: This template includes both the head and the modifier in the same regular expression. A corresponding 5-gram template for a NC *Amateur-Championship* is shown in Table 1.

Head <*> <*> <*>Mod	*championship* conducted for the *amateurs*
Head <*><*> Mod <*>	*championship* for all *amateur* players
Head <*>Mod <*><*>	*championship* where *amateur* is competing

Table 1: Templates for paraphrase extraction

The paraphrases obtained from the above template are quite useful, but scarce. To overcome the issue of coverage of verb paraphrases, a loosely coupled analysis and representation of compounds can be employed, as suggested by (Li et.al, 2010). We retrieve the partial triplets from the n-gram corpus in the form of *"Head Para"* and *"Para Modifier"*.

$$(Head,\ Para,\ Mod) \longrightarrow \begin{cases} (Head,\ Para,\ ?) \\ (?,\ Para,\ Mod) \end{cases}$$

Head Template: Head <*> <*>

Mod Template: <*> <*> Mod; <*> Mod <*>

But the process of generating paraphrases from head and the modifier n-gram incorporates a huge amount of noise and produces a lot of irrelevant paraphrases. Therefore, these partial paraphrases are not directly used for generating the paraphrases but are instead used to diagnose the compatibility of the selected verb with the head and the modifier of the given NC in Section 2.2.2. We also extract paraphrases from ANC and BNC corpus.

2.2 Verb Prediction Module

This module is the heart of our system. It implements two models for predicting the verb paraphrases: a Verb Co-occurrence model and a Relation Prediction model. The decision of selection of model for verb prediction is based on the size of the seed list. If the number of seed paraphrases is above the threshold value, the verb co-occurrence model is used whereas the relation prediction model is used if it is below the threshold value.

2.2.1 Verb Co-occurrence Model

This model uses the seed paraphrases extracted from the corpus to predict other verb paraphrases by computing their co-occurrences. The model gains insights from the UCD-PN system (Nulty and Costello, 2010) which tries to identify a more general paraphrase by computing the co-occurrence of a paraphrase with other paraphrases. But the task of generating paraphrases has two subtle but significant differences: (i) The list of seed verb paraphrases for a given NC is usually small, with each seed verb having a corresponding probability of occurrence; and (ii) Not all the seed verbs have legitimate representation of the noun compound. Our system incorporates these distinctions in the co-occurrence model discussed below.

Using the training data at hand, we build a Verb-Verb co-occurrence matrix, a 2-D matrix where each cell (i,j) represents the probability of occurrence of V_j when V_i has already occurred.

$$P(V_j|V_i) = \frac{P(V_i, V_j)}{P(V_i)} = \frac{Count(V_i, V_j)}{Count(V_i)}$$

The verbs used in co-occurrence matrix are stored in a List A. Now, for a given test NC, the model extracts the seed list of verb paraphrases (referred as List B) from the corpus with their corresponding probabilities. The above model calculates a score for each verb in List A, by computing its co-occurrence with the verbs in List B.

$$score_{a\in A}(V_a) = \sum_{b\in B} P(V_a|V_b) * P(V_b)$$

The term $P(V_b)$ in the above equation represents the relative occurrence of the verb V_b with the given NC. The relevance of this term becomes evident in the next model. The verbs achieving higher score are selected, suggesting a higher probability of co-occurrence with the seed verbs.

2.2.2 Semantic Relation Prediction Model

This module describes the second model of the two-way model, and is used by the system when the verbs extracted from the corpus are less than the threshold. In this model, we use prepositional paraphrases, having a pretty good coverage in the corpus, to predict the semantic relation of the compound which helps us in predicting the other paraphrases. The intuition behind using semantic class for predicting paraphrases is that they tend to capture the behavior of the noun compound and can be represented by general paraphrases.

Noun Compound	**Relation**	**Paraphrase Sel.**	
		Prep	**Verb**
Garden Party	Location	In, At	Held
Community Life	Theme	**Of**, In	Made
Advertising Agency	Purpose	**For**, Of, In	Doing

Table 2: Occurrence of Prepositional Paraphrases

Relation Annotation: Since a supervised approach is used for identifying the semantic relation of the noun compound, we manually annotate the noun compounds with a semantic relation. We tag each noun compound with one semantic relation from the set used in (Moldovan et. al. 2004).

Prep-Rel and Verb-Rel Co-occurrence: A Prep-Rel co-occurrence matrix similar to Verb-Verb co-occurrence matrix discussed in last subsection. This 2-D matrix consists of co-occurrence probabilities between the prepositional paraphrases and the semantic relation of the compound, where each cell (i,j) represents the probability of occurrence of preposition P_j with relation R_i. This matrix is used as a model to identify semantic relation using prepositional paraphrases extracted from the corpus.
The Verb-Relation co-occurrence matrix is used to predict the most co-occurring verbs with the identified relation. Each cell (i,j) in the matrix represents the probability of the verb V_j co-occurring with relation R_i.

Relation Extraction: Research focusing on semantic relation extraction has followed two directions: (i) Statistical approaches to using very large corpus (Berland and Charniak (1999); Hearst (1998)); and (ii) Ontology based approaches using hierarchical structure of wordnet (Moldovan et. al., 2004). We employ a statistical model based on the Preposition-Relation co-occurrence for identifying the relation. The model is quite similar to the one used in Section 2.2, but it is here that the model reveals its actual power. Since two or more relations can be represented by same set of prepositional paraphrases, as *Theme* and *Purpose* in Table 2, it is important to take into account the probabilities with which the extracted prepositions occur in the corpus. In Table 2, the NC *Community Life (Theme)* occurs frequently with preposition '*of*' whereas the NC *Advertising Agency (Purpose)* is mostly represented by preposition '*for*' in the corpus. The term $P(P_p)$ in the equation below captures this phenomenon and classifies these two NCs in their respective classes.

$$score_{r\in R}(r) = \sum_{p\in P} P(r|P_p) * P(P_p)$$

The relation with the highest score is selected as the semantic class of the noun compound. A set of verbs highly co-occurring with that class are selected, and their compatibility with the corresponding noun compound is judged from their occurrences with the partial head and the modifier paraphrases as discussed in Section 2.1. The above classifier performs moderately and classifies a given NC with 42.5% accuracy. We have also tried the Wordnet based Semantic Scattering model (Moldovan et. al., 2004), trained on a set of 400 instances, but achieved an accuracy of 38%, the reason for which can be attributed to the small training set. Since the accuracy of identifying the correct relation is low, we select some paraphrases from the 2nd most probable relation, as assigned by the probabilistic classifier.

2.3 Paraphrase Generator Module

After predicting a set of verb for a test noun compound, we use the following templates to generate the paraphrases:

a) *Head VP Mod*
b) *Head VP PP Mod*
c) *Head [that|which] VP PP Mod*

The paraphrases that are extracted from the corpus are also cleaned using the POS templates extracted from the training data.

2.4 Paraphrase Ranker Module

Motivated by the observations from Nulty and Costello (2010) that "people tend to use general, semantically light paraphrases more often than detailed, semantically heavy ones", we perform ranking of the paraphrases in two steps: (i) Assigning different weights to different type of paraphrases, i.e. a light weight prepositional paraphrases achieving higher score than the verb paraphrases; and (ii) Ranking a more general paraphrase with the same category higher. A paraphrase A is more general that paraphrase B (Nulty and Costello, 2010) if

$$P(A|B) > P(B|A)$$

For a list of paraphrases A generated for a given compound, each paraphrase b in that list is scored using the below eq., where more general paraphrase achieves a high score and is ranked higher.

$$score(b) = \sum_{a \in A} P(b|a)$$

The seed paraphrases extracted from the corpus are ranked higher than the predicted paraphrases.

3 Algorithm

This section presents the implementation of the overall system.

```
// Training Phase – Build Co-occurrence Matrices
Verb_Co-occur = 2-D Matrix
Prep-Rel_Co-occur = 2-D Matrix
Verb-Rel_Co-occur = 2-D Matrix
Verb_List = Verb List extracted from training corpus

// Testing – Extract paraphrases with probabilities
Ext_Verb = List of extracted verb paraphrase
VProb = Probability of each Ext_Verb
Ext_Prep = List of extracted prepositional paraphrases
PProb = Probability of each Ext_Prep

Prob_Verb = List // Verbs with their selection score
Prob_Rel = List // Relations with their selection score
Threshold = 3 // Verb threshold for two-way model

if count( Ext_Verb ) > Threshold
  Candidate_Verbs = {Verb_List } - { Ext_Verbs }
  foreach Candidate_Verbs V_i :
    Prob_Verb[V_i] = 0
    foreach Ext_Verb V_j :
      Prob_Verb[V_i] += Verb_Co-occur [V_i][V_j] *
                        VProb[V_j]
else
  foreach Prep-Rel_Co-occur as rel :
    Prob_Rel[rel] = 0
    foreach Ext_Prep as prep :
      Prob_Rel[rel] += Prep-Rel_Co-occur[rel][prep]
                       * PProb[prep]
      Rel=select highestProb(Prob_Rel)
      Prob_Verb = Verb-Rel_Co-occur[Rel]

sort(Prob_Verb)
Verb_Predicted = select top(N)
Paraphrase = generate_paraphrase(verb_predicted)
rank(Paraphrase)
```

4 Results

The set of generated paraphrases are evaluated on two metrics: a) Isomorphic; b) Non-isomorphic. In the isomorphic setting, the test paraphrase is matched to the closest reference paraphrases, but the reference paraphrase is removed from the set whereas in non-isomorphic setting, the reference paraphrase which is mapped to a test paraphrase can still be used for matching other test paraphrases. Table 3 presents the scores of the 3 participating teams who have submitted total of 4 systems.

Systems	Isomorphic	Non-Isomorphic
SFS	0.2313	0.1794
IIITH	*0.2309*	*0.2583*
MELODI-Pri	0.1298	0.5484
MELODI-Cont	0.1357	0.536

Table 3: Results of the submitted systems

Our system achieves an isomorphic score of 0.23, just below the SFS system maintaining a score of 0.26 for the non-isomorphic system. The two variants of MELODI system get a high score for the non-isomorphic metric but low scores for isomorphic metric as compared to other systems.

5 Conclusion

We have described a system for automatically generating a set of paraphrases for a given noun compound, based on the co-occurrences of the paraphrases. The system describes an approach for handling those 38% cases (calculated for optimum threshold value) of NCs where it is not convenient to predict the verbs using their co-occurrences with the seed verbs, because the size of the seed list is below a threshold value. For other cases, the verb co-occurrence model is used to predict the verbs for NC paraphrasing. The optimum value of threshold parameter investigated from experiments is found to be 3, showing that atleast 3 verb paraphrases are necessary to capture the concept of a NC.

References

Matthew Berland and Eugene Charniak. 1999. *Finding parts in very large*. In Proceeding of ACL 1999

T. Brants and A. Franz. 2006. *Web 1T 5-gram Version1*. Linguistic Data Consortium

Cristina Butnariu, Su Nam Kim, Preslav Nakov, Diarmuid O S′ eaghdha, Stan Szpakowicz, and Tony-Veale. 2010. *Semeval-2 task 9: The interpreta-tion of noun compounds using paraphrasing verbs and prepositions*. In Proceedings of the 5th SIGLEX Workshop on Semantic Evaluation

Cristina Butnariu, Su Nam Kim, Preslav Nakov, Diarmuid O S′eaghdha, Stan Szpakowicz, and Tony-Veale. 2013. *Semeval'13 task 4: Free Paraphrases of Noun Compounds*. In Proceedings of the International Workshop on Semantic Evaluation, Atlanta, Georgia

Marti Hearst. 1998. *Automated Discovery of Word-Net relations*. In An Electronic Lexical Database and-Some of its Applications. MIT Press, Cambridge MA

Mark Lauer. 1995. *Designing Statistical Language-Learners: Experiments on Noun Compounds*. Ph.D. Thesis, Macquarie University

Guofu Li, Alejandra Lopez-Fernandez and Tony Veale. 2010. *UCD-Goggle: A Hybrid System for Noun Compound Paraphrasing*. In Proceedings of the 5th International Workshop on Semantic Evaluation (SemEval-2), Uppsala, Sweden

Dan Moldovan, Adriana Badulescu, Marta Tatu, Daniel Antohe, and Roxana Girju. 2004. *Models for the Semantic Classification of Noun Phrases*. In Proceedings of the HLT-NAACL-04 Workshop on Computational Lexical Semantics, pages 60–67, Boston, MA

Paul Nulty and Fintan Costello. 2010. *UCD-PN: Selecting general paraphrases using conditional probability*. In Proceedings of the 5th International Workshop on Semantic Evaluation (SemEval-2), Uppsala, Sweden

SemEval-2013 Task 10: Cross-lingual Word Sense Disambiguation

Els Lefever[1,2] **and Véronique Hoste**[1,3]

[1]LT3, Language and Translation Technology Team, University College Ghent
Groot-Brittanniëlaan 45, 9000 Gent, Belgium
[2]Department of Applied Mathematics, Computer Science and Statistics, Ghent University
Krijgslaan 281 (S9), 9000 Gent, Belgium
[3]Department of Linguistics, Ghent University
Blandijnberg 2, 9000 Gent, Belgium

{Els.Lefever,Veronique.Hoste}@hogent.be

Abstract

The goal of the Cross-lingual Word Sense Disambiguation task is to evaluate the viability of multilingual WSD on a benchmark lexical sample data set. The traditional WSD task is transformed into a multilingual WSD task, where participants are asked to provide contextually correct translations of English ambiguous nouns into five target languages, viz. French, Italian, English, German and Dutch. We report results for the 12 official submissions from 5 different research teams, as well as for the ParaSense system that was developed by the task organizers.

1 Introduction

Lexical ambiguity remains one of the major problems for current machine translation systems. In the following French sentence "Je cherche des idées pour manger de l'avocat"[1], the word "avocat" is clearly referring to the fruit, whereas both Google Translate[2] as well as Babelfish[3] translate the word as "lawyer". Although "lawyer" is a correct translation of the word "avocat", it is the wrong translation in this context. Other language technology applications, such as Question Answering (QA) systems or information retrieval (IR) systems, also suffer from the poor contextual disambiguation of word senses. Word sense disambiguation (WSD) is still considered one of the most challenging problems within language technology today. It requires the construction of an artificial text understanding as the system should detect the correct word sense based on the context of the word. Different methodologies have been investigated to solve the problem; see for instance Agirre and Edmonds (2006) and Navigli (2009) for a detailed overview of WSD algorithms and evaluation.

This paper reports on the second edition of the "Cross-Lingual Word Sense Disambiguation" (CLWSD) task, that builds further on the insights we gained from the SemEval-2010 evaluation (Lefever and Hoste, 2010b) and for which new test data were annotated. The task is an unsupervised Word Sense Disambiguation task for English nouns, the sense label of which is composed of translations in different target languages (viz. French, Italian, Spanish, Dutch and German). The sense inventory is built up on the basis of the Europarl parallel corpus; all translations of a polysemous word were manually grouped into clusters, which constitute different senses of that given word. For the test data, native speakers assigned a translation cluster(s) to each test sentence and gave their top three translations from the predefined list of Europarl translations, in order to assign weights to the set of gold standard translations.

The decision to recast the more traditional monolingual WSD task into a cross-lingual WSD task was motivated by the following arguments. Firstly, using multilingual unlabeled parallel corpora contributes to clearing the data acquisition bottleneck for WSD, because using translations as sense labels excludes the need for manually created sense-tagged corpora

[1]English translation: "I'm looking for ideas to eat avocado".
[2]http://translate.google.com
[3]http://be.bing.com/translator/

*Second Joint Conference on Lexical and Computational Semantics (*SEM), Volume 2: Seventh International Workshop on Semantic Evaluation (SemEval 2013)*, pages 158–166, Atlanta, Georgia, June 14-15, 2013.

and sense inventories such as WordNet (Fellbaum, 1998) or EuroWordNet (Vossen, 1998). Moreover, as there is fairly little linguistic knowledge involved, the framework can be easily deployed for a variety of different languages. Secondly, a cross-lingual approach also deals with the sense granularity problem; finer sense distinctions are only relevant as far as they get lexicalized in different translations of the word. If we take the English word "head" as an example, we see that this word is always translated as "hoofd" in Dutch (both for the "chief" and for the 'body part" sense of the word). At the same time, the subjectivity problem is tackled that arises when lexicographers have to construct a fixed set of senses for a particular word that should fit all possible domains and applications. In addition, the use of domain-specific corpora allows to derive sense inventories that are tailored towards a specific target domain or application and to train a dedicated CLWSD system using these particular sense inventories. Thirdly, working immediately with translations instead of more abstract sense labels allows to bypass the need to map abstract sense labels to corresponding translations. This makes it easier to integrate a dedicated WSD module into real multilingual applications such as machine translation (Carpuat and Wu, 2007) or information retrieval (Clough and Stevenson, 2004).

Many studies have already shown the validity of a cross-lingual approach to Word Sense Disambiguation (Brown et al., 1991; Gale and Church, 1993; Ng et al., 2003; Diab, 2004; Tufiş et al., 2004; Chan and Ng, 2005; Specia et al., 2007; Apidianaki, 2009). The Cross-lingual WSD task contributes to this research domain by the construction of a dedicated benchmark data set where the ambiguous words were annotated with the senses from a multilingual sense inventory extracted from a parallel corpus. This benchmark data sets allows a detailed comparison between different approaches to the CLWSD task.

The remainder of this paper is organized as follows. Section 2 focuses on the task description and briefly recapitalizes the construction of the sense inventory and the annotation procedure of the test sentences. Section 3 presents the participating systems to the task, whereas Section 4 gives an overview of the experimental setup and results. Section 5 concludes this paper.

2 Task set up

The "Cross-lingual Word Sense Disambiguation" (CLWSD) task was organized for the first time in the framework of SemEval-2010 (Lefever and Hoste, 2010b) and resulted in 16 submissions from five different research teams. Many additional research teams showed their interest and downloaded the trial data, but did not manage to finish their systems in time. In order to gain more insights into the complexity and the viability of cross-lingual WSD, we proposed a second edition of the task for SemEval-2013 for which new test data were annotated.

The CLWSD task is an unsupervised Word Sense Disambiguation task for a lexical sample of twenty English nouns. The sense label of the nouns is composed of translations in five target languages (viz. Spanish, French, German, Italian and Dutch) and the sense inventory is built up on the basis of the Europarl parallel corpus[4]. This section briefly describes the data construction process for the task. For a more detailed description of the gold standard creation and data annotation process, we refer to Lefever and Hoste (2010a; 2010b).

2.1 Sense inventory

The starting point for the gold standard sense inventory creation was the parallel corpus Europarl. We selected six languages from Europarl (English and the five target languages) and only considered the 1-1 sentence alignments between English and the five target languages[5]. In order to obtain the multilingual sense inventory we:

1. performed word alignment on the parallel corpus in order to find all possible translations for our set of ambiguous focus nouns

2. clustered the resulting translations by meaning and manually lemmatized all translations

The resulting sense inventory was then used to annotate the sentences in the test set that was developed for the SemEval-2013 CLWSD task.

[4] http://www.statmt.org/europarl/

[5] This six-lingual sentence-aligned subcorpus of Europarl can be downloaded from http://lt3.hogent.be/semeval/.

2.2 Test data

For the creation of the test data set, we manually selected 50 sentences per ambiguous focus word from the part of the ANC corpus that is publicly available[6]. In total, 1000 sentences were annotated using the sense inventory that was described in Section 2.1. Three annotators per target language were asked to first select the correct sense cluster and next to choose the three contextually most appropriate translations from this sense cluster. They could also provide fewer translations in case they could not find three good translations for this particular occurrence of the test word. These translations were used to (1) compose the set of gold standard translations per test instance and (2) to assign frequency weights to all translations in the gold standard (e.g. translations that were chosen by all three annotators get a frequency weight of 3 in the gold standard).

2.3 Evaluation tasks

Two subtasks were proposed for the Cross-lingual WSD task: a *best evaluation* and an *Out-of-five* evaluation task. For the *best* evaluation, systems can propose as many guesses as the system believes are correct, but the score is divided by the number of guesses. In case of the *Out-of-five* evaluation, systems can propose up to five guesses per test instance without being penalized for wrong translation suggestions. Both evaluation tasks are explained in more detail in Section 4.1.

3 Systems

3.1 Systems participating to the official CLWSD evaluation campaign

Five different research teams participated to the CLWSD task and submitted up to three different runs of their system, resulting in 12 different submissions for the task. All systems took part in both the *best* and the *Out-of-five* evaluation tasks. These systems took very different approaches to solve the task, ranging from statistical machine translation, classification and sense clustering to topic model based approaches.

The XLING team (Tan and Bond, 2013) submitted three runs of their system for all five target languages. The first version of the system presents a topic matching and translation approach to CLWSD (*TnT* run), where LDA is applied on the Europarl sentences containing the ambiguous focus word in order to train topic models. Each sentence in the training corpus is assigned a topic that contains a list of associated words with the topic. The topic of the test sentence is then inferred and compared to the matching training sentences by means of the cosine similarity between the training and test vectors. WordNet (WN) is used as a fallback in case the system returns less than 5 answers. The second - and best performing - flavor of the system (*SnT* run) calculates the cosine similarity between the context words of the test and training sentences. The output of the system then contains the translation that results from running word alignment on the focus word in the training corpus. As a fallback, WordNet is again used. The WN senses are sorted by frequency in the SemCor corpus and the corresponding translation is selected from the aligned WordNet in the target language. The third run of the system (*merged*) combines the output from the other two flavors of the system.

The LIMSI system (Apidianaki, 2013) applies an unsupervised CLWSD method that was proposed in (Apidianaki, 2009) for three target languages, viz. Spanish, Italian and French. First, word alignment is applied on the parallel corpus and three bilingual lexicons are built, containing for each focus word the translations in the three target languages. In a next step, a vector is built for each translation of the English focus word, using the cooccurrences of the word in the sentences in which it gets this particular translation. A clustering algorithm then groups the feature vectors using the Weighted Jaccard measure. New instances containing the ambiguous focus word are then compared to the training feature vectors and assigned to one of the sense clusters. In case the highest-ranked translation in the cluster has a score below the threshold, the system falls back to the most frequent translation.

Two very well performing systems take a classification-based approach to the CLWSD task: the HLTDI and WSD2 systems. The HLTDI system (Rudnick et al., 2013) performs word alignment on the intersected Europarl corpus to locate training instances containing the ambiguous focus words. The first flavor of the system (*l1*) uses a maxent clas-

[6] `http://www.americannationalcorpus.org/`

sifier that is trained over local context features. The L2 model (*l2* run) also adds translations of the focus word into the four other target languages to the feature vector. To disambiguate new test instances, these translations into the four other languages are estimated using the classifiers built in the first version of the system (l1). The third system run (*mrf*) builds a Markov network of L1 classifiers in order to find the best translation into all five target languages jointly. The nodes of this network correspond to the distribution produced by the L1 classifiers, while the edges contain pairwise potentials derived from the joint probabilities of translation labels occurring together in the training data.

Another classification-based approach is presented by the WSD2 system (van Gompel and van den Bosch, 2013), that uses a k-NN classifier to solve the CLWSD task. The first configuration of the system (*c1l*) uses local context features for a window of three words containing the focus word. Parameters were optimized on the trial data. The second flavor of the system (*c1lN*) uses the same configuration of the system, but without parameter optimization. The third configuration of the system (*var*) is heavily optimized on the trial data, selecting the winning configuration per trial word and evaluation metric. In addition to the local context features, also global bag-of-word context features are considered for this version of the system.

A completely different approach is taken by the NRC-SMT system (Carpuat, 2013), that uses a statistical machine translation approach to tackle the CLWSD task. The baseline version of the system (*SMTbasic*) represents a standard phrase-based SMT baseline, that is trained only on the intersected Europarl corpus. Translations for the test instances are extracted from the top hypothesis (for the *best* evaluation) or from the 100-best list (for the *Out-of-five* evaluation). The optimized version of the system (*SMTadapt2*) is trained on the Europarl corpus and additional news data, and uses mixture models that are developed for domain adaptation in SMT.

In addition to the five systems that participated to the official evaluation campaign, the organizers also present results for their ParaSense system, which is described in the following section.

3.2 ParaSense system

The ParaSense system (Lefever et al., 2013) is a multilingual classification-based approach to CLWSD. A combination of both local context information and translational evidence is used to discriminate between different senses of the word, the underlying hypothesis being that using multilingual information should be more informative than only having access to monolingual or bilingual features. The local context features contain the word form, lemma, part-of-speech and chunk information for a window of seven words containing the ambiguous focus word. In addition, a set of bag-of-words features is extracted from the aligned translations that are not the target language of the classifier. Per ambiguous focus word, a list of all content words (nouns, adjectives, adverbs and verbs) that occurred in the linguistically preprocessed aligned translations of the English sentences containing this word, were extracted. Each content word then corresponds to exactly one binary feature per language. For the construction of the translation features for the training set, we used the Europarl aligned translations. As we do not dispose of similar aligned translations for the test instances for which we only have the English test sentences at our disposal, we used the Google Translate API[7] to automatically generate translations for all English test instances in the five target languages.

As a classifier, we opted for the k Nearest neighbor method as implemented in TIMBL (Daelemans and van den Bosch, 2005). As most classifiers can be initialized with a wide range of parameters, we used a genetic algorithm to optimize the parameter settings for our classification task.

4 Results

4.1 Experimental set up

Test set The lexical sample contains 50 English sentences per ambiguous focus word. All instances were manually annotated per language, which resulted in a set of gold standard translation labels per instance. For the construction of the test dataset, we refer to Section 2.

[7] `http://code.google.com/apis/language/`

Evaluation metric The BEST precision and recall metric was introduced by (McCarthy and Navigli, 2007) in the framework of the SemEval-2007 competition. The metric takes into account the frequency weights of the gold standard translations: translations that were picked by different annotators received a higher associated frequency which is incorporated in the formulas for calculating precision and recall. For the BEST precision and recall evaluation, the system can propose as many guesses as the system believes are correct, but the resulting score is divided by the number of guesses. In this way, systems that output many guesses are not favored and systems can maximize their score by guessing the most frequent translation from the annotators. We also calculate Mode precision and recall, where precision and recall are calculated against the translation that is preferred by the majority of annotators, provided that one translation is more frequent than the others.

The following variables are used for the BEST precision and recall formulas. Let H be the set of annotators, T the set of test words and h_i the set of translations for an item $i \in T$ for annotator $h \in H$. Let A be the set of words from T where the system provides at least one answer and a_i the set of guesses from the system for word $i \in A$. For each i, we calculate the multiset union (H_i) for all h_i for all $h \in H$ and for each unique type (res) in H_i that has an associated frequency ($freq_{res}$). Equation 1 lists the BEST precision formula, whereas Equation 2 lists the formula for calculating the BEST recall score:

$$Precision = \frac{\sum_{a_i:i \in A} \frac{\frac{\sum_{res \in a_i} freq_{res}}{|a_i|}}{|H_i|}}{|A|} \quad (1)$$

$$Recall = \frac{\sum_{a_i:i \in T} \frac{\frac{\sum_{res \in a_i} freq_{res}}{|a_i|}}{|H_i|}}{|T|} \quad (2)$$

Most Frequent translation baseline As a baseline, we selected the most frequent lemmatized translation that resulted from the automated word alignment (GIZA++) for all ambiguous nouns in the training data. This baseline is inspired by the most frequent sense baseline often used in WSD evaluations. The main difference between the most frequent sense baseline and our baseline is that the latter is corpus-dependent: we do not take into account the overall frequency of a word as it would be measured based on a large general purpose corpus, but calculate the most frequent sense (or translation in this case) based on our training corpus.

4.2 Experimental results

For the system evaluation results, we show precision and Mode precision figures for both evaluation types (*best* and *Out-of-five*). In our case, precision refers to the number of correct translations in relation to the total number of translations generated by the system, while recall refers to the number of correct translations generated by the classifier. As all participating systems predict a translation label for all sentences in the test set, precision and recall will give identical results. As a consequence, we do not list the recall and Mode recall figures that are in this case identical to the corresponding precision scores.

Table 1 lists the averaged *best* precision scores for all systems, while Table 2 gives an overview of the *best* Mode precision figures for all five target languages, viz. Spanish (Es), Dutch (Nl), German (De), Italian (It) and French (Fr). We list scores for all participating systems in the official CLWSD evaluation campaign, as well as for the organizers' system *ParaSense*, that is not part of the official SemEval competition. The best results for the *best* precision evaluation are achieved by the NRC-SMTadapt2 system for Spanish and by the WSD2 system for the other four target languages, closely followed by the HLTDI system. The latter two systems also obtain the best results for the *best* Mode precision metric.

Table 3 lists the averaged *Out-of-five* precision scores for all systems, while Table 4 gives an overview of the *Out-of-five* Mode precision figures for all five target languages, viz. Spanish (Es), Dutch (Nl), German (De), Italian (It) and French (Fr). For the *Out-of-five* evaluation, where systems are allowed to generate up to five unique translations without being penalized for wrong translations, again the HLTDI and WSD2 systems obtain the best classification performance.

Although the winning systems use different approaches (statistical machine translation and classification algorithms), they have in common that they only use a parallel corpus to extract disambiguating information, and do not use external resources such as WordNet. As a consequence, this makes the systems very flexible and language-independent. The ParaSense system, that incorporates translation information from four other languages, outperforms all other systems, except for the *best* precision metric in Spanish, where the NRC-SMT system obtains the overall best results. This confirms the hypothesis that a truly multilingual approach to WSD, which incorporates translation information from multiple languages into the feature vector, is more effective than only using monolingual or bilingual features. A possible explanation could be that the differences between the different languages that are integrated in the feature vector enable the system to refine the obtained sense distinctions. We indeed see that the ParaSense system outperforms the classification-based bilingual approaches which exploit similar information (e.g. training corpora and machine learning algorithms).

	Es	Nl	De	It	Fr
Baseline					
	23.23	20.66	17.43	20.21	25.74
results for the HLTDI **system**					
hltdi-l1	29.01	21.53	19.50	24.52	27.01
hltdi-l2	28.49	22.36	19.92	23.94	28.23
hltdi-mrf	29.36	21.61	19.76	24.62	27.46
results for the XLING **system**					
merged	11.09	4.91	4.08	6.93	9.57
snt	19.59	9.89	8.13	12.74	17.33
tnt	18.60	7.40	5.29	10.70	16.48
results for the LIMSI **system**					
limsi	24.70			21.20	24.56
results for the NRC-SMT **system**					
basic	27.24				
adapt2	**32.16**				
results for the WSD2 **system**					
c1l	28.40	23.14	20.70	25.43	29.88
c1lN	28.65	**23.61**	**20.82**	**25.66**	**30.11**
var	23.31	17.17	16.20	20.38	25.89
results for the PARASENSE **system**					
	31.72	25.29	24.54	28.15	31.21

Table 1: BEST precision scores averaged over all twenty test words for Spanish (Es), Dutch (Nl), German (De), Italian (It) and French (Fr).

	Es	Nl	De	It	Fr
Baseline					
	27.48	24.15	15.30	19.88	20.19
results for the HLTDI **system**					
hltdi-l1	36.32	25.39	24.16	26.52	21.24
hltdi-l2	**37.11**	25.34	**24.74**	26.65	21.07
hltdi-mrf	36.57	25.72	24.01	26.26	21.24
results for the XLING **system**					
merged	24.31	8.54	5.82	7.54	11.63
snt	21.36	9.56	10.36	11.27	11.57
tnt	24.31	8.54	5.82	7.54	11.63
results for the LIMSI **system**					
limsi	32.09			23.06	22.16
results for the NRC-SMT **system**					
basic	32.28				
adapt2	36.2				
results for the WSD2 **system**					
c1l	33.89	26.32	24.73	**31.61**	**26.62**
c1lN	33.70	**27.96**	24.27	30.67	25.27
var	27.98	18.74	21.74	20.69	16.71
results for the PARASENSE **system**					
	40.26	30.29	25.48	30.11	26.33

Table 2: BEST Mode precision scores averaged over all twenty test words for Spanish (Es), Dutch (Nl), German (De), Italian (It) and French (Fr).

	Es	Nl	De	It	Fr
Baseline					
	53.07	43.59	38.86	42.63	51.36
results for the HLTDI **system**					
hltdi-l1	**61.69**	46.55	**43.66**	**53.57**	57.76
hltdi-l2	59.51	46.36	42.32	53.05	58.20
hltdi-mrf	9.89	5.69	4.15	3.91	7.11
results for the XLING **system**					
merged	43.76	24.30	19.83	33.95	38.15
snt	44.83	27.11	23.71	32.38	38.44
tnt	39.52	23.27	19.13	33.28	35.30
results for the LIMSI **system**					
limsi	49.01			40.25	45.37
results for the NRC-SMT **system**					
basic	37.98				
adapt2	41.65				
results for the WSD2 **system**					
c1l	58.23	**47.83**	43.17	52.22	59.07
c1lN	57.62	47.62	43.24	52.73	**59.80**
var	55.70	46.85	41.46	51.18	59.19

Table 3: OUT-OF-FIVE precision scores averaged over all twenty test words for Spanish (Es), Dutch (Nl), German (De), Italian (It) and French (Fr).

	Es	Nl	De	It	Fr
Baseline					
	57.35	41.97	44.35	41.69	47.42
results for the HLTDI system					
hltdi-l1	**64.65**	**47.34**	53.50	**56.61**	51.96
hltdi-l2	62.52	44.06	49.03	54.06	53.57
hltdi-mrf	11.39	5.09	3.14	3.87	7.79
results for the XLING system					
merged	48.63	23.64	24.64	31.74	30.11
snt	50.04	27.30	30.57	29.17	32.45
tnt	44.96	22.98	23.54	29.61	28.02
results for the LIMSI system					
limsi	51.41			47.21	39.54
results for the NRC-SMT system					
basic	42.92				
adapt2	45.38				
results for the WSD2 system					
c1l	63.75	45.27	50.11	54.13	**57.57**
c1lN	63.80	44.53	**50.26**	54.37	56.40
var	61.51	41.82	49.23	54.73	54.97

Table 4: OUT-OF-FIVE Mode precision scores averaged over all twenty test words for Spanish (Es), Dutch (Nl), German (De), Italian (It) and French (Fr).

In general, we notice that French and Spanish have the highest scores, while Dutch and German seem harder to tackle. Italian is situated somewhere in between the Romance and Germanic languages. This trend confirms the results that were obtained during the first SemEval Cross-lingual WSD task (Lefever and Hoste, 2010b). As pointed out after the first competition, the discrepancy between the scores for the Romance and Germanic languages can probably be explained by the number of classes (or translations in this case) the systems have to choose from. Germanic languages are typically characterized by a very productive compounding system, where compounds are joined together in one orthographic unit, which results in a much higher number of different class labels. As the Romance languages typically write compounds in separate orthographic units, they dispose of a smaller number of different translations for each ambiguous noun.

We can also notice large differences between the scores for the individual words. Figure 1 illustrates this by showing the *best* precision scores in Spanish for the different test words for the best run per system. Except for some exceptions (e.g. *coach* in the NRC-SMT system), most system performance scores follow a similar curve. Some words (e.g. *match, range*) are particularly hard to disambiguate, while others obtain very high scores (e.g. *mission, soil*). One possible explanation for the very good scores for some words (e.g. *soil*) can be attributed to a very generic translation which accounts for all senses of the word even though there might be more suitable translations for each of the senses depending on the context. Because the manual annotators were able to select three good translations for each test instance, the most generic translation is often part of the gold standard translations. This is also reflected in the high baseline scores for these words. For the words performing badly in most systems, an inspection of the training data properties revealed two possible explanations for these poor classification results. Firstly, there seems to be a link with the number of training instances, corresponding to the frequency of the word in the training corpus. Both for *coach* and *match*, two words consistently performing bad in all systems, there are very few training examples in the corpus (66 and 109 respectively). This could also explain why the NRC-SMT system, that also uses additional parallel data, achieves better results for *coach* than all other systems. Secondly, the ambiguity or number of valid translations per word in the training data also seems to play a role in the classification results. Both *job* and *range* appear very hard to classify correctly, and both words are very ambiguous, with no fewer than 121 and 125 translations, respectively, to choose from in Spanish.

5 Conclusion

The Cross-lingual Word Sense Disambiguation task attempts to address three important challenges for WSD, namely (1) the data acquisition bottleneck, which is caused by the lack of manually created resources, (2) the sense granularity and subjectivity problem of the existing sense inventories and (3) the need to make WSD more suited for practical applications. The task contributes to the WSD research domain by the construction of a dedicated benchmark data set that allows to compare different approaches to the Cross-lingual WSD task.

The evaluation results lead to the following observations. Firstly, languages which make exten-

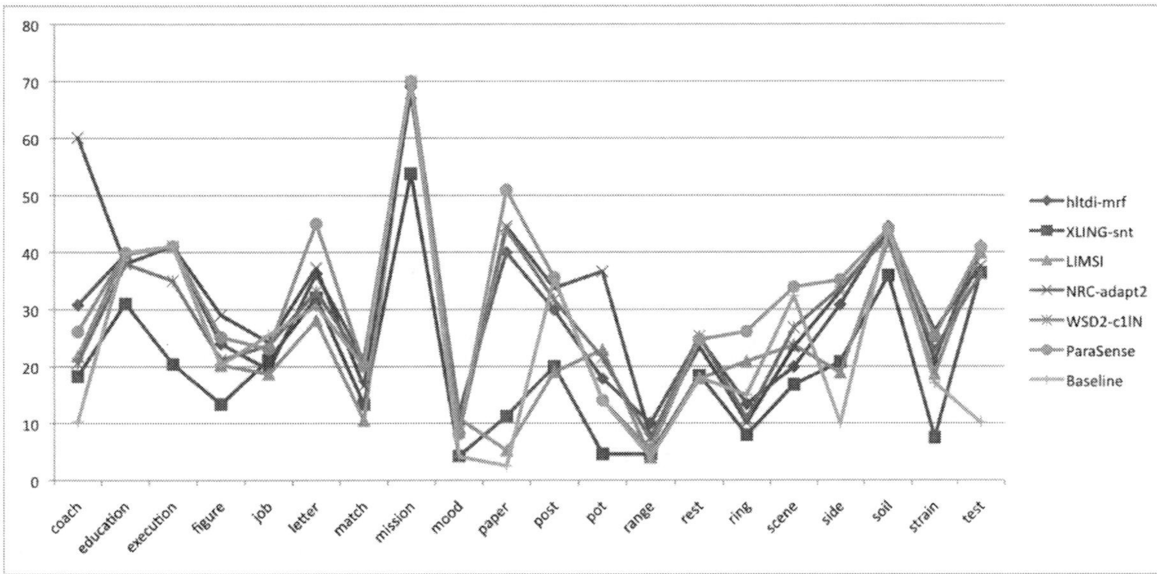

Figure 1: Spanish *best* precision scores for all systems per ambiguous focus word.

sive use of single word compounds seem harder to tackle, which can probably be explained by the higher number of translations these classifiers have to choose from. Secondly, we can notice large differences between the performances of the individual test words. For the words that appear harder to disambiguate, both the number of training instances as well as the ambiguity of the word seem to play a role for the classification performance. Thirdly, both the ParaSense system as well as the two winning systems from the competition extract all disambiguating information from the parallel corpus and do not use any external resources. As a result, these systems are very flexible and can be easily extended to other languages and domains. In addition, the good scores of the ParaSense system, that incorporates information from four additional languages, confirms the hypothesis that a truly multilingual approach is an effective way to tackle the CLWSD task.

Acknowledgments

We would like to thank all annotators for their hard work.

References

Eneko Agirre and Philip Edmonds. 2006. *Word Sense Disambiguation. Algorithms and Applications.* Text, Speech and Language Technology. Springer.

M. Apidianaki. 2009. Data-driven semantic analysis for multilingual WSD and lexical selection in translation. In *Proceedings of the 12th Conference of the European Chapter of the Association for Computational Linguistics (EACL)*, pages 77–85, Athens, Greece.

Marianna Apidianaki. 2013. LIMSI : Cross-lingual Word Sense Disambiguation using Translation Sense Clustering. In *Proceedings of the 7th International Workshop on Semantic Evaluation (SemEval 2013), in conjunction with the Second Joint Conference on Lexical and Computational Semantcis (*SEM 2013)*, Atlanta, USA.

P.F. Brown, S.A.D. Pietra, V.J.D. Pietra, and R.L. Mercer. 1991. Word-sense disambiguation using statistical methods. In *Proceedings of the 29th Annual Meeting of the Association for Computational Linguistics*, pages 264–270, Berkeley, California.

M. Carpuat and D. Wu. 2007. Improving statistical machine translation using word sense disambiguation. In *Proceedings of the 2007 Joint Conference on Empirical Methods in Natural Language Processing and Computational Natural Language Learning (EMNLP-CoNLL)*, pages 61–72, Prague, Czech Republic.

Marine Carpuat. 2013. NRC: A Machine Translation Approach to Cross-Lingual Word Sense Disambiguation (SemEval-2013 Task 10). In *Proceedings of the 7th International Workshop on Semantic Evaluation (SemEval 2013), in conjunction with the Second Joint Conference on Lexical and Computational Semantcis (*SEM 2013)*, Atlanta, USA.

Y.S. Chan and H.T. Ng. 2005. Scaling Up Word Sense Disambiguation via Parallel Texts. In *Proceedings of the 20th National Conference on Artificial Intelligence (AAAI 2005)*, pages 1037–1042, Pittsburgh, Pennsylvania, USA.

P. Clough and M. Stevenson. 2004. Cross-language information retrieval using eurowordnet and word sense disambiguation. In *Advances in Information Retrieval, 26th European Conference on IR Research (ECIR)*, pages 327–337, Sunderland, UK.

W. Daelemans and A. van den Bosch. 2005. *Memory-based Language Processing*. Cambridge University Press.

M. Diab. 2004. *Word Sense Disambiguation within a Multilingual Framework*. Phd, University of Maryland, USA.

C. Fellbaum. 1998. *WordNet: An Electronic Lexical Database*. MIT Press.

W.A. Gale and K.W. Church. 1993. A program for aligning sentences in bilingual corpora. *Computational Linguistics*, 19(1):75–102.

E. Lefever and V. Hoste. 2010a. Construction of a Benchmark Data Set for Cross-Lingual Word Sense Disambiguation. In Nicoletta Calzolari, Khalid Choukri, Bente Maegaard, Joseph Mariani, Jan Odijk, Stelios Piperidis, and Daniel Tapias, editors, *Proceedings of the seventh International Conference on Language Resources and Evaluation (LREC'10)*, Valletta, Malta, May. European Language Resources Association (ELRA).

E. Lefever and V. Hoste. 2010b. SemEval-2010 Task 3: Cross-Lingual Word Sense Disambiguation. In *Proceedings of the 5th International Workshop on Semantic Evaluation, ACL 2010*, pages 15–20, Uppsala, Sweden.

E. Lefever, V. Hoste, and M. De Cock. 2013. Five languages are better than one: an attempt to bypass the data acquisition bottleneck for wsd. In *In Alexander Gelbukh (ed.), CICLing 2013, Part I, LNCS 7816*, pages 343–354. Springer-Verlag Berlin Heidelberg.

D. McCarthy and R. Navigli. 2007. SemEval-2007 Task 10: English Lexical Substitution Task. In *Proceedings of the 4th International Workshop on Semantic Evaluations (SemEval-2007)*, pages 48–53, Prague, Czech Republic.

R. Navigli. 2009. Word Sense Disambiguation: a Survey. *ACM Computing Surveys*, 41(2):1–69.

H.T. Ng, B. Wang, and Y.S. Chan. 2003. Exploiting parallel texts for word sense disambiguation: An empirical study. In *41st Annual Meeting of the Association for Computational Linguistics (ACL)*, pages 455–462, Sapporo, Japan.

Alex Rudnick, Can Liu, and Michael Gasser. 2013. HLTDI: CL-WSD Using Markov Random Fields for SemEval-2013 Task 10. In *Proceedings of the 7th International Workshop on Semantic Evaluation (SemEval 2013), in conjunction with the Second Joint Conference on Lexical and Computational Semantcis (*SEM 2013)*, Atlanta, USA.

L. Specia, M.G.V. Nunes, and M. Stevenson. 2007. Learning Expressive Models for Word Sense Disambiguation. In *Proceedings of the 45th Annual Meeting of the Association of Computational Linguistics*, pages 41–48, Prague, Czech Republic.

Liling Tan and Francis Bond. 2013. XLING: Matching Query Sentences to a Parallel Corpus using Topic Models for WSD. In *Proceedings of the 7th International Workshop on Semantic Evaluation (SemEval 2013), in conjunction with the Second Joint Conference on Lexical and Computational Semantcis (*SEM 2013)*, Atlanta, USA.

D. Tufiş, R. Ion, and N. Ide. 2004. Fine-Grained Word Sense Disambiguation Based on Parallel Corpora, Word Alignment, Word Clustering and Aligned Wordnets. In *Proceedings of the 20th International Conference on Computational Linguistics (COLING 2004)*, pages 1312–1318, Geneva, Switzerland, August. Association for Computational Linguistics.

Maarten van Gompel and Antal van den Bosch. 2013. Parameter optimisation for Memory-based Cross-Lingual Word-Sense Disambiguation. In *Proceedings of the 7th International Workshop on Semantic Evaluation (SemEval 2013), in conjunction with the Second Joint Conference on Lexical and Computational Semantcis (*SEM 2013)*, Atlanta, USA.

P. Vossen, editor. 1998. *EuroWordNet: a multilingual database with lexical semantic networks*. Kluwer Academic Publishers, Norwell, MA, USA.

XLING: Matching Query Sentences to a Parallel Corpus using Topic Models for Word Sense Disambiguation

Liling Tan and **Francis Bond**
Division of Linguistics and Multilingual Studies,
Nanyang Technological University
14 Nanyang Drive, Singapore 637332
alvations@gmail.com, bond@ieee.org

Abstract

This paper describes the XLING system participation in SemEval-2013 Crosslingual Word Sense Disambiguation task. The XLING system introduces a novel approach to skip the sense disambiguation step by matching query sentences to sentences in a parallel corpus using topic models; it returns the word alignments as the translation for the target polysemous words. Although, the topic-model base matching underperformed, the matching approach showed potential in the simple cosine-based surface similarity matching.

1 Introduction

This paper describes the XLING system, an unsupervised Cross-Lingual Word Sense Disambiguation (CLWSD) system based on matching query sentence to parallel corpus using topic models. CLWSD is the task of disambiguating a word given a context by providing the most appropriate translation in different languages (Lefever and Hoste, 2013).

2 Background

Topic models assume that latent topics exist in texts and each semantic topic can be represented with a multinomial distribution of words and each document can be classified into different semantic topics (Hofmann, 1999). Blei et al. (2003b) introduced a Bayesian version of topic modeling using Dirichlet hyper-parameters, Latent Dirichlet Allocation (LDA). Using LDA, a set of topics can be generated to classify documents within a corpus. Each topic will contain a list of all the words in the vocabulary of the corpus where each word is assigned a probability of occurring given a particular topic.

3 Approach

We hypothesized that sentences with different senses of a polysemous word will be classified into different topics during the LDA process. By matching the query sentence to the training sentences by LDA induced topics, the most appropriate translation for the polysemous word in the query sentence should be equivalent to translation of word in the matched training sentence(s) from a parallel corpus. By pursuing this approach, we escape the traditional mode of disambiguating a sense using a sense inventory.

4 System Description

The XLING_TnT system attempts the matching subtask in three steps (1) **Topicalize**: matching the query sentence to the training sentences by the most probable topic. (2) **Rank**: the matching sentences were ranked according to the cosine similarity between the query and matching sentences. (3) **Translate**: provides the translation of the polysemous word in the matched sentence(s) from the parallel corpus.

4.1 Preprocessing

The Europarl version 7 corpus bitexts (English-German, English-Spanish, English-French, English-Italian and English-Dutch) were aligned at word-level with GIZA++ (Och and Ney, 2003). The translation tables from the word-alignments were used to provide the translation of the polysemous word in the **Translate** step.

The English sentences from the bitexts were lemmatized using a dictionary-based lemmatiz-

*Second Joint Conference on Lexical and Computational Semantics (*SEM), Volume 2: Seventh International Workshop on Semantic Evaluation (SemEval 2013)*, pages 167–170, Atlanta, Georgia, June 14-15, 2013.

er: `xlemma`[1]. After the lemmatization, English stopwords[2] were removed from the sentences. The lemmatized and stop filtered sentences were used as document inputs to train the LDA topic model in the **`Topicalize`** step.

Previously, topic models had been incorporated as global context features into a modified naive Bayes network with traditional WSD features (Cai et al. 2007). We try a novel approach of integrating local context (N-grams) by using pseudo-word sentences as input for topic induction. Here we neither lemmatize or remove stops words. For example:

Original Europarl sentence: "*Education and cultural policies are important tools for creating these values*"

Lemmatized and stopped: "*education cultural policy be important tool create these values*"

Ngram pseudo-word: "*education_and_cultural and_cultural_policies cultural_policies_are are_important_tools important_tools_for tools_for_creating for_creating_these creating_these_values*"

4.2 Topicalize and Match

The **`Topicalize`** step of the system first (i) induced a list of topics and trained a topic model for each polysemous word using LDA, then (ii) allocated the topic with the highest probability to each training sentence.

Finally, at evaluation, (iii) the query sentences were assigned the most probable topic inferred using the trained topic models. Then the training sentences allocated with the same topic were considered as matching sentences for the next **`Rank`** step.

4.2.1 Topic Induction

Topic models were trained using Europarl sentences that contain the target polysemous words; one model per target word. The topic models were induced using LDA by setting the number of topics (*#topics*) as 50, and the alpha and beta hyper-parameters were symmetrically set at 1.0/*#topics*. Blei et al. (2003) had shown that the perplexity plateaus when *#topics* $\geq$ 50; higher perplexity means more computing time needed to train the model.

4.2.2 Topic Allocation

Each sentence was allocated the most probable topic induced by LDA. An induced topic contained a ranked list of tuples where the 2nd element in each tuple is a word that associated with the topic, the 1st element is the probability that the associated word will occur given the topic. The probabilities are generatively output using Variational Bayes algorithm as described in Hoffman et al. (2010). For example:

[*(0.0208, 'sport'), (0.0172, 'however'), (0.0170, 'quite'), (0.0166, 'maritime'), (0.0133, 'field'), (0.0133, 'air-transport'), (0.0130, 'appear'), (0.0117, 'arrangement'), (0.0117, 'pertain'), (0.0111, 'supervision')*]

4.2.3 Topic Inference

With the trained LDA model, we inferred the most probable topic of the query sentence. Then we extracted the top-10 sentences from the training corpus that shared the same top ranking topic.

The topic induction, allocation and inference were done separately on the lemmatized and stopped sentences and on the pseudo-word sentence, resulting in two sets of matching sentences. Only the sentences that were in both sets of matches are considered for the **`Rank`** step.

4.3 Rank

Matched sentences from the **`Topicalize`** step were converted into term vectors. The vectors were reweighted using tf-idf and ranked according to the cosine similarity with the query sentences. The top five sentences were piped into the `Translate` step.

4.4 Translate

From the matching sentences, the **`Translate`** step simply checks the `GIZA++` word alignment table and outputs the translation(s) of the target polysemous word. Each matching sentence,

[1] http://code.google.com/p/xlemma/

[2] Using the Page and Article Analyzer stopwords from http://www.ranks.nl/resources/stopwords.html

could output more than 1 translation depending on the target word alignment. As a simple way of filtering stop-words from target European languages, translations with less than 4 characters were removed. This effectively distills misaligned non-content words, such as articles, pronouns, prepositions, etc. To simplify the lemmatization of Spanish and French plural noun suffixes, the '*-es*' and '*-s*' are stemmed from the translation outputs.

The `XLING_TnT` system outputs one translation for each query sentence for the best result evaluation. It output the top 5 translations for the *out-of-five* evaluation.

4.5 Fallback

For the *out-of-five* evaluation, if the query returned less than 5 answers, the first fallback[3] appended the lemma of the Most Frequent Sense (according to Wordnet) of the target polysemous word in their respective language from the Open Multilingual Wordnet.[4] If the first fallback was insufficient, the second fallback appended the most frequent translation of the target polysemous word to the queries' responses.

4.6 Baseline

We also constructed a baseline for matching sentences by cosine similarity between the lemmas of the query sentence and the lemmas of each English sentence in the training corpus.[5] The baseline system is named `XLING_SnT` (Similar and Translate). The cosine similarity is calculated from the division of the vector product of the query and training sentence (i.e. numerator) by the root product of the vector's magnitude squared.

5 Results

Tables 1 and 2 present the results for the XLING system for best and out-of-five evaluation. Our system did worse than the task's baseline, i.e. the Most Frequent Translation (MFT) of the target word for all languages. Moreover the topic model based matching did worse than the cosine similarity matching baseline. The results show that matching on topics did not help. However, Li et al. (2010) and Anaya-Sanchez et al. (2007) had shown that pure topic model based unsupervised system for WSD should perform a little better than Most Frequent Sense baseline in coarse-grain English WSD. Hence it was necessary to perform error analysis and tweaking to improve the XLING system.

BEST	German	Spanish	French	Italian	Dutch
SnT	**8.13**	**19.59**	**17.33**	**12.74**	**9.89**
	(10.36)	(24.31)	(11.57)	(11.27)	(9.56)
TnT	5.28	18.60	16.48	10.70	7.40
	(5.82)	(24.31)	(11.63)	(7.54)	(8.54)
MFT	17.43	23.23	25.74	20.21	20.66
	(15.30)	(27.48)	(20.19)	(19.88)	(24.15)

Table 1: Precision and (Mood) for the best evaluation

OOF	German	Spanish	French	Italian	Dutch
SnT	**23.71**	**44.83**	**38.44**	32.38	**27.11**
	(30.57)	(50.04)	(32.45)	(29.17)	(27.31)
TnT	19.13	39.52	35.3	**33.28**	23.27
	(23.54)	(44.96)	(28.02)	(29.61)	(22.98)
MFT	38.86	53.07	51.36	42.63	43.59
	(44.35)	(57.35)	(47.42)	(41.69)	(41.97)

Table 2: Precision and (Mood) for the oof evaluation

6 Error Analysis and Modifications

Statistically, we could improve the robustness of the topic models in the **`Topicalize`** step by (i) tweaking the Dirichlet hyper-parameters to *alpha = 50/#topics, beta = 0.01* as suggested by Wang et al. (2009).

	BEST		OOF	
	Precision	**Mood**	**Precision**	**Mood**
German	6.50	6.71	20.98	25.18
Spanish	**14.77**	**19.43**	**40.22**	**45.67**
French	10.79	7.95	31.26	23.37
Italian	13.10	10.95	36.56	31.94
Dutch	7.42	7.47	21.66	20.42

Table 3: Evaluations on Hyper-parameter tweaks

Although the hyperparameters tweaks improves the scores for German and Dutch evaluations it brings the overall precision and mood precision of the other three languages down. Since the documents from each language are parallel, this

3 Code sample for the fallback can be found at http://goo.gl/PbdK7

4 http://www.casta-net.jp/~kuribayashi/multi/

5 Code-snippet for the baseline can be found at http://pythonfiddle.com/surface-cosine-similarity

suggests that there is some language-dependency for LDA's hyperparameters.

By going through the individual queries and responses, several issues in the `translate` step need to be resolved to achieve higher precision; (i) German-English and Dutch-English word alignments containing compound words need to be segmented (e.g. *kraftomnibusverkehr* →*kraft omnibus verkehr)* and realigned such that the target word *coach* only aligns to *omnibus*, (ii) lemmatization of Italian, German and Dutch is crucial is getting the gold answers of the task (e.g. XLING answers *omnibussen* while the gold answers allowed *omnibus*). The use of target language lemmatizers, such as TreeTagger (Schmid, 1995) would have benefited the system.

7 Discussion

The main advantage of statistical language independent approaches is the ability to scale the system in any possible language. However language dependent processing remains crucial in building an accurate system, especially lemmatization in WSD tasks (e.g. *kraftomnibusverkehr*). We also hypothesize that more context would have improved the results of using topics: disambiguating senses solely from sentential context is artificially hard.

8 Conclusion

Our system has approached the CLWSD task in an unconventional way of matching query sentences to parallel corpus using topic models. Given no improvement from hyper-parameter tweaks, it reiterates Boyd-Graber, Blei and Zhu's (2007) assertion that while topic models capture polysemous use of words, they do not carry explicit notion of senses that is necessary for WSD. Thus our approach to match query sentences by topics did not perform beyond the MFT baseline in the CLWSD evaluation.

However, the surface cosine baseline, without any incorporation of any sense knowledge, had surprisingly achieved performance closer to MFT It provides a pilot platform for future work to approach the CLWSD as a vector-based document retrieval task on parallel corpora and providing the translation from the word alignments.

References

Henry Anaya-Śanchez, Aurora Pons-Porrata, and Rafael Berlanga-Llavori. 2007. Tkb-uo: Using sense clustering for wsd. In *Proceedings of the Fourth International Workshop on Semantic Evaluations (SemEval-2007)*, pp. 322–325.

Jordan Boyd-Graber, David M. Blei, and Xiaojin Zhu. 2007. A Topic Model for Word Sense Disambiguation. In *Proc. of Empirical Methods in Natural Language Processing(EMNLP)*.

David M. Blei, Andrew Y. Ng, and Michael L. Jordan. 2003. Latent Dirichlet allocation. *Journal of Machine Learning Research*, 3:993–1022.

Jun-Fu Cai, Wee-Sun Lee and Yee-Whye Teh. 2007. Improving word sense disambiguation using topic features. In *Proceedings of the 2007 Joint Conference on Empirical Methods in Natural Language Processing and Computational Natural Language Learning (EMNLP-CoNLL)*, pp. 1015–1023.

Christiane Fellbaum. (ed.) (1998) *WordNet: An Electronic Lexical Database*, MIT Press

Thomas Hofmann. 1999. Probabilistic latent semantic indexing. In *Proceedings of SIGIR '99*, Berkeley, CA, USA.

Matthew Hoffman, David Blei and Francis Bach. 2010. Online Learning for Latent Dirichlet Allocation. In Proceedings of NIPS 2010.

Els Lefever and Véronique Hoste. 2013. SemEval-2013 Task 10: Cross-Lingual Word Sense Disambiguation, In *Proceedings SemEval 2013, in conjunction with *SEM 2013*, Atlanta, USA.

Linlin Li, Benjamin Roth and Caroline Sporleder. Topic Models for Word Sense Disambiguation and Token-based Idiom Detection. In *Proc. of The 48th Annual Meeting of the Association for Computational Linguistics (ACL)*, 2010. Uppsala, Sweden.

Franz Josef Och, Hermann Ney. 2003. A Systematic Comparison of Various Statistical Alignment Models. *Computational Linguistics* 29:1. pp. 19-51.

Helmut Schmid. 1995. Improvements in Part-of-Speech Tagging with an Application to German. *Proceedings of the ACL SIGDAT-Workshop*. Dublin, Ireland.

Yi Wang, Hongjie Bai, Matt Stanton, Wen-Yen Chen, Edward Y. Chang. 2009. Plda: Parallel latent dirichlet allocation for large-scale applications. In *Proc. of 5th International Conference on Algorithmic Aspects in Information and Management*.

HLTDI: CL-WSD Using Markov Random Fields for SemEval-2013 Task 10

Alex Rudnick, Can Liu and Michael Gasser
Indiana University, School of Informatics and Computing
{alexr,liucan,gasser}@indiana.edu

Abstract

We present our entries for the SemEval-2013 cross-language word-sense disambiguation task (Lefever and Hoste, 2013). We submitted three systems based on classifiers trained on local context features, with some elaborations. Our three systems, in increasing order of complexity, were: maximum entropy classifiers trained to predict the desired target-language phrase using only monolingual features (we called this system L1); similar classifiers, but with the desired target-language phrase for the other four languages as features (L2); and lastly, networks of five classifiers, over which we do loopy belief propagation to solve the classification tasks jointly (MRF).

1 Introduction

In the cross-language word-sense disambiguation (CL-WSD) task, given an instance of an ambiguous word used in a context, we want to predict the appropriate translation into some target language. This setting for WSD has an immediate application in machine translation, since many words have multiple possible translations. Framing the resolution of lexical ambiguities as an explicit classification task has a long history, and was considered in early SMT work at IBM (Brown et al., 1991). More recently, Carpuat and Wu have shown how to use CL-WSD techniques to improve modern phrase-based SMT systems (Carpuat and Wu, 2007), even though the language model and phrase-tables of these systems mitigate the problem of lexical ambiguities somewhat.

In the SemEval-2013 CL-WSD shared task (Lefever and Hoste, 2013), entrants are asked to build a system that can provide translations for twenty ambiguous English nouns, given appropriate contexts – here the particular usage of the ambiguous noun is called the *target* word. The five target languages of the shared task are Spanish, Dutch, German, Italian and French. In the evaluation, for each of the twenty ambiguous nouns, systems are to provide translations for the target word in each of fifty sentences or short passages. The translations of each English word may be single words or short phrases in the target language, but in either case, they should be lemmatized.

Following the work of Lefever and Hoste (2011), we wanted to make use of multiple bitext corpora for the CL-WSD task. ParaSense, the system of Lefever and Hoste, takes into account evidence from all of the available parallel corpora. Let S be the set of five target languages and t be the particular target language of interest at the moment; ParaSense creates bag-of-words features from the translations of the target sentence into the languages $S - \{t\}$. Given corpora that are parallel over many languages, this is straightforward at training time. However, at testing time it requires a complete MT system for each of the four other languages, which is computationally prohibitive. Thus in our work, we learn from several parallel corpora but require neither a locally running MT system nor access to an online translation API.

We presented three systems in this shared task, all of which were variations on the theme of a maximum entropy classifier for each ambiguous noun, trained on local context features similar to those used in previous work and familiar from the WSD literature. The first system, L1 ("layer one"), uses maximum entropy classifiers trained on local con-

*Second Joint Conference on Lexical and Computational Semantics (*SEM), Volume 2: Seventh International Workshop on Semantic Evaluation (SemEval 2013)*, pages 171–177, Atlanta, Georgia, June 14-15, 2013.

text features. The second system, L2 ("layer two"), is the same as the L1 system, with the addition of the correct translations into the other target languages as features, which at testing time are predicted with L1 classifiers. The third system, MRF ("Markov random field") uses a network of interacting classifiers to solve the classification problem for all five target languages jointly. Our three systems are all trained from the same data, which we extracted from the Europarl Intersection corpus provided by the shared task organizers.

At the time of the evaluation, our simplest system had the top results in the shared task for the out-of-five evaluation for three languages (Spanish, German, and Italian). However, after the evaluation deadline, we fixed a simple bug in our MRF code, and the MRF system then achieved even better results for the *oof* evaluation. For the *best* evaluation, our two more sophisticated systems posted better results than the L1 version. All of our systems beat the "most-frequent sense" baseline in every case.

In the following sections, we will describe our three systems[1], our training data extraction process, the results on the shared task, and conclusions and future work.

2 L1

The "layer one" classifier, L1, is a maximum entropy classifier that uses only monolingual features from English. Although this shared task is described as unsupervised, the L1 classifiers are trained with supervised learning on instances that we extract programmatically from the Europarl Intersection corpus; we describe the preprocessing and training data extraction in Section 5.

Having extracted the relevant training sentences from the aligned bitext for each of the five language pairs, we created training instances with local context features commonly used in WSD systems. These are described in Figure 1. Each instance is assigned the lemma of the translation that was extracted from the training sentence as its label.

We trained one L1 classifier for each target language and each word of interest, resulting in $20*5=$ 100 classifiers. Classifiers were trained with the MEGA Model optimization package [2] and its corresponding NLTK interface (Bird et al., 2009). Upon training, we cache these classifiers with Python pickles, both to speed up L1 experiments and also because they are used as components of the other models.

- target word features
  - literal word form
  - POS tag
  - lemma
- window unigram features (within 3 words)
  - word form
  - POS tag
  - word with POS tag
  - word lemma
- window bigram features (within 5 words)
  - bigrams
  - bigrams with POS tags

Figure 1: Features used in our classifiers

We combined the word tokens with their tags in some features so that the classifier would not treat them independently, since maximum entropy classifiers learn a single weight for each feature. Particularly, the "POS tag" feature is distinct from the "word with tag" feature; for the tagged word "house/NN", the "POS tag" feature would be NN, and the "word with tag" feature is $house\_NN$.

3 L2

The "layer two" classifier, L2, is an extension to the L1 approach, with the addition of multilingual features. Particularly, L2 makes use of the translations of the target word into the four target languages other than the one we are currently trying to predict. At training time, since we have the translations of each of the English sentences into the other target languages, the appropriate features are extracted from the corresponding sentences in those languages. This is the same as the process by which labels are given to training instances, described in Section 5. At testing time, since translations of the

[1] Source is available at `http://github.iu.edu/alexr/semeval2013`

[2] `http://www.umiacs.umd.edu/~hal/megam/`

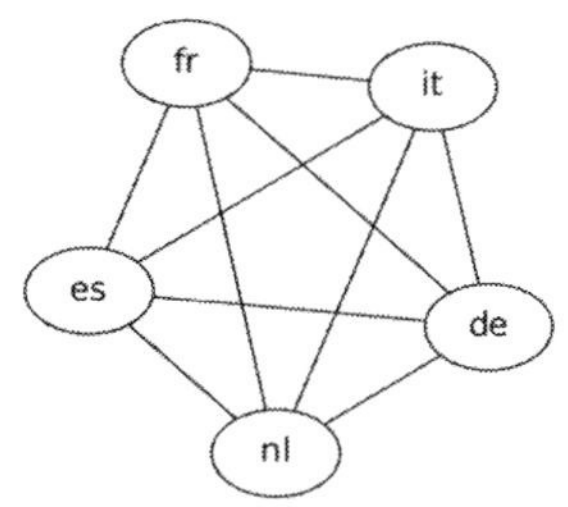

Figure 2: The network structure used in the MRF system: a complete graph with five nodes where each node represents a variable for the translation into a target language

test sentences are not given, we estimate the translations for the target word in the four other languages using the cached L1 classifiers.

Lefever and Hoste (2011) used the Google Translate API to translate the source English sentences into the four other languages, and extracted bag-of-words features from these complete sentences. The L2 classifiers make use of a similar intuition, but they do not rely on a complete MT system or an available online MT API; we only include the translations of the specific target word as features.

4 MRF

Our MRF model builds a Markov network (often called a "Markov random field") of L1 classifiers in an effort to find the best translation into all five target languages jointly. This network has nodes that correspond to the distributions produced by the L1 classifiers, given an input sentence, and edges with pairwise potentials that are derived from the joint probabilities of target-language labels occurring together in the training data. Thus the task of finding the optimal translations into five languages jointly is framed as a MAP (Maximum A Posteriori) inference problem, where we try to maximize the joint probability $P(w_{fr}, w_{es}, w_{it}, w_{de}, w_{nl})$, given the evidence of the features extracted from the source-language sentence. The inference process is performed using loopy belief propagation (Murphy et al., 1999), which is an approximate but tractable inference algorithm that, while it gives no guarantees, often produces good solutions in practice.

The intuition behind using a Markov network for this task is that, since we must make five decisions for each source-language sentence, we should make use of the correlations between the target-language words. Correlations might occur in practice due to cognates – the languages in the shared task are fairly closely related – or they may simply reflect ambiguities in the source language that are resolved in two target languages.

So by building a Markov network in which all of the classifiers can communicate (see Figure 2), we allow nodes to influence the translation decisions of their neighbors, but only proportionally to the correlation between the translations that we observe in the two languages.

We frame the MAP inference task as a minimization problem; we want to find an assignment that minimizes the sum of all of our penalty functions, which we will describe next. First, we have a unary function from each of the five L1 classifiers, which correspond to nodes in the network. These functions each assign a penalty to each possible label for the target word in the corresponding language; that penalty is simply the negative log of the probability of the label, as estimated by the classifier.

Formally, a unary potential ϕ_i, for some fixed set of features f and a particular language i, is a function from a label l to some positive penalty value.

$$\phi_i(l) = -logP(L_i = l|F = f)$$

Secondly, for each unordered pair of classifiers (i, j) (*i.e.*, each edge in the graph) there is a pairwise potential function $\phi_{(i,j)}$ that assigns a penalty to any assignment of that pair of variables.

$$\phi_{(i,j)}(l_i, l_j) = -logP(L_i = l_i, L_j = l_j)$$

Here by $P(L_i = l_i, L_j = l_j)$, we mean the probability that, for a fixed ambiguous input word, language i takes the label l_i and language j takes the label l_j. These joint probabilities are estimated from the training data; we count the number of times each pair of labels l_i and l_j co-occurs in the training sentences and divide, with smoothing to avoid zero probabilities and thus infinite penalties.

When it comes time to choose translations, we want to find a complete assignment to the five variables that minimizes the sum of all of the penalties assigned by the ϕ functions. As mentioned earlier, we do this via loopy belief propagation, using the formulation for pairwise Markov networks that passes messages directly between the nodes rather than first constructing a cluster graph (Koller and Friedman, 2009, §11.3.5.1).

As we are trying to compute the minimum-penalty assignment to the five variables, we use the *min-sum* version of loopy belief propagation. The messages are mappings from the possible values that the recipient node could take to penalty values.

At each time step, every node passes to each of its neighbors a message of the following form:

$$\delta_{i\rightarrow j}^{t}(L_j) = \min_{l_i \in L_i} \Big[\phi_i(l_i) + \phi_{(i,j)}(l_i, l_j) + \sum_{k \in S-\{i,j\}} \delta_{k\rightarrow i}^{t-1}(l_i)\Big]$$

By this expression, we mean that the message from node i to node j at time t is a function from possible labels for node j to scalar penalty values. Each penalty value is determined by minimizing over the possible labels for node i, such that we find the label l_i that minimizes sum of the unary cost for that label, the binary cost for l_i and l_j taken jointly, and all of the penalties in the messages that node i received at the previous time step, except for the one from node j.

Intuitively, these messages inform a given neighbor about the estimate, from the perspective of the sending node and what it has heard from its other neighbors, of the minimum penalty that would be incurred if the recipient node were to take a given label. As a concrete example, when the *nl* node sends a message to the *fr* node at time step 10, this message is a table mapping from all possible French translations of the current target word to their associated penalty values. The message depends on three things: the function ϕ_{nl} (itself dependent on the probability distribution output by the L1 classifier), the binary potential function $\phi_{(nl,fr)}$, and the messages from *es*, *it* and *de* from time step 9. Note that the binary potential functions are symmetric because they are derived from joint probabilities.

Loopy belief propagation is an approximate inference algorithm, and it is neither guaranteed to find a globally optimal solution, nor even to converge at all, but it does often find good solutions in practice. We run it for twenty iterations, which empirically works well. After the message-passing iterations, each node chooses the value that minimizes the sum of the penalties from messages and from its own unary potential function. To avoid accumulating very large penalties, we normalize the outgoing messages at each time step and give a larger weight to the unary potential functions. These normalization and weighting parameters were set by hand, but seem to work well in practice.

5 Training Data Extraction

For simplicity and comparability with previous work, we worked with the Europarl Intersection corpus provided by the task organizers. Europarl (Koehn, 2005) is a parallel corpus of proceedings of the European Parliament, currently available in 21 European languages, although not every sentence is translated into every language. The Europarl Intersection is the intersection of the sentences from Europarl that are available in English and all five of the target languages for the task.

In order to produce the training data for the classifiers, we first tokenized the text for all six languages with the default NLTK tokenizer and tagged the English text with the Stanford Tagger (Toutanova et al., 2003). We aligned the untagged English with each of the target languages using the Berkeley Aligner (DeNero and Klein, 2007) to get one-to-many alignments from English to target-language words, since the target-language labels may be multi-word phrases. We used nearly the default settings for Berkeley Aligner, except that we ran 20 iterations each of IBM Model 1 and HMM alignment.

We used TreeTagger (Schmid, 1995) to lemmatize the text. At first this caused some confusion in our pipeline, as TreeTagger by default re-tokenizes input text and tries to recognize multi-word expressions. Both of these, while sensible behaviors, were unexpected, and resulted in a surprising number of tokens in the TreeTagger output. Once we turned off these behaviors, TreeTagger provided useful lemmas for all of the languages.

Given the tokenized and aligned sentences, with their part-of-speech tags and lemmas, we used a number of heuristics to extract the appropriate target-language labels for each English-language input sentence. For each target word, we extracted a sense inventory V_i from the gold standard answers from the 2010 iteration of this task (Lefever and Hoste, 2009). Then, for each English sentence that contains one of the target words used as a noun, we examine the alignments to determine whether that word is aligned with a sense present in V_i , or whether the words aligned to that noun are a subsequence of such a sense. The same check is performed both on the lemmatized and unlemmatized versions of the target-language sentence. If we do find a match, then that sense from the gold standard V_i is taken to be the label for this sentence. While a gold standard sense inventory will clearly not be present for general translation systems, there will be some vocabulary of possible translations for each word, taken from a bilingual dictionary or the phrase table in a phrase-based SMT system.

If a label from V_i is not found with the alignments, but some other word or phrase is aligned with the ambiguous noun, then we trust the output of the aligner, and the lemmatized version of this target-language phrase is assigned as the label for this sentence. In this case we used some heuristic functions to remove stray punctuation and attached articles (such as *d'* from French or *nell'* from Italian) that were often left appended to the tokens by the default NLTK English tokenizer.

We dropped all of the training instances with labels that only occurred once, considering them likely alignment errors or other noise.

6 Results

There were two settings for the evaluation, *best* and *oof*. In either case, systems may present multiple possible answers for a given translation, although in the *best* setting, the first answer is given more weight in the evaluation, and the scoring encourages only returning the top answer. In the *oof* setting, systems are asked to return the top-five most likely translations. In both settings, the answers are compared against translations provided by several human annotators for each test sentence, who provided a number of possible target-language translations in lemmatized form, and more points are given for matching the more popular translations given by the annotators. In the "mode" variant of scoring, only the one most common answer for a given test sentence is considered valid. For a complete explanation of the evaluation and its scoring, please see the shared task description (Lefever and Hoste, 2013).

The scores for our systems[3] are reported in Figure 3. In all of the settings, our systems posted some of the top results among entrants in the shared task, achieving the best scores for some evaluations and some languages. For every setting and language, our systems beat the most-frequent sense baseline, and our best results usually came from either the L2 or MRF system, which suggests that there is some benefit in using multilingual information from the parallel corpora, even without translating the whole source sentence.

For the *best* evaluation, considering only the mode gold-standard answers, our L2 system achieved the highest scores in the competition for Spanish and German. For the *oof* evaluation, our MRF system – with its post-competition bug fix – posted the best results for Spanish, German and Italian in both complete and mode variants. Also, curiously, our L1 system posted the best results in the competition for Dutch in the *oof* variant.

For the *best* evaluation, our results were lower than those posted by ParaSense, and in the standard *best* setting, they were also lower than those from the *c1lN* system (van Gompel and van den Bosch, 2013) and *adapt1* (Carpuat, 2013). This, combined with the relatively small difference between our simplest system and the more sophisticated ones, suggests that there are many improvements that could be made to our system; perhaps

[3]The *oof* scores for the MRF system reflect a small bug fix after the competition.

system	es	nl	de	it	fr
MFS	23.23	20.66	17.43	20.21	25.74
best	32.16	23.61	20.82	25.66	30.11
PS	31.72	25.29	24.54	28.15	31.21
L1	29.01	21.53	19.5	24.52	27.01
L2	28.49	**22.36**	**19.92**	23.94	**28.23**
MRF	**29.36**	21.61	19.76	**24.62**	27.46

(a) *best* evaluation results: precision

system	es	nl	de	it	fr
MFS	53.07	43.59	38.86	42.63	51.36
best	62.21	47.83	44.02	53.98	59.80
L1	61.69	46.55	43.66	53.57	57.76
L2	59.51	46.36	42.32	53.05	**58.20**
MRF	***62.21***	**46.63**	***44.02***	***53.98***	57.83

(b) *oof* evaluation results: precision

system	es	nl	de	it	fr
MFS	27.48	24.15	15.30	19.88	20.19
best	37.11	27.96	24.74	31.61	26.62
PS	40.26	30.29	25.48	30.11	26.33
L1	36.32	25.39	24.16	26.52	**21.24**
L2	***37.11***	25.34	***24.74***	**26.65**	21.07
MRF	36.57	**25.72**	24.01	26.26	**21.24**

(c) *best* evaluation results: mode precision

system	es	nl	de	it	fr
MFS	57.35	41.97	44.35	41.69	47.42
best	65.10	47.34	53.75	57.50	57.57
L1	64.65	***47.34***	53.50	56.61	51.96
L2	62.52	44.06	49.03	54.06	**53.57**
MRF	***65.10***	47.29	***53.75***	***57.50***	52.14

(d) *oof* evaluation results: mode precision

Figure 3: Task results for our systems. Scores in **bold** are the best result for that language and evaluation out of our systems, and those in ***bold italics*** are the best posted in the competition. For comparison, we also give scores for the most-frequent-sense baseline ("MFS"), ParaSense ("PS"), the system developed by Lefever and Hoste, and the best posted score for competing systems this year ("best").

we could integrate ideas from the other entries in the shared task this year.

7 Conclusions and future work

Our systems had a strong showing in the competition, always beating the MFS baseline, achieving the top score for three of the five languages in the *oof* evaluation, and for two languages in the *best* evaluation when considering the mode gold-standard answers. The systems that took into account evidence from multiple sources had better performance than the one using monolingual features: our top result in every language came from either the L2 or the MRF classifier for both evaluations. This suggests that it is possible to make use of the evidence in several parallel corpora in a CL-WSD task without translating every word in a source sentence into many target languages.

We expect that the L2 classifier could be improved by adding features derived from more classifiers and making use of information from many disparate sources. We would like to try adding classifiers trained on the other Europarl languages, as well as completely different corpora. The L2 classifier approach only requires that the first-layer classifiers make *some* prediction based on text in the source language. They need not be trained from the same source text, depend on the same features, or even output words as labels. In future work we will explore all of these variations. One could, for example, train a monolingual WSD system on a sense-tagged corpus and use this as an additional information source for an L2 classifier.

There remain a number of avenues that we would like to explore for the MRF system; thus far, we have used the joint probability of two labels to set the binary potentials. We would like to investigate other functions, especially ones that do not incur large penalties for rare labels, as the joint probability of two labels that often co-occur but are both rare will be low. Also, in the current system, the relative weights of the binary potentials and the unary potentials were set by hand, with a very small amount of empirical tuning. We could, in the future, tune the weights with a more principled optimization strategy, using a development set.

As with the L2 classifiers, it would be helpful in the future for the MRF system to not require many mutually parallel corpora for training – however, the current approach for estimating the edge potentials requires the use of bitext for each edge in the network. Perhaps these correlations could be estimated in a semi-supervised way, with high-confidence automatic labels being used to estimate the joint distribution over target-language phrases. We would also like to investigate approaches to jointly disambiguate many words in the same sentence, since lexical ambiguity is not just a problem for a few nouns.

Aside from improvements to the design of our CL-WSD system itself, we want to use it in a practical system for translating into under-resourced languages. We are now working on integrating this project with our rule-based MT system, L^3 (Gasser, 2012). We had experimented with a similar, though less sophisticated, CL-WSD system for Quechua (Rudnick, 2011), but in the future, L^3 with the integrated CL-WSD system should be capable of translating Spanish to Guarani, either as a standalone system, or as part of a computer-assisted translation tool.

References

Steven Bird, Ewan Klein, and Edward Loper. 2009. *Natural Language Processing with Python*. O'Reilly Media.

Peter F. Brown, Stephen A. Della Pietra, Vincent J. Della Pietra, and Robert L. Mercer. 1991. Word-Sense Disambiguation Using Statistical Methods. In *Proceedings of the 29th Annual Meeting of the Association for Computational Linguistics*, pages 264–270.

Marine Carpuat and Dekai Wu. 2007. How Phrase Sense Disambiguation Outperforms Word Sense Disambiguation for Statistical Machine Translation. In *11th Conference on Theoretical and Methodological Issues in Machine Translation*.

Marine Carpuat. 2013. NRC: A Machine Translation Approach to Cross-Lingual Word Sense Disambiguation (SemEval-2013 Task 10). In *Proceedings of the 7th International Workshop on Semantic Evaluation (SemEval 2013)*, Atlanta, USA.

John DeNero and Dan Klein. 2007. Tailoring Word Alignments to Syntactic Machine Translation. In *Proceedings of the 45th Annual Meeting of the Association of Computational Linguistics*, pages 17–24, Prague, Czech Republic, June. Association for Computational Linguistics.

Michael Gasser. 2012. Toward a Rule-Based System for English-Amharic Translation. In *LREC-2012: SALTMIL-AfLaT Workshop on Language technology for normalisation of less-resourced languages*.

Philipp Koehn. 2005. Europarl: A Parallel Corpus for Statistical Machine Translation. In *Proceedings of The Tenth Machine Translation Summit*, Phuket, Thailand.

D. Koller and N. Friedman. 2009. *Probabilistic Graphical Models: Principles and Techniques*. MIT Press.

Els Lefever and Véronique Hoste. 2009. SemEval-2010 Task 3: Cross-lingual Word Sense Disambiguation. In *Proceedings of the Workshop on Semantic Evaluations: Recent Achievements and Future Directions (SEW-2009)*, pages 82–87, Boulder, Colorado, June. Association for Computational Linguistics.

Els Lefever and Véronique Hoste. 2013. SemEval-2013 Task 10: Cross-Lingual Word Sense Disambiguation. In *Proceedings of the 7th International Workshop on Semantic Evaluation (SemEval 2013)*, Atlanta, USA.

Els Lefever, Véronique Hoste, and Martine De Cock. 2011. ParaSense or How to Use Parallel Corpora for Word Sense Disambiguation. In *Proceedings of the 49th Annual Meeting of the Association for Computational Linguistics: Human Language Technologies*, pages 317–322, Portland, Oregon, USA, June. Association for Computational Linguistics.

Kevin P. Murphy, Yair Weiss, and Michael I. Jordan. 1999. Loopy Belief Propagation for Approximate Inference: An Empirical Study. In *UAI '99: Proceedings of the Fifteenth Conference on Uncertainty in Artificial Intelligence*, Stockholm, Sweden.

Alex Rudnick. 2011. Towards Cross-Language Word Sense Disambiguation for Quechua. In *Proceedings of the Second Student Research Workshop associated with RANLP 2011*, pages 133–138, Hissar, Bulgaria, September. RANLP 2011 Organising Committee.

Helmut Schmid. 1995. Improvements In Part-of-Speech Tagging With an Application To German. In *Proceedings of the ACL SIGDAT-Workshop*, pages 47–50.

Kristina Toutanova, Dan Klein, Christopher D. Manning, and Yoram Singer. 2003. Feature-Rich Part-of-Speech Tagging with a Cyclic Dependency Network. In *PROCEEDINGS OF HLT-NAACL*, pages 252–259.

Maarten van Gompel and Antal van den Bosch. 2013. WSD2: Parameter optimisation for Memory-based Cross-Lingual Word-Sense Disambiguation. In *Proceedings of the 7th International Workshop on Semantic Evaluation (SemEval 2013)*, Atlanta, USA.

LIMSI : Cross-lingual Word Sense Disambiguation using Translation Sense Clustering

Marianna Apidianaki
LIMSI-CNRS
Rue John Von Neumann
91403 Orsay Cedex, France
marianna@limsi.fr

Abstract

We describe the LIMSI system for the SemEval-2013 Cross-lingual Word Sense Disambiguation (CLWSD) task. Word senses are represented by means of translation clusters in different languages built by a cross-lingual Word Sense Induction (WSI) method. Our CLWSD classifier exploits the WSI output for selecting appropriate translations for target words in context. We present the design of the system and the obtained results.

1 Introduction

This paper describes the LIMSI system that participated in the Cross-Lingual Word Sense Disambiguation (CLWSD) task of SemEval-2013. The goal of CLWSD is to predict semantically correct translations for ambiguous words in context (Resnik and Yarowsky, 2000; Carpuat and Wu, 2007; Apidianaki, 2009). The CLWSD task of the SemEval-2013 evaluation campaign is a lexical sample task for English nouns and is divided into two subtasks: the *best* subtask where systems are asked to provide a unique good translation for words in context; the *out-of-five* (oof) subtask where systems can propose up to five semantically related translations for each target word instance (Lefever and Hoste, 2013). The CLWSD lexical sample contains 20 nouns and the test set is composed of 50 instances per noun. System performance is evaluated by comparing the system output to a set of gold standard annotations in five languages: French, Spanish, Italian, Dutch and German. Participating systems have to provide contextually appropriate translations for target words in context in each or a subset of the target languages.

We apply the CLWSD method proposed by Apidianaki (2009) to three bilingual tasks: English-Spanish, English-French and English-Italian. The method exploits the translation clusters generated in the three target languages by a cross-lingual Word Sense Induction (WSI) method. The WSI method clusters the translations of target words in a parallel corpus using source language context vectors. The same vectors are exploited during disambiguation in order to select the most appropriate translations for new instances of the target words in context.

2 System Description

2.1 Translation clustering

Contrary to monolingual WSI methods which group the instances of the words into clusters describing their senses, the cross-lingual WSI method used here clusters the translations of words in a parallel corpus. The corpus used for French consists of the English-French parts of Europarl (version 7) (Koehn, 2005) and of the JRC-Acquis corpus (Steinberger et al., 2006), joined together. For English-Spanish and English-Italian we only use the corresponding parts of Europarl. The corpora are first tokenized and lowercased using the Moses scripts, then lemmatized and tagged by part-of-speech (PoS) using the TreeTagger (Schmid, 1994). Words in the corpus are replaced by a lemma and PoS tag pair before word alignment, to resolve categorical ambiguities in context. The corpus is aligned in both translation directions with GIZA++ (Och and Ney, 2000)

*Second Joint Conference on Lexical and Computational Semantics (*SEM), Volume 2: Seventh International Workshop on Semantic Evaluation (SemEval 2013)*, pages 178–182, Atlanta, Georgia, June 14-15, 2013.

Target word	French	Spanish	Italian
range	{ensemble, diversité, palette, nombre} {domaine} {portée} {éventail, nombre, gamme, série, ensemble}	{gama, serie, abanico, diversidad, variedad, espectro, conjunto} {cantidad, alcance, àmbito, número, tipo, espectro, rango} {amplitud}	{serie, gamma, spettro, numero, ventaglio} {ampiezza, portata} {settore, ambito} {diversitá, fascia}
mood	{climat, atmosphère}, {esprit, atmosphère, ambiance, humeur} {opinion} {volonté} {attitude}	{clima, atmòsfera, ambiente} {ànimo, sentimiento} {talante} {ànimo, clima, ambiente} {ànimo, humor, ambiente}	{clima} {atmosfera} {chiarezza, predisposizione} {opinione} {atteggiamento}
mission	{opération, mandat} {délégation, commission} {délégation, tâche, voyage, opération}	{función, cometido, objetivo, tarea} {viaje, tarea, delegación} {tarea, mandato, cometido}	{mandato, obiettivo, compito, mission, funzione, operazione,} {viaggio, mission, commissione, delegazione}

Table 1: Sense clusters generated by the WSI method in the three languages.

and three bilingual lexicons are built from the alignment results (one for each language pair) containing intersecting alignments. The lexicons contain noun translations of each English target word in the three languages. We keep French translations that translate the target words at least 10 times in the training corpus; for Spanish and Italian, where the corpus was smaller, the translation frequency threshold was set to 5.

For each translation T_i of a word w, we extract the content words that occur in the same sentence as w whenever it is translated by T_i. These constitute the features of the vector built for the translation. Let N be the number of features retained for each T_i from the corresponding source contexts. Each feature F_j ($1 \leq j \leq N$) receives a total weight $\text{tw}(F_j, T_i)$ defined as the product of the feature's global weight, $\text{gw}(F_j)$, and its local weight with that translation, $\text{lw}(F_j, T_i)$. The global weight of a feature F_j is a function of the number N_i of translations (T_i's) to which F_j is related, and of the probabilities (p_{ij}) that F_j co-occurs with instances of w translated by each of the T_i's:

$$\text{gw}(F_j) = 1 - \frac{\sum_{T_i} p_{ij} \log(p_{ij})}{N_i} \quad (1)$$

Each of the p_{ij}'s is computed as the ratio between the co-occurrence frequency of F_j with w when translated as T_i, denoted as $\text{cooc\_frequency}(F_j, T_i)$, and the total number of features (N) seen with T_i:

$$p_{ij} = \frac{\text{cooc\_frequency}(F_j, T_i)}{N} \quad (2)$$

The local weight $\text{lw}(F_j, T_i)$ between F_j and T_i directly depends on their co-occurrence frequency:

$$\text{lw}(F_j, T_i) = \log(\text{cooc\_frequency}(F_j, T_i)) \quad (3)$$

The pairwise similarity of the translation vectors is calculated using the Weighted Jaccard Coefficient (Grefenstette, 1994). The similarity score of each translation pair is compared to a threshold locally defined for each w, which serves to distinguish strongly related translations from semantically unrelated ones. The semantically related translations of a word w are then grouped into clusters. Translation pairs with a score above the threshold form a set of initial clusters that might be further enriched with other translations through an iterative procedure, provided that there are other translations that are strongly related to the elements in the cluster.[1] The clustering stops when all the translations of w have been clustered and all their relations have been checked. The algorithm performs a soft clustering so translations might be found in different clusters. Final clusters are characterized by global connectivity, meaning that all their elements are linked by pertinent relations. Table 1 gives examples of clusters generated for CLWSD target words in the three languages. The clusters group translations carrying the same sense and their overlaps describe relations between senses. The translation clusters serve as the target words' candidate senses from which one has to be selected during disambiguation.

[1] The thresholding procedure and the clustering algorithm are described in detail in Apidianaki and He (2010).

Subtask	Metric	Spanish			French			Italian		
		LIMSI	Baseline	Best system	LIMSI	Baseline	Best system	LIMSI	Baseline	Best system
Best	P/R	24,7	23,23	32,16	24,56	25,73	30,11	21,2	20,21	25,66
	Mode P/R	32,09	27,48	37,11	22,16	20,19	26,62	23,06	19,88	31,61
OOF	P/R	49,01	53,07	61,69	45,37	51,35	59,8	40,25	42,62	53,57
	Mode P/R	51,41	57,34	64,65	39,54	47,42	57,57	47,21	41,68	56,61
OOF (dupl)	P/R	98,6	-	-	101,75	-	-	90,23	-	-
	Mode P/R	51,41	-	-	39,54	-	-	47,21	-	-

Table 2: Results at the SemEval 2013 CLWSD task.

2.2 Word Sense Disambiguation

The vectors used for clustering the translations also serve for disambiguating new instances of the target words in context. The new contexts are tokenized, lowercased, PoS tagged and lemmatized to facilitate comparison with the vectors. We use the features shared by each pair of clustered translations, or the vector corresponding to the translation in an one-element cluster. If no CFs exist between the new context and a pair of translations, WSD is performed by comparing context information separately to the vector of each clustered translation. Once the common features (CFs) between the vectors and the new context are identified, a score is calculated corresponding to the mean of the weights of the CFs with the translations (weights assigned to the features during WSI). In formula 4, CF_j is the set of CFs and N_{CF} is the number of translations T_i characterized by a CF.

$$wsd\_score = \frac{\sum_{i=1}^{N_{CF}} \sum_j w(T_i, CF_j)}{N_{CF} \cdot |CF_j|} \quad (4)$$

The cluster containing the highest ranked translation or translation pair is selected and assigned to the new target word instance. If the translations are present in more than one clusters, a new score is calculated using equation 4 and by taking into account the weights of the CFs with the other translations (T_i's) in the cluster.

3 Evaluation

Systems participating to the CLWSD task have to provide the most plausible translation for a word in context in the *best* subtask, and five semantically correct translations in *oof*. The baselines provided by the organizers are based on the output of GIZA++ alignments on Europarl. The *best* baseline corresponds to the most frequent translation of the target word in the corpus and the *oof* baseline to the five most frequent translations. Our CLWSD system makes predictions in three languages for all 1000 test instances. If the selected cluster contains five translations, all of them are proposed in the *oof* subtask while if it is bigger, the five most frequent translations are selected. In case of smaller clusters, the *best* translation is repeated in the output until reaching five suggestions. Duplicate suggestions were allowed in previous cross-lingual SemEval tasks as a means to boost translations with high confidence (Mihalcea et al., 2010). However, as in this year's CLWSD task the *oof* system output has been post-processed by the organizers to keep only unique translations, the number of predictions made by our system for some words has been significantly reduced. This has had a negative impact on the *oof* results, as we will show in the next section.

For selecting *best* translations, each translation of a target word w is scored separately by comparing its vector to the new context. In case the highest-ranked translation has a score lower than 1, the system falls back to using the most frequent translation (MFT). To note that frequency information differs from the one used in the MFT baseline because words in our corpus were replaced by a lemma and PoS tag pair prior to alignment. The discrepancy is more apparent in French where MFT is the most frequent translation of the target word in the joint Europarl and JRC-Acquis corpus. Five teams participated to the CLWSD task with a varying number of systems: twelve systems provided output for Spanish and ten for French and Italian.

4 Results

The results obtained by our system for the *best* and *oof* evaluations in the three languages (Spanish, French and Italian) are presented in Table 2. We contrast them with the baselines provided by the organizers and with the score of the system that performed best in each subtask. Our system made suggestions for all test instances, so recall (R) coincides with precision (P). The baselines are quite challenging, as noted in Lefever and Hoste (2010), especially the *oof* one which contains the five most frequent Europarl translations. These often correspond to the most frequent translations from different sense clusters and cover multiple senses of the target word.

Our system outperforms the *best* baseline in all languages except for French, where the *best* score lies near below the baseline. This is not surprising given that the training corpus for French is the joint Europarl and JRC-Acquis corpus, which causes a discrepancy between the selected *best* translations and the baseline. The mode precision and recall scores reflect the capacity of the system to predict the translations that were most frequently selected by the annotators for each instance and are thus considered as the most plausible ones. Our system outperforms the mode *best* baselines for all languages.

In the *oof* task, the system has been penalized by the elimination of duplicate translations from the output after submission. In previous work, the CLWSD system gave very good results when applied, with some slight variations, to the *out-of-ten* subtask of the SemEval-2010 Cross-Lingual Lexical Substitution task where duplicates served to promote translations with high confidence (Mihalcea et al., 2010; Apidianaki, 2011). Here, after the post-processing step, *oof* suggestions contain in many cases less than five translations which explains the low scores. In Table 2 we provide *oof* results before and after post-processing the output and show how the system was affected by this change in evaluation. By boosting plausible translations, precision and recall scores get higher while mode scores are naturally not affected.[2] As the other systems might have been impacted to different extents by this change, we cannot estimate how this affects the global system ranking.

[2]Precision scores might be inflated, as in the case of French, because the credit for each item is not divided by the number of predictions and the annotation frequencies are used.

5 Discussion and future work

We presented a CLWSD system that uses translation clusters as candidate senses. Disambiguation is performed by comparing the feature vectors that served for clustering to the context of new target word instances. We observe that the use of a bigger corpus – as in the case of French – not only does not help in this task but actually has a negative impact on the results. This is due to the inclusion of translations that are not present in the gold standard (built from Europarl) and to the discrepancy between most frequent translations in the large corpus and the Europarl MFT baselines. This discrepancy affects all three languages, as words in the training corpora were replaced by lemma and PoS tag pairs prior to alignment.

It is important to note that our CLWSD method exploits the output of another unsupervised semantic analysis method (WSI) which groups the translations into clusters. This is an important feature of the system and affects the results in two ways. First, the translation clusters of a word constitute its candidate senses from which the CLWSD method selects the most appropriate one for a given context. This means that no variation regarding the contents of a cluster is permitted and that different instances are tagged by the same set of translations, contrary to the gold standard annotations which might, at the same time, be very close and contain some variations. In the system output, this is the case only when overlapping clusters are selected for different instances. Moreover, given that the WSI method is automatic and that the clusters are not manually validated, the noise that might be introduced during clustering is propagated and reflected in the disambiguation results. So, if a cluster contains one or more noisy translations, these occur in the disambiguation output and naturally count as wrong predictions. However, in an application setting like Machine Translation (MT), the translation clusters could be filtered using information from the target language context. Future work will focus on integrating this method into MT systems and examining ways for optimally taking advantage of CLWSD predictions in this context.

References

Marianna Apidianaki and Yifan He. 2010. An algorithm for cross-lingual sense clustering tested in a MT evaluation setting. In *Proceedings of the 7th International Workshop on Spoken Language Translation (IWSLT-10)*, pages 219–226, Paris, France.

Marianna Apidianaki. 2009. Data-driven Semantic Analysis for Multilingual WSD and Lexical Selection in Translation. In *Proceedings of the 12th Conference of the European Chapter of the Association for Computational Linguistics (EACL-09)*, pages 77–85, Athens, Greece.

Marianna Apidianaki. 2011. Unsupervised Cross-Lingual Lexical Substitution. In *Proceedings of the First workshop on Unsupervised Learning in NLP in conjunction with EMNLP*, pages 13–23, Edinburgh, Scotland, July. Association for Computational Linguistics.

Marine Carpuat and Dekai Wu. 2007. Improving statistical machine translation using word sense disambiguation. In *EMNLP-CoNLL*, pages 61–72.

Gregory Grefenstette. 1994. *Explorations in Automatic Thesaurus Discovery*. Kluwer Academic Publishers, Norwell, MA.

Philipp Koehn. 2005. Europarl: A Parallel Corpus for Statistical Machine Translation. In *Proceedings of MT Summit X*, pages 79–86, Phuket, Thailand.

Els Lefever and Veronique Hoste. 2010. SemEval-2010 Task 3: Cross-lingual Word Sense Disambiguation. In *Proceedings of the 5th International Workshop on Semantic Evaluations (SemEval-2), ACL 2010*, pages 15–20, Uppsala, Sweden.

Els Lefever and Véronique Hoste. 2013. SemEval-2013 Task 10: Cross-Lingual Word Sense Disambiguation. In *Proceedings of the 7th International Workshop on Semantic Evaluation (SemEval 2013), in conjunction with the Second Joint Conference on Lexical and Computational Semantcis (*SEM 2013)*, pages 63–72, Atlanta, USA.

Rada Mihalcea, Ravi Sinha, and Diana McCarthy. 2010. SemEval-2010 Task 2: Cross-Lingual Lexical Substitution. In *Proceedings of the 5th International Workshop on Semantic Evaluations (SemEval-2), ACL 2010*, pages 9–14, Uppsala, Sweden.

Franz Josef Och and Hermann Ney. 2000. Improved statistical alignment models. In *Proceedings of the 38th Annual Meeting of the Association for Computational Linguistics (ACL'00)*, pages 440–447, Hongkong, China.

Philip Resnik and David Yarowsky. 2000. Distinguishing Systems and Distinguishing Senses: New Evaluation Methods for Word Sense Disambiguation. *Natural Language Engineering*, 5(3):113–133.

Helmut Schmid. 1994. Probabilistic Part-of-Speech Tagging Using Decision Trees. In *Proceedings of the International Conference on New Methods in Language Processing*, pages 44–49, Manchester, UK.

Ralf Steinberger, Bruno Pouliquen, Anna Widiger, Camelia Ignat, Tomaž Erjavec, and Dan Tufiş. 2006. The JRC-Acquis: A multilingual aligned parallel corpus with 20+ languages. In *Proceedings of the 5th International Conference on Language Resources and Evaluation (LREC'2006)*, pages 2142–2147.

WSD2: Parameter optimisation for Memory-based Cross-Lingual Word-Sense Disambiguation

Maarten van Gompel and Antal van den Bosch
Centre for Language Studies, Radboud University Nijmegen
proycon@anaproy.nl, a.vandenbosch@let.ru.nl

Abstract

We present our system WSD2 which participated in the Cross-Lingual Word-Sense Disambiguation task for SemEval 2013 (Lefever and Hoste, 2013). The system closely resembles our winning system for the same task in SemEval 2010. It is based on k-nearest neighbour classifiers which map words with local and global context features onto their translation, i.e. their cross-lingual sense. The system participated in the task for all five languages and obtained winning scores for four of them when asked to predict the best translation(s). We tested various configurations of our system, focusing on various levels of hyperparameter optimisation and feature selection. Our final results indicate that hyperparameter optimisation did not lead to the best results, indicating overfitting by our optimisation method in this aspect. Feature selection does have a modest positive impact.

1 Introduction

WSD2 is a rewrite and extension of our previous system (van Gompel, 2010) that participated in the Cross-Lingual Word Sense Disambiguation task in SemEval 2010 (Lefever and Hoste, 2010). In WSD2 we introduce and test a new level of hyperparameter optimisation. Unlike the previous occasion, we participate in all five target languages (Dutch, Spanish, Italian, French, and German). The task presents twenty polysemous nouns with fifty instances each to be mapped onto normalised (lemmatised) translations in all languages. The task is described in detail by Lefever and Hoste (2013).

Trial data is provided and has been used to optimise system parameters. Due to the unsupervised nature of the task, no training data is provided. However, given that the gold standard of the task is based exclusively on the Europarl parallel corpus (Koehn, 2005), we select that same corpus to minimise our chances of delivering translations that the human annotators preparing the test data could have never picked.

Systems may output several senses per instance, rather than producing just one sense prediction. These are evaluated in two different ways. The scoring type "**best**" expects that the system outputs the sense it considers the most likely, or a number of senses in the order of its confidence in these senses being correct. Multiple guesses are penalised, however. In contrast, the scoring type "**out of five**" expects five guesses, in which each answer carries the same weight. These metrics are more extensively described in Mihalcea et al. (2010) and Lefever and Hoste (2013).

2 System Description

The WSD2 system, like its predecessor, distributes the task over word experts. Each word expert is a k-nearest neighbour classifier specialising in the disambiguation of a single of the twenty provided nouns. This is implemented using the Tilburg Memory Based Learner (TiMBL) (Daelemans et al., 2009). The classifiers are trained as follows: First the parallel corpus which acts as training data is tokenised using Ucto (van Gompel et al., 2012), for all five language pairs. Then, a word-alignment between sentence pairs in the Europarl training data is established, for which we use GIZA++ (Och and Ney, 2000). We use the intersection of both translation directions, as we know the sense reposi-

*Second Joint Conference on Lexical and Computational Semantics (*SEM), Volume 2: Seventh International Workshop on Semantic Evaluation (SemEval 2013)*, pages 183–187, Atlanta, Georgia, June 14-15, 2013.

tory from which the human annotators preparing the task's test data can select their translations is created in the same fashion.

Whilst the word alignment is computed on the actual word forms, we also need lemmas for both the source language (English) as well as for all of the five target languages. The English nouns in the test data can be either singular or plural, and both forms may occur in the input. Second, the target translations all have to be mapped to their lemma forms. Moreover, to be certain we are dealing with nouns in the source language, a Part-of-Speech tagger is also required. PoS tagging and lemmatisation is conducted using Freeling (Atserias et al., 2006) for English, Spanish and Italian; Frog (van den Bosch et al., 2007) for Dutch, and TreeTagger (Schmid, 1994) for German and French.

With all of this data generated, we then iterate over all sentences in the parallel corpus and extract occurrences of any of the twenty nouns, along with the translation they are aligned to according to the word alignment. We extract the words themselves and compute the lemma and the part-of-speech tag, and do the same for a specified number of words to the left and to the right of the found occurrence. These constitute the *local context* features.

In addition to this, *global context* features are extracted; these are a set of keywords per lemma and per translation which are found occurring above certain occurrence thresholds at arbitrary positions in the same sentence, as this is the widest context supplied in the task data. The global context features are represented as a binary bag-of-words model in which the presence of each of the keywords that may be indicative for a given mapping of the focus word to a sense is represented by a boolean value. Such a set of keywords is constructed for each of the twenty nouns, per language.

The method used to extract these keywords (k) is proposed by Ng and Lee (1996) and used also by Hoste et al. (2002). Assume we have a focus word f, more precisely, a lemma of one of the target nouns. We also have one of its aligned translations/senses s, also a lemma. We can now estimate $P(s|k)$, the probability of sense s, given a keyword k. Let $N_{s,k_{local}}$. be the number of occurrences of a possible local context word k with particular focus word lemma-PoS combination and with a particular sense s. Let $N_{k_{local}}$ be the number of occurrences of a possible local context keyword k with a particular focus word-PoS combination regardless of its sense. If we also take into account the frequency of a possible keyword k in the complete training corpus ($N_{k_{corpus}}$), we get:

$$P(s|k) = \frac{N_{s,k_{local}}}{N_{k_{local}}}\left(\frac{1}{N_{k_{corpus}}}\right) \qquad (1)$$

Hoste et al. (2002) select a keyword k for inclusion in the bag-of-words representation if that keyword occurs more than T_1 times in that sense s, and if $P(s|k) \geq T_2$. Both T_1 and T_2 are predefined thresholds, which by default were set to 3 and 0.001 respectively. In addition, WSD2 and its predecessor WSD1 contain an extra parameter which can be enabled to automatically adjust the T_1 threshold when it yields too many or too few keywords. The selection of bag-of-word features is computed prior to the extraction of the training instances, as this information is a prerequisite for the successful generation of both training and test instances.

3 Feature and Hyperparameter Optimisation

The size of the local context, the inclusion of global context features, and the inclusion of syntactic features are all features that can be selected, changed, or disabled, allowing for a variety of combinations to be tested. In addition, each word expert is a k-nearest neighbour classifier that can take on many hyperparameters beyond k. In the present study we performed both optimisations for all word experts, but the optimisations were performed independently to reduce complexity: we optimised classifier hyperparameters on the basis of the training examples extracted from our parallel corpus, producing optimal accuracy on each word-expert. We optimised feature selection on the basis of the trial data provided for the task. As has been argued before (Hoste et al., 2002), the joint search space of feature selection and hyperparameters is prohibitively large. Our current setup runs the risk of finding hyperparameters that are not optimal for the feature selection in the second optimisation step. Our final results indeed show that only feature selection produced improved results. We choose the feature selection with the high-

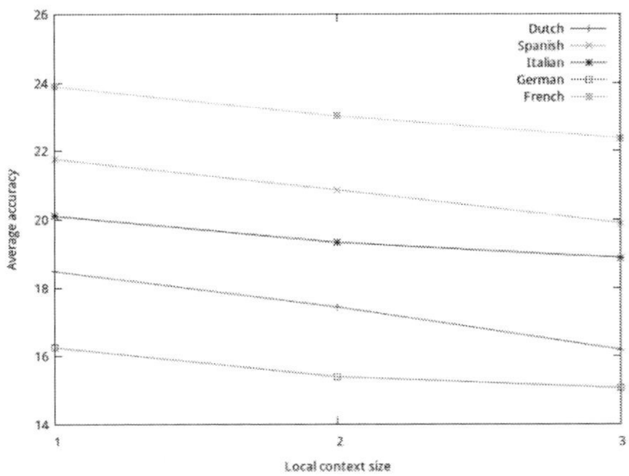

Figure 1: Average accuracy for different local context sizes

est score on the trial set, for each of the nouns and separately for both evaluation metrics in the task.

To optimise the choice of hyperparameters per word expert, a heuristic parameter search algorithm (van den Bosch, 2004)[1] was used that implements wrapped progressive sampling using cross-validation: it performs a large number of experiments with many hyperparameter setting combinations on small samples of training data, and then progressively zooms in on combinations estimated to perform well with larger samples of the training data. As a control run we also trained word experts with default hyperparameters, i.e. with $k = 1$ and with all other hyperparameters at their default values as specified in the TiMBL implementation.

4 Experiments & Results

To assess the accuracy of a certain configuration of our system as a whole, we take the average over all word experts. An initial experiment on the trial data explores the impact of different context sizes, with hyperparameter optimisation on the classifiers. The results, shown in Figure 1, clearly indicate that on average the classifiers perform best with a local context of just one word to the left and one to the right of the word to be disambiguated. Larger context sizes have a negative impact on average accuracy. These tests include hyperparameter optimisation, but the same trend shows without.

[1] http://ilk.uvt.nl/paramsearch/

BEST	**ES**	**FR**	**IT**	**NL**	**DE**
baseline	19.65	21.23	15.17	15.75	13.16
plain	21.76	23.89	20.10	18.47	16.25
+lem (`c1l`)	21.88	**23.93**	**19.90**	**18.61**	**16.43**
+pos	22.09	23.91	19.95	18.02	15.37
lem+pos	**22.12**	23.61	19.82	18.18	15.48
glob.context	20.57	23.34	17.76	17.06	16.05
OUT-OF-5	**ES**	**FR**	**IT**	**NL**	**DE**
baseline	48.34	45.99	34.51	38.59	32.90
plain	49.81	**50.91**	42.30	41.74	**36.86**
+lem (`c1l`)	**49.91**	50.65	**42.41**	**41.83**	36.45
+pos	47.86	49.72	41.91	41.31	35.93
lem+pos	47.90	49.75	41.49	41.31	35.80
glob.ccontext	48.09	49.68	40.87	37.70	34.47

Table 1: Feature exploration on the trial data

BEST	**ES**	**FR**	**IT**	**NL**	**DE**
c1lN	22.60	24.09	19.87	18.70	16.43
c1l	21.88	23.93	19.90	18.61	16.43
var	23.79	**25.66**	**21.65**	**20.19**	**19.06**
varN	**23.90**	25.65	21.52	19.92	18.96
OUT-OF-5	**ES**	**FR**	**IT**	**NL**	**DE**
c1lN	50.14	50.98	42.92	42.08	36.45
c1l	49.91	50.65	42.41	41.83	36.45
var	51.95	**53.66**	45.59	**44.66**	**39.81**
varN	**52.91**	53.61	**45.92**	44.32	39.40

Table 2: Results on the trial data

We submitted three configurations of our system to the shared task, the maximum number of runs. Adding lemma features to the local context window of three words proves beneficial in general, as shown in Table 1. This is therefore the first configuration we submitted (`c1l`). As second configuration (`c1lN`) we submitted the same configuration without parameter optimisation on the classifiers. Note that neither of these include global context features.

The third configuration (`var`) we submitted includes feature selection, and selects per word expert the configuration that has the highest score on the trial data, and thus tests all kinds of configurations. Note that hyperparameter optimisation is also enabled for this configuration. Due to the feature selection on the trial data, we by definition obtain the highest scores on this trial data, but this carries the risk of overfitting. Results on the trial data are shown in Table 2.

The hyperparameter optimisation on classifier accuracy has a slightly negative impact, suggesting overfitting on the training data. Therefore a fourth configuration (`varN`) was tried later to independently assess the idea of feature selection, without hyperparameter optimisation on the classifiers. This proves to be a good idea. However, the fourth configuration was not yet available for the actual competition. This incidentally would have had no impact on the final ranking between competitors. When we run these systems on the actual test data of the shared task, we obtain the results in Table 3. The best score amongst the other competitors is mentioned in the last row for reference, this is the HLTDI team (Rudnick et al., 2013) for all but Best-Spanish, which goes to the NRC contribution (Carpuat, 2013).

BEST	**ES**	**FR**	**IT**	**NL**	**DE**
baseline	23.23	25.74	20.21	20.66	17.42
c1l	28.40	29.88	25.43	23.14	20.70
c1lN	28.65	30.11	**25.66**	**23.61**	20.82
var	23.3	25.89	20.38	17.17	16.2
varN	29.05	**30.15**	24.90	23.57	**21.98**
best.comp	**32.16**	28.23	24.62	22.36	19.92
OUT-OF-5	**ES**	**FR**	**IT**	**NL**	**DE**
baseline	53.07	51.36	42.63	43.59	38.86
c1l	58.23	59.07	52.22	**47.83**	43.17
c1lN	57.62	**59.80**	52.73	47.62	43.24
var	55.70	59.19	51.18	46.85	41.46
varN	58.61	59.26	50.89	50.42	43.34
best.comp	**61.69**	58.20	**53.57**	46.55	**43.66**

Table 3: Results on the test set

A major factor in this task is the accuracy of lemmatisation, and to lesser extent of PoS tagging. We conducted additional experiments on German and French without lemmatisation, tested on the trial data. Results immediately fell below baseline.

Another main factor is the quality of the word alignments, and the degree to which the found word alignments correspond with the translations the human annotators could choose from in preparing the gold standard. An idea we tested is, instead of relying on the mere intersection of word alignments, to use a phrase-translation table generated by and for the Statistical Machine Translation system Moses (Koehn et al., 2007), which uses the grow-diag-final heuristic to extract phrase pairs. This results in more phrases, and whilst this is a good idea for MT, in the current task it has a detrimental effect, as it creates too many translation options and we do not have an MT decoder to discard ineffective options in this task. The grow-diag-final heuristic incorporates unaligned words to the end of a translation in the translation option, a bad idea for CLWSD.

5 Conclusion

In this study we have taken parameter optimisation one step further compared to our previous research (van Gompel, 2010), namely by selecting system parameters per word expert from the best configurations on the trial data. Optimising the hyperparameter of the classifiers on the training data proves to have a slightly negative effect, especially when combined with the selection of features. This is likely due to the fact that feature selection was performed after hyperparameter optimisation, causing certain optimisations to be rendered ineffective.

We can furthermore uphold the conclusion from previous research that including lemma features is generally a good idea. As to the number of local context features, we observed that a context size of one feature to the left, and one to the right, has the best overall average accuracy. Eventually, due to our feature selection without hyperparameter optimisation on the classifier not being available yet at the time of submission, our simplest system `c1lN` emerged as best in the contest.

When asked to predict the best translation(s), our system comes out on top for four out of five languages; only for Spanish we are surpassed by two competitors. Our out-of-five predictions win for two out of five languages, and are fairly close the the best competitor for the others, except again for Spanish.

We assumed independence between hyperparameter optimisation and feature selection, where the former was conducted using cross-validation on the training data rather than on the development set. As this independence assumption is a mere simplification to reduce algorithmic complexity, future research could focus on a more integrated approach and test hyperparameter optimisation of the classifiers on the trial set which may produce better scores.

The WSD2 system is available as open-source under the GNU Public License v3. It is implemented in Python (van Rossum, 2006) and can be obtained from http://github.com/proycon/wsd2[2]. The experimental data and results are included in the git repository as well.

[2] git commit f10e796141003d8a2fbaf8c463588a6d7380c05e represents a fair state of the system at the time of submission

References

J. Atserias, B. Casas, E. Comelles, M. Gonzlez, L. Padró, and M. Padró. 2006. FreeLing 1.3: Syntactic and semantic services in an open-source NLP library . In *Proceedings of the Fifth International Conference on Language Resources and Evaluation (LREC 2006)*, Genoa, Italy. ELRA.

M. Carpuat. 2013. NRC: A Machine Translation Approach to Cross-Lingual Word Sense Disambiguation (semeval-2013 task 10). In *Proceedings of the 7th International Workshop on Semantic Evaluation (SemEval 2013), in conjunction with the Second Joint Conference on Lexical and Computational Semantics.*

W. Daelemans, J. Zavrel, K. Van der Sloot, and A. Van den Bosch. 2009. TiMBL: Tilburg memory based learner, version 6.2, reference guide. Technical Report ILK 09-01, ILK Research Group, Tilburg University.

V. Hoste, I. Hendrickx, W. Daelemans, and A. Van den Bosch. 2002. Parameter optimization for machine learning of word sense disambiguation. *Natural Language Engineering*, 8(4):311–325.

P. Koehn, H. Hoang, A. Birch, C. Callison-Burch, M. Federico, N. Bertoldi, B. Cowan, W. Shen, C. Moran, R. Zens, C. Dyer, O. Bojar, A. Constantin, and E. Herbst. 2007. Moses: Open source toolkit for statistical machine translation. In *Proceedings of the 45th Annual Meeting of the Association for Computational Linguistics Companion Volume Proceedings of the Demo and Poster Sessions*, pages 177–180, Prague, Czech Republic, June. Association for Computational Linguistics.

P. Koehn. 2005. Europarl: A parallel corpus for statistical machine translation. In *In Proceedings of the Machine Translation Summit X ([MT]'05).*, pages 79–86.

E. Lefever and V. Hoste. 2010. Semeval-2010 task 3: Cross-lingual word sense disambiguation. In *Proceedings of the 5th International Workshop on Semantic Evaluation*, SemEval '10, pages 15–20, Stroudsburg, PA, USA. Association for Computational Linguistics.

E. Lefever and V. Hoste. 2013. SemEval-2013 Task 10: Cross-Lingual Word Sense Disambiguation. In *Proceedings of the 7th International Workshop on Semantic Evaluation (SemEval 2013), in conjunction with the Second Joint Conference on Lexical and Computational Semantics.*

R. Mihalcea, R. Sinha, and D. McCarthy. 2010. Semeval 2010 task 2: Cross-lingual lexical substitution. In *Proceedings of the 5th International Workshop on Semantic Evaluations (SemEval-2010)*, Uppsala, Sweden.

H. Tou Ng and H. Beng Lee. 1996. Integrating multiple knowledge sources to disambiguate word sense: An exemplar-based approach. In *ACL*, pages 40–47.

F.J. Och and H. Ney. 2000. Giza++: Training of statistical translation models. Technical report, RWTH Aachen, University of Technology.

A. Rudnick, C. Liu, and M. Gasser. 2013. HLTDI: CL-WSD using Markov Random Fields for SemEval-2013 Task 10. In *Proceedings of the 7th International Workshop on Semantic Evaluation (SemEval 2013), in conjunction with the Second Joint Conference on Lexical and Computational Semantics.*

H Schmid. 1994. Probabilistic part-of-speech tagging using decision trees.

A. van den Bosch, G.J. Busser, S. Canisius, and W. Daelemans. 2007. An efficient memory-based morpho-syntactic tagger and parser for Dutch. In P. Dirix, I. Schuurman, V. Vandeghinste, , and F. Van Eynde, editors, *Computational Linguistics in the Netherlands: Selected Papers from the Seventeenth CLIN Meeting*, pages 99–114, Leuven, Belgium.

A. van den Bosch. 2004. Wrapped progressive sampling search for optimizing learning algorithm parameters. In R. Verbrugge, N. Taatgen, and L. Schomaker, editors, *Proceedings of the Sixteenth Belgian-Dutch Conference on Artificial Intelligence*, pages 219–226, Groningen, The Netherlands.

M. van Gompel, K. van der Sloot, and A. van den Bosch. 2012. Ucto: Unicode tokeniser. version 0.5.3. Reference Guide. Technical Report ILK 12-05, ILK Research Group, Tilburg University.

M. van Gompel. 2010. UvT-WSD1: A cross-lingual word sense disambiguation system. In *SemEval '10: Proceedings of the 5th International Workshop on Semantic Evaluation*, pages 238–241, Morristown, NJ, USA. Association for Computational Linguistics.

G. van Rossum. 2006. Python reference manual, release 2.5. Technical report, Amsterdam, The Netherlands, The Netherlands.

NRC: A Machine Translation Approach to Cross-Lingual Word Sense Disambiguation (SemEval-2013 Task 10)

Marine Carpuat
National Research Council
Ottawa, Canada
Marine.Carpuat@nrc.gc.ca

Abstract

This paper describes the NRC submission to the Spanish Cross-Lingual Word Sense Disambiguation task at SemEval-2013. Since this word sense disambiguation task uses Spanish translations of English words as gold annotation, it can be cast as a machine translation problem. We therefore submitted the output of a standard phrase-based system as a baseline, and investigated ways to improve its sense disambiguation performance. Using only local context information and no linguistic analysis beyond lemmatization, our machine translation system surprisingly yields top precision score based on the best predictions. However, its top 5 predictions are weaker than those from other systems.

1 Introduction

This paper describes the systems submitted by the National Research Council Canada (NRC) for the Cross-Lingual Word Sense Disambiguation task at SemEval 2013 (Lefever and Hoste, 2013). As in the previous edition (Lefever and Hoste, 2010), this word sense disambiguation task asks systems to disambiguate English words by providing translations in other languages. It is therefore closely related to machine translation. Our work aims to explore this connection between machine translation and cross-lingual word sense disambiguation, by providing a machine translation baseline and investigating ways to improve the sense disambiguation performance of a standard machine translation system.

Machine Translation (MT) has often been used indirectly for SemEval Word Sense Disambiguation (WSD) tasks: as a tool to automatically create training data (Guo and Diab, 2010, for instance) ; as a source of parallel data that can be used to train WSD systems (Ng and Chan, 2007; van Gompel, 2010; Lefever et al., 2011); or as an application which can use the predictions of WSD systems developed for SemEval tasks (Carpuat and Wu, 2005; Chan et al., 2007; Carpuat and Wu, 2007). This SemEval shared task gives us the opportunity to compare the performance of machine translation systems with other submissions which use very different approaches. Our goal is to provide machine translation output which is representative of state-of-the-art approaches, and provide a basis for comparing its strength and weaknesses with that of other systems submitted to this task. We submitted two systems to the Spanish Cross-Lingual WSD (CLWSD) task:

1. BASIC, a baseline machine translation system trained on the parallel corpus used to define the sense inventory;
2. ADAPT, a machine translation system that has been adapted to perform better on this task.

After describing these systems in Sections 2 and 3, we give an overview of the results in Section 4.

2 BASIC: A Baseline Phrase-Based Machine Translation System

We use a phrase-based SMT (PBSMT) architecture, and set-up our system to perform English-to-Spanish translation. We use a standard SMT system set-up, as for any translation task. The fact that this PBSMT system is intended to be used for CLWSD only influences data selection and pre-processing.

*Second Joint Conference on Lexical and Computational Semantics (*SEM), Volume 2: Seventh International Workshop on Semantic Evaluation (SemEval 2013)*, pages 188–192, Atlanta, Georgia, June 14-15, 2013.

2.1 Model and Implementation

In order to translate an English sentence e into Spanish, PBSMT first segments the English sentence into phrases, which are simply sequences of consecutive words. Each phrase is translated into Spanish according to the translations available in a translation lexicon called phrase-table. Spanish phrases can be reordered to account for structural divergence between the two languages. This simple process can be used to generate Spanish sentences, which are scored according to translation, reordering and language models learned from parallel corpora. The score of a Spanish translation given an English input sentence e segmented into J phrases is defined as follows: $score(s,e) = \sum_i \sum_j \lambda_i log(\phi_i(s_j, e_j)) + \lambda_{LM}\phi_{LM}(s)$

Detailed feature definitions for phrase-based SMT models can be found in Koehn (2010). In our system, we use the following standard feature functions ϕ to score English-Spanish phrase pairs:

- 4 phrase-table scores, which are conditional translation probabilities and HMM lexical probabilities in both directions translation directions (Chen et al., 2011)

- 6 hierarchical lexicalized reordering scores, which represent the orientation of the current phrase with respect to the previous block that could have been translated as a single phrase (Galley and Manning, 2008)

- a word penalty, which scores the length of the output sentence

- a word-displacement distortion penalty, which penalizes long-distance reorderings.

In addition, fluency of translation is ensured by a monolingual Spanish language model ϕ_{LM}, which is a 5-gram model with Kneser-Ney smoothing.

Phrase translations are extracted based on IBM-4 alignments obtained with GIZA++ (Och and Ney, 2003). The λ weights for these features are learned using the batch lattice-MIRA algorithm (Cherry and Foster, 2012) to optimize BLEU-4 (Papineni et al., 2002) on a tuning set. We use PORTAGE, our internal PBSMT decoder for all experiments. PORTAGE uses a standard phrasal beam-search algorithm with cube pruning. The main differences between this set-up and the popular open-source Moses system (Koehn et al., 2007), are the use of hierarchical reordering (Moses only supports non-hierarchical lexicalized reordering by default) and smoothed translation probabilities (Chen et al., 2011).

As a result, disambiguation decisions for the CLWSD task are based on the following sources of information:

- **local source context**, represented by source phrases of length 1 to 7 from the translation and reordering tables

- **local target context**, represented by the 5-gram language model.

Each English sentence in the CLWSD task is translated into Spanish using our PBSMT system. We keep track of the phrasal segmentation used to produce the translation hypothesis and identify the Spanish translation of the English word of interest. When the English word is translated into a multi-word Spanish phrase, we output the Spanish word within the phrase that has the highest IBM1 translation probability given the English target word.

For the BEST evaluation, we use this process on the top PBSMT hypothesis to produce a single CLWSD translation candidate. For the Out-Of-Five evaluation, we produce up to five CLWSD translation candidates from the top 1000 PBSMT translation hypotheses.

2.2 Data and Preprocessing

Training the PBSMT system requires a two-step process with two distinct sets of parallel data.

First, the translation, reordering and language models are learned on a large parallel corpus, the **training set**. We use the sentence pairs extracted from Europarl by the organizers for the purpose of selecting translation candidates for the gold annotation. Training the SMT system on the exact same parallel corpus ensures that the system "knows" the same translations as the human annotators who built the gold standard. This corpus consists of about 900k sentence pairs.

Second, the feature weights λ in the PBSMT are learned on a smaller parallel corpus, the **tuning set**. This corpus should ideally be drawn from the test domain. Since the CLWSD task does not provide parallel data in the test domain, we construct the tuning set using corpora publicly released for the WMT2012 translation task[1]. Since sentences provided in the trial data appeared to come from a wide variety of genres and domains, we decided to build our tuning set using data from the news-commentary domain, rather then the more narrow Europarl domain used for training. We selected the top 3000 sentence pairs from the WMT 2012 development test sets, based on their distance to the CLWSD trial and test sentences as measured by cross-entropy (Moore and Lewis, 2010).

All Spanish and English corpora were processed using FreeLing (Padró and Stanilovsky, 2012). Since the CLWSD targets and gold translations are lemmatized, we lemmatize all corpora. While FreeLing can provide a much richer linguistic analysis of the input sentences, the PBSMT sytem only makes use of their lemmatized representation. Our systems therefore contrast with previous approaches to CLWSD (van Gompel, 2010; Lefever et al., 2011, for instance), which use richer sources of information such as part-of-speech tags.

3 ADAPT: Adapting the MT system to the CLWSD task

Our ADAPT system simply consists of two modifications to the BASIC PBSMT system.

First, it uses a shorter maximum English phrase length. Instead of learning a translation lexicons for phrases of length 1 to 7 as in the BASIC system, the ADAPT system only uses phrases of length 1 and 2. While this dramatically reduces the amount of source side context available for disambiguation, it also reduces the amount of noise due to incorrect word alignments. In addition, there is more evidence to estimate reliable translation probabilities for short phrase, since they tend to occur more frequently than longer phrases.

Second, the ADAPT system is trained on larger and more diverse data sets. Since MT systems are known to perform better when they can learn from larger amounts of relevant training data, we augment our training set with additional parallel corpora from the WMT-12 evaluations. We learn translation and reordering models for (1) the Europarl subset used by the CLWSD organizers (900k sentence pairs, as in the BASIC system), and (2) the news commentary corpus from WMT12 (which comprises 150k sentence pairs). For the language model, we use the Spanish side of these two corpora, as well as that of the full Europarl corpus from WMT12 (which comprises 1.9M sentences). Models learned on different data sets are combined using linear mixtures learned on the tuning set (Foster and Kuhn, 2007).

We also attempted other variations on the BASIC system which were not as successful. For instance, we tried to update the PBSMT tuning objective to be better suited to the CLWSD task. When producing translation of entire sentences, the PBSMT system is expected to produce hypotheses that are simultaneously fluent and adequate, as measured by BLEU score. In contrast, CLWSD measures the adequacy of the translation of a single word in a given sentence. We therefore attempted to tune for BLEU-1, which only uses unigram precision, and therefore focuses on adequacy rather than fluency. However, this did not improve CLWSD accuracy.

4 Results

Table 1 gives an overview of the results per target word for both systems, as measured by all official metrics (see Lefever and Hoste (2010) for a detailed description.) According to the BEST Precision scores, the ADAPT system outperforms the BASIC system for almost all target words. Using only the dominant translation picked by the human annotators as a reference (Mode), the precision for BEST scores yield more heterogeneous results. This is not surprising since the ADAPT system uses more heterogeneous training data, which might make it harder to learn a reliable estimate of a single dominant translation. When evaluating the precision out of the top 5 candidates (OOF), all systems improve, indicating that PBSMT systems can usually produce some correct alternatives to their top hypothesis.

Table 2 lets us compare the average performance of the BASIC and ADAPT systems with other participating systems. The ADAPT system surprisingly yields the top performance based on the Precision BEST evaluation setting, suggesting that, even with relatively poor models of context, a PBSMT sys-

[1] http://www.statmt.org/wmt12/translation-task.html

Precision:	Best	Best	Best Mode	Best Mode	OOF	OOF	OOF Mode	OOF Mode
Systems:	**BASIC**	**ADAPT**	**BASIC**	**ADAPT**	**BASIC**	**ADAPT**	**BASIC**	**ADAPT**
coach	22.30	60.10	13.64	59.09	38.30	66.30	31.82	63.64
education	36.07	38.01	73.08	84.62	42.36	42.80	84.62	84.62
execution	41.07	41.07	32.00	32.00	41.57	41.57	36.00	36.00
figure	23.43	29.02	33.33	37.04	31.15	36.12	37.04	44.44
job	13.45	24.26	0.00	37.23	26.52	37.57	27.27	54.55
letter	35.35	37.23	66.67	64.10	37.22	41.20	66.67	66.67
match	15.07	16.53	2.94	2.94	20.70	20.90	5.88	8.82
mission	67.98	67.98	85.29	85.29	67.98	67.98	85.29	85.29
mood	7.18	8.97	0.00	0.00	26.99	29.90	11.11	11.11
paper	31.33	44.59	29.73	40.54	50.45	55.61	45.95	51.35
post	32.26	33.72	23.81	19.05	50.67	53.28	57.14	42.86
pot	34.20	36.63	35.00	32.50	36.12	37.13	32.50	25.00
range	5.41	7.56	10.00	0.00	10.39	17.47	10.00	20.00
rest	20.91	23.44	12.00	8.00	27.44	25.89	16.00	16.00
ring	15.87	10.10	18.92	10.81	42.80	43.14	48.65	45.95
scene	15.86	23.42	43.75	62.50	38.35	37.53	81.25	81.25
side	24.63	33.14	13.04	17.39	36.84	44.03	21.74	39.13
soil	43.88	43.63	66.67	66.67	51.73	57.15	66.67	66.67
strain	24.00	26.24	35.71	35.71	38.37	36.58	42.86	35.71
test	34.45	37.51	50.00	28.57	43.61	40.86	50.00	28.57
Average	27.24	**32.16**	32.28	**36.20**	37.98	**41.65**	42.92	**45.38**

Table 1: Precision scores by target word for the BASIC and ADAPT systems

Precision:	Best	Best Mode	OOF	OOF Mode
System				
Best	32.16	37.11	61.69	57.35
ADAPT	32.16	36.20	41.65	45.38
BASIC	27.24	32.28	37.98	42.92
Baseline	23.23	27.48	53.07	64.65

Table 2: Overview of official results: comparison of the precision scores of the ADAPT and BASIC systems with the best system according to each metric and with the official baseline

tem can succeed in learning useful disambiguating information for its top candidate. Despite the problems stemming from learning good dominant translations from heterogeneous data, ADAPT ranks near the top using the Best Mode metric. The rankings in the out-of-five settings are strikingly different: the difference between BEST and OOF precisions are much smaller for BASIC and ADAPT than for all other participating systems (including the baseline.) This suggests that our PBSMT system only succeeds in learning to disambiguate one or two candidates per word, but does not do a good job of a estimating the full translation probability distribution of a word in context. As a result, there is potentially much to be gained from combining PBSMT systems with the approaches used by other systems, which typically use richer feature representation and context models. Further exploration of the role of context in PBSMT performance and a comparison with dedicated classifiers trained on the same word-aligned parallel data can be found in (Carpuat, 2013).

5 Conclusion

We have described the two systems submitted by the NRC to the Cross-Lingual Word Sense Disambiguation task at SemEval-2013. We used phrase-based machine translation systems trained on lemmatized parallel corpora. These systems are unsupervised and do not use any linguistic analysis beyond lemmatization. Disambiguation decisions are based on the local source context available in the phrasal translation lexicon and the target n-gram language model. This simple approach gives top performance when measuring the precision of the top predictions. However, the top 5 predictions are interestingly not as good as those of other systems.

(Carpuat, 2013)

References

Marine Carpuat and Dekai Wu. 2005. Word Sense Disambiguation vs. Statistical Machine Translation. In *Proceedings of the Annual Meeting of the Association for Computational Linguistics (ACL-05)*, pages 387–394, Ann Arbor, Michigan.

Marine Carpuat and Dekai Wu. 2007. Improving Statistical Machine Translation using Word Sense Disambiguation. In *Proceedings of the 2007 Joint Conference on Empirical Methods in Natural Language Processing and Computational Natural Language Learning (EMNLP-CoNLL 2007)*, pages 61–72, Prague, June.

Marine Carpuat. 2013. A semantic evaluation of machine translation lexical choice. In *Proceedings of the 7th Workshop on Syntax, Semantics and Structure in Statistical Translation*, Atlanta, USA, May.

Yee Seng Chan, Hwee Tou Ng, and David Chiang. 2007. Word Sense Disambiguation improves Statistical Machine Translation. In *45th Annual Meeting of the Association for Computational Linguistics (ACL-07)*, Prague, June.

Boxing Chen, Roland Kuhn, George Foster, and Howard Johnson. 2011. Unpacking and transforming feature functions: New ways to smooth phrase tables. In *Proceedings of Machine Translation Summit*.

Colin Cherry and George Foster. 2012. Batch tuning strategies for statistical machine translation. In *Proceedings of the 2012 Conference of the North American Chapter of the Association for Computational Linguistics: Human Language Technologies*, pages 427–436, Montréal, Canada, June.

George Foster and Roland Kuhn. 2007. Mixture-model adaptation for SMT. In *Proceedings of the Second Workshop on Statistical Machine Translation*, pages 128–135, Prague, Czech Republic, June.

Michel Galley and Christopher D. Manning. 2008. A simple and effective hierarchical phrase reordering model. In *Proceedings of the Conference on Empirical Methods in Natural Language Processing*, EMNLP '08, pages 848–856.

Weiwei Guo and Mona Diab. 2010. COLEPL and COLSLM: An unsupervised wsd approach to multilingual lexical substitution, tasks 2 and 3 semeval 2010. In *Proceedings of the 5th International Workshop on Semantic Evaluation*, pages 129–133, Uppsala, Sweden, July.

Philipp Koehn, Hieu Hoang, Alexandra Birch, Chris Callison-Burch, Marcello Federico, Nicola Bertoldi, Brooke Cowan, Wade Shen, Christine Moran, Richard Zens, Chris Dyer, Ondrej Bojar, Alexandra Constantin, and Evan Herbst. 2007. Moses: Open Source Toolkit for Statistical Machine Translation. In *Annual Meeting of the Association for Computational Linguistics (ACL), demonstration session*, Prague, Czech Republic, June.

Philipp Koehn. 2010. *Statistical Machine Translation*. Cambridge University Press.

Els Lefever and Véronique Hoste. 2010. Semeval-2010 task 3: Cross-lingual word sense disambiguation. In *Proceedings of the 5th International Workshop on Semantic Evaluation*, pages 15–20, Uppsala, Sweden, July.

Els Lefever and Véronique Hoste. 2013. Semeval-2013 task 10: Cross-lingual word sense disambiguation. In *Proceedings of the 7th International Workshop on Semantic Evaluation (SemEval 2013)*, Atlanta, USA, May.

Els Lefever, Véronique Hoste, and Martine De Cock. 2011. Parasense or how to use parallel corpora for word sense disambiguation. In *Proceedings of the 49th Annual Meeting of the Association for Computational Linguistics: Human Language Technologies*, pages 317–322, Portland, Oregon, USA, June.

Robert C. Moore and William Lewis. 2010. Intelligent selection of language model training data. In *Proceedings of the ACL 2010 Conference Short Papers*, ACLShort '10, pages 220–224, Stroudsburg, PA, USA.

Hwee Tou Ng and Yee Seng Chan. 2007. SemEval-2007 Task 11: English Lexical Sample Task via English-Chinese Parallel Text. In *Proceedings of the 4th International Workshop on Semantic Evaluations (SemEval 2007)*, pages 54–58, Prague, Czech Republic. SIGLEX.

Franz Josef Och and Hermann Ney. 2003. A Systematic Comparison of Various Statistical Alignment Models. *Computational Linguistics*, 29(1):19–52.

Lluís Padró and Evgeny Stanilovsky. 2012. FreeLing 3.0: Towards wider multilinguality. In *Proceedings of the Language Resources and Evaluation Conference (LREC 2012)*, Istanbul, Turkey, May.

Kishore Papineni, Salim Roukos, Todd Ward, and Wei-Jing Zhu. 2002. BLEU: a method for automatic evaluation of machine translation. In *Proceedings of the 40th Annual Meeting of the Association for Computational Linguistics*, Philadelphia, PA, July.

Maarten van Gompel. 2010. Uvt-wsd1: A cross-lingual word sense disambiguation system. In *Proceedings of the 5th International Workshop on Semantic Evaluation*, pages 238–241, Uppsala, Sweden, July.

SemEval-2013 Task 11: Word Sense Induction & Disambiguation within an End-User Application

Roberto Navigli and **Daniele Vannella**
Dipartimento di Informatica
Sapienza Università di Roma
Viale Regina Elena, 295 – 00161 Roma Italy
{navigli,vannella}@di.uniroma1.it

Abstract

In this paper we describe our Semeval-2013 task on Word Sense Induction and Disambiguation within an end-user application, namely Web search result clustering and diversification. Given a target query, induction and disambiguation systems are requested to cluster and diversify the search results returned by a search engine for that query. The task enables the end-to-end evaluation and comparison of systems.

1 Introduction

Word ambiguity is a pervasive issue in Natural Language Processing. Two main techniques in computational lexical semantics, i.e., Word Sense Disambiguation (WSD) and Word Sense Induction (WSI) address this issue from different perspectives: the former is aimed at assigning word senses from a predefined sense inventory to words in context, whereas the latter automatically identifies the meanings of a word of interest by clustering the contexts in which it occurs (see (Navigli, 2009; Navigli, 2012) for a survey).

Unfortunately, the paradigms of both WSD and WSI suffer from significant issues which hamper their success in real-world applications. In fact, the performance of WSD systems depends heavily on which sense inventory is chosen. For instance, the most popular computational lexicon of English, i.e., WordNet (Fellbaum, 1998), provides fine-grained distinctions which make the disambiguation task quite difficult even for humans (Edmonds and Kilgarriff, 2002; Snyder and Palmer, 2004), although disagreements can be solved to some extent with graph-based methods (Navigli, 2008). On the other hand, although WSI overcomes this issue by allowing unrestrained sets of senses, its evaluation is particularly arduous because there is no easy way of comparing and ranking different representations of senses. In fact, all the proposed measures in the literature tend to favour specific cluster shapes (e.g., singletons or all-in-one clusters) of the senses produced as output. Indeed, WSI evaluation is actually an instance of the more general and difficult problem of evaluating clustering algorithms.

Nonetheless, many everyday tasks carried out by online users would benefit from intelligent systems able to address the lexical ambiguity issue effectively. A case in point is Web information retrieval, a task which is becoming increasingly difficult given the continuously growing pool of Web text of the most wildly disparate kinds. Recent work has addressed this issue by proposing a general evaluation framework for injecting WSI into Web search result clustering and diversification (Navigli and Crisafulli, 2010; Di Marco and Navigli, 2013). In this task the search results returned by a search engine for an input query are grouped into clusters, and diversified by providing a reranking which maximizes the meaning heterogeneity of the top ranking results.

The Semeval-2013 task described in this paper[1] adopts the evaluation framework of Di Marco and Navigli (2013), and extends it to both WSD and WSI systems. The task is aimed at overcoming the well-known limitations of *in vitro* evaluations, such as those of previous SemEval tasks on the topic (Agirre

[1]http://www.cs.york.ac.uk/semeval-2013/task11/

*Second Joint Conference on Lexical and Computational Semantics (*SEM), Volume 2: Seventh International Workshop on Semantic Evaluation (SemEval 2013)*, pages 193–201, Atlanta, Georgia, June 14-15, 2013.

and Soroa, 2007; Manandhar et al., 2010), and enabling a fair comparison between the two disambiguation paradigms. Key to our framework is the assumption that search results grouped into a given cluster are semantically related to each other and that each cluster is expected to represent a specific meaning of the input query (even though it is possible for more than one cluster to represent the same meaning). For instance, consider the target query *apple* and the following 3 search result snippets:

1. *Apple* Inc., formerly Apple Computer, Inc., is...
2. The science of *apple* growing is called pomology...
3. *Apple* designs and creates iPod and iTunes...

Participating systems were requested to produce a clustering that groups snippets conveying the same meaning of the input query *apple*, i.e., ideally $\{1, 3\}$ and $\{2\}$ in the above example.

2 Task setup

For each ambiguous query the task required participating systems to cluster the top ranking snippets returned by a search engine (we used the Google Search API). WSI systems were required to identify the meanings of the input query and cluster the snippets into semantically-related groups according to their meanings. Instead, WSD systems were requested to sense-tag the given snippets with the appropriate senses of the input query, thereby implicitly determining a clustering of snippets (i.e., one cluster per sense).

2.1 Dataset

We created a dataset of 100 ambiguous queries. The queries were randomly sampled from the AOL search logs so as to ensure that they had been used in real search sessions. Following previous work on the topic (Bernardini et al., 2009; Di Marco and Navigli, 2013) we selected those queries for which a sense inventory exists as a disambiguation page in the English Wikipedia[2]. This guaranteed that the selected queries consisted of either a single word or a multiword expression for which we had a collaboratively-edited list of meanings, including lexicographic and encyclopedic ones. We discarded all queries made

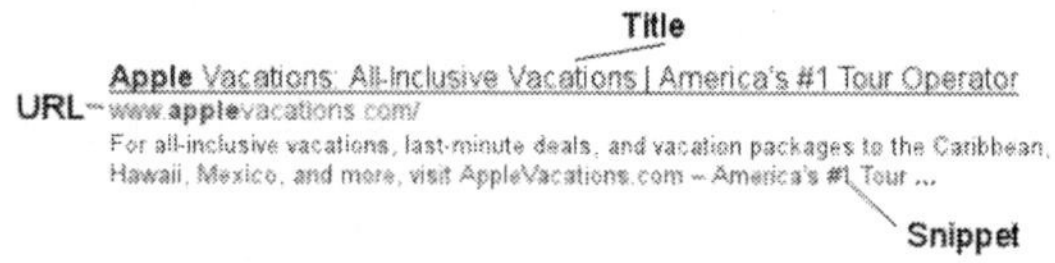

Figure 1: An example of search result for the *apple* query, including: page title, URL and snippet.

query length	1	2	3	4
AOL logs	45.89	40.98	10.98	2.32
our dataset	40.00	40.00	15.00	5.00

Table 1: Percentage distribution of AOL query lengths (first row) vs. the queries sampled for our task (second row).

up of > 4 words, since the length of the great majority of queries lay in the range $[1, 4]$. In Table 1 we compare the percentage distribution of 1- to 4-word queries in the AOL query logs against our dataset of queries. Note that we increased the percentage of 3- and 4-word queries in order to have a significant coverage of those lengths. Anyhow, in both cases most queries contained from 1 to 2 words. Note that the reported percentage distributions of query length is different from recent statistics for two reasons: first, over the years users have increased the average number of words per query in order to refine their searches; second, we selected only queries which were either single words (e.g., *apple*) or multi-word expressions (e.g., *mortal kombat*), thereby discarding several long queries composed of different words (such as *angelina jolie actress*).

Finally, we submitted each query to Google search and retrieved the 64 top-ranking results returned for each query. Therefore, overall the dataset consists of 100 queries and 6,400 results. Each search result includes the following information: page title, URL of the page and snippet of the page text. We show an example of search result for the *apple* query in Figure 1.

2.2 Dataset Annotation

For each query q we used Amazon Mechanical Turk[3] to annotate each query result with the

[2] http://en.wikipedia.org/wiki/Disambiguation_page

[3] https://www.mturk.com

most suitable sense. The sense inventory for q was obtained by listing the senses available in the Wikipedia disambiguation page of q augmented with additional options from the classes obtained from the section headings of the disambiguation page plus the OTHER catch-all meaning. For instance, consider the *apple* query. We show its disambiguation page in Figure 2. The sense inventory for *apple* was made up of the senses listed in that page (e.g., MALUS, APPLE INC., APPLE BANK, etc.) plus the set of generic classes OTHER PLANTS AND PLANT PARTS, OTHER COMPANIES, OTHER FILMS, plus OTHER.

For each query we ensured that three annotators tagged each of the 64 results for that query with the most suitable sense among those in the sense inventory (selecting OTHER if no sense was appropriate). Specifically, each Turker was provided with the following instructions: "The goal is annotating the search result snippets returned by Google for a given query with the appropriate meaning among those available (obtained from the Wikipedia disambiguation page for the query). You have to select the meaning that you consider most appropriate". No constraint on the age, gender and citizenship of the annotators was imposed. However, in order to avoid random tagging of search results, we provided 3 gold-standard result annotations per query, which could be shown to the Turker more than once during the annotation process. In the case (s)he failed to annotate the gold items, the annotator was automatically excluded.

2.3 Inter-Annotator Agreement and Adjudication

In order to determine the reliability of the Turkers' annotations, we calculated the individual values of Fleiss' kappa κ (Fleiss, 1971) for each query q and then averaged them:

$$\overline{\kappa} = \frac{\sum_{q \in Q} \kappa_q}{|Q|}, \tag{1}$$

where κ_q is the Fleiss' kappa agreement of the three annotators who tagged the 64 snippets returned by the Google search engine for the query $q \in Q$, and Q is our set of 100 queries. We obtained an average value of $\overline{\kappa} = 0.66$, which according to Landis and Koch (1977) can be seen as substantial agreement, with a standard deviation $\sigma = 0.185$.

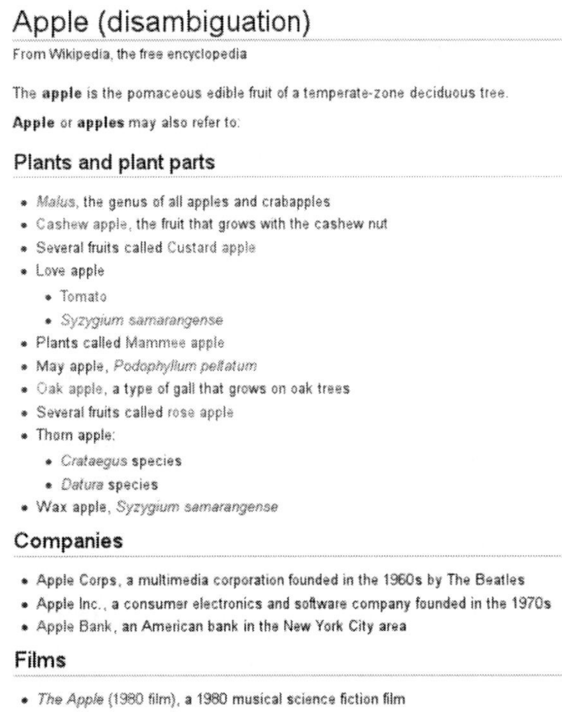
Apple (disambiguation)

From Wikipedia, the free encyclopedia

The **apple** is the pomaceous edible fruit of a temperate-zone deciduous tree.

Apple or **apples** may also refer to:

Plants and plant parts

- *Malus*, the genus of all apples and crabapples
- Cashew apple, the fruit that grows with the cashew nut
- Several fruits called Custard apple
- Love apple
  - Tomato
  - *Syzygium samarangense*
- Plants called Mammee apple
- May apple, *Podophyllum peltatum*
- Oak apple, a type of gall that grows on oak trees
- Several fruits called rose apple
- Thorn apple:
  - *Crataegus* species
  - *Datura* species
- Wax apple, *Syzygium samarangense*

Companies

- Apple Corps, a multimedia corporation founded in the 1960s by The Beatles
- Apple Inc., a consumer electronics and software company founded in the 1970s
- Apple Bank, an American bank in the New York City area

Films

- *The Apple* (1980 film), a 1980 musical science fiction film

Figure 2: The Wikipedia disambiguation page of Apple.

In Table 2 we show the agreement distribution of our 6400 snippets, distinguishing between full agreement (3 out of 3), majority agreement (2 out of 3), and no agreement. Most of the items were annotated with full or majority agreement, indicating that the manual annotation task was generally doable for the layman. We manually checked all the cases of majority agreement, correcting only 7.92% of the majority adjudications, and manually adjudicated all the snippets for which there was no agreement. We observed during adjudication that in many cases the disagreement was due to the existence of subtle sense distinctions, like between MORTAL KOMBAT (VIDEO GAME) and MORTAL KOMBAT (2011 VIDEO GAME), or between THE DA VINCI CODE and INACCURACIES IN THE DA VINCI CODE.

The average number of senses associated with the search results of each query was 7.69 (higher than in previous datasets, such as AMBIENT[4]+MORESQUE[5], which associates 5.07 senses

[4]http://credo.fub.it/ambient

[5]http://lcl.uniroma1.it/moresque

	Full agr.	Majority	Disagr.
% snippets	66.70	25.85	7.45

Table 2: Percentage of snippets with full agreement, majority agreement and full disagreement.

per query on average).

3 Scoring

Following Di Marco and Navigli (2013), we evaluated the systems' outputs in terms of the snippet clustering quality (Section 3.1) and the snippet diversification quality (Section 3.2). Given a query $q \in Q$ and the corresponding set of 64 snippet results, let $\mathcal{C}$ be the clustering output by a given system and let $\mathcal{G}$ be the gold-standard clustering for those results. Each measure $M(\mathcal{C}, \mathcal{G})$ presented below is calculated for the query q using these two clusterings. The overall results on the entire set of queries Q in the dataset is calculated by averaging the values of $M(\mathcal{C}, \mathcal{G})$ obtained for each single test query $q \in Q$.

3.1 Clustering Quality

The first evaluation concerned the quality of the clusters produced by the participating systems. Since clustering evaluation is a difficult issue, we calculated four distinct measures available in the literature, namely:

- Rand Index (Rand, 1971);
- Adjusted Rand Index (Hubert and Arabie, 1985);
- Jaccard Index (Jaccard, 1901);
- F1 measure (van Rijsbergen, 1979).

The *Rand Index* (RI) of a clustering $\mathcal{C}$ is a measure of clustering agreement which determines the percentage of correctly bucketed snippet pairs across the two clusterings $\mathcal{C}$ and $\mathcal{G}$. RI is calculated as follows:

$$RI(\mathcal{C}, \mathcal{G}) = \frac{\text{TP} + \text{TN}}{\text{TP} + \text{FP} + \text{FN} + \text{TN}}, \qquad (2)$$

where TP is the number of true positives, i.e., snippet pairs which are in the same cluster both in $\mathcal{C}$ and $\mathcal{G}$, TN is the number of true negatives, i.e., pairs which are in different clusters in both clusterings, and FP and FN are, respectively, the number of false positives and false negatives. RI ranges between 0 and 1, where 1 indicates perfect correspondence.

$\mathcal{G}$ \ $\mathcal{C}$	C_1	C_2	$\cdots$	C_m	**Sums**
G_1	n_{11}	n_{12}	$\cdots$	n_{1m}	a_1
G_2	n_{21}	n_{22}	$\cdots$	n_{2m}	a_2
$\vdots$	$\vdots$	$\vdots$	$\ddots$	$\vdots$	$\vdots$
G_g	n_{g1}	n_{g2}	$\cdots$	n_{gm}	a_g
Sums	b_1	b_2	$\cdots$	b_m	N

Table 3: Contingency table for the clusterings $\mathcal{G}$ and $\mathcal{C}$.

Adjusted Rand Index (ARI) is a development of Rand Index which corrects the RI for chance agreement and makes it vary according to expectaction:

$$ARI(\mathcal{C}, \mathcal{G}) = \frac{RI(\mathcal{C}, \mathcal{G}) - E(RI(\mathcal{C}, \mathcal{G}))}{\max RI(\mathcal{C}, \mathcal{G}) - E(RI(\mathcal{C}, \mathcal{G}))}. \qquad (3)$$

where $E(RI(\mathcal{C}, \mathcal{G}))$ is the expected value of the RI. Using the contingency table reported in Table 3 we can quantify the degree of overlap between $\mathcal{C}$ and $\mathcal{G}$, where n_{ij} denotes the number of snippets in common between G_i and C_j (namely, $n_{ij} = |G_i \cap C_j|$), a_i and b_j represent, respectively, the number of snippets in G_i and C_j, and N is the total number of snippets, i.e., $N = 64$. Now, the above equation can be reformulated as:

$$ARI(\mathcal{C}, \mathcal{G}) = \frac{\sum_{ij}\binom{n_{ij}}{2} - [\sum_i \binom{a_i}{2} \sum_j \binom{b_j}{2}]/\binom{N}{2}}{\frac{1}{2}[\sum_i \binom{a_i}{2} + \sum_j \binom{b_j}{2}] - [\sum_i \binom{a_i}{2} \sum_j \binom{b_j}{2}]/\binom{N}{2}}. \qquad (4)$$

The ARI ranges between -1 and $+1$ and is 0 when the index equals its expected value.

Jaccard Index (JI) is a measure which takes into account only the snippet pairs which are in the same cluster both in $\mathcal{C}$ and $\mathcal{G}$, i.e., the true positives (TP), while neglecting true negatives (TN), which are the vast majority of cases. JI is calculated as follows:

$$JI(\mathcal{C}, \mathcal{G}) = \frac{\text{TP}}{\text{TP} + \text{FP} + \text{FN}}. \qquad (5)$$

Finally, the *F1 measure* calculates the harmonic mean of precision (P) and recall (R). Precision determines how accurately the clusters of $\mathcal{C}$ represent the query meanings in the gold standard $\mathcal{G}$, whereas recall measures how accurately the different meanings in $\mathcal{G}$ are covered by the clusters in $\mathcal{C}$. We follow Crabtree et al. (2005) and define the precision of a cluster $C_j \in \mathcal{C}$ as follows:

$$P(C_j) = \frac{|C_j^s|}{|C_j|}, \tag{6}$$

where C_j^s is the intersection between $C_j \in \mathcal{C}$ and the gold cluster $G_s \in \mathcal{G}$ which maximizes the cardinality of the intersection. The recall of a query sense s is instead calculated as:

$$R(s) = \frac{|\bigcup_{C_j \in \mathcal{C}^s} C_j^s|}{n_s}, \tag{7}$$

where $\mathcal{C}^s$ is the subset of clusters of $\mathcal{C}$ whose majority sense is s, and n_s is the number of snippets tagged with query sense s in the gold standard. The total precision and recall of the clustering $\mathcal{C}$ are then calculated as:

$$P = \frac{\sum_{C_j \in \mathcal{C}} P(C_j)|C_j|}{\sum_{C_j \in \mathcal{C}} |C_j|}; \quad R = \frac{\sum_{s \in \mathcal{S}} R(s) n_s}{\sum_{s \in \mathcal{S}} n_s} \tag{8}$$

where $\mathcal{S}$ is the set of senses in the gold standard $\mathcal{G}$ for the given query (i.e., $|\mathcal{S}| = |\mathcal{G}|$). The two values of P and R are then combined into their harmonic mean, namely the F1 measure:

$$F1(\mathcal{C}, \mathcal{G}) = \frac{2PR}{P+R}. \tag{9}$$

3.2 Clustering Diversity

Our second evaluation is aimed at determining the impact of the output clustering on the diversification of the top results shown to a Web user. To this end, we applied an automatic procedure for flattening the clusterings produced by the participating systems to a list of search results. Given a clustering $\mathcal{C} = (C_1, C_2, \ldots, C_m)$, we add to the initially empty list the first element of each cluster C_j ($j = 1, \ldots, m$); then we iterate the process by selecting the second element of each cluster C_j such that $|C_j| \geq 2$, and so on. The remaining elements returned by the search engine, but not included in any cluster of $\mathcal{C}$, are appended to the bottom of the list in their original order. Note that systems were asked to sort snippets within clusters, as well as clusters themselves, by relevance.

Since our goal is to determine how many different meanings are covered by the top-ranking search results according to the output clustering, we used the measures of S-recall@K (Subtopic recall at rank K) and S-precision@r (Subtopic precision at recall r) (Zhai et al., 2003).

S-recall@K determines the ratio of different meanings for a given query q in the top-K results returned:

$$\text{S-recall@}K = \frac{|\{sense(r_i) : i \in \{1, \ldots, K\}\}|}{g}, \tag{10}$$

where $sense(r_i)$ is the gold-standard sense associated with the i-th snippet returned by the system, and g is the total number of distinct senses for the query q in our gold standard.

S-precision@r instead determines the ratio of different senses retrieved for query q in the first K_r snippets, where K_r is the minimum number of top results for which the system achieves recall r. The measure is defined as follows:

$$\text{S-precision@}r = \frac{|\cup_{i=1}^{K_r} sense(r_i)|}{K_r}. \tag{11}$$

3.3 Baselines

We compared the participating systems with two simple baselines:

- SINGLETONS: each snippet is clustered as a separate singleton cluster (i.e., $|\mathcal{C}| = 64$).
- ALL-IN-ONE: all snippets are clustered into a single cluster (i.e., $|\mathcal{C}| = 1$).

These baselines are important in that they make explicit the preference of certain quality measures towards clusterings made up with a small or large number of clusters.

4 Systems

5 teams submitted 10 systems, out of which 9 were WSI systems, while 1 was a WSD system, i.e., using the Wikipedia sense inventory for performing the disambiguation task. All systems could exploit the information provided for each search result, i.e., URL, page title and result snippet. WSI systems were requested to use unannotated corpora only.

	System	URLs	Snippets	Wikipedia	YAGO Hierarchy	Distr. Thesaurus	Other
WSI	HDP-CLUSTERS-LEMMA		✓	✓			
	HDP-CLUSTERS-NOLEMMA		✓	✓			
	DULUTH.SYS1.PK2		✓				
	DULUTH.SYS7.PK2		✓				
	DULUTH.SYS9.PK2						Gigaword
	UKP-WSI-WP-LLR2	✓		✓		✓	WaCky
	UKP-WSI-WP-PMI	✓		✓		✓	WaCky
	UKP-WSI-WACKY-LLR	✓		✓		✓	WaCky
	SATTY-APPROACH1		✓				
WSD	RAKESH				✓		DBPedia

Table 4: Resources used for WSI/WSD.

We asked each team to provide information about their systems. In Table 4 we report the resources used by each system. The HDP and UKP systems use Wikipedia as raw text for sampling word counts; DULUTH-SYS9-PK2 uses the first 10,000 paragraphs of the Associated Press wire service data from the English Gigaword Corpus (Graff, 2003, 1st edition), whereas DULUTH-SYS1-PK2 and DULUTH-SYS7-PK2 both use the snippets for inducing the query senses. Finally, the UKP systems were the only ones to retrieve the Web pages from the corresponding URLs and exploit them for WSI purposes. They also use WaCky (Baroni et al., 2009) and a distributional thesaurus obtained from the Leipzig Corpora Collection[6] (Biemann et al., 2007). SATTY-APPROACH1 just uses snippets.

The only participating WSD system, RAKESH, uses the YAGO hierarchy (Suchanek et al., 2008) together with DBPedia abstracts (Bizer et al., 2009).

5 Results

We show the results of RI and ARI in Table 5. The best performing systems are those from the HDP team, with considerably higher RI and ARI. The next best systems are SATTY-APPROACH1, which uses only the words in the snippets, and the only WSD system, i.e., RAKESH. SINGLETONS perform well with RI, but badly when chance agreement is taken into account.

As for F1 and JI, whose values are shown in Table 6, the two HDP systems again perform best in terms of F1, and are on par with UKP-WSI-WACKY-LLR in terms of JI. The third best approach in terms of F1 is again SATTY-APPROACH1, which however performs badly in terms of JI. The SINGLETONS baseline clearly obtains the best F1 performance, but the worst JI results. The ALL-IN-ONE baseline outperforms all other systems with the JI measure, because TN are not considered, which favours large clusters.

	System	RI	ARI
WSI	HDP-CLUSTERS-LEMMA	**65.22**	21.31
	HDP-CLUSTERS-NOLEMMA	64.86	**21.49**
	SATTY-APPROACH1	59.55	7.19
	DULUTH.SYS9.PK2	54.63	2.59
	DULUTH.SYS1.PK2	52.18	5.74
	DULUTH.SYS7.PK2	52.04	6.78
	UKP-WSI-WP-LLR2	51.09	3.77
	UKP-WSI-WP-PMI	50.50	3.64
	UKP-WSI-WACKY-LLR	50.02	2.53
WSD	RAKESH	58.76	8.11
BL	SINGLETONS	**60.09**	0.00
	ALL-IN-ONE	39.90	0.00

Table 5: Results for Rand Index (RI) and Adjusted Rand Index (ARI), sorted by RI.

To get more insights into the performance of the various systems, we calculated the average number of clusters per clustering produced by each system and compared it with the gold standard average. We also computed the average cluster size, i.e., the average number of snippets per cluster. The statistics are shown in Table 7. Interestingly, the best performing systems are those with the cluster number and average number of clusters closest to the gold standard ones. This finding is also confirmed by Figure 3, where we draw each system according to its average values regarding cluster number and size: again the distance from the gold standard is meaningful.

We now move to the diversification perfor-

[6]http://corpora.uni-leipzig.de/

	System	JI	F1
WSI	UKP-WSI-WACKY-LLR	**33.94**	58.26
	HDP-CLUSTERS-NOLEMMA	33.75	68.03
	HDP-CLUSTERS-LEMMA	33.02	**68.30**
	DULUTH.SYS1.PK2	31.79	56.83
	UKP-WSI-WP-LLR2	31.77	58.64
	DULUTH.SYS7.PK2	31.03	58.78
	UKP-WSI-WP-PMI	29.32	60.48
	DULUTH.SYS9.PK2	22.24	57.02
	SATTY-APPROACH1	15.05	67.09
WSD	RAKESH	30.52	39.49
BL	SINGLETONS	0.00	**100.00**
	ALL-IN-ONE	**39.90**	54.42

Table 6: Results for Jaccard Index (JI) and F1 measure.

	System	# cl.	ACS
	GOLD STANDARD	7.69	11.56
WSI	HDP-CLUSTERS-LEMMA	**6.63**	**11.07**
	HDP-CLUSTERS-NOLEMMA	**6.54**	**11.68**
	SATTY-APPROACH1	9.90	6.46
	UKP-WSI-WP-PMI	5.86	30.30
	DULUTH.SYS7.PK2	3.01	25.15
	UKP-WSI-WP-LLR2	4.17	21.87
	UKP-WSI-WACKY-LLR	3.64	32.34
	DULUTH.SYS9.PK2	3.32	19.84
	DULUTH.SYS1.PK2	2.53	26.45
WSD	RAKESH	9.07	2.94

Table 7: Average number of clusters (# cl.) and average cluster size (ACS).

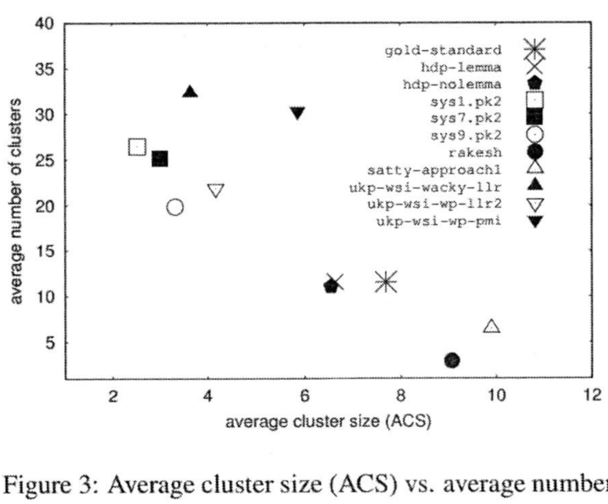

Figure 3: Average cluster size (ACS) vs. average number of clusters.

mance, calculated in terms of S-recall@K and S-precision@r, whose results are shown in Tables 8

	System	*K*			
		5	10	20	40
WSI	HDP-CL.-NOLEMMA	**50.80**	63.21	**79.26**	**92.48**
	HDP-CL.-LEMMA	48.13	**65.51**	78.86	91.68
	UKP-WACKY-LLR	41.19	55.41	68.61	83.90
	UKP-WP-LLR2	41.07	53.76	68.87	85.87
	UKP-WP-PMI	40.45	56.25	68.70	84.92
	SATTY-APPROACH1	38.97	48.90	62.72	82.14
	DULUTH.SYS7.PK2	38.88	53.79	70.38	86.23
	DULUTH.SYS9.PK2	37.15	49.90	68.91	83.65
	DULUTH.SYS1.PK2	37.11	53.29	71.24	88.48
WSD	RAKESH	46.48	62.36	78.66	90.72

Table 8: S-recall@K.

	System	*r*			
		50	60	70	80
WSI	HDP-CL.-LEMMA	**48.85**	42.93	**35.19**	27.62
	HDP-CL.-NOLEMMA	48.18	**43.88**	34.85	**29.30**
	UKP-WP-PMI	42.83	33.40	26.63	22.92
	UKP-WACKY-LLR	42.47	31.73	25.39	22.71
	UKP-WP-LLR2	42.06	32.04	26.57	22.41
	DULUTH.SYS1.PK2	40.08	31.31	26.73	24.51
	DULUTH.SYS7.PK2	39.11	30.42	26.54	23.43
	DULUTH.SYS9.PK2	35.90	29.72	25.26	21.26
	SATTY-APPROACH1	34.94	26.88	23.55	20.40
WSD	RAKESH	48.00	39.04	32.72	27.92

Table 9: S-precision@r.

and 9, respectively. Here we find that, again, the HDP team obtains the best performance, followed by RAKESH. We note however that not all systems optimized the order of clusters and cluster snippets by relevance.

We also graph the diversification performance trend of S-recall@K and S-precision@r in Figures 4 and 5 for $K = 1, \ldots, 25$ and $r \in \{40, 50, \ldots, 100\}$.

6 Conclusions and Future Directions

One of the aims of the SemEval-2013 task on Word Sense Induction & Disambiguation within an End User Application was to enable an objective comparison of WSI and WSD systems when integrated into Web search result clustering and diversification. The task is a hard one, in that it involves clustering, but provides clear-cut evidence that our end-to-end application framework overcomes the limits of previous in-vitro evaluations. Indeed, the systems which create good clusters and better diversify search results, i.e., those from the HDP team, achieve good performance across all the proposed measures, with no contradictory evidence.

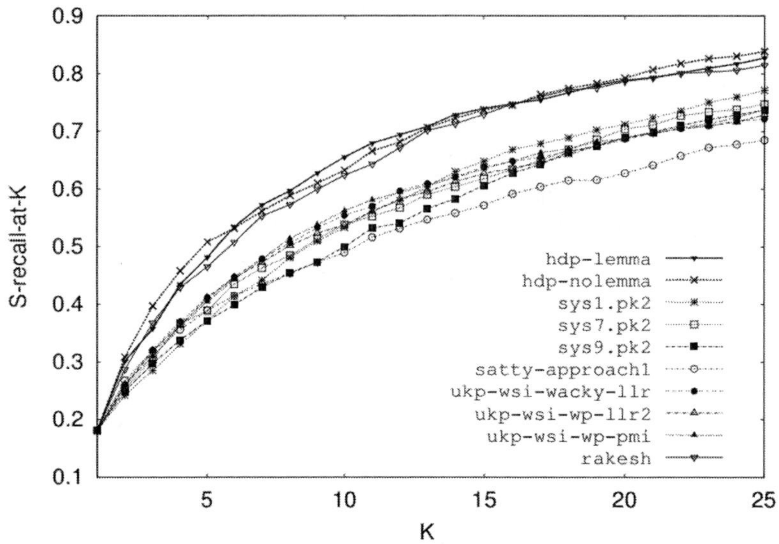

Figure 4: S-recall@K.

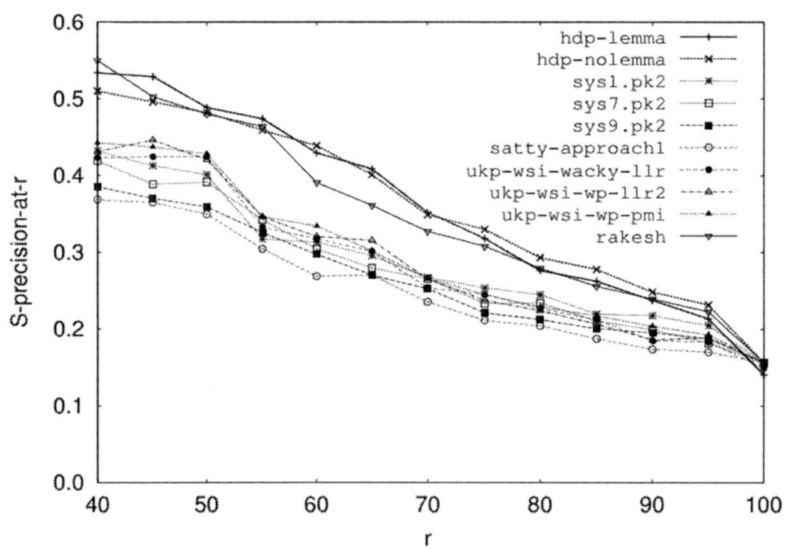

Figure 5: S-precision@r.

Our annotation experience showed that the Wikipedia sense inventory, augmented with our generic classes, is a good choice for semantically tagging search results, in that it covers most of the meanings a Web user might be interested in. In fact, only 20% of the snippets was annotated with the OTHER class.

Future work might consider large-scale multilingual lexical resources, such as BabelNet (Navigli and Ponzetto, 2012), both as sense inventory and for performing the search result clustering and diversification task.

Acknowledgments

erc The authors gratefully acknowledge the support of the ERC Starting Grant MultiJEDI No. 259234.

We thank Antonio Di Marco and David A. Jurgens for their help.

References

Eneko Agirre and Aitor Soroa. 2007. Semeval-2007 task 02: Evaluating word sense induction and discrimination systems. In *Proceedings of the 4th International Workshop on Semantic Evaluations (SemEval-2007)*, pages 7–12, Prague, Czech Republic.

Marco Baroni, Silvia Bernardini, Adriano Ferraresi, and Eros Zanchetta. 2009. The WaCky Wide Web: A collection of very large linguistically processed web-crawled corpora. *Language Resources and Evaluation*, 43(3):209–226.

Andrea Bernardini, Claudio Carpineto, and Massimiliano D'Amico. 2009. Full-subtopic retrieval with keyphrase-based search results clustering. In *Proceedings of Web Intelligence 2009*, volume 1, pages 206–213, Los Alamitos, CA, USA.

Chris Biemann, Gerhard Heyer, Uwe Quasthoff, and Matthias Richter. 2007. The Leipzig corpora collection - monolingual corpora of standard size. In *Proceedings of Corpus Linguistic 2007*, Birmingham, UK.

Christian Bizer, Jens Lehmann, Georgi Kobilarov, Sören Auer, Christian Becker, Richard Cyganiak, and Sebastian Hellmann. 2009. Dbpedia - a crystallization point for the web of data. *J. Web Sem.*, 7(3):154–165.

Daniel Crabtree, Xiaoying Gao, and Peter Andreae. 2005. Improving web clustering by cluster selection. In *Proceedings of the 2005 IEEE/WIC/ACM International Conference on Web Intelligence*, pages 172–178, Washington, DC, USA.

Antonio Di Marco and Roberto Navigli. 2013. Clustering and diversifying web search results with graph-based word sense induction. *Computational Linguistics*, 39(4).

Philip Edmonds and Adam Kilgarriff. 2002. Introduction to the special issue on evaluating word sense disambiguation systems. *Journal of Natural Language Engineering*, 8(4):279–291.

Christiane Fellbaum, editor. 1998. *WordNet: An Electronic Database*. MIT Press, Cambridge, MA, USA.

Joseph L. Fleiss. 1971. Measuring nominal scale agreement among many raters. In *Psychological Bulletin*, volume 76, page 378–382.

David Graff. 2003. English Gigaword. In *Technical Report, LDC2003T05, Linguistic Data Consortium*, Philadelphia, PA, USA.

Lawrence Hubert and Phipps Arabie. 1985. Comparing Partitions. *Journal of Classification*, 2(1):193–218.

Paul Jaccard. 1901. Étude comparative de la distribution florale dans une portion des alpes et des jura. In *Bulletin de la Sociétè Vaudoise des Sciences Naturelles*, volume 37, page 547–579.

J Richard Landis and Gary G Koch. 1977. The measurement of observer agreement for categorical data. *biometrics*, pages 159–174.

Suresh Manandhar, Ioannis P. Klapaftis, Dmitriy Dligach, and Sameer S. Pradhan. 2010. SemEval-2010 task 14: Word sense induction & disambiguation. In *Proceedings of the 5th International Workshop on Semantic Evaluation*, pages 63–68, Uppsala, Sweden.

Roberto Navigli and Giuseppe Crisafulli. 2010. Inducing word senses to improve web search result clustering. In *Proceedings of the 2010 Conference on Empirical Methods in Natural Language Processing*, pages 116–126, Boston, USA.

Roberto Navigli and Simone Paolo Ponzetto. 2012. BabelNet: The automatic construction, evaluation and application of a wide-coverage multilingual semantic network. *Artificial Intelligence*, 193:217–250.

Roberto Navigli. 2008. A structural approach to the automatic adjudication of word sense disagreements. *Journal of Natural Language Engineering*, 14(4):293–310.

Roberto Navigli. 2009. Word Sense Disambiguation: a survey. *ACM Computing Surveys*, 41(2):1–69.

Roberto Navigli. 2012. A quick tour of word sense disambiguation, induction and related approaches. In *Proceedings of the 38th Conference on Current Trends in Theory and Practice of Computer Science (SOFSEM)*, pages 115–129.

William M. Rand. 1971. Objective criteria for the evaluation of clustering methods. *Journal of the American Statistical association*, 66(336):846–850.

Benjamin Snyder and Martha Palmer. 2004. The English all-words task. In *Proceedings of the 3rd International Workshop on the Evaluation of Systems for the Semantic Analysis of Text (Senseval-3)*, pages 41–43, Barcelona, Spain.

Fabian M. Suchanek, Gjergji Kasneci, and Gerhard Weikum. 2008. YAGO: A large ontology from wikipedia and wordnet. *Journal of Web Semantics*, 6(3):203–217.

Cornelis Joost van Rijsbergen. 1979. *Information Retrieval*. Butterworths, second edition.

ChengXiang Zhai, William W. Cohen, and John Lafferty. 2003. Beyond independent relevance: Methods and evaluation metrics for subtopic retrieval. In *Proceedings of the 26th annual international ACM SIGIR conference on Research and development in informaion retrieval*, pages 10–17, Toronto, Canada.

Duluth : Word Sense Induction Applied to Web Page Clustering

Ted Pedersen
Department of Computer Science
University of Minnesota
Duluth, MN 55812 USA
tpederse@d.umn.edu
http://senseclusters.sourceforge.net

Abstract

The Duluth systems that participated in task 11 of SemEval–2013 carried out word sense induction (WSI) in order to cluster Web search results. They relied on an approach that represented Web snippets using second–order co–occurrences. These systems were all implemented using SenseClusters, a freely available open source software package.

1 Introduction

The goal of task 11 of SemEval–2013 was to cluster Web search results (Navigli and Vannella, 2013). The test data consisted of the top 64 Google results for each of 100 potentially ambiguous queries, for a total of 6,400 test instances. The Web snippets returned for each query were clustered and evaluated separately, with an overall evaluation score provided for each system.

The problem of Web page clustering is one of the use cases envisioned for SenseClusters (Pedersen and Kulkarni, 2007; Pedersen, 2010a), a freely available open source software package developed at the University of Minnesota, Duluth starting in 2002. It supports first and second–order clustering of contexts using both co–occurrence matrices (Purandare and Pedersen, 2004; Kulkarni and Pedersen, 2005) and Latent Semantic Analysis (Landauer and Dumais, 1997).

SenseClusters has participated in various forms at different SenseEval and SemEval shared tasks, including SemEval-2007 (Pedersen, 2007), SemEval-2010 (Pedersen, 2010b) and also in an i2b2 clinical medicine task (Pedersen, 2006).

2 Duluth System

While we refer to three Duluth systems (sys1, sys7, and sys9), in reality these are all variations of the same overall system. All three are based on second–order context clustering as provided in SenseClusters. The query terms are treated exactly like any other word in the snippets, which is called *headless* clustering in SenseClusters.

2.1 Common aspects to all systems

The input to sys1, sys7, and sys9 consists of 64 Web search snippets, each approximately 25 words in length. All text was converted to upper case prior to processing. The goal was to group the 64 snippets for each query into k distinct clusters, where k was automatically determined by the PK2 method of SenseClusters (Pedersen and Kulkarni, 2006a; Pedersen and Kulkarni, 2006b). Each discovered cluster represents a different underlying meaning of the given query term that resulted in those snippets being returned. Word sense induction was carried out separately on the Web snippets associated with each query term, meaning that the algorithm was run 100 times and clustered 64 Web page snippets each time.

In second–order context clustering, the words in a context (i.e., Web snippet) to be clustered are replaced by vectors that are derived from some corpus of text. The corpora used are among the main differences in the Duluth systems. Once the words in a context are replaced by vectors, those vectors are averaged together to create a new representation of the context. That representation is said to be *second–order* because each word is represented by its direct or first order co–occurrences, and simi-

*Second Joint Conference on Lexical and Computational Semantics (*SEM), Volume 2: Seventh International Workshop on Semantic Evaluation (SemEval 2013)*, pages 202–206, Atlanta, Georgia, June 14-15, 2013.

larities between words in the same Web snippet are captured by the set of words that mutually co–occur with them.

If *car* is represented by the vector *[motor, magazine, insurance]*, and if *life* is represented by the vector *[sentence, force, insurance]*, then *car* and *life* are said to be second–order co-occurrences because they both occur with *insurance*. A second–order co-occurrence can capture more indirect relationships between words, and so these second–order connections tend to be more numerous and more subtle than first–order co–occurrences (which would require that *car* and *life* co–occur near or adjacent to each other in a Web snippet to establish a relationship).

The co-occurrence matrix is created by finding bigrams that occur more than a given number of times (this varies per system) and have a log-likelihood ratio greater than 3.84.[1] Then, the first word in a bigram is represented in the rows of the matrix, the second word is represented in the columns. The value in the corresponding cell is the log-likelihood score. This matrix is therefore not symmetric, and has different entries for *old age* and *age old*. Also, any bigram that includes one or two stop words (e.g., *to fire, running to, for the*) will be excluded and not included in the co-occurrence matrix and will not be included in the overall sample count used for computing the log–likelihood ratio. To summarize then, words in a Web snippet are represented by the words with which they occur in bigrams, where the context word is the first word in the bigram, and the vector is the set of words that follow it in bigrams.

Once the co–occurrence matrix is created, it may be optionally reduced by Singular Value Decomposition. The result of this will be a matrix with the same number of rows prior to SVD, but a reduced number of columns. The goal of SVD is to compress together columns of words with similar co–occurrence patterns, and thereby reduce the size and noisiness of the data. Whether the matrix is reduced or not, then each word in each snippet to be clustered is replaced by a vector from that matrix. A word is replaced by the row in the co-occurrence matrix to which it corresponds. Any words that do not have an entry in the co-occurrence matrix will not be represented. Then, the contexts are clustered using the method of repeated bisections (Zhao and Karypis, 2004), where the number of clusters is automatically discovered using the PK2 method.

[1]This value corresponds with a p-value of 0.05 when testing for significance, meaning that bigrams with log-likelihood at least equal to 3.84 have at least a 95% chance of having been drawn from a population where their co-occurrence is not by chance.

2.2 Differences among systems

The main difference among the systems was the corpora used to create their co-occurrence matrices.

The smallest corpus was used by sys7, which simply treated the 64 snippets returned by each query as the corpus for creating a co–occurrence matrix. Thus, each query term had a unique co-occurrence matrix that was created from the Web snippets returned by that query. This results in a very small amount of data per query (approx. 25 words/snippet * 64 snippets = 1600 words), and so bigrams were allowed to have up to three intervening words that were skipped (in order to increase the number of bigrams used to create the co–occurrence matrix). Bigrams were excluded if they only occurred 1 time, had a log–likelihood ratio of less than 3.84, or were made up of one or two stop words. Even with this more flexible definition of bigram, the resulting co–occurrence matrices were still quite small. The largest resulting co–occurrence matrix for any query was 221 x 222, with 602 non–zero values (meaning there were 602 different bigrams used as features). The smallest of the co-occurrence matrices was 102 x 113 with 242 non–zero values. Given these small sizes, SVD was not employed in sys7.

sys1 and sys9 used larger corpora, and therefore required bigrams to be made up of adjacent words that occurred 5 or more times, had log–likelihood ratio scores of 3.84 or above, and contained no stop words. Rather than having a different co–occurrence matrix for each query, sys1 and sys9 created a single co-occurrence matrix for all queries.

In sys1, all the Web snippet results for all 100 queries were combined into a single corpus. Thus, the co–occurrence matrix was based on bigram features found in a corpus of 6,400 Web snippets that consisted of approximately 160,000 words. This resulted in a co–occurrence matrix of size 771 x 952 with 1,558 non–zero values prior to SVD. After SVD the matrix was 771 x 90, and all cells had non-zero values (as a result of SVD). Note that if there are less than 3,000 columns in a co-occurrence matrix, the columns are reduced down to 10% of their original size. If there are more than 3,000 columns then it is reduced to 300 dimensions. This follows recommendations for SVD given for Latent Semantic Analysis (Landauer and Dumais, 1997).

Rather than using task data, sys9 uses the first 10,000 paragraphs of Associated Press newswire (APW) that appear in the English Gigaword corpus (1st edition) (Graff and Cieri, 2003). This created a corpus of approximately 3.6 million words which resulted in a co-occurrence matrix prior to SVD of 9,853 x 10,995 with 43,199 non-zero values. After SVD the co–occurrence matrix was 9,853 by 300.

3 Results

Various measures were reported by the task organizers, including F1 (F1-13), the Rand Index (RI), the Adjusted Rand Index (ARI), and the Jaccard Coefficient. More details can be found in (Di Marco and Navigli, 2013).

In addition we computed the paired F-Score (F-10) (Artiles et al., 2009) as used in the 2010 SemEval word sense induction task (Manandhar et al., 2010) and the F-Measure (F-SC), which is provided by SenseClusters. This allows for the comparison of results from this task with the 2010 task and various results from SenseClusters.

The organizers also provided scores for S-recall and S-precision (Zhai et al., 2003), however for these to be meaningful the results for each cluster must be output in ranked order. The Duluth systems did not make a ranking distinction among the instances in each cluster, and so these scores are not particularly meaningful for the Duluth systems.

3.1 Comparisons to Baselines

Table 1 includes the results of the three submitted Duluth systems, plus numerous baselines. **RandX** designates a random baseline where senses were assigned by randomly assigning a value between 1 and X. In word sense induction, the labels assigned to discovered clusters are arbitrary, so a random baseline is a convenient sanity check. **MFS** replicates the most frequent sense baseline from supervised learning by simply assigning all instances for a word to a single cluster. This is sometimes also known as the "all–in–one" baseline. **Gold** are the evaluation results when the gold standard data is provided as input (and compared to itself).

The various baselines give us a sense of the characteristics of the different evaluation measures, and a few points emerge. We have argued previously (Pedersen, 2010a) that any evaluation measure used for word sense induction needs to be able to expose random baselines and distinguish them from more systematic results. By this standard a number of measures are found to be lacking. In SemEval–2010 we demonstrated that the V-Measure (Rosenberg and Hirschberg, 2007) had an overwhelming bias towards systems that produce larger numbers of clusters – as a result it scored random baselines that generated larger number of clusters (like Rand25 and Rand50) very highly.

The Rand Index (**RI**), which does not correct for chance agreement, also scores random baselines higher than both non–random systems and MFS. The Adjusted Rand Index (**ARI**) corrects for chance and scores random systems near 0, but it also scores MFS near 0. According to ARI, random systems and MFS perform at essentially the same level. This is a troublesome tendency when evaluating word sense induction systems, since MFS is often considered a reasonable baseline that provides useful results. Many words have relatively skewed distributions where they are mostly used in one sense, and this is exactly what is approximated by MFS.

Of the measures included in Table 1, the paired FScore (F-10), the F-Measure (F-SC), and the Jaccard Coefficient provide results that seem most appropriate for word sense induction. This is because these measures score random baselines lower than MFS, and that RandX scores lower than RandY, when ($X > Y$). The paired FScore (F-10) and the Jaccard Coefficient arrived at similar results, where Rand50 received an extremely low score, and MFS scored the highest. The F-measure (F-SC) had a similar profile, except that the decline in evaluation scores as X grows in RandX is somewhat less.

The paired F-Score (F-10), the F-Measure (F-SC), and F1 (F1-13) all score MFS at approximately 54%, which is intuitively appealing since that is the percentage of instances correctly clustered if all instances are placed into a single cluster. However, in

Table 1: Experimental Results

System	F-10	F-SC	Jaccard	F1-13	RI	ARI	clusters	size
sys1	46.53	46.90	31.79	56.83	52.18	5.75	2.5	26.5
sys7	45.89	44.03	31.03	58.78	52.04	**6.78**	3.0	25.2
sys9	35.56	37.21	22.24	57.02	54.63	2.59	3.3	19.8
Rand2	41.49	42.86	26.99	54.89	50.06	-0.04	2.0	32.0
Rand5	25.17	31.28	14.52	56.73	56.13	0.12	5.0	12.8
Rand10	15.05	28.71	8.18	59.67	58.10	0.02	10.0	6.4
Rand25	7.01	26.78	3.63	66.89	59.24	-0.15	23.2	2.8
Rand50	4.07	25.97	2.00	**76.19**	**59.73**	0.10	35.9	1.8
MFS	**54.06**	**54.42**	**39.90**	54.42	39.90	0.0	1.0	64.0
Gold	100.00	100.00	100.00	100.00	100.00	99.0	7.7	11.6

other cases these measures begin to diverge. F1 (F1-13) tends to score random baselines even higher than MFS, and Rand50 gets a higher score than Rand2, which is somewhat counter intuitive. In fact according to F1 (F1-13), Rand50 would have been the top ranked system in task 11. It appears that F1 (F1-13) is strongly influenced by cluster purity, but does not penalize a system for creating too many clusters. Thus, as the number of clusters increases, F1 (F1-13) will consistently improve since smaller clusters are nearly always more pure than larger ones.

Interestingly enough, the Rand Index (RI) and the Jaccard Coefficient both score MFS at 39%. This number does not have an intuitively appealing interpretation, and thereafter RI and Jaccard diverge. RI scores random baselines higher than MFS, whereas the Jaccard Coefficient takes the more reasonable path of scoring random baselines well below MFS.

3.2 Duluth Systems Evaluation

The FScore (F-10), F-Measure (F-SC), and Jaccard Coefficient result in a comparable and consistent view of the system results. sys1 was found to be the most accurate, followed closely by sys7. All three measures showed that sys9 lagged considerably.

While all three systems relied on second–order co-occurrences, sys7 used the least amount of data, while sys9 used the most. This shows that better results can be obtained using the Web snippets to be clustered as the source of the co–occurrence data (as sys1 and sys7 did) rather than larger amounts of possibly less relevant text (as sys9 did).

Each of these systems created a roughly comparable number of clusters (on average, per query term, shown in the column labeled *clusters*). sys7 created 2.53, while sys9 created 3.01, and sys1 found 3.32. The average number of web snippets in the discovered clusters (shown in the column labeled *size*) are likewise somewhat consistent: sys1 was the largest at 26.5, sys7 had 25.2, and sys9 was the smallest with 19.8. The gold standard found an average of 7.7 queries per cluster and 11.6 snippets per cluster.

After the competition sys1 and sys9 were run without SVD. There was no significant difference in results with or without SVD. This is consistent with previous work that found SVD had relatively little impact in name discrimination experiments (Pedersen et al., 2005).

4 Conclusions

sys7 achieved the best results by using very small co-occurrence matrices of approximately one to two hundred rows and columns. While small, this data was most relevant to the task since it was made up of the Web snippets to be clustered. sys1 increased the size of the co–occurrence matrix to 771 x 96 by using all of the test data, but saw no increase in performance. sys9 used the largest corpus, which resulted in a co–occurrence matrix of 9,853 x 300, and had the poorest results of the Duluth systems.

Sixty–four instances is a small amount of data for clustering. In future we will augment each query with additional unannotated web snippets that will be discarded after clustering. Hopefully the core 64 instances that remain will be clustered more effectively given the cushion provided by the extra data.

References

J. Artiles, E. Amigó, and J. Gonzalo. 2009. The role of named entities in Web People Search. In *Proceedings of the 2009 Conference on Empirical Methods in Natural Language Processing*, pages 534–542, Singapore, August.

A. Di Marco and R. Navigli. 2013. Clustering and diversifying web search results with graph-based word sense induction. *Computational Linguistics*, 39(4):1–46.

D. Graff and C. Cieri. 2003. English Gigaword. Linguistic Data Consortium, Philadelphia.

A. Kulkarni and T Pedersen. 2005. SenseClusters: Unsupervised discrimination and labeling of similar contexts. In *Proceedings of the Demonstration and Interactive Poster Session of the 43rd Annual Meeting of the Association for Computational Linguistics*, pages 105–108, Ann Arbor, MI, June.

T. Landauer and S. Dumais. 1997. A solution to Plato's problem: The Latent Semantic Analysis theory of acquisition, induction and representation of knowledge. *Psychological Review*, 104:211–240.

S. Manandhar, I. Klapaftis, D. Dligach, and S. Pradhan. 2010. SemEval-2010 Task 14: Word sense induction and disambiguation. In *Proceedings of the SemEval 2010 Workshop : the 5th International Workshop on Semantic Evaluations*, Uppsala, Sweden, July.

R. Navigli and D. Vannella. 2013. Semeval-2013 task 11: Evaluating word sense induction and disambiguation within an end-user application. In *Proceedings of the 7th International Workshop on Semantic Evaluation (SemEval 2013), in conjunction with the Second Joint Conference on Lexical and Computational Semantics (*SEM-2013)*, Atlanta, June.

T. Pedersen and A. Kulkarni. 2006a. Automatic cluster stopping with criterion functions and the gap statistic. In *Proceedings of the Demonstration Session of the Human Language Technology Conference and the Sixth Annual Meeting of the North American Chapter of the Association for Computational Linguistics*, pages 276–279, New York City, June.

T. Pedersen and A. Kulkarni. 2006b. Selecting the right number of senses based on clustering criterion functions. In *Proceedings of the Posters and Demo Program of the Eleventh Conference of the European Chapter of the Association for Computational Linguistics*, pages 111–114, Trento, Italy, April.

T. Pedersen and A. Kulkarni. 2007. Discovering identities in web contexts with unsupervised clustering. In *Proceedings of the IJCAI-2007 Workshop on Analytics for Noisy Unstructured Text Data*, pages 23–30, Hyderabad, India, January.

T. Pedersen, A. Purandare, and A. Kulkarni. 2005. Name discrimination by clustering similar contexts. In *Proceedings of the Sixth International Conference on Intelligent Text Processing and Computational Linguistics*, pages 220–231, Mexico City, February.

T. Pedersen. 2006. Determining smoker status using supervised and unsupervised learning with lexical features. In *Working Notes of the i2b2 Workshop on Challenges in Natural Language Processing for Clinical Data*, Washington, DC, November.

T. Pedersen. 2007. UMND2 : SenseClusters applied to the sense induction task of Senseval-4. In *Proceedings of the Fourth International Workshop on Semantic Evaluations (SemEval-2007)*, pages 394–397, Prague, Czech Republic, June.

T. Pedersen. 2010a. Computational approaches to measuring the similarity of short contexts. Technical report, University of Minnesota Supercomputing Institute Research Report UMSI 2010/118, October.

T. Pedersen. 2010b. Duluth-WSI: SenseClusters applied to the sense induction task of semEval-2. In *Proceedings of the SemEval 2010 Workshop : the 5th International Workshop on Semantic Evaluations*, pages 363–366, Uppsala, July.

A. Purandare and T. Pedersen. 2004. Word sense discrimination by clustering contexts in vector and similarity spaces. In *Proceedings of the Conference on Computational Natural Language Learning*, pages 41–48, Boston, MA.

A. Rosenberg and J. Hirschberg. 2007. V-measure: A conditional entropy-based external cluster evaluation measure. In *Proceedings of the 2007 Joint Conference on Empirical Methods in Natural Language Processing and Computational Natural Language Learning*, pages 410–420, Prague, Czech Republic, June.

C. X. Zhai, W. Cohen, and J. Lafferty. 2003. Beyond independent relevance: methods and evaluation metrics for subtopic retrieval. In *Proceedings of the 26th Annual International ACM SIGIR Conference on Research and Development in Information Retrieval*, pages 10–17. ACM.

Y. Zhao and G. Karypis. 2004. Empirical and theoretical comparisons of selected criterion functions for document clustering. *Machine Learning*, 55:311–331.

SATTY : Word Sense Induction Application in Web Search Clustering*

Satyabrata Behera
IIT Bombay
Mumbai, India
satty@cse.iitb.ac.in

Upasana Gaikwad
IIT Bombay
Mumbai, India
upasana@cse.iitb.ac.in

Ramakrishna Bairi
IIT Bombay
Mumbai, India
bairi@cse.iitb.ac.in

Ganesh Ramakrishnan
IIT Bombay
Mumbai, India
ganesh@cse.iitb.ac.in

Abstract

The aim of this paper is to perform Word Sense induction (WSI); which clusters web search results and produces a diversified list of search results. It describes the WSI system developed for Task 11 of SemEval - 2013. This paper implements the idea of *monotone submodular* function optimization using greedy algorithm.

1 Introduction

Two different types of systems were submitted under Task 11 of SemEval - 2013 (Roberto Navigli and Daniele Vannella, 2013). The two system types are WSI (Word Sense Induction) and WSD (Word Sense Disambiguation). WSD is the task of automatically associating meaning with words. In WSD the possible meanings for a given word are drawn from an existing sense inventory. In contrast, WSI aims at automatically identifying the meanings of a given word from raw text. A WSI system will be asked to identify the meaning of the input query and cluster the search results into semantically-related groups according to their meanings. Instead, a WSD system will be requested to sense-tag the above search results with the appropriate senses of the input query and this, again, will implicitly determine a clustering of snippets (i.e., one cluster per sense).

Our system implements the idea given in (Jingrui He and Hanghang Tong and Qiaozhu Mei and Boleslaw Szymanski, 2012). This developed system uses the concept of submodularity. The task is treated as a submodular function maximization which has its benefits. On the one hand, there exists a simple greedy algorithm for monotone submodular function maximization where the solution obtained is guaranteed to be almost as good as the best possible solution according to an objective. More precisely, the greedy algorithm is a constant factor approximation to the cardinality constrained version of the problem, so that the approximate soultion is in the bound of $(1 - 1/e)$ of optimal solution. It is also important to note that this is a worst case bound, and in most cases the quality of the solution obtained will be much better than this bound suggests. In our system, monotone submodular objective of (Jingrui He and Hanghang Tong and Qiaozhu Mei and Boleslaw Szymanski, 2012) was implemented to find the top k simultaneously relevant and diversified list of search results. Once these top k results are obtained, they are used as centroids to form clusters by classifying each of remaining search results to one of the centroid with maximum similarity, producing k clusters. Those results which are not similar to any of the centroids are either put in a different cluster or are assigned to cluster with highest similarity.

2 Background on Submodularity

Our system uses the concept of submodularity. Given a set of objects $V = v_1, ..., v_n$ and a function $F : 2^V \rightarrow \mathbf{R}$ that returns a real value for any subset

*This system was designed and submitted in the competition SemEval-2013 under task 11 : Evaluating Word Sense Induction & Disambiguation within An End-User Application (Roberto Navigli and Daniele Vannella2013). http://www.cs.york.ac.uk/semeval-2013/.

*Second Joint Conference on Lexical and Computational Semantics (*SEM), Volume 2: Seventh International Workshop on Semantic Evaluation (SemEval 2013)*, pages 207–211, Atlanta, Georgia, June 14-15, 2013.

$S \subseteq V$. The function F is said to be submodular if it satisfies the property of *diminishing returns*, i.e., $A \subseteq B \subseteq V \setminus v$, a submodular function F must satisfy $F(A+v) - F(A) \geq F(B+v) - F(B)$. A set function F is *monotone nondecreasing* if $\forall A \subseteq B, F(A) \geq F(B)$. A *monotone nondecreasing* submodular function is referred to as monotone submodular.

We need to find the subset of bounded size $|S| \leq k$ that maximizes the function F, e.g. $argmax_{S \subseteq V}\ F(S)$. In general, this operation is intractable. As shown in (G.L. Nemhauser and L.A. Wolsey, 1978), if function F is monotone submodular, then a simple greedy algorithm finds an approximate solution which is guaranteed to be within $(1 - 1/e) \sim 0.63$ of optimal solution. Many properties of submodular functions are common with convex and concave functions (L. Lovász, 1983). One of those is that they are closed under a number of common combination operations such as summation, certain compositions, restrictions etc.

Previous work on submodularity is in (Hui Lin and Jeff Bilmes, 2011) where a monotone submodular objective is maximized using a greedy algorithm for document summarization. The objective function is:

$$F(S) = L(S) + \lambda R(S)$$

where $L(S)$ measures the coverage of summary set S to the document V and $R(S)$ measures diversity in S, which are properties of a good summary. $\lambda \geq 0$ is trade-off coefficient. V represents all the sentences (or other linguistic units) in a document (or document collection). Also $L(S)$ and $R(S)$ are monotone submodular functions. This work was again extended in (Hui Lin and Jeff A. Bilmes, 2012) where the submodular objective is itself a weighted combination of several submodular functions, where the weights are learnt in a max-margin setting. This work also demonstrates the use of this idea for document summarization.

3 System Description

The system works in 2 stages:

1. The first stage produces top k diversified and relevant set of search results.
2. The second stage forms k clusters of search results treating top k results as centroids.

The problem of finding top k diversified and relevant search results is posed as an optimization problem. This optimization function has the property of diminishing returns and monotonicity, which is a **monotone submodular function**. This enables to design a scalable, greedy algorithm to find the $(1 - 1/e)$ near-optimal solution. The optimization function is taken from (Jingrui He and Hanghang Tong and Qiaozhu Mei and Boleslaw Szymanski, 2012) and presented below.

Objective Function : The aim is to find a subset T of k search results which optimizes the objective function.

$$argmax_{|T|=k}\ w \sum_{i \in T} q_i r_i - \sum_{i,j \in T} r_i S_{ij} r_j$$

where, T is the subset of search results. $q = S.r$ is a nx1 vector. Intuitively, its ith element q_i measures the importance of ith search result. To be specific, if x_i is similar to many search results that are highly relevant to the query, it is more important than the search results whose neighbours are less relevant. S is a nxn similarity matrix between search results. r is a nx1 relevance vector of search results to query. w is a regularization parameter which defines trade-off between two terms.

The first term of the objective function measures the total weighted relevance of T with respect to query. It favours relevant search results from big clusters. In other words, if two search results are equally relevant to the query, one from a big cluster and the other isolated, by using weighted relevance, it prefers the former.

The second term measures the similarity among the search results within T such that it penalizes the selection of multiple relevant search results that are very similar to each other. By including this term in the objective function, we try to find a set of search results which are highly relevant to the query and also dissimilar to each other.

As the objective function is monotone submodular, the greedy algorithm finds the top k search results (i.e. near optimal solution) with approximation guarantee of $(1 - 1/e)$.

The second stage performs clustering using results of previous stage. The top k search results output by the previous stage are treated as centroids and the remaining search results are assigned to the centroid with the maximum similarity.

4 Experimental Results

The implemented system was tested on data given by SemEval - 2013[1](Roberto Navigli and Daniele Vannella, 2013). Data contains 100 queries, each with 64 search results. Each search result contains title, url and snippet.

Only title and snippet information was used. The relevance between query and a search result is calculated using weighted Jaccard. Cosine similarity is used to calculate the similarity between search results using only title and snippet. It was just bag of words (i.e. unigram) approach and no other preprocessing of data was done. In the first stage, system produces top 10 diversified search results which are then used as centroids to form 10 clusters. Those results which are not similar to any of the centroids are put in a different cluster, sometimes resulting in 11 clusters.

The evaluation method required : (i) to rank the search results within each cluster according to the confidence with which they belong to that cluster, (ii) to rank the clusters according to their diversity.

The cluster ranking is kept same as the rank of their centroids in top 10 results returned in first stage of the system.

Also search results within each cluster are then ranked by their average similarity to rest of the search results in the same cluster, in descending order with respect to the ranking score. The ranking score of search result x_i in cluster C is calculated as below, which is used in our system :

$$score(x_i) = \frac{1}{|C| - 1} \sum_{j:j \in C, i \neq j} S_{ij}$$

[1] http://www.cs.york.ac.uk/semeval-2013/task11/index.php?id=data

The other way of ranking search results within a cluster can be ranking by their relevance to the query. In that case, it depends on how good the relevance scores are. This ranking affects the ability of the system to diversify search results, i.e., *Subtopic Recall@K* and *Subtopic Precision@r* measures. The clustering quality is measured by measures of Rand Index (RI), Adjusted Rand Index (ARI), F1-measure (F1) and Jaccard Index (JI). All these evaluation metrics used are described in (Antonio Di Marco and Roberto Navigli, 2013). All the given evaluation metric values are obtained for the described data using the java evaluator provided by SemEval - 2013 (Roberto Navigli and Daniele Vannella, 2013). Our system's evaluation measures along with other systems, submitted in SemEval - 2013 are shown in tables 1, 2 and 3. Our system's name is task11-satty-approach1.

The clustering quality was found to be good as indicated by F1 and RI while scoring low for ARI, JI. In terms of diversification of search results, it did not perform that well indicating that either ranking of search results within each cluster or cluster ranking or both were not that good.

5 Conclusion

In this paper Word Sense Induction was implemented on web search clustering. The developed system evaluated with respect to different evaluation metrics. The system's clustering quality was found to be good while its ability to diversify search results was not that good. Better ranking of clusters as well as ranking of search results within each cluster can improve the system's ability to diversify search results.

The similarity score between search results were calculated using only title and snippet, but it can also be evaluated by fetching whole document. Since the relevance score of each search result to the query was not available, it was calculated by considering occurrence frequency of query words in search results (i.e. title and snippet). If a better relevance score were available by the search engine, the system might have performed better. These two aspects can be tested in further work.

System	Type	F1	ARI	RI	Jaccard	Avg. No. of Clusters	Avg. Cluster Size
hdp-clusters-lemma	WSI	**0.683**	0.2131	**0.6522**	0.3302	6.63	11.0756
hdp-clusters-nolemma	WSI	0.6803	**0.2149**	0.6486	0.3375	6.54	11.6803
task11-satty-approach1	WSI	0.6709	0.0719	0.5955	0.1505	9.9	6.4631
task11-ukp-wsi-wp-pmi	WSI	0.6048	0.0364	0.505	0.2932	5.86	30.3098
task11.duluth.sys7.pk2	WSI	0.5878	0.0678	0.5204	0.3103	3.01	25.1596
task11-ukp-wsi-wp-llr2	WSI	0.5864	0.0377	0.5109	0.3177	4.17	21.8702
task11-ukp-wsi-wacky-llr	WSI	0.5826	0.0253	0.5002	**0.3394**	3.64	32.3434
task11.duluth.sys9.pk2	WSI	0.5702	0.0259	0.5463	0.2224	3.32	19.84
task11.duluth.sys1.pk2	WSI	0.5683	0.0574	0.5218	0.3179	2.53	26.4533
rakesh	WSD	0.3949	0.0811	0.5876	0.3052	9.07	2.9441
singleton		1.0000	0.0000	0.6009	0.0000	64.0000	1.0000
allinone		0.5442	0.0000	0.3990	0.3990	1.0000	64.0000
gold		1.0000	0.9900	1.0000	1.0000	7.6900	11.5630

Table 1: The best result for each column is presented in boldface. **singleton** and **allinone** are baseline systems and **gold** is the theoretical upper-bound for the task. WSI : Word Sense Induction, WSD : Word Sense Disambiguation

System	Type	K=5	K=10	K=20	K=40	K=60
hdp-clusters-nolemma	WSI	0.508	0.6321	0.7926	0.9248	0.9821
hdp-clusters-lemma	WSI	0.4813	0.6551	0.7886	0.9168	0.9856
task11-ukp-wsi-wacky-llr	WSI	0.4119	0.5541	0.6861	0.839	0.9691
task11-ukp-wsi-wp-llr2	WSI	0.4107	0.5376	0.6887	0.8587	0.983
task11-ukp-wsi-wp-pmi	WSI	0.4045	0.5625	0.687	0.8492	0.978
task11-satty-approach1	WSI	0.3897	0.489	0.6272	0.8214	0.9745
task11.duluth.sys7.pk2	WSI	0.3888	0.5379	0.7038	0.8623	0.9844
task11.duluth.sys9.pk2	WSI	0.3715	0.499	0.6891	0.8365	0.9734
task11.duluth.sys1.pk2	WSI	0.3711	0.5329	0.7124	0.8848	0.9849
rakesh	WSD	0.4648	0.6236	0.7866	0.9072	0.9903

Table 2: S-recall@K for different values of K averaged over 100 queries.

System	Type	r=0.5	r=0.6	r=0.7	r=0.8	r=0.9
hdp-clusters-lemma	WSI	0.4885	0.4293	0.3519	0.2762	0.2376
hdp-clusters-nolemma	WSI	0.4818	0.4388	0.3485	0.293	0.2485
task11-ukp-wsi-wp-pmi	WSI	0.4283	0.334	0.2663	0.2292	0.2039
task11-ukp-wsi-wacky-llr	WSI	0.4247	0.3173	0.2539	0.2271	0.1849
task11-ukp-wsi-wp-llr2	WSI	0.4206	0.3204	0.2657	0.2241	0.1858
task11.duluth.sys1.pk2	WSI	0.4008	0.3131	0.2673	0.2451	0.2177
task11.duluth.sys7.pk2	WSI	0.3911	0.3042	0.2654	0.2343	0.1995
task11.duluth.sys9.pk2	WSI	0.359	0.2972	0.2526	0.2126	0.1951
task11-satty-approach1	WSI	0.3494	0.2688	0.2355	0.204	0.1736
rakesh	WSD	0.48	0.3904	0.3272	0.2792	0.2394

Table 3: S-precision@r for different values of r averaged over 100 queries.

References

Hui Lin and Jeff Bilmes. 2011. *A class of submodular functions for document summarization.* The 49th Annual Meeting of the Association for Computational Linguistics: Human Language Technologies (ACL-HLT), Portland, OR, June.

Hui Lin and Jeff A Bilmes. 2012. *Learning mixtures of submodular shells with application to document summarization.* arXiv preprint arXiv:1210.4871.

Jingrui He and Hanghang Tong and Qiaozhu Mei and Boleslaw Szymanski. 2012. *GenDeR: A Generic Diversified Ranking Algorithm.* Advances in Neural Information Processing Systems 25.

Antonio Di Marco and Roberto Navigli. 2013. *Clustering and Diversifying Web Search Results with Graph-Based Word Sense Induction.* Computational Linguistics, 39(4), MIT Press.

Roberto Navigli and Daniele Vannella. 2013. *SemEval-2013 Task 11: Evaluating Word Sense Induction Disambiguation within An End-User Application.* Proceedings of the 7th International Workshop on Semantic Evaluation (SemEval 2013), in conjunction with the Second Joint Conference on Lexical and Computational Semantcis (*SEM 2013), Atlanta, USA, 2013.

L. Lovász. 1983. *Submodular functions and convexity.* Mathematical programming-The state of the art,(eds. A. Bachem, M. Grotschel and B. Korte) Springer, pages 235257.

G.L. Nemhauser and L.A. Wolsey. 1978 *An analysis of approximations for maximizing submodular set functions I.* Mathematical Programming, 14(1):265294.

UKP-WSI: UKP Lab Semeval-2013 Task 11 System Description

Hans-Peter Zorn† and Iryna Gurevych†‡

†Ubiquitous Knowledge Processing Lab (UKP-TUDA)
Department of Computer Science, Technische Universität Darmstadt
‡Ubiquitous Knowledge Processing Lab (UKP-DIPF)
German Institute for Educational Research and Educational Information
www.ukp.tu-darmstadt.de

Abstract

In this paper, we describe the UKP Lab system participating in the Semeval-2013 task "Word Sense Induction and Disambiguation within an End-User Application". Our approach uses preprocessing, co-occurrence extraction, graph clustering, and a state-of-the-art word sense disambiguation system. We developed a configurable pipeline which can be used to integrate and evaluate other components for the various steps of the complex task.

1 Introduction

The task "Evaluating Word Sense Induction and Word Sense Disambiguation in an End-User Application" of SemEval-2013 (Navigli and Vannella, 2013) aims at an extrinsic evaluation scheme for WSI to overcome the difficulties inherent to WSI evaluation. The task requires building a WSI system and combining it with a WSD step to assign the induced sentences to example instances.

Word sense disambiguation (WSD) is the task of determining the correct meaning for an ambiguous word from its context. WSD algorithms usually choose one sense out of a given set of possible senses for each word. A resource that enumerates possible senses for each word is called a sense inventory. Manually created inventories come usually in form of lexical semantic resources, such as WordNet or more specifically created inventories such as OntoNotes (Hovy et al., 2006).

Word sense induction (WSI) on the other hand aims to create such an inventory from a corpus in an unsupervised manner. For each word that should be disambiguated, a WSI algorithm creates a set of context clusters that will be used to define and describe the senses.

We build our system upon the open-source DKPro framework [1] and a corresponding WSD component (upcoming).

Input for the task comes as two files. One contains the search queries, also referred as topics. Sense induction will be performed for each of those topics. The second file contains 6400 entries from the result pages of a search engine. Each entry consists of the title, a snippet and the URL of the corresponding web page.

2 Related Work

One of the early approaches to WSI (Schütze, 1998) maps words into a vector space and represents word contexts as vector-sums and use cosine vector similarity, clustering is performed by expectation maximization (EM) clustering. Dorow and Widdows (2003) use the BNC to build a co-occurrence graph for nouns, based on a co-occurrence frequency threshold. They perform Markov clustering on this graph. Pantel and Lin (2002) proposes a clustering approach called clustering by committee (CBC). This algorithm first selects the words with the highest similarity based on mutual information and then builds groups of highly connected words called committees. It then iteratively assigns the remaining words to one of the committee clusters by comparing them to the averaged the com-

[1] http://code.google.com/p/dkpro-core-asl/

*Second Joint Conference on Lexical and Computational Semantics (*SEM), Volume 2: Seventh International Workshop on Semantic Evaluation (SemEval 2013)*, pages 212–216, Atlanta, Georgia, June 14-15, 2013.

mittee feature vectors. This exploits the assumption that two or more words together disambiguate each other, Bordag (2006) extends on this idea by using word triples to form non-ambiguous seed-clusters. Many approaches use a variety of graph clustering algorithms for WSI: Others (Klapaftis and Manandhar, 2010) use hierarchical agglomerative clustering on hierarchical random graphs created from word co-occurrences. Di Marco and Navigli (2013) use word sense induction for web search result clustering. They introduce a maximum spanning tree algorithm that operates on co-occurrence graphs built from large corpora, such as ukWaC (Baroni et al., 2009). The system by Pedersen (2010) employs clustering first- and second-order co-occurrences as well as singular value decomposition on the co-occurrence matrix, which is clustered using repeated bisections. Jurgens (2011) employ a graph-based community detection algorithm on a co-occurrence graph. Distributional approaches for WSI include LSA Apidianaki and Van de Cruys (2011) or LDA (Brody and Lapata, 2009).

3 Our Approach

Our system consists of two independent parts. The first is a batch process that creates database containing co-occurrence statistics derived from a background corpus. The second is the actual WSI and WSD pipeline doing the result clustering. Both parts include identical preprocessing steps for segmentation and lemmatization.

The pipeline (Figure 1) first performs Word Sense Induction, resulting in an induced sense inventory. A WSD algorithm then uses this inventory to disambiguate all instances of the search query within a web-page. A majority voting finally assigns a sense to each result-snippet.

The sense induction algorithm is based on graph clustering on a co-occurrence graph, similar to the approach by Di Marco and Navigli (2013). Our approach differs from previous work in the way we perform a greedy search for additional context and how it combines WSI with an advanced WSD step using lexical expansions. Moreover, we consider our generic UIMA-based WSD and WSI system as a useful basis for experimentation and evaluation of WSI systems.

	# words	# co-occurrences
Wikipedia	3,011,397	96,979,920
ukWaC	8,687,711	441,005,478

Table 1: Size of co-occurrence databases

3.1 Preprocessing

The pipeline first reads topics and snippets. If the web-page can be downloaded at the URL that corresponds to the result, it is cleaned by an HTML parser and the plain text is appended to the snippet. As further steps we segment and lemmatize the input. We apply the same preprocessing to snippets, queries and the corpora.

3.2 Co-occurrence Extraction

We calculate the log-likelihood ratio (LLR) (Dunning, 1993) and point-wise mutual information (PMI) (Church and Hanks, 1990) of a word pair co-occurring at sentence level using a modified version of the collocation statistics implemented in Apache Mahout [2]. Even when sorting the co-occurrences by PMI, we employ a minimum support cut-off based on the LLR, which is based on significance. All pairs with a log-likelihood ratio < 1 are discarded. This value is lower than the significance level of $\tilde{3}.8$ we found in the literature, but because in the expand step (see algorithm 2) we require more than two words to co-occur with the target word, we used a lower value. We use the English Wikipedia [3] and ukWaC (Baroni et al., 2009) as background corpus. Table 1 gives an overview about the obtained co-occurrence pairs.

3.3 Clustering Algorithm

The algorithm is a two-step approach that first creates an initial clustering of a graph $G = (V, E)$ and then improves this clustering in a second step. The initial step (Algorithm 1) starts by retrieving the top $n = 150$ most similar terms for the target word by querying the co-occurrence database we created in section 3.2. These represent vertices in a graph. We then construct [4] a minimum spanning tree (mst)

[2]http://mahout.apache.org

[3]Dump from April 2011

[4]For all of our graph operations, we employ the *igraph* library for R, http://igraph.sf.net

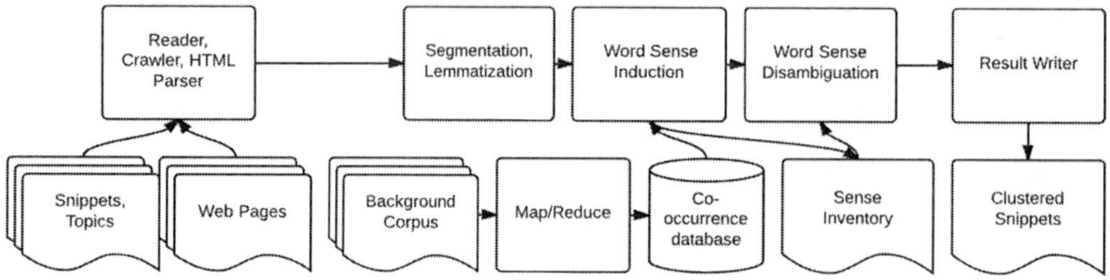

Figure 1: WSI and WSD Pipeline

by inserting edges $\{v_i, v_j\}$ from the co-occurrence database. The weight $w(\{v_i, v_j\})$ of each edge is set to the inverse of the used similarity measure $dist$ (LLR or PMI) between those terms. The minimum spanning tree then is cut into subtrees be iteratively removing the edge with the highest edge-betweenness (Freeman, 1977) ($betweeness$) until the size of the largest component of G falls below a threshold $S_{initial}$.

Algorithm 1 initialClusters

$V(G_0) \leftarrow$ top n most similar words to target word
$w(v_i, v_j) \leftarrow dist(term_i, term_j)$
$G \leftarrow mst(G_0)$
$V(G) \leftarrow V(G) \setminus v_{target}$
while $\max(|C(G)|) > S_{intitial}$ **do**
  $E(G) \leftarrow E(G) \setminus \arg\max_e(betweeness(e))$
end while

The resulting partitioning of the graph is the starting point for the second phase of the algorithm, which we call *expand/join* step (Algorithm 2). During this step, the algorithm looks iteratively at all clusters C_{small} of size s smaller than $S_{max} = 9$ (determined empirically), starting with the largest ones. From each of these clusters, it constructs a query to the co-occurrence database, retrieving all terms that significantly co-occur together with all terms in the respective cluster ($query_s$) and with the target word (E). This list of terms is then compared to all clusters C_{large} with $|C| > s$. If the normalized intersection between one of those C_{large} is above a threshold $t = 0.3$ (determined empirically), we assume that the C_{small} represents the same sense as the C_{large} and merge those clusters. If this is not the case for any of the larger clusters, we assume that C_{small} represents a sense of its own extend the cluster by adding edges between vertices representing the expansion terms and C_{small}.

Algorithm 2 expandJoin

Require: G is a minimum spanning forest
for $s = S_{max} \rightarrow 1$ **do**
  for all $C_{small}(G), |C_{small}| = s$ **do**
    $E \leftarrow query_s(v_1, .., v_i)$
    for all $C_{large} \in G, |C_{large}| > s$ **do**
      if $|C_{large} \cap E| / |C_{large}| > t$ **then**
        $C_{large} \leftarrow C_{large} \cup C_{small}$
      else
        $C_{small} \leftarrow C_{small} \cup E$
      end if
    end for
  end for
end for

3.4 Word Sense Disambiguation

We use the DKPro WSD framework, which implements various WSD algorithms, with the same system configuration as reported by Miller et al. (2012). It uses a variant of the Simplified Lesk Algorithm (Kilgarriff et al., 2000). This algorithm measures the overlap between a words context and the textual descriptions of senses within a machine readable dictionary, such as WordNet. The senses that have been induced in the previous step are provided to the framework as a sense inventory. Instead of using sense descriptions, we now compute the overlap between the sense clusters and the context of the target word. The WSD system expands both the word context and the sense clusters with synonyms from a distributional thesaurus (DT), similar to Lin (1998). The DT has been created from 10M dependency-parsed sentences of English newswire

Run	F_1	ARI	RI	JI	# clusters	avg cl. size
wacky-llr	0.5826	0.0253	0.5002	0.3394	3.6400	32.3434
wp-llr	0.5864	0.0377	0.5109	0.3177	4.1700	21.8702
wp-pmi	0.6048	0.0364	0.5050	0.2932	5.8600	30.3098

Table 2: Results for the submitted runs

from the Leipzig Corpora Collection (Biemann et al., 2007) for word similarity[5]. Besides knowledge-based WSD, the DT also has been successfully used for improving the performance of semantic text similarity (Bär et al., 2012). The WSD component disambiguates each instance of the search query within the snippet and web page individually.

4 Results

The clustering was evaluated using four different metrics as described by Di Marco and Navigli (2013). The Rand index and its chance-adjusted variant ARI are common cluster evaluation metrics. The adjusted rand index gives special weight to less frequent senses. The Jaccard index (JI) disregards the cases where two results are assigned to different clusters in the gold standard, therefore it is less sensitive to the granularity of the clustering. The F_1-Measure gives more attention to the individual clusters and how they cover the topics in the gold standard.

We submitted several runs for different configurations of the co-occurrence extraction (Table 2). Between runs, we did not modify the configuration of the sense induction or disambiguation step. The first run used collocations extracted from ukWaC scored by LLR metric (wacky-llr), and two others used Wikipedia as background corpus. One of the WP-based runs used PMI as association metric (wp-pmi), the other one used LLR (wp-llr). The run on the larger ukWaC corpus scored best with regard to the Jaccard measure, but worst in the adjusted Rand index measure. We attribute low scores for ARI to the fact that our system did not induce certain less frequent senses, resulting in small average number of clusters. The coarse grained clusters however, have been assigned quite well by our WSD system, as shown by relatively high Jaccard Index. For the WP-based runs, the clustering based on PMI produced more clusters and therefore scored higher on the F_1 measure than the LLR-based run. From an exploratory analysis of the created clusters, we assume that the WP-based runs have a higher chance to find more rare senses in this specific task, since the gold standard was also based on Wikipedia disambiguation pages.

5 Conclusion

We presented our word sense induction and disambiguation pipeline for search result clustering. Our contribution is a sense induction algorithm that incrementally retrieves more context from a co-occurrence database and the integration of WSI and WSD into a UIMA-based pipeline for easy experimentation. The system scored best with regard to Jaccard similarity of clusters, while performing low especially with the adjusted rand index. We assume that our sense granularity was too low for this task and failed to create clusters for rare senses. This could be improved by making the merge phase of the induction algorithm less eager. Furthermore, increasing the size of the background corpus, e.g. by combining the both corpora that have been used could increase the size of the context clusters especially for rare senses, which should further improve the performance in these cases. We attribute the good results with regard to the F_1 and Jaccard measures also to our state-of-the-art word sense disambiguation step and the use of the distributional thesaurus.

6 Acknowledgements

We thank Tristan Miller for helping us with the DKPro WSD framework and Chris Biemann for providing the distributional thesaurus. This work has been supported by the Volkswagen Foundation as part of the Lichtenberg-Professorship Program under grant No. I/82806.

[5]The software used to create the DT is available from http://www.jobimtext.org

References

Marianna Apidianaki and Tim Van de Cruys. 2011. Latent Semantic Word Sense Induction and Disambiguation. In *ACL HLT 2011*, pages 1476–1485, June.

Daniel Bär, Chris Biemann, Iryna Gurevych, and Torsten Zesch. 2012. UKP: Computing Semantic Textual Similarity by Combining Multiple Content Similarity Measures. In *Proceedings of First Joint Conference on Lexical and Computational Semantics (*SEM)*, pages 435–440.

Marco Baroni, Silvia Bernardini, Adriano Ferraresi, and Eros Zanchetta. 2009. The WaCky wide web: a collection of very large linguistically processed web-crawled corpora. *Language Resources and Evaluation*, 43(3):209–226, February.

Chris Biemann, Gerhard Heyer, Uwe Quasthoff, and Matthias Richter. 2007. The Leipzig Corpora Collection - Monolingual corpora of standard size. In *Proceedings of Corpus Linguistic 2007*, Birmingham, UK.

Stefan Bordag. 2006. Word Sense Induction: Triplet-Based Clustering and Automatic Evaluation. In *Proceedings of the 11th Conference of the European Chapter of the Association for Computational Linguistics*, pages 137–144, Trento, Italy.

Samuel Brody and Mirella Lapata. 2009. Bayesian word sense induction. In *Proceedings of the 12th Conference of the European Chapter of the Association for Computational Linguistics*, EACL '09, pages 103–111, Stroudsburg, PA, USA. Association for Computational Linguistics.

Kenneth Ward Church and Patrick Hanks. 1990. Word association norms, mutual information, and lexicography. *Computational Linguistics*, 16(1):22–29, March.

Antonio Di Marco and Roberto Navigli. 2013. Clustering and Diversifying Web Search Results with Graph-Based Word Sense Induction. *Computational Linguistics*, 39(4):1–46, November.

Beate Dorow and Dominic Widdows. 2003. Discovering corpus-specific word senses. In *Proceedings of the Tenth Conference on European Chapter of the Association for Computational Linguistics - EACL '03*, volume 2, page 79, Morristown, NJ, USA, April. Association for Computational Linguistics.

Ted Dunning. 1993. Accurate Methods for the Statistics of Surprise and Coincidence. *Computational Linguistics*, 19(1):61 – 74.

Linton C Freeman. 1977. A set of measures of centrality based on betweenness. *Sociometry*, 40(1):35–41.

Eduard Hovy, Mitchell Marcus, Martha Palmer, Lance Ramshaw, and Ralph Weischedel. 2006. OntoNotes: the 90% solution. In *Proceedings of the Human Language Technology Conference of the NAACL, Companion Volume: Short Papers*, NAACL-Short '06, pages 57–60, Stroudsburg, PA, USA. Association for Computational Linguistics.

David Jurgens. 2011. Word Sense Induction by Community Detection. In *HLT '11: Proceedings of the 49th Annual Meeting of the Association for Computational Linguistics Human Language Technologies*, pages 24–28, Portland, Oregon.

Adam Kilgarriff, Brighton England, and Joseph Rosenzweig. 2000. English Senseval: Report and Results. In *Proceedings of the 2nd International Conference on Language Resources and Evaluation*, Athens, Greece.

Ioannis P. Klapaftis and Suresh Manandhar. 2010. Word sense induction & disambiguation using hierarchical random graphs. In *Proceedings of the 2010 Conference on Empirical Methods in Natural Language Processing*, pages 745–755, Cambridge, Massachusetts, October. Association for Computational Linguistics.

Dekang Lin. 1998. Automatic retrieval and clustering of similar words. In *Proceedings of the 36th annual meeting on Association for Computational Linguistics*, pages 768–774, Morristown, NJ, USA, August. Association for Computational Linguistics.

Tristan Miller, Chris Biemann, Torsten Zesch, and Iryna Gurevych. 2012. Using Distributional Similarity for Lexical Expansion in Knowledge-based Word Sense Disambiguation. In *Proceedings of the 24th International Conference on Computational Linguistics (COLING 2012)*.

Roberto Navigli and Daniele Vannella. 2013. SemEval-2013 Task 11: Evaluating Word Sense Induction & Disambiguation within An End-User Application. In *Proceedings of the 7th International Workshop on Semantic Evaluation (SemEval 2013), in conjunction with the Second Joint Conference on Lexical and Computational Semantcis (*SEM 2013)*, Atlanta, USA.

Patrick Pantel and Dekang Lin. 2002. Discovering word senses from text. In *Proceedings of the eighth ACM SIGKDD international conference on Knowledge discovery and data mining - KDD '02*, page 613, New York, New York, USA, July. ACM Press.

Ted Pedersen. 2010. Duluth-WSI: SenseClusters applied to the sense induction task of SemEval-2. In *Proceedings of the 5th International Workshop on Semantic Evaluation*, pages 363–366, Stroudsburg, PA, USA, July. Association for Computational Linguistics.

Hinrich Schütze. 1998. Automatic word sense discrimination. *Computational Linguistics*, 24(1):97–123, March.

unimelb: Topic Modelling-based Word Sense Induction for Web Snippet Clustering

Jey Han Lau, Paul Cook and **Timothy Baldwin**
Department of Computing and Information Systems
The University of Melbourne
jhlau@csse.unimelb.edu.au, paulcook@unimelb.edu.au,
tb@ldwin.net

Abstract

This paper describes our system for Task 11 of SemEval-2013. In the task, participants are provided with a set of ambiguous search queries and the snippets returned by a search engine, and are asked to associate senses with the snippets. The snippets are then clustered using the sense assignments and systems are evaluated based on the quality of the snippet clusters. Our system adopts a pre-existing Word Sense Induction (WSI) methodology based on Hierarchical Dirichlet Process (HDP), a non-parametric topic model. Our system is trained over extracts from the full text of English Wikipedia, and is shown to perform well in the shared task.

1 Introduction

The basic premise behind research on word sense disambiguation (WSD) is that there exists a static, discrete set of word senses that can be used to label distinct usages of a given word (Agirre and Edmonds, 2006; Navigli, 2009). There are various pitfalls underlying this premise, including: (1) what sense inventory is appropriate for a particular task (given that sense inventories can vary considerably in their granularity and partitioning of word usages)? (2) given that word senses tend to take the form of prototypes, is discrete labelling a felicitous representation of word usages, especially for non-standard word usages? (3) how should novel word usages be captured under this model? and (4) given the rapid pace of language evolution on real-time social media such as Twitter and Facebook, is it reasonable to assume a static sense inventory? Given this backdrop, there has been a recent growth of interest in the task of word sense induction (WSI), where the word sense representation for a given word is automatically inferred from a given data source, and word usages are labelled (often probabilistically) according to that data source. While WSI has considerable appeal as a task, intrinsic cross-comparison of WSI systems is fraught with many of the same issues as WSD (Agirre and Soroa, 2007; Manandhar et al., 2010), leading to a move towards task-based WSI evaluation, such as in Task 11 of SemEval-2013, titled "Evaluating Word Sense Induction & Disambiguation within an End-User Application".

This paper presents the UNIMELB system entry to SemEval-2013 Task 11. Our method is based heavily on the WSI methodology proposed by Lau et al. (2012) for novel word sense detection. Largely the same methodology was also applied to SemEval-2013 Task 13 on WSI (Lau et al., to appear).

2 System Description

Our system is based on the WSI methodology proposed by Lau et al. (2012) for the task of novel word sense detection. The core machinery of our system is driven by a Latent Dirichlet Allocation (LDA) topic model (Blei et al., 2003). In LDA, the model learns latent topics for a collection of documents, and associates these latent topics with every document in the collection. A topic is represented by a multinomial distribution of words, and the association of topics with documents is represented by a multinomial distribution of topics, with one distribution per document. The generative process of LDA

*Second Joint Conference on Lexical and Computational Semantics (*SEM), Volume 2: Seventh International Workshop on Semantic Evaluation (SemEval 2013)*, pages 217–221, Atlanta, Georgia, June 14-15, 2013.

for drawing word w in document d is as follows:

1. draw latent topic z from document d;

2. draw word w from the chosen latent topic z.

The probability of selecting word w given a document d is thus given by:

$$P(w|d) = \sum_{z=1}^{T} P(w|t=z)P(t=z|d).$$

where t is the topic variable, and T is the number of topics.

The number of topics, T, is a parameter in LDA, and the model tends to be highly sensitive to this setting. To remove the need for parameter tuning over development data, we make use of a non-parametric variant of LDA, in the form of a Hierarchical Dirichlet Process (HDP: Teh et al. (2006)). HDP learns the number of topics based on data, and the concentration parameters γ and α_0 control the variability of topics in the documents (for details of HDP please refer to the original paper, Teh et al. (2006)).

To apply HDP in the context of WSI, the latent topics are interpreted as the word senses, and the documents are usages that contain the target word of interest (or search query in the case of Task 11). That is, given a search query (e.g. *Prince of Persia*), a "document" in our application is a sentence/snippet containing the target word. In addition to the bag of words surrounding the target word, we also include positional context word information, as used in the original methodology of Lau et al. (2012). That is, we introduce an additional word feature for each of the three words to the left and right of the target word. An example of the topic model features for a context sentence is given in Table 1.

2.1 Background Corpus and Preprocessing

As part of the task setup, we were provided with snippets for each search query, constituting the documents for the topic model for that query (each search query is topic-modelled separately). Our system uses only the text of the snippets as features, and ignores the URL information. The text of the snippets is tokenised and lemmatised using OpenNLP and Morpha (Minnen et al., 2001).

As there are only 64 snippets for each query in the test dataset, which is very small by topic modelling standards, we turn to English Wikipedia to expand the data, by extracting all context sentences that contain the search query in the full collection of Wikipedia articles.[1] Each extracted usage is a three-sentence context containing the search query: the original sentence that contains the actual usage and its preceding and succeeding sentences. The extraction of usages from Wikipedia significantly increases the amount of information for the topic model to learn the senses for the search queries. To give an estimate: for very ambiguous queries such as *queen* we extracted almost 150,000 usages from Wikipedia; for most queries, however, this number tends to be a few thousand usages.

To summarise, for each search query we apply the HDP model to the combined collection of the 64 snippets and the extracted usages from Wikipedia. The topic model learns the senses/topics for all documents in the collection, but we only use the sense/topic distribution for the 64 snippets as they are the documents that are evaluated in the shared task.

Our English Wikipedia collection is tokenised and lemmatised using OpenNLP and Morpha (Minnen et al., 2001). The search queries provided in the task, however, are not lemmatised. Two approaches are used to extract the usages of search queries from Wikipedia:

HDP-CLUSTERS-LEMMA Search queries are lemmatised using Morpha (Minnen et al., 2001), and both the original and lemmatised forms are used for extraction;[2]

HDP-CLUSTERS-NOLEMMA Search queries are not lemmatised and only their original forms are used for extraction.

[1] The Wikipedia dump was retrieved on November 28th 2009.

[2] Morpha requires the part-of-speech (POS) of a given word, which is determined by the majority POS aggregated over all of that word's occurrences in Wikipedia.

Search query	*dogs*
Context sentence	Most breeds of *dogs* are at most a few hundred years old
Bag-of-word features	most, breeds, of, are, at, most, a, few, hundred, years, old
Positional word features	most_#-3, breeds_#-2, of_#-1, are_#1, at_#2, most_#3

Table 1: An example of topic model features.

System	F1	ARI	RI	JI	Avg. No. of Clusters	Avg. Cluster Size
HDP-CLUSTERS-LEMMA	**0.6830**	0.2131	**0.6522**	0.3302	6.6300	11.0756
HDP-CLUSTERS-NOLEMMA	0.6803	**0.2149**	0.6486	0.3375	6.5400	11.6803
TASK11.DULUTH.SYS1.PK2	0.5683	0.0574	0.5218	0.3179	2.5300	26.4533
TASK11.DULUTH.SYS7.PK2	0.5878	0.0678	0.5204	0.3103	3.0100	25.1596
TASK11.DULUTH.SYS9.PK2	0.5702	0.0259	0.5463	0.2224	3.3200	19.8400
TASK11-SATTY-APPROACH1	0.6709	0.0719	0.5955	0.1505	9.9000	6.4631
TASK11-UKP-WSI-WACKY-LLR	0.5826	0.0253	0.5002	**0.3394**	3.6400	32.3434
TASK11-UKP-WSI-WP-LLR2	0.5864	0.0377	0.5109	0.3177	4.1700	21.8702
TASK11-UKP-WSI-WP-PMI	0.6048	0.0364	0.5050	0.2932	5.8600	30.3098
RAKESH	0.3949	0.0811	0.5876	0.3052	9.0700	2.9441
SINGLETON	1.0000	0.0000	0.6009	0.0000	64.0000	1.0000
ALLINONE	0.5442	0.0000	0.3990	0.3990	1.0000	64.0000
GOLD	1.0000	0.9900	1.0000	1.0000	7.6900	11.5630

Table 2: Cluster quality results for all systems. The best result for each column is presented in boldface. SINGLETON and ALLINONE are baseline systems and GOLD is the theoretical upper-bound for the task.

3 Experiments and Results

Following Lau et al. (2012), we use the default parameters ($\gamma = 0.1$ and $\alpha_0 = 1.0$) for HDP.[3] For each search query, we apply HDP to induce the senses, and a distribution of senses is produced for each "document" in the model. As the snippets in the test dataset correspond to the documents in the model and evaluation is based on "hard" clusters of snippets, we assign a sense to each snippet based on the sense (= topic) which has the highest probability for that snippet.

The task requires participants to produce a ranked list of snippets for each induced sense, based on the relative fit between the snippet and the sense. We induce the ranking based on the sense probabilities assigned to the senses, such that snippets that have the highest probability of the induced sense are ranked highest, and snippets with lower sense probabilities are ranked lower.

Two classes of evaluation are used in the shared task:

1. cluster quality measures: Jaccard Index (JI), RandIndex (RI), Adjusted RandIndex (ARI) and F1;
2. diversification of search results: Subtopic Recall@K and Subtopic Precision@r.

Details of the evaluation measures are described in Navigli and Vannella (2013).

The idea behind the second form of evaluation (i.e. diversification of search results) is that search engine results should cluster the results based on senses (of the query term in the documents) given an ambiguous query. For example, if a user searches for *apple*, the search engine may return results related to both the computer brand sense and the fruit sense of *apple*. Given this assumption, the best WSI/WSD system is the one that can correctly identify the diversity of senses in the snippets.

[3] Our implementation can be accessed via `https://github.com/jhlau/hdp-wsi`.

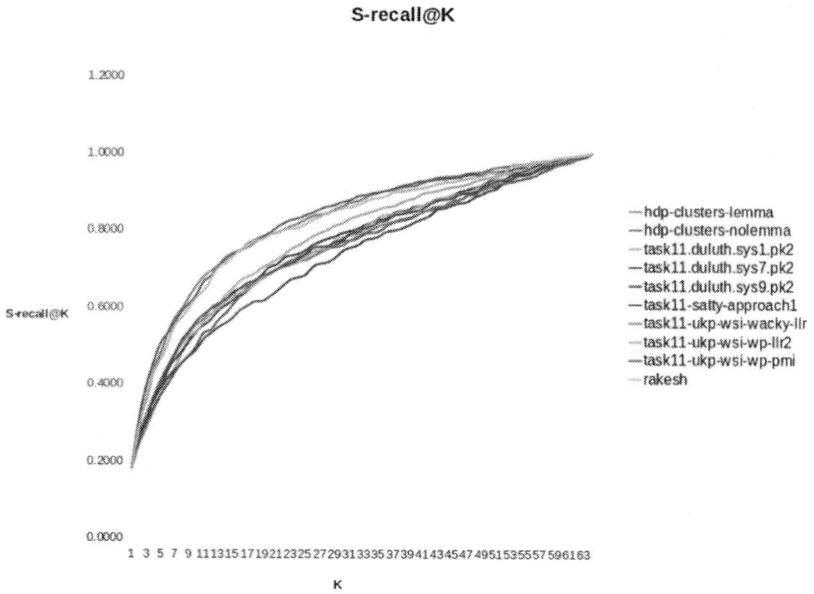

Figure 1: Subtopic Recall@K for all participating systems.

Cluster quality, subtopic recall@K and subtopic precision@r results for all systems entered in the task are presented in Table 2, Figure 1 and Figure 2, respectively.

In terms of cluster quality, our systems (HDP-CLUSTERS-LEMMA and HDP-CLUSTERS-NOLEMMA) consistently outperform the other teams for all measures except for the Jaccard Index (where we rank second and third, by a narrow margin). The average number of induced clusters and the average cluster size of our systems are similar to those of the gold standard system (GOLD), indicating that our systems are learning an appropriate sense granularity.

In terms of diversification of search results, our systems perform markedly better than most teams, other than RAKESH which trails closely behind our systems (despite a relatively low ranking in terms of the cluster quality evaluation). Overall, the results are encouraging and our system performs very well over the task.

4 Discussion and Conclusion

Our system adopts the WSI system proposed in Lau et al. (2012) with no parameters tuned for this task, and performs very well over it. Parameter tuning and exploiting URL information in the snippets could potentially boost the system performance further. Other background corpora (such as news articles) could also be used to increase the size of the training data. We leave these ideas for future work.

Inspecting the difference between the HDP-CLUSTERS-LEMMA and HDP-CLUSTERS-NOLEMMA approaches, only 6 out of the 100 lemmas have a lemmatised form which differs from the original query composition: *pods* (*pod*), *ten commandments* (*ten commandment*), *guild wars* (*guild war*), *stand by me* (*stand by i*), *sisters of mercy* (*sister of mercy*) and *lord of the flies* (*lord of the fly*). In most cases, including the lemmatised query results in the extraction of additional useful usages, e.g. using only the original form *lord of the flies* would extract no usages from Wikipedia (because this corpus has itself been lemmatised). In other cases, however, including the lemmatised forms results in many common noun usages, e.g. the number of usages of the lemmatised *pod* is significantly greater than that of the original form *pods* (which corresponds to proper noun usages in the lemmatised corpus), resulting in senses being induced only for common noun usages of *pods*. The

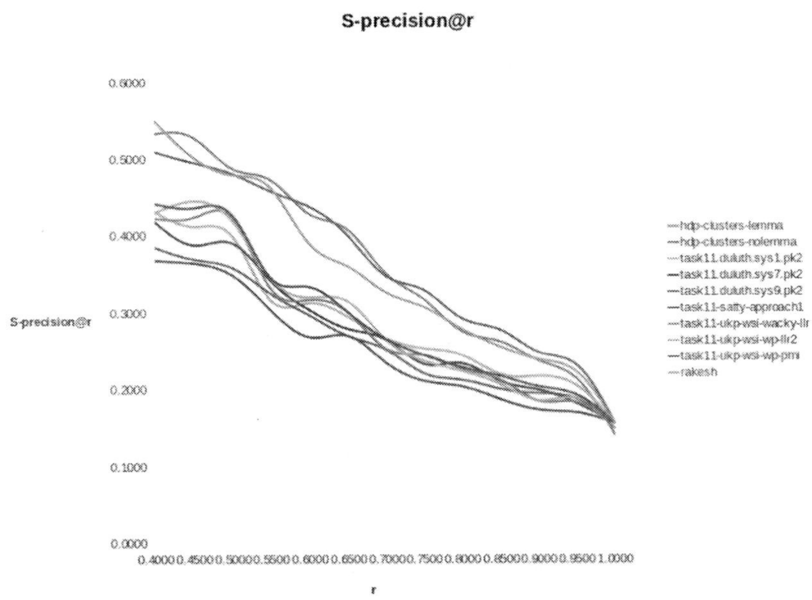

Figure 2: Subtopic Precision@r for all participating systems.

advantages and disadvantages of both approaches are reflected in the results: performance is mixed and no one method clearly outperforms the other.

To conclude, we apply a topic model-based WSI methodology to the task of web result clustering, using English Wikipedia as an external resource for extracting additional usages. Our system is completely unsupervised and requires no annotated resources, and appears to perform very well on the task.

References

Eneko Agirre and Philip Edmonds. 2006. *Word Sense Disambiguation: Algorithms and Applications*. Springer, Dordrecht, Netherlands.

Eneko Agirre and Aitor Soroa. 2007. SemEval-2007 task 02: Evaluating word sense induction and discrimination systems. In *Proc. of the 4th International Workshop on Semantic Evaluations*, pages 7–12, Prague, Czech Republic.

David M. Blei, Andrew Y. Ng, and Michael I. Jordan. 2003. Latent Dirichlet allocation. *Journal of Machine Learning Research*, 3:993–1022.

Jey Han Lau, Paul Cook, Diana McCarthy, David Newman, and Timothy Baldwin. 2012. Word sense induction for novel sense detection. In *Proc. of the 13th Conference of the EACL (EACL 2012)*, pages 591–601, Avignon, France.

Jey Han Lau, Paul Cook, and Timothy Baldwin. to appear. unimelb: Topic modelling-based word sense induction. In *Proc. of the 7th International Workshop on Semantic Evaluation (SemEval 2013)*.

Suresh Manandhar, Ioannis Klapaftis, Dmitriy Dligach, and Sameer Pradhan. 2010. SemEval-2010 Task 14: Word sense induction & disambiguation. In *Proceedings of the 5th International Workshop on Semantic Evaluation*, pages 63–68, Uppsala, Sweden.

Guido Minnen, John Carroll, and Darren Pearce. 2001. Applied morphological processing of English. *Natural Language Engineering*, 7(3):207–223.

Roberto Navigli and Daniele Vannella. 2013. SemEval-2013 task 11: Evaluating word sense induction & disambiguation within an end-user application. In *Proceedings of the 7th International Workshop on Semantic Evaluation (SemEval 2013), in conjunction with the Second Joint Conference on Lexical and Computational Semantcis (*SEM 2013)*, Atlanta, USA.

Roberto Navigli. 2009. Word sense disambiguation: A survey. *ACM Computing Surveys*, 41(2).

Yee Whye Teh, Michael I. Jordan, Matthew J. Beal, and David M. Blei. 2006. Hierarchical Dirichlet processes. *Journal of the American Statistical Association*, 101:1566–1581.

SemEval-2013 Task 12: Multilingual Word Sense Disambiguation

Roberto Navigli, David Jurgens and **Daniele Vannella**
Dipartimento di Informatica
Sapienza Università di Roma
Viale Regina Elena, 295 – 00161 Roma Italy
{navigli,jurgens,vannella}@di.uniroma1.it

Abstract

This paper presents the SemEval-2013 task on multilingual Word Sense Disambiguation. We describe our experience in producing a multilingual sense-annotated corpus for the task. The corpus is tagged with BabelNet 1.1.1, a freely-available multilingual encyclopedic dictionary and, as a byproduct, WordNet 3.0 and the Wikipedia sense inventory. We present and analyze the results of participating systems, and discuss future directions.

1 Introduction

Word Sense Disambiguation (WSD), the task of automatically assigning predefined meanings to words occurring in context, is a fundamental task in computational lexical semantics (Navigli, 2009; Navigli, 2012). Several Senseval and SemEval tasks have been organized in the past to study the performance and limits of disambiguation systems and, even more importantly, disambiguation settings. While an ad-hoc sense inventory was originally chosen for the first Senseval edition (Kilgarriff, 1998; Kilgarriff and Palmer, 2000), later tasks (Edmonds and Cotton, 2001; Snyder and Palmer, 2004; Mihalcea et al., 2004) focused on WordNet (Miller et al., 1990; Fellbaum, 1998) as a sense inventory. In 2007 the issue of the fine sense granularity of WordNet was addressed in two different SemEval disambiguation tasks, leading to the beneficial creation of coarser-grained sense inventories from WordNet itself (Navigli et al., 2007) and from OntoNotes (Pradhan et al., 2007).

In recent years, with the exponential growth of the Web and, consequently, the increase of non-English speaking surfers, we have witnessed an upsurge of interest in multilinguality. SemEval-2010 tasks on cross-lingual Word Sense Disambiguation (Lefever and Hoste, 2010) and cross-lingual lexical substitution (Mihalcea et al., 2010) were organized. While these tasks addressed the multilingual aspect of sense-level text understanding, they departed from the traditional WSD paradigm, i.e., the automatic assignment of senses from an existing inventory, and instead focused on lexical substitution (McCarthy and Navigli, 2009). The main factor hampering traditional WSD from going multilingual was the lack of a freely-available large-scale multilingual dictionary.

The recent availability of huge collaboratively-built repositories of knowledge such as Wikipedia has enabled the automated creation of large-scale lexical knowledge resources (Hovy et al., 2013). Over the past few years, a wide-coverage multilingual "encyclopedic" dictionary, called BabelNet, has been developed (Navigli and Ponzetto, 2012a). BabelNet[1] brings together WordNet and Wikipedia and provides a multilingual sense inventory that currently covers 6 languages. We therefore decided to put the BabelNet 1.1.1 sense inventory to the test and organize a traditional Word Sense Disambiguation task on a given English test set translated into 4 other languages (namely, French, German, Spanish and Italian). Not only does BabelNet enable multilinguality, but it also provides coverage for both lexicographic (e.g., apple as fruit) and encyclopedic

[1] http://babelnet.org

*Second Joint Conference on Lexical and Computational Semantics (*SEM), Volume 2: Seventh International Workshop on Semantic Evaluation (SemEval 2013)*, pages 222–231, Atlanta, Georgia, June 14-15, 2013.

meanings (e.g., Apple Inc. as company). In this paper we describe our task and disambiguation dataset and report on the system results.

2 Task Setup

The task required participating systems to annotate nouns in a test corpus with the most appropriate sense from the BabelNet sense inventory or, alternatively, from two main subsets of it, namely the WordNet or Wikipedia sense inventories. In contrast to previous all-words WSD tasks we did not focus on the other three open classes (i.e., verbs, adjectives and adverbs) since BabelNet does not currently provide non-English coverage for them.

2.1 Test Corpus

The test set consisted of 13 articles obtained from the datasets available from the 2010, 2011 and 2012 editions of the workshop on Statistical Machine Translation (WSMT).[2] The articles cover different domains, ranging from sports to financial news.

The same article was available in 4 different languages (English, French, German and Spanish). In order to cover Italian, an Italian native speaker manually translated each article from English into Italian, with the support of an English mother tongue advisor. In Table 1 we show for each language the number of words of running text, together with the number of multiword expressions and named entities annotated, from the 13 articles.

2.2 Sense Inventories

2.2.1 BabelNet inventory

To semantically annotate all the single- and multiword expressions, as well as the named entities, occurring in our test corpus we used BabelNet 1.1.1 (Navigli and Ponzetto, 2012a). BabelNet is a multilingual "encyclopedic dictionary" and a semantic network currently covering 6 languages, namely: English, Catalan, French, German, Italian and Spanish. BabelNet is obtained as a result of a novel integration and enrichment methodology. This resource is created by linking the largest multilingual Web encyclopedia – i.e., Wikipedia – to the most popular computational lexicon – i.e., WordNet 3.0. The integration is performed via an automatic mapping and by filling in lexical gaps in resource-poor languages with the aid of Machine Translation (MT).

Its lexicon includes lemmas which denote both lexicographic meanings (e.g., *balloon*) and encyclopedic ones (e.g., *Montgolfier brothers*). The basic meaning unit in BabelNet is the Babel synset, modeled after the WordNet synset (Miller et al., 1990; Fellbaum, 1998). A Babel synset is a set of synonyms which express a concept in different languages. For instance, { Globus aerostàtic$_{\mathrm{CA}}$, Balloon$_{\mathrm{EN}}$, Aérostation$_{\mathrm{FR}}$, Ballon$_{\mathrm{DE}}$, Pallone aerostatico$_{\mathrm{IT}}$, . . . , Globo aerostático$_{\mathrm{ES}}$ } is the Babel synset for the balloon aerostat, where the language of each synonym is provided as a subscript label. Thanks to their multilingual nature, we were able to use Babel synsets as interlingual concept tags for nouns occurring within text written in any of the covered languages.

2.2.2 WordNet and Wikipedia inventories

Since BabelNet 1.1.1 is a superset of the WordNet 3.0 and Wikipedia sense inventories,[3] once text is annotated with Babel synsets, it turns out to be annotated also according to either WordNet or Wikipedia, or both. In fact, in order to induce the WordNet annotations, one can restrict to those lexical items annotated with Babel synsets which contain WordNet senses for the target lemma; similarly, for Wikipedia, we restrict to those items tagged with Babel synsets which contain Wikipedia pages for the target lemma.

2.3 BabelNet sense inventory validation

Because BabelNet is an automatic integration of WordNet and Wikipedia, the resulting Babel synsets may contain WordNet and Wikipedia entries about different meanings of the same lemma. The underlying cause is a wrong mapping between the two original resources. For instance, in BabelNet 1.1 the WordNet synset { arsenic, As, atomic number 33 } was mapped to the Wikipedia page AS (ROMAN COIN), and therefore the same Babel synset mixed the two meanings.

In order to avoid an inconsistent semantic tagging of text, we decided to manually check all the mappings in BabelNet 1.1 between Wikipedia pages

[2] `http://www.statmt.org/wmt12/`

[3] For version 1.1.1 we used the English Wikipedia database dump from October 1, 2012.

Language	Instances	Single-words	Multiword expressions	Named Entities	Mean senses per instance	Mean senses per lemma
			BabelNet			
English	1931	1604	127	200	1.02	1.09
French	1656	1389	89	176	1.05	1.15
German	1467	1267	21	176	1.00	1.05
Italian	1706	1454	211	41	1.22	1.27
Spanish	1481	1103	129	249	1.15	1.19
			Wikipedia			
English	1242	945	102	195	1.15	1.16
French	1039	790	72	175	1.18	1.14
German	1156	957	21	176	1.07	1.08
Italian	1977	869	85	41	1.20	1.18
Spanish	1103	758	107	248	1.11	1.10
			WordNet			
English	1644	1502	85	57	1.01	1.10

Table 1: Statistics for the sense annotations of the test set.

and WordNet senses involving lemmas in our English test set for the task. Overall, we identified 8306 synsets for 978 lemmas to be manually checked. We recruited 8 annotators in our research group and assigned each lemma to two annotators. Each annotator was instructed to check each Babel synset and determine whether any of the following three operations was needed:

- **Delete** a mapping and separate the WordNet sense from the Wikipedia page (like in the *arsenic* vs. AS (ROMAN COIN) example above);
- **Add** a mapping between a WordNet sense and a Wikipedia page (formerly available as two separate Babel synsets);
- **Merge** two Babel synsets which express the same concept.

After disagreement adjudication carried out by the first author, the number of delete, add and merge operations was 493, 203 and 43, respectively, for a total of 739 operations (i.e., 8.8% of synsets corrected). As a result of our validation of BabelNet 1.1, we obtained version 1.1.1, which is currently available online.

2.4 Sense Annotation

To ensure high quality annotations, the annotation process was completed in three phases. Because BabelNet is a superset of both the WordNet and Wikipedia sense inventories, all annotators used the BabelNet 1.1.1 sense inventory for their respective language. These BabelNet annotations were then projected into WordNet and Wikipedia senses. Annotation was performed by one native speaker each for English, French, German and Spanish and, for Italian, by two native speakers who annotated different subsets of the corpus.

In the first phase, each annotator was instructed to inspect each instance to check that (1) the lemma was tagged with the correct part of speech, (2) lemmas were correctly annotated as named entity or multiword expressions, and (3) the meaning of the instance's lemma had an associated sense in BabelNet. Based on these criteria, annotators removed dozens of instances from the original data.

In the second phase, each instance in the English dataset was annotated using BabelNet senses. To reduce the time required for annotation in the other languages, the sense annotations for the English dataset were then projected onto the other four

Language	Projected instances	Valid projections	Invalid projections
French	1016	791	225
German	592	373	219
Italian	1029	774	255
Spanish	911	669	242

Table 2: Statistics when using the English sense annotations to project the correct sense of a lemma in another language of the sentence-aligned test data.

languages using the sense translation API of BabelNet (Navigli and Ponzetto, 2012d). The projection operated as follows, using the aligned sentences in the English and non-English texts. For an instance in the non-English text, all of the senses for that instance's lemma were compared with the sense annotations in the English sentence. If any of that lemma's senses was used in the English sentence, then that sense was selected for the non-English instance. The matching procedure operates at the sentence-aligned level because the instances themselves are not aligned; i.e., different languages have different numbers of instances per sentence, which are potentially ordered differently due to language-specific construction. Ultimately, this projection labeled approximately 50-70% of the instances in the other four languages. Given the projected senses, the annotators for the other four languages were then asked to (1) correct the projected sense labels and (2) annotate those still without senses.[4] These annotations were recorded in text in a stand-off file; no further annotation tools were used.

The resulting sense projection proved highly useful for selecting the correct sense. Table 2 shows the number of corrections made by the annotators to the projected senses, who changed only 22-37% of the labels. While simple, the projection method offers significant potential for generating good quality sense-annotated data from sentence-aligned multilingual text.

In the third phase, an independent annotator reviewed the labels for the high-frequency lemmas for all languages to check for systematic errors and discuss possible changes to the labeling. This review resulted in only a small number of changes to less than 5% of the total instances, except for German which had a slightly higher percentage of changes.

Table 1 summarizes the sense annotation statistics for the test set. Annotators were allowed to use multiple senses in the case of ambiguity, but encouraged to use a single sense whenever possible. In rare cases, a lemma was annotated with senses from a different lemma. For example, WordNet does not contain a sense for "card" that corresponds to the penalty card meaning (as used in sports such as football). In contrast, BabelNet has a sense for "penalty card" from Wikipedia which, however, is not mapped to the lemma "card". In such cases, we add both the closest meaning from the original lemma (e.g., the rectangual piece of paper sense in WordNet) and the most suitable sense that may have a different lemma form (e.g., PENALTY CARD).

Previous annotation studies have shown that, when a fine-grained sense inventory is used, annotators will often label ambiguous instances with multiple senses if allowed (Erk and McCarthy, 2009; Jurgens and Klapaftis, 2013). Since BabelNet is a combination of a fine-grained inventory (WordNet) and contains additional senses from Wikipedia, we analyzed the average number of BabelNet sense annotations per instance, shown in column six of Table 1. Surprisingly, Table 1 suggests that the rate of multiple sense annotation varies significantly between languages.

BabelNet may combine multiple Wikipedia pages into a single BabelNet synset. As a result, when Wikipedia is used as a sense inventory, instances are annotated with all of the Wikipedia pages associated with each BabelNet synset. Indeed, Table 1 shows a markedly increased multi-sense annotation rate for three languages when using Wikipedia.

As a second analysis, we considered the observed level of polysemy for each of the unique lemmas. The last column of Table 1 shows the average number of different senses seen for each lemma across the test sets. In all languages, often only a single sense of a lemma was used. Because the test set is constructed based on topical documents, infrequent lemmas mostly occurred within a single document where they were used with a consistent interpreta-

[4] During the second phase, annotators were also allowed to add and remove instances that were missed during the first phase, which resulted in small number of changes.

tion. However, we note that in the case of lemmas that were only seen with a single sense, this sense does not always correspond to the most frequent sense as seen in SemCor.

3 Evaluation

Task 12 uses the standard definitions of precision and recall for WSD evaluation (see, e.g., (Navigli, 2009)). Precision measures the percentage of the sense assignments provided by the system that are identical to the gold standard; Recall measures the percentage of instances that are correctly labeled by the system. When a system provides sense labels for all instances, precision and recall are equivalent. Systems using BabelNet and WordNet senses are compared against the Most Frequent Sense (MFS) baseline obtained by using the WordNet most frequent sense. For the Wikipedia sense inventory, we constructed a pseudo-MFS baseline by selecting (1) the Wikipedia page associated with the highest ranking WordNet sense, as ranked by SemCor frequency, or (2) when no synset for a lemma was associated with a WordNet sense, the first Wikipedia page sorted using BabelNet's ordering criteria, i.e., lexicographic sorting. We note that, in the second case, this procedure frequently selected the page with the same name as the lemma itself. For instance, the first sense of *Dragon Ball* is the cartoon with title DRAGON BALL, followed by two films (DRAGON BALL (1990 FILM) and DRAGON BALL EVOLUTION).

Systems were scored separately for each sense inventory. We note that because the instances in each test set are filtered to include only those that can be labeled with the respective inventory, both the Wikipedia and WordNet test sets are subsets of the instances in the BabelNet test set.

4 Participating Systems

Three teams submitted a total of seven systems for the task, with at least one participant attempting all of the sense inventory and language combinations. Six systems participated in the WSD task with BabelNet senses; two teams submitted four systems using WordNet senses; and one team submitted three systems for Wikipedia-based senses. Notably, all systems used graph-based approaches for sense disambiguation, either using WordNet or BabelNet's synset graphs. We summarize the teams' systems as follows.

DAEBAK! DAEBAK! submitted one system called PD (Peripheral Diversity) based on BabelNet path indices from the BabelNet synset graph. Using a ± 5 sentence window around the target word, a graph is constructed for all senses of co-occurring lemmas following the procedure proposed by Navigli and Lapata (2010). The final sense is selected based on measuring connectivity to the synsets of neighboring lemmas. The MFS is used as a backoff strategy when no appropriate sense can be picked out.

GETALP GETALP submitted three systems, two for BabelNet and one for WordNet, all based on the ant-colony algorithm of (Schwab et al., 2012), which uses the sense inventory network structure to identify paths connecting synsets of the target lemma to the synsets of other lemmas in context. The algorithm requires setting several parameters for the weighting of the structure of the context-based graph, which vary across the three systems. The BN1 system optimizes its parameters from the trial data, while the BN2 and WN1 systems are completely unsupervised and optimize their parameters directly from the structure of the BabelNet and WordNet graphs.

UMCC-DLSI UMCC-DLSI submitted three systems based on the ISR-WN resource (Gutiérrez et al., 2011), which enriches the WordNet semantic network using edges from multiple lexical resources, such as WordNet Domains and the eXtended WordNet. WSD was then performed using the ISR-WN network in combination with the algorithm of Gutiérrez (2012), which is an extension of the Personalized PageRank algorithm for WSD (Agirre and Soroa, 2009) which includes senses frequency. The algorithm requires initializing the PageRank algorithm with a set of seed synsets (vertices) in the network; this initialization represents the key variation among UMCC's three approaches. The RUN-1 system performs WSD using all noun instances from the sentence context. In contrast, the RUN-2 works at the discourse level and initializes the PageRank using the synsets of all

Team	System	English	French	German	Italian	Spanish
DAEBAK!	PD	0.604	0.538	0.591	0.613	0.600
GETALP	BN-1	0.263	0.261	0.404	0.324	-
GETALP	BN-2	0.266	0.257	0.400	0.324	0.371
UMCC-DLSI	RUN-1	0.677	**0.605**	0.618	0.657	0.705
UMCC-DLSI	RUN-2	**0.685**	**0.605**	**0.621**	**0.658**	**0.710**
UMCC-DLSI	RUN-3	0.680	-	-	-	-
MFS		0.665	0.453	0.674	0.575	0.645

Table 3: System performance, reported as F1, for all five languages in the test set when using BabelNet senses. Top performing systems are marked in bold.

nouns in the document. Finally, the RUN-3 system initializes using all words in the sentence.

5 Results and Discussion

All teams submitted at least one system using the BabelNet inventory, shown in Table 3. The UMCC-DLSI systems were consistently able to outperform the MFS baseline (a notoriously hard-to-beat heuristic) in all languages except German. Additionally, the DAEBAK! system outperformed the MFS baseline on French and Italian. The UMCC-DLSI RUN-2 system performed the best for all languages. Notably, this system leverages the single-sense per discourse heuristic (Yarowsky, 1995), which uses the same sense label for all occurrences of a lemma in a document.

UMCC-DLSI submitted the only three systems to use Wikipedia-based senses. Table 4 shows their performance. Of the three sense inventories, Wikipedia had the most competitive MFS baseline, scoring at least 0.694 on all languages. Notably, the Wikipedia-based system has the lowest recall of all systems. Despite having superior precision to the MFS baseline, the low recall brought the resulting F1 measure below the MFS.

Two teams submitted four total systems for WordNet, shown in Table 5. The UMCC-DLSI RUN-2 system was again the top-performing system, underscoring the benefit of using discourse information in selecting senses. The other two UMCC-DLSI systems also surpassed the MFS baseline. Though still performing worse than the MFS baseline, when using the WordNet sense graph, the GETALP system sees a noticeable improvement of 0.14 over its performance on English data when using the WordNet sense graph.

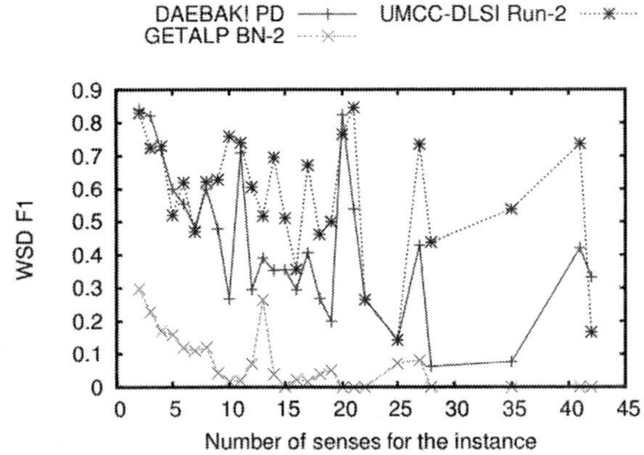

Figure 1: F1 measure according to the degree of instance polysemy, reported when at least ten instances have the specified polysemy.

The disambiguation task encompasses multiple types of entities. Therefore, we partitioned the BabelNet test data according to the type of instance being disambiguated; Table 6 highlights the results per instance type, averaged across all languages.[5] Both multiword expressions and named entities are less polysemous, resulting in a substantially higher MFS baseline that no system was able to outperform on the two classes. However, for instances made of a single term, both of the UMCC-DLSI systems were able to outperform the MFS baseline.

BabelNet adds many Wikipedia senses to the existing WordNet senses, which increases the poly-

[5]We omit the UMCC-DLSI Run-3 system from analysis, as it participated in only a single language.

		English			French			German			Italian			Spanish		
Team	System	Prec.	Rec.	F1	Prec.	Rec.	F1	Prec.	Rec.	F1	Prec.	Rec.	F1	Prec.	Rec.	F1
UMCC-DLSI	Run-1	0.619	0.484	0.543	0.817	0.480	0.605	0.758	0.460	0.572	0.785	0.458	0.578	0.773	0.493	0.602
UMCC-DLSI	Run-2	0.620	0.487	0.546	0.815	0.478	0.603	0.769	0.467	0.581	0.787	0.463	0.583	0.778	0.502	0.610
UMCC-DLSI	Run-3	0.622	0.489	0.548	-	-	-	-	-	-	-	-	-	-	-	-
MFS		0.860	0.753	0.803	0.698	0.691	0.694	0.836	0.827	0.831	0.833	0.813	0.823	0.830	0.819	0.824

Table 4: The F1 measure for each system across all five languages in the test set when using Wikipedia-based senses.

Team	System	Precision	Recall	F1
GETALP	WN-1	0.406	0.406	0.406
UMCC-DLSI	Run-1	0.639	0.635	0.637
UMCC-DLSI	Run-2	**0.649**	**0.645**	**0.647**
UMCC-DLSI	Run-3	0.642	0.639	0.640
MFS		0.630	0.630	0.630

Table 5: System performance when using WordNet senses. Top performing systems are marked in bold.

Team	System	Single term	Multiword expression	Named Entity
DAEBAK!	PD	0.502	0.801	**0.910**
GETALP	BN-1	0.232	0.724	0.677
GETALP	BN-2	0.235	0.740	0.656
UMCC-DLSI	Run-1	0.582	0.806	0.865
UMCC-DLSI	Run-2	**0.584**	**0.809**	0.864
MFS		0.511	0.853	0.920

Table 6: System F1 per instance type, averaged across all submitted languages, with the highest system scores in bold.

		English			French			German			Italian			Spanish		
Team	System	Prec.	Rec.	F1	Prec.	Rec.	F1	Prec.	Rec.	F1	Prec.	Rec.	F1	Prec.	Rec.	F1
DAEBAK	PD	0.769	0.364	0.494	0.747	0.387	0.510	0.762	0.307	0.438	0.778	0.425	0.550	0.778	0.450	0.570
GETALP	BN-2	0.793	0.111	0.195	0.623	0.130	0.215	0.679	0.124	0.210	0.647	0.141	0.231	0.688	0.177	0.282
UMCC-DLSI	Run-1	0.787	0.421	0.549	0.754	0.441	0.557	0.741	0.330	0.457	0.796	0.461	0.584	0.830	0.525	0.643
UMCC-DLSI	Run-2	0.791	0.419	0.548	0.760	0.436	0.554	0.746	0.332	0.460	0.799	0.453	0.578	0.837	0.530	0.649

Table 7: System performance when the system's annotations are restricted to only those senses that it also uses in the aligned sentences of at least two other languages.

semy of most instances. As a further analysis, we consider the relationship between the polysemy of an instance's target and system performance. Instances were grouped according to the number of BabelNet senses that their lemma had; following, systems were scored on each grouping. Figure 1 shows the performance of the best system from each team on each polysemy-based instance grouping, with a general trend of performance decay as the number of senses increases. Indeed, all systems' performances are negatively correlated with the degree of polysemy, ranging from -0.401 (UMCC-DLSI Run-1) to -0.654 (GETALP BN-1) when measured using Pearson's correlation. All systems' correlations are significant at $p < 0.05$.

Last, we note that all systems operated by sense-annotating each language individually without taking advantage of either the multilingual structure of BabelNet or the sentence alignment of the test data. For example, the sense projection method used to create the initial set of multilingual annotations on our test data (cf. Table 2) suggests that the sense translation API could be used as a reliable source for estimating the correctness of an annotation; specifically, given the sense annotations for each language, the translation API could be used to test whether the sense is also present in the aligned sentence in the other languages.

Therefore, we performed a post-hoc analysis of the benefit of multilingual sense alignment using the results of the four systems that submitted for all languages in BabelNet. For each language, we filter the sense annotations such that an annotation for an instance is retained only if the system assigned the same sense to some word in the aligned sentence from at least two other languages.

Table 7 shows the resulting performance for the four systems. As expected, the systems exhibit significantly lower recall due to omitting all language-specific instances. However, the resulting precision is significantly higher than the original performance, shown in Table 3. Additionally, we analyzed the set of instances reported for each system and confirmed that the improvement is not due to selecting only monosemous lemmas. Despite the GETALP system having the lower performance of the four systems when all instances are considered, the system obtains the highest precision for the English dataset. Furthermore, the UMCC-DLSI systems still obtain moderate recall, while enjoying 0.106-0.155 absolute improvements in precision across all languages. While the resulting F1 is lower due to a loss of recall, we view this result as a solid starting point for other methods to sense-tag the remaining instances. Overall, these results corroborate previous studies suggesting that highly precise sense annotations can be obtained by leveraging multiple languages (Navigli and Ponzetto, 2012b; Navigli and Ponzetto, 2012c).

6 Conclusion and Future Directions

Following recent SemEval efforts with word senses in multilingual settings, we have introduced a new task on multilingual WSD that uses the recently released BabelNet 1.1.1 sense inventory. Using a data set of 13 articles in five languages, all nominal instances were annotated with BabelNet senses. Because BabelNet is a superset of WordNet and Wikipedia, the task also facilitates analysis in those sense inventories.

Three teams submitted seven systems, with all systems leveraging the graph-based structure of WordNet and BabelNet. Several systems were able to outperform the competitive MFS baseline, except in the case of Wikipedia, but current performance leaves significant room for future improvement. In addition, we believe that future research could leverage sense parallelism available in sentence-aligned multilingual corpora, together with enriched information available in future versions of BabelNet. All of the resources for this task, including the newest 1.1.1 version of BabelNet, were released on the task website.[6]

Acknowledgments

erc The authors gratefully acknowledge the support of the ERC Starting Grant MultiJEDI No. 259234.

A large group of people assisted with SemEval-2013 Task 12, and without whose help this task would not have been possible. In particular, we would like to thank Philipp Cimiano, Maud Erhmann, Sascha Hinte, Jesús Roque Campaña Gómez, and Andreas Soos for their assistance in sense annotation; our fellow LCL team members: Moreno De Vincenzi, Stefano Faralli, Tiziano Flati, Marc Franco Salvador, Andrea Moro, Silvia Necşulescu, and Taher Pilehvar for their invaluable assistance in creating BabelNet 1.1.1, preparing and validating sense annotations, and sense-tagging the Italian corpus; last, we thank Jim McManus for his help in producing the Italian test data.

[6] `http://www.cs.york.ac.uk/semeval-2013/task12/`

References

Eneko Agirre and Aitor Soroa. 2009. Personalizing PageRank for Word Sense Disambiguation. In *Proceedings of EACL, Athens, Greece*, pages 33–41.

Philip Edmonds and Scott Cotton. 2001. Senseval-2: Overview. In *Proceedings of The Second International Workshop on Evaluating Word Sense Disambiguation Systems*, pages 1–6, Toulouse, France.

Katrin Erk and Diana McCarthy. 2009. Graded word sense assignment. In *Proceedings of Empirical Methods in Natural Language Processing*, pages 440–449, Singapore.

Christiane Fellbaum, editor. 1998. *WordNet: An Electronic Database*. MIT Press, Cambridge, MA.

Yoan Gutiérrez, Antonio Fernández Orquín, Sonia Vázquez, and Andrés Montoyo. 2011. Enriching the integration of semantic resources based on wordnet. *Procesamiento del Lenguaje Natural*, 47:249–257.

Yoan Gutiérrez. 2012. *Análisis semántico multidimensional aplicado a la desambiguación del lenguaje natural.* Ph.D. thesis, Universidad de Alicante.

Eduard H. Hovy, Roberto Navigli, and Simone Paolo Ponzetto. 2013. Collaboratively built semi-structured content and artificial intelligence: The story so far. *Artificial Intelligence*, 194:2–27.

David Jurgens and Ioannis Klapaftis. 2013. Semeval-2013 task 13: Word sense induction for graded and non-graded senses. In *Proceedings of the 7th International Workshop on Semantic Evaluation.*

Adam Kilgarriff and Martha Palmer. 2000. Introduction to the special issue on senseval. *Computers and the Humanities*, 34(1-2):1–13.

Adam Kilgarriff. 1998. Senseval: An exercise in evaluating word sense disambiguation programs. In *Proceedings of the First International Conference on Language Resources and Evaluation*, pages 1255–1258, Granada, Spain.

Els Lefever and Veronique Hoste. 2010. Semeval-2010 task 3: Cross-lingual word sense disambiguation. In *Proceedings of the 5th International Workshop on Semantic Evaluation*, pages 15–20, Uppsala, Sweden. Association for Computational Linguistics.

Diana McCarthy and Roberto Navigli. 2009. The English lexical substitution task. *Language Resources and Evaluation*, 43(2):139–159.

Rada Mihalcea, Timothy Chklovski, and Adam Kilgarriff. 2004. The Senseval-3 English lexical sample task. In *Proceedings of the 3rd International Workshop on the Evaluation of Systems for the Semantic Analysis of Text (SENSEVAL-3) at ACL-04, Barcelona, Spain, 25–26 July 2004*, pages 25–28.

Rada Mihalcea, Ravi Sinha, and Diana McCarthy. 2010. Semeval-2010 task 2: Cross-lingual lexical substitution. In *Proceedings of the 5th international workshop on semantic evaluation*, pages 9–14, Uppsala, Sweden. Association for Computational Linguistics.

George A. Miller, R.T. Beckwith, Christiane D. Fellbaum, D. Gross, and K. Miller. 1990. WordNet: an online lexical database. *International Journal of Lexicography*, 3(4):235–244.

Roberto Navigli and Mirella Lapata. 2010. An experimental study on graph connectivity for unsupervised Word Sense Disambiguation. *IEEE Transactions on Pattern Analysis and Machine Intelligence*, 32(4):678–692.

Roberto Navigli and Simone Paolo Ponzetto. 2012a. BabelNet: The automatic construction, evaluation and application of a wide-coverage multilingual semantic network. *Artificial Intelligence*, 193:217–250.

Roberto Navigli and Simone Paolo Ponzetto. 2012b. BabelRelate! a joint multilingual approach to computing semantic relatedness. In *Proceedings of the Twenty-Sixth AAAI Conference on Artificial Intelligence (AAAI)*, Toronto, Ontario, Canada.

Roberto Navigli and Simone Paolo Ponzetto. 2012c. Joining forces pays off: Multilingual Joint Word Sense Disambiguation. In *Proceedings of EMNLP-CoNLL*, pages 1399–1410, Jeju Island, Korea.

Roberto Navigli and Simone Paolo Ponzetto. 2012d. Multilingual WSD with just a few lines of code: the BabelNet API. In *Proceedings of the 50th Annual Meeting of the Association for Computational Linguistics (ACL 2012)*, Jeju, Korea.

Roberto Navigli, Kenneth C. Litkowski, and Orin Hargraves. 2007. SemEval-2007 Task 07: Coarse-grained English all-words task. In *Proceedings of the 4th International Workshop on Semantic Evaluations (SemEval-2007), Prague, Czech Republic*, pages 30–35.

Roberto Navigli. 2009. Word Sense Disambiguation: A survey. *ACM Computing Surveys*, 41(2):1–69.

Roberto Navigli. 2012. A quick tour of Word Sense Disambiguation, Induction and related approaches. In *Proceedings of the 38th Conference on Current Trends in Theory and Practice of Computer Science (SOFSEM)*, pages 115–129.

Sameer Pradhan, Edward Loper, Dmitriy Dligach, and Martha Palmer. 2007. SemEval-2007 Task-17: English lexical sample, SRL and all words. In *Proceedings of the 4th International Workshop on Semantic Evaluations (SemEval-2007), Prague, Czech Republic*, pages 87–92.

Didier Schwab, Jérôme Goulian, Andon Tchechmedjiev, and Hervé Blanchon. 2012. Ant colony algorithm for the unsupervised word sense disambiguation of texts: Comparison and evaluation. In *Proceedings of the* 24th *International Conference on Computational Linguistics (COLING)*, pages 8–15, Mumbai, India.

Benjamin Snyder and Martha Palmer. 2004. The english all-words task. In *Proceedings of ACL 2004 SENSEVAL-3 Workshop*, pages 41–43, Barcelona, Spain.

David Yarowsky. 1995. Unsupervised word sense disambiguation rivaling supervised methods. In *Proceedings of the* 33rd *Annual Meeting of the Association for Computational Linguistics*, pages 189–196, Cambridge, MA, USA.

GETALP: Propagation of a Lesk Measure through an Ant Colony Algorithm

Didier Schwab, Andon Tchechmedjiev, Jérôme Goulian,
Mohammad Nasiruddin, Gilles Sérasset, Hervé Blanchon
LIG-GETALP
Univ. Grenoble Alpes
`http://getalp.imag.fr/WSD`
`firstname.lastname@imag.fr`

Abstract

This article presents the GETALP system for the participation to SemEval-2013 Task 12, based on an adaptation of the Lesk measure propagated through an Ant Colony Algorithm, that yielded good results on the corpus of Semeval 2007 Task 7 (WordNet 2.1) as well as the trial data for Task 12 SemEval 2013 (BabelNet 1.0). We approach the parameter estimation to our algorithm from two perspectives: edogenous estimation where we maximised the sum the local Lesk scores; exogenous estimation where we maximised the F1 score on trial data. We proposed three runs of out system, exogenous estimation with BabelNet 1.1.1 synset id annotations, endogenous estimation with BabelNet 1.1.1 synset id annotations and endogenous estimation with WordNet 3.1 sense keys. A bug in our implementation led to incorrect results and here, we present an amended version thereof. Our system arrived third on this task and a more fine grained analysis of our results reveals that the algorithms performs best on general domain texts with as little named entities as possible. The presence of many named entities leads the performance of the system to plummet greatly.

1 Introduction

Out team is mainly interested in Word Sense Disambiguation (WSD) based on semantic similarity measures. This approach to WSD is based on a local algorithm and a global algorithm. The local algorithm corresponds to a semantic similarity measure (for example (Wu and Palmer, 1994), (Resnik, 1995) or (Lesk, 1986)), while the global algorithm propagates the values resulting from these measures at the level of a text, in order to disambiguate the words that compose it. For two years, now, our team has focussed on researching global algorithms. The local algorithm we use, a variant of the Lesk algorithm that we have evaluated with several global algorithms (Simulated Annealing (SA), Genetic Algorithms (GA) and Ant Colony Algorithms (ACA)) (Schwab et al., 2012; Schwab et al., 2013), has shown its robustness with WordNet 3.0. For the present campaign, we chose to work with an ant colony based global algorithms that has proven its efficiency (Schwab et al., 2012; Tchechmedjiev et al., 2012).

Presently, for this SemEval 2013 Task 12 (Navigli et al., 2013), the objective is to disambiguate a set of target words (nouns) in a corpus of 13 texts in 5 Languages (English, French, German, Italian, Spanish) by providing, for each sense the appropriate sense labels. The evaluation of the answers is performed by comparing them to a gold standard annotation of the corpus in all 5 languages using three possible sense inventories and thus sense tags: BabelNet 1.1.1 Synset ids (Navigli and Pozetto, 2012), Wikipedia page names and Wordnet sense keys (Miller, 1995).

Our ant colony algorithm is a stochastic algorithm that has several parameters that need to be selected and tuned. Choosing the values of the parameters based on linguistic criteria remains an open and difficult problem, which is why we wanted to automatize the parameter search process. There are two ways to go about this process: exogenous estima-

*Second Joint Conference on Lexical and Computational Semantics (*SEM), Volume 2: Seventh International Workshop on Semantic Evaluation (SemEval 2013)*, pages 232–240, Atlanta, Georgia, June 14-15, 2013.

tion, when the parameter values are selected so as to maximise the F-score on a small training annotated corpus and then used to disambiguate another corpus (weakly supervised); endogenous estimation, when the parameters are chosen so as to maximise the global similarity score on a text or corpus (unsupervised). Our first experiment and system run consists in tuning the parameters on the trial corpus of the campaign and running the system with the BabelNet sense inventory. Our second and third experiments consist in endogenous parameter estimation, the first using BabelNet as a sense inventory and the second using WordNet. Unfortunately, the presence of an implementation issue prevented us from obtaining scores up to par with the potential of our system and thus we will present indicative results of the performance of the system after the implementation issue was fixed.

2 The GETALP System: Propagation of a Lesk Measure through an Ant Colony Algorithm

In this section we will first describe the local algorithm we used, followed by a quick overview of global algorithms and our own Ant Colony Algorithm.

2.1 The Local Algorithm: a Lesk Measure

Our local algorithm is a variant of the Lesk Algorithm (Lesk, 1986). Proposed more than 25 years ago, it is simple, only requires a dictionary and no training. The score given to a sense pair is the number of common words (space separated strings) in the definition of the senses, without taking into account neither the word order in the definitions (bag-of-words approach), nor any syntactic or morphological information. Variants of this algorithm are still today among the best on English-language texts (Ponzetto and Navigli, 2010).

Our local algorithm exploits the links provided by WordNet: it considers not only the definition of a sense but also the definitions of the linked senses (using all the semantic relations for WordNet, most of them for BabelNet) following (Banerjee and Pedersen, 2002), henceforth referred as $ExtLesk$[1] Contrarily to Banerjee, however, we do not consider the sum of squared sub-string overlaps, but merely a bag-of-words overlap that allows us to generate a dictionary from WordNet, where each word contained in any of the word sense definitions is indexed by a unique integer and where each resulting definition is sorted. Thus we are able to lower the computational complexity from $O(mn)$ to $O(m)$, where m and n are the respective length of two definitions and $m \geq n$. For example for the definition: "Some kind of evergreen tree", if we say that *Some* is indexed by 123, *kind* by 14, *evergreen* by 34, and tree by 90, then the indexed representation is $\{14, 34, 90, 123\}$.

2.2 Global Algorithm : Ant Colony Algorithm

We will first review the principles pertaining to global algorithms and then a more detailed account of our Ant Colony algorithm.

2.2.1 Global algorithms, Global scores and Configurations

A global algorithm is a method that allows to propagate a local measure to a whole text in order to assign a sense label to each word. In the similarity-based WSD perspective, the algorithms require some *fitness* measure to evaluate how good a configuration is. With this in mind, the score of the selected sense of a word can be expressed as the sum of the local scores between that sense and the selected senses of all the other words of a context. Hence, in order to obtain a *fitness* value (*global score*) for the whole configuration, it is possible to simply sum the scores for all selected senses of the words of the context: $Score(C) = \sum_{i=1}^{m} \sum_{j=i}^{m} ExtLesk(w_{i,C[i]}, w_{j,C[j]})$.

For a given text, the chosen configuration is the one which maximizes the global score among the evaluated ones. The simplest approach is the exhaustive evaluation of sense combinations (BF), used for example in (Banerjee and Pedersen, 2002), that assigns a score to each word sense combination in a given context (window or whole text) and selects the one with the highest score. The main issue with this approach is that it leads to a combi-

[1] All dictionaries and Java implementations of all algorithms of our team can be found on our WSD page `http://getalp.imag.fr/WSD` and more specifically for SemEval 2013 Task 12 on the following page `http://getalp.imag.fr/static/wsd/GETALP-WSD-ACA/`

natorial explosion in the length of the context window or text. The number of combinations is indeed $\prod_{i=1}^{|T|}(|s(w_i)|)$, where $s(w_i)$ is the set of possible senses of word i of a text T. For this reason it is very difficult to use the BF approach on an analysis window larger than a few words. In our work, we consider the whole text as context. In this perspective, we studied several methods to overcome the combinatorial explosion problem.

2.2.2 Complete and Incomplete Approaches

Several approximation methods can be used in order to overcome the combinatorial explosion issue. On the one hand, *complete approaches* try to reduce dimensionality using pruning techniques and sense selection heuristics. Some examples include: (Hirst and St-Onge, 1998), based on lexical chains that restrict the possible sense combinations by imposing constraints on the succession of relations in a taxonomy (e.g. WordNet); or (Gelbukh et al., 2005) that review general pruning techniques for Lesk-based algorithms; or yet (Brody and Lapata, 2008) who exploit distributional similarity measures extracted from corpora (information content).

On the other hand, *incomplete approaches* generally use stochastic sampling techniques to reach a local maximum by exploring as little as necessary of the search space. Our present work focuses on such approaches. Furthermore, we can distinguish two possible variants:

- local neighbourhood-based approaches (new configurations are created from existing configurations) among which are some approaches from artificial intelligence such as genetic algorithms or optimization methods such as simulated annealing;
- constructive approaches (new configurations are generated by iteratively adding new elements of solutions to the configuration under construction), among which are for example ant colony algorithms.

2.2.3 Principle of our Ant Colony Algorithm

In this section, we briefly describe out Ant Colony Algorithm so as to give a general idea of how it operates. However, readers are strongly encouraged to read the detailed papers (Schwab et al., 2012; Schwab et al., 2013) for a more detailed description of the system, including examples of how the graph is built, of how the algorithm operates step by step as well all pseudo code listing.

Ant colony algorithms (ACA) are inspired from nature through observations of ant social behavior. Indeed, these insects have the ability to collectively find the shortest path between their nest and a source of food (energy). It has been demonstrated that cooperation inside an ant colony is self-organised and allows the colony to solve complex problems. The environment is usually represented by a graph, in which virtual ants exploit pheromone trails deposited by others, or pseudo-randomly explore the graph. ACAs are a good alternative for the resolution of optimization problems that can be encoded as graphs and allow for a fast and efficient exploration on par with other search heuristics. The main advantage of ACAs lies in their high adaptivity to dynamically changing environments. Readers can refer to (Dorigo and Stützle, 2004) or (Monmarché, 2010) for a state of the art.

In this article we use a simple hierarchical graph (text, sentence, word) that matches the structure of the text and that exploits no external linguistic information. In this graph we distinguish two types of nodes: nests and plain nodes. Following (Schwab et al., 2012), each possible word sense is associated to a nest. Nests produce ants that move in the graph in order to find energy and bring it back to their mother nest: the more energy is brought back by ants, the more ants can be produced by the nest in turn. Ants carry an odour (a vector) that contains the words of the definition of the sense of its mother nest. From the point of view of an ant, a node can be: (1) *its mother nest*, where it was born; (2) *an enemy nest* that corresponds to another sense of the same word; (3) *a potential friend nest*: any other nest; (4) a *plain node*: any node that is not a nest. Furthermore, to each plain node is also associated an odour vector of a fixed length that is initially empty.

Ant movement is function of the scores given by the local algorithm, of the presence of energy, of the passage of other ants (when passing on an edge ants leave a pheromone trail that evaporates over time) and of the nodes' odour vectors (ants deposit a part of their odour on the nodes they go through). When an ant arrives onto the nest of another word (that corresponds to a sense thereof), it can either continue its exploration or, depending on the score between this nest and its mother nest, decide to build a bridge between them and to follow it home. Bridges behave like normal edges except that if at any given time the concentration of pheromone reaches 0, the bridge collapses. Depending on the lexical information present and the structure of the graph, ants will favor following bridges between more closely related senses. Thus, the more closely related the senses of the nests are, the more bridges between them will contribute to their mutual reinforcement and to the sharing of resources between them (thus forming *meta-nests*); while the bridges between more distant senses will tend to fade away. We are thus able to build interpretative paths (possible interpretations of the text) through emergent behaviour and to suppress the need to use a complete graph that includes all the links between the senses from the start (as is usually the case with classical graph-based optimisation approaches).

Through the emergence of interpretative paths, sense pairs that are closer semantically benefit from an increased ant traffic and thus tend to capture most of the energy of the system at a faster pace, thus favouring a faster convergence over an algorithm that uses a local neighbourhood graph (nodes are senses interconnected so as to represent all sense combinations in a context window) without sacrificing the quality of the results.

The selected answers correspond, for each word to the nest node with the highest energy value. The reason for this choice over using the pheromone concentration is that empirically, the energy level better correlates with the actual F1 scores. In turn, the global Lesk score of a selected sense combination correlates even better with the F1 score, which is why, we keep the sense combinations resulting from each iteration of the algorithm (highest energy nests at each iteration) and select the one with the highest global Lesk score as the final solution.

2.3 Parameters

This version of our ant algorithm has seven parameters (ω, E_a, E_{max}, E_0, δ_v, δ, L_V) which have an influence on the emergent phenomena in the system:

- The maximum amount of energy an ant can carry, E_{max} and E_a the amount of energy an ant can take on a node, influences how much an ant explores the environment. Ants cannot go back through an edge they just crossed and have to make circuits to come back to their nest (if the ant does not die before that). The size of the circuits depend on the moment the ants switch to return mode, hence on E_{max}.
- The evaporation rate of the pheromone between cycles (δ) is one of the memories of the system. The higher the rate is, the least the trails from previous ants are given importance and the faster interpretative paths have to be confirmed (passed on) by new ants in order not to be forgotten by the system.
- The initial amount of energy per node (E_0) and the ant life-span (ω) influence the number of ants that can be produced and therefore the probability of reinforcing less likely paths.
- The odour vector length (L_v) and the proportion of odour components deposited by an ant on a plain node (δ_V) are two dependent parameters that influence the global system memory. The higher the length of the vector, the longer the memory of the passage of an ant is kept. On the other hand, the proportion of odour components deposited has the opposite effect.

Given the lack of an analytical way of determining the optimal parameters of the ant colony algorithm, they have to be estimated experimentally, which is detailed in the following section.

3 Acquisition of Parameter Values

The algorithms we are interested in have a certain number of parameters that need tuning in order to obtain the best possible score on the evaluation corpus. There are three possible approaches:

- Make an educated guess about the value ranges based on *a priori* knowledge about the dynamics of the algorithm;
- Test manually (or semi-manually) several combinations of parameters that *appear* promising and determine the influence of making small adjustments to the values ;
- Use a learning algorithm to automate acquisition of parameters values. We present that approach in the following part.

3.1 Automated Parameter Estimation

Two methods can be used to automatically acquire parameters. The first one consists in maximizing the F-score on an sense-annotated corpus (weak approach) while the second one consist in maximizing the global Lesk score (unsupervised approach).

3.1.1 Generalities

Both approaches are based on the same principle (Tchechmedjiev et al., 2012). We use a simulated annealing algorithm (Laarhoven and Aarts, 1987) combined with a non-parametric statistical (Mann-Whitney-U test (Mann and Whitney, 1947)) test with a p-value adapted for multiple comparisons through False Discovery Rate control (FDR) (Benjamini and Hochberg, 1995). The estimation algorithm operates on all the parameters of the ant colony algorithm described above and attempts to maximise the objective function (Global score, F1). The reason why we need to use a statistical test and FDR rather than using the standard SA algorithm, is that the Ant Colony Algorithm is stochastic in nature and requires tuning to be performed over the distribution of possible answers for a given set of parameter values. Indeed, there is no guarantee that the value resulting from one execution is representative at all of the distribution. The exact nature of the distribution of answers is unknown and thus we take a sampling of the distribution as precise as can be afforded. Thus, we require the statistical test to ascertain the significance between the scores for two parameter configurations.

3.1.2 Exogenous parameter tuning

If we have a sense-annotated corpus at our disposal, it is possible to directly use the F1 value obtained by the system on this reference to tune the parameters of the systems so as to maximise said F1 score. The main issues that arise from such methods are the fact that gold standards are expensive to produce and that there is no guarantee on the generality of the contents of the gold standard. Thus, in languages with little resources we may be unable to obtain a gold standard and in the case one is available, there is a potentially strong risk of over fitting. Furthermore due to the nature of the training, taking training samples in a random order for cross-validation becomes tricky. This is why we also want to test another method that can tune the parameters without using labelled examples. For the evaluation, we estimated parameters on the F1 score on the test corpus for English and French (the only ones available). We used the parameters estimated for English for our English results for our first system run `GETALP-BN1` and the French parameters for the results on French, German, Italian, Spanish.

For English we found: $\omega = 26$, $E_a = 14$, $E_{max} = 3$, $E_0 = 34$, $\delta_v = 0.9775$, $\delta = 0.3577$, $L_V = 25$.

For French: $\omega = 19$, $E_a = 9$, $E_{max} = 3$, $E_0 = 32$, $\delta_v = 0.9775$, $\delta = 0.3577$, $L_V = 25$.

3.1.3 Endogenous parameter tuning

In the context of the evaluation campaign, the absence of an example gold standard on the same version of the resource (synset id mismatch between BabelNet 1.0 and 1.1.1 [2]) made dubious the prospect of using parameters estimated from a gold standard. Consequently, we set out to investigate the relation between the F1 score of the gold standard and the Global Lesk Score of successive solutions throughout the execution of the algorithm.

We observed that the Lesk score is highly correlated to the F1 score and can be used as an estimator thereof. The main quality criterion being the discriminativeness of the Lesk score compared to the F1 score (average ratio between the number of possible F1 score values for a single Lesk score value), for which the correlation is a possible indicator. We make the hypothesis based on the correlation that for a given specific local measure, the global score will be an adequate estimator of the F1 score. Our second system run `GETALP-WSD-BN2` is based on the endogenous parameter estimation. We will not list all the parameters here, as there is a different set of parameters for each text and each language.

3.2 Voting

In previous experiment, as can be expected, we have observed a consistent rise the F1 score when applying a majority vote method on the output of several executions (Schwab et al., 2012). Consequently we followed the same process here, and for all the runs of our system we performed 100 executions and applied a majority vote (For each word, our of all se-

[2] `http://lcl.uniroma1.it/babelnet/`

lected senses, take the one that has been selected the most over all the executions) on all 100 answer files. The result of this process is a single answer file and comes with the advantage of greatly reducing the variability of the answers. Say this voting process is repeated over and over again 100 times, then the standard deviation of F1 scores around the mean is much smaller. Thus, we also have a good solutions to the problem of selecting the answer that yields the highest score, without actually having access to the gold standard.

4 Runs for SemEval 2013 task 12

In this section we will describe the various runs we performed in the context of Task 12. We will first present our methodologies relating to the BabelNet tagged gold standard followed by the methodologies relating to the WordNet tagged gold standard.

4.1 BabelNet Gold Standard Evaluation

In the context of the BabelNet gold standard evaluation, we need to tag the words of the corpus with BabelNet synset ids. Due to the slow speed of retrieving Babel synsets and extracting glosses, especially in the context of our extended Lesk Approach, we pre-generate a dictionary for each language that contains entries for each word of the corpus and then for each possible sense (as per BabelNet). In the short time allotted for the competition, we restrict ourselves to building dictionaries only for the words of the corpus, but the process described can be applied to pre-generate a dictionary for the whole of BabelNet.

Each BabelNet synset for a word is considered as a possible sense in the dictionary. For each synset we retrieve the Babel senses and retain the ones that are in the appropriate language. Then, we retrieve the Glosses corresponding to each selected sense and combine them in as the definition corresponding to that particular BabelNet synset. Furthermore, we also retrieve certain of the related synsets and repeat the same process so as to add the related definitions to the BabelNet synset being considered. In our experiments on the test corpus, we determined that what worked best (i.e. English and French) was to use only relations coming from WordNet, all the while excluding the `r`, `gdis`, `gmono` relation added by BabelNet. We observed a similar increase in disambiguation quality with the Degree (Navigli and Lapata, 2010) algorithm implementation that comes with BabelNet. The `r` relation correspond to the relations in BabelNet extracted from Wikipedia, whereas `gdis` and `gmono` corresponds to relation created using a disambiguation algorithm (respectively for monosemous and polysemous words).

4.2 WordNet Gold Standard Evaluation

In the context of the WordNet gold standard evaluation, we initially thought the purpose would be to annotate the corpus in all five languages with WordNet sense keys through alignments extracted from BabelNet. As a consequence, we exploited BabelNet as a resource, merely obtaining WordNet sense keys through the *main senses* expressed in BabelNet, that correspond to WordNet synsets. Although we were able to produce annotations for all languages, as it turns out, the WordNet evaluation was merely aimed at evaluating monolingual systems that do not support BabelNet at all. For reference, we subsequently generated a dictionary from WordNet only, to gauge the performance of our system on the evaluation as intended by the organisers.

5 Results

We will first present the general results pertaining to Task 12, followed by a more detailed analysis on a text by text basis, as well as the comparison with results obtained on the Semeval 2007 WSD task in terms of specific parts of speech.

5.1 General Results for Semeval-2013 Task 12

Important: implementation issue during the evaluation period During the evaluation period, we had an implementation issue, where a parameter that limited the size of definition was not disabled properly. As a consequence, when we experimented to determine the appropriate relations to consider for the context expansion of the glosses, we arrived at the experimental conclusion that using all relations worked best. However, since it was already the case with WordNet (Schwab et al., 2011), we readily accepted that our experimental conclusion was indeed correct. The issue was indirectly resolved as an unforeseen side effect of another hot-fix applied shortly before the start of the evaluation period.

Given that we were not aware of the presence of a limitation on the definition length before the hot-fix, we performed all the experiments under an incorrect hypothesis which led us to an incorrect conclusion, that itself led to the results we obtained for the campaign. Indeed, with no restrictions on the size of the definition, our official results for this task were consistently inferior to the random baseline across the board. After a thorough analysis of our runs we observed that the sum of local measures (global lesk score) that correlated inversely with the gold standard F1 score, the opposite of what it should have been. We immediately located and corrected this bug when we realized what had caused these bad results that did not correspond at all with what we obtained on the test corpus. After the fix, we strictly ran the same experiment without exploiting the gold standard, so as to obtain the results we would have obtained had the bug not been present in the first place.

Run	Lang.	P	R	F1	MFS
BN1	EN	58.3	58.3	58.3	65.6
	FR	48.3	48.2	48.3	50.1
	DE	52.3	52.3	52.3	68.6
	ES	57.6	57.6	57.6	64.4
	IT	52.6	52.5	52.6	57.2
BN2	EN	56.8	56.8	56.8	65.6
	FR	48.3	48.2	48.3	50.1
	DE	51.9	51.9	51.9	68.6
	ES	57.8	57.8	57.8	64.4
	IT	52.8	52.8	52.8	57.2
WN1	EN	51.4	51.4	51.4	63.0

Table 1: Results after fixing the implementation issue for all three of our runs, compared to the Most Frequent Sense baseline (MFS).

We can see in Table 1, that after the removal of the implementation issues, the scores become more competitive and meaningful compared to the other system, although we remain third of the evaluation campaign. We can observe that there is no large difference between the exogenous results (using a small annotated corpus) and endogenous results. Except for the English corpus where there is a 2% increase. The endogenous estimation, since it is performed on a text by text basis is much slower and resource consuming. Given that the exogenous estimation offers slightly better results and that it requires very little annotated data, we can conclude that in most cases the exogenous estimation will be much faster to obtain.

5.2 A more detailed analysis

In this section we will first make a more detailed analysis for each text on the English corpus, by looking where our algorithm performed best. We restrict ourselves on one language for this analysis for the sake of brevity. As we can see in Table 2, the results can vary greatly depending on the text (within a twofold range). The system consistently performs better on texts from the general domain (T 4, 6, 10), often beating the first sense baseline. For more specialized texts, however, (T 2, 7, 8, 11, 12, 13) the algorithm performs notably lower than the baseline. The one instance where the algorithm truly fails, is when the text in question contains many ambiguous entities. Indeed for text 7, which is about football, many of the instance words to disambiguate are the names of players and of clubs. Intuitively, this behaviour is understandable and can be mainly attributed to the local Lesk algorithm. Since we use glosses from the resource, that mostly remain in the general domain, a better performance in matching texts is likely. As for named entities, the Lesk algorithm is mainly meant to capture the similarity between concepts and it is much more difficult to differentiate two football players from a definition over concepts (often more general).

To further outline the strength of our approach, we need to look back further at a setting with all parts of speech being considered, namely Task 7 from SemEval 2007. As can be seen in Table 3, even though for adjectives and adverbs the system is slightly below the MFS (respectively), it has a good performance compared to graph based WSD approaches that would be hindered by the lack of taxonomical relations. For verbs the performance is lower as is consistently observed with WSD algorithms due to the high degree of polysemy of verbs. For example, in the case of Degree (Navigli and Pozetto, 2012), nouns are the part of speech for which the system performs the best, while the scores for other parts of speech are somewhat lower. Thus, we can hypoth-

Text	Descr.	Len.	F1	MFS	Diff.
1	Gen. Env.	228	61.4	68.9	-7.5
2	T. Polit.	84	51.2	66.7	-15.5
3	T. Econ.	84	52.4	56.0	- 3.6
4	News. Gen.	119	58.8	58.0	0.8
5	T. Econ.	74	39.2	36.5	2.7
6	Web Gen.	210	67.1	64.3	2.8
7	T. Sport.	190	34.2	60.5	-26.3
8	Sci.	153	63.4	67.3	-3.9
9	Geo. Econ.	190	63.2	74.2	-11
10	Gen. Law.	160	61.9	61.9	0
11	T. Sport.	125	56.8	64.0	-7.2
12	T. Polit.	185	64.3	73.0	-8.7
13	T. Econ.	130	68.5	72.6	-4.1

Table 2: Text by text F1 scores compared to the MFS baseline for the English corpus (T.= Translated, Gen.= General, Env.= Environment, Polit.= Politics, Econ.= Economics, Web= Internet, Sport.= Sports, Geo.= Geopolitics, Sci.= Science).

A	P.O.S.	F1	MFS F1	Diff
1108	Noun	79.42	77.4	+1.99
591	Verb	74.78	75.3	-0.51
362	Adj.	82.66	84.3	-1.59
208	Adv.	86.95	87.5	-0.55
2269	All	79.42	78.9	+0.53

Table 3: Detailed breakdown of F1 score per part of speech category for Semeval-2007 Task 7, over results resulting from a vote over 100 executions

esise that using a different local measure depending on the part of speech may constitute an interesting development while allowing a return to a more general all-words WSD task where all parts of speech are considered, even when the resource does not offer taxonomical relation for the said parts of speech.

6 Conclusions & Perspectives

In this paper, we present a method based on a Lesk inspired local algorithm and a global algorithm based on ant colony optimisation. An endogenous version (parameter estimation based on the maximisation of the F-score on an annotated corpus) and an exogenous version (parameter estimation based on the maximisation of the global Lesk score on the corpus) of the latter algorithm do not exhibit a significant difference in terms of the F-score of the result. After a more detailed analysis on a text by text basis, we found that the algorithm performs best on general domain texts with as little named entities as possible (around or above the MFS baseline). For texts of more specialized domain the algorithm consistently performs below the MFS baseline, and for texts with many named entities, the performance plummets greatly slightly above the level of a random selection. We also show that with our Lesk measure the system is best suited for WSD in a more general setting with all parts of speech, however in the context of just nouns, it is not the most suitable local measure. As we have seen from the other systems, graph based local measures may be the appropriate answer to reach the level of the best systems on this task, however it is important not to dismiss the potential of other approaches. The quality of the results depend on the global algorithm, however they are also strongly bounded by the local measure considered. Our team, is headed towards investigating local semantic similarity measures and towards exploiting multilingual features so as to improve the disambiguation quality.

7 Acknowledgements

The work presented in this paper was conducted in the context of the Formicae project funded by the University Grenoble 2 (Université Pierre Mendès France) and the Videosense project, funded by the French National Research Agency (ANR) under its CONTINT 2009 programme (grant ANR-09-CORD-026).

References

[Banerjee and Pedersen2002] Satanjee Banerjee and Ted Pedersen. 2002. An adapted lesk algorithm for word sense disambiguation using wordnet. In *CICLing 2002*, Mexico City, February.

[Benjamini and Hochberg1995] Yoav Benjamini and Yosef Hochberg. 1995. Controlling the False Discovery Rate: A Practical and Powerful Approach to Multiple Testing. *Journal of the Royal Statistical Society. Series B (Methodological)*, 57(1):289–300.

[Brody and Lapata2008] Samuel Brody and Mirella Lapata. 2008. Good neighbors make good senses: Exploiting distributional similarity for unsupervised

WSD. In *Proceedings of the 22nd International Conference on Computational Linguistics (Coling 2008)*, pages 65–72, Manchester, UK.

[Dorigo and Stützle2004] Dorigo and Stützle. 2004. *Ant Colony Optimization*. MIT-Press.

[Gelbukh et al.2005] Alexander Gelbukh, Grigori Sidorov, and Sang-Yong Han. 2005. On some optimization heuristics for Lesk-like WSD algorithms. In *International Conference on Applications of Natural Language to Information Systems – NLDB'05*, pages 402–405, Alicante, Spain.

[Hirst and St-Onge1998] G. Hirst and David D. St-Onge. 1998. Lexical chains as representations of context for the detection and correction of malapropisms. *WordNet: An electronic Lexical Database. C. Fellbaum. Ed. MIT Press. Cambridge. MA*, pages 305–332. Ed. MIT Press.

[Laarhoven and Aarts1987] P.J.M. Laarhoven and E.H.L. Aarts. 1987. *Simulated annealing: theory and applications*. Mathematics and its applications. D. Reidel.

[Lesk1986] Michael Lesk. 1986. Automatic sense disambiguation using mrd: how to tell a pine cone from an ice cream cone. In *Proceedings of SIGDOC '86*, pages 24–26, New York, NY, USA. ACM.

[Mann and Whitney1947] H. B. Mann and D. R. Whitney. 1947. On a Test of Whether one of Two Random Variables is Stochastically Larger than the Other. *The Annals of Mathematical Statistics*, 18(1):50–60.

[Miller1995] George A. Miller. 1995. Wordnet: A lexical database. *ACM*, Vol. 38(No. 11):p. 1–41.

[Monmarché2010] N. Monmarché. 2010. *Artificial Ants*. Iste Series. John Wiley & Sons.

[Navigli and Lapata2010] Roberto Navigli and Mirella Lapata. 2010. An experimental study of graph connectivity for unsupervised word sense disambiguation. *IEEE Trans. Pattern Anal. Mach. Intell.*, 32:678–692, April.

[Navigli and Pozetto2012] Roberto Navigli and Simone Paolo Pozetto. 2012. Babelnet: The automatic construction, evaluation and application of a wide-coverage multilingual semantic network. *Artificial Intelligence*, 193:217–250. http://dx.doi.org/10.1016/j.artint.2012.07.004.

[Navigli et al.2013] Roberto Navigli, David Jurgens, and Daniele Vannella. 2013. Semeval-2013 task 12: Multilingual word sense disambiguation. In *Proceedings of the 7th International Workshop on Semantic Evaluation (SemEval 2013), in conjunction with the Second Joint Conference on Lexical and Computational Semantics (*SEM 2013)*, Atlanta, Georgia, 14-15 June.

[Ponzetto and Navigli2010] Simone Paolo Ponzetto and Roberto Navigli. 2010. Knowledge-rich word sense disambiguation rivaling supervised systems. In *Proceedings of the 48th Annual Meeting of the Association for Computational Linguistics*, pages 1522–1531.

[Resnik1995] Philip Resnik. 1995. Using information content to evaluate semantic similarity in a taxonomy. In *Proceedings of the 14th international joint conference on Artificial intelligence - Volume 1*, IJCAI'95, pages 448–453, San Francisco, CA, USA. Morgan Kaufmann Publishers Inc.

[Schwab et al.2011] Didier Schwab, Jérôme Goulian, and Nathan Guillaume. 2011. Désambiguïsation lexicale par propagation de mesures semantiques locales par algorithmes a colonies de fourmis. In *TALN*, Montpellier (France), Juillet.

[Schwab et al.2012] Didier Schwab, Jérôme Goulian, Andon Tchechmedjiev, and Hervé Blanchon. 2012. Ant colony algorithm for the unsupervised word sense disambiguation of texts: Comparison and evaluation. In *Proceedings of COLING'2012*, Mumbai (India), December. To be published.

[Schwab et al.2013] Didier Schwab, Jerôme Goulian, and Andon Tchechmedjiev. 2013. Theoretical and empirical comparison of artificial intelligence methods for unsupervised word sense disambiguation. *Int. J. of Web Engineering and Technology*. In Press.

[Tchechmedjiev et al.2012] Andon Tchechmedjiev, Jérôme Goulian, Didier Schwab, and Gilles Sérasset. 2012. Parameter estimation under uncertainty with simulated annealing applied to an ant colony based probabilistic wsd algorithm. In *Proceedings of the First International Workshop on Optimization Techniques for Human Language Technology*, pages 109–124, Mumbai, India, December. The COLING 2012 Organizing Committee.

[Wu and Palmer1994] Zhibiao Wu and Martha Palmer. 1994. Verbs semantics and lexical selection. In *Proceedings of the 32nd annual meeting of Association for Computational Linguistics*, ACL '94, pages 133–138, Stroudsburg, PA, USA. Association for Computational Linguistics.

UMCC_DLSI: Reinforcing a Ranking Algorithm with Sense Frequencies and Multidimensional Semantic Resources to solve Multilingual Word Sense Disambiguation

Yoan Gutiérrez, Yenier Castañeda, Andy González, Rainel Estrada, Dennys D. Piug, Jose I. Abreu, Roger Pérez
DI, University of Matanzas
Matanzas, Cuba
{yoan.gutierrez, yenier.castaneda, rainel.estrada, dennys.puig, jose.abreu, roger.perez}@umcc.cu, andy.gonzalez@infonet.umcc.cu

Antonio Fernández Orquín, Andrés Montoyo, Rafael Muñoz
DLSI, University of Alicante
Alicante, Spain
antonybr@yahoo.com, {montoyo,rafael}@dlsi.ua.es

Franc Camara
Independent Consultant
USA
info@franccamara.com

Abstract

This work introduces a new unsupervised approach to multilingual word sense disambiguation. Its main purpose is to automatically choose the intended sense (meaning) of a word in a particular context for different languages. It does so by selecting the correct Babel synset for the word and the various Wiki Page titles that mention the word. BabelNet contains all the output information that our system needs, in its Babel synset. Through Babel synset, we find all the possible Synsets for the word in WordNet. Using these Synsets, we apply the disambiguation method Ppr+Freq to find what we need. To facilitate the work with WordNet, we use the ISR-WN which offers the integration of different resources to WordNet. Our system, recognized as the best in the competition, obtains results around 69% of Recall.

1 Introduction

Word Sense Disambiguation (WSD) focuses on resolving the semantic ambiguity of a given word. This is an important task in Natural Language Processing (NLP) because in many applications, such as Automatic Translation, it is essential to know the exact meaning of a word in a given context. In order to solve semantic ambiguity, different systems have been developed. However, we can categorize them in two main groups: supervised and unsupervised systems. The supervised ones need large quantity of hand-tagged data in order to gather enough information to build rules, train systems, and so on. Unsupervised systems, on the other hand, do not need such a large amount of hand-tagged datasets. This means that, when there aren't enough corpora to train the systems, an unsupervised system is a good option.

A sub-task of WSD is Multilingual Word Sense Disambiguation (MWSD) (Navigli *et al.*, 2013) that aims at resolving ambiguities in different languages.

In a language, there are words that have only one sense (or meaning), but in other languages, the same words can have different senses. For example, "patient" is a word that in English can be either a noun or an adjective, but in German, it only has one sense - "viz" (a person that needs treatment). This shows that the information obtained by combining two languages can be more useful for WSD because the word senses in each language can complement each other. For it to be useful, MWSD needs a multilingual resource that contains different languages, such as BabelNet (Navigli and Ponzetto, 2010; 2012) and EuroWordNet (Vossen, 1998).

*Second Joint Conference on Lexical and Computational Semantics (*SEM), Volume 2: Seventh International Workshop on Semantic Evaluation (SemEval 2013)*, pages 241–249, Atlanta, Georgia, June 14-15, 2013. ©2013 Association for Computational Linguistics

As the preferred disambiguation method, we decided to use the Ppr+Freq (Personalized Page Rank combined with Frequencies of senses) (Gutiérrez, 2012) method because, among unsupervised systems, graph-based methods have obtained more promising results.

It is worth mentioning the relevant approaches used by the scientific community to achieve promising results. One approach used is structural interconnections, such as Structural Semantic Interconnections (SSI), which create structural specifications of the possible senses for each word in a context (Navigli and Velardi, 2005). The other approaches used are "Exploring the integration of WordNet" (Miller *et al.*, 1990), FrameNet (Laparra *et al.*, 2010) and those using Page-Rank such as (Sinha and Mihalcea, 2007) and (Agirre and Soroa, 2009).

The aforementioned types of graph based approaches have achieved relevant results in both the SensEval-2 and SensEval-3 competitions (see Table 1).

Algorithm	**Recall**
TexRank (Mihalcea, 2005)	54.2%
(Sinha and Mihalcea, 2007)	56.4%
(Tsatsaronis *et al.*, 2007)	49.2%
Ppr (Agirre and Soroa, 2009)	58.6%

Table 1. Relevant WSD approaches. Recall measure is calculated recalls using SensEval-2 (English All Word task) guidelines over.

Experiments using SensEval-2 and SensEval-3 corpora suggest that Ppr+Freq (Gutiérrez, 2012) can lead to better results by obtaining over 64% of Recall. Therefore we selected Ppr+Freq as the WSD method for our system.

The key proposal for this work is an unsupervised algorithm for MWSD, which uses an unsupervised method, Ppr+Freq, for semantic disambiguation with resources like BabelNet (as sense inventory only) (Navigli and Ponzetto, 2010) and ISR-WN (as knowledge base) (Gutiérrez *et al.*, 2011a; 2010a).

ISR-WN was selected as the default knowledge base because of previous NLP research, which included: (Fernández *et al.*, 2012; Gutiérrez *et al.*, 2010b; Gutiérrez *et al.*, 2012; 2011b; 2011c; 2011d), which achieved relevant results using ISR-WN as their knowledge base.

2 System architecture

By using one of BabelNet (BN) features, our technique begins by looking for all the Babel synsets (Bs) linked to the lemma of each word in the sentence that we need to disambiguate. Through the Bs offsets, we can get its corresponding WordNet Synset (WNS), which would be retrieved from WordNet (WN) using the ISR-WN resource. As a result, for each lemma, we have a WordNet Synset List (WNSL) from which our Word Sense Disambiguation method obtains one WNS as the correct meaning.

Our WSD method consists of applying a modification of the Personalizing PageRank (Ppr) algorithm (Agirre and Soroa, 2009), which involves the senses frequency. More specifically, the key proposal is known as Ppr+Freq (see Section 2.3).

Given a set of WNSLs of WNSL, as words window, we applied the Synsets ranking method, Ppr+Freq, which ranks in a descending order, the Synsets of each lemma according to a calculated factor of relevance. The first Synset (WNS) of each WNSL (the most relevant) is established as the correct one and its associated Babel synset (Bs) is also tagged as correct. To determine the Wiki Page Titles (WK), we examine the WIKI (Wikipedia pages) and WIKIRED (Wikipedia pages redirections) in the correct Babel synset obtained.

Figure 1 shows a general description of our system that is made up of the following steps:

I. Obtaining lemmas
II. Obtaing WN Synset of selected lemmas
III. Applying Ppr+Freq method
IV. Assigning Synset, Babel synset and Wiki page title

Note that ISR-WN contains WN as its nucleus. This allows linking both resources, BabelNet and ISR-WN.

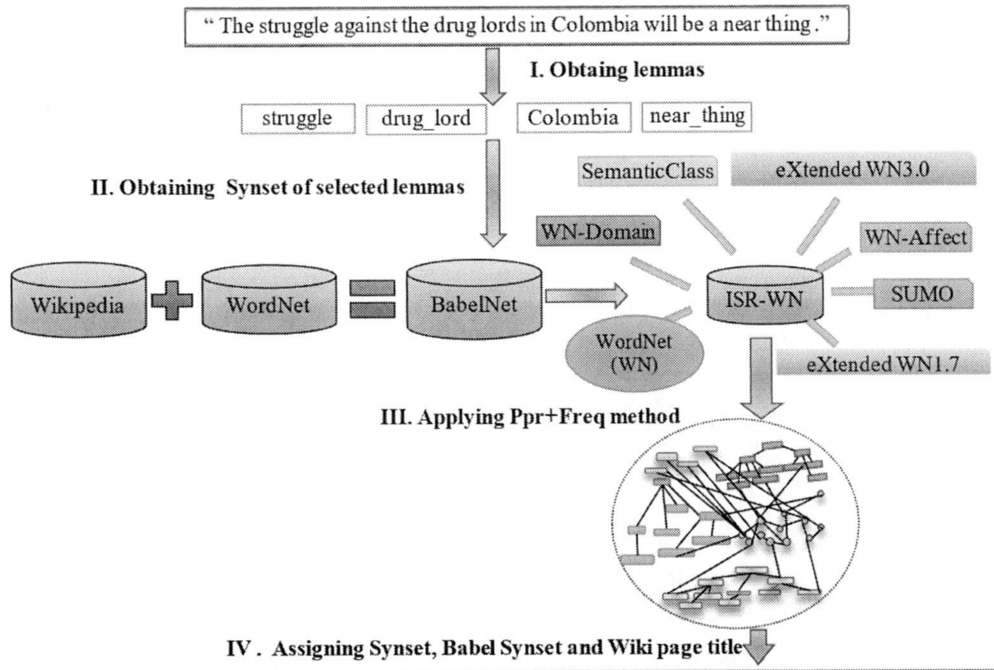

WN key	struggle%1:04:01::	drug_lord%1:18:00::	colombia%1:15:00::	near_thing%1:04:00::
BS	bn:00009079n	bn:00028876n	bn:00020697n	bn:00057109n
WK	-	Drug_Lord	Colombia	-
	struggle	**drug_lord**	**Colombia**	**near_thing**

Figure 1. General process description taking as instance a sentence provided by the trial dataset.

2.1 Obtaining lemmas

For each input sentence, we extract the labeled lemmas. As an example, for the sentence, "The struggle against the drug lords in Colombia will be a near thing," the selected lemmas are: "struggle," "drug_lord," "Colombia", and "near_thing."

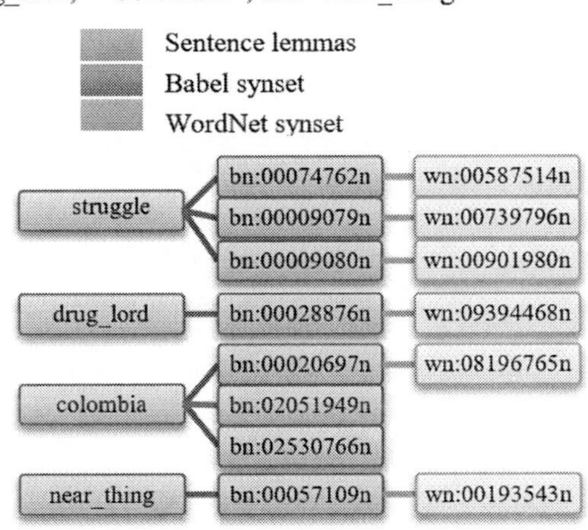

Figure 2. Obtaining synset of lemmas.

2.2 Obtaing WN Synset of selected lemmas

For each lemma obtained in the previous section, we look through BabelNet to recover the Bs that contains the lemma among its labels. When BSs are mapped to WN, we use the ISR-WN resource to find the corresponding Synset. Since a lemma can appear in a different Bs, it can be mapped with several WNS. Thus, we get a Synset list for each lemma in the sentence. In case the lemma does not have an associated Bs, its list would be empty. An example of this step is shown on Figure 2.

2.3 Applying Ppr+Freq method

In the above case, Ppr+Freq modifies the "classic" Page Rank approach instead of assigning the same weight for each sense of WN in the disambiguation graph (G_D).

The PageRank (Brin and Page, 1998) adaptation, Ppr , which was popularized by (Agirre

and Soroa, 2009) in Word Sense Disambiguation thematic, and which has obtained relevant results, was an inspiration to us in our work. The main idea behind this algorithm is that, for each edge between v_i and v_j in graph G, a vote is made from v_i to v_j. As a result, the relevance of v_j is increased.
On top of that, the vote strength from i to j depends on $v_i's$ relevance. The philosophy behind it is that, the more important the vertex is, the more strength the voter would have. Thus, PageRank is generated by applying a random walkthrough from the internal interconnection of G, where the final relevance of v_i represents the random walkthrough probability over G, and ending on v_i.

Ppr+Freq includes the existent semantic and frequency patterns of each sense of the word to disambiguate while finding a way to connect each one of these words in a knowledge base.

The new graph-based approach of WSD generates a graph of disambiguated words for each input sentence. For that reason, it is necessary to classify the word senses according to the other words that compose the context. The general method is shown in Figure 3. This method is divided into three steps:

I. Creation of a disambiguation graph
II. Application of Ppr+Freq in the generated graph
III. Selection of the correct answer

Creation of a disambiguation graph: In the first step, a disambiguation graph is built by means of a Breath First Search (BFS) over the "super" graph composed by all the resources integrated into ISR-WN. The components involved in this process are: WordNet, SUMO (Zouaq *et al.*, 2009) WordNet Domains (Magnini and Cavaglia, 2000) WordNet Affects (Strapparava and Valitutti, 2004) Semantic Classes (Izquierdo *et al.*, 2007) and eXtended WordNet (XWN) relations (Moldovan and Rus, 2001). This search aims to recover all senses (nodes), domain labels (from WordNet Domain and WordNet Affects), SUMO categories, and Semantic Classes labels through the shortest path between every pair of senses in the WNSL set associated with the input sentence. Using ISR-WN as the KB, through experimentation, we obtained the shortest paths with a length of five edges. For a better understanding of this process, see (Gutiérrez, 2012).

Application of Ppr+Freq in the generated graph: In the second step, we use the weighted Personalized PageRank. Here, all the vertices from vector v in G_D are initialized with the value $\frac{1}{N}$; where N is the number of nodes in G_D. On the other hand, the vertices that represent word senses in the analyzed sentence are not initialized with this value. Instead, they are initialized with values in the range [0…1], which are associated to their occurrence frequency in SemCor[1] (Corpus and sense frequencies knowledge). In the last step, after applying the Ppr+Freq algorithm over G_D, we get a representative vector which contains ISR-WN nodes in G_D sorted in a descending order by a ranking score computed by this algorithm. For a better description, see (Gutiérrez, 2012).

Selection of the correct answer: As the correct sense, we take the highest ranked sense of each target word involved in this vector. Note that domain labels, SUMO categories, semantic class labels, and affect labels are ranked too. They could be used in the future to determine relevant conceptualizations that would be useful for text classification and more.

In our system, we assume the following configuration: dumping factor $c = 0.85$ and like in (Agirre and Soroa, 2009) we used 30 iterations. A detailed explanation about PageRank algorithm can be found in (Agirre and Soroa, 2009).

Table 2 shows an example that analyzes the Synset for each word in the sentence and also shows how the higher ranked Synsets of the target words are selected as the correct ones. For a detailed explanation of Ppr+Freq, see (Gutiérrez, 2012).

2.4 Assigning Synset, Babel synset and Wiki Pages

In this step, English is handled differently from other languages because WordNet Synsets are available only for English. The following sections explain how we proceed in each case. Once the Synsets list is obtained for each lemma in section 2.3, selecting the correct answer for the lemma is all that's left to do.

[1] http://www.cse.unt.edu/~rada/downloads.html

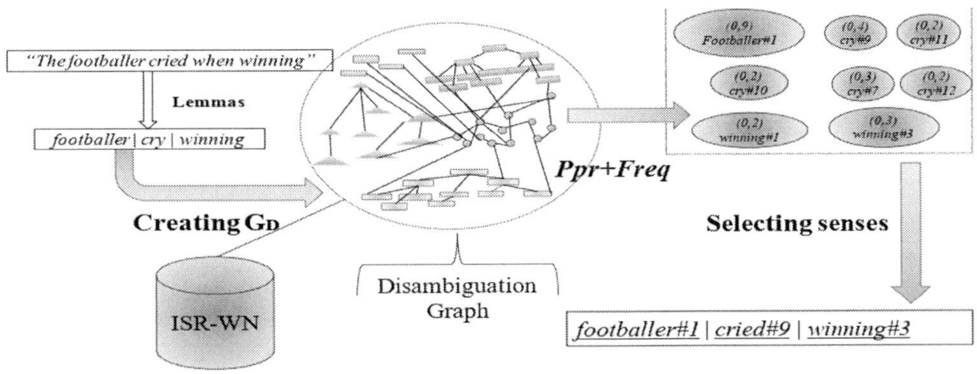

Figure 3. General process of WSD with Ppr+Freq.

2.4.1 English

Given a lemma, we go through its Synset list from beginning to end looking for the first Synset that contains a key[2] for the lemma. If such Synset exists, it is designated as the Synset for the lemma. Otherwise, no Synset is assigned.

As already explained, each Synset in the list is connected to a Bs. Therefore, the lemma linked with the correct WNS selected in the previous step, is chosen as the correct lemma. In case no Synsets were designated as the correct ones, we take the first Bs in BN, which contains the lemma among its labels.

To determine the Wiki pages titles (WK) we examine the WIKIRED and WIKI labels in the correct Bs selected in the preceding step. This search is restricted only to labels corresponding to the analyzed language and discriminating upper and lower case letters. Table 2 shows some sample results of the WSD process.

Lemma	**struggle**	**drug_lord**
WNS	00739796n	09394468n
WN key	struggle%1:04:01::	drug_lord%1:18:00::
Bs	bn:00009079n	bn:00028876n
WK	-	Drug_Lord
Lemma	**colombia**	**near_thing**
WNS	08196765n	00193543n
WN key	colombia%1:15:00::	near_thing%1:04:00::
Bs	bn:00020697n	bn:00057109n
WK	Colombia	-

Table 2 : Example of English Language.

[2]A sense_key is the best way to represent a sense in semantic tagging or other systems that refer to WordNet senses. sense_key's are independent of WordNet sense numbers and synset_offset's, which vary between versions of the database.

2.4.2 Other languages

For this scenario, we introduce a change in the first step discussed in the previous section. The reason is that the Synsets do not contain any keys in any other language than English. Thus, the correct Synset for the lemma is the first in the Synset list for the lemma obtained, as described, in section 2.3.

3 Results

We tested three versions (runs) of the proposed approach and evaluated them through a trial dataset provided by Task12[3] of Semeval-2013 using babelnet-1.0.1. Table 3 shows the result for each run. Note that the table results were calculated with the traditional WSD recall measure, being this measure which has ranked WSD systems on mostly Semeval competitions. On the other hand, note that our precision and recall results are different because the coverage is not 100%. See Table 5.

	English			**French**	
Runs	WNS	Bs	WK	Bs	WK
Run1	0.70	0.71	0.77	0.59	0.85
Run2	**0.70**	**0.71**	**0.78**	**0.60**	**0.85**
Run3	0.69	0.70	0.77	-	-

Table 3 : Results of runs with trial recall values.

As can be noticed on Table 3, results of different versions do not have big differences, but in general, Run2 achieves the best results; it's better

[3] http://www.cs.york.ac.uk/semeval-2013/task12

than Run1 in the WK with a 78% in English and Bs with 60% in French. The best results are in the WK in French with a value of 85%.

Since we can choose to include different resources into ISR-WN, it is important to analyze how doing so would affect the results. Table 4 shows comparative results for Run 2 of a trial dataset with BabelNet version 1.1.1.

As can be observed in Table 4, the result does not have a significant change even though we used the ISR-WN with all resources.

A better analysis of Ppr+Freq in, as it relates to the influence of each resource involved in ISR-WN (similar to Table 4 description) assessing SensEval-2 and SensEval-3 dataset, is shown in (Gutiérrez, 2012). There are different resource combinations showing that only XWN1.7 and all ISR-WN resources obtain the highest performance. Other analysis found in (Gutiérrez, 2012) evaluates the influence of adding the sense frequency for Ppr+Freq.

By excluding the Factotum Domain, we obtain the best result in Bs 54% for French (only 1% more than the version used in the competition). The other results are equal, with a 69% in WNS, 66% in Bs, 64% in WK for English, and 69% in WK for French.

								English			**French**	
WN	**Domains**	**Sumo**	**Affect**	**Factotum Domain**	**SemanticClass**	**XWN3.0**	**XWN1.7**	**WNS**	**Bs**	**WK**	**Bs**	**WK**
X	X	X	X	X	X	X	X	0.69	0.66	0.64	0.53	0.69
X	X		X	X	X	X	X	0.69	0.66	0.64	0.53	0.69
X				X	X	X	X	0.68	0.65	0.64	0.52	0.69
X	X	X	X		X	X	X	**0.69**	**0.66**	**0.64**	**0.54**	**0.69**
X	X	X	X		X		X	0.68	0.65	0.65	0.53	0.69

Table 4. Influence of different resources that integrate ISR-WN in our technique.

		Wikipedia			BabelNet			WordNet		
System	Language	Precision	Recall	F-score	Precision	Recall	F-score	Precision	Recall	F-score
MFS	DE	**0.836**	**0.827**	**0.831**	**0.676**	**0.673**	**0.686**	-	-	-
	EN	**0.86**	**0.753**	**0.803**	0.665	0.665	0.656	0.63	0.63	0.63
	ES	**0.83**	**0.819**	**0.824**	0.645	0.645	0.644	-	-	-
	FR	0.698	**0.691**	**0.694**	0.455	0.452	0.501	-	-	-
	IT	**0.833**	**0.813**	**0.823**	0.576	0.574	0.572	-	-	-
Run1	DE	0.758	0.46	0.572	0.619	0.617	0.618	-	-	-
	EN	0.619	0.484	0.543	0.677	0.677	0.677	0.639	0.635	0.637
	ES	0.773	0.493	0.602	0.708	0.703	0.705	-	-	-
	FR	**0.817**	0.48	0.605	**0.608**	**0.603**	**0.605**	-	-	-
	IT	0.785	0.458	0.578	**0.659**	0.656	0.657	-	-	-
Run2	DE	0.769	0.467	0.581	0.622	0.62	0.621	-	-	-
	EN	0.62	0.487	0.546	**0.685**	**0.685**	**0.685**	**0.649**	**0.645**	**0.647**
	ES	0.778	0.502	0.61	**0.713**	**0.708**	**0.71**	-	-	-
	FR	0.815	0.478	0.603	**0.608**	**0.603**	**0.605**	-	-	-
	IT	0.787	0.463	0.583	**0.659**	**0.657**	**0.658**	-	-	-
Run3	EN	0.622	0.489	0.548	0.68	0.68	0.68	0.642	0.639	0.64

Table 5. Results of Runs for Task12 of semeval-2013 using the test dataset.

3.1 Run1

In this Run, WNSLs consist of all the target words involved in each sentence. This run is applied at the sentence level. The results for the competition are shown in Table 5. For this Run, the best result was obtained for Spanish with a 70.3% in Bs and 49.3% in WK of Recall. As we can see, for Run1 the precision is high for Wikipedia disambiguation, obtaining for French the best result of the ranking. The low Recall in Wikipedia is due to the exact mismatching of labels between our system output and the gold standard. This fact, affects the rest of our runs.

3.2 Run2

In this Run, WNSLs consist of all the target words involved in each domain. We can obtain the target words because the training and test dataset contain the sentences grouped by topics. For instance, for English, 13 WNSLs are established. This Run is applied at the corpora level. The results for the competition are shown in Table 5. It is important to emphasize that our best results ranked our algorithm as first place among all proposed approaches for the MWSD task.

For this run, the best Recall was obtained for Spanish with a 70.8% in Bs and 50.2% in WK. This Run also has the best result of the three runs. For the English competition, it ended up with a 64.5% in WNS, 68.5% in Bs, and 48.7% in WK.

This Run obtained promising results, which took first place in the competition. It also had better results than that of the First Sense (Most Frequent Sense) baseline in Bs results for all languages, except for German. In Bs, it only obtained lower results in German with a 62% of Recall for our system and 67.3% for the First Sense baseline.

3.3 Run3

In this run, WNSLs consist of all the words included in each sentence. This run uses target words and non-target words of each sentence, as they are applied to the sentence level. The results for the competition are shown in Table 5.

As we can see, the behavior of this run is similar to the previous runs.

4 Conclusions and Future work

The above results suggest that our proposal is a promising approach. It is also important to notice that a richer knowledgebase can be built by combining different resources such as BabelNet and ISR-WN, which can lead to an improvement of the results. Notwithstanding, our system has been recognized as the best in the competition, obtaining results around 70% of Recall.

According to the Task12 results[4], only the baseline Most Frequent Sense (MFS) could improve our scores in order to achieve better WK and German (DE) disambiguation. Therefore, we plan to review this point to figure out why we obtained better results in other categories, but not for this one. At the same time, further work will use the internal Babel network to run the Ppr+Freq method in an attempt to find a way to enrich the semantic network obtained for each target sentence to disambiguate. On top of that, we plan to compare Ppr (Agirre and Soroa, 2009) with Ppr+Freq using the Task12 dataset.

Availability of our Resource

In case researchers would like to use our resource, it is available at the GPLSI[5] home page or by contacting us via email.

Acknowledgments

This research work has been partially funded by the Spanish Government through the project TEXT-MESS 2.0 (TIN2009-13391-C04), "Análisis de Tendencias Mediante Técnicas de Opinión Semántica" (TIN2012-38536-C03-03) and "Técnicas de Deconstrucción en la Tecnologías del Lenguaje Humano" (TIN2012-31224); and by the Valencian Government through the project PROMETEO (PROMETEO/2009/199).

References

Agirre, E. and A. Soroa. Personalizing PageRank for Word Sense Disambiguation. Proceedings of the 12th conference of the European chapter of the Association for Computational Linguistics (EACL-2009), Athens, Greece, 2009.

[4] http://www.cs.york.ac.uk/semeval-2013/task12/index.php?id=results

[5] http://gplsi.dlsi.ua.es/

Fernández, A.; Y. Gutiérrez; H. Dávila; A. Chávez; A. González; R. Estrada; Y. Castañeda; S. Vázquez; A. Montoyo and R. Muñoz. UMCC_DLSI: Multidimensional Lexical-Semantic Textual Similarity. {*SEM 2012}: The First Joint Conference on Lexical and Computational Semantics -- Volume 1: Proceedings of the main conference and the shared task, and Volume 2: Proceedings of the Sixth International Workshop on Semantic Evaluation {(SemEval 2012)}, Montreal, Canada, Association for Computational Linguistics, 2012. 608--616 p.

Gutiérrez, Y. Análisis Semántico Multidimensional aplicado a la Desambiguación del Lenguaje Natural. Departamento de Lenguajes y Sistemas Informáticos. Alicante, Alicante, 2012. 189. p.

Gutiérrez, Y.; A. Fernández; A. Montoyo and S. Vázquez. Integration of semantic resources based on WordNet. XXVI Congreso de la Sociedad Española para el Procesamiento del Lenguaje Natural, Universidad Politécnica de Valencia, Valencia, SEPLN 2010, 2010a. 161-168 p. 1135-5948.

Gutiérrez, Y.; A. Fernández; A. Montoyo and S. Vázquez. UMCC-DLSI: Integrative resource for disambiguation task. Proceedings of the 5th International Workshop on Semantic Evaluation, Uppsala, Sweden, Association for Computational Linguistics, 2010b. 427-432 p.

Gutiérrez, Y.; A. Fernández; A. Montoyo and S. Vázquez Enriching the Integration of Semantic Resources based on WordNet Procesamiento del Lenguaje Natural, 2011a, 47: 249-257.

Gutiérrez, Y.; S. Vázquez and A. Montoyo. Improving WSD using ISR-WN with Relevant Semantic Trees and SemCor Senses Frequency. Proceedings of the International Conference Recent Advances in Natural Language Processing 2011, Hissar, Bulgaria, RANLP 2011 Organising Committee, 2011b. 233--239 p.

Gutiérrez, Y.; S. Vázquez and A. Montoyo. Sentiment Classification Using Semantic Features Extracted from WordNet-based Resources. Proceedings of the 2nd Workshop on Computational Approaches to Subjectivity and Sentiment Analysis (WASSA 2.011), Portland, Oregon., Association for Computational Linguistics, 2011c. 139--145 p.

Gutiérrez, Y.; S. Vázquez and A. Montoyo. Word Sense Disambiguation: A Graph-Based Approach Using N-Cliques Partitioning Technique. en: Natural Language Processing and Information Systems. MUÑOZ, R.;MONTOYO, A.et al, Springer Berlin / Heidelberg, 2011d. 6716: 112-124.p.

Gutiérrez, Y.; S. Vázquez and A. Montoyo. A graph-Based Approach to WSD Using Relevant Semantic Trees and N-Cliques Model. CICLing 2012, New Delhi, India, 2012. 225-237 p.

Izquierdo, R.; A. Suárez and G. Rigau A Proposal of Automatic Selection of Coarse-grained Semantic Classes for WSD Procesamiento del Lenguaje Natural, 2007, 39: 189-196.

Laparra, E.; G. Rigau and M. Cuadros. Exploring the integration of WordNet and FrameNet. Proceedings of the 5th Global WordNet Conference (GWC'10), Mumbai, India, 2010.

Magnini, B. and G. Cavaglia. Integrating Subject Field Codes into WordNet. Proceedings of Third International Conference on Language Resources and Evaluation (LREC-2000), 2000. 1413--1418 p.

Mihalcea, R. Unsupervised large-vocabulary word sense disambiguation with graph-based algorithms for sequence data labeling. Proceedings of HLT05, Morristown, NJ, USA., 2005.

Miller, G. A.; R. Beckwith; C. Fellbaum; D. Gross and K. Miller. Five papers on WordNet. Princenton University, Cognositive Science Laboratory, 1990.

Moldovan, D. I. and V. Rus Explaining Answers with Extended WordNet ACL, 2001.

Navigli, R.; D. Jurgens and D. Vannella. SemEval-2013 Task 12: Multilingual Word Sense Disambiguation. . Proceedings of the 7th International Workshop on Semantic Evaluation (SemEval 2013), in conjunction with the Second Joint Conference on Lexical and Computational Semantics (*SEM 2013), Atlanta, Georgia, 2013.

Navigli, R. and S. P. Ponzetto. BabelNet: Building a Very Large Multilingual Semantic Network. Proceedings of the 48th Annual Meeting of the Association for Computational Linguistics, Uppsala, Sweden, Association for Computational Linguistics, 2010. 216--225 p.

Navigli, R. and S. P. Ponzetto BabelNet: The automatic construction, evaluation and application of a wide-coverage multilingual semantic network Artif. Intell., 2012, 193: 217-250.

Navigli, R. and P. Velardi Structural Semantic Interconnections: A Knowledge-Based Approach to Word Sense Disambiguation IEEE Transactions on Pattern Analysis and Machine Intelligence, 2005, 27(7): 1075-1086.

Sinha, R. and R. Mihalcea. Unsupervised Graph-based Word Sense Disambiguation Using Measures of Word Semantic Similarity. Proceedings of the IEEE International Conference on Semantic Computing (ICSC 2007), Irvine, CA, 2007.

Strapparava, C. and A. Valitutti. WordNet-Affect: an affective extension of WordNet. Proceedings of the 4th International Conference on Language Resources and Evaluation (LREC 2004), Lisbon, 2004. 1083-1086 p.

Tsatsaronis, G.; M. Vazirgiannis and I. Androutsopoulos. Word sense disambiguation with spreading activation networks generated from thesauri. IJCAI, 2007.

Vossen, P. EuroWordNet: A Multilingual Database with Lexical Semantic Networks. Dordrecht, Kluwer Academic Publishers, 1998.

Zouaq, A.; M. Gagnon and B. Ozell. A SUMO-based Semantic Analysis for Knowledge Extraction. Proceedings of the 4th Language & Technology Conference, Poznań, Poland, 2009.

DAEBAK!: Peripheral Diversity for Multilingual Word Sense Disambiguation

Steve L. Manion
University of Canterbury
Christchurch, New Zealand
steve.manion
@pg.canterbury.ac.nz

Raazesh Sainudiin
University of Canterbury
Christchurch, New Zealand
r.sainudiin
@math.canterbury.ac.nz

Abstract

We introduce Peripheral Diversity (PD) as a knowledge-based approach to achieve multilingual Word Sense Disambiguation (WSD). PD exploits the frequency and diverse use of word senses in semantic subgraphs derived from larger sense inventories such as BabelNet, Wikipedia, and WordNet in order to achieve WSD. PD's f-measure scores for SemEval 2013 Task 12 outperform the Most Frequent Sense (MFS) baseline for two of the five languages: English, French, German, Italian, and Spanish. Despite PD remaining under-developed and under-explored, it demonstrates that it is robust, competitive, and encourages development.

1 Introduction

By reading out aloud "A *minute* is a *minute* division of time" (Nelson, 1976), we can easily make the distinction between the two *senses* of the homograph *minute*. For a machine this is a complex task known as Word Sense Disambiguation (WSD). Task 12 of SemEval 2013 (Navigli et al., 2013) calls for a language-independent solution to WSD that utilises a multilingual sense inventory.

Supervised approaches to WSD have dominated for some time now (Màrquez et al., 2007). Homographs such as *minute* are effortlessly disambiguated and more polysemous words such as *bar* or *line* can also be disambiguated with reasonable competence (Agirre and Edmonds, 2007). However our approach is purely knowledge-based and employs semantic graphs. This allows us to avoid the notorious predicament Gale et al. (1992) name the *information bottleneck*, in which supervised approaches fail to be portable across alternative languages and domains if the annotated corpora do not exist. Conversely, knowledge-based approaches for WSD are usually applicable to all words in unrestricted text (Mihalcea, 2007). It is this innate scalability that motivates us to pursue knowledge-based approaches. Regardless of whether sense inventories can maintain *knowledge-richness* as they grow, their continued refinement by contributors is directly beneficial.

Knowledge-based approaches that employ semantic graphs increasingly rival leading supervised approaches to WSD. They can beat a Random or LESK (Lesk, 1986) baseline (*see* Mihalcea (2005), Navigli and Lapata (2007), Sinha and Mihalcea (2007), Navigli and Lapata (2010)) and can compete with or even beat the Most Frequent Sense (MFS) baseline in certain contexts which is by no means an easy task (*see* Navigli et al. (2007), Eneko Agirre and Aitor Soroa (2009), Navigli and Ponzetto (2012a)).

2 Methodology

PD is a framework for knowledge-based WSD approaches that employ semantic graphs. However before we can elaborate we must first cover the fundamental resources it is built upon.

2.1 Fundamental Resource Definitions

2.1.1 Lemma Sequences

At a glance across the text of any language, we absorb meaning and new information through its *lexical composition*. Depending on the length of text

*Second Joint Conference on Lexical and Computational Semantics (*SEM), Volume 2: Seventh International Workshop on Semantic Evaluation (SemEval 2013)*, pages 250–254, Atlanta, Georgia, June 14-15, 2013.

we are reading, we could interpret it as one of many structural subsequences of writing such as a *paragraph, excerpt, quote, verse, sentence*, among many others. Let $\mathcal{W} = (w_a, ..., w_b)$ be this subsequence of words, which we will utilise as a sliding window for PD. Again let $\mathbb{W} = (w_1, ..., w_m)$ be the larger body of text of length m, such as a *book, newspaper*, or *corpus of text*, that our sliding window of length $b-a$ moves through.

In SemEval Task 12 on Multilingual Word Sense Disambiguation all words are *lemmatised*, which is the process of unifying the different inflected forms of a word so they can be analysed as a consolidated *lemma* (or *headword*). Therefore words (or *lexemes*) such as *runs* and *ran* are all mapped to their unifying lemma *run*[1].

To express this, let $\ell_w : \mathcal{W} \rightarrow \mathcal{L}$ be a *many-to-one* mapping from the sequence of words $\mathcal{W}$ to the sequence of lemmas $\mathcal{L}$, in which $(w_a, ..., w_b) \mapsto (\ell_{w_a}, ..., \ell_{w_b}) = (\ell_a, ..., \ell_b)$. To give an example from the test data set[2], the word sequence $\mathcal{W}$ = (*And, it, 's, nothing, that, runs, afoul, of, ethics, rules, .*) maps to the lemma sequence $\mathcal{L}$ = (*and, it, be, nothing, that, run, afoul, of, ethic, rule, .*). In order to complete this SemEval task we disambiguate a large sequence of lemmas $\mathbb{L} = (\ell_1, ..., \ell_m)$, via our lemma-based sliding window $\mathcal{L} = (\ell_a, ..., \ell_b)$.

2.1.2 Synsets

Each lemma $\ell_i \in \mathcal{L}$ may refer up to k senses in $S(\ell_i) = \{s_{i,1}, s_{i,2}, ..., s_{i,k}\} = \mathcal{S}$. Furthermore each sense $s_{i,j} \in \mathcal{S}$ maps to a set of unique concepts in the human lexicon. To clarify let us consider one of the earliest examples of modern ambiguity taken from Bar-Hillel's (1960) critique of Machine Translation: $\mathcal{W}$ = (*The, box, was, in, the, pen, .*). The sense of *pen* could be either *a)* a certain writing *utensil* or *b)* an *enclosure* where small children can play, therefore $\{s_{\text{enclosure}}, s_{\text{utensil}}\} \subset S(\ell_{\text{pen}}) = \mathcal{S}$. Humans can easily resolve the ambiguity between the possible senses of *pen* by accessing their own internal lexicon and knowledge of the world they have built up over time.

In the same vein, when accessing sense inventories such as BabelNet, WordNet (Fellbaum, 1998), and Wikipedia which are discrete representations of the human lexicon, we refer to each sense $s_{i,j} \in \mathcal{S}$ as a synset. Depending on the sense inventory the synset belongs to, it may contain alternative or translated lexicalisations, glosses, links to other semantic resources, among a collection of semantically defined relations to other synsets.

2.1.3 Subgraphs

PD makes use of subgraphs derived from a directed graph $\mathcal{G} = (\mathcal{V}, \mathcal{E})$ that can be crafted from a sense inventory, such as BabelNet, WordNet, or Wikipedia. We construct subgraphs using the BabelNet API which accesses BabelNet[3] and Babel synset paths[4] indexed into Apache Lucene[5] to ensure speed of subgraph construction. This process is described in Navigli and Ponzetto (2012a) and demonstrated in Navigli and Ponzetto (2012b). Our formalisation of subgraphs is adapted into our own notation from the original papers of Navigli and Lapata (2007) and Navigli and Lapata (2010). We refer the reader to these listed sources if they desire an extensive explanation of our subgraph construction as we have built PD on top of the same code base therefore we do not deviate from it.

For a given lemma sequence $\mathcal{L} = (\ell_i, ..., \ell_n)$ and directed graph $\mathcal{G} = (\mathcal{V}, \mathcal{E})$ we construct our subgraph $\mathcal{G}_\mathcal{L} = (\mathcal{V}_\mathcal{L}, \mathcal{E}_\mathcal{L})$ in two steps:

1. Initialize $\mathcal{V}_\mathcal{L} := \bigcup_{i=1}^{n} S(\ell_i)$ and $\mathcal{E}_\mathcal{L} := \emptyset$.

2. For each node $v \in \mathcal{V}_\mathcal{L}$, we perform a depth-first search (DFS) of $\mathcal{G}$, such that, every time we encounter a node $v' \in \mathcal{V}_\mathcal{L}$ $(v' \neq v)$ along a path $v, v_1, ..., v_k, v'$ of length $\leq L$ in $\mathcal{G}$, we add all intermediate nodes and edges on the path from v to v', i.e., $\mathcal{V}_\mathcal{L} := \mathcal{V}_\mathcal{L} \cup \{v_1, ..., v_k\}$ and $\mathcal{E}_\mathcal{L} := \mathcal{E}_\mathcal{L} \cup \{\{v, v_1\}, ..., \{v_k, v'\}\}$.

2.2 Interpretation of Problem

For the lemmatisation of any word $w_i \mapsto \ell_i : w_i \in \mathcal{W}, \ell_i \in \mathcal{L}$, we must estimate the most appropriate synset $s_{i,*} \in S(\ell_i) = \{s_{i,1}, s_{i,2}, ..., s_{i,k}\}$. Our system associates a PD score $\phi(s_{i,j})$ for each

[1]While all words are lemmatised, this task strictly focuses on the WSD of noun phrases.

[2]This is sentence `d010.s014` in the English test data set.

[3]BabelNet 1.1.1 API & Sense Inventory - `http://lcl.uniroma1.it/babelnet/download.jsp`

[4]BabelNet 1.0.1 Paths - `http://lcl.uniroma1.it/babelnet/data/babelnet_paths.tar.bz2`

[5]Apache Lucene - `http://lucene.apache.org`

$s_{i,j} \in S(\ell_i)$ by taking $\mathcal{G}_\mathcal{L}$ as input. We estimate $s_{i,*}$, the most appropriate sense for ℓ_i, by $\hat{s}_{i,*} = \arg\max_{s_{i,j} \in S(\ell_i)} \phi(s_{i,j})$. It's worth noting here that $\mathcal{G}_\mathcal{L}$ ensures the estimation of $\hat{s}_{i,*}$ is not an independent scoring rule, since $\mathcal{G}_\mathcal{L}$ embodies the context surrounding ℓ_i via our sliding lemma-based window $\mathcal{L}$.

2.3 Peripheral Diversity Framework

PD is built on the following two ideas that are explained in the following subsections:

1. For a subgraph derived from one lone lemma ℓ_i, in which no other lemmas can provide context, the synset $s_{i,j} \in \mathcal{G}_{\ell_i}$ that has the largest and most semantically diverse set of peripheral synset nodes is assumed to be the MFS for ℓ_i.

2. For a larger subgraph derived from a sliding lemma window $\mathcal{L}$, in which other lemmas can provide context, the synset $s_{i,j} \in \mathcal{G}_\mathcal{L}$ that observes the largest increase in size and semantic diversity of its peripheral synset nodes is estimated to be $s_{i,*}$, the most appropriate synset for lemma ℓ_i.

Therefore PD is merely a framework that exploits these two assumptions. Now we will go through the process of estimating $s_{i,*}$ for a given lemma ℓ_i.

2.3.1 Pairwise Semantic Dissimilarity

First, for each synset $s_{i,j} \in \mathcal{S}$, we need to acquire a set of its peripheral synsets. We do this by travelling a depth of up to d (stopping if the path ends), then adding the synset we reach to our set of peripheral synsets $\mathcal{P}^{\leq d} = \{s_{j,1}, s_{j,2}, ..., s_{j,k'}\}$.

Next for every pair of synsets v and v' that are not direct neighbours in $\mathcal{P}^{\leq d}$ such that $v \neq v'$, we calculate their Pairwise Semantic Dissimilarity (PSD) $\delta(v, v')$ which we require for a synset's PD score. To generate our results for this task we have used the complement to Cosine Similarity, commonly known as the Cosine Distance as our PSD measure:

$$\delta(v, v') =$$

$$\begin{cases} 1 - \left(\frac{|O(v) \cap O(v')|}{\sqrt{|O(v)|}\sqrt{|O(v')|}} \right), & \text{if } |O(v)||O(v')| \neq 0 \\ 1, & \text{otherwise,} \end{cases}$$

where $O(v)$ is the outgoing (out-neighbouring) synsets for $v \in \mathcal{P}^{\leq d}$, and $|O(v)|$ denotes the number of elements in $O(v)$.

2.3.2 Peripheral Diversity Score

Once we have PSD scores for every permitted pairing of v and v', we have a number of ways to generate our $\phi(s_{i,j})$ values. To generate our results for this task, we chose to score synsets on the *sum of their minimum PSD values*, which is expressed formally below:

$$\phi(s_{i,j}) = \sum_{v \in \mathcal{P}^{\leq d}(s_{i,j})} \min_{\substack{v' \neq v \\ v' \in \mathcal{P}^{\leq d}(s_{i,j})}} \delta(v, v')$$

The idea is that this summing over the peripheral synsets in $\mathcal{P}^{\leq d}(s_{i,j})$ accounts for how frequently synset $s_{i,j}$ is used, then each increment in size is weighted by a peripheral synset's minimumal PSD across all synsets in $\mathcal{P}^{\leq d}(s_{i,j})$. Therefore peripheral set size and semantic diversity are rewarded simultaneously by ϕ. To conclude, the final estimated synset sequence for a given lemma sequence $(\ell_1, ..., \ell_m)$ based on ϕ is $(\hat{s}_{1,*}, \hat{s}_{2,*}, ..., \hat{s}_{m,*})$.

2.3.3 Strategies, Parameters, & Filters

Wikipedia's *Did You Mean?* We account for deviations and errors in spelling to ensure lemmas have the best chance of being mapped to a synset. Absent synsets in subgraph $\mathcal{G}_\mathcal{L}$ will naturally degrade system output. Therefore if $\ell_i \mapsto \emptyset$, we make an HTTP call to Wikipedia's *Did you mean?* and parse the response for any alternative spellings. For example in the test data set[6] the misspelt lemma: "feu_de_la_rampe" is corrected to "*feux*_de_la_rampe".

Custom Back-off Strategy As *back-off strategies*[7] have proved useful in (Navigli and Ponzetto, 2012a) and (Navigli et al., 2007), we designed our own back-off strategy. In the event our system provides a `null` result, the Babel synset $s_{i,j} \in S(\ell_i) = \mathcal{S}$ with the most senses associated with it will be chosen with preference to its region in BabelNet such that WIKIWN $\succ$ WN $\succ$ WIKI.

[6] Found in sentence `d001.s002.t005` in the French test data set.

[7] In the event the WSD technique fails to provide an answer, a back-off strategy provides one for the system to output.

Input Parameters We set our sliding window length $(b - a)$ to encompass 5 sentences at a time, in which the step size is also 5 sentences. For subgraph construction the maximum length $L = 3$. Finally we set our peripheral search depth $d = 3$.

Filters For the purposes of reproducibility only we briefly mention two filters we apply to our subgraphs that ship with the BabelNet API. We remove WordNet contributed domain relations with the `ILLEGAL_POINTERS` filter and apply the `SENSE_SHIFTS` filter. For more information on these filters we suggest the reader consult the BabelNet API documentation.

3 Results & Discussion

3.1 Results of SemEval Submission

	Language	DAEBAK!	$MFS_{Baseline}$	+/-
DE	*German*	59.10	68.60	-9.50
EN	*English*	60.40	65.60	-5.20
ES	*Spanish*	60.00	64.40	-4.40
FR	*French*	53.80	50.10	+3.70
IT	*Italian*	61.30	57.20	+4.10
	Mean	58.92	61.18	-2.26

Table 1: DAEBAK! vs MFS Baseline on BabelNet

As can be seen in Table 1, the results of our single submission were varied and competitive. The worst result was for German in which our system fell behind the MFS baseline by a margin of 9.50. Again for French and Italian we exceeded the MFS baseline by a margin of 3.70 and 4.10 respectively. Our Daebak back-off strategy contributed anywhere between 1.12% (for French) to 2.70% (for Spanish) in our results, which means our system outputs a result without the need for a back-off strategy at least 97.30% of the time. Overall our system was slightly outperformed by the MFS baseline by a margin of 2.26. Overall PD demonstrated to be robust across a range of European languages. With these preliminary results this surely warrants further investigation of what can be achieved with PD.

3.2 Exploratory Results

The authors observed some inconsistencies in the task answer keys across different languages as Table 2 illustrates. For each Babel synset ID found in the answer key, we record where its original source synsets are from, be it Wikipedia (WIKI), WordNet (WN), or both (WIKIWN).

	Language	WIKI	WN	WIKIWN
DE	*German*	43.42%	5.02%	51.55%
EN	*English*	10.36%	32.11%	57.53%
ES	*Spanish*	30.65%	5.40%	63.94%
FR	*French*	40.81%	6.55%	52.64%
IT	*Italian*	38.80%	7.33%	53.87%

Table 2: BabelNet Answer Key Breakdown

This is not a critical observation but rather an empirical enlightenment on the varied mechanics of different languages and the amount of development/translation effort that has gone into the contributing subparts of BabelNet: Wikipedia and WordNet. The heterogeneity of hybrid sense inventories such as BabelNet creates new obstacles for WSD, as seen in (Medelyan et al., 2013) it is difficult to create a disambiguation policy in this context. Future work we would like to undertake would be to investigate the heterogenous nature of BabelNet and how this affects various WSD methods.

4 Conclusion & Future Directions

To conclude PD has demonstrated in its early stages that it can perform well and even outperform the MFS baselines in certain experimental contexts. Furthermore it leaves a lot left to be explored in terms of what this approach is capable of via adjusting subgraph filters, strategies, and input parameters across both heterogenous and homogenous semantic graphs.

Acknowledgments

This research was completed with the help of the Korean Foundation Graduate Studies Fellowship[8].

5 Resources

The code base for this work can be found in the near future at `http://www.stevemanion.com/`.

[8]KF Graduate Studies Fellowship - `http://www.kf.or.kr/eng/01_sks/sks_fel_sfb01.asp`

References

Eneko Agirre and Philip Edmonds. 2007. Introduction. *Word Sense Disambiguation Algorithms and Applications*, Chapter 1:1-28. Springer, New York.

Eneko Agirre and Aitor Soroa. 2009. Personalizing PageRank for Word Sense Disambiguation. *In Proceedings of the 12th Conference of the European Chapter of the ACL*, April:33–41. Association for Computational Linguistics.

Yehoshua Bar-Hillel. 1960. The Present Status of Automatic Translation of Languages. *Advances in Computers*, 1:91–163.

Christiane Fellbaum. 1998, ed. *WordNet: An Electronic Lexical Database.*, Cambridge, MA: MIT Press.

William A Gale, Kenneth W Church, David Yarowsky. 1992. A Method for Disambiguating Word Senses in a Large Corpus. *Computers and the Humanities*, 26(5–6):415–439.

Michael Lesk. 1986. Automatic Sense Disambiguation Using Machine Readable Dictionaries: How to Tell a Pine Cone from an Ice Cream Cone. *Proceedings of the 5th Annual International Conference on System Documentation.*, 24–26. ACM.

Llus Màrquez, Gerard Escudero, David Martínez, German Rigau. 2007. Supervised Corpus-Based Methods for WSD. *Word Sense Disambiguation Algorithms and Applications*, Chapter 7:167-216. Springer, New York.

Rada Mihalcea. 2005. Unsupervised Large-Vocabulary Word Sense Disambiguation with Graph-based Algorithms for Sequence Data Labeling. *Proceedings of the conference on Human Language Technology and Empirical Methods in Natural Language Processing*, 411-418. Association for Computational Linguistics.

Rada Mihalcea. 2007. Knowledge-Based Methods for WSD. *Word Sense Disambiguation Algorithms and Applications*, Chapter 5:107–131. Springer, New York.

Alyona Medelyan, Steve Manion, Jeen Broekstra, Anna Divoli, Anna-lan Huang, and Ian H Witten. 2013. Constructing a Focused Taxonomy from a Document Collection *Extended Semantic Web Conference*, (Accepted, in press)

Roberto Navigli and Mirella Lapata. 2007. Graph connectivity measures for unsupervised word sense disambiguation. *IJCAI'07 Proceedings of the 20th International Joint Conference on Artifical Intelligence*, 1683–1688.

Roberto Navigli, Kenneth C Litkowski, and Orin Hargraves. 2007. SemEval-2007 Task 07: Coarse-Grained English All-Words Task. *In Proceedings of the 4th International Workshop on Semantic Evaluations*, 30–35.

Roberto Navigli and Mirella Lapata. 2010. An Experimental Study of Graph Connectivity for Unsupervised Word Sense Disambiguation. *IEEE transactions on pattern analysis and machine intelligence*, 32(4):678–692.

Roberto Navigli and Simone Paolo Ponzetto. 2012. BabelNet: The automatic construction, evaluation and application of a wide-coverage multilingual semantic network. *Artificial Intelligence*, 193:217–250.

Roberto Navigli and Simone Paolo Ponzetto. 2012. Multilingual WSD with Just a Few Lines of Code: the BabelNet API. *In Proceedings of the 50th Annual Meeting of the Association for Computational Linguistics*, 67–72.

Roberto Navigli, David Jurgens, and Daniele Vannella. 2013. SemEval-2013 Task 12: Multilingual Word Sense Disambiguation. *Proceedings of the 7th International Workshop on Semantic Evaluation (SemEval 2013), in conjunction with the Second Joint Conference on Lexical and Computational Semantcis (*SEM 2013).*

Frederic Nelson. 1976. Homographs *American Speech*, 51(3):296–297.

Ravi Sinha and Rada Mihalcea. 2007. Unsupervised Graph-based Word Sense Disambiguation Using Measures of Word Semantic Similarity. *Proceedings of IEEE International Conference on Semantic Computing.*

SemEval-2013 Task 3: Spatial Role Labeling

Oleksandr Kolomiyets[†], **Parisa Kordjamshidi**[†],
Steven Bethard[‡] and **Marie-Francine Moens**[†]
[†]KU Leuven, Celestijnenlaan 200A, Heverlee 3001, Belgium
[‡]University of Colorado, Campus Box 594 Boulder, Colorado, USA

Abstract

Many NLP applications require information about locations of objects referenced in text, or relations between them in space. For example, the phrase *a book on the desk* contains information about the location of the object *book*, as *trajector*, with respect to another object *desk*, as *landmark*. Spatial Role Labeling (SpRL) is an evaluation task in the information extraction domain which sets a goal to automatically process text and identify objects of spatial scenes and relations between them. This paper describes the task in Semantic Evaluations 2013, annotation schema, corpora, participants, methods and results obtained by the participants.

1 Introduction

Spatial Role Labeling at SemEval-2013 is the second iteration of the task, which was initially introduced at SemEval-2012 (Kordjamshidi et al., 2012a). The second iteration extends the previous work with an additional training corpus, which contains besides "static" spatial relations, annotated motions. Motion detection is a novel task for annotating trajectors (objects, which are moving), landmarks (spatial context in which the motion is performed), motion indicators (lexical triggers which signals trajector's motion), paths (a path along which the motion is performed), directions (absolute or relative directions of trajector's motion) and distances (a distance as a product of motion). For annotating motions the existing annotation scheme has been adapted with additional markables which are, all together, described below.

2 Spatial Annotation Schema

In this Section we describe the annotation format of spatial markables in text, and annotation guidelines for the annotators.

2.1 Spatial Annotation Format

Building upon the previous work, we used the notions of trajectors, landmarks and spatial indicators as introduced by Kordjamshidi *et al.* (2010). In addition, we further expanded the set of spatial roles labels with motion indicators, paths, directions and distances to capture fine-grained spatial semantics of *static* spatial relations (as the ones which do not involve motions), and to accommodate *dynamic* spatial relations (the ones which do involve motions).

2.1.1 Static Spatial Relations and their Roles

Static spatial relations are defined as relations between still objects, whereas one object plays a central role in the spatial scene, which is called *trajector*, and the second one plays a secondary role, and it is called *landmark*. In language, a spatial relation between two objects is usually implemented by a preposition (*in*, *on*, *at*, etc.) or a prepositional phrase (*on top of*, *inside of*, etc.).

A static spatial relation is defined as a tuple that contains a trajector, a landmark and a spatial indicator. In the annotation schema, these annotations are defined as follows:

Trajector: Trajector is a spatial role label assigned to a word or a phrase that denotes a central object of a spatial scene. For example:

- [$_{Trajector}$ *a lake*] *in the forest*

*Second Joint Conference on Lexical and Computational Semantics (*SEM), Volume 2: Seventh International Workshop on Semantic Evaluation (SemEval 2013)*, pages 255–262, Atlanta, Georgia, June 14-15, 2013.

- $[_{Trajector}$ *a flag*$]$ *on top of the building*

Landmark: Landmark is a spatial role label assigned to a word or a phrase that denotes a secondary object of a spatial scene, to which a possible spatial relation (as between two objects in space) can be established. For example:

- *a lake in* $[_{Landmark}$ *the forest*$]$
- *a flag on top of* $[_{Landmark}$ *the building*$]$

Spatial Indicator: Spatial Indicator is a spatial role label assigned to a word or a phrase that signals a spatial relation between objects (trajectors and landmarks) of a spatial scene. For example:

- *a lake* $[_{Sp\ indicator}$ *in*$]$ *the forest*
- *a flag*$]$ $[_{Sp\ indicator}$ *on top of*$]$ *the building*

Spatial Relation: Spatial Relation is a relation that holds between spatial markables in text as, e.g., between a trajector and a landmark and triggered by a spatial indicator. In spatial information theory the relations and properties are usually grouped into the domains of topological, directional, and distance relations and also shape (Stock, 1998). Three semantic classes for spatial relations were proposed:

- **Region.** This type refers to a region of space which is always defined in relation to a landmark, e.g., the interior or exterior. For example:

  a lake in the forest $\Longrightarrow$ ⟨Region, $[_{Sp\ indicator}$ *in*$]$, $[_{Trajector}$ *a lake*$]$, $[_{Landmark}$ *the forest*$]$⟩

- **Direction.** This relation type denotes a direction along the axes provided by the different frames of reference, in case the trajector of motion is not characterized in terms of its relation to the region of a landmark. For example:

  a flag on top of the building $\Longrightarrow$ ⟨Direction, $[_{Sp\ indicator}$ *on top of*$]$, $[_{Trajector}$ *a flag*$]$, $[_{Landmark}$ *the building*$]$⟩

- **Distance.** Type *Distance* states information about the spatial distance of the objects and could be a qualitative expression, such as *close*, far or quantitative, such as *12 km*. For example:

  the kids are close to the blackboard $\Longrightarrow$ ⟨Distance, $[_{Distance}$ *close*$]$, $[_{Trajector}$ *the kids*$]$, $[_{Landmark}$ *the blackboard*$]$⟩

2.1.2 Dynamic Spatial Relations

In addition to static spatial relations and their roles, SpRL-2013 introduces new spatial roles to capture *dynamic* spatial relations which involve motions. Let us demonstrate this with the following example:

(1) *In Brazil coming from the North-East I stepped into the small forest and followed down a dried creek.*

The text above describes a motion, and the reader can identify a number of concepts which are peculiar for motions: there is an object whose location is changing, the motion is performed in a specific spatial context, with a specific direction, and with a number of locations related to the object's motion.

There has been an enormous effort in formalizing and annotating motions in natural language. While annotating motions was out of scope for the previous SpRL task and SpatialML (Mani et al., 2010), the most recent work on the Dynamic Interval Temporal Logic (DITL) (Pustejovsky and Moszkowicz, 2011) presents a framework for modeling motions as a change of state, which adapts linguistic background considering path constructions and *manner-of-motion* constructions. On this basis the Spatiotemporal Markup Language (STML) has been introduced for annotating motions in natural language. In STML, a motion is treated as a change of location over time, while differentiating between a number of spatial configurations along the path. Being well-defined for the formal representations of motion and reasoning, in which representations either take explicit reference to temporal frames or reify a spatial object for a path, all the previous work seems to be difficult to apply in practice when annotating motions in natural language. It can be attributed to possible vague descriptions of path in natural language when neither clear temporal event ordering, nor distinction between the start, end or intermediate path point can be made.

In SpRL-2013, we simplify the previously introduced notion of path in order to provide practical motion annotations. For dynamic spatial relations we introduce the following roles:

Trajector: Trajector is a spatial role label assigned to a word or a phrase which denotes an object which moves, starts, interrupts, resumes a motion, or is forcibly involved in a motion. For example:

- ... *coming from the North-East* [$_{Trajector}$ *I*] *stepped into ...*

Motion Indicator: Motion indicator is a spatial role label assigned to a word or a phrase which signals a motion of the trajector along a path. In Example (1), a number of motion indicators can be identified:

- ... [$_{Motion}$ *coming*] *from the North-East I* [$_{Motion}$ *stepped into*] ... *and* [$_{Motion}$ *followed down*] ...

Path: Path is a spatial role label assigned to a word or phrase that denotes the path of the motion as the trajector is moving along, starting in, arriving in or traversing it. In SpRL-2013, as opposite to STML, the notion of path does not have the temporal dimension, thus whenever the motion is performed along a path, for which either a start, an intermediate, an end path point, or an entire path can be identified in text, they are labeled as path. In Example (1), a number of path labels can be identified:

- ... *coming* [$_{Path}$ *from the North-East*] *I stepped into* [$_{Path}$ *the small forest*] *and followed down* [$_{Path}$ *a dried creek*].

Landmark: The notion of path should not be confused with landmarks. For spatial annotations, landmark has been introduced as a spatial role label for a secondary object of the spatial scene. Being of great importance for static spatial relations, in dynamic spatial relations, landmarks are used to capture a spatial context of a motion as for example:

- *In* [$_{Landmark}$ *Brazil*] *coming from the North-East ...*

Distance: In contrast to the previous SpRL annotation standard, in which distances and directions have been uniformly treated as signals, in SpRL-2013 if the motion is performed for a certain distance, and such a distance is mentioned in text, the corresponding textual span is labeled as distance. Distance is a spatial role label assigned to a word or a phrase that denotes an absolute or relative distance of motion, or the distance between a trajector and a landmark in case of a static spatial scene. For example:

- [$_{Distance}$ *25 km*]
- [$_{Distance}$ *about 100 m*]
- [$_{Distance}$ *not far away*]
- [$_{Distance}$ *25 min by car*]

Direction: Additionally, if the motion is performed in a certain (absolute or relative) direction, and such a direction is mentioned in text, the corresponding textual span is annotated as direction. Direction is a spatial role label assigned to a word or a phrase that denotes an absolute or relative direction of motion, or a spatial arrangement between a trajector and a landmark. For example:

- [$_{Direction}$ *the North-West*]
- [$_{Direction}$ *northwards*]
- [$_{Direction}$ *west*]
- [$_{Direction}$ *the left-hand side*]

Spatial Relation: Similarly to static spatial relations, dynamic spatial relations are annotated by relations that hold between a number of spatial roles. The major difference to static spatial relations is the mandatory motion indicator[1]. For example:

- *In Brazil coming from the North-East I ...* $\Longrightarrow$ ⟨Direction, [$_{Sp\ indicator}$ *In*], [$_{Trajector}$ *I*], [$_{Landmark}$ *Brazil*], [$_{Motion}$ *coming*],[$_{Path}$ *from the North-East*]⟩
- ... *I stepped into the small forest and ...* $\Longrightarrow$ ⟨Direction, [$_{Trajector}$ *I*], [$_{Motion}$ *stepped into*],[$_{Path}$ *the small forest*]⟩
- ... *I* [...] *and followed down a dried creek.* $\Longrightarrow$ ⟨Direction, [$_{Trajector}$ *I*], [$_{Motion}$ *followed down*],[$_{Path}$ *a dried creek*]⟩

[1]All dynamic spatial relations were annotated with type *Direction*.

Corpus		Files	Sent.	TR	LM	SI	MI	Path	Dir	Dis	Relation
IAPR TC-12	Training	1	600	716	661	670	-	-	-	-	765
	Evaluation	1	613	872	743	796	-	-	-	-	940
Confluence Project	Training	95	1422	1701	1037	879	1039	945	223	307	2105
	Evaluation	22	367	497	316	247	305	240	37	87	598

Table 1: Corpus statistics for SpRL-2013 with respect to annotated spatial roles (trajectors (TR), landmarks (LM), spatial indicators (SI), motion indicators (MI), paths (Path), directions (Dir) and distances (Dis)) and spatial relations.

3 Corpora

The data for the shared task comprises two different corpora.

3.1 IAPR TC-12 Image Benchmark Corpus

The first corpus is a subset of the IAPR TC-12 image benchmark corpus (Grubinger et al., 2006). It contains 613 text files that include 1213 sentences in total, and represents an extension of the dataset previously used in (Kordjamshidi et al., 2011). The original corpus was available free of charge and without copyright restrictions. The corpus contains images taken by tourists with descriptions in different languages. The texts describe objects, and their absolute and relative positions in the image. This makes the corpus a rich resource for spatial information, however, the descriptions are not always limited to spatial information. Therefore, they are less domain-specific and contain free explanations about the images. For training we released 600 sentences (about 50% of the corpus), and used remaining 613 sentences for evaluations.

3.2 Confluence Project Corpus

The second corpus comes from the Confluence project that targets the description of locations situated at each of the latitude and longitude integer degree intersection in the world. This corpus contains user-generated content produced by, sometimes, non-native English speakers. We gathered the content by keeping the original orthography and formating. In addition, we stored the URLs of the descriptions and extracted the coordinates of the described confluence point, which might be interesting for further research. In total, the entire corpus contains 117 files with 1789 sentences (about 40,000 tokens). For training we released 95 annotated files with 1422 sentences, 2105 annotated relations in total. For evaluation we used 22 annotated files with 367 sentences. The statistics on both corpora are provided in Table 1.

3.3 Data Format

One important change to the data was made in SpRL-2013. In contrast to SpRL-2012, where spatial roles were annotated over "head words" whose indexes were part of unique identifiers, in SpRL-2013 we switched to span-based annotations. Moreover, in order to provide a single data format for the task, we transformed SpRL-2012 data into span-based annotations, in course of which, we identified a number of annotation errors and made further improvements for about 50 annotations.

For annotating the Confluence Project corpus we used a freely available annotation tool MAE created by Amber Stubbs (Stubbs, 2011). The resulting data format uses the same annotation tags as in SpRL-2012, but each role annotation refers to a character offset in the original text[2]. Spatial relations are composed of references to annotations by their unique identifiers. Similarly to SpRL-2012, we allowed annotators to provide non-consuming annotations, where entity mentions, for which spatial roles can be identified, are omitted in text but necessary for a spatial relation triggered by either a spatial indicator or a motion indicator. Two spatial roles are eligible for non-consuming annotations: trajectors and landmarks.

4 Tasks Descriptions

For the sake of consistency with SpRL-2012, in SpRL-2013 we proposed the following tasks:

[2]Due to paper length constraints we omit the BNF specifications for spatial roles and relations. For further data format information we refer the reader to the task description web page: `www.cs.york.ac.uk/semeval-2013/task3/`

- Task A: Identification of markable spans for **three types** of spatial annotations such as trajector, landmark and spatial indicator.

- Task B: Identification of tuples (triplets) that connect trajectors, landmarks and spatial indicators identified in Task A into spatial relations. That is, identification of spatial relations with **three markables** connected, and **without** semantic relation classification.

- Task C: Identification of markable spans for **all** spatial annotations such as trajector, landmark, spatial indicator, motion indicator, path, direction and distance.

- Task D: Identification of *n-tuples* that connect spatial markables identified in Task C into spatial relations. That is, identification of spatial relations **with as many participating markables as possible**, and **without** semantic relation classification.

- Task E: **Semantic classification** of spatial relations identified in Task D.

5 Evaluation Criteria and Metrics

System outputs were evaluated against the gold annotations, which had to conform to the role's Backus-Naur form. For Tasks A and C, the system annotations are spatial roles: spans of text associated with spatial role types. A system annotation of a role is considered correct if it has a minimal overlap of one character with a gold annotation and matches the role type of the gold annotation. For Tasks B and D, the system annotations are spatial relation tuples (of length 3 in task B, of length 3 to 5 in Task D) of references to markable annotations. A system annotation of a spatial relation tuple is considered correct if it is of the same length as the gold annotation, and if each spatial role in the system tuple matches each role in the gold tuple. A spatial role estimated by a system is considered correct if it matches a gold reference when having the same character offsets and markable types (strict evaluation settings). In addition we introduced relaxed evaluation settings, in which a minimal overlap of one character between a system and a gold markable references is required for a positive match under condition that the roles match. For Task E, the system annotations are spatial relation tuples of length 3 to 5, along with relation type labels. A system annotation of a spatial relation is considered correct if the spatial relation tuple is correct under the evaluation of Task D and the relation type of the system relation is the same as the relation type of the gold relation.

Systems were evaluated for each of the tasks in terms of precision (*P*), recall (*R*) and *F1*-score which are defined as follows:

$$Precision = \frac{tp}{tp + fp} \tag{1}$$

$$Recall = \frac{tp}{tp + fn} \tag{2}$$

where tp is the number of true positives (the number of instances that are correctly found), fp is the number of false positives (number of instances that are predicted by the system but not a true instance), and fn is the number of false negatives (missing results).

$$F_1 = 2 \cdot \frac{Precision \cdot Recall}{Precision + Recall} \tag{3}$$

6 System Description and Evaluation Results

UNITOR. The UNITOR-HMM-TK system addressed Tasks A,B and C (Bastianelli et al., 2013).

In Tasks A and C, roles are labeled by a sequence-based classifier: each word in a sentence is classified with respect to the possible spatial roles. An approach based on the SVM-HMM learning algorithm, formulated in (Tsochantaridis et al., 2006), was used. It is in line with other methods based on sequence-based classifier for Spatial Role Labeling, such as Conditional Random Fields (Kordjamshidi et al., 2011), and the same SVM-HMM learning algorithm (Kordjamshidi et al., 2012b). UNITOR's labeling approach has been inspired by the work in (Croce et al., 2012), where an SVM-HMM learning algorithm has been applied to the classical FrameNet-based Semantic Role Labeling. The main contribution of the proposed approach is the adoption of shallow grammatical features instead of the full syntax of the sentence, in order to avoid over-fitting on the training data. Moreover, lexical information has been generalized through the use

Run	Task	Evaluation	Label	P	R	F_1-score
UNITOR.Run1.1	Task A	relaxed	TR	0.684	0.681	0.682
			LM	0.741	0.835	0.785
			SI	0.967	0.889	0.926
	Task B	relaxed	Relation	0.551	0.391	0.458
		strict	Relation	0.431	0.306	0.358
UNITOR.Run1.2	Task A	relaxed	TR	0.682	0.493	0.572
			LM	0.801	0.560	0.659
			SI	0.968	0.585	0.729
	Task B	relaxed	Relation	0.551	0.391	0.458
		strict	Relation	0.431	0.306	0.358
UNITOR.Run2.1	Task A	relaxed	TR	0.565	0.317	0.406
			LM	0.661	0.476	0.554
			SI	0.612	0.481	0.538
	Task C	relaxed	TR	0.565	0.317	0.406
			LM	0.662	0.476	0.554
			SI	0.609	0.479	0.536
			MI	0.892	0.294	0.443
			Path	0.775	0.295	0.427
			Dir	0.312	0.229	0.264
			Dis	0.946	0.331	0.490

Table 2: Results of UNITOR for SpRL-2013 tasks (Task A, B and C).

of Word Space – a Distributional Model of Lexical Semantics derived from the unsupevised analysis of an unlabeled large-scale corpus (Sahlgren, 2006). Similarly to the approaches demonstrated in SpRL-2012, the proposed approach first classifies spatial and motion indicators, then, using these outcomes further spatial roles are determined. For classifying indicators, the classifier makes use of lexical and grammatical features like lemmas, part-of-speech tags and lexical context representations. The remaining spatial roles are estimated by another classifier additionally employing the lemma of the indicator, distance and relative position to the indicator, and the number of tokens composing the indicator as features.

In Task B, all roles found in a sentence for Task A are combined to generate candidate relations, which are verified by a Support Vector Machine (SVM) classifier. As the entire sentence is informative to determine the proper conjunction of all roles, a Smoothed Partial Tree Kernel (SPTK) within the classifier that enhances both syntactic and lexical information of the examples was applied (Croce et al., 2011). This is a convolution kernel that measures the similarity between syntactic structures, which are partially similar and whose nodes can be different, but are, nevertheless, semantically related. Each example is represented as a tree-structure which is directly derived from the sentence dependency parse, and thus allows for avoiding manual feature engineering as in contrast to the work of Roberts and Harabagiu (2012). In the end, the similarity score between lexical nodes is measured by the Word Space model.

UNITOR submitted two runs for the IAPR TC-12 Image benchmark corpus (we refer to them as to UNITOR.Run1.1 and UNITOR.Run1.2) and one run for the Confluence Project corpus (UNITOR.Run2.1), based on the models individually trained on the different corpora. The difference between UNITOR.Run1.1 and UNITOR.Run1.2 is that for UNITOR.Run1.1 the results are obtained for all spatial roles (also the ones that have no spatial relation), and UNITOR.Run1.2 only provided the roles for which also spatial relations were identified. The results are presented in Table 2.

Although, not directly comparable to the results in SpRL-2012, one may observe some common trends. First, similarly to the previous findings, the performance for recognition of landmarks and spatial indicators (Task A) on the IAPR TC-12 Image benchmark corpus is better than trajectors (F_1-scores of 0.785, 0.926 and 0.682 respectively), and spatial indicators is the "easiest" spatial role to recognize (F_1-score of 0.926).

In contrast, spatial role labeling on the Confluence Project corpus performs worse than on the IAPR TC-12 Image benchmark corpus (with F_1-scores of 0.406, 0.538 and 0.554 for trajectors, spatial indicators and landmarks respectively). Interestingly, the performance for landmarks is generally higher than for trajectors, which is in line with previous findings in SpRL-2012. The performance drop on the new corpus can be attributed to more complex text and descriptions, whereas multiple roles can be identified for the same span (for example, a path which spans over trajectors, landmarks and spatial indicators). For the new spatial roles of motion indicators, paths, directions and distances, the performance levels are overall higher than for trajectors with an exception of directions. Yet, the precision levels for new roles is much higher than the recall (0.892 vs. 0.294 for motion indicators, 0.775 vs. 0.295 for paths and 0.946 vs. 0.331 for distances). Directions turned out to be the most difficult role to classify (0.312, 0.229 and 0.264 for P, R and F_1-score respectively).

7 Conclusion

In this paper we described an evaluation task on Spatial Role Labeling in the context of Semantic Evaluations 2013. The task sets a goal to automatically process text and identify objects of spatial scenes and relations between them. Building largely upon the previous evaluation campaign, SpRL-2012, in SpRL-2013 we introduced additional spatial roles and relations for capturing motions in text. In addition, a new annotated corpus for spatial roles (including annotated motions) was produced and released to the participants. It comprises a set of 117 files with about 40,000 tokens in total.

With the registered number of 10 participants and the final number of submissions (only one) we can conclude that spatial role labeling is an interesting task within the research community, however sometimes underestimated in its complexity. Our further steps in promoting spatial role labeling will be a detailed description of the annotation scheme and annotation guidelines, analysis of the corpora and obtained results.

Acknowledgments

The presented research was supporter by the PARIS project (IWT - SBO 110067), TERENCE (EU FP7–257410) and MUSE (EU FP7–296703).

References

Emanuele Bastianelli, Danilo Croce, Roberto Basili, and Daniele Nardi. 2013. UNITOR-HMM-TK: Structured Kernel-based learning for Spatial Role Labeling. In *Proceedings of the Seventh International Workshop on Semantic Evaluation (SemEval 2013)*. Association for Computational Linguistics.

Danilo Croce, Alessandro Moschitti, and Roberto Basili. 2011. Structured Lexical Similarity via Convolution Kernels on Dependency Trees. In *Proceedings of the Conference on Empirical Methods in Natural Language Processing*, pages 1034–1046. Association for Computational Linguistics.

Danilo Croce, Giuseppe Castellucci, and Emanuele Bastianelli. 2012. Structured Learning for Semantic Role Labeling. *Intelligenza Artificiale*, 6(2):163–176.

Michael Grubinger, Paul Clough, Henning Müller, and Thomas Deselaers. 2006. The IAPR TC-12 Benchmark: A New Evaluation Resource for Visual Information Systems. In *International Workshop OntoImage*, pages 13–23.

Parisa Kordjamshidi, Marie-Francine Moens, and Martijn van Otterlo. 2010. Spatial Role Labeling: Task Definition and Annotation Scheme. In *Proceedings of the Seventh Conference on International Language Resources and Evaluation (LREC'10)*, pages 413–420.

Parisa Kordjamshidi, Martijn Van Otterlo, and Marie-Francine Moens. 2011. Spatial Role Labeling: Towards Extraction of Spatial Relations from Natural Language. *ACM Transactions on Speech and Language Processing (TSLP)*, 8(3):4.

Parisa Kordjamshidi, Steven Bethard, and Marie-Francine Moens. 2012a. Semeval-2012 Task 3: Spatial Role Labeling. In *Proceedings of the Sixth International Workshop on Semantic Evaluation*, pages 365–373. Association for Computational Linguistics.

Parisa Kordjamshidi, Paolo Frasconi, Martijn Van Otterlo, Marie-Francine Moens, and Luc De Raedt.

2012b. Relational Learning for Spatial Relation Extraction from Natural Language. In *Inductive Logic Programming*, pages 204–220. Springer.

Inderjeet Mani, Christy Doran, Dave Harris, Janet Hitzeman, Rob Quimby, Justin Richer, Ben Wellner, Scott Mardis, and Seamus Clancy. 2010. SpatialML: Annotation Scheme, Resources, and Evaluation. *Language Resources and Evaluation*, 44(3):263–280.

James Pustejovsky and Jessica L Moszkowicz. 2011. The Qualitative Spatial Dynamics of Motion in Language. *Spatial Cognition & Computation*, 11(1):15–44.

Kirk Roberts and Sanda M Harabagiu. 2012. UTD-SpRL: A Joint Approach to Spatial Role Labeling. In *Proceedings of the Sixth International Workshop on Semantic Evaluation*, pages 419–424. Association for Computational Linguistics.

Magnus Sahlgren. 2006. *The Word-space Model*. Ph.D. thesis, Stockholm University.

Oliviero Stock. 1998. *Spatial and Temporal Reasoning*. Springer-Verlag New York Incorporated.

Amber Stubbs. 2011. MAE and MAI: Lightweight Annotation and Adjudication Tools. In *Proceedings of the 5th Linguistic Annotation Workshop*, LAW V '11, pages 129–133, Stroudsburg, PA, USA. Association for Computational Linguistics.

Ioannis Tsochantaridis, Thorsten Joachims, Thomas Hofmann, Yasemin Altun, and Yoram Singer. 2006. Large Margin Methods for Structured and Interdependent Output Variables. *Journal of Machine Learning Research*, 6(2):1453.

SemEval-2013 Task 7: The Joint Student Response Analysis and 8th Recognizing Textual Entailment Challenge

Myroslava O. Dzikovska
School of Informatics, University of Edinburgh
Edinburgh, United Kingdom
m.dzikovska@ed.ac.uk

Rodney D. Nielsen
University of North Texas
Denton, TX, USA
Rodney.Nielsen@UNT.edu

Chris Brew
Nuance Communications
USA
cbrew@acm.org

Claudia Leacock
CTB McGraw-Hill
USA
claudia_leacock@mheducation.com

Danilo Giampiccolo
CELCT
Italy
giampiccolo@celct.it

Luisa Bentivogli
CELCT and FBK
Italy
bentivo@fbk.eu

Peter Clark
Vulcan Inc.
USA
peterc@vulcan.com

Ido Dagan
Bar-Ilan University
Israel
dagan@cs.biu.ac.il

Hoa Trang Dang
NIST
hoa.dang@nist.gov

Abstract

We present the results of the Joint Student Response Analysis and 8th Recognizing Textual Entailment Challenge, aiming to bring together researchers in educational NLP technology and textual entailment. The task of giving feedback on student answers requires semantic inference and therefore is related to recognizing textual entailment. Thus, we offered to the community a 5-way student response labeling task, as well as 3-way and 2-way RTE-style tasks on educational data. In addition, a partial entailment task was piloted. We present and compare results from 9 participating teams, and discuss future directions.

1 Introduction

One of the tasks in educational NLP systems is providing feedback to students in the context of exam questions, homework or intelligent tutoring. Much previous work has been devoted to the automated scoring of essays (Attali and Burstein, 2006; Shermis and Burstein, 2013), error detection and correction (Leacock et al., 2010), and classification of texts by grade level (Petersen and Ostendorf, 2009; Sheehan et al., 2010; Nelson et al., 2012). In these applications, NLP methods based on shallow features and supervised learning are often highly effective. However, for the assessment of responses to short-answer questions (Leacock and Chodorow, 2003; Pulman and Sukkarieh, 2005; Nielsen et al., 2008a; Mohler et al., 2011) and in tutorial dialog systems (Graesser et al., 1999; Glass, 2000; Pon-Barry et al., 2004; Jordan et al., 2006; VanLehn et al., 2007; Dzikovska et al., 2010) deeper semantic processing is likely to be appropriate.

Since the task of making and testing a full educational dialog system is daunting, Dzikovska et al. (2012) identified a key subtask and proposed it as a new shared task for the NLP community. Student response analysis (henceforth SRA) is the task of labeling student answers with categories that could

*Second Joint Conference on Lexical and Computational Semantics (*SEM), Volume 2: Seventh International Workshop on Semantic Evaluation (SemEval 2013)*, pages 263–274, Atlanta, Georgia, June 14-15, 2013. ©2013 Association for Computational Linguistics

Example 1	QUESTION	You used several methods to separate and identify the substances in mock rocks. How did you separate the salt from the water?
	REF. ANS.	The water was evaporated, leaving the salt.
	STUD. ANS.	The water dried up and left the salt.
Example 2	QUESTION	Georgia found one brown mineral and one black mineral. How will she know which one is harder?
	REF. ANS.	The harder mineral will leave a scratch on the less hard mineral. If the black mineral is harder, the brown mineral will have a scratch.
	STUD. ANS.	The harder will leave a scratch on the other.

Figure 1: Example questions and answers

help a full dialog system to generate appropriate and effective feedback on errors. System designers typically create a repertoire of questions that the system can ask a student, together with reference answers (see Figure 1 for an example). For each student answer, the system needs to decide on the appropriate tutorial feedback, either confirming that the answer was correct, or providing additional help to indicate how the answer is flawed and help the student improve. This task requires semantic inference, for example, to detect when the student answers are explaining the same content but in different words, or when they are contradicting the reference answers.

Recognizing Textual Entailment (RTE) is a series of highly successful challenges used to evaluate tasks related to semantic inference, held annually since 2005. Initial challenges used examples from information retrieval, question answering, machine translation and information extraction tasks (Dagan et al., 2006; Giampiccolo et al., 2008). Later challenges started to explore the applicability and impact of RTE technology on specific application settings such as Summarization and Knowledge Base Population (Bentivogli et al., 2009; Bentivogli et al., 2010; Bentivogli et al., 2011). The SRA Task offers a similar opportunity.

We therefore organized a joint challenge at SemEval-2013, aiming to bring together the educational NLP and the semantic inference communities. The goal of the challenge is to compare approaches for student answer assessment and to evaluate the methods typically used in RTE on data from educational applications.

We present the corpus used in the task (Section 2) and describe the Main task, including educational NLP and textual entailment perspectives and data set creation (Section 3). We discuss evaluation metrics and results in Section 4. Section 5 describes the Pilot task, including data set creation and evaluation results. Section 6 presents conclusions and future directions.

2 Student Response Analysis Corpus

We used the Student Response Analysis corpus (henceforth SRA corpus) (Dzikovska et al., 2012) as the basis for our data set creation. The corpus contains manually labeled student responses to explanation and definition questions typically seen in practice exercises, tests, or tutorial dialogue.

Specifically, given a question, a known correct 'reference answer' and a 1- or 2-sentence 'student answer', each student answer in the corpus is labelled with one of the following judgments:

- 'Correct', if the student answer is a complete and correct paraphrase of the reference answer;
- 'Partially_correct_incomplete', if it is a partially correct answer containing some but not all information from the reference answer;
- 'Contradictory', if the student answer explicitly contradicts the reference answer;
- 'Irrelevant' if the student answer is talking about domain content but not providing the necessary information;
- 'Non_domain' if the student utterance does not include domain content, e.g., "I don't know", "what the book says", "you are stupid".

The SRA corpus consists of two distinct subsets: BEETLE data, based on transcripts of students interacting with BEETLE II tutorial dialogue system (Dzikovska et al., 2010), and SCIENTSBANK data, based on the corpus of student answers to assessment questions collected by Nielsen et al. (2008b).

The BEETLE corpus consists of 56 questions in the basic electricity and electronics domain requiring 1- or 2- sentence answers, and approximately 3000 student answers to those questions. The SCIENTSBANK corpus contains approximately 10,000 answers to 197 assessment questions in 15 different science domains (after filtering, see Section 3.3)

Student answers in the BEETLE corpus were manually labeled by trained human annotators using a scheme that straightforwardly mapped into SRA annotations. The annotations in the SCIENTSBANK corpus were converted into SRA labels from a substantially more fine-grained scheme by first automatically labeling them using a set of question-specific heuristics and then manually revising them according to the class definitions (Dzikovska et al., 2012). We further filtered and transformed the corpus to produce training and test data sets as discussed in the next section.

3 Main Task

3.1 Educational NLP perspective

The 5-way SRA task focuses on associating student answers with categorical labels that can be used in providing tutoring feedback. Most NLP research on short answer scoring reports agreement with a numeric score (Leacock and Chodorow, 2003; Pulman and Sukkarieh, 2005; Mohler et al., 2011), which is a potential contrast with our task. However, the majority of the NLP work makes use of underlying representations in terms of concepts, so the 5-way task is still likely to mesh well with the available technology. Research on tutorial dialog has emphasized generic methods that use latent semantic analysis or other machine learning methods to determine when text strings express similar concepts (Hu et al., 2003; Jordan et al., 2004; VanLehn et al., 2007; McCarthy et al., 2008). Most of these methods, like the NLP methods, (with the notable exception of (Nielsen et al., 2008a)), are however strongly dependent on domain expertise for the definitions of the concepts. In educational applications, there would be great value in a system that could operate more or less unchanged across a range of domains and question-types, requiring only a question text and a reference answer supplied by the instructional designers. Thus, the 5-way classification task at SemEval was set up to evaluate the feasibility of such answer assessment, either by adapting the existing educational NLP methods to the categorical labeling task or by employing the RTE approaches.

3.2 RTE perspective and 2- and 3-way Tasks

According to the standard definition of Textual Entailment, given two text fragments called *Text* (T) and *Hypothesis* (H), it is said that T entails H if, typically, a human reading T would infer that H is most likely true (Dagan et al., 2006).

In a typical answer assessment scenario, we expect that a correct student answer would entail the reference answer, while an incorrect answer would not. However, students often skip details that are mentioned in the question or may be inferred from it, while reference answers often repeat or make explicit information that appears in or is implied from the question, as in Example 2 in Figure 1. Hence, a more precise formulation of the task in this context considers the entailing text T as consisting of both the original question and the student answer, while H is the reference answer.

We carried out a feasibility study to check how well the entailment judgments in this formulation align with the annotated response assessment, by annotating a sample of the data used in the SRA task with entailment judgments. We found that some answers labeled as "correct" implied inferred or assumed pieces of information not present in the text. These reflected the teachers' assessment of student understanding but would not be considered entailed from the traditional RTE perspective. However, we observed that in most such cases, a substantial part of the hypothesis was still implied by the text. Moreover, answers assigned labels other than "correct" were always judged as "not entailed".

Overall, we concluded that the correlation between assessment judgments of the two types was sufficiently high to consider an RTE approach. The challenge for the textual entailment community was to address the answer assessment task at varying levels of granularity, using textual entailment techniques, and explore how well these techniques can help in this real-world educational setting.

In order to make the setup more similar to previous RTE tasks, we introduced 3-way and 2-way versions of the task. The data for those tasks were obtained by automatically collapsing the 5-way labels. In the 3-way task, the systems were required to classify the student answer as either (i) *correct*; (ii) *contradictory*; or (iii) *incorrect* (combining the categories partially correct but incomplete, irrelevant and not in the domain from the 5-way classification).

In the two-way task, the systems were required to classify the student answer as either correct or incorrect (combining the categories contradictory and incorrect from the 3-way classification)

3.3 Data Preparation and Training Data

In preparation of the task four of the organizers examined all questions in the SRA corpus, and decided that to remove some of the questions to make the dataset more uniform.

We observed two main issues. First, a number of questions relied on external material, e.g., charts and graphs. In some cases, the information in the reference answer was sufficient to make a reasonable assessment of student answer correctness, but in other cases the information contained in the questions was deemed insufficient and the questions were removed.

Second, some questions in the SCIENTSBANK dataset could have multiple possible correct answers, e.g., a question asking for any example out of two or more unrelated possibilities. Such questions were also removed as they do not align well with the RTE perspective.

Finally, parts of the data were re-checked for reliability. In BEETLE data, a second manual annotation pass was carried out on a subset of questions to check for consistency. In SCIENTSBANK, we manually re-checked the test data. The automatic conversion from the original SCIENTSBANK annotations into SRA labels was not perfectly accurate (Dzikovska et al., 2012). We did not have the resources to check the entire data set. However, four of the organizers jointly hand-checked approximately 100 examples to establish consensus, and then one organizer hand-checked all of the test data set.

3.4 Test Data

We followed the evaluation methodology of Nielsen et al. (2008a) for creating the test data. Since our goal is to support systems that generalize across problems and domains (see Section 3.1), we created three distinct test sets:

1. **Unseen answers (UA)**: a held-out set to assess system performance on the answers to questions contained in the training set (for which the system has seen example student answers). It was created by setting aside a subset if randomly selected learner answers to each question included in the training data set.

2. **Unseen questions (UQ)**: a test set to assess system performance on responses to previously unseen questions but which still fall within the application domains represented in the training data. It was created by holding back all student answers to a subset of randomly selected questions in each dataset.

3. **Unseen domains (UD)**: a domain-independent test set of responses to topics not seen in the training data, available only in the SCIENTSBANK dataset. It was created by setting aside the complete set of questions and answers from three science modules from the fifteen modules in the SCIENTSBANK data.

The final label distribution for train and test data is shown in Table 1.

4 Main Task Results

4.1 Participants

The participants were invited to submit up to three runs in any combination of the tasks. Nine teams participated in the main task, most choosing to attempt all subtasks (5-way, 3-way and 2-way), with 1 team entering only the 5-way and 1 team entering only the 2-way task.

At least 6 (CNGL, CoMeT, CU, BIU, EHUALM, LIMSI) of the 9 systems used some form of syntactic processing, in most cases going beyond parts of speech to dependencies or constituency structure. CNGL emphasized this as an important aspect of the system. At least 5 (CoMeT, CU, EHUALM, ETS UKP) of the 9 systems used a system combination approach, with several components feeding into a final decision made by some form of stacked classifier. The majority of the systems used some kind

label	Beetle				SciEntsBank				
	train (%)	UA	UQ	Test-Total (%)	train (%)	UA	UQ	UD	Test-Total (%)
correct	1665 (0.42)	176	344	520 (0.41)	2008 (0.40)	233	301	1917	2451 (0.42)
pc_inc	919 (0.23)	112	172	284 (0.23)	1324 (0.27)	113	175	986	1274 (0.22)
contra	1049 (0.27)	111	244	355 (0.28)	499 (0.10)	58	64	417	539 (0.09)
irrlvnt	113 (0.03)	17	19	36 (0.03)	1115 (0.22)	133	193	1222	1548 (0.27)
non_dom	195 (0.05)	23	40	63 (0.05)	23 (0.005)	3	0	20	23 (0.004)
incorr-3way	1227 (0.31)	152	231	383 (0.30)	2462 (0.495)	249	368	2228	2845 (0.49)
incorr-2way	2276 (0.58)	263	475	538 (0.59)	2961 (0.596)	307	432	2645	3384 (0.58)

Table 1: Label distribution. Percentages in parentheses. UA, UQ, UD correspond to individual test sets.

of measure of text-to-text similarity, whether the inspiration was LSA, MT measures such as BLEU or in-house methods. These methods were emphasized as especially important by Celi, ETS and SoftCardinality. These impressions are based on short summaries sent to us by the participants prior to the availability of the full system descriptions. Check the individual system papers for detail.

4.2 Evaluation Metrics

For each evaluation data set (test set), we computed the per-class precision, recall and F_1 score. We also computed three main summary metrics: accuracy, macro-average F_1 and weighted average F_1.

Accuracy is the overall percentage of correctly classified examples.

Macroaverage is the average value of each metric (precision, recall, F_1) across classes, without taking class size into account. It is defined as $1/N_c \sum_c metric(c)$, where N_c is the number of classes (2, 3, or 5 depending on the task). Note that in the 5-way SciEntsBank dataset the 'non-domain' class is severely underrepresented, with only 23 examples out of 4335 total (see Table 1). Therefore, we calculated macro-averaged P/R/F_1 over only 4 classes (i.e. excluding the 'non-domain' class) for SciEntsBank 5-way data.

Weighted Average (or simply *weighted*) is the average value for each metric weighted by class size, defined as $1/N \sum_c |c| * metric(c)$ where N is the total number of test items and $|c|$ is the number of items labeled as c in gold-standard data.[1]

In general, macro-averaging favors systems that perform well across all classes regardless of class size. Accuracy and weighted average prefer systems that perform best on the largest number of examples, favoring higher performance on the most frequent classes. In practice, only a small number of the systems were ranked differently by the different metrics. We discuss this further in Section 4.7. Results for all metrics are available online, and this paper focuses on two metrics for brevity: weighted and macro-average F_1 scores.

4.3 Results

The evaluation results for all metrics and all participant runs are provided online.[2] The tables in this paper present the F_1 scores for the best system runs. Results are shown separately for each test set (TS), with the simple mean over the five TSs reported in the final column.

We used two baselines: the majority (most frequent) class baseline and a lexical overlap baseline described in detail in (Dzikovska et al., 2012). The performance of the baselines is presented jointly with system scores in the results tables.

For each participant, we report the single run with the best average TS performance, identified by the subscript in the run title, with the exception of ETS. With all other participants, there was almost always one run that performed best for a given metric on *all* the TSs. In the small number of cases where another run performed best on a given TS, we instead report that value and indicate its run with a subscript (these changes never resulted in meaningful changes in the performance rankings). ETS, on the other hand, sub-

[1]This metric is called *microaverage* in (Dzikovska et al., 2012). However, *microaverage* is used to define a different metric in tasks where more than one label can be associated with each data item (Tsoumakas et al., 2010). therefore, we use *weighted* average to match the terminology used by the `Weka` toolkit. The micro-average precision, recall and F_1 computed using the multi-label metric are all equal and mathematically equivalent to accuracy.

[2]`http://bit.ly/11a7QpP`

Dataset:	BEETLE		SCIENTSBANK			
Run	UA	UQ	UA	UQ	UD	Mean
$CELI_1$	0.423	0.386	0.372	0.389	0.367	0.387
$CNGL_2$	*0.547*	0.469	0.266	0.297	0.294	0.375
$CoMeT_1$	***0.675***	0.445	***0.598***	0.299	0.252	0.454
$EHUALM_2$	*0.566*	0.416_3	*0.525_3*	0.446	*0.437*	0.471
ETS_1	*0.552*	*0.547*	*0.535*	***0.487***	*0.447*	0.514
ETS_2	***0.705***	***0.614***	***0.625***	0.356	*0.434*	0.547
$LIMSIILES_1$	0.505	0.424	0.419	***0.456***	*0.422*	0.445
$SoftCardinality_1$	*0.558*	0.450	*0.537*	***0.492***	***0.471***	0.502
$UKP\text{-}BIU_1$	0.448	0.269	***0.590***	0.397_2	0.407	0.418
Median	0.552	0.445	0.535	0.397	0.422	0.454
Baselines:						
Lexical	0.483	0.463	0.435	0.402	0.396	0.436
Majority	0.229	0.248	0.260	0.239	0.249	0.245

Table 2: Five-way task weighted-average F_1

Dataset:	BEETLE 5way		SCIENTSBANK 4way			
Run	UA	UQ	UA	UQ	UD	Mean
$CELI_1$	0.315	0.300	0.278	0.286	0.269	0.270
$CNGL_2$	0.431	0.382	0.252	0.262	0.239	0.274
$CoMeT_1$	***0.569***	0.300	***0.551***	0.201	0.151	0.312
$EHUALM_2$	*0.526*	0.370_3	*0.447_3*	**0.353**	*0.340*	0.382
ETS_1	0.444	0.461	*0.467*	***0.372***	*0.334*	0.377
ETS_2	***0.619***	***0.552***	***0.581***	0.274	*0.339*	0.428
$LIMSIILES_1$	0.327	0.280	0.335	**0.361**	*0.337*	0.308
$SoftCardinality_1$	0.455	0.436	*0.474*	***0.384***	***0.375***	0.389
$UKP\text{-}BIU_1$	0.423	0.285	***0.560***	0.325_2	*0.348*	0.364
Median	0.444	0.370	0.467	0.325	0.337	0.367
Baselines:						
Lexical	0.424	0.414	0.375	0.329	0.311	0.333
Majority	0.114	0.118	0.151	0.146	0.148	0.129

Table 3: Five-way task macro-average F_1

mitted results for systems that were substantially different from one another, with performance varying from being the top rank to nearly the lowest. Hence, it seemed more appropriate to report two separate runs.[3] In the rest of the discussion *system* is used to refer to a row in the tables as just described.

Systems with performance that was not statistically different from the best results for a given TS are all shown in **bold** (significance was not calculated for the TS mean). Systems with performance statistically better than the lexical baseline are displayed in *italics*. Statistical significance tests were conducted using approximate randomization test (Yeh, 2000) with 10,000 iterations; $p \leq 0.05$ was considered statistically significant.

4.4 Five-way Task

The results for the five-way task are shown in Tables 2 and 3.

Comparison to baselines All of the systems performed substantially better than the majority class baseline ("correct" for both BEETLE and SCIENTSBANK), on average exceeding it on the TS mean by 0.21 on the weighted F_1 and 0.24 on the macro-average F_1. Six systems outperformed the lexical baseline on the mean TS results for the weighted F_1 and five for the macro-average F_1. Nearly all of the top results on a given TS (shown in bold in the tables) were statistically better than corresponding lexical baselines according to significance tests (indicated by italics in the tables).

Comparing UA and UQ/UD performance The BEETLE UA (BUA) and SCIENTSBANK UA (SUA) test sets represent questions with example answers in training data, while the UQ and UD test sets represent transfer performance to new questions and new domains respectively.

The top performers on UA test sets were $CoMeT_1$ and ETS_2, with the addition of $UKP\text{-}BIU_1$ on SUA. However, there was not a single best performer on UQ and UD sets. ETS_2 performed statistically better than all other systems on BEETLE UQ (BUQ), but it performed *statistically worse* than the lexical baseline on SCIENTSBANK UQ (SUQ), resulting in no overlap in the top performing systems on the two UQ test sets. $SoftCardinality_1$ performed statistically better than all other systems on SUD and was among the three or four top performers on SUQ, but was not a top performer on the other three TSs, generally not performing statistically better than the lexical baseline on the BEETLE TSs.

Group performance The two UA TSs had more systems that performed statistically better than the lexical baseline (generally six systems) than did the UQ TSs where on average only two systems performed statistically better than the lexical baseline. Over twice as many systems outperformed the lexical baseline on UD as on the UQ TSs. The top performing systems according to the macro-average F_1 were nearly identical to the top performing systems according to the weighted F_1.

[3]In a small number of cases, ETS's third run performed marginally better, see full results online.

4.5 Three-way Task

The results for the three-way task are shown in Tables 4 and 5.

Comparison to baselines All of the systems performed substantially better than the majority baseline ("correct" for BEETLE and "incorrect" for SCIENTSBANK), on average exceeding it on the TS mean by 0.28 on the weighted F_1 and 0.31 on the macro-average F_1. Five of the eight systems outperformed the lexical baseline on the mean TS results for the weighted F_1 and five on the macro-average F_1, and all top systems outperformed the lexical baseline with statistical significance.

Comparing UA and UQ/UD performance The top performers on both BUA and SUA were CoMeT_1 and ETS_2. As for the 5-way task there was no single best performer for UQ and UD sets, and no overlap in top performing systems on BUQ and SUQ test sets, with ETS_2 being the top performer on BUQ, but statistically worse than the baseline on SUQ and SUD. On the weighted F_1, SoftCardinality_1 performed statistically better than all other systems on SUD and was among the two statistically best systems on SUQ, but was not a top performer on BUQ or BUA/SUA TSs. On the macro-average F_1, UKP-BIU_1 became one of the statistically best performers on all SCIENTSBANK TSs but, along with SoftCardinality_1, never performed statistically better than the lexical baseline on the BEETLE TSs.

Group performance With the exception of SUA, only around two systems performed statistically better than the lexical baseline on each TS. The top performing systems were nearly the same according to the weighted F_1 and the macro-average F_1.

4.6 Two-way Task

The results for the two-way task are shown in Table 6. Because the labels are roughly balanced in the two-way task, the results on the weighted and macro-average F_1 are very similar and the top performing systems are identical. Hence this section will focus only on the macro-average F_1.

As in the previous tasks, all of the systems performed substantially better than the majority baseline ("incorrect" for all sets), on average exceeding it on the TS mean by 0.25 on the weighted F_1 and 0.30 on the macro-average F_1. However, just four of the nine systems in the two-way task outperformed the lexical baseline on the mean TS results. In fact, the average performance fell below the lexical baseline. The differences in the macro-average F_1 between the top results on a SCIENTSBANK TS and the corresponding lexical baselines were all statistically significant. Two of the top results on BUA were not statistically better than the lexical baseline, and all systems performed below the baseline on BUQ.

Dataset:	BEETLE		SCIENTSBANK			
Run	UA	UQ	UA	UQ	UD	Mean
CELI_1	0.519	0.463	0.500	0.555	0.534	0.514
CNGL_2	0.592	0.471	0.383	0.367	0.360	0.435
CoMeT_1	***0.728***	0.488	***0.707***	0.522	0.550	0.599
ETS_1	0.619	0.542	*0.603*	***0.631***	*0.600*	0.599
ETS_2	***0.723***	***0.597***	***0.709***	0.537	0.505	0.614
LIMSIILES_1	0.587	0.454	0.532	0.553	0.564	0.538
SoftCardinality_1	0.616	0.451	*0.647*	***0.634***	***0.620***	0.594
UKP-BIU_1	0.472	0.313	*0.670*	*0.573*	*0.577*$_2$	0.521
Median	0.604	0.467	0.625	0.554	0.557	0.566
Baselines:						
Lexical	0.578	0.500	0.523	0.520	0.554	0.535
Majority	0.229	0.248	0.260	0.239	0.249	0.245

Table 4: Three-way task weighted-average F_1

Dataset:	BEETLE		SCIENTSBANK			
Run	UA	UQ	UA	UQ	UD	Mean
CELI_1	0.494	0.441	0.373	0.412	0.415	0.427
CNGL_2	0.567	0.450	0.330	0.308	0.311	0.393
CoMeT_1	***0.715***	0.466	***0.640***	0.380	0.404	0.521
ETS_1	0.592	*0.521*	*0.477*	***0.459***	*0.439*	0.498
ETS_2	***0.710***	***0.585***	***0.643***	0.389	0.367	0.539
LIMSIILES_1	0.563	0.431	0.404	0.409	0.429	0.447
SoftCardinality_1	0.596	0.439	*0.555*	***0.469***	***0.486***	0.509
UKP-BIU_1	0.468	0.333	***0.620***	***0.458***	***0.487***	0.473
Median	0.580	0.446	0.516	0.411	0.422	0.485
Baselines:						
Lexical	0.552	0.477	0.405	0.390	0.416	0.448
Majority	0.191	0.197	0.201	0.194	0.197	0.196

Table 5: Three-way task macro-average F_1

4.7 Discussion

All of the systems consistently outperformed the most frequent class baseline. Beating the lexical overlap baseline proved to be more challenging, being achieved by just over half of the results with about half of those being statistically significant improvements. This underscores the fact that there is still a considerable opportunity to improve student

Dataset:	BEETLE		SCIENTSBANK			
Run	UA	UQ	UA	UQ	UD	Mean
$CELI_1$	0.640	0.656	0.588	0.619	0.615	0.624
$CNGL_2$	**0.800**	0.666	0.591_1	0.561	0.556	0.635
$CoMeT_1$	***0.833***	**0.695**	***0.768***	0.579	*0.670*	0.709
CU_1	0.778	**0.689**	0.603	0.638	*0.673*	0.676
ETS_1	**0.802**	**0.720**	*0.705*	*0.688*	*0.683*	0.720
ETS_2	***0.833***	**0.702**	***0.762***	0.602	0.543	0.688
$LIMSIILES_1$	0.723	0.641	0.583	0.629	0.648	0.645
$SoftCardinality_1$	0.774	0.635	*0.715*	***0.737***	***0.705***	0.713
$UKP\text{-}BIU_1$	0.608	0.481	0.726	0.669	0.666_2	0.630
Median	0.778	0.666	0.705	0.629	0.666	0.676
Baselines:						
Lexical	0.788	**0.725**	0.617	0.630	0.650	0.682
Majority	0.375	0.367	0.362	0.371	0.367	0.368

Table 6: Two-way task macro-average F_1

response assessment systems.

The set of top performing systems on the weighted F_1 for a given TS were also always in the top on the macro-average F_1, but a small number of additional systems joined the top performing set on the macro-average F_1. Specifically, one, three, and two results joined the top set in the five-way, three-way, and two-way tasks, respectively. In principle, the metrics could differ substantially, because of the treatment of minority classes, but in practice they rarely did. Only one pair of participants swap adjacent TS mean rankings on the macro-average F_1 relative to the weighted F_1 on the two-way task. On the five-way task, two pairs swap rankings and another participant moved up two positions in the ranking, ending at the median value.

Most (28/34) rank changes were only one position and most (21/34) were in positions at or below the median ranking. In the five-way task, a pair of systems, $UKP\text{-}BIU_1$ and ETS_1, had a meaningful performance rank swap on the macro-average F_1 relative to the weighted F_1 on the UD test set. Specifically, $UKP\text{-}BIU_1$ moved up four positions from rank 6, where it was not statistically better than the lexical baseline, to the second best performance.

Not surprisingly, performance on UA was substantially higher than on UQ and UD, since the UA is the only set which contains questions with example answers in training data. Performance on BUA was usually better than performance on SUA, most likely because BUA contains more similar questions and answers, focusing on a single science area, Electricity and Magnetism, compared to 12 distinct science topics in SUA). In addition, the BEETLE study participants may have used simpler language, since they were aware that they were talking to a computer system instead of writing down answers for human teachers to assess as in SCIENTSBANK.

Performance on BUQ versus SUQ was much more varied, presumably since there was no direct training data for either TS. For the five-way task, the best performance on the weighted F_1 measure for BUQ is 0.09 below the best result for BUA and the analogous decrease from SUA to SUQ is 0.13, with an additional 0.02 drop on SUD. On the two-way task, the best weighted F_1 for BUQ drops 0.11 from the best BUA value, but the decrease from SUA to SUQ is just 0.03, with another 0.03 drop to SUD. While the drop in performance is fairly similar from BUA to BUQ on all tasks and either metric, the decrease from SUA to SUQ seems to potentially be dependent on the task, ranging from 0.13 on the five-way task to 0.08 on the three-way task and 0.03 on the two-way task.

5 Pilot Task on Partial Entailment

The SCIENTSBANK corpus was originally developed to assess student answers at a very fine-grained level and contains additional annotations that break down the answers into "facets", or low-level concepts and relationships connecting them (henceforth, SCIENTSBANK Extra). This annotation aims to support educational systems in recognizing when specific parts of a reference answer are expressed in the student answer, even if the reference answer is not entailed as a whole (Nielsen et al., 2008b). The task of recognizing such partial entailment relationships may also have various uses in applications such as summarization or question answering, but it has not been explored in previous RTE challenges.

Therefore, we proposed a pilot task on partial entailment, in which systems are required to recognize whether the semantic relation between specific parts of the Hypothesis is expressed by the Text, directly or by implication, even though entailment might not be recognized for the Hypothesis as a whole, based on the SCIENTSBANK facet annotation.

Each reference answer in SCIENTSBANK data is broken down into facets, where a facet is a triplet consisting of two key terms (both single words and multi-words, e.g. *carbon dioxide, each other, burns out*) and a relation linking them, as shown in Figure 2. The student answers were then annotated with regards to each reference answer facet in order to indicate whether the facet was (i) expressed, either explicitly or by assumption or easy inference; (ii) contradicted; or (iii) left unaddressed. Considering the SCIENTSBANK reference answers as Hypotheses, the facets capture their atomic components, and facet annotations may correspond to the judgments on the sub-parts of the H which are entailed by T.

We carried out a feasibility study to explore this idea and to verify how well the facet annotations align with traditional entailment judgments. We focused on the reference answer facets labeled in the gold standard annotation as *Expressed* or *Unaddressed*. The working hypothesis was that *Expressed* labels assigned in SCIENTSBANK annotations corresponded to *Entailed* judgments in traditional textual entailment annotations, while *Unaddressed* labels corresponded to *No-entailment* judgments.

Similarly to the feasibility study reported in Section 3.2, we concluded that the correspondence between educational labels and entailment judgments was not perfect due to the difference in educational and textual entailment perspectives. Nevertheless, the two classes of assessment appeared to be sufficiently well correlated so as to offer a good testbed for partial entailment in a natural setting.

5.1 Task Definition

Given (i) a text T, made up of a Question and a Student Answer; (ii) a hypothesis H, i.e. the Reference Answer for that question and (iii) a facet, i.e. a pair of key terms in H, the task consists of determining whether T expresses, either directly or by implication, the same relationship between the facet words as in H. In other words, for each of H's facets the system assign one of the following judgments: *Expressed*, if the Student Answer expresses the same relationship between the meaning of the facet terms as in H; *Unaddressed*, if it does not.

Consider the example shown in Figure 2. For facet 3, the system must decide whether the same relation between the two terms *'contains'* and *'seeds'* in H (the reference answer) is expressed, explicitly or implicitly, in T (the combination of question and student response). If the student answer is '*The part of a plant you are observing is a fruit if it has seeds.*', the answer to the question is *'yes'* and the correct judgment is *'Expressed'*. But if the student says '*My rule is has to be sweet.*', T does not express the same semantic relationship between *'contains'* and *'seeds'* exhibited in H, thus the correct judgment is *'Unaddressed'*. Note that even though this is an exercise in textual entailment, student response assessment labels were used instead of traditional entailment judgments, due to the partial mismatch between the two assessment classes found in the feasibility study.

5.2 Dataset

We used a subset of the SCIENTSBANK Extra corpus (Nielsen et al., 2008b) with the same problematic questions filtered out as the main task (see Section 3.3). We further filtered out all the student answer facets which were labeled other than *'Expressed'* or *'Unaddressed'* in the gold standard annotation; the facets in which the relationship between the two key terms, as classified in the manual annotation, proved to be problematic to define and judge, namely *Topic, Agent, Root, Cause, Quantifier, Neg*; and inter-propositional facets, i.e. facets that expressed relations between higher-level propositions. Finally, the facet relations were removed from the dataset, leaving the relationship between the two facet terms unspecified so as to allow a more fuzzy approach to the inference problem posed by the exercise.

We used the same training/test split as reported in Section 3.4. The training set created from the Training SCIENTSBANK Extra corpus contains 13,145 reference answer facets, 5,939 of which were labeled as *'Expressed'* in the student answers and 7,206 as *'Unaddressed'*. The Test set was created from the SCIENTSBANK Extra unseen data and is divided into the same subsets as the main task (Unseen Answers, Unseen Questions and Unseen Domains). It contains 16,263 facets total, with 5,945 instances labeled as *'Expressed'*, and 10,318 labeled as *'Unaddressed'*.

5.3 Evaluation Metrics and Baselines

The metrics used in the Pilot task were the same as in the Main task, i.e. Overall Accuracy, Macroaverage

QUESTION:	What is your "rule" for deciding if the part of a plant you are observing is a fruit?
REFERENCE ANSWER:	If a part of the plant contains seeds, that part is the fruit.
FACET 1:	Relation *NMod_of* Term1 *part* Term2 *plant*
FACET 2:	Relation *Theme* Term1 *contains* Term2 *part*
FACET 3:	Relation *Material* Term1 *contains* Term2 *seeds*
FACET 4:	Relation *Be* Term1 *fruit* Term2 *part*

Figure 2: Example of facet annotations supporting the partial entailment task

Run	UA	UQ	UD	UA	UQ	UD
	Weighted Averaged			*Macro Average*		
Run1	0.756	0.71	0.76	0.7370	0.686	0.755
Run 2	0.782	0.765	0.816	0.753	0.73	0.804
Run 3	0.744	0.733	0.77	0.719	0.7050	0.761
Baseline	0.54	0.547	0.478	0.402	0.404	0.384

Table 7: Weighted-average and macro-average F_1 scores (*UA: Unseen Answers; UQ: Unseen Questions; UD Unseen Domains*)

.

and Weighted Average Precision, Recall and F_1, and computed as described in Section 4.2. We used only a majority class baseline, which labeled all facets as *'Unaddressed'*. Its performance is presented in Section 5.4 jointly with the system results.

5.4 Participants and results

Only one participant, UKP-BIU, participated in the Partial Entailment Pilot task. The UKP-BIU system is a hybrid of two semantic relationship approaches, namely (i) computing semantic textual similarity by combining multiple content similarity measures (Bär et al., 2012), and (ii) recognizing textual entailment with BIUTEE (Stern and Dagan, 2011). The two approaches are combined by generating indicative features from each one and then applying standard supervised machine learning techniques to train a classifier. The system used several lexical-semantic resources as part of the BIUTEE entailment system, together with SCIENTSBANK dependency parses and ESA semantic relatedness indexes from Wikipedia.

The team submitted the maximum allowed of 3 runs. Table 7 shows Weighted Average and Macro Average F_1 scores respectively, also for the majority baseline. The system outperformed the majority baseline on both metrics. The best performance was observed on Run 2, with the highest results on the Unseen Domains test set.

6 Conclusions and Future Work

The Joint Student Response Analysis and 8th Recognizing Textual Entailment challenge has proven to be a useful, interdisciplinary task using a realistic dataset from the educational domain. In almost all cases the best systems significantly outperformed the lexical overlap baseline, sometimes by a large margin, showing that computational linguistics approaches can contribute to educational tasks. However, the lexical baseline was not trivial to beat, particularly in the 2-way task. These results are consistent with similar findings in previous RTE exercises. Moreover, there is still significant room for improvement in the absolute scores, reflecting the interesting challenges that both educational data and RTE tasks present to computational linguistics.

The educational setting places new stresses on semantic inference technology because the educational notion of *'Expressed'* and the RTE notion of *'Entailed'* are slightly different. This raises the educational question of whether RTE can work in this setting, and the RTE question of whether this setting is meaningful for evaluating RTE system performance. The experimental results suggests that the answer to both questions is 'yes', a significant finding for both educators and RTE technologists going forward.

The Pilot task, aimed at exploring notions of partial entailment, so far not explored in the series of RTE challenges, has proven to be an interesting, though challenging exercise. The novelty of the task, namely performing textual entailment not on a pair of full texts, but between a text and a hypothesis consisting of a pair of words, may have represented a more complex task than expected for some textual entailment engines. Despite this, the encouraging results obtained by the team which carried out the exercise has shown that this partial entailment task is worthy of further investigation.

Acknowledgments

The research reported here was supported by the US ONR award N000141010085 and by the Institute of Education Sciences, U.S. Department of Education, through Grant R305A120808 to the University of North Texas. The opinions expressed are those of the authors and do not represent views of the Institute or the U.S. Department of Education. The RTE-related activities were partially supported by the Pascal-2 Network of Excellence, ICT-216886-NOE. We would also like to acknowledge the contribution of Alessandro Marchetti and Giovanni Moretti from CELCT to the organization of the challenge.

References

Yigal Attali and Jill Burstein. 2006. Automated essay scoring with e-rater v.2. *The Journal of Technology, Learning, and Assessment*, 4(3), February.

Daniel Bär, Chris Biemann, Iryna Gurevych, and Torsten Zesch. 2012. Ukp: Computing semantic textual similarity by combining multiple content similarity measures. In *Proceedings of the 6th International Workshop on Semantic Evaluation, held in conjunction with the 1st Joint Conference on Lexical and Computational Semantics*, pages 435–440, Montreal, Canada, June.

Luisa Bentivogli, Ido Dagan, Hoa Trang Dang, Danilo Giampiccolo, and Bernando Magnini. 2009. The fifth PASCAL recognizing textual entailment challenge. In *Proceedings of Text Analysis Conference (TAC) 2009.*

Luisa Bentivogli, Peter Clark, Ido Dagan, Hoa Trang Dang, and Danilo Giampiccolo. 2010. Thesixth PASCAL recognizing textual entailment challenge. In *Notebook papers and results, Text Analysis Conference (TAC).*

Luisa Bentivogli, Peter Clark, Ido Dagan, Hoa Trang Dang, and Danilo Giampiccolo. 2011. The seventh PASCAL recognizing textual entailment challenge. In *Notebook papers and results, Text Analysis Conference (TAC).*

Ido Dagan, Oren Glickman, and Bernardo Magnini. 2006. The pascal recognising textual entailment challenge. In J. Quiñonero-Candela, I. Dagan, B. Magnini, and F. d'Alché Buc, editors, *Machine Learning Challenges*, volume 3944 of *Lecture Notes in Computer Science*. Springer.

Myroslava O. Dzikovska, Johanna D. Moore, Natalie Steinhauser, Gwendolyn Campbell, Elaine Farrow, and Charles B. Callaway. 2010. Beetle II: a system for tutoring and computational linguistics experimentation. In *Proc. of ACL 2010 System Demonstrations*, pages 13–18.

Myroslava O. Dzikovska, Rodney D. Nielsen, and Chris Brew. 2012. Towards effective tutorial feedback for explanation questions: A dataset and baselines. In *Proc. of 2012 Conference of NAACL: Human Language Technologies*, pages 200–210.

Danilo Giampiccolo, Hoa Trang Dang, Bernardo Magnini, Ido Dagan, Elena Cabrio, and Bill Dolan. 2008. The fourth PASCAL recognizing textual entailment challenge. In *Proceedings of Text Analysis Conference (TAC) 2008*, Gaithersburg, MD, November.

Michael Glass. 2000. Processing language input in the CIRCSIM-Tutor intelligent tutoring system. In *Papers from the 2000 AAAI Fall Symposium, Available as AAAI technical report FS-00-01*, pages 74–79.

A. C. Graesser, K. Wiemer-Hastings, P. Wiemer-Hastings, and R. Kreuz. 1999. Autotutor: A simulation of a human tutor. *Cognitive Systems Research*, 1:35–51.

Xiangen Hu, Zhiqiang Cai, Max Louwerse, Andrew Olney, Phanni Penumatsa, and Art Graesser. 2003. A revised algorithm for latent semantic analysis. In *Proceedings of the 18th International Joint Conference on Artificial intelligence (IJCAI'03)*, pages 1489–1491, San Francisco, CA, USA. Morgan Kaufmann Publishers Inc.

Pamela W. Jordan, Maxim Makatchev, and Kurt VanLehn. 2004. Combining competing language understanding approaches in an intelligent tutoring system. In *Proc. of Intelligent Tutoring Systems Conference*, pages 346–357.

Pamela Jordan, Maxim Makatchev, Umarani Pappuswamy, Kurt VanLehn, and Patricia Albacete. 2006. A natural language tutorial dialogue system for physics. In *Proc. of 19th Intl. FLAIRS conference*, pages 521–527.

Claudia Leacock and Martin Chodorow. 2003. C-rater: Automated scoring of short-answer questions. *Computers and the Humanities*, 37(4):389–405.

Claudia Leacock, Martin Chodorow, Michael Gamon, and Joel R. Tetreault. 2010. *Automated Grammatical Error Detection for Language Learners*. Synthesis Lectures on Human Language Technologies. Morgan & Claypool Publishers.

Philip M. McCarthy, Vasile Rus, Scott A. Crossley, Arthur C. Graesser, and Danielle S. McNamara. 2008. Assessing forward-, reverse-, and average-entailment indices on natural language input from the intelligent tutoring system, iSTART. In *Proc. of 21st Intl. FLAIRS conference*, pages 165–170.

Michael Mohler, Razvan Bunescu, and Rada Mihalcea. 2011. Learning to grade short answer questions using semantic similarity measures and dependency graph alignments. In *Proceedings of the 49th Annual Meeting of the Association for Computational Linguistics: Human Language Technologies*, pages 752–762, Portland, Oregon, USA, June. Association for Computational Linguistics.

Jessica Nelson, Charles Perfetti, David Liben, and Meredith Liben. 2012. Measures of text difficulty: Testing their predictive value for grade levels and student performance. Technical report, Student Achievement Partners. `http://www.ccsso.org/Documents/2012/Measures%20ofText%20Difficulty_fina%l.2012.pdf`.

Rodney D. Nielsen, Wayne Ward, and James H. Martin. 2008a. Learning to assess low-level conceptual understanding. In *Proc. of 21st Intl. FLAIRS Conference*, pages 427–432.

Rodney D. Nielsen, Wayne Ward, James H. Martin, and Martha Palmer. 2008b. Annotating students' understanding of science concepts. In *Proceedings of the Sixth International Language Resources and Evaluation Conference, (LREC08)*, Marrakech, Morocco.

Sarah Petersen and Mari Ostendorf. 2009. A machine learning approach to reading level assessment. *Computer, Speech and Language*, 23(1):89–106.

Heather Pon-Barry, Brady Clark, Karl Schultz, Elizabeth Owen Bratt, and Stanley Peters. 2004. Advantages of spoken language interaction in dialogue-based intelligent tutoring systems. In *Proc. of ITS-2004 Conference*, pages 390–400.

Stephen G Pulman and Jana Z Sukkarieh. 2005. Automatic short answer marking. In *Proceedings of the Second Workshop on Building Educational Applications Using NLP*, pages 9–16, Ann Arbor, Michigan, June. Association for Computational Linguistics.

Kathryn M. Sheehan, Irene Kostin, Yoko Futagi, and Michael Flor. 2010. Generating automated text complexity classifications that are aligned with targeted text complexity standards. Technical Report RR-10-28, Educational Testing Service.

Mark D. Shermis and Jill Burstein, editors. 2013. *Handbook on Automated Essay Evaluation: Current Applications and New Directions*. Routledge.

Asher Stern and Ido Dagan. 2011. A confidence model for syntactically-motivated entailment proofs. In *Recent Advances in Natural Language Processing (RANLP 2011)*, pages 455–462, Hissar, Bulgaria, September.

Grigorios Tsoumakas, Ioannis Katakis, and Ioannis Vlahavas. 2010. Mining multi-label data. In Oded Maimon and Lior Rokach, editors, *Data Mining and Knowledge Discovery Handbook*, pages 667–685. Springer US.

Kurt VanLehn, Pamela Jordan, and Diane Litman. 2007. Developing pedagogically effective tutorial dialogue tactics: Experiments and a testbed. In *Proc. of SLaTE Workshop on Speech and Language Technology in Education*, Farmington, PA, October.

Alexander Yeh. 2000. More accurate tests for the statistical significance of result differences. In *Proceedings of the 18th International Conference on Computational linguistics (COLING 2000)*, pages 947–953, Stroudsburg, PA, USA. Association for Computational Linguistics.

ETS: Domain Adaptation and Stacking for Short Answer Scoring*

Michael Heilman and **Nitin Madnani**
Educational Testing Service
660 Rosedale Road
Princeton, NJ 08541, USA
{mheilman,nmadnani}@ets.org

Abstract

Automatic scoring of short text responses to educational assessment items is a challenging task, particularly because large amounts of labeled data (i.e., human-scored responses) may or may not be available due to the variety of possible questions and topics. As such, it seems desirable to integrate various approaches, making use of model answers from experts (e.g., to give higher scores to responses that are similar), prescored student responses (e.g., to learn direct associations between particular phrases and scores), etc. Here, we describe a system that uses stacking (Wolpert, 1992) and domain adaptation (Daume III, 2007) to achieve this aim, allowing us to integrate item-specific n-gram features and more general text similarity measures (Heilman and Madnani, 2012). We report encouraging results from the Joint Student Response Analysis and 8th Recognizing Textual Entailment Challenge.

1 Introduction

In this paper, we address the problem of automatically scoring short text responses to educational assessment items for measuring content knowledge.

Many approaches can be and have been taken to this problem—e.g., Leacock and Chodorow (2003), Nielsen et al. (2008), *inter alia*. The effectiveness of any particular approach likely depends on the the availability of data (among other factors). For example, if thousands of prescored responses are available, then a simple classifier using n-gram features may suffice. However, if only model answers (i.e., reference answers) or rubrics are available, more general semantic similarity measures (or even rule-based approaches) would be more effective.

It seems likely that, in many cases, there will be model answers as well as a modest number of prescored responses available, as was the case for the Joint Student Response Analysis and 8th Recognizing Textual Entailment Challenge (§2). Therefore, we desire to incorporate both task-specific features, such as n-grams, as well as more general features such as the semantic similarity of the response to model answers.

We also observe that some features may themselves require machine learning or tuning on data from the domain, in addition to any machine learning required for the overall system.

In this paper, we describe a machine learning approach to short answer scoring that allows us to incorporate both item-specific and general features by using the domain adaptation technique of Daume III (2007). In addition, the approach employs stacking (Wolpert, 1992) to support the integration of components that require tuning or machine learning.

2 Task Overview

In this section, we describe the task to which we applied our system: the Joint Student Response Analysis and 8th Recognizing Textual Entailment Challenge (Dzikovska et al., 2013), which was task 7 at SemEval 2013.

The aim of the task is to classify student responses to assessment items from two datasets represent-

*System description papers for SemEval 2013 are required to have a team ID (e.g., "ETS") as a prefix.

*Second Joint Conference on Lexical and Computational Semantics (*SEM), Volume 2: Seventh International Workshop on Semantic Evaluation (SemEval 2013)*, pages 275–279, Atlanta, Georgia, June 14-15, 2013.

ing different science domains: the Beetle dataset, which pertains to basic electricity and electronics (Dzikovska et al., 2010), and the Science Entailments corpus (SciEntsBank) (Nielsen et al., 2008), which covers a wider range of scientific topics.

Responses were organized into five categories: correct, partially correct, contradictory, irrelevant, and non-domain. The SciEntsBank responses were converted to this format as described by Dzikovska et al. (2012).

The Beetle training data had about 4,000 student answers to 47 questions. The SciEntsBank training data had about 5,000 prescored student answers to 135 questions from 12 domains (different learning modules). For each item, one or more model responses were provided by the task organizers.

There were three different evaluation scenarios: "unseen answers", for scoring new answers to items represented in the training data; "unseen questions", for scoring answers to new items from domains represented in the training data; and "unseen domains", for scoring answers to items from new domains (only for SciEntsBank since Beetle focused on a single domain).

Performance was evaluated using accuracy, macro-average F_1 scores, and weighted average F_1 scores.

For additional details, see the task description paper (Dzikovska et al., 2013).

3 System Details

In this section, we describe the short answer scoring system we developed, and the variations of it that comprise our submissions to task 7. We begin by describing our statistical modeling approach. Thereafter, we describe the features used by the model (§3.1), including the PERP feature that relies on stacking (Wolpert, 1992), and then the domain adaptation technique we used (§3.2).

Our system is a logistic regression model with ℓ_2 regularization. It uses the implementation of logistic regression from the scikit-learn toolkit (Pedregosa et al., 2011).[1] To tune the C hyperparameter, it uses a 5-fold cross-validation grid search (with $C \in 10^{\{-3,-2,\ldots,3\}}$).

During development, we evaluated performance using 10-fold cross-validation, with the 5-fold cross-validation grid search still used for tuning within each training partition (i.e., each set of 9 folds used for training during cross-validation).

3.1 Features

Our full system includes the following features.

3.1.1 Baseline Features

It includes all of the baseline features generated with the code provided by the task organizers.[2] There are four types of lexically-driven text similarity measures, and each is computed by comparing the learner response to both the expected answer(s) and the question, resulting in eight features in total. They are described more fully by Dzikovska et al. (2012).

3.1.2 Intercept Feature

The system includes an intercept feature that is always equal to one, which, in combination with the domain adaptation technique described in §3.2, allows the system to model the *a priori* distribution over classes for each domain and item. Having these explicit intercept features effectively saves the learning algorithm from having to use other features to encode the distribution over classes.

3.1.3 Word and Character n-gram Features

The system includes binary indicator features for the following types of n-grams:

- lowercased word n-grams in the response text for $n \in \{1, 2, 3\}$.
- lowercased word n-grams in the response text for $n \in \{4, 5, \ldots, 11\}$, grouped into 10,000 bins by hashing and using a modulo operation (i.e., the "hashing trick") (Weinberger et al., 2009).
- lowercased character n-grams in the response text for $n \in \{5, 6, 7, 8\}$

[1] The scikit-learn toolkit uses a one-versus-all scheme, using multiple binary logistic regression classifiers, rather than a single multiclass logistic regression classifier.

[2] At the time of writing, the baseline code could be downloaded at http://www.cs.york.ac.uk/semeval-2013/task7/.

3.1.4 Text Similarity Features

The system includes the following text similarity features that compare the student response either to a) the reference answers for the appropriate item, or b) the student answers in the training set that are labeled "correct".

- the maximum of the smoothed, uncased BLEU (Papineni et al., 2002) scores obtained by comparing the student response to each correct reference answer. We also include the word n-gram precision and recall values for $n \in \{1, 2, 3, 4\}$ for the maximally similar reference answer.
- the maximum of the smoothed, uncased BLEU scores obtained by comparing the student response to each correct training set student answer. We also include the word n-gram precision and recall values for $n \in \{1, 2, 3, 4\}$ for the maximally similar student answer.
- the maximum PERP (Heilman and Madnani, 2012) score obtained by comparing the student response to the correct reference answers.
- the maximum PERP score obtained by comparing the student response to the correct student answers.

PERP is an edit-based approach to text similarity. It computes the similarity of sentence pairs by finding sequences of edit operations (e.g., insertions, deletions, substitutions, and shifts) that convert one sentence in a pair to the other. Then, using various features of the edits and weights for those features learned from labeled sentence pairs, it assigns a similarity score. Heilman and Madnani (2012) provide a detailed description of the original PERP system. In addition, Heilman and Madnani (To Appear) describe some minor modifications to PERP used in this work.

To estimate weights for PERP's edit features, we need labeled sentence pairs. First, we describe how these labeled sentence pairs are generated from the task data, and then we describe the stacking approach used to avoid training PERP on the same data it will compute features for.

For the reference answer PERP feature, we use the Cartesian product of the set of correct reference answers ("good" or "best" for Beetle) and the set of student answers, using 1 as the similarity score (i.e., the label for training PERP) for pairs where the student answer is labeled "correct" and 0 for all others. For the student answer PERP feature, we use the Cartesian product of the set of correct student answers and the set of all student answers, using 1 as the similarity score for pairs where both student answers are labeled "correct" and 0 for all others.[3] We use 10 iterations for training PERP.

In order to avoid training PERP on the same responses it will compute features for, we use 10-fold stacking (Wolpert, 1992). In this process, the training data are split up into ten folds. To compute the PERP features for the instances in each fold, PERP is trained on the other nine folds. After all 10 iterations, there are PERP features for every example in the training set. This process is similar to 10-fold cross-validation.

3.2 Domain Adaptation

The system uses the domain adaptation technique from Daume III (2007) to support generalization across items and domains.

Instead of having a single weight for each feature, following Daume III (2007), the system has multiple copies with potentially different weights: a generic copy, a domain-specific copy, and an item-specific copy. For an answer to an unseen item (i.e., question) from a new domain in the test set, only the generic feature will be active. In contrast, for an answer to an item represented in the training data, the generic, domain-specific, and item-specific copies of the feature would be active and contribute to the score.

For our submissions, this feature copying approach was not used for the baseline features (§3.1.1) or the BLEU and PERP text similarity features (§3.1.4), which are less item-specific. Those features had only general copies. We did not test whether doing so would affect performance.

[3]The Cartesian product of the sets of correct student answers and of all student answers will contain some pairs of identical correct answers. We decided to simply include these when training PERP, since we felt it would be desirable for PERP to learn that identical sentences should be considered similar.

	Beetle		SciEntsBank		
Submission	**A**	**Q**	**A**	**Q**	**D**
Run 1	.5520	.5470	.5350	.4870	.4470
Run 2	**.7050**	**.6140**	.6250	.3560	.4340
Run 3	.7000	.5860	**.6400**	.4110	.4140
maximum	.7050	.6140	.6400	.4920	.4710
mean	.5143	.3978	.4568	.3769	.3736

Table 1: Weighted average F_1 scores for 5-way classification for our SemEval 2013 task 7 submissions, along with the maximum and mean performance, for comparison. "A" = unseen answers, "Q" = unseen questions, "D" = unseen domains (see §2 for details). Results that were the maximum score among submissions for part of the task are in bold.

3.3 Submissions

We submitted three variations of the system. For each variation, a separate model was trained for Beetle and for SciEntsBank.

- **Run 1**: This run included the baseline (§3.1.1), intercept (§3.1.2), and the text-similarity features (§3.1.4) that compare student responses to reference answers (but not those that compare to scored student responses in the training set).
- **Run 2**: This run included the baseline (§3.1.1), intercept (§3.1.2), and n-gram features (§3.1.3).
- **Run 3**: This run included all features.

4 Results

Table 1 presents the weighted averages of F_1 scores across the five categories for the 5-way subtask, for each dataset and scenario. The maximum and mean scores of all the submissions are included for comparison. These results were provided to us by the task organizers.

For conciseness, we do not include accuracy or macro-average F_1 scores here. We observed that, in general, the results from different evaluation metrics were very similar to each other. We refer the reader to the task description paper (Dzikovska et al., 2013) for a full report of the task results.

Interestingly, the differences in performance between the unseen answers task and the other tasks was somewhat larger for the SciEntsBank dataset than for the Beetle dataset. We speculate that this result is because the SciEntsBank data covered a more diverse set of topics.

Note that Runs 1 and 2 use subsets of the features from the full system (Run 3). While Runs 1 and 2 are not directly comparable to each other, Runs 1 and 3 can be compared to measure the effect of the features based on other previously scored student responses (i.e., n-grams, and the PERP and BLEU features based on student responses). Similarly, Runs 2 and 3 can be compared to measure the combined effect of all BLEU and PERP features.

It appears that features of the other student responses improve performance for the unseen answers task. For example, the full system (Run 3) performed better than Run 1, which did not include features of other student responses, on the unseen answers task for both Beetle and SciEntsBank.

However, it is not clear whether the PERP and BLEU features improve performance. The full system (Run 3) did not always outperform Run 2, which did not include these features.

We leave to future work various additional questions, such as whether student response features or reference answer similarity features are more useful in general, and whether there are any systematic differences between human-machine and human-human disagreements.

5 Conclusion

We have presented an approach for short answer scoring that uses stacking (Wolpert, 1992) and domain adaptation (Daume III, 2007) to support the integration of various types of task-specific and general features. Evaluation results from task 7 at SemEval 2013 indicate that the system achieves relatively high levels of agreement with human scores, as compared to other systems submitted to the shared task.

Acknowledgments

We would like to thank the task organizers for facilitating this research and Dan Blanchard for helping with scikit-learn.

References

Hal Daume III. 2007. Frustratingly easy domain adaptation. In *Proceedings of the 45th Annual Meeting of the Association of Computational Linguistics*, pages 256–263, Prague, Czech Republic, June. Association for Computational Linguistics.

Myroslava O. Dzikovska, Diana Bental, Johanna D. Moore, Natalie Steinhauser, Gwendolyn Campbell, Elaine Farrow, and Charles B. Callaway. 2010. Intelligent tutoring with natural language support in the BEETLE II system. In *Proceedings of Fifth European Conference on Technology Enhanced Learning (EC-TEL 2010)*.

Myroslava O. Dzikovska, Rodney D. Nielsen, and Chris Brew. 2012. Towards effective tutorial feedback for explanation questions: A dataset and baselines. In *Proceedings of the 2012 Conference of the North American Chapter of the Association for Computational Linguistics: Human Language Technologies*, pages 200–210, Montréal, Canada, June. Association for Computational Linguistics.

Myroslava O. Dzikovska, Rodney Nielsen, Chris Brew, Claudia Leacock, Danilo Giampiccolo, Luisa Bentivogli, Peter Clark, Ido Dagan, and Hoa Trang Dang. 2013. Semeval-2013 task 7: The joint student response analysis and 8th recognizing textual entailment challenge. In **SEM 2013: The First Joint Conference on Lexical and Computational Semantics*, Atlanta, Georgia, USA, 13-14 June. Association for Computational Linguistics.

Michael Heilman and Nitin Madnani. 2012. ETS: Discriminative edit models for paraphrase scoring. In **SEM 2012: The First Joint Conference on Lexical and Computational Semantics – Volume 1: Proceedings of the main conference and the shared task, and Volume 2: Proceedings of the Sixth International Workshop on Semantic Evaluation (SemEval 2012)*, pages 529–535, Montréal, Canada, 7-8 June. Association for Computational Linguistics.

Michael Heilman and Nitin Madnani. To Appear. Henry: Domain adapation and stacking for text similarity. In **SEM 2013: The Second Joint Conference on Lexical and Computational Semantics*. Association for Computational Linguistics.

C. Leacock and M. Chodorow. 2003. c-rater: Scoring of short-answer questions. *Computers and the Humanities*, 37.

Rodney D. Nielsen, Wayne Ward, and James H. Martin. 2008. Classification errors in a domain-independent assessment system. In *Proceedings of the Third Workshop on Innovative Use of NLP for Building Educational Applications*, pages 10–18, Columbus, Ohio, June. Association for Computational Linguistics.

Kishore Papineni, Salim Roukos, Todd Ward, and Wei-Jing Zhu. 2002. Bleu: a method for automatic evaluation of machine translation. In *Proceedings of 40th Annual Meeting of the Association for Computational Linguistics*, pages 311–318, Philadelphia, Pennsylvania, USA, July. Association for Computational Linguistics.

F. Pedregosa, G. Varoquaux, A. Gramfort, V. Michel, B. Thirion, O. Grisel, M. Blondel, P. Prettenhofer, R. Weiss, V. Dubourg, J. Vanderplas, A. Passos, D. Cournapeau, M. Brucher, M. Perrot, and E. Duchesnay. 2011. Scikit-learn: Machine learning in Python. *Journal of Machine Learning Research*, 12:2825–2830.

Kilian Weinberger, Anirban Dasgupta, John Langford, Alex Smola, and Josh Attenberg. 2009. Feature hashing for large scale multitask learning. In *Proceedings of the 26th Annual International Conference on Machine Learning*, ICML '09, pages 1113–1120, New York, NY, USA. ACM.

David H. Wolpert. 1992. Stacked generalization. *Neural Networks*, 5:241–259.

SOFTCARDINALITY: Hierarchical Text Overlap for Student Response Analysis

Sergio Jimenez, Claudia Becerra
Universidad Nacional de Colombia
Ciudad Universitaria,
edificio 453, oficina 114
Bogotá, Colombia
sgjimenezv@unal.edu.co
cjbecerrac@unal.edu.co

Alexander Gelbukh
CIC-IPN
Av. Juan Dios Bátiz, Av. Mendizábal,
Col. Nueva Industrial Vallejo
CP 07738, DF, México
gelbukh@gelbukh.com

Abstract

In this paper we describe our system used to participate in the Student-Response-Analysis task-7 at SemEval 2013. This system is based on text overlap through the soft cardinality and a new mechanism for weight propagation. Although there are several official performance measures, taking into account the overall accuracy throughout the two availabe data sets (Beetle and SciEntsBank), our system ranked first in the *2 way* classification task and second in the others. Furthermore, our system performs particularly well with "unseen-domains" instances, which was the more challenging test set. This paper also describes another system that integrates this method with the lexical-overlap baseline provided by the task organizers obtaining better results than the best official results. We concluded that the soft cardinality method is a very competitive baseline for the automatic evaluation of student responses.

1 Introduction

The Student-Response-Analysis (SRA) task consist in provide assessments of the correctness of student answers (A), considering their corresponding questions (Q) and reference answers (RA) (Dzikovska et al., 2012). SRA is the task-7 in the SemEval 2013 evaluation campaign (Dzikovska et al., 2013). The method used in our participation was basically text overlap based on the soft cardinality (Jimenez et al., 2010) plus a machine learning classifier. This method did not use any information external to the data sets except for a stemmer and a list of stop words.

The soft cardinality is a general model for object comparison that has been tested at text applications. Particularly, this text overlap approach has provided strong baselines for several applications, i.e. entity resolution (Jimenez et al., 2010), semantic textual similarity (Jimenez et al., 2012a), cross-lingual textual entailment (Jimenez et al., 2012b), information retrieval, textual entailment and paraphrase detection (Jimenez and Gelbukh, 2012). A brief description of the soft cardinality is presented in the next section.

The data for SRA consist of two data sets *Beetle* (5,199 instances) and *SciEntsBank* (10,804 instances) divided into training and test sets (76%-24% for *Beetle* and 46%-54% *SciEntsBank*). In addition, the test part of *Beetle* data set was divided into two test sets: "unseen answers" (35%) and "unseen questions" (65%). Similarity, *SciEntsBank* test part is divided into "unseen answers" (9%), "unseen questions" (13%) and "unseen domains" (78%). All texts are in English.

The challenge consists in predicting for each instance triple (Q, A, RA) an assessment of correctness for the student's answer. Three levels of detail are considered for this assessment: 2 way (*correct* and *incorrect*), 3 way (*correct*, *contradictory* and *incorrect*) and 5 way (*correct*, *incomplete*, *contradictory*, *irrelevant* and *non-in-the-domain*).

Section 3 presents the method used for the extraction of features from texts using the soft cardinality to provide a vector representation. In Section 4, the details of the system used to produce our predic-

*Second Joint Conference on Lexical and Computational Semantics (*SEM), Volume 2: Seventh International Workshop on Semantic Evaluation (SemEval 2013)*, pages 280–284, Atlanta, Georgia, June 14-15, 2013.

tions are presented. Besides, in that section a system that integrates our system with the lexical-overlap baseline proposed by the task organizers is also presented. This combined system was motivated by the observation that our system performed well in the *SciEntsBank* data set but poorly in *Beetle* in comparison with the lexical-overlap baseline. The results obtained by both systems are also presented in that section.

Finally in Section 5 the conclusions of our participation in this evaluation campaign are presented.

2 Soft Cardinality

The soft cardinality (Jimenez et al., 2010) of a collection of elements S is calculated with the following expression:

$$|S|' = \sum_{i=1}^{n} w_i \cdot \left(\sum_{j=1}^{n} \mathbf{sim}(s_i, s_j)^p \right)^{-1} \quad (1)$$

Having $S = \{s_1, s_2, \ldots, s_n\}$; $w_i \geq 0$; $p \geq 0$; $1 > \mathbf{sim}(x, y) \geq 0$, $x \neq y$; and $\mathbf{sim}(x, x) = 1$. The parameter p controls the degree of "softness" of the cardinality (the larger the "harder"). In fact, when $p \to \infty$ the soft cardinality is equivalent to classical set cardinality. The default value for this parameter is $p = 1$. The coefficients w_i are weights associated with each element, which can represent the importance or informative character of each element. The function **sim** is a similarity function that compares pairs of elements in the collection S.

3 Features from Cardinalities

It is commonly accepted that it is possible to make a fair comparison of two objects if they are of the same nature. If the objects are instances of a compositional hierarchy, they should belong to the same class to be comparable. Clearly, a house is comparable with another house, a wall with another wall and a brick with another brick, but walls and bricks are not comparable (at least not directly). Similarly, in text applications documents should be compared with documents, sentences with sentences, words with words, and so on.

However, a comparison measure between a sentence and a document can be obtained with different approaches. First, using the information retrieval approach, the document is considered like a very long sentence and the comparison is then straight forward. Another approach is to make pairwise comparisons between the sentence and each sentence in the document. Then, the similarity scores of these comparisons can be aggregated in a single score using average, max or min functions. These approaches have issues, the former ignores the sentence subdivision of the document and the later ignores the similarities among the sentences in the document.

In the task at hand, each instance is composed of a question Q, a student answer A, which are sentences, and a collection of reference answers RA, which could be considered as a multi-sentence document. The soft cardinality can be used to provide values for $|Q|'$, $|A|'$, $|RA|'$, $|Q \cap A|'$, $|A \cap RA|'$ and $|Q \cap RA|'$. The intersections that involve RA require a special treatment to tackle the aforementioned issues.

Let's start defining a word-similarity function. Two words (or terms) t_1 and t_2 can be compared dividing them into character q-grams (Kukich, 1992). The representation in q-grams of t_i can be denoted as $t_i^{[q]}$. Similarly, a combined representation using a range of q-grams of different length can be denoted as $t_i^{[q_1:q_2]}$. For instance, if t_1 ="home" then $t_1^{[2:3]}$={"ho","om","me","hom","ome"}. Thus, $t_1^{[q_1:q_2]}$ and $t_2^{[q_1:q_2]}$ representations can be compared using the Dice's coefficient to build a word-similarity function:

$$\mathbf{sim_{words}}(t_1, t_2) = \frac{2 \cdot \left| t_1^{[q_1:q_2]} \cap t_2^{[q_1:q_2]} \right|}{\left| t_1^{[q_1:q_2]} \right| + \left| t_1^{[q_1:q_2]} \right|} \quad (2)$$

Note that in eq. 2 the classical set cardinality was used, i.e $|x|$ means classical cardinality and $|x|'$ soft cardinality.

The function $\mathbf{sim_{words}}$ can be plugged in eq.1 to obtain the soft cardinality of a sentence S (using unitary weights $w_i = 1$ and $p = 1$):

$$|S|' = \sum_{i=1}^{|S|} \left(\sum_{j=1}^{|S|} \mathbf{sim_{word}}(t_i, t_j) \right)^{-1} \quad (3)$$

$\lvert X\rvert$		$\lvert Y\rvert$		$\lvert X\cup Y\rvert$	
BF1:	$\lvert Q\rvert'$	BF2:	$\lvert A\rvert'$	BF3:	$\lvert Q\cup A\rvert'$
BF2:	$\lvert A\rvert'$	BF4:	$\lvert RA\rvert''$	BF5:	$\lvert RA\cup A\rvert''$
BF1:	$\lvert Q\rvert'$	BF4:	$\lvert RA\rvert''$	BF6:	$\lvert RA\cup Q\rvert''$

Table 1: Basic feature set

Where t_i are the words in the sentence S .

The sentence-soft-cardinality function can be used to build a sentence-similarity function to compare two sentences S_1 and S_2 using again the Dice's coefficient:

$$\mathbf{sim}_{\mathbf{sent.}}(S_1,S_2)=\frac{2\cdot(|S_1|'+|S_2|'-|S_1\cup S_2|')}{|S_1|+|S_2|} \quad (4)$$

In this formulation $S_1\cup S_2$ is the concatenation of both sentences.

The eq. 4 can be plugged again into eq. 1 to obtain the soft cardinality of a "document" RA, which is a collection of sentences $RA=\{S_1,S_2\ldots,S_{|RA|}\}$:

$$|RA|''=\sum_{i=1}^{|RA|}|S_i|'\cdot\left(\sum_{j=1}^{|RA|}\mathrm{sim}(S_i,S_j)\right)^{-1} \quad (5)$$

Note that the soft cardinalities of the sentences $|S_i|'$ were re-used as importance weights w_i in eq. 1. These weights are propagations of the unitary weights assigned to the words, which in turn were aggregated by the soft cardinality at sentence level (eq. 3). This soft cardinality is denoted with double apostrophe because is a function recursively based in the single-apostrophized soft cardinality.

The proposed soft cardinality expressions are used to obtain the basic feature set presented in Table 1. The soft cardinalities of $|Q|'$, $|A|'$ and $|Q\cup A|'$ are calculated with eq. 3. The soft cardinalities $|RA|''$, $|RA\cup A|''$ and $|RA\cup Q|''$ are calculated with eq. 5. Recall that $Q\cup A$ is the concatenation of the question and answer sentences. Similarly, $RA\cup A$ and $RA\cup Q$ are the collection of reference answers adding A xor Q .

Starting from the basic feature set, an extended set, showed in Table 2, can be obtained from each one of the three rows in Table 1. Recall that $|X\cap Y|=|X|+|Y|-|X\cup Y|$ and $|X\setminus Y|=|X|-|X\cap Y|$. Consequently, the total number of features is 6 basic features plus 12 extended features multiplied by 3, i.e. 42 features.

EF1:	$\lvert X\cap Y\rvert$	EF2:	$\lvert X\setminus Y\rvert$
EF3:	$\lvert Y\setminus X\rvert$	EF4:	$\frac{\lvert X\cap Y\rvert}{\lvert X\rvert}$
EF5:	$\frac{\lvert X\cap Y\rvert}{\lvert Y\rvert}$	EF6:	$\frac{\lvert X\cap Y\rvert}{\lvert X\cup Y\rvert}$
EF7:	$\frac{2\cdot\lvert X\cap Y\rvert}{\lvert X\rvert+\lvert Y\rvert}$	EF8:	$\frac{\lvert X\cap Y\rvert}{\sqrt{\lvert X\rvert\cdot\lvert Y\rvert}}$
EF9:	$\frac{\lvert X\cap Y\rvert}{\min(\lvert X\rvert,\lvert Y\rvert)}$	EF10:	$\frac{\lvert X\cap Y\rvert}{\max(\lvert X\rvert,\lvert Y\rvert)}$
EF11:	$\frac{\lvert X\cap Y\rvert\cdot(\lvert X\rvert+\lvert Y\rvert)}{2\cdot\lvert X\rvert\cdot\lvert Y\rvert}$	EF12:	$\lvert X\cup Y\rvert-\lvert X\cap Y\rvert$

Table 2: Extended feature set

4 Systems Description

4.1 Submitted System

First, each text in the SRA data was preprocessed by tokenizing, lowercasing, stop-words[1] removing and stemming with the Porter's algorithm (Porter, 1980). Second, each stemmed word t was represented in q-grams: $t^{[3:4]}$ for *Beetle* and $t^{[4]}$ for *SciEntsBank*. These representations obtained the best accuracies in the training data sets.

Two vector data sets were obtained extracting the 42 features–described in Section 3–for each instance in *Beetle* and *SciEntsBank* separately. Then, three classification models (*2 way*, *3way* and *5 way*) were learned from the training partitions on each vector data set using a J48 graft tree (Webb, 1999). All 6 resulting classification models were boosted with 15 iterations of bagging (Breiman, 1996). The used implementation of this classifier was that included in WEKA v.3.6.9 (Hall et al., 2009). The results obtained by this system are shown in Table 3 in the rows labeled with "Soft Cardinality-run1".

4.2 An Improved System

At the time when the official results were released, we observed that our submitted system performed pretty well in *SciEntsBank* but poorly in *Beetle*. Moreover, the lexical-overlap baseline outperformed our system in *Beetle*. Firstly, we decided to include in our feature set the 8 features of the lexical overlap baseline described by Dzikovska et al. (2012)

[1]those provided by `nltk.org`

		Beetle			SciEntsBank					
Task	System	UA[1]	UQ[2]	All	UA[1]	UQ[2]	UD[3]	All	All	Rank
2 way	*Soft Cardinality-unofficial*	*0.797*	*0.725*	*0.750*	*0.717*	*0.733*	*0.726*	*0.726*	***0.730***	-
	Soft Cardinality-run1	0.781	0.667	0.707	0.724	0.745	0.711	0.716	0.715	1
	ETS-run1	0.811	0.741	0.765	0.722	0.711	0.698	0.702	0.713	2
	CU-run1	0.786	0.718	0.742	0.656	0.674	0.693	0.687	0.697	3
	Lexical overlap baseline	0.797	0.740	0.760	0.661	0.674	0.676	0.674	0.690	6
3 way	*Soft Cardinality-unofficial*	*0.608*	*0.532*	*0.559*	*0.656*	*0.671*	*0.646*	*0.650*	***0.634***	-
	ETS-run1	0.633	0.551	0.580	0.626	0.663	0.632	0.635	0.625	1
	Soft Cardinality-run1	0.624	0.453	0.513	0.659	0.652	0.637	0.641	0.618	2
	CoMeT-run1	0.731	0.518	0.592	0.713	0.546	0.579	0.587	0.588	3
	Lexical overlap baseline	0.595	0.512	0.541	0.556	0.540	0.577	0.570	0.565	8
5way	*Soft Cardinality-unofficial*	*0.572*	*0.476*	*0.510*	*0.552*	*0.520*	*0.534*	*0.534*	***0.530***	-
	ETS-run1	0.574	0.560	0.565	0.543	0.532	0.501	0.509	0.519	1
	Soft Cardinality-run1	0.576	0.451	0.495	0.544	0.525	0.512	0.517	0.513	2
	ETS-run2	0.715	0.621	0.654	0.631	0.401	0.476	0.481	0.512	3
	Lexical overlap baseline	0.519	0.480	0.494	0.437	0.413	0.415	0.417	0.430	11
Total number of test instances		439	819	1,258	540	733	4,562	5,835	7,093	

TEST SETS: unseen answers[1], unseen questions[2], unseen domains[3].

Table 3: Official results for the top-3 performing systems (among 15), the lexical overlap baseline in the SRA task SemEval 2013 and unofficial results of the soft cardinality system combined with the lexical overlap (in italics). Performance measure used: overall accuracy.

(see Text::Similarity::Overlaps[2] package for more details).

Secondly, the lexical overlap baseline aggregates the pairwise scores between each reference answer and the student answer by taking the maximum value of the pairwise scores. So, we decided to use this aggregation mechanism instead of the aggregation proposed through eq. 3.

Thirdly, only at that time we realized that, unlike *Beetle*, in *SciEntsBank* all instances have only one reference answer. Consequently, the only effect of eq. 5 in *SciEntsBank* was in the calculation of $|RA \cup A|''$ (and $|RA \cup Q|''$) by $|X \cup Y|'' = \frac{|X|'+|Y|'}{1+\mathbf{sim}_{\mathbf{sent.}}(X,Y)}$. As a result, this transformation induced a boosting effect in $X \cap Y$ making $|X \cap Y|'' \geq |X \cap Y|'$ for any X, Y. We decided to use this intersection-boosting effect not only in $RA \cap A$, $RA \cap Q$, but in $Q \cap A$. This intersecton boosting effect works similarly to the Lesk's measure (Lesk, 1986) included in the lexical overlap baseline.

The individual effect in the performance of each of the previous decisions was positive in all three cases. The results obtained using an improved system that implemented those three decisions are shown in Table 3–in italics. This system would have obtained the best general overall accuracy in the official ranking.

5 Conclusions

We participated in the Student-Response-Analysis task-7 in SemEval 2013 with a text overlap system based on the soft cardinality. This system obtained places 1st (*2 way* task) and 2nd (*3 way* and *5 way*) considering the overall accuracy across all data sets and test sets. Particularly, our system was the best in the largest and more challenging test set, namely "unseen domains". Moreover, we integrated the lexical overlap baseline to our system obtaining even better results.

As a conclusion, the text overlap method based on the soft cardinality is very challenging base line for the SRA task.

[2]http://search.cpan.org/dist/Text-Similarity/lib/Text/Similarity/Overlaps.pm

Acknowledgments

This research was funded in part by the Systems and Industrial Engineering Department, the Office of Student Welfare of the National University of Colombia, Bogotá, and through a grant from the Colombian Department for Science, Technology and Innovation, Colciencias, proj. 1101-521-28465 with funding from "El Patrimonio Autónomo Fondo Nacional de Financiamiento para la Ciencia, la Tecnología y la Innovación, Francisco José de Caldas." The third author recognizes the support from Mexican Government (SNI, COFAA-IPN, SIP 20131702, CONACYT 50206-H) and CONACYT–DST India (proj. 122030 "Answer Validation through Textual Entailment").

References

Leo Breiman. 1996. Bagging predictors. *Machine Learning*, 24(2):123–140.

Myroslava O. Dzikovska, Rodney D. Nielsen, and Chris Brew. 2012. Towards effective tutorial feedback for explanation questions: a dataset and baselines. In *Proceedings of the 2012 Conference of the North American Chapter of the Association for Computational Linguistics: Human Language Technologies*, NAACL HLT '12, page 200–210, Stroudsburg, PA, USA. Association for Computational Linguistics.

Myroslava O. Dzikovska, Rodney D. Nielsen, Chris Brew, Claudia Leacock, Danilo Giampiccolo, Luisa Bentivogli, Peter Clark, Ido Dagan, and Hoa Trang Dang. 2013. SemEval-2013 task 7: The joint student response analysis and 8th recognizing textual entailment challenge. In *Proceedings of the 7th International Workshop on Semantic Evaluation (SemEval 2013), in conjunction with the Second Joint Conference on Lexical and Computational Semantcis (*SEM 2013)*, Atlanta, Georgia, USA, June. Association for Computational Linguistics.

Mark Hall, Frank Eibe, Geoffrey Holmes, and Bernhard Pfahringer. 2009. The WEKA data mining software: An update. *SIGKDD Explorations*, 11(1):10–18.

Sergio Jimenez and Alexander Gelbukh. 2012. Baselines for natural language processing tasks. *Appl. Comput. Math.*, 11(2):180–199.

Sergio Jimenez, Fabio Gonzalez, and Alexander Gelbukh. 2010. Text comparison using soft cardinality. In Edgar Chavez and Stefano Lonardi, editors, *String Processing and Information Retrieval*, volume 6393 of *LNCS*, pages 297–302. Springer, Berlin, Heidelberg.

Sergio Jimenez, Claudia Becerra, and Alexander Gelbukh. 2012a. Soft cardinality: A parameterized similarity function for text comparison. In *Proceedings of the 6th International Workshop on Semantic Evaluation (SemEval, *SEM 2012)*, Montreal, Canada.

Sergio Jimenez, Claudia Becerra, and Alexander Gelbukh. 2012b. Soft cardinality+ ML: learning adaptive similarity functions for cross-lingual textual entailment. In *Proceedings of the 6th International Workshop on Semantic Evaluation (SemEval, *SEM 2012)*, Montreal, Canada. ACL.

Karen Kukich. 1992. Techniques for automatically correcting words in text. *ACM Computing Surveys*, 24:377–439, December.

Michael Lesk. 1986. Automatic sense disambiguation using machine readable dictionaries: how to tell a pine cone from an ice cream cone. In *Proceedings of the 5th annual international conference on Systems documentation*, SIGDOC '86, page 24–26, New York, NY, USA. ACM.

Martin Porter. 1980. An algorithm for suffix stripping. *Program*, 3(14):130–137, October.

Geoffrey I. Webb. 1999. Decision tree grafting from the all-tests-but-one partition. In *Proceedings of the 16th international joint conference on Artificial intelligence - Volume 2*, IJCAI'99, pages 702–707, San Francisco, CA, USA. Morgan Kaufmann Publishers Inc.

UKP-BIU: Similarity and Entailment Metrics for Student Response Analysis

Torsten Zesch[†] **Omer Levy**[§] **Iryna Gurevych**[†] **Ido Dagan**[§]

† Ubiquitous Knowledge Processing Lab
Computer Science Department
Technische Universität Darmstadt

§ Natural Language Processing Lab
Computer Science Department
Bar-Ilan University

Abstract

Our system combines text similarity measures with a textual entailment system. In the main task, we focused on the influence of lexicalized versus unlexicalized features, and how they affect performance on unseen questions and domains. We also participated in the pilot partial entailment task, where our system significantly outperforms a strong baseline.

1 Introduction

The Joint Student Response Analysis and 8th Recognizing Textual Entailment Challenge (Dzikovska et al., 2013) brings together two important dimensions of Natural Language Processing: real-world applications and semantic inference technologies. The challenge focuses on the domain of middle-school quizzes, and attempts to emulate the meticulous marking process that teachers do on a daily basis. Given a question, a reference answer, and a student's answer, the task is to determine whether the student answered correctly. While this is not a new task in itself, the challenge focuses on employing textual entailment technologies as the backbone of this educational application. As a consequence, we formalize the question "Did the student answer correctly?" as "Can the reference answer be inferred from the student's answer?". This question can (hopefully) be answered by a textual entailment system (Dagan et al., 2009).

The challenge contains two tasks: In the **main task**, the system must analyze each answer as a whole. There are three settings, where each one defines "correct" in a different resolution. The highest-resolution setting defines five different classes or "correctness values": correct, partially correct, contradictory, irrelevant, non-domain. In the **pilot task**, critical elements of the answer need to be analyzed separately. Each such element is called a *facet*, and is defined as a pair of words that are critical in answering the question. As there is a substantial difference between the two tasks, we designed sibling architectures for each task, and divide the main part of the paper accordingly.

Our goal is to provide a robust architecture for student response analysis, that can generalize and perform well in multiple domains. Moreover, we are interested in evaluating how well general-purpose technologies will perform in this setting. We therefore approach the challenge by combining two such technologies: **DKPro Similarity** –an extensive suite of text similarity measures– that has been successfully applied in other settings like the SemEval 2012 task on semantic textual similarity (Bär et al., 2012a) or reuse detection (Bär et al., 2012b).

BIUTEE, the Bar-Ilan University Textual Entailment Engine (Stern and Dagan, 2011), which has shown state-of-the-art performance on recognizing textual entailment challenges. Our systems use both technologies to extract features, and combine them in a supervised model. Indeed, this approach works relatively well (with respect to other entries in the challenge), especially in unseen domains.

2 Background

2.1 Text Similarity

Text similarity is a bidirectional, continuous function which operates on pairs of texts of any length and returns a numeric score of how similar one text is to the other. In previous work (Mihalcea et al.,

*Second Joint Conference on Lexical and Computational Semantics (*SEM), Volume 2: Seventh International Workshop on Semantic Evaluation (SemEval 2013)*, pages 285–289, Atlanta, Georgia, June 14-15, 2013.

2006; Gabrilovich and Markovitch, 2007; Landauer et al., 1998), only a single text similarity measure has typically been applied to text pairs. However, as recent work (Bär et al., 2012a; Bär et al., 2012b) has shown, text similarity computation can be much improved when a variety of measures are combined.

In recent years, UKP lab at TU Darmstadt has developed DKPro Similarity[1], an open source toolkit for analyzing text similarity. It is part of the DKPro framework for natural language processing (Gurevych et al., 2007). DKPro Similarity excels at the tasks of measuring semantic textual similarity (STS) and detecting text reuse (DTR), having achieved the best performance in previous challenges (Bär et al., 2012a; Bär et al., 2012b).

2.2 Textual Entailment

The *textual entailment* paradigm is a generic framework for applied semantic inference (Dagan et al., 2009). The most prevalent task of textual entailment is to recognize whether the meaning of a target natural language statement (H for hypothesis) can be inferred from another piece of text (T for text). Apparently, this core task underlies semantic inference in many text applications. The task of analyzing student responses is one such example. By assigning the student's answer as T and the reference answer as H, we are basically asking whether one can infer the correct (reference) answer from the student's response. In recent years, Bar-Ilan University has developed BIUTEE (Stern and Dagan, 2011), an extensive textual entailment recognition engine. BIUTEE tries to convert T (represented as a dependency tree) to H. It does so by applying a series of knowledge-based transformations, such as synonym substitution, active-passive conversion, and more. BIUTEE is publicly available as open source.[2]

3 Main Task

In this section, we explain how we approached the main task, in which the system needs to analyze each answer as a whole. After describing our system's architecture, we explain how we selected training data for the different scenarios in the main task. We then provide the details for each submitted run, and finally, our empirical results.

3.1 System Description

We build a system based on the Apache UIMA framework (Ferrucci and Lally, 2004) and DKPro Lab (Eckart de Castilho and Gurevych, 2011). We use DKPro Core[3] for preprocessing. Specifically, we used the default DKPro segmenter, TreeTagger POS tagger and chunker, Jazzy Spell Checker, and the Stanford parser.[4] We trained a supervised model (Naive Bayes) using Weka (Hall et al., 2009) with feature extraction based on clearTK (Ogren et al., 2008). The following features have been used:

BOW features Bag-of-word features are based on the assumption that certain words need to appear in a correct answer. We used a mixture of token unigrams, bigrams, and trigrams, where each n-gram is a binary feature that can either be true or false for a document.[5] Additionally, we also used the number of tokens in the student answer as another feature in this group.

Syntactic Features We extend BOW features with syntactic functions by adding dependency and phrase n-grams. Dependency n-grams are combinations of two tokens and their dependency relation. Phrase n-grams are combinations of the main verb and the noun phrase left and right of the verb. In both cases, we use the 10 most frequent n-grams.

Basic Similarity Features This group of features computes the similarity between the reference answer and the student answer. In case there is more than one reference answer, we compute all pairwise similarity scores and add the minimum, maximum, average, and median similarity.[6]

Semantic Similarity Features are very similar to the basic similarity features, except that we use semantic similarity measures in order to bridge a possible vocabulary gap between the student and reference answer. We use the ESA measure (Gabrilovich

[1] `code.google.com/p/dkpro-similarity-asl`

[2] `cs.biu.ac.il/~nlp/downloads/biutee`

[3] `code.google.com/p/dkpro-core-asl/`

[4] DKPro Core v1.4.0, TreeTagger models v20130204.0, Stanford parser PCFG model v20120709.0.

[5] Using the 750 most frequent n-grams gave good results on the training set, so we also used this number for the test runs.

[6] As basic similarity measures, we use greedy string tiling (Wise, 1996) with $n = 3$, longest common subsequence and longest common substring (Allison and Dix, 1986), and word n-gram containment(Lyon et al., 2001) with $n = 2$.

and Markovitch, 2007) based on concept vectors build from WordNet, Wiktionary, and Wikipedia.

Spelling Features As spelling errors might be indicative of the answer quality, we use the number of spelling errors normalized by the text length as an additional feature.

Entailment Features We run BIUTEE (Stern and Dagan, 2011) on the test instance (as T) with each reference answer (as H), which results in an array of numerical entailment confidence values. If there is more than one reference answer, we compute all pairwise confidence scores and add the minimum, maximum, average, and median confidence.

3.2 Data Selection Regime

There are three scenarios under which our system is expected to perform. For each one, we chose (a-priori) a different set of examples for training.

Unseen Answers Classify new answers to familiar questions. Train on instances that have the same question as the test instance.

Unseen Questions Classify new answers to unseen (but related) questions. Partition the questions according to their IDs, creating sets of related questions, and then train on all the instances that share the same partition as the test instance.

Unseen Domains Classify new answers to unseen questions from unseen domains. Use all available training data from the same dataset.

3.3 Submitted Runs

The runs represent the different levels of lexicalization of the model which we expect to have strong influence in each scenario:

Run 1 uses all features as described above. We expect the BOW features to be helpful for the *Unseen Answers* setting, but to be misleading for unseen questions or domains, as the same word indicating a correct answer for one question might correspond to a wrong answer for another question.

Run 2 uses only non-lexicalized features, i.e. all features except the BOW and syntactic features, in order to assess the impact of the lexicalization that overfits on the topic of the questions. We expect this run to be less sensitive to the topic changes in the *Unseen Questions* and *Unseen Domains* settings.

Run 3 uses only the basic similarity and the entailment features. It should indicate the baseline performance that can be expected without targeting the system towards a certain topic.

Task	Run	Unseen Answers	Unseen Questions	Unseen Domains
2-way	1	**.734**	**.678**	.671
	2	.665	.644	.677
	3	.662	.625	.677
3-way	1	**.670**	**.573**	.572
	2	.595	.561	.577
	3	.574	.540	.576
5-way	1	**.590**	.376	**.407**
	2	.495	**.397**	.371
	3	.461	.394	.376

Table 1: Main task performance for the SciEntsBank test set. We show weighted average F_1 for the three scenarios.

	Cor.	Par	Con.	Irr.	Non.
Correct	**903**	463	164	309	78
Partially Correct	219	**261**	93	333	80
Contradictory	61	126	**91**	103	36
Irrelevant	209	229	119	**476**	189
Non-Domain	0	0	0	2	**18**

Table 2: Confusion matrix of *Run 1* in the 5-way *Unseen Domains* scenario. The vertical axis is the real class, the horizontal axis is the predicted class.

3.4 Empirical Results

Table 1 shows the F_1-measure (weighted average) of the three runs. As was expected for the *Unseen Answers* scenario, *Run 1* using a lexicalized model outperformed the other two runs. However, in the other scenarios *Run 1* is not significantly better, as lexicalized features do not have the same impact if the question or the domain changes.

Table 2 shows the confusion matrix of *Run 1* in the 5-way *Unseen Domains* scenario. The *Correct* category was classified quite reliably, but the *Irrelevant* category was especially hard. While the reference answer provides some clues for what is correct or incorrect, the range of things that are "irrelevant" for a given question is potentially very big and thus cannot be easily learned. We also see that the system ability to distinguish *Correct* and *Partially Correct* answers need to be improved.

It is difficult to provide an exact assessment of our system's performance (with respect to other systems in the challenge), since there are multiple tasks, scenarios, datasets, and even metrics. However, we can safely say that our system performed above average in most settings, and showed competitive results in the *Unseen Domains* scenario.

4 Pilot Task

In the pilot task each facet needs to be analyzed separately, which requires some changes in the system architecture.

4.1 System Description

We segmented and lemmatized the input data using the default DKPro segmenter and the TreeTagger lemmatizer. The partial entailment system is composed of three methods: *Exact*, *WordNet*, and *BIUTEE*. These were combined in different combinations to form the different runs.

Exact In this baseline method, we represent a student answer as a bag-of-words containing all tokens and lemmas appearing in the text. Lemmas are used to account for minor morphological differences, such as tense or plurality. We then check whether both facet words appear in the set.

WordNet checks whether both facet words, or their semantically related words, appear in the student's answer. We use WordNet (Fellbaum, 1998) with the Resnik similarity measure (Resnik, 1995) and count a facet term as matched if the similarity score exceeds a certain threshold (0.9, empirically determined on the training set).

BIUTEE processes dependency trees instead of bags of words. We therefore added a pre-processing stage that extracts a path in the dependency parse that represents the facet. This is done by first parsing the entire reference answer, and then locating the two nodes mentioned in the facet. We then find their lowest common ancestor (LCA), and extract the path from the facet's first word to the second through the LCA. BIUTEE can now be given the student answer and the pre-processed facet, and try to recognize whether the former entails the latter.

4.2 Submitted Runs

In preliminary experiments using the provided training data, we found that the very simple *Exact Match* baseline performed surprisingly well, with 0.96 precision and 0.32 recall on positive class instances (expressed facets). We therefore decided to use this feature as an initial filter, and employ the others for classifying the "harder" cases. Training BIUTEE only on these cases, while dismissing easy ones, improved our system's performance significantly.

Run 1: *Exact* OR *WordNet* This is essentially just the *WordNet* feature on its own, because every instance that *Exact* classifies as positive is also positive by *WordNet*.

Run 2: *Exact* OR (*BIUTEE* AND *WordNet*) If the instance is non-trivial, this configuration requires that both *BIUTEE* and *WordNet Match* agree on positive classification. Equivalent to the majority rule.

Run 3: *Exact* OR *BIUTEE* *BIUTEE* increases recall of expressed facets at the expense of precision.

	Unseen Answers	Unseen Questions	Unseen Domains
Baseline	.670	.688	.731
Run 1	.756	.710	.760
Run 2	**.782**	**.765**	**.816**
Run 3	.744	.733	.770

Table 3: Pilot task performance across different scenarios. The scores are F_1-measures (weighted average).

4.3 Empirical Results

Table 3 shows the F_1-measure (weighted average) of each run in each scenario, including *Exact Match* as a quite strong baseline. In the majority of cases, *Run 2* that combines entailment and WordNet-based lexical matching, significantly outperformed the other two. It is interesting to note that the systems' performance does not degrade in "harder" scenarios; this is a result of the non-lexicalized nature of our methods. Unfortunately, our system was the only submission in this track, so we do not have any means to perform relative comparison.

5 Conclusion

We combined semantic textual similarity with textual entailment to solve the problem of student response analysis. Though our features were not tailored for this task, they proved quite indicative, and adapted well to unseen domains. We believe that additional generic features and knowledge resources are the best way to improve on our results, while retaining the same robustness and generality as our current architecture.

Acknowledgements

This work has been supported by the Volkswagen Foundation as part of the Lichtenberg-Professorship Program under grant No. I/82806, and by the European Community's Seventh Framework Programme (FP7/2007-2013) under grant agreement no. 287923 (EXCITEMENT). We would like to thank the Minerva Foundation for facilitating this cooperation with a short term research grant.

References

Lloyd Allison and Trevor I. Dix. 1986. A bit-string longest-common-subsequence algorithm. *Information Processing Letters*, 23:305–310.

Daniel Bär, Chris Biemann, Iryna Gurevych, and Torsten Zesch. 2012a. UKP: Computing semantic textual similarity by combining multiple content similarity measures. In *Proceedings of the 6th International Workshop on Semantic Evaluation and the 1st Joint Conference on Lexical and Computational Semantics*, pages 435–440, June.

Daniel Bär, Torsten Zesch, and Iryna Gurevych. 2012b. Text reuse detection using a composition of text similarity measures. In *Proceedings of the 24th International Conference on Computational Linguistics (COLING 2012)*, pages 167–184, December.

Ido Dagan, Bill Dolan, Bernardo Magnini, and Dan Roth. 2009. Recognizing textual entailment: Rationale, evaluation and approaches. *Natural Language Engineering*, 15(4):i–xvii.

Myroslava O. Dzikovska, Rodney Nielsen, Chris Brew, Claudia Leacock, Danilo Giampiccolo, Luisa Bentivogli, Peter Clark, Ido Dagan, and Hoa Trang Dang. 2013. Semeval-2013 task 7: The joint student response analysis and 8th recognizing textual entailment challenge. In **SEM 2013: The First Joint Conference on Lexical and Computational Semantics*, Atlanta, Georgia, USA, 13-14 June. Association for Computational Linguistics.

Richard Eckart de Castilho and Iryna Gurevych. 2011. A lightweight framework for reproducible parameter sweeping in information retrieval. In *Proceedings of the 2011 workshop on Data infrastructurEs for supporting information retrieval evaluation (DESIRE '11)*, New York, NY, USA. ACM.

Christiane Fellbaum, editor. 1998. *WordNet: An Electronic Lexical Database*. MIT Press, Cambridge, MA.

David Ferrucci and Adam Lally. 2004. UIMA: An architectural approach to unstructured information processing in the corporate research environment. *Natural Language Engineering*, 10(3-4):327–348.

Evgeniy Gabrilovich and Shaul Markovitch. 2007. Computing semantic relatedness using Wikipedia-based explicit semantic analysis. In *Proceedings of the 20th International Joint Conference on Artificial Intelligence (IJCAI 2007)*, pages 1606–1611.

Iryna Gurevych, Max Mühlhäuser, Christof Müller, Jürgen Steimle, Markus Weimer, and Torsten Zesch. 2007. Darmstadt Knowledge Processing Repository based on UIMA. In *Proceedings of the 1st Workshop on Unstructured Information Management Architecture at Biannual Conference of the Society for Computational Linguistics and Language Technology*, Tübingen, Germany, April.

Mark Hall, Eibe Frank, Geoffrey Holmes, Bernhard Pfahringer, Peter Reutemann, and Ian H. Witten. 2009. The WEKA Data Mining Software: An Update. *SIGKDD Explorations*, 11(1).

Thomas K. Landauer, Peter W. Foltz, and Darrell Laham. 1998. An introduction to latent semantic analysis. *Discourse Processes*, 25(2&3):259–284.

Caroline Lyon, James Malcolm, and Bob Dickerson. 2001. Detecting short passages of similar text in large document collections. In *Proceedings of the 6th Conference on Empirical Methods in Natural Language Processing (EMNLP 2001)*, pages 118–125, Pittsburgh, PA USA.

Rada Mihalcea, Courtney Corley, and Carlo Strapparava. 2006. Corpus-based and knowledge-based measures of text semantic similarity. In *Proceedings of the 21st National Conference on Artificial Intelligence*, pages 775–780, Boston, MA.

Philip V. Ogren, Philipp G. Wetzler, and Steven Bethard. 2008. ClearTK: A UIMA Toolkit for Statistical Natural Language Processing. In *Towards Enhanced Interoperability for Large HLT Systems: UIMA for NLP workshop at Language Resources and Evaluation Conference (LREC)*.

Philip Resnik. 1995. Using information content to evaluate semantic similarity in a taxonomy. In *Proceedings of the 14th International Joint Conference on Artificial Intelligence (IJCAI 1995)*, pages 448–453.

Asher Stern and Ido Dagan. 2011. A confidence model for syntactically-motivated entailment proofs. In *Proceedings of the 8th International Conference on Recent Advances in Natural Language Processing (RANLP 2011)*, pages 455–462.

Michael J. Wise. 1996. YAP3: Improved detection of similarities in computer program and other texts. In *Proceedings of the 27th SIGCSE Technical Symposium on Computer Science Education (SIGCSE 1996)*, pages 130–134, Philadelphia, PA.

SemEval-2013 Task 13: Word Sense Induction for Graded and Non-Graded Senses

David Jurgens
Dipartimento di Informatica
Sapienza Università di Roma
jurgens@di.uniroma1.it

Ioannis Klapaftis
Search Technology Center Europe
Microsoft
ioannisk@microsoft.com

Abstract

Most work on word sense disambiguation has assumed that word usages are best labeled with a single sense. However, contextual ambiguity or fine-grained senses can potentially enable multiple sense interpretations of a usage. We present a new SemEval task for evaluating Word Sense Induction and Disambiguation systems in a setting where instances may be labeled with multiple senses, weighted by their applicability. Four teams submitted nine systems, which were evaluated in two settings.

1 Introduction

Word Sense Disambiguation (WSD) attempts to identify which of a word's meanings applies in a given context. A long-standing task, WSD is fundamental to many NLP applications (Navigli, 2009). Typically, each usage of a word is treated as expressing only a single sense. However, contextual ambiguity as well as the relatedness of certain meanings can potentially elicit multiple sense interpretations. Recent work has shown that annotators find multiple applicable senses in a given target word context when using fine-grained sense inventories such as WordNet (Véronis, 1998; Murray and Green, 2004; Erk et al., 2009; Passonneau et al., 2012b; Jurgens, 2013; Navigli et al., 2013). Such contexts would be better annotated with multiple sense labels, weighting each sense according to its applicability (Erk et al., 2009; Jurgens, 2013), in effect allowing ambiguity or multiple interpretations to be explicitly modeled. Accordingly, the first goal of this task is to evaluate WSD systems in a setting where instances may be labeled with one or more senses, weighted by their applicability.

WSD methods are ultimately defined and potentially restricted by their choice in sense inventory; for example, a sense inventory may have insufficient sense-annotated data to build WSD systems for specific types of text (e.g., social media), or the inventory may lack domain-specific senses. Word Sense Induction (WSI) has been proposed as a method for overcoming such limitations by learning the senses automatically from text. In essence, a WSI algorithm acts as a lexicographer by grouping word usages according to their shared meaning. The second goal of this task is to assess the performance of WSI algorithms when they are able to model multiple meanings of a usage with graded senses.

Task 12 focuses on disambiguating senses for 50 target lemmas: 20 nouns, 20 verbs, and 10 adjectives (Sec. 2). Since the Task evaluates only unsupervised systems, no training data was provided; however, to enable more comparison, Unsupervised WSD systems were also allowed to participate. Participating systems were evaluated in two settings (Sec. 3), depending on whether they used induced senses or WordNet 3.1 senses for their annotations. The results (Sec. 5) demonstrate a substantial improvement over the competitive most frequent sense baseline.

2 Task Description

This task required participating systems to annotate instances of nouns, verb, and adjectives using WordNet 3.1 (Fellbaum, 1998), which was selected due to its fine-grained senses. Participants could label each instance with one or more senses, weighting

*Second Joint Conference on Lexical and Computational Semantics (*SEM), Volume 2: Seventh International Workshop on Semantic Evaluation (SemEval 2013)*, pages 290–299, Atlanta, Georgia, June 14-15, 2013.

We all are relieved to lay aside our fight-or-flight reflexes and to commemorate our births from out of the **dark** centers of the women, to feel the complexity of our love and frustration with each other, to stretch our cognition to encompass the thoughts of every entity we know.
`dark%3:00:01::` – devoid of or deficient in light or brightness; shadowed or black `dark%3:00:00::` – secret
I **ask** because my practice has always been to allow about five minutes grace, then remove it.
`ask%2:32:02::` – direct or put; seek an answer to `ask%2:32:04::` – address a question to and expect an answer from

Table 1: Example instances with multiple senses due to intended double meanings (top) or contextual ambiguity (bottom). Senses are specified using their WordNet 3.1 sense keys.

each by their applicability. Table 1 highlights two example contexts where multiple senses apply. The first example shows a case of an intentional double meaning that evokes both the physical aspect of *dark.a* as being devoid of light and the causal result of being secret. In contrast, the second example shows a case of multiple interpretations from ambiguity; a different preceding context could generate the alternate interpretations "I ask [*you*] because" (sense `ask%2:32:04::`) or "I ask [*the question*] because" (sense `ask%2:32:02::`).

2.1 Data

Three datasets were provided with the task. The trial dataset provided weighted word sense annotations using the data gathered by Erk et al. (2009). The trial dataset consisted of 50 contexts for eight words, where each context was labeled with WordNet 3.0 sense ratings from three untrained lexicographers.

Due to the unsupervised nature of the task, participants were not provided with sense-labeled training data. However, WSI systems were provided with the ukWaC corpus (Baroni et al., 2009) to use in inducing senses. Previous SemEval WSI tasks had provided participants with corpora specific to the task's target terms; in contrast, this task opted to use a large corpus to enable WSI methods that require corpus-wide statistics, e.g., statistical associations.

Test data was drawn from the Open American National Corpus (Ide and Suderman, 2004, OANC) across a variety of genres and from both the spoken and written portions of the corpus, summarized in Table 2. All contexts were manually inspected to ensure that the lemma being disambiguated was of the correct part of speech and had an interpretation that matched at least one WordNet 3.1 sense. This filtering also removed instances that were in a collocation, or had an idiomatic meaning. Ultimately, 4664 contexts were used as test data, with a minimum of 22 and a maximum of 100 contexts per word.

2.2 Sense Annotation

Recent work proposes to gather sense annotations using crowdsourcing in order to reduce the time and cost of acquiring sense-annotated corpora (Biemann and Nygaard, 2010; Passonneau et al., 2012b; Rumshisky et al., 2012; Jurgens, 2013). Therefore, we initially annotated the Task's data using the method of Jurgens (2013), where workers on Amazon Mechanical Turk (AMT) rated all senses of a word on a Likert scale from one to five, indicating the sense does not apply at all or completely applies, respectively. Twenty annotators were assigned per instance, with their ratings combined by selecting the most frequent rating. However, we found that while the annotators achieved moderate inter-annotator agreement (IAA), the resulting annotations were not of high enough quality to use in the Task's evaluations. Specifically, for some senses and contexts, AMT annotators required more information about sense distinctions than was feasible to integrate into the AMT setting, which led to consistent but incorrect sense assignments.

Therefore, the test data was annotated by the two authors, with the first author annotating all instances and the second author annotating a 10% sample of each lemma's instances in order to calculate IAA. IAA was calculated using Krippendorff's α (Krippendorff, 1980; Artstein and Poesio, 2008), which is an agreement measurement that adjusts for chance,

Genre	Spoken		Written						
	Face-to-face	Telephone	Fiction	Journal	Letters	Non-fiction	Technical	Travel Guides	*All*
Instances	52	699	127	2403	103	477	611	192	4664
Tokens	1742	30,700	3438	69,479	2238	11,780	17,337	4490	141,204
Mean senses/inst.	1.17	1.08	1.15	1.13	1.31	1.10	1.11	1.11	1.12

Table 2: Test data used in Task 12, divided according to source type

ranging in $(-1, 1]$ for interval data, where 1 indicates perfect agreement and -1 indicates systematic disagreement; two random annotations have an expected α of zero. We treat each sense and instance combination as a separate item to rate. The total IAA for the dataset was 0.504, and on individual words, ranged from 0.903 for *number.n* to 0.00 for *win.v*. While this IAA is less than the 0.8 recommended by Krippendorff (2004), it is consistent with the IAA distribution for the sense annotations of MASC on other parts of the OANC corpus: Passonneau et al. (2012a) reports an α of 0.88 to -0.02 with the MASI statistic (Passonneau et al., 2006).

Table 2 summarizes the annotation statistics for the Task's data. The annotation process resulted in far fewer senses per instance in the trial data, which we attribute to using trained annotators. An analysis across the corpora genres showed that the multiple-sense annotation rates were similar. Due to the variety of contextual sources, all lemmas were observed with at least two distinct senses.

3 Evaluation

We adopt a two-part evaluation setting used in previous SemEval WSI and WSD tasks (Agirre and Soroa, 2007; Manandhar et al., 2010). The first evaluation uses a traditional WSD task that directly compares WordNet sense labels. For WSI systems, their induced sense labels are converted to WordNet 3.1 labels via a mapping procedure. The second evaluation performs a direct comparison of the two sense inventories using clustering comparisons.

3.1 WSD Task

In the first evaluation, we adopt a WSD task with three objectives: (1) detecting which senses are applicable, (2) ranking senses by their applicability, and (3) measuring agreement in applicability ratings with human annotators. Each objectives uses a specific measurement: (1) the Jaccard Index, (2) positionally-weighted Kendall's τ similarity, and (3) a weighted variant of Normalized Discounted Cumulative Gain, respectively. Each measure is bounded in $[0, 1]$, where 1 indicates complete agreement with the gold standard. We generalize the traditional definition of WSD Recall such that it measures the average score for each measure across *all* instances, including those not labeled by the system. Systems are ultimately scored using the F1 measure between each objective's measure and Recall.

3.1.1 Transforming Induced Sense Labels

In the WSD setting, induced sense labels may be transformed into a reference inventory (e.g., WordNet 3.1) using a sense mapping procedure. We follow the 80/20 setup of Manandhar et al. (2010), where the corpus is randomly divided into five partitions, four of which are used to learn the sense mapping; the sense labels for the held-out partition are then converted and compared with the gold standard. This process is repeated so that each partition is tested once. For learning the sense mapping function, we use the distribution mapping technique of Jurgens (2012), which takes into account the sense applicability weights in both labelings.

3.1.2 Jaccard Index

Given two sets of sense labels for an instance, X and Y, the Jaccard Index is used to measure the agreement: $\frac{|X \cap Y|}{|X \cup Y|}$. The Jaccard Index is maximized when X and Y use identical labels, and is minimized when the sets of sense labels are disjoint.

3.1.3 Positionally-Weighted Kendall's τ

Rank correlations have been proposed for evaluating a system's ability to order senses by applicability; in previous work, both Erk and McCarthy (2009) and Jurgens (2012) propose rank correlation coefficients that assume all positions in the ranking are equally important. However, in the case of graded sense evaluation, often only a few senses are applicable, with the applicability ratings of the remaining senses being relatively inconsequential. Therefore, we consider an alternate rank scoring based on Kumar and Vassilvitskii (2010), which weights the penalty of reordering the lower positions less than the penalty of reordering the first ranks.

Kendall's τ distance, K, is a measure of the number of item position swaps required to make two sequences identical. Kumar and Vassilvitskii (2010) extend this distance definition using a variable penalty function δ for the cost of swapping two positions, which we denote K_δ. By using an appropriate δ, K_δ can be biased towards the correctness of higher ranks by assigning a smaller δ to lower ranks. Because K_δ is a distance measure, its value range will be different depending on the number of ranks used. Therefore, to convert the measure to a similarity we normalize the distance to $[0, 1]$ by dividing by the maximum K_δ distance and then subtracting the distance from one. Given two rankings x and y where x is the reference by which y is to be measured, we may compute the normalized similarity using

$$K_\delta^{\text{sim}} = 1 - \frac{K_\delta(x, y)}{K_\delta^{\text{max}}(x)}. \quad (1)$$

Equation 1 has its maximal value of one when ranking y is identical to ranking x, and its minimal value of zero when y is in the reverse order as x. We refer to this value as the positionally-weighted Kendall's τ similarity, K_δ^{sim}. As defined, K_δ^{sim} does not account for ties. Therefore, we arbitrarily break ties in a deterministic fashion for both rankings. Second, we define δ to assign higher cost to the first ranks: the cost to move an item into position i, δ_i, is defined as $\frac{n-(i+1)}{n}$, where n is the number of senses.

3.1.4 Weighted NDCG

To compare the applicability ratings for sense annotations, we recast the annotation process in an Information Retrieval setting: Given an example context acting as a query over a word's senses, the task is to retrieve all applicable senses, ranking and scoring them by their applicability. Moffat and Zobel (2008) propose using Discounted Cumulative Gain (DCG) as a method to compare a ranking against a baseline. Given (1) a gold standard weighting of the k senses applicable to a context, where w_i denotes the applicability for sense i in the gold standard, and (2) a ranking of the k senses by some method, the DCG may be calculated as $\sum_{i=1}^{k} \frac{2^{w_i+1}-1}{log_2(i+1)}$. DCG is commonly normalized to $[0, 1]$ so that the value is comparable when computed on rankings with different k and weight values. To normalize, the maximum value is calculated by first computing the DCG on the ranking when the k items are sorted by their weights, referred as the Ideal DCG (IDCG), and then normalizing as $NDCG = \frac{DCG}{IDCG}$.

The DCG only considers the weights assigned in the gold standard, which potentially masks importance differences in the weights assigned to the senses. Therefore, we propose weighting the DCG by the relative difference in the two weights. Given an alternate weighting of the k items, denoted as $\hat{w}_i$,

$$WDCG = \sum_{i=1}^{k} \frac{\frac{min(w_i, \hat{w}_i)}{max(w_i, \hat{w}_i)} \left(2^{w_i+1} - 1\right)}{log_2(i)}. \quad (2)$$

The key impact in Equation 2 comes from weighting an item's contribution to the score by its relative deviation in absolute weight. A set of weights that achieves an equivalent ranking may have a low WDCG if the weights are significantly higher or lower than the reference. Equation 2 may be normalized in the same way as the DCG. We refer to this final normalized measure as the Weighted Normalized Discounted Cumulative Gain (WNDCG).

3.2 Sense Cluster Comparisons

Sense induction can be viewed as an unsupervised clustering task where usages of a word are grouped into clusters, each representing uses of the same meaning. In previous SemEval tasks on sense induction, instances were labeled with a single sense, which yields a *partition* over the instances into disjoint sets. The proposed partition can then be compared with a gold-standard partition using many existing clustering comparison methods, such as the V-Measure (Rosenberg and Hirschberg, 2007) or paired FScore (Artiles et al., 2009). Such cluster comparison methods measure the degree of similarity between the sense boundaries created by lexicographers and those created by WSI methods.

In the present task, instances are potentially labeled both with multiple senses and with weights reflecting the applicability. This type of sense labeling produces a fuzzy clustering: An instance may belong to one or more sense clusters with its cluster membership relative to its weight for that sense. Formally, we refer to (1) a solution where the sets of instances overlap as a *cover* and (2) a solution where the sets overlap and instances may have partial memberships in a set as *fuzzy cover*.

We propose two new fuzzy measures for comparing fuzzy sense assignments: Fuzzy B-Cubed and Fuzzy Normalized Mutual Information. The two measures provide complementary information. B-Cubed summarizes the performance per instance and therefore provides an estimate of how well a system would perform on a new corpus with a similar sense distribution. In contrast, Fuzzy NMI is measured based on the clusters rather than the instances, thereby providing a performance analysis that is independent of the corpus sense distribution.

3.2.1 Fuzzy B-Cubed

Bagga and Baldwin (1998) proposed a clustering evaluation known as B-Cubed, which compares two partitions on a per-item basis. Amigó et al. (2009) later extended the definition of B-Cubed to compare overlapping clusters (i.e., covers). We generalize B-Cubed further to handle the case of fuzzy covers. B-Cubed is based on precision and recall, which estimate the fit between two clusterings, X and Y at the item level. For an item i, precision reflects how many items sharing a cluster with i in X appear in its cluster in Y; conversely, recall measures how many items sharing a cluster in Y with i also appear in its cluster in X. The final B-Cubed value is the harmonic mean of the two scores.

To generalize B-Cubed to fuzzy covers, we adopt the formalization of Amigó et al. (2009), who define item-based precision and recall functions, P and R, in terms of a correctness function, $C \to \{0, 1\}$. For notational brevity, let avg be a function that returns the mean value of a series, and $\mu_x(i)$ denote the set of clusters in clustering X of which item i is a member. B-Cubed precision and recall may therefore calculated over all n items:

$$\text{B-Cubed Precision} = \underset{i}{\text{avg}}[\underset{j \neq i \in \cup \mu_y(i)}{\text{avg}} P(i,j)] \quad (3)$$

$$\text{B-Cubed Recall} = \underset{i}{\text{avg}}[\underset{j \neq i \in \cup \mu_x(i)}{\text{avg}} R(i,j)]. \quad (4)$$

When comparing partitions, P and R are defined as 1 if two items cluster labels are identical. To generalize B-Cubed for fuzzy covers, we redefine P and R to account for differences in the partial cluster membership of items. Let $\ell_X(i)$ denote the set of clusters of which i is a member, and $w_k(i)$ denote the membership weight of item i in cluster k in X. We therefore define C with respect to X of two items as

$$\text{C}(i, j, X) = \sum_{k \in \ell_X(i) \cup \ell_X(j)} 1 - |w_k(i) - w_k(j)|. \quad (5)$$

Equation 5 is maximized when i and j have identical membership weights in the clusters of which they are members. Importantly, Equation 5 generalizes to the correctness operations both when comparing partitions and covers, as defined by Amigó et al. (2009). Item-based Precision and Recall are then defined using Equation 5 as $P(i,j,X) = \frac{\text{Min}(\text{C}(i,j,X),\text{C}(i,j,Y))}{\text{C}(i,j,X)}$ and $R(i,j,X) = \frac{\text{Min}(\text{C}(i,j,X),\text{C}(i,j,Y))}{\text{C}(i,j,Y)}$, respectively. These fuzzy generalizations are used in Equations 3 and 4.

3.2.2 Fuzzy Normalized Mutual Information

Mutual information measures the dependence between two random variables. In the context of clustering evaluation, mutual information treats the sense labels as random variables and measures the level of agreement in which instances are labeled with the same senses (Danon et al., 2005). Formally, mutual information is defined as $I(X;Y) = H(X) - (H(X|Y)$ where $H(X)$ denotes the entropy of the random variable X that represents a partition, i.e., the sets of instances assigned to each sense. Typically, mutual information is normalized to $[0, 1]$ in order to facilitate comparisons between multiple clustering solutions on the same scale (Luo et al., 2009), with $Max(H(X), H(Y))$ being the recommended normalizing factor (Vinh et al., 2010).

In its original formulation Mutual information is defined only to compare non-overlapping cluster partitions. Therefore, we propose a new definition of mutual information between fuzzy covers using extension of Lancichinetti et al. (2009) for calculating the normalized mutual information between covers. In the case of partitions, a clustering is represented as a discrete random variable whose states denote the probability of being assigned to each cluster. In the fuzzy cover setting, each item may be assigned to multiple clusters and no longer has a binary assignment to a cluster, but takes on a value in $[0, 1]$. Therefore, each cluster X_i can be represented separately as a continuous random variable, with the entire fuzzy cover denoted as the variable $\mathbf{X}_{1...k}$, where the ith entry of $\mathbf{X}$ is the continuous random variable for cluster i. However, by modeling clusters using continuous domain, differential entropy must be used for the continuous variables; importantly, differential entropy does not obey the same properties as discrete entropy and may be negative.

To avoid calculating entropy in the continuous domain, we therefore propose an alternative method of computing mutual information based on discretizing the continuous values of X_i in the fuzzy setting. For the continuous random variable X_i, we discretize the value by dividing up probability mass into discrete bins. That is, the support of X_i is partitioned into disjoint ranges, each of which represents a discrete outcome of X_i. As a result, X_i becomes a *categorical distribution* over a set of weights ranges $\{w_1, \ldots, w_n\}$ that denote the strength of membership in the fuzzy set. With respect to sense annotation, this discretization process is analogous to having an annotator rate the applicability of a sense for an instance using a Likert scale instead of using a rational number within a fixed bound.

Discretizing the continuous cluster membership ratings into bins allows us to avoid the problematic interpretation of entropy in the continuous domain while still expanding the definition of mutual information from a binary cluster membership to one of degrees. Using the definition of X_i and Y_j as a categorical variables over discrete ratings, we may then estimate the entropy and joint entropy as follows.

$$H(X_i) = \sum_{i=1}^{n} p(w_i) \log_2 p(w_i) \quad (6)$$

where $p(w_i)$ is the probability of an instance being labeled with rating w_i Similarly, we may define the joint entropy of two fuzzy clusters as

$$H(X_k, Y_l) = \sum_{i=1}^{n} \sum_{j=1}^{m} p(w_i, w_j) \log_2 p(w_i, w_j) \quad (7)$$

where $p(w_i, w_j)$ is the probability of an instance being labeled with rating w_i in cluster X_k and w_j in cluster Y_l, and m denotes the number of bins for Y_l. The conditional entropy between two clusters may then be calculated as

$$H(X_k|Y_l) = H(X_k, Y_l) - H(Y_l).$$

Together, Equations 6 and 7 may be used to define $I(X, Y)$ as in the original definition. We then normalize using the method of McDaid et al. (2011). Based on the limited range of fuzzy memberships in $[0, 1]$, we selected uniformly distributed bins in $[0, 1]$ at 0.1 intervals when discretizing the membership weights for sense labelings.

3.3 Baselines

Task 12 included multiple baselines based on modeling different types of WSI and WSD systems. Due to space constraints, we include only the four most descriptive here: (1) **Semcor MFS** which labels each instance with the most frequent sense of that lemma in SemCor, (2) **Semcor Ranked Senses** baseline, which labels each instance with all of the target lemma's senses, ranked according to their frequency in SemCor, using weights $\frac{n-i+1}{n}$, where n is the number of senses and i is the rank, (3) **1c1inst** which labels each instance with its own induced sense and (4) **All-instances, One sense** which labels all instances with the same induced sense. The first two baselines directly use WordNet 3.1 senses, while the last two use induced senses.

4 Participating Systems

Four teams submitted nine systems, seven of which used induced sense inventories. **AI-KU** submitted three WSI systems based on a lexical substitution method; a language model is built from the target word's contexts in the test data and the ukWaC corpus and then Fastsubs (Yuret, 2012) is used to identify lexical substitutes for the target. Together, the contexts of the target and substitutes are used to build a distributional model using the S-CODE algorithm (Maron et al., 2010). The resulting contextual distributions are then clustered using K-means to identify word senses. The University of Melbourne (**Unimelb**) team submitted two WSI systems based on the approach of Lau et al. (2012). Their systems use a Hierarchical Dirichlet Process (Teh et al., 2006) to automatically infer the number of senses from contextual and positional features. Un-

Team	System	WSD F1			Cluster Comparison			
		Jac. Ind.	K_{δ}^{sim}	WNDCG	Fuzzy NMI	Fuzzy B-Cubed	#Cl	#S
AI-KU	Base	0.197	0.620	**0.387**	**0.065**	0.390	7.76	6.61
AI-KU	add1000	0.197	0.606	0.215	0.035	0.320	7.76	6.61
AI-KU	remove5-add1000	**0.244**	**0.642**	0.332	0.039	0.451	3.12	5.33
Unimelb	5p	0.218	0.614	0.365	0.056	0.459	2.37	5.97
Unimelb	50k	0.213	0.620	0.371	0.060	**0.483**	2.48	6.08
UoS	#WN Senses	0.192	0.596	0.315	0.047	0.201	8.08	6.77
UoS	top-3	0.232	0.625	0.374	0.045	0.448	3.00	5.44
La Sapienza	system-1	0.149	0.507	0.311	-	-	-	8.69
La Sapienza	system-2	0.149	0.510	0.383	-	-	-	8.67
All-instances, One sense		0.192	0.609	0.288	0.0	0.623	1.00	6.62
1c1inst		0.0	0.0	0.0	0.071	0.0	1.00	0.0
Semcor MFS		0.455	0.465	0.339	-	-	-	1.00
Semcor Ranked Senses		0.149	0.559	0.489	-	-	-	8.66

Table 3: Performance on the five evaluation measures for all system and selected baselines. Top system performances are marked in bold.

like other teams, the Unimelb systems were trained on a Wikipedia corpus instead of the ukWaC corpus. The University of Sussex (**UoS**) team submitted two WSI systems that use dependency-parsed features from the corpus, which are then clustered into senses using the MaxMax algorithm (Hope and Keller, 2013); the resulting fine-grained clusters are then combined based on their degree of separability. The **La Sapienza** team submitted two Unsupervised WSD systems based applying Personalized Page Rank (Agirre and Soroa, 2009) over a WordNet-based network to compare the similarity of each sense with the similarity of the context, ranking each sense according to its similarity.

Team	System	F1	NMI	B-Cubed
AI-KU	Base	**0.641**	**0.045**	0.351
AI-KU	add1000	0.601	0.023	0.288
AI-KU	remove5-add1000	0.628	0.026	0.421
Unimelb	5p	0.596	0.035	0.421
Unimelb	50k	0.605	0.039	**0.441**
UoS	#WN Senses	0.574	0.031	0.180
UoS	top-3	0.600	0.028	0.414
La Sapienza	System-1	0.204	-	-
La Sapienza	System-2	0.217	-	-
All-instances, One sense		0.569	0.0	0.570
1c1inst		0.0	0.018	0.0
Semcor MFS		0.477	0.0	0.570

Table 4: System performance in the single-sense setting. Top system performances are marked in bold.

5 Results and Discussion

Table 3 shows the main results for all instances. Additionally, we report the number of induced clusters used to label each sense as #Cl and the number of resulting WordNet 3.1 senses for each sense with #S. As in previous WSD tasks, the MFS baseline was quite competitive, outperforming all systems on detecting which senses were applicable, measured using the Jaccard Index. However, most systems were able to outperform the MFS baseline on ranking senses and quantifying their applicability.

Previous cluster comparison evaluations often faced issues with the measures being biased either towards the 1c1inst baseline or labeling all instances with the same sense. However, Table 3 shows that systems are capable of performing well in both the Fuzzy NMI and Fuzzy B-Cubed measures, thereby avoiding the extreme performance of either baseline.

An analysis of the systems' results showed that many systems labeled instances with a high number of senses, which could have been influenced by the trial data having significantly more instances labeled with multiple senses than the test data. Therefore, we performed a second analysis that partitioned the test set into two sets: those labeled with a single sense and those with multiple senses. For single-sense set, we modified the test setting to have systems also label instances with a single sense: (1) the sense mapping function for WSI systems (Sec. 3.1.1) was modified so that after the mapping,

		WSD F1			Cluster Comparison	
Team	System	Jac. Ind.	$K_{\delta}^{\mathrm{sim}}$	WNDCG	Fuzzy NMI	Fuzzy B-Cubed
AI-KU	Base	0.394	0.617	0.317	0.029	0.078
AI-KU	add1000	0.394	0.620	0.214	0.014	0.061
AI-KU	remove5-add1000	0.434	0.585	0.290	0.004	0.116
Unimelb	5p	**0.436**	0.585	0.286	0.019	0.130
Unimelb	5000k	0.414	0.602	0.298	0.021	**0.134**
UoS	#WN Senses	0.367	0.627	0.313	**0.036**	0.037
UoS	top-3	0.421	0.574	0.302	0.006	0.113
La Sapienza	system-1	0.263	0.660	0.447	-	-
La Sapienza	system-2	0.412	**0.694**	**0.536**	-	-
All-instances, One sense		0.387	0.635	0.254	0.0	0.130
1c1inst		0.0	0.0	0.0	0.300	0.0
Semcor MFS		0.283	0.373	0.197		
Semcor Ranked Senses		0.263	0.593	0.395		

Table 5: System performance on all instances labeled with multiple senses. Top system performances are marked in bold.

only the highest-weighted WordNet 3.1 sense was used, and (2) the La Sapienza system output was modified to retain only the highest weighted sense. In this single-sense setting, systems were evaluated using the standard WSD Precision and Recall measures; we report the F1 measure of Precision and Recall. The remaining subset of instances annotated with multiple senses were evaluated separately.

Table 4 shows the systems' performance on single-sense instances, revealing substantially increased performance and improvement over the MFS baseline for WSI systems. Notably, the performance of the best sense-remapped WSI systems surpasses the performance of many supervised WSD systems in previous WSD evaluations (Kilgarriff, 2002; Mihalcea et al., 2004; Pradhan et al., 2007; Agirre et al., 2010). This performance suggests that WSI systems using graded labels provide a way to leverage huge amounts of unannotated corpus data for finding sense-related features in order to train semi-supervised WSD systems.

Table 5 shows the performance on the subset of instances that were annotated with multiple senses. We note that in this setting, the mapping procedure transforms the All-Instances One Sense baseline into the average applicability rating for each sense in the test corpus. Notably, the La Sapienza systems sees a significant performance increase in this setting; their systems label each instance with all of the lemma's senses, which significantly degrades performance in the most common case where only a single sense applies. However, when multiple senses are known to be present, their method for quantifying sense applicability appears closest to the gold standard judgments. Furthermore, the majority of WSI systems are able to surpass all four baselines on identifying which senses are present and quantifying their applicability.

6 Conclusion

We have introduced a new evaluation setting for WSI and WSD systems where systems are measured by their ability to detect and weight multiple applicable senses for a single context. Four teams submitted nine systems, annotating a total of 4664 contexts for 50 words from the OANC. Many systems were able to surpass the competitive MFS baseline. Furthermore, when WSI systems were trained to produce only a single sense label, the performance of resulting semi-supervised WSD systems surpassed that of many supervised systems in previous WSD evaluations. Future work may assess the impact of graded sense annotations in a task-based setting. All materials have been released on the task website.[1]

Acknowledgments

We thank Rebecca Passonneau for her feedback and suggestions for target lemmas used in this task.

[1] http://www.cs.york.ac.uk/semeval-2013/task13/

References

Eneko Agirre and Aitor Soroa. 2007. Semeval-2007 task 2: Evaluating word sense induction and discrimination systems. In *Proceedings of the Fourth International Workshop on Semantic Evaluations*, pages 7–12. ACL.

Eneko Agirre and Aitor Soroa. 2009. Personalizing PageRank for Word Sense Disambiguation. In *Proceedings of EACL*, pages 33–41. ACL.

Eneko Agirre, Oier López De Lacalle, Christine Fellbaum, Andrea Marchetti, Antonio Toral, and Piek Vossen. 2010. SemEval-2010 task 17: All-words word sense disambiguation on specific domains. In *Proceedings of SemEval-2010*. ACL.

Enrique Amigó, Julio Gonzalo, Javier Artiles, and Felisa Verdejo. 2009. A comparison of extrinsic clustering evaluation metrics based on formal constraints. *Information Retrieval*, 12(4):461–486.

Javier Artiles, Enrique Amigó, and Julio Gonzalo. 2009. The role of named entities in web people search. In *Proceedings of EMNLP*, pages 534–542. Association for Computational Linguistics.

Ron Artstein and Massimo Poesio. 2008. Inter-coder agreement for computational linguistics. *Computational Linguistics*, 34(4):555–596.

Amit Bagga and Breck Baldwin. 1998. Algorithms for scoring coreference chains. In *Proceedings of the Linguistic Coreference Workshop at LREC*, pages 563–566.

Marco Baroni, Silvia Bernardini, Adriano Ferraresi, and Eros Zanchetta. 2009. The WaCky wide web: A collection of very large linguistically processed web-crawled corpora. *Language Resources and Evaluation*, 43(3):209–226.

Chris Biemann and Valerie Nygaard. 2010. Crowdsourcing wordnet. In *The 5th International Conference of the Global WordNet Association (GWC-2010)*.

Leon Danon, Albert Díaz-Guilera, Jordi Duch, and Alex Arenas. 2005. Comparing community structure identification. *Journal of Statistical Mechanics: Theory and Experiment*, 2005(09):P09008.

Katrin Erk and Diana McCarthy. 2009. Graded word sense assignment. In *Proceedings of Empirical Methods in Natural Language Processing (EMNLP)*, pages 440–449. ACL.

Katrin Erk, Diana McCarthy, and Nicholas Gaylord. 2009. Investigations on word senses and word usages. In *Proceedings of the Joint Conference of the 47th Annual Meeting of the ACL and the 4th International Joint Conference on Natural Language Processing of the AFNLP*, pages 10–18. ACL.

Christine Fellbaum, editor. 1998. *WordNet: An Electronic Lexical Database*. The MIT Press.

David Hope and Bill Keller. 2013. MaxMax: A Graph-Based Soft Clustering Algorithm Applied to Word Sense Induction. In *Proceedings of CICLing*, pages 368–381.

Nancy Ide and Keith Suderman. 2004. The american national corpus first release. In *Proceedings of the Fourth Language Resources and Evaluation Conference*, pages 1681–1684.

David Jurgens. 2012. An Evaluation of Graded Sense Disambiguation using Word Sense Induction. In *Proceedings of *SEM, the First Joint Conference on Lexical and Computational Semantics*. ACL.

David Jurgens. 2013. Embracing Ambiguity: A Comparison of Annotation Methodologies for Crowdsourcing Word Sense Labels. In *Proceedings of the North American Chapter of the Association for Computational Linguistics (NAACL)*. ACL.

Adam Kilgarriff. 2002. English lexical sample task description. In *Proceedings of ACL-SIGLEX SENSEVAL-2 Workshop*.

Klaus Krippendorff. 1980. *Content Analysis: An Introduction to Its Methodology*. Sage, Beverly Hills, CA.

Klaus Krippendorff. 2004. *Content Analysis: An Introduction to Its Methodology*. Sage, Thousand Oaks, CA, second edition.

Ravi Kumar and Sergei Vassilvitskii. 2010. Generalized distances between rankings. In *Proceedings of the 19th International Conference on World Wide Web (WWW)*, pages 571–580. ACM.

Andrea Lancichinetti, Santo Fortunato, and János Kertész. 2009. Detecting the overlapping and hierarchical community structure in complex networks. *New Journal of Physics*, 11(3):033015.

Jey Han Lau, Paul Cook, Diana McCarthy, David Newman, and Timothy Baldwin. 2012. Word sense induction for novel sense detection. In *Proceedings of the 13th Conference of the European Chapter of the Association for computational Linguistics (EACL 2012)*.

Ping Luo, Hui Xiong, Guoxing Zhan, Junjie Wu, and Zhongzhi Shi. 2009. Information-theoretic distance measures for clustering validation: Generalization and normalization. *IEEE Transactions on Knowledge and Data Engineering*, 21(9):1249–1262.

Suresh Manandhar, Ioannis P. Klapaftis, Dmitriy Dligach, and Sameer S. Pradhan. 2010. SemEval-2010 task 14: Word sense induction & disambiguation. In *Proceedings of the 5th International Workshop on Semantic Evaluation*, pages 63–68. ACL.

Yariv Maron, Michael Lamar, and Elie Bienenstock. 2010. Sphere embedding: An application to part-of-speech induction. In *Proceedings of Advances in Neural Information Processing Systems (NIPS)*.

Aaron F. McDaid, Derek Greene, and Neil Hurley. 2011. Normalized mutual information to evaluate overlapping community finding algorithms. arXiv:1110.2515.

Rada Mihalcea, Timothy Chklovski, and Adam Kilgarriff. 2004. The Senseval-3 English lexical sample task. In *Senseval-3: Third International Workshop on the Evaluation of Systems for the Semantic Analysis of Text*, pages 25–28. ACL.

Alistair Moffat and Justin Zobel. 2008. Rank-biased precision for measurement of retrieval effectiveness. *ACM Transactions on Information Systems (TOIS)*, 27(1):2.

G. Craig Murray and Rebecca Green. 2004. Lexical knowledge and human disagreement on a wsd task. *Computer Speech & Language*, 18(3):209–222.

Roberto Navigli, David Jurgens, and Daniele Vanilla. 2013. Semeval-2013 task 12: Multilingual word sense disambiguation. In *Proceedings of the 7th International Workshop on Semantic Evaluation*.

Roberto Navigli. 2009. Word Sense Disambiguation: A Survey. *ACM Computing Surveys*, 41(2):1–69.

Rebecca Passonneau, Nizar Habash, and Owen Rambow. 2006. Inter-annotator agreement on a multilingual semantic annotation task. In *Proceedings of the Fifth International Conference on Language Resources and Evaluation (LREC)*, pages 1951–1956.

Rebecca J Passonneau, Collin Baker, Christiane Fellbaum, and Nancy Ide. 2012a. The MASC word sense sentence corpus. In *Proceedings of LREC*.

Rebecca J. Passonneau, Vikas Bhardwaj, Ansaf Salleb-Aouissi, and Nancy Ide. 2012b. Multiplicity and word sense: evaluating and learning from multiply labeled word sense annotations. *Language Resources and Evaluation*, pages 1–34.

Sameer S. Pradhan, Edward Loper, Dmitriy Dligach, and Martha Palmer. 2007. SemEval-2007 task 17: English lexical sample, SRL, and all-words. In *Proceedings of the 4th International Workshop on Semantic Evaluations*. ACL.

Andrew Rosenberg and Julia Hirschberg. 2007. V-measure: A conditional entropy-based external cluster evaluation measure. In *Proceedings of the 2007 Joint Conference on Empirical Methods in Natural Language Processing and Computational Natural Language Learning (EMNLP-CoNLL)*. ACL.

Anna Rumshisky, Nick Botchan, Sophie Kushkuley, and James Pustejovsky. 2012. Word sense inventories by non-experts. In *Proceedings of the 8th International Conference on Language Resources and Evaluation (LREC)*.

Yee Whye Teh, Michael I. Jordan, Matthew J. Beal, and David M. Blei. 2006. Hierarchical dirichlet processes. *Journal of the American Statistical Association*, 101(476):1566–1581.

Jean Véronis. 1998. A study of polysemy judgments and inter-annotator agreement. In *Program and advanced papers of the Senseval workshop*.

Nguyen Xuan Vinh, Julien Epps, and James Bailey. 2010. Information theoretic measures for clusterings comparison: Variants, properties, normalization and correction for chance. *The Journal of Machine Learning Research*, 11:2837–2854.

Deniz Yuret. 2012. FASTSUBS: An Efcient Admissible Algorithm for Finding the Most Likely Lexical Substitutes Using a Statistical Language Model. *Computing Research Repository (CoRR)*.

AI-KU: Using Substitute Vectors and Co-Occurrence Modeling for Word Sense Induction and Disambiguation

Osman Başkaya **Enis Sert** **Volkan Cirik** **Deniz Yuret**

Artificial Intelligence Laboratory
Koç University, İstanbul, Turkey
{obaskaya,esert,vcirik,dyuret}@ku.edu.tr

Abstract

Word sense induction aims to discover different senses of a word from a corpus by using unsupervised learning approaches. Once a sense inventory is obtained for an ambiguous word, word sense discrimination approaches choose the best-fitting single sense for a given context from the induced sense inventory. However, there may not be a clear distinction between one sense and another, although for a context, more than one induced sense can be suitable. Graded word sense method allows for labeling a word in more than one sense. In contrast to the most common approach which is to apply clustering or graph partitioning on a representation of first or second order co-occurrences of a word, we propose a system that creates a substitute vector for each target word from the most likely substitutes suggested by a statistical language model. Word samples are then taken according to probabilities of these substitutes and the results of the co-occurrence model are clustered. This approach outperforms the other systems on graded word sense induction task in SemEval-2013.

1 Introduction

There exists several drawbacks of representing the word senses with a fixed-list of definitions of a manually constructed lexical database. There is no guarantee that they reflect the exact meaning of a target word in a given context since they usually contain definitions that are too general (Véronis, 2004). More so, lexical databases often include many rare senses while missing corpus/domain-specific senses (Pantel and Lin, 2004). The goal of Word Sense Induction (WSI) is to solve these problems by automatically discovering the meanings of a target word from a text, not pre-defined sense inventories. Word Sense Discrimination (WSD) approaches determine best-fitting sense among the meanings that are discovered for an ambiguous word. However, (Erk et al., 2009) suggested that annotators often gave high ratings to more than one WordNet sense for the same occurrence. They introduced a novel annotation paradigm allowing that words have more than one sense with a degree of applicability.

Unlike previous SemEval tasks in which systems labeled a target word's meaning with only one sense, word sense induction task in SemEval-2013 relaxes this by allowing a target word to have more than one sense if applicable.

Word sense induction approaches can be categorized into graph based models, bayesian, and vector-space ones. In graph-based approaches, every context word is represented as a vertex and if two context words co-occur in one or more instances of a target word, then two vertices are connected with an edge. When the graph is obtained, one of the graph clustering algorithm is employed. As a result, different partitions indicate the different senses of a target word (Véronis, 2004). Agirre et al. (2006) explored the use of two graph algorithms for unsupervised induction and tagging of nominal word senses based on corpora. Recently, Korkontzelos and Manandhar (2010) proposed a graph-based model which achieved good results on word sense induction and discrimination task in SemEval-2010.

*Second Joint Conference on Lexical and Computational Semantics (*SEM), Volume 2: Seventh International Workshop on Semantic Evaluation (SemEval 2013)*, pages 300–306, Atlanta, Georgia, June 14-15, 2013.

Brody and Lapata (2009) proposed a Bayesian approach modeling the contexts of the ambiguous word as samples from a multinomial distribution over senses which are in turn characterized as distributions over words.

Vector-space models, on the other hand, typically create context vector by using first or second order co-occurrences. Once context vector has been constructed, different clustering algorithms may be applied. However, representing the context with first or second order co-occurrences can be difficult since there are plenty of parameters to be considered such as the order of occurrence, context window size, statistical significance of words in the context window and so on. Instead of dealing with these, we suggest representing the context with the most likely substitutes determined by a statistical language model. Statistical language models based on large corpora has been examined in (Yuret, 2007; Hawker, 2007; Yuret and Yatbaz, 2010) for unsupervised word sense disambiguation and lexical substitution. Moreover, the best results in unsupervised part-of-speech induction achieved by using substitute vectors (Yatbaz et al., 2012).

In this paper, we propose a system that represents the context of each target word by using high probability substitutes according to a statistical language model. These substitute words and their probabilities are used to create word pairs (instance id - substitute word) to feed our co-occurrence model. The output of the co-occurrence model is clustered by k-means algorithm. Our systems perform well among other submitted systems in SemEval-2013.

Rest of the paper is organized as follows. Section 2 describes the provided datasets and evaluation measures of the task. Section 3 gives details of our algorithm and is divided into five contiguous subsections that correspond to each step of our system. In Section 4 we present the differences between our three systems and their performances. Finally, Section 5 summarizes our work in this task. The code to replicate this work is available at `http://goo.gl/jPTZQ`.

2 Data and Evaluation Methodology

The test data for the graded word sense induction task in SemEval-2013 includes 50 terms containing 20 verbs, 20 nouns and 10 adjectives. There are a total of 4664 test instances provided. All evaluation was performed on test instances only. In addition, the organizers provided sense labeled trial data which can be used for tuning. This trial data is a redistribution of the Graded Sense and Usage data set provided by Katrin Erk, Diana McCarthy, and Nicholas Gaylord (Erk et al., 2009). It consists of 8 terms; 3 verbs, 3 nouns, and 2 adjectives all with moderate polysemy (4-7 senses). Each term in trial data has 50 contexts, in total 400 instances provided. Lastly, participants can use ukWaC[1], a 2-billion word web-gathered corpus, for sense induction. Furthermore, unlike in previous WSI tasks, organizers allow participants to use additional contexts not found in the ukWaC under the condition that they submit systems for both using only the ukWaC and with their augmented corpora.

The gold-standard of test data was prepared using WordNet 3.1 by 10 annotators. Since WSI systems report their annotations in a different sense inventory than WordNet 3.1, a mapping procedure should be used first. The organizers use the sense mapping procedure explained in (Jurgens, 2012). This procedure has adopted the supervised evaluation setting of past SemEval WSI Tasks, but the main difference is that the former takes into account applicability weights for each sense which is a necessary for graded word sense.

Evaluation can be divided into two categories: (1) a traditional WSD task for Unsupervised WSD and WSI systems, (2) a clustering comparison setting that evaluates the similarity of the sense inventories for WSI systems. WSD evaluation is made according to three objectives:

- Their ability to detect which senses are applicable (Jaccard Index is used)
- Their ability to rank the applicable senses according to the level of applicability (Weighted Kendall's τ is used)
- Their ability to quantify the level of applicability for each sense (Weighted Normalized Discounted Cumulative Gain is used)

Clustering comparison is made by using:

[1] Available here: http://wacky.sslmit.unibo.it

- Fuzzy Normalized Mutual Information: It captures the alignment of the two clusterings independent of the cluster sizes and therefore serves as an effective measure of the ability of an approach to accurately model rare senses.

- Fuzzy B-Cubed: It provides an item-based evaluation that is sensitive to the cluster size skew and effectively captures the expected performance of the system on a dataset where the cluster (i.e., sense) distribution would be equivalent.

More details can be found on the task website.[2]

3 Algorithm

In this section, we explain our algorithm. First, we describe data enrichment procedure then we will answer how each instance's substitute vector was constructed. In contrast to common practice which is clustering the context directly, we first performed word sampling on the substitute vectors and created instance id - substitute word pairs as explained in Subsection 3.3. These pairs were used in the co-occurrence modeling step described in Subsection 3.4. Finally, we clustered these co-occurrence modeling output with the k-means clustering algorithm. It is worth noting that this pipeline is performed on each target word separately.

SRILM (Stolcke, 2002) is employed on entire ukWaC corpus for the 4-gram language model to conduct all experiments.

3.1 Data Enrichment

Data enrichment aims to increase the number of instances of target words. Our preliminary experiments on the trial data showed that additional contexts increase the performance of our systems.

Assuming that our target word is *book* in noun form. We randomly fetch 20,000 additional contexts from ukWaC where our target word occurs with the same part-of-speech tag. This implies that we skip those sentences in which the word *book* functions as a verb. These additional contexts are labeled with unique numbers so that we can distinguish actual instances in the test data. We follow this procedure for every target word in the test data. In total, 1 million additional instances were fetched from ukWac. Hereafter we refer to this new dataset with as an expanded dataset.

[2]www.cs.york.ac.uk/semeval-2013/task13/

Substitute	Probability
solve	0.305
complete	0.236
meet	0.096
overcome	0.026
counter	0.022
tackle	0.014
address	0.012
...	...
...	...

Table 1: The most likely substitutes for **meet**

3.2 Substitute Vectors

Unlike other WSI methods which rely on the first or the second order co-occurrences (Pedersen, 2010), we represent the context of each target word instance by finding the most likely substitutes suggested by the 4-gram language model we built from ukWaC corpus. The high probability substitutes reflect both semantic and syntactic properties of the context as seen in Table 1 for the following example:

> And we need Your help to **meet** the challenge!

For every instance in our expanded dataset, we use three tokens each on the left and the right side of a target word as a context when estimating the probabilities for potential lexical substitutes. This tight window size might seem limited, however, tight context windows give better scores for semantic similarity, while larger context windows or second-order context words are better for modeling general topical relatedness (Sahlgren, 2006; Peirsman et al., 2008).

Fastsubs (Yuret, 2012) was used for this process and the top 100 most likely substitutes were used for representing each instance since the rest of the substitutes had negligible probabilities. These top 100 probabilities were normalized to add up to 1.0 giving us a final substitute vector for a particular target word's instance. Note that the substitute vector is a

Instance ID	Substitute Word
$meet_1$	complete
$meet_1$	solve
$meet_1$	solve
$meet_1$	overcome
...	...
...	...
$meet_1$	meet
$meet_1$	complete
$meet_1$	solve
$meet_1$	solve

Table 2: Substitute word sampling for instance $meet_1$

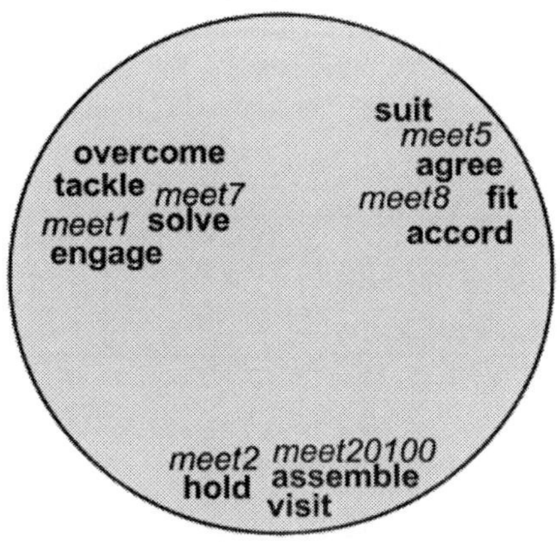

Figure 1: Co-Occcurrence Embedding Sphere for **meet**

function of the context only and is indifferent to the target word.

At the end of this step, we had 1,004,466 substitute vectors. The next common step might be to cluster these vectors either locally, which means every target word will be clustered separately; or globally, which indicates all instances (approximately 1 million) will be clustered together. Both approaches led us to lower scores than the presented method. Therefore, instead of clustering substitute vectors directly, we relied on co-occurrence modeling.

3.3 Substitute Word Sampling

Before running S-CODE (Maron et al., 2010) to model co-occurrence statistics, we needed to perform the substitute word sampling. For each target word's instance, we sample 100 substitutes from its substitute vector. Assuming that our target word is *meet* and its substitute vector is the one shown in

Instance ID	Substitute Word
$meet_1$	complete
$meet_1$	solve
...	...
$meet_2$	hold
$meet_2$	visit
...	...
$meet_{20100}$	assemble
...	...
$meet_{20100}$	gather

Table 3: Substitute sampling for a target word **meet**. Instance ID - Substitute word pairs

Table 1. We choose 100 substitutes from this instance's substitute vector by using individual probabilities of substitutes. As seen in Table 2, those substitutes which have high probabilities dominate the right column. Recall that Table 2 illustrates only one instance (subscript denotes the instance number) for the target word *meet* which has 20,000 and 100 instances from the context enrichment procedure and the test, respectively. We followed the same procedure for every instance of each target word. Table 3 depicts instance id - substitute word pairs for the target word *meet* rather than for only one instance shown in Table 2.

3.4 Co-Occurrence Modeling

After sampling, we had approximately 20,000 instance id - substitute word pairs. These pairs were used to feed S-CODE. The premise is that words with similar meanings will occur in similar contexts (Harris, 1954), and at the end this procedure enables us to put together words with similar meanings as well as making the clustering procedure more accurate. If two different instances have similar substitute word pairs (i.e, similar contexts) then these two word pairs attract each other and they will be located closely on the unit sphere, otherwise they will repel and eventually be far away from each other (see Figure 1).

3.5 Clustering

We used k-means clustering on S-CODE sphere. Note that the procedures explained in the foregone subsections were repeated for each target

	System	JI	WKT	WNDCG
All Instances	ai-ku	0.759	0.804	0.432
	ai-ku(a1000)	0.759	0.794	0.612
	ai-ku(r5-a1000)	0.760	0.800	0.541
	MFS	0.381	0.655	0.337
	All-Senses	0.757	0.745	0.660
	All-Senses-freq-ranked	0.757	0.789	0.671
	All-Senses-avg-ranked	0.757	0.806	0.706
	Random-3	0.776	0.784	0.306
	Random-n	0.795	0.747	0.301

Table 4: Supervised results on the trial set using median gold-standard (JI: Jaccard Index FScore, WKT: Weighted Kendall's Tau FScore, WNDCG: Weighted Normalized Discounted Cumulative Gain FScore)

word. More precisely, the substitute sampling, co-occurrence modeling and clustering were performed one by one for each target word.

We picked 22 as k value since the test set contained words with 3 to 22 senses. After all word pairs were labeled, we counted all class labels for each instance in the test set. For example, if meet_1's 50 word pairs are labeled with c_1 and 30 word pairs are labeled with c_2 and finally 20 word pairs are labeled with c_3, then this particular instance would have 50% sense_1, 30% sense_2 and 20% sense_3.

4 Evaluation Results

In this section, we will discuss evaluation scores and the characteristics of the test and the trial data.

All three AI-KU systems followed the same procedures described in Section 3. After clustering, some basic post-processing operations were performed for *ai-ku(a1000)* and *ai-ku(r5-a1000)*. For *ai-ku(a1000)*, we added 1000 to all sense labels which were obtained from the clustering procedure; for *ai-ku(r5-a1000)*, those sense labels occurred less than 5 times in clustering were removed since we considered them to be unreliable labels, afterwards we added 1000 for all remaining sense labels.

Supervised Metrics: Table 5 shows the performance of our systems on the test data using all instances (verbs, nouns, adjectives) for all supervised measures and in comparison with the systems that performed best and worst, most frequent sense (MFS), all senses equally weighted, all senses average weighted, random-3, and random-n baselines. Bold numbers indicate that ai-ku achieved best scores among all submitted systems. Our systems performed generally well for all three supervised measures and slightly better for all submitted systems. On the other hand, baselines achieved better scores than all participants. More precisely, on sense detection objective, MFS baseline obtained 0.552 which is the top score, while the best submitted system could reach only 0.244. Why is it the case that MFS had one of the worst sense detection score on trial data (see Table 4), but best on test data? Unlike the trial data, test data largely consists of only one sense instances, MFS usually gives correct answer. Table 6 illustrates the characteristics of the test and trial data. Instances annotated with multiple sense had a very small fraction in the test data. In fact, 517 instances in the test set were annotated with two senses (11%) and only 25 were annotated with three senses (0.5%). However, trial data provided by the organizers had almost 5 senses per instance on the average. A similar results can be observed in All-Senses baselines. On sense ranking objec-

	System	JI	WKT	WNDCG
All Instances	ai-ku	0.197	0.620	**0.387**
	ai-ku(a1000)	0.197	0.606	0.215
	ai-ku(r5-a1000)	**0.244**	**0.642**	0.332
	Submitted-Best	0.244	0.642	0.387
	All-Best	0.552	0.787	0.499
	All-Worst	0.149	0.465	0.215
	MFS	0.552	0.560	0.412
	All-Senses-eq-weighted	0.149	0.787	0.436
	All-Senses-avg-ranked	0.187	0.613	0.499
	Random-3	0.244	0.633	0.287
	Random-n	0.290	0.638	0.286

Table 5: Supervised results on the test set. (Submitted-Best indicates the best scores among all submitted system. All-Best indicates the best scores among all submitted systems and baselines. JI: Jaccard Index FScore, WKT: Weighted Kendall's Tau FScore, WNDCG: Weighted Normalized Discounted Cumulative Gain FScore)

	Trial Data	Test Data
Number of Sense	4.97	1.19
Sense Perplexity	5.79	3.78

Table 6: Average number of senses and average sense perplexity for trial and test data

	System	FScore	FNMI	FB-Cubed
All Single-sense Instances	ai-ku	**0.641**	**0.045**	0.351
	ai-ku(a1000)	0.601	0.023	0.288
	ai-ku(r5-a1000)	0.628	0.026	0.421
	Submitted-Best	0.641	0.045	0.441
	All-Best	0.641	0.048	0.570
	All-Worst	0.477	0.006	0.180
	MFS	0.578	-	-
	SemCor-MFS	0.477	-	-
	One Sense	0.569	0.0	0.570
	Random-3	0.555	0.010	0.359
	Random-n	0.533	0.006	0.223

Table 7: Supervised and unsupervised results on the test set using instances which have only one sense. Bold numbers indicate that ai-ku achieved the best submitted system scores. (FScore: Supervised FScore, FNMI: Fuzzy Normalized Mutual Information, FB-Cubed: Fuzzy B-Cubed FScore)

	System	Fuzzy NMI	Fuzzy B-Cubed
All Instances	ai-ku	**0.065**	0.390
	ai-ku(a1000)	0.035	0.320
	ai-ku(r5-a1000)	0.039	0.451
	Submitted-Best	0.065	0.483
	All-Best	0.065	0.623
	All-Worst	0.016	0.201
	Random-2	0.028	0.474
	Random-3	0.018	0.382
	Random-n	0.016	0.245

Table 8: Scores on clustering measures (Fuzzy NMI: Fuzzy Normalized Mutual Information, Fuzzy B-Cubed: Fuzzy B-Cubed FScore)

	All instances
ai-ku	7.72
ai-ku(a1000)	7.72
ai-ku(r5-a1000)	3.11

Table 9: Average number of senses for each ai-ku systems on test data

tives, *All-Sense-eq-weighted* outperformed all other systems. The reason is the same as the above. This baseline ranks all senses equally and since most instances had been annotated only one sense, the other wrong senses were tied and placed at the second position in ranking. As a result, this baseline achieved the highest score. Finally, for quantifying the level of applicability for each sense, Weighted NDCG was employed. *ai-ku* outperformed other submitted systems, but top score was achieved by all-sense-avg-weighted baseline. Addition to these results, organizers provided scores for instances which have only one sense. This setting contains 89% of the test data. Table 7 shows supervised and unsupervised scores for all single-sense instances. Our base system, *ai-ku*, outperformed all other system and all baselines for FScore. Moreover, it also achieved the second best score (0.045) for Fuzzy NMI. Only one baseline (*one sense per instance*) obtained slightly better score (0.048) for this metric. For Fuzzy B-Cubed, *ai-ku(r5-a1000)* obtained 0.421 which is the third best score.

Clustering Comparison: This evaluation setting aims to measure the similarity of the induced sense inventories for WSI systems. Unlike supervised metrics, it avoids potential loss of sense information since this setting does not require any sense mapping procedure to convert induced senses to a WordNet sense. *ai-ku* performed best for Fuzzy NMI among other systems included baselines. For Fuzzy B-Cubed, *ai-ku(r5a1000)* outperformed random-3 and random-n baselines. Table 8 depicts the performance of our systems, best and worst systems as well as the random baselines.

The best scores for the graded word sense induction task in SemEval-2013 are mostly achieved by baselines in supervised setting. Major problem is that there is huge sense differences between test and trial data regarding to number of sense distribution. Participants that used trial data as for parameter tuning and picking the best algorithm achieved lower scores than baselines since test data does not show properties of trial data. Consequently, *ai-ku* systems produce significantly more senses than the gold-standard (see Table 9), and this mainly deteriorates our performance.

5 Conclusion

In this paper, we presented substitute vector representation and co-occurrence modeling on WSI task. Clustering substitute vectors directly gives lower scores. Thus, taking samples from each target's substitute vector, we obtained instance id - substitute word pairs. These pairs were used by S-CODE. Finally we run k-means on the S-CODE. Although our systems were highly ranked among the other submitted systems, no system showed better performance than the top baselines for all metrics. One explanation is that trial data does not reflect the characteristics of test data according to their number of sense distributions. Systems used trial data biased to return more than one sense for each instance since average number of sense is almost five in trial data. In addition, baselines (except random ones) know true sense distribution in the test data beforehand which make them harder to beat.

References

Eneko Agirre, David Martínez, Oier López de Lacalle and Aitor Soroa. 2006. Two graph-based algorithms for state-of-the-art WSD. In *Proceedings of the 2006 Conference on Empirical Methods in Natural Language Processing,* pages 585-593.

Samuel Brody and Mirella Lapata. 2009. Bayesian Word Sense Induction. In *Proceedings of the 12th Conference of the European Chapter of the ACL (EACL 2009),* pages 103-111, Athens, Greece.

Katrin Erk, Diana McCarthy, Nicholas Gaylord. 2009. Investigations on Word Senses and Word Usages, In *Proceedings of ACL-09* Singapore.

Zellig S. Harris. 2012. Distributional structure. *Word,* Vol. 10, pages 146-162.

Tobias Hawker. 2007. USYD: WSD and lexical substitution using the Web 1T corpus In *Proceedings of the Fourth International Workshop on Semantic Evaluations (SemEval-2007),* pages 207214, Prague, Czech Republic, June. Association for Computational Linguistics.

Ioannis Korkontzelos and Suresh Manandhar. 2010. UoY: Graphs of Unambiguous Vertices for Word Sense Induction and Disambiguation. In *Proceedings of the 5th International Workshop on Semantic Evaluation.* Uppsala, Sweden.

David Jurgens. 2012. An Evaluation of Graded Sense Disambiguation using Word Sense Induction. In *SemEval '12 Proceedings of the First Joint Conference on Lexical and Computational Semantics.* pages 189-198.

Yariv Maron, Michael Lamar, and Elie Bienenstock. 2012. Sphere embedding: An application to part-of-speech induction. In J. Lafferty, C. K. I. Williams, J. Shawe-Taylor, R.S. Zemel, and A. Culotta, editors, In *Advances in Neural Information Processing Systems 23,* pages 1567-1575.

Patrick Pantel and Dekang Lin. 2002. Discovering Word Senses from Text. In *Proceedings of the 8th ACM SIGKDD Conference,* pages 613-619, New York, NY, USA. ACM.

Ted Pedersen. 2010. Duluth-WSI: SenseClusters Applied to the Sense Induction Task of SemEval-2. In *Proceedings of the 5th International Workshop on Semantic Evaluation.* pages 363-366, Uppsala, Sweden.

Yves Peirsman, Kris Heylen and Dirk Geeraerts. 2008. Size Matters. Tight and Loose Context Definitions in English Word Space Models. *In Proceedings of the ESSLLI Workshop on Distributional Lexical Semantics,* Hamburg, Germany.

Magnus Sahlgren. 2002. The Word-Space Model: Using distributional analysis to represent syntagmatic and paradigmatic relations between words in high-dimensional vector spaces. *Ph.D. dissertation, Department of Linguistics, Stockholm University.*

Andreas Stolcke. 2002. SRILM - An Extensible Language Modeling Toolkit. *Proceedings International Conference on Spoken Language Processing,* pages 257286.

Jean Véronis. 2004. HyperLex: Lexical Cartography for Information Retrieval. *Computer Speech & Language,* 18(3):223-252.

Mehmet Ali Yatbaz, Enis Sert and Deniz Yuret. 2012. Learning Syntactic Categories Using Paradigmatic Representations of Word Context. In *Proceedings of the 2012 Joint Conference on Empirical Methods in Natural Language Processing and Computational Natural Language Learning, EMNLP-CoNLL 2012,* July 12-14, 2012, Jeju Island, Korea.

Deniz Yuret. 2012. FASTSUBS: An Efficient Admissible Algorithm for Finding the Most Likely Lexical Substitutes Using a Statistical Language Model. *Computing Research Repository (CoRR).*

Deniz Yuret. 2007. KU: Word sense disambiguation by substitution. In *Proceedings of the Fourth International Workshop on Semantic Evaluations (SemEval-2007),* pages 207214, Prague, Czech Republic, June. Association for Computational Linguistics.

Deniz Yuret and Mehmet Ali Yatbaz. 2010. The noisy channel model for unsupervised word sense disambiguation. *Computational Linguistics,* Volume 36 Issue 1, March 2010, pages 111-127.

unimelb: Topic Modelling-based Word Sense Induction

Jey Han Lau, Paul Cook and **Timothy Baldwin**
Department of Computing and Information Systems
The University of Melbourne
jhlau@csse.unimelb.edu.au, paulcook@unimelb.edu.au,
tb@ldwin.net

Abstract

This paper describes our system for shared task 13 "Word Sense Induction for Graded and Non-Graded Senses" of SemEval-2013. The task is on word sense induction (WSI), and builds on earlier SemEval WSI tasks in exploring the possibility of multiple senses being compatible to varying degrees with a single contextual instance: participants are asked to *grade* senses rather than selecting a single sense like most word sense disambiguation (WSD) settings. The evaluation measures are designed to assess how well a system perceives the different senses in a contextual instance. We adopt a previously-proposed WSI methodology for the task, which is based on a Hierarchical Dirichlet Process (HDP), a nonparametric topic model. Our system requires no parameter tuning, uses the English ukWaC as an external resource, and achieves encouraging results over the shared task.

1 Introduction

In our previous work (Lau et al., 2012) we developed a word-sense induction (WSI) system based on topic modelling, specifically a Hierarchical Dirichlet Process (Teh et al., 2006). In evaluations over the SemEval-2007 and SemEval-2010 WSI tasks we achieved performance on par with the current state-of-the art. The SemEval-2007 and SemEval-2010 WSI tasks assumed that each usage of a word has a single gold-standard sense. In this paper we apply this WSI method "off-the-shelf", with no adaptation, to the novel SemEval-2013 task of "Word Sense Induction for Graded and Non-Graded Senses". Given that the topic model allocates a multinomial distribution over topics to each word usage ("document", in topic modelling terms), the SemEval-2013 WSI task is an ideal means for evaluating this aspect of the topic model.

2 System Description

Our system is based on the WSI methodology proposed by Lau et al. (2012), and also applied to SemEval-2013 Task 11 on WSI for web snippet clustering (Lau et al., to appear). The core machinery of our system is driven by a Latent Dirichlet Allocation (LDA) topic model (Blei et al., 2003). In LDA, the model learns latent topics for a collection of documents, and associates these latent topics with every document in the collection. A topic is represented by a multinomial distribution of words, and the association of topics with documents is represented by a multinomial distribution of topics, a distribution for each document. The generative process of LDA for drawing word w in document d is as follows:

1. draw latent topic z from document d;
2. draw word w from the chosen latent topic z.

The probability of selecting word w given a document d is thus given by:

$$P(w|d) = \sum_{z=1}^{T} P(w|t=z)P(t=z|d).$$

where t is the topic variable, and T is the number of topics.

*Second Joint Conference on Lexical and Computational Semantics (*SEM), Volume 2: Seventh International Workshop on Semantic Evaluation (SemEval 2013)*, pages 307–311, Atlanta, Georgia, June 14-15, 2013. ©2013 Association for Computational Linguistics

The number of topics, T, is a parameter in LDA. We relax this assumption by extending the model to be non-parametric, using a Hierarchical Dirichlet Process (HDP: (Teh et al., 2006)). HDP learns the number of topics based on data, with the concentration parameters γ and α_0 controlling the variability of topics in the documents (for details of HDP please refer to the original paper).

To apply HDP to WSI, the latent topics are interpreted as the word senses, and the documents are usages that contain the target word of interest. That is, given a target word (e.g. *paper*), a "document" in our application is a sentence context surrounding the target word. In addition to the bag of words surrounding the target word, we also include positional context word information, which was used in our earlier work (Lau et al., 2012). That is, we introduce an additional word feature for each of the three words to the left and right of the target word. An example of the topic model features is given in Table 1.

2.1 Background Corpus and Preprocessing

The test dataset provides us with contextual instances for each target word, and these instances constitute the documents for the topic model. The text of the test data is tokenised and lemmatised using OpenNLP and Morpha (Minnen et al., 2001).

Note, however, that there are only 100 instances for most target words in the test dataset, and as such the dataset may be too small for the topic model to induce meaningful senses. To this end, we turn to the English ukWaC — a web corpus of approximately 1.9 billion tokens — to expand the data, by extracting context sentences that contain the target word. Each extracted usage is a three-sentence context containing the target word: the original sentence that contains the actual usage and its preceding and succeeding sentences. The extraction of usages from the ukWaC significantly increases the amount of information for the topic model to learn the senses for the target words from. However, HDP is computationally intensive, so we limit the number of extracted usages from the ukWaC using two sampling approaches:

UNIMELB (5P) Take a 5% random sample of usages;

UNIMELB (50K) Limit the maximum number of randomly-sampled usages to 50,000 instances.

The usages from the ukWaC are tokenised and lemmatised using TreeTagger (Schmid, 1994), as provided by the corpus.

To summarise, for each target word we apply the HDP model to the combined collection of the test instances (provided by the shared task) and the extracted usages from the English ukWaC (noting that each instance/usage corresponds to a topic model "document"). The topic model learns the senses/topics for all documents in the collection, but we only use the sense/topic distribution for the test instances as they are the ones evaluated in the shared task.

3 Experiments and Results

Following Lau et al. (2012), we use the default parameters ($\gamma = 0.1$ and $\alpha_0 = 1.0$) for HDP.[1] For each target word, we apply HDP to induce the senses, and a distribution of senses is produced for each "document" in the model. To grade the senses for the instances in the test dataset, we apply the sense probabilities learnt by the topic model as the sense weights without any modification.

To illustrate the senses induced by our model, we present the top-10 words of the induced senses for the verb *strike* in Table 2. Although 13 senses in total are induced and some of them do not seem very coherent, only the first 8 senses — the more coherent ones — are observed (i.e., have non-zero probability for any usage) in the test dataset.

Two forms of evaluation are used in the task: WSD evaluation and clustering comparison. For WSD evaluation, three measures are used: (1) Jaccard Index (JI), which measures the degree of overlap between the induced senses and the gold senses; (2) positionally-weighted Kendall's tau (KT: (Kumar and Vassilvitskii, 2010)), which measures the correlation between the ranking of the induced senses and that of the gold senses; and (3) normalised discounted cumulative gain (NDCG), which

[1] These settings were considered "vague" priors in Teh et al. (2006). They were tested in Lau et al. (2012) and the model was shown to be robust under different parameter settings. As such we decided to keep the settings. The implementation of our WSI system can be accessed via GitHub: `https://github.com/jhlau/hdp-wsi`.

Target word	*dogs*
Context sentence	Most breeds of *dogs* are at most a few hundred years old
Bag-of-word features	most, breeds, of, are, at, most, a, few, hundred, years, old
Positional word features	most_#-3, breeds_#-2, of_#-1, are_#1, at_#2, most_#3

Table 1: An example of the topic model features.

Sense Num	Top-10 Terms
1	strike @card@ worker union war iraq week pay government action
2	strike hand god head n't look face fall leave blow
3	strike @card@ balance court company case need balance_#1 order claim
4	strike ball @card@ minute game goal play player shot half
5	strike @card@ people fire disaster area road car ship lightning
6	@card@ strike new news post deal april home business week
7	strike n't people thing think way life book find new
8	@card@ strike coin die john church police age house william
9	div ukl syn color hunter text-decoration australian verb condom font-size
10	invent rocamadour cost mp3 terminal total wav honor omen node
11	training run rush kata performance marathon exercise technique workout interval
12	wrong qha september/2000 sayd — hawksmoor thyna pan salt common
13	zidane offering stone blow zidane_#-1 type type_#2 zidane_#1 blow_#3 materials

Table 2: The top-10 terms for each of the senses induced for the verb *strike* by the HDP model.

measures the correlation between the weights of the induced senses and that of the gold senses. For clustering comparison, fuzzy normalised mutual information (FNMI) and fuzzy b-cubed (FBC) are used. Note that the WSD systems participating in this shared task are not evaluated with clustering comparison metrics, as they do not induce senses/clusters in the same manner as WSI systems.

WSI systems produce senses that are different to the gold standard sense inventory (WordNet 3.1), and the induced senses are mapped to the gold standard senses using the 80/20 validation setting. Details of this mapping procedure are described in Jurgens (2012).

Results for all test instances are presented in Table 3. Note that many baselines are used, only some of which we present in this paper, namely: (1) RANDOM — label instances with one of three random induced senses; (2) SEMCOR MFS — label instances with the most frequently occurring sense in Semcor; (3) TEST MFS — label instances with the most frequently occurring sense in the test dataset. To benchmark our method, we present one or two of the best systems from each team.

Looking at Table 3, our system performs encouragingly well. Although not the best system, we achieve results close to the best system for each evaluation measure.

Most of the instances in the data were annotated with only one sense; only 11% were annotated with two senses, and 0.5% with three. As a result, the task organisers categorised the instances into single-sense instances and multi-sense instances to better analyse the performance of participating systems. Results for single-sense and multi-sense instances are presented in Table 4 and Table 5, respectively. Note that for single-sense instances, only precision is used for WSD evaluation as the Jaccard Index, positionally-weighted Kendall's tau and normalised discounted cumulative gain are not applicable. Our system performs relatively well, and trails marginally behind the best system in most cases.

4 Conclusion

We adopt a WSI methodology from Lau et al. (2012) for the task of grading senses in a WSD setting.

System	JI	KT	NDCG	FNMI	FBC
RANDOM	0.244	0.633	0.287	0.018	0.382
SEMCOR MFS	0.455	0.465	0.339	—	—
TEST MFS	0.552	0.560	0.412	—	—
AI-KU	0.197	0.620	**0.387**	**0.065**	0.390
AI-KU (REMOVE5-AD1000)	**0.244**	**0.642**	0.332	0.039	0.451
LA SAPIENZA (2)	0.149	0.510	0.383	—	—
UoS (TOP-3)	0.232	0.625	0.374	0.045	0.448
UNIMELB (5P)	0.218	0.614	0.365	0.056	0.459
UNIMELB (50K)	0.213	0.620	0.371	0.060	**0.483**

Table 3: Results for all instances. The best-performing system is indicated in boldface.

System	Precision	FNMI	FBC
RANDOM	0.555	0.010	0.359
SEMCOR MFS	0.477	—	—
TEST MFS	0.578	—	—
AI-KU	**0.641**	**0.045**	0.351
AI-KU (REMOVE5-AD1000)	0.628	0.026	0.421
UoS (TOP-3)	0.600	0.028	0.414
UNIMELB (5P)	0.596	0.035	0.421
UNIMELB (50K)	0.605	0.039	**0.441**

Table 4: Results for single-sense instances. The best-performing system is indicated in boldface.

System	JI	KT	NDCG	FNMI	FBC
RANDOM	0.429	0.548	0.236	0.006	0.113
SEMCOR MFS	0.283	0.373	0.197	—	—
TEST MFS	0.354	0.426	0.248	—	—
AI-KU	0.394	0.617	0.317	0.029	0.078
AI-KU (REMOVE5-AD1000)	**0.434**	0.586	0.291	0.004	0.116
LA SAPIENZA (2)	0.263	0.531	**0.365**	—	—
UoS (#WN SENSES)	0.387	**0.628**	0.314	**0.036**	0.037
UNIMELB (5P)	0.426	0.586	0.287	0.019	0.130
UNIMELB (50K)	0.414	0.602	0.299	0.021	**0.134**

Table 5: Results for multi-sense instances. The best-performing system is indicated in boldface.

With no parameter tuning and using only the English ukWaC as an external resource, our system performs relatively well at the task.

References

David M. Blei, Andrew Y. Ng, and Michael I. Jordan. 2003. Latent Dirichlet allocation. *Journal of Machine Learning Research*, 3:993–1022.

David Jurgens. 2012. An evaluation of graded sense disambiguation using word sense induction. In *Proc. of the First Joint Conference on Lexical and Computational Semantics (*SEM 2012)*, pages 189–198, Montréal, Canada.

Ravi Kumar and Sergei Vassilvitskii. 2010. Generalized distances between rankings. In *Proc. of the 19th International Conference on the World Wide Web (WWW 2010)*, pages 571–580, Raleigh, USA.

Jey Han Lau, Paul Cook, Diana McCarthy, David Newman, and Timothy Baldwin. 2012. Word sense induction for novel sense detection. In *Proc. of the 13th Conference of the EACL (EACL 2012)*, pages 591–601, Avignon, France.

Jey Han Lau, Paul Cook, and Timothy Baldwin. to appear. unimelb: Topic modelling-based word sense induction for web snippet clustering. In *Proc. of the 7th International Workshop on Semantic Evaluation (SemEval 2013)*.

Guido Minnen, John Carroll, and Darren Pearce. 2001. Applied morphological processing of English. *Natural Language Engineering*, 7(3):207–223.

Helmut Schmid. 1994. Probabilistic part-of-speech tagging using decision trees. In *Proc. of the Conference on New Methods in Natural Language Processing*, Manchester, 1994.

Yee Whye Teh, Michael I. Jordan, Matthew J. Beal, and David M. Blei. 2006. Hierarchical Dirichlet processes. *Journal of the American Statistical Association*, 101:1566–1581.

SemEval-2013 Task 2: Sentiment Analysis in Twitter

Preslav Nakov
QCRI, Qatar Foundation
pnakov@qf.org.qa

Sara Rosenthal
Columbia University
sara@cs.columbia.edu

Zornitsa Kozareva
USC Information Sciences Institute
kozareva@isi.edu

Veselin Stoyanov
JHU HLTCOE
ves@cs.jhu.edu

Alan Ritter
University of Washington
aritter@cs.washington.edu

Theresa Wilson
JHU HLTCOE
taw@jhu.edu

Abstract

In recent years, sentiment analysis in social media has attracted a lot of research interest and has been used for a number of applications. Unfortunately, research has been hindered by the lack of suitable datasets, complicating the comparison between approaches. To address this issue, we have proposed *SemEval-2013 Task 2: Sentiment Analysis in Twitter*, which included two subtasks: A, an expression-level subtask, and B, a message-level subtask. We used crowdsourcing on Amazon Mechanical Turk to label a large Twitter training dataset along with additional test sets of Twitter and SMS messages for both subtasks. All datasets used in the evaluation are released to the research community. The task attracted significant interest and a total of 149 submissions from 44 teams. The best-performing team achieved an F1 of 88.9% and 69% for subtasks A and B, respectively.

1 Introduction

In the past decade, new forms of communication, such as microblogging and text messaging have emerged and become ubiquitous. Twitter messages (tweets) and cell phone messages (SMS) are often used to share opinions and sentiments about the surrounding world, and the availability of social content generated on sites such as Twitter creates new opportunities to automatically study public opinion.

Working with these informal text genres presents new challenges for natural language processing beyond those encountered when working with more traditional text genres such as newswire.

Tweets and SMS messages are short in length: a sentence or a headline rather than a document. The language they use is very informal, with creative spelling and punctuation, misspellings, slang, new words, URLs, and genre-specific terminology and abbreviations, e.g., RT for re-tweet and #hashtags.[1] How to handle such challenges so as to automatically mine and understand the opinions and sentiments that people are communicating has only very recently been the subject of research (Jansen et al., 2009; Barbosa and Feng, 2010; Bifet et al., 2011; Davidov et al., 2010; O'Connor et al., 2010; Pak and Paroubek, 2010; Tumasjan et al., 2010; Kouloumpis et al., 2011).

Another aspect of social media data, such as Twitter messages, is that they include rich structured information about the individuals involved in the communication. For example, Twitter maintains information about who follows whom. Re-tweets (reshares of a tweet) and tags inside of tweets provide discourse information. Modeling such structured information is important because it provides means for empirically studying social interactions where opinion is conveyed, e.g., we can study the properties of persuasive language or those associated with influential users.

Several corpora with detailed opinion and sentiment annotation have been made freely available, e.g., the MPQA corpus (Wiebe et al., 2005) of newswire text. These corpora have proved very valuable as resources for learning about the language of sentiment in general, but they did not focus on social media.

[1]Hashtags are a type of tagging for Twitter messages.

*Second Joint Conference on Lexical and Computational Semantics (*SEM), Volume 2: Seventh International Workshop on Semantic Evaluation (SemEval 2013)*, pages 312–320, Atlanta, Georgia, June 14-15, 2013.

Twitter	RT @tash_jade: That's really sad, Charlie RT "Until tonight I never realised how fucked up I was" - Charlie Sheen #sheenroast
SMS	Glad to hear you are coping fine in uni... So, wat interview did you go to? How did it go?

Table 1: Examples of sentences from each corpus that contain subjective phrases.

While some Twitter sentiment datasets have already been created, they were either small and proprietary, such as the i-sieve corpus (Kouloumpis et al., 2011), or they were created only for Spanish like the TASS corpus[2] (Villena-Román et al., 2013), or they relied on noisy labels obtained from emoticons and hashtags. They further focused on message-level sentiment, and no Twitter or SMS corpus with expression-level sentiment annotations has been made available so far.

Thus, the primary goal of our SemEval-2013 task 2 has been to promote research that will lead to a better understanding of how sentiment is conveyed in Tweets and SMS messages. Toward that goal, we created the SemEval Tweet corpus, which contains Tweets (for both training and testing) and SMS messages (for testing only) with sentiment expressions annotated with contextual phrase-level polarity as well as an overall message-level polarity. We used this corpus as a testbed for the system evaluation at SemEval-2013 Task 2.

In the remainder of this paper, we first describe the task, the dataset creation process, and the evaluation methodology. We then summarize the characteristics of the approaches taken by the participating systems and we discuss their scores.

2 Task Description

We had two subtasks: an expression-level subtask and a message-level subtask. Participants could choose to participate in either or both subtasks. Below we provide short descriptions of the objectives of these two subtasks.

Subtask A: Contextual Polarity Disambiguation

Given a message containing a marked instance of a word or a phrase, determine whether that instance is positive, negative or neutral in that context. The boundaries for the marked instance were provided: this was a classification task, not an entity recognition task.

Subtask B: Message Polarity Classification

Given a message, decide whether it is of positive, negative, or neutral sentiment. For messages conveying both a positive and a negative sentiment, whichever is the stronger one was to be chosen.

Each participating team was allowed to submit results for two different systems per subtask: one constrained, and one unconstrained. A constrained system could only use the provided data for training, but it could also use other resources such as lexicons obtained elsewhere. An unconstrained system could use any additional data as part of the training process; this could be done in a supervised, semi-supervised, or unsupervised fashion.

Note that constrained/unconstrained refers to the data used to train a classifier. For example, if other data (excluding the test data) was used to develop a sentiment lexicon, and the lexicon was used to generate features, the system would still be constrained. However, if other data (excluding the test data) was used to develop a sentiment lexicon, and this lexicon was used to automatically label additional Tweet/SMS messages and then used with the original data to train the classifier, then such a system would be unconstrained.

3 Dataset Creation

In the following sections we describe the collection and annotation of the Twitter and SMS datasets.

3.1 Data Collection

Twitter is the most common micro-blogging site on the Web, and we used it to gather tweets that express sentiment about popular topics. We first extracted named entities using a Twitter-tuned NER system (Ritter et al., 2011) from millions of tweets, which we collected over a one-year period spanning from January 2012 to January 2013; we used the public streaming Twitter API to download tweets.

[2]http://www.daedalus.es/TASS/corpus.php

Instructions: Subjective words are ones which convey an opinion. Given a sentence, identify whether it is objective, positive, negative, or neutral. Then, identify each subjective word or phrase in the context of the sentence and mark the position of its start and end in the text boxes below. The number above each word indicates its position. The word/phrase will be generated in the adjacent textbox so that you can confirm that you chose the correct range. Choose the polarity of the word or phrase by selecting one of the radio buttons: positive, negative, or neutral. If a sentence is not subjective please select the checkbox indicating that "There are no subjective words/phrases". Please read the examples and invalid responses before beginning if this is your first time answering this hit.

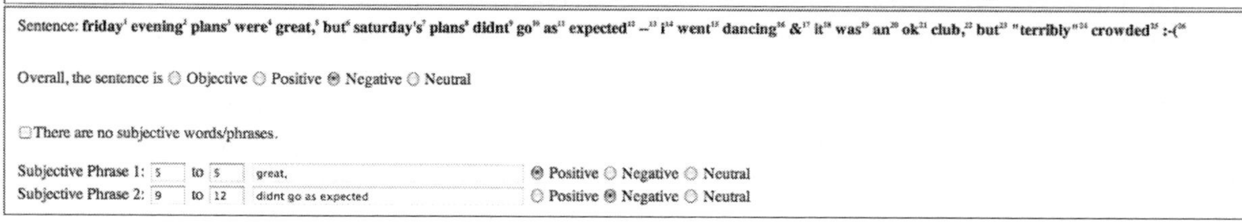

Figure 1: Instructions provided to workers on Mechanical Turk followed by a screenshot.

	Average # of		Total Phrase Count			Vocabulary
Corpus	**Words**	**Characters**	**Positive**	**Negative**	**Neutral**	**Size**
Twitter - Training	25.4	120.0	5,895	3,131	471	20,012
Twitter - Dev	25.5	120.0	648	430	57	4,426
Twitter - Test	25.4	121.2	2,734	1,541	160	11,736
SMS - Test	24.5	95.6	1,071	1,104	159	3,562

Table 2: Statistics for Subtask A.

We then identified popular topics as those named entities that are frequently mentioned in association with a specific date (Ritter et al., 2012). Given this set of automatically identified topics, we gathered tweets from the same time period which mentioned the named entities. The testing messages had different topics from training and spanned later periods.

To identify messages that express sentiment towards these topics, we filtered the tweets using SentiWordNet (Baccianella et al., 2010). We removed messages that contained no sentiment-bearing words, keeping only those with at least one word with positive or negative sentiment score that is greater than 0.3 in SentiWordNet for at least one sense of the words. Without filtering, we found class imbalance to be too high.[3]

Twitter messages are rich in social media features, including out-of-vocabulary (OOV) words, emoticons, and acronyms; see Table 1. A large portion of the OOV words are hashtags (e.g., `#sheenroast`) and mentions (e.g., `@tash_jade`).

Corpus	**Positive**	**Negative**	**Objective / Neutral**
Twitter - Training	3,662	1,466	4,600
Twitter - Dev	575	340	739
Twitter - Test	1,573	601	1,640
SMS - Test	492	394	1,208

Table 3: Statistics for Subtask B.

We annotated the same Twitter messages with annotations for subtask A and subtask B. However, the final training and testing datasets overlap only partially between the two subtasks since we had to throw away messages with low inter-annotator agreement, and this differed between the subtasks. For testing, we also annotated SMS messages, taken from the NUS SMS corpus[4] (Chen and Kan, 2012). Tables 2 and 3 show statistics about the corpora we created for subtasks A and B.

[3] Filtering based on an existing lexicon does bias the dataset to some degree; however, note that the text still contains sentiment expressions outside those in the lexicon.

[4] `http://wing.comp.nus.edu.sg/SMSCorpus/`

	A			B
	Lower	**Avg.**	**Upper**	**Avg.**
Twitter - Train	64.7	82.4	90.8	82.7
Twitter - Dev	51.2	74.7	87.8	78.4
Twitter - Test	68.8	83.6	90.9	76.9
SMS - Test	66.5	88.5	81.2	77.6

Table 4: Bounds for datasets in subtasks A and B.

3.2 Annotation Guidelines

The instructions provided to the annotators, along with an example, are shown in Figure 1. We provided several additional examples to the annotators, shown in Table 5.

In addition, we filtered spammers by considering the following kinds of annotations invalid:

- containing overlapping subjective phrases;
- subjective but without a subjective phrase;
- marking every single word as subjective;
- not having the overall sentiment marked.

3.3 Annotation Process

Our datasets were annotated for sentiment on Mechanical Turk. Each sentence was annotated by five Mechanical Turk workers (Turkers). In order to qualify for the hits, the Turker had to have an approval rate greater than 95% and have completed 50 approved hits. Each Turker was paid three cents per hit. The Turker had to mark all the subjective words/phrases in the sentence by indicating their start and end positions and say whether each subjective word/phrase was positive, negative, or neutral (subtask A). They also had to indicate the overall polarity of the sentence (subtask B).

Figure 1 shows the instructions and an example provided to the Turkers. The first five rows of Table 6 show an example of the subjective words/phrases marked by each of the workers.

For subtask A, we combined the annotations of each of the workers using intersection as indicated in the last row of Table 6. A word had to appear in 2/3 of the annotations in order to be considered subjective. Similarly, a word had to be labeled with a particular polarity (positive, negative, or neutral) 2/3 of the time in order to receive that label.

We also experimented with combining annotations by computing the union of the sentences, and taking the sentence of the worker who annotated the most hits, but we found that these methods were not as accurate. Table 4 shows the lower, average, and upper bounds for all the hits by computing the bounds for each hit and averaging them together. This gives a good indication about how well we can expect the systems to perform. For example, even if we used the best annotator each time, it would still not be possible to get perfect accuracy.

For subtask B, the polarity of the entire sentence was determined based on the majority of the labels. If there was a tie, the sentence was discarded. In order to reduce the number of sentences lost, we combined the objective and the neutral labels, which Turkers tended to mix up. Table 4 shows the average bound for subtask B by computing the bounds for each hit and averaging them together. Since the polarity is chosen based on the majority, the upper bound is 100%.

4 Scoring

For both subtasks, the participating systems were required to perform a three-way classification – a particular marked phrase (for subtask A) or an entire message (for subtask B) was to be classified as *positive*, *negative*, or *objective*. For each system, we computed a score for predicting positive/negative phrases/messages vs. the other two classes.

For instance, to compute positive precision, P_{pos}, we find the number of phrases/messages that a system correctly predicted to be positive, and we divide that number by the total number of messages it predicted to be positive. To compute recall, for the positive class, R_{pos}, we find the number of messages correctly predicted to be positive and we divide that number by the total number of positive messages in the gold standard.

We then calculate F-score for the positive labels, the harmonic average of precision and recall as follows $F_{pos} = 2\frac{P_{pos}R_{pos}}{P_{pos}+R_{pos}}$. We carry out a similar computation to calculate F_{neg}, which is F1 for negative messages.

The overall score for each system run is then given by the average of the F1-scores for the positive and negative classes: $F = (F_{pos} + F_{neg})/2$.

Authorities are *only too aware* that Kashgar is 4,000 kilometres (2,500 miles) from Beijing but *only* a tenth of the distance from the Pakistani border, and are *desperate* to *ensure instability or militancy* does not leak over the frontiers.
Taiwan-made products *stood a good chance* of becoming *even more competitive thanks to* wider access to overseas markets and lower costs for material imports, he said.
"March *appears* to be a *more reasonable* estimate while earlier admission *cannot be entirely ruled out*," according to Chen, also Taiwan's chief WTO negotiator.
friday evening plans were great, but saturday's plans *didnt go as expected* – i went dancing & it was an *ok* club, but *terribly crowded :-(*
WHY THE *HELL* DO YOU GUYS ALL HAVE MRS. KENNEDY! SHES A FUCKING DOUCHE
AT&T was *okay* but whenever they do something *nice* in the name of customer service it seems like a favor, while T-Mobile makes that a *normal everyday thin*
obama should be *impeached* on *TREASON* charges. Our Nuclear arsenal was TOP Secret. Till HE told our enemies what we had. *#Coward #Traitor*
My graduation speech: "I'd like to *thanks* Google, Wikipedia and my computer! *:D* #iThingteens

Table 5: List of example sentences with annotations that were provided to the annotators. All subjective phrases are italicized. Positive phrases are in green, negative phrases are in red, and neutral phrases are in blue.

Worker 1	***I would love*** to watch Vampire Diaries ***:)*** and some Heroes! ***Great combination***	9/13
Worker 2	I would love to watch Vampire Diaries :) and some ***Heroes! Great*** combination	11/13
Worker 3	I ***would love*** to watch Vampire Diaries ***:)*** and some Heroes! ***Great*** combination	10/13
Worker 4	I would ***love*** to watch Vampire Diaries :) and some Heroes! ***Great*** combination	13/13
Worker 5	I would love to watch Vampire Diaries :) and some Heroes! ***Great*** combination	11/13
Intersection	I would ***love*** to watch Vampire Diaries :) and some Heroes! ***Great*** combination	

Table 6: Example of a sentence annotated for subjectivity on Mechanical Turk. Words and phrases that were marked as subjective are italicized and highlighted in bold. The first five rows are annotations provided by Turkers, and the final row shows their intersection. The final column shows the accuracy for each annotation compared to the intersection.

Note that ignoring $F_{neutral}$ does not reduce the task to predicting positive vs. negative labels only (even though some participants have chosen to do so) since the gold standard still contains neutral labels which are to be predicted: F_{pos} and F_{neg} would suffer if these examples are labeled as positive and/or negative instead of neutral.

We provided participants with a scorer. In addition to outputting the overall F-score, it produced a confusion matrix for the three prediction classes (*positive*, *negative*, and *objective*), and it also validated the data submission format.

5 Participants and Results

The results for subtask A are shown in Tables 7 and 8 for Twitter and for SMS messages, respectively; those for subtask B are shown in Table 9 for Twitter and in Table 10 for SMS messages. Systems are ranked by their scores for the constrained runs; the ranking based on scores for unconstrained runs is shown as a subindex.

For both subtasks, there were teams that only submitted results for the Twitter test set. Some teams submitted both a constrained and an unconstrained version (e.g., AVAYA and teragram). As one would expect, the results on the Twitter test set tended to be better than those on the SMS test set since the SMS data was out-of-domain with respect to the training (Twitter) data.

Moreover, the results for subtask A were significantly better than those for subtask B, which shows that it is a much easier task, probably because there is less ambiguity at the phrase-level.

5.1 Subtask A: Contextual Polarity

Table 7 shows that subtask A, Twitter, attracted 23 teams, who submitted 21 constrained and 7 unconstrained systems. Five teams submitted both a constrained and an unconstrained system, and two other teams submitted constrained systems that are on the boundary between being constrained and unconstrained.

Run	Const-rained	Unconst-rained	Use Neut.?	Super-vised?
NRC-Canada	88.93		yes	yes
AVAYA	86.98	$87.38_{(1)}$	yes	yes
BOUNCE	86.79		yes	yes
LVIC-LIMSI	85.70		yes	yes
FBM	85.50		yes	semi
GU-MLT-LT	85.19		yes	yes
°UNITOR	84.60		yes	yes
USNA	81.31		yes	yes
Serendio	80.04		yes	yes
◇ECNUCS	79.48	$80.15_{(2)}$	yes	yes
TJP	78.16		yes	yes
°columbia-nlp	74.94		yes	yes
teragram		$74.89_{(3)}$	yes	yes
sielers	74.41		yes	yes
KLUE	73.74		yes	yes
OPTWIMA	69.17	$36.91_{(6)}$	yes	yes
swatcs	67.19	$63.86_{(5)}$	no	yes
Kea	63.94		yes	yes
senti.ue-en	62.79	$71.38_{(4)}$	yes	yes
uottawa	60.20		yes	yes
IITB	54.80		yes	yes
SenselyticTeam	53.88		yes	yes
SU-sentilab		$34.73_{(7)}$	no	yes
Majority Baseline	38.10		N/A	N/A

Table 7: Results for subtask A on the Twitter dataset. The ° marks a team that includes a task coorganizer, and the ◇ indicates a system submitted as constrained but which used additional Tweets or additional sentiment-annotated text to collect statistics that were then used as a feature.

Run	Const-rained	Unconst-rained	Use Neut.?	Super-vised?
GU-MLT-LT	88.37		yes	yes
NRC-Canada	88.00		yes	yes
*AVAYA	83.94	$85.79_{(1)}$	yes	yes
◇UNITOR	82.49		yes	yes
TJP	81.23		yes	yes
LVIC-LIMSI	80.16		yes	yes
USNA	79.82		yes	yes
◇ECNUCS	76.69	$77.34_{(2)}$	yes	yes
sielers	73.48		yes	yes
FBM	72.95		no	semi
teragram	72.83	$72.83_{(4)}$	yes	yes
KLUE	70.54		yes	yes
°columbia-nlp	70.30		yes	yes
senti.ue-en	66.09	$74.13_{(3)}$	yes	yes
swatcs	66.00	$67.68_{(5)}$	no	yes
Kea	63.27		yes	yes
uottawa	55.89		yes	yes
SU-sentilab		$55.38_{(6)}$	no	yes
SenselyticTeam	51.13		yes	yes
OPTWIMA	37.32	$36.38_{(7)}$	yes	yes
Majority Baseline	31.50		N/A	N/A

Table 8: Results for subtask A on the SMS dataset. The * indicates a late submission, the ° marks a team that includes a task co-organizer, and the ◇ indicates a system submitted as constrained but which used additional Tweets or additional sentiment-annotated text to collect statistics that were then used as a feature.

One system was semi-supervised, and the rest were supervised. The supervised systems used classifiers such as SVM (8 systems), Naive Bayes (7 systems), and Maximum Entropy (3 systems). Other approaches used include an ensemble of classifiers, manual rules, and a linear classifier. Two of the systems chose not to predict neutral as a possible classification label.

The average F1-measure on the Twitter test set was 74.1% for constrained systems and 60.5% for unconstrained ones; this does not mean that using additional data does not help, it just shows that the best teams only participated with a constrained system. NRC-Canada had the best constrained system with an F1-measure of 88.9%, and AVAYA had the best unconstrained one with F1=87.4%.

Table 8 shows the results for the SMS test set, where 20 teams submitted 19 constrained and 7 unconstrained systems (again, this included two teams that submitted boundary systems, marked accordingly). The average F-measure on this test set was 70.8% for constrained systems and 65.7% for unconstrained systems. The best constrained system was that of GU-MLT-LT with an F-measure of 88.4%, and AVAYA had the best unconstrained system with an F1 of 85.8%.

5.2 Subtask B: Message Polarity

Table 9 shows that subtask B, Twitter, attracted 38 teams, who submitted 36 constrained and 15 unconstrained systems (and two boundary ones).

The average F1-measure was 53.7% for the constrained and 54.6% for the unconstrained systems.

Run	Const-rained	Unconst-rained	Use Neut.?	Super-vised?
NRC-Canada	69.02		yes	yes
GU-MLT-LT	65.27		yes	yes
teragram	64.86	$64.86_{(1)}$	yes	yes
BOUNCE	63.53		yes	yes
KLUE	63.06		yes	yes
AMI&ERIC	62.55	$61.17_{(3)}$	yes	yes/semi
FBM	61.17		yes	yes
AVAYA	60.84	$64.06_{(2)}$	yes	yes/semi
SAIL	60.14	$61.03_{(4)}$	yes	yes
UT-DB	59.87		yes	yes
FBK-irst	59.76		yes	yes
nlp.cs.aueb.gr	58.91		yes	yes
◇UNITOR	58.27	$59.50_{(5)}$	yes	semi
LVIC-LIMSI	57.14		yes	yes
Umigon	56.96		yes	yes
NILC_USP	56.31		yes	yes
DataMining	55.52		yes	semi
◇ECNUCS	55.05	$58.42_{(6)}$	yes	yes
nlp.cs.aueb.gr	54.73		yes	yes
ASVUniOfLeipzig	54.56		yes	yes
SZTE-NLP	54.33	$53.10_{(9)}$	yes	yes
CodeX	53.89		yes	yes
Oasis	53.84		yes	yes
NTNU	53.23	$50.71_{(10)}$	yes	yes
UoM	51.81	$45.07_{(15)}$	yes	yes
SSA-UO	50.17		yes	no
SenselyticTeam	50.10		yes	yes
UMCC_DLSI_(SA)	49.27	$48.99_{(12)}$	yes	yes
bwbaugh	48.83	$54.37_{(8)}$	yes	yes/semi
senti.ue-en	47.24	$47.85_{(13)}$	yes	yes
SU-sentilab		$45.75_{(14)}$	yes	yes
OPTWIMA	45.40	$54.51_{(7)}$	yes	yes
REACTION	45.01		yes	yes
uottawa	42.51		yes	yes
IITB	39.80		yes	yes
IIRG	34.44		yes	yes
sinai	16.28	$49.26_{(11)}$	yes	yes
Majority Baseline	29.19		N/A	N/A

Table 9: Results for subtask B on the Twitter dataset. The ◇ indicates a system submitted as constrained but which used additional Tweets or additional sentiment-annotated text to collect statistics that were then used as a feature.

These averages are much lower than those for subtask A, which indicates that subtask B is harder, probably because a message can contain parts expressing both positive and negative sentiment.

Run	Const-rained	Unconst-rained	Use Neut.?	Super-vised?
NRC-Canada	68.46		yes	yes
GU-MLT-LT	62.15		yes	yes
KLUE	62.03		yes	yes
AVAYA	60.00	$59.47_{(1)}$	yes	yes/semi
teragram		$59.10_{(2)}$	yes	yes
NTNU	57.97	$54.55_{(6)}$	yes	yes
CodeX	56.70		yes	yes
FBK-irst	54.87		yes	yes
AMI&ERIC	53.63	$52.62_{(7)}$	yes	yes/semi
◇ECNUCS	53.21	$54.77_{(5)}$	yes	yes
UT-DB	52.46		yes	yes
SAIL	51.84	$51.98_{(8)}$	yes	yes
◇UNITOR	51.22	$48.88_{(10)}$	yes	semi
SZTE-NLP	51.08	$55.46_{(3)}$	yes	yes
SenselyticTeam	51.07		yes	yes
NILC_USP	50.12		yes	yes
REACTION	50.11		yes	yes
SU-sentilab		$49.57_{(9)}$	no	yes
nlp.cs.aueb.gr	49.41	$55.28_{(4)}$	yes	yes
LVIC-LIMSI	49.17		yes	yes
FBM	47.40		yes	yes
ASVUniOfLeipzig	46.50		yes	yes
senti.ue-en	44.65	$46.72_{(12)}$	yes	yes
SSA_UO	44.39		yes	no
UMCC_DLSI_(SA)	43.39	$40.67_{(14)}$	yes	yes
UoM	42.22	$35.22_{(15)}$	yes	yes
OPTWIMA	40.98	$47.15_{(11)}$	yes	yes
uottawa	40.51		yes	yes
bwbaugh	39.73	$43.43_{(13)}$	yes	yes/semi
IIRG	22.16		yes	yes
Majority Baseline	19.03		N/A	N/A

Table 10: Results for subtask B on the SMS dataset. The ◇ indicates a system submitted as constrained but which used additional Tweets or additional sentiment-annotated text to collect statistics that were then used as a feature.

Once again, NRC-Canada had the best constrained system with an F1-measure of 69%, followed by teragram, which had the best unconstrained system with an F1-measure of 64.9%.

As Table 10 shows, the average F1-measure on the SMS test set was 50.2% for constrained and 50.3% for unconstrained systems. NRC-Canada had the best constrained system with an F1=68.5%, and AVAYA had the best unconstrained one with F1-measure of 59.5%.

5.3 Overall

Overall, the results achieved by the best teams were very strong, especially for the simpler subtask A:

- F1=88.93, NRC-Canada on subtask A, Twitter;
- F1=88.37, GU-MLT-LT on subtask A, SMS;
- F1=69.02, NRC-Canada on subtask B, Twitter;
- F1=68.46, NRC-Canada on subtask B, SMS.

We can see that the strongest team overall was that of NRC-Canada, which was ranked first on three of the four conditions; and it was second on subtask A, SMS. There were two other teams that were strong across both tasks and on both test sets: GU-MLT-LT and AVAYA. Three other teams, namely teragram, BOUNCE and KLUE, were ranked in the top-3 in at least one subtask and test set.

6 Discussion

We have seen that most participants restricted themselves to the provided data and submitted constrained systems. Indeed, the best systems for each of the two subtasks and for each of the two testing datasets were constrained systems; of course, this does not mean that additional data would not be useful. Curiously, in some cases where a team submitted a constrained and unconstrained run, the unconstrained run actually performed worse.

Not surprisingly, most systems were supervised; there were only five semi-supervised systems, and there was only one unsupervised system. One additional team declared their system as unsupervised since it was not making use of the training data; we still classified it as supervised though since it did use supervision – in the form of manual rules.

Most participants predicted all three labels (positive, negative and neutral), even though some participants opted for not predicting neutral, which made some sense since the final F1-score was averaged over the positive and the negative predictions only.

The most popular classifiers included SVM, MaxEnt, linear classifier, Naive Bayes; in some cases, manual rules or ensembles of classifiers were used.

A variety of features were used, including word-related (e.g., words, stems, n-grams, word clusters), word-shape (e.g., punctuation, capitalization), syntactic (e.g., POS tags, dependency relations), Twitter-specific (e.g., repeated characters, emoticons, URLs, hashtags, slang, abbreviations), and sentiment-related (e.g., negation); one team also used discourse relations. Almost all participants relied heavily of various sentiment lexicons, the most popular ones being MPQA and SentiWordNet, as well as AFINN and Bing Liu's Opinion Lexicon; some participants used their own lexicons – preexisting or built from the provided data.

Given that Twitter messages are noisy, most participants did some preprocessing, including tokenization, stemming, lemmatization, stopword removal, normalization/removal of URLs, hashtags, users, slang, emoticons, repeated vowels, punctuation; some even did pronoun resolution.

7 Conclusion

We have described a new task that entered SemEval-2013: task 2 on Sentiment Analysis on Twitter. The task has attracted a very high number of participants: 149 submissions from 44 teams.

We believe that the datasets that we have created as part of the task and which we have released to the community[5] under a Creative Commons Attribution 3.0 Unported License,[6] will be found useful by researchers beyond SemEval.

Acknowledgments

The authors would like to thank Kathleen McKeown for her insight in creating the Amazon Mechanical Turk annotation task.

Funding for the Amazon Mechanical Turk annotations was provided by the JHU Human Language Technology Center of Excellence and by the Office of the Director of National Intelligence (ODNI), Intelligence Advanced Research Projects Activity (IARPA), through the U.S. Army Research Lab. All statements of fact, opinion or conclusions contained herein are those of the authors and should not be construed as representing the official views or policies of IARPA, the ODNI or the U.S. Government.

[5]http://www.cs.york.ac.uk/semeval-2013/task2/
[6]http://creativecommons.org/licenses/by/3.0/

References

Stefano Baccianella, Andrea Esuli, and Fabrizio Sebastiani. 2010. SentiWordNet 3.0: An enhanced lexical resource for sentiment analysis and opinion mining. In Nicoletta Calzolari (chair), Khalid Choukri, Bente Maegaard, Joseph Mariani, Jan Odijk, Stelios Piperidis, Mike Rosner, and Daniel Tapias, editors, *Proceedings of the Seventh International Conference on Language Resources and Evaluation*, LREC '10, pages 2200–2204, Valletta, Malta.

Luciano Barbosa and Junlan Feng. 2010. Robust sentiment detection on Twitter from biased and noisy data. In *Proceedings of the 23rd International Conference on Computational Linguistics: Posters*, COLING '10, pages 36–44, Beijing, China.

Albert Bifet, Geoffrey Holmes, Bernhard Pfahringer, and Ricard Gavaldà. 2011. Detecting sentiment change in Twitter streaming data. *Journal of Machine Learning Research - Proceedings Track*, 17:5–11.

Tao Chen and Min-Yen Kan. 2012. Creating a live, public short message service corpus: the NUS SMS corpus. *Language Resources and Evaluation*, pages 1–37.

Dmitry Davidov, Oren Tsur, and Ari Rappoport. 2010. Semi-supervised recognition of sarcastic sentences in Twitter and Amazon. In *Proceedings of the Fourteenth Conference on Computational Natural Language Learning*, CoNLL '10, pages 107–116, Uppsala, Sweden.

Bernard J. Jansen, Mimi Zhang, Kate Sobel, and Abdur Chowdury. 2009. Twitter power: Tweets as electronic word of mouth. *J. Am. Soc. Inf. Sci. Technol.*, 60(11):2169–2188.

Efthymios Kouloumpis, Theresa Wilson, and Johanna Moore. 2011. Twitter sentiment analysis: The Good the Bad and the OMG! In Lada A. Adamic, Ricardo A. Baeza-Yates, and Scott Counts, editors, *Proceedings of the Fifth International Conference on Weblogs and Social Media*, ICWSM' 11, pages 538-541, Barcelona, Spain.

Brendan O'Connor, Ramnath Balasubramanyan, Bryan R. Routledge, and Noah A. Smith. 2010. From tweets to polls: Linking text sentiment to public opinion time series. In William W. Cohen and Samuel Gosling, editors, *Proceedings of the Fourth International Conference on Weblogs and Social Media*, ICWSM '10, Washington, DC, USA.

Alexander Pak and Patrick Paroubek. 2010. Twitter based system: Using Twitter for disambiguating sentiment ambiguous adjectives. In *Proceedings of the 5th International Workshop on Semantic Evaluation*, SemEval '10, pages 436–439, Los Angeles, CA, USA.

Alan Ritter, Sam Clark, Mausam, and Oren Etzioni. 2011. Named entity recognition in tweets: an experimental study. In *Proceedings of the Conference on Empirical Methods in Natural Language Processing*, EMNLP '11, pages 1524–1534, Edinburgh, United Kingdom.

Alan Ritter, Mausam, Oren Etzioni, and Sam Clark. 2012. Open domain event extraction from twitter. In *Proceedings of the 18th ACM SIGKDD international conference on Knowledge discovery and data mining*, KDD '12, pages 1104–1112, Beijing, China.

Andranik Tumasjan, Timm O. Sprenger, Philipp G. Sandner, and Isabell M. Welpe. 2010. Predicting elections with Twitter: What 140 characters reveal about political sentiment. In William W. Cohen and Samuel Gosling, editors, *Proceedings of the Fourth International Conference on Weblogs and Social Media*, ICWSM '10, pages 178–185, Washington, DC, USA. The AAAI Press.

Julio Villena-Román, Sara Lana-Serrano, Eugenio Martínez-Cámara, and José Carlos González Cristóbal. 2013. TASS - Workshop on Sentiment Analysis at SEPLN. *Procesamiento del Lenguaje Natural*, 50:37–44.

Janyce Wiebe, Theresa Wilson, and Claire Cardie. 2005. Annotating expressions of opinions and emotions in language. *Language Resources and Evaluation*, 39(2-3):165–210.

NRC-Canada: Building the State-of-the-Art in Sentiment Analysis of Tweets

Saif M. Mohammad, Svetlana Kiritchenko, and Xiaodan Zhu
National Research Council Canada
Ottawa, Ontario, Canada K1A 0R6
{saif.mohammad,svetlana.kiritchenko,xiaodan.zhu}@nrc-cnrc.gc.ca

Abstract

In this paper, we describe how we created two state-of-the-art SVM classifiers, one to detect the sentiment of messages such as tweets and SMS (message-level task) and one to detect the sentiment of a term within a message (term-level task). Among submissions from 44 teams in a competition, our submissions stood first in both tasks on tweets, obtaining an F-score of 69.02 in the message-level task and 88.93 in the term-level task. We implemented a variety of surface-form, semantic, and sentiment features. We also generated two large word–sentiment association lexicons, one from tweets with sentiment-word hashtags, and one from tweets with emoticons. In the message-level task, the lexicon-based features provided a gain of 5 F-score points over all others. Both of our systems can be replicated using freely available resources.[1]

1 Introduction

Hundreds of millions of people around the world actively use microblogging websites such as Twitter. Thus there is tremendous interest in sentiment analysis of tweets across a variety of domains such as commerce (Jansen et al., 2009), health (Chew and Eysenbach, 2010; Salathé and Khandelwal, 2011), and disaster management (Verma et al., 2011; Mandel et al., 2012).

In this paper, we describe how we created two state-of-the-art SVM classifiers, one to detect the sentiment of messages such as tweets and SMS (message-level task) and one to detect the sentiment of a term within a message (term-level task). The sentiment can be one out of three possibilities: positive, negative, or neutral. We developed these classifiers to participate in an international competition organized by the Conference on Semantic Evaluation Exercises (SemEval-2013) (Wilson et al., 2013).[2] The organizers created and shared sentiment-labeled tweets for training, development, and testing. The distributions of the labels in the different datasets is shown in Table 1. The competition, officially referred to as *Task 2: Sentiment Analysis in Twitter*, had 44 teams (34 for the message-level task and 23 for the term-level task). Our submissions stood first in both tasks, obtaining a macro-averaged F-score of 69.02 in the message-level task and 88.93 in the term-level task.

The task organizers also provided a second test dataset, composed of Short Message Service (SMS) messages (no training data of SMS messages was provided). We applied our classifiers on the SMS test set without any further tuning. Nonetheless, the classifiers still obtained the first position in identifying sentiment of SMS messages (F-score of 68.46) and second position in detecting the sentiment of terms within SMS messages (F-score of 88.00, only 0.39 points behind the first ranked system).

We implemented a number of surface-form, semantic, and sentiment features. We also generated two large word–sentiment association lexicons,

[1]The three authors contributed equally to this paper. Svetlana Kiritchenko developed the system for the message-level task, Xiaodan Zhu developed the system for the term-level task, and Saif Mohammad led the overall effort, co-ordinated both tasks, and contributed to feature development.

[2]http://www.cs.york.ac.uk/semeval-2013/task2

*Second Joint Conference on Lexical and Computational Semantics (*SEM), Volume 2: Seventh International Workshop on Semantic Evaluation (SemEval 2013)*, pages 321–327, Atlanta, Georgia, June 14-15, 2013.

Table 1: Class distributions in the training set (Train), development set (Dev) and testing set (Test). The Train set was accessed through tweet ids and a download script. However, not all tweets were accessible. Below is the number of Train examples we were able to download. The Dev and Test sets were provided by FTP.

Dataset	Positive	Negative	Neutral	Total
Tweets				
Message-level task:				
Train	3,045 (37%)	1,209 (15%)	4,004 (48%)	8,258
Dev	575 (35%)	340 (20%)	739 (45%)	1,654
Test	1,572 (41%)	601 (16%)	1,640 (43%)	3,813
Term-level task:				
Train	4,831 (62%)	2,540 (33%)	385 (5%)	7,756
Dev	648 (57%)	430 (38%)	57 (5%)	1,135
Test	2,734 (62%)	1,541 (35%)	160 (3%)	4,435
SMS				
Message-level task:				
Test	492 (23%)	394 (19%)	1,208 (58%)	2,094
Term-level task:				
Test	1,071 (46%)	1,104 (47%)	159 (7%)	2,334

one from tweets with sentiment-word hashtags, and one from tweets with emoticons. The automatically generated lexicons were particularly useful. In the message-level task for tweets, they alone provided a gain of more than 5 F-score points over and above that obtained using all other features. The lexicons are made freely available.[3]

2 Sentiment Lexicons

Sentiment lexicons are lists of words with associations to positive and negative sentiments.

2.1 Existing, Automatically Created Sentiment Lexicons

The manually created lexicons we used include the NRC Emotion Lexicon (Mohammad and Turney, 2010; Mohammad and Yang, 2011) (about 14,000 words), the MPQA Lexicon (Wilson et al., 2005) (about 8,000 words), and the Bing Liu Lexicon (Hu and Liu, 2004) (about 6,800 words).

2.2 New, Tweet-Specific, Automatically Generated Sentiment Lexicons

2.2.1 NRC Hashtag Sentiment Lexicon

Certain words in tweets are specially marked with a hashtag (#) to indicate the topic or sentiment. Mohammad (2012) showed that hashtagged emotion words such as joy, sadness, angry, and surprised are good indicators that the tweet as a whole (even without the hashtagged emotion word) is expressing the same emotion. We adapted that idea to create a large corpus of positive and negative tweets.

We polled the Twitter API every four hours from April to December 2012 in search of tweets with either a positive word hashtag or a negative word hashtag. A collection of 78 seed words closely related to *positive* and *negative* such as *#good, #excellent, #bad,* and *#terrible* were used (32 positive and 36 negative). These terms were chosen from entries for *positive* and *negative* in the Roget's Thesaurus.

A set of 775,000 tweets were used to generate a large word–sentiment association lexicon. A tweet was considered positive if it had one of the 32 positive hashtagged seed words, and negative if it had one of the 36 negative hashtagged seed words. The association score for a term w was calculated from these pseudo-labeled tweets as shown below:

$$score(w) = PMI(w, positive) - PMI(w, negative) \quad (1)$$

where PMI stands for pointwise mutual information. A positive score indicates association with positive sentiment, whereas a negative score indicates association with negative sentiment. The magnitude is indicative of the degree of association. The final lexicon, which we will refer to as the *NRC Hashtag Sentiment Lexicon* has entries for 54,129 unigrams and 316,531 bigrams. Entries were also generated for unigram–unigram, unigram–bigram, and bigram–bigram pairs that were not necessarily contiguous in the tweets corpus. Pairs with certain punctuations, '@' symbols, and some function words were removed. The lexicon has entries for 308,808 non-contiguous pairs.

2.2.2 Sentiment140 Lexicon

The sentiment140 corpus (Go et al., 2009) is a collection of 1.6 million tweets that contain positive and negative emoticons. The tweets are labeled positive or negative according to the emoticon. We generated a sentiment lexicon from this corpus in the same manner as described above (Section 2.2.1). This lexicon has entries for 62,468 unigrams, 677,698 bigrams, and 480,010 non-contiguous pairs.

[3] www.purl.com/net/sentimentoftweets

3 Task: Automatically Detecting the Sentiment of a Message

The objective of this task is to determine whether a given message is positive, negative, or neutral.

3.1 Classifier and features

We trained a Support Vector Machine (SVM) (Fan et al., 2008) on the training data provided. SVM is a state-of-the-art learning algorithm proved to be effective on text categorization tasks and robust on large feature spaces. The linear kernel and the value for the parameter C=0.005 were chosen by cross-validation on the training data.

We normalized all URLs to http://someurl and all userids to @someuser. We tokenized and part-of-speech tagged the tweets with the Carnegie Mellon University (CMU) Twitter NLP tool (Gimpel et al., 2011). Each tweet was represented as a feature vector made up of the following groups of features:

- word ngrams: presence or absence of contiguous sequences of 1, 2, 3, and 4 tokens; non-contiguous ngrams (ngrams with one token replaced by *);
- character ngrams: presence or absence of contiguous sequences of 3, 4, and 5 characters;
- all-caps: the number of words with all characters in upper case;
- POS: the number of occurrences of each part-of-speech tag;
- hashtags: the number of hashtags;
- lexicons: the following sets of features were generated for each of the three manually constructed sentiment lexicons (NRC Emotion Lexicon, MPQA, Bing Liu Lexicon) and for each of the two automatically constructed lexicons (Hashtag Sentiment Lexicon and Sentiment140 Lexicon). Separate feature sets were produced for unigrams, bigrams, and non-contiguous pairs. The lexicon features were created for all tokens in the tweet, for each part-of-speech tag, for hashtags, and for all-caps tokens. For each token w and emotion or polarity p, we used the sentiment/emotion score $score(w,p)$ to determine:
  - total count of tokens in the tweet with $score(w,p) > 0$;
  - total score = $\sum_{w \in tweet} score(w,p)$;
  - the maximal score = $max_{w \in tweet} score(w,p)$;
  - the score of the last token in the tweet with $score(w,p) > 0$;
- punctuation:
  - the number of contiguous sequences of exclamation marks, question marks, and both exclamation and question marks;
  - whether the last token contains an exclamation or question mark;
- emoticons: The polarity of an emoticon was determined with a regular expression adopted from Christopher Potts' tokenizing script:[4]
  - presence or absence of positive and negative emoticons at any position in the tweet;
  - whether the last token is a positive or negative emoticon;
- elongated words: the number of words with one character repeated more than two times, for example, 'soooo';
- clusters: The CMU pos-tagging tool provides the token clusters produced with the Brown clustering algorithm on 56 million English-language tweets. These 1,000 clusters serve as alternative representation of tweet content, reducing the sparcity of the token space.
  - the presence or absence of tokens from each of the 1000 clusters;
- negation: the number of negated contexts. Following (Pang et al., 2002), we defined a negated context as a segment of a tweet that starts with a negation word (e.g., *no, shouldn't*) and ends with one of the punctuation marks: ',', '.', ':', ';', '!', '?'. A negated context affects the ngram and lexicon features: we add '_NEG' suffix to each word following the negation word ('perfect' becomes 'perfect_NEG'). The '_NEG' suffix is also added to polarity and emotion features ('POLARITY_positive' becomes 'POLARITY_positive_NEG'). The list of negation words was adopted from Christopher Potts' sentiment tutorial.[5]

[4]http://sentiment.christopherpotts.net/tokenizing.html
[5]http://sentiment.christopherpotts.net/lingstruc.html

3.2 Experiments

We trained the SVM classifier on the set of 9,912 annotated tweets (8,258 in the training set and 1,654 in the development set). We applied the model to the test set of 3,813 unseen tweets. The same model was applied unchanged to the other test set of 2,094 SMS messages as well. The bottom-line score used by the task organizers was the macro-averaged F-score of the positive and negative classes. The results obtained by our system on the training set (ten-fold cross-validation), development set (when trained on the training set), and test sets (when trained on the combined set of tweets in the training and development sets) are shown in Table 2. The table also shows baseline results obtained by a majority classifier that always predicts the most frequent class as output. Since the bottom-line F-score is based only on the F-scores of positive and negative classes (and not on neutral), the majority baseline chose the most frequent class among positive and negative, which in this case was the positive class. We also show baseline results obtained using an SVM and unigram features alone. Our system (SVM and all features) obtained a macro-averaged F-score of 69.02 on the tweet set and 68.46 on the SMS set. In the SemEval-2013 competition, our submission ranked first on both datasets. There were 48 submissions from 34 teams for this task.

Table 3 shows the results of the ablation experiments where we repeat the same classification process but remove one feature group at a time. The most influential features for both datasets turned out to be the sentiment lexicon features: they provided gains of more than 8.5%. It is interesting to note that tweets benefited mostly from the automatic sentiment lexicons (NRC Hashtag Lexicon and the Sentiment140 Lexicon) whereas the SMS set benefited more from the manual lexicons (MPQA, NRC Emotion Lexicon, Bing Liu Lexicon). Among the automatic lexicons, both the Hashtag Sentiment Lexicon and the Sentiment140 Lexicon contributed to roughly the same amount of improvement in performance on the tweet set.

The second most important feature group for the message-level task was that of ngrams (word and character ngrams). Expectedly, the impact of ngrams on the SMS dataset was less extensive since the classifier model was trained only on tweets.

Table 2: Message-level Task: The macro-averaged F-scores on different datasets.

	Classifier	Tweets	SMS
Training set:	Majority	26.94	-
	SVM-all	67.20	-
Development set:	Majority	26.85	-
	SVM-all	68.72	-
Test set:	Majority	29.19	19.03
	SVM-unigrams	39.61	39.29
	SVM-all	**69.02**	**68.46**

Table 3: Message-level Task: The macro-averaged F-scores obtained on the test sets with one of the feature groups removed. The number in the brackets is the difference with the *all features* score. The biggest drops are shown in bold.

Experiment	Tweets	SMS
all features	69.02	68.46
all - lexicons	60.42 (**-8.60**)	59.73 (**-8.73**)
all - manual lex.	67.45 (-1.57)	65.64 (-2.82)
all - auto. lex.	63.78 (-5.24)	67.12 (-1.34)
all - Senti140 lex.	65.25 (-3.77)	67.33 (-1.13)
all - Hashtag lex.	65.22 (-3.80)	70.28 (1.82)
all - ngrams	61.77 (-7.25)	67.27 (-1.19)
all - word ngrams	64.64 (-4.38)	66.56 (-1.9)
all - char. ngrams	67.10 (-1.92)	68.94 (0.48)
all - negation	67.20 (-1.82)	66.22 (-2.24)
all - POS	68.38 (-0.64)	67.07 (-1.39)
all - clusters	69.01 (-0.01)	68.10 (-0.36)
all - encodings (elongated, emoticons, punctuations, all-caps, hashtags)	69.16 (0.14)	68.28 (-0.18)

Attention to negations improved performance on both datasets. Removing the sentiment encoding features like hashtags, emoticons, and elongated words, had almost no impact on performance, but this is probably because the discriminating information in them was also captured by some other features such as character and word ngrams.

4 Task: Automatically Detecting the Sentiment of a Term in a Message

The objective of this task is to detect whether a term (a word or phrase) within a message conveys a positive, negative, or neutral sentiment. Note that the same term may express different sentiments in different contexts.

4.1 Classifier and features

We trained an SVM using the LibSVM package (Chang and Lin, 2011) and a linear kernel. In ten-fold cross-validation over the training data, the linear kernel outperformed other kernels implemented in LibSVM as well as a maximum-entropy classifier. Our model leverages a variety of features, as described below:

- word ngrams:
  - presence or absence of unigrams, bigrams, and the full word string of a target term;
  - leading and ending unigrams and bigrams;
- character ngrams: presence or absence of two- and three-character prefixes and suffixes of all the words in a target term (note that the target term may be a multi-word sequence);
- elongated words: presence or absence of elongated words (e.g., 'sooo');
- emoticons: the numbers and categories of emoticons that a term contains[6];
- punctuation: presence or absence of punctuation sequences such as '?!' and '!!!';
- upper case:
  - whether all the words in the target start with an upper case letter followed by lower case letters;
  - whether the target words are all in uppercase (to capture a potential named entity);
- stopwords: whether a term contains only stopwords. If so, separate features indicate whether there are 1, 2, 3, or more stop-words;
- lengths:
  - the length of a target term (number of words);
  - the average length of words (number of characters) in a term;
  - a binary feature indicating whether a term contains long words;
- negation: similar to those described for the message-level task. Whenever a negation word was found immediately before the target or within the target, the polarities of all tokens after the negation term were flipped;
- position: whether a term is at the beginning, end, or another position;
- sentiment lexicons: we used automatically created lexicons (NRC Hashtag Sentiment Lexicon, Sentiment140 Lexicon) as well as manually created lexicons (NRC Emotion Lexicon, MPQA, Bing Liu Lexicon).
  - total count of tokens in the target term with sentiment score greater than 0;
  - the sum of the sentiment scores for all tokens in the target;
  - the maximal sentiment score;
  - the non-zero sentiment score of the last token in the target;
- term splitting: when a term contains a hashtag made of multiple words (e.g., #biggestdaythisyear), we split the hashtag into component words;
- others:
  - whether a term contains a Twitter user name;
  - whether a term contains a URL.

The above features were extracted from target terms as well as from the rest of the message (the context). For unigrams and bigrams, we used four words on either side of the target as the context. The window size was chosen through experiments on the development set.

4.2 Experiments

We trained an SVM classifier on the 8,891 annotated terms in tweets (7,756 terms in the training set and 1,135 terms in the development set). We applied the model to 4,435 terms in the tweets test set. The same model was applied unchanged to the other test set of 2,334 terms in unseen SMS messages as well. The bottom-line score used by the task organizers was the macro-averaged F-score of the positive and negative classes.

[6]http://en.wikipedia.org/wiki/List_of_emoticons

The results on the training set (ten-fold cross-validation), the development set (trained on the training set), and the test sets (trained on the combined set of tweets in the training and development sets) are shown in Table 4. The table also shows baseline results obtained by a majority classifier that always predicts the most frequent class as output, and an additional baseline result obtained using an SVM and unigram features alone. Our submission obtained a macro-averaged F-score of 88.93 on the tweet set and was ranked first among 29 submissions from 23 participating teams. Even with no tuning specific to SMS data, our SMS submission still obtained second rank with an F-score of 88.00. The score of the first ranking system on the SMS set was 88.39. A post-competition bug-fix in the bigram features resulted in a small improvement: F-score of 89.10 on the tweets set and 88.34 on the SMS set.

Note that the performance is significantly higher in the term-level task than in the message-level task. This is largely because of the ngram features (see unigram baselines in Tables 2 and 4). We analyzed the labeled data provided to determine why ngrams performed so strongly in this task. We found that the percentage of test tokens already seen within training data targets was 85.1%. Further, the average ratio of instances pertaining to the most dominant polarity of a target term to the total number of instances of that target term was 0.808.

Table 5 presents the ablation F-scores. Observe that the ngram features were the most useful. Note also that removing just the word ngram features or just the character ngram features results in only a small drop in performance. This indicates that the two feature groups capture similar information.

The sentiment lexicon features are the next most useful group—removing them leads to a drop in F-score of 3.95 points for the tweets set and 4.64 for the SMS set. Modeling negation improves the F-score by 0.72 points on the tweets set and 1.57 points on the SMS set.

The last two rows in Table 5 show the results obtained when the features are extracted only from the target (and not from its context) and when they are extracted only from the context of the target (and not from the target itself). Observe that even though the context may influence the polarity of the target, using target features alone is substantially more useful than using context features alone. Nonetheless, adding context features improves the F-scores by roughly 2 to 4 points.

Table 4: Term-level Task: The macro-averaged F-scores on the datasets. The official scores of our submission are shown in bold. SVM-all* shows results after a bug fix.

	Classifier	Tweets	SMS
Training set:	Majority	38.38	-
	SVM-all	86.80	-
Development set:	Majority	36.34	-
	SVM-all	86.49	-
Test set:	Majority	38.13	32.11
	SVM-unigrams	80.28	78.71
	official SVM-all	**88.93**	**88.00**
	SVM-all*	89.10	88.34

Table 5: Term-level Task: The F-scores obtained on the test sets with one of the feature groups removed. The number in brackets is the difference with the *all features* score. The biggest drops are shown in bold.

Experiment	Tweets	SMS
all features	89.10	88.34
all - ngrams	83.86 (**-5.24**)	80.49 (**-7.85**)
all - word ngrams	88.38 (-0.72)	87.37 (-0.97)
all - char. ngrams	89.01 (-0.09)	87.31 (-1.03)
all - lexicons	85.15 (-3.95)	83.70 (-4.64)
all - manual lex.	87.69 (-1.41)	86.84 (-1.5)
all - auto lex.	88.24 (-0.86)	86.65 (-1.69)
all - negation	88.38 (-0.72)	86.77 (-1.57)
all - stopwords	89.17 (0.07)	88.30 (-0.04)
all - encodings (elongated words, emoticons, punctns., uppercase)	89.16 (0.06)	88.39 (0.05)
all - target	72.97 (**-16.13**)	68.96 (**-19.38**)
all - context	85.02 (-4.08)	85.93 (-2.41)

5 Conclusions

We created two state-of-the-art SVM classifiers, one to detect the sentiment of messages and one to detect the sentiment of a term within a message. Our submissions on tweet data stood first in both these subtasks of the SemEval-2013 competition 'Detecting Sentiment in Twitter'. We implemented a variety of features based on surface form and lexical categories. The sentiment lexicon features (both manually created and automatically generated) along with ngram features (both word and character ngrams) led to the most gain in performance.

Acknowledgments

We thank Colin Cherry for providing his SVM code and for helpful discussions.

References

Chih-Chung Chang and Chih-Jen Lin. 2011. LIBSVM: A library for support vector machines. *ACM Transactions on Intelligent Systems and Technology*, 2(3):27:1–27:27.

Cynthia Chew and Gunther Eysenbach. 2010. Pandemics in the Age of Twitter: Content Analysis of Tweets during the 2009 H1N1 Outbreak. *PLoS ONE*, 5(11):e14118+, November.

R.-E. Fan, K.-W. Chang, C.-J. Hsieh, X.-R. Wang, and Lin C.-J. 2008. LIBLINEAR: A Library for Large Linear Classification. *Journal of Machine Learning Research*, 9:1871–1874.

Kevin Gimpel, Nathan Schneider, Brendan O'Connor, Dipanjan Das, Daniel Mills, Jacob Eisenstein, Michael Heilman, Dani Yogatama, Jeffrey Flanigan, and Noah A. Smith. 2011. Part-of-Speech Tagging for Twitter: Annotation, Features, and Experiments. In *Proceedings of the Annual Meeting of the Association for Computational Linguistics*.

Alec Go, Richa Bhayani, and Lei Huang. 2009. Twitter Sentiment Classification using Distant Supervision. In *Final Projects from CS224N for Spring 2008/2009 at The Stanford Natural Language Processing Group*.

Minqing Hu and Bing Liu. 2004. Mining and summarizing customer reviews. In *Proceedings of the tenth ACM SIGKDD international conference on Knowledge discovery and data mining*, KDD '04, pages 168–177, New York, NY, USA. ACM.

Bernard J. Jansen, Mimi Zhang, Kate Sobel, and Abdur Chowdury. 2009. Twitter power: Tweets as electronic word of mouth. *Journal of the American Society for Information Science and Technology*, 60(11):2169–2188.

Benjamin Mandel, Aron Culotta, John Boulahanis, Danielle Stark, Bonnie Lewis, and Jeremy Rodrigue. 2012. A demographic analysis of online sentiment during hurricane irene. In *Proceedings of the Second Workshop on Language in Social Media*, LSM '12, pages 27–36, Stroudsburg, PA, USA. Association for Computational Linguistics.

Saif M. Mohammad and Peter D. Turney. 2010. Emotions Evoked by Common Words and Phrases: Using Mechanical Turk to Create an Emotion Lexicon. In *Proceedings of the NAACL-HLT 2010 Workshop on Computational Approaches to Analysis and Generation of Emotion in Text*, LA, California.

Saif Mohammad and Tony Yang. 2011. Tracking Sentiment in Mail: How Genders Differ on Emotional Axes. In *Proceedings of the 2nd Workshop on Computational Approaches to Subjectivity and Sentiment Analysis (WASSA 2.011)*, pages 70–79, Portland, Oregon. Association for Computational Linguistics.

Saif Mohammad. 2012. #Emotional Tweets. In *Proceedings of the First Joint Conference on Lexical and Computational Semantics (*SEM)*, pages 246–255, Montréal, Canada. Association for Computational Linguistics.

Bo Pang, Lillian Lee, and Shivakumar Vaithyanathan. 2002. Thumbs up?: Sentiment Classification Using Machine Learning Techniques. In *Proceedings of the Conference on Empirical Methods in Natural Language Processing*, pages 79–86, Philadelphia, PA.

Marcel Salathé and Shashank Khandelwal. 2011. Assessing vaccination sentiments with online social media: Implications for infectious disease dynamics and control. *PLoS Computational Biology*, 7(10).

Sudha Verma, Sarah Vieweg, William Corvey, Leysia Palen, James Martin, Martha Palmer, Aaron Schram, and Kenneth Anderson. 2011. Natural language processing to the rescue? extracting "situational awareness" tweets during mass emergency. In *International AAAI Conference on Weblogs and Social Media*.

Theresa Wilson, Janyce Wiebe, and Paul Hoffmann. 2005. Recognizing contextual polarity in phrase-level sentiment analysis. In *Proceedings of the conference on Human Language Technology and Empirical Methods in Natural Language Processing*, HLT '05, pages 347–354, Stroudsburg, PA, USA. Association for Computational Linguistics.

Theresa Wilson, Zornitsa Kozareva, Preslav Nakov, Sara Rosenthal, Veselin Stoyanov, and Alan Ritter. 2013. SemEval-2013 task 2: Sentiment analysis in twitter. In *Proceedings of the International Workshop on Semantic Evaluation*, SemEval '13, Atlanta, Georgia, USA, June.

GU-MLT-LT: Sentiment Analysis of Short Messages using Linguistic Features and Stochastic Gradient Descent

Tobias Günther
University of Gothenburg
Olof Wijksgatan 6
41255 Göteborg, Sweden
email@tobias.io

Lenz Furrer
University of Zurich
Binzmühlestrasse 14
8050 Zürich, Switzerland
lenz.furrer@gmail.com

Abstract

This paper describes the details of our system submitted to the SemEval-2013 shared task on sentiment analysis in Twitter. Our approach to predicting the sentiment of Tweets and SMS is based on supervised machine learning techniques and task-specific feature engineering. We used a linear classifier trained by stochastic gradient descent with hinge loss and elastic net regularization to make our predictions, which were ranked first or second in three of the four experimental conditions of the shared task. Furthermore, our system makes use of social media specific text preprocessing and linguistically motivated features, such as word stems, word clusters and negation handling.

1 Introduction

Sentiment analysis, also known as opinion mining, is a research field in the area of text mining and natural language processing, which investigates the automated detection of opinions in language. In written text, an opinion is a person's attitude towards some topic, pronounced by verbal (e.g. choice of words, rhetorical figures) or non-verbal means (e.g. emoticons, emphatic spelling). More formally, Liu (2012) defines an opinion as the quintuple $(e_i, a_{ij}, s_{ijkl}, h_k, t_l)$ where "e_i is the name of an entity, a_{ij} is an aspect of e_i, s_{ijkl} is the sentiment on aspect a_{ij} of entity e_i, h_k is the opinion holder, and t_l is the time when the opinion is expressed by h_k. The sentiment s_{ijkl} is positive, negative, or neutral, or expressed with different strength/intensity levels [...]. When an opinion is on the entity itself as a whole, the special aspect GENERAL is used to denote it. [...] e_i and a_{ij} together represent the opinion target" (Liu, 2012).

With the massively growing importance of social media in everyday life, being able to automatically find and classify attitudes in written text allows for estimating the mood of a large group of people, e.g. towards a certain event, service, product, matter of fact or the like. As working with the very short and informal texts typical for social networks poses challenges not encountered in more traditional text genres, the International Workshop on Semantic Evaluation (SemEval) 2013 has a shared task on sentiment analysis in microblogging texts, which is detailed in Wilson et al. (2013). The task requires sentiment analysis of Twitter[1] and SMS messages and comprises two subtasks, one of which deals with determining the sentiment of a given message fragment depending on its context (Task A) and one on overall message polarity classification (Task B).

We treat both tasks as document-level sentiment classification tasks, which we define according to Liu (2012) as determining the opinion $(\_, \text{GENERAL}, s, \_, \_)$ of a given message, where $s \in \{\text{positive, negative, neutral}\}$ and "the entity e, opinion holder h, and time of opinion t are assumed known or irrelevant" (Liu, 2012). For Task A we only consider the marked fraction of the message to be given.

This introduction is followed by sections discussing related work (2), details of our system (3), experiments (4) and results and conclusion (5).

[1] a popular microblogging service on the Internet, see http://twitter.com

*Second Joint Conference on Lexical and Computational Semantics (*SEM), Volume 2: Seventh International Workshop on Semantic Evaluation (SemEval 2013)*, pages 328–332, Atlanta, Georgia, June 14-15, 2013.

2 Related Work

Previous approaches to sentiment analysis of microblogging texts make use of a wide range of features, including unigrams, n-grams, part-of-speech tags and polarity values from (usually hand-crafted) sentiment lexicons. O'Connor et al. (2010) examine tweets concerned with the 2009 US presidential elections, relying solely on the occurrence of words from a sentiment lexicon. Nielsen (2011) investigates the impact of including internet slang and obscene language when building a sentiment lexicon. Barbosa and Feng (2010) make use of three different sentiment detection websites to label Twitter data, while Davidov et al. (2010), Kouloumpis et al. (2011) and Pak and Paroubek (2010) use Twitter hashtags and emoticons as labels. Speriosu et al. (2011) propagate information from seed labels along a linked structure that includes Twitter's follower graph, and Saif et al. (2012) specifically address the data-sparsity problem by using semantic smoothing and topic extraction.

3 System Description

In this section we present the details of our sentiment analysis system, which was implemented in the Python programming language and is publicly available online.[2] We used the same preprocessing, feature extraction and learning algorithm for both subtasks, only the hyperparameters of the machine learning algorithm were adjusted to the respective dataset.

3.1 Preprocessing

Tokenization of the messages was done using a simple regular expression, which matches either URLs, alphanumeric character sequences (plus apostrophe) or non-alphanumeric non-whitespace character sequences. This way punctuation sequences like emoticons are preserved, while still being separated from words in case of missing whitespace. The same happens to hashtags, so "#liiike:)" gets separated into the three tokens `#`, `liiike` and `:)`, which can then be processed separately or as n-grams. While this strategy performed reasonably well for us, more sophisticated tokenizers for social media messages that handle more special cases like emoticons including letters are thinkable.

To address the large variety in spelling typical for social networks we store three different variants of each token:

a) The *raw* token found in the message

b) A *normalized* version, in which all characters are converted to lowercase and all digits to 0

c) A *collapsed* version, in which all adjacent duplicate characters are removed from the normalized version, if it is not present in an English word list. That way "school" stays "school", but "liiike" gets converted to "like".

3.2 Features

We explored a wide variety of linguistic and lexical features. In our final submission we used the following set of features for each message:

- The **normalized tokens** [boolean]
- The **stems** of the collapsed tokens, which were computed using the Porter stemming algorithm (Porter, 1980) implemented in the Python Natural Language Toolkit (Bird et al., 2009). [boolean]
- The **word cluster** IDs of raw, normalized and collapsed tokens. The clusters were obtained via unsupervised Brown clustering (Brown et al., 1992) of 56,345,753 Tweets by Owoputi et al. (2013) and are available on the web.[3] [boolean]
- The accumulated (summed) positive and accumulated negative **SentiWordNet** scores (Baccianella et al., 2010) of all synsets matching the collapsed token strings. [continuous]

Furthermore, the normalized tokens and stems were marked with a special **negation** prefix, if they occurred after a negation word or word cluster of negation words. If a punctuation token occurred before the end of the message the marking was discontinued at that point.

[2] `http://tobias.io/semevaltweet`

[3] `http://www.ark.cs.cmu.edu/TweetNLP`

3.3 Machine Learning Methods

For the classification of the messages into the positive, negative and neutral classes we use three linear models, which were trained in an one-vs.-all manner. At prediction time we simply choose the label with the highest score. All training was done using the open-source machine learning toolkit *scikit-learn*,[4] which provides a consistent Python API to fast implementations of various machine learning algorithms (Pedregosa et al., 2011).

The linear models were trained using *stochastic gradient descent* (SGD), which is a gradient descent optimization method that minimizes a given loss function. The term "stochastic" refers to the fact that the weights of the model are updated for each training example, which is an approximation of batch gradient descent, in which all training examples are considered to make a single step. This way SGD is very fast to train, which was important to us to be able to rapidly evaluate different feature combinations and hyperparameter settings using cross-validation.

Algorithm 1 Stochastic gradient descent with hinge loss and elastic net regularization

1: $t \leftarrow 1/(\eta\,\alpha)$
2: $u \leftarrow 0$
3: Initialize w_j and q_j with 0 for all j
4: **for** *epoch* to N_{ITER} **do**
5:     **for** i to N_{SAMPLES} **do**
6:         $s \leftarrow w^T x^{(i)}$
7:         $\eta \leftarrow 1/(\alpha\,t)$
8:         $c \leftarrow \text{CLASSWEIGHT}(y^{(i)})$
9:         $u \leftarrow u + ((1-\rho)\,\eta\,\alpha)$
10:         **for** j to N_{FEATURES} **do**
11:             $\frac{\partial \ell}{\partial w_j} \leftarrow \begin{cases} -y^{(i)} x_j^{(i)} & \text{if } y^{(i)} s < 1 \\ 0 & \text{otherwise} \end{cases}$
12:             $w_j \leftarrow (1-\rho\,\eta\,\alpha)\,w_j - \eta\,c\,\frac{\partial \ell}{\partial w_j}$
13:             $z \leftarrow w_j$
14:             **if** $w_j > 0$ **then**
15:                 $w_j \leftarrow \max(0, w_j - (u + q_j))$
16:             **else if** $w_j < 0$ **then**
17:                 $w_j \leftarrow \min(0, w_j + (u - q_j))$
18:             $q_j \leftarrow q_j + (w_j - z)$
19:         $t \leftarrow t + 1$

[4] Version 0.13.1, `http://scikit-learn.org`

Hyperparameter	Task A	Task B
N_{ITER}	1000	1000
$\text{CLASSWEIGHT}(y^{(i)})$	1	auto[5]
α	0.0001	0.001
ρ	0.15	0.15

Table 1: Hyperparameters used for final model training

The loss function we used was *hinge loss*, which is a large-margin loss function known for its use in support vector machines. To avoid overfitting the training set we employed *elastic net regularization*, which is a combination of L1 and L2 regularization.

A simplified version of the SGD learning procedure implemented in *scikit-learn* is shown in Algorithm 1, where w is the weight vector of the model, $x^{(i)}$ the feature vector of sample i, $y^{(i)} \in \{-1, +1\}$ the ground truth label of sample i, η the learning rate, α the regularization factor and ρ the elastic net mixing parameter. Be aware that we did not pick samples at random or shuffle the data, which is crucial in case of training data which is sorted by classes. The initial learning rate is set heuristically and updated following Shalev-Shwartz et al. (2007).[6] The way of applying the L1 penalty (lines 13 to 18) is published as "cumulative L1 penalty" in Tsuruoka et al. (2009). The final settings for the hyperparameters were determined by running a cross-validated grid search on the combined training and development sets and can be found in Table 1.

4 Experiments

For our experiments and the final model training we used the combined training and development set of the shared task. For Task A we removed messages labeled "objective" prior to training, while we merged them into the "neutral" class for Task B. This left us with 9419 training samples (5855 positive, 457 neutral, 3107 negative) for Task A and 10368 training samples (3855 positive, 4889 neutral, 1624 negative) for Task B. As the shared task was evaluated on average F_1 of the positive and negative class, disregarding the neutral class, we also provide our results in these measures in the following.

[5] inversely proportional to class frequency

[6] This is achieved by choosing "optimal" as setting for the learning rate for *scikit-learn's SGDClassifier*.

	Negative		Positive		Avg.
	Prec	**Rec**	**Prec**	**Rec**	$\mathbf{F_1}$
ALL	53.86	62.68	77.88	68.95	65.54
-stem	-0.38	**-1.10**	-0.07	-0.08	-0.385
-wc	**-0.74**	-0.30	+0.13	**-2.05**	**-0.835**
-swn	-0.15	-0.73	-0.27	+0.10	-0.23
-neg	+0.04	-0.92	**-1.06**	+0.44	-0.30
bow	-4.03	-7.01	-0.44	-3.68	-3.83

Table 2: Feature ablation study (Task B)

During the process of preparing our submission we used 10-fold cross-validation to evaluate different combinations of features, machine learning algorithms and their hyperparameter settings. While we found the features described in section 3.2 to be useful, we did not find further improvement by using n-grams and part-of-speech tags, despite using the Twitter-specific part-of-speech tagger by Owoputi et al. (2013). Table 2 shows a cross-validated ablation study on the features, removing one group of features at a time to see their contribution to the model. Using only normalized tokens is referred to as bag-of-words (bow). One can see that word clusters are the most important for our model, causing the highest overall loss in F_1 performance when being removed. Nevertheless, all other features contribute to the performance of the model as well.

Further improvement can be made by carefully picking a machine learning algorithm and tuning its hyperparameters. For this task we found linear models to perform better than other classification methods such as naive bayes, decision tree / random forest and k-nearest neighbor. Figure 1 shows that models trained with the method described in section 3.3 (marked SGD) clearly outperforms models trained with the popular perceptron algorithm (which could be described as stochastic gradient descent with zero-one loss, no regularization and constant learning rate, marked PER) with increasing training set size. The values were obtained by training on different portions of the training set of Task B and testing on the previously unseen Task B Twitter test set (3813 samples). Starting from a certain amount of available training data, the choice of the training algorithm becomes even more important than the choice of features.

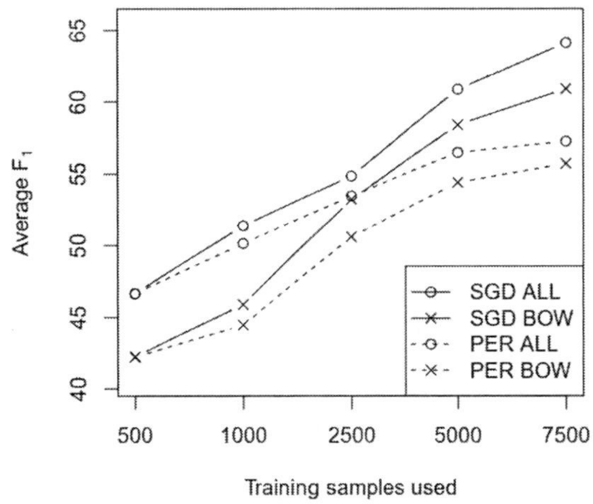

Figure 1: Effect of training set size on different classifiers

5 Results and Conclusion

The results of our submission for the four hidden test sets of the shared task can be found in Table 3. Given the relatively small deviation from the results of the cross-validation on combined training and development set and the good ranks obtained in the shared task system ranking, we conclude that the method for sentiment analysis in microblogging messages presented in this paper yields competitive results.

We showed that the performance for this task can be improved by using linguistically motivated features as well as carefully choosing a learning algorithm and its hyperparameter settings.

Task	Prec	Rec	$\mathbf{F_1}$ (Rank)
A SMS	86.09	91.01	88.37 (1)
A Twitter	85.06	85.43	85.19 (7)
B SMS	55.83	72.55	62.15 (2)
B Twitter	70.21	61.49	65.27 (2)

Table 3: Final results of our submission

Acknowledgments

We would like to thank the organizers of the shared task for their effort, Peter Prettenhofer for his help with getting to the bottom of the SGD implementation in *scikit-learn* and Richard Johansson as well as the anonymous reviewers for their helpful comments on the paper.

References

Stefano Baccianella, Andrea Esuli, and Fabrizio Sebastiani. 2010. Sentiwordnet 3.0: An enhanced lexical resource for sentiment analysis and opinion mining. In *Proceedings of the 7th conference on International Language Resources and Evaluation (LREC'10), Valletta, Malta.*

Luciano Barbosa and Junlan Feng. 2010. Robust Sentiment Detection on Twitter from Biased and Noisy Data. In *COLING (Posters)*, pages 36–44.

Steven Bird, Ewan Klein, and Edward Loper. 2009. *Natural Language Processing with Python.* O'Reilly Media.

Peter F Brown, Peter V Desouza, Robert L Mercer, Vincent J Della Pietra, and Jenifer C Lai. 1992. Class-based n-gram models of natural language. *Computational linguistics*, 18(4):467–479.

Dmitry Davidov, Oren Tsur, and Ari Rappoport. 2010. Enhanced Sentiment Learning Using Twitter Hashtags and Smileys. In *COLING (Posters)*, pages 241–249.

Efthymios Kouloumpis, Theresa Wilson, and Johanna Moore. 2011. Twitter Sentiment Analysis: The Good the Bad and the OMG! In *Fifth International AAAI Conference on Weblogs and Social Media*, ICWSM.

Bing Liu. 2012. *Sentiment Analysis and Opinion Mining.* Synthesis Lectures on Human Language Technologies. Morgan & Claypool Publishers.

Finn Årup Nielsen. 2011. A new ANEW: Evaluation of a word list for sentiment analysis in microblogs. In *Proceedings of the ESWC2011 Workshop on 'Making Sense of Microposts': Big things come in small packages*, volume 718 of *CEUR Workshop Proceedings*, pages 93–98.

Brendan O'Connor, Ramnath Balasubramanyan, Bryan R. Routledge, and Noah A. Smith. 2010. From Tweets to Polls: Linking Text Sentiment to Public Opinion Time Series. In *Fourth International AAAI Conference on Weblogs and Social Media*, ICWSM.

Olutobi Owoputi, Brendan O'Connor, Chris Dyer, Kevin Gimpel, Nathan Schneider, and Noah A Smith. 2013. Improved part-of-speech tagging for online conversational text with word clusters. In *Proceedings of NAACL 2013.*

Alexander Pak and Patrick Paroubek. 2010. Twitter as a Corpus for Sentiment Analysis and Opinion Mining. In *Proceedings of the 7th conference on International Language Resources and Evaluation*, volume 2010, pages 1320–1326.

Fabian Pedregosa, Gaël Varoquaux, Alexandre Gramfort, Vincent Michel, Bertrand Thirion, Olivier Grisel, Mathieu Blondel, Peter Prettenhofer, Ron Weiss, Vincent Dubourg, Jake Vanderplas, Alexandre Passos, David Cournapeau, Matthieu Brucher, Matthieu Perrot, and Édouard Duchesnay. 2011. Scikit-learn: Machine learning in Python. *Journal of Machine Learning Research*, 12:2825–2830.

Martin F Porter. 1980. An algorithm for suffix stripping. *Program: electronic library and information systems*, 14(3):130–137.

Hassan Saif, Yulan He, and Harith Alani. 2012. Alleviating data sparsity for twitter sentiment analysis. In *Proceedings of the 2nd Workshop on Making Sense of Microposts.*

Shai Shalev-Shwartz, Yoram Singer, and Nathan Srebro. 2007. Pegasos: Primal estimated sub-gradient solver for svm. In *Proceedings of the 24th international conference on Machine learning*, pages 807–814. ACM.

Michael Speriosu, Nikita Sudan, Sid Upadhyay, and Jason Baldridge. 2011. Twitter Polarity Classification with Label Propagation over Lexical Links and the Follower Graph. In *Proceedings of the 2011 Conference on Empirical Methods in Natural Language Processing*, EMNLP '11, page 53–63.

Yoshimasa Tsuruoka, Jun'ichi Tsujii, and Sophia Ananiadou. 2009. Stochastic gradient descent training for l1-regularized log-linear models with cumulative penalty. In *Proceedings of the Joint Conference of the 47th Annual Meeting of the ACL and the 4th International Joint Conference on Natural Language Processing of the AFNLP: Volume 1-Volume 1*, pages 477–485. Association for Computational Linguistics.

Theresa Wilson, Zornitsa Kozareva, Preslav Nakov, Alan Ritter, Sara Rosenthal, and Veselin Stoyanov. 2013. Semeval-2013 task 2: Sentiment analysis in twitter. In *Proceedings of the 7th International Workshop on Semantic Evaluation.* Association for Computational Linguistics.

AVAYA: Sentiment Analysis on Twitter with Self-Training and Polarity Lexicon Expansion

Lee Becker, George Erhart, David Skiba and Valentine Matula
Avaya Labs Research
1300 West 120th Avenue
Westminster, CO 80234, USA
{beckerl,gerhart,dskiba,matula}@avaya.com

Abstract

This paper describes the systems submitted by Avaya Labs (AVAYA) to SemEval-2013 Task 2 - Sentiment Analysis in Twitter. For the constrained conditions of both the message polarity classification and contextual polarity disambiguation subtasks, our approach centers on training high-dimensional, linear classifiers with a combination of lexical and syntactic features. The constrained message polarity model is then used to tag nearly half a million unlabeled tweets. These automatically labeled data are used for two purposes: 1) to discover prior polarities of words and 2) to provide additional training examples for self-training. Our systems performed competitively, placing in the top five for all subtasks and data conditions. More importantly, these results show that expanding the polarity lexicon and augmenting the training data with unlabeled tweets can yield improvements in precision and recall in classifying the polarity of non-neutral messages and contexts.

1 Introduction

The past decade has witnessed a massive expansion in communication from long-form delivery such as e-mail to short-form mechanisms such as microblogging and short messaging service (SMS) text messages. Simultaneously businesses, media outlets, and investors are increasingly relying on these messages as sources of real-time information and are increasingly turning to sentiment analysis to discover product trends, identify customer preferences, and categorize users. While a variety of corpora exist for developing and evaluating sentiment classifiers for long-form texts such as product reviews, there are few such resources for evaluating sentiment algorithms on microblogs and SMS texts.

The organizers of SemEval-2013 task 2, have begun to address this resource deficiency by coordinating a shared evaluation task for Twitter sentiment analysis. In doing so they have assembled corpora in support of the following two subtasks:

Task A - Contextual Polarity Disambiguation *"Given a message containing a marked instance of a word or phrase, determine whether that instance is positive, negative or neutral in that context."*

Task B - Message Polarity Classification *"Given a message, classify whether the message is of positive, negative, or neutral sentiment. For messages conveying both a positive and negative sentiment, whichever is the stronger sentiment should be chosen."*

This paper describes the systems submitted by Avaya Labs for participation in subtasks A and B. Our goal for this evaluation was to investigate the usefulness of dependency parses, polarity lexicons, and unlabeled tweets for sentiment classification on short messages. In total we built four systems for SemEval-2013 task 2. For task B we developed a constrained model using supervised learning, and an unconstrained model that used semi-supervised learning in the form of self-training and polarity lexicon expansion. For task A the constrained system utilized supervised learning, while the unconstrained model made use of the expanded lexicon

*Second Joint Conference on Lexical and Computational Semantics (*SEM), Volume 2: Seventh International Workshop on Semantic Evaluation (SemEval 2013)*, pages 333–340, Atlanta, Georgia, June 14-15, 2013.

from task B. Output from these systems were submitted to all eight evaluation conditions. For a complete description of the data, tasks, and conditions, please refer to Wilson et al. (2013). The remainder of this paper details the approaches, experiments and results associated with each of these models.

2 Related Work

Over the past few years sentiment analysis has grown from a nascent topic in natural language processing to a broad research area targeting a wide range of text genres and applications. There is now a significant body of work that spans topics as diverse as document level sentiment classification (Pang and Lee, 2008), induction of word polarity lexicons (Hatzivassiloglou and McKeown, 1997; Turney, 2002; Esuli and Sebastiani, 2006; Mohammad and Turney, 2011) and even election prediction (Tumasjan et al., 2010).

Efforts to train sentiment classifiers for Twitter messages have largely relied on using emoticons and hashtags as proxies of the true polarity (Barbosa and Feng, 2010; Davidov et al., 2010b; Pak and Paroubek, 2010; Agarwal et al., 2011; Kouloumpis et al., 2011; Mohammad, 2012). Classification of word and phrase sentiment with respect to surrounding context (Wilson et al., 2005) has yet to be explored for the less formal language often found in microblog and SMS text. Semi-supervised learning has been applied to polarity lexicon induction (Rao and Ravichandran, 2009), and sentiment classification at the sentence level (Täckström and McDonald, 2011) and document level (Sindhwani and Melville, 2008; He and Zhou, 2011); however to the best of our knowledge self-training and other semi-supervised learning has seen only minimal use in classifying Twitter texts (Davidov et al., 2010a; Zhang et al., 2012).

3 System Overview

Given our overarching goal of combining polarity lexicons, syntactic information and unlabeled data, our approach centered on first building strong constrained models and then improving performance by adding additional data and resources. For both tasks, our data-constrained approach combined standard features for document classification with dependency parse and word polarity features into a weighted linear classifier. For our data-unconstrained models we used pointwise mutual information for lexicon expansion in conjunction with self-training to increase the size of the feature space.

$conj \rightarrow conj\_\langle conjunction\rangle$
$pobj \rightarrow prep\_\langle preposition\rangle$
$pcomp \rightarrow prepc\_\langle preposition\rangle$
$prep\|punct\|cc \rightarrow \emptyset$

Table 1: Collapsed Dependency Transformation Rules

4 Preprocessing and Text Normalization

Our systems were built with ClearTK (Ogren et al., 2008) a framework for developing NLP components built on top of Apache UIMA. Our preprocessing pipeline utilized ClearTK's wrappers for ClearNLP's (Choi and McCallum, 2013) tokenizer, lemmatizer, part-of-speech (POS) tagger, and dependency parser. ClearNLP's ability to retain emoticons and emoji as individual tokens made it especially attractive for sentiment analysis. POS tags were mapped from Penn Treebank-style tags to the simplified, Twitter-oriented tags introduced by Gimpel et al. (2011). Dependency graphs output by ClearNLP were also transformed to the Stanford Collapsed dependencies representation (de Marneffe and Manning, 2012) using our own transformation rules (table 1). Input normalization consisted solely of replacing all usernames and URLs with common placeholders.

5 Sentiment Resources

A variety of our classifier features rely on manually tagged sentiment lexicons and word lists. In particular we make use of the MPQA Subjectivity Lexicon (Wiebe et al., 2005) as well as manually-created negation and emoticon dictionaries[1]. The negation word list consisting of negation words such as *no* and *not*. Because tokenization splits contractions, the list includes the sub-word token *n't* as well as the apostrophe-less version of 12 contractions (e.g. *cant*, *wont*, etc ...). To support emoticon-specific features we created a dictionary, which paired 183 emoticons with either a positive or negative polarity.

[1]http://leebecker.com/resources/semeval-2013

6 Message Polarity Classification

6.1 Features

Polarized Bag-of-Words Features: Instead of extracting raw bag-of words (BOW), we opted to integrate negation directly into the word representations following the approaches used by Das and Chen (2001) and Pang et al. (2002). All words between a negation word and the first punctuation mark after the negation word were suffixed with a **_NOT** tag – essentially doubling the number of BOW features. We extended this polarized BOW paradigm to include not only the raw word forms but all of the following combinations: raw word, raw word+PTB POS tag, raw word+simplified POS tag, lemma+simplified POS tag.

Word Polarity Features: Using a subjectivity lexicon, we extracted features for the number of positive, negative, and neutral words as well as the net polarity based on these counts. Individual word polarities were inverted if the word had a child dependency relation with a negation (*neg*) label. Constrained models use the MPQA lexicon, while unconstrained models use an expanded lexicon that is described in section 6.2.

Emoticon Features: Similar to the word polarity features, we computed features for the number of positive, negative, and neutral emoticons, and the net emoticon polarity score.

Microblogging Features: As noted by Kouloumpis et al. (2011), the emotional intensity of words in social media messages is often emphasized by changes to the word form such as capitalization, character repetition, and emphasis characters (asterisks, dashes). To capture this intuition we compute features for the number of fully-capitalized words, words with characters repeated more than 3 times (e.g. *booooo*), and words surround by asterisks or dashes (e.g. **yay**). We also created a binary feature to indicate the presence of a winning score or winning record within the target span (e.g. *Oh yeah #Nuggets **15-0***).

Part-of-Speech Tag Features: Counts of the Penn Treebank POS tags provide a rough measure of the content of the message.

Syntactic Dependency Features: We extracted dependency pair features using both standard and collapsed dependency parse graphs. Extracted head/child relations include: raw word/raw word, lemma/lemma, lemma/simplified POS tag, simplified POS tag/lemma. If the head node of the relation has a child negation dependency, the pair's relation label is prefixed with a **NEG_** tag.

6.2 Expanding the Polarity Lexicon

Unseen words pose a recurring challenge for both machine learning and dictionary-based approaches to sentiment analysis. This problem is even more prevalent in social media and SMS messages where text lengths are often limited to 140 characters or less. To expand our word polarity lexicon we adopt a framework similar to the one introduced by Turney (2002). Turney's unsupervised approach centered on computing pointwise mutual information (PMI) between highly polar seed words and bigram phrases extracted from a corpus of product reviews.

Instead of relying solely on seed words for polarity, we use the constrained version of the message polarity classifier to tag a corpus of approximately 475,000 unlabeled, English language tweets. These tweets were collected over the period from November 2012 to February 2013. To reduce the number of noisy instances and to obtain a more balanced distribution of sentiment labels, we eliminated all tweets with classifier confidence scores below 0.9, 0.7, and 0.8 for *positive*, *negative* and *neutral* instances respectively. Applying the threshold, reduced the tweet count to 180,419 tweets (50,789 positive, 59,029 negative, 70,601 neutral). This filtered set of automatically labeled tweets was used to accumulate co-occurrence statistics between the words in the tweets and their corresponding sentiment labels. These statistics are then used to compute word-sentiment PMI (equation 1), which is the joint probability of a word and sentiment co-occurring divided by the probability of each of the events occurring independently. A word's net polarity is computed as the signum (sgn) of the difference between a its positive and negative PMI values (equation 2). It should be noted that polarities were deliberately limited to values of $\{-1, 0, +1\}$ to ensure consistency with the existing MPQA lexicon, and to dampen the bias of any single word.

$$PMI(word, sentiment) = log_2 \frac{p(word, sentiment)}{p(word)p(sentiment)} \quad (1)$$

$$polarity(word) = sgn(PMI(word, positive) - PMI(word, negative)) \quad (2)$$

Words with fewer than 10 occurrences, words with neutral polarities, numbers, single characters, and punctuation were then removed from this PMI-derived polarity dictionary. Lastly, this dictionary was merged with the dictionary created from the MPQA lexicon yielding a final polarity dictionary with 11,740 entries. In cases where an entry existed in both dictionaries, the MPQA polarity value was retained. This final polarity dictionary was used by the unconstrained models for task A and B.

6.3 Model Parameters and Training

Constrained Model: Models were trained using the LIBLINEAR classification library (Fan et al., 2008). L2 regularized logistic regression was chosen over other LIBLINEAR loss functions because it not only gave improved performance on the development set but also produced calibrated outcomes for confidence thresholding. Training data for the constrained model consisted of all 9829 examples from the training (8175 examples) and development (1654 examples) set released for SemEval 2013. Cost and label-specific cost weight parameters were selected via experimentation on the development set to maximize the average positive and negative F_1 values. The c values ranged over $\{0.1, 0.5, 1, 2, 5, 10, 20, 100\}$ and the label weights $w_{polarity}$ ranged over $\{0.1, 1, 2, 5, 10, 20, 25, 50, 100\}$. Final parameters for the constrained model were cost $c = 1$ and weights $w_{positive} = 1$, $w_{negative} = 25$, and $w_{neutral} = 1$.

Unconstrained Model: In addition to using the expanded polarity dictionary described in 6.2 for feature extraction, the unconstrained model also makes use of automatically labeled tweets for self-training (Scudder, 1965). In contrast to preparation of the expanded polarity dictionary, the self-training placed no threshold on the examples. Combining the self-labeled tweets, with the official training and development set yielded a new training set consisting of 485,112 examples. Because the self-labeled instances were predominantly tagged *neutral*, the LIBLINEAR cost parameters were adjusted to heavily discount *neutral* while emphasizing *positive* and *neutral* instances. The size and cost of training this model prevented extensive parameter tuning and instead were chosen based on experience with the constrained model and to maximize recall on positive and negative items. Final parameters for the unconstrained model were cost $c = 1$ and category weights $w_{positive} = 2$, $w_{negative} = 5$, and $w_{neutral} = 0.1$.

7 Contextual Polarity Disambiguation

7.1 Features

The same base set of features used for message polarity classification were used for the contextual polarity classification, with the exception of the syntactic dependency features. To better express the in-context and out-of-context relation these additional feature classes were added:

Scoped Dependency Features: Because this task focuses on a smaller context within the message, collapsed dependencies are less useful as the compression may cross over context boundaries. Instead the standard syntactic dependency features described above were modified to account for their relation to the context. All governing relations for the words contained within the contact were extracted. Relations wholly contained within the boundaries of the context were prefixed with an **IN** tag, whereas those that crossed outside of the context were prefixed with an **OUT** tag. Additionally counts of IN and OUT relations were included as features.

Dependency Path Features: Like the single dependency arcs, a dependency path can provide additional information about the syntactic and semantic role of the context in the sentence. Our path features consisted of two varieties: 1) POS-path and 2) Sentiment-POS-path. The POS-path consisted of the PTB POS tags and dependency relation labels for all nodes between the head of the context and the root node of the parent sentence. The Sentiment-POS-path follows the same path but omits the dependency relation labels, uses the simplified POS tags and appends word polarities (POS/NEG/NTR) to the POS tags along the path.

	System	Positive			Negative			Neutral			F_{avg}	Rank
		P	R	F	P	R	F	P	R	F	+/-	
Tweet	NRC-Canada (top)	0.814	0.667	0.733	0.697	0.604	0.647	0.677	0.826	0.744	0.690	1
Tweet	AVAYA-Unconstrained	0.751	0.655	0.700	0.608	0.557	0.582	0.665	0.768	0.713	0.641	5
Tweet	AVAYA-Constrained	0.791	0.580	0.669	0.593	0.509	0.548	0.636	0.832	0.721	0.608	12
Tweet	*Mean of submissions*	0.687	0.591	0.626	0.491	0.456	0.450	0.612	0.663	0.615	0.538	-
SMS	NRC-Canada (top)	0.731	0.730	0.730	0.554	0.754	0.639	0.852	0.753	0.799	0.685	1
SMS	AVAYA-Constrained	0.630	0.667	0.648	0.526	0.581	0.553	0.802	0.756	0.778	0.600	4
SMS	AVAYA-Unconstrained	0.609	0.659	0.633	0.494	0.637	0.557	0.814	0.710	0.759	0.595	5
SMS	*Mean of submissions*	0.512	0.620	0.546	0.462	0.518	0.456	0.754	0.578	0.627	0.501	-

Table 2: Message Polarity Classification (Task B) Results

	System	Positive			Negative			Neutral			F_{avg}	Rank
		P	R	F	P	R	F	P	R	F	+/-	
Tweet	NRC-Canada (top)	0.889	0.932	0.910	0.866	0.871	0.869	0.455	0.063	0.110	0.889	1
Tweet	AVAYA-Unconstrained	0.892	0.905	0.898	0.834	0.865	0.849	0.539	0.219	0.311	0.874	2
Tweet	AVAYA-Constrained	0.882	0.911	0.896	0.844	0.843	0.843	0.493	0.225	0.309	0.870	3
Tweet	*Mean of submissions*	0.837	0.745	0.773	0.745	0.656	0.677	0.159	0.240	0.115	0.725	-
SMS	GUMLTLT (top)	0.814	0.924	0.865	0.908	0.896	0.902	0.286	0.050	0.086	0.884	1
SMS	AVAYA-Unconstrained	0.815	0.871	0.842	0.853	0.896	0.874	0.448	0.082	0.138	0.858	3
SMS	AVAYA-Constrained	0.777	0.875	0.823	0.859	0.852	0.856	0.364	0.076	0.125	0.839	4
SMS	*Mean of submissions*	0.734	0.722	0.710	0.807	0.663	0.698	0.144	0.184	0.099	0.704	-

Table 3: Contextual Polarity Disambiguation (Task A) Results

For example given the bold-faced context in the sentence:

> *@User Criminals killed Sadat, and in the process they killed* ***Egypt. . . they*** *destroyed the future of young & old Egyptians..*

the extracted POS-path feature would be:

> {NNP} dobj <{VBD} conj <{VBD} ccomp <{VBD} root <{TOP}

while the Sentiment-POS path would be:

> {^/pos}{V/neg}{V/neg}{V/neg}{TOP}.

Paths with depth greater than 4 dependency relations were truncated to reduce feature sparsity. In addition to these detailed path features, we include two binary features to indicate if any part of the path contains subject or object relations.

7.2 Model Parameters and Training

Like with message polarity classification, the contextual polarity disambiguation systems rely on LIBLINEAR's L2 regularized logistic regression for model training. Both constrained and unconstrained models use identical parameters of cost $c = 1$ and weights $w_{positive} = 1$, $w_{negative} = 2$, and $w_{neutral} = 1$. They vary only in the choice of polarity lexicon. The constrained model uses the MPQA subjectivity lexicon, while the unconstrained model uses the expanded dictionary derived via computation of PMI, which ultimately differentiates these models through the variation in the sentiment path and word polarity features.

8 Experiments and Results

In this section we report results for the series of Sentiment Analysis in Twitter tasks at SemEval 2013. Please refer to refer to Wilson et al. (2013) for the exact details about the corpora, evaluation conditions, and methodology.

We submitted polarity output for the Message Polarity Classification (task B) and the Contextual Polarity Disambiguation (task A). For each task we submitted system output from our constrained and unconstrained models. As stated above, the constrained models made use of only the training data released for the task, whereas the unconstrained models trained on additional tweets. Each subtask had two test sets one comprised of tweets and the other comprised of SMS messages. Final task 2

	S	G	Message / Context
1	+	/	*Going to Helsinki tomorrow or on the day after tomorrow,yay!*
2	/	+	*Eric Decker catches his second TD pass from Manning. This puts Broncos up 31-7 with 14:54 left in the 4th.*
3	-	/	*So, crashed a wedding reception and Andy Lee's bro was in the bridal party. How'd you spend your Saturday night? #longstory*
4	-	+	*Aiyo... **Dun worry** la, they'll let u change one... Anyway, sleep early, nite nite...*
5	+	-	***Sori** I haven't done anything for today's meeting.. pls pardon me. Cya guys later at 10am.*
6	+	-	*these PSSA's are just gonna be the icing to another horrible monday. #fmlll **#ihateschool***

Table 4: Example Classification Errors: S=System, G=Gold, +=positive, −=negative, /=neutral. Bold-faced text indicates the span for contextual polarities.

evaluation is based on the average positive and negative F-score. Task B results are listed in table 2, and task A results are shown in table 3. For comparison these tables also include the top-ranked system in each category as well as the mean scores across all submissions.

9 Error Analysis

To better understand our systems' limitations we manually inspected misclassified output. Table 4 lists errors representative of the common issues uncovered in our error analysis.

Though some degree of noise is expected in sentiment analysis, we found several instances of annotation error or ambiguity where it could be argued that the system was actually correct. The message in #1 was annotated as neutral, whereas the presence of the word "yay" suggests an overall positive polarity. The text in #2 could be interpreted as positive, negative or neutral depending on the author's disposition.

Unseen vocabulary and unexpected usages were the largest category of error. For example in #3 "crashed" means to attend without an invitation instead of the more negative meaning associated with car accidents and airplane failures. Although POS features can disambiguate word senses, in this case more sophisticated features for word sense disambiguation could help. While the degradation in performance between the Tweet and SMS test sets might be explained by differences in medium, errors like those found in #4 and #5 suggest that this may have more to do with the dialectal differences between the predominantly American and British English found in the Tweet test set and the Colloquial Singaporean English (aka Singlish) found in the SMS test set. Error #6 illustrates both how hashtags composed of common words can easily become a problem when assigning a polarity to a short context. Hashtag segmentation presents one possible path to reducing this source of error.

10 Conclusions and Future Work

The results and rankings reported in section 8 suggest that our systems were competitive in assigning sentiment across the varied tasks and data conditions. We performed particularly well in disambiguating contextual polarities finishing second overall on the Tweet test set. We hypothesize this performance is largely due to the expanded vocabulary obtained via unlabeled data and the richer syntactic context captured with dependency path representations.

Looking forward, we expect that term recall and unseen vocabulary will continue to be key challenges for sentiment analysis on social media. While larger amounts of data should assist in that pursuit, we would like to explore how a more iterative approach to self-training and lexicon expansion may provide a less noisy path to attaining such recall.

11 Acknowledgments

We would like to thank the organizers of SemEval 2013 and the Sentiment Analysis in Twitter task for their time and energy. We also would like to express our appreciation to the anonymous reviewers for their helpful feedback and suggestions.

References

Apoorv Agarwal, Boyi Xie, Ilia Vovsha, Owen Rambow, and Rebecca Passonneau. 2011. Sentiment analysis of twitter data. In *Proceedings of the Workshop on Language in Social Media (LSM 2011)*.

Luciano Barbosa and Junlan Feng. 2010. Robust sentiment detection on twitter from biased and noisy data.

In *Proceedings of the 23rd International Conference on Computational Linguistics*, COLING '10, pages 36–44, Stroudsburg, PA, USA. Association for Computational Linguistics.

Jinho D. Choi and Andrew McCallum. 2013. Transition-based dependency parsing with selectional branching. In *Proceedings of the 51st Annual Meeting of the Association for Computational Linguistics (ACL'13)*.

Sanjiv Das and Mike Chen. 2001. Yahoo! for amazon: extracting market sentiment from stock message boards. In *Proceedings of the 8th Asia Pacific Finance Association Annual Conference*.

Dmitry Davidov, Oren Tsur, and Ari Rappaport. 2010a. Semi-supervised recognition of sarcastic sentences in twitter and amazon. In *Proceedings of the Fourteenth Conference on Computational Natural Language Learning*.

Dmitry Davidov, Oren Tsur, and Ari Rappoport. 2010b. Enhanced sentiment learning using twitter hashtags and smileys. In *Coling 2010*, pages 241–249.

Marie-Catherine de Marneffe and Christopher D. Manning, 2012. *Stanford typed dependencies manual*. Stanford University, v2.0.4 edition, November.

Andrea Esuli and Fabrizio Sebastiani. 2006. SENTIWORDNET: A Publicly Available Lexical Resource for Opinion Mining. In *Proceedings of the 5th Conference on Language Resources and Evaluation (LREC'06)*.

Rong-En Fan, Kai-Wei Chang, Cho-Jui Hsieh, Xiang-Rui Wang, and Chih-Jen Lin. 2008. LIBLINEAR: A Library for Large Linear Classication. *Journal of Machine Learning Research*, 9:1871–1874.

Kevin Gimpel, Nathan Schneider, Brendan O'Connor, Dipanjan Das, Daniel Mills, Jacob Eisenstein, Michael Heilman, Dani Yogatama, Jeffrey Flanigan, and Noah A. Smith. 2011. Part-of-speech tagging for twitter: Annotation, features, and experiments. In *Proceedings of the 49th Annual Meeting of the Association for Computational Linguistics: Human Language Technologies ACL:HLT 2011*.

Vasileios Hatzivassiloglou and Kathleen R. McKeown. 1997. Predicting the semantic orientation of adjectives. In *Proceedings of the 35th Annual Meeting of the Association for Computational Linguistics (ACL 1997)*.

Yulan He and Deyu Zhou. 2011. Self-training from labeled features for sentiment analysis. *Information Processing and Management*, 47(4):606–616.

Efthymios Kouloumpis, Theresa Wilson, and Johanna Moore. 2011. Twitter Sentiment Analysis: The Good the Bad and the OMG! In *Proceedings of the Fifth International AAAI Conference on Weblogs and Social Media (ICWSM 2011)*.

Saif M. Mohammad and Peter D. Turney. 2011. Crowdsourcing a word-emotion association lexicon. *Computational Intelligence*, 59(000).

Saif M. Mohammad. 2012. #emotional tweets. In *Proceedings of the First Joint Conference on Lexical and Computational Semantics (*SEM)*.

Philip V. Ogren, Philipp G. Wetzler, and Steven Bethard. 2008. ClearTK: A UIMA toolkit for statistical natural language processing. In *Towards Enhanced Interoperability for Large HLT Systems: UIMA for NLP workshop at Language Resources and Evaluation Conference (LREC '08)*, 5.

Alexander Pak and Patrick Paroubek. 2010. Twitter as a corpus for sentiment analysis and opinion mining. In Nicoletta Calzolari (Conference Chair), Khalid Choukri, Bente Maegaard, Joseph Mariani, Jan Odijk, Stelios Piperidis, Mike Rosner, and Daniel Tapias, editors, *Proceedings of the Seventh International Conference on Language Resources and Evaluation (LREC'10)*.

Bo Pang and Lillian Lee. 2008. Opinion mining and sentiment analysis. *Foundations and Trends in Information Retrieval*, 2(1-2):1–135.

Bo Pang, Lillian Lee, and Shivakumar Vaithyanathan. 2002. Thumbs up? Sentiment Classification Using Machine Learning Techniques. In *Proceedings of the Conference on Empirical Methods in Natural Language Processing (EMNLP 2002)*.

Delip Rao and Deepak Ravichandran. 2009. Semi-supervised polarity lexicon induction. In *Proceedings of the 12th Conference of the European Chapter of the ACL (EACL 2009)*.

H. J. Scudder. 1965. Probability of error of some adaptive pattern-recognition machine. *IEEE Transactions on Information Theory*, 11:363–371.

Vikas Sindhwani and Prem Melville. 2008. Document-word co-regularization for semi-supervised sentiment analysis. In *Proceedings of the 2008 Eighth IEEE International Conference on Data Mining*, ICDM '08, pages 1025–1030.

Oscar Täckström and Ryan McDonald. 2011. Semi-supervised latent variable models for sentence-level sentiment analysis. In *Proceedings of the 49th Annual Meeting of the Association for Computational Linguistics (ACL 2011)*.

Andranik Tumasjan, Timm O. Sprenger, Philipp G. Sandner, and Isabell M. Welpe. 2010. Predicting elections with twitter what 140 characters reveal about political sentiment. In *Proceedings of the Fourth International AAAI Conference on Weblogs and Social Media (ICWSM 2010)*.

Peter Turney. 2002. Thumbs up or thumbs down? semantic orientation applied to unsupervised classification of reviews. In *Proceedings of the 40th Annual*

Meeting of the Association for Computational Linguistics (ACL 2002).

Janyce Wiebe, Theresa Wilson, and Claire Cardie. 2005. Annotating expressions of opinions and emotions in language. *Language Resources and Evaluation*, 39:165–210.

Theresa Wilson, Janyce Wiebe, and Paul Hoffman. 2005. Recognizing contextual polarity in phrase-level sentiment analysis. In *Proceedings of Human Language Technology Conference and Conference on Empirical Methods in Natural Language Processing (HLT/EMNLP)*.

Theresa Wilson, Zornitsa Kozareva, Preslav Nakov, Alan Ritter, Sara Rosenthal, and Veselin Stoyanov. 2013. SemEval-2013 task 2: Sentiment analysis in twitter. In *Proceedings of the 7th International Workshop on Semantic Evaluation*. Association for Computation Linguistics.

Xiuzhen Zhang, Yun Zhou, James Bailey, and Kotagiri Ramamohanarao. 2012. Sentiment analysis by augmenting expectation maximisation with lexical knowledge. *Proceedings of the 13th International Conference on Web Information Systems Engineering (WISE2012)*.

SemEval-2013 Task 9 : Extraction of Drug-Drug Interactions from Biomedical Texts (DDIExtraction 2013)

Isabel Segura-Bedmar, Paloma Martínez, María Herrero-Zazo
Universidad Carlos III de Madrid
Av. Universidad, 30, Leganés 28911, Spain
{isegura,pmf}@inf.uc3m.es, mhzazo@pa.uc3m.es

Abstract

The DDIExtraction 2013 task concerns the recognition of drugs and extraction of drug-drug interactions that appear in biomedical literature. We propose two subtasks for the DDIExtraction 2013 Shared Task challenge: 1) the recognition and classification of drug names and 2) the extraction and classification of their interactions. Both subtasks have been very successful in participation and results. There were 14 teams who submitted a total of 38 runs. The best result reported for the first subtask was F1 of 71.5% and 65.1% for the second one.

1 Introduction

The definition of drug-drug interaction (DDI) is broadly described as a change in the effects of one drug by the presence of another drug (Baxter and Stockely, 2010). The detection of DDIs is an important research area in patient safety since these interactions can become very dangerous and increase health care costs. Drug interactions are frequently reported in journals, making medical literature the most effective source for their detection (Aronson, 2007). Therefore, Information Extraction (IE) can be of great benefit in the pharmaceutical industry allowing identification and extraction of relevant information on DDIs and providing an interesting way of reducing the time spent by health care professionals on reviewing the literature.

The DDIExtraction 2013 follows up on a first event organized in 2011, DDIExtraction 2011 (Segura-Bedmar et al., 2011b) whose main goal was the detection of drug-drug interactions from biomedical texts. The new edition includes in addition to DDI extraction also a supporting task, the recognition and classification of pharmacological substances. DDIExtraction 2013 is designed to address the extraction of DDIs as a whole, but divided into two subtasks to allow separate evaluation of the performance for different aspects of the problem. The shared task includes two challenges:

- Task 9.1: Recognition and classification of pharmacological substances.
- Task 9.2: Extraction of drug-drug interactions.

Additionally, while the datasets used for the DDIExtraction 2011 task were composed by texts describing DDIs from the DrugBank database(Wishart et al., 2006), the new datasets for DDIExtraction 2013 also include MedLine abstracts in order to deal with different types of texts and language styles.

This shared task has been conceived with a dual objective: advancing the state-of-the-art of text-mining techniques applied to the pharmacological domain, and providing a common framework for evaluation of the participating systems and other researchers interested in the task.

In the next section we describe the DDI corpus used in this task. Sections 3 and 4 focus on the description of the task 9.1 and 9.2 respectively. Finally, Section 5 draws the conclusions and future work.

2 The DDI Corpus

The DDIExtraction 2013 task relies on the DDI corpus, which is a semantically annotated corpus of

*Second Joint Conference on Lexical and Computational Semantics (*SEM), Volume 2: Seventh International Workshop on Semantic Evaluation (SemEval 2013)*, pages 341–350, Atlanta, Georgia, June 14-15, 2013.

documents describing drug-drug interactions from the DrugBank database and MedLine abstracts on the subject of drug-drug interactions.

The DDI corpus consists of 1,017 texts (784 DrugBank texts and 233 MedLine abstracts) and was manually annotated with a total of 18,491 pharmacological substances and 5,021 drug-drug interactions (see Table 1). A detailed description of the method used to collect and process documents can be found in (Segura-Bedmar et al., 2011a). The corpus is distributed in XML documents following the unified format for PPI corpora proposed by Pyysalo et al., (2008) (see Figure 1). A detailed description and analysis of the DDI corpus and its methodology are included in an article currently under review by BioInformatics journal.[1]

The corpus was split in order to build the datasets for the training and evaluation of the different participating systems. Approximately 77% of the DDI corpus documents were randomly selected for the training dataset and the remaining (142 DrugBank texts and 91 MedLine abstracts) was used for the test dataset. The training dataset is the same for both subtasks since it contains entity and DDI annotations. The test dataset for the task 9.1 was formed by discarding documents which contained DDI annotations. Entity annotations were removed from this dataset to be used by participants. The remaining documents (that is, those containing some interaction) were used to create the test dataset for task 9.2. Since entity annotations are not removed from these documents, the test dataset for the task 9.2 can also be used as additional training data for the task 9.1.

		Training	Test for task 9.1	Test for task 9.2
DDI-DrugBank	documents	572	54	158
	sentences	5675	145	973
	drug	8197	180	1518
	group	3206	65	626
	brand	1423	53	347
	drug_n	103	5	21
	mechanism	1260	0	279
	effect	1548	0	301
	advice	819	0	215
	int	178	0	94
DDI-MedLine	documents	142	58	33
	sentences	1301	520	326
	drug	1228	171	346
	group	193	90	41
	brand	14	6	22
	drug_n	401	115	119
	mechanism	62	0	24
	effect	152	0	62
	advice	8	0	7
	int	10	0	2

Table 1: Basic statistics on the DDI corpus.

3 Task 9.1: Recognition and classification of pharmacological substances.

This task concerns the named entity extraction of pharmacological substances in text. This named entity task is a crucial first step for information extraction of drug-drug interactions. In this task, four types of pharmacological substances are defined: *drug* (generic drug names), *brand* (branded drug names), *group* (drug group names) and *drug-n* (active substances not approved for human use). For a more detailed description, the reader is directed to our annotation guidelines.[2]

For evaluation, a part of the DDI corpus consisting of 52 documents from DrugBank and 58 MedLine abstracts, is provided with the gold annotation hidden. The goal for participating systems is to recreate the gold annotation. Each participant system must output an ASCII list of reported entities, one per line, and formatted as:

IdSentence|startOffset-endOffset|text|type

Thus, for each recognized entity, each line must contain the id of the sentence where this entity appears, the position of the first character and the one of the last character of the entity in the sentence, the text of the entity, and its type. When the entity is a discontinuous name (eg. *aluminum* and magnesium *hydroxide*), this second field must contain the start and end positions of all parts of the entity separated by semicolon. Multiple mentions from the same sentence should appear on separate lines.

3.1 Evaluation Metrics

This section describes the methodology that is used to evaluate the performance of the participating systems in task 9.1.

The major forums of the Named Entity Recognition and Classification (NERC) research community (such as MUC-7 (Chinchor and Robinson, 1997), CoNLL 2003 (Tjong Kim Sang and De Meulder, 2003) or ACE07 have proposed several techniques to assess the performance of NERC systems. While

[1]M. Herrero-Zazo, I. Segura-Bedmar, P. Martínez. 2013. The DDI Corpus: an annotated corpus with pharmacological substances and drug-drug interactions, submitted to BioInformatics

[2]http://www.cs.york.ac.uk/semeval-2013/task9/

```
-<document id="DDI-DrugBank.d372">
 -<sentence id="DDI-DrugBank.d372.s0" text="Cytadren accelerates the metabolism of dexamethasone;">
    <entity id="DDI-DrugBank.d372.s0.e0" charOffset="0-7" type="brand" text="Cytadren"/>
    <entity id="DDI-DrugBank.d372.s0.e1" charOffset="39-51" type="drug" text="dexamethasone"/>
    <pair id="DDI-DrugBank.d372.s0.p0" e1="DDI-DrugBank.d372.s0.e0" e2="DDI-DrugBank.d372.s0.e1" ddi="true" type="mechanism"/>
  </sentence>
 -<sentence id="DDI-DrugBank.d372.s1" text="therefore, if glucocorticoid replacement is needed, hydrocortisone should be prescribed.">
    <entity id="DDI-DrugBank.d372.s1.e0" charOffset="14-27" type="group" text="glucocorticoid"/>
    <entity id="DDI-DrugBank.d372.s1.e1" charOffset="52-65" type="drug" text="hydrocortisone"/>
    <pair id="DDI-DrugBank.d372.s1.p0" e1="DDI-DrugBank.d372.s1.e0" e2="DDI-DrugBank.d372.s1.e1" ddi="false"/>
  </sentence>
 -<sentence id="DDI-DrugBank.d372.s2" text="Aminoglutethimide diminishes the effect of coumarin and warfarin.">
    <entity id="DDI-DrugBank.d372.s2.e0" charOffset="0-16" type="drug" text="Aminoglutethimide"/>
    <entity id="DDI-DrugBank.d372.s2.e1" charOffset="43-50" type="group" text="coumarin"/>
    <entity id="DDI-DrugBank.d372.s2.e2" charOffset="56-63" type="drug" text="warfarin"/>
    <pair id="DDI-DrugBank.d372.s2.p0" e1="DDI-DrugBank.d372.s2.e0" e2="DDI-DrugBank.d372.s2.e1" ddi="true" type="effect"/>
    <pair id="DDI-DrugBank.d372.s2.p1" e1="DDI-DrugBank.d372.s2.e0" e2="DDI-DrugBank.d372.s2.e2" ddi="true" type="effect"/>
    <pair id="DDI-DrugBank.d372.s2.p2" e1="DDI-DrugBank.d372.s2.e1" e2="DDI-DrugBank.d372.s2.e2" ddi="false"/>
  </sentence>
</document>
```

Figure 1: Example of an annotated document of the DDI corpus.

	Team	Affiliation	Description
Task 9.1	LASIGE(Grego et al., 2013)	University of Lisbon, Portugal	Conditional random fields
	NLM_LHC	National Library of Medicine, USA	Dictionary-based approach
	UEM_UC3M(Sanchez-Cisneros and Aparicio, 2013)	European U. of Madrid, Carlos III University of Madrid, Spain	Ontology-based approach
	UMCC_DLSI(Collazo et al., 2013)	Matanzas University, Cuba	j48 classifier
	UTurku(Björne et al., 2013)	University of Turku, Finland	SVM classifier (TEES system)
	WBI_NER(Rocktäschel et al., 2013)	Humboldt University of Berlin, Germany	Conditional random fields
Task 9.2	FBK-irst (Chowdhury and Lavelli, 2013c)	FBK-irst, Italy	hybrid kernel + scope of negations and semantic roles
	NIL_UCM(Bokharaeian, 2013)	Complutense University of Madrid, Spain	SVM classifier (Weka SMO)
	SCAI(Bobić et al., 2013)	Fraunhofer SCAI, Germany	SVM classifier (LibLINEAR)
	UC3M(Sanchez-Cisneros, 2013)	Carlos III University of Madrid, Spain	Shallow Linguistic Kernel
	UCOLORADO_SOM(Hailu et al., 2013)	University of Colorado School of Medicine, USA	SVM classifier (LIBSVM)
	UTurku(Björne et al., 2013)	University of Turku, Finland	SVM classifier (TEES system)
	UWM-TRIADS(Rastegar-Mojarad et al., 2013)	University of Wisconsin-Milwaukee, USA	Two-stage SVM
	WBI_DDI(Thomas et al., 2013)	Humboldt University of Berlin, Germany	Ensemble of SVMs

Table 2: Short description of the teams.

ACE evaluation is very complex because its scores are not intuitive, MUC and CoNLL 2003 used the standard precision/recall/f-score metrics to compare their participating systems. The main shared tasks in the biomedical domain have continued using these metrics to evaluate the outputs of their participant teams.

System performance should be scored automatically by how well the generated pharmacological substance list corresponds to the gold-standard annotations. In our task, we evaluate the results of the participating systems according to several evaluation criteria. Firstly, we propose a strict evaluation, which does not only demand exact boundary match, but also requires that both mentions have the same entity type. We are aware that this strict criterion may be too restrictive for our overall goal (extraction of drug interactions) because it misses partial matches, which can provide useful information for a DDI extraction system. Our evaluation metrics should score if a system is able to identify the exact span of an entity (regardless of the type) and if it is able to assign the correct entity type (regardless of the boundaries). Thus, our evaluation script will output four sets of scores according to:

1. Strict evaluation (exact-boundary and type matching).

2. Exact boundary matching (regardless to the type).

3. Partial boundary matching (regardless to the type).

4. Type matching (some overlap between the tagged entity and the gold entitity is required).

Evaluation results are reported using the standard precision/recall/f-score metrics. We refer the reader to (Chinchor and Sundheim, 1993) for a more detailed description of these metrics.

These metrics are calculated over all entities and on both axes (type and span) in order to evaluate the performance of each axe separately. The final score is the micro-averaged F-measure, which is calculated over all entity types without distinction. The main advantage of the micro-average F1 is that it takes into account all possible types of errors made by a NERC system.

Additionally, we calculate precision, recall and f-measure for each entity type and then their macro-average measures are provided. Calculating these metrics for each entity type allows us to evaluate the level of difficulty of recognizing each entity type. In addition to this, since not all entity types have the same frequency, we can better assess the performance of the algorithms proposed by the participating systems. This is mainly because the results achieved on the most frequent entity type have a much greater impact on overall performance than those obtained on the entity types with few instances.

3.2 Results and Discussion

Participants could send a maximum of three system runs. After downloading the test datasets, they had a maximum of two weeks to upload the results. A total of 6 teams participated, submitting 16 system runs. Table 2 lists the teams, their affiliations and a brief description of their approaches. Due to the lack of space we cannot describe them in this paper. Tables 3, 4 and 5 show the F1 scores for each run in alphabetic order. The reader can find the full ranking information on the SemEval-2013 Task 9 website[3].

The best results were achieved by the WBI team with a conditional random field. They employed a domain-independent feature set along with features generated from the output of ChemSpot (Rocktäschel et al., 2012), an existing chemical named entity recognition tool, as well as a collection of domain-specific resources. Its model was trained on the training dataset as well as on entities of the test dataset for task 9.2. The second top best performing team developed a dictionary-based approach combining biomedical resources such as DrugBank, the ATC classification system,[4] or MeSH,[5] among others. Regarding the classification of each entity type, we observed that brand drugs were easier to recognize than the other types. This could be due to the fact that when a drug is marketed by a pharmaceutical company, its brand name is carefully selected to be short, unique and easy to remember (Boring, 1997). On the other hand, substances not approved for human use (*drug-n*) were more difficult, due to the greater variation and complexity in their naming. In fact, the UEM_UC3M team was the only team who obtained an F1 measure greater than 0 on the DDI-DrugBank dataset. Also, this may indicate that this type is less clearly defined than the others in the annotation guidelines. Another possible reason is that the presence of such substances in this dataset is very scarce (less than 1%). It is interesting that almost every participating system was better in detecting and classifying entities of a particular class compared to all other systems. For instance, on the whole dataset the dictionary-based system from NLM_LHC had it strengths at *drug* entities, UEM_UC3M at *drug_N* entities, UTurku at *brand* entities and WBI_NER at *group* entities.

Finally, the results on the DDI-DrugBank dataset are much better than those obtained on the DDI-MedLine dataset. While DDI-DrugBank texts focus on the description of drugs and their interactions, the main topic of DDI-MedLine texts would not necessarily be on DDIs. Coupled with this, it is not always trivial to distinguish between substances that should be classified as pharmacological substances and those who should not. This is due to the ambiguity of some pharmacological terms. For example, *insulin* is a hormone produced by the pancreas, but can also be synthesized in the laboratory and used as drug to treat insulin-dependent diabetes mellitus. The participating systems should be able to determine if the text is describing a substance originated within the organism or, on the contrary, it describes a process in which the substance is used for a specific purpose and thus should be identified as pharmacological substance.

4 Task 9.2: Extraction of drug-drug interactions.

The goal of this subtask is the extraction of drug-drug interactions from biomedical texts. However, while the previous DDIExtraction 2011 task focused on the identification of all possible pairs of interacting drugs, DDIExtraction 2013 also pursues the classification of each drug-drug interaction according to one of the following four types: *advice*, *effect*, *mechanism*, *int*. A detailed description of these

[3]http://www.cs.york.ac.uk/semeval-2013/task9/

[4]http://www.whocc.no/atc_ddd_index/

[5]http://www.ncbi.nlm.nih.gov/mesh

Team	Run	Rank	STRICT	EXACT	PARTIAL	TYPE	DRUG	BRAND	GROUP	DRUG_N	MAVG
LASIGE	1	6	0,656	0,781	0,808	0,69	0,741	0,581	0,712	0,171	0,577
	2	9	0,639	0,775	0,801	0,672	0,716	0,541	0,696	0,182	0,571
	3	10	0,612	0,715	0,741	0,647	0,728	0,354	0,647	0,16	0,498
NLM_LHC	1	4	0,698	0,784	0,801	0,722	0,803	0,809	0,646	0	0,57
	2	3	0,704	0,792	0,807	0,726	**0,81**	0,846	0,643	0	0,581
UMCC_DLSI	1,2,3	14,15,16	0,275	0,3049	0,367	0,334	0,297	0,313	0,257	0,124	0,311
UEM_UC3M	1	13	0,458	0,528	0,585	0,51	0,718	0,075	0,291	0,185	0,351
	2	12	0,529	0,609	0,669	0,589	0,752	0,094	0,291	**0,264**	0,38
UTurku	1	11	0,579	0,639	0,719	0,701	0,721	0,603	0,478	0,016	0,468
	2	8	0,641	0,659	0,731	0,766	0,784	0.901	0,495	0,015	0,557
	3	7	0,648	0,666	0,743	**0,777**	0,783	**0,912**	0,485	0,076	0,604
WBI	1	5	0,692	0,772	0,807	0,729	0,768	0,787	0,761	0,071	0,615
	2	2	0,708	0,831	0,855	0,741	0,786	0,803	0,757	0,134	**0,643**
	3	1	**0,715**	**0,833**	**0,856**	0,748	0,79	0,836	**0,776**	0,141	0,652

Table 3: F1 scores for task 9.1 on the whole test dataset (DDI-MedLine + DDI-DrugBank). (MAVG for macro-average). Each run is ranked by STRICT performance.

Team	Run	Rank	STRICT	EXACT	PARTIAL	TYPE	DRUG	BRAND	GROUP	DRUG_N	MAVG
LASIGE	1	8	0,771	0,834	0,855	0,799	0,817	0.571	**0,833**	0	0,563
	2	9	0,771	0,831	0,852	0,799	0,823	0,553	0,824	0	0,568
	3	11	0,682	0,744	0,764	0,713	0,757	0,314	0,756	0	0,47
NLM_LHC	1	2	0,869	0,902	**0,922**	0,902	0,909	0,907	0,766	0	0,646
	2	3	0,869	**0,903**	0,919	0,896	0,911	0,907	0,754	0	0,644
UMCC_DLSI	1,2,3	14,15,16	0,424	0,4447	0,504	0,487	0.456	0,429	0,371	0	0,351
UEM_UC3M	1	13	0,561	0,632	0,69	0,632	0,827	0,056	0,362	0,022	0,354
	2	12	0,595	0,667	0,721	0,667	0,842	0,063	0,366	**0,028**	0,37
UTurku	1	10	0,739	0,753	0,827	0,864	0,829	0,735	0,553	0	0,531
	2	6	0,785	0,795	0,863	**0,908**	0,858	0,898	0,559	0	0,581
	3	7	0,781	0,787	0,858	0,905	0,847	**0,911**	0,551	0	0,578
WBI	1	5	0,86	0,877	0,9	0,89	0,905	0,857	0,782	0	0,636
	2	4	0,868	0,894	0,914	0,897	0,909	0,865	0,794	0	0,642
	3	1	**0,878**	0,901	0,917	**0,908**	**0,912**	0,904	0,806	0	**0,656**

Table 4: F1 scores for task 9.1 on the DDI-DrugBank test data. (MAVG for macro-average). Each run is ranked by STRICT performance.

Team	Run	Rank	STRICT	EXACT	PARTIAL	TYPE	DRUG	BRAND	GROUP	DRUG_N	MAVG
LASIGE	1	4	0,567	0,74	0,772	0,605	0,678	0,667	0,612	0,183	**0,577**
	2	8	0,54	0,733	0,763	0,576	0,631	0,444	0,595	0,196	0,512
	3	6	0,557	0,693	0,723	0,596	0,702	0,667	0,56	0,171	0,554
NLM_LHC	1	5	0,559	0,688	0,702	0,575	0,717	0,429	0,548	0	0,462
	2	3	0,569	0,702	0,715	0,586	**0,726**	0,545	0,555	0	0,486
UMCC_DLSI	1,2,3	14,15,16	0,187	0,2228	0,287	0,245	0,2	0,091	0,191	0,13	0,23
UEM_UC3M	1	13	0,39	0,461	0,516	0,431	0,618	0,111	0,238	0,222	0,341
	2	11	0,479	0,564	0,628	0,529	0,665	0,182	0,233	**0,329**	0,387
UTurku	1	12	0,435	0,538	0,623	0,556	0,614	0,143	0,413	0,016	0,328
	2	10	0,502	0,528	0,604	0,628	0,703	**0,923**	0,436	0,016	0,533
	3	9	0,522	0,551	0,634	**0,656**	0,716	**0,923**	0,426	0,08	0,582
WBI	1	7	0,545	0,681	0,726	0,589	0,634	0,353	0,744	0,074	0,479
	2	2	0,576	**0,779**	**0,807**	0,612	0,673	0,444	0,729	0,14	0,534
	3	1	**0,581**	0,778	0,805	0,617	0,678	0,444	**0,753**	0,147	0,537

Table 5: F1 scores for task 9.1 on the DDI-MedLine test data. (MAVG for macro-average). Each run is ranked by STRICT performance.

types can be found in our annotation guidelines[6].

Gold standard annotations (correct, human-created annotations) of pharmacological substances are provided to participants both for training and test data. The test data for this subtask consists of 158 DrugBank documents and 33 MedLine abstracts. Each participant system must output an ASCII list including all pairs of drugs in each sentence, one per line (multiple DDIs from the same sentence should appear on separate lines), its prediction (1 if the pair is a DDI and 0 otherwise) and its type (label *null* when the prediction value is 0), and formatted as:

IdSentence|IdDrug1|IdDrug2|prediction|type

4.1 Evaluation Metrics

Evaluation is relation-oriented and based on the standard precision, recall and F-score metrics. A DDI is correctly detected only if the system is able to assign the correct prediction label and the correct type to it. In other words, a pair is correct only if both prediction and type are correct. The performance of systems to identify those pairs of drugs interacting (regardless of the type) is also evaluated. This allows us to assess the progress made with regard to the previous edition, which only dealt with the detection of DDIs.

Additionally, we are interested in assessing which drug interaction types are most difficult to detect. Thus, we calculate precision, recall and F1 for each DDI type and then their macro-average measures are provided. While micro-averaged F1 is calculated by constructing a global contingency table and then calculating precision and recall, macro-averaged F-score is calculated by first calculating precision and recall for each type and then taking the average of these results.

Evaluating each DDI type separately allows us to assess the level of difficulty of detecting and classifying each type of interaction. Additionally, it is important to note that the scores achieved on the most frequent DDI type have a much greater impact on overall performance than those achieved on the DDI types with few instances. Therefore, by calculating scores for each type of DDI, we can better assess the performance of the algorithms proposed by the participating systems.

4.2 Results and Discussion

The task of extracting drug-drug interactions from biomedical texts has attracted the participation of 8 teams (see Table 2) who submitted 22 runs. Tables 6, 7 and 8 show the results for each run in alphabetic order. Due to the lack of space, the performance information is only shown in terms of F1 score. The reader can find the full ranking information on the SemEval-2013 Task 9 website[7].

Most of the participating systems were built on support vector machines. In general, approaches based on non-linear kernels methods achieved better results than linear SVMs. As in the previous edition of DDIExtraction, most systems have used primarily syntactic information. However, semantic information has been poorly used.

The best results were submitted by the team from FBK-irst. They applied a novel hybrid kernel based RE approach described in Chowdhury (2013a). They also exploited the scope of negations and semantic roles for negative instance filtering as proposed in (Chowdhury and Lavelli, 2013b) and (Chowdhury and Lavelli, 2012). The second best results were obtained by the WBI team from the Humboldt University of Berlin. Its system combines several kernel methods (APG (Airola et al., 2008) and Shallow Linguistic Kernel (SL) (Giuliano et al., 2006) among others), the Turku Event Extraction system (TEES) (Björne et al., 2011)[8] and the Moara system (Neves et al., 2009). These two teams were also the top two ranked teams in DDIExtraction 2011. For a more detailed description, the reader is encouraged to read the papers of the participants in the proceedings book.

While the DDIExtraction 2011 shared task concentrated efforts on the detection of DDIs, this new DDIExtraction 2013 task involved not only the detection of DDIs, but also their classification. Although the results of DDIExtraction 2011 are not directly comparable with the ones reported in DDIExtraction 2013 due to the use of different training and test datasets in each edition, it should be noted that there has been a significant improvement in the de-

[6]http://www.cs.york.ac.uk/semeval-2013/task9/

[7]http://www.cs.york.ac.uk/semeval-2013/task9/

[8]http://jbjorne.github.io/TEES/

Team	Run	Rank	CLA	DEC	MEC	EFF	ADV	INT	MAVG
FBK-irst	1	3	0.638	**0.8**	**0.679**	**0.662**	**0.692**	0.363	0.602
	2	1	**0.651**	**0.8**	**0.679**	0.628	**0.692**	**0.547**	**0.648**
	3	2	0.648	**0.8**	0.627	**0.662**	**0.692**	**0.547**	0.644
NIL_UCM	1	12	0.517	0.588	0.515	0.489	0.613	0.427	0.535
	2	10	0.548	0.656	0.531	0.556	0.61	0.393	0.526
SCAI	1	14	0.46	0.69	0.446	0.459	0.562	0.02	0.423
	2	16	0.452	0.683	0.441	0.44	0.559	0.021	0.448
	3	15	0.458	0.704	0.45	0.462	0.54	0.02	0.411
UC3M	1	11	0.529	0.676	0.48	0.547	0.575	0.5	0.534
	2	21	0.294	0.537	0.268	0.286	0.325	0.402	0.335
UCOLORADO_SOM	1	22	0.214	0.492	0.109	0.25	0.219	0.097	0.215
	2	20	0.334	0.504	0.361	0.311	0.381	0.333	0.407
	3	19	0.336	0.491	0.335	0.313	0.42	0.329	0.38
UTurku	1	9	0.581	0.684	0.578	0.585	0.606	0.503	0.572
	2	7	0.594	0.696	0.582	0.6	0.63	0.507	0.587
	3	8	0.582	0.699	0.569	0.593	0.608	0.511	0.577
UWM-TRIADS	1	17	0.449	0.581	0.413	0.446	0.502	0.397	0.451
	2	13	0.47	0.599	0.446	0.449	0.532	0.421	0.472
	3	18	0.432	0.564	0.442	0.383	0.537	0.292	0.444
WBI	1	6	0.599	0.736	0.602	0.604	0.618	0.516	0.588
	2	5	0.601	0.745	0.616	0.595	0.637	0.49	0.588
	3	4	0.609	0.759	0.618	0.61	0.632	0.51	0.597

Table 6: F1 scores for Task 9.2 on the whole test dataset (DDI-MedLine + DDI-DrugBank). DEC for Detection, CLA for detection and classification, MEC for *mechanism* type, EFF for *effect* type, ADV for *advice* type, INT for *int* type and MAVG for macro-average. Each run is ranked by CLA performance.

Team	Run	Rank	CLA	DEC	MEC	EFF	ADV	INT	MAVG
FBK-irst	1	3	0.663	**0.827**	**0.705**	**0.699**	**0.705**	0.376	0.624
	2	1	**0.676**	**0.827**	**0.705**	0.664	**0.705**	**0.545**	**0.672**
	3	2	0.673	**0.827**	0.655	**0.699**	**0.705**	**0.545**	0.667
NIL_UCM	1	12	0.54	0.615	0.527	0.525	0.625	0.444	0.565
	2	10	0.573	0.68	0.552	0.597	0.619	0.408	0.55
SCAI	1	15	0.464	0.711	0.449	0.459	0.57	0.021	0.461
	2	16	0.463	0.71	0.445	0.458	0.569	0.021	0.46
	3	14	0.473	0.734	0.468	0.482	0.551	0.021	0.439
UC3M	1	11	0.555	0.703	0.493	0.593	0.59	0.51	0.561
	2	21	0.306	0.549	0.274	0.302	0.334	0.426	0.352
UCOLORADO_SOM	1	22	0.218	0.508	0.115	0.251	0.24	0.098	0.228
	2	20	0.341	0.518	0.373	0.313	0.398	0.344	0.425
	3	19	0.349	0.511	0.353	0.324	0.429	0.327	0.394
UTurku	1	8	0.608	0.712	0.6	0.63	0.617	0.522	0.6
	2	7	0.62	0.724	0.605	0.644	0.638	0.522	0.614
	3	9	0.608	0.726	0.591	0.635	0.617	0.522	0.601
UWM-TRIADS	1	17	0.462	0.596	0.43	0.459	0.509	0.405	0.463
	2	13	0.485	0.616	0.467	0.466	0.536	0.425	0.486
	3	18	0.445	0.573	0.469	0.39	0.544	0.29	0.46
WBI	1	6	0.624	0.762	0.621	0.645	0.634	0.52	0.61
	2	5	0.627	0.775	0.636	0.636	0.652	0.5	0.611
	3	4	0.632	0.783	0.629	0.652	0.65	0.513	0.617

Table 7: F1 scores for task 9.2 on the DDI-DrugBank test dataset. Each run is ranked by CLA performance.

Team	Run	Rank	CLA	DEC	MEC	EFF	ADV	INT	MAVG
FBK-irst	1	4	0.387	**0.53**	0.383	0.436	0.286	0.211	0.406
	2	3	0.398	**0.53**	0.383	0.407	0.286	**0.571**	0.436
	3	2	0.398	**0.53**	0.339	0.436	0.286	**0.571**	**0.44**
NIL_UCM	1	20	0.19	0.206	0.286	0.186	0	0	0.121
	2	19	0.219	0.336	0.143	0.271	0	0	0.11
SCAI	1	1	**0.42**	0.462	0.412	**0.458**	0.2	0	0.269
	2	8	0.323	0.369	0.389	0.333	0	0	0.182
	3	6	0.341	0.474	0.31	0.379	0.222	0	0.229
UC3M	1	15	0.274	0.406	0.333	0.267	0	0.364	0.268
	2	22	0.186	0.421	0.222	0.171	0.143	0	0.149
UCOLORADO_SOM	1	21	0.188	0.37	0.042	0.241	0	0	0.073
	2	14	0.275	0.394	0.258	0.302	0.138	0	0.177
	3	17	0.244	0.356	0.194	0.255	0.222	0.4	0.272
UTurku	1	18	0.242	0.339	0.258	0.256	0.2	0	0.18
	2	16	0.262	0.344	0.214	0.278	0.364	0	0.224
	3	13	0.286	0.376	0.286	0.289	0.333	0	0.232
UWM-TRIADS	1	10	0.312	0.419	0.233	0.36	0.267	0	0.219
	2	9	0.319	0.436	0.233	0.34	**0.421**	0.333	0.345
	3	11	0.306	0.479	0.247	0.326	0.381	0.333	0.33
WBI	1	7	0.336	0.456	0.368	0.344	0.154	0.4	0.334
	2	12	0.304	0.406	0.343	0.318	0.167	0	0.209
	3	5	0.365	0.503	**0.476**	0.347	0.143	0.4	0.353

Table 8: F1 scores for task 9.2 on the DDI-MedLine test dataset. Each run is ranked by CLA performance.

tection of DDIs: F1 has a remarkable increase from 65.74% (the best F1-score in DDIExtraction 2011) to 80% (see *DEC* column of Table 6). The increase of the size of the corpus made for DDIExtraction 2013 and of the quality of their annotations may have contributed significantly to this improvement.

However, the results for the detection and classification for DDIs did not exceed an F1 of 65.1%. Table 6 suggests that some type of DDIs are more difficult to classify than others. The best F1 ranges from 69.2% for *advice* to 54.7% for *int*. One possible explanation for this could be that recommendations or advice regarding a drug interaction are typically described by very similar text patterns such as *DRUG should not be used in combination with DRUG* or *Caution should be observed when DRUG is administered with DRUG*.

Regarding results for the *int* relationship, it should be noted that the proportion of instances of this relationship (5.6%) in the DDI corpus is much smaller than those of the rest of the relations (41.1% for *effect*, 32.3% for *mechanism* and 20.9% for *advice*).

As stated earlier, one of the differences from the previous edition is that the corpus developed for DDIExtraction 2013 is made up of texts from two different sources: MedLine and the DrugBank database. Thus, the different approaches can be evaluated on two different styles of biomedical texts. While MedLine abstracts are usually written in extremely scientific language, texts from DrugBank are written in a less technical form of the language (similar to the language used in package inserts). Indeed, this may be the reason why the results on the DDI-DrugBank dataset are much better than those obtained on the DDI-MedLine dataset (see Tables 7 and 8).

5 Conclusions

The DDIExtraction 2011 task concentrated efforts on the novel aspects of the DDI extraction task, the drug recognition was assumed and the annotations for drugs were provided to the participants. This new DDIExtraction 2013 task pursues the detection and classification of drug interactions as well as the recognition and classification of pharmacological substances. The task attracted broad interest from the community. A total of 14 teams from 7 different countries participated, submitted a total of 38 runs, exceeding the participation of DDIExtraction 2011 (10 teams). The participating systems demonstrated substantial progress at the established DDI extraction task on DrugBank texts and showed that their methods also obtain good results for MedLine abstracts.

The results that the participating systems have reported show successful approaches to this difficult task, and the advantages of non-linear kernel-based methods over linear SVMs for extraction of DDIs. In the named entity task, the participating systems perform well in recognizing generic drugs, brand drugs and groups of drugs, but they fail in recognizing active substances not approved for human use. Although the results are positive, there is still much room to improve in both subtasks. We have accomplished our goal of providing a framework and a benchmark data set to allow for comparisons of methods for the recognition of pharmacological substances and detection and classification of drug-drug interactions from biomedical texts.

We would like that our test dataset can still serve as the basis for fair and stable evaluation after the task. Thus, we have decided that the full gold annotations for the test data are not available for the moment. We plan to make available a web service where researchers can test their methods on the test dataset and compare their results with the DDIExtraction 2013 task participants.

Acknowledgments

This research work has been supported by the Regional Government of Madrid under the Research Network MA2VICMR (S2009/TIC-1542), by the Spanish Ministry of Education under the project MULTIMEDICA (TIN2010-20644-C03-01). Additionally, we would like to thank all participants for their efforts and to congratulate them to their interesting work.

References

A. Airola, S. Pyysalo, J. Bjorne, T. Pahikkala, F. Ginter, and T. Salakoski. 2008. All-paths graph kernel for protein-protein interaction extraction with evaluation of cross-corpus learning. *BMC bioinformatics*, 9(Suppl 11):S2.

JK. Aronson. 2007. Communicating information about drug interactions. *British Journal of Clinical Pharmacology*, 63(6):637–639, June.

K. Baxter and I.H. Stockely. 2010. *Stockley's drug interactions.8th ed.* London:Pharmaceutical Press.

J. Björne, J. Heimonen, F. Ginter, A. Airola, T. Pahikkala, and T. Salakoski. 2011. Extracting contextualized complex biological events with graph-based feature sets. *Computational Intelligence*, 27(4):541–557.

J. Björne, S. Kaewphan, and T. Salakoski. 2013. UTurku: Drug Named Entity Detection and Drug-drug Interaction Extraction Using SVM Classification and Domain Knowledge. In *Proceedings of the 7th International Workshop on Semantic Evaluation (SemEval 2013)*.

T. Bobić, J. Fluck, and M. Hofmann-Apitius. 2013. SCAI: Extracting drug-drug interactions using a rich feature vector. In *Proceedings of the 7th International Workshop on Semantic Evaluation (SemEval 2013)*.

A. Bokharaeian, B.and Díaz. 2013. NIL_UCM: Extracting Drug-Drug interactions from text through combination of sequence and tree kernels. In *Proceedings of the 7th International Workshop on Semantic Evaluation (SemEval 2013)*.

D. Boring. 1997. The development and adoption of nonproprietary, established, and proprietary names for pharmaceuticals. *Drug information journal*, 31(3):621–634.

N. Chinchor and P. Robinson. 1997. Muc-7 named entity task definition. In *Proceedings of the 7th Conference on Message Understanding*.

N. Chinchor and B. Sundheim. 1993. Muc-5 evaluation metrics. In *Proceedings of the 5th conference on Message understanding*, pages 69–78. Association for Computational Linguistics.

MFM. Chowdhury and A. Lavelli. 2012. Impact of less skewed distributions on efficiency and effectiveness of biomedical relation extraction. In *Proceedings of COLING 2012*.

MFM. Chowdhury and A. Lavelli. 2013b. Exploiting the scope of negations and heterogeneous features for relation extraction: Case study drug-drug interaction extraction. In *Proceedings of NAACL 2013*.

M.F.M. Chowdhury and A. Lavelli. 2013c. FBK-irst : A Multi-Phase Kernel Based Approach for Drug-Drug Interaction Detection and Classification that Exploits Linguistic Information. In *Proceedings of the 7th International Workshop on Semantic Evaluation (SemEval 2013)*.

MFM. Chowdhury. 2013a. *Improving the Effectiveness of Information Extraction from Biomedical Text*. Ph.d. dissertation, University of Trento.

A. Collazo, A. Ceballo, D Puig, Y. Gutiérrez, J. Abreu, J Pérez, A. Fernández-Orquín, A. Montoyo, R. Muñoz, and F. Camara. 2013. UMCC_DLSI-(DDI): Semantic and Lexical features for detection and classification Drugs in biomedical texts. In *Proceedings of the 7th International Workshop on Semantic Evaluation (SemEval 2013)*.

C. Giuliano, A. Lavelli, and L. Romano. 2006. Exploiting shallow linguistic information for relation extraction from biomedical literature. In *Proceedings of the Eleventh Conference of the European Chapter of the Association for Computational Linguistics (EACL-2006)*, pages 401–408.

T. Grego, F. Pinto, and F.M. Couto. 2013. LASIGE: using Conditional Random Fields and ChEBI ontology. In *Proceedings of the 7th International Workshop on Semantic Evaluation (SemEval 2013)*.

N.D. Hailu, L.E. Hunter, and K.B. Cohen. 2013. UColorado_SOM: Extraction of Drug-Drug Interactions from Biomedical Text using Knowledge-rich and Knowledge-poor Features. In *Proceedings of the 7th International Workshop on Semantic Evaluation (SemEval 2013)*.

ML. Neves, JM. Carazo, and A. Pascual-Montano. 2009. Extraction of biomedical events using case-based reasoning. In *Proceedings of the Workshop on BioNLP: Shared Task*, pages 68–76. Association for Computational Linguistics.

S. Pyysalo, A. Airola, J. Heimonen, J. Bjorne, F. Ginter, and T. Salakoski. 2008. Comparative analysis of five protein-protein interaction corpora. *BMC bioinformatics*, 9(Suppl 3):S6.

M. Rastegar-Mojarad, R. D. Boyce, and R. Prasad. 2013. UWM-TRIADS: Classifying Drug-Drug Interactions with Two-Stage SVM and Post-Processing. In *Proceedings of the 7th International Workshop on Semantic Evaluation (SemEval 2013)*.

T. Rocktäschel, M. Weidlich, and U. Leser. 2012. Chemspot: a hybrid system for chemical named entity recognition. *Bioinformatics*, 28(12):1633–1640.

T. Rocktäschel, T. Huber, M. Weidlich, and U. Leser. 2013. WBI-NER: The impact of domain-specific features on the performance of identifying and classifying mentions of drugs. In *Proceedings of the 7th International Workshop on Semantic Evaluation (SemEval 2013)*.

D. Sanchez-Cisneros and F. Aparicio. 2013. UEM-UC3M: An Ontology-based named entity recognition system for biomedical texts. In *Proceedings of the 7th International Workshop on Semantic Evaluation (SemEval 2013)*.

D. Sanchez-Cisneros. 2013. UC3M: A kernel-based approach for identify and classify DDIs in biomedical texts. In *Proceedings of the 7th International Workshop on Semantic Evaluation (SemEval 2013)*.

I. Segura-Bedmar, P. Martínez, and C. de Pablo-Sánchez. 2011a. Using a shallow linguistic kernel for drug-drug interaction extraction. *Journal of Biomedical Informatics*, 44(5):789 – 804.

I. Segura-Bedmar, P. Martınez, and D. Sánchez-Cisneros. 2011b. The 1st ddiextraction-2011 challenge task: Extraction of drug-drug interactions from biomedical texts. In *Proceedings of DDIExtraction-2011 challenge task*, pages 1–9.

P. Thomas, M. Neves, T. Rocktäschel, and U. Leser. 2013. WBI-DDI: Drug-Drug Interaction Extraction using Majority Voting. In *Proceedings of the 7th International Workshop on Semantic Evaluation (SemEval 2013)*.

E.F. Tjong Kim Sang and F. De Meulder. 2003. Introduction to the CoNLL-2003 shared task: Language-independent named entity recognition. In *Proceedings of the seventh conference on Natural language learning at HLT-NAACL 2003-Volume 4*, pages 142–147. Association for Computational Linguistics.

D.S. Wishart, C. Knox, A.C. Guo, S. Shrivastava, M. Hassanali, P. Stothard, Z. Chang, and J. Woolsey. 2006. Drugbank: a comprehensive resource for in silico drug discovery and exploration. *Nucleic acids research*, 34(suppl 1):D668–D672.

FBK-irst : A Multi-Phase Kernel Based Approach for Drug-Drug Interaction Detection and Classification that Exploits Linguistic Information

Md. Faisal Mahbub Chowdhury [†‡] **and Alberto Lavelli** [‡]
[‡] Fondazione Bruno Kessler (FBK-irst), Italy
[†] University of Trento, Italy
fmchowdhury@gmail.com, lavelli@fbk.eu

Abstract

This paper presents the multi-phase relation extraction (RE) approach which was used for the DDI Extraction task of SemEval 2013. As a preliminary step, the proposed approach indirectly (and automatically) exploits the scope of negation cues and the semantic roles of involved entities for reducing the skewness in the training data as well as discarding possible negative instances from the test data. Then, a state-of-the-art hybrid kernel is used to train a classifier which is later applied on the instances of the test data not filtered out by the previous step. The official results of the task show that our approach yields an F-score of 0.80 for DDI detection and an F-score of 0.65 for DDI detection and classification. Our system obtained significantly higher results than all the other participating teams in this shared task and has been ranked 1st.

1 Introduction

Drug-drug interaction (DDI) is a condition when one drug influences the level or activity of another. The extraction of DDIs has significant importance for public health safety. It was reported that about 2.2 million people in USA, age 57 to 85, were taking potentially dangerous combinations of drugs (Landau, 2009). Another report mentioned that deaths from accidental drug interactions rose by 68 percent between 1999 and 2004 (Payne, 2007). The DDIExtraction 2011 and DDIExtraction 2013 shared tasks underline the importance of DDI extraction.

The DDIExtraction 2013 task concerns the recognition of drugs and the extraction of drug-drug interactions from biomedical literature. The dataset of the shared task is composed by texts from the DrugBank database as well as MedLine abstracts in order to deal with different type of texts and language styles. Participants were asked to not only extract DDIs but also classify them into one of four predefined classes: advise, effect, mechanism and int. A detailed description of the task settings and data can be found in Segura-Bedmar et al. (2013).

The system that we used in this shared task combines various techniques proposed in our recent research activities for relation extraction (RE) (Chowdhury and Lavelli, 2012a; Chowdhury and Lavelli, 2012b; Chowdhury and Lavelli, 2013).[1]

2 DDI Detection

Our system performs DDI detection and classification in two separate steps. In this section, we explain how DDI detection (i.e. whether two drug mentions participate in a DDI) is accomplished. DDI classification will be described in Section 3.

There are three phases for DDI detection: (i) discard less informative sentences, (ii) discard less informative instances, and (iii) train the system (a single model regardless of DDI types) on the remaining training instances and identify possible DDIs from the remaining test instances. These phases are described below.

2.1 Exploiting the scope of negations for sentence filtering

Negation is a linguistic phenomenon where a *negation cue* (e.g. *not*) can alter the meaning of a partic-

[1] Available in *https://github.com/fmchowdhury/HyREX*.

*Second Joint Conference on Lexical and Computational Semantics (*SEM), Volume 2: Seventh International Workshop on Semantic Evaluation (SemEval 2013)*, pages 351–355, Atlanta, Georgia, June 14-15, 2013.

ular text segment or of a fact. This text segment (or fact) is said to be inside the *scope of such negation (cue)*. In one of our recent papers (Chowdhury and Lavelli, 2013), we proposed how to exploit the scope of negations for RE. We hypothesize that a classifier trained solely on features related to the scope of negations can be used to pro-actively filter groups of instances which are less informative and mostly negative.

To be more precise, we propose to train a classifier (which will be applied before using the kernel based RE classifier mentioned in Section 2.3) that would check whether all the target entity mentions inside a sentence along with possible relation clues (or trigger words), if any, fall (directly or indirectly) under the scope of a negation cue. If such a sentence is found, then it would be identified as less informative and discarded (i.e. the candidate mention pairs inside such sentence would not be considered). During training (and testing), we group the instances by sentences. *Any sentence that contains at least one relation of interest is considered by the less informative sentence (LIS) classifier as a positive (training/test) instance.* The remaining sentences are considered as negative instances.

We use a number of features related to negation scopes to train a binary SVM classifier that filters out less informative sentences. These features are basically contextual and shallow linguistic features. Due to space limitation, we do not report these features here. Interested readers are referred to Chowdhury and Lavelli (2013).

The objective of the classifier is to decide whether all target entity mentions as well as any possible evidence inside the corresponding sentence fall under the scope of a negation cue in such a way that the sentence is unlikely to contain the relation of interest (e.g. DDI). If the classifier finds such a sentence, then it is assigned the negative class label. At present, we focus only on the first occurrence of the negation cues "no", "n't" or "not". These cues usually occur more frequently and generally have larger negation scope than other negation cues.

The LIS classifier is trained using a linear SVM classifier. Its hyper-parameters are tuned during training for obtaining maximum recall. In this way we minimize the number of false negatives (i.e. sentences that contain relations but are wrongly filtered out). Once the classifier is trained using the training data, we apply it on both the training and test data. However, if the recall of the LIS classifier is found to be below a *threshold value* (we set it to 70.0) during cross validation on the training data of a corpus, it is not used for sentence filtering on such corpus.

Any (training/test) sentence that is classified as negative is considered as a less informative sentence and is filtered out. In other words, such a sentence is not considered for RE. However, it should be noted that, if such a sentence is a test sentence and it contains positive RE instances, then *all these filtered positive RE instances are automatically considered as false negatives during the calculation of RE performance*.

We rule out sentences (i.e. we consider them neither positive nor negative instances for training the classifier that filters less informative sentences) during both training and testing if any of the following conditions holds:

- The sentence contains less than two target entity mentions (such sentence would not contain the relation of interest anyway).
- It has any of the following phrases – "not recommended", "should not be" or "must not be".[2]
- There is no "no", "n't" or "not" in the sentence.
- No target entity mention appears in the sentence after "no", "n't' or "not".

2.2 Discarding instances using semantic roles and contextual evidence

For identifying less informative negative instances, we exploit static (i.e. already known, heuristically motivated) and dynamic (i.e. automatically collected from the data) knowledge which has been proposed in Chowdhury and Lavelli (2012b). This knowledge is described by the following criteria:

- **C1:** If each of the two entity mentions (of a candidate pair) has *anti-positive governors* (see Section 2.2.1) with respect to the type of the relation, then they are not likely to be in a given relation.

[2] These expressions often provide clues that one of the drug entity mentions negatively influences the level of activity of the other.

- **C2:** If two entity mentions in a sentence refer to the same entity, then it is unlikely that they would have a relation between themselves.

- **C3:** If a mention is the abbreviation of another mention (i.e. they refer to the same entity), then they are unlikely to be in a relation.

Criteria C2 and C3 (static knowledge) are quite intuitive. For criterion C1, we construct on the fly a list of *anti-positive governors* (dynamic knowledge) taken from the training data and use them for detecting pairs that are unlikely to be in relation. As for criterion C2, we simply check whether two mentions have the same name and there is more than one character between them. For criterion C3, we look for any expression of the form "Entity1 (Entity2)" and consider "Entity2" as an abbreviation or alias of "Entity1".

The above criteria are used to filter instances from both training and test data. *Any positive test instance filtered out by these criteria is automatically considered as a false negative during the calculation of RE performance.*

2.2.1 Anti-positive governors

The semantic roles of the entity mentions may indirectly contribute either to relate or not to relate them in a particular relation type (e.g. PPI) in the corresponding context. To put it differently, the semantic roles of two mentions in the same context could provide an indication whether the relation of interest does *not* hold between them. Interestingly, the word on which a certain entity mention is (syntactically) dependent (along with the dependency type) could often provide a clue of the semantic role of such mention in the corresponding sentence.

Our goal is to automatically identify the words (if any) that tend to prevent mentions, which are directly dependent on those words, from participating in a certain relation of interest with any other mention in the same sentence. We call such words ***anti-positive governors*** and assume that they could be exploited to identify negative instances (i.e. negative entity mention pairs) in advance. Interested readers are referred to Chowdhury and Lavelli (2012b) for example and description of how anti-positive governors are automatically collected from the training data.

2.3 Hybrid Kernel based RE Classifier

As RE classifier we use the following hybrid kernel that has been proposed in Chowdhury and Lavelli (2013). It is defined as follows:

$$K_{Hybrid}(R_1, R_2) = K_{HF}(R_1, R_2) + K_{SL}(R_1, R_2) + w * K_{PET}(R_1, R_2)$$

where K_{HF} is a feature based kernel (Chowdhury and Lavelli, 2013) that uses a heterogeneous set of features, K_{SL} is the Shallow Linguistic (SL) kernel proposed by Giuliano et al. (2006), and K_{PET} stands for the Path-enclosed Tree (PET) kernel (Moschitti, 2004). w is a multiplicative constant that allows the hybrid kernel to assign more (or less) weight to the information obtained using tree structures depending on the corpus. We exploit the SVM-Light-TK toolkit (Moschitti, 2006; Joachims, 1999) for kernel computation. The parameters are tuned by doing 5-fold cross validation on the training data.

3 DDI Type Classification

The next step is to classify the extracted DDIs into different categories. We train 4 separate models for each of the DDI types (one Vs all) to predict the class label of the extracted DDIs. During this training, all the negative instances from the training data are removed. The filtering techniques described in Sections 2.1 and 2.2 are not used in this stage.

The extracted DDIs are assigned a default DDI class label. Once the above models are trained, they are applied on the extracted DDIs from the test data. The class label of the model which has the highest confidence score for an extracted DDI instance is assigned to such instance.

4 Data Pre-processing and Experimental Settings

The Charniak-Johnson reranking parser (Charniak and Johnson, 2005), along with a self-trained biomedical parsing model (McClosky, 2010), has been used for tokenization, POS-tagging and parsing of the sentences. Then the parse trees are processed by the Stanford parser (Klein and Manning, 2003) to obtain syntactic dependencies. The Stanford parser often skips some syntactic dependencies in output. We use the rules proposed in Chowdhury and Lavelli (2012a) to recover some of such dependencies. We use the same techniques for unknown characters (if any) as described in Chowdhury and Lavelli (2011).

Our system uses the SVM-Light-TK toolkit[3] (Moschitti, 2006; Joachims, 1999) for computation of the hybrid kernels. The ratio of negative and positive examples has been used as the value of the cost-ratio-factor parameter. The SL kernel is computed using the jSRE tool[4].

The K_{HF} kernel can exploit non-target entities to extract important clues (Chowdhury and Lavelli, 2013). So, we use a publicly available state-of-the-art NER system called BioEnEx (Chowdhury and Lavelli, 2010) to automatically annotate both the training and the test data with disease mentions.

The DDIExtraction 2013 shared task data include two types of texts: texts taken from the DrugBank database and texts taken from MedLine abstracts. During training we used both types together.

5 Experimental Results

Table 1 shows the results of 5-fold cross validation for DDI detection on the training data. As we can see, the usage of the LIS and LII filtering techniques improves both precision and recall.

We submitted three runs for the DDIExtraction 2013 shared task. The only difference between the three runs concerns the default class label (i.e. the class chosen when none of the separate models assigns a class label to a predicted DDI). Such default class label is "int", "effect" and "mechanism" for run 1, 2 and 3 respectively. According to the official results provided by the task organisers, our best result was obtained by run 2 (shown in Table 2).

According to the official results, the performance for "advise" is very low (F_1 0.29) in MedLine texts, while the performance for "int" is comparatively much higher (F_1 0.57) with respect to the one of the other DDI types. In comparison, the performance for "int" is much lower (F_1 0.55) in DrugBank texts with respect to the one of the other DDI types.

In MedLine test data, the number of "effect" (62) and "mechanism" (24) DDIs is much higher than that of "advise" (7) and "int" (2). On the other hand, in DrugBank test data, the different DDIs are more evenly distributed – "effect" (298), "mechanism" (278), "advise" (214) and "int" (94).

Initially, it was not clear to us why our system (as well as other participants) achieves so much higher results on the DrugBank sentences in comparison to MedLine sentences. Statistics of the average number of words show that the length of the two types of training sentences are substantially similar (DrugBank : 21.2, MedLine : 22.3). It is true that the number of the training sentences for the former is almost 5.3 times higher than the latter. But it could not be the main reason for such high discrepancies.

So, we turned our attention to the presence of the cue words. In the 4,683 sentences of the DrugBank training set (which have at least one drug mention), we found that the words "increase" and "decrease" are present in 721 and 319 sentences respectively. While in the 877 sentences of the MedLine training set (which have at least one drug mention), we found that the same words are present in only 67 and 40 sentences respectively. In other words, the presence of these two important cue words in the

	P	R	F_1
K_{Hybrid}	0.66	0.80	0.72
LIS filtering + K_{Hybrid}	0.67	0.80	0.73
LIS filtering + LII filtering + K_{Hybrid}	**0.68**	**0.82**	**0.74**

Table 1: Comparison of results for DDI detection on the training data using 5-fold cross validation. Parameter tuning is not done during these experiments.

	P	R	F_1
All text			
DDI detection only	0.79	0.81	0.80
Detection and Classification	0.65	0.66	0.65
DrugBank text			
DDI detection only	0.82	0.84	0.83
Detection and Classification	0.67	0.69	0.68
MedLine text			
DDI detection only	0.56	0.51	0.53
Detection and Classification	0.42	0.38	0.40

Table 2: Official results of the best run (run 2) of our system in the DDIExtraction 2013 shared task.

[3] http://disi.unitn.it/moschitti/Tree-Kernel.htm
[4] http://hlt.fbk.eu/en/technology/jSRE

DrugBank sentences is twice more likely than that in the MedLine sentences. We assume similar observations might be also possible for other cue words. Hence, this is probably the main reason why the results are so much better on the DrugBank sentences.

6 Conclusion

In this paper, we have described a novel multi-phase RE approach that outperformed all the other participating teams in the DDI Detection and Classification task at SemEval 2013. The central component of the proposed approach is a state-of-the-art hybrid kernel. Our approach also indirectly (and automatically) exploits the scope of negation cues and the semantic roles of the involved entities.

Acknowledgments

This work is supported by the project "eOnco - Pervasive knowledge and data management in cancer care". The authors would like to thank Alessandro Moschitti for his help in the use of SVM-Light-TK.

References

E Charniak and M Johnson. 2005. Coarse-to-fine n-best parsing and MaxEnt discriminative reranking. In *Proceedings of the 43rd Annual Meeting of the Association for Computational Linguistics (ACL 2005)*.

MFM Chowdhury and A Lavelli. 2010. Disease mention recognition with specific features. In *Proceedings of the 2010 Workshop on Biomedical Natural Language Processing*, pages 83–90, Uppsala, Sweden, July.

MFM Chowdhury and A Lavelli. 2011. Drug-drug interaction extraction using composite kernels. In *Proceedings of the 1st Challenge task on Drug-Drug Interaction Extraction (DDIExtraction 2011)*, pages 27–33, Huelva, Spain, September.

MFM Chowdhury and A Lavelli. 2012a. Combining tree structures, flat features and patterns for biomedical relation extraction. In *Proceedings of the 13th Conference of the European Chapter of the Association for Computational Linguistics (EACL 2012)*, pages 420–429, Avignon, France, April.

MFM Chowdhury and A Lavelli. 2012b. Impact of Less Skewed Distributions on Efficiency and Effectiveness of Biomedical Relation Extraction. In *Proceedings of the 24th International Conference on Computational Linguistics (COLING 2012)*, Mumbai, India, December.

MFM Chowdhury and A Lavelli. 2013. Exploiting the Scope of Negations and Heterogeneous Features for Relation Extraction: A Case Study for Drug-Drug Interaction Extraction. In *Proceedings of the 2013 Conference of the North American Chapter of the Association for Computational Linguistics: Human Language Technology (NAACL 2013)*, Atlanta, USA, June.

C Giuliano, A Lavelli, and L Romano. 2006. Exploiting shallow linguistic information for relation extraction from biomedical literature. In *Proceedings of the 11th Conference of the European Chapter of the Association for Computational Linguistics (EACL 2006)*, pages 401–408.

T Joachims. 1999. Making large-scale support vector machine learning practical. In *Advances in kernel methods: support vector learning*, pages 169–184. MIT Press, Cambridge, MA, USA.

D Klein and C Manning. 2003. Accurate unlexicalized parsing. In *Proceedings of the 41st Annual Meeting of the Association for Computational Linguistics (ACL 2003)*, pages 423–430, Sapporo, Japan.

E Landau. 2009. Jackson's death raises questions about drug interactions [Published in CNN; June 26, 2009]. `http://edition.cnn.com/2009/HEALTH/06/26/jackson.drug.interaction.caution/index.html`.

D McClosky. 2010. *Any Domain Parsing: Automatic Domain Adaptation for Natural Language Parsing*. Ph.D. thesis, Department of Computer Science, Brown University.

A Moschitti. 2004. A study on convolution kernels for shallow semantic parsing. In *Proceedings of the 42nd Annual Meeting of the Association for Computational Linguistics*, ACL '04, Barcelona, Spain.

A Moschitti. 2006. Making tree kernels practical for natural language learning. In *Proceedings of 11th Conference of the European Chapter of the Association for computational Linguistics (EACL 2006)*, pages 113–120, Trento, Italy.

JW Payne. 2007. A Dangerous Mix [Published in The Washington Post; February 27, 2007]. `http://www.washingtonpost.com/wp-dyn/content/article/2007/02/23/AR2007022301780.html`.

I Segura-Bedmar, P Martínez, and M Herrero-Zazo. 2013. SemEval-2013 task 9: Extraction of drug-drug interactions from biomedical texts. In *Proceedings of the 7th International Workshop on Semantic Evaluation (SemEval 2013)*, Atlanta, USA, June.

WBI-NER: The impact of domain-specific features on the performance of identifying and classifying mentions of drugs

Tim Rocktäschel **Torsten Huber** **Michael Weidlich** **Ulf Leser**
Humboldt-Universität zu Berlin
Knowledge Management in Bioinformatics
Unter den Linden 6
Berlin, 10099, Germany
{trocktae,thuber,weidlich,leser}@informatik.hu-berlin.de

Abstract

Named entity recognition (NER) systems are often based on machine learning techniques to reduce the labor-intensive development of hand-crafted extraction rules and domain-dependent dictionaries. Nevertheless, time-consuming feature engineering is often needed to achieve state-of-the-art performance. In this study, we investigate the impact of such domain-specific features on the performance of recognizing and classifying mentions of pharmacological substances. We compare the performance of a system based on general features, which have been successfully applied to a wide range of NER tasks, with a system that additionally uses features generated from the output of an existing chemical NER tool and a collection of domain-specific resources. We demonstrate that acceptable results can be achieved with the former system. Still, our experiments show that using domain-specific features outperforms this general approach. Our system ranked first in the SemEval-2013 Task 9.1: Recognition and classification of pharmacological substances.

1 Introduction

The accurate identification of drug mentions in text is an important prerequisite for many applications, including the retrieval of information about substances in drug development (*e.g.* Roberts and Hayes (2008)), the identification of adverse drug effects (*e.g.* Leaman et al. (2010)) and the recognition of drug-drug interactions (*e.g.* Thomas et al. (2011)). Given that most of the information related to drug research is covered by medical reports and pharmacological publications, computational methods for information extraction should be used to support this task.

The SemEval-2013 Task 9.1 competition[1] (Segura-Bedmar et al., 2013) aims at a fair assessment on the state-of-the-art of tools that recognize and classify mentions of pharmacological substances in natural language texts – a task referred to as drug named entity recognition (NER). The goal of participating teams is to recreate the gold annotation on a held-out part of an annotated corpus. Four classes of entities have to be identified: `Drug`, `DrugN`, `Group` and `Brand`. Entities of class `Drug` denote any kind of drug that is approved for use in humans, whereas `DrugN` denotes substances that are not approved. `Group` are terms describing a group of drugs and `Brand` stands for drug names introduced by a pharmaceutical company.

The aim of this study is to examine whether it is worthwhile to implement domain-specific features for supporting drug NER. The question we attempt to answer is whether such features really help in identifying and classifying mentions of drugs or whether a mostly domain-independent feature set, which can be applied to many other tasks, achieves a comparable performance.

2 Related work

Various NER systems for identifying different classes of chemical entities, including mentions of drugs, trivial names and IUPAC terms, have been proposed.

[1] `http://www.cs.york.ac.uk/semeval-2013/task9/` (accessed 2013-04-29)

*Second Joint Conference on Lexical and Computational Semantics (*SEM), Volume 2: Seventh International Workshop on Semantic Evaluation (SemEval 2013)*, pages 356–363, Atlanta, Georgia, June 14-15, 2013.

Klinger et al. (2008) trained a conditional random field (CRF) (Lafferty et al., 2001) for extracting mentions of IUPAC and IUPAC-like entities. They report an F_1 measure of 85.6% on a hand-annotated corpus consisting of MEDLINE abstracts.

Segura-Bedmar et al. (2008) introduced DrugNER, which is based on UMLS MetaMap Transfer (MMTx) and nomenclature rules by the World Health Organization International Nonproprietary Names (INNs). Their system extracts and classifies mentions of drugs and achieves a precision of 99.1% and a recall of 99.8% on a silver-standard corpus.

OSCAR (Open-Source Chemistry Analysis Routines) (Corbett and Murray-Rust, 2006; Jessop et al., 2011) extracts mentions of a wide range of chemicals using a maximum entropy Markov model (McCallum et al., 2000). It achieves an F_1 of 83.2% on a corpus consisting of PubMed abstracts and 80.7% on a corpus consisting of chemistry papers (Corbett and Copestake, 2008).

Hettne et al. (2009) compiled Jochem (the joint chemical dictionary) from ChemIDplus, ChEBI, DrugBank, PubChem, HMDB, KEGG, MeSH and CAS Registry IDs. Jochem was used with Peregrine (Schuemie et al., 2007), a dictionary-based NER tool, achieving an F_1 of 50% on the SCAI corpus (Kolárik et al., 2008).

We developed ChemSpot (Rocktäschel et al., 2012), a system for extracting mentions of various kinds of chemicals from text. We applied a CRF for extracting mentions of IUPAC entities based on the work of Klinger et al. (2008) and used Jochem (Hettne et al., 2009) with an adapted matching-mechanism for identifying trivial names, drugs and brands. ChemSpot v1.0 achieved an overall F_1 of 68.1% on the SCAI corpus. In the meantime, we have worked on several enhancements (see Section 3.1).

The SemEval-2013 Task 9.1 poses new challenges on NER tools. Instead of targeting all kinds of chemicals, it focuses on drugs, *i.e.*, pharmacological substances that affect humans and are used for administration. Moreover, entities need to be classified into the four categories mentioned above.

3 Methods

Our approach is based on a linear-chain CRF with mostly domain-independent features commonly applied to NER tasks. In addition, we employ various domain-specific features derived from the output of ChemSpot's components, as well as Jochem, the PHARE ontology (Coulet et al., 2011) and the ChEBI ontology (De Matos et al., 2010). In the following, we first explain extensions to ChemSpot. Subsequently, we give a brief introduction to linear-chain CRFs before describing the general and domain-specific features used by our system. Finally, we explain the experimental setup and discuss our results.

3.1 Improvements of ChemSpot

To improve ChemSpot's chemical NER performance, we extend it by two components and modify its match-expansion mechanism.

The first addition is a pattern-based tagger for chemical formulae. In its basic form it extracts mentions matching the regular expression `(S N?(\+|-)?)+` where `S` denotes a chemical symbol and `N` a natural number greater one.[2] This pattern is augmented by filters to comply with other naming conventions, such as correct grouping of compounds with parentheses.

The second extension targets ambiguous abbreviations. For example, the abbreviation "DAG" could denote "diacylglycerol" or "directed acyclic graph". We use ABBREV, an algorithm proposed by Schwartz and Hearst (2003), for extracting such abbreviations and their definitions (*e.g.* "diacylglycerol (DAG)"). Note that the position of the long form (LF) and short form (SF) is interchangeable. To disambiguate between chemical and non-chemical abbreviations, we apply the following two rules to the mentions extracted by ChemSpot: (1) For a given pair of LF and SF, we check whether the LF was found to be a chemical but the SF was not. In this case we add a new annotation for every occurrence of the SF in the document. (2) Contrary to that, if only the SF was tagged as a chemical but the LF was not, we assume that the abbreviation does not refer to a chemical and remove all annotations of the SF in the document.

ChemSpot's match-expansion often leads to the extraction of non-chemical suffixes corresponding to verbs, *e.g.*, "-induced", "-enriched" or "-mediated".

[2] By convention, 1 is ommited (*e.g.* CO_2 instead of C_1O_2).

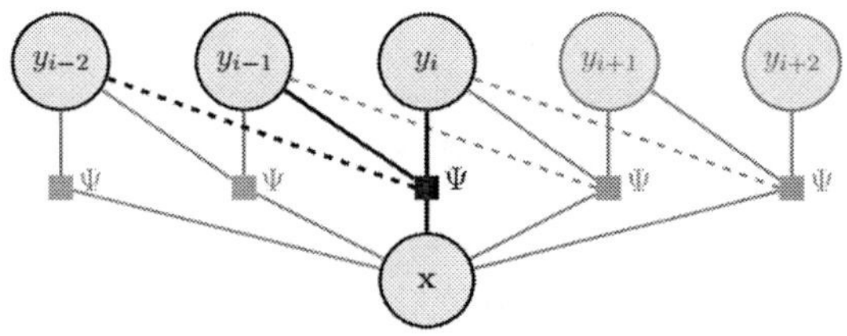

Figure 1: A factor graph for a 1st-order linear-chain CRF (2nd-order with dashed edges). Note that for each feature function f_j in the factor Ψ, the same weight θ_j is used at all other positions (gray) in the sequence (parameter tying).

To tackle this issue we stop the expansion at tokens whose part-of-speech tag refers to a verb form. Furthermore, we integrated OPSIN (Lowe et al., 2011) to normalize entity mentions to InChI strings.

The current v1.5 release of ChemSpot achieves an overall F_1 of 74.2% on the SCAI corpus, improving the performance by 6.1 percentage points (pp) F1 compared to ChemSpot v1.0.

3.2 Linear-chain conditional random fields

Contrary to the hybrid strategy used in ChemSpot, we follow a purely machine learning based approach for drug NER in this work. NER can be formulated as a sequence labeling task where the goal is to find a sequence of labels $\mathbf{y} = \{y_1, \ldots, y_n\}$ given a sequence $\mathbf{x} = \{x_1, \ldots, x_n\}$ of observed input tokens. Labels commonly follow the `IOB` format, where `B` denotes a token at the beginning of an entity mention, `I` denotes the continuation of a mention and `O` corresponds to tokens that are not part of a mention. Extracting entity mentions from a tokenized text $\mathbf{x}$ then amounts to finding $\mathbf{y}^* = \arg\max_{\mathbf{y}} p(\mathbf{y} \mid \mathbf{x})$.

Linear-chain CRFs are well-known discriminative undirected graphical models that encode the conditional probability $p(\mathbf{y} \mid \mathbf{x})$ of a *set* of input variables $\mathbf{x}$ and a *sequence* of output variables $\mathbf{y}$ (see Wallach (2004) or Klinger and Tomanek (2007) for an introduction). In the case of NER, $\mathbf{x}$ is a *sequence* of n tokens and $\mathbf{y}$ a sequence of n corresponding labels. Linear-chain CRFs of order k factorize $p(\mathbf{y} \mid \mathbf{x})$ into a product of factors Ψ, globally normalized by an input-dependent partition function $Z(\mathbf{x})$:

$$p(\mathbf{y} \mid \mathbf{x}) = \frac{1}{Z(x)} \prod_{i=1}^{n} \Psi(y_{i-k}, \ldots, y_{i-1}, y_i, \mathbf{x}, i).$$

A factor Ψ is commonly defined as the exponential function of a sum of weighted feature functions $\{f_1, \ldots, f_m\}$:

$$\frac{1}{Z(\mathbf{x})} \prod_{i=1}^{n} \exp\left(\sum_{j=1}^{m} \theta_j f_j(y_{i-k}, \ldots, y_{i-1}, y_i, \mathbf{x}, i) \right).$$

The feature function weights $\{\theta_j\}$ can be learned from training data and are shared across all positions i (*parameter tying*).

The factorization of a CRF can be illustrated by a factor graph (Kschischang et al., 2001). A factor graph is a bipartite graph, where one set of nodes corresponds to random variables and the other to factors. Each factor is connected to the variables of its domain, making the factorization of the model apparent. Figure 1 shows a factor graph for a segment of a linear-chain CRF of order one and two respectively. In a linear-chain CRF of order k, the label of a token at position i is connected via feature functions of a factor to the input sequence $\mathbf{x}$ as well as the previous k labels. For example, in a first-order linear-chain CRF, one of the feature functions could be $f_{[\text{O}\rightarrow\text{B,capital}]}(y_{i-1}, y_i, \mathbf{x}, i)$, which evaluates to 1 if $y_{i-1} = \texttt{O}$, $y_i = \texttt{B}$ and $\mathbf{x}_i$ starts with a capital letter (otherwise it yields 0). Multiplication with the weight $\theta_{[\text{O}\rightarrow\text{B,capital}]}$ yields an unnormalized local score that indicates how favorable a transition from `O` to `B` is provided that the token at position i starts with a capital letter. Note that the terms *feature function* and *feature* are often used synonymously and the case differentiation for different labels is implicit. In this work a feature f_{capital} denotes its corresponding set of first-order feature functions $\{f_{[\text{s}\rightarrow\text{t,capital}]}(y_{i-1}, y_i, \mathbf{x}, i) \mid (s,t) \in \{(\texttt{B},\texttt{B}), (\texttt{B},\texttt{I}), (\texttt{B},\texttt{O}), (\texttt{I},\texttt{B}), (\texttt{I},\texttt{I}), (\texttt{I},\texttt{O}), (\texttt{O},\texttt{B}), (\texttt{O},\texttt{O})\}\}$[3] (similarly for second-order).

We employ MALLET (McCallum, 2002) as underlying CRF implementation and use a second-order linear-chain CRF with offset conjunctions of order two. Offset conjunctions of order k adds features around a window of k to the features at a particular position, providing more contextual information. Akin to Klinger et al. (2008), we perform fine-grained tokenization, splitting at special characters and transitions from alphanumeric characters to digits. An exemplary tagging sequence is shown in Table 1.

[3]Transitions from `O` to `I` are invalid.

i	0	1	2	3	4	5	6	7	8	9	10
y	O	B-DrugN	O	B-DrugN	I-DrugN	I-DrugN	O	B-Group	O	O	O
x	Both	ibogaine	and	18	-	MC	ameliorate	opioid	withdrawal	signs	.

Table 1: Example label sequence for the tokenized sentence MedLine.d110.s4 of the training corpus.

	Feature Class	Description
	f_{CHEMSPOT}	part of a prediction by ChemSpot
	f_{IUPAC}	part of an IUPAC entity
F_C	f_{FORMULA}	part of a chemical formula
	$f_{\text{DICTIONARY}}$	part of a dictionary match
	f_{ABBREV}	part of a chemical abbreviation
	f_{JOCHEM}	dictionaries in Jochem
F_J	f_{PREFIX}	frequent chemical prefix
	f_{SUFFIX}	frequent chemical suffix
	f_{PHARE}	PHARE ontology
F_O	$f_{\text{CHEBDESCS}}$	#descendants in ChEBI ontology
	$f_{\text{CHEBDEPTH}}$	average depth in ChEBI ontology
	f_{KLINGER}	see Klinger et al. (2008)
F_G	f_{BANNER}	see Leaman and Gonzalez (2008)
	f_{ABNER}	see Settles (2005)
	$f_{\text{UPPERCASESENT.}}$	part of an upper-case sentence
F_F	$f_{\text{PREVWINDOW}}$	text of preceding four tokens
	$f_{\text{NEXTWINDOW}}$	text of succeeding four tokens

Table 2: Overview of features used for identifying and classifying mentions of pharmacological substances.

Note that the sequence-labeling approach in the described form cannot cope with discontinuous entity mentions. Since only a tiny fraction ($\approx 0.3\%$) of entities in the training corpus are discontinuous, we simply neglect these for training and tagging.

3.3 Feature sets

An overview of the features used by our system is shown in Table 2. Our first two submissions for the SemEval-2013 Task 9.1 differ only in that they use different subsets of these features. Run 1 employs a feature set assembled from common general features used for biomedical NER ($F_G \cup F_F$), whereas Run 2 additionally uses features tailored for extracting mentions of chemicals ($F_C \cup F_J \cup F_O$).

3.3.1 Run 1: general features F_G and F_F

We employ a union of common, rather domain-independent features published by Klinger et al. (2008), Settles (2005) and Leaman and Gonzalez (2008). Note that these feature sets have been successfully applied to a wide range of different biomedical NER tasks, *e.g.*, identifying mentions of DNA sequences, genes, diseases, mutations, IUPAC terms, cell lines and cell types. They encompass morphological, syntactic and orthographic features, such as the text of the token itself, token character n-grams of length 2 and 3, prefixes and suffixes of length 2, 3, and 4, characters left and right to a token and part-of-speech tags. Furthermore, they contain various regular expressions that capture, for instance, whether a token starts with a capital letter or contains digits.

In addition, we employ features based on NER examples in FACTORIE (McCallum et al., 2009). Specifically, we use the text of the four preceding and succeeding tokens and whether a token is part of a sentence that contains only upper-case characters. The latter is commonly the case for headlines, which likely contain an entity mention.

3.3.2 Run 2: domain-specific features

In addition to the features of Run 1, we use predictions of our improved version of ChemSpot, as well as features derived from Jochem, PHARE and ChEBI.

ChemSpot-based features F_C: When a token is part of a mention extracted by one of ChemSpot's components (*i.e.* IUPAC entity, chemical formula, dictionary match or chemical abbreviation), we use the name of the respective component as feature. In addition, we determine whether a token is part of an entity predicted by ChemSpot after match-expansion, boundary-correction and resolution of overlapping entities. Using the output of ChemSpot as features for our system could be framed as *stacking* (see Wolpert (1992)).

Jochem-based features F_J: For every dictionary contained in Jochem, we check whether a token is part of an entity in that dictionary and use the name of the dictionary as feature. Furthermore, we compile a list of frequent chemical suffixes and prefixes of length three from Jochem.

Ontology-based features F_O: It is often hard to determine whether a mention refers to a specific chemical entity or rather an abstract term denoting a group of chemicals. To distinguish between these two cases, we calculate the average depth and the number of descendants of a term in the ChEBI ontology and use the binned count as feature. The idea behind these features is that the specificity of an entity correlates positively with its depth in the ontology (*e.g.* leaf nodes are likely specific chemicals) and negatively with the number of descendants (*i.e.* having few descendants indicates a specific entity).

Further ontology-based features are derived from PHARE, which consists of 200 curated relations. If possible, we map a token to a term in that ontology and use its label as feature.

3.4 Experiments

We perform document-level 10-fold cross-validation (CV) on the training corpus to measure the impact of domain-specific features. To ensure comparability between Run 1 and Run 2, we use the same splits for evaluation. Furthermore, we train models on the complete training corpus and evaluate on the test corpus of DDI Task 9.1 for each run respectively. In addition, we train a third model based on the best feature set determined with CV and use the entity mentions of the Task 9.2 test corpus, which also contains annotations of drug-drug interactions, as additional training data (Run 3). Following the SemEval-2013 Task 9.1 metrics, we evaluate *exact* matching performance (correct entity boundaries) and *strict* matching performance (correct boundaries and correct type).

4 Results

Table 3 shows micro-average CV results for identifying and classifying mentions of pharmacological substances in the training corpus. The performance varies drastically between different entity classes regardless of the feature set, *e.g.*, Run 1 achieves an F_1 of 91.0% for `Drug`, but only 15.9% F_1 for `DrugN`.

Run 2 outperforms Run 1 for entities of class `Drug` (+1.2 pp F_1) and `DrugN` (+4.9 pp F_1), but yields a lower performance for `Brand` (−0.9 pp F_1) and no change for `Group` entities. Overall, the micro-average F_1 measure increases by 0.8 pp for strict matching and 1.4 pp F_1 for exact matching.

	Run 1			Run 2			
	P	R	F_1	P	R	F_1	ΔF_1
`Drug`	92.1	89.9	91.0	92.0	92.3	92.2	+1.2
`DrugN`	54.7	9.3	15.9	62.4	12.5	20.8	+4.9
`Group`	87.2	82.5	84.8	87.3	82.3	84.8	0.0
`Brand`	87.8	70.8	78.4	87.1	69.8	77.5	−0.9
Exact	93.9	86.9	90.3	94.5	89.0	91.7	+1.4
Strict	90.3	83.6	86.8	90.3	85.1	87.6	+0.8

Table 3: Document-level 10-fold cross-validation micro-average results on the training corpus.

The performance on the test corpus (see Table 4) is drastically lower compared to CV results (*e.g.* 17.6 pp F_1 for strict evaluation of Run 1). Except for entities of class `Group`, using domain-specific features leads to a superior performance for identifying and classifying mentions of pharmacological substances. Run 2 outperforms Run 1 by 1.6 pp F_1 for strict evaluation and 5.9 pp F_1 for exact evaluation. Using entity mentions of the Task 9.2 test corpus as additional training data (Run 3) further boosts the performance by 0.7 pp F_1 for strict evaluation.

5 Discussion

Our results show a clear performance advantage when using domain-specific features tailored for identifying mentions of chemicals. CV results and results on the test corpus show an increase in precision and recall for exact matching and an increase in recall for strict matching. The considerably higher recall for exact matching can be attributed to a higher coverage of chemical entities by features that exploit domain-knowledge.

It is striking that the performance for `DrugN` entities is extremely low compared to the other classes. We believe that this might be due to two reasons. First, entities of this class are underrepresented in the training corpus ($\approx$ 3%). Since machine learning based methods tend to favor the majority class, it is likely that many `DrugN` entities were classified as mentions of one of the much larger classes `Drug` ($\approx$ 64%) or `Group` ($\approx$ 23%). This can be confirmed by the large differences between strict and exact matching results shown in Table 3 and Table 4.

	#	Run 1 P	Run 1 R	Run 1 F_1	Run 2 P	Run 2 R	Run 2 F_1	Run 2 ΔF_1	Run 3 P	Run 3 R	Run 3 F_1	Run 3 ΔF_1
Drug	351	74.2	79.5	76.8	72.9	85.2	78.6	+1.8	73.6	85.2	79.0	+0.4
DrugN	121	25.0	4.1	7.1	35.7	8.3	13.4	+6.3	31.4	9.1	14.1	+0.7
Group	155	77.3	74.8	76.1	78.1	73.5	75.7	−0.4	79.2	76.1	77.6	+1.9
Brand	59	76.2	81.4	78.7	77.8	83.1	80.3	+1.6	81.0	86.4	83.6	+3.3
Exact	686	82.1	72.9	77.2	85.6	80.8	83.1	+5.9	85.5	81.3	83.3	+0.2
Strict	686	73.6	65.3	69.2	73.0	68.8	70.8	+1.6	73.4	69.8	71.5	+0.7
DrugBank (Strict)	304	86.9	85.2	86.0	87.3	86.2	86.8	+0.8	88.1	87.5	87.8	+1.0
MEDLINE (Strict)	382	60.8	49.5	54.5	60.5	55.0	57.6	+3.1	60.7	55.8	58.1	+0.5

Table 4: Results on the test corpus. ΔF_1 denotes the F_1 pp difference to the preceding Run and # the number of annotated mentions

Second, `DrugN` denotes substances that have an effect on humans, but are not approved for medical use – a property that is rarely stated along with the entity mention and can thus often only be determined with domain-knowledge.

We think it is also important to point to the large difference between results obtained by 10-fold CV on the training corpus and test results (*e.g.* up to 17.6 pp F_1 for Run 1). One reason might be the large fraction ($\approx 83\%$) of entity mentions that appear more than once in the training corpus compared to presumably many unseen entities in the test corpus. For 10-fold CV this means that an entity in the evaluation fold has already been seen with a high probability in one of the nine training folds, yielding results that overestimate the generalization performance. Moreover, our results indicate that identifying and classifying pharmacological substances is much harder for MEDLINE documents than for DrugBank documents with a difference of up to 31.5 pp F_1 (*cf.* the last two rows of Table 4). Hence, another apparent reason for the performance differences is the substantial skew in the ratio of DrugBank to MEDLINE documents in the training corpus (roughly 4:1) compared to the test corpus (roughly 1:1). Since both sets of documents stem from different resources, this can be referred to as domain-adaptation problem.

In additional experiments we found that the general-purpose chemical NER tool ChemSpot achieves an F_1 of 65.5% for exact matching on the test corpus. This is 17.8 pp F_1 below our best results obtained with a machine learning based system (*cf.* Run 3) that is able to exploit properties of the task-specific annotations of the corpora.

6 Conclusion

We described our contribution to the SemEval-2013 Task 9.1: Recognition and classification of pharmacological substances. We found that a system based on rather general features commonly used for a wide range of biomedical NER tasks yields competetive results. Implementing this system needed no domain-adaptation and its performance could be sufficient for applications building upon drug NER. Nevertheless, adding domain-specific features boosts the performance considerably. Further improvements can be achieved by using entity annotations of the Task 9.2 test corpus as additional training data.

We identified two limitations of our approach. First, we found that entities of the minority class (`DrugN`) are very hard to classify correctly. Second, differences between DrugBank and MEDLINE documents probably cause a domain-adaptation problem. For future work, one could investigate whether the latter can be addressed by domain-adaptation techniques (*e.g.* Satpal and Sarawagi (2007)). To cope with `DrugN` entities, one could implement features derived from those resources that were used by the annotators for deciding whether a substance is approved for use in humans, *e.g.*, Drugs@FDA[4] and the WHO ATC[5] classification system.

[4] `http://www.accessdata.fda.gov/scripts/cder/drugsatfda/` (accessed 2013-04-29)

[5] `http://www.whocc.no/atc_ddd_index/` (accessed 2013-04-29)

Acknowledgements

We thank Philippe Thomas for preparing a simplified format of the corpora. We thank him and Roman Klinger for fruitful discussions.

Funding: Tim Rocktäschel is funded by the German Federal Ministry of Economics and Technology (BMWi) [KF2205209MS2], Torsten Huber and Michael Weidlich are funded by the German Federal Ministry of Education and Research (BMBF) [0315746].

References

Peter Corbett and Ann Copestake. 2008. Cascaded classifiers for confidence-based chemical named entity recognition. *BMC Bioinf.*, 9(Suppl 11):S4.

Peter Corbett and Peter Murray-Rust. 2006. High-throughput identification of chemistry in life science texts. In *Proc. of CompLife 2006*, pages 107–118.

Adrien Coulet, Yael Garten, Michel Dumontier, Russ B. Altman, Mark A. Musen, and Nigam H. Shah. 2011. Integration and publication of heterogeneous text-mined relationships on the Semantic Web. *J. Biomed. Semantics*, 2(Suppl 2):S10.

Paula De Matos, Rafael Alcántara, Adriano Dekker, Marcus Ennis, Janna Hastings, Kenneth Haug, Inmaculada Spiteri, Steve Turner, and Christoph Steinbeck. 2010. Chemical Entities of Biological Interest: an update. *Nucleic Acids Res.*, 38:D249–D254.

Kristina M. Hettne, Rob H. Stierum, Martijn J. Schuemie, Peter J.M. Hendriksen, Bob J.A. Schijvenaars, Erik M. Van Mulligen, Jos Kleinjans, and Jan A. Kors. 2009. A dictionary to identify small molecules and drugs in free text. *Bioinformatics*, 25(22):2983–2991.

David M. Jessop, Sam E. Adams, Egon L. Willighagen, Lezan Hawizy, and Peter Murray-Rust. 2011. OSCAR4: a flexible architecture for chemical text-mining. *J. Cheminf.*, 3(1):41.

Roman Klinger, Corinna Kolárik, Juliane Fluck, Martin Hofmann-Apitius, and Christoph M. Friedrich. 2008. Detection of IUPAC and IUPAC-like chemical names. In *Proc. of ISMB. Bioinformatics*, volume 24, pages i268–i276.

Roman Klinger and Katrin Tomanek. 2007. Classical Probabilistic Models and Conditional Random Fields. *Algorithm Engineering Report TR07-2-013*. Department of Computer Science, Dortmund University of Technology. ISSN 1864-4503.

Corinna Kolárik, Roman Klinger, Christoph M. Friedrich, Martin Hofmann-Apitius, and Juliane Fluck. 2008. Chemical names: terminological resources and corpora annotation. In *Proc. of the Workshop on Building and evaluating resources for biomedical text mining*, pages 51–58.

Frank R. Kschischang, Brendan J. Frey, and Hans-Andrea Loeliger. 2001. Factor graphs and the sum-product algorithm. *IEEE Trans. Inf. Theory*, 47(2):498–519.

John Lafferty, Andrew McCallum, and Fernando Pereira. 2001. Conditional Random Fields : Probabilistic Models for Segmenting and Labeling Sequence Data. In *Proc. of ICML-2001*, pages 282–289.

Robert Leaman and Graciela Gonzalez. 2008. BANNER: an executable survey of advances in biomedical named entity recognition. In *Proc. of Pac Symp Biocomput*, pages 652–663.

Robert Leaman, Laura Wojtulewicz, Ryan Sullivan, Annie Skariah, Jian Yang, and Graciela Gonzalez. 2010. Towards internet-age pharmacovigilance: extracting adverse drug reactions from user posts to health-related social networks. In *Proc. of Workshop BioNLP*, pages 117–125. ACL.

Daniel M. Lowe, Peter T. Corbett, Peter Murray-Rust, and Robert C. Glen. 2011. Chemical name to structure: Opsin, an open source solution. *J. Chem. Inf. Model.*, 51(3):739–753.

Andrew K. McCallum. 2002. MALLET: A Machine Learning for Language Toolkit. http://mallet.cs.umass.edu.

Andrew K. McCallum, Dayne Freitag, and Fernando. Pereira. 2000. Maximum entropy Markov models for information extraction and segmentation. In *Proc. of ICML-2000*, pages 591–598.

Andrew K. McCallum, Karl Schultz, and Sameer Singh. 2009. FACTORIE: Probabilistic programming via imperatively defined factor graphs. In *Proc. of Neural Information Processing Systems (NIPS)*.

Phoebe M. Roberts and William S. Hayes. 2008. Information needs and the role of text mining in drug development. In *Proc. of Pac Symp Biocomput*, pages 592–603.

Tim Rocktäschel, Michael Weidlich, and Ulf Leser. 2012. ChemSpot: A Hybrid System for Chemical Named Entity Recognition. *Bioinformatics*, 28(12):1633–1640.

Sandeepkumar Satpal and Sunita Sarawagi. 2007. Domain adaptation of conditional probability models via feature subsetting. In *Knowledge Discovery in Databases: PKDD 2007*, pages 224–235. Springer.

Martijn J. Schuemie, Rob Jelier, and Jan A. Kors. 2007. Peregrine: Lightweight gene name normalization by dictionary lookup. In *Proc. of the Second BioCreative Challenge*, volume 2, pages 131–133.

Ariel S. Schwartz and Marti A. Hearst. 2003. A simple algorithm for identifying abbreviation definitions in biomedical text. In *Proc. of Pac Symp Biocomput*, volume 8, pages 451–462.

Isabel Segura-Bedmar, Paloma Martínez, and María Herrero-Zazo. 2013. Semeval-2013 task 9: Extraction of drug-drug interactions from biomedical texts. In

Proc. of the 7th International Workshop on Semantic Evaluation (SemEval 2013).

Isabel Segura-Bedmar, Paloma Martínez, and María Segura-Bedmar. 2008. Drug name recognition and classification in biomedical texts. A case study outlining approaches underpinning automated systems. *Drug Discovery Today*, 13(17-18):816–823.

Burr Settles. 2005. ABNER: an open source tool for automatically tagging genes, proteins and other entity names in text. *Bioinformatics*, 21(14):3191–3192.

Philippe Thomas, Mariana Neves, Illés Solt, Domonkos Tikk, and Ulf Leser. 2011. Relation extraction for drug-drug interactions using ensemble learning. In *Proc. of the 1st Challenge Task on Drug-Drug Interaction Extraction 2011*, pages 11–18.

Hanna M. Wallach. 2004. Conditional Random Fields: An Introduction. *Technical Report MS-CIS-04-21*. Department of Computer and Information Science, University of Pennsylvania.

David H. Wolpert. 1992. Stacked generalization. *Neural Networks*, 5(2):241–259.

AMI&ERIC: How to Learn with Naive Bayes and Prior Knowledge: an Application to Sentiment Analysis

Mohamed Dermouche[1,2], Leila Khouas[1], Julien Velcin[2] and Sabine Loudcher[2]

[1]AMI Software R&D
1475 av. A. Einstein
34000 Montpellier, France
mde@amisw.com
lkh@amisw.com

[2]Université de Lyon, ERIC (Lyon 2)
5 av. P. Mendès-France
69676 Bron Cedex, France
julien.velcin@univ-lyon2.fr
sabine.loudcher@univ-lyon2.fr

Abstract

In this paper, we describe our system that participated in SemEval-2013, Task 2.B (sentiment analysis in Twitter). Our approach consists of adapting Naive Bayes probabilities in order to take into account prior knowledge (represented in the form of a sentiment lexicon). We propose two different methods to efficiently incorporate prior knowledge. We show that our approach outperforms the classical Naive Bayes method and shows competitive results with SVM while having less computational complexity.

1 Introduction

With the advent of Internet microblogging, social networks, like Twitter[1] and Facebook[2], have brought about a real revolution in our way of communicating. People share their opinions of everyday life without taboos or restrictions thanks to the anonymity offered by these tools, which makes them a valuable source of information rather rich of subjective data. These data can be mined using sentiment analysis as a means to understand people's feelings towards a political cause or what people are thinking about a product or a service. Recent works showed that Twitter sentiments can be correlated to box-office revenues (Asur and Huberman, 2010) or political polls (O'Connor et al., 2010).

Machine learning methods, like Naive Bayes (NB) and Support Vector Machines (SVM), have been widely used in sentiment analysis (Pang et al., 2002; Pak and Paroubek, 2010). One major problem with these methods, and in particular NB, is that the model is built only on the learning data which can lead to overfitting. In this paper, we describe our approach that participated in SemEval-2013, Task 2.B (sentiment analysis in Twitter) (Wilson et al., 2013). Our approach consists of learning with both NB and prior knowledge. We show that our approach outperforms the classical NB method and gives competitive results compared to SVM while having less computational complexity.

The remainder of this paper is organized as follows: prior works on sentiment analysis are discussed in Section 2. The proposed approach is detailed in Section 3. Then, experiments and results are given in Section 4 and 5.

2 Background

Sentiment analysis is a text mining task which deals with the feelings expressed explicitly or implicitly in a textual content. It concerns subjectivity analysis (subjective/objective), opinion mining (positive/negative/neutral), strength analysis, etc. Although the term "sentiment analysis" includes all these tasks, it often refers to opinion mining. Sentiment analysis methods can be categorized into machine learning, linguistic and hybrid methods.

Machine learning methods are usually supervised. A model is built based on a learning dataset composed of annotated texts and represented by a bag of words. The model is then deployed to classify new texts. Pang et al. (2002) use machine learning methods (NB, SVM and MaxEnt) to detect sentiments on movie reviews. Pak and Paroubek (2010) use NB to

[1]http://www.twitter.com/

[2]http://www.facebook.com/

*Second Joint Conference on Lexical and Computational Semantics (*SEM), Volume 2: Seventh International Workshop on Semantic Evaluation (SemEval 2013)*, pages 364–368, Atlanta, Georgia, June 14-15, 2013. ©2013 Association for Computational Linguistics

perform sentiment analysis on Twitter data.

Linguistic methods use lexicons and manually-crafted rules to detect sentiments. Kennedy and Inkpen (2006) use syntactic analysis to capture language aspects like negation and contextual valence shifters. Other works (Turney and Littman, 2003; Kamps et al., 2004) propose to use a term similarity measure which can be statistical (e.g., Mutual Information, LSA) or semantic (e.g., WordNet-based).

Hybrid methods use both statistical and linguistic approaches. Esuli and Sebastiani (2011), which is the closest work to ours, propose to use annotated lexical resources to improve opinion extraction. The bag-of-word text representation is enriched by new tags (e.g. subjectivity, polarity). Then, an SVM-based system is used for opinion classification.

3 Our approach

NB is a machine learning method that builds a classification model based only on the learning data which makes it highly dependent on this data. For example, in a sentiment analysis task, if the term `actor` appears more frequently within a negative context than in a positive one, it will be classified as negative while actually it is not. Moreover, NB tends sometimes to predict the class of majority (observed on learning data) which increases classification errors on unbalanced data. Our approach consists of incorporating prior knowledge into the NB model to make it less dependent on learning data.

To be efficiently used, prior knowledge must be represented in a structured form. We choose, here, to represent it by a sentiment lexicon (a set of positive and negative terms). Several lexicons have already been developed to address sentiment analysis issues. Some of them are publicly available like the MPQA subjectivity lexicon (Wilson et al., 2005), Liu's opinion lexicon (Ding et al., 2008), SentiWordNet (Esuli and Sebastiani, 2006). We believe that such knowledge can be quite useful if used correctly and efficiently by machine learning methods.

In the following, we settle for a 2-way classification task (positive vs. negative). Texts are represented by a vector space model (Salton et al., 1975) and terms are weighted according to their presence/absence in the text because previous works (Pang et al., 2002; Pak and Paroubek, 2010) showed that Boolean model performs better than other weighting schemes in sentiment analysis. We denote by w and $\bar{w}$ the presence, respectively absence, modality of a word w. A "term" stands, here, for any type of text features (smileys, n-grams).

3.1 Sentiment lexicon

We represent the prior knowledge by a 2-class sentiment lexicon: a list of subjective terms (words, n-grams and smileys) manually annotated with two scores: positive ($score_{c_+}$) and negative ($score_{c_-}$). Each term has a score of 1 on a class polarity (we call it right class) and 0 on the other one (wrong class). For example, the word `good` has $score_{c_+} = 1$ and $score_{c_-} = 0$. Then, c_+ is the right class of the word `good` and c_- is the wrong class.

3.2 NB method

NB is based on calculating class-wise term probabilities on a learning dataset D where each text $d \in D$ is annotated with a class $c \in \{c_+, c_-\}$. In the learning step, probability values $p(w|c)$ are estimated from D as follows:

$$p(w|c) = \frac{1}{nb(c)} \cdot nb(w, c) \qquad (1)$$

Where $nb(c)$ denotes the number of texts of class c and $nb(w, c)$ is the number of texts of class c that contain the term w.

Once these probabilities are calculated for each couple (w, c), the model can be used to classify new texts. We choose to assign a new text d to the class that maximizes the probability $p(c|d)$. Using Bayes' theorem and independence assumption between term distributions, this probability is calculated as follows (the denominator can be dropped because it is not dependent on the class c):

$$p(c|d) = \frac{p(c) \cdot \prod_{w \in d} p(w|c)}{p(d)} \qquad (2)$$

3.3 Incorporating prior knowledge

Prior knowledge is incorporated by adapting NB formulas. We propose two different methods to do this: Add & Remove and Transfer. These methods differ in the way to calculate the class-wise term probabilities $p(w|c)$ but use the same classification rule: $class(d) = \arg\max_{c \in \{c_+, c_-\}} p(c|d)$.

Add & Remove. This method consists of artificially adding some occurrences of term w to the right class and removing some occurrences from the wrong class. The lexicon is used to determine for each term its right and wrong classes. To ensure that probability values do not exceed 1, we introduce $nb(\bar{w}, c)$, the number of texts of class c that do not contain the term w, which is also equal to the maximum number of occurrences of w that can be added to the class c. Thus, the number of added occurrences is a ratio α_c of this maximum ($0 \leq \alpha_c \leq 1$). Likewise, if c was the wrong class of w, the number of removed occurrences from the class c is a ratio β_c of the maximum number that can be removed from the class c, $nb(w, c)$, with $0 \leq \beta_c \leq 1$. Formally, term probabilities are calculated as follows:

$$p(w|c) = \frac{1}{nb(c)} \cdot [nb(w,c) + \alpha_c \cdot score_c(w) \cdot nb(\bar{w}, c) - \beta_c \cdot score_{\bar{c}}(w) \cdot nb(w,c)] \quad (3)$$

Transfer. This method consists of transferring some occurrences of a term w from the wrong class to the right class. The number of transferred occurrences is such that the final probability is not greater than 1 and the number of transferred occurrences is not greater than the actual number of occurrences in the wrong class. To meet these constraints, we introduce $max(w, c)$: the maximum number of occurrences of w that can be transferred to the class c from the other class $\bar{c}$. This number must not be greater than both the number of texts from $\bar{c}$ containing w and the number of texts from c not containing w.

$$max(w, c) = \min\{nb(w, \bar{c}), nb(\bar{w}, c)\} \quad (4)$$

Finally, the number of occurrences actually transferred is a ratio α_c of $max(w, c)$ with $0 \leq \alpha_c \leq 1$. Term probabilities are estimated as follows:

$$p(w|c) = \frac{1}{nb(c)} \cdot [nb(w,c) + \alpha_c \cdot score_c(w) \cdot max(w,c) - \alpha_c \cdot score_{\bar{c}}(w) \cdot max(w, \bar{c})] \quad (5)$$

Both methods, Add & Remove and Transfer, consist of removing occurrences from the wrong class and adding occurrences to the right class with the difference that in Transfer, the number of added occurrences is exactly the number of removed ones.

4 Experiment

4.1 Sentiment lexicon

For SemEval-2013 contest (Wilson et al., 2013), we have developed our own lexicon based on Liu's opinion lexicon (Ding et al., 2008) and enriched with some "microblogging style" terms (e.g., `luv`, `xox`, `gd`) manually collected on the Urban Dictionary[3]. The whole lexicon contains 7720 English terms (words, 2-grams, 3-grams and smileys) where 2475 are positive and 5245 negative.

4.2 Dataset and preprocessing

To evaluate the proposed approach, we use SemEval-2013 datasets: TW (tweets obtained by merging learn and development data) and SMS, in addition to MR (English movie reviews of Pang and Lee (2004)). Concerning SMS, the classification is performed using the model learned on tweets (TW) in order to assess how it generalizes on SMS data. Note that our approach is adapted to binary classification but can be used for 3-way classification (which is the case of TW and SMS). We do this by adapting only positive and negative probabilities, neutral ones remain unchanged.

Texts are preprocessed by removing stopwords, numerics, punctuation and terms that occur only once (to reduce vocabulary size and data sparseness). Texts are then stemmed using Porter stemmer (Porter, 1997). We also remove URLs and Twitter keywords (`via`, `RT`) from tweets.

4.3 Tools

As we compare our approach to SVM method, we have used SVM^{multiclass} (Crammer and Singer, 2002). For a compromise between processing time and performance, we set the trade-off parameter c to 4 on MR dataset and 20 on TW and SMS (based on empirical results).

5 Results and discussion

In addition to the two proposed methods: Add & Remove (A&R) and Transfer (TRA), texts are classified using NB and SVM with two kernels: linear (SVM-L) and polynomial of degree 2 (SVM-P). All the scores given below correspond to the average

[3]http://www.urbandictionary.com/

F-score of positive and negative classes, even for 3-way classification. This measure is also used in SemEval-2013 result evaluation and ranking (Wilson et al., 2013).

5.1 General results

General results are obtained only with unigrams and smileys. Figure 1 presents the results obtained on the different datasets on both 2-way (left) and 3-way (right) classifications. For 2-way classification, neutral texts are ignored and the model is evaluated using a 5-fold cross validation. For 3-way classification, the model is evaluated on the provided test data. Compared with NB, our approach performs better on all datasets. It also outperforms SVM, that achieves poor results, except on MR.

Method	2-class		3-class	
	TW	MR	TW	SMS
NB	74.07	73.06	59.43	48.80
SVM-L	49.79	74.56	37.56	32.13
SVM-P	49.74	**84.64**	37.56	32.13
A&R	**76.05**	80.57	**60.57**	49.42
TRA	76.00	75.53	60.27	**51.35**

Figure 1: General results (unigrams and smileys)

Parameter effect. To examine the effect of parameters, we perform a 2-way classification on TW and MR datasets using 5-fold cross validation (Figure 2). We take, for A&R method, $\beta_{c_+} = \beta_{c_-} = 0$ and for both methods, $\alpha_{c_+} = \alpha_{c_-}$ (denoted α). This configuration does not necessarily give the best scores. However, empirical tests showed that scores are not significantly lower than the best ones. We choose this configuration for simplicity (only one parameter to tune).

Figure 2 shows that best scores are achieved with different values of α depending on the used method (A&R, TRA) and the data. Therefore, parameters must be fine-tuned for each dataset separately.

5.2 SemEval-2013 results

For SemEval-2013 contest, we have enriched text representation by 2-grams and 3-grams and used A&R method with: $\alpha_{c_+} = \alpha_{c_-} = 0.003$, $\beta_{c_+} = 0.04$ and $\beta_{c_-} = 0.02$. All of these parameters have been fine-tuned using the development data. We have also made an Information Gain-based feature

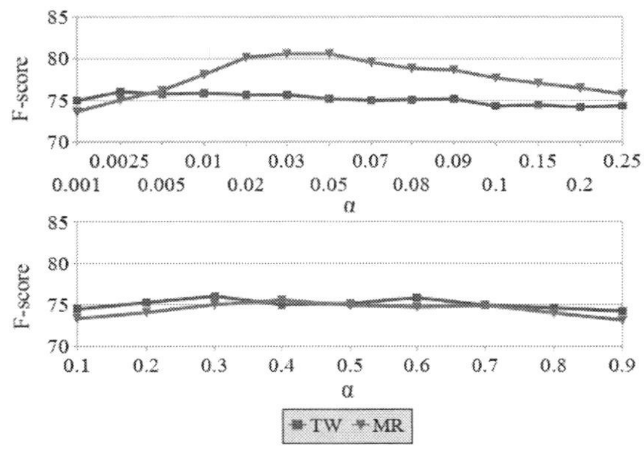

Figure 2: Effect of the parameter α on a 2-way classification using methods: A&R (top) and TRA (bottom)

selection (Mitchell, 1997). Only the best 2000 terms are kept to which we have added terms of the lexicon. Under these conditions, our approach achieved the scores 62.55% on tweets (ranked 6th/35) and 53.63% on SMS (ranked 9th/28).

Dataset	Class	Pecision	Recall	F-score
TW	positive	62.12	74.49	67.75
	negative	46.23	75.54	57.36
	neutral	76.74	44.27	56.15
SMS	positive	39.59	78.86	52.72
	negative	45.64	67.77	54.55
	neutral	90.93	39.82	55.38

Figure 3: SemEval-2013 results (A&R method)

Regarding F-score of each class (Figure 3), our approach gave better results on the negative class (under-represented in the learning data) than NB (49.09% on TW and 47.63% on SMS).

6 Conclusion

In this paper, we have presented a novel approach to sentiment analysis by incorporating prior knowledge into NB model. We showed that our approach outperforms NB and gives competitive results with SVM while better handling unbalanced data.

As a future work, further processing may be required on Twitter data. Tweets, in contrast to traditional text genres, show many specificities (short size, high misspelling rate, informal text, etc.). Moreover, tweets rely on an underlying structure (re-tweets, hashtags) that may be quite useful to build more accurate analysis tools.

References

Sitaram Asur and Bernardo A. Huberman. Predicting the future with social media. In *Proceedings of the 2010 IEEE/WIC/ACM International Conference on Web Intelligence and Intelligent Agent Technology (WI-IAT'10)*, pages 492–499, Washington, DC, USA, 2010. IEEE Computer Society.

Koby Crammer and Yoram Singer. On the algorithmic implementation of multiclass kernel-based vector machines. *The Journal of Machine Learning Research*, 2:265–292, 2002.

Xiaowen Ding, Bing Liu, and Philip S. Yu. A holistic lexicon-based approach to opinion mining. In *Proceedings of the 2008 International Conference on Web Search and Data Mining (WSDM '08)*, pages 231–240, New York, NY, USA, 2008. ACM.

Andrea Esuli and Fabrizio Sebastiani. Sentiwordnet: A publicly available lexical resource for opinion mining. In *Proceedings of the 5th Conference on Language Resources and Evaluation (LREC06)*, pages 417–422, Genova, IT, 2006.

Andrea Esuli and Fabrizio Sebastiani. Enhancing opinion extraction by automatically annotated lexical resources. In *Proceedings of the 4th conference on Human language technology: challenges for computer science and linguistics (LTC'09)*, pages 500–511, Poznan, Poland, 2011. Springer-Verlag.

Vasileios Hatzivassiloglou and Kathleen R Mckeown. Predicting the Semantic Orientation of Adjectives. In *Proceedings of the eighth conference of the European chapter of the Association for Computational Linguistics (EACL'97)*, pages 174–181, Madrid, Spain, 1997. ACL.

Jaap Kamps, Maarten Marx, Robert J. Mokken, and Maarten de Rijke. Using WordNet to measure semantic orientations of adjectives. In *Proceedings of the 4th International Conference on Language Resources and Evaluation (LREC-04)*, pages 1115–1118, Lisbon, PT, 2004.

Alistair Kennedy and Diana Inkpen. Sentiment classification of movie reviews using contextual valence shifters. *Computational Intelligence*, 22(2):110–125, May 2006.

Brendan O'Connor, Ramnath Balasubramanyan, Bryan R. Routledge, and Noah A. Smith. From tweets to polls: Linking text sentiment to public opinion time series. In *Proceedings of the 4th International AAAI Conference on Weblogs and Social Media*, Washington, DC, USA, 2010.

Alexander Pak and Patrick Paroubek. Twitter as a corpus for sentiment analysis and opinion mining. In *Proceedings of the Seventh conference on International Language Resources and Evaluation (LREC'10)*, pages 1320–1326, Valletta, Malta, 2010. ELRA.

Bo Pang, Lillian Lee, and Shivakumar Vaithyanathan. Thumbs up?: sentiment classification using machine learning techniques. In *Proceedings of the ACL-02 conference on Empirical methods in natural language processing (EMNLP'02)*, pages 79–86. ACL, 2002.

Bo Pang and Lillian Lee. A sentimental education: Sentiment analysis using subjectivity summarization based on minimum cuts. In *Proceedings of the 42nd Annual Meeting on Association for Computational Linguistics (ACL'04)*, pages 271–278, Barcelona, Catalonia, Spain, 2004. ACL.

Thomas M. Mitchell. *Machine Learning*. McGraw-Hill, Inc., New York, NY, USA, 1 edition, 1997.

Martin F. Porter. An algorithm for suffix stripping. In *Readings in information retrieval*, number 3, pages 313–316. Morgan Kaufmann Publishers Inc., San Francisco, CA, USA, 1997.

Peter D. Turney and Michael L. Littman. Measuring praise and criticism: Inference of semantic orientation from association. *ACM Transactions on Information Systems (TOIS)*, 21(4):315–346, 2003.

Gerard Salton, Andrew K. C. Wong, and Chung S. Yang. A vector space model for automatic indexing. *Communications of the ACM*, 18(11):613–620, 1975.

Theresa Wilson, Janyce Wiebe, and Paul Hoffmann. Recognizing contextual polarity in phrase-level sentiment analysis. In *Proceedings of the conference on Human Language Technology and Empirical Methods in Natural Language Processing (HLT/EMNLP-2005)*, pages 347–354, Vancouver, British Columbia, Canada, 2005. ACL.

Theresa Wilson, Zornitsa Kozareva, Preslav Nakov, Sara Rosenthal, Veselin Stoyanov, and Alan Ritter. SemEval-2013 Task 2: Sentiment Analysis in Twitter. *In Proceedings of the International Workshop on Semantic Evaluation (SemEval'13)*, Atlanta, Georgia, USA, 2013. ACL.

UNITOR: Combining Syntactic and Semantic Kernels for Twitter Sentiment Analysis

Giuseppe Castellucci[(†)], Simone Filice[(‡)], Danilo Croce[(⋆)], Roberto Basili[(⋆)]

(†) Dept. of Electronic Engineering
(‡) Dept. of Civil Engineering and Computer Science Engineering
(⋆) Dept. of Enterprise Engineering
University of Rome, Tor Vergata
Rome, Italy
{castellucci,filice,croce,basili}@info.uniroma2.it

Abstract

In this paper, the UNITOR system participating in the SemEval-2013 *Sentiment Analysis in Twitter* task is presented. The polarity detection of a tweet is modeled as a classification task, tackled through a Multiple Kernel approach. It allows to combine the contribution of complex kernel functions, such as the Latent Semantic Kernel and Smoothed Partial Tree Kernel, to implicitly integrate syntactic and lexical information of annotated examples. In the challenge, UNITOR system achieves good results, even considering that no manual feature engineering is performed and no manually coded resources are employed. These kernels in-fact embed distributional models of lexical semantics to determine expressive generalization of tweets.

1 Introduction

Web 2.0 and Social Networks technologies allow users to generate contents on blogs, forums and new forms of communication (such as micro-blogging) writing their opinion about facts, things, events. The analysis of this information is crucial for companies, politicians or other users in order to learn what people think, and consequently to adjust their strategies. In such a scenario, the interest in the analysis of the sentiment expressed by people is rapidly growing. Twitter[1] represents an intriguing source of information as it is used to share opinions and sentiments about brands, products, or situations (Jansen et al., 2009).

On the other hand, tweet analysis represents a challenging task for natural language processing systems. Let us consider the following tweets, evoking a *positive* (1), and *negative* (2) polarity, respectively.

Porto amazing as the sun sets... http://bit.ly/c28w (1)

@knickfan82 Nooooo ;(they delayed the knicks game until Monday! (2)

Tweets are short, informal and characterized by their own particular language with "Twitter syntax", e.g. retweets ("*RT*"), user references ("@"), hashtags ("*#*") or other typical web abbreviations, such as emoticons or acronyms.

Classical approaches to sentiment analysis (Pang et al., 2002; Pang and Lee, 2008) are not directly applicable to tweets: most of them focus on relatively large texts, e.g. movie or product reviews, and performance drops are experimented in tweets scenario. Some recent works tried to model the sentiment in tweets (Go et al., 2009; Pak and Paroubek, 2010; Kouloumpis et al., 2011; Davidov et al., 2010; Bifet and Frank, 2010; Croce and Basili, 2012; Barbosa and Feng, 2010; Agarwal et al., 2011). Specific approaches and feature modeling are used to achieve good accuracy levels in tweet polarity recognition. For example, the use of n-grams, POS tags, polarity lexicon and tweet specific features (e.g. hashtag, retweet) are some of the component exploited by these works in combination with different machine learning algorithms (e.g. Naive Bayes (Pak and Paroubek, 2010), k-NN strategies (Davidov et al., 2010), SVM and Tree Kernels (Agarwal et al., 2011)).

In this paper, the UNITOR system participating

[1]http://www.twitter.com

*Second Joint Conference on Lexical and Computational Semantics (*SEM), Volume 2: Seventh International Workshop on Semantic Evaluation (SemEval 2013)*, pages 369–374, Atlanta, Georgia, June 14-15, 2013.

in the SemEval-2013 *Sentiment Analysis in Twitter* task (Wilson et al., 2013) models the sentiment analysis stage as a classification task. A Support Vector Machine (SVM) classifier learns the association between short texts and polarity classes (i.e. *positive*, *negative*, *neutral*). Different kernel functions (Shawe-Taylor and Cristianini, 2004) have been used: each kernel aims at capturing specific aspects of the semantic similarity between two tweets, according to syntactic and lexical information. In particular, in line with the idea of using convolution tree kernels to model complex semantic tasks, e.g. (Collins and Duffy, 2001; Moschitti et al., 2008; Croce et al., 2011), we adopted the *Smoothed Partial Tree Kernel* (Croce et al., 2011) (SPTK). It is a state-of-the-art convolution kernel that allows to measure the similarity between syntactic structures, which are partially similar and whose nodes can differ but are nevertheless semantically related. Moreover, a Bag-of-Word and a Latent Semantic Kernel (Cristianini et al., 2002) are also combined with the SPTK in a multi-kernel approach.

Our aim is to design a system that exhibits wide applicability and robustness. This objective is pursued by adopting an approach that avoids the use of any manually coded resource (e.g. a polarity lexicon), but mainly exploits distributional analysis of unlabeled corpora: the generalization of words meaning is achieved through the construction of a Word Space (Sahlgren, 2006), which provides an effective distributional model of lexical semantics.

In the rest of the paper, in Section 2 we will deeply explain our approach. In Section 3 the results achieved by our system in the SemEval-2013 challenge are described and discussed.

2 System Description

This section describes the approach behind the `UNITOR` system. Tweets pre-processing and linguistic analysis is described in Section 2.1, while the core modeling is described in 2.2.

2.1 Tweet Preprocessing

Tweets are noisy texts and a pre-processing phase is required to reduce data sparseness and improve the generalization capability of the learning algorithms. The following set of actions is performed before applying the natural language processing chain:

- fully capitalized words are converted in their lowercase counterparts;
- reply marks are replaced with the pseudo-token `USER`, and POS tag is set to `$USR`;
- hyperlinks are replaced by the token `LINK`, whose POS is `$URL`;
- *hashtags* are replaced by the pseudo-token `HASHTAG`, whose POS is imposed to `$HTG`;
- characters consecutively repeated more than three times are cleaned as they cause high levels of lexical data sparseness (e.g. *"nooo!!!!!"* and *"nooooo!!!"* are both converted into *"noo!!"*);
- all emoticons are replaced by `SML_CLS`, where `CLS` is an element of a list of classified emoticons (113 emoticons in 13 classes).

For example, the tweet in the example 2 is normalized in '*user noo sml_cry they delayed the knicks game until monday*'. Then, we apply an almost standard NLP chain with *Chaos* (Basili and Zanzotto, 2002). In particular, we process each tweet to produce *chunks*. We adapt the POS Tagging and Chunking phases in order to correctly manage the pseudo-tokens introduced in the normalization step. This is necessary because tokens like `SML_SAD` are tagged as nouns, and they influence the chunking quality.

2.2 Modeling Kernel Functions

Following a summary of the employed kernel functions is provided.

Bag of Word Kernel (BOWK) A basic kernel function that reflects the lexical overlap between tweets. Each text is represented as a vector whose dimensions correspond to different words. Each dimension represents a boolean indicator of the presence or not of a word in the text. The kernel function is the cosine similarity between vector pairs.

Lexical Semantic Kernel (LSK) A kernel function is obtained to generalize the lexical information of tweets, without exploiting any manually coded resource. Basic lexical information is obtained by a co-occurrence Word Space built accordingly to the methodology described in (Sahlgren, 2006) and (Croce and Previtali, 2010). A word-by-context matrix M is obtained through a large scale corpus analysis. Then the *Latent Semantic Analysis* (Landauer and Dumais, 1997) technique is applied as follows. The matrix M is decomposed through Singular Value Decomposition (SVD) (Golub and Kahan, 1965) into the product of three new matrices: U, S, and V so that S is diagonal and $M = USV^T$. M is then approximated by $M_k = U_k S_k V_k^T$, where only the first k columns of U and V are used, corresponding to the first k greatest singular values. The original statistical information about M is captured by the new k-dimensional space, which preserves the global structure while removing low-variant dimensions, i.e. distribution noise. The result is that every word is projected in the reduced Word Space and an entire tweet is represented by applying an *additive linear combination*. Finally, the resulting kernel function is the cosine similarity between vector pairs, in line with (Cristianini et al., 2002).

Smoothed Partial Tree Kernel (SPTK) In order to exploit the syntactic information of tweets, the *Smoothed Partial Tree Kernel* proposed in (Croce et al., 2011) is adopted. Tree kernels exploit syntactic similarity through the idea of convolutions among substructures. Any tree kernel evaluates the number of common substructures between two trees T_1 and T_2 without explicitly considering the whole fragment space. Its general equation is reported hereafter:

$$TK(T_1, T_2) = \sum_{n_1 \in N_{T_1}} \sum_{n_2 \in N_{T_2}} \Delta(n_1, n_2), \quad (3)$$

where N_{T_1} and N_{T_2} are the sets of the T_1's and T_2's nodes, respectively and $\Delta(n_1, n_2)$ is equal to the number of common fragments rooted in the n_1 and n_2 nodes. The function Δ determines the nature of the kernel space. In the SPTK formulation (Croce et al., 2011) this function emphasizes lexical nodes. It computes the similarity between lexical nodes as the similarity between words in the Word Space. So, this kernel allows a generalization both from the syntactic and the lexical point of view.

However, tree kernel methods are biased by parsing accuracy and standard NLP parsers suffer accuracy loss in this scenario (Foster et al., 2011). It is mainly due to the complexities of the language adopted in tweets. In this work, we do not use a representation that depends on full parse trees. A syntactic representation derived from tweets chunking (Tjong Kim Sang and Buchholz, 2000) is here adopted, as shown in Figure 1.

Notice that no explicit manual feature engineering is applied. On the contrary we expect that discriminative lexical and syntactic information (e.g. negation) is captured by the kernel in the implicit feature space, as discussed in (Collins and Duffy, 2001).

A multiple kernel approach Kernel methods are appealing as they can be integrated in various machine learning algorithms, such as SVM. Moreover a combination of kernels is still a kernel function (Shawe-Taylor and Cristianini, 2004). We employed a linear combination αBOWK + βLSK + γSPTK in order to exploit the lexical properties captured by BOWK (and generalized by LSK) and the syntactic information of the SPTK. In our experiments, the kernel weights α, β and γ are set to 1.

3 Results and Discussion

In this section experimental results of the `UNITOR` system are reported.

3.1 Experimental setup

In the *Sentiment Analysis in Twitter* task, two subtasks are defined: `Contextual Polarity Disambiguation` (Task A), and `Message Polarity Classification` (Task B). The former deals with the polarity classification (*positive*, *negative* or *neutral*) of a marked occurrence of a word or phrase in a tweet context. For example the adjective "*amazing*" in example 1 expresses a positive marked word. The latter deals with the classification of an entire tweet with respect to the three classes *positive*, *negative* and *neutral*. In both subtasks, we computed a fixed (80%-20%) split of the training data for classifiers parameter tuning. Tuned parameters are the *regularization parameter* and the *cost factor* (Morik et al., 1999) of the SVM formulation. The former represents the trade off between a training error and the margin. The latter controls the trade off between positive and negative examples. The learning phase is made available by an extended version of SVM-LightTK[2], implementing the smooth matching between tree nodes.

We built a Word Space based on about 1.5 million of tweets downloaded during the challenge period using the topic name from the trial material as

[2] `http://disi.unitn.it/moschitti/Tree-Kernel.htm`

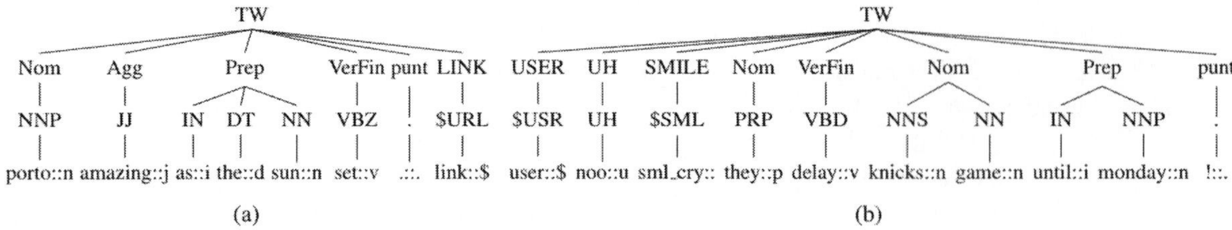

Figure 1: Chunk-based tree derived from examples (1) and (2)

query terms. We normalized and analyzed tweets as described in section 2.1. Words occurring more than 100 times in the source corpus are represented as vectors. The $10,000$ most frequent words in the corpus are considered as contexts and the co-occurrence scores are measured in a window of size $n = \pm 5$. Vector components are weighted through the Pointwise Mutual Information (PMI), and dimensionality reduction is applied through SVD with a cut of $k = 250$.

The task requires to classify two different texts: tweets and sms. Sms classification is intended to verify how well a system can scale on a different domain. In the testing phase two types of submissions are allowed. *Constrained* results refer to the case where systems are trained only with the released data. *Unconstrained* results refer to the case where additional training material is allowed. Evaluation metrics adopted to compare systems are *Precision, Recall* and *F1-Measure. Average F1* of the *positive* and *negative* classes is then used to generate ranks. Further information about the task is available in (Wilson et al., 2013).

3.2 Results over Contextual Polarity Disambiguation

We tackled Task A with a multi-kernel approach combining the kernel functions described in Section 2.2. The final kernel is computed as the linear combination of the kernels, as shown in Equation 4.

$$k(t_1, t_2) = SPTK(\phi_A(t_1), \phi_A(t_2)) + BOWK(\psi_A(t_1), \psi_A(t_2)) + LSK(\tau_A(t_1), \tau_A(t_2)) \quad (4)$$

where t_1, t_2 are two tweet examples. The $\phi_A(x)$ function extracts the 4-level chunk tree from the tweet x; nodes (except leaves) covering the marked instance in x are highlighted in the tree with `-POL`. The $\psi_A(x)$ function extracts the vector representing the Bag-of-Word of the words inside the marked instance of x, while τ_A builds the LSA vectors of the words occurring within the marked span of x. Referring to example 1, both $\psi_A(x)$ and τ_A point to the "*amazing*" adjective. Finally, $k(t_1, t_2)$ returns the similarity between t_1 and t_2 accordingly to our modeling. As three polarity classes are considered, we adopt a multi-classification schema accordingly to a *One-Vs-All* strategy (Rifkin and Klautau, 2004): the final decision function consists in the selection of the category associated with the maximum SVM margin.

Rank	4/19	class	precision	recall	f1
		positive	.8375	.7750	.8050
Avg-F1	.8249	negative	.8103	.8822	.8448
		neutral	.3475	.3082	.3267

Table 1: Task A results for the sms dataset

Rank	7/21	class	precision	recall	f1
		positive	.8739	.8844	.8791
Avg-F1	.8460	negative	.8273	.7988	.8128
		neutral	.2778	.3125	.2941

Table 2: Task A results for the twitter dataset

Tables 1 and 2 report the results of the `UNITOR` system in the Task A. Only the constrained setting has been submitted. The performance of the proposed approach is among the best ones and we ranked 4th and 7th among about 20 systems.

The system seems to be able to generalize well from the provided training data, and results are remarkable, especially considering that no manual annotated lexical resources were adopted and no manual feature engineering is exploited. It demonstrates that a multi-kernel approach, with the proposed shallow syntactic representation, is able to correctly classify the sentiment in out-of-domain contexts too. Syntax is well captured by the SPTK and the lexical generalization provided by the Word Space allows to generalize in the sms scenario.

3.3 Results over Message Polarity Classification

A multi-kernel approach is adopted for this task too, as described in the following Equation 5:

$$k(t_1, t_2) = SPTK(\phi_B(t_1), \phi_B(t_2)) + BOWK(\psi_B(t_1), \psi_B(t_2)) + LSK(\tau_B(t_1), \tau_B(t_2)) \quad (5)$$

The $\phi_B(x)$ function extracts a tree representation of x. In this case no nodes in the trees are marked. The $\psi_B(x)$ function extracts Bag-of-Word vectors for all the words in the tweet x, while $\tau_B(x)$ extracts the linear combination of vectors in the Word Space for adjectives, nouns, verbs and special tokens (e.g. hashtag, smiles) of the words in x. Again, a *One-Vs-All* strategy (Rifkin and Klautau, 2004) is applied.

Constrained run. Tables 3 and 4 report the result in the constrained case. In the sms dataset our system suffers more with respect to the tweet one. In both cases, the system shows a performance drop on the *negative* class. It seems that the multi-kernel approach needs more examples to correctly disambiguate elements within this class. Indeed, *negative* class cardinality was about 15% of the training data, while the *positive* and *neutral* classes approximately equally divided the remaining 85%. Moreover, it seems that our system confuses polarized classes with the *neutral* one. For example, the tweet "*going Hilton hotel on Thursday for #cantwait*" is classified as *neutral* (the gold label is *positive*). In this case, the hashtag is the sentiment bearer, and our model is not able to capture this information.

Rank	13/29	class	precision	recall	f1
		positive	.5224	.7358	.6110
Avg-F1	.5122	negative	.6019	.3147	.4133
		neutral	.7883	.7798	.7840

Table 3: Task B results for the sms dataset in the constrained case

Rank	13/36	class	precision	recall	f1
		positive	.7394	.6514	.6926
Avg-F1	.5827	negative	.6366	.3760	.4728
		neutral	.6397	.8085	.7142

Table 4: Task B results for the twitter dataset in the constrained case

Unconstrained run. In the unconstrained case we trained our system adding 2000 *positive* examples and 2000 *negative* examples to the provided training set. These additional tweets were downloaded from Twitter during the challenge period using *positive* and *negative* emoticons as query terms. The underlying hypothesis is that the polarity of the emoticons can be extended to the tweet (Pak and Paroubek, 2010; Croce and Basili, 2012). In tables 5 and 6 performance measures in this setting are reported.

Rank	10/15	class	precision	recall	f1
		positive	.4337	.7317	.5446
Avg-F1	.4888	negative	.3294	.6320	.4330
		neutral	.8524	.3584	.5047

Table 5: Task B results for the sms dataset in the unconstrained case

Rank	5/15	class	precision	recall	f1
		positive	.7375	.6399	.6853
Avg-F1	.5950	negative	.5729	.4509	.5047
		neutral	.6478	.7805	.7080

Table 6: Task B results for the twitter dataset in the unconstrained case

In this scenario, sms performances are again lower than the twitter case. This is probably due to the fact that the sms context is quite different from the twitter one. This is not true for Task A: polar expressions are more similar in sms and tweets. Again, we report a performance drop on the *negative* class. However, using more negative tweets seems to be beneficial. The F1 for this class increased of about 3 points for both datasets. Our approach thus needs more examples to better generalize from data.

In the future, we should check the redundancy and novelty of the downloaded material, as early discussed in (Zanzotto et al., 2011). Moreover, we will explore the possibility to automatically learn the kernel linear combination coefficients in order to optimize the balancing between kernel contributions (Gönen and Alpaydin, 2011).

Acknowledgements

This work has been partially funded by the Italian Ministry of Industry within the "Industria 2015" Framework, under the project DIVINO (MI01_00234).

References

Apoorv Agarwal, Boyi Xie, Ilia Vovsha, Owen Rambow, and Rebecca Passonneau. 2011. Sentiment analysis of twitter data. In *Proceedings of the Workshop on Languages in Social Media*, pages 30–38, Stroudsburg, PA, USA. Association for Computational Linguistics.

Luciano Barbosa and Junlan Feng. 2010. Robust sentiment detection on twitter from biased and noisy data. In *COLING*, pages 36–44, Stroudsburg, PA, USA. Association for Computational Linguistics.

Roberto Basili and Fabio Massimo Zanzotto. 2002. Parsing engineering and empirical robustness. *Nat. Lang. Eng.*, 8(3):97–120, June.

Albert Bifet and Eibe Frank. 2010. Sentiment knowledge discovery in twitter streaming data. In *Proceedings of the 13th international conference on Discovery science*, pages 1–15, Berlin, Heidelberg. Springer-Verlag.

Michael Collins and Nigel Duffy. 2001. Convolution kernels for natural language. In *Proceedings of Neural Information Processing Systems (NIPS'2001)*, pages 625–632.

Nello Cristianini, John Shawe-Taylor, and Huma Lodhi. 2002. Latent semantic kernels. *J. Intell. Inf. Syst.*, 18(2-3):127–152.

Danilo Croce and Roberto Basili. 2012. Grammatical feature engineering for fine-grained ir tasks. In *IIR*, pages 133–143.

Danilo Croce and Daniele Previtali. 2010. Manifold learning for the semi-supervised induction of framenet predicates: an empirical investigation. In *GEMS 2010*, pages 7–16, Stroudsburg, PA, USA. Association for Computational Linguistics.

Danilo Croce, Alessandro Moschitti, and Roberto Basili. 2011. Structured lexical similarity via convolution kernels on dependency trees. In *Proceedings of EMNLP*, Edinburgh, Scotland, UK.

Dmitry Davidov, Oren Tsur, and Ari Rappoport. 2010. Enhanced sentiment learning using twitter hashtags and smileys. In *COLING*, pages 241–249, Stroudsburg, PA, USA. Association for Computational Linguistics.

Jennifer Foster, Özlem Çetinoglu, Joachim Wagner, Joseph Le Roux, Stephen Hogan, Joakim Nivre, Deirdre Hogan, and Josef van Genabith. 2011. #hardtoparse: Pos tagging and parsing the twitterverse. In *Analyzing Microtext*.

Alec Go, Richa Bhayani, and Lei Huang. 2009. Twitter sentiment classification using distant supervision.

G. Golub and W. Kahan. 1965. Calculating the singular values and pseudo-inverse of a matrix. *Journal of the Society for Industrial and Applied Mathematics: Series B, Numerical Analysis*, 2(2):pp. 205–224.

Mehmet Gönen and Ethem Alpaydin. 2011. Multiple kernel learning algorithms. *Journal of Machine Learning Research*, 12:2211–2268.

Bernard J. Jansen, Mimi Zhang, Kate Sobel, and Abdur Chowdury. 2009. Twitter power: Tweets as electronic word of mouth. *J. Am. Soc. Inf. Sci. Technol.*, 60(11):2169–2188, November.

Efthymios Kouloumpis, Theresa Wilson, and Johanna Moore. 2011. Twitter sentiment analysis: The good the bad and the omg! In *ICWSM*.

Tom Landauer and Sue Dumais. 1997. A solution to plato's problem: The latent semantic analysis theory of acquisition, induction and representation of knowledge. *Psychological Review*, 104.

Katharina Morik, Peter Brockhausen, and Thorsten Joachims. 1999. Combining statistical learning with a knowledge-based approach - a case study in intensive care monitoring. In *ICML*, pages 268–277, San Francisco, CA, USA. Morgan Kaufmann Publishers Inc.

Alessandro Moschitti, Daniele Pighin, and Robert Basili. 2008. Tree kernels for semantic role labeling. *Computational Linguistics*, 34.

Alexander Pak and Patrick Paroubek. 2010. Twitter as a corpus for sentiment analysis and opinion mining. In *LREC*.

Bo Pang and Lillian Lee. 2008. Opinion mining and sentiment analysis. *Found. Trends Inf. Retr.*, 2(1-2):1–135, January.

Bo Pang, Lillian Lee, and Shivakumar Vaithyanathan. 2002. Thumbs up?: sentiment classification using machine learning techniques. In *EMNLP*, volume 10, pages 79–86, Stroudsburg, PA, USA. Association for Computational Linguistics.

Ryan Rifkin and Aldebaro Klautau. 2004. In defense of one-vs-all classification. *J. Mach. Learn. Res.*, 5:101–141, December.

Magnus Sahlgren. 2006. *The Word-Space Model*. Ph.D. thesis, Stockholm University.

John Shawe-Taylor and Nello Cristianini. 2004. *Kernel Methods for Pattern Analysis*. Cambridge University Press, New York, NY, USA.

Erik F. Tjong Kim Sang and Sabine Buchholz. 2000. Introduction to the conll-2000 shared task: chunking. In *ConLL '00*, pages 127–132, Stroudsburg, PA, USA. Association for Computational Linguistics.

Theresa Wilson, Zornitsa Kozareva, Preslav Nakov, Alan Ritter, Sara Rosenthal, and Veselin Stoyonov. 2013. Semeval-2013 task 2: Sentiment analysis in twitter. In *Proceedings of the 7th International Workshop on Semantic Evaluation*. Association for Computational Linguistics.

Fabio Massimo Zanzotto, Marco Pennacchiotti, and Kostas Tsioutsiouliklis. 2011. Linguistic redundancy in twitter. In *EMNLP*, pages 659–669.

TJP: Using Twitter to Analyze the Polarity of Contexts

Tawunrat Chalothorn
University of Northumbria at Newcastle
Pandon Building, Camden Street
Newcastle Upon Tyne, NE2 1XE, UK
Tawunrat.chalothorn@unn.ac.uk

Jeremy Ellman
University of Northumbria at Newcastle
Pandon Building, Camden Street
Newcastle Upon Tyne, NE2 1XE, UK
Jeremy.ellman@unn.ac.uk

Abstract

This paper presents our system, TJP, which participated in SemEval 2013 Task 2 part A: Contextual Polarity Disambiguation. The goal of this task is to predict whether marked contexts are positive, neutral or negative. However, only the scores of positive and negative class will be used to calculate the evaluation result using F-score. We chose to work as 'constrained', which used only the provided training and development data without additional sentiment annotated resources. Our approach considered unigram, bigram and trigram using Naïve Bayes training model with the objective of establishing a simple-approach baseline. Our system achieved F-score 81.23% and F-score 78.16% in the results for SMS messages and Tweets respectively.

1 Introduction

Natural language processing (NLP) is a research area comprising various tasks; one of which is sentiment analysis. The main goal of sentiment analysis is to identify the polarity of natural language text (Shaikh et al., 2007). Sentiment analysis can be referred to as opinion mining, as study peoples' opinions, appraisals and emotions towards entities and events and their attributes (Pang and Lee, 2008). Sentiment analysis has become a popular research area in NLP with the purpose of identifying opinions or attitudes in terms of polarity.

This paper presents TJP, a system submitted to SemEval 2013 for Task 2 part A: Contextual Polarity Disambiguation (Wilson et al., 2013). TJP was focused on the 'constrained' task, which used only training and development data provided. This avoided both resource implications and potential advantages implied by the use of additional data containing sentiment annotations. The objective was to explore the relative success of a simple approach that could be implemented easily with open-source software.

The TJP system was implemented using the Python Natural Language Toolkit (NLTK, Bird et al., 2009). We considered several basic approaches. These used a preprocessing phase to expand contractions, eliminate stopwords, and identify emoticons. The next phase used supervised machine learning and n-gram features. Although we had two approaches that both used n-gram features, we were limited to submitting just one result. Consequently, we chose to submit a unigram based approach followed by naive Bayes since this performed better on the data.

The remainder of this paper is structured as follows: section 2 provides some discussion on the related work. The methodology of corpus collection and data classification are provided in section 3. Section 4 outlines details of the experiment and results, followed by the conclusion and ideas for future work in section 5.

2 Related Work

The micro-blogging tool Twitter is well-known and increasingly popular. Twitter allows its users to post messages, or 'Tweets' of up to 140 characters each time, which are available for immediate

*Second Joint Conference on Lexical and Computational Semantics (*SEM), Volume 2: Seventh International Workshop on Semantic Evaluation (SemEval 2013)*, pages 375–379, Atlanta, Georgia, June 14-15, 2013.

download over the Internet. Tweets are extremely interesting to marketing since their rapid public interaction can either indicate customer success or presage public relations disasters far more quickly than web pages or traditional media. Consequently, the content of tweets and identifying their sentiment polarity as positive or negative is a current active research topic.

Emoticons are features of both SMS texts, and tweets. Emoticons such as :) to represent a smile, allow emotions to augment the limited text in SMS messages using few characters. Read (2005) used emoticons from a training set that was downloaded from Usenet newsgroups as annotations (positive and negative). Using the machine learning techniques of Naïve Bayes and Support Vector Machines Read (2005) achieved up to 70 % accuracy in determining text polarity from the emoticons used.

Go et al. (2009) used distant supervision to classify sentiment of Twitter, as similar as in (Read, 2005). Emoticons have been used as noisy labels in training data to perform distant supervised learning (positive and negative). Three classifiers were used: Naïve Bayes, Maximum Entropy and Support Vector Machine, and they were able to obtain more than 80% accuracy on their testing data.

Aisopos et al. (2011) divided tweets in to three groups using emoticons for classification. If tweets contain positive emoticons, they will be classified as positive and vice versa. Tweets without positive/negative emoticons will be classified as neutral. However, tweets that contain both positive and negative emoticons are ignored in their study. Their task focused on analyzing the contents of social media by using n-gram graphs, and the results showed that n-gram yielded high accuracy when tested with C4.5, but low accuracy with Naïve Bayes Multinomial (NBM).

3 Methodology

3.1 Corpus

The training data set for SemEval was built using Twitter messages training and development data. There are more than 7000 pieces of context. Users usually use emoticons in their tweets; therefore, emoticons have been manually collected and labeled as positive and negative to provide some context (Table 1), which is the same idea as in Aisopos et al. (2011).

Negative emoticons	:(:-(:d :< D: :\ /: etc.
Positive emoticons	:) ;) :-) ;-) :P ;P (: (; :D ;D etc.

Table 1: Emoticon labels as negative and positive

Furthermore, there are often features that have been used in tweets, such as hashtags, URL links, etc. To extract those features, the following processes have been applied to the data.

1. Retweet (RT), twitter username (@panda), URL links (e.g. y2u.be/fiKKzdLQvFo), and special punctuation were removed.
2. Hashtags have been replaced by the following word (e.g. # love was replaced by love, # exciting was replaced by exciting).
3. English contraction of 'not' was converted to full form (e.g. don't -> do not).
4. Repeated letters have been reduced and replaced by 2 of the same character (e.g. happpppppy will be replaced by happy, coollllll will be replaced by cooll).

3.2 Classifier

Our system used the NLTK Naïve Bayes classifier module. This is a classification based on Bayes's rule and also known as the state-of-art of the Bayes rules (Cufoglu et al., 2008). The Naïve Bayes model follows the assumption that attributes within the same case are independent given the class label (Hope and Korb, 2004).

Tang et al. (2009) considered that Naïve Bayes assigns a context X_i(represented by a vector X_i^*) to the class C_j that maximizes $P(C_j|X_i^*)$ by applying Bayes's rule, as in (1).

$$P(C_j|X_i^*) = \frac{P(C_j)P(X_i^*|C_j)}{P(X_i^*)} \quad (1)$$

where $P(X_i^*)$ is a randomly selected context X. The representation of vector is X_j^*. $P(C)$ is the random select context that is assigned to class C.

To classify the term $P(X_i^*|C_j)$, features in X_i^* were assumed as f_j from $j = 1\ to\ m$ as in (2).

$$P(C_j|X_i^*) = \frac{P(C_j)\prod_{j=1}^{m} P(f_j|C_j)}{P(X_i^*)} \qquad (2)$$

There are many different approaches to language analysis using syntax, semantics, and semantic resources such as WordNet. That may be exploited using the NLTK (Bird et al. 2009). However, for simplicity we opted here for the n-gram approach where texts are decomposed into term sequences. A set of single sequences is a unigram. The set of two word sequences (with overlapping) are bigrams, whilst the set of overlapping three term sequences are trigrams. The relative advantage of the bi-and trigram approaches are that coordinates terms effectively disambiguate senses and focus content retrieval and recognition.

N-grams have been used many times in contents classification. For example, Pang et al. (2002) used unigram and bigram to classify movie reviews. The results showed that unigram gave better results than bigram. Conversely, Dave et al. (2003) reported gaining better results from trigrams rather than bigram in classifying product reviews. Consequently, we chose to evaluate unigrams, bigrams and trigrams to see which will give the best results

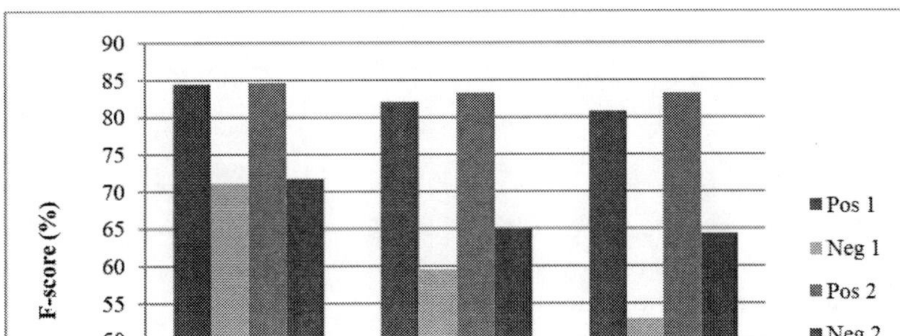

	Unigram	Bigram	Trigram
Pos 1	84.46	82.09	80.8
Neg 1	71.08	59.53	52.91
Pos 2	84.62	83.31	83.25
Neg 2	71.70	65.00	64.34

Figure 1: Comparison of Twitter messages from two approaches

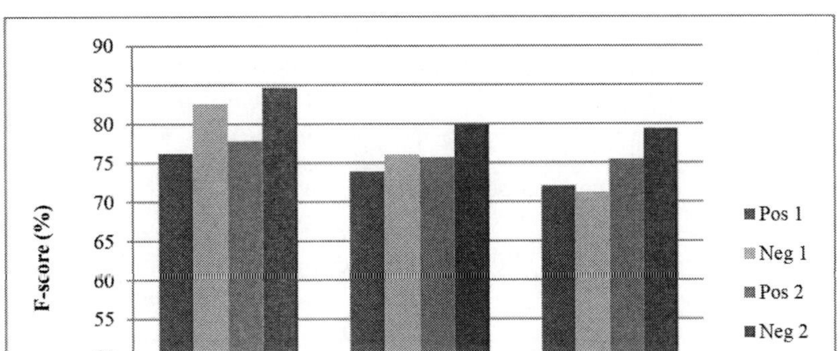

	Unigram	Bigram	Trigram
Pos 1	76.23	73.89	72.02
Neg 1	82.61	76.04	71.19
Pos 2	77.81	75.69	75.42
Neg 2	84.66	79.94	79.37

Figure 2: Comparison of SMS messages from two approaches

in the polarity classification. Our results are described in the next section.

4 Experiment and Results

In this experiment, we used the distributed data from Twitter messages and the F-measure for system evaluation. As at first approach, the corpora were trained directly in the system, while stopwords (e.g. a, an, the) were removed before training using the python NLTK for the second approach. The approaches are demonstrated on a sample context in Table 2 and 3.

After comparing both approaches (Figure 1), we were able to obtain an F-score 84.62% of positive and 71.70% of negative after removing stopwords. Then, the average F-score is 78.16%, which was increased from the first approach by 0.50%. The results from both approaches showed that, unigram achieved higher scores than either bigrams or trigrams.

Moreover, these experiments have been tested with a set of SMS messages to assess how well our system trained on Twitter data can be generalized to other types of message data. The second approach still achieved the better scores (Figure 2), where we were able to obtain an F-score of 77.81% of positive and 84.66% of negative; thus, the average F-score is 81.23%.

The results of unigram from the second approach submitted to SemEval 2013 can be found in Figure 3. After comparing them using the average F-score from positive and negative class, the results showed that our system works better for SMS messaging than for Twitter.

gonna miss some of my classes.		
Unigram	**Bigram**	**Trigram**
gonna miss some of my classes	gonna miss miss some some of of my my classes	gonna miss some miss some of some of my of my classes

Table 2: Example of context from first approach

gonna miss (*some of*) my classes.		
Unigram	**Bigram**	**Trigram**
gonna miss my classes	gonna miss miss my my classes	gonna miss my miss my classes

Table 3: Example of context from second approach. Note 'some' and 'of' are listed in NLTK stopwords.

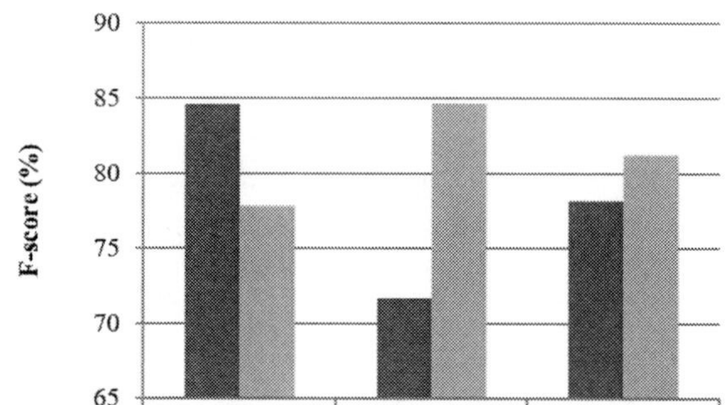

	Pos	Neg	Average
Twitter	84.62	71.70	78.16
SMS	77.81	84.66	81.23

Figure 3: Results of unigram of Twitter and SMS in the second approach

5 Conclusion and Future Work

A system, TJP, has been described that participated in SemEval 2013 Task 2 part A: Contextual Polarity Disambiguation (Wilson et al., 2013). The system used the Python NLTK (Bird et al 2009) Naive Bayes classifier trained on Twitter data. Furthermore, emoticons were collected and labeled as positive and negative in order to classify contexts with emoticons. After analyzing the Twitter message and SMS messages, we were able to obtain an average F-score of 78.16% and 81.23% respectively during the SemEval 2013 task. The reason that, our system achieved better scores with SMS message then Twitter message might be due to our use of Twitter messages as training data. However this is still to be verified experimentally.

The experimental performance on the tasks demonstrates the advantages of simple approaches. This provides a baseline performance set to which more sophisticated or resource intensive techniques may be compared.

For future work, we intend to trace back to the root words and work with the suffix and prefix that imply negative semantics, such as 'dis-', 'un-', '-ness' and '-less'. Moreover, we would like to collect more shorthand texts than that used commonly in microblogs, such as gr8 (great), btw (by the way), pov (point of view), gd (good) and ne1 (anyone). We believe these could help to improve our system and achieve better accuracy when classifying the sentiment of context from microblogs.

References

Alec Go, Richa Bhayani and Lei Huang. 2009. Twitter sentiment classification using distant supervision. *CS224N Project Report*, Stanford, 1-12.

Ayse Cufoglu, Mahi Lohi and Kambiz Madani. 2008. *Classification accuracy performance of Naive Bayesian (NB), Bayesian Networks (BN), Lazy Learning of Bayesian Rules (LBR) and Instance-Based Learner (IB1) - comparative study*. Paper presented at the Computer Engineering & Systems, 2008. ICCES 2008. International Conference on.

Bo Pang, Lillian Lee and Shivakumar Vaithyanathan. 2002. *Thumbs up?: sentiment classification using machine learning techniques*. Paper presented at the Proceedings of the ACL-02 conference on Empirical methods in natural language processing - Volume 10.

Fotis Aisopos, George Papadakis and Theodora Varvarigou. 2011. *Sentiment analysis of social media content using N-Gram graphs*. Paper presented at the Proceedings of the 3rd ACM SIGMM international workshop on Social media, Scottsdale, Arizona, USA.

Huifeng Tang, Songbo Tan and Xueqi Cheng. 2009. A survey on sentiment detection of reviews. *Expert Systems with Applications*, 36(7), 10760-10773.

Jonathon. Read. 2005. *Using emoticons to reduce dependency in machine learning techniques for sentiment classification*. Paper presented at the Proceedings of the ACL Student Research Workshop, Ann Arbor, Michigan.

Kushal Dave, Steve Lawrence and David M. Pennock. 2003. *Mining the peanut gallery: opinion extraction and semantic classification of product reviews*. Paper presented at the Proceedings of the 12th international conference on World Wide Web, Budapest, Hungary.

Lucas R. Hope and Kevin B. Korb. 2004. *A bayesian metric for evaluating machine learning algorithms*. Paper presented at the Proceedings of the 17th Australian joint conference on Advances in Artificial Intelligence, Cairns, Australia.

Mostafa Al Shaikh, Helmut Prendinger and Ishizuka Mitsuru. 2007. *Assessing Sentiment of Text by Semantic Dependency and Contextual Valence Analysis*. Paper presented at the Proceedings of the 2nd international conference on Affective Computing and Intelligent Interaction, Lisbon, Portugal.

Pang Bo and Lillian Lee. 2008. Opinion Mining and Sentiment Analysis. *Found. Trends Inf. Retr.*, 2(1-2), 1-135.

Steven Bird, Ewan Klein and Edward Loper. 2009. *Natural language processing with Python*: O'Reilly.

Theresa Wilson, Zornitsa Kozareva, Preslav Nakov, Sara Rosenthal, Veselin Stoyanov and Alan Ritter. 2013. SemEval-2013 Task 2: Sentiment Analysis in Twitter *Proceedings of the 7th International Workshop on Semantic Evaluation*: Association for Computational Linguistics.

uOttawa: System description for SemEval 2013 Task 2 Sentiment Analysis in Twitter

Hamid Poursepanj, Josh Weissbock, and Diana Inkpen
School of Electrical Engineering and Computer Science
University of Ottawa
Ottawa, K1N6N5, Canada
{hpour099, jweis035, Diana.Inkpen}@uottawa.ca

Abstract

We present two systems developed at the University of Ottawa for the SemEval 2013 Task 2. The first system (for Task A) classifies the polarity / sentiment orientation of one target word in a Twitter message. The second system (for Task B) classifies the polarity of whole Twitter messages. Our two systems are very simple, based on supervised classifiers with bag-of-words feature representation, enriched with information from several sources. We present a few additional results, besides results of the submitted runs.

1 Introduction

The Semeval 2013 Task 2 focused on classifying Twitter messages ("tweets") as expressing a positive opinion, a negative opinion, a neutral opinion, or no opinion (objective). In fact, the neutral and objective were joined in one class for the requirements of the shared task. Task A contained target words whose sense had to be classified in the context, while Task B was to classify each text into one of the three classes: positive, negative, and neutral/objective. The training data that was made available for each task consisted in annotated Twitter message. There were two test sets for each task, one composed of Twitter messages and one of SMS message (even if there was no specific training data for SMS messages). See more details about the datasets in (Wilson et al., 2013).

2 System Description

We used supervised learning classifiers from Weka (Witten and Frank, 2005). Initially we extracted simple bag-of-word features (BOW). For the submitted systems, we also used features calculated based on SentiWordNet information (Baccianella et al., 2010). SentiWordNet contains positivity, negativity, and objectivity scores for each sense of a word. We explain below how this information was used for each task.

As classifiers, we used Support Vector Machines (SVM) (SMO and libSVM from Weka with default values for parameters), because SVM is known to perform well on many tasks, and Multinomial Naive Bayes (MNB), because MNB is known to perform well on text data and it is faster than SVM.

2.1 Task A

Our system for Task A involved two parts: the expansion of our training data and the classification. The expansion was done with information from SentiWordNet. Stop words and words that appeared only once in the training data were filtered out. Then the classification was completed with algorithms from Weka.

As mentioned, the first task was to expand all of the tweets that were provided as training data. This was doing using Python and the Python NLTK library, as well as SentiWordNet. SentiWordNet provides a score of the sentient state for each word (for each sense, in case the word has more than

*Second Joint Conference on Lexical and Computational Semantics (*SEM), Volume 2: Seventh International Workshop on Semantic Evaluation (SemEval 2013)*, pages 380–383, Atlanta, Georgia, June 14-15, 2013.

one sense). As an example, the word "want" can mean "a state of extreme poverty" with the SentiWordNet score of (Positive: 0 Objective: 0.75 Negative: 0.25). The same word could also mean "a specific feeling of desire" with a score of (Positive: 0.5 Objective: 0.5 Negative: 0). We also used for expansion the definitions and synonyms of each word sense, from WordNet.

The tweets in the training data are labeled with their sentiment type (Positive, Negative, Objective and Neutral). Neutral and Objective are treated the same. The provided training data has the target word marked, and also the sentiment orientation of the word in the context of the tweeter message. These target words were the ones expanded by our method. When the target was a multi-word expression, if the expression was found in WordNet, then the expansion was done directly; if not, each word was expanded in a similar fashion and concatenated to the original tweet. These target words were looked up in SentiWordNet and matched with the definition that had the highest score that also matched their sentiment label in the training data.

Original Tweet	The great Noel Gallagher is about to hit the stage in St. Paul. Plenty of room here so we're 4th row center. Plenty of room. Pretty fired up
Key Words	Great
Sentiment	Positive
Definition	very good; "he did a bully job"; "a neat sports car"; "had a great time at the party"; "you look simply smashing"
Synonyms	Swell, smashing, slap-up, peachy, not_bad, nifty, neat, keen, groovy, dandy, cracking, corking, bully, bang-up
Expanded Tweet	The great Noel Gallagher is about to hit the stage in St. Paul. Plenty of room here so were 4th row center. Plenty of room. Pretty fired up swell smashing slap-up peachy not_bad nifty neat keen groovy dandy cracking corking bully bang-up very good he did a bully job a neat sports car had a great time at the party you look simply smashing

Table 1: Example of tweet expansion for Task A

The target word's definition and synonyms were then concatenated to the original tweet. No additional changes were made to either the original tweet or the features that were added from SentiWordNet. An example follows in Table 1. The test data (Twitter and SMS) was not expanded, because there are no labels in the test data to be able to choose the sense with corresponding sentiment.

2.2 Task B

For this task, we used the following resources: SentiwordNet (Baccianella et al, 2010), the Polarity Lexicon (Wilson et al., 2005), the General Inquirer (Stone et al., 1966), and the Stanford NLP tools (Toutanova et al., 2003) for preprocessing and feature selection. The preprocessing of Twitter messages is implemented in three steps namely, stop-word removal, stemming, and removal of words with occurrence frequency of one. Several extra features will be used: the number of positive words and negative words identified by three lexical resources mentioned above, the number of emoticons, the number of elongated words, and the number of punctuation tokens (single or repeated exclamation marks, etc.). As for SentiWordNet, for each word a score is calculated that shows the positive or negative weight of that word. No sense disambiguation is done (the first sense is used), but the scores are used for the right part-of-speech (in case a word has more than one possible part-of-speech). Part-of-Speech tagging was done with the Stanford NLP Tools. As for General Inquirer and Polarity Lexicon, we simply used the list positive and negative words from these resources in order to count how many positive and how many negative terms appear in a message.

3 Results

3.1 Task A

For classification, we first trained on our expanded training data using 10-fold cross-validation and using the SVM (libSVM) and Multinomial NaiveBayes classifiers from Weka, using their default settings. The training data was represented as a bag of words (BOW). These classifiers were chosen as they have given us good results in the past for text classification. The classifiers were run with 10-fold cross-validation. See Table 2 for the results. Without expanding the tweets, the accuracy of the SVM classifier was equal to the baseline of classifying everything into the most frequent class, which was "positive" in the training data. For MNB, the results were lower than the baseline. After expanding the tweets, the accuracy increased to 73% for SVM and to 80.36% for MNB. We concluded that MNB works better for Task A. This is why the submitted runs used the MNB model that was created from the expanded training data. Then we used this to classify the Twitter and SMS test data. The average F-score for the positive and the negative class for our submitted runs can be seen in Table 3, compared to the other systems that participated in the task. We report this measure because it was the official evaluation measure used in the task.

System	SVM	MNB
Baseline	66.32%	66.32%
BOW features	66.32%	33.23%
BOW+ text expansion	73.00%	**80.36%**

Table 2: Accuracy results for task A by 10-fold cross-validation on the training data

System	Tweets	SMS
uOttawa system	0.6020	0.5589
Median system	0.7489	0.7283
Best system	0.8893	0.8837

Table 3: Results for Task A for the submitted runs (Average F-score for positive/negative class)

The precision, recall and F-score on the Twitter and SMS test data for our submitted runs can be seen in Tables 4 and 5, respectively. All our submitted runs were for the "constrained" task; no additional training data was used.

Class	Precision	Recall	F-Score
Positive	0.6934	0.7659	0.7278
Negative	0.5371	0.4276	0.4762
Neutral	0.0585	0.0688	0.0632

Table 4: Results for Tweet test data for Task A, for each class.

Class	Precision	Recall	F-Score
Positive	0.5606	0.5705	0.5655
Negative	0.5998	0.5118	0.5523
Neutral	0.1159	0.2201	0.1518

Table 5: Results for SMS test data for Task A, for each class.

3.2 Task B

First we present results on the training data (10-fold cross-validation), then we present the results for the submitted runs (also without any additional training data).

Table 6 shows the overall accuracy for BOW features for two classifiers, evaluated based on 10-fold cross validation on the training data, for two classifiers: SVM (SMO in Weka) and Multidimensional Naïve Bays (MNB in Weka). The BOW plus SentiWordNet features also include the number of positive and negative words identified from SentiWordNet. The BOW plus extra features representation includes the number of positive and negative words identified from SentiWordNet, General Inquirer, and Polarity Lexicon (six extra features). The last row of the table shows the overall accuracy for BOW features plus all the extra features mentioned in Section 2.2, including information extracted from SentiWordNet, Polarity Lexicon, and General Inquirer. We can see that the SentiWordNet features help, and that when including all the extra features, the results improve even more. We noticed that the features from the Polarity Lexicon contributed the most. When we removed GI, the accuracy did not change much; we believe this is because GI has too small coverage.

System	SVM	MNB
Baseline	48.50%	48.50%
BOW features	58.75%	59.56%
BOW+ SentiWordNet	69.43%	63.30%
BOW+ extra features	**82.42%**	73.09%

Table 6: Accuracy results for task B by 10-fold cross-validation on the training data

The baseline in Table 6 is the accuracy of a trivial classifier that puts everything in the most frequent class, which is neutral/objective for the training data (ZeroR classifier in Weka).

The results of the submitted runs are in Table 7 for the two data sets. The features representation was BOW plus SentiWordNet information. The official evaluation measure is reported (average F-score for the positive and negative class). The detailed results for each class are presented in Tables 8 and 9.

In Table 7, we added an extra row for a new uOttawa system (SVM with BOW plus extra features) that uses the best classifier that we designed (as chosen based on the experiments on the training data, see Table 6). This classifier uses SVM with BOW and all the extra features.

System	Tweets	SMS
uOttawa submitted system	0.4251	0.4051
uOttawa new system	**0.8684**	**0.9140**
Median system	0.5150	0.4523
Best system	0.6902	0.6846

Table 7: Results for Task B for the submitted runs (Average F-score for positive/negative).

Class	Precision	Recall	F-score
Positive	0.6206	0.5089	0.5592
Negative	0.4845	0.2080	0.2910
Neutral	0.5357	0.7402	0.6216

Table 8: Results for each class for task B, for the submitted system (SVM with BOW plus SentiWordNet features) for the Twitter test data.

Class	Precision	Recall	F-score
Positive	0.4822	0.5508	0.5142
Negative	0.5643	0.2005	0.2959
Neutral	0.6932	0.7988	0.7423

Table 9: Results for each class for task B, for the submitted system (SVM with BOW plus SentiWordNet features) for the SMS test data.

4 Conclusions and Future Work

In Task A, we expanded upon the Twitter messages from the training data using their keyword's definition and synonyms from SentiWordNet. We showed that the expansion helped improve the classification performance. In future work, we would like to try an SVM using asymmetric soft-boundaries to try and penalize the classifier for missing items in the neutral class, the class with the least items in the Task A training data.

The overall accuracy of the classifiers for Task B increased a lot when we introduced the extra features discussed in section 2.2. The overall accuracy of SVM increased from 58.75% to 82.42% (as measures by cross-validation on the training data). When applying this classifier on the two test data sets, the results were very surprisingly good (even higher that the best system submitted by the SemEval participants for Task B[1]).

References

Stefano Baccianella, Andrea Esuli and Fabrizio Sebastiani. SentiWordNet 3.0: An Enhanced Lexical Resource for Sentiment Analysis and Opinion Mining. In Proceedings of the Seventh International Conference on Language Resources and Evaluation (LREC'10), Valletta, Malta, May 2010.

Philip J. Stone, Dexter C. Dunphy, Marshall S. Smith, and Daniel M. Ogilvie. The General Inquirer: A computer approach to content analysis. MIT Press, 1966.

Kristina Toutanova, Dan Klein, Christopher Manning, and Yoram Singer. Feature-Rich Part-of-Speech Tagging with a Cyclic Dependency Network. In Proceedings of HLT-NAACL 2003, pp. 252-259, 2003.

Theresa Wilson, Zornitsa Kozareva, Preslav Nakov, Sara Rosenthal, Veselin Stoyanov and Alan Ritter. SemEval-2013 Task 2: Sentiment Analysis in Twitter. In Proceedings of the International Workshop on Semantic Evaluation SemEval '13, Atlanta, Georgia, June 2013.

Theresa Wilson, Janyce Wiebe and Paul Hoffmann. Recognizing contextual polarity in phrase- level sentiment analysis. In Proceedings of HLT/ EMNLP 2005.

Ian H. Witten and Eibe Frank. Data Mining: Practical Machine Learning Tools and Techniques, 2nd edition, Morgan Kaufmann, San Francisco, 2005.

[1] Computed with the provided scoring script.

UT-DB: An Experimental Study on Sentiment Analysis in Twitter

Zhemin Zhu Djoerd Hiemstra Peter Apers Andreas Wombacher
CTIT Database Group, University of Twente
Drienerlolaan 5, 7500 AE, Enschede, The Netherlands
{z.zhu, d.hiemstra, p.m.g.apers, A.Wombacher}@utwente.nl

Abstract

This paper describes our system for participating SemEval2013 Task2-B (Kozareva et al., 2013): Sentiment Analysis in Twitter. Given a message, our system classifies whether the message is *positive*, *negative* or *neutral* sentiment. It uses a co-occurrence rate model. The training data are constrained to the data provided by the task organizers (No other tweet data are used). We consider 9 types of features and use a subset of them in our submitted system. To see the contribution of each type of features, we do experimental study on features by leaving one type of features out each time. Results suggest that unigrams are the most important features, bigrams and POS tags seem not helpful, and stopwords should be retained to achieve the best results. The overall results of our system are promising regarding the constrained features and data we use.

1 Introduction

The past years have witnessed the emergence and popularity of short messages such as tweets and SMS messages. Comparing with the traditional genres such as newswire data, tweets are very short and use informal grammar and expressions. The shortness and informality make them a new genre and bring new challenges to sentiment analysis (Pang et al., 2002) as well as other NLP applications such named entity recognition (Habib et al., 2013).

Recently a wide range of *methods* and *features* have been applied to sentimental analysis over tweets. Go et al. (2009) train sentiment classifiers using machine learning methods, such as Naive Bayes, Maximum Entropy and SVMs, with different combinations of features such as unigrams, bigrams and Part-of-Speech (POS) tags. Microblogging features such as hashtags, emoticons, abbreviations, all-caps and character repetitions are also found helpful (Kouloumpis et al., 2011). Saif et al. (2012) train Naive Bayes models with semantic features. Also the lexicon prior polarities have been proved very useful (Agarwal et al., 2011). Davidov et al. (2010) utilize hashtags and smileys to build a large-scale annotated tweet dataset automatically. This avoids the need for labour intensive manual annotation. Due to the fact that tweets are generated constantly, sentiment analysis over tweets has some interesting applications, such as predicting stock market movement (Bollen et al., 2011) and predicting election results (Tumasjan et al., 2010; O'Connor et al., 2010).

But there are still some unclear parts in the literature. For example, it is unclear whether using POS tags improves the sentiment analysis performance or not. Conflicting results are reported (Pak and Paroubek, 2010; Go et al., 2009). It is also a little surprising that *not* removing stopwords increases performance (Saif et al., 2012). In this paper, we build a system based on the concept of co-occurrence rate. 9 different types of features are considered. We find that using a subset of these features achieves the best results in our system, so we use this subset of features rather than all the 9 types of features in our submitted system. To see the contribution of each type of features, we perform experiments by leaving one type of features out each time. Results show that unigrams are the most important

*Second Joint Conference on Lexical and Computational Semantics (*SEM), Volume 2: Seventh International Workshop on Semantic Evaluation (SemEval 2013)*, pages 384–389, Atlanta, Georgia, June 14-15, 2013.

features, bigrams and POS tags seem not helpful, and retaining stopwords makes the results better. The overall results of our system are also promising regarding the constrained features and data we use.

2 System Description

2.1 Method

We use a supervised method which is similar to the Naive Bayes classifier. The score of a tweet, denoted by t, and a sentiment category, denoted by c, is calculated according to the following formula:

$$Score(t, c) = [\sum_{i=1}^{n} \log CR(f_i, c)] + \log P(c),$$

where f_i is a feature extracted from t. The sentiment category c can be *positive*, *negative* or *neutral*. And $CR(f_i, c)$ is Co-occurrence Rate (CR) of f_i and c which can be obtained as follows:

$$CR(f, c) = \frac{P(f_i, c)}{P(f_i)P(c)} \propto \frac{\#(f_i, c)}{\#(f_i)\#(c)},$$

where $\#(*)$ is the number of times that the pattern $*$ appears in the training dataset. Then the category of the highest score $\arg\max_c Score(t, c)$ is the prediction.

This method assumes all the features are independent which is also the assumption of the Naive Bayes model. But our model excludes $P(f_i)$ because they are observations. Hence comparing with Naive Bayes, our model saves the effort to model feature distributions $P(f_i)$. Also this method can be trained efficiently because it only depends on the empirical distributions.

2.2 Features

To make our system general, we constrain to the text features. That is we do not use the features outside the tweet texts such as features related to the user profiles, discourse information or links. The following 9 types of features are considered:

1. Unigrams. We use lemmas as the form of unigrams. The lemmas are obtained by the Stanford CoreNLP[1] (Toutanova et al., 2003). Hashtags and emoticons are also considered as unigrams. Some of the unigrams are stopwords which will be discussed in the next section.

2. Bigrams. We consider two adjacent lemmas as bigrams.

3. Named entities. We use the CMU Twitter Tagger (Gimpel et al., 2011; Owoputi et al., 2013)[2] to recognize named entities. The tokens covered by a named entity are not considered as unigrams any more. Instead a named entity as a whole is treated as a single feature.

4. Dependency relations. Dependency relations are helpful to the sentiment prediction. Here we give an example to explain this type of features. In the tweet "I may not be able to vote from Britain but I COMPLETLEY support you!!!!", the dependency relation between the word 'not' and 'able' is 'NEG' which stands for negation, and the dependency relation between the word 'COMPLETELY' and 'support' is 'ADVMOD' which means adverb modifier. For this example, we add 'NEG able' and 'completely support' as dependency features to our system. We use Stanford CoreNLP (Klein and Manning, 2003a; Klein and Manning, 2003b) to obtain dependencies. And we only consider two types of dependencies 'NEG' and 'ADVMOD'. Other dependency relations are not helpful.

5. Lexicon prior polarity. The prior polarity of lexicons have been proved very useful to sentiment analysis. Many lexicon resources have been developed. But for a single lexicon resource, the coverage is limited. To achieve better coverage, we merge three lexicon resources. The first one is SentiStrength[3] (Kucuktunc et al., 2012). SentiStrength provides a fine-granularity system for grading lexicon polarity which ranges from -5 (most negative) to $+5$ (most positive). Our grading system consists of three categories: *negative*, *neutral* and *positive*. So we map the words ranging from -5 to -1 in SentiStrength to *negative* in our grading system, and the words ranging from

[1] http://nlp.stanford.edu/software/corenlp.shtml

[2] http://www.ark.cs.cmu.edu/TweetNLP/

[3] http://sentistrength.wlv.ac.uk/

$+1$ to $+5$ to *positive*. The rest are mapped to *neutral*. We do the same for the other two lexicon resources: OpinionFinder[4] (Wiebe et al., 2005) and SentiWordNet[5] (Esuli and Sebastiani, 2006; Baccianella and Sebastiani, 2010).

6. Intensifiers. The tweets containing intensifiers are more likely to be non-neutral. In the submitted system, we merge the boosters in SentiStrength and the intensifiers in OpinionFinder to form a list of intensifiers. Some of these intensifiers strengthen emotion (e.g. 'definitely'), but others weaken emotion (e.g. 'slightly'). They are distinguished and assigned with different labels {`intensifier_strengthen`, `intensifier_weaken`}.

7. All-caps and repeat characters. All-caps[6] and repeat characters are common expressions in tweets to make emphasis on the applied tokens. They can be considered as implicit intensifiers. In our system, we first normalize the repeat characters. For example, `happyyyy` is normalized to `happy` as there are ≥ 3 consequent `y`. Then they are treated in the same way as intensifier features discussed above.

8. Interrogative sentence. Interrogative sentences are more likely to be neutral. So we add if a tweet includes interrogative sentences as a feature to our system. The sentences ending with a question mark '?' are considered as interrogative sentences. We first use the Stanford CoreNLP to find the sentence boundaries in a tweet, then check the ending mark of each sentence.

9. Imperative sentence. Intuitively, imperative sentences are more likely to be negative. So if a tweet contains imperative sentences can be a feature. We consider the sentences start with a verb as imperative sentences. The verbs are identified by the CMU Twitter Tagger.

We further filter out the low-frequency features which have been observed less than 3 times in the training data. Because these features are not stable indicators of sentiment. Our experiments show that removing these low-frequency features increases the accuracy.

2.3 Pre-processing

The pre-processing of our system includes two steps. In the first step, we replace the abbreviations as described in Section 2.3.1. In the second step, we use the CMU Twitter Tagger to extract the features of emoticons (e.g. `:)`), hashtags (e.g. `#Friday`), reciepts (e.g. `@Peter`) and URLs, and remove these symbols from tweet texts for further processing.

2.3.1 Replacing Abbreviations

Abbreviations are replaced by their original expressions. We use the Internet Lingo Dictionary (Wasden, 2010) to obtain the original expressions of abbreviations. This dictionary originally contains 748 acronyms. But we do not use the acronyms in which all characters are digits. Because we find they are more likely to be numbers than acronyms. This results in 735 acronyms.

3 Experiments

Our system is implemented in Java and organized as a pipeline consisting of a sequence of annotators and extractors. This architecture is very similar to the framework of UIMA (Ferrucci and Lally, 2004). With such an architecture, we can easily vary the configurations of our system.

3.1 Datasets

We use the standard dataset provided by SemEval2013 Task2-B (Kozareva et al., 2013) for training and testing. The training and development data provided are merged together to train our model. Originally, the training and development data contain 9,684 and 1,654 instances, respectively. But due to the policy of Twitter, only the tweet IDs can be released publicly. So we need to fetch the actual tweets by their IDs. Some of the tweets are no longer existing after they were downloaded for annotation. So the number of tweets used for training is less than the original tweets provided by the organizers. In our case, we obtained 10,370 tweets for training our model.

[4] https://code.google.com/p/opinionfinder/

[5] http://sentiwordnet.isti.cnr.it/

[6] All characters of a token are in upper case.

Class	Precision	Recall	F-Score
Positive	74.86	60.05	66.64
Negative	47.80	59.73	53.11
Neutral	67.02	73.60	70.15
Avg (Pos & Neg)	61.33	59.89	**59.87**

Table 1: Submitted System on Twitter Data

Class	Precision	Recall	F-Score
Positive	54.81	57.93	56.32
Negative	37.87	67.77	48.59
Neutral	80.78	58.11	67.60
Avg (Pos & Neg)	46.34	62.85	**52.46**

Table 2: Submitted System on SMS Data

Feature	Y(T)	N(T)	Y(sms)	N(sms)
Stopword	59.87	58.19	52.64	51.00
POS Tag	58.68	59.87	51.87	52.64
Bigram	58.47	59.87	51.94	52.64
Unigram	59.87	41.22	52.64	35.09
$3 \leq$	59.87	57.66	52.64	51.20
Intensifier	59.87	59.47	52.64	52.39
Lexicon	59.87	58.33	52.64	51.26
Named Ent.	59.87	59.71	52.64	51.80
Interrogative	59.87	59.67	52.64	52.93
Imperative	59.87	59.54	52.64	52.14
Dependence	59.87	59.37	52.64	52.08

Table 3: Avg (Pos & Neg) of Leave-one-out Experiments

There are two test datasets: Twitter and SMS. The first dataset consists of 3,813 twitter messages and the second dataset contains 2,094 SMS messages. The purpose of having a separate test set of SMS messages is to see how well systems trained on twitter data will generalize to other types of data.

3.2 Results of Our Submitted System

We use a subset of features described in Section 2.2 in our submitted system: unigrams, named entities, dependency relations, lexicon prior polarity, intensifiers, all-caps and repeat characters, interrogative and imperative sentences. The official results on the two datasets are given in Table (1, 2). Our system is ranked as #14/51 on the Twitter dataset and #18/44 on the SMS dataset.

3.3 Feature Contribution Analysis

To see the contribution of each type of features, we vary the configuration of our system by leaving one type of features out each time. The results are listed in Table 3.

In Table 3, 'Y(T)' means the corresponding feature is used and the test dataset is the Twitter Data, and 'N(sms)' means the corresponding feature is left out and the test dataset is SMS Data.

From Table 3, we can see that unigrams are the most important features. Leaving out unigrams leads to a radical decrease of F-scores. On the Twitter dataset, the F-score drops from 59.87 to 41.44, and on the SMS dataset, the F-score drops from 52.64 to 35.09. And also filtering out the low-frequency features which happens less than 3 times increases the F-scores on Twitter data from 57.66 to 59.87, and on SMS data from 51.20 to 52.64. Removing stopwords decreases the scores by 1.66 percent. This result is consistent with that reported by Saif et al. (2012). By taking a close look at the stopwords we use, we find that some of the stopwords are highly related to the sentiment polarity, such as 'can', 'no', 'very' and 'want', but others are not, such as 'the', 'him' and 'on'. Removing the stopwords which are related to the sentiment is obviously harmful. This means the stopwords which originally developed for the purpose of information retrieval are not suitable for sentimental analysis. Dependency relations are also helpful features which increase F-scores by about 0.5 percent. The POS tags and bigrams seem not helpful in our experiments, which is consistent with the results reported by (Kouloumpis et al., 2011).

4 Conclusions

We described the method and features used in our system. We also did analysis on feautre contribution. Experiment results suggest that unigrams are the most important features, POS tags and bigrams seem not helpful, filtering out the low-frequency features is helpful and retaining stopwords makes the results better.

Acknowledgements

This work has been supported by the Dutch national program COMMIT.

References

Apoorv Agarwal, Boyi Xie, Ilia Vovsha, Owen Rambow, and Rebecca Passonneau. 2011. Sentiment analysis of twitter data. In *Proceedings of the Workshop on Languages in Social Media*, LSM '11, pages 30–38, Stroudsburg, PA, USA. Association for Computational Linguistics.

Andrea Esuli Stefano Baccianella and Fabrizio Sebastiani. 2010. Sentiwordnet 3.0: An enhanced lexical resource for sentiment analysis and opinion mining. In *Proceedings of the Seventh conference on International Language Resources and Evaluation (LREC'10)*, Valletta, Malta, May. European Language Resources Association (ELRA).

J. Bollen, H. Mao, and X. Zeng. 2011. Twitter mood predicts the stock market. *Journal of Computational Science*.

Dmitry Davidov, Oren Tsur, and Ari Rappoport. 2010. Enhanced sentiment learning using twitter hashtags and smileys. In *Proceedings of the 23rd International Conference on Computational Linguistics: Posters*, COLING '10, pages 241–249, Stroudsburg, PA, USA. Association for Computational Linguistics.

Andrea Esuli and Fabrizio Sebastiani. 2006. Sentiwordnet: A publicly available lexical resource for opinion mining. In *In Proceedings of the 5th Conference on Language Resources and Evaluation (LREC06*, pages 417–422.

David Ferrucci and Adam Lally. 2004. Uima: an architectural approach to unstructured information processing in the corporate research environment. *Nat. Lang. Eng.*, 10(3-4):327–348, September.

Kevin Gimpel, Nathan Schneider, Brendan O'Connor, Dipanjan Das, Daniel Mills, Jacob Eisenstein, Michael Heilman, Dani Yogatama, Jeffrey Flanigan, and Noah A. Smith. 2011. Part-of-speech tagging for twitter: annotation, features, and experiments. In *Proceedings of the 49th Annual Meeting of the Association for Computational Linguistics: Human Language Technologies: short papers - Volume 2*, HLT '11, pages 42–47, Stroudsburg, PA, USA. Association for Computational Linguistics.

Alec Go, Richa Bhayani, and Lei Huang. 2009. Twitter sentiment classification using distant supervision. Technical report, Stanford University.

M. B. Habib, M. van Keulen, and Z. Zhu. 2013. Concept extraction challenge: University of twente at #msm2013. In *Proceedings of the 3rd workshop on 'Making Sense of Microposts' (#MSM2013), Rio de Janeiro, Brazil*, Brazil, May. CEUR.

Dan Klein and Christopher D. Manning. 2003a. Accurate unlexicalized parsing. In *Proceedings of the 41st Annual Meeting on Association for Computational Linguistics - Volume 1*, ACL '03, pages 423–430, Stroudsburg, PA, USA. Association for Computational Linguistics.

Dan Klein and Christopher D. Manning. 2003b. Fast exact inference with a factored model for natural language parsing. In *Advances in Neural Information Processing Systems*, volume 15. MIT Press.

Efthymios Kouloumpis, Theresa Wilson, and Johanna Moore. 2011. Twitter sentiment analysis: The good the bad and the omg! In Lada A. Adamic, Ricardo A. Baeza-Yates, and Scott Counts, editors, *ICWSM*. The AAAI Press.

Zornitsa Kozareva, Preslav Nakov, Alan Ritter, Sara Rosenthal, Veselin Stoyonov, and Theresa Wilson. 2013. Sentiment analysis in twitter. In *Proceedings of the 7th International Workshop on Semantic Evaluation*. Association for Computation Linguistics.

Onur Kucuktunc, B. Barla Cambazoglu, Ingmar Weber, and Hakan Ferhatosmanoglu. 2012. A large-scale sentiment analysis for yahoo! answers. In *Proceedings of the fifth ACM international conference on Web search and data mining*, WSDM '12, pages 633–642, New York, NY, USA. ACM.

Brendan O'Connor, Ramnath Balasubramanyan, Bryan R. Routledge, and Noah A. Smith. 2010. From tweets to polls: Linking text sentiment to public opinion time series. In *Proceedings of the Fourth International Conference on Weblogs and Social Media, ICWSM 2010, Washington, DC, USA, May 23-26, 2010*.

Olutobi Owoputi, Brendan OConnor, Chris Dyer, Kevin Gimpel, Nathan Schneider, and Noah A. Smith. 2013. Hello, who is calling?: Can words reveal the social nature of conversations? In *Proceedings of the 2013 Conference of the North American Chapter of the Association for Computational Linguistics: Human Language Technologies*. Association for Computational Linguistics, June.

Alexander Pak and Patrick Paroubek. 2010. Twitter as a corpus for sentiment analysis and opinion mining. In Nicoletta Calzolari (Conference Chair), Khalid Choukri, Bente Maegaard, Joseph Mariani, Jan Odijk, Stelios Piperidis, Mike Rosner, and Daniel Tapias, editors, *Proceedings of the Seventh International Conference on Language Resources and Evaluation (LREC'10)*, Valletta, Malta, may. European Language Resources Association (ELRA).

Bo Pang, Lillian Lee, and Shivakumar Vaithyanathan. 2002. Thumbs up?: sentiment classification using machine learning techniques. In *Proceedings of the ACL-02 conference on Empirical methods in natural language processing - Volume 10*, EMNLP '02, pages 79–

86, Stroudsburg, PA, USA. Association for Computational Linguistics.

Hassan Saif, Yulan He, and Harith Alani. 2012. Semantic sentiment analysis of twitter. In *Proceedings of the 11th international conference on The Semantic Web - Volume Part I*, ISWC'12, pages 508–524, Berlin, Heidelberg. Springer-Verlag.

Kristina Toutanova, Dan Klein, Christopher D. Manning, and Yoram Singer. 2003. Feature-rich part-of-speech tagging with a cyclic dependency network. In *Proceedings of the 2003 Conference of the North American Chapter of the Association for Computational Linguistics on Human Language Technology - Volume 1*, NAACL '03, pages 173–180, Stroudsburg, PA, USA. Association for Computational Linguistics.

A. Tumasjan, T.O. Sprenger, P.G. Sandner, and I.M. Welpe. 2010. Predicting elections with twitter: What 140 characters reveal about political sentiment. In *Proceedings of the Fourth International AAAI Conference on Weblogs and Social Media*, pages 178–185.

Lawrence Wasden. 2010. Internet lingo dictionary: A parents guide to codes used in chat rooms, instant messaging, text messaging, and blogs. Technical report, Attorney General.

Janyce Wiebe, Theresa Wilson, and Claire Cardie. 2005. Annotating expressions of opinions and emotions in language. *Language Resources and Evaluation*, 1(2):0.

USNA: A Dual-Classifier Approach to Contextual Sentiment Analysis

Ganesh Harihara and **Eugene Yang** and **Nathanael Chambers**
United States Naval Academy
Annapolis, MD 21401, USA
nchamber@usna.edu

Abstract

This paper describes a dual-classifier approach to contextual sentiment analysis at the SemEval-2013 Task 2. Contextual analysis of polarity focuses on a word or phrase, rather than the broader task of identifying the sentiment of an entire text. The Task 2 definition includes target word spans that range in size from a single word to entire sentences. However, the context of a single word is dependent on the word's surrounding syntax, while a phrase contains most of the polarity within itself. We thus describe separate treatment with two independent classifiers, outperforming the accuracy of a single classifier. Our system ranked 6th out of 19 teams on SMS message classification, and 8th of 23 on twitter data. We also show a surprising result that a very small amount of word context is needed for high-performance polarity extraction.

1 Introduction

A variety of approaches to sentiment analysis have been proposed in the literature. Early work sought to identify the general sentiment of entire documents, but a recent shift to social media has provided a large quantity of publicly available data, and private organizations are increasingly interested in how a population "feels" toward its products. Identifying the polarity of language toward a particular topic, however, no longer requires identifying the sentiment of an entire text, but rather the *contextual sentiment* surrounding a target phrase.

Identifying the polarity of text toward a phrase is significantly different from a sentence's overall polarity, as seen in this example from the SemEval-2013 Task 2 (Wilson et al., 2013) training set:

> *I had a severe* ***nosebleed*** *last night.* ***I think my iPad caused it as I was browsing for a few hours on it.*** *Anyhow, its stopped, which is good.*

An ideal sentiment classifier would classify this text as overall positive (the nosebleed stopped!), but this short snippet actually contains three types of polarity (positive, negative, and neutral). The middle sentence about the iPad is not positive, but neutral. The word 'nosebleed' has a very negative polarity in this context, and the phrase 'its stopped' is positive. Someone interested in specific health concerns, such as nosebleeds, needs a contextual classifier to identify the desired polarity in this context.

This example also illustrates how phrases of different sizes require unique handling. Single token phrases, such as 'nosebleed', are highly dependent on the surrounding context for its polarity. However, the polarity of the middle iPad sentence is contained within the phrase itself. The surrounding context is not as important. This paper thus proposes a dual-classifier that trains two separate classifiers, one for single words, and another for phrases. We empirically show that unique features apply to both, and both benefit from independent training. In fact, we show a surprising result that a very small window size is needed for the context of single word phrases. Our system performs well on the SemEval task, placing 8th of 23 systems on twitter text. It also shows strong generalization to SMS text messages, placing 6th of 19.

*Second Joint Conference on Lexical and Computational Semantics (*SEM), Volume 2: Seventh International Workshop on Semantic Evaluation (SemEval 2013)*, pages 390–394, Atlanta, Georgia, June 14-15, 2013.

2 Previous Work

Sentiment analysis is a large field applicable to many genres. This paper focuses on social media (microblogs) and contextual polarity, so we only address the closest work in those areas. For a broader perspective, several survey papers are available (Pang and Lee, 2008; Tang et al., 2009; Liu and Zhang, 2012; Tsytsarau and Palpanas, 2012).

Microblogs serve as a quick way to measure a large population's mood and opinion. Many different sources have been used. O'Connor et al. (2010) used Twitter data to compute a ratio of positive and negative words to measure consumer confidence and presidential approval. Kramer (2010) counted lexicon words on Facebook for a general 'happiness' measure, and Thelwall (2011) built a general sentiment model on MySpace user comments. These are general sentiment algorithms.

Specific work on microblogs has focused on finding noisy training data with distant supervision. Many of these algorithms use emoticons as semantic indicators of polarity. For instance, a tweet that contains a sad face likely contains a negative polarity (Read, 2005; Go et al., 2009; Bifet and Frank, 2010; Pak and Paroubek, 2010; Davidov et al., 2010; Kouloumpis et al., 2011). In a similar vein, hashtags can also serve as noisy labels (Davidov et al., 2010; Kouloumpis et al., 2011). Most work on *distant supervision* relies on a variety of syntactic and word-based features (Marchetti-Bowick and Chambers, 2012). We adopt many of these features.

Supervised learning for *contextual* sentiment analysis has not been thoroughly investigated. Labeled data for specific words or queries is expensive to generate, so Jiang et al. (2011) is one of the few approaches with labeled training data. Earlier work on product reviews sought the sentiment toward particular product features. These systems used rule based approaches based on parts of speech and other surface features (Nasukawa and Yi, 2003; Hu and Liu, 2004; Ding and Liu, 2007).

Finally, topic identification in microblogs is also related. The first approaches are somewhat simple, selecting single keywords (e.g., "Obama") to represent the topic (e.g., "US President"), and retrieve tweets that contain the word (O'Connor et al., 2010; Tumasjan et al., 2010; Tan et al., 2011). These systems then classify the polarity of *the entire tweet*, and ignore the question of polarity toward the particular topic. This paper focuses on the particular keyword or phrase, and identifies the sentiment toward that phrase, not the overall sentiment of the text.

3 Dataset

This paper uses three polarity classes: positive, negative, and neutral. We developed all algorithms on the 'Task A' corpora provided by SemEval-2013 Task 2 (Wilson et al., 2013). Both training and development sets were provided, and an unseen test set was ultimately used to evaluate the final systems. The number of tweets in each set are shown here:

	positive	negative	neutral
training	5348	2817	422
development	648	430	57
test (tweet)	2734	1541	160
test (sms)	1071	1104	159

4 Contextual Sentiment Analysis

Contextual sentiment analysis focuses on the disposition of a certain word or groups of words. Most data-driven approaches rely on a labeled corpus to drive the learning process, and this paper is no different. However, we propose a novel approach to contextual analysis that differentiates between *single words* and *phrases*.

The semantics of a single word in context from that of a phrase are fundamentally different. Since one word will have multiple contexts and is heavily influenced by the surrounding words, more consideration is given to adjacent words. A phrase often carries its own semantics, so has less variability in its meaning based on its context. Context is still important, but we propose separate classifiers in order to learn weights unique to tokens and phrases. The following describes the two unique feature sets. We trained a Maximum Entropy classifier for each set.

4.1 Text Pre-Processing

All text is lowercased, and twitter usernames (e.g., *@user*) and URLs are replaced with placeholder tokens. The text is then split on whitespace. We also prepend the occurrence of token "not" to the subsequent token, merging the two (e.g., "not happy" becomes "not-happy"). We also found that removing prefix and affix punctuation from each token, and storing the punctuation for later use in punctuation features boosts performance. These cleaned tokens are the input to the features described below.

4.2 Single Word Sentiment Analysis

Assigning polarity to a single word mainly requires features that accurately capture the surrounding context. In fact, many single words do no carry any polarity in isolation, but solely require context. Take the following two examples:

> ***Justin*** *LOVE YA so excited for the concert in october MEXICO LOVES YOU*
>
> *Im not getting on twitter tomorrow because all my TL will consist of is a bunch of girls talking about* ***Justin*** *Beiber*

In these examples, Justin is the name of a singer who does not carry an initial polarity. The first tweet is clearly positive toward him, while the second is not. Our single-token classifier used the following set of features to capture these different contexts:

Target Token: The first features are the unigram and bigram ending with the target token. We attach a unique string to each to distinguish it from the text's other n-grams. We also include a feature for any punctuation that was attached to the end of the token (e.g., 'Justin!' generates '!' as a feature).

Target Patterns: This feature generalizes the n-grams that include the target word. It replaces the target word with a variable in an effort to capture general patterns that indicate sentiment. For instance, using the first tweet above, we add the trigram '*<s> __ LOVE*' and two bigrams, '*<s> __*' and '*__ LOVE*'.

Unigrams, Bigrams, Trigrams: We include all other n-grams in the text within a window of size n from the target token.

Dictionary Matching: We have two binary features, *postivemood* and *negativemood*, that indicate if any word in the text appears in a sentiment lexicon's positive or negative list. We use Bing Liu's Opinion Lexicon[1].

[1] http://www.cs.uic.edu/~liub/FBS/sentiment-analysis.html\#lexicon

Punctuation Features: We included a binary feature for the presence or absence of exclamation marks anywhere in the text. Further, we generate a feature for punctuation at the end of the text.

Emoticons: We included two binary features for the presence or absence of a smiley face and sad face emoticon.

4.3 Phrasal Sentiment Analysis

We adopted several single word features for use in phrases, including punctuation, dictionary matching, and emoticons. However, since phrasal analysis is often less dependent on context and more dependent on the phrase itself, we altered the n-gram features to be unique to the phrase. The following features are solely used for target phrases, not single words:

Unigrams, Bigrams, Trigrams: We include all n-grams *in the target phrase* only. This differs from the single token features that included n-grams from a surrounding window.

Phrasal Punctuation: If the *target phrase* ends with any type of punctuation, we include it as a feature.

5 Experiments

Initial model design and feature tuning was conducted on the SemEval-2013 Task 2 training set for training, and its dev set for evaluation. We split the data into two parts: tweets with single word targets, and tweets with target phrases. We trained two MaxEnt classifiers using the Stanford JavaNLP toolkit[2]. Each datum in the test set is labeled using the appropriate classifier based on the target phrase's length.

The first experiments are ablation over the features described in Section 4, separately improving the single token and phrasal classifiers. Results are reported in Table 1 using simple accuracy on the development set. We initially do not split off punctuation, and use only unigram features for phrases. The window size is initally infinite (i.e., the entire text is used for n-grams). Bigrams and trigrams hurt performance and are not shown. Reducing the window size to a single token (ignore the entire tweet) increased performance by 1.2%, and stripping punctuation off tokens by another 1.9%. The perfor-

[2] http://nlp.stanford.edu/software/index.shtml

Single Token Features

Just Unigrams	70.5
+ Target Token Patterns	70.4
+ Sentiment Lexicon	71.5
+ Target Token N-Grams	73.3
+ EOS punctuation	73.2
+ Emoticons	73.3
Set Window Size = 1	74.5
Strip punctuation off tokens	76.4

Phrasal Features

Just Unigrams	76.4
+ Emoticons	76.3
+ EOS punctuation	76.6
+ Exclamation Marks	76.5
+ Sentiment Lexicon	77.7

Table 1: Feature ablation in order. Single token features begin with unigrams only, holding phrasal features constant at unigrams only. The phrasal table picks up where the single token table finishes. Each row uses all features added in previous rows.

Dual-Classifier Comparison

Single Classifier	76.6%
Dual-Classifier	77.7%

Table 2: Performance increase from splitting into two classifiers. Accuracy reported on the development set.

mance increase with phrasal features is 1.3% absolute, whereas token features contributed 5.9%.

After choosing the optimum set of features based on ablation, we then retrained the classifiers on both the training and development sets as one large training corpus. The SemEval-2013 Task 2 competition included two datasets for testing: tweets and SMS messages. Official results for both are given in Table 3 using the F1 measure.

Finally, we compare our dual-classifier to a single standard classifier. We use the same features used in Table 1, train on the training set, and report accuracy on the development set. See Table 2. Our dual classifier improves relative accuracy by 1.4%.

6 Discussion

One of the main surprises from our experiments was that a large portion of text could be ignored without hurting classification performance. We reduced

Twitter Dataset

	F1 Score
Top System (1st)	88.9
This Paper (8th)	**81.3**
Majority Baseline (20th)	61.6
Bottom System (24th)	34.7

SMS Dataset

	F1 Score
Top System (1st)	88.4
This Paper (6th)	**79.8**
Majority Baseline (19th)	47.3
Min System (20th)	36.4

Table 3: Performance on Twitter and SMS Data.

the window size in which n-grams are extracted to size one, and performance actually increases 1.2%. At least for single word target phrases, including n-grams of the entire tweet/sms is not helpful. We only used n-gram patterns that included the token and its two immediate neighbors. A nice side benefit is that the classifier contains fewer features, and trains faster as a result.

The decision to use two separate classifiers helped performance, improving by 1.4% relative accuracy on the development set. The decision was motivated by the observation that the polarity of a token is dependent on its surrounding context, but a longer phrase is dependent more on its internal syntax. This allowed us to make finer-grained feature decisions, and the feature ablation experiments suggest our observation to be true. Better feature weights are ultimately learned for the unique tasks.

Finally, the feature ablation experiments revealed a few key takeaways for feature engineering: bigrams and trigrams hurt classification, using a window size is better than the entire text, and punctuation should always be split off tokens. Further, a sentiment lexicon reliably improves both token and phrasal classification.

Opportunities for future work on contextual analysis exist in further analysis of the feature window size. Why doesn't more context help token classification? Do n-grams simply lack the deeper semantics needed, or are these supervised algorithms still suffering from sparse training data? Better sentence and phrase detection may be a fruitful focus.

References

Albert Bifet and Eibe Frank. 2010. Sentiment knowledge discovery in twitter streaming data. In *Lecture Notes in Computer Science*, volume 6332, pages 1–15.

Dmitry Davidov, Oren Tsur, and Ari Rappoport. 2010. Enhanced sentiment learning using twitter hashtags and smileys. In *Proceedings of the 23rd International Conference on Computational Linguistics (COLING 2010)*.

Xiaowen Ding and Bing Liu. 2007. The utility of linguistic rules in opinion mining. In *Proceedings of SIGIR-2007*, pages 23–27.

Alec Go, Richa Bhayani, and Lei Huang. 2009. Twitter sentiment classification using distant supervision. Technical report.

Minqing Hu and Bing Liu. 2004. Mining and summarizing customer reviews. In *Proceedings of the ACM SIGKDD International Conference on Knowledge Discovery and Data Mining*.

Long Jiang, Mo Yu, Ming Zhou, Xiaohua Liu, and Tiejun Zhao. 2011. Target-dependent twitter sentiment classification. In *Proceedings of the Association for Computational Linguistics (ACL-2011)*.

Efthymios Kouloumpis, Theresa Wilson, and Johanna Moore. 2011. Twitter sentiment analysis: The good the bad and the omg! In *Proceedings of the Fifth International AAAI Conference on Weblogs and Social Media*.

Adam D. I. Kramer. 2010. An unobtrusive behavioral model of 'gross national happiness'. In *Proceedings of the 28th International Conference on Human Factors in Computing Systems (CHI 2010)*.

Bing Liu and Lei Zhang. 2012. A survey of opinion mining and sentiment analysis. *Mining Text Data*, pages 415–463.

Micol Marchetti-Bowick and Nathanael Chambers. 2012. Learning for microblogs with distant supervision: Political forecasting with twitter. In *Proceedings of the 13th Conference of the European Chapter of the Association for Computational Linguistics*.

Tetsuya Nasukawa and Jeonghee Yi. 2003. Sentiment analysis: capturing favorability using natural language processing. In *Proceedings of K-CAP*.

Brendan O'Connor, Ramnath Balasubramanyan, Bryan R. Routledge, and Noah A. Smith. 2010. From tweets to polls: Linking text sentiment to public opinion time series. In *Proceedings of the AAAI Conference on Weblogs and Social Media*.

Alexander Pak and Patrick Paroubek. 2010. Twitter as a corpus for sentiment analysis and opinion mining. In *Proceedings of the Seventh International Conference On Language Resources and Evaluation (LREC)*.

B. Pang and L. Lee. 2008. Opinion mining and sentiment analysis. *Foundations and Trends in Information Retrieval*.

Jonathon Read. 2005. Using emoticons to reduce dependency in machine learning techniques for sentiment classification. In *Proceedings of the ACL Student Research Workshop (ACL-2005)*.

Chenhao Tan, Lillian Lee, Jie Tang, Long Jiang, Ming Zhou, and Ping Li. 2011. User-level sentiment analysis incorporating social networks. In *Proceedings of the 17th ACM SIGKDD Conference on Knowledge Discovery and Data Mining*.

H. Tang, S. Tan, and X. Cheng. 2009. A survey on sentiment detection of reviews. *Expert Systems with Applications*.

Mike Thelwall, Kevan Buckley, and Georgios Paltoglou. 2011. Sentiment in twitter events. *Journal of the American Society for Information Science and Technology*, 62(2):406–418.

M. Tsytsarau and T. Palpanas. 2012. Survey on mining subjective data on the web. *Data Mining and Knowledge Discovery Journal*, 24(3):478–514.

Andranik Tumasjan, Timm O. Sprenger, Philipp G. Sandner, and Isabell M. Welpe. 2010. Election forecasts with twitter: How 140 characters reflect the political landscape. *Social Science Computer Review*.

Theresa Wilson, Zornitsa Kozareva, Preslav Nakov, Alan Ritter, Sara Rosenthal, and Veselin Stoyanov. 2013. Semeval-2013 task 2: Sentiment analysis in twitter. In *Proceedings of the 7th International Workshop on Semantic Evaluation*. Association for Computational Linguistics.

KLUE: Simple and robust methods for polarity classification

Thomas Proisl and **Paul Greiner** and **Stefan Evert** and **Besim Kabashi**
Friedrich-Alexander-Universität Erlangen-Nürnberg
Department Germanistik und Komparatistik
Professur für Korpuslinguistik
Bismarckstr. 6
91054 Erlangen, Germany
{thomas.proisl,paul.greiner,stefan.evert,besim.kabashi}@fau.de

Abstract

This paper describes our approach to the SemEval-2013 task on "Sentiment Analysis in Twitter". We use simple bag-of-words models, a freely available sentiment dictionary automatically extended with distributionally similar terms, as well as lists of emoticons and internet slang abbreviations in conjunction with fast and robust machine learning algorithms. The resulting system is resource-lean, making it relatively independent of a specific language. Despite its simplicity, the system achieves competitive accuracies of 0.70–0.72 in detecting the sentiment of text messages. We also apply our approach to the task of detecting the context-dependent sentiment of individual words and phrases within a message.

1 Introduction

The SemEval-2013 task on "Sentiment Analysis in Twitter" (Wilson et al., 2013) focuses on polarity classification, i. e. the problem of determining whether a textual unit, e. g. a document, paragraph, sentence or phrase, expresses a positive, negative or neutral sentiment (for a review of research topics and recent developments in the field of sentiment analysis see Liu (2012)). There are two subtasks: in task B, "Message Polarity Classification", whole messages have to be classified as being of positive, negative or neutral sentiment; in task A, "Contextual Polarity Disambiguation", a marked instance of a word or phrase has to be classified in the context of a whole message.

The training data for task B consist of approximately 10 200 manually annotated Twitter messages, the training data for task A of approximately 9 500 marked instances in approximately 6 300 Twitter messages.[1] The test data consist of in-domain Twitter messages (3 813 messages for task B and 4 435 marked instances in 2 826 messages for task A) and out-of-domain SMS text messages (2 094 messages for task B, 2 334 marked instances in 1 437 messages for task A). The distribution of messages and marked instances over sentiment categories in the training and test sets is shown in Tab. 1.

	pos	neg	neu	total
train-B	3 783	1 600	4 832	10 215
test-B Twitter	1 572	601	1 640	3 813
test-B SMS	492	394	1 208	2 094
train-A	5 862	3 166	463	9 491
test-A Twitter	2 734	1 541	160	4 435
test-A SMS	1 071	1 104	159	2 334

Table 1: The data sets for both tasks

The main focus of the current paper lies on experimenting with resource-lean and robust methods for task B, the classification of whole messages. We do, however, apply our approach also to task A.

2 Features used for polarity classification

Our general approach is quite simple: we extract feature vectors from the training data (based on the

[1] These figures indicate the amount of training data we were actually able to use. Due to Twitter's licensing conditions, the training data could only be made available as a collection of IDs. Even when using the official Twitter API for collecting the actual messages rather than the screen-scraping approach suggested by the task organizers, ca. 10% of the data were not (or no longer) available.

*Second Joint Conference on Lexical and Computational Semantics (*SEM), Volume 2: Seventh International Workshop on Semantic Evaluation (SemEval 2013)*, pages 395–401, Atlanta, Georgia, June 14-15, 2013.

original messages and a small number of additional resources) and feed them into fast and robust supervised machine learning algorithms implemented in the Python machine learning library scikit-learn (Pedregosa et al., 2011). For task B, the features are computed on the basis of the whole message; for task A, we use essentially the same features, but compute them once for the marked word or phrase and once for the rest of the message. All the features we use are described in some more detail in the following subsections.

2.1 Bag of words

We experimented with three different sets of bag-of-words features: unigrams, unigrams and bigrams, and an extended unigram model that includes a simple treatment of negation. For all three models we simply use the word frequencies as feature weights.

Our preprocessing pipeline starts with a simple preliminary tokenization step (lowercasing the whole message and splitting it on whitespace). In the resulting list of tokens, all user IDs and web URLs are replaced with placeholders.[2] Any remaining punctuation is stripped from the tokens and empty tokens are deleted. In the extended unigram model, up to three tokens following a negation marker are then prefixed with `not_` (fewer tokens if another negation marker or the end of the message is reached). Finally all words are stemmed using the Snowball stemmer.[3]

For a token unigram or bigram to be included in the bag of words models, it has to occur in at least five messages.

As an additional feature we include the total number of tokens per message.

2.2 Features based on a sentiment dictionary

Widely-used algorithms such as SentiStrength (Thelwall et al., 2010) rely heavily on dictionaries containing sentiment ratings of words and/or phrases. We use features based on an extended version of AFINN-111 (Nielsen, 2011).[4]

The AFINN sentiment dictionary contains sentiment ratings ranging from -5 (very negative) to 5 (very positive) for 2 476 word forms. In order to obtain a better coverage, we extended the dictionary with distributionally similar words. For this purpose, large-vocabulary distributional semantic models (DSM) were constructed from a version of the English Wikipedia[5] and the Google Web 1T 5-Grams database (Brants and Franz, 2006). The Wikipedia DSM consists of 122 281 case-folded word forms as target terms and 30 484 mid-frequency content words (lemmatised) as feature terms; the Web1T5 DSM of 241 583 case-folded word forms as target terms and 100 063 case-folded word forms as feature terms. Both DSMs use a context window of two words to the left and right, and were reduced to 300 latent dimensions using randomized singular value decomposition (Halko et al., 2009).

For each AFINN entry, the 30 nearest neighbours according to each DSM were considered as extension candidates. Sentiment ratings for the new candidates were computed by averaging over the 30 nearest neighbours of the respective candidate term (with scores set to 0 for all neighbours not listed in AFINN), and rescaling to the range $[-5,5]$.[6] After some initial experiments, only candidates with a computed rating ≤ -2.5 or ≥ 2.5 were retained, resulting in an extended dictionary of 2 820 word forms.

As with the bag of words model, we make use of a simple heuristic treatment of negation: following a negation marker, the polarity of the next sentiment-carrying token up to a distance of at most four tokens is multiplied by -1.

The sentiment dictionary is used to extract four features: I) the number of tokens that express a positive sentiment, II) the number of tokens that express a negative sentiment, III) the total number of tokens that express a sentiment according to our sentiment dictionary and IV) the arithmetic mean of all the sentiment scores from the sentiment dictionary in the message.

[2] The regular expression for matching web URLs has been taken from `http://daringfireball.net/2010/07/improved_regex_for_matching_urls`.

[3] `http://snowball.tartarus.org/`

[4] `http://www2.imm.dtu.dk/pubdb/p.php?6010`

[5] We used the pre-processed and linguistically annotated Wackypedia corpus available from `http://wacky.sslmit.unibo.it/`.

[6] Scaling coefficients were determined by regression on extension candidates that were already listed in AFINN.

2.3 Features based on emoticons and internet slang abbreviations

In addition to the sentiment dictionary we use a list of 212 emoticons and 95 internet slang abbreviations from Wikipedia. We manually classified these 307 emotion markers as negative (−1), neutral (0) or positive (1).

The extracted features based on this list are similar to the ones based on the sentiment dictionary. We use I) the number of positive emotion markers, II) the number of negative emotion markers, III) the total number of emotion markers and IV) the arithmetic mean of all the emotion markers in the message.

3 Experiments

In this section we evaluate different classifiers (multinomial Naive Bayes,[7] Linear SVM[8] and Maximum Entropy[9]) and various combinations of features on the gold test sets. We vary the bag-of-words model (bow), the use of AFINN (sent), our extensions to the sentiment dictionary (ext) and the list of emotion markers (emo). To present as clear a picture of the classifiers' performances as possible, we report F-scores for each of the three classes, the weighted average of all three F-scores (F_w), the (unweighted) average of the positive and negative F-scores ($F_{pos+neg}$; this is the value shown in the official task results and used for ranking systems), as well as accuracy.

Results for submitted systems are typeset in italics, the best results in each column are typeset in bold font.

3.1 Task B: Message Polarity Classification

Experiments with just a simple unigram bag-of-words model show that for both the Twitter (Tab. 3) and the SMS data (Tab. 4) the Maximum Entropy classifier outperforms multinomial Naive Bayes and Linear SVM by a considerable margin. For comparison, we also include some weak baselines (Tab. 2). The random baselines classify messages randomly,[10] the majority baselines simply assign all messages to the most frequent category in the training data.[11] As one would expect, all three learning algorithms are vastly superior to those baselines. Using both unigrams and bigrams in the bag-of-words model improves classifier peformance; so does the extended unigram model with negations.

For the Twitter data, adding the sentiment dictionary, the dictionary extensions and the list of emotion markers further improves classifier performance, with the best results being achieved by a combination of all these features with a uni- and bigram bag-of-words model. The best combination of features would have been the fourth best system out of 35 constrained systems (sixth best out of all 51 systems), one rank higher than our task submission.[12]

For the SMS data, adding the sentiment dictionary and the dictionary extensions seems to improve the official score $F_{pos+neg}$, but slightly decreases weighted average F-score and accuracy. This might be due to the greater orthographical variation in SMS texts. Emotion markers seem to be a much better sentiment indicator in the SMS data. But while just combining the list of emotion markers with the extended unigram bag-of-words model leads to the best weighted average F-score and accuracy, $F_{pos+neg}$ is best when a combination of all features is used. This is also the system we submitted, being the third best system (out of 44) for that task.

3.2 Task A: Contextual Polarity Disambiguation

The results for task A are similar to those for task B in that Maximum Entropy is the best classifier for the unigram bag-of-words model for both the Twitter (Tab. 5) and the SMS data (Tab. 6). Adding negation treatment to the bag-of-words model increases classifier performance, as do the inclusion of AFINN and the use of emotion markers. Interestingly, extending the sentiment dictionary based on distributional similarity leads to slightly worse results. Therefore,

[7] We always use the default setting `alpha = 1.0`.

[8] In all experiments, we use the following parameters: `penalty = 'l1', dual = False, C = 1.0`.

[9] We use the following parameter settings in our experiments: `penalty = 'l1', C = 1.0`.

[10] $random_{uniform}$ assumes a uniform probability distribution (all categories have equal probabilities), $random_{weighted}$ has learned the probability distribution from the training data, $random_{weighted,binary}$ uses the same probability distribution but classifies messages only as either positive or negative.

[11] majority classifies all messages as neutral, as this is the most frequent category in the training data, $majority_{binary}$ does binary classification and thus classifies all messages as positive.

[12] Evaluation results for all SemEval-2013 tasks are available online: `http://www.cs.york.ac.uk/semeval-2013/index.php?id=evaluation-results`.

classifier	F_{pos}	F_{neg}	F_{neu}	F_w	$F_{pos+neg}$	Acc
$random_{uniform}$	0.3666	**0.2128**	0.3745	0.3458	0.2897	0.3318
$random_{weighted}$	0.3912	0.1681	0.4521	**0.3820**	0.2796	0.3835
$random_{weighted,binary}$	0.5186	0.2042	0.000	0.2460	**0.3614**	0.3349
majority	0.0000	0.0000	**0.6015**	0.2587	0.0000	**0.4301**
$majority_{binary}$	**0.5838**	0.0000	0.0000	0.2407	0.2919	0.4123

Table 2: Some weak baselines for task B, Twitter test set

classifier	bow	sent	ext	emo	F_{pos}	F_{neg}	F_{neu}	F_w	$F_{pos+neg}$	Acc
Multin. NB	uni	-	-	-	0.6355	0.5093	0.6898	0.6390	0.5724	0.6423
LinearSVM	uni	-	-	-	0.6412	0.4884	0.6876	0.6371	0.5648	0.6418
MaxEnt	uni	-	-	-	0.6705	0.5109	0.7212	0.6671	0.5907	0.6761
MaxEnt	uni+bi	-	-	-	0.6845	0.5192	0.7257	0.6762	0.6019	0.6845
MaxEnt	uni_{neg}	-	-	-	0.6797	0.5284	0.7242	0.6750	0.6041	0.6824
MaxEnt	uni_{neg}	+	-	-	0.6860	0.5661	0.7284	0.6854	0.6261	0.6911
MaxEnt	uni_{neg}	-	-	+	0.6807	0.5393	0.7229	0.6766	0.6100	0.6835
MaxEnt	uni_{neg}	+	+	-	0.6841	0.5529	0.7258	0.6814	0.6185	0.6874
MaxEnt	uni_{neg}	+	+	+	*0.6963*	*0.5650*	*0.7325*	*0.6912*	*0.6306*	*0.6968*
MaxEnt	uni_{neg}	+	-	+	0.6952	**0.5753**	0.7338	0.6929	0.6353	0.6984
MaxEnt	uni+bi	+	-	+	0.7034	0.5706	0.7358	0.6964	0.6370	0.7018
MaxEnt	uni+bi	+	+	+	**0.7052**	0.5720	**0.7371**	**0.6979**	**0.6386**	**0.7031**
MaxEnt	-	+	+	+	0.6920	0.3532	0.6533	0.6220	0.5226	0.6370

Table 3: Evaluation results for task B on the Twitter test set

classifier	bow	sent	ext	emo	F_{pos}	F_{neg}	F_{neu}	F_w	$F_{pos+neg}$	Acc
Multin. NB	uni	-	-	-	0.4918	0.4773	0.5541	0.5250	0.4845	0.5153
LinearSVM	uni	-	-	-	0.5833	0.5046	0.7229	0.6490	0.5440	0.6442
MaxEnt	uni	-	-	-	0.6260	0.5015	0.7903	0.6974	0.5638	0.7015
MaxEnt	uni+bi	-	-	-	0.6003	0.5380	0.7658	0.6840	0.5692	0.6829
MaxEnt	uni_{neg}	-	-	-	0.6528	0.5412	0.7884	0.7100	0.5970	0.7125
MaxEnt	uni_{neg}	+	-	-	0.6399	**0.5955**	0.7744	0.7092	0.6177	0.7073
MaxEnt	uni_{neg}	-	-	+	**0.6596**	0.5507	**0.8033**	**0.7220**	0.6052	**0.7259**
MaxEnt	uni_{neg}	+	+	-	0.6374	0.5905	0.7731	0.7068	0.6140	0.7049
MaxEnt	uni_{neg}	+	+	+	*0.6506*	*0.5900*	*0.7903*	*0.7198*	***0.6203***	*0.7197*
MaxEnt	uni_{neg}	+	-	+	0.6556	0.5833	0.7908	0.7200	0.6195	0.7202
MaxEnt	uni+bi	+	-	+	0.6318	0.5896	0.7750	0.7064	0.6107	0.7044
MaxEnt	uni+bi	+	+	+	0.6341	0.5783	0.7746	0.7047	0.6062	0.7030
MaxEnt	-	+	+	+	0.5961	0.3421	0.7179	0.6186	0.4691	0.6342

Table 4: Evaluation results for task B on the SMS test set

classifier	bow	sent	ext	emo	F_{pos}	F_{neg}	F_{neu}	F_w	$F_{pos+neg}$	Acc
Multin. NB	uni	-	-	-	0.7799	0.6164	0.0498	0.6967	0.6981	0.7067
LinearSVM	uni	-	-	-	0.7759	0.6046	0.0576	0.6905	0.6902	0.6949
MaxEnt	uni	-	-	-	0.7974	0.6155	0.0110	0.7059	0.7065	0.7218
MaxEnt	uni+bi	-	-	-	0.8071	0.6320	0.0222	0.7179	0.7195	0.7335
MaxEnt	uni_{neg}	-	-	-	0.8058	0.6380	0.0110	0.7188	0.7219	0.7342
MaxEnt	uni_{neg}	+	-	-	**0.8160**	0.6610	0.0317	0.7339	0.7385	0.7479
MaxEnt	uni_{neg}	+	+	-	0.8153	0.6583	0.0316	0.7325	0.7368	0.7466
MaxEnt	uni_{neg}	+	+	+	*0.8141*	*0.6608*	*0.0330*	*0.7326*	*0.7374*	*0.7468*
MaxEnt	uni_{neg}	+	-	+	0.8153	**0.6664**	**0.0331**	**0.7353**	**0.7409**	**0.7493**

Table 5: Evaluation results for task A on the Twitter test set

classifier	bow	sent	ext	emo	F_{pos}	F_{neg}	F_{neu}	F_w	$F_{pos+neg}$	Acc
Multin. NB	uni	-	-	-	0.6766	0.6657	0.0213	0.6268	0.6712	0.6452
LinearSVM	uni	-	-	-	0.6628	0.6533	0.0365	0.6157	0.6581	0.6290
MaxEnt	uni	-	-	-	0.6829	0.6630	0.0117	0.6277	0.6729	0.6491
MaxEnt	uni+bi	-	-	-	0.6825	0.6504	0.0230	0.6224	0.6665	0.6435
MaxEnt	uni_{neg}	-	-	-	0.7008	0.6770	0.0120	0.6427	0.6889	0.6654
MaxEnt	uni_{neg}	+	-	-	**0.7127**	0.6962	**0.0238**	0.6579	0.7044	0.6804
MaxEnt	uni_{neg}	+	+	-	0.7108	0.6954	**0.0238**	0.6568	0.7031	0.6791
MaxEnt	uni_{neg}	+	+	+	*0.7090*	*0.7017*	*0.0237*	*0.6589*	*0.7054*	*0.6808*
MaxEnt	uni_{neg}	+	-	+	0.7114	**0.7034**	**0.0238**	**0.6608**	**0.7074**	**0.6829**

Table 6: Evaluation results for task A on the SMS test set

we could have improved upon our task submission by excluding the sentiment dictionary extensions – however, the gains are very small and the system's ranks would still be the same (17/28 for the Twitter data, 16/26 for the SMS data).

		predicted					
		pos		neg		neu	
gold	pos	979	352	70	40	523	100
	neg	70	47	287	213	244	134
	neu	191	191	58	75	1391	942

Table 7: Task B, confusion matrix for tweets/SMS

4 Discussion

4.1 Error analysis

4.1.1 Task B: Message Polarity Classification

The most prominent problem, according to the confusion matrix in Tab. 7, is that a lot of negative messages are classified as neutral; the same problem exists to a lesser extent for positive messages.

A qualitative analysis of mis-classified messages for which the MaxEnt classifier indicated high confidence suggests that the human annotators did not clearly distinguish between sentiment expressed by the authors of messages and their own response to message content. For example, the messages shown in (1) and (2) report a negative and positive event, respectively, in a neutral way and should therefore be annotated with neutral sentiment. However, in the test data they are labelled as negative and positive by the human annotators.

(1) MT @LccSy #Syria, Deir Ezzor | Marba'eh: Aerial shelling dropped explosive barrels on residential buildings in the town. Tue, 23 October.

(2) European Exchanges open with a slight rise: (AGI) Rome, October 24 - European Exchanges opened with a slight ris... http://t.co/mAljf6eT

This problem is probably a major factor in the misclassification of many negative and positive messages as neutral. In order to better reproduce the human annotations, the system would additionally have to decide whether a reported event is of a negative, positive or neutral nature *per se* – a quite different task that would require external training data and world knowledge.

An analysis of mis-classified positive messages further suggests that certain punctuation marks, especially multiple exclamation marks, might be useful as additional features.

4.1.2 Task A: Contextual Polarity Disambiguation

The confusion matrix in Tab. 8 shows that messages marked as negative in the test data often misclassified as positive and vice versa, while neutral instances are overwhelmingly classified as positive or negative. This suggests that for the classifiers we use, there might be too few neutral instances in the training data (cf. Tab. 1).

		predicted					
		pos		neg		neu	
gold	pos	2329	826	397	239	8	6
	neg	550	341	980	761	11	2
	neu	109	92	48	65	3	2

Table 8: Task A, confusion matrix for tweets/SMS

4.2 Conclusion and future work

We use a resource-lean approach, relying only on three external resources: a stemmer, a relatively small sentiment dictionary and an even smaller list of emotion markers. Stemmers are already available for many languages and both kinds of lexical resources can be gathered relatively easily for other languages. The list of emotion markers should apply to most languages. This makes our whole system relatively language-independent, provided that a similar amount of manually labelled training data is available.[13] In fact, the learning curve for our system (Fig. 1) suggests that even as few as 3 000–3 500 labelled messages might be sufficient. The similar

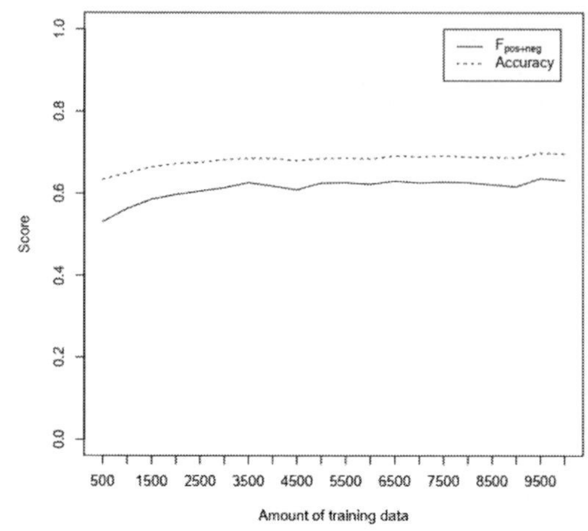

Figure 1: Learning curve of our system for the "Message Polarity Classification" task, evaluated on the Twitter data

evaluation results for the Twitter and the SMS data show that not relying on Twitter-specific features like hashtags pays off: by making our system as generic as possible, it is robust, not overfitted to the training data, and generalizes well to other types of data. The methods discussed in the current paper are particularly well suited to the "Message Polarity Classification" task, our system ranking amongst the best. It turns out, however, that simply applying the same approach to the "Contextual Polarity Disambiguation" task yields only mediocre results.

In the future, we would like to experiment with a couple of additional features. Determining the nearest neighbors of a message based on Latent Semantic Analysis might be a useful addition, as might be the use of part-of-speech tags created by an in-domain POS tagger (Gimpel et al., 2011)[14]. We would also like to find out whether a heuristic treatment of intensifiers and detensifiers, the normalization of character repetitions, or the inclusion of some punctuation-based features could further improve classifier performance.

[13]For task B, even the extended unigram bag-of-words model by itself, without any additional resources, would have performed quite well as the 9th best constrained system on the Twitter test set (13th best system overall) and the 5th best system on the SMS test set.

[14]`http://www.ark.cs.cmu.edu/TweetNLP/`

References

Thorsten Brants and Alex Franz. 2006. *Web 1T 5-gram Version 1*. Linguistic Data Consortium, Philadelphia, PA.

Kevin Gimpel, Nathan Schneider, Brendan O'Connor, Dipanjan Das, Daniel Mills, Jacob Eisenstein, Michael Heilman, Dani Yogatama, Jeffrey Flanigan, and Noah A. Smith. 2011. Part-of-speech tagging for Twitter: Annotation, features, and experiments. In *Proceedings of the 49th Annual Meeting of the Association for Computational Linguistics*, pages 42–47, Portland, Oregon. Association for Computational Linguistics.

N. Halko, P. G. Martinsson, and J. A. Tropp. 2009. Finding structure with randomness: Stochastic algorithms for constructing approximate matrix decompositions. Technical Report 2009-05, ACM, California Institute of Technology, September.

Bing Liu. 2012. *Sentiment Analysis and Opinion Mining*. Synthesis Lectures on Human Language Technologies. Morgan & Claypool.

Finn Årup Nielsen. 2011. A new ANEW: Evaluation of a word list for sentiment analysis in microblogs. In *Proceedings of the ESWC2011 Workshop on 'Making Sense of Microposts': Big things come in small packages*, number 718 in CEUR Workshop Proceedings, pages 93–98, Heraklion.

F. Pedregosa, G. Varoquaux, A. Gramfort, V. Michel, B. Thirion, O. Grisel, M. Blondel, P. Prettenhofer, R. Weiss, V. Dubourg, J. Vanderplas, A. Passos, D. Cournapeau, M. Brucher, M. Perrot, and E. Duchesnay. 2011. Scikit-learn: Machine learning in Python. *Journal of Machine Learning Research*, 12:2825–2830.

Mike Thelwall, Kevan Buckley, Georgios Paltoglou, Di Cai, and Arvid Kappas. 2010. Sentiment in short strength detection informal text. *Journal of the American Society for Information Science and Technology*, 61(12):2544–2558.

Theresa Wilson, Zornitsa Kozareva, Preslav Nakov, Alan Ritter, Sara Rosenthal, and Veselin Stoyanov. 2013. SemEval-2013 task 2: Sentiment analysis in Twitter. In *Proceedings of the 7th International Workshop on Semantic Evaluation (SemEval 2013)*. Association for Computational Linguistics.

SINAI: Machine Learning and Emotion of the Crowd for Sentiment Analysis in Microblogs

E. Martínez-Cámara
SINAI research group
University of Jaén
E-23071, Jaén (Spain)
emcamara@ujaen.es

A. Montejo-Ráez
SINAI research group
University of Jaén
E-23071, Jaén (Spain)
amontejo@ujaen.es

M. T. Martín-Valdivia
SINAI research group
University of Jaén
E-23071, Jaén (Spain)
maite@ujaen.es

L. A. Ureña-López
SINAI research group
University of Jaén
E-23071, Jaén (Spain)
laurena@ujaen.es

Abstract

This paper describes the participation of the SINAI research group in the 2013 edition of the International Workshop SemEval. The SINAI research group has submitted two systems, which cover the two main approaches in the field of sentiment analysis: supervised and unsupervised.

1 Introduction

In the last years, the sentiment analysis (SA) research community wants to go one step further, which consists in studying different texts that usually can be found in commerce websites or opinions websites. Currently, the users publish their opinions through other platforms, being one of the most important the microblogging platform Twitter[1]. Thus, the SA research community is focused on the study of opinions that users publish through Twitter. This interest is shown in several workshops focused on the study of SA in Twitter:

1. RepLab 2012 at CLEF[2] (Amigó et al., 2012): Competition carried out within the CLEF conference, where the participants had to develop a system for measuring the reputation of commercial brands.
2. TASS 2012 at SEPLN[3](Villena-Román et al., 2013): Satellite event of the SEPLN 2012 Conference to foster the research in the field of SA in social media, specifically focused on the Spanish language.

In this paper is described the participation of the SINAI[4] research group in the second task of the 2013 edition of the International Workshop SemEval (Wilson et al., 2013). We have submitted two systems (constrained and unconstrained). The constrained system follows a supervised approach, while the unconstrained system is based on an unsupervised approach which used two linguistic resources: the Sentiment Analysis Lexicon[5] (Hu and Liu, 2004) and WeFeelFine[6] (Kamvar and Harris, 2011).

The paper is organized as follows: first we present a description of the preparing data process. Then the constrained system is outlined. The participation overview finishes with the description of the unconstrained system.

2 Preparing data

The organizers provided two sets of data, one for training and another for the development. The data was concerned by a set of identification number of tweets with their corresponding polarity label. We used the script provided by the organizers to download the two sets of tweets.

[1] http://twitter.com

[2] http://limosine-project.eu/events/replab2012

[3] http://www.daedalus.es/TASS/

[4] http://sinai.ujaen.es

[5] http://www.cs.uic.edu/~liub/FBS/opinion-lexicon-English.rar

[6] http://wefeelfine.org

*Second Joint Conference on Lexical and Computational Semantics (*SEM), Volume 2: Seventh International Workshop on Semantic Evaluation (SemEval 2013)*, pages 402–407, Atlanta, Georgia, June 14-15, 2013.

The python script was no able to download all the tweets. The training set was composed by 8,633 tweets and the development set by 1,053 tweets.

The data preparation is a step in the workflow of most data mining tasks. Also, in Natural Language Processing is usual the preparation of the documents or the texts for their further processing. Internet is usually the source of texts for SA tasks, so the application of a specific processing to those texts with the aim of extracting their polarity is recommended. The texts published in Twitter have several issues that must be resolved before processing them:

1. The linguistic style of tweets is usually informal, with a intensive usage of abbreviations, idioms, and jargon.

2. The users do not care about the correct use of grammar, which increases the difficulty of carrying out a linguistic analysis.

3. Because the maximum length of a tweet is 140 characters, the users normally refer to the same concept with a large variety of short and irregular forms. This problems is known as data sparsity, and it is a challenge for the sentiment-topic task.

4. The lack of context, which makes difficult to extract the semantics of these sort pieces of text.

Before applying a cleaning process to the corpus with the aim of overcoming the issues described above, we have studied the different kinds of marks, like emoticons, question and exclamation marks or hashtags in the tweets.

Regarding the issues listed above and the marks in the tweets, we have carried out a cleaning and a normalization process which imply the following operations:

1. The uppercase characters have been exchanged by lowercase characters.

2. Links have been replaced by the token "_ULR_".

3. Question and exclamation marks have been switched to the tokens "_QUESTION_" and "_EXCLAMATION_" respectively.

4. Mentions[7] have been exchanged by the token "_MENTION_".

5. All the HTML tags have been removed.

6. The hashtags[8] have been normalized with the token "_HASHTAG_".

7. Tokens that express laughing (hahaha, hehehe...) have been normalized with the token "_LAUGH_".

8. Users usually write expressions or abbreviations for surprise phrases like *omg*. All these kind of expressions are replaced by the token "_SURPRISE_".

9. Positive emoticons like :), ;) or :, have been normalized with the token "_HAPPY_".

10. Negative emoticons like :(, :'(or :-(have been normalized with the token "_SAD_".

11. Twitter users usually repeat letters to emphasize the idea that they want to express. Therefore, all the words with a letter repeated more than two times have been reduced to only two instances. For example, the word "aaaamaaaaaziiiing" in tweet 111733236627025920 is transformed into "aamaaziing".

After applying a normalization process to the training and development sets, we have used for the constrained system and the unconstrained system a dataset of 9,686 tweets.

3 Constrained System

The guidelines of the task define a constrained system as a system that only can use the train data provided by the organizers. Due to this restriction we decided to follow a supervised approach. It is required to define a set of parameters when the supervised method is the elected. The first step is to choose the minimum unit of information, i.e. what segments of text are considered as features. Pang et al. (2002) assert that

[7]A twitter mention is a reference to another user which has the pattern "*@user_name*"

[8]A hashtag is the way to refer a topic in Twitter, which has the pattern "*#topic_name*"

Class	Precision	Recall	F1-score
Positive	0.6983	0.6295	0.6621
Neutral	0.6591	0.8155	0.7290
Negative	0.5592	0.2710	0.3651
Average			0.6652

Table 1: Assessment with TF-IDF weighting scheme

Class	Precision	Recall	F1-score
positive	0.7037	0.6335	0.6668
neutral	0.6506	0.8313	0.7299
negative	0.5890	0.2105	0.3112
Average			0.6654

Table 2: Assessment with a binary weighting scheme

opinions or reviews should be represented with unigrams, but other work shows bigrams and trigrams outperformed the unigrams features (Dave et al., 2003). Therefore, there is not agreement in the SA research community about what is the best choice, unigrams or n-grams. Before several validations on the training set of the task we decided to use unigrams as feature for the polarity classification process. Thus, for the supervised algorithm, we have represented each tweet as a vector of unigrams.

The next decision was about the application of a stemmer process and getting rid off the English stop words. We only have applied stemmer process to the data because in previous works (Martínez-Cámara et al., 2013a) we did not reach good results removing the stop words in texts from Twitter. Another topic of discussion in the SA research community is the weighting scheme. Pang et al. (2002) weighted each unigram following a binary scheme. Also, in the most cited survey about SA (Pang and Lee, 2008) the authors indicated that the overall sentiment may not usually be highlighted through repeated use of the same terms. On the other hand, Martínez-Cámara et al. (2011) achieved the best results using TF-IDF as weighting scheme. Due to the lack of agreement in the SA research community about the use of a specific weight scheme, we have carried out several assessments with aim of deciding the most suitable one for the task. The machine learning algorithm selected for the evaluation was SVM. The results are shown in Tables 1 and 2.

The results achieved with the two weighting schemes are very similar. Regarding the positive class, the binary weighting scheme obtains better results than the TF-IDF one, so the presence of positive keywords is more useful than the frequent occurrence of those keywords. For the neutral class, regarding precision and F1-score, the TF-IDF scheme outperformed the binary scheme, but the recall had a higher value when the terms are weighted binary. The precision of the classification for the neutral class is only 1.2% better than the case where TF-IDF is used, while recall and the F1-score is better when the weighting of the features is binary. Although the negative class has a similar performance to that of the positive one with the two weighting schemes, we highlighted the high difference between the other two classes and the negative. The difference is more evident in the recall value, while the neutral class has a value of 0.8313 (binary), the negative one has a value of 0.2105 (binary). Therefore, due to the fact that the binary weighting scheme achieved better results in average, we decided to use it in the final system.

The last step in the configuration of a supervised approach based on machine learning is the selection of the algorithm. The algorithm selected was Support Vector Machine (SVM) (Cortes and Vapnik, 1995). Our decision is based on the widely used SVM by the research community of SA. The first application of SVM for SA was in (Pang et al., 2002) with good results. Since the publication of the previous work, other researchers have used SVM, and some of them are: (Zhang et al., 2009), (Pang and Lee, 2004) and (Jindal and Liu, 2006). Also, the algorithm SVM has been used to classify the polarity over tweets (Go et al., 2009) (Zhang et al., 2011) (Jiang et al., 2011). A broader review of the research about SA in Twitter can be found in (Martínez-Cámara et al., 2013b). Furthermore, our decision is supported by previous in-house experimentation.

For the experimentation we have used the framework for data mining RapidMiner[9]. In RapidMiner there are several implementations of SVM, among which we have selected LibSVM[10](Chang and Lin, 2011) with built-in default parametrization.

To sum up, the configuration of the SINAI constrained system is:

1. Machine learning approach: Supervised
2. Features: Unigrams.
3. Weighted scheme: Binary. If the term is presence the value is 1, 0 in other case.
4. Stemmer: Yes
5. Stopper: No
6. Algorithm: SVM.

The results reached during the development period are shown in Table 2

4 Unconstrained System

Our unconstrained system follows a two level categorization approach, determining whether the tweet is subjective or not at a first stage, and, for the subjective classified ones, whether the tweet is positive or negative. Both classification phases are fully based on knowledge resources. A predefined list of affective words is used for subjectivity detection, and a search process over the collection of emotions generated from a web resource is applied for final polarity classification. Figure 1 shows a general diagram of the system.

4.1 Step 1: determining subjectivity

The system based in WeFeelFine only categorizes between positive and negative texts, so a preliminary classification into subjective and objective (i.e. neutral) must be performed. To this end, a lexical approach is followed: those tweets containing at least one affective term from a list of predefined ones are considered subjective. If affective terms are not found, then the tweet is directly labeled as neutral. This list is called *Sentiment Analysis Lexicon* (SAL), which is defined in the work of Bing Liu (Hu and Liu, 2004). The list has two differentiated groups: a list of positive terms (*agile*, *enjoy*, *improving*) and another with negative ones (*anger*, *refusing*, *unable*...). At this phase, the polarity is not considered, so both lists are merged into a list of around 6,800 subjectivity terms.

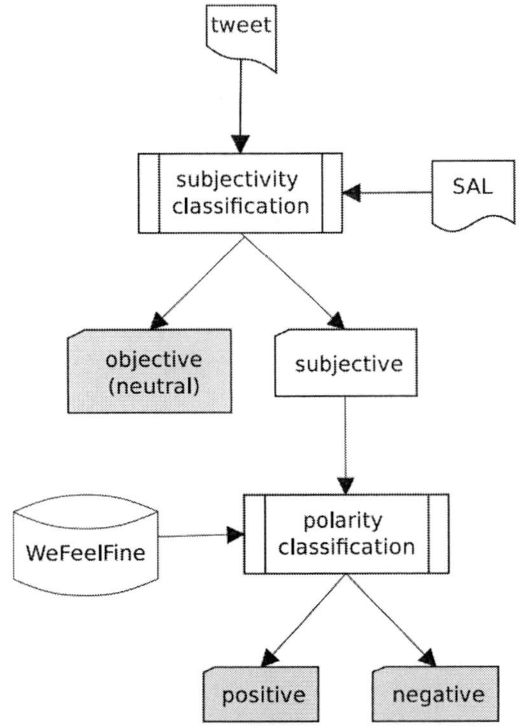

Figure 1: Unconstrained system general diagram

4.2 Step 2: determining polarity

The WeFeelFine project (Kamvar and Harris, 2011) has been used as knowledge base for polarity classification following the approach proposed by (Montejo-Ráez, 2013). WeFeelFine[11] gathers affective texts from several blogs, creating a huge database of mood-related expressions. Almost two millions "feelings" are collected and indexed by the system. It is possible to retrieve related sentences and expressions by using its API. In this way, we have obtained the

[9] http://rapid-i.com/

[10] http://www.csie.ntu.edu.tw/~cjlin/libsvm/

[11] http://wefeelfine.org

top 200 most frequent feelings. For each feeling, about 1,500 sentences are include in a document that represents such a feeling. Then, using the Lucene[12] search engine, these documents have been indexed. In this way, we can use an incoming tweet as query and retrieve a ranked list of feelings, as shown in Figure 2.

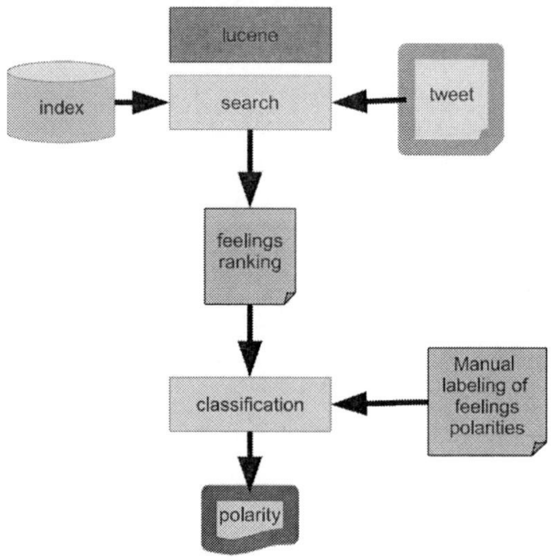

Figure 2: Polarity classification

The ranked list with the top 100 feelings (i.e. those feelings more related to the tweet) is taken for computing the final polarity by a summation of the manually assigned polarity of the feeling weighted with the score value returned by the engine, as shown in Equation 1.

$$p(t) = \frac{1}{|R|} \sum_{r \in R} RSV_r \cdot l_r \quad (1)$$

where
$p(t)$ is the polarity of tweet t
R is the list of retrieved feelings
l_r is the polarity label of feeling r
RSV_r is the *Ranking Status Value* of the feeling determined by Lucene.

As we did with the constrained system, we also assess the unconstrained system before applying the test data. The results reached during the evaluation phase are shown in Table 3. It is remarkable the fact that the precision value of the unconstrained system is a bit higher than the one

[12] `http://lucene.apache.org/`

Class	Precision	Recall	F1-score
positive	0.5004	0.6341	0.5593
neutral	0.6772	0.5416	0.6018
negative	0.3580	0.3456	0.3516
Average			0.5094

Table 3: Assessment of the unconstrained system

reached by the constrained configuration. Thus, SAL is a good resource for subjective classification tasks. The unconstrained system reached worse results with positive and negative classes, but it is an expected result because supervised approaches usually obtain better results than the unsupervised and knowledge based approaches. However, the polarity classification has reached acceptable results, so it encourage us to follow improving the method based of the use of WeFeelFine.

Acknowledgments

This work has been partially supported by a grant from the Fondo Europeo de Desarrollo Regional (FEDER), TEXT-COOL 2.0 project (TIN2009-13391-C04-02) and ATTOS project (TIN2012-38536-C03-0) from the Spanish Government. Also, this paper is partially funded by the European Commission under the Seventh (FP7 - 2007-2013) Framework Programme for Research and Technological Development through the FIRST project (FP7-287607). This publication reflects the views only of the authors, and the Commission cannot be held responsible for any use which may be made of the information contained therein.

References

Enrique Amigó, Adolfo Corujo, Julio Gonzalo, Edgar Meij, and Md Rijke. 2012. Overview of replab 2012: Evaluating online reputation management systems. In *CLEF 2012 Labs and Workshop Notebook Papers*.

Chih-Chung Chang and Chih-Jen Lin. 2011. Libsvm: A library for support vector machines. *ACM Trans. Intell. Syst. Technol.*, 2(3):27:1–27:27, May.

Corinna Cortes and Vladimir Vapnik. 1995. Support-vector networks. *Machine Learning*, 20:273–297.

Kushal Dave, Steve Lawrence, and David M. Pennock. 2003. Mining the peanut gallery: opinion extraction and semantic classification of product reviews. In *Proceedings of the 12th international conference on World Wide Web*, WWW '03, pages 519–528, New York, NY, USA. ACM.

Alec Go, Richa Bhayani, and Lei Huang. 2009. Twitter sentiment classification using distant supervision. *CS224N Project Report, Stanford*, pages 1–12.

Minqing Hu and Bing Liu. 2004. Mining and summarizing customer reviews. In *Proceedings of the tenth ACM SIGKDD international conference on Knowledge discovery and data mining*, KDD '04, pages 168–177, New York, NY, USA. ACM.

Long Jiang, Mo Yu, Ming Zhou, Xiaohua Liu, and Tiejun Zhao. 2011. Target-dependent twitter sentiment classification. In *Proceedings of the 49th Annual Meeting of the Association for Computational Linguistics: Human Language Technologies - Volume 1*, HLT '11, pages 151–160, Stroudsburg, PA, USA. Association for Computational Linguistics.

Nitin Jindal and Bing Liu. 2006. Identifying comparative sentences in text documents. In *Proceedings of the 29th annual international ACM SIGIR conference on Research and development in information retrieval*, SIGIR '06, pages 244–251, New York, NY, USA. ACM.

Sepandar D. Kamvar and Jonathan Harris. 2011. We feel fine and searching the emotional web. In *Proceedings of the fourth ACM international conference on Web search and data mining*, WSDM '11, pages 117–126, New York, NY, USA. ACM.

Eugenio Martínez-Cámara, M. Teresa Martín-Valdivia, José M. Perea-Ortega, and L. Alfonso Ure na López. 2011. Opinion classification techniques applied to a spanish corpus. *Procesamiento de Lenguaje Natural*, 47.

Eugenio Martínez-Cámara, M. Teresa Martín-Valdivia, L. Alfonso Ure na López, and Ruslan Mitkov. 2013a. Detecting sentiment polarity in spanish tweets. *Information Systems Management*, In Press.

Eugenio Martínez-Cámara, M. Teresa Martín-Valdivia, L. Alfonso Ure na López, and Arturo Montejo-Ráez. 2013b. Sentiment analysis in twitter. *Natural Language Engineering*, FirstView:1–28, 2.

Arturo Montejo-Ráez. 2013. Wefeelfine as resource for unsupervised polarity classification. *Procesamiento del Lenguaje Natural*, 50:29–35.

Bo Pang and Lillian Lee. 2004. A sentimental education: sentiment analysis using subjectivity summarization based on minimum cuts. In *Proceedings of the 42nd Annual Meeting on Association for Computational Linguistics*, ACL '04, Stroudsburg, PA, USA. Association for Computational Linguistics.

Bo Pang and Lillian Lee. 2008. Opinion mining and sentiment analysis. *Found. Trends Inf. Retr.*, 2(1-2):1–135, January.

Bo Pang, Lillian Lee, and Shivakumar Vaithyanathan. 2002. Thumbs up?: Sentiment classification using machine learning techniques. In *Proceedings of the ACL-02 conference on Empirical methods in natural language processing - Volume 10*, EMNLP '02, pages 79–86, Stroudsburg, PA, USA. Association for Computational Linguistics.

Julio Villena-Román, Sara Lana-Serrano, Eugenio Martínez-Cámara, and José Carlos González-Cristóbal. 2013. Tass - workshop on sentiment analysis at sepln. *Procesamiento del Lenguaje Natural*, 50(0).

Theresa Wilson, Zornitsa Kozareva, Preslav Nakov, Sara Rosenthal, Veselin Stoyanov, and Alan Ritter. 2013. SemEval-2013 task 2: Sentiment analysis in twitter. In *Proceedings of the International Workshop on Semantic Evaluation*, SemEval '13, June.

Changli Zhang, Daniel Zeng, Jiexun Li, Fei-Yue Wang, and Wanli Zuo. 2009. Sentiment analysis of chinese documents: From sentence to document level. *Journal of the American Society for Information Science and Technology*, 60(12):2474–2487.

Ley Zhang, Riddhiman Ghosh, Mohamed Dekhil, Meichun Hsu, and Bing Liu. 2011. Combining lexiconbased and learning-based methods for twitter sentiment analysis. *HP Laboratories, Technical Report HPL-2011-89*.

ECNUCS: A Surface Information Based System Description of Sentiment Analysis in Twitter in the SemEval-2013 (Task 2)

Tian Tian ZHU and **Fang Xi ZHANG** and **Man LAN***
Department of Computer Science and Technology
East China Normal University
51111201046,51111201041@ecnu.edu.cn; mlan@cs.ecnu.edu.cn

Abstract

This paper briefly reports our submissions to the two subtasks of Semantic Analysis in Twitter task in SemEval 2013 (Task 2), i.e., the Contextual Polarity Disambiguation task (an expression-level task) and the Message Polarity Classification task (a message-level task). We extract features from surface information of tweets, i.e., content features, Micro-blogging features, emoticons, punctuation and sentiment lexicon, and adopt SVM to build classifier. For subtask A, our system on twitter data ranks 2 on unconstrained rank and on SMS data ranks 1 on unconstrained rank.

1 Introduction

Micro-blogging today has become a very popular communication tool among Internet users. Millions of messages are appearing daily in popular web sites that provide services for Micro-blogging and one popularly known is Twitter[1]. Through the twitter platform, users share either information or opinions about personalities, politicians, products, companies, events (Prentice and Huffman, 2008) etc. As a result of the rapidly increasing number of tweets, mining sentiments expressed in tweets has attracted more and more attention, which is also one of the basic analysis utility functions needed by various applications.

The task of Sentiment Analysis in Twitter is to identify the sentiment of tweets and get a better understanding of how sentiment is conveyed in tweets and texts, which consists of two sub-tasks, i.e., the Contextual Polarity Disambiguation task (an expression-level task) and the Message Polarity Classification task (a message-level task). The contextual polarity disambiguation task (subtask A) is to determine whether a given message containing a marked instance of a word or a phrase is positive, negative or neutral in that context. The message polarity classification task (subtask B) is to decide whether a given message is of positive, negative, or neutral sentiment and for messages conveying both a positive and negative sentiment, whichever is the stronger sentiment should be chosen (Wilson et al., 2013). We participate in these two tasks.

In recent years, many researchers have proposed methods to analyze sentiment in twitter. For example, (Pak and Paroubek, 2010) used a Part of Speech (POS) tagger on the tweets and found that some POS taggers can help identify the sentiment of tweets. They found that objective tweets often contain more nouns than subjective tweets. However, subjective tweets may carry more adjectives and adverbs than objective tweets. Besides, (Davidov et al., 2010) proved that emoticon and punctuation like exclamation mark are good features when distinguishing the sentiment of tweets. In addition, some sentiment lexicons like SentiWordNet (Baccianella et al., 2010) and MPQA Subjectivity Lexicon (Wilson et al., 2009) have been adopted to calculate the sentiment score of tweets (Zirn et al., 2011).

The rest of this paper is organized as follows. Section 2 describes our approach for subtask 1, i.e., the Contextual Polarity Disambiguation task. Section 3 describes our approach for subtask 2, i.e., the

[1]http://www.twitter.com

*Second Joint Conference on Lexical and Computational Semantics (*SEM), Volume 2: Seventh International Workshop on Semantic Evaluation (SemEval 2013)*, pages 408–413, Atlanta, Georgia, June 14-15, 2013. ©2013 Association for Computational Linguistics

message polarity classification task. Concluding remarks is in Section 4.

2 System Description of Contextual Polarity Disambiguation

For the Contextual Polarity Disambiguation task, we first extract features from multiple aspects, i.e., punctuation, emoticons, POS tags, instance length and sentiment lexicon features. Then we adopt polynomial SVM to build classification models. According to the definition of this task, the given instance has been marked by a start position and an end position rather than a whole tweet. So we first record the frequency of the first three kinds of features in this given instance. To avoid interference from the number of words in given instance, we then normalize the feature values by the length of instance.

2.1 Preprocessing

Typically, most tweets contain informal language expressions, with creative spelling and punctuation, misspellings, slang, new words, URLs, and genre-specific terminology and abbreviations, such as, "RT" for "re-tweet" and #hashtags, which are a type of tagging for Twitter messages. Therefore, working with these informal text genres presents challenges for natural language processing beyond those typically encountered when working with more traditional text genres, such as newswire data. So we perform text preprocessing in order to remedy as many informal texts as possible. Firstly, we perform normalization to convert creative spelling and misspelling into its right spelling. For example, any repetition of more than 3 continuous letters are reduced back to 1 letter (e.g. "noooo" is reduced to "no"). In addition, according to the Internet slang dictionary[2], we convert each slang to its complete form, for example, "aka" is rewritten as "also known as". After that, we use the Stanford parser[3] for tokenization and the Stanford POS Tagger[4] for POS tagging. Finally, Natural Language Toolkit[5] is used for WordNet based Lemmatization.

[2]http://www.noslang.com

[3]http://nlp.stanford.edu/software/lex-parser.shtml

[4]http://nlp.stanford.edu/software/tagger.shtml

[5]http://nltk.org/

2.2 Features

2.2.1 Punctuation

Typically, punctuation may express user's sentiment to a certain extent. For example, many exclamation marks (!) in tweet may indicate strong feelings or high volume (shouting). Therefore, given a marked instance, we record the frequency of the following four types of punctuation: (1) exclamation mark (!), (2) question mark (?), (3) double or single quotation marks(" and ""), (4) sum of the above three punctuation. Then the punctuation feature value is normalized by the length of instance.

2.2.2 Emoticons

We create two features that capture the number of positive and negative emoticons. Table 1 lists the two types of emoticons. We also use the union of the two emoticon sets as a feature. In total, we have three emoticon features.

Positive Emoticons	Negative Emoticons
:-) :) :D :-D =) ;)	:(:-(: (;(
;-) ;) ;D ;-D (; :)	;-(; ():
:-P ;-P XD (-: (-; :o) ;o)	-/ :/ ;-/ ;/
:0) ;0) ^_^	T_T T0T ToT

Table 1: List of emoticons

2.2.3 POS

According to the finding of (Pak and Paroubek, 2010), POS taggers help to identify the sentiment of tweets. Therefore, we record the frequency of the following four POS features, i.e., noun ("NN", "NNP", "NNS" and "NNPS" POS tags are grouped into noun feature), verb ("VB", "VBD", "VBG", "VBN", "VBP" and "VBZ" POS tags are grouped into verb feature), adjective ("JJ", "JJR" and "JJS" POS tags are grouped into adjective feature) and adverb ("RB", "RBR" and "RBS" POS tags are grouped into adverb feature). Then we normalize them by the length of given instance.

2.2.4 Sentiment lexicon Features

For each word in a given instance, we use three sentiment lexicons to identify its sentiment polarity and calculate its sentiment weight, i.e., SentiWordNet (Baccianella et al., 2010), MPQA Subjectivity Lexicon (Wilson et al., 2009) and an Unigram Lexicon made from the Large Movie Review Dataset v1.0 (Maas et al., 2011). To calculate the sentiment score for this instance, we use the following formula to sum up the sentiment score of each word:

$$Senti(I) = \sum_{w \in I} \frac{Num(w) * Senti\_weight}{Length(I)} \quad (1)$$

where I represents the given instance and w represents each word in I. The $Senti\_weight$ is calculated based on the word in the instance and the chosen sentiment lexicon. That is, for each word in the instance, we have different $Senti\_weight$ values for it since we use different sentiment lexicons. Below we describe the calculation of $Senti\_weight$ values for a word in three sentiment lexicons. Note that $Num(w)$ is always 1 since most words appear one time in a instance.

SentiWordNet. SentiWordNet is a lexical resource for sentiment analysis, which assigns each synset of WordNet (Stark and Riesenfeld, 1998) three sentiment scores: positivity, negativity, objectivity (e.g. living#a#3, positivity: 0.5, negativity: 0.125, objectivity: 0.375), where sum of these three scores is always 1. For one concept, if its positive score and negative score are all 0, we treat it as objective concept; otherwise, we treat it as subjective concept. And we take the first sense as the concept of each word.

We extract three features from SentiWordNet, i.e., $SUB_{WordNet}$, $POS_{WordNet}$ and $NEG_{WordNet}$. The $Senti\_weight$ of $SUB_{WordNet}$ records whether a word is subjective. If it is subjective, we set $Senti\_weight$ as 1, otherwise 0. Similarly, the $Senti\_weight$ values of $POS_{WordNet}$ and $NEG_{WordNet}$ indicate the positive score and the negative score of the given word. Considering some negation terms may reverse the sentiment orientation of instance, we manually generate a negation term list (e.g. "not", "never", etc.,) and if a negation term appears in the instance, we switch the $POS_{WordNet}$ to $NEG_{WordNet}$ and vice versa. Besides, we adopt another feature to record the ratio of $POS_{WordNet}/NEG_{WordNet}$. If the denominator is 0, i.e., $NEG_{WordNet} = 0$, that means, the word has the strongest positive sentiment orientation, then we set 10*$POS_{WordNet}$ as its feature value.

MPQA. The MPQA Subjectivity Lexicon contains about $8,000$ subjective words. Each word in the lexicon has two types of sentiment strength: strong subjective and weak subjective, and four kinds of sentiment polarity: positive, negative, both (positive and negative) and neutral. Therefore we calculate three features from this lexicon, i.e., SUB_{MPQA}, POS_{MPQA} and NEG_{MPQA}. For the SUB_{MPQA} feature, if the word has strong or weak subjective, we set its $Senti\_weight$ as 1 or 0.5 accordingly. For the POS_{MPQA} (NEG_{MPQA}) feature, we set $Senti\_weight$ as 1, or 0.5 or 0 if the word has strong positive (negative), or weak positive (negative) or neutral. We also reverse the sentiment orientation of POS_{MPQA} and NEG_{MPQA} if a negation term appears.

Unigram Lexicon. Unlike the above two lexicons in themselves which provide sentiment polarity and sentiment strength for each word, we also utilize the third lexicon to calculate the sentiment information statistically. Therefore we generate an unigram lexicon by ourselves from a large Movie Review data set(Maas et al., 2011) which contains $25,000$ positive and $25,000$ negative movie reviews. We calculate the $Senti\_weight$ of each word appears in the data set as the ratio of the frequency of this word in positive reviews to that in negative reviews and record this feature as $Senti_{UL}$.

Clearly, since we use additional data set to develop a sentiment lexicon which is used to generate this $Senti_{UL}$ feature, this feature is worked with all other features to train the unconstrained system.

2.2.5 Other features

In addition, we collect three other features: (1) length of instance, (2) uppercase word (e.g. "WTO" or "Machine Learning"), (3) URL. For the uppercase word and URL features, we record the frequency of them and then normalize them by the instance length as well.

2.3 Experiment and Results

2.3.1 Classification Algorithm

We adopt LibSVM[6] to build polynomial kernel-based SVM classifiers. We have also tried linear kernel but get no improvement. To obtain the optimal parameters for SVM, such as c and g, we perform grid search with 10-fold cross validation on training

[6]http://www.csie.ntu.edu.tw/ cjlin/libsvm/

data.

2.3.2 Results and Discussion

In section 2, we obtained 22 features in total. To train the constrained model, we used the above described 21 features (except $Senti_{UL}$) and used all above 22 features to train the unconstrained model. We combined the provided training and development data by the organizers as our final training data. And we should apologize for our misunderstanding of the definitions of the constrained and unconstrained condition. As the official definition of unconstrained model, participates are allowed to add other data to expand the training data sets, but our unconstrained model only adds one feature ($Senti_{UL}$) which is got from other data set. Therefore, we actually submitted two results of constrained model. But we still refer this model trained on all features as unconstrained model for it appeared in the unconstrained list of official results. There are two kinds of test data: $4,435$ twitter instances and $2,334$ SMS message instances. Table 2 list the F-score and averaged F-score of positive, negative and neutral class of each test data set.

On one hand, from the table we can see that whether on constrained or unconstrained model, the results on twitter data are slightly better than those of SMS data. However, this difference is not significant. This indicates that the model trained on twitter data performs well on SMS data. And it also shows that twitter data and SMS data are linguistically similar with each other in nature. On the other hand, we find that on each test data set, there is little difference between the constrained model and the unconstrained model, which indicates the $Senti_{UL}$ feature does not have discriminating power by itself. However, since we had not used other labeled or unlabeled data to extend the training data set, we cannot draw a conclusion on this. Besides, our results contain no neutral items even though the classifier we used is multivariate. One reason may be the neutral instances in training data is too sparse for the classifier to learn.

On twitter data, our system ranks 2 under unconstrained model and ranks 10 under constrained model. On SMS data, our system ranks first under unconstrained model and ranks 7 under constrained model.

3 System Description of Message Polarity Classification

Unlike the previous subtask, the Message Polarity classification task focuses on the whole tweet rather than a marked sequence of given instance. Firstly, we perform text preprocessing as Task A. Besides the previous described features, we also extract following features.

3.1 Features

3.1.1 Micro-blogging features

We adopted three tweet domain-specific features, i.e., #hashtags, @USERS, URLs. We calculate the frequency of the three features and normalize them by the length of instance.

3.1.2 *n*-gram features

We used unigrams to capture the content of tweets.

3.2 Classification Algorithm

We adopted two different classifiers in preliminary experiments, i.e., maximum entropy and SVM. We used the Mallet tool (McCallum, 2002) to perform Maximum Entropy classification and LibSVM[7] with a linear kernel, where the default setting is adopted in all experiments.

3.3 Results on Training Data

In the first experiment, we used only content features and LibSVM classifier to do our experiments. The results were listed in Table 3. From Table 3, we found that the system with unigram without removing stop words performs the best. The possible reason was that Microblogs are always short (constrained in 140 words) and removing stop words would cause information missing in such a short text. In addition, although bigrams improved the performance to some extern, they added the feature space many more and might affect other features. So in our final systems, we used only unigram feature and did not remove stop words.

In the second experiment, we compared all features described before with two learning algorithms. The results were shown in Table 4, where 1 indicates unigram, 2 indicates micro-blog, 3 indicates

[7] http://www.csie.ntu.edu.tw/ cjlin/libsvm/

System	F-pos	F-neg	F-neu	average F(pos and neg)
twitter-constrained	0.8506	0.7390	0.0	0.7948
twitter-unconstrained	0.8561	0.7468	0.0	**0.8015**
SMS-constrained	0.7727	0.7611	0.0	0.7669
SMS-unconstrained	0.7645	0.7824	0.0	**0.7734**

Table 2: Results of our systems on subtask A test data

features	F-pos	F-neg	F-neu	average F(pos and neg)	acc(%)
unigrams	**0.6356**	0.3381	**0.7122**	0.4869	**63.75**
unigrams(remove stop words)	0.6046	0.3453	0.6988	0.4750	62.13
bigrams	0.5186	0.0196	0.6625	0.2691	55.85
unigrams+bigrams	0.6234	**0.3724**	0.7043	**0.4979**	63.18

Table 3: Results of our systems on on subtask B training data using content features

features	F-pos		F-neg		F-neu		average F(pos and neg)		acc(%)	
	MaxEnt	SVM	MaxEnt	SVM	MaxEnt	SVM	MaxEnt	SVM	MaxEnt	SVM
1	0.6178	0.6356	0.3696	0.3381	0.6848	0.7122	0.4937	0.4869	61.56	63.75
1+2	0.6403	0.6339	0.4207	0.4310	0.6990	0.7184	0.5305	0.5324	63.75	64.89
1+2+3	0.6328	0.6512	0.4051	0.4371	0.6975	0.7232	0.5190	0.5442	63.18	65.75
1+2+3+4	**0.6488**	**0.6593**	**0.4587**	**0.4481**	**0.7083**	**0.7288**	**0.5538**	**0.5537**	**64.89**	**66.41**
2+3+4	0.5290	0.5201	0.2897	0.2643	0.6503	0.6411	0.4093	0.3922	55.85	54.80

Table 4: Results of our systems on subtask B training data using all features and two learning algorithms

punctuation, 4 indicates sentiment lexicon features. From Table 4, the best performance was obtained by using all these features. Since the performance of Maximum Entropy and SVM in terms of F-score was comparable to each other, we finally chose SVM since it achieved a better accuracy than MaxEnt.

3.4 Results on Test Data

We combined the provided training and development data by the organizers as our final training data. There were two kinds of test data: 3,813 tweets and 2,094 SMS messages . Table 5 listed the results of our final systems on the tweet and SMS data sets by using all above described features and SVM algorithm.

From Table 5, on one hand, we can see that the overall performance of SMS test data is inferior to twitter data, for the reason may be that the domain of features are all based on twitter data, and maybe not quite suitable for SMS data. However, this different is not significant. On the other hand, we also can find that there is no obvious distinction between the constrained and the unconstrained model on each test data.Also from Table 5, the F-score for positive instances is higher than negative instances, and it is interesting that most of other participants'systems results show the same consequence. One of the reason may be the positive instance in training data are more than negative instances both in training data and test data.

Our result on twitter message is 0.5842 , while on SMS is 0.5477. Compared with the highest average F-score 0.6902 in twitter data and 0.6848 in SMS data, our system does not perform very well. On the one hand , pre-processing was roughly , then features extracted were not suited in classification stage. On the other hand, in classification stage all parameters were default when used LibSVM. These might cause low performance. In future, we may overcome the insufficient described above and take hashtags' sentiment inclination and the source files of URLs into consideration to enhance the performance.

System	F-pos	F-neg	F-neu	average F(pos and neg)
twitter-constrained	0.6671	0.4338	0.7124	0.5505
twitter-unconstrained	**0.6775**	0.4908	0.7204	**0.5842**
SMS-constrained	0.5796	0.4846	**0.7801**	0.5321
SMS-unconstrained	0.5818	**0.5137**	0.7612	0.5477

Table 5: Results of our systems on subtask B test data

4 Conclusion

In this work we extracted features from four aspects, including surface information of twitters and sentiment lexicons like SentiWordNet and MPQA Lexicon. On the contextual polarity disambiguation task, our system ranks 2 on twitter (unconstrained) rank and ranks 1 on SMS (unconstrained) rank.

Acknowledgements

The authors would like to thank the organizers and reviewers for this interesting task and their helpful suggestions and comments, which improves the final version of this paper. This research is supported by grants from National Natural Science Foundation of China (No.60903093), Shanghai Pujiang Talent Program (No.09PJ1404500), Doctoral Fund of Ministry of Education of China (No. 20090076120029) and Shanghai Knowledge Service Platform Project (No. ZF1213).

References

Stefano Baccianella, Andrea Esuli, and Fabrizio Sebastiani. 2010. Sentiwordnet 3.0: An enhanced lexical resource for sentiment analysis and opinion mining. In Nicoletta Calzolari (Conference Chair), Khalid Choukri, Bente Maegaard, Joseph Mariani, Jan Odijk, Stelios Piperidis, Mike Rosner, and Daniel Tapias, editors, *Proceedings of the Seventh International Conference on Language Resources and Evaluation (LREC'10)*, Valletta, Malta, may. European Language Resources Association (ELRA).

Dmitry Davidov, Oren Tsur, and Ari Rappoport. 2010. Enhanced sentiment learning using twitter hashtags and smileys. In *Proceedings of the 23rd International Conference on Computational Linguistics: Posters*, pages 241–249. Association for Computational Linguistics.

Andrew L. Maas, Raymond E. Daly, Peter T. Pham, Dan Huang, Andrew Y. Ng, and Christopher Potts. 2011. Learning word vectors for sentiment analysis. In *Proceedings of the 49th Annual Meeting of the Association for Computational Linguistics: Human Language Technologies*, pages 142–150, Portland, Oregon, USA, June. Association for Computational Linguistics.

Andrew Kachites McCallum. 2002. Mallet: A machine learning for language toolkit. http://mallet.cs.umass.edu.

Alexander Pak and Patrick Paroubek. 2010. Twitter as a corpus for sentiment analysis and opinion mining. In *Proceedings of LREC*, volume 2010.

Sara Prentice and Ethan Huffman. 2008. Social medias new role in emergency management. *Idaho National Laboratory*, pages 1–5.

Michael M Stark and Richard F Riesenfeld. 1998. Wordnet: An electronic lexical database. In *Proceedings of 11th Eurographics Workshop on Rendering*. Citeseer.

Theresa Wilson, Janyce Wiebe, and Paul Hoffmann. 2009. Recognizing contextual polarity: An exploration of features for phrase-level sentiment analysis. *Computational linguistics*, 35(3):399–433.

Theresa Wilson, Zornitsa Kozareva, Preslav Nakov, Alan Ritter, Sara Rosenthal, and Veselin Stoyanov. 2013. Semeval-2013 task 2: Sentiment analysis in twitter. In *Proceedings of the 7th International Workshop on Semantic Evaluation*. Association for Computational Linguistics.

Căcilia Zirn, Mathias Niepert, Heiner Stuckenschmidt, and Michael Strube. 2011. Fine-grained sentiment analysis with structural features. In *Proceedings of the 5th international Joint conference on natural Language Processing (iJcnLP-2011)*, volume 167.

Umigon: sentiment analysis for tweets based on lexicons and heuristics

Clement Levallois
Department of Marketing Management, Rotterda School of Management
and Erasmus Studio, Erasmus University Rotterdam
The Netherlands.
clevallois@rsm.nl

Abstract

Umigon is developed since December 2012 as a web application providing a service of sentiment detection in tweets. It has been designed to be fast and scalable. Umigon also provides indications for additional semantic features present in the tweets, such as time indications or markers of subjectivity. Umigon is in continuous development, it can be tried freely at www.umigon.com. Its code is open sourced at: https://github.com/seinecle/Umigon

1. General principle of operation

Umigon belongs to the family of lexicon based sentiment classifiers (Davidov et al. 2010, Kouloumpis et al. 2011). It is specifically designed to detect sentiment (positive, negative or neutral) in tweets. The "sentiment detection engine" of Umigon consists of 4 main parts, which are detailed below:

- detection of semantic features in the entire tweet. Smileys and onomatopes are given special attention.
- evaluation of hashtags.
- decomposition of the tweet into a list of its n-grams (up to 4-grams), comparison of each n-gram with the terms in lexicons. In case of a match, a heuristic is applied.
- final series of heuristics at the level of the entire tweet, taking advantage of the semantic features detected in the previous steps. A final, unique sentiment (pos, neg or neut) is ascribed to the tweet.

2. The four steps of the classification engine

We refer in footnotes to the Java classes which implement the processes described here.

2.1 Global heuristics

Smileys and onomatopes carry strong indications of sentiment, but also come in a variety of orthographic forms which require methods devoted to their treatment[1].

Onomatopes and exclamations often include repeated vowels and consonants, as in yeaaaaahhhh (repeated "a" and "h"), but also yeaah (repeated "a"), or yeeeeaaaaah (repeated "e" and "a"). We list the most common exclamations and use regular expressions to capture the variety of forms they can assume. If such a form is found in the tweet, the related sentiment (positive or negative) is saved, and will be evaluated at a final stage for the global sentiment of the entire tweet.

Similarly, smileys are frequently spelled in multiple variations: :-) can also be found as :-)) or :-))))))) . For this reason here also the flexibility of regular expressions is used to detect spelling variations. In addition, we consider that a smiley positioned at the very end of a tweet gives an unambiguous signal as to the sentiment of the tweet. For instance:

@mydearfriend You got to see Lady Gaga live, so lucky! Hate you :)))

Here, whatever the negative sentiments (Hate you) signaled in the tweet, the final smiley has an overriding effect and signals the strongest sentiment in the tweet. For this reason smileys located in final positions are recorded as such.

2.2 Evaluation of hashtags

Hashtags are of special interest as they single out a semantic unit of special significance in the tweet. Exploiting the semantics in a hashtag faces the issue that a hashtag can conflate several terms, as in #greatstuff or #notveryexciting. Umigon applies a series

[1] https://github.com/seinecle/Umigon/blob/master/src/java/Heuristics/SentenceLevelHeuristicsPre.java

*Second Joint Conference on Lexical and Computational Semantics (*SEM), Volume 2: Seventh International Workshop on Semantic Evaluation (SemEval 2013)*, pages 414–417, Atlanta, Georgia, June 14-15, 2013. ©2013 Association for Computational Linguistics

of heuristics matching parts of the hashtag with lexicons[2]. In the case of #notveryexciting , the starting letters not will be identified as one of the terms in the lexicon for negative terms. Similarly, the letters very will be identified as one of the terms present in the lexicon for "strength of sentiment". exciting will be detected as one of the terms in the lexicon for positive sentiment. Taken together, not very exciting will lead to an evaluation of a negative sentiment for this hashtag. This evaluation is recorded and will be combined with the evaluation of other features of the tweet at a later stage.

2.3 Decomposition in ngrams

The text of the tweet is decomposed in a list of unigrams, bigrams, trigrams and quadrigrams. For example, the tweet This service leaves to be desired will be decomposed in list of the following expressions:

"This, service, leaves, to, be, desired, This service, service leaves, leaves to, to be, be desired, This service leaves, service leaves to, leaves to be, to be desired, This service leaves to, service leaves to be, leaves to be desired"

The reason for this decomposition is that some markers of sentiment are contained in expressions made of several terms. In the example above, to be desired is a marker of negative judgment recorded as such in the lexicon for negative sentiment, while desired is a marker of positive sentiment. Umigon loops through all the n-grams of the tweet and checks for their presence in several lexicons[3].

If an n-gram is indeed found to be listed in one of the lexicons, the heuristic attached to this term in this lexicon is executed, returning a classification (positive sentiment, negative sentiment, or another semantic feature). Heuristics attached to terms in the lexicons are described in detail in section 3.

2.4 Post-processing: a last look at the entire tweet .

At this stage, the methods described above may have returned a large number of (possibly conflicting) sentiment categories for a single tweet. For instance, in the example This service leaves to be desired, the examination of the n-grams has returned a positive sentiment classification (desired) and also negative (to be desired). A series of heuristics adjucates which of the conflicting indications for sentiments should be retained in the end. In the case above, the co-presence of negative and positive sentiments without any further indication is resolved as the tweet being of a negative sentiment. If the presence of a moderator is detected in the tweet (such as but, even if, though), rules of a more complex nature are applied[4].

3. A focus on lexicons and heuristics

Four lexicons are used for sentiment analysis (number of terms in the lexicons in brackets): "positive tone" (332), "negative tone" (630), "strength of sentiment" (59), "negations" (45). These lexicons have been created manually by the inspection of thousands of tweets, and continue to be expanded on a regular basis. Note that the same term can appear in different lexicons (if rarely in practice). For example, the term fucking appears in the lexicon for negative tone and in the lexicon for strong sentiments. Each term in a lexicon is accompanied by a heuristics and a decision rule.

3.1 Simple case from the "negative sentiments" lexicon:

Term	sadfaced
Heuristics	None
Decision Rule	012

If a tweet contains the term sadfaced, Umigon will directly add the code "012" (which stands for negative sentiment) to the tweet[5].

3.2 More complex case from the "positive sentiments" lexicon:

Term	Satisfied
Heuristics	!isImmediatelyPrecededBy ANegation
Decision Rule	011|012

If the term satisfied is present in a tweet, the heuristics !isImmediatelyPrecededByANegation is applied. This s a method checking whether the term immediately

2 https://github.com/seinecle/Umigon/blob/master/src/java/Heuristics/HashtagLevelHeuristics.java

3 https://github.com/seinecle/Umigon/blob/master/src/java/Classifier/ClassifierMachine.java

4 https://github.com/seinecle/Umigon/blob/master/src/java/Heuristics/SentenceLevelHeuristicsPost.java

5 See this class for the full list of possible classifications: https://github.com/seinecle/Umigon/blob/master/src/java/Classifier/Categories.java

preceding satisfied in the tweet is a negation or not[6]. This method returns a Boolean (true / false). The Boolean returned by this heuristics will determine the outcome of the decision rule. Here, the decision rule is a simple binary choice: codify as 011 (meaning, a positive sentiment) if satisfied is not preceded by a negation; codify it as 012 (negative sentiment) otherwise.

3.3 Complex case from the "negative sentiments" lexicon:

Term	hard
Heuristics	!isImmediatelyPrecededByANegation+++!isImmediatelyFollowedBySpecificTerm///work|disk
Decision Rule	A?(B?(012):011)

This example shows how several heuristics (separated by +++) can be combined, leading to complex rules of decision. In this example, whenever the term hard is detected in a tweet, 2 heuristics are evaluated: is the term preceded by a negation? Is the term followed by specific terms – work or disk, in this case? Each of these heuristics returns a Boolean. The Booleans are fed into the interpreter of the decision rule, where A and B represent the 2 Booleans[7]. Depending on their value, the decision tree takes a different branch, leading to the selection of one codification. In the example:
If A is false, return 011: a positive sentiment.
Example: not hard
If A is true and B is true, return 012: a negative sentiment. Example: it is hard
If A is true and B is false, returns null: nothing (a neutral sentiment).
Example: this is a hard disk

While in practice it is rarely needed to write up rules of such complexity, they offer an extra flexibility to exploit the semantic features of terms in varying contexts.

[6] The method actually checks the two terms before, in order to capture cases such as "not very satisfied", where a negative term is present but not immediately preceding the term under review. See the details of all heuristics here: https://github.com/seinecle/Umigon/blob/master/src/java/Heuristics/Heuristic.java

[7] The class for the interpreter is: https://github.com/seinecle/Umigon/blob/master/src/java/RuleInterpreter/Interpreter.java

4. Performance

4.1 Accuracy

Umigon was formally evaluated in a semantic evaluation task proposed by SemEval-2013, the International Workshop on Semantic Evaluation (Wilson et al., 2013). The task consisted in classifying 3,813 tweets as positive, negative or neutral in polarity (task B). The results:

class	Pos	neg	neut
prec	0.7721	0.4407	0.6471
rec	0.5604	0.5507	0.7579
fscore	0.6495	0.4896	0.6981

average(pos and neg) 0.5696

For reference, the best performing participant in this task obtained the following results (Mohammad et al., 2013):

class	pos	neg	neut
prec	0.8138	0.6967	0.6765
rec	0.6673	0.604	0.8262
fscore	0.7333	0.6471	0.7439

average(pos and neg) 0.6902

We see that Umigon had an especially poor precision for tweets of a negative sentiment (results greyed in the table). This means that Umigon failed to identify many negative tweets as such. One reason accounting for this poor performance is the definition we adopt for what a negative sentiment is. For example, the SemEval task included this negative tweet:
"Renewed fighting rocks Syria: An early morning explosion rocked the flashpoint city of Deir Ezzor on Saturday in..."
By design, Umigon has not been conceived to classify such a tweet as negative because if it contains negative elements of a *factual* nature (explosion, fighting), but contains no marker of a negative *attitude*. This question aside, the accuracy of Umigon should be improved by increasing the number of terms and heuristics in the lexicons, which is an ongoing process.

4.2 Speed

Tested on a dataset provided by sentiment140.com[8], Umigon performs the classification of 1.6 million tweets in less than 15 minutes. We believe that not relying on Part of Speech tagging makes it a specially

[8] http://help.sentiment140.com/for-students

fast solution for lexicon-based sentiment classifiers. The classifier engine is implemented in such a way that the presence of absence of n-grams in the terms lists is checked through look-ups on hashsets (is this n-gram contained in a set?), not loops through these sets. Since look-ups in hashsets is typically of O(1) compexity[9], this insures that the performance of Umigon will not degrade even with expanded lexicons.

References

Davidov, D., Tsur, O., and Rappoport, A. 2010. Enhanced sentiment learning using twitter hashtags and smileys. Proceedings of Coling.

Kouloumpis, E., Wilson, T., and Moore, J. 2011. Twitter Sentiment Analysis: The Good the Bad and the OMG! Proceedings of ICWSM.

Mohammad, S., Kiritchenko, S. and Zhu, X. 2013. NRC-Canada: Building the State-of-the-Art in Sentiment Analysis of Tweets. In *Proceedings of the International Workshop on Semantic Evaluation*, SemEval '13, June 2013, Atlanta, Georgia.

Wilson, T., Kozareva, Z., Nakov, P., Rosenthal, S. Stoyanov, V. and Alan Ritter. 2013. SemEval-2013 Task 2: Sentiment Analysis in Twitter. In *Proceedings of the International Workshop on Semantic Evaluation*, SemEval '13, June 2013, Atlanta, Georgia.

[9] http://stackoverflow.com/questions/6574916/hashset-look-up-complexity

[LVIC-LIMSI]: Using Syntactic Features and Multi-polarity Words for Sentiment Analysis in Twitter

Morgane Marchand[1,2], **Alexandru Lucian Ginsca**[1], **Romaric Besançon**[1], **Olivier Mesnard**[1]
(1) CEA-LIST, DIASI, LVIC
CEA SACLAY - Nano-INNOV - Bt. 861 - Point courrier 173
91191 Gif-sur-Yvette Cedex, France
(2) LIMSI-CNRS
Bat 508, BP133,91403 Orsay Cedex
morgane.marchand@cea.fr; alexandru.ginsca@cea.fr
romaric.besancon@cea.fr; olivier.mesnard@cea.fr

Abstract

This paper presents the contribution of our team at task 2 of SemEval 2013: Sentiment Analysis in Twitter. We submitted a constrained run for each of the two subtasks. In the Contextual Polarity Disambiguation subtask, we use a sentiment lexicon approach combined with polarity shift detection and tree kernel based classifiers. In the Message Polarity Classification subtask, we focus on the influence of domain information on sentiment classification.

1 Introduction

In the past decade, new forms of communication, such as microblogging and text messaging have emerged and became ubiquitous. These short messages are often used to share opinions and sentiments. The *Sentiment Analysis in Twitter* task promotes research that will lead to a better understanding of how sentiment is conveyed in tweets and texts. In this paper, we describe our contribution at task 2 of SemEval 2013 (Wilson et al., 2013). For the *Contextual Polarity Disambiguation* subtask, covered in section 2, we use a system that combines a lexicon based approach to sentiment detection with two types of supervised learning methods, one used for polarity shift identification and one for tweet segment classification in the absence of lexicon words. The third section presents the *Message Polarity Classification* subtask. We focus here on the influence of domain information on sentiment classification by detecting words that change their polarity across domains.

2 Task A: Contextual Polarity Disambiguation

In this section we present our approach for the contextual polarity disambiguation task in which, given a message containing a marked instance of a word or a phrase, the system has to determine whether that instance is positive, negative or neutral in that context. For this task, we submitted a single run using only the tweets provided by the organizers.

2.1 System description

Based on the predominant strategy, sentiment analysis systems can be divided into those that focus on sentiment lexicons together with a set of rules and those that rely on machine learning techniques. For this task, we use a mixed approach in which we first filter the tweets based on the occurrences of words from a sentiment lexicon and then apply different supervised learning methods on the grounds of this initial classification. In Figure 1 we detail the workflow of our system. We use the $+$, $-$ and $*$ symbols to denote a positive, negative and neutral tweet segment, respectively. Also, we use the $a \rightarrow b$ notation when referring to a polarity shift from a to b.

2.1.1 Data preprocessing

The language used in Twitter presents some particularities, such as the use of hashtags or user mentions. In order to maximize the efficiency of language processing methods, such as lemmatization and syntactic parsing, we perform several normalization steps. We remove the # symbol, all @ mentions and links and perform lower case conversion. Also, if a vowel is repeated more than 3 times in a word, we reduce it to

*Second Joint Conference on Lexical and Computational Semantics (*SEM), Volume 2: Seventh International Workshop on Semantic Evaluation (SemEval 2013)*, pages 418–424, Atlanta, Georgia, June 14-15, 2013.

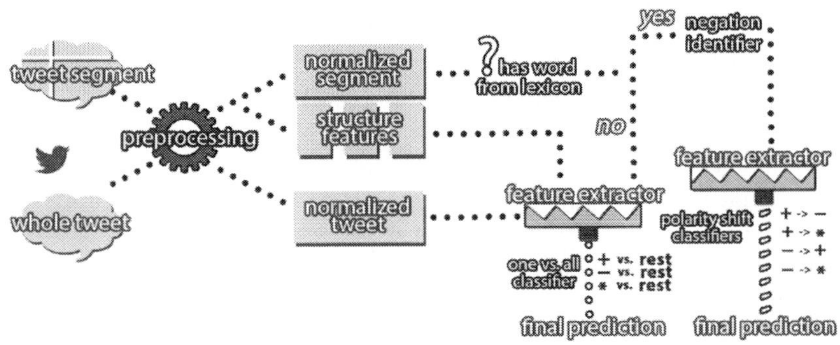

Figure 1: Contextual polarity disambiguation task system description

a single occurrence and we reduce multiple consecutive punctuation marks to a single one. Finally, we lemmatize the normalized text.

Emoticons have been successfully used as sentiment indicators in tweets (Davidov et al., 2010). In our approach, we map a set of positive emoticons to the word *good* and a set of negative emoticons to the word *bad*. We use the following sets of emoticons:

- Positive emoticons: :) , :-) , :D , =) , :’) , :o) , :P , >:) , :”>, >:|, <3 , ;>, ;) , ;-) , ;>, (: , (;
- Negative emoticons: :(, : (, :-(, :’(, :/ , :<, ;(

Traits of informal language have been used as features in Twitter sentiment classification tasks (Go et al., 2009). In order to avoid the loss of possible useful information, we keep record of the performed normalizations as binary features associated to a tweet segment. We retain the following set of features: *hasPositiveEmoticon, hasNegativeEmoticon, hasHashtag, hasAtSign, hasConsecutivePunctuation, hasConsecutiveVowels, hasUpperCaseWords.*

2.1.2 Classification methods

In a first step, we select tweet segments that contain at least one word from a lexicon and assign to it the polarity of that word. If there are more than one sentiment words with different polarities in the segment, we keep the most frequent polarity and in the few cases where there is an equal number of positive and negative words, we take the polarity of the last one. Next, we look for negation indicators (e.g. *not, ’t*) using a set of words and rules and replace them with the *NEG* token. We then identify instances where there is a shift between the polarity predicted from the lexicon and the one from the ground truth. In order to account for the unbalanced datasets(e.g. 192 instances where there is a $+ \rightarrow -$ shift and 3188 where the positive instance was correctly identified from the lexicon) we use cost sensitive classifiers. We define a cost matrix in which the cost of the classifier making a false positive error is three times higher than a false negative error. Using this approach we guide the classifier to provide less but more confident predictions for the existence of a polarity shift while allowing it to make more errors when predicting the absence of a shift. For these classifiers, we use a *Bag of Words* representation of the lemmatized segments. When a word from the sentiment lexicon does not appear in the tweet segment, we use a *one vs. all* classification approach with a SVM classifier and tree kernels. The tree kernel is a function between two trees that computes a normalized similarity score in the range *[0,1]* (Culotta and Sorensen, 2004). For our task, we use an implementation of tree kernels for syntactic parse trees (Moschitti, 2006) that is built on top of the SVM-Light library (Joachims, 1999) in a similar manner to that presented in (Ginsca, 2012). We build the syntactic parse trees with the Stanford CoreNLP library (Klein and Manning, 2003).

2.2 Evaluation and Results

For the experiments presented in this section, we merge the training and development datasets and for the polarity shift and sentiment classification experiments we report the results using a 5-fold cross validation technique over the resulting dataset.

2.2.1 Lexicon choice influence

Considering that the selection of a lexicon plays an important role on the performance of our system, we tested 3 widely used sentiment lexicons: SentiWordNet 3 (Baccianella et al., 2010), Bing Liu's Opinion Lexicon (Hu and Liu, 2004) and MPQA Subjectivity Lexicon (Wilson et al., 2005). Different combinations of these lexicons were tried and in Table 1 we present the top performing ones. Besides the F-Measure for positive (*Fp*) and negative (*Fn*) instances, we also list the percentage of instances in which appears at least one word from the lexicon. SentiWordnet appoints polarity weights to words, ranging from 0 to 1. An important parameter is the threshold over which a word is considered to have a certain polarity. We tested several values (from 0.5 to 0.9 with a step of 0.05) and the best results in terms of F-Measure were obtained for a threshold of 0.75. Our finding is consistent with the value suggested in (Chen et al., 2012).

Lexicon	Found(%)	Fp	Fn
Liu	55.7	0.93	0.85
MPQA	61.4	0.89	0.76
SentWN	79.4	0.86	0.78
Liu+MPQA	67.1	0.89	0.78
Liu+SentWN	79.4	0.87	0.81
Liu+MPQA+SentWN	79.4	0.86	0.81

Table 1: Influence of lexicon on the F-Measure for positive and negative segments

2.2.2 Polarity shift experiments

We tested several classifiers using the Weka toolkit (Hall et al., 2009) and found that the best results were obtained with the Sequential Minimal Optimization (SMO) classifier. For instance, when classifying $+ \rightarrow -$ shifts, SMO correctly identified 91 out of 192 polarity shifts in contrast with 68 and 41 detected by a Random Forests and a Naive Bayes classifier, respectively. For the $+ \rightarrow *$ classification, the SMO classifier finds 2 out of 34 shifts, for $- \rightarrow +$, 15 out of 238 and for $- \rightarrow *$, 2 out of 32 shifts are found. After changing the polarity of sentiment segments as found by the 4 classifiers, we obtain an increase in F-Measure from 0.930 to **0.947** for positive segments and from 0.851 to **0.913** for negative segments. Our choice of the *Bag of Words* model instead of a parse tree representation for these classifiers is justified by the poor performance of tree kernels when dealing with unbalanced data.

2.2.3 Sentiment classification experiments

Model	Class	Avg. F-score
Basic Tree	positive	0.780
	negative	0.645
	neutral	0.227
Tree + Numeric	positive	0.768
	negative	0.590
	neutral	0.132
Tree + Context_2	positive	0.801
	negative	0.676
	neutral	0.231

Table 2: Comparison between different models used for segment polarity classification

In a series of preliminary experiments, we tested several classifiers trained on a *Bag of Words* model and an SVM classifier with a tree kernel. We found that the parse tree representation of a tweet segment provided a higher accuracy. This shows that although small, when a segment contains more than one word, its syntactic structure becomes a relevant feature.
In Table 2 we compare the results of 3 tree based models. In the *Basic Tree* model, we use only the syntactic parse tree representation of a tweet segment. For the *Tree + Numeric* model, we use the initial tree kernel together with a polynomial kernel on the binary structure features presented in section 2.1.1. In the *Tree + Context* model, we include in the parse tree, besides the given section, *k* tokens (words, punctuation) from the whole tweet that surround the selected segment. We performed tests with *k* from *1* to *5* and obtained the best results with a *k* value of 2.

2.2.4 Competition results

For the Twitter dataset, we ranked **4th** out of 23 groups that submitted constrained runs. When combining the results of the constrained and unconstrained submissions, our run was ranked **5th** out of a total of 29 submissions. For the SMS dataset, we ranked **5th** out of a total of 18 groups for the constrained setting and our submission was ranked **5th** out of 24 combined runs. In Table 3, we detail the results we obtained on the competition test datasets.

Class	P	R	F-score
Twitter_positive	0.8623	0.9140	0.8874
Twitter_negative	0.8453	0.8086	0.8265
Twitter_neutral	0.4127	0.1625	0.2332
SMS_positive	0.7107	0.8945	0.7921
SMS_negative	0.8687	0.7609	0.8112
SMS_neutral	0.3684	0.0440	0.0787

Table 3: Competition results overview on the Twitter and SMS datasets

2.3 Discussion

The robustness of our approach is proved by the low standard deviation of the F-Measure scores obtained over each of the the 5 folds used for evaluation (0.026) but also by the small difference between the results we obtained during the development phase and those reported on the competition test dataset. The choice of lexicons results in a trade-off between the percentage of instances classified with either the lexicon and polarity shift or the supervised learning method. Although the first one yields better results and it is apparently desirable to have a better coverage of lexicon terms, this would reduce the number of instances for training a classifier leading to a poorer performance of this approach.

3 Task B: Message Polarity Classification

In this section, we present our approach for the message polarity classification task in which, given a message, the system has to determine whether it expresses a positive, negative, or neutral sentiment. As for Task A, we submitted a single constrained run.

3.1 Preprocessing of the corpora

We use as training corpora the training data, merged with the development data. After the deletion of tweets no longer available, our final training set contains 10402 tweets: 3855 positive, 1633 negative and 4914 objective or neutral. In the preprocessing step, we first remove the web addresses from the tweets to reduce the noise. Then, we extract the emoticons and create new features with the number of occurrences of each type of emoticon. The different emoticons types are presented in Table 4. Then, we lemmatize the text using LIMA, a linguistic analyzer of CEA LIST (Besançon et al., 2010).

:-) :) =) X) x)	Smile
:-(:(=(	Sadness
:-D :D =D X-D XD x-D xD :')	Laugh
;-) ;)	Wink
< 3	Heart
:'-(:'(='(	Tear

Table 4: Common emoticon types

3.2 Boostexter baseline

To classify the tweets, we used the BoosTexter[1] classifier (Schapire and Singer, 2000) in its discrete AdaBoost.MH version, setting the number of iterations to 1000. We used two types of features: a *Bag of Words* of lemmatized uni-, bi- and tri-grams and the number of occurrences of each emoticon type.

Bog of words features	Emoticon type feature
wow lady gaga be great	Smile 1

Table 5: Example of tweet representation

Boostexter is designed to maximize the accuracy, not the F-score, which is the chosen evaluation metric for this task. As the training data contain few negative examples, the classifier tends to under-detect this class. In order to favour the negative class detection, we balance the training corpora. So our final system is trained on 4899 tweets (1633 of each class, chosen randomly). The accuracy results are not presented here. However, the gain between our baseline and our final system has the same order of magnitude.

3.3 Integration of domain information

Some words can change their polarity between two different domains (Navigli, 2012; Yoshida et al., 2011). For example, the word "return" is positive in "I can't wait to return to my book". However, it is often very negative when we are talking about some electronics device, as in "I had to return my phone to the store". This phenomenon happens even in more closely related domains: "I was laughing all the time" is a good point for a comedy film but a bad one for a horror film. We call such words or expressions "multi-polarity words". This phenomenon is different

[1]BoosTexter is a general purpose machine-learning program based on boosting for building a classifier from text.

from polysemy, as a word can keep the same meaning across domains while changing its polarity and it can lead to classification error (Wilson et al., 2009). In (Marchand, 2013), we have shown, on a corpus of reviews, that a sensible amount of multi-polarity words influences the results of common opinion classifiers. Their deletion or their differentiation leads to better classification results. Here, we test this approach on a corpus of tweets.

3.3.1 Domain generation with LDA

In order to apply our method, we need to assign domains to tweets. For that purpose, we use Latent Dirichlet Allocation (LDA) (Blei et al., 2003). We used the Mallet LDA implementation (McCallum, 2002). The framework uses Gibbs sampling to constitute the sample distributions that are exploited for the creation of the topic models. The models are built using the lemmatized tweets from the training and development data. We performed tests with a number of domains ranging from 5 to 25, with a step of 5. Each LDA representation of a tweet is encoded by inferring a domain distribution. For example, if a model with 5 domains is used, we generate a vector of length 5, where each the i-th value is the proportion of terms belonging to the i-th domain.

Domain 1	tonight, watch, time, today
Domain 2	win, vote, obama, black
Domain 3	game, play, win, team
Domain 4	apple, international, sun, anderson
Domain 5	ticket, show, open, live

Table 6: Most representative words of each domain (5 domains version)

In first experiments with crossvalidation on training data, the 5 domains version, presented in Table 6, appears to be the most efficient. Therefore, in the rest of the paper, results are shown only for this version.

3.3.2 Detection of multi-polarity words

For detecting the multi-polarity words, we use the positive and negative labels of the training data. We make the assumption that positive words will mostly appear in positive tweets and negative words in negative tweets. Between two different corpora, we determine words with different polarity across corpora by using a χ^2 test on their profile of occurrence in positive and negative tweets in both corpora. The risk of false positive is set to 0.05. The words are also selected only if they occur more often than a given threshold. For the SemEval task B, we apply this detection for each domain. Each time, we detect the words that change their polarity between a specific domain and all the others. For example, the word "black" is detected as positive in the second domain, related to the election of Barack Obama, and neutral in the rest of the tweets. At the end of this procedure, we have 5 collections of words which change their polarity (one different collection for each domain). These collections are rather small: from 21 to 61 multi-polarity words are detected depending on the domain and the parameters.

3.3.3 Differentiation of multi-polarity words

We tested different strategies in order to integrate the domain information in the Sentiment Classification in Twitter task.

- Domain-specific: 5 different classifiers are trained on the domain specific subpart of the tweets, without change on the data.
- Diff-topic: 5 different classifiers are trained on the whole corpus, where the detected multi-polarity words are differentiated into "word-domainX" and "word-other".
- Change-all: only 1 classifier is trained. Similar to the previous one, except all the differentiations are made at the same time.
- Keep-topic: 5 different classifiers are trained. The detected multi-polarity words are kept inside their domain and deleted in the others.
- Remove-all: 5 different classifiers are trained. The detected multi-polarity words are deleted inside and outside their domain.

For the *change-all* version, we use only one classifier: all test tweets are classified using the same classifier. In the other versions, we obtain 5 classifiers. For each test tweet, we determine its domain profile using topic models of LDA. Then we use a mix of all the classifiers with weighting according to the LDA mixture[2]. The *domain-specific* version gives worse

[2]The weight is the exponential of the LDA score.

results than the baseline trained on the whole original corpus and is not represented on the figures.

Figure 2: Average F-measure results for the best set of parameters for each method.

We tested all these versions with two training sets: first, using all the training tweets to train the classifiers (Figure 2) and secondly, only the tweets for which a domain can be confidently attributed (at least a 75% score from the LDA model) (Figure 3). In this case, the training set contains 2889 tweets. The run submitted to SemEval corresponds to the *change-all* version, trained with all the training tweets.

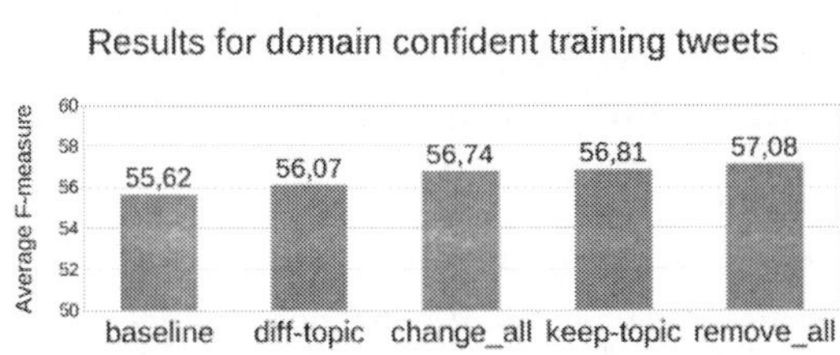

Figure 3: Average F-measure results for the best set of parameters for each method.

Empirically, we set the threshold for the number of occurrences to 10 in the first experiment and only to 5 in the domain confident experiment, due to the smallest size of the training corpora.

3.4 Analysis of the result and discussion

Using a boosting method with lemma trigrams and emoticons features is a good fully automatic baseline. We are in the mid range of results of all the participants (19th out of 48 submissions for the tweets and 26th out of 42 submissions for the SMS). We try to include domain information to improve the opinion classification. As we don't have a reference domain differentiation for the tweets, we separate them using the LDA method. The *domain-specific* version, which does not take into account the multi-polarity words, degrades the performances(-1.85% in the first experiment, -2.8% in the second). On the contrary, all our versions which use multi-polarity words, especially remove-all version, improve the F-measure. The final improvement is small but it has to be related to the small number of multi-polarity words we have detected (in average, 36 words per domain). We think that the tweet collection is too small for the χ_2 test to detect a lot of words with enough confidence. For comparison, in our experiment on reviews, we detected about 400 multi-polarity words per domain. It is also worth noticing that for the domain confident experiment, the improvement is more sensible (+1.46% versus +0.70%) even if the absolute value of the score is not better, due to a much smaller training data. It's a good argument for our method. Another question is about the method used to separate the tweets into different domains. We plan to have more control on the domains by using a more supervised method based on the categories of Wikipedia.

4 Conclusion

In this paper, we presented our contribution to SemEval 2013 task 2: Sentiment Analysis in Twitter. For the Contextual Polarity Disambiguation subtask, we described a very efficient and robust method based on a sentiment lexicon associated with a polarity shift detector and a tree based classification. As for the Message Polarity Classification, we focused on the impact of domain information. With only 4899 training tweets, we achieve good performances and we demonstrate that words with changing polarity can influence the classification performance.
One of the challenges of this SemEval task was to see how well sentiment analysis models trained using Twitter data would generalize to a SMS dataset. Looking at our result but also at the submissions of other participants, a drop of performance can be observed between the results on the Twitter and SMS test datasets. In (Hu et al., 2013), the authors perform a thorough study on the differences between the language used on Twitter and that of SMS messages and chat. They find that Twitter language is more conservative and less informal than SMS and online chat and that the language of Twitter can be seen as a projection of a formal register in a restricted space. This is a good indicator to the difficulty of using a Twitter centered system on a SMS dataset.

Acknowledgments

This work was partly supported by the MUCKE project (http://ifs.tuwien.ac.at/~mucke/) through a grant from the French National Research Agency (ANR), FP7 CHIST-ERA Programme (ANR-12-CHRI-0007-04).

References

Stefano Baccianella, Andrea Esuli, and Fabrizio Sebastiani. 2010. Sentiwordnet 3.0: An enhanced lexical resource for sentiment analysis and opinion mining. In *Proceedings of the 7th conference on International Language Resources and Evaluation (LREC10), Valletta, Malta, May.*

Romaric Besançon, Gaël de Chalendar, Olivier Ferret, Faiza Gara, Olivier Mesnard, Meriama Lab, and Nasredine Semmar. 2010. Lima : A multilingual framework for linguistic analysis and linguistic resources development and evaluation. In Nicoletta Calzolari (Conference Chair), Khalid Choukri, Bente Maegaard, Joseph Mariani, Jan Odijk, Stelios Piperidis, Mike Rosner, and Daniel Tapias, editors, *Proceedings of LREC'10*, Valletta, Malta, may. European Language Resources Association (ELRA).

David M Blei, Andrew Y Ng, and Michael I Jordan. 2003. Latent dirichlet allocation. *the Journal of machine Learning research*, 3:993–1022.

Lu Chen, Wenbo Wang, Meenakshi Nagarajan, Shaojun Wang, and Amit P Sheth. 2012. Extracting diverse sentiment expressions with target-dependent polarity from twitter. *Proceedings of ICWSM*.

Aron Culotta and Jeffrey Sorensen. 2004. Dependency tree kernels for relation extraction. In *Proceedings of the 42nd Annual Meeting on Association for Computational Linguistics*, page 423. Association for Computational Linguistics.

Dmitry Davidov, Oren Tsur, and Ari Rappoport. 2010. Enhanced sentiment learning using twitter hashtags and smileys. In *Proceedings of the 23rd International Conference on Computational Linguistics: Posters*, pages 241–249. Association for Computational Linguistics.

Alexandru Lucian Ginsca. 2012. Fine-grained opinion mining as a relation classification problem. In *2012 Imperial College Computing Student Workshop*, volume 28, pages 56–61. Schloss Dagstuhl–Leibniz-Zentrum fuer Informatik.

Alec Go, Richa Bhayani, and Lei Huang. 2009. Twitter sentiment classification using distant supervision. *CS224N Project Report, Stanford*, pages 1–12.

Mark Hall, Eibe Frank, Geoffrey Holmes, Bernhard Pfahringer, Peter Reutemann, and Ian H Witten. 2009. The weka data mining software: an update. *ACM SIGKDD Explorations Newsletter*, 11(1):10–18.

Minqing Hu and Bing Liu. 2004. Mining and summarizing customer reviews. In *Proceedings of the tenth ACM SIGKDD international conference on Knowledge discovery and data mining*, pages 168–177. ACM.

Yuheng Hu, Kartik Talamadupula, and Subbarao Kambhampati. 2013. Dude, srsly?: The surprisingly formal nature of twitters language. *Proceedings of ICWSM*.

Thorsten Joachims. 1999. Making large scale svm learning practical.

Dan Klein and Christopher D Manning. 2003. Accurate unlexicalized parsing. In *Proceedings of the 41st Annual Meeting on Association for Computational Linguistics-Volume 1*, pages 423–430. Association for Computational Linguistics.

Morgane Marchand. 2013. Fouille dopinion: ces mots qui changent de polarité selon le domaine. In *Proceedings of the 8e Rencontres Jeunes Chercheurs en Recherche dInformation (RJCRI)*.

Andrew Kachites McCallum. 2002. Mallet: A machine learning for language toolkit.

Alessandro Moschitti. 2006. Making tree kernels practical for natural language learning. In *Proceedings of EACL*, volume 6, pages 113–120.

R. Navigli. 2012. A quick tour of word sense disambiguation, induction and related approaches. *SOFSEM 2012: Theory and Practice of Computer Science*, pages 115–129.

Robert E Schapire and Yoram Singer. 2000. Boostexter: A boosting-based system for text categorization. *Machine learning*, 39(2-3):135–168.

Theresa Wilson, Janyce Wiebe, and Paul Hoffmann. 2005. Recognizing contextual polarity in phrase-level sentiment analysis. In *Proceedings of the conference on Human Language Technology and Empirical Methods in Natural Language Processing*, pages 347–354. Association for Computational Linguistics.

Theresa Wilson, Janyce Wiebe, and Paul Hoffmann. 2009. Recognizing contextual polarity: An exploration of features for phrase-level sentiment analysis. *Computational Linguistics*, 35.

Theresa Wilson, Zornitsa Kozareva, Preslav Nakov, Alan Ritter, Sara Rosenthal, and Veselin Stoyanov. 2013. Semeval-2013 task 2: Sentiment analysis in twitter. In *Proceedings of the 7th International Workshop on Semantic Evaluation*. Association for Computational Linguistics.

Yasuhisa Yoshida, Tsutomu Hirao, Tomoharu Iwata, Masaaki Nagata, and Yuji Matsumoto. 2011. Transfer learning for multiple-domain sentiment analysis - identifying domain dependent/independent word polaritys. In *AAAI*.

SwatCS: Combining simple classifiers with estimated accuracy

Sam Clark and **Richard Wicentowski**
Department of Computer Science
Swarthmore College
Swarthmore, PA 19081 USA
sclark2@sccs.swarthmore.edu and richardw@cs.swarthmore.edu

Abstract

This paper is an overview of the SwatCS system submitted to SemEval-2013 Task 2A: Contextual Polarity Disambiguation. The sentiment of individual phrases within a tweet are labeled using a combination of classifiers trained on a range of lexical features. The classifiers are combined by estimating the accuracy of the classifiers on each tweet. Performance is measured when using only the provided training data, and separately when including external data.

1 Introduction

Spurred on by the wide-spread use of the social networks to communicate with friends, fans and customers around the globe, Twitter has been adopted by celebrities, athletes, politicians, and major companies as a platform that mitigates the interaction between individuals.

Analysis of this Twitter data can provide insights into how users express themselves. For example, many new forms of expression and language features have emerged on Twitter, including expressions containing mentions, hashtags, emoticons, and abbreviations. This research leverages the lexical features in tweets to predict whether a phrase within a tweet conveys a positive or negative sentiment.

2 Related Work

A common goal of past research has been to discover and extract features from tweets that accurately indicate sentiment (Liu, 2010). The importance of feature selection and machine learning in sentiment analysis has been explored prior to the rise of social networks. For example, Pang and Lee (2004) apply machine learning techniques to extracted features from movie reviews.

More recent feature-based systems include a lexicon-based approach (Taboada et al., 2011), and a more focused study on the importance of both adverbs and adjectives in determining sentiment (Benamara et al., 2007). Other examples include using looser descriptions of sentiment rather than rigid positive/negative labelings (Whitelaw et al., 2005) and investigating how connections between users can be used to predict sentiment (Tan et al., 2011).

This task differs from past work in sentiment analysis of tweets because we aim to build a model capable of predicting the sentiment of sub-phrases within the tweet rather than considering the entire tweet. Specifically, "given a message containing a marked instance of a word or a phrase, determine whether that instance is positive, negative or neutral in that context" (Wilson et al., 2013). Research on context-oriented polarity predates the emergence of social networks: (Nasukawa and Yi, 2003) predict sentiment of subsections in a larger document.

N-gram features, part of speech features and "micro-blogging features" have been used as accurate indicators of polarity (Kouloumpis et al., 2011). The "micro-blogging features" are of particular interest as they provide insight into how users have adapted Twitter tokens to natural language to portray sentiment. These features include hashtags and emoticons (Kouloumpis et al., 2011).

*Second Joint Conference on Lexical and Computational Semantics (*SEM), Volume 2: Seventh International Workshop on Semantic Evaluation (SemEval 2013)*, pages 425–429, Atlanta, Georgia, June 14-15, 2013.

3 Data

The task organizers provided a manually-labeled set of tweets. For parts of this study, their data was supplemented with external data (Go et al., 2009).

As part of pre-processing, all tweets were part-of-speech tagged using the ARK TweetNLP tools (Owoputi et al., 2013). All punctuation was stripped, except for `#hashtags`, `@mentions`, emoticons `:)`, and exclamation marks. All hyperlinks were replaced with a common string, "URL".

3.1 Common Data

The provided training data was a collection of approximately 15K tweets, manually labeled for sentiment (positive, negative, neutral, or objective) (Wilson et al., 2013). These sentiment labels applied to a specific phrase within the tweet and did not necessarily match the sentiment of the entire tweet. Each tweet had at least one labeled phrase, though some tweets had multiple phrases labeled individually. Overall, 37% of tweets had one labeled phrase, with an average of 2.58 labeled phrases per tweet.

Each of our classifiers were binary classifiers, labeling phrases as either positive or negative. As such, approximately 10.5K phrases labeled as objective or neutral were pruned from the training data, resulting in a final training set containing 5362 labeled phrases, 3445 positive and 1917 negative.

The test data consisted of tweets and SMS messages, although the training data contained only tweets. The test set for the phrase-level task (Task A) contained 4435 tweets and 2334 SMS messages.

3.2 Outside Data

Task organizers allowed two submissions, a constrained submission using only the provided training data, and an unconstrained submission allowing the use of external data. For the unconstrained submission, we used a data set built by Go et al. (2009). The data set was automatically labeled using emoticons to predict sentiment. We used a 50K tweet subset containing 25K positive and 25K negative tweets.

3.3 Phrase Isolation

For tweets containing a single labeled phrase, we use the entire tweet as the context for the phrase. For tweets containing two labeled phrases, we use the context from the start of the tweet to the end of the first phrase as the context for the first phrase, and the context from the start of the second phrase to the end of the tweet for the second phrase. If more than two phrases are present, the context for any phrase in the middle of the tweet is limited to only the words in the labeled phrase.

unigram	label	**bigram**	label
happy	pos	not going	neg
good	pos	looking forward	pos
great	pos	happy birthday	pos
love	pos	last episode	neg
best	pos	i'm mad	neg

Table 1: The 5 most influential unigram and bigrams ranked by information gain.

4 Classifiers

The system uses a combination of naive Bayes classifiers to label the input. Each classifier is trained on a single feature extracted from the tweet. The classifiers are combined using a confidence-weighted voting scheme. The system applies a simple negation scheme to all of the language features used by the classifiers. Any word following a negation term in the phrase has the substring "NOT" prefixed to it. This negation scheme was applied to n-gram features and lexicon features.

4.1 N-gram Features

Rather than use all of the n-grams as features, we ranked each n-gram (w/POS tags) by calculating its chi-square-based information gain. The top 2000 n-grams (1000 positive, 1000 negative) are used as features in the n-gram classifier. Both a unigram and bigram classifier use these ranked (word/POS) features. Table 1 shows the highest ranked unigrams and bigrams using this method.

4.2 Sentiment Lexicon Features

A second classifier uses the MPQA subjectivity lexicon (Wiebe et al., 2005). We extract both the polarity and the polarity strength for each word/POS in the lexicon matching a word/POS in the phrase's context. We refer to this classifier as the *lexicon classifier*.

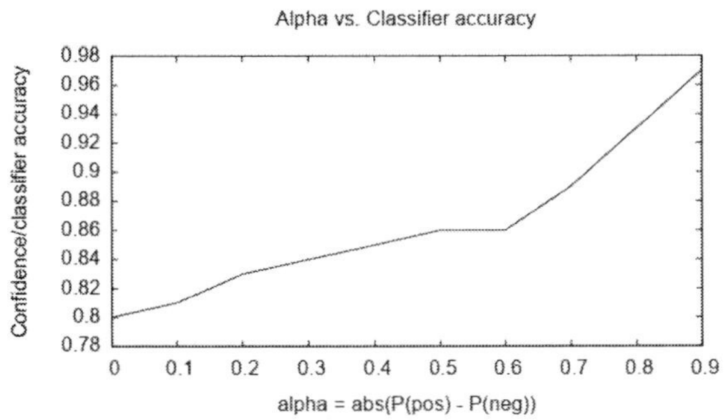

Figure 1: Classifier accuracy increases as the difference between the probabilities of the labelings increases.

rank	classifier	data	polarity	acc
1	unigrams	(C)	positive	0.89
2	unigrams	(U)	positive	0.88
3	lexicon	(C)	negative	0.83
4	lexicon	(U)	negative	0.81
5	tagcount	(C)	positive	0.78
6	bigrams	(C)	positive	0.75
7	tagcount	(U)	novote	<0.65
8	bigrams	(U)	novote	<0.65

Table 2: An example of the polarity and corresponding accuracy output for each classifier for a single tweet. The labels (C) and (U) indicate whether the classifier was trained on constrained training data or on unconstrained data (Go et al., 2009).

4.3 Part of Speech and Special Token Features

Three additional classifiers were built using features extracted from the tweets. Our third classifier uses only the raw counts of specific part of speech tags: adjectives, adverbs, interjections, and emoticons. The fourth classifier uses the emoticons as a feature. To reduce the noise in the emoticon feature set, many (over 25) different emoticons are mapped to the basic ":)" and ":(" expressions. Some emoticons such as "xD" did not map to these basic expressions. A fifth classifier gives added weight to words with extraneous repeated letters. Words containing two or more repeated letters (that are not in a dictionary, e.g. "heyyyyy", "sweeeet") are mapped to their presumed correct spelling (e.g. "hey", "sweet").

5 Confidence-Based Classification

To combine all of the classifiers, the system estimates the confidence of each classifier and only accepts the classification output if the confidence is higher than a specified baseline. To establish a classifier's confidence, we take the absolute value of the difference between a classifier's positive output probability and negative output probability, which we call alpha. Alpha values close to 1 indicate high confidence in the predicted label; values close to 0 indicate low confidence in the predicted label.

5.1 Classifier Voting

The predicted accuracy of each classifier is determined after the trained classifiers are evaluated using a development set with known labels. Using the dev set, we calculate the accuracy of each classifier at alpha values between 0 and 1. The result is a trained classifier with an approximation of overall classification accuracy at a given alpha value. Figure 1 shows the relationship between alpha value and overall classifier accuracy. As expected, classification accuracy increases as confidence increases.

Table 2 shows the breakdown of classifier accuracy for a single tweet using both provided and external data. The accuracy listed is the classifier-specific accuracy determined by the alpha value for that phrase in the tweet. Using a dev set, we experimentally established the most effective baseline to be 0.65. In the voting system described below, only classifiers with confidence above the baseline (per marked phrase) are used. Therefore, the specific combination of classifiers used for each phrase may be different.

An unlabeled phrase is assigned a polarity and confidence value from each classifier. These probabilities are combined using a voting system to determine a single output. This voting system calculates the final labeling by computing the average probability for each label only for those classifiers with estimated accuracies above the baseline. The label with the highest overall probability is selected.

6 Results

The constrained submission only allowed for training on the provided data and placed 17 out of 23 entries. The unconstrained submission was trained on both the provided data and the external data and placed 6 out of 8 entries. Both submissions were

unigram	label	**bigram**	label	**lexicon**	label
aint	neg	school tomorrow	neg	bad	neg
excited	pos	not going	neg	excited	pos
sucks	neg	didn't get	neg	tired	neg
sick	neg	might not	neg	dead	neg
poor	neg	gonna miss	neg	poor	neg
smh	pos	still haven't	neg	happy	pos
tough	pos	breakout kings	neg	black	neg
greatest	pos	work tomorrow	neg	good	pos
f*ck	neg	ray lewis	pos	hate	neg
nets	neg	can't wait	pos	sorry	neg

Table 3: The most influential features from the unigram, bigram, and lexicon classifiers.

evaluated using the Twitter and SMS data described in Section 3.1. As mentioned, our system used a binary classifier, predicting only positive and negative labels, making no neutral classifications.

The constrained system evaluated on the Twitter test set had an F-measure of .672, with a high disparity between the F-measure for tweets labeled as positive versus those labeled as negative (.79 vs .53). The unconstrained system on the Twitter test set underperformed our constrained system, with an F-measure of only .639.

The constrained system on the SMS test set yielded an F-measure of .660; the unconstrained system on the same data yielded an F-measure of .679.

6.1 Features Extracted

The most important features extracted by the unigram, bigram and lexicon classifiers are shown in Table 3. Features such as "ray lewis", "smh", "school tomorrow", "work tomorrow", "breakout kings" and "nets" demonstrate that the classifiers formed a relationship between sentiment and colloquial language. An example of this understanding is assigning a strong negative sentiment to "sucks" (as the verb "to suck" does not carry sentiment). The bigrams "breakout kings", "ray lewis" and "nets" are interesting features because their sentiment is highly cultural: "breakout kings" is a popular TV show that was canceled, "ray lewis" a high profile player for an NFL team, and "nets" a reference to the struggling NBA basketball team. Expressions such as "smh" (a widely-used abbreviation for "shaking my head") show how detecting tweet- and SMS-specific language is important to understanding sentiment in this domain.

7 Discussion

This supervised system combines many features to classify positive and negative sentiment at the phrase-level. Phrase-based isolation (Section 3.3) limits irrelevant context in the model. By estimating classifier confidence on a per-phrase basis, the system can prioritize confident classifiers and ignore less-confident ones before combination.

Similar results on the Twitter and SMS data sets indicates the similarity between the domains. The external data improved the system on the SMS data and reduced system accuracy on the Twitter data. This difference in performance may be an indication that the supplemental data set was noisier than we expected, or that it was more applicable to the SMS domain (SMS) than we anticipated.

There was a noticeable difference between positive and negative classification accuracy for all of the submissions. This difference is likely due to either a positive bias in training set used (the provided training data is 64% positive, 36% negative) or a selection of features that favored positive sentiment.

7.1 Improvements and Future Work

Unfortunately, the time constraints of the evaluation exercise led to a programming bug that wasn't caught until after the submission deadline. In preprocessing, we accidentally stripped most of the emoticon features out of the text. While it is unclear how much this would have effected our final performance, such features have been demonstrated as valuable in similar tasks. After fixing this bug the system performs better in both constrained and unconstrained situations (as evaluated on the development set).

We would like to increase the size of external data set to include all of the approximately 380K tweets (rather than the 50K subset we used). This expanded training set would likely improve the robustness of the system. Specifically, we would expect classifiers with limited coverage, such as the repeat-letter classifier, to yield increased performance.

References

Farah Benamara, Carmine Cesarano, Antonio Picariello, Diego Reforgiato, and V Subrahmanian. 2007. Sentiment analysis: Adjectives and adverbs are better than adjectives alone. In *Proceedings of the International Conference on Weblogs and Social Media (ICWSM)*.

A. Go, R. Bhayani, and Huang. L. 2009. Twitter sentiment classification using distant supervision. Technical report, Stanford University.

Efthymios Kouloumpis, Theresa Wilson, and Johanna Moore. 2011. Twitter sentiment analysis: The good the bad and the omg. In *Proceedings of the Fifth International AAAI Conference on Weblogs and Social Media*, pages 538–541.

Bing Liu. 2010. Sentiment analysis and subjectivity. *Handbook of natural language processing*, 2:568.

Tetsuya Nasukawa and Jeonghee Yi. 2003. Sentiment analysis: capturing favorability using natural language processing. In *Proceedings of the 2nd international conference on Knowledge capture*, K-CAP '03, pages 70–77.

Olutobi Owoputi, Brendan O'Connor, Chris Dyer, Kevin Gimpel, Nathan Schneider, and Noah A. Smith. 2013. Improved part-of-speech tagging for online conversational text with word clusters. In *Proceedings of NAACL 2013*.

Bo Pang and Lillian Lee. 2004. A sentimental education: sentiment analysis using subjectivity summarization based on minimum cuts. In *Proceedings of the 42nd Annual Meeting on Association for Computational Linguistics*, ACL '04, Stroudsburg, PA, USA. Association for Computational Linguistics.

Maite Taboada, Julian Brooke, Milan Tofiloski, Kimberly Voll, and Manfred Stede. 2011. Lexicon-based methods for sentiment analysis. *Computational linguistics*, 37(2):267–307.

Chenhao Tan, Lillian Lee, Jie Tang, Long Jiang, Ming Zhou, and Ping Li. 2011. User-level sentiment analysis incorporating social networks. In *Proceedings of the 17th ACM SIGKDD international conference on Knowledge discovery and data mining*, pages 1397–1405.

Casey Whitelaw, Navendu Garg, and Shlomo Argamon. 2005. Using appraisal groups for sentiment analysis. In *Proceedings of the 14th ACM international conference on Information and knowledge management*, CIKM '05, pages 625–631.

Janyce Wiebe, Theresa Wilson, and Claire Cardie. 2005. Annotating expressions of opinions and emotions in language. *Language Resources and Evaluation*, 39(2-3):165–210.

Theresa Wilson, Zornitsa Kozareva, Preslav Nakov, Sara Rosenthal, Veselin Stoyanov, and Alan Ritter. 2013. SemEval-2013 task 2: Sentiment analysis in twitter. In *Proceedings of the International Workshop on Semantic Evaluation*, SemEval'13.

NTNU: Domain Semi-Independent Short Message Sentiment Classification

Øyvind Selmer **Mikael Brevik** **Björn Gambäck** **Lars Bungum**
Department of Computer and Information Science
Norwegian University of Science and Technology (NTNU)
Sem Sælands vei 7–9, NO–7491 Trondheim, Norway
{oyvinsel,mikaelbr}@stud.ntnu.no {gamback,larsbun}@idi.ntnu.no

Abstract

The paper describes experiments using grid searches over various combinations of machine learning algorithms, features and preprocessing strategies in order to produce the optimal systems for sentiment classification of microblog messages. The approach is fairly domain independent, as demonstrated by the systems achieving quite competitive results when applied to short text message data, i.e., input they were not originally trained on.

1 Introduction

The informal texts in microblogs such as Twitter and on other social media represent challenges for traditional language processing systems. The posts ("tweets") are limited to 140 characters and often contain misspellings, slang and abbreviations. On the other hand, the posts are often opinionated in nature as a very result of their informal character, which has led Twitter to being a gold mine for sentiment analysis (SA). SA for longer texts, such as movie reviews, has been explored since the 1990s;[1] however, the limited amount of attributes in tweets makes the feature vectors shorter than in documents and the task of analysing them closely related to phrase- and sentence-level SA (Wilson et al., 2005; Yu and Hatzivassiloglou, 2003). Hence there are no guarantees that algorithms that perform well on document-level SA will do as well on tweets. On the other hand, it is possible to exploit some of the special features of the web language, e.g., emoticons and emotionally loaded abbreviations. Thus the data will normally go through some preprocessing before any classification is attempted, e.g., by filtering out Twitter specific symbols and functions, in particular retweets (reposting another user's tweet), mentions ('@', tags used to mention another user), hashtags ('#', used to tag a tweet to a certain topic), emoticons, and URLs (linking to an external resource, e.g., a news article or a photo). The first system to really use Twitter as a corpus was created as a student course project at Stanford (Go et al., 2009). Pak and Paroubek (2010) experimented with sentiment classification of tweets using Support Vector Machines and Conditional Random Fields, benchmarked with a Naïve Bayes Classifier baseline, but were unable to beat the baseline. Later, and as Twitter has grown in popularity, many other systems for Twitter Sentiment Analysis (TSA) have been developed (see, e.g., Maynard and Funk, 2011; Mukherjee et al., 2012; Saif et al., 2012; Chamlertwat et al., 2012).

Clearly, it is possible to classify the sentiment of tweets in a single step; however, the approach to TSA most used so far is a two-step strategy where the first step is subjectivity classification and the second step is polarity classification. The goal of *subjectivity classification* is to separate subjective and objective statements. Pak and Paroubek (2010) counted word frequencies in a subjective vs an objective set of tweets; the results showed that interjections and personal pronouns are the strongest indicators of subjectivity. In general, these word classes, adverbs and (in particular) adjectives (Hatzivassiloglou and Wiebe, 2000) have shown to be good subjectivity indicators, which has made part-

[1] See Pang and Lee (2008); Feldman (2013) for overviews.

*Second Joint Conference on Lexical and Computational Semantics (*SEM), Volume 2: Seventh International Workshop on Semantic Evaluation (SemEval 2013)*, pages 430–437, Atlanta, Georgia, June 14-15, 2013.

of-speech (POS) tagging a reasonable technique for filtering out objective tweets. Early research on TSA showed that the challenging vocabulary made it harder to accurately tag tweets; however, Gimpel et al. (2011) report on using a POS tagger for marking tweets, performing with almost 90% accuracy.

Polarity classification is the task of separating the subjective statements into positives and negatives. Kouloumpis et al. (2011) tried different solutions for tweet polarity classification, and found that the best performance came from using n-grams together with lexicon and microblog features. Interestingly, performance dropped when a POS tagger was included. They speculate that this can be due to the accuracy of the POS tagger itself, or that POS tagging just is less effective for analysing tweet polarity.

In this paper we will explore the application of a set of machine learning algorithms to the task of Twitter sentiment classification, comparing one-step and two-step approaches, and investigate a range of different preprocessing methods. What we explicitly will not do, is to utilise a sentiment lexicon, even though many methods in TSA rely on lexica with a sentiment score for each word. Nielsen (2011) manually built a sentiment lexicon specialized for Twitter, while others have tried to induce such lexica automatically with good results (Velikovich et al., 2010; Mohammad et al., 2013). However, sentiment lexica — and in particular specialized Twitter sentiment lexica — make the classification more domain dependent. Here we will instead aim to exploit domain independent approaches as far as possible, and thus abstain from using sentiment lexica. The rest of the paper is laid out as follows: Section 2 introduces the twitter data sets used in the study. Then Section 3 describes the system built for carrying out the twitter sentiment classification experiments, which in turn are reported and discussed in Sections 4 and 5.

2 Data

Manually collecting information from Twitter would be a tedious task, but Twitter offers a well documented Representational State Transfer Application Programming Interface (REST API) which allows users to collect a corpus from the microblogosphere. Most of the data used in TSA research is collected through the Twitter API, either by searching for a certain topic/keyword or by streaming realtime data. Four different data sets were used in the experiments described below. three were supplied by the organisers of the SemEval'13 shared task on Twitter sentiment analysis (Wilson et al., 2013), in the form of a training set, a smaller initial development set, and a larger development set. All sets consist of manually annotated tweets on a range of topics, including different products and events.

	Training		Dev 1		Dev 2		NTNU	
Class	Num	%	Num	%	Num	%	Num	%
Negative	1288	15	176	21	340	26	86	19
Neutral	4151	48	144	45	739	21	232	50
Positive	3270	37	368	35	575	54	142	31
Total	8709		688		1654		461	

Table 1: The data sets used in the experiments

Tweet-level classification (Task 2B) was split into two subtasks in SemEval'13, one allowing training only on the data sets supplied by the organisers (*constrained*) and one allowing training also on external data (*unconstrained*). To this end, a web application[2] for manual annotation of tweets was built and used to annotate a small fourth data set ('NTNU'). Each of the 461 tweets in the 'NTNU' data set was annotated by one person only.

The distribution of target classes in the data sets is shown in Table 1. The data was neither preprocessed nor filtered, and thus contain hashtags, URLs, emoticons, etc. However, all the data sets provided by SemEval'13 had more than three target classes (e.g., 'objective', 'objective-OR-neutral'), so tweets that were not annotated as 'positive' or 'negative' were merged into the 'neutral' target class.

Due to Twitter's privacy policy, the given data sets do not contain the tweet text, but only the tweet ID which in turn can be used to download the text. The Twitter API has a limit on the number of downloads per hour, so SemEval'13 provided a Python script to scrape texts from `https://twitter.com`. This script was slow and did not download the texts for all tweet IDs in the data sets, so a faster and more precise download script[3] for node.js was implemented and submitted to the shared task organisers.

[2] `http://tinyurl.com/tweetannotator`
[3] `http://tinyurl.com/twitscraper`

3 Experimental Setup

In order to run sentiment classification experiments, a general system was built. It has a Sentiment Analysis API Layer which works as a thin extension of the Twitter API, sending all tweets received in parallel to a Sentiment Analysis Classifier server. After classification, the SA API returns the same JSON structure as the Twitter API sends out, only with an additional attribute denoting the tweet's sentiment. The Sentiment Analysis Classifier system consists of preprocessing and classification, described below.

3.1 Preprocessing

As mentioned in the introduction, most approaches to Twitter sentiment analysis start with a preprocessing step, filtering out some Twitter specific symbols and functions. Go et al. (2009) used ':)' and ':(' as labels for the polarity, so did not remove these emoticons, but replaced URLs and user names with placeholders. Kouloumpis et al. (2011) used both an emoticon set and a hashtagged set. The latter is a subset of the Edinburgh Twitter corpus which consists of 97 million tweets (Petrović et al., 2010). Some approaches have also experimented with normalizing the tweets, and removing redundant letters, e.g., "loooove" and "crazyyy", that are used to express a stronger sentiment in tweets. Redundant letters are therefore often not deleted, but words rather trimmed down to one additional redundant letter, so that the stronger sentiment can be taken into consideration by a score/weight adjustment for that feature.

To find the best features to use, a set of eight different combinations of preprocessing methods was designed, as detailed in Table 2. These include no preprocessing ($P0$, not shown in the table), where all characters are included as features; full remove ($P4$), where all special Twitter features like user names, URLs, hashtags, retweet (RT) tags, and emoticons are stripped; and replacing Twitter features with placeholder texts to reduce vocabulary. The "hashtag as word" method transforms a hashtag to a regular word and uses the hashtag as a feature. "Reduce letter duplicate" removes redundant characters more than three ("happyyyyyyyy!!!!!!" $\rightarrow$ "happyyy!!!"). Some methods, like $P1$, $P2$, $P4$, $P5$ and $P7$ remove user names from the text, as they most likely are just noise for the sentiment. Still,

Method	$P1$	$P2$	$P3$	$P4$	$P5$	$P6$	$P7$
Remove Usernames	✓	✓		✓	✓		✓
Username placeholder			✓				
Remove URLs		✓		✓	✓		✓
URL placeholder			✓				
Remove hashtags				✓	✓		
Hashtag as word		✓					
Hashtag placeholder			✓				
Remove RT-tags		✓		✓	✓		
Remove emoticons				✓	✓		
Reduce letter duplicate		✓		✓		✓	✓
Negation attachment				✓		✓	✓

Table 2: Overview of the preprocessing methods

the fact that there are references to URLs and user names might be relevant for the sentiment. To make these features more informative for the machine learning algorithms, a preprocessing method ($P3$) was implemented for replacing them with placeholders. In addition, a very rudimentary treatment of negation was added, in which the negation is attached to the preceding and following words, so that they will also reflect the change in sentence polarity.

Even though this preprocessing obviously is Twitter-specific, the results after it will still be domain semi-independent, in as far as the strings produced after the removal of URLs, user names, etc., will be general, and can be used for system training.

3.2 Classification

The classification step currently supports three machine learning algorithms from the Python `scikit-learn`[4] package: Naïve Bayes (NB), Maximum Entropy (MaxEnt), and Support Vector Machines (SVM). These are all among the supervised learners that previously have been shown to perform well on TSA, e.g., by Bermingham and Smeaton (2010) who compared SVM and NB for microblogs. Interestingly, while the SVM technique normally beats NB and MaxEnt on longer texts, that comparison indicated that it has some trouble with outperforming NB when feature vectors are shorter. Three different models were implemented:

1. *One-step model*: a single algorithm classifies tweets as negative, neutral or positive.
2. *Two-step model*: the tweets are first classified as either subjective or neutral. Those that are

[4] `http://scikit-learn.org`

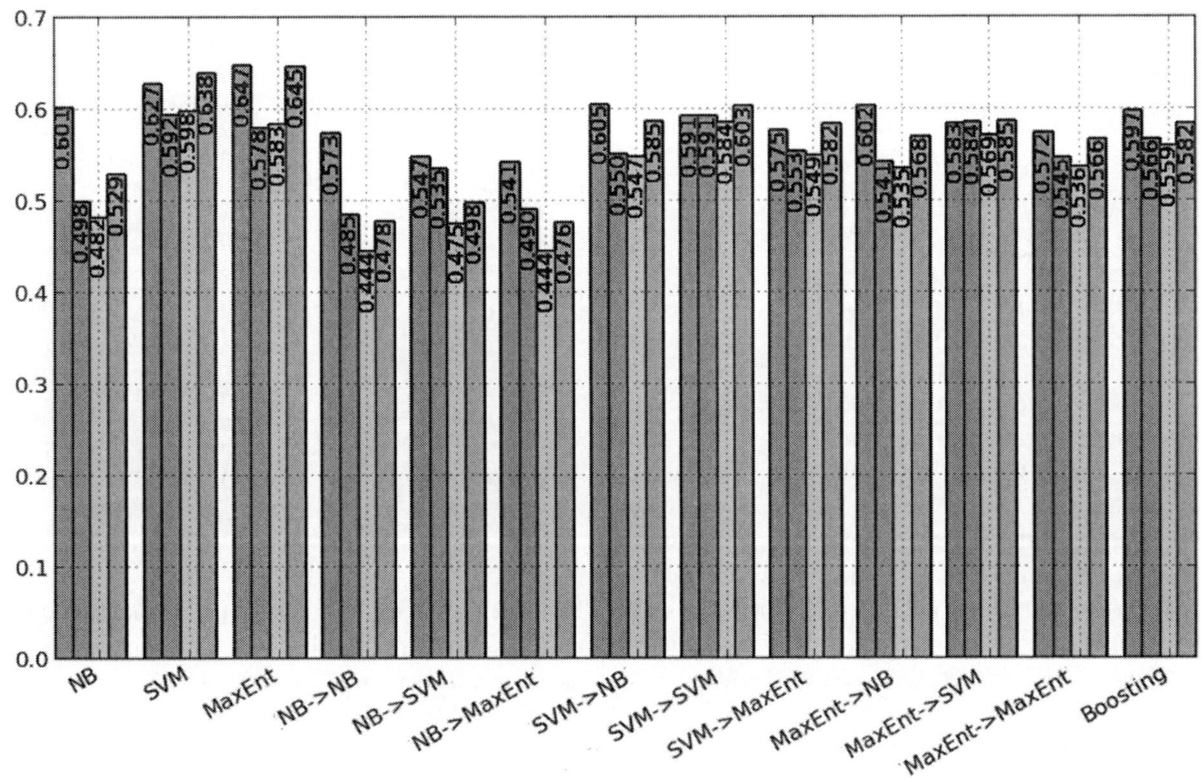

Figure 1: Performance across all models (red=precision, blue=recall, green=F_1-score, brown=accuracy)

classified as subjective are then sent to polarity classification (i.e., negative or positive).

3. *Boosting* (Freund and Schapire, 1997): a way to combine classifiers by generating a set of sub-models, each of which predicts a sentiment on its own and then sends it to a voting process that selects the sentiment with highest score.

In all cases, the final classification is returned to the API Layer sentiment provider.

4 Experimental Results

Experiments were carried out using the platform introduced in the previous section, with models built on the training set of Table 1. The testing system generates and trains different models based on a set of parameters, such as classification algorithm, preprocessing methods, whether or not to use inverse document frequency (IDF) or stop words. A grid search option can be activated, so that a model is generated with the best possible parameter set for the given algorithm, using 10-fold cross validation.

4.1 Selection of Learners and Features

An extensive grid search was conducted. This search cycled through different algorithms, parameters and preprocessing techniques. The following parameters were included in the search. Three binary (`Yes/No`) parameters: `Use IDF`, `Use Smooth IDF`, and `Use Sublinear IDF`, together with `ngram` (`unigram/bigram/trigram`). SVM and MaxEnt models in addition included `C` and NB models `alpha` parameters, all with the value ranges `[0.1/0.3/0.5/0.7/0.8/1.0]`. SVM and MaxEnt models also had `penalty` (`L1/L2`).

Figure 1 displays the precision, recall, F_1-score, and accuracy for each of the thirteen classifiers with the Dev 2 data set (see Table 1) used for evaluation. Note that most classifiers involving the NB algorithm perform badly, both in terms of accuracy and F-score. This was observed for the other data sets as well. Further, we can see that one-step classifiers did better than two-step models, with MaxEnt obtaining the best accuracy, but SVM a slightly better F-score.

Data set	Dev 2		Dev 1	
Learner	SVM	MaxEnt	SVM	MaxEnt
Precision	0.627	**0.647**	**0.700**	0.561
Recall	**0.592**	0.578	**0.726**	0.589
F_1-score	**0.598**	0.583	**0.707**	0.556
Accuracy	0.638	**0.645**	**0.728**	0.581

Table 3: Best classifier performance (bold=best score; all classifiers were trained on the training set of Table 1)

A second grid search with the two best classifiers from the first search was performed instead using the smaller Dev 1 data set for evaluation. The results for both the SVM and MaxEnt classifiers are shown in Table 3. With the Dev 1 data set, SVM performs much better than MaxEnt. The larger Dev 2 development set contains more neutral tweets than the Dev 1 set, which gives us reasons to believe that evaluating on the Dev 2 set favours the MaxEnt classifier.

A detailed error analysis was conducted by inspecting the confusion matrices of all classifiers. In general, classifiers involving SVM tend to give better confusion matrices than the others. Using SVM only in a one-step model works well for positive and neutral tweets, but a bit poorer for negative. Two-step models with SVM-based subjectivity classification exhibit the same basic behaviour. The one-step MaxEnt model classifies more tweets as neutral than the other classifiers. Using MaxEnt for subjectivity classification and either MaxEnt or SVM for polarity classification performs well, but is too heavy on the positive class. Boosting does not improve and behaves in a fashion similar to two-step MaxEnt models. All combinations involving NB tend to heavily favour positive predictions; only the two-step models involving another algorithm for polarity classification gave some improvement for negative tweets.

The confusion matrices of the two best learners are shown in Figures 2a-2d, where a learner is shown to perform better if it has redish colours on the main diagonal and blueish in the other fields, as is the case for SVM on the Dev 1 data set (Figure 2c).

As a part of the grid search, all preprocessing methods were tested for each classifier. Figure 3 shows that $P2$ (removing user names, URLs, hashtags prefixes, retweet tokens, and redundant letters) is the preprocessing method which performs best

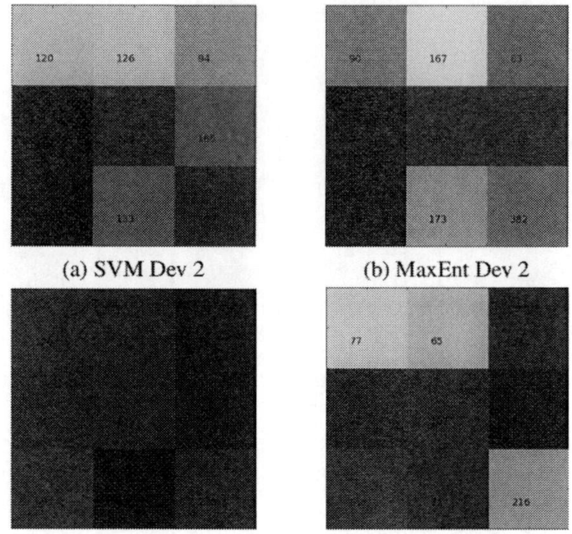

(a) SVM Dev 2 (b) MaxEnt Dev 2

(c) SVM Dev 1 (d) MaxEnt Dev 1

Figure 2: SVM and MaxEnt confusion matrices (output is shown from left-to-right: negative-neutral-positive; the correct classes are in the same order, top-to-bottom. "Hotter" colours (red) indicate that more instances were assigned; "colder" colours (blue) mean fewer instances.)

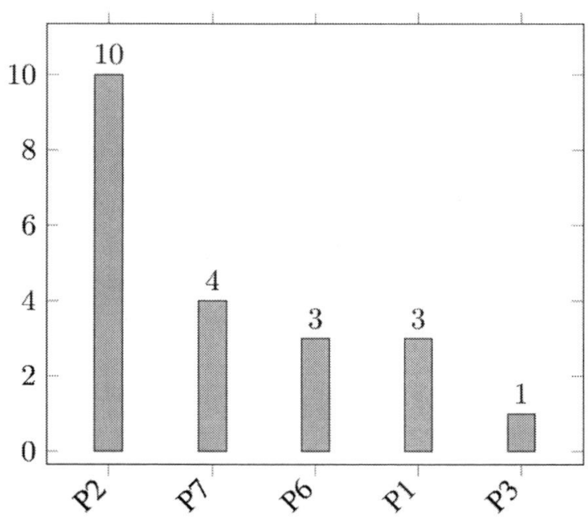

Figure 3: Statistics of preprocessing usage

(gives the best accuracy) and thus used most often (10 times). Figure 3 also indicates that URLs are noisy and do not contain much sentiment, while hashtags and emoticons tend to be more valuable features ($P2$ and $P7$ — removing URLs — perform best, while $P4$ and $P5$ — removing hashtags and emoticons in addition to URLs — perform badly).

Data set	Twitter		SMS	
System	NTNUC	NTNUU	NTNUC	NTNUU
Precision	**0.652**	0.633	**0.659**	0.623
Recall	**0.579**	0.564	**0.646**	0.623
F_1-score	**0.590**	0.572	**0.652**	0.623
$F_1 +/-$	**0.532**	0.507	**0.580**	0.546

Table 4: The NTNU systems in SemEval'13

4.2 SemEval'13 NTNU Systems and Results

Based on the information from the grid search, two systems were built for SemEval'13. Since one-step SVM-based classification showed the best performance on the training data, it was chosen for the system participating in the *constrained* subtask, **NTNUC**. The preprocessing also was the one with the best performance on the provided data, $P2$ which involves lower-casing all letters; reducing letter duplicates; using hashtags as words (removing #); and removing all URLs, user names and RT-tags.

Given the small size of the in-house ('NTNU') data set, no major improvement was expected from adding it in the *unconstrained* task. Instead, a radically different set-up was chosen to create a new system, and train it on both the in-house and provided data. **NTNUU** utilizes a two-step approach, with SVM for subjectivity and MaxEnt for polarity classification, a combination intended to capture the strengths of both algorithms. No preprocessing was used for the subjectivity step, but user names were removed before attempting polarity classification.

As further described by Wilson et al. (2013), the SemEval'13 shared task involved testing on a set of 3813 tweets (1572 positive, 601 negative, and 1640 neutral). In order to evaluate classification performance on data of roughly the same length and type, but from a different domain, the evaluation data also included 2094 Short Message Service texts (SMS; 492 positive, 394 negative, and 1208 neutral).

Table 4 shows the results obtained by the NTNU systems on the SemEval'13 evaluation data, in terms of average precision, recall and F-score for all three classes, as well as average F-score for positive and negative tweets only ($F_1 +/-$; i.e., the measure used to rank the systems participating in the shared task).

5 Discussion and Conclusion

As can be seen in Table 4, the extra data available to train the NTNUU system did not really help it: it gets outperformed by NTNUC on all measures. Notably, both systems perform well on the out-of-domain data represented by the SMS messages, which is encouraging and indicates that the approach taken really is domain semi-independent. This was also reflected in the rankings of the two systems in the shared task: both were on the lower half among the participating systems on Twitter data ($24^{th}/36$ resp. $10^{th}/15$), but near the top on SMS data, with NTNUC being ranked 5th of 28 constrained systems and NTNUU 6th of 15 unconstrained systems.

Comparing the results to those shown in Table 3 and Figure 1, NTNUC's (SVM) performance is in line with that on Dev 2, but substantially worse than on Dev 1; NTNUU (SVM→MaxEnt) performs slightly worse too. Looking at system output with and without the 'NTNU' data, both one-step SVM and MaxEnt models and SVM→MaxEnt classified more tweets as negative when trained on the extra data; however, while NTNUC benefited slightly from this, NTNUU even performed better without it.

An obvious extension to the present work would be to try other classification algorithms (e.g., Conditional Random Fields or more elaborate ensembles) or other features (e.g., character n-grams). Rather than the very simple treatment of negation used here, an approach to automatic induction of scope through a negation detector (Councill et al., 2010) could be used. It would also be possible to relax the domain-independence further, in particular to utilize sentiment lexica (including twitter specific), e.g., by automatic phrase-polarity lexicon extraction (Velikovich et al., 2010). Since many users tweet from their smartphones, and a large number of them use iPhones, several tweets contain iPhone-specific smilies ("Emoji"). Emoji are implemented as their own character set (rather than consisting of characters such as ':)' and ':(', etc.), so a potentially major improvement could be to convert them to character-based smilies or to emotion-specific placeholders.

Acknowledgements

Thanks to Amitava Das for initial discussions and to the human annotators of the 'NTNU' data set.

References

Bermingham, A. and Smeaton, A. F. (2010). Classifying sentiment in microblogs: Is brevity an advantage? In *Proceedings of the 19th International Conference on Information and Knowledge Management*, pages 1833–1836, Toronto, Canada. ACM.

Chamlertwat, W., Bhattarakosol, P., Rungkasiri, T., and Haruechaiyasak, C. (2012). Discovering consumer insight from Twitter via sentiment analysis. *Journal of Universal Computer Science*, 18(8):973–992.

Councill, I. G., McDonald, R., and Velikovich, L. (2010). What's great and what's not: learning to classify the scope of negation for improved sentiment analysis. In *Proceedings of the 48th Annual Meeting of the Association for Computational Linguistics*, pages 51–59, Uppsala, Sweden. ACL. Workshop on Negation and Speculation in Natural Language Processing.

Feldman, R. (2013). Techniques and applications for sentiment analysis. *Communications of the ACM*, 56(4):82–89.

Freund, Y. and Schapire, R. E. (1997). A decision-theoretic generalization of on-line learning and application to boosting. *Journal of Computer and System Sciences*, 55(1):119–139.

Gimpel, K., Schneider, N., O'Connor, B., Das, D., Mills, D., Eisenstein, J., Heilman, M., Yogatama, D., Flanigan, J., and Smith, N. A. (2011). Part-of-speech tagging for Twitter: Annotation, features, and experiments. In *Proceedings of the 49th Annual Meeting of the Association for Computational Linguistics: Human Language Technologies*, volume 2: short papers, pages 42–47, Portland, Oregon. ACL.

Go, A., Huang, L., and Bhayani, R. (2009). Twitter sentiment analysis. Technical Report CS224N Project Report, Department of Computer Science, Stanford University, Stanford, California.

Hatzivassiloglou, V. and Wiebe, J. M. (2000). Effects of adjective orientation and gradability on sentence subjectivity. In *Proceedings of the 18th International Conference on Computational Linguistics*, pages 299–305, Saarbrücken, Germany. ACL.

HLT10 (2010). *Proceedings of the 2010 Human Language Technology Conference of the North American Chapter of the Association for Computational Linguistics*, Los Angeles, California. ACL.

Kouloumpis, E., Wilson, T., and Moore, J. (2011). Twitter sentiment analysis: The good the bad and the OMG! In *Proceedings of the 5th International Conference on Weblogs and Social Media*, pages 538–541, Barcelona, Spain. AAAI.

Maynard, D. and Funk, A. (2011). Automatic detection of political opinions in tweets. In #MSM2011 (2011), pages 81–92.

Mohammad, S., Kiritchenko, S., and Zhu, X. (2013). NRC-Canada: Building the state-of-the-art in sentiment analysis of tweets. In SemEval'13 (2013).

#MSM2011 (2011). *Proceedings of the 1st Workshop on Making Sense of Microposts (#MSM2011)*, Heraklion, Greece.

Mukherjee, S., Malu, A., Balamurali, A., and Bhattacharyya, P. (2012). TwiSent: A multistage system for analyzing sentiment in Twitter. In *Proceedings of the 21st International Conference on Information and Knowledge Management*, pages 2531–2534, Maui, Hawaii. ACM.

Nielsen, F. Å. (2011). A new ANEW: Evaluation of a word list for sentiment analysis in microblogs. In #MSM2011 (2011), pages 93–98.

Pak, A. and Paroubek, P. (2010). Twitter as a corpus for sentiment analysis and opinion mining. In *Proceedings of the 7th International Conference on Language Resources and Evaluation*, Valetta, Malta. ELRA.

Pang, B. and Lee, L. (2008). Opinion mining and sentiment analysis. *Foundations and Trends in Information Retrieval*, 2(1-2):1–135.

Petrović, S., Osborne, M., and Lavrenko, V. (2010). The Edinburgh Twitter corpus. In HLT10 (2010), pages 25–26. Workshop on Computational Linguistics in a World of Social Media.

Saif, H., He, Y., and Alani, H. (2012). Semantic sentiment analysis of Twitter. In *Proceedings of the 11th International Semantic Web Conference*, pages 508–524, Boston, Massachusetts. Springer.

SemEval'13 (2013). *Proceedings of the International Workshop on Semantic Evaluation*, SemEval '13, Atlanta, Georgia. ACL.

Velikovich, L., Blair-Goldensohn, S., Hannan, K., and McDonald, R. (2010). The viability of web-derived polarity lexicons. In HLT10 (2010), pages 777–785.

Wilson, T., Kozareva, Z., Nakov, P., Ritter, A., Rosenthal, S., and Stoyanov, V. (2013). SemEval-2013 Task 2: Sentiment analysis in Twitter. In SemEval'13 (2013).

Wilson, T., Wiebe, J., and Hoffmann, P. (2005). Recognizing contextual polarity in phrase-level sentiment analysis. In *Proceedings of the 2005 Human Language Technology Conference and Conference on Empirical Methods in Natural Language Processing*, pages 347–354, Vancouver, British Columbia, Canada. ACL.

Yu, H. and Hatzivassiloglou, V. (2003). Towards answering opinion questions: Separating facts from opinions and identifying the polarity of opinion sentences. In Collins, M. and Steedman, M., editors, *Proceedings of the 2003 Conference on Empirical Methods in Natural Language Processing*, pages 129–136, Sapporo, Japan. ACL.

SAIL: A hybrid approach to sentiment analysis

Nikolaos Malandrakis[1], **Abe Kazemzadeh**[2], **Alexandros Potamianos**[3], **Shrikanth Narayanan**[1]
[1] Signal Analysis and Interpretation Laboratory (SAIL), USC, Los Angeles, CA 90089, USA
[2] Annenberg Innovation Laboratory (AIL), USC, Los Angeles, CA 90089, USA
[3]Department of ECE, Technical University of Crete, 73100 Chania, Greece
malandra@usc.edu, kazemzad@usc.edu, potam@telecom.tuc.gr, shri@sipi.usc.edu

Abstract

This paper describes our submission for SemEval2013 Task 2: Sentiment Analysis in Twitter. For the limited data condition we use a lexicon-based model. The model uses an affective lexicon automatically generated from a very large corpus of raw web data. Statistics are calculated over the word and bigram affective ratings and used as features of a Naive Bayes tree model. For the unconstrained data scenario we combine the lexicon-based model with a classifier built on maximum entropy language models and trained on a large external dataset. The two models are fused at the posterior level to produce a final output. The approach proved successful, reaching rankings of 9th and 4th in the twitter sentiment analysis constrained and unconstrained scenario respectively, despite using only lexical features.

1 Introduction

The analysis of the emotional content of text, is relevant to numerous natural language processing (NLP), web and multi-modal dialogue applications. To that end there has been a significant scientific effort towards tasks like product review analysis (Wiebe and Mihalcea, 2006; Hu and Liu, 2004), speech emotion extraction (Lee and Narayanan, 2005; Lee et al., 2002; Ang et al., 2002) and pure text word (Esuli and Sebastiani, 2006; Strapparava and Valitutti, 2004) and sentence (Turney and Littman, 2002; Turney and Littman, 2003) level emotion extraction.

The rise of social media in recent years has seen a shift in research focus towards them, particularly twitter. The large volume of text data available is particularly useful, since it allows the use of complex machine learning methods. Also important is the interest on the part of companies that are actively looking for ways to mine social media for opinions and attitudes towards them and their products. Similarly, in journalism there is interest in sentiment analysis for a way to process and report on the public opinion about current events (Petulla, 2013).

Analyzing emotion expressed in twitter borrows from other tasks related to affective analysis, but also presents unique challenges. One common issue is the breadth of content available in twitter: a more limited domain would make the task easier, however there are no such bounds. There is also a significant difference in the form of language used in tweets. The tone is informal and typographical and grammatical errors are very common, making even simple tasks, like Part-of-Speech tagging much harder. Features like hashtags and emoticons can also be helpful (Davidov et al., 2010).

This paper describes our submissions for SemEval 2013 task 2, subtask B, which deals primarily with sentiment analysis in twitter. For the constrained condition (using only the organizer-provided twitter sentences) we implemented a system based on the use of an affective lexicon and part-of-speech tag information, which has been shown relevant to the task (Pak and Paroubek, 2010). For the unconstrained condition (including external sources of twitter sentences) we combine the constrained model with a maximum entropy language

*Second Joint Conference on Lexical and Computational Semantics (*SEM), Volume 2: Seventh International Workshop on Semantic Evaluation (SemEval 2013)*, pages 438–442, Atlanta, Georgia, June 14-15, 2013.

model trained on external data.

2 Experimental procedure

We use two separate models, one for the constrained condition and a combination for the unconstrained condition. Following are short descriptions.

2.1 Lexicon-based model

The method used for the constrained condition is based on an affective lexicon containing out-of-context affective ratings for all terms contained in each sentence. We use an automated algorithm of affective lexicon expansion based on the one presented in (Malandrakis et al., 2011), which in turn is an expansion of (Turney and Littman, 2002).

We assume that the continuous (in $[-1,1]$) valence and arousal ratings of any term can be represented as a linear combination of its semantic similarities to a set of seed words and the affective ratings of these words, as follows:

$$\hat{v}(w_j) = a_0 + \sum_{i=1}^{N} a_i \, v(w_i) \, d_{ij}, \qquad (1)$$

where w_j is the term we mean to characterize, $w_1...w_N$ are the seed words, $v(w_i)$ is the valence rating for seed word w_i, a_i is the weight corresponding to seed word w_i (that is estimated as described next), d_{ij} is a measure of semantic similarity between w_i and w_j. For the purposes of this work, the semantic similarity metric is the cosine similarity between context vectors computed over a corpus of 116 million web snippets collected by posing one query for every word in the Aspell spellchecker's vocabulary to the Yahoo! search engine and collecting up to 500 of the top results.

Given a starting, manually annotated, lexicon we can select part of it to serve as seed words and then use 1 to create a system of linear equations where the only unknowns are the weights a_i. The system is solved using Least Squares Estimation. That provides us with an equation that can generate affective ratings for every term (not limited to words), as long as we can estimate the semantic similarity between it and the seed words.

Seed word selection is performed by a simple heuristic (though validated through experiments): we want seed words to have extreme affective ratings (maximum absolute value) and we want the set to be as closed to balanced as possible (sum of seed ratings equal to zero).

Given these term ratings, the next step is combining them through statistics. To do that we use simple statistics (mean, min, max) and group by part of speech tags. The results are statistics like "maximum valence among adjectives", "mean arousal among proper nouns" and "number of verbs and nouns". The dimensions used are: valence, absolute valence and arousal. The grouping factors are the 39 Penn treebank pos tags plus higher order tags (adjectives, verbs, nouns, adverbs and combinations of 2,3 and 4 of them). The statistics extracted are: mean, min, max, most extreme, sum, number, percentage of sentence coverage. In the case of bigram terms no part-of-speech filtering/grouping is applied. These statistics form the feature vectors.

Finally we perform feature selection on the massive set of candidates and use them to train a model. The model selected is a Naive Bayes tree, a tree with Naive Bayes classifiers on each leaf. The motivation comes by considering this a two stage problem: subjectivity detection and polarity classification, making a hierarchical model a natural choice. NB trees proved superior to other types of trees during our testing, presumably due to the smoothing of observation distributions.

2.2 N-gram language model

The method used for the unconstrained condition is based on a combination of the automatically expanded affective lexicon described in the previous section together with a bigram language model based on the work of (Wang et al., 2012), which uses a large set of twitter data from the U.S. 2012 Presidential election. As a part of the unconstrained system, we were able to leverage external annotated data apart from those provided by the SEMEVAL 2013 sentiment task dataset. Of the 315 million tweets we collected about the election, we annotated a subset of 40 thousand tweets using Amazon Mechanical Turk. The annotation labels that we used were "positive", "negative", "neutral", and "unsure", and additionally raters could mark tweets for sarcasm and humor. We excluded tweets marked as "unsure" as well as tweets that had disagreement in labels if they were annotated by more than one annotator. To extract the bigram features, we used a twitter-specific tokenizer (Potts, 2011), which marked uniform resource locators (URLs), emoticons, and repeated characters, and which lowercased words that began with capital letters followed by lowercase letters (but left words in all capitals). The bigram features were computed as presence or absense in the tweet rather than counts due to the small number of words in tweets. The machine learning model used to classify the tweets was the Megam maximum entropy classifier (Daumé III, 2004) in the Natural Language Toolkit (NLTK) (Bird et al., 2009).

2.3 Fusion

The submitted system for the unconstrained condition leverages both the lexicon-based and bigram language models. Due to the very different nature of the models we opt to not fuse them at the feature level, using a late fusion scheme instead. Both partial models are probabilistic, therefore we can use their per-class posterior probabilities as features of a fusion model. The fusion model is a linear kernel SVM using six features, the three posteriors from each partial model, and trained on held out data.

3 Results

Following are results from our method, evaluated on the testing sets (of sms and twitter posts) of SemEval2013 task 2. We evaluate in terms of 3-class classification, polarity classification (positive vs. negative) and subjectivity detection (neutral vs. other). Results shown in terms of per category f-measure.

3.1 Constrained

The preprocessing required for the lexicon-based model is just part-of-speech tagging using Treetagger (Schmid, 1994). The lexicon expansion method is used to generate valence and arousal ratings for all words and ngrams in all datasets and the part of speech tags are used as grouping criteria to generate statistics. Finally, feature selection is performed using a correlation criterion (Hall, 1999) and the resulting feature set is used to train a Naive Bayes tree model. The feature selection and model training/classification was conducted using Weka (Witten and Frank, 2000).

The final model uses a total of 72 features, which can not be listed here due to space constraints. The vast majority of these features are necessary to detect the neutral category: positive-negative separation can be achieved with under 30 features.

One aspect of the model we felt worth investigating, was the type of model to be used. Using a multi-stage model, performing subjectivity detection before positive-negative classification, has been shown to provide an improvement, however single models have also been used extensively. We compared some popular models: Naive Bayes, linear kernel SVM, CART-trained tree and Naive Bayes tree, all using the same features, on the twitter part of the SemEval testing data. The results are shown in Table 1. The two Naive Bayes-based models proved significantly better, with NBTree being clearly the best model for these features.

Results from the submitted constrained model are shown in Table 2. Looking at the twitter data results and comparing the positive-negative vs the

Table 1: F-measure results for the lexicon-based model, using different machine learning methods, evaluated on the 3-class twitter testing data.

model	per-class F-measure		
	neg	neu	pos
Nbayes	0.494	0.652	0.614
SVM	0.369	0.677	0.583
CART	0.430	0.676	0.593
NBTree	0.561	0.662	0.643

Table 2: F-measure results for the constrained condition, evaluated on the testing data.

set	classes	per-class F-measure		
		neg	neu	pos/other
twitter	3-class	0.561	0.662	0.643
	pos vs neg	0.679		0.858
	neu vs other		0.685	0.699
sms	3-class	0.506	0.709	0.531
	pos vs neg	0.688		0.755
	neu vs other		0.730	0.628

3-class results, it appears the main weakness of this model is subjectivity detection, mostly on the neutral-negative side. It is not entirely clear to us whether that is an artifact of the model (the negative class has the lowest prior probability, thus may suffer compared to neutral) or of the more complex forms of negativity (sarcasm, irony) which we do not directly address. There is a definite drop in performance when using the same twitter-trained model on sms data, which we would not expect, given that the features used are not twitter-specific. We believe this gap is caused by lower part-of-speech tagger performance: visual inspection reveals the output on twitter data is fairly bad.

Overall this model ranked 9th out of 35 in the twitter set and 11th out of 28 in the sms set, among all constrained submissions.

3.2 Unconstrained

Table 3: F-measure results for the maximum entropy model with bigram features, evaluated on the testing data.

set	classes	per-class F-measure		
		neg	neu	pos/other
twitter	3-class	0.403	0.661	0.623
	pos vs neg	0.586		0.804
	neu vs other		0.661	0.704
sms	3-class	0.390	0.587	0.542
	pos vs neg	0.710		0.648
	neu vs other		0.587	0.641

Table 4: F-measure results for the unconstrained condition, evaluated on the testing data.

set	classes	per-class F-measure		
		neg	neu	pos/other
twitter	3-class	0.565	0.679	0.655
	pos vs neg	0.672		0.881
	neu vs other		0.667	0.732
sms	3-class	0.502	0.723	0.538
	pos vs neg	0.625		0.772
	neu vs other		0.710	0.637

In order to create the submitted unconstrained model we train an SVM model using the lexicon-based and bigram language model posterior probabilities as features. This fusion model is trained on held-out data (the development set of the SemEval data). The results of classification using the bigram language model alone are shown in Table 3 and the results from the final fused model are shown in Table 4. Looking at relative per-class performance, the results follow a form most similar to the constrained model, though there are gains in all cases. These gains are less significant when evaluated on the sms data, resulting in a fair drop in ranks: the bigram language model (expectedly) suffers more when moving to a different domain, since it uses words as features rather than the more abstract affective ratings used by the lexicon-based model. Also, because the external data used to train the bigram language model was from discussions of politics on Twitter, the subject matter also varied in terms of prior sentiment distribution in that the negative class was predominant in politics, which resulted in high recall but low precision for the negative class.

This model ranked 4th out of 16 in the twitter set and 7th out of 17 in the sms set, among all unconstrained submissions.

4 Conclusions

We presented a system of twitter sentiment analysis combining two approaches: a hierarchical model based on an affective lexicon and a language modeling approach, fused at the posterior level. The hierarchical lexicon-based model proved very successful despite using only n-gram affective ratings and part-of-speech information. The language model was not as good individually, but provided a noticeable improvement to the lexicon-based model. Overall the models achieved good performance, ranking 9th of 35 and 4th of 16 in the constrained and unconstrained twitter experiments respectively, despite using only lexical information.

Future work will focus on incorporating improved tokenization (including part-of-speech tagging), making better use of twitter-specific features like emoticons and hashtags, and performing affective lexicon generation on twitter data.

References

J. Ang, R. Dhillon, A. Krupski, E. Shriberg, and A. Stolcke. 2002. Prosody-based automatic detection of annoyance and frustration in human-computer dialog. In *Proc. ICSLP*, pages 2037–2040.

S. Bird, E. Klein, and E. Loper. 2009. *Natural Language Processing with Python*. O'Reilly Media.

H. Daumé III. 2004. Notes on cg and lm-bfgs optimization of logistic regression. *Paper available at http://pub. hal3. name# daume04cg-bfgs, implementation available at http://hal3. name/megam.*

D. Davidov, O. Tsur, and A. Rappoport. 2010. Enhanced sentiment learning using twitter hashtags and smileys. In *Proc. COLING*, pages 241–249.

A. Esuli and F. Sebastiani. 2006. Sentiwordnet: A publicly available lexical resource for opinion mining. In *Proc. LREC*, pages 417–422.

M. A. Hall. 1999. *Correlation-based feature selection for machine learning*. Ph.D. thesis, The University of Waikato.

M. Hu and B. Liu. 2004. Mining and summarizing customer reviews. In *Proc. SIGKDD*, KDD '04, pages 168–177. ACM.

C. M. Lee and S. Narayanan. 2005. Toward detecting emotions in spoken dialogs. *IEEE Transactions on Speech and Audio Processing*, 13(2):293–303.

C. M. Lee, S. Narayanan, and R. Pieraccini. 2002. Combining acoustic and language information for emotion recognition. In *Proc. ICSLP*, pages 873–876.

N. Malandrakis, A. Potamianos, E. Iosif, and S. Narayanan. 2011. Kernel models for affective lexicon creation. In *Proc. Interspeech*, pages 2977–2980.

A. Pak and P. Paroubek. 2010. Twitter as a corpus for sentiment analysis and opinion mining. In *Proc. LREC*, pages 1320–1326.

S. Petulla. 2013. Feelings, nothing more than feelings: The measured rise of sentiment analysis in journalism. *Neiman Journalism Lab*, January.

C. Potts. 2011. Sentiment symposium tutorial: Tokenizing. Technical report, Stanford Linguistics.

H. Schmid. 1994. Probabilistic part-of-speech tagging using decision trees. In *Proc. International Conference on New Methods in Language Processing*, volume 12, pages 44–49.

C. Strapparava and A. Valitutti. 2004. WordNet-Affect: an affective extension of WordNet. In *Proc. LREC*, volume 4, pages 1083–1086.

P. Turney and M. L. Littman. 2002. Unsupervised Learning of Semantic Orientation from a Hundred-Billion-Word Corpus. Technical report ERC-1094 (NRC 44929). National Research Council of Canada.

P. Turney and M. L. Littman. 2003. Measuring praise and criticism: Inference of semantic orientation from association. *ACM Transactions on Information Systems*, 21:315–346.

H. Wang, D. Can, A. Kazemzadeh, F. Bar, and S. Narayanan. 2012. A system for real-time twitter sentiment analysis of 2012 u.s. presidential election cycle. In *Proc. ACL*, pages 115–120.

J. Wiebe and R. Mihalcea. 2006. Word sense and subjectivity. In *Proc. COLING/ACL*, pages 1065–1072.

Ian H. Witten and Eibe Frank. 2000. *Data Mining: Practical Machine Learning Tools and Techniques*. Morgan Kaufmann.

UMCC_DLSI-(SA): Using a ranking algorithm and informal features to solve Sentiment Analysis in Twitter

Yoan Gutiérrez, Andy González, Roger Pérez, José I. Abreu
University of Matanzas, Cuba
{yoan.gutierrez, roger.perez ,jose.abreu}@umcc.cu, andy.gonzalez@infonet.umcc.cu

Antonio Fernández Orquín, Alejandro Mosquera, Andrés Montoyo, Rafael Muñoz
University of Alicante, Spain
antonybr@yahoo.com, {amosquera, montoyo, rafael}@dlsi.ua.es

Franc Camara
Independent Consultant
USA
info@franccamara .com

Abstract

In this paper, we describe the development and performance of the supervised system UMCC_DLSI-(SA). This system uses corpora where phrases are annotated as Positive, Negative, Objective, and Neutral, to achieve new sentiment resources involving word dictionaries with their associated polarity. As a result, new sentiment inventories are obtained and applied in conjunction with detected informal patterns, to tackle the challenges posted in Task 2b of the Semeval-2013 competition. Assessing the effectiveness of our application in sentiment classification, we obtained a 69% F-Measure for neutral and an average of 43% F-Measure for positive and negative using Tweets and SMS messages.

1 Introduction

Textual information has become one of the most important sources of data to extract useful and heterogeneous knowledge from. Texts can provide factual information, such as: descriptions, lists of characteristics, or even instructions to opinion-based information, which would include reviews, emotions, or feelings. These facts have motivated dealing with the identification and extraction of opinions and sentiments in texts that require special attention.

Many researchers, such as (Balahur *et al.*, 2010; Hatzivassiloglou *et al.*, 2000; Kim and Hovy, 2006; Wiebe *et al.*, 2005) and many others have been working on this and related areas.

Related to assessment Sentiment Analysis (SA) systems, some international competitions have taken place. Some of those include: Semeval-2010 (Task 18: Disambiguating Sentiment Ambiguous Adjectives [1]) NTCIR (*Multilingual Opinion Analysis Task* (MOAT[2])) TASS[3] (Workshop on Sentiment Analysis at SEPLN workshop) and Semeval-2013 (Task 2[4] Sentiment Analysis in Twitter) (Kozareva *et al.*, 2013).

In this paper, we introduce a system for Task 2 b) of the Semeval-2013 competition.

1.1 Task 2 Description

In participating in "Task 2: Sentiment Analysis in Twitter" of Semeval-2013, the goal was to take a given message and its topic and classify whether it had a positive, negative, or neutral sentiment towards the topic. For messages conveying, both a positive and negative sentiment toward the topic, the stronger sentiment of the two would end up as the classification. Task 2 included two sub-tasks. Our team focused on Task 2 b), which provides two training corpora as described in Table 3, and two test corpora: 1) sms-test-input-B.tsv (with 2094 SMS) and 2) twitter-test-input-B.tsv (with 3813 Twit messages).

The following section shows some background approaches. Subsequently, in section 3, we describe the UMCC_DLSI-(SA) system that was used in Task 2 b). Section 4 describes the assessment of the obtained resource from the Sentiment Classification task. Finally, the conclusion and future works are presented in section 5.

2 Background

The use of sentiment resources has proven to be a necessary step for training and evaluating systems that implement sentiment analysis, which also

[1] http://semeval2.fbk.eu/semeval2.php
[2] http://research.nii.ac.jp/ntcir/ntcir-ws8/meeting/
[3] http://www.daedalus.es/TASS/
[4] http://www.cs.york.ac.uk/semeval-2013/task2/

*Second Joint Conference on Lexical and Computational Semantics (*SEM), Volume 2: Seventh International Workshop on Semantic Evaluation (SemEval 2013)*, pages 443–449, Atlanta, Georgia, June 14-15, 2013.

include fine-grained opinion mining (Balahur, 2011).

In order to build sentiment resources, several studies have been conducted. One of the first is the relevant work by (Hu and Liu, 2004) using lexicon expansion techniques by adding synonymy and antonym relations provided by WordNet (Fellbaum, 1998; Miller *et al.*, 1990) Another one is the research described by (Hu and Liu, 2004; Liu *et al.*, 2005) which obtained an Opinion Lexicon compounded by a list of positive and negative opinion words or sentiment words for English (around 6800 words).

A similar approach has been used for building WordNet-Affect (Strapparava and Valitutti, 2004) which expands six basic categories of emotion; thus, increasing the lexicon paths in WordNet.

Nowadays, many sentiment and opinion messages are provided by Social Media. To deal with the informalities presented in these sources, it is necessary to have intermediary systems that improve the level of understanding of the messages. The following section offers a description of this phenomenon and a tool to track it.

2.1 Text normalization

Several informal features are present in opinions extracted from Social Media texts. Some research has been conducted in the field of lexical normalization for this kind of text. TENOR (Mosquera and Moreda, 2012) is a multilingual text normalization tool for Web 2.0 texts with an aim to transform noisy and informal words into their canonical form. That way, they can be easily processed by NLP tools and applications. TENOR works by identifying out-of-vocabulary (OOV) words such as slang, informal lexical variants, expressive lengthening, or contractions using a dictionary lookup and replacing them by matching formal candidates in a word lattice using phonetic and lexical edit distances.

2.2 Construction of our own Sentiment Resource

Having analyzed the examples of SA described in section 2, we proposed building our own sentiment resource (Gutiérrez *et al.*, 2013) by adding lexical and informal patterns to obtain classifiers that can deal with Task 2b of Semeval-2013. We proposed the use of a method named RA-SR (using Ranking Algorithms to build Sentiment Resources) (Gutiérrez *et al.*, 2013) to build sentiment word inventories based on senti-semantic evidence obtained after exploring text with annotated sentiment polarity information. Through this process, a graph-based algorithm is used to obtain auto-balanced values that characterize sentiment polarities, a well-known technique in Sentiment Analysis. This method consists of three key stages: **(I)** Building contextual word graphs; **(II)** Applying a ranking algorithm; and **(III)** Adjusting the sentiment polarity values.

These stages are shown in the diagram in Figure 1, which the development of sentimental resources starts off by giving four corpora of annotated sentences (the first with neutral sentences, the second with objective sentences, the third with positive sentences, and the last with negative sentences).

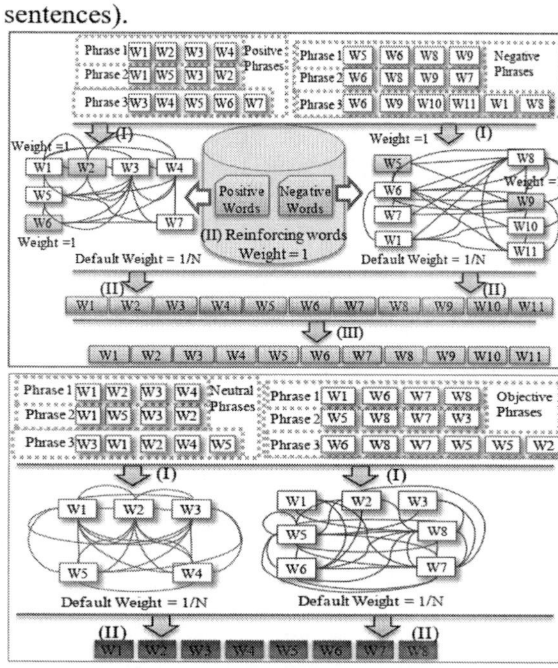

Figure 1. Resource walkthrough development process.

2.3 Building contextual word graphs

Initially, text preprocessing is performed by applying a Post-Tagging tool (using Freeling (Atserias *et al.*, 2006) tool version 2.2 in this case) to convert all words to lemmas[5]. After that, all obtained lists of lemmas are sent to RA-SR, then divided into four groups: neutral, objective, positive, and negative candidates. As the first set

[5] Lemma denotes canonic form of the words.

of results, four contextual graphs are obtained: $Gneu$, $Gobj$, $Gpos$, and $Gneg$, where each graph includes the words/lemmas from the neutral, objective, positive and negative sentences respectively. These graphs are generated after connecting all words for each sentence into individual sets of annotated sentences in concordance with their annotations (Pos, Neg, Obj, Neu).

Once the four graphs representing neutral, objective, positive and negative contexts are created, we proceed to assign weights to apply graph-based ranking techniques in order to auto-balance the particular importance of each vertex v_i into $Gneu$, $Gobj$, $Gpos$ and $Gneg$.

As the primary output of the graph-based ranking process, the positive, negative, neutral, and objective values are calculated using the PageRank algorithm and normalized with equation (1). For a better understanding of how the contextual graph was built see (Gutiérrez *et al.*, 2013).

2.4 Applying a ranking algorithm

To apply a graph-based ranking process, it is necessary to assign weights to the vertices of the graph. Words involved into $Gneu$, $Gobj$, $Gpos$ and $Gneg$ take the default of $1/N$ as their weight to define the weight of v vector, which is used in our proposed ranking algorithm. In the case where words are identified on the sentiment repositories (see Table 4) as positive or negative, in relation to their respective graph, a weight value of 1 (in a range $[0 \dots 1]$) is assigned. N represents the maximum quantity of words in the current graph. After that, a graph-based ranking algorithm is applied in order to structurally raise the graph vertexes' voting power. Once the reinforcement values are applied, the proposed ranking algorithm is able to increase the significance of the words related to these empowered vertices.

The PageRank (Brin and Page, 1998) adaptation, which was popularized by (Agirre and Soroa, 2009) in Word Sense Disambiguation thematic, and which has obtained relevant results, was an inspiration to us in our work. The main idea behind this algorithm is that, for each edge between v_i and v_j in graph G, a vote is made from v_i to v_j. As a result, the relevance of v_j is increased.

On top of that, the vote strength from i to j depends on v_i's relevance. The philosophy behind it is that, the more important the vertex is, the more strength the voter would have. Thus, PageRank is generated by applying a random walkthrough from the internal interconnection of G, where the final relevance of v_i represents the random walkthrough probability over G, and ending on v_i.

In our system, we apply the following configuration: dumping factor $c = 0.85$ and, like in (Agirre and Soroa, 2009) we used 30 iterations. A detailed explanation about the PageRank algorithm can be found in (Agirre and Soroa, 2009)

After applying PageRank, in order to obtain standardized values for both graphs, we normalize the rank values by applying the equation (1), where $Max(\mathbf{Pr})$ obtains the maximum rank value of $\boldsymbol{Pr}$ vector (rankings' vector).

$$\mathbf{Pr}_i = \mathbf{Pr}_i / Max(\mathbf{Pr}) \quad (1)$$

2.5 Adjusting the sentiment polarity values

After applying the PageRank algorithm on$Gneu$, $Gobj$, $Gpos$ and $Gneg$, having normalized their ranks, we proceed to obtain a final list of lemmas (named Lf) while avoiding repeated elements. Lf is represented by Lf_i lemmas, which would have, at that time, four assigned values: Neutral, Objective, Positive, and Negative, all of which correspond to a calculated rank obtained by the PageRank algorithm.

At that point, for each lemma from Lf, the following equations are applied in order to select the definitive subjectivity polarity for each one:

$$Pos = \begin{cases} Pos - Neg\,; & Pos > Neg \\ 0 & ; otherwise \end{cases} \quad (2)$$

$$Neg = \begin{cases} Neg - Pos\,; & Neg > Pos \\ 0 & ; otherwise \end{cases} \quad (3)$$

Where Pos is the Positive value and Neg the Negative value related to each lemma in Lf.

In order to standardize again the Pos and Neg values and making them more representative in a $[0 \dots 1]$ scale, we proceed to apply a normalization process over the Pos and Neg values.

From there, based on the objective features commented by (Baccianella *et al.*, 2010), we assume the same premise to establish an alternative objective value of the lemmas. Equation (4) is used for that:

$$ObjAlt = 1 - |Pos - Neg| \quad (4)$$

Where $ObjAlt$ represents the alternative objective value.

As a result, each word obtained in the sentiment resource has an associated value of: positivity (Pos, see equation (2)), negativity (Neg, see equation (3)), objectivity ($Real\_obj$, obtained by PageRank over $Gobj$ and normalized with equation (1)), calculated-objectivity ($ObjAlt$, now cited as $obj\_measured$) and neutrality (Neu, obtained by PageRank over $Gneu$ and normalized with equation (1)).

3 System Description

The system takes annotated corpora as input from which two models are created. One model is created by using only the data provided at Semeval-2013 (Restricted Corpora, see Table 3), and the other by using extra data from other annotated corpora (Unrestricted Corpora, see Table 3). In all cases, the phrases are pre-processed using Freeling 2.2 pos-tagger (Atserias *et al.*, 2006) while a dataset copy is normalized using TENOR (described in section 2.1).

The system starts by extracting two sets of features. The Core Features (see section 3.1) are the Sentiment Measures and are calculated for a standard and normalized phrase. The Support Features (see section 3.2) are based on regularities, observed in the training dataset, such as emoticons, uppercase words, and so on.

The supervised models are created using Weka[6] and a Logistic classifier, both of which the system uses to predict the values of the test dataset. The selection of the classifier was made after analyzing several classifiers such as: Support Vector Machine, J48 and REPTree. Finally, the Logistic classifier proved to be the best by increasing the results around three perceptual points.

The test data is preprocessed in the same way the previous corpora were. The same process of feature extraction is also applied. With the aforementioned features and the generated models, the system proceeds to classify the final values of Positivity, Negativity, and Neutrality.

3.1 The Core Features

The Core Features is a group of measures based on the resource created early (see section 2.2). The system takes a sentence preprocessed by Freeling 2.2 and TENOR. For each lemma of the analyzed sentence, pos, neg, $obj\_measured$, $real\_obj$, and neu are calculated by using the respective word values assigned in RA-SR. The obtained values correspond to the sum of the corresponding values for each intersecting word between the analyzed sentence (lemmas list) and the obtained resource by RA-SR. Lastly, the aforementioned attributes are normalized by dividing them by the number of words involved in this process.

Other calculated attributes are: pos_count, neg_count, $obj\_measured\_count$, obj_real_count and neu_count. These attributes count each involved iteration for each feature type (Pos, Neg, $Real\_obj$, $ObjAlt$ and Neu respectively, where the respective value may be greater than zero.

Attributes cnp and cnn are calculated by counting the amount of lemmas in the phrases contained in the Sentiment Lexicons (Positive and Negative respectively).

All of the 12 attributes described previously are computed for both, the original, and the normalized (using TENOR) phrase, totaling 24 attributes. The Core features are described next.

Feature Name	Description
pos	Sum of respective value of each word.
neg	
obj_measured	
real_obj	
neu	
pos_count	Counts the words where its respective value is greater than zero
neg_count	
obj_measured_count	
real_obj_count	
neu_count	
cnp (to positive)	Counts the words contained in the Sentiment Lexicons for their respective polarities.
cnn (to negative)	

Table 1. Core Features

3.2 The Support Features

The Support Features is a group of measures based on characteristics of the phrases, which may help with the definition on extreme cases. The *emotPos* and *emotNeg* values are the amount of Positive and Negative Emoticons found in the phrase. The *exc* and *itr* are the amount of exclamation and interrogation signs in the phrase. The following table shows the attributes that represent the support features:

Feature Name	Description
emotPos	Counts the respective Emoticons
emotNeg	
exc (exclamation marks ("!"))	Counts the respective marks
itr (question marks ("?"))	
WORDS_count	Counts the uppercase words
WORDS_pos	Sums the respective values of the Uppercase words
WORDS_neg	
WORDS_pos_count_res (to	Counts the Uppercase words

[6] http://www.cs.waikato.ac.nz/

positivity)	contained in their respective Graph
WORDS_neg_count_res(to negativity)	
WORDS_pos_count_dict (to positivity)	Counts the Uppercase words contained in the Sentiment Lexicons [7] for their respective polarity
WORDS_neg_count_dict (to negativity)	
wooords_count	Counts the words with repeated chars
wooords_pos	Sums the respective values of the words with repeated chars
wooords_neg	
wooords_neg_count_dict (in negative lexical resource)	Counts the words with repeated chars contained in the respective lexical resource
wooords_pos_count_dict (in positive lexical resource)	
wooords_pos_count_res (in positive graph)	Counts the words with repeated chars contained in the respective graph
wooords_neg_count_res (in negative graph)	

Table 2. The Support Features

4 Evaluation

In the construction of the sentiment resource, we used the annotated sentences provided by the corpora described in Table 3. The resources listed in Table 3 were selected to test the functionality of the words annotation proposal with subjectivity and objectivity. Note that the shadowed rows correspond to constrained runs corpora: tweeti-b-sub.dist_out.tsv [8] (dist), b1_tweeti-objorneu-b.dist_out.tsv [9] (objorneu), twitter-dev-input-B.tsv[10] (dev).

The resources from Table 3 that include unconstrained runs corpora are: all the previously mentioned ones, Computational-intelligence[11] (CI) and stno[12] corpora.

The used sentiment lexicons are from the WordNetAffect_Categories[13] and opinion-words[14] files as shown in detail in Table 4.

Some issues were taken into account throughout this process. For instance, after obtaining a contextual graph G, factotum words are present in most of the involved sentences (i.e., verb *"to be")*. This issue becomes very dangerous after applying the PageRank algorithm because the algorithm strengthens the nodes possessing many linked elements. For that reason, the subtractions $Pos - Neg$ and $Neg - Pos$ are applied, where the most frequent words in all contexts obtain high values. The subtraction becomes a dumping factor.

As an example, when we take the verb *"to be"*, before applying equation (1), the verb achieves the highest values in each subjective context graph ($Gpos$ and $Gneg$) namely, 9.94 and 18.67 rank values respectively. These values, once equation (1) is applied, are normalized obtaining both $Pos = 1$ and $Neg = 1$ in a range [0...1]. At the end, when the following steps are executed (Equations (2) and (3)), the verb *"to be"* achieves $Pos = 0$, $Neg = 0$ and therefore $ObjAlt = 1$. Through this example, it seems as though we subjectively discarded words that appear frequently in both contexts (Positive and Negative).

Corpus	**N**	**P**	**O**	**Neu**	**Obj or Neu**	**Unk**	**T**	**C**	**UC**
dist	176	368	110	34	-	-	688	X	X
objorneu	828	1972	788	1114	1045	-	5747	X	X
dev	340	575	-	739	-	-	1654	X	X
CI	6982	6172	-	-	-	-	13154		X
stno[15]	1286	660	-	384	-	10000	12330		X
T	9272	9172	898	1532	1045	10000	31919		

Table 3. Corpora used to apply RA-SR. Positive (P), Negative (N), Objective (Obj/O), Unknow (Unk), Total (T), Constrained (C), Unconstrained (UC).

Sources	**P**	**N**	**T**
WordNet-Affects_Categories (Strapparava and Valitutti, 2004)	629	907	1536
opinion-words (Hu and Liu, 2004; Liu *et al.*, 2005)	2006	4783	6789
Total	2635	5690	8325

Table 4. Sentiment Lexicons. Positive (P), Negative (N) and Total (T).

			Precision (%)			**Recall (%)**			**Total (%)**		
	C	**Inc**	**P**	**N**	**Neu**	**P**	**N**	**Neu**	**Prec**	**Rec**	**F1**
Run1	8032	1631	80,7	83,8	89,9	90,9	69,5	86,4	**84,8**	**82,3**	**82,9**
Run2	19101	4671	82,2	77,3	89,4	80,7	81,9	82,3	**83,0**	**81,6**	**80,4**

Table 5. Training dataset evaluation using cross-validation (Logistic classifier (using 10 folds)). Constrained (Run1), Unconstrained (Run2), Correct(C), Incorrect (Inc).

4.1 The training evaluation

In order to assess the effectiveness of our trained classifiers, we performed some evaluation tests. Table 5 shows relevant results obtained after applying our system to an environment (specific domain). The best results were obtained with the

[7] Resources described in Table 4.

[8]Semeval-2013 (Task 2. Sentiment Analysis in Twitter, subtask b).

[9]Semeval-2013 (Task 2. Sentiment Analysis in Twitter, subtask b).

[10] http://www.cs.york.ac.uk/semeval-2013/task2/

[11]A sentimental corpus obtained applying techniques developed by GPLSI department. See (http://gplsi.dlsi.ua.es/gplsi11/allresourcespanel)

[12]NTCIR Multilingual Opinion Analysis Task (MOAT) http://research.nii.ac.jp/ntcir/ntcir-ws8/meeting/

[13] http://wndomains.fbk.eu/wnaffect.html

[14] http://www.cs.uic.edu/~liub/FBS/sentiment-analysis.html

[15] NTCIR Multilingual Opinion Analysis Task (MOAT) http://research.nii.ac.jp/ntcir/ntcir-ws8/meeting/

restricted corpus. The information used to increase the knowledge was not balanced or perhaps is of poor quality.

4.2 The test evaluation

The test dataset evaluation is shown in Table 6, where system results are compared with the best results in each case. We notice that the constrained run is better in almost every aspect. In the few cases where it was lower, there was a minimal difference. This suggests that the information used to increase our Sentiment Resource was unbalanced (high difference between quantity of tagged types of annotated phrases), or was of poor quality. By comparing these results with the ones obtained by our system on the test dataset, we notice that on the test dataset, the results fell in the middle of the effectiveness scores. After seeing these results (Table 5 and Table 6), we assumed that our system performance is better in a controlled environment (or specific domain). To make it more realistic, the system must be trained with a bigger and more balanced dataset.

Table 6 shows the results obtained by our system while comparing them to the best results of Task 2b of Semeval-2013. In Table 5, we can see the difference between the best systems. They are the ones in bold and underlined as target results. These results have a difference of around 20 percentage points. The grayed out ones correspond to our runs.

			Precision (%)			Recall (%)			Total		
Runs	**C**	**Inc**	**P**	**N**	**Neu**	**P**	**N**	**Neu**	**Prec**	**Rec**	**F 1**
1_tw	2082	1731	60,9	46,5	52,8	49,8	41,4	64,1	53,4	51,8	**49,3**
1_tw_cnd	2767	1046	81,4	69,7	67,7	66,7	60,4	82,6	72,9	69,9	69,0
2_tw	2026	1787	58,0	42,2	42,2	52,2	43,9	57,4	47,4	51,2	49,0
2_tw_ter	2565	1248	71,1	54,6	68,6	74,7	59,4	63,1	64,8	65,7	64,9
1_sms	1232	862	43,9	46,1	**69,5**	55,9	31,7	**68,9**	53,2	52,2	**43,4**
1_sms_cnd	1565	529	73,1	55,4	85,2	73,0	75,4	75,3	71,2	74,5	68,5
2_sms	1023	1071	38,4	31,4	68,3	60,0	38,3	47,8	46,0	48,7	40,7
2_sms_ava	1433	661	60,9	49,4	81,4	65,9	63,7	71,0	63,9	66,9	59,5

Table 6. Test dataset evaluation using official scores. Corrects(C), Incorrect (Inc).

Table 6 run descriptions are as follows:

- UMCC_DLSI_(SA)-B-twitter-constrained (1_tw),
- NRC-Canada-B-twitter-constrained (1_tw_cnd),
- UMCC_DLSI_(SA)-B-twitter-unconstrained (2_tw),
- teragram-B-twitter-unconstrained (2_tw_ter),
- UMCC_DLSI_(SA)-B-SMS-constrained (1_sms),
- NRC-Canada-B-SMS-constrained (1_sms_cnd), UMCC_DLSI_(SA)-B-SMS-unconstrained (2_sms),
- AVAYA-B-sms-unconstrained (2_sms_ava).

As we can see in the training and testing evaluation tables, our training stage offered more relevant scores than the best scores in Task2b (Semaval-2013). This means that we need to identify the missed features between both datasets (training and testing).

For that reason, we decided to check how many words our system (more concretely, our Sentiment Resource) missed. Table 7 shows that our system missed around 20% of the words present in the test dataset.

	hits	miss	miss (%)
twitter	23807	1591	6,26%
sms	12416	2564	17,12%
twitter nonrepeat	2426	863	**26,24%**
sms norepeat	1269	322	**20,24%**

Table 7. Quantity of words used by our system over the test dataset.

5 Conclusion and further work

Based on what we have presented, we can say that we could develop a system that would be able to solve the SA challenge with promising results. The presented system has demonstrated election performance on a specific domain (see Table 5) with results over 80%. Also, note that our system, through the SA process, automatically builds sentiment resources from annotated corpora.

For future research, we plan to evaluate RA-SR on different corpora. On top of that, we also plan to deal with the number of neutral instances and finding more words to evaluate the obtained sentiment resource.

Acknowledgments

This research work has been partially funded by the Spanish Government through the project TEXT-MESS 2.0 (TIN2009-13391-C04), "Análisis de Tendencias Mediante Técnicas de Opinión Semántica" (TIN2012-38536-C03-03) and “Técnicas de Deconstrucción en la Tecnologías del Lenguaje Humano” (TIN2012-31224); and by the Valencian Government through the project PROMETEO (PROMETEO/2009/199).

References

Agirre, E. and A. Soroa. Personalizing PageRank for Word Sense Disambiguation. Proceedings of the 12th conference of the European chapter of the Association for Computational Linguistics (EACL-2009), Athens, Greece, 2009.

Atserias, J.; B. Casas; E. Comelles; M. González; L. Padró and M. Padró. FreeLing 1.3: Syntactic and semantic services in an opensource NLP library. Proceedings of LREC'06, Genoa, Italy, 2006.

Baccianella, S.; A. Esuli and F. Sebastiani. SENTIWORDNET 3.0: An Enhanced Lexical Resource for Sentiment Analysis and Opinion Mining. 7th Language Resources and Evaluation Conference, Valletta, MALTA., 2010. 2200-2204 p.

Balahur, A. Methods and Resources for Sentiment Analysis in Multilingual Documents of Different Text Types. Department of Software and Computing Systems. Alacant, Univeristy of Alacant, 2011. 299. p.

Balahur, A.; E. Boldrini; A. Montoyo and P. Martinez-Barco. The OpAL System at NTCIR 8 MOAT. Proceedings of NTCIR-8 Workshop Meeting, Tokyo, Japan., 2010. 241-245 p.

Brin, S. and L. Page The anatomy of a large-scale hypertextual Web search engine Computer Networks and ISDN Systems, 1998, 30(1-7): 107-117.

Fellbaum, C. WordNet. An Electronic Lexical Database. University of Cambridge, 1998. p. The MIT Press.

Gutiérrez, Y.; A. González; A. F. Orquín; A. Montoyo and R. Muñoz. RA-SR: Using a ranking algorithm to automatically building resources for subjectivity analysis over annotated corpora. 4th Workshop on Computational Approaches to Subjectivity, Sentiment & Social Media Analysis (WASSA 2013), Atlanta, Georgia, 2013.

Hatzivassiloglou; Vasileios and J. Wiebe. Effects of Adjective Orientation and Gradability on Sentence Subjectivity. International Conference on Computational Linguistics (COLING-2000), 2000.

Hu, M. and B. Liu. Mining and Summarizing Customer Reviews. Proceedings of the ACM SIGKDD International Conference on Knowledge Discovery and Data Mining (KDD-2004), USA, 2004.

Kim, S.-M. and E. Hovy. Extracting Opinions, Opinion Holders, and Topics Expressed in Online News Media Text. In Proceedings of workshop on sentiment and subjectivity in text at proceedings of the 21st international conference on computational linguistics/the 44th annual meeting of the association for computational linguistics (COLING/ACL 2006), Sydney, Australia, 2006. 1-8 p.

Kozareva, Z.; P. Nakov; A. Ritter; S. Rosenthal; V. Stoyonov and T. Wilson. Sentiment Analysis in Twitter. in: Proceedings of the 7th International Workshop on Semantic Evaluation. Association for Computation Linguistics, 2013.

Liu, B.; M. Hu and J. Cheng. Opinion Observer: Analyzing and Comparing Opinions on the Web. Proceedings of the 14th International World Wide Web conference (WWW-2005), Japan, 2005.

Miller, G. A.; R. Beckwith; C. Fellbaum; D. Gross and K. Miller. Five papers on WordNet. Princenton University, Cognositive Science Laboratory, 1990.

Mosquera, A. and P. Moreda. TENOR: A Lexical Normalisation Tool for Spanish Web 2.0 Texts. in: Text, Speech and Dialogue - 15th International Conference (TSD 2012). Springer, 2012.

Strapparava, C. and A. Valitutti. WordNet-Affect: an affective extension of WordNet. Proceedings of the 4th International Conference on Language Resources and Evaluation (LREC 2004), Lisbon, 2004. 1083-1086 p.

Wiebe, J.; T. Wilson and C. Cardie. Annotating Expressions of Opinions and Emotions in Language. Kluwer Academic Publishers, Netherlands, 2005.

ASVUniOfLeipzig: Sentiment Analysis in Twitter using Data-driven Machine Learning Techniques

Robert Remus
Natural Language Processing Group,
Department of Computer Science,
University of Leipzig, Germany
rremus@informatik.uni-leipzig.de

Abstract

This paper describes University of Leipzig's approach to SemEval-2013 task 2B on Sentiment Analysis in Twitter: message polarity classification. Our system is designed to function as a baseline, to see what we can accomplish with well-understood and purely data-driven lexical features, simple generalizations as well as standard machine learning techniques: We use one-against-one Support Vector Machines with asymmetric cost factors and linear "kernels" as classifiers, word uni- and bigrams as features and additionally model negation of word uni- and bigrams in word n-gram feature space. We consider generalizations of URLs, user names, hash tags, repeated characters and expressions of laughter. Our method ranks 23 out of all 48 participating systems, achieving an averaged (positive, negative) F-Score of 0.5456 and an averaged (positive, negative, neutral) F-Score of 0.595, which is above median and average.

1 Introduction

In SemEval-2013's task 2B on *Sentiment Analysis in Twitter*, given a Twitter message, i.e. a tweet, the goal is to classify whether this tweet is of positive, negative, or neutral polarity (Wilson et al., 2013), i.e. the task is a ternary polarity classification.

Due to Twitter's growing popularity, the availability of large amounts of data that go along with that and the fact, that many people freely express their opinion on virtually everything using Twitter, research on sentiment analysis in Twitter has received a lot of attention lately (Go et al., 2009; Pak and Paroubek, 2010). Language is usually used casually in Twitter and exhibits interesting properties. Therefore, some studies specifically address certain issues, e.g. a tweet's length limitation of 140 characters, some studies leverage certain language characteristics, e.g. the presence of emoticons etc.

Davidov et al. (2010) identify various "sentiment types" defined by Twitter hash tags (e.g. `#bored`) and smileys (e.g. `:S`) using words, word n-grams, punctuation marks and patterns as features. Barbosa and Feng (2010) map words to more general representations, i.e. part of speech (POS) tags and the words' prior subjectivity and polarity. Additionally, they count the number of re-tweets, hash tags, replies, links etc. They then combine the outputs of 3 online sources of labeled but noisy and biased Twitter data into a more robust classification model. Saif et al. (2012) also address data sparsity via word clustering methods, i.e. semantic smoothing and sentiment-topics extraction. Agarwal et al. (2011) contrast a word unigram model, a tree kernel model and a model of various features, e.g. POS tag counts, summed up prior polarity scores, presence or absence of capitalized text, all applied to binary and ternary polarity classification. Kouloumpis et al. (2011) show that Twitter-specific feature engineering, e.g. representing the presence or absence of abbreviations and character repetitions improves model quality. Jiang et al. (2011) focus on target-dependent polarity classification regarding a given user query.

While various models and features have been proposed, word n-gram models proved to be competitive in many studies (Barbosa and Feng, 2010; Agar-

*Second Joint Conference on Lexical and Computational Semantics (*SEM), Volume 2: Seventh International Workshop on Semantic Evaluation (SemEval 2013)*, pages 450–454, Atlanta, Georgia, June 14-15, 2013.

wal et al., 2011; Saif et al., 2012) yet are straightforward to implement. Moreover, word n-gram models do not rely on hand-crafted and generally {genre, domain}-non-specific resources, e.g. prior polarity dictionaries like *SentiWordNet* (Esuli and Sebastiani, 2006) or *Subjectivity Lexicon* (Wiebe et al., 2005). In contrast, purely data-driven word n-gram models are *domain-specific* per se: they "let the data speak for themselves". Therefore we believe that carefully designing such a baseline using well-understood and purely data-driven lexical features, simple generalizations as well as standard machine learning techniques is a worthwhile endeavor.

In the next Section we describe our system. In Section 3 we discuss its results in SemEval-2013 task 2B and finally conclude in Section 4.

2 System Description

We approach the ternary polarity classification via one-against-one (Hsu and Lin, 2002) Support Vector Machines (SVMs) (Vapnik, 1995; Cortes and Vapnik, 1995) using a linear "kernel" as implemented by *LibSVM*[1]. To deal with the imbalanced class distribution of positive (+), negative (−) and neutral-or-objective (0) instances, we use asymmetric cost factors C_+, C_-, C_0 that allow for penalizing false positives and false negatives differently inside the one-against-one SVMs. While the majority class' C_0 is set to 1.0, the minority classes' $C_{\{+,-\}}$s are set as shown in (1)

$$C_{\{+,-\}} = \frac{\#(0\text{-class instances})}{\#(\{+,-\}\text{-class instances})} \quad (1)$$

similar to Morik et al. (1999)'s suggestion.

2.1 Data

To develop our system, we use all training data available to us for training and all development data available to us for testing, after removing 75 duplicates from the training data and 2 duplicates from the development data. Please note that 936 tweets of the originally provided training data and 3 tweets of the originally provided development data were not available at our download time[2]. Table 1 summarizes the used data's class distribution after duplicate removal.

Data	+	−	0	Σ
Training	3,263	1,278	4,132	8,673
Development	384	197	472	1,053
Σ	3,647	1,475	4,604	9,726

Table 1: Class distribution of positive (+), negative (−) and neutral-or-objective (0) instances in training and development data after duplicate removal.

For sentence segmentation and tokenization of the data we use *OpenNLP*[3]. An example tweet of the provided training data is shown in (1):

(1) #nacamam @naca you have to try Skywalk Deli on the 2nd floor of the Comerica building on Monroe! #bestlunche http://instagr.am/p/Rfv-RfTI-3/.

2.2 Model Selection

To select an appropriate model, we experiment with different feature sets (cf. Section 2.2.1) and different combinations of generalizations (cf. Section 2.2.2).

2.2.1 Features

We consider the following feature sets:

a. word unigrams

b. word unigrams plus negation modeling for word unigrams

c. word uni- and bigrams

d. word uni- and bigrams plus negation modeling for word unigrams

e. word uni- and bigrams plus negation modeling for word uni- and bigrams

Word uni- and bigrams are induced data-driven, i.e. directly extracted from the textual data. We perform no feature selection; neither stop words nor punctuation marks are removed. We simply encode the presence or absence of word n-grams.

[1] `http://www.csie.ntu.edu.tw/~cjlin/libsvm/`

[2] Training data was downloaded on February 21, 2013, 9:18 a.m. and development data was downloaded on February 28, 2013, 10:41 a.m. using the original download script.

[3] `http://opennlp.apache.org`

Whether a word uni- or bigram is negated, i.e. appears inside of a negation scope (Wiegand et al., 2010), is detected by *LingScope*[4] (Agarwal and Yu, 2010), a state-of-the-art negation scope detection based on Conditional Random Fields (Lafferty et al., 2001). We model the negation of word n-grams in an augmented word n-gram feature space as detailedly described in Remus (2013): In this feature space, each word n-gram is either represented as present ($[1, 0]$), absent ($[0, 0]$), present inside a negation scope ($[0, 1]$) and present both inside and outside a negation scope ($[1, 1]$).

We trained a model for each feature set and chose the one that yields the highest accuracy: word uni- and bigrams plus negation modeling for word uni- and bigrams.

2.2.2 Generalizations

To account for Twitter's typical language characteristics, we consider all possible combinations of generalizations of the following character sequences, inspired by (Montejo-Ráez et al., 2012):

a. User names, that mark so-called mentions in a Tweet, expressed by `@username`.

b. Hash tags, that mark keywords or topics in a Tweet, expressed by `#keyword`.

c. URLs, that mark links to other web pages.

d. Twitpic URLs, that mark links to pictures hosted by `twitpic.com`.

e. Repeated Characters, e.g. `woooow`. We collapse characters re-occuring more than twice, e.g. `woooow` is replaced by `woow`.

f. Expressions of laughter, e.g. `hahaha`. We generalize derivatives of the "base forms" `haha`, `hehe`, `hihi` and `huhu`. A derivative must contain the base form and may additionally contain arbitrary uppercased and lowercased letters at its beginning and its end. We collapse these derivatives. E.g., `hahahah` and `HAHAhaha` and `hahaaa` are all replaced by their base form `haha`, `eheheh` and `heheHE` are all replaced by `hehe` etc.

[4] `http://sourceforge.net/projects/lingscope/`

User names, hash tags, URLs and Twitpic URLs are generalized by either simply removing them (mode I) or by replacing them with a single unique token (mode II), i.e. by forming an equivalence class. Repeated characters and expressions of laughter are generalized by collapsing them as described above.

There are $1 + \sum_{k=1}^{6} \binom{6}{k} = 64$ possible combinations of generalizations including no generalization at all. We trained a word uni- and bigram plus negation modeling for word uni- and bigrams model (cf. Section 2.2.1) for each combination and both mode I and mode II and chose the one that yields the highest accuracy: Generalization of URLs (mode I), repeated characters and expressions of laughter.

Although it may appear counterintuitive not to generalize hash tags and user names, the training data contains several re-occuring hash tags, that actually convey sentiment, e.g. `#love`, `#cantwait`, `#excited`. Similarly, the training data contains several re-occuring mentions of "celebrities", that may hint at sentiment which is usually associated with them, e.g. `@justinbieber` or `@MittRomney`.

3 Results & Discussion

To train our final system, we use all available training and development data (cf. Table 1). The SVM's "base" cost factor C is optimized via 10-fold cross validation, where in each fold 9/10th of the available data are used for training, the remaining 1/10th is used for testing. C values are chosen from $\{2 \cdot 10^{-3}, 2 \cdot 10^{-2}, 2 \cdot 10^{-1}, 2 \cdot 10^{0}, 2 \cdot 10^{1}, 2 \cdot 10^{2}, 2 \cdot 10^{3}\}$. Internally, the asymmetric cost factors C_+, C_-, C_0 (cf. Section 2) are then set to $C_{\{+,-,0\}} := C \cdot C_{\{+,-,0\}}$.

The final system is then applied to both Twitter and SMS test data (cf. Table 2). Please note

Test Data	$+$	$-$	0	Σ
Twitter	1,572	601	1,640	3,813
SMS	492	394	1,208	2,094

Table 2: Class distribution of positive (+), negative (−) and neutral-or-objective (0) instances in Twitter and SMS testing data.

that we only participate in the *constrained* setting of SemEval-2013 task 2B (Wilson et al., 2013) as we did not use any additional training data.

Detailed evaluation results on Twitter test data are shown in Table 3, results on SMS test data are shown in Table 4. The ranks we achieved in the constrained only-ranking and the full constrained and unconstrained-ranking are shown in Table 5.

Class	P	R	F
$+$	0.7307	0.5833	0.6487
$-$	0.5795	0.3577	0.4424
0	0.6072	0.8098	0.6940
$+,-$	0.6551	0.4705	*0.5456*
$+,-,0$	0.6391	0.5836	0.5950

Table 3: Precision P, Recall R and F-Score F of University of Leipzig's approach to SemEval-2013 task 2B on Twitter test data distinguished by classes ($+$, $-$, 0) and averages of $+,-$ and $+,-,0$.

Class	P	R	F
$+$	0.5161	0.5854	0.5486
$-$	0.5174	0.3020	0.3814
0	0.7289	0.7881	0.7574
$+,-$	0.5168	0.4437	*0.4650*
$+,-,0$	0.5875	0.5585	0.5625

Table 4: Precision P, Recall R and F-Score F of University of Leipzig's approach to SemEval-2013 task 2B on SMS test data distinguished by classes ($+$, $-$, 0) and averages of $+,-$ and $+,-,0$.

Test data	Constr.	Un/constr.
Twitter	18 of 35	23 of 48
SMS	20 of 28	31 of 42

Table 5: Ranks of University of Leipzig's approach to SemEval-2013 task 2B on Twitter and SMS test data in the constrained only (Constr.) and the constrained and unconstrained setting (Un/constr.).

On Twitter test data our system achieved an averaged $(+,-)$ F-Score of 0.5456, which is above the average (0.5382) and above the median (0.5444). Our system ranks 23 out of 48 participating systems in the full constrained and unconstrained-ranking. Averaging over over $+,-,0$ it yields an F-Score of 0.595.

On SMS test data our system performs quite poorly compared to other participating systems as (i) we did not adapt our model to the SMS data at all, e.g. we did not consider more appropriate or other generalizations, and (ii) its class distribution is quite different from our training data (cf. Table 1 vs. 2). Our system achieved an averaged $(+,-)$ F-Score of 0.465, which is below the average (0.5008) and below the median (0.5060). Our system ranks 31 out of 42 participating systems in the full constrained and unconstrained-ranking. Averaging over over $+,-,0$ it yields an F-Score of 0.5625.

4 Conclusion

We described University of Leipzig's contribution to SemEval-2013 task 2B on Sentiment Analysis in Twitter. We approached the message polarity classification via well-understood and purely data-driven lexical features, negation modeling, simple generalizations as well as standard machine learning techniques. Despite being designed as a baseline, our system ranks midfield on both Twitter and SMS test data.

As even the state-of-the-art system achieves $(+,-)$ averaged F-Scores of 0.6902 and 0.6846 on Twitter and SMS test data, respectively, polarity classification of tweets and short messages still proves to be a difficult task that is far from being solved. Future enhancements of our system include the use of more data-driven features, e.g. features that model the distribution of abbreviations, punctuation marks or capitalized text as well as fine-tuning our generalization mechanism, e.g. by (i) generalizing only low-frequency hash tags and usernames, but not generalizing high-frequency ones, (ii) generalizing acronyms that express laughter, such as `lol` ("laughing out loud") or `rofl` ("rolling on the floor laughing").

References

S. Agarwal and H. Yu. 2010. Biomedical negation scope detection with conditional random fields. *Journal of the American Medical Informatics Association*, 17(6):696–701.

A. Agarwal, B. Xie, I. Vovsha, O. Rambow, and R. Passonneau. 2011. Sentiment analysis of twitter data. In *Proceedings of the Workshop on Languages in Social Media (LSM*, pages 30–38.

L. Barbosa and J. Feng. 2010. Robust sentiment detection on twitter from biased and noisy data. In *Proceed-*

ings of the 23rd International Conference on Computational Linguistics (COLING), pages 36–44.

C. Cortes and V. Vapnik. 1995. Support-vector networks. *Machine Learning*, 20(3):273–297.

D. Davidov, O. Tsur, and A. Rappoport. 2010. Enhanced sentiment learning using twitter hashtags and smileys. In *Proceedings of the 23rd International Conference on Computational Linguistics (COLING)*, pages 241–249.

A. Esuli and F. Sebastiani. 2006. SentiWordNet: A publicly available lexical resource for opinion mining. In *Proceedings of the 5th International Conference on Language Resources and Evaluation (LREC)*, pages 417–422.

A. Go, R. Bhayani, and L. Huang. 2009. Twitter sentiment classification using distant supervision. CS224N project report, Stanford University.

C. Hsu and C. Lin. 2002. A comparison of methods for multiclass support vector machines. *IEEE Transactions on Neural Networks*, 13(2):415–425.

L. Jiang, M. Yu, M. Zhou, X. Liu, and T. Zhao. 2011. Target-dependent twitter sentiment classification. In *Proceedings of the 49th Annual Meeting of the Association for Computational Linguistics (ACL)*, pages 151–160.

E. Kouloumpis, T. Wilson, and J. Moore. 2011. Twitter sentiment analysis: The good the bad and the OMG. In *Proceedings of the 5th International Conference on Weblogs and Social Media (ICWSM)*, pages 538–541.

J. Lafferty, A. McCallum, and F. Pereira. 2001. Conditional random fields: Probabilistic models for segmenting and labeling sequence data. In *Proceedings of the 18th International Conference on Machine Learning (ICML)*, pages 282–289.

A. Montejo-Ráez, E. Martınez-Cámara, M.T. Martın-Valdivia, and L.A. Urena-López. 2012. Random walk weighting over sentiwordnet for sentiment polarity detection on twitter. In *Proceedings of the 3rd Workshop on Computational Approaches to Subjectivity and Sentiment Analysis (WASSA)*, pages 3–10.

K. Morik, P. Brockhausen, and T. Joachims. 1999. Combining statistical learning with a knowledge-based approach – a case study in intensive care monitoring. In *Proceedings of the 16th International Conference on Machine Learning (ICML)*, pages 268–277.

A. Pak and P. Paroubek. 2010. Twitter as a corpus for sentiment analysis and opinion mining. In *Proceedings of the 7th International Conference on Language Resources and Evaluation (LREC)*.

R. Remus. 2013. Negation modeling in machine learning-based sentiment analysis. In *forthcoming*.

H. Saif, Y. He, and H. Alani. 2012. Alleviating data sparsity for twitter sentiment analysis. In *Proceedings of the 2nd Workshop on Making Sense of Microposts (#MSM)*.

V. Vapnik. 1995. *The Nature of Statistical Learning*. Springer New York, NY.

J. Wiebe, T. Wilson, and C. Cardie. 2005. Annotating expressions of opinions and emotions in language. *Language Resources and Evaluation*, 1(2):165–210.

M. Wiegand, A. Balahur, B. Roth, D. Klakow, and A. Montoyo. 2010. A survey on the role of negation in sentiment analysis. In *Proceedings of the 2010 Workshop on Negation and Speculation in Natural Language Processing (NeSp-NLP)*, pages 60–68.

T. Wilson, Z. Kozareva, P. Nakov, A. Ritter, S. Rosenthal, and V. Stoyanov. 2013. SemEval-2013 task 2: Sentiment analysis in twitter. In *Proceedings of the 7th International Workshop on Semantic Evaluation (SemEval)*.

Experiments with DBpedia, WordNet and SentiWordNet as resources for sentiment analysis in micro-blogging

Hussam Hamdan[*,**,***]
hussam.hamdan@lsis-.org
*LSIS
Aix-Marseille Université CNRS
Av. Esc. Normandie Niemen,
13397 Marseille Cedex 20,
France

Frederic Béchet[**]
frederic.bechet@lif-.univ-mrs.fr
**LIF
Aix-Marseille Université CNRS
Avenue de Luminy
13288 Marseille Cedex 9,
France

Patrice Bellot[*,***]
patrice.bellot@lsis-.org
***OpenEdition
Aix-Marseille Université CNRS
3 pl. V. Hugo, case n°86
13331 Marseille Cedex 3,
France

Abstract

Sentiment Analysis in Twitter has become an important task due to the huge user-generated content published over such media. Such analysis could be useful for many domains such as Marketing, Finance, Politics, and Social. We propose to use many features in order to improve a trained classifier of Twitter messages; these features extend the feature vector of uni-gram model by the concepts extracted from DBpedia, the verb groups and the similar adjectives extracted from WordNet, the Senti-features extracted using SentiWordNet and some useful domain specific features. We also built a dictionary for emotion icons, abbreviation and slang words in tweets which is useful before extending the tweets with different features. Adding these features has improved the f-measure accuracy 2% with SVM and 4% with NaiveBayes.

1 Introduction

In recent years, the explosion of social media has changed the relation between the users and the web. The world has become closer and more "real-time" than ever. People have increasingly been part of virtual society where they have created their content, shared it, interacted with others in different ways and at a very increasingly rate. Twitter is one of the most important social media, with 1 billion tweets[1] posted per week and 637 million users[2].

With the availability of such content, it attracts the attention from who want to understand the opinion and interestingness of individuals. Thus, it would be useful in various domains such as politics, financing, marketing and social. In this context, the efficacy of sentiment analysis of twitter has been demonstrated at improving prediction of box-office revenues of movies in advance of their release (Asur and Huberman, 2010). Sentiment Analysis has been used to study the impact of 13 twitter accounts of celebrated person on their followers (Bae and Lee, 2012) and for forecasting the interesting tweets which are more probably to be reposted by the followers many times (Naveed, Gottron *et al.*, 2011).

However, sentiment analysis of microblogs faces several challenges, the limited size of posts (e.g., maximum 140 characters in Twitter), the informal language of such content containing slang words and non-standard expressions (e.g. *gr8* instead of *great*, *LOL* instead of *laughing out loud*, *goooood* etc.), and the high level of noise in the posts due to the absence of correctness verification by user or spelling checker tools.

Three different approaches can be identified in the literature of Sentiment Analysis, the first approach is the lexicon based which uses specific types of lexicons to derive the polarity of a text, this approach is suffering from the limited size of lexicon and requires human expertise to build the lexicon (Joshi, Balamurali *et al.*, 2011). The second one is machine learning approach which uses annotated texts with a given label to learn a statistical model and an early work was done on a movie review dataset (Pang, Lee et al., 2002). Both lexicon and machine learning approaches can be

1http://blog.kissmetrics.com/twitter-statistics/
2http://twopcharts.com/twitter500million.php

*Second Joint Conference on Lexical and Computational Semantics (*SEM), Volume 2: Seventh International Workshop on Semantic Evaluation (SemEval 2013)*, pages 455–459, Atlanta, Georgia, June 14-15, 2013.

combined to achieve a better performance (Khuc, Shivade et al. 2012). The third one is social approach which exploits social network properties and data for enhancing the accuracy of the classification (Speriosu, Sudan *et al.*, 2011; Tan, Lee et al. 2011; Hu, Tang *et al.*, 2013) (Hu, Tang et al., 2013) (Tan, Lee *et al.*, 2011).

In this paper, we employ machine learning. Each text is represented by a vector in which the features have to be selected carefully. They can be the words of the text, their POS tags (part of speech), or any other syntactic or semantic features.

We propose to exploit some additional features (section 3) for sentiment analysis that extend the representation of tweets by:

- the concepts extracted from DBpedia[3],
- the related adjectives and verb groups extracted from WordNet[4],
- some "social" features such as the number of happy and bad emotion icons,
- the number of exclamation and question marks,
- the existence of URL (binary feature),
- if the tweet is re-tweeted (binary feature),
- the number of symbols the tweet contains,
- the number of uppercase words,
- some other senti-features extracted from SentiWordNet[5] such as the number of positive, negative and neutral words that allow estimating a score of the negativity, positivity and objectivity of the tweets, their polarity and subjectivity.

We extended the unigram model with these features (section 4.2). We also constructed a dictionary for the abbreviations and the slang words used in Twitter in order to overcome the ambiguity of the tweets.

We tested various combinations (section 4.2) of these features, and then we chose the one that gave the highest F-measure for negative and positive classes (submission for Tweet subtask B of sentiment analysis in twitter task of SemEval2013 (Wilson, Kozareva et al. 2013)). We tested different machine learning models: Naïve Bayes, SVM, IcsiBoost[6] but the submitted runs exploited SVM only[6].

[3] http://dbpedia.org/About
[4] http://wordnet.princeton.edu/
[5] http://sentiwordnet.isti.cnr.it/
[6] http://code.google.com/p/icsiboost/

The rest of this paper is organized as follows. Section 2 outlines existing work of sentiment analysis over Twitter. Section 3 presents the features we used for training a classifier. Our experiments are described in section 4 and future work is presented in section 5.

2 Related Work

We can identify three main approaches for sentiment analysis in Twitter. The lexicon based approaches which depend on dictionaries of positive and negative words and calculate the polarity according to the positive and negative words in the text. Many dictionaries have been created manually such as ANEW (Aaffective Norms for English Words) or automatically such as SentiWordNet (Baccianella, Esuli et al. 2010). Four lexicon dictionaries were used to overcome the lack of words in each one (Joshi, Balamurali et al. 2011; Mukherjee, Malu et al. 2012). Automatically construction of a Twitter lexicon was implemented by Khuc, Shivade *et al.* (2012).

Machine learning approaches were employed from annotated tweets by using Naive Bayes, Maximum Entropy *MaxEnt* and Support Vector Machines (SVM) (Go, Bhayani et al. 2009). Go *et al.* (2009) reported that SVM outperforms other classifiers. They tried a unigram and a bigram model in conjunction with parts-of-speech (POS) features; they noted that the unigram model outperforms all other models when using SVM and that POS features decline the results. N-gram with lexicon features and microbloging features were useful but POS features were not (Kouloumpis, Wilson et al. 2011). In contrast, Pak & Paroubek (2010) reported that POS and bigrams both help. Barbosa & Feng (2010) proposed the use of syntax features of tweets like retweet, hashtags, link, punctuation and exclamation marks in conjunction with features like prior polarity of words and POS of words, Agarwal *et al.* (2011) extended their approach by using real valued prior polarity and by combining prior polarity with POS. They build models for classifying tweets into positive, negative and neutral sentiment classes and three models were proposed: a unigram model, a feature based model and a tree kernel based model which presented a new tree representation for tweets. Both combining unigrams with their features and combining the features with the tree kernel outperformed the unigram baseline. Saif *et al.* (2012) proposed to use the semantic features, therefore they extracted the hidden concepts in the tweets. They demonstrated that incorporating semantic features extracted using AlchemyAPI[7] improves the accuracy of sentiment classification through three different tweet corpuses.

The third main approach takes into account the influence of users on their followers and the relation between the users and the tweets they wrote. Using the Twitter follower graph might improve the polarity classification. Speriosu, Sudan et al. (2011) demonstrated that using label propagation with Twitter follower graph improves the polarity classification. Tan, Lee et al. (2011) employed social relation for user-level sentiment analysis. Hu, Tang et al. (2013) proposed a sociological approach to handling the noisy and short text (SANT) for supervised sentiment classification, they reported that social theories such as Sentiment Consistency and Emotional Contagion could be helpful for sentiment analysis.

3 Feature Extraction

We used different types of features in order to improve the accuracy of sentiment classification.

— Bag of words (uni-gram)

The most commonly used features in text analysis are the bag of words which represent a text as unordered set of words. It assumes that words are independent from each other and also disregards their order of appearance. We used these features as a baseline model.

— Domain specific features

We extracted some domain specific features of tweets which are: presence of an URL or not, the tweet was retweeted or not, the number of "*Not*", the number of happy emotion icons, the number of sad emotion icons, exclamation and question marks, the number of words starting by a capital letter, the number of @.

— DBpedia features

We used the DBpedia Spotlight[8] Web service to extract the concepts of each tweet. For example, for the previous tweet, the DBpedia concepts for Chapel Hill are (*Settlement, PopulatedPlace, Place*). Therefore, if we suppose that people post positively about settlement, it would be more probable to post positively about Chapel Hill.

— WordNet features

We used WordNet for extracting the synonyms of nouns, verbs and adjectives, the verb groups (the hierarchies in which the verb synsets are arranged), the similar adjectives (synset) and the concepts of nouns which are related by the relation is-a in WordNet.

We chose the first synonym set for each noun, adjective and verb, then the concepts of the first noun synonym set, the similar adjectives of the first adjective synonym set and the verb group of the first verb synonym set. We think that those features would improve the accuracy because they could overcome the ambiguity and the diversity of the vocabulary.

- Senti-features

We used SentiWordNet for extracting the number and the scores of positive, negative and neutral words in tweets, the polarity (the number of positive words divided by the number of negative ones incremented by one) and subjectivity (the number of positive and negative words divided by the neutral ones incremented by one).

4 Evaluations

4.1 Data collection

We used the data set provided in SemEval 2013 for subtask B of sentiment analysis in Twitter (Wilson, Kozareva et al. 2013). The participants were provided with training tweets annotated positive, negative or neutral. We downloaded these tweets using the given script. Among 9646 tweets, we could only download 8498 of them because of protected profiles and deleted tweets. Then, we used the development set containing 1654 tweets for evaluating our methods. The method which gave the highest accuracy for the average of positive and negative classes was chosen for the submitted runs. Lastly, we combined the development set with training set and built a new model which predicted the labels of the 3813 tweets in the test set.

[7] http://www.alchemyapi.com/

[8] http://dbpedia-spotlight.github.io/

4.2 Experiments

We have done various experiments using the features presented in Section 3 with SVM model using linear kernel and the following parameters: weighting value=1, degree=3, cost=1, nu=0.5 and seed=1. We firstly constructed feature vector of tweet terms which gave 0.52% for f-measure of the negative and positive classes. Then, we augmented this vector by the similar adjectives of WordNet which improves a little the f-measure, particularly for the positive class. After that, we added the concepts of DBpedia which also improved the quality of the positive class and declined the negative one. Finally, we added all the verb groups, senti-features and domain specific features which improved the f-measure for both negative and positive classes but particularly for the positive one. Table 1 presents the results for each kind of feature vector.

	Feature vector	Uni-gram	+adjectives	+DBpedia	+verb groups+ syntactic + senti-features
f-measure	**Positive**	0.603	0.619	0.622	**0.637**
	Negative	**0.443**	0.436	0.417	0.440
	Neutral	0.683	0.685	**0.691**	0.689
	Avg neg+pos	0.523	0.527	0.520	**0.538**

Table 1. The results of different feature vectors using linear SVM model (degree=3, weight=1, nu=0.5)

	Feature vector	Uni-gram	+adjectives	+DBpedia	+verb groups+ syntactic + senti-features
f-measure	**Positive**	0.514	**0.563**	0.562	0.540
	Negative	0.397	0.422	**0.427**	0.424
	Neutral	0.608	**0.652**	0.648	0.636
	Avg neg+pos	0.456	0.493	**0.495**	0.482

Table 2. The results of different feature vectors using a NaiveBayes approach.

We remark that the DBpedia concepts improved the accuracy, and just the similar adjectives and group verbs of WordNet improved it, but the other synonyms and concepts declined it. The reason may be linked to a perturbation added by the synonyms. Moreover, the first synonym set is not necessary to be the most suitable one. Many domain specific and Senti-WordNet features improved the accuracy, but others did not, such as the number of neutral words, whether the tweet is reposted or not, the number of @ and the number of #. So we excluded the features that declined the accuracy.

We have done some experiments using NaiveBayes (Table 2). Naïve Bayes improved the accuracy of the negative and positive classes, and the highest f-measure was obtained by adding the adjectives and the DBpedia concepts. Using such features improved the f-measure for the positive and negative classes: about 2% with SVM and 4% with NaiveBayes. The improvement given by means of the Naïve Bayes model was more significant than the one obtained with SVM and needed fewer features, but the higher accuracy was obtained by SVM.

5 Discussion and Future Work

In this paper we experimented the value of using DBpedia, WordNet and SentiWordNet for the sentiment classification of tweets. We extended the feature vector of tweets by the concepts of DBpedia, verb groups and similar adjectives from WordNet, the senti-features from SentiWordNet and other domain specific features. We think that using other lexicon dictionaries with SentiWordNet is more useful, we did not use POS Tagger for detecting the part of speech. We augmented the feature vector by all these features. In fact, for some tweets this expansion is not the best strategy. However, it will be important to find out a way for selecting only the features that improve the accuracy.

We verified that the adjectives are useful features and we should now focus on extracting the suitable and similar adjectives. For the abbreviation *LOL* (loud of laughing), it might be more useful to replace it by *funny* or by another adjective that reflects the sentiment of the writer. However, we could enhance our dictionary by these adjectives. We could handle the emotion icons in a similar way.

We also plan to combine the results of different classifiers for improving the total accuracy.

References

Agarwal, A., B. Xie, et al. (2011). Sentiment analysis of Twitter data.Proceedings of the Workshop on Languages in Social Media. Portland, Oregon, Association for Computational Linguistics: 30-38.

Asur, S. and B. A. Huberman (2010). Predicting the Future with Social Media. Proceedings of the 2010 IEEE/WIC/ACM International Conference on Web Intelligence and Intelligent Agent Technology - Volume 01, IEEE Computer Society: 492-499.

Baccianella, S., A. Esuli, et al. (2010). SentiWordNet 3.0: An Enhanced Lexical Resource for Sentiment Analysis and Opinion Mining. Proceedings of the Seventh Conference on International Language Resources and Evaluation (LREC'10), European Language Resources Association (ELRA).

Bae, Y. and H. Lee (2012). "Sentiment analysis of twitter audiences: Measuring the positive or negative influence of popular twitterers." J. Am. Soc. Inf. Sci. Technol.63(12): 2521-2535.

Barbosa, L. and J. Feng (2010). Robust sentiment detection on Twitter from biased and noisy data.Proceedings of the 23rd International Conference on Computational Linguistics: Posters. Beijing, China, Association for Computational Linguistics: 36-44.

Go, A., R. Bhayani, et al. (2009). Twitter Sentiment Classification using Distant Supervision.

Hu, X., L. Tang, et al. (2013). Exploiting social relations for sentiment analysis in microblogging. Proceedings of the sixth ACM international conference on Web search and data mining.Rome, Italy, ACM: 537-546.

Joshi, A., A. R. Balamurali, et al. (2011). C-Feel-It: a sentiment analyzer for micro-blogs. Proceedings of the 49th Annual Meeting of the Association for Computational Linguistics: Human Language Technologies: Systems Demonstrations. Portland, Oregon, Association for Computational Linguistics: 127-132.

Khuc, V. N., C. Shivade, et al. (2012). Towards building large-scale distributed systems for twitter sentiment analysis. Proceedings of the 27th Annual ACM Symposium on Applied Computing. Trento, Italy, ACM: 459-464.

Kouloumpis, E., T. Wilson, et al. (2011).Twitter Sentiment Analysis: The Good the Bad and the OMG! Fifth International AAAI Conference on Weblogs and Social Media.

Mukherjee, S., A. Malu, et al. (2012).TwiSent: a multistage system for analyzing sentiment in twitter. Proceedings of the 21st ACM international conference on Information and knowledge management.Maui, Hawaii, USA, ACM: 2531-2534.

Naveed, N., T. Gottron, et al. (2011). Bad News Travels Fast: A Content-based Analysis of Interestingness on Twitter. Proc. Web Science Conf.

Pak, A. and P. Paroubek (2010). Twitter as a corpus for sentiment analysis and opinion mining.

Pang, B., L. Lee, et al. (2002). Thumbs up?: sentiment classification using machine learning techniques. Proceedings of the ACL-02 conference on Empirical methods in natural language processing - Volume 10, Association for Computational Linguistics: 79-86.

Saif, H., Y. He, et al. (2012).Semantic sentiment analysis of twitter.Proceedings of the 11th international conference on The Semantic Web - Volume Part I. Boston, MA, Springer-Verlag: 508-524.

Speriosu, M., N. Sudan, et al. (2011). Twitter polarity classification with label propagation over lexical links and the follower graph. Proceedings of the First Workshop on Unsupervised Learning in NLP. Edinburgh, Scotland, Association for Computational Linguistics: 53-63.

Tan, C., L. Lee, et al. (2011). User-level sentiment analysis incorporating social networks. Proceedings of the 17th ACM SIGKDD international conference on Knowledge discovery and data mining. San Diego, California, USA, ACM: 1397-1405.

Khuc, V. N., C. Shivade, et al. (2012). Towards building large-scale distributed systems for twitter sentiment analysis. Proceedings of the 27th Annual ACM Symposium on Applied Computing. Trento, Italy, ACM: 459-464.

Wilson, T., Z. Kozareva, et al. (2013). "SemEval-2013 Task 2: Sentiment Analysis in Twitter." Proceedings of the 7th International Workshop on Semantic Evaluation. Association for Computational Linguistics.

OPTWIMA: Comparing Knowledge-rich and Knowledge-poor Approaches for Sentiment Analysis in Short Informal Texts

Alexandra Balahur
European Commission Joint Research Centre
Via E. Fermi 2749
21027 Ispra (VA), Italy
{alexandra.balahur}@jrc.ec.europa.eu

Abstract

The fast development of Social Media made it possible for people to no loger remain mere spectators to the events that happen in the world, but become part of them, commenting on their developments and the entities involved, sharing their opinions and distributing related content. This phenomenon is of high importance to news monitoring systems, whose aim is to obtain an informative snapshot of media events and related comments.

This paper presents the strategies employed in the OPTWIMA participation to SemEval 2013 Task 2-Sentiment Analysis in Twitter. The main goal was to evaluate the best settings for a sentiment analysis component to be added to the online news monitoring system.

We describe the approaches used in the competition and the additional experiments performed combining different datasets for training, using or not slang replacement and generalizing sentiment-bearing terms by replacing them with unique labels.

The results regarding tweet classification are promising and show that sentiment generalization can be an effective approach for tweets and that SMS language is difficult to tackle, even when specific normalization resources are employed.

1 Introduction

Sentiment analysis is the Natural Language Processing (NLP) task dealing with the detection and classification of sentiments in texts. Usually, the classes considered are "positive", "negative" and "neutral", although in some cases finer-grained categories are added (e.g. "very positive" and "very negative") or only the "positive" and "negative" classes are taken into account.

This task has received a lot of interest from the research community in the past years. The work done regarded the manner in which sentiment can be classified from texts pertaining to different genres and distinct languages, in the context of various applications, using knowledge-based, semi-supervised and supervised methods [Pang and Lee, 2008]. The result of the analyses performed have shown that the different types of text require specialized methods for sentiment analysis, as, for example, sentiments are not conveyed in the same manner in newspaper articles and in blogs, reviews, forums or other types of user-generated contents [Balahur et al., 2010].

In the light of these findings, dealing with sentiment analysis in tweets and SMS (that we can generally call "short informal texts") requires an analysis of the characteristics of such texts and the design of adapted methods.

Our participation in the SemEval 2013 Task 2 [Wilson et al., 2013] had as objective to test how well our proposed methods for sentiment analysis for short informal texts (especially tweets) would perform. The two subtasks proposed in this competition were: a) the classification of sentiment from snippets from tweets and SMS marked as start and end position and b) the classification of sentiment from entire tweets and SMS. Each team could submit 2 runs for each dataset and task, one employing as training data only the data provided within the competition ("constrained") and the second em-

*Second Joint Conference on Lexical and Computational Semantics (*SEM), Volume 2: Seventh International Workshop on Semantic Evaluation (SemEval 2013)*, pages 460–465, Atlanta, Georgia, June 14-15, 2013.

ploying any additional data ("unconstrained"). We submitted 2 of such runs for each of the subtasks and datasets.

The main requirements for the system we implemented were: a) not to use language-specific NLP processing tools (since our final goal is to make the present system work for many more languages); and b) to work fast, so that it can be integrated in a near real time media monitoring system.

2 Related Work and Contribution

One of the first studies on the classification of polarity in tweets was Go et al. [2009]. The authors conducted a supervised classification study on tweets in English, using the emoticons (e.g. ":)", ":(", etc.) as markers of positive and negative tweets. Read [2005] employed this method to generate a corpus of positive tweets, with positive emoticons ":)", and negative tweets with negative emoticons ":(". Subsequently, they employ different supervised approaches (SVM, Naïve Bayes and Maximum Entropy) and various sets of features and conclude that the simple use of unigrams leads to good results, but it can be slightly improved by the combination of unigrams and bigrams.

In the same line of thinking, Pak and Paroubek [2010] also generated a corpus of tweets for sentiment analysis, by selecting positive and negative tweets based on the presence of specific emoticons. Subsequently, they compare different supervised approaches with n-gram features and obtain the best results using Naïve Bayes with unigrams and part-of-speech tags.

Another approach on sentiment analysis in tweet is that of Zhang et al. [2011]. Here, the authors employ a hybrid approach, combining supervised learning with the knowledge on sentiment-bearing words, which they extract from the DAL sentiment dictionary [Whissell, 1989]. Their pre-processing stage includes the removal of retweets, translation of abbreviations into original terms and deleting of links, a tokenization process, and part-of-speech tagging. They employ various supervised learning algorithms to classify tweets into positive and negative, using n-gram features with SVM and syntactic features with Partial Tree Kernels, combined with the knowledge on the polarity of the words appearing in the tweets. The authors conclude that the most important features are those corresponding to sentiment-bearing words. Finally, Jiang et al. [2011] classify sentiment expressed on previously-given "targets" in tweets. They add information on the context of the tweet to its text (e.g. the event that it is related to). Subsequently, they employ SVM and General Inquirer and perform a three-way classification (positive, negative, neutral).

The main contributions of the approaches considered for the competition reside in the evaluation of different strategies to adapt sentiment analysis methods to the language employed in short informal texts.

The methods employed in our system are simple, work fast and efficient and can be easily adapted to other languages. The main adaptations we consider are part of a pre-processing step, in which the language in these short informal texts is normalized (brought to a dictionary form).

Finally, the methods presented are compared on different configurations and training sets, so that the conclusions drawn are relevant to the phenomena found in this type of informal texts.

3 Methods Employed by OPTWIMA in SemEval 2013 Task 2

We employ two different approaches: a) one based on supervised learning using Support Vector Machines Sequential Minimal Optimization (SVM SMO) using unigram and bigram features; and b) a hybrid approach, based on supervised learning with a SVM SMO linear kernel, on unigram and bigram features, but exploiting as features sentiment dictionaries, emoticon lists, slang lists and other social media-specific features. SVM SMO was preferred due to the computation speed. We do not employ any specific language analysis software. The aim is to be able to apply, in a straightforward manner, the same approach to as many languages as possible. The approach can be extended to other languages by using similar dictionaries that have been created in our team Steinberger et al. [2011].

The sentiment analysis process contains two stages: preprocessing and sentiment classification.

3.1 Preprocessing of Short Informal Texts

The language employed in short informal texts such as tweets and SMS is different from the one found in other types of texts, such as newspaper articles and the form of the words employed is sometimes not the one we may find in a dictionary. Further on, users writing on Twitter or SMS-ing on their cell phone employ a special "slang" (i.e. informal language, with special expressions, such as "lol", "omg"), emoticons, and often emphasize words by repeating some of their letters. Additionally, the language employed in Twitter has specific characteristics, such as the markup of tweets that were reposted by other users with "RT", the markup of topics using the "#" (hash sign) and of the users using the "@" sign.

All these aspects must be considered at the time of processing tweets and, to some extent, SMS.

As such, before applying supervised learning to classify the sentiment of the short informal texts considered, we preprocess them, to normalize the language they contain and try to abstract on the concepts that are sentiment-bearing, by replacing them with labels, according to their polarity[1]. In case of SMS messages, the slang employed, the short forms of words and the acronyms make these texts non processable without prior replacement and normalization of the slang. The preprocessing stage contains the following steps:

- Repeated punctuation sign normalization (RPSN).

  In the first step of the preprocessing, we detect repetitions of punctuation signs (".", "!" and "?"). Multiple consecutive punctuation signs are replaced with the labels "multistop", for the fullstops, "multiexclamation" in the case of exclamation sign and "multiquestion" for the question mark and spaces before and after.

- Emoticon replacement (ER).

  In the second step of the preprocessing, we employ the annotated list of emoticons from SentiStrength[2] and match the content of the tweets against this list. The emoticons found are replaced with their polarity ("positive" or "negative") and the "neutral" ones are deleted.

- Lower casing and tokenization (LCN).

  Subsequently, the tweets are lower cased and split into tokens, based on spaces and punctuation signs.

- Slang replacement (SR).

  The next step involves the normalization of the language employed. In order to be able to include the semantics of the expressions frequently used in Social Media, we employed the list of slang expressions from dedicated sites [3]. This step is especially relevant to SMS texts, whose language in their original form has little to do with language employed in ordinary texts.

- Word normalization (WN).

  At this stage, the tokens are compared to entries in Roget's Thesaurus. If no match is found, repeated letters are sequentially reduced to two or one until a match is found in the dictionary (e.g. "perrrrrrrrrrrrrrrrrrfeeect" becomes "perrfeect", "perfeect", "perrfect" and subsequently "perfect"). The words used in this form are maked as "stressed".

- Affect word matching (AWM).

  Further on, the tokens in the tweet are matched against three different sentiment lexicons: General Inquirer, LIWC and MicroWNOp, which were previously split into four different categories ("positive", "high positive", "negative" and "high negative"). Matched words are replaced with their sentiment label - i.e. "positive", "negative", "hpositive" and "hnegative".

- Modifier word matching (MWM).

  Similar to the previous step, we employ a list of expressions that negate, intensify or diminish the intensity of the sentiment expressed to detect such words in the tweets. If such a word is matched, it is replaced with "negator", "intensifier" or "diminisher", respectively.

[1] The preprocessing steps involving the use of affect dictionaries and modifier replacement are used only in one of the two methods considered

[2] http://sentistrength.wlv.ac.uk/

[3] www.noslang.com/dictionary, www.smsslang.com

- User and topic labeling (UTL).

  Finally, the users mentioned in the tweet, which are marked with "@", are replaced with "PERSON" and the topics which the tweet refers to (marked with "#") are replaced with "TOPIC".

3.2 Sentiment Classification of Short Informal Texts

Once the texts are preprocessed, they are passed on to the sentiment classification module.

We employed supervised learning using Support Vector Machines Sequential Minimal Optimization (SVM SMO) [Platt, 1998] with a linear kernel, employing boolean features - the presence or absence of unigrams and bigrams determined from the training data (tweets that were previousely preprocessed as described above) that appeared at least twice. Bigrams are used especially to spot the influence of modifiers (negations, intensifiers, diminishers) on the polarity of the sentiment-bearing words. We tested different parameters for the kernel and modified only the C constant to the best value determined on the training data (5.0)/

We tested the approach on different datasets and dataset splits, using the Weka data mining software [4]. The training models are built on a cluster of computers (4 cores, 5000MB of memory each).

4 Evaluation and Discussion

We participated in SemEval 2013 in Task 2 with two versions of the system, for each of the two subtasks (A and B). The main difference among them is the use of dictionaries for affect and modifier word matching and replacement. As such, in the first method (denoted as "Dict"), we perform all the preprocessing steps mentioned above, while the second method is applied on the data on which the AWM and MWM are not performed (i.e. words that are associated with a sentiment in a lexicon are not replaced with labels). This second method will be denoted "NoDict".

Another difference between the different evaluations we performed are the datasets employed for training. We created different models, employing:

1) For both the "Constrained" and "Unconstrained" submissions, the development and training data from the corresponding subtask (i.e. using as training the data in subtask A - the sets given as training and development together - to train a classifier for the test data in task A; the same for subtask B). In this case, the training data is marked with the corresponding subtask (i.e. training data "A", training data "B");

2) For both the "Constrained" and "Unconstrained" submissions, the development and training data from both subtasks - both training and development sets - to train one classifier which is used for both subtasks. This training set is denoted as "A+B";

3) For the "Unconstrained" submissions, we added to the joint training and development data from both subtasks the set of MySpace comments provided by [Thelwall et al., 2010]. This small set contains 1300 short texts from the MySpace social network[5]. The motivation behind this choice is that texts from this source are very similar in language and structure to tweets and (after slang replacement) SMS.

Finally, we trained different classifiers on the training sets described, with and without replacing the affective and modifier words and with and without employing the slang replacement pre-processing step.

The results are presented in Tables 1, 2, 3, 4, in terms of average F-measure of the positive and negative classes (as used by the organizers). The runs submitted in the competition are marked with an asterisk ("*"). We did not perform all the experiments for the sets of SMS without slang replacement, as the first results were very low.

As we can see from the results, our approach performed better in classifying the overall sentiment of texts than small snippets. The results were significantly better for the classification of tweets in comparison to SMS, whose language (even with slang replacement) made them difficult to tackle. We can also see that the joint use of slang replacement and dictionaries for tweets leads to significantly lower results, meaning that this step (at least with the resources we employed for slang treatment), is not necessary for the treatment of tweets. Instead, for these texts, the use of affect dictionaries and modifier lists and their generalizaton lead to better re-

[4]http://www.cs.waikato.ac.nz/ml/weka/

[5]http://www.myspace.com/

	Trained on A+B with slang replacement (Constrained)	
Test set	Dict	NoDict
Task A Tweets	0.35	0.37
Task A SMS	0.35	0.37*
Task B Tweets	0.45*	0.54
Task B SMS	0.40*	0.47

Table 1: Results obtained using A+B (train and developement data) as training set and replacing the slang.

	Trained on A+B+MySpace with slang replacement (Unconstrained)	
Test Set	Dict	NoDict
Task A Tweets	0.36	0.39*
Task A SMS	0.37*	0.37
Task B Tweets	0.46	0.54*
Task B SMS	0.40	0.37*

Table 2: Results obtained using A+B+MySpace (train and developement data) as training set and replacing the slang.

sults. This proves that such a generalization, in the context of "legible" texts, is a useful tool for sentiment analysis. Further on, the results showed that adding a small quantity of training data led to no significant growth in performance (for the data in which slang was replaced). Additional evaluations could be made to quantify the effect of this data when other methods to generalize are not applied. As an observation, our results were balanced for all three classes, with even higher scores for the neutral class. We believe this class should have been considered as well, since in real-world settings systems for sentiment analysis must also be able to classify texts pertaining to this category.

Finally, we can see that in the case of SMS, the difference between the use of slang with or without affect label generalizations is insignificant. We believe this is due to the fact that the expressions with which the slang is replaced are very infrequent in traditional sentiment dictionaries (such as the ones we employed). Even by replacing the short forms and slang with their equivalents, the texts obtained contain words that are infrequent in other types of texts, even tweets. However, we will perform additional experiments with other lists of slang and add, as much as it is possible, the informal sentiment-bearing expressions to create new affect resources for this types of texts.

5 Conclusions and Future Work

In this article, we presented and evaluated the approaches considered for our participation in the SemEval 2013 Task 2. We evaluated different combinations of features, resources and training sets and applied different methods to tackle the issues brought by the informal language used in tweets and SMS.

As future work, we would like to extend the system to more languages, using the dictionaries created by Steinberger et al. [2011] and analyze and include new features that are particular to social media - especially tweets - to improve the performance of the sentiment analysis component. Further on, we would like to quantify the influence of using linguistic processing tools to perform lemmatizing, POS-tagging and the inclusion of corresponding features on the final performance of the system. Finally, we would like to explore additional resources to deal with the issue of language informality in tweets and further explore the problems posed by the peculiar language employed in SMS.

References

Alexandra Balahur, Ralf Steinberger, Mijail Kabadjov, Vanni Zavarella, Erik van der Goot, Matina Halkia, Bruno Pouliquen, and Jenya Belyaeva. Sentiment analysis in the news. In *Proceedings*

	Trained on data of subtask (A or B) with slang replacement	
Test Set	Dict	NoDict
Task A Tweets	0.36	0.37
Task A SMS	0.36	0.37
Task B Tweets	0.5	0.55
Task B SMS	0.49	0.53

Table 3: Results obtained using A (train and developement data) or B (train and developement data) as training set and replacing the slang.

	Trained on data of subtask (A or B), no slang replacement		Trained on A+B, no slang replacement	
Test Set	Dict	NoDict	Dict	NoDict
Task A Tweets	0.69*	0.59	0.6	0.69
Task B Tweets	0.59	0.51	0.62	0.44

Table 4: Results obtained for tweet classification using A+B or A or B as training set and not replacing the slang.

of the Seventh International Conference on Language Resources and Evaluation (LREC'10), Valletta, Malta, may 2010.

Alec Go, Richa Bhayani, and Lei Huang. Twitter sentiment classification using distant supervision. *Processing*, pages 1–6, 2009.

Long Jiang, Mo Yu, Ming Zhou, Xiaohua Liu, and Tiejun Zhao. Target-dependent twitter sentiment classification. In *Proceedings of the 49th Annual Meeting of the Association for Computational Linguistics: Human Language Technologies*, HLT '11, pages 151–160. ACL, 2011. ISBN 978-1-932432-87-9.

Alexander Pak and Patrick Paroubek. Twitter as a corpus for sentiment analysis and opinion mining. In *Proceedings of the Seventh conference on International Language Resources and Evaluation (LREC'10)*, Valletta, Malta; ELRA, may 2010. ELRA. ISBN 2-9517408-6-7. 19-21.

Bo Pang and Lillian Lee. Opinion mining and sentiment analysis. *Found. Trends Inf. Retr.*, 2(1-2): 1–135, January 2008. ISSN 1554-0669.

John C. Platt. Sequential minimal optimization: A fast algorithm for training support vector machines. Technical report, Advances in Kernel Methods - Support Vector Learning, 1998.

Jonathon Read. Using emoticons to reduce dependency in machine learning techniques for sentiment classification. In *Proceedings of the ACL Student Research Workshop*, ACLstudent '05, pages 43–48, Stroudsburg, PA, USA, 2005.

J. Steinberger, P. Lenkova, M. Ebrahim, M. Ehrmann, A. Hurriyetoglu, M. Kabadjov, R. Steinberger, H. Tanev, V. Zavarella, and S. Vázquez. Creating sentiment dictionaries via triangulation. In *Proceedings of WASSA 2011*, WASSA '11, pages 28–36. ACL, 2011.

Mike Thelwall, Kevan Buckley, Georgios Paltoglou, Di Cai, and Arvid Kappas. Sentiment in short strength detection informal text. *Journal of the American Society for Information Science and Technology*, 61(12):2544–2558, December 2010.

Cynthia Whissell. The Dictionary of Affect in Language. In Robert Plutchik and Henry Kellerman, editors, *Emotion: theory, research and experience*, volume 4, The measurement of emotions. Academic Press, London, 1989.

Theresa Wilson, Zornitsa Kozareva, Preslav Nakov, Sara Rosenthal, Veselin Stoyanov, and Alan Ritter. SemEval-2013 task 2: Sentiment analysis in twitter. In *Proceedings of the International Workshop on Semantic Evaluation*, SemEval '13, June 2013.

Ley Zhang, Riddhiman Ghosh, Mohamed Dekhil, Meichun Hsu, and Bing Liu. Combining lexicon-based and learning-based methods for twitter sentiment analysis. Technical Report HPL-2011-89, HP, 21/06/2011 2011.

FBK: Sentiment Analysis in Twitter with Tweetsted

Md. Faisal Mahbub Chowdhury
FBK and University of Trento, Italy
fmchowdhury@gmail.com

Marco Guerini
Trento RISE, Italy
marco.guerini@trentorise.eu

Sara Tonelli
FBK, Trento, Italy
satonelli@fbk.eu

Alberto Lavelli
FBK, Trento, Italy
lavelli@fbk.eu

Abstract

This paper presents the *Tweetsted* system implemented for the SemEval 2013 task on Sentiment Analysis in Twitter. In particular, we participated in Task B on Message Polarity Classification in the Constrained setting. The approach is based on the exploitation of various resources such as SentiWordNet and LIWC. Official results show that our approach yields a F-score of 0.5976 for Twitter messages (11th out of 35) and a F-score of 0.5487 for SMS messages (8th out of 28 participants).

1 Introduction

Microblogging is currently a very popular communication tool where millions of users share opinions on different aspects of life. For this reason it is a valuable source of data for opinion mining and sentiment analysis.

Working with such type of texts presents challenges for NLP beyond those typically encountered when dealing with more traditional texts, such as newswire data. Tweets are short, the language used is very informal, with creative spelling and punctuation, misspellings, slang, new words, URLs, genre-specific terminology and abbreviations, and #hashtags. These characteristics need to be handled with specific approaches.

This paper presents the approach adopted for the SemEval 2013 task on Sentiment Analysis in Twitter, in particular Task B on Message Polarity Classification in the Constrained setting (i.e., using the provided training data only).

The goal of Task B on Message Polarity Classification is the following: given a message, decide whether it expresses a positive, negative, or neutral sentiment. For messages conveying both a positive and a negative sentiment, whichever is the stronger sentiment should be chosen.

Two modalities are possible: (1) Constrained (using the provided training data only; other resources, such as lexica, are allowed; however, it is not allowed to use additional tweets/SMS messages or additional sentences with sentiment annotations); and (2) Unconstrained (using additional data for training, e.g., additional tweets/SMS messages or additional sentences annotated for sentiment). We participated in the Constrained modality.

We adopted a supervised machine learning (ML) approach based on various contextual and semantic features. In particular, we exploited resources such as SentiWordNet (Esuli and Sebastiani, 2006), LIWC (Pennebaker and Francis, 2001), and the lexicons described in Mohammad et al. (2009).

Critical features include: whether the message contains intensifiers, adjectives, interjections, presence of positive or negative emoticons, possible message polarity based on SentiWordNet scores (Esuli and Sebastiani, 2006; Gatti and Guerini, 2012), scores based on LIWC categories (Pennebaker and Francis, 2001), negated words, etc.

2 System Description

Our supervised ML-based approach relies on Support Vector Machines (SVMs). The SVM implementation used in the system is LIBSVM (Chang

*Second Joint Conference on Lexical and Computational Semantics (*SEM), Volume 2: Seventh International Workshop on Semantic Evaluation (SemEval 2013)*, pages 466–470, Atlanta, Georgia, June 14-15, 2013.

and Lin, 2001) for training SVM models and testing. Moreover, in the preprocessing phase we used TweetNLP (Owoputi et al., 2013), a POS tagger explicitly tailored for working on tweets.

We adopted a 2 stage approach: (1) during stage 1, we performed a binary classification of messages according to the classes *neutral* vs *subjective*; (2) in stage 2, we performed a binary classification of subjective messages according to the classes *positive* vs *negative*. We performed various experiments on the training and development sets exploring the use of different features (see Section 2.1) to find the best configurations for the official submission.

2.1 Feature list

We implement several features divided into three groups: contextual features, semantic features from context and semantic features from external resources. The complete list is reported in Table 1.

Contextual features are features computed by considering only the tokens in the tweets/SMS and the associated part of speech.

Semantic Features from Context are features based on words polarity. Emoticons were recognized through a list of emoticons extracted from Wikipedia[1] and then manually labeled as positive or negative. Negated words (feature n. 18) are any token occurring between *n't, not, no* and a comma, excluding those tagged as function words. Feature n. 19 captures tokens (or sequences of tokens) labeled with a positive or negative polarity in the resource described in Mohammad et al. (2009). The intensifiers considered for Feature n. 20 have been identified by implementing a simple algorithm that detects tokens containing anomalously repeated characters (e.g. *happyyyyy*). Feature n. 21 was computed by training the system on the training data and predicting labels for the test data, and then using these labels as new features to train the system again.

Semantic Features from external resources include word classes from the Linguistic Inquiry and Word Count (LIWC), a tool that calculates the degree to which people use different categories of words related to psycholinguistic processes (Pennebaker and Francis, 2001). LIWC includes about 2,200 words and stems grouped into 70 broad categories relevant to psychological processes (e.g., EMOTION, COGNITION). Sample words are shown in Table 2.

For each non-zero valued LIWC category of a corresponding tweet/SMS, we added a feature for that category and used the category score as the value of that feature. We call this *LWIC string* feature. Alternatively, we also added a separate feature for each non-zero valued LIWC category and set 1 as the value of that feature. This feature is called *LWIC boolean*.

We also used words prior polarity - i.e. if a word out of context evokes something positive or negative. For this, we relied on SentiWordNet, a broad-coverage resource that provides polarities for (almost) every word. Since words can have multiple senses, we compute the prior polarity of a word starting from the polarity of each sense and returning its *polarity strength* as an index between -1 and 1. We tested 14 formulae that combine posterior polarities in different ways to obtain a word prior polarity, as reported in (Gatti and Guerini, 2012).

For the *SWNscoresMaximum* feature, we select the prior polarity of the word in a tweet/SMS having the maximum absolute score among all words (of that tweet/SMS). For *SWNscoresPolarityCount*, we select the polarity (positive, negative or neutral) that is assigned to the majority of the words. As for *SWNscoresSum*, it corresponds to the sum of the prior polarities associated with all words in the tweet/SMS.

3 Experimental Setup

In order to select the best performing feature set, we carried out several 5-fold cross validation experiments on the training data. We report in Table 3 the best performing feature set. In particular, we adopted a 2 stage approach:

1. during the first stage we performed a binary classification of messages according to the classes *neutral* vs *subjective*;
2. in the second stage, we performed a binary classification of subjective messages according to the classes *positive* vs *negative*.

We opted for a two stage binary classification approach, since we observed that it produces slightly

[1]`http://en.wikipedia.org/wiki/List_of_emoticons`

Contextual Features	
1. noOfAdjectives	num
2. adjective list	string
3. interjection list	string
4. firstInterj	string
5. lastInterj	string
6. bigramList	string
7. beginsWithRT	boolean
8. hasRTinMiddle	boolean
9. endsWithLink	boolean
10. endsWithHashtag	boolean
11. hasQuestion	boolean
Semantic Features from Context	
12. noOfPositiveEmoticons	num
13. noOfNegativeEmoticons	num
14. beginsWithPosEmoticon	boolean
15. beginsWithNegEmoticon	boolean
16. endsWithPosEmoticon	boolean
17. endsWithNegEmoticon	boolean
18. negatedWords	string
19. indexOfChunksWithPolarity	string
20. containsIntensifier	boolean
21. labelPredictedBySystem	pos./neg./neut.
Semantic Features from External Resources	
22. LIWC string	string
23. LIWC boolean	string
24. SWNscoresMaximum	pos./neg./neut.
25. SWNscoresPolarityCount	pos./neg./neut.
26. SWNscoresSum	pos./neg./neut.

Table 1: Complete feature list.

LABEL	*Sample words*
CERTAIN	all, very, fact*, exact*, certain*, completely
DISCREP	but, if, expect*, should
TENTAT	or, some, may, possib*, probab*
SENSES	observ*, discuss*, shows, appears
SELF	we, our, I, us
SOCIAL	discuss*, interact*, suggest*, argu*
OPTIM	best, easy*, enthus*, hope, pride
ANGER	hate, kill, annoyed
INHIB	block, constrain, stop

Table 2: Word categories along with sample words

better results than a single stage multi-class approach (i.e. *neutral* vs *positive* vs *negative*).[2] Different combinations of classifiers were explored obtaining comparable results. Here we will report only the best results.

[2]The average F-scores (pos and neg) for two stage and single stage approaches obtained using the official scorer, by training on the training data and testing on the development data, are 0.5682 and 0.5611 respectively.

STAGE 1. The best result for stage (1), *neutral* vs *subjective*, obtained with 5-fold cross validation on training set only, accounts for an accuracy of 69.6%. Instead, the best result for stage (1), obtained with training on training data and testing on development data, accounts for an accuracy of 72.67%.

The list of best features is reported in Table 3. Feature selection was performed by starting from a small set of basic features, and then by adding the remaining features incrementally.

Contextual Features	
2. adjective list	string
3. interjection list	string
5. lastInterj	string
Semantic Features from Context	
12. noOfPositiveEmoticons	num
13. noOfNegativeEmoticons	num
18. negatedWords	string
19. indexOfChunksWithPolarity	string
20. containsIntensifier	boolean
Semantic Features from external resources	
23. LIWC boolean	string
24. SWNscoresMaximum	posi./neg./neut.

Table 3: Best performing feature set.

STAGE 2. In stage (2), *positive* vs *negative*, we started from the best feature set obtained from stage (1) and added the remaining features one by one incrementally. In this case, we kept *SWNscoresMaximum* without testing again other formulae; in particular, to compute words prior polarity, we also kept the *first sense* approach, that assigns to every word the SWN score of its most frequent sense and proved to be the most discriminative in the first stage *neutral* vs. *subjective*. We found that none of the feature sets produced better results than that obtained using the best feature set selected from stage (1). So, the best feature set for stage (2) is unchanged. We trained the system on the training data and tested it on the development data, achieving an accuracy of 80.67%.

4 Evaluation

The SemEval task organizers (Wilson et al., 2013) provided two test sets on which the systems were to be evaluated: one included Twitter messages, i.e. the same type of texts included in the training set, while the other comprised SMS messages, i.e. texts having more or less the same length as the Twitter data but (supposedly) a different style. We applied the same model, trained both on the training and the development set, on the two types of data, without any specific adaptation.

The *Twitter test set* was composed of 3,813 tweets. Official results show that our approach yields an F-score of 0.5976 for Twitter messages (11th out of 35), while the best performing system obtained an F-score of 0.6902. The confusion matrix is reported in Table 4, while the score details in Table 5. The latter table shows that our system achieves the lowest results on negative tweets, both in terms of precision and of recall.

gs/pred	positive	negative	neutral
positive	946	101	525
negative	90	274	237
neutral	210	70	1360

Table 4: Confusion matrix for Twitter task

class	prec	recall	F-score
positive	0.7592	0.6018	0.6714
negative	0.6157	0.4559	0.5239
neutral	0.6409	0.8293	0.7230
average(pos and neg)			0.5976

Table 5: Detailed results for Twitter task

The *SMS test set* for the competition was composed of 2,094 SMS. Official results provided by the task organizers show that our approach yields an F-score of 0.5487 for SMS messages (8th out of 28 participants), while the best performing system obtained an F-score of 0.6846. The confusion matrix is reported in Table 6, while the score details in Table 7. Also in this case the recognition of negative messages achieves by far the poorest performance.

A comparison of the results on the two test sets shows that, as expected, our system performs better on tweets than on SMS. However, precision achieved by the system on neutral SMS is 0.12 points better on text messages than on tweets.

Interestingly, it appears from the results in Tables 5 and 7 (and from the distribution of the classes in the data sets) that there may be a correlation between the number of tweets/SMS for a particular class and the performance obtained for such class. We plan to further investigate this issue.

gs/pred	positive	negative	neutral
positive	320	44	128
negative	66	171	157
neutral	208	64	936

Table 6: Confusion matrix for SMS task

class	prec	recall	F-score
positive	0.5387	0.6504	0.5893
negative	0.6129	0.4340	0.5082
neutral	0.7666	0.7748	0.7707
average(pos and neg)			0.5487

Table 7: Detailed results for SMS task

5 Conclusions

In this paper, we presented *Tweetsted*, the system developed by FBK for the SemEval 2013 task on Sentiment Analysis. We trained a classifier performing a two-step binary classification, i.e. first neutral vs. subjective data, and then positive vs. negative ones. We implemented a set of features including contextual and semantic ones. We also integrated in our feature representation external knowledge from SentiWordNet, LIWC and the resource by Mohammad et al. (2009). On both test sets (i.e., Twitter messages and SMS) of the constrained modality of the challenge, we achieved a good performance, being among the top 30% of the competing systems. In the near future, we plan to perform an error analysis of the wrongly classified data to investigate possible classification issues, in particular the lower performance on negative tweets and SMS.

Acknowledgments

This work is supported by "eOnco - Pervasive knowledge and data management in cancer care" and "Trento RISE PerTe" projects.

References

Chih-Chung Chang and Chih-Jen Lin, 2001. *LIBSVM: a library for support vector machines*. Software available at `http://www.csie.ntu.edu.tw/~cjlin/libsvm`.

A. Esuli and F. Sebastiani. 2006. SentiWordNet: A publicly available lexical resource for opinion mining. In *Proceedings of the 5th International Conference on Language Resources and Evaluation (LREC 2006)*, Genoa, Italy.

Lorenzo Gatti and Marco Guerini. 2012. Assessing sentiment strength in words prior polarities. In *Proceedings of COLING 2012: Posters*, pages 361–370, Mumbai, India, December. The COLING 2012 Organizing Committee.

Saif Mohammad, Bonnie Dorr, and Cody Dunne. 2009. Generating High-Coverage Semantic Orientation Lexicons From Overtly Marked Words and a Thesaurus. In *Proceedings of the Conference on Empirical Methods in Natural Language Processing*.

Olutobi Owoputi, Brendan O'Connor, Chris Dyer, Kevin Gimpel, Nathan Schneider, and Noah A. Smith. 2013. Improved part-of-speech tagging for online conversational text with word clusters. In *Proceedings of NAACL 2013*, Atlanta, Georgia, June.

J. Pennebaker and M. Francis. 2001. Linguistic inquiry and word count: LIWC. Erlbaum Publishers.

Theresa Wilson, Zornitsa Kozareva, Preslav Nakov, Sara Rosenthal, Veselin Stoyanov, and Alan Ritter. 2013. SemEval-2013 task 2: Sentiment analysis in twitter. In *Proceedings of the International Workshop on Semantic Evaluation*, SemEval '13, June.

SU-Sentilab : A Classification System for Sentiment Analysis in Twitter

Gizem Gezici, Rahim Dehkharghani, Berrin Yanikoglu, Dilek Tapucu, Yucel Saygin
Sabanci University
Istanbul, Turkey 34956
{gizemgezici,rdehkharghani,berrin,dilektapucu,ysaygin}@sabanciuniv.edu

Abstract

Sentiment analysis refers to automatically extracting the sentiment present in a given natural language text. We present our participation to the SemEval2013 competition, in the sentiment analysis of Twitter and SMS messages. Our approach for this task is the combination of two sentiment analysis subsystems which are combined together to build the final system. Both subsystems use supervised learning using features based on various polarity lexicons.

1 Introduction

Business owners are interested in the feedback of their customers about the products and services provided by businesses. Social media networks and micro-blogs such as Facebook and Twitter play an important role in this area. Micro-blogs allow users share their ideas with others in terms of small sentences; while Facebook updates may indicate an opinion inside a longer text. Automatic sentiment analysis of text collected from social media makes it possible to quantitatively analyze this feedback.

In this paper we describe our sentiment analysis system identified as SU-Sentilab in the SemEval 2013 competition, Task 2: Sentiment analysis in Twitter. One or the problems in this competition was to label a given tweet or sms message with the correct sentiment orientation, as positive, negative or neutral. In the second task of the same competition, the polarity of a given word or word sequence in the message was asked. Details are described in (Manandhar and Yuret, 2013).

We participated in both of these tasks using a classifier combination consisting of two sub-systems that are based on (Dehkharghani et al., 2012)(Gezici et al., 2012) and adapted to the tweet domain. Both sub-systems use supervised learning in which the system is trained using tweets with known polarities and used to predict the label (polarity) of tweets in the test set. Both systems use features that are based on well-known polarity resources namely SentiWordNet (Baccianella et al., 2010), SenticNet (Cambria et al., 2012) and NRC Emotion Lexicon (Mohammad, 2012). Also a set of positive and negative seed words (Liu et al., 2005) is used in feature extraction.

The remainder of paper is organized as follows: Related works are presented in Section 2; the proposed approach is described in Section 3 and experimental evaluation is presented in Section 4.

2 Related Works

There has been much work on sentiment analysis in the last ten years (Riloff and Wiebe, 2003) (Wilson et al., 2009) (Taboada et al., 2011) (Pang and Lee, 2008). The two fundamental methods for sentiment analysis are lexicon-based and supervised methods. The lexicon-based technique adopts the idea of determining the review sentiment by obtaining word polarities from a lexicon, such as the SentiWordNet (Baccianella et al., 2010), SenticNet (Cambria et al., 2012). This lexicon can be domain-independent or domain-specific. One can use a domain-specific lexicon whenever available, to get a better performance by obtaining the correct word polarities in the given domain (e.g., the word 'small' has a positive mean-

*Second Joint Conference on Lexical and Computational Semantics (*SEM), Volume 2: Seventh International Workshop on Semantic Evaluation (SemEval 2013)*, pages 471–477, Atlanta, Georgia, June 14-15, 2013.

ing in cell phone domain, while it has a negative meaning in hotel domain). On the other hand, establishing a domain-specific lexicon is costly, so many systems use a domain-independent lexicon, such as the SentiWordNet, shortly SWN, (Baccianella et al., 2010) and SenticNet (Cambria et al., 2012). Part of Speech (POS) information is commonly indicated in polarity lexicons, partly to overcome word-sense disambiguity and therefore help achieve a better sentiment classification performance.

Alternatively, supervised methods use machine learning techniques to build models or discriminators for the different classes (e.g. positive reviews), using a large corpus. For example, in (Pang et al., 2002) (Yu and Hatzivassiloglou, 2003), the Naive Bayes algorithm is used to separate positive reviews from negative ones. Note that supervised learning techniques can also use a lexicon in the feature extraction stage. They also generally perform better compared to lexicon-based approaches; however collecting a large training data may be an issue.

In estimating the sentiment of a given natural language text, many issues are considered. For instance one important problem is determining the subjectivity of a given sentence. In an early study, the effects of adjective orientation and gradability on sentence subjectivity was studied (Hatzivassiloglou and Wiebe, 2000). Wiebe et al. (Wiebe et al., 2004) presents a broad survey on subjectivity recognition and the key elements that may have an impact on it.

In estimating the sentiment polarity, the use of higher-order n-grams is also studied. Pang et. al report results where unigrams work better than bigrams for sentiment classification on a movie dataset (Pang et al., 2002). Similarly, occurrence of rare words (Yang et al., 2006) or the position of words in a text are examined for usefulness (Kim and Hovy, 2006)(Pang et al., 2002). In connection with the occurrences of rare words, different variations of delta tf*idf scores of words, indicating the difference in occurrences of words in different classes (positive or negative reviews), have been suggested (Paltoglou and Thelwall, 2010).

In addition to sentiment classification, obtaining the opinion strength is another issue which may be of interest. Wilson et al. (Wilson et al., 2004) for instance, attempts to determine clause-level opinion strength. Since this is a difficult task, one of the recent studies also investigated the relations between word disambiguation and subjectivity, in order to obtain sufficient information for a better sentiment classification (Wiebe and Mihalcea, 2006). A recent survey describing the fundamental approaches can be found in (Liu, 2012).

Two sub-systems combined to form the SU-Sentilab submission are slightly modified from our previous work (Gezici et al., 2012) (Dehkharghani et al., 2012) (Demiroz et al., 2012). For subsystem SU1, we presented some new features in addition to the ones suggested in (Dehkharghani et al., 2012). For subsystem SU2, we combined two systems (Demiroz et al., 2012) (Gezici et al., 2012). The detailed descriptions for our subsystems SU1 and SU2 as well as our combined system can be found in the following sections.

3 System Description

We built two sentiment analysis systems using supervised learning techniques with labelled tweets for training. Then, another classifier was trained for combining the two systems, which is what is submitted to SemEval-2013 Task 2. The subsystems, SU1 and SU2, and also the combination method are explained in the following subsections.

3.1 Subsystem SU1

Subsystem SU1 uses subjectivity based features that are listed in Table 1. These features are divided into two groups:

- F_1 through F_8, using domain independent resources SenticNet (SN) (Cambria et al., 2012), SentiWordNet (SWN) (Baccianella et al., 2010) and the NRC Emotion lexicons (NRC) (Mohammad, 2012),
- F_9 through F_{13} using the seed word list (called SubjWords).

In the remainder of this subsection, we describe the features which are grouped according to the lexical resource used.

SentiWordNet In SentiWordNet (Baccianella et al., 2010), three scores are assigned to each connotation of a word: positivity, negativity and objectivity.

The summation of these three scores equals to one:

$$Pos(w) + Neg(w) + Obj(w) = 1 \quad (1)$$

where w stands for a given word; and the three scores stand for its positivity, negativity and objectivity scores, respectively. Furthermore, we define the the polarity of a word w as:

$$Pol(w) = Pos(w) - Neg(w) \quad (2)$$

We also do not do word sense disambiguation (WSD) because it is an ongoing problem that has not been completely solved. The average polarity of all words in a review, r, denoted by $AP(r)$ is computed as in (3).

$$AP(r) = \frac{1}{|r|} \sum_{w_i \in r} Pol(w_i) \quad (3)$$

where $|r|$ is the number of words in tweet r and $Pol(w_i)$ is the polarity of the word w_i as defined above.

Feature name
F_1: Avg. polarity of all words using SWN
F_2: Avg. polarity of negative words using SWN
F_3: Avg. polarity of positive words using SWN
F_4: Avg. polarity of negative words using SN
F_5: Avg. polarity of positive words using SN
F_6: term frequency of negative words using NRC
F_7: term frequency of positive words using NRC
F_8: term frequency of swear words
F_9: Cumulative frequency of positive SubjWords
F_{10}: Cumulative frequency of negative SubjWords
F_{11}: Proportion of positive to negative SubjWords
F_{12}: Weighted probability of positive SubjWords
F_{13}: Weighted probability of negative SubjWords

Table 1: Features extracted for each tweet in subsystem SU1

The first three features (F_1, F_2, F_3) are based on the average polarity concept (AP). A word w is decided as positive if $Pol(w) > 0$, and decided as negative if $Pol(w) < 0$.

SenticNet SenticNet (Cambria et al., 2012) is a polarity lexicon that assigns numerical values between -1 and +1 to a *phrase*.

Unlike SentiWordNet (Baccianella et al., 2010), we did not need to do word sense disambiguation for SenticNet. Two features, F_4 and F_5 use the average polarity of negative and positive words extracted from SenticNet. A term is considered as positive if its overall polarity score is greater than 0 and is considered as negative if this score is lower than 0.

NRC Emotion Lexicon The NRC Emotion Lexicon (Mohammad, 2012) is similar to SenticNet in terms of considering different emotions such as anger and happiness; but it is different from SenticNet because it only assigns a binary value (0 or 1) to words. Features F_6 and F_7 use the number of negative and positive words seen according to this lexicon.

Feature F_8 is an isolated feature from other groups which is the list of English swear words collected from the Internet. As an indication to negative sentiment, we counted the number of appearances of those swear words in tweets and used it as a feature.

Subjective Words (SubjWords) We also use a set of seed words which is a subset of the seed word list proposed in (Liu et al., 2005), which we called *SubjWords*. The filtering of the original set of subjective words, for a particular domain, is done through a supervised learning process, where words that are not seen in any tweet in the training set are eliminated. Specifically, we add a positive seed word to the positive subset of SubjWords if it has been seen in at least one positive tweet; and similarly a negative seed word is added to negative subset if it has been seen in a negative tweet.

The number of positive and negative words in the initial set before filtering is 2005 and 4783 respectively. Those numbers decrease to 387 positive and 558 negative words after filtering. Note that this filtering helps us to make the seed word sets domain-specific, which in turn helps increase the accuracy of sentiment classification.

The mentioned filtered seed words are used in features F_9 through F_{13} in different ways. For F_9 and F_{10}, we compute the cumulative term frequency of positive and negative seed words for each tweet in the training set, respectively.

$$F_9(r) = \sum_{t_i \in PS} tf(t_i, r) \quad (4)$$

$$F_{10}(r) = \sum_{t_i \in NS} tf(t_i, r) \quad (5)$$

The feature F_{11} is the proportion of positive seed words (the number of occurrences) to the negative ones in a review (tweet):

$$F_{11}(r) = \frac{p+1}{n+1} \quad (6)$$

where p and n are the number of positive and negative seed words, respectively.

Finally features F_{12} and F_{13} are the weighted probabilities of positive and negative words in a review, calculated as follows:

$$F_{12}(r) = p * (1 - P_{+}(p)) \quad (7)$$

$$F_{13}(r) = n * (1 - P_{-}(n)) \quad (8)$$

where p is the number of positive seed words in review r and $P_{+}(p)$ is the probability of seeing p positive words in a review. Similarly, $F_{13}(r)$ is the weighted probability of negative words in a review r; n is the number of negative seed words in the review, and $P_{-}(n)$ is the probability of seeing n negative words in a review. Probabilities $P_{+}(p)$ and $P_{-}(n)$ are calculated from training set. Table 2 presents the values of $P_{+}(p)$ for $n = 1 \ldots 5$. For instance, the probability of seeing at least one positive subjective word in a positive tweet is 0.87, while seeing three positive words is only 0.47.

p	1	2	3	4	5
$P_{+}(p)$	0.87	0.69	0.47	0.17	0.06

Table 2: The probability of seeing p positive words in a positive tweet.

Classifier The extracted features are fed into a logistic regression classifier, chosen for its simplicity and successful use in many problems. We have used WEKA 3.6 (Hall et al., 2009) implementation for this classifier, all with default parameters.

3.2 Subsystem SU2

Subsystem SU2 uses word-based and sentence-based features proposed in (Gezici et al., 2012) and summarized in Table 3. For adapting to the tweet domain, we also added some new features regarding smileys.

The features consist of an extensive set of 24 features that can be grouped in five categories: (1) basic features, (2) features based on subjective word occurrence statistics, (3) delta-tf-idf weighting of word polarities, (4) punctuation based features, and (5) sentence-based features. They are as follows:

Basic Features In this group of features, we exploit word-based features and compute straightforward features which were proposed several times before in the literature (e.g. avg. review polarity and review purity). Moreover, smileys which are crucial symbols in Twitter are also included here.

Seed Words Features In the second group of features, we have two seed sets as positive and negative seed words. These seed words are the words that are obviously positive or negative irrelevant of the context. As seed words features, we make calculations related to their occurrences in a review to capture several clues for sentiment determination.

Δtf-idf Features This group consists of features based on the Δtf-idf score of a word-sense pair, indicating the relative occurrence of a word-sense among positive and negative classes (Demiroz et al., 2012).

Punctuation-based Features This group contains the number of question and exclamation marks in the message, as they may give some information about the sentiment of a review, especially for the Twitter domain.

Sentence-based Features In this last group of features, we extract features based on sentence type (e.g. subjective, pure, and non-irrealis) (Taboada et al., 2011) and sentence position (e.g. first line and last line) (Zhao et al., 2008). Features include several basic ones such as the average polarity of the first sentence and the average polarity of subjective or pure sentences. We also compute Δtf-idf scores on sentence level.

Finally, we consider the number of sentences which may be significant in SMS messages and the estimated review subjectivity as a feature derived from sentence-level processing. The review is considered subjective if it contains at least one subjective sentence. In turn, a sentence is subjective if and only if it contains at least one subjective word-sense pair or contains at least one smiley. A word-sense pair is subjective if and only if the sum of its positive and negative polarity taken from SentiWordNet (Baccianella et al., 2010) is bigger than 0.5 (Zhang and Zhang, 2006). These features are described in detail in (Gezici et al., 2012).

Feature name
F_1: Average review polarity
F_2: Review purity
F_3: # of positive smileys
F_4: # of negative smileys
F_5: Freq. of seed words
F_6: Avg. polarity of seed words
F_7: Std. of polarities of seed words
F_8: Δtf-idf weighted avg. polarity of words
F_9: Δtf-idf scores of words
F_{10}: # of Exclamation marks
F_{11}: # of Question marks
F_{12}: Avg. First Line Polarity
F_{13}: Avg. Last Line Polarity
F_{14}: First Line Purity
F_{15}: Last Line Purity
F_{16}: Avg. pol. of subj. sentences
F_{17}: Avg. pol. of pure sentences
F_{18}: Avg. pol. of non-irrealis sentences
F_{19}: Δtf-idf weighted polarity of first line
F_{20}: Δtf-idf scores of words in the first line
F_{21}: Δtf-idf weighted polarity of last line
F_{22}: Δtf-idf scores of words in the last line
F_{23}: Review subjectivity (0 or 1)
F_{24}: Number of sentences in review

Table 3: Features extracted for each tweet in subsystem SU2

Obtaining Polarities from SentiWordNet For all the features in subsystem SU2, we use SentiWordNet (Baccianella et al., 2010) as a lexicon. Although, we use the same lexicon for our two subsystems, the way we include the lexicon to our subsystems differs. In this subsystem, we obtain the dominant polarity of the word-sense pair from the lexicon and use the sign for the indication of polarity direction. The dominant polarity of a word w, denoted by $Pol(w)$, is calculated as:

$$Pol(w) = \begin{cases} 0 & \text{if } max(p^{=}, p^{+}, p^{-}) = p^{=} \\ p^{+} & \text{else if } p^{+} \geq p^{-} \\ -p^{-} & \text{otherwise} \end{cases}$$

where p^{+}, $p^{=}$ and p^{-} are the positive, objective and negative polarities of a word w, respectively.

After obtaining the dominant polarities of words from SentiWordNet (Baccianella et al., 2010), we update these polarities using our domain adaptation technique (Demiroz et al., 2012). The $\Delta tf - idf$ scores of words are computed and if there is a disagreement between the $\Delta tf - idf$ and the dominant polarity of a word indicated by the lexicon, then the polarity of the word is updated. This adaptation is described in detail in one of our previous works (Demiroz et al., 2012).

Classifier The extracted features are fed into a Naive Bayes classifier, also chosen for its simplicity and successful use in many problems. We have used WEKA 3.6 (Hall et al., 2009) implementation for this classifier, where the Kernel estimator parameter was set to true.

3.3 Combination of Subsystems

As we had two independently developed systems that were only slightly adapted for this competition, we wanted to apply a sophisticated classifier combination technique. Rather than averaging the outputs of the two classifiers, we used the development set to train a new classifier, to learn how to best combine the two systems. Note that in this way the combiner takes into account the different score scales and accuracies of the two sub-systems automatically.

The new classifier takes as features the probabilities assigned by the systems to the three possible classes (positive, objective, negative) and another feature which is an estimate of subjectivity of the tweet or SMS messages. We trained the system using these 7 features obtained from the development data for which we had the groundtruth, with the goal of predicting the actual class label based on the estimates of the two subsystems.

4 Evaluation

4.1 Competition Tasks

There were two tasks in this competition: 1) Task A where the aim was to determine the sentiment of a phrase within the message and 2) Task B where the aim was to obtain the overall sentiment of a message. In each task, the classification involves the assignment of one of the three sentiment classes, positive, negative and objective/neutral. There were two different datasets for each task, namely tweet and SMS datasets (Manandhar and Yuret, 2013). Due to the different nature of tweets and SMS and the two tasks (A and B), we in fact considered this as four different tasks.

4.2 Submitted Systems

Due to time constraints, we mainly worked on TaskB where we had some prior experience, and only submitted participated in TaskA for completeness.

As we did not use any outside labelled data (tweets or SMS), we trained our systems on the available training data which consisted only of tweets and submitted them on both tweets and SMS sets. In fact, we separated part of the training data as validation set and comparison of the two subsystems.

Since only one system is allowed for each task, we selected the submitted system from our 3 systems (SU1, SU2, combined) based on their performance on the validation set. The performances of these systems are summarized in Table 4.

Finally, we re-trained the selected system with the full training data, to use all available data.

For the implementation, we used C# for subsystem SU1 and Java & Stanford NLP Parser (De Marneffe and Manning, 2008) for subsystem SU2 and WEKA (Hall et al., 2009) for the classification part for both of the systems.

4.3 Results

In order to evaluate and compare the performances of our two systems, we separated a portion of the training data as validation set, and kept it separate. Then we trained each system on the training set and tested it on the validation set. These test results are given in Table 4.

We obtained 75.60% accuracy on the validation set with subsystem SU1 on TaskA_twitter using logistic regression. For the same dataset, we obtained 70.74% accuracy on the validation set with subsystem SU2 using a Naive Bayes classifier.

For TaskB_Twitter dataset on the other hand, we benefited from our combined system in order to get better results. With this combined system using logistic regression as a classifier, we achieved 64% accuracy on the validation set. The accuracies obtained by the individual subsystems on this task was 63.10% by SU1 and 62.92% by SU2.

Dataset	System	Accuracy
TaskA_Twitter	SU1	75.60%
	SU2	70.74%
TaskB_Twitter	SU1	63.10%
	SU2	62.92%
	Combined	64.00%

Table 4: Performance of Our Systems on Validation Data

4.4 Discussion & Future Work

The accuracy of our submitted systems for different tasks are not very high due to many factors. First of all, both domains (tweets and SMSs) were new to us as we had only worked on review polarity estimation on hotel and movie domains before.

For tweets, the problem is quite difficult due to especially short message length; misspelled words; and lack of domain knowledge (e.g. 'Good Girl, Bad Girl' does not convey a sentiment, rather it is a stage play's name). As for the SMS data, there were no training data for SMSs, so we could not tune or retrain our existing systems, either. Finally, for Task A, we had some difficulty with the phrase index, due to some ambiguity in the documentation. Nonetheless, we thank the organizers for a chance to evaluate ourselves among others.

This was our first experience with this competition and with the Twitter and SMS domains. Given the nature of tweets, we used simple features extracted from term polarities obtained from domain-independent lexicons. In the future, we intend to use more sophisticated algorithms, both in the natural language processing stage, as well as the machine learning algorithms.

References

Stefano Baccianella, Andrea Esuli, and Fabrizio Sebastiani. 2010. Sentiwordnet 3.0: An enhanced lexical resource for sentiment analysis and opinion mining. In *Proc. of LREC*.

Erik Cambria, Catherine Havasi, and Amir Hussain. 2012. Senticnet 2: A semantic and affective resource for opinion mining and sentiment analysis. In G. Michael Youngblood and Philip M. McCarthy, editors, *FLAIRS Conf.* AAAI Press.

Marie-Catherine De Marneffe and Christopher D Manning. 2008. Stanford typed dependencies manual. *URL http://nlp. stanford. edu/software/dependencies_manual. pdf.*

Rahim Dehkharghani, Berrin Yanikoglu, Dilek Tapucu, and Yucel Saygin. 2012. Adaptation and use of subjectivity lexicons for domain dependent sentiment classification. In *Data Mining Workshops (ICDMW), 2012 IEEE 12th International Conf.*, pages 669–673.

Gulsen Demiroz, Berrin Yanikoglu, Dilek Tapucu, and Yucel Saygin. 2012. Learning domain-specific polarity lexicons. In *Data Mining Workshops (ICDMW), 2012 IEEE 12th International Conf. on*, pages 674–679.

Gizem Gezici, Berrin Yanikoglu, Dilek Tapucu, and Yücel Saygın. 2012. New features for sentiment analysis: Do sentences matter? In *SDAD 2012 The 1st International Workshop on Sentiment Discovery from Affective Data*, page 5.

Mark Hall, Eibe Frank, Geoffrey Holmes, Bernhard Pfahringer, Peter Reutemann, and Ian H Witten. 2009. The weka data mining software: an update. *ACM SIGKDD Explorations Newsletter*, 11(1):10–18.

Vasileios Hatzivassiloglou and Janyce M Wiebe. 2000. Effects of adjective orientation and gradability on sentence subjectivity. In *Proc. of the 18th Conf. on Comp. Ling.-Volume 1*, pages 299–305.

Soo-Min Kim and Eduard Hovy. 2006. Automatic identification of pro and con reasons in online reviews. In *Proc. of the COLING/ACL Main Conf. Poster Sessions*, pages 483–490.

Bing Liu, Minqing Hu, and Junsheng Cheng. 2005. Opinion observer: analyzing and comparing opinions on the web. In *WWW '05: Proc. of the 14th International Conf. on World Wide Web*.

Bing Liu. 2012. Sentiment analysis and opinion mining. *Synthesis Lectures on Human Language Technologies*, 5(1):1–167.

Suresh Manandhar and Deniz Yuret. 2013. Semeval tweet competition. In *Proc. of the 7th International Workshop on Semantic Evaluation (SemEval 2013) in conjunction with the Second Joint Conference on Lexical and Comp.Semantics (*SEM 2013)*.

Saif Mohammad. 2012. #emotional tweets. In **SEM 2012: The First Joint Conf. on Lexical and Comp. Semantics*, pages 246–255. Association for Comp. Ling.

Georgios Paltoglou and Mike Thelwall. 2010. A study of information retrieval weighting schemes for sentiment analysis. In *Proc. of the 48th Annual Meeting of the Association for Comp. Ling.*, pages 1386–1395.

Bo Pang and Lillian Lee. 2008. Opinion mining and sentiment analysis. *Foundations and Trends in Information Retrieval*, 2(1-2):1–135, January.

Bo Pang, Lillian Lee, and Shivakumar Vaithyanathan. 2002. Thumbs up? sentiment classification using machine learning techniques. In *Proc. of EMNLP*, pages 79–86.

Ellen Riloff and Janyce Wiebe. 2003. Learning extraction patterns for subjective expressions. In *Proc. of the 2003 Conf. on Empirical methods in natural language processing*, pages 105–112, Morristown, NJ, USA. Association for Comp. Ling.

Maite Taboada, Julian Brooke, Milan Tofiloski, Kimberly Voll, and Manfred Stede. 2011. Lexicon-based methods for sentiment analysis. *Comput. Linguist.*, 37(2):267–307.

Janyce Wiebe and Rada Mihalcea. 2006. Word sense and subjectivity. In *ACL*.

Janyce Wiebe, Theresa Wilson, Rebecca F. Bruce, Matthew Bell, and Melanie Martin. 2004. Learning subjective language. *Comp. Ling.*, 30(3):277–308.

Theresa Wilson, Janyce Wiebe, and Rebecca Hwa. 2004. Just how mad are you? finding strong and weak opinion clauses. In *Proc. of the 19th national Conf. on Artifical intelligence*, AAAI'04, pages 761–767.

Theresa Wilson, Janyce Wiebe, and Paul Hoffmann. 2009. Recognizing contextual polarity: An exploration of features for phrase-level sentiment analysis. *Comp. Ling.*, pages 399–433.

Kiduk Yang, Ning Yu, Alejandro Valerio, and Hui Zhang. 2006. Widit in trec-2006 blog track. In *Proc. of TREC*, pages 27–31.

Hong Yu and Vasileios Hatzivassiloglou. 2003. Towards answering opinion questions: Separating facts from opinions and identifying the polarity of opinion sentences. In *Proc. of the 2003 Conf. on Empirical methods in natural language processing*, pages 129–136. Association for Comp. Ling.

Ethan Zhang and Yi Zhang. 2006. Ucsc on trec 2006 blog opinion mining. In *Text Retrieval Conference*.

Jun Zhao, Kang Liu, and Gen Wang. 2008. Adding redundant features for crfs-based sentence sentiment classification. In *Proc. of the conference on empirical methods in natural language processing*, pages 117–126. Association for Comp. Ling.

Columbia_NLP: Sentiment Detection of Subjective Phrases in Social Media

Sara Rosenthal
Department of Computer Science
Columbia University
New York, NY 10027, USA
sara@cs.columbia.edu

Kathleen McKeown
Department of Computer Science
Columbia University
New York, NY 10027, USA
kathy@cs.columbia.edu

Abstract

We present a supervised sentiment detection system that classifies the polarity of subjective phrases as positive, negative, or neutral. It is tailored towards online genres, specifically Twitter, through the inclusion of dictionaries developed to capture vocabulary used in online conversations (e.g., slang and emoticons) as well as stylistic features common to social media. We show how to incorporate these new features within a state of the art system and evaluate it on subtask A in SemEval-2013 Task 2: Sentiment Analysis in Twitter.

1 Introduction

People use social media to write openly about their personal experiences, likes and dislikes. The following sentence from Twitter is a typical example: "*Tomorrow I'm coming back from Barcelona...I don't want! :(((*". The ability to detect the sentiment expressed in social media can be useful for understanding what people think about the restaurants they visit, the political viewpoints of the day, and the products they buy. These sentiments can be used to provided targeted advertising, automatically generate reviews, and make various predictions, such as political outcomes.

In this paper we develop a sentiment detection algorithm for social media that classifies the polarity of sentence phrases as positive, negative, or neutral and test its performance in Twitter through the participation in the expression level task (subtask A) of the SemEval-2013 Task 2: Sentiment Analysis in Twitter (Wilson et al., 2013) which the authors helped organize. To do so, we build on previous work on sentiment detection algorithms for the more formal news genre, notably the work of Agarwal et al (2009), but adapt it for the language of social media, in particular Twitter. We show that exploiting lexical-stylistic features and dictionaries geared toward social media are useful in detecting sentiment.

In this rest of this paper, we discuss related work, including the state of the art sentiment system (Agarwal et al., 2009) our method is based on, the lexicons we used, our method, and experiments and results.

2 Related Work

Several recent papers have explored sentiment analysis in Twitter. Go et al (2009) and Pak and Paroubek (2010) classify the sentiment of tweets containing emoticons using n-grams and POS. Barbosa and Feng (2010) detect sentiment using a polarity dictionary that includes web vocabulary and tweet-specific social media features. Bermingham and Smeaton (2010) compare polarity detection in twitter to blogs and movie reviews using lexical features. Agarwal et al (2011) perform polarity sentiment detection on the entire tweet using features that are somewhat similar to ours: the DAL, lexical features (e.g. POS and n-grams), social media features (e.g. slang and hashtags) and tree kernel features. In contrast to this related work, our approach is geared towards predicting sentiment is at the phrase level as opposed to the tweet level.

3 Lexicons

Several lexicons are used in our system. We use the DAL and expand it with WordNet, as it was used in

*Second Joint Conference on Lexical and Computational Semantics (*SEM), Volume 2: Seventh International Workshop on Semantic Evaluation (SemEval 2013)*, pages 478–482, Atlanta, Georgia, June 14-15, 2013.

Corpus	DAL	NNP (Post DAL)	Word Length-ening	WordNet	Wiktionary	Emoticons	Punctuation & Numbers	Not Covered
Twitter - Train	42.9%	19.2%	1.4%	10.2%	12.7%	0.3%	1.5%	11.7%
Twitter - Dev	57.3%	13.8%	1.1%	7.1%	12.2%	0.4%	2.7%	5.4%
Twitter - Test	49.9%	15.6%	1.4%	9.6%	12.1%	0.5%	1.6%	9.3%
SMS - Test	60.1%	3.6%	0.6%	7.9%	14.7%	0.6%	1.9%	10.3%

Table 1: Coverage for each of the lexicons in the training and test corpora's.

the original work (Agarwal et al., 2009), and expand it further to use Wiktionary and an emoticon lexicon. We consider proper nouns that are not in the DAL to be objective. We also shorten words that are lengthened to see if we can find the shortened version in the lexicons (e.g. sweeeet → sweet). The coverage of the lexicons for each corpus is shown in Table 1.

3.1 DAL

The Dictionary of Affect and Language (DAL) (Whissel, 1989) is an English language dictionary of 8742 words built to measure the emotional meaning of texts. In addition to using newswire, it was also built from individual sources such as interviews on abuse, students' retelling of a story, and adolescent's descriptions of emotions. It therefore covers a broad set of words. Each word is given three scores (pleasantness - also called evaluation (ee), activeness (aa), and imagery (ii)) on a scale of 1 (low) to 3 (high). We compute the polarity of a chunk in the same manner as the original work (Agarwal et al., 2009), using the sum of the AE Space Score's ($|\sqrt{ee^2 + aa^2}|$) of each word within the chunk.

3.2 WordNet

The DAL does cover a broad set of words, but we will still often encounter words that are not included in the dictionary. Any word that is not in the DAL and is not a proper noun is accessed in WordNet (Fellbaum, 1998) [1] and, if it exists, the DAL scores of the synonyms of its first sense are used in its place. In addition to the original approach, if there are no synonyms we look at the hypernym. We then compute the average scores (ee, aa, and ii) of all the words and use that as the score for the word.

[1]We cannot use SentiWordNet because we are interested in the DAL scores

3.3 Wiktionary

We use Wiktionary, an online dictionary, to supplement the common words that are not found in WordNet and the DAL. We first examine all "form of" relationships for the word such as "doesnt" is a "misspelling of" "doesn't", and 'tonite" is an "alternate form of" "tonight". If no "form of" relationships exist, we take all the words in the definitions that have their own Wiktionary page and look up the scores for each word in the DAL. (e.g., the verb definition for *LOL* (laugh out loud) in Wiktionary is *"To laugh out loud"* with *"laugh"* having its own Wiktionary definition; it is therefore looked up in the DAL and the score for "laugh" is used for *"LOL"*.) We then compute the average scores (ee, aa, and ii) of all the words and use that as the score for the word.

3.4 Emoticon Dictionary

emoticon	:)	:D	<3	:(	;)
definition	happy	laughter	love	sad	wink

Table 2: Popular emoticons and their definitions

We created a simple lexicon to map common emoticons to a definition in the DAL. We looked at over 1000 emoticons gathered from several lists on the internet[2] and computed their frequencies within a LiveJournal blog corpus. (In the future we would like to use an external Twitter corpus). We kept the 192 emoticons that appeared at least once and mapped each emoticon to a single word definition. The top 5 emoticons and their definitions are shown in Table 2. When an emoticon is found in a tweet we look up its definition in the DAL.

4 Methods

We run our data through several pre-processing steps to preserve emoticons and expand contractions. We

[2]www.chatropolis.com, www.piology.org, en.wikipedia.org

General		Social Media	
Feature	**Example**	**Feature**	**Example**
Capital Words	Hello	Emoticons	:)
Out of Vocabulary	duh	Acronyms	LOL
Punctuation	.	Repeated Questions	???
Repeated Punctuation	#@.	Exclamation Points	!
Punctuation Count	5	Repeated Exclamations	!!!!
Question Marks	?	Word Lengthening	sweeeet
Ellipses	...	All Caps	HAHA
Avg Word Length	5	Links/Images	www.url.com

Table 3: List of lexical-stylistic features and examples.

then pre-process the sentences to add Part-of-Speech tags (POS) and chunk the sentences using the CRF tagger and chunker (Phan, 2006a; Phan, 2006b). The chunker uses three labels, 'B' (beginning), 'I' (in), and 'O' (out). The 'O' label tends to be applied to punctuation which one typically wants to ignore. However, in this context, punctation can be very important (e.g. exclamation points, and emoticons). Therefore, we append words/phrases tagged as O to the prior B-I chunk.

We apply the dictionaries to the preprocessed sentences to generate lexical, syntactic, and stylistic features. All sets of features were reduced using chi-square in Weka (Hall et al., 2009).

4.1 Lexical and Syntactic Features

We include POS tags and the top 500 n-gram features(Agarwal et al., 2009). We experimented with different amounts of n-grams and found that more than 500 n-grams reduced performance.

The DAL and other dictionaries are used along with a negation state machine(Agarwal et al., 2009) to determine the polarity for each word in the sentence. We include all the features described in the original system (Agarwal et al., 2009).

4.2 Lexical-Stylistic Features

We include several lexical-stylistic features (see Table 3) that can occur in all datasets. We divide these features into two groups, **general**: ones that are common across online and traditional genres, and **social media**: one that are far more common in online genres. Examples of general style features are exclamation points and ellipses. Examples of social media style features are emoticons and word lengthening. Word lengthening is a common phenomenon in social media where letters are repeated to indicate emphasis (e.g. sweeeet). It is particularly common in opinionated words (Brody and Diakopoulos, 2011). The count values of each feature was normalized by the number of words in the phrase.

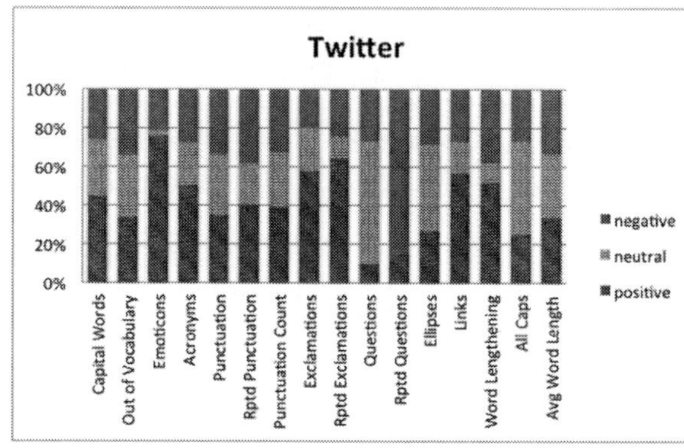

Figure 1: Percentage of lexical-stylistic features that are negative (top), neutral (middle), and positive (bottom) in the Twitter training corpus.

The percentage of lexical-stylistic features that are positive/negative/neutral is shown in Figure 1. For example, emoticons tend to indicate a positive phrase in Twitter. Each stylistic feature accounts for less than 2% of the sentence but at least one of the stylistic features exists in 61% of the Tweets.

We also computed the most frequent emoticons (*<3, :D*), acronyms (*lol*), and punctuation symbols (*#*) within a subset of the Twitter training set and included those as additional features.

5 Experiments and Results

This task was evaluated on the Twitter dataset provided by Semeval-2013 Task 2, subtask A, which the authors helped organize. Therefore, a large portion of time was spent on creating the dataset.

Experiment	Twitter		SMS
	Dev	Test	
Majority	36.3	38.1	31.5
Just DAL	70.1	72.3	67.1
WordNet	72.2	**73.6**	67.7
Wiktionary	**72.8**	**73.7**	**68.7**
Style	71.5	**73.7**	**69.7**
n-grams	**75.2**	**75.7**	**72.5**
WordNet+Style	73.2	74.6	**70.1**
Dictionaries+Style	**74.0**	**75.0**	**70.2**
Dictionaries+Style+n-grams	**75.8**	**77.6**	**73.3**

Table 4: Experiments using the Twitter corpus. Results are shown using average F-measure of the positive and negative class. All experiments include the DAL. The dictionaries refer to WordNet, Wiktionary, and Emoticon. Style refers to Lexical-Stylistic features. All results exceed the majority baseline significantly.

We ran all of our experiments in Weka (Hall et al., 2009) using Logistic Regression. We also experimented with other learning methods but found that this worked best. All results are shown using the average F-measure of the positive and negative class.

We tuned our system for Semeval-2013 Task 2, subtask A, using the provided development set and ran it on the provided Twitter and SMS test data. Our results are shown in Table 4 with all results being statistically significant over a majority baseline. We also use the DAL as a baseline to indicate how useful lexical-stylistic features (specifically those geared towards social media) and the dictionaries are in improving the performance of sentiment detection of phrases in online genres in contrast to using just the DAL. The results that are statistically significant (computed using the Wilcoxon's test, $p \leq .02$) shown in bold. Our best results for each dataset include all features with an average F-measure of 77.6% and 73.3% for the Twitter and SMS test sets respectively resulting in a significant improvement of more than 5% for each test set over the DAL baseline.

At the time of submission, we had not experimented with n-grams, and therefore chose the Dictionaries+Style system as our final version for the official run resulting in a rank of 12/22 (75% F-measure) for Twitter and 13/19 (70.2% F-measure) for SMS. Our rank with the best system, which includes n-grams, would remain the same for Twitter, but bring our rank up to 10/19 for SMS.

We looked more closely at the impact of our new features and as one would expect, feature selection found the general and social media style features (e.g. emoticons, :(, lol, word lengthening) to be useful in Twitter and SMS data. Using additional online dictionaries is useful in Twitter and SMS, which is understandable because they both have poor coverage in the DAL and WordNet. In all cases using n-grams was the most useful which indicates that context is most important. Using Dictionaries and Style in addition to n-grams did provide a significant improvement in the Twitter test set, but not in the Twitter Dev and SMS test set.

6 Conclusion and Future Work

We have explored whether social media features, Wiktionary, and emoticon dictionaries positively impact the accuracy of polarity detection in Twitter and other online genres. We found that social media related features can be used to predict sentiment in Twitter and SMS. In addition, Wiktionary helps improve the word coverage and though it does not provide a significant improvement over WordNet, it can be used in place of WordNet. On the other hand, we found that using the DAL and n-grams alone does almost as well as the best system. This is encouraging as it indicates that content is important and domain independent sentiment systems can do a good job of predicting sentiment in social media.

The results of the SMS messages dataset indicate that even though the online genres are different, the training data in one online genre can indeed be used to predict results with reasonable accuracy in the other online genre. These results show promise for further work on domain adaptation across different kinds of social media.

7 Acknowledgements

This research was partially funded by (a) the ODNI, IARPA, through the U.S. Army Research Lab and (b) the DARPA DEFT Program. All statements of fact, opinion or conclusions contained herein are those of the authors and should not be construed as representing the official views, policies, or positions of IARPA, the ODNI, the Department of Defense, or the U.S. Government.

References

Apoorv Agarwal, Fadi Biadsy, and Kathleen R. Mckeown. 2009. Contextual phrase-level polarity analysis using lexical affect scoring and syntactic n-grams. In *Proceedings of the 12th Conference of the European Chapter of the Association for Computational Linguistics*, EACL '09, pages 24–32, Stroudsburg, PA, USA. Association for Computational Linguistics.

Apoorv Agarwal, Boyi Xie, Ilia Vovsha, Owen Rambow, and Rebecca Passonneau. 2011. Sentiment analysis of twitter data. In *Proceedings of the Workshop on Language in Social Media (LSM 2011)*, pages 30–38, Portland, Oregon, June. Association for Computational Linguistics.

Luciano Barbosa and Junlan Feng. 2010. Robust sentiment detection on twitter from biased and noisy data. In *COLING (Posters)*, pages 36–44.

Adam Bermingham and Alan F. Smeaton. 2010. Classifying sentiment in microblogs: is brevity an advantage? In Jimmy Huang, Nick Koudas, Gareth J. F. Jones, Xindong Wu, Kevyn Collins-Thompson, and Aijun An, editors, *CIKM*, pages 1833–1836. ACM.

Samuel Brody and Nicholas Diakopoulos. 2011. Cooooooooooooooollllllllllllll!!!!!!!!!!!!!! using word lengthening to detect sentiment in microblogs. In *Proceedings of the 2011 Conference on Empirical Methods in Natural Language Processing*, pages 562–570, Edinburgh, Scotland, UK., July. Association for Computational Linguistics.

Christiane Fellbaum, editor. 1998. *WordNet An Electronic Lexical Database*. The MIT Press, Cambridge, MA ; London, May.

Alec Go, Richa Bhayani, and Lei Huang. 2009. Twitter sentiment classification using distant supervision. *Processing*, pages 1–6.

Mark Hall, Eibe Frank, Geoffrey Holmes, Bernhard Pfahringer, Peter Reutemann, and Ian H. Witten. 2009. The weka data mining software: an update. *SIGKDD Explor. Newsl.*, 11(1):10–18, November.

Alexander Pak and Patrick Paroubek. 2010. Twitter as a corpus for sentiment analysis and opinion mining. In Nicoletta Calzolari (Conference Chair), Khalid Choukri, Bente Maegaard, Joseph Mariani, Jan Odijk, Stelios Piperidis, Mike Rosner, and Daniel Tapias, editors, *Proceedings of the Seventh International Conference on Language Resources and Evaluation (LREC'10)*, Valletta, Malta, may. European Language Resources Association (ELRA).

Xuan-Hieu Phan. 2006a. Crfchunker: Crf english phrase chunker.

Xuan-Hieu Phan. 2006b. Crftagger: Crf english phrase tagger.

C. M. Whissel. 1989. The dictionary of affect in language. In *R. Plutchik and H. Kellerman, editors, Emotion: theory research and experience*, volume 4, London. Acad. Press.

Theresa Wilson, Zornitsa Kozareva, Preslav Nakov, Alan Ritter, Sara Rosenthal, and Veselin Stoyanov. 2013. Semeval-2013 task 2: Sentiment analysis in twitter. In *Proceedings of the 7th International Workshop on Semantic Evaluation*. Association for Computational Linguistics.

FBM: Combining lexicon-based ML and heuristics for Social Media Polarities

Carlos Rodríguez-Penagos, Jordi Atserias, Joan Codina-Filbà, David García-Narbona, Jens Grivolla, Patrik Lambert, Roser Saurí
Barcelona Media
Av. Diagonal 177, Barcelona 08018
Corresponding author: `carlos.rodriguez@barcelonamedia.org`

Abstract

This paper describes the system implemented by Fundació Barcelona Media (FBM) for classifying the polarity of opinion expressions in tweets and SMSs, and which is supported by a UIMA pipeline for rich linguistic and sentiment annotations. FBM participated in the SEMEVAL 2013 Task 2 on polarity classification. It ranked 5th in Task A (constrained track) using an ensemble system combining ML algorithms with dictionary-based heuristics, and 7th (Task B, constrained) using an SVM classifier with features derived from the linguistic annotations and some heuristics.

1 Introduction

We introduce the FBM system for classifying the polarity of short user-generated text (tweets and SMSs), which participated in the two subtasks of SEMEVAL 2013 Task 2 on *Sentiment Analysis in Twitter*. These are: *Task A*. Contextual Polarity Disambiguation, and *Task B*. Message Polarity Classification. The former aimed at classifying the polarity of already identified opinion expressions (or cues), whereas the latter consisted in classifying the polarity of the whole text (Wilson et al., 2013).

The literature agrees on two main approaches for classifying opinion expressions: using supervised learning methods and applying dictionary/rule-based knowledge (see (Liu, 2012) for an overview). Each of them on its own has been used in workable systems, and a principled combination of both of them can yield good results on noisy data, since generally one (dictionaries/rules) offers good precision while the other (ML) is able to discover unseen examples and thus enhances recall.

FBM combined both approaches in order to benefit from their respective strengths and compensating as much as possible their weaknesses. For Task A we used linguistic (lexical and syntactic) annotations to implement both types of approaches. On the one hand, we built machine learning classifiers based on Support Vector Machines (SVMs) and Conditional Random Fields (CRFs). On the other, we implemented a basic classification system mainly based on polarity dictionaries and negation information, as well as simple decision tree-like heuristics extracted from the training data. For task B we trained an SVM classifier using some of the annotations from Task A.

The paper first presents the process of data compilation and preprocessing (section 2), and then describes the systems for Tasks A (section 3) and B (section 4). Results and conclusions are discussed in the last section.

2 Data Compilation and Processing

2.1 Making data available

The **corpus of SMSs** was provided to the participants by the organizers of the task. As for the **corpus of tweets**, legal restrictions on twitter data distribution required the participants to download the textual contents of the corpus from a list of tweet ids. We retrieved the tweet text using the official twitter API instead of script provided by the organizers, but not all the tweets were available for download

*Second Joint Conference on Lexical and Computational Semantics (*SEM), Volume 2: Seventh International Workshop on Semantic Evaluation (SemEval 2013)*, pages 483–489, Atlanta, Georgia, June 14-15, 2013.

due to restrictions of different types (e.g. geographical), or because the twitter account was temporarily suspended. In total, we managed to retrieve 10,764 tweets out of 11,777 ids provided by the organizers (91.4%). It is worth pointing out that the restrictions on tweets distribution can become an issue for future users of the dataset, as the amount of available tweets will diminish over time. By contrast, the twitter test corpus was distributed with the full text to avoid those problems.

2.2 Leveraging the data with rich linguistic information

We applied the same linguistic processing to both corpora (SMSs and tweets), even though the SMS test data presents very different characteristics from the twitter data, not only because of what can be appreciated as genre differences, but also due to the fact that is apparently written in Singaporean English, which differs significantly from American or British English. No efforts were made to adapt our linguistic processing modules and dictionaries to this data.

Tweets and SMSs were processed with a UIMA[1]-based pipeline consisting of a set of linguistic and opinion-oriented modules, which includes:

Basic linguistic processing: Sentence segmentation, tokenization, POS-tagging, lemmatization.

Syntax: Dependency parsing.

Lexicon-based annotations:

- *Basic polarity*, distinguishing among: *positive*, *negative*, and *neutral*, as encoded in Wilson et al. (2010).
- *Polarity strength*, using the score for positive and negative polarity in SentiWordnet 3.0 (Baccianella et al., 2010). Each SentiWordNet synset has an associated triplet of numerical scores (`positive`, `negative`, and `objective`) expressing the intensity of positive, negative and objective polarity of the terms it contains. They range from 0.0 to 1.0, and their sum is 1.0 for each synset (Esuli and Sebastiani, 2007). We selected only the synset with positive or negative scores higher than 0.5, containing a total of 16,791 words.
- *Subjectiviy* clues, from Wilson et al. (2010), which are classified as *weak* or *strong* depending on their degree of subjectivity.
- *Sentiment* expressions, from the Linguistic Inquiry and Word Count (LIWC) 2001 Dictionary (Pennebaker et al., 2001).
- In-house compiled lexicons of *negation markers* (such as 'no', 'never', 'none') and *quantifiers* ('all', 'many', etc.), the latter further classified into *low*, *medium* and *high* according to their quantification degree.

The different classifiers employed by FBM constructed their vectors from this output to learn global and contextual polarities.

3 Task A: Ensemble System

Our system combined Machine Learning and rule-based approaches. The aim was to combine the strengths of each individual component while avoiding as much as possible their weaknesses. In what follows we describe each system component as well as the way the ensemble system worked out the collective decisions.

3.1 Conditional Random Fields

One of the classifiers uses the Conditional Random Fields implementation of a biomedical Named Entity Recognition system (JNET from JulieLab) [2], exploiting the classification capabilities of the system (rather than its span detection) by strongly associating already defined "marked instances" with a polarity, and exploring a 5-word window. It uses dependency labels, POS tags, polar words, sentiwordnet and LWIC sentiment annotations, as well as indications for quantifiers and negation markers.

3.2 Support Vector Machines

This classifier was implemented using an SVM algorithm with a linear kernel and the C parameter set to 0.2 (determined using a 5 fold cross-validation). The features set includes those that we used in RepLab

[1] http://uima.apache.org/uima-specification.html

[2] http://www.julielab.de

2012 (Chenlo et al., 2012) (including number of: characters, words, links, hashtags, positive and negative emoticons, question-exclamation marks, adjectives, nouns, verbs, adverbs, uppercased words, words with duplicated vowels), plus a set of new features at tweet level obtained from the linguistic annotations: number of high/medium/low polarity quantifiers, number of positive and negative polar words, sentiwordnet applied to both the cue and the whole tweet.

Moreover, the RepLab polarity calculation based on different dictionaries was modified to take into account negation (in a 3-word window) potentially inverting the polarity (negPol). This polarity measure was applied to the cue and to the whole tweet, thus generating two additional features.

3.3 Heuristic Approach

In task A, in parallel to the supervised learning system, we developed a method (named Heur) based on polarity dictionary lookup and simple heuristics (see Figure 1) taking into account opinion words as well as negation markers and quantifiers. These heuristics were implemented so as to maximize the number of correct positive and negative labels in the training data. To this end, we calculated the aggregate polarity of a cue segment as the sum of word polarities found in the polarity lexicon. The aggregate values in the training set ranged from -3 to +3, taking respectively 1, 0 and -1 as the polarity of positive, neutral and negative words. The label distribution of cue segments with an aggregate polarity value of -1 is shown in Table 1.

Aggregate polarity	-1	
Negation	no	yes
negative	1,032	30
neutral	37	4
positive	178	71

Table 1: Cue segment polarity statistics in training data for an aggregate polarity value of -1.

In this case, if no negation is present in the cue segment, a majority (1,032) of examples had the negative label. In case there was at least a negation, a majority (71) of examples had a positive label. This behaviour was observed with all negative aggregate

```
1:  if has_polar_word(CUE) then
2:      polarity= lex(P)-0.5*lex(QP)
3:                -lex(N)+0.5*lex(QN)
4:      if polarity>0 then
5:          if has_negation(CUE) then negative
6:          else positive
7:          end if
8:      else if polarity<0 then
9:          if has_negation(CUE) then positive
10:         else negative
11:         end if
12:     else
13:         if has_negation(CUE) then positive
14:         else negative
15:         end if
16:     end if
17: else if has_negation(CUE) then negative
18: else
19:     polarity= tlex(P)-0.5*tlex(QP)
20:               -tlex(N)+0.5*tlex(QN)
21:     if polarity<0 then negative
22:     else if tlex(NEU)>0 then neutral
23:     else if polarity>0 then positive
24:     else if has_negemo(CUE) then negative
25:     else if has_posemo(CUE) then positive
26:     else unknwn
27:     end if
28: end if
```

Figure 1: Heuristics used by the lexicon-based system to classify the polarity of a segment marked up as opinion cue (Task A).

polarity values in training data, yielding the rule in lines 8 to 11 of Figure 1. Similar rules were extracted for the other aggregate polarity values (lines 4 to 16 of Figure 1).

Figure 1 details the complete classification algorithm. Note (lines 1 to 17) that we first rely on the basic polarity lexicon annotations (described in section 2). The final aggregate polarity formula (lines 2-3) was refined to distinguish sentiment words which act as quantifiers, such as *pretty* in *pretty mad.* The word *pretty* is both a positive polar word and a quantifier. We want its polarity to be positive in case it occurs in isolation, but less than one so that the sum with a following negative polar word (such as *mad*) be negative. We thus give this kind of words a polarity of 0.5 by substracting 0.5 for each polar word which is also a quantifier. In the polarity formula of lines 2-3, `lex(X)` refers to the number of words annotated as X, P and N refer respectively to positive and negative polar words, and QP and

QN refer to positive and negative polar words which are also quantifiers. Quantifiers which are not polar words are not taken into account because they are not likely to change the opinion polarity.

In case that no annotations from the basic polarity, quantifiers, and negative markers lexicons are found (lines 18 to 28), we look up in dictionaries built from the training data (`tlex` in lines 19-20). To build these dictionaries, we counted how many times each word was labeled positive, negative and neutral. We considered that a word has a given polarity if the number of times it was assigned to this class is greater than the number of times it was assigned to any other class by a given threshold. We calculated the polarity in the same way as before, but now with the counts from the lexicon automatically compiled from the training data. To improve the recall of the dictionary lookup, we performed some text normalization: lowercasing, deletion of repeated characters (such as *gooood*) and deletion of the hashtag "#" character. Finally, if no polar word is found in the automatically compiled lexicon, we look at the sentiment annotations (extracted from the LIWC dictionary).

3.4 Ensemble Voting Algorithm

As already mentioned, we combined the results from the described polarity methods to build a collective decision. Table 2 shows the performance (in terms of F1 measure) of the different single methods over the tweet test data.

	SVM	Heur	Heur+	CRF
Test	80.74	83.47	84.62	62.85

Table 2: Twitter Task A results for different methods

Although the heuristic method outperforms the ML methods, they are not only different in nature (ML vs. heuristic) but also use different information (see Table 5). This suggests that the ensemble solution will be complementary and capable of obtaining better results than any of the individual methods by itself.

The development set was used to calculate the ensemble response given the individual votes of the different systems in a way similar to the behavior knowledge space method (Huang and Suen, 1993). Table 3 shows an example of how the assemble voting is built. For each method vote combination (SVM-Heuristics-CRF) the number of positives / negatives / neutral is calculated in the development data. The ensemble (EV) selects the vote that maximizes the number of correct votes in the development data (in bold).

SVM	Heur	CRF	EV	# Instances		
				pos	neg	neu
−	+	−	−	0	**6**	0
−	−	+	−	1	**23**	2
−	−	−	−	3	**125**	2
−	u	+	+	**1**	0	0
+	u	n	−	0	**1**	0
+	−	+	+	**17**	13	2
+	+	+	+	**314**	18	17
+	−	n	+	**3**	1	0

Table 3: Oracle building example (EV: Ensemble Vote, +:positive, −:negative, n:neutral, u:unknown)

The test data contains some combination of votes that were not seen in the development data. Thus, in order to deal with these unseen combinations of votes in the test set we use the following backup heuristics based on the preformance figures of the individual methods: Use the vote of the heuristic method. If this method does not vote (u), then select the SVM vote.

Table 4 shows the results of the proposed ensemble method, the well-known majority voting and the upper bound of this ensemble method (calculated with the same strategy over the test data), over the development and test tweet data

	Ensemble Voting	Majority Voting	Upper Bound
Dev	85.48	81.31	85.48
Test	85.50	82.70	89.37

Table 4: Results for different ensemble strategies

In the development corpus, the upper bound and ensemble results are the same, given that they apply the same knowledge. The difference is in the test dataset, where the ensemble voting is calculated based on the knowledge obtained from the development corpus, while the upper bound uses the knowledge that can be derived from the test corpus.

Table 5 illustrates the features used by each component.

	SVM (task A)	SVM (task B)	CRF	Heur
word	•		•	•
lemma				
pos	•		•	
deps			•	
pol	•	•	•	•
polW		•		
sent	•		•	•
sentiwn	•	•	•	
quant	•	•	•	•
neg	•	•	•	•
links	•			
hashTags	•			

Table 5: Information used (pos: part-of-speech; deps: dependencies; pol: basic polarity classification; polW: basic polarity word; sent: LIWC sentiments; sentwn: SentiWordnet; quant/neg: quantifiers and negation markers.)

4 Task B: A Support Vector Machine-based System

The system presented for task B is based on ML using a SVM model. The feature vector used as input for the SVM component is composed of the annotations provided by the linguistic annotation pipeline, extended with a feature obtained by applying negation to the next polar words (window of size 3).

The features used do not include the words (or their lemmas) because the number of tweets available for training is small (10^4) compared to the number of different words ($4 \cdot 10^4$). A model based on bag-of-words would suffer from overfitting and thus be very domain and time-dependent. If the train and test sets were randomly selected from a bigger set, the use of words could increase the model's accuracy, but the model would also be too narrowly applied to this specific dataset.

From the annotation pipeline we extracted as features: the polar words (PolW) and their basic polarity (Pol); the sentiment annotations from LIWC (Sent); the negation markers (Neg) and quantifiers (Quant). The model was trained using Weka (Hall et al., 2009).

The model used is SVM with the C parameter set to 1.0 and applying a 10 fold cross-validation. The option of doing first a model to discriminate polar and neutral tweets was discarded because Weka already does that when training classifiers for more than two training classes, and the combination of the two classifiers (a first one between polar and opinionated and a second one between positive and negative) would produce the same results.

5 Results and Discussion

The results of our system in each subcorpus and task are presented in Table 5 (average of the F1-measure over the classes positive and negative, constrained track), with the ranking achieved in the competition in parentheses.

	Tweet Corpus	SMS Corpus
Task A	0.86 (5th)	0.73 (11th)
Task B	0.61 (7th)	0.47 (28th)

Table 6: FBM system performance (F1 average over positive and negative classes, constrained track) and rankings

Given the differences in style and vocabularies between the SMS and tweet corpora, and the fact that we made not effort whatsoever to adapt our system or models to them, the drop in performance from one to the other is considerable, but to be expected since domain customization is an important aspect of opinion mining.

Task A: The confusion matrix in Table 7 shows an acceptable performance for the most frequent classes in the corpus (with an error of 7.75% and 19.5% for postive and negative cues, respectively) and a very poor job for neutral cues (98.1% of error), clearly a minority class in the training corpus (5% of the data).

	GOLD:	Pos	Neg	Neu
SYSTEM:	**Pos**	2,522	296	126
	Neg	206	1,240	31
	Neu	6	5	3

Table 7: Task A confusion matrix

Given the skewed distribution of polarity categories in the test corpus, however, neutral mistakes amount to only 23% of our system error, and so we focus our analysis on the problems in positive and negative cues, respectively amounting to 31.7% and 44.8% of the total error. There are 2 main sources of error:

- *Limitations of the dictionaries* employed, which were short in covering somewhat frequent slang words (e.g., *wacky, baddest, shitloads*), expressions (e.g., *ouch, yukk, C'MON*), or phrases (e.g., *over the top*), some of which express a particular polarity but contain a word expressing just the opposite (*have a blast, to want something bad/ly*).
- *Problems in UGC processing*, mainly related to normalization (e.g., *foooooool*) and tokenization (*Perfect...not sure*), which put at risk the correct identification of lexical elements that are crucial for polarity classification.

Task B: The average F-score of positive and negative classes was 0.62 in the development set (that was included in the training set) and the averaged F-score for the test set was 0.61 (so they are very similar). If focusing on precision and recall, the positive and negative classes have higher precision but lower recall in the test set. We think that this low degradation of perfomance indicates the model's potential for generalization.

6 Conclusions

From our results, we can conclude that the use of ensemble combination of orthogonal methods provides good performance for Task A. Similar results could be expected for Task B (judging from mixing dictionaries and ML in similar tasks at RepLab 2012 (Chenlo et al., 2012)). The ML methods that we applied for Task B are essentially additive, and hence have difficulties in applying features such as polarity shifters. To overcome this, one of the features includes negation of polar words when a polarity shifter is near.

Overall, the SemEval Tasks have make evident the usual challenges when mining opinions from Social Media channels: noisy text, irregular grammar and orthography, highly specific lingo, etc. Moreover, temporal dependencies can affect the performance if the training and test data have been gathered at different times, as is the case with text of such a volatile nature as tweets and SMSs.

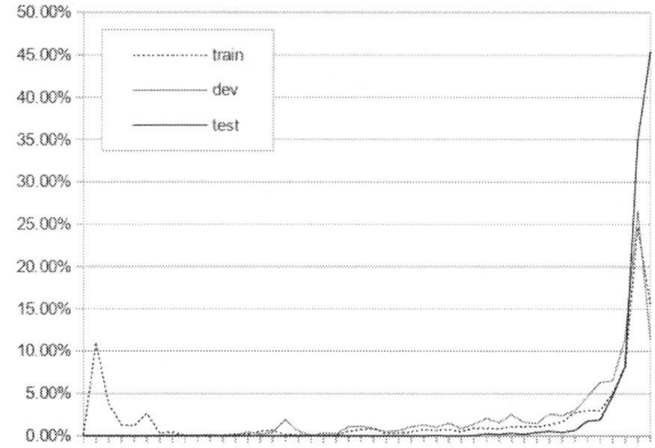

Figure 2: Distribution of tweets over time

The histogram in Figure 2 shows that this also applies to the Semeval tweets dataset. It illustrates the distribution of tweets over time (extrapolated from the sequential ids) in the 3 subcorpora (train, development and test), showing some divergence between the test corpus on the one hand, and the development and training corpora on the other. Nevertheless, our system shows little performance degradation between development and testing results, as attested in Table 4 (ensemble voting column).

Our work here and at other competitions already cited validate a system that combines stochastic and symbolic methodologies in a principled, data-driven approach. Time and domain dependencies of Social Media data make system and model generalization highly desirable, and our system hybrid nature also contribute to this objective.

Acknowledgments

This work has been partially funded by the Spanish Government project *Holopedia*, TIN2010-21128-C02-02, the CENIT program project *Social Media*, CEN-20101037, and the Marie Curie Reintegration Grant PIRG04-GA-2008-239414.

References

Baccianella, Stefano, Andrea Esuli and Fabrizio Sebastiani. 2010. SentiWordNet 3.0: An enhanced lexical resource for sentiment analysis and opinion mining. In *Proceedings of the 7th conference on International Language Resources and Evaluation*, Valletta, Malta.

Chenlo, Jose M., Jordi Atserias, Carlos Rodríguez-Penagos and Roi Blanco. 2012. FBM-Yahoo! at RepLab 2012. In: P. Forner, J. Karlgren, C. Womser-Hacker (eds.) *CLEF 2012 Evaluation Labs and Workshop, Online Working Notes*. http://clef2012.org/index.php?page=Pages/proceedings.php.

Esuli, Andrea and Fabrizio Sebastiani. 2007. SENTIWORDNET: a high-coverage lexical resource for opinion mining. Technical Report ISTI-PP-002/2007, Institute of Information Science and Technologies (ISTI) of the Italian National Research Council (CNR).

Hall, Mark, Frank Eibe, Geoffrey Holmes, Bernhard Pfahringer, Peter Reutemann and Ian H. Witten. 2009. The WEKA data mining software: an update. In: *ACM* SIGKDD Explorations Newsletter, 1: 10–18.

Huang, Y. S. and C. Y. Suen. 1993. Behavior-knowledge space method for combination of multiple classifiers. In *Proceedings of IEEE Computer Vision and Pattern Recognition*, 347–352.

Liu, Bing. 2012. Sentiment analysis and opinion mining. *Synthesis Lectures on Human Language Technologies*, (5-1), 1–167.

Pennebaker, James W., Martha E. Francis and Roger J. Booth. 2001. Linguistic inquiry and word count: LIWC 2001. *Mahway: Lawrence Erlbaum Associates*.

Wilson, Theresa, Zornitsa Kozareva, Preslav Nakov, Sara Rosenthal, Veselin Stoyanov and Alan. Ritter. 2013. SemEval-2013 task 2: Sentiment analysis in twitter. In *Proceedings of the International Workshop on Semantic Evaluation*, SemEval '13.

Wilson, Theresa, Janyce Wiebe and Paul Hoffmann. 2010. Recognizing contextual polarity: An exploration of features for phrase-level sentiment analysis. *Computational Linguistics*, *35*(3), 399–433.

REACTION: A naive machine learning approach for sentiment classification

Silvio Moreira
IST/INESC-ID
Rua Alves Redol, 9
1000-029 Lisboa
Portugal
samir@inesc-id.pt

João Filgueiras
INESC-ID
Rua Alves Redol, 9
1000-029 Lisboa
Portugal
jfilgueiras@inesc-id.pt

Bruno Martins
IST/INESC-ID
Rua Alves Redol, 9
1000-029 Lisboa
Portugal
bruno.g.martins@ist.utl.pt

Francisco Couto
LASIGE - FCUL
Edifício C6 Piso 3
Campo Grande
1749 - 016 Lisboa
Portugal
fcouto@di.fc.ul.pt

Mário J. Silva
IST/INESC-ID
Rua Alves Redol, 9
1000-029 Lisboa
Portugal
mjs@inesc-id.pt

Abstract

We evaluate a naive machine learning approach to sentiment classification focused on Twitter in the context of the sentiment analysis task of SemEval-2013. We employ a classifier based on the Random Forests algorithm to determine whether a tweet expresses overall positive, negative or neutral sentiment. The classifier was trained only with the provided dataset and uses as main features word vectors and lexicon word counts. Our average F-score for all three classes on the Twitter evaluation dataset was 51.55%. The average F-score of both positive and negative classes was 45.01%. For the optional SMS evaluation dataset our overall average F-score was 58.82%. The average between positive and negative F-scores was 50.11%.

1 Introduction

Sentiment Analysis is a growing research field, especially on web social networks. In this setting, users share very diverse messages such as real-time reactions to news, events and daily experiences. The ability to tap on a vast repository of opinions, such as Twitter, where there is great diversity of topics, has become an important goal for many different applications. However, due to the nature of the text, NLP systems face additional challenges in this context. Shared messages, such as tweets, are very short and users tend to resort to highly informal an noisy speech.

Following this trend, the 2013 edition of SemEval[1] included a sentiment analysis on Twitter task (SemEval-2013 Task 2). Participants were asked to implement a system capable of determining whether a given tweet expresses positive, negative or neutral sentiment. To help in the development of the system, an annotated training corpus was released. Systems that used only the given corpus for training were considered *constrained*, while others were considered *unconstrained*. The submitted prototypes were evaluated in a dataset consisting of around 3700 tweets of several topics. The metric used was the average F-score between the positive and negative classes.

Our goal with this participation was to create a baseline system from which we can build upon and perform experiments to compare new approaches with the state-of-the-art.

2 Related Work

The last decade saw a growing interest in systems to automatically process sentiment in text. Many approaches to detect subjectivity and determine

[1] Proceedings of the 7th International Workshop on Semantic Evaluation (SemEval 2013), in conjunction with the Second Joint Conference on Lexical and Computational Semantics (*SEM 2013)

*Second Joint Conference on Lexical and Computational Semantics (*SEM), Volume 2: Seventh International Workshop on Semantic Evaluation (SemEval 2013)*, pages 490–494, Atlanta, Georgia, June 14-15, 2013.

polarity of opinions in news articles, weblogs and product reviews have been proposed (Pang et al., 2002; Pang et al., 2004; Wiebe et al., 2005; Wilson et al., 2005). This sub-field of NLP, known as Sentiment Analysis is presented in great depth in (Liu, 2012).

The emergence and proliferation of microblog platforms created a medium where people express and convey all kinds of information. In particular, these platforms are a rich source of subjective and opinionated text, which has motivated the application of similar techniques to this domain. However, in this context, messages tend to be very short and highly informal, full of typos, slang and unconventional spelling, posing additional challenges to NLP systems. In fact, early experiments in Sentiment Analysis in the context of Twitter (Barbosa et al., 2010; Davidov et al., 2010; Koulompis et al., 2011; Pak et al., 2010; Bifet et al., 2010) show that the techniques that proved effective in other domains are not sufficient in the microblog setting. In the spirit of these approaches, we included a preprocessing step, followed by feature extraction focusing on word, lexical and Twitter-specific features. Finally, we use annotated data to train an automatic classifier based on the Random Forests (Breiman, 2001) and BESTrees (Sun et al., 2011) learning algorithms.

3 Resources

Two annotated datasets were made available to participants of SemEval-2013 Task 2: one for training purposes which was to contain 8000 to 12000 tweets; and another, for development, containing 2000. The combined datasets ended up amounting to a little over 7500 tweets. The distribution of positives, negatives and neutrals for the combined datasets can be found in Table 1. Nearly half of all tweets belonged to the neutral class, and negatives represent just 15% of these datasets.

Class	Number
Positive	37%
Negative	15%
Neutral	48%

Table 1: Class distribution of annotated data.

Random examples of each class drawn from the datasets are shown in Table 2.

Positive:
1 *Louis inspired outfit on Monday and Zayn inspired outfit today..4/5 done just need Harry*
2 *waking up to a Niners win, makes Tuesday get off to a great start! 21-3 over the cards and 2 games clear in the NFC West.*

Negative:
3 *Sitting at home on a Saturday night doing absolutely nothing... Guess I'll just watch Greys Anatomy all night. #lonerproblems #greysanatomy*
4 *Life just isn't the same when there is no Pretty Little Liars on Tuesday nights.*

Neutral:
5 *Won the match #getin . Plus, tomorrow is a very busy day, with Awareness Day's and debates. Gulp. Debates*
6 *@_Nenaah oh cause my friend got something from china and they said it will take at least 6 to 8 weeks and it came in the 2nd week :P*

Table 2: Random examples of annotated tweets.

4 Approach

Given our goal of creating a baseline system, we experimented with a common set of features used in sentiment analysis. The messages were modelled as a combination of binary (or presence) unigrams, lexical features and Twitter-specific features. We decided to follow a supervised approach by learning a Random Forests classifier from the annotated data provided by the organisers of the workshop (see Section 3). In summary, the development of our system consisted of four steps: 1) preprocessing of the data, 2) feature extraction, 3) learning the classifier, and 4) applying the classifier to the test set.

4.1 Preprocessing

The lexical variation introduced by typos, abbreviations, slang and unconventional spelling, leads to very large vocabularies. The resulting sparse vector representations with few non-zero values hamper the learning process. In order to tackle this problem, we replaced user mentions (@<username>) with a fixed tag <USER> and URLs with the tag <URL>. Then, each sentence was normalised by converting to lower-case and reducing character repetitions to at most 3 characters (e.g. *"heelloooooo!"* would be normalised to *"heellooo!"*). Finally, we performed the lemmatisation of the sentence using the Morphadorner[2] software.

4.2 Feature Extraction

After the preprocessing step, we extract a vector consisting of the top uni-grams present in the training set and represent individual messages in terms of this vector. For each message we also compute the frequency of smileys and words with prior sentiment polarity using a sentiment lexicon. Finally, we include the harmonic mean of positive and negative words. Next we explain each feature in more detail.

Word vector: a sparse word vector containing the top 25.000 most frequent words that occur in the training set. This feature aims at capturing relations between certain words and overall message polarity. The vector was extracted using the Weka toolkit (Hall et al., 2009) with the stop word list option.

Lexicon word count: positive and negative sentiment word counts. When the word is preceded by a negation particle we invert the polarity. We used Bing Liu's Opinion Lexicon[3] that includes 2006 positive and 4783 negative words and is especially tailored for social media because it considers misspellings, slang and other domain specific variations.

Smileys count: a count of positive and negative smileys that appear in the tweet. We take advantage of these constructs being especially indicative of the overall expressed sentiment in a text (Davidov et al., 2010). Although there are smiley lexicons, such as the one used on SentiStrength[4], we used regular expressions to capture most common smileys in a flexible way.

Hashtag count: a count of positive and negative hashtags. This feature also uses Bing Liu's lexicon to determine wether a word contained in an hashtag is positive or negative. The rationale behind this feature is that positive or negative words in the form of hashtags can have a stronger meaning than regular words (Davidov et al., 2010).

Positive/negative harmonic mean: harmonic mean between positive and negative token counts, including words and hashtags.

In an attempt to further reduce the dimensionality of the feature space we computed the principal components of the word vector using the Principal Components Analysis filter in Weka but observed that this yielded worse results.

4.3 Learning the classifier

To implement our classifier we used the Weka machine learning framework and experimented with two ensemble algorithms: Random Forests and BESTrees. We eventually dropped the use of BESTrees as initial results were worse.

We attempted to use most of the data while being able to effectively measure the performance of the classifier. Therefore we used the totality of both sets for training and evaluated using 10 fold cross-validation.

Since we used only the annotated dataset that was provided for this task, our approach is considered constrained.

5 Results

Our results with 10 fold cross-validation using the submitted classifier, are presented in Table 3.

Class	Precision	Recall	F-score
positive	61.0%	63.9%	62.4%
negative	54.1%	26.8%	35.8%
neutral	**64.7%**	**72.4%**	**68.3%**
average F-score (pos/neg)			49.1%

Table 3: Cross-validation results using the training set.

Task evaluation results are presented in Table 4 for tweets. Our approach ranked 44th out of 48 participants. The evaluation dataset had a similar class distribution to the annotated datasets,

[2] http://morphadorner.northwestern.edu/

[3] http://www.cs.uic.edu/~liub/FBS/sentiment-analysis.html

[4] http://sentistrength.wlv.ac.uk

with almost half being neutral, and just 14% negative. Preliminary results with cross-validation were similar to those of the final evaluation for Twitter.

Class	Precision	Recall	F-score
positive	**62.52%**	55.28%	58.68%
negative	55.74%	21.80%	31.34%
neutral	56.54%	**75.43%**	**64.63%**
average F-score (pos/neg)			45.01%

Table 4: Task evaluation results for Tweets.

Also included in SemEval-2013 Task 2 was an evaluation using a SMS dataset to understand if a classifier trained using tweets could be applied to SMS messages. SMS results are shown in Table 5. In this case our approach ranked 23th out of 42 participants. The SMS evaluation dataset was composed of more than half neutral messages (58%), and similarly distributed positives (23%) and negatives (19%).

Class	Precision	Recall	F-score
positive	53.66%	59.50%	56.45%
negative	60.54%	34.26%	43.76%
neutral	**72.91%**	**79.90%**	**76.27%**
average F-score (pos/neg)			50.11%

Table 5: Task evaluation results for SMS.

6 Discussion and Conclusions

As expected, our naive approach performs poorly in the context of Twitter messages. The obtained results are in line with similar approaches described in the literature and we found that Random Forests achieve the same performance as other learning algorithms tried for the same task (Kouloumpis et al., 2011).

The uneven distribution of classes in the data may have also contributed to the low performance of the classifier. Although the neutral class was not considered in the evaluation, the datasets had a great predominance of neutral messages whereas the negative examples only accounted for 15% of the corpus. This suggests that it could be useful to use a minority class over-sampling method, such as SMOTE (Chawla, 2002), to reduce the effect of this imbalance on the data. We used n-grams to model the words that compose each message. However, this approach leads to very sparse representations, thus becoming important to consider techniques that reduce feature space. We experimented with PCA, without success, but we still believe that applying feature selection algorithms or denser word representations (Turian et al., 2010) could improve performance in this task.

We find that our classifier performs better on the SMS dataset. This might be explained by the fact that SMS messages tend to be more direct, whereas the same tweet can express, or show signs of, contradictory sentiments. In fact, our naive approach outperforms other systems that had better results in the Twitter dataset, but it is difficult to say why, given that we do not have access to the SMS test set annotations.

Despite the poor ranking results, we achieved our goal of performing basic experiments in the task of sentiment analysis in Twitter and developed a baseline system that will serve as a starting point for future research.

Acknowledgments

This work was partially supported by FCT (Portuguese research funding agency) under project grants UTA-Est/MAI/0006/2009 (REACTION) and PTDC/CPJ-CPO/116888/2010 (POPSTAR). FCT also supported scholarship SFRH/BD/89020/2012. This research was also funded by the PIDDAC Program funds (INESC-ID multi annual funding) and the LASIGE multi annual support.

References

Barbosa, L., and Feng, J. 2010. *Robust sentiment detection on twitter from biased and noisy data.* Proceedings of the 23rd International Conference on Computational Linguistics: Posters, pp. 36-44.

Bifet, A., and Frank, E. 2010. *Sentiment knowledge discovery in twitter streaming data.* Discovery Science.

Breiman, L. 2001. Random forests. *Machine learning*, 45(1), 5-32.

Chawla, N. V., Bowyer, K. W., Hall, L. O., and Kegelmeyer, W. P. 2002 *SMOTE: synthetic minority over-sampling technique*. Journal of Artificial Intelligence Research, 16, 321-357.

Davidov, D., Tsur, O., and Rappoport, A. 2010 *Enhanced sentiment learning using twitter hashtags and smileys*. Proceedings of the 23rd International Conference on Computational Linguistics: Posters. Pages 241-249. Association for Computational Linguistics.

Hall, M., Frank, E., Holmes, G., Pfahringer, B., Reutemann, P., and Witten, I. H. 2009. *The WEKA Data Mining Software: An Update* SIGKDD Explorations, Volume 11, Issue 1.

Kouloumpis, E., Wilson, T., and Moore, J. 2011. *Twitter sentiment analysis: The good the bad and the omg*. Proceedings of the Fifth International AAAI Conference on Weblogs and Social Media, 538541.

Liu, B. 2012. *Sentiment Analysis and Opinion Mining*. Synthesis Lectures on Human Language Technologies, 5(1), 1167.

Pak, A., and Paroubek, P. 2010. *Twitter as a corpus for sentiment analysis and opinion mining*. Proceedings of LREC.

Pang, B., Lee, L., and Vaithyanathan, S. 2002. *Thumbs up?: sentiment classification using machine learning techniques*. Proceedings of the ACL-02 conference on Empirical methods in natural language processing. Volume 10, pp. 79-86. Association for Computational Linguistics.

Pang, B. and Lee, L. 2004. *A sentimental education: Sentiment analysis using subjectivity summarization based on minimum cuts*. Proceedings of the 42nd annual meeting on Association for Computational Linguistics.

Sun, Q. and Pfahringer, B. 2011. *Bagging Ensemble Selection*. Proceedings of the 24th Australasian Joint Conference on Artificial Intelligence (AI'11), Perth, Australia, pages 251-260. Springer.

Turian, J., Ratinov, L., and Bengio, Y. 2010. *Word representations: a simple and general method for semi-supervised learning*. Proceedings of the 48th Annual Meeting of the Association for Computational Linguistics (pp. 384-394). Association for Computational Linguistics.

Wiebe, J. and Riloff, E. 2005. *Creating subjective and objective sentence classifiers from unannotated texts*. Computational Linguistics and Intelligent Text Processing, pages 486-497, Springer.

Wilson, T., Wiebe, J., and Hoffmann, P. 2005. *Recognizing contextual polarity in phrase-level sentiment analysis*. Proceedings of the conference on Human Language Technology and Empirical Methods in Natural Language Processing, pp. 347-354. Association for Computational Linguistics.

IITB-Sentiment-Analysts: Participation in Sentiment Analysis in Twitter SemEval 2013 Task

Karan Chawla, Ankit Ramteke, Pushpak Bhattacharyya
Dept. of Computer Science and Engineering, IIT Bombay
{chawlakaran,ankitr,pb}@cse.iitb.ac.in

Abstract

We propose a method for using discourse relations for polarity detection of tweets. We have focused on unstructured and noisy text like tweets on which linguistic tools like parsers and POS-taggers don't work properly. We have showed how conjunctions, connectives, modals and conditionals affect the sentiments in tweets. We have also handled the commonly used abbreviations, slangs and collocations which are usually used in short text messages like tweets. This work focuses on a Web based application which produces results in real time. This approach is an extension of the previous work (Mukherjee et al. 2012).

1. Introduction

Discourse relation is an important component of natural language processing which connects phrases and clauses together to establish a coherent relation. Linguistic constructs like conjunctions, connectives, modals, conditionals and negation do alter the sentiments of a sentence. For example, *the movie had* ***quite a few memorable moments*** *but I still* ***did not like it***. The overall polarity of the sentence is negative even though it has one positive and one negative clause. This is because of the presence of the conjunction **but** which gives more weightage to the clause following the conjunction.

Traditional works in discourse analysis use a discourse parser (Marcu et al., 2003; Polanyi et al., 2004; Wolf et al., 2005; Welner et al., 2006; Narayanan et al., 2009; Prasad et al., 2010). Many of these works and some other works in discourse (Taboada et al., 2008; Zhou et al., 2011) build on the Rhetorical Structure Theory (RTS) proposed by Mann et al. (1988) which tries to identify the relations between the nucleus and satellite in the sentence.

Most of the work is based on well-structured text and the methods applied on that text is not suitable for the discourse analysis on micro-blogs because of the following reasons:

1. Micro-blogs like Twitter restricts a post (tweet) to be of only 140 characters. Thus, users do not use formal language to discuss their views. Thus, there are abundant spelling mistakes, abbreviations, slangs, collocations, discontinuities and grammatical errors.
These differences cause NLP tools like POS-taggers and parsers to fail frequently, as these tools are built for well-structured text. Thus, most of the methods described in the previous works are not well suited for discourse analysis on Micro-blogs like text.
2. The web-based applications require a fast response time. Using a heavy linguistic resource like parsing increases the processing time and slows down the application.

Most of the previous work on discourse analysis does not take into consideration the conjunctions, connectives, modals, conditionals etc and are based on bag-of-words model with features like part-of-speech information, unigrams, bigrams etc. along with other domain-specific features like emoticons, hashtags etc. Our work harness the importance of discourse connectives like conjunctions, connectives, modals, conditionals etc and show that along with bag-of-words model, it gives better sentiment classification accuracy. This work is the extension of (Mukherjee et al. 2012).

The roadmap for the rest of the paper is as follows: Section 2 studies the effect of discourse relations on sentiment analysis and identifies the

*Second Joint Conference on Lexical and Computational Semantics (*SEM), Volume 2: Seventh International Workshop on Semantic Evaluation (SemEval 2013)*, pages 495–500, Atlanta, Georgia, June 14-15, 2013.

critical ones. Section 3 talks about the semantic operators which influence the discourse relations. Section 4 discusses the lexicon based classification approach. Section 5 describes the feature engineering of the important features. Section 6 gives the list of experiments conducted and analysis of the results. Conclusion and Future Work is presented in Section 7.

2. Discourse Relations Critical for Sentiment Analysis

(Mukherjee et al. 2012) showed that that the following discourse relations are critical for SA as all relations are not useful for SA. Table 1 provides examples of various discourse relations.

Violated Expectations and Contrast: In Example 2, a simple bag-of-words feature based classifier will classify it as positive. However, it actually represents a negative sentiment. Such cases need to be handled separately. In Example 5, "memorable" has (+1) score and "not like" has (-1) score and overall polarity is 0 or objective whereas it should be negative as the final verdict following "but" is the deciding factor.

These kinds of sentences refute the neighboring clause. They can be classified as Conj_Prev in which the clause preceding the conjunction is preferred and Conj_Fol in which the clause following the conjunction is preferred.

Conclusive or Inferential Conjunctions: These are the set of conjunctions, Conj_infer, that tend to draw a conclusion or inference. Hence, the discourse segment following them (subsequently in Example 11) should be given more weight.

Conditionals: In Example 3, "amazing" represent a positive sentiment. But the final polarity should be objective as we are talking of a hypothetical situation.

Other Discourse Relations: Sentences under Cause-Effect, Similarity, Temporal Sequence, Attribution, Example, Generalization and Elaboration, provide no contrasting, conflicting or hypothetical information. They can be handled by taking a simple bag-of-words model.

3. Semantic Operators Influencing Discourse Relations

There are connectives or semantic operators present in the sentences which influence the discourse relation within a sentence. For example, in the sentence *the cannon camera may bad despite good battery life.* The connective *despite* increases the weightage of the previous discourse element *i.e.* bad is weighted up but *may* introduces a certain kind of uncertainty which cannot be ignored.

1. (I did not study anything throughout the semester), **so** (I failed in the exams).
2. (Sourav failed to deliver in the penultimate test) **despite** (great expectations).
3. If (I had bought the amazing Nokia phone), I would not be crying).
4. (I love Cannon) **and** (I also love Sony).
5. (The movie had quite a few memorable moments) **but** (I still did not like it).
6. (The theater became interesting) **after a while**.
7. According (to the reviews), (the movie must be bad).
8. (Salman is a bad guy), **for instance** (he is always late).
9. In addition (to the bad battery life), (the camera is also very costly).
10. In general, (cameras from cannon (take great pictures).
11. (They were not in favour of that camera) and **subsequently** (decided not to buy it).

Table 1: Examples of Discourse Coherent Relations

Similarity, in the sentence *He gave his best in the movie, but still it was not good enough to win an Oscar.* The connective *but* increases the weight of the following discourse *i.e. good* and *win* are weighted up but presence of negation operator also cannot be ignored.

1. Modals: Events that are happening or are bound to happen are called *realis events*. And those events that have possibly occurred or have some probability to occur in distant future are known as *irrealis events*. And it is important to distinguish between the two as it also alters the sentiments in a piece of text. Modals depict irrealis events and just cannot be handled by simple majority valence model.

(Mukherjee et al. 2012) divided modals into two categories: Strong_Mod and Weak_Mod.

Strong_Mod is the set of modals that express a higher degree of uncertainty in any situation. Weak_Mod is the set of modals that express lesser degree of uncertainty and more emphasis on certain events or situations.

Like conditionals, sentences with strong modals express higher degree of uncertainty, thus discourse elements near strong modals are weighted down. Thus, in the previous example *the cannon camera may bad despite good battery life* bad is toned down.

Relations	Attributes
Conj_Fol	but, however, nevertheless, otherwise, yet, still, nonetheless
Conj_Prev	till, until, despite, in spite, though, although
Conj_Inf	therefore, furthermore, consequently, thus, as a result, subsequently, eventually, hence
Conditionals	If
Strong_Mod	might, could, can, would, may
Weak_Mod	should, ought to, need not, shall, will, must
Neg	not, neither, never, no, nor

Table 2: Discourse Relations and Semantic Operators Essential for Sentiment Analysis

2. Negation: The negation operator inverts the polarity of the sentence following it. Usually, to handle negation a window (typically 3-5 words) is considered and the polarities of all the words are reversed. We have considered the window size to be 5 and reverse the polarities of all the words within the window, till either a conjunction comes or window size exceeds. For example In the sentence *He gave his best in the movie, but still it was not good enough to win an Oscar* polarities of good and win are reversed.

4. Lexicon Based Classification

We have used Senti-WordNet (Esuli et al. 2006), Inquirer (Stone et. al 1996) and the Bing Liu sentiment lexicon (Hu et al. 2004) to find out the word polarities. To compensate the bias effects introduced by the individual lexicons, we have used three different lexicons. The polarities of the reviews are given by (Mukherjee et al. 2012)

$$sign\left(\sum_{i=1}^{m}\sum_{i=1}^{n_i} f_{ij} * flip_{ij} * p(w_{ij})\right)$$

$$where\ p(w_{ij}) = pol(w_{ij})\ if\ hyp_{ij} = 0$$

$$= \frac{pol(w_{ij})}{2}\ if\ hyp_{ij} = 1$$

Above equation finds the weighted, signed polarity of a review. The polarity of each word, $pol(w_{ij})$ being $+1$ or -1, is multiplied with its discourse weight f_{ij} and all the weighted polarities are added. $Flip_{ij}$ indicates if the polarity of w_{ij} is to be negated.
In case there is any conditional or strong modal in the sentence (indicated by $hyp_{ij} = 1$), then the polarity of every word in the sentence is toned down, by considering half of its assigned polarity $(\frac{+1}{2}, \frac{-1}{2})$
Thus, if *good* occurs in the user post twice, it will contribute a polarity of $+1 \times 2 = +2$ to the overall review polarity, if $hyp_{ij} = 0$. In the presence of a *strong modal* or *conditional*, it will contribute a polarity of $\frac{+1}{2} * 2 = +1$.

All the stop words, discourse connectives and modals are ignored during the classification phase, as they have a zero polarity in the lexicon. We have handled commonly used slangs, abbreviations and collocations by manually tagging them as positive, negative or neutral.

5. Feature Engineering

The features specific for lexicon based classification for the task sentiment Analysis, identified in Section 2.4, are handled as follows:

a) The words following the Conj_Fol (Table 2) are given more weightage. Hence their frequency count is incremented by 1.
We follow a naive weighting scheme whereby we give a (+1) weightage to every word we consider important. In Example 5, “memorable" gets (+1) score, while “did not like" gets a (-2) score, making the overall score (-1) i.e. the example suggests a negative sentiment.

b) The weightage of the words occurring before the Conj_Prev (Table 2) is increased by 1. In Example 2, “failed" will have polarity (-2) instead of (-1) and “great expectations" will have polarity (+1), making the overall polarity (-1), which conforms to the overall sentiment.

c) The weightage of the words in the sentences containing conditionals (if) and strong modals (might, could, can, would, may) are toned down.

e) The polarity of all words appearing within a window of 5 from the occurrence of a negation operator (not, neither, nor, no, never) and before the occurrence of a violating expectation conjunction is reversed.

f) Exploiting sentence position information, the words appearing in the first k and last k sentences, are given more weightage. The value of k is set empirically.

g) The Negation Bias factor is treated as a parameter which is learnt from a small set of negative polarity tagged documents. The frequency count of all the negative words (in a rule based system) is multiplied with this factor to give negative words more weightage than positive words.

6. Experiments and Evaluation

For the lexicon-based approach, we performed two types of experiments- sentiment pertaining to a particular instance in a tweet (SemEval-2013 Task A) and generic sentiment analysis of a tweet (SemEval-2013 Task B). We treat both the tasks similarly.

6.1 Dataset

We performed experiments on two Datasets:

1) SemEval-2013-task 2 Twitter Dataset A containing 4435 tweets without any external data.
2) SemEval-2013-task 2 Twitter Dataset B containing 3813 tweets without any external data.

6.2 Results on the Twitter Dataset A and B

The system performs best for the positive class tweets as shown in Table 3 and Table 4 and performs badly for the negative class which is due to the fact that negative tweets can contain sarcasm which is a difficult phenomenon to capture. Also the results of the neutral category are very less which suggests that our system is biased towards subjective tweets and we wish to give the majority sentiment in the tweets.

Class	Precision	Recall	F-score
Positive	0.6706	0.5958	**0.6310**
Negative	0.4124	0.5328	0.4649
Neutral	0.0667	0.0063	0.0114

Table 3: Results on Twitter Dataset A

Class	Precision	Recall	F-score
Positive	0.4809	0.5941	**0.5316**
Negative	0.1753	0.5374	0.2643
Neutral	0.6071	0.0104	0.0204

Table 4: Results on Twitter Dataset B

6.3 Discussion

The lexicon based classifier suffers from the problem of lexeme space where it is not able handle all the word senses. Also, short-noisy text like tweets often contain various spelling mistakes like *great* can be grt, g8t *etc.* or *tomorrow* can be tom, tomm, tommrrw *etc.* which will not be detected and handled properly.

We suggest that a supervised approach comprising of the discourse features along with the bag-of-words model and the sense based features will improve the results.

7. Conclusion and Future Work

We have showed that discourse connectives, conjunctions, negations and conditionals do alter the sentiments of a piece of text. Most of the work on Micro-blogs like twitter is build on bag-of-words model and does not incorporate discourse relations. We discussed an approach where we can incorporate discourse relations along-with bag-of-words model for a web-application where parsers and taggers cannot be used as the results are required in real time.

We need to take into consideration word senses and a supervised approach to use all the features collectively. Also, a spell checker would really help in the noisy text like in tweets.

References

A Agarwal and Pushpak Bhattacharyya. 2005. Sentiment Analysis: A New Approach for Effective Use of Linguistic Knowledge and Exploiting Similarities in a Set of Documents to be classified. *International Conference on Natural Language Processing (ICON 05)*, IIT Kanpur, India, December

AR Balamurali, Aditya Joshi and Pushpak Bhattacharyya. 2011. Harnessing WordNet Senses for Supervised Sentiment Classification. *In Proceedings of Empirical Methods in Natural Language Processing (EMNLP).*

A Esuli and F Sebastiani, 2006. SentiWordNet: A Publicly Available Lexical Resource for Opinion Mining. *In Proceedings from International Conference on Language Resources and Evaluation (LREC),* Genoa.

Minqing Hu and Bing Liu. 2004. Mining and summarizing customer reviews. *In Proc. of ACM SIGKDD.*

Aditya Joshi, AR Balamurali, Pushpak Bhattacharyya and R Mohanty. 2010. C-Feel-It: A Sentiment Analyzer for Micro-blogs', *Annual Meeting of the Association of Computational Linguistics (ACL 2011)*, Oregon, USA.

William C. Mann and Sandra A. Thompson. Rhetorical Structure Theory: Toward a functional theory of text organization. Text, 8 (3), 243-281. 1988

R Narayanan, Bing Liu and A Choudhary. 2009. Sentiment Analysis of Conditional Sentences. *In Proceedings of Conference on Empirical Methods in Natural Language Processing (EMNLP-09).*

L Polanyi and A Zaenen. 2004. Contextual Valence Shifters. *In James G. Shanahan, Yan Qu, Janyce Wiebe (eds.), Computing Attitude and Affect in Text: Theory and Applications*, pp. 1-10.

BP Ramesh, R Prasad and H Yu. 2010. Identifying explicit discourse connective in biomedical text. *In Annual Symposium proceedings, AMIA Symposium*, Vol. 2010, pp. 657-661.

R Soricut and D Marcu. 2003. Sentence level discourse parsing using syntactic and lexical information. *In Proc. of HLT-NAACL*

PJ Stone, DC Dunphy, MS Smith, DM Ogilvie and Associates. 1996. The General Inquirer: A Computer Approach to Content Analysis. *The MIT Press*

Subhabrata Mukherjee and Pushpak Bhattacharyya. 2012. Sentiment Analysis in Twitter with Lightweight Discourse Analysis. *In Proceedings of COLING 2012*

Subhabrata Mukherjee and Pushpak Bhattacharyya. 2012. Sentiment Analysis in Twitter with Lightweight Discourse Analysis. *In Proceedings of the 21st ACM Conference on Information and Knowledge Management (CIKM)*, short paper.

Subhabrata Mukherjee, AR Balamurali, Akshat Malu and Pushpak Bhattacharyya. 2012. TwiSent: A Robust Multistage System for Analyzing Sentiment on Twitter. *In Proceedings of the 21st ACM Conference on Information and Knowledge Management (CIKM),* poster paper.

Maite Taboada, Julian Brooke and Kimberly Voll. 2008. *Extracting Sentiment as a Function of Discourse Structure and Topicality.* Simon Fraser Univeristy School of Computing Science Technical Report.

B Wellner, J Pustejovski, A Havasi, A Rumshiskym and R Suair. 2006. Classification of discourse coherence relations: An exploratory study using multiple knowledge sources. *In Proc. of SIGDIAL*

F Wolf and E Gibson. 2005. Representing Discourse Coherence: A Corpus-based Study. *Computational Linguistics,* 31(2), pp. 249-287.

Lanjun Zhou, Binyang Li, Wei Gao, Zhongyu Wei and Kam-Fai Wong. 2011. Unsupervised discovery of discourse relations for eliminating intra-sentence polarity ambiguities. *In Proceedings of EMNLP.*

SSA-UO: Unsupervised Twitter Sentiment Analysis

Reynier Ortega, Adrian Fonseca
CERPAMID, University of Oriente
Ave Patricio Lumumba S/N
Santiago de Cuba, Cuba

Yoan Gutiérrez
DI, University of Matanzas
Autopista a Varadero Km $3\frac{1}{2}$
Matanzas, Cuba

Andrés Montoyo
DLSI, University of Alicante
Carretera de San Vicente S/N
Alicante,Spain

Abstract

This paper describes the specifications and results of SSA-UO, unsupervised system, presented in SemEval 2013 for Sentiment Analysis in Twitter (Task 2) (Wilson et al., 2013). The proposal system includes three phases: data preprocessing, contextual word polarity detection and message classification. The preprocessing phase comprises treatment of emoticon, slang terms, lemmatization and POS-tagging. Word polarity detection is carried out taking into account the sentiment associated with the context in which it appears. For this, we use a new contextual sentiment classification method based on coarse-grained word sense disambiguation, using WordNet (Miller, 1995) and a coarse-grained sense inventory (sentiment inventory) built up from SentiWordNet (Baccianella et al., 2010). Finally, the overall sentiment is determined using a rule-based classifier. As it may be observed, the results obtained for Twitter and SMS sentiment classification are good considering that our proposal is unsupervised.

1 Introduction

The explosion of Web 2.0 has marked a new age for the human society. The huge use of Social Media such as Facebook[1] , MySpace[2] , LinkedIn[3] and Twitter[4] , offers a place for people to share information in real time. Twitter is one of the most popular social network websites and has been growing at a very fast pace. The number of active users exceeds 500 million and the number of tweets posted by day exceeds 500 million (as of May 2012)[5]. Through the twitter applications, users shared opinions about personalities, politicians, products, companies, events, etc. This has been attracting the attention of different research communities interested in analyzing its content and motivated many natural language tasks, such as sentiment analysis, emotions detection, opinions retrieval, product recommendation or opinion summarization.

One of the most popular sentiment analysis tasks is polarity classification. This task is a new field that classifies opinion texts as positive, negative or neutral (Pang et al., 2002; Turney, 2002; Esuli and Sebastiani, 2006; Wilson et al., 2006; Wiegand et al., 2010). Determining polarity might seem an easy task, as many words have some polarity by themselves. However, words do not always express the same sentiment, and in most cases the polarity of a word depends on the context in which the word is used. So, terms that clearly denote negative feelings can be neutral, or even positive, depending on their context. Hence, sentiment analysis systems should include semantic-level analysis in order to solve word ambiguity and correctly capture the meaning of each word according to its context. Also, complex linguistic processing is needed to deal with problems such as the effect of negations and informal language. Moreover, understanding the sentimental meaning of the different textual units is important to accurately determine the overall polarity

[1]https://www.facebook.com
[2]http://www.myspace.com/
[3]http://www.linkedin.com
[4]https://www.twitter.com/
[5]http://www.statisticbrain.com/twitter-statistics/

*Second Joint Conference on Lexical and Computational Semantics (*SEM), Volume 2: Seventh International Workshop on Semantic Evaluation (SemEval 2013)*, pages 501–507, Atlanta, Georgia, June 14-15, 2013.

of a text.

In this paper, we present a system that has as main objective to analyze the sentiments of tweets and classify these as positive, negative or neutral. The proposal system includes three phases: data preprocessing, contextual word polarity detection and message classification. The preprocessing phase comprises treatment of emoticons, spell-errors, slang terms, lemmatization and POS-tagging. Word polarity detection is carried out taking into account the sentiment associated with the context within which it appears. For this, we use a new contextual sentiment classification method based on coarse-grained word sense disambiguation, using WordNet (Miller, 1995) and a coarse-grained sense inventory (sentiment inventory) built up from SentiWordNet (Baccianella et al., 2010). Finally, the polarity is determined using a rule-based classifier. The paper is organized as follows. Section 2 describes of SSA-UO system. In Section 3 we evaluate our proposal and discuss the results obtained in the SemEval 2013 Task No. 2. Finally, section 4 provides concluding remarks.

2 SSA-UO System

We use an unsupervised strategy consisting in a coarse-grained clustering-based word sense disambiguation (WSD) method that differentiates positive, negative, highly positive, highly negative and objective uses of every word on context which it occurs. The proposal method uses WordNet and a coarse-grained sense inventory (sentiment inventory) built up from SentiWordNet. The overall architecture of our sentiment classifier is shown in Figure 1.

Firstly, data preprocessing is done to eliminate incomplete, noisy or inconsistent information. A Sentiment Word Sense Disambiguation method (Section 2.3) is then applied to content words (nouns, adjectives, verbs and adverbs). Once all content words are disambiguated, we apply a rule-based classifier (Section 2.4) to decide whether the tweet is positive, negative or neutral.

Unsupervised word sense disambiguation method proposed by (Anaya-Sánchez et al., 2006) was adapted for sentiment word sense disambiguation. Unlike the authors, who aim to obtain the correct sense of a word, we use the method to determine

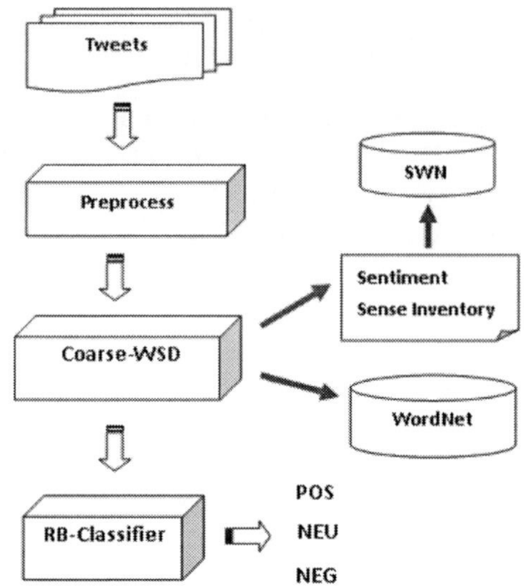

Figure 1: Overall architecture of Sentiment Classifier

when a word is used with highly positive (HP), positive (P), highly negative (HN), negative (N) or objective (O) meaning based on a sentiment sense inventory. We make sentiment sense inventory based on sense-level annotation in SentiWordNet. Finally, we apply a rule-based classifier to determine the overall sentiment in tweet.

2.1 Data Preprocessing

The tweets differ from the text in articles, books, or even spoken language. It is limited to 140 characters, also includes many idiosyncratic uses, such as emoticons, slang terms, misspellings, URLs, "RT" for re-tweet, "@" for user mentions, "#" for hashtags, and character repetitions. Therefore it is necessary to preprocess the text, in order to reduce the noise information. The preprocessing step involve the following task. The text is tokenized and URL, re-tweets and author mentions are removed. Hashtag tokens frequently contain relevant information related to the topic of the tweet, this is included as part of the text but without the "#" character. We replace emoticon tokens by emotion words using an emoticons dictionary, obtained from Wikipedia

[6]. Each emoticon was manually annotated with an emotion word and polarity value. Emoticons that suggest positive emotions - ":-)", ":)", "X-D" - are annotated with the emotion word *"happy"* and negative emoticons - ":-(", ":-c", ":,(" - are annotated with the emotion word *"sad"*. The presence of abbreviations within a tweet is noted, therefore abbreviations are replaced by their meaning (e.g., LOL – laughing out loud) using a dictionary[7]. Finally the text is POS-tagged and lemmatized using TreeTagger (Schmid, 1994) and stopwords are discarded.

2.2 Sentiment Sense Inventory

We considered SentiWordNet for building sentiment coarse-grained sense inventory. SentiWordNet contain positive, negative and objective scores between 0 and 1 for all senses in WordNet. Based on this sense level annotation, we define a new rule (*SentiS*) for classifying senses in five sentiment class. The senses are classified in the following manner (Alexandra et al., 2009): senses whose positive score is greater than or equal to 0.75 are considered to be highly positive (HP), senses with positive score greater than or equal to 0.5 and lower than 0.75 are considered positive (P), senses with negative score greater than or equal 0.75 are considered highly negative (HN), whereas those whose negative score is lower than 0.75 and greater than or equal to 0.5 are considered to be negative (N). In the remaining cases, the senses are considered to be objective (O) (see equation(1)).

$$sentiS(s) = \begin{cases} HP\ if\ ScoreP(s) \geq 0.75 \\ HN\ if\ ScoreN(s) \geq 0.75 \\ P\ if\ ScoreP(s) < 0.75\ and\ ScoreP(s) \geq 0.5 \\ N\ if\ ScoreN(s) < 0.75\ and\ ScoreN(s) \geq 0.5 \\ O\ in\ other\ case \end{cases} \quad (1)$$

Table 1 summarizes the distribution of the five sentiment classes once classified all senses of SentiWordNet.

A notable unbalance can be observed between the number of highly positive, highly negative, positive, negative and objective senses.

[6]http://en.wikipedia.org/wiki/List_of_emoticons
[7]http://www.noslang.com/dictionary/

Once all senses were classified in a five sentiment sense class, we create a coarse sense inventory based on this classification. This inventory is defined in the following manner: For each word in SentiWordNet we grouped its senses with the same sentiment class in a single sense (coarse-sense), in case of objective senses these are kept separated.

2.3 Contextual Word Polarity Detection

Much work on sentiment analysis have been directed to determine the polarity of opinion using anotated lexicons with prior polarity (Hatzivassiloglou and McKeown, 1997; Kamps and Marx, 2002; Turney, 2002). However a word can modify your prior polarity in relation to the context within which it is invoked. For example the word "earthquake" is used with negative meaning in the sentence :

"Selling the company caused an earthquake amount the employees".

Whereas it is used in an neutral meaning in the sentence:

"An earthquake is the result of a sudden release of energy in the Earth's crust that creates seismic waves".

For this reason, our system uses a coarse-grained WSD method for obtaining the contextual polarity of all words in tweets. The selected disambiguation method (Anaya-Sánchez et al., 2006) was developed for the traditional WSD task. In this WSD method, the senses are represented as topic signatures (Lin and Hovy, 2000) built from the repository of concepts of WordNet. The disambiguation process starts from a clustering distribution of all possible senses of the ambiguous words by applying the Extended Star clustering algorithm (Gil-García et al., 2003). Such a clustering tries to identify cohesive groups of word senses, which are assumed to represent different meanings for the set of words.

Resource	HP	HN	P	N	O
SWN	310	938	2242	2899	109035

Table 1: Senses highly positive, highly negative, positive, negative and objective distributions.

Then, clusters that match the best with the context are selected. If the selected clusters disambiguate all words, the process stops and the senses belonging to the selected clusters are interpreted as the disambiguating ones. Otherwise, the clustering is performed again (regarding the remaining senses) until a complete disambiguation is achieved. It does not distinguish between highly positive, positive, negative, highly negative or objective meaning of a word. In this paper, we propose a strategy to built a coarse-grained sense representation. Firstly, a topic signatures for all senses into WordNet is built and the topic signatures for coarse-grained senses is the sum of the topic signatures of the corresponding fine-grained senses that was grouped.

We explain coarse-grained sense representation using the following example:

Let us consider the adjective *"sad"*. This adjective has three word senses into WordNet 2.0

sad#a#1 – *experiencing or showing sorrow or unhappiness*
sad#a#2 – *of things that make you feel sad*
sad#a#3 – *bad; unfortunate*

Firstly the topic signature are built for each word sense:

$$vector1 = topicSignature(sad\#a\#1)$$
$$vector2 = topicSignature(sad\#a\#2)$$
$$vector3 = topicSignature(sad\#a\#3)$$

The senses are classified using equation (1)(in Section 2.2), sense 1 and 3 were considered as highly negative, whereas the sense 2 is objective. The topic signature associated to highly negative coarse-grained sense is computed as:

$$topicSignature(sad\#a\#HN) = sum(vector1 + vector3)$$

and objective coarse-grained sense is kept as vector2

$$topicSignature(sad\#a\#O) = vector2$$

2.4 Rule-based Sentiment Classifier

We use a rule-based classifier to classify tweets into positive, negative or neutral. A polarity value is assigned to each word, based on equation 2, after these were disambiguated. It is necessary to clarify that emotion words that replaced emoticons in the pre-processing phase, are not disambiguated. Instead, we give a prior polarity value equal to 4 if emotion word is *"happy"* and -4 in case that emotion word is *"sad"*. It is important to mention that the polarity of a word is forced into the opposite class if it is preceded by a valence shifter (obtained from the Negate category in GI (Stone et al., 1966)).

$$polarity(w) = \begin{cases} 4 & if\ w\ is\ disambiguated\ as\ HP \\ -4 & if\ w\ is\ disambiguated\ as\ HN \\ 2 & if\ w\ is\ disambiguated\ as\ P \\ -2 & if\ w\ is\ disambiguated\ as\ N \\ 0 & if\ w\ is\ disambiguated\ as\ O \end{cases} \tag{2}$$

The polarity of the tweet is determined from the scores of positive and negative words it contains. To sum up, for each tweet the overall positive ($PosS(t)$) value and overall negative value ($NegS(t)$) , are computed as:

$$PosS(t) = \sum_{w_i \in W_P} polarity(w_i) \tag{3}$$

W_P: Words disambiguated as highly positive or positive in tweet t

$$NegS(t) = \sum_{w_i \in W_N} polarity(w_i) \tag{4}$$

W_N: Words disambiguated as highly negative or negative in tweet t

If $PosS(t)$ is greater than $NegS(t)$ then the tweet is considered as positive. On the contrary, if $PosS(t)$ is less than $NegS(t)$ the tweet is negative. Finally, if $PosS(t)$ is equal to $NegS(t)$ the tweet is considered as neutral.

2.5 A Tweet Sentiment Classification Example

The general operation of the algorithm is illustrated in the following example:

Let us consider the following tweet:

@JoeyMarchant: I really love Jennifer Aniston :-) #loving, she is very cooooollll and sexy. I'm married to her... LOL, http://t.co/2RShsRNSDW

After applying the preprocessing phase, we obtain the following normalized text:

I really love Jennifer Aniston "happy" loving, she is very cooll and sexy. I'm married to her... lots of laughs.

When the text is lemmatized and stopwords are removed, we obtain the following bag of words (for each word we show: lemma and part-of-speech *n-noun, v-verb, a-adjective, r-adverb and u-unknown*):

really#r love#v jennifer#a aniston#n "happy"#a loving#a cooll#a sexy#a marry#v lot#n laugh#n.

After contextual word polarity detection, we obtain the following result (for each word we shown lemma, part-of-speech and sentiment sense, *HP-highly positive, HN-highly negative, P-positive, N-negative and O-objective*).

really#r#P love#v#P jennifer#a#O aniston#n#O "happy"#a loving#a#HP cooll#a#O sexy#a#P marry#v#O lot#n#O laugh#n#P

Once that all words were disambiguated we obtained their polarities using the equation 2 introduced in section 2.4. We show the polarities values assigned to each word, in Table 2.

Word	POS	Sentiment	Polarity
really	r	P	2
love	v	P	2
jennifer	a	O	0
aniston	n	O	0
"happy"	a	-	4
loving	a	HP	4
cooll	a	O	0
sexy	a	P	2
marry	a	O	0
lot	n	O	0
laugh	n	P	2

Table 2: Polarity assigned to each word

Note that the word "happy" has not been disambiguated, its polarity is assigned according to the emoticon associated in the original tweet. Afterward we compute overall positive and negative polarity value:

$$NegS(t) = 0$$

$$PosS(t) = 2+2+4+4+2+2 = 16$$

Therefore, the tweet t is classified as positive.

3 Results

This section presents the evaluation of our system in the context of SemEval 2013 Task No.2 Subtask B (Sentiment Analysis in Twitter). For evaluating the participant's systems two unlabeled datasets were provided, one composed of Twitter messages and another of SMS messages. For each dataset two runs can be submitted, the first (constrained), the system can only be used the provided training data and other resources such as lexicons. In the second (unconstrained), the system can use additional data for training. Our runs are considered as constrained because SSA-UO only use lexical resources for sentiment classification.

Runs	Dataset	F1	all runs Rank
twitter-1	Twitter	50.17	33(48)
sms-1	SMS	44.39	33 (42)

Table 3: SSA-UO results in polarity classification, all runs summited

Runs	Dataset	F1	constrained runs Rank
twitter-1	Twitter	50.17	25 (35)
sms-1	SMS	44.39	22 (28)

Table 4: SSA-UO results in polarity classification, constrained runs summited

In Table 3 we summarize the results obtained by SSA-UO system. As may be observed average F1 measure for Twitter dataset is the 50.17 and 44.39 for the SMS dataset. A total of 48 runs were submitted by all systems participant's in Twitter and 42 for SMS dataset. Our runs were ranked 33th for both datasets.

In Table 4 we compare our results with those runs that can be considered as constrained. A total of 35 runs for Twitter and 28 for SMS were submitted , ours runs were ranked in 25th and 22th respectively. It's worth mentioning that, the results obtained can be considered satisfactory, considering the complexity of the task and that our system is unsupervised.

4 Conclusion

In this paper, we have described the SSA-UO system for Twitter Sentiment Analysis Task at SemEval-2013. This knowledge driven system relies on unsupervised coarse-grained WSD to obtain the contextual word polarity. We used a rule-based classifier for determining the polarity of a tweet. The experimental results show that our proposal is accurate for Twitter sentiment analysis considering that our system does not use any corpus for training.

Acknowledgments

This research work has been partially funded by the Spanish Government through the project TEXT-MESS 2.0 (TIN2009-13391-C04), "Análisis de Tendencias Mediante Técnicas de Opinión Semántica" (TIN2012-38536-C03-03) and "Técnicas de Deconstrucción en la Tecnologías del Lenguaje Humano" (TIN2012-31224); and by the Valencian Government through the project PROMETEO (PROMETEO/2009/199).

References

Balahur Alexandra, Steinberger Ralf, Goot Erik van der, Pouliquen Bruno, and Kabadjov Mijail. 2009. Opinion mining on newspaper quotations. In *Proceedings of the 2009 IEEE/WIC/ACM International Joint Conference on Web Intelligence and Intelligent Agent Technology - Volume 03*, WI-IAT '09, pages 523–526, Washington, DC, USA. IEEE Computer Society.

Henry Anaya-Sánchez, Aurora Pons-Porrata, and Rafael Berlanga-Llavori. 2006. Word sense disambiguation based on word sense clustering. In *Proceedings of the 2nd international joint conference, and Proceedings of the 10th Ibero-American Conference on AI 18th Brazilian conference on Advances in Artificial Intelligence*, IBERAMIA-SBIA'06, pages 472–481, Berlin, Heidelberg. Springer-Verlag.

Stefano Baccianella, Andrea Esuli, and Fabrizio Sebastiani. 2010. Sentiwordnet 3.0: An enhanced lexical resource for sentiment analysis and opinion mining. In Nicoletta Calzolari (Conference Chair), Khalid Choukri, Bente Maegaard, Joseph Mariani, Jan Odijk, Stelios Piperidis, Mike Rosner, and Daniel Tapias, editors, *Proceedings of the Seventh International Conference on Language Resources and Evaluation (LREC '10)*, Valletta, Malta, may. European Language Resources Association (ELRA).

Andrea Esuli and Fabrizio Sebastiani. 2006. Sentiwordnet: A publicly available lexical resource for opinion mining. In *In Proceedings of the 5th Conference on Language Resources and Evaluation (LREC'06*, pages 417–422.

R. Gil-García, J. M. Badía-Contelles, and A. Pons-Porrata. 2003. Extended Star Clustering Algorithm. In *CIARP 2003, LNCS, vol. 2905*, pages 480–487.

Vasileios Hatzivassiloglou and Kathleen R. McKeown. 1997. Predicting the semantic orientation of adjectives. In *Proceedings of the eighth conference on European chapter of the Association for Computational Linguistics*, EACL '97, pages 174–181, Stroudsburg, PA, USA. Association for Computational Linguistics.

Jaap Kamps and Maarten Marx. 2002. Words with attitude. In *First International WordNet conference*.

Chin-Yew Lin and Eduard Hovy. 2000. The automated acquisition of topic signatures for text summarization. In *Proceedings of the 18th conference on Computational linguistics - Volume 1*, COLING '00, pages 495–501, Stroudsburg, PA, USA. Association for Computational Linguistics.

George A. Miller. 1995. Wordnet: A lexical database for english. *Communications of the ACM*, 38:39–41.

Bo Pang, Lillian Lee, and Shivakumar Vaithyanathan. 2002. Thumbs up? sentiment classification using machine learning techniques. In *Proceeding of Empirical Methods in Natural Language Processing*, pages 79–86.

Helmut Schmid. 1994. Probabilistic part-of-speech tagging using decision trees.

Philip J. Stone, Dexter C. Dunphy, Marshall S. Smith, and Daniel M. Ogilvie. 1966. *The General Inquirer: A Computer Approach to Content Analysis*. MIT Press, Cambridge, MA.

Peter Turney. 2002. Thumbs up or thumbs down? semantic orientation applied to unsupervised classification of reviews. pages 417–424.

Michael Wiegand, Alexandra Balahur, Benjamin Roth, Dietrich Klakow, and Andrés Montoyo. 2010. A survey on the role of negation in sentiment analysis. In *Proceedings of the Workshop on Negation and Speculation in Natural Language Processing*, NeSp-NLP '10, pages 60–68, Stroudsburg, PA, USA. Association for Computational Linguistics.

Theresa Wilson, Janyce Wiebe, and Rebecca Hwa. 2006. Recognizing strong and weak opinion clauses. *Computational Intelligence*, 22:73–99.

Theresa Wilson, Zornitsa Kozareva, Preslav Nakov, Sara Rosenthal, Veselin Stoyanov, and Alan Ritter. 2013. SemEval-2013 task 2: Sentiment analysis in twitter. In *Proceedings of the International Workshop on Semantic Evaluation*, SemEval '13, June.

senti.ue-en: an approach for informally written short texts in SemEval-2013 Sentiment Analysis task

José Saias
DI - ECT - Universidade de Évora
Rua Romão Ramalho, 59
7000-671 Évora, Portugal
jsaias@uevora.pt

Hilário Fernandes
Cortex Intelligence
Rua Sebastião Mendes Bolas, 2 K
7005-872 Évora, Portugal
hilario.fernandes@cortex-intelligence.com

Abstract

This article describes a Sentiment Analysis (SA) system named `senti.ue-en`, built for participation in SemEval-2013 Task 2, a Twitter SA challenge. In both challenge subtasks we used the same supervised machine learning approach, including two classifiers in pipeline, with 22 semantic oriented features, such as polarized term presence and index, and negation presence. Our system achieved a better score on Task A (0.7413) than in the Task B (0.4785). In the first subtask, there is a better result for SMS than the obtained for the more trained type of data, the tweets.

1 Introduction

This paper describes the participation of a group led by Universidade de Évora's Computer Science Department in SemEval-2013 Task 2 (Wilson et al., 2013), using `senti.ue-en` system. Having previous experience in NLP tasks, such as question answering (Saias, 2010; Saias and Quaresma, 2012), this was the authors first attempt to implement a system for Sentiment Analysis (SA) in English language. We have a recent work (Fernandes, 2013) involving SA but it is geared towards Portuguese language, and thought for regular text. It was based on rules on the outcome of linguistic analysis, which did not work well for tweets, because the morphosyntactic analyzer misses much, due to the abundance of writing errors, symbols and abbreviations. Moreover, in that work we began by detecting named entities and afterwards classify the sentiment being expressed about them. For SemEval the goal is different, being target-independent. In both A and B subtasks, systems must work on sentiment polarity, in a certain context or full message, but the target entity (or the opinion topic) will not appear in the output. Thus, we have decided that `senti.ue-en` system would be implemented from scratch, for English language and according to the objectives of this challenge, in particular the Task B.

2 Related Work

Microblogging and social networks are platforms where people express opinions. In recent years many papers have been published on social media content SA. Pang et al. (2002) applied machine learning based classifiers for sentiment classification on movie reviews. Their experimental results using Naive Bayes, Maximum Entropy, and Support Vector Machines (SVM) algorithms achieved best results with SVM and unigram presence as features.
Some target-dependent approaches are sensitive to the entity that is receiving each sentiment. A sentence can have a positive sentiment about an entity and a negative for another. Such classification can be performed with rules on the occurrence of nouns, verbs and adjectives, as done in (Nasukawa and Yi, 2003). It is common to use parsers and part-of-speech tagging. Barbosa and Feng (2010) explore tweet writting details and meta-information in feature selection. Instead of using many unigrams as features, the authors propose the use of 20 features (related to POS tags, emoticons, upper case usage, word polarity and negation), achieving faster training and test times. A two-phase approach first clas-

*Second Joint Conference on Lexical and Computational Semantics (*SEM), Volume 2: Seventh International Workshop on Semantic Evaluation (SemEval 2013)*, pages 508–512, Atlanta, Georgia, June 14-15, 2013.

sifies messages as subjective and objective, and then the polarity is classified as positive or negative for tweets having subjectivity. Groot (2012) builds a feature vector with polarized words and frequently occurring words being taken as predictive for Twitter messages. Supervised learning algorithms as SVM and Naive Bayes are then used to create a prediction model. The work (Gebremeskel, 2011) is focused on tweets about news. Authors report an accuracy of 87.78% for a three-classed sentiment classification using unigram+bigram presence features and Multinomial Naive Bayes classifier. In Jiang et al. (2011) work, Twitter SA starts with a query, identifying a target, and classifies sentiment in the query result tweets, related to that target. Instead of considering only the text of a tweet, their context-aware approach also considers related tweets and target-dependent features. With precise criteria for the context of a tweet, authors seek to reduce ambiguity and report performance gains.

3 Methodology

As in most systems described in the literature, in this area, our `senti.ue-en` system is based on supervised machine learning. To handle the data format, in the input and on the outcome of the system, we chose to use Python and the Natural Language Toolkit (NLTK), a platform with resources and programming libraries suitable for linguistic processing (Bird, 2006). Task A asks us to classify the sentiment in a word or phrase in the context of the message to which it belongs. For Task B, we had to classify the overall sentiment expressed in each message. Since tweets are short messages, we early have chosen to apply the same system for both tasks, admitting some possible difference in training or parameterization. As the fine control of the correspondence between each sentiment expression and its target entity is not sought, Task A is treated as a special case of Task B, and our system does not consider the text around the expression to classify. The organization prepared a message corpus for training and another to be used as a development-time evaluation dataset. We merged the training corpus with the development corpus, and our development test set was dynamically formed by random selection of instances for each class (positive, negative and neutral). Some tweets were not downloaded properly. For message polarity classification, we ended up with 9191 labeled messages, which we split into training and test sets.

Text processing started with tokenization, that was white space or punctuation based. Some experiments also included lemmatization, done with the NLTK WordNet Lemmatizer. In the first approach to Task B, we applied the Naive Bayes classification algorithm using term presence features. The test set was formed by random selection of 200 instances of each class. After several experiments with this system configuration, the average accuracy for the 3 classes was close to 45%. Looking for better results, instead of the bag-of-words approach, we chose a smaller set of semantic oriented features:

- presence of polarized term
- overall value of sentiment in text
- negation presence
- negation before polarized expression
- presence of polarized task A n-grams
- overall value of polarized task A n-grams
- overall and presence of similar to Task A n-grams
- first and last index of polarized terms

Checking for the presence of positive and negative polarized terms produces two features for each of the three sentiment lexicons used by our system. AFINN (Nielsen, 2011) is a sentiment lexicon containing a list of English words rated between minus five (negative) and plus five (positive). The words have been manually labeled by Finn Årup Nielsen, from 2009 to 2011. SentiWordNet (Baccianella et al., 2010) is a lexical resource for opinion mining that assigns sentiment scores to each synset of WordNet (Princeton University, 2010). After some experimentation with this resource, we decided to apply a threshold, disregarding terms whose score absolute value is less than 0.3. Another sentiment lexicon, from Liu et al. (2005), derived from a work on online customer reviews of products. The overall text sentiment value is calculated by adding the sentiment value in each word. This is the way chosen to handle more than one sentiment in a single tweet. Our system creates a separated overall sentiment value feature for AFINN, SentiWordNet and Liu's lexicons, because each resource uses a different range of values. Each of these features is calculated by summing the sentiment value in each word of the text classify. Detection of denial in the text also gave rise to a feature. Thinking in cases like *"This meal was not good*", we created features for the presence of denial before positive and negative expressions, where the adjective's sentiment value is inverted by negation. In these two features, an expression is polarized if it is included in any of the sentiment lexicons. The training corpus for Task A included words or phrases marked as positive or negative. We created two more features to signal the presence of polarized words or n-grams in the texts to be classified. To complement, another feature accounts for the overall Task A polarized n-grams value, adding 1 for each positive occurrence and subtracting 1 every negative occurrence in the tweet. Because a term can arise in inflected form, we added another three features to assess the same on Task A data, but accepting variations in words or expressions. Using lemmatization and synonyms, we seek more flexibility in n-gram verification. The last four features identify the text token index for the first and the last occurrence, for each sentiment flavor, positive and negative, according to any used sentiment lexicon. Emoticons are present in sentiment lexicons, so it was not created a specific feature for them.

Using these 22 features with Naive Bayes, the average overall accuracy was 60%. When analyzed by class, the lower accuracy happens on neutral class, near 50%. Accuracy por positive class was 68%, and for negative it was 63%. For the next iteration, the NLTK classifier was set up for Decision Tree algorithm. After several runs, we noticed that while the overall accuracy remained identical, the poorest results came now for the negative class, having 54% accuracy. The run average accuracy for classes positive and neutral, was respectively 59% and 64%. In the latest evolution the system applies two classifiers in sequence. Each tweet is first classified with Naive Bayes. This creates a new feature for the second classifier, which is considered along with the previous ones by the Decision Tree algorithm. This configuration led us to the best overall accuracy in the development stage, with 62%, and was the version applied to Task B in constrained mode.

The unconstrained mode allowed systems to use additional data for training. The IMDB dataset (Maas et al., 2011) contains movie reviews with their associated binary sentiment polarity labels. We chose a subset of this corpus consisting of 500 positive and 500 negative reviews with less than 350 characters.

T	Data	Mode	Positive	Negative	Neutral
A	sms	C	0.8079	0.8985	0.1130
		U	0.8695	0.9206	0.1348
	twitter	C	0.9190	0.8162	0.0588
		U	0.9412	0.8411	0.0705
B	sms	C	0.4676	0.4356	0.7168
		U	0.4625	0.4161	0.7293
	twitter	C	0.6264	0.3996	0.5538
		U	0.6036	0.3589	0.5621

Table 1: `senti.ue-en` precision in Tasks A and B

Sanders used a Naive Bayes classifier and token-based feature extraction to create a corpus (Sanders, 2011) for SA on Twitter. We were able to discharge only part of the corpus, from which we selected 250 positive tweets and the same number of negative ones. In unconstrained mode, `senti.ue-en` has the same configuration, but uses extra instances from these two corpus for training.

Task A is treated with the same mechanism. The system classifies the sentiment for the text inside the given boundaries. Because many of these cases have a single word, our system uses a third extra corpus for training in unconstrained mode. Each word on AFINN lexicon is added to training set, with positive or negative class, depending on its sentiment value.

4 Results

We submitted our system's result for each of the eight expected runs. Each run was a combination of subtask (A or B), dataset (Twitter or SMS) and training mode (constrained or unconstrained). After the deadline for submission, the organization evaluated the results. The precision in our system's output is indicated in Table 1. The use of more training instances in unconstrained mode leads to an improvement of precision in Task A, for all classes. In Task B we notice the opposite effect, with a slight drop in precision for positive and negative classes, and about 1% improvement in neutral class precision. We also note that precision has lower values in neutral class for Task A, whereas in Task B it is the class negative that has the lowest precision.

Table 2 shows the recall obtained for the same results. This metric also shows a gain in Task A, for positive and negative classes using unconstrained mode. For subtask B, the constrained mode had bet-

T	Data	Mode	Positive	Negative	Neutral
A	sms	C	0.5341	0.5453	0.6792
		U	0.6471	0.6196	0.6730
	twitter	C	0.4898	0.4958	0.7500
		U	0.6203	0.5704	0.7000
B	sms	C	0.5711	0.3350	0.7061
		U	0.5386	0.4594	0.6556
	twitter	C	0.5515	0.3245	0.6555
		U	0.5280	0.4359	0.5854

Table 2: `senti.ue-en` recall in Tasks A and B

T	Data	Mode	Positive	Negative	Neutral
A	sms	C	0.6431	0.6787	0.1937
		U	0.7420	0.7407	0.2246
	twitter	C	0.6390	0.6169	0.1090
		U	0.7478	0.6798	0.1281
B	sms	C	0.5142	0.3788	0.7114
		U	0.4977	0.4367	0.6905
	twitter	C	0.5866	0.3581	0.6004
		U	0.5633	0.3937	0.5735

Table 3: `senti.ue-en` F-measure in Tasks A and B

T	Data	Mode	Score
A	sms	C	0.6609
		U	0.7413
	twitter	C	0.6279
		U	0.7138
B	sms	C	0.4465
		U	0.4672
	twitter	C	0.4724
		U	0.4785

Table 4: `senti.ue-en` score

ter recall for positive and neutral classes. But recall varies in the opposite direction in the negative class when using our extra training instances.

Using the F-measure metric to evaluate our results, we get the values in Table 3. This balanced assessment between precision and recall confirms the improvement of results in Task A when using the unconstrained mode. We note, for Task B, a small loss in unconstrained mode on positive class, but that is outweighed by the gain on the negative class.

In SemEval-2013 Task 2, the participating systems are ranked by their score. This corresponds to the average F-measure in positive and negative classes. Table 4 shows the score obtained by our system. The score is in line with our forecasts in the Task A, but below what we wanted in Task B. Looking at Table 3 we see that positive and negative classes' F-measure values are substantially lower than the values for neutral class, in Task B and in both constrained and unconstrained mode. For Task B, most correct results were in the class less relevant for the score.

5 Conclusions

With our participation in SemEval-2013 Task 2 we intended to build a real-time SA system for the English used nowadays in social media content. This goal was achieved and we experienced the use of important English linguistic resources to support this task, such as corpora and sentiment lexicons.

We had some problems detected only after the close of submission. Lemmatization did not always work well. In 'last index of polarized term' feature, we noticed a problem that ironically came precisely at the version used to submit, where the last index was counted from the start of text, and it should be counted from the end.

We think that the difference in system performance between Task A and Task B has to do with the amount of noise present in the text. Because many of the texts to classify in Task A had a single word or a short phrase, the system was more likely to succeed. Another reason is the fact that our system has not been tuned to maximize the score (F-measure in positive and negative classes). During development we took into account only the overall accuracy seen in NLTK classifier result. Perhaps the overall system performance may have been affected by our decision of merge the training and the development corpus as training set. We used a class balanced set for development-time evaluation, smaller than the given development set, and the final test set had a different class distribution (Wilson et al., 2013).

By reviewing the system, we feel that the classification algorithms in the pipeline system should swap. Now we would use first the Decision Tree classifier, and after, receiving an extra feature, the Naive Bayes classifier, which as mentioned in section 3, suggested slightly better results for positive and negative classes. For the future, we intend to evolve the system in order to become more precise and target-aware. For the first part we need to review and evaluate the actual contribution of the current features. As for the second, we intend to introduce named entity recognition, so that each sentiment can be associated with its target entity.

References

Andrew L. Maas, Raymond Daly, Peter Pham, Dan Huang, Andrew Ng and Christopher Potts. 2011. *Learning Word Vectors for Sentiment Analysis.* In Proceedings of the 49th Annual Meeting of the Association for Computational Linguistics: Human Language Technologies, pp: 142-150. ACL. Portland, USA.

Bing Liu, Minqing Hu and Junsheng Cheng. 2005. *Opinion Observer: Analyzing and Comparing Opinions on the Web.* In Proceedings of the 14th International World Wide Web conference (WWW-2005). Chiba, Japan.

Bo Pang, Lillian Lee, Shivakumar Vaithyanathan. 2002. *Thumbs up? Sentiment Classification using Machine Learning Techniques.* In Proceedings of EMNLP. pp: 79–86.

Finn Årup Nielsen. 2011. *A New ANEW: Evaluation of a Word List for Sentiment Analysis in Microblogs.* In Proceedings, 1st Workshop on Making Sense of Microposts (#MSM2011): Big things come in small packages. pp: 93-98. Greece. http://arxiv.org/abs/1103.2903

Gebrekirstos Gebremeskel. 2011. *Sentiment Analysis of Twitter Posts About news.* Master's thesis. University of Malta.

Hilário Fernandes. 2013. *Sentiment Detection and Classification in Non Structured Information Sources.* Master's thesis, ECT - Universidade de Évora.

José Saias. 2010. *Contextualização e Activação Semântica na Selecção de Resultados em Sistemas de Pergunta-Resposta.* PhD thesis, Universidade de Évora.

José Saias and Paulo Quaresma. 2012. Di@ue in clef2012: question answering approach to the multiple choice qa4mre challenge. In *Proceedings of CLEF 2012 Evaluation Labs and Workshop - Working Notes Papers*, Rome, Italy.

Long Jiang, Mo Yu, Ming Zhou, Xiaohua Liu, and Tiejun Zhao. 2011. Target-dependent twitter sentiment classification. In *Proceedings of the 49th Annual Meeting of the Association for Computational Linguistics: Human Language Technologies - Volume 1*, HLT '11, pages 151–160. Association for Computational Linguistics. USA.

Luciano Barbosa and Junlan Feng. 2010. *Robust Sentiment Detection on Twitter from Biased and Noisy Data.* Coling 2010. pages 36–44. Beijing.

Niek J. Sanders. 2011. *Sanders-Twitter Sentiment Corpus.* Sanders Analytics LLC

Princeton University. 2010. "About WordNet." WordNet. http://wordnet.princeton.edu

Roy de Groot. 2012. *Data mining for tweet sentiment classification.* Master's thesis, Faculty of Science - Utrecht University.

Stefano Baccianella, Andrea Esuli and Fabrizio Sebastiani. 2010. *SentiWordNet 3.0: An Enhanced Lexical Resource for Sentiment Analysis and Opinion Mining.* In Proceedings of the Seventh conference on International Language Resources and Evaluation - LREC'10. European Language Resources Association. Malta.

Steven Bird. 2006. *NLTK: the natural language toolkit.* In Proceedings of the COLING'06/ACL on Interactive presentation sessions. Australia. http://nltk.org

Tetsuya Nasukawa, Jeonghee Yi. 2003. *Sentiment analysis: capturing favorability using natural language processing.* In Proceedings of the 2nd International Conference on Knowledge Capture(K-CAP). USA.

Theresa Wilson, Zornitsa Kozareva, Preslav Nakov, Alan Ritter, Sara Rosenthal and Veselin Stoyanov. 2013. SemEval-2013 task 2: Sentiment analysis in twitter. In *Proceedings of the 7th International Workshop on Semantic Evaluation.* Association for Computation Linguistics.

teragram:
Rule-based detection of sentiment phrases using SAS Sentiment Analysis

Hilke Reckman, Cheyanne Baird, Jean Crawford, Richard Crowell, Linnea Micciulla, Saratendu Sethi, and Fruzsina Veress
SAS Institute
10 Fawcett Street
Cambridge, MA 02138, USA
hilke.reckman@sas.com

Abstract

For SemEval-2013 Task 2, A and B (Sentiment Analysis in Twitter), we use a rule-based pattern matching system that is based on an existing 'Domain Independent' sentiment taxonomy for English, essentially a highly phrasal sentiment lexicon. We have made some modifications to our set of rules, based on what we found in the annotated training data that was made available for the task. The resulting system scores competitively, especially on task B.

1 Introduction

SAS taxonomies for sentiment analysis are primarily topic-focused. They are designed to track sentiment around brands, entities, or other topics and subtopics in a domain (Lange and Sethi, 2011; Lakkaraju and Sethi, 2012; Albright and Lakkaraju, 2011). Domain-independent taxonomies have a second function. In addition to performing topic-focused tasks, they can be set up to perform sentiment analysis at the document level, classifying the whole document as positive, negative, or neutral. In this task all sentiment expressions are taken into account, rather than only those which are related to the tracked topic. This second function is becoming increasingly important. It allows for a broader perspective that is complementary to topic-focused opinion mining.

We participated in both subtask A and B of SemEval-2013 Task 2: Sentiment Analysis in Twitter (Wilson et al., 2013) with an adaptation of our existing system. For task B, identifying the overall sentiment of a tweet, our taxonomy mainly needed some fine-tuning to specifically accommodate Twitter data. (Normally tweets only make up a small part of the data we work with.) We also made a few adaptations to focus entirely on document level sentiment, whereas originally the main focus of our system was on tracking sentiment around products. For task A, identifying the sentiment of ambiguous phrases in a tweet, a few more modifications were needed.

Our system is entirely rule-based, and the rules are hand-written. In some cases, statistical text mining approaches are used for the discovery of topics and terms to facilitate rule writing. Our sentiment analysis software does offer a statistical component, but our experience is that purely rule-based models work better for our typical sentiment analysis tasks.

Advantages of rules are that problems observed in the output can be targeted directly, and the model can become more and more refined over time. Also, they allow for simple customization. In our brand-centered work, we customize our taxonomies for one or more brands that we want to track. When we build a taxonomy for a new domain, we build upon work we have done before in other domains. The assignment of sentiment to certain phrases can be sensitive to context where it needs to be. The canceled task C, identifying sentiment related to a topic, could have been approached successfully with a rule-based approach, as our rules are specifically designed to connect sentiment to targeted topics.

Section 2 describes the basic architecture of our system, followed by a section on related work. Then sections 4 and 5 describe the adaptations made for

*Second Joint Conference on Lexical and Computational Semantics (*SEM), Volume 2: Seventh International Workshop on Semantic Evaluation (SemEval 2013)*, pages 513–519, Atlanta, Georgia, June 14-15, 2013.

each subtask and present the results. This is followed by a more general discussion of our approach in the light of these results in section 6, and the conclusion in section 7.

2 The base system

The datasets we normally use for the development of our taxonomies include blogs, forums, news, and Twitter. When developing a domain-specific taxonomy, we collect data for that particular domain, e.g. Banking, Retail, Hospitality. We build the taxonomy with the terms we encounter in those documents, and test on a new set of documents. The Domain Independent taxonomy started out as the common base derived from several of these taxonomies, and was then built out and tested using a wider range of English-language documents. Since we used some other tweets in the development of the original system, our submission is considered unconstrained.

Our rules are patterns that match words or sequences of words, which makes our approach essentially lexicon-based. Matching occurs left-to-right and longer matches take precedence over shorter ones. The top level rules in our sentiment taxonomy are set up to recognize positive and negative word-sequences. There is also a set of 'neutral' rules at that level that block the assignment of positive or negative sentiment in certain cases.

A positive or negative sequence can consist of a single word from the positive or negative word-lists, or a spelled out phrase from the positive or negative phrase-lists. Alternatively, it can be built up out of multiple components, for example an emphatic modifier and a sentiment term, or a negation and a sentiment term. We call these sequences Positive and Negative 'Contexts', since they are contexts for the topic-terms that we normally track.

Documents are preprocessed by an in-house POS-tagger. Rules can require a word to have a particular part of speech.

The words in the word-list, or in any of the other rules, can be marked with an '@'-sign to enable morphological expansion, and in that case they will match any of the forms in their paradigm. For example 'love@' will match *love*, *loves*, *loved*, and *loving*. This functionality is supported by a morphological dictionary that links these forms to their stem.

The rules are organized into lists that represent useful concepts, which can be referred to in other rules as a means of abstraction. For example the rule:

_def{Negation} _def{PositiveAdjectives}

matches phrases that are composed of a negation (as defined in the list named *Negation*) and a positive adjective (as defined in the list named *PositiveAdjectives*). *Negation* includes rules like 'hasn't been', 'doesnt'[sic], 'not exactly the most', etc., and *PositiveAdjectives* contains a rule that matches words in *PositiveWords* if they are also tagged as adjectives. For efficiency reasons the dependencies cannot be circular, hence not allowing for recursion.

Distance rules can be used to capture a longer span, matching a specified pattern at the beginning and at the end, including arbitrary intervening words up to a specified number. They can also be used to make matching a term dependent on specified terms in the context. For example,

(SENT, (DIST_4, "_a{_def{HigherIsBetter}}", "_a{_def{Lowering}}"))

will capture phrases that say a company's profit (*HigherIsBetter*) went down (*Lowering*). The SENT-operator prevents matching across sentence boundaries.

(ORDDIST_7, "_def{PositiveContext}", "_a{_def{PositiveAmbig}}")

will capture ambiguous positive expressions when they follow an unambiguously positive sequence within a distance of 7 words.

This ensemble of lists and rules has grown relatively organically, and is motivated by the data we encounter. We introduce new distinctions when we feel it will make a difference in terms of results, or sometimes for ease of development and maintenance.

Usually each sentiment expression has the same weight, and one positive and one negative expression cancel each other out. However at the top level we can introduce weights, and we have done so in this model. We have created lists of weak positive and negative expressions, and we gave those very

Positive:

- (ORDDIST_2, "_a{exceed@}", "_a{expectation@}")
- :Pro could not be happier
- blown away by
- _def{Negation} want@ it to end
- above and beyond
- break@ down barriers
- can't go wrong with
- dying to _def{Consume}
- save@ me _def{Money}
- (ALIGNED, "_c{treat@}", ":N")

Negative:

- _def{Negation} find _def{NounPhrases} _def{PositivePhrases}
- (SENT, (ORDDIST_7, "_a{disappointed that}", "_a{_def{PositivePhrases}}"))
- I would have loved
- _def{Negation} accept@
- breach of _def{PositiveWords}
- _def{Money} magically disappears
- lack of training
- make@ no sense
- subject@ me to
- fun dealing with

Figure 1: Examples of rules for positive and negative phrases and patterns.

low weights, so that they would only matter if there were no regular-strength expressions present. We limited some of those weak sentiment rules to subtask A only, but they clearly helped with recall there.

Negations in the default case turn positives into negatives and negatives into neutrals. In addition to negations we also have sentiment reversers, which turn negatives into positives. Simple negations normally scope over a right-adjacent word or phrase, for example a noun phrase or a verb. A special class of clausal negations (*I don't think that*) by approximation take scope over a clause.

This system contains roughly 2500 positive words and 2000 positive phrases, and roughly 7500 negative words and 3000 negative phrases. Some examples are given in Figure 1. The neutral list also contains about 2000 rules. Other helper lists such as *Negation*, *EmphaticModifiers*, and *Money* typically contain about a hundred rules each.

A system like this takes about six to eight weeks to build for a new language. This requires a developer who is already familiar with the methodology, and assumes existing support for the language, including a morphological dictionary and a part-of-speech tagger.

3 Related work

In tasks that are not topic-related, purely rule-based models are rare, although the winning system of SemEval-2010 Task 18 (Wu and Jin, 2010), somewhat similar to task A, was rule-based (Yang and Liu, 2010). Liu (2010) suggests that more rule-based work may be called for. However, there are many other systems with a substantial rule-based component (Nasukawa and Yi, 2003; Choi and Cardie, 2008; Prabowo and Thelwall, 2009; Wilson et al., 2005). Systems commonly have some rules in place that account for the effect of negation (Wiegand et al., 2010) and modifiers. Sentiment lexicons are widely used, but mainly contain single words (Baccianella et al., 2010; Taboada et al., 2011). For topic-related tasks, rule-based systems are a bit more common (Ding et al., 2008).

4 Task A

Task A was to assign sentiment to a target in context. The target in isolation would often be ambiguous. It was a novel challenge to adapt our model for this subtask.

Since we normally track sentiment around specific topics, we can usually afford to ignore highly ambiguous phrases. Typical examples of this are ambiguous emoticons and comments like *no joke* at the end a sentence, or directly following it. When these are used and could be disambiguated, usually there is a less ambiguous term available that occurs closer to the topic-term that we are interested in. (In some cases we do use the topic as disambiguating context.)

Also, we generally place slightly more emphasis on precision than on recall, assuming that with enough data the important trends will emerge, even if we ignore some of the unclear cases and outliers. This makes the output cleaner and more pleasant to work with for follow-up analysis.

4.1 Model adaptations and processing

We adapted our model to task A by introducing lists of ambiguous positive and negative terms that were then disambiguated in context, e.g. if there was another sentiment term of a specified polarity nearby. We also added some larger patterns that included an ambiguous term, but as a whole had a much clearer polarity. Below are some examples of rules for the word *like*, which is highly ambiguous in English.

1. (ALIGNED, "_c{like@}", ":V") (pos)
2. likes (pos)
3. I like (pos)
4. like magic (pos)
5. give it a "like" (pos)
6. kinda like it (weakpos)
7. doesn't seem like (hypothetical)
8. How can you like (neg)
9. don't like (neg)
10. like to pretend (neg)
11. treated like a number (neg)
12. Is it like (neutral)
13. a bit like (neutral)
14. the likes of (neutral)

A seemingly obvious rule for *like* is (1), restricting it to usage as a verb. However, disambiguating *like* is a difficult task for the tagger too, and the result is not always correct. Therefore this rule is a fall-back case, when none of the longer rules apply. Inflected forms such as (2) are pretty safe, with a few exceptions, which can be caught by neutralizing rules, such as (14). The hypothetical case, (7), is not used in task A, but it is in task B.

A potential issue for our results on this task is that our system only returns the longest match. So in a sentence such as '*I didn't like it*', if you ask people to annotate *like*, they may say it is positive, whereas the longer phrase *didn't like* is negative. In the output of our system, *like* will only be part of a negative sequence. The information that it was originally recognized as a positive word cannot be retrieved at the output level.

We found that the annotators for task A were in general much more liberal in assigning sentiment than we normally are. We made major gains by removing some of our neutralizing rules, for example those that neutralize sentiment in hypothetical contexts, and by classifying negations that were not part of a larger recognized phrase as weak negatives.

The annotations in the development data were sometimes confusing (see also section 6). We had some difficulty in figuring out when certain terms such as *hope* or *miss you* should be considered positive and when negative. The verb *apologize* turned out to be annotated sometimes positive and sometimes negative in near identical tweets.

The test items were processed as follows:

1. run the sentiment model on the text (tweet/SMS)
2. identify the target phrase as a character span
3. collect detected sentiment that overlaps with the target phrase
   (a) if there is no overlapping sentiment expression, the sentiment is neutral
   (b) if there is exactly one overlapping sentiment expression, that expression determines the sentiment
   (c) if there is more than one sentiment expression that overlaps with the target, compute which sentiment has more weight (and in case of a draw, assign neutral)

4.2 Results

We get a higher precision for positive and negative sentiment on task A than any of the other teams, but we generally under-predict sentiment. Precision on neutral sentiment is very low. Detecting neutral phrases did not seem to be a very important goal in the final version of this task, though. The results of our predictions on the Twitter portion of the data are shown in Figure 2.

These results are slightly different from what we submitted, as we did not realize at the time of submission that the encoding of the text was different in the test data than it had been in the previously released data. The submitted results are included in the summarizing Table 1 at the end of the discussion section.

Some targets are easily missed. We do not have a good coverage of hashtags yet, for example. We incorporate frequent misspellings that are common in Twitter and SMS. However, we have no general strategy in place to systematically recognize unconventionally spelled words (Eisenstein, 2013). For

gs \ pred	positive	negative	neutral	
positive	1821	77	888	2734
negative	47	1091	403	1541
neutral	11	6	143	160
	1879	990	1382	4435

class	precision	recall	f-score
positive	0.9691	0.6661	0.7895
negative	0.9293	0.7080	0.8037
neutral	0.1035	0.8938	0.1855
average(pos and neg)			**0.7966**

Figure 2: Confusion table and scores on task **A**, tweets

a project that processes Twitter data it would also make sense to periodically scan for new hashtags and add them to the rules if they carry sentiment. However, a sentiment lexicon is never quite complete.

Therefore we experimented with a guessing component. If we do not detect any sentiment in the target sequence, we let our model make a guess, based on the overall sentiment it assigns to the document, assuming that an ambiguous target overall is more likely to be positive in a positive context and negative in a negative context. (Note that this is different from our disambiguation rules, which only apply to explicitly listed items.) This gives us substantial gains on this subtask (Figure 3). However, this may not hold up in a similar task where there are more neutral instances than there were here, as we see a decrease in precision on positive and negative.

gs \ pred	positive	negative	neutral	
positive	2147	230	357	2734
negative	137	1249	155	1541
neutral	50	33	77	160
	2334	1512	589	4435

class	precision	recall	f-score
positive	0.9199	0.7853	0.8473
negative	0.8261	0.8105	0.8182
neutral	0.1307	0.4813	0.2056
average(pos and neg)			**0.8327**

Figure 3: Confusion table and scores on task **A**, tweets, with guessing

5 Task B

Task B was to predict the overall sentiment of a tweet. This was much closer to the task our taxonomy is designed for, and yet it turned out to be different in subtle ways.

5.1 Model adaptations and processing

We quickly found that running the model as we had adapted it for subtask A over-predicted sentiment on subtask B. We therefore put most of our neutralizing rules back in place for this subtask, and restricted a subset of the weak sentiment terms to subtask A only. We disabled the mechanism that helped us catch ambiguous terms in subtask A (see section 4.1).

For processing we used our standard method, comparing the added weights of the positive and of the negative sequences found. The highest score wins. In case of a draw, the document is classified as neutral. 'Unclassified' (no sentiment terms found) also maps to neutral for this task. A confidence score is computed, but not used here.

5.2 Results

Our system compares positively to those of the other teams. Originally we were in 3rd place as a team on the Twitter data. After correcting for the encoding problem we rise to second (assuming the other teams did not have the same problem). Among unconstrained systems only, we are first on tweets and second on SMS. The results, after the correction, are shown in Figure 4. As for task A, the original results are included in the final summarizing Table 1.

gs \ pred	positive	negative	neutral	
positive	1188	88	296	1572
negative	66	373	162	601
neutral	408	202	1030	1640
	1662	663	1488	3813

class	precision	recall	f-score
positive	0.7148	0.7557	0.7347
negative	0.5626	0.6206	0.5902
neutral	0.6922	0.6280	0.6586
average(pos and neg)			**0.6624**

Figure 4: Confusion table and scores on task **B**, tweets

6 Discussion

We modified an existing rule-based system for SemEval Task 2. While the development of this existing system was a considerable time investment, the modifications for the two SemEval subtasks took no more than about 2 person-weeks in total. The models used in task A and B have a large common base, and our rule-based approach measures up well against other systems. This shows that if the work is done once, it can be re-used, modified, and refined.

As mentioned in section 4.1, the annotations did not always seem consistent. The guidelines did not ask the annotators to keep in mind a particular task or purpose for their annotations. However, the correct annotation of a tweet or fragment can vary depending on the purpose of the annotation. Non-arbitrary choices have to be made as to what counts as sentiment: *Do you try to identify cases of implicit sentiment? Do you count cases of quoted or reported '3rd-party'-sentiment? ...* Ultimately it depends on what you are interested in: *Do you want to: -track sentiment around certain topics? -know how authors are feeling? -assess the general mood? -track distressing versus optimistic messages in the news? ...* While manual rule writing allows us to choose a consistent strategy, it was not obvious what the optimal strategy was in this SemEval task.

There were considerable differences in annotation strategy between task A and task B, which shared the same tweets. The threshold for detecting sentiment appeared to be considerably lower in task A than in task B. This suggests that different choices had been made. These choices probably reflect how the annotators perceived the tasks.

In our core business, we primarily track sentiment around brands. One of the choices we made was to also include good and bad news about the brand (such as that the company's stock went up or down) where no explicit sentiment is expressed, because the circulation of such messages reflects on the reputation of the brand. (Liu (2010) points out that a lot of sentiment is implicit.) In task B, we noticed that 'newsy' tweets had a tendency to be annotated as neutral. We did not have the time to thoroughly adapt our model for that interpretation.

Both manually annotating training data for supervised machine learning and using training data for manual rule writing require a lot of work. Both can be crowd-sourced to a large extent if the process is made simple enough, and the instructions are clear enough. All methods that use lists of sentiment terms benefit from automatically extracting such terms from a corpus (Qiu et al., 2009; Wiebe and Riloff, 2005). As those methods become more sophisticated, the work of rule writers becomes easier. Since the correct annotation depends on the task at hand, and there are many different choices that can be made, annotated data can be hard to reuse for a slightly different task than the one for which it was created. In rule-based models it is easier to leverage earlier work and to slightly modify the model for a new task. Both the rules and the model's decision-making process are human-interpretable.

Table 1 (next page) summarizes our results on the various portions of the task, and under different conditions. The results on SMS-data are consistently lower than their counterparts on tweets, but they follow the same pattern. We conclude that the model generalizes to SMS, but not perfectly. This is not surprising, since we have never looked at SMS-data before, and the genre does appear to have some idiosyncrasies.

7 Conclusion

Our model is essentially a highly phrasal sentiment lexicon. Ways of defining slightly more abstract patterns keep the amount of work and the number of rules manageable. The model is applied through pattern matching on text, and returns a sentiment prediction based on the number of positive and negative expressions found, based on the sum of their weights. This is not mediated by any machine learning.

Slightly different versions of this system were employed in subtasks A and B. It turned out to be a strong competitor in Task 2 of SemEval-2013, especially on subtask B, where it scored in the top three.

References

Russell Albright and Praveen Lakkaraju. 2011. Combining knowledge and data mining to understand sentiment: A practical assessment of approaches. Technical report, SAS White Paper, January.

	Task A Twitter		Task A SMS		Task B Twitter		Task B SMS	
	F-score	rank	F-score	rank	F-score	rank	F-score	rank
Submitted	0.7489	*3 of 7*	0.7283	*4 of 7*	0.6486	***1 of 15***	0.5910	***2 of 15***
		13 of 23		*11 of 19*		*3 of 34*		*5 of 29*
After fixing encoding	0.7966	*3 of 7*	0.7454	*3 of 7*	0.6624	***1 of 15***	0.6014	***1 of 15***
		11 of 23		*8 of 19*		***2 of 34***		*4 of 29*
With guessing	0.8327	*(2 of 7)*	0.7840	*(2 of 7)*	NA		NA	
		(8 of 23)		*(7 of 19)*				

Table 1: Summary of results. The first rank indication is relative to the other systems in the unconstrained category. The second is relative to the total number of participating teams (by highest scoring system).

Stefano Baccianella, Andrea Esuli, and Fabrizio Sebastiani. 2010. Sentiwordnet 3.0: An enhanced lexical resource for sentiment analysis and opinion mining. In *Proceedings of the 7th conference on International Language Resources and Evaluation (LREC10), Valletta, Malta, May*.

Yejin Choi and Claire Cardie. 2008. Learning with compositional semantics as structural inference for subsentential sentiment analysis. In *Proceedings of the Conference on Empirical Methods in Natural Language Processing*, pages 793–801. Association for Computational Linguistics.

Xiaowen Ding, Bing Liu, and Philip S Yu. 2008. A holistic lexicon-based approach to opinion mining. In *Proceedings of the international conference on Web search and web data mining*, pages 231–240. ACM.

Jacob Eisenstein. 2013. What to do about bad language on the internet. In *Proc. of NAACL*.

Praveen Lakkaraju and Saratendu Sethi. 2012. Correlating the analysis of opinionated texts using sas text analytics with application of sabermetrics to cricket statistics. In *Proceedings of SAS Global Forum 2012*, number 136.

Kathy Lange and Saratendu Sethi. 2011. What are people saying about your company, your products, or your brand? In *Proceedings of SAS Global Forum 2011*, number 158.

Bing Liu. 2010. Sentiment analysis and subjectivity. *Handbook of natural language processing*, 2:568.

Tetsuya Nasukawa and Jeonghee Yi. 2003. Sentiment analysis: Capturing favorability using natural language processing. In *Proceedings of the 2nd international conference on Knowledge capture*, pages 70–77. ACM.

Rudy Prabowo and Mike Thelwall. 2009. Sentiment analysis: A combined approach. *Journal of Informetrics*, 3(2):143–157.

Guang Qiu, Bing Liu, Jiajun Bu, and Chun Chen. 2009. Expanding domain sentiment lexicon through double propagation. In *Proceedings of the 21st international jont conference on Artifical intelligence*, pages 1199–1204.

Maite Taboada, Julian Brooke, Milan Tofiloski, Kimberly Voll, and Manfred Stede. 2011. Lexicon-based methods for sentiment analysis. *Computational linguistics*, 37(2):267–307.

Janyce Wiebe and Ellen Riloff. 2005. Creating subjective and objective sentence classifiers from unannotated texts. In *Computational Linguistics and Intelligent Text Processing*, pages 486–497. Springer.

Michael Wiegand, Alexandra Balahur, Benjamin Roth, Dietrich Klakow, and Andrés Montoyo. 2010. A survey on the role of negation in sentiment analysis. In *Proceedings of the workshop on negation and speculation in natural language processing*, pages 60–68. Association for Computational Linguistics.

Theresa Wilson, Paul Hoffmann, Swapna Somasundaran, Jason Kessler, Janyce Wiebe, Yejin Choi, Claire Cardie, Ellen Riloff, and Siddharth Patwardhan. 2005. Opinionfinder: A system for subjectivity analysis. In *Proceedings of HLT/EMNLP on Interactive Demonstrations*, pages 34–35. Association for Computational Linguistics.

Theresa Wilson, Zornitsa Kozareva, Preslav Nakov, Alan Ritter, Sara Rosenthal, and Veselin Stoyanov. 2013. SemEval-2013 task 2: Sentiment analysis in twitter. In *Proceedings of the 7th International Workshop on Semantic Evaluation*. Association for Computational Linguistics.

Yunfang Wu and Peng Jin. 2010. Semeval-2010 task 18: Disambiguating sentiment ambiguous adjectives. In *Proceedings of the 5th International Workshop on Semantic Evaluation*, pages 81–85. Association for Computational Linguistics.

Shi-Cai Yang and Mei-Juan Liu. 2010. Ysc-dsaa: An approach to disambiguate sentiment ambiguous adjectives based on saaol. In *Proceedings of the 5th International Workshop on Semantic Evaluation*, pages 440–443. Association for Computational Linguistics.

CodeX: Combining an SVM Classifier and Character N-gram Language Models for Sentiment Analysis on Twitter Text

Qi Han, Junfei Guo and **Hinrich Schütze**
Institute for Nature Language Processing
University of Stuttgart
Stuttgart, Germany
{hanqi, guojf}@ims.uni-stuttgart.de

Abstract

This paper briefly reports our system for the SemEval-2013 Task 2: sentiment analysis in Twitter. We first used an SVM classifier with a wide range of features, including bag of word features (unigram, bigram), POS features, stylistic features, readability scores and other statistics of the tweet being analyzed, domain names, abbreviations, emoticons in the Twitter text. Then we investigated the effectiveness of these features. We also used character n-gram language models to address the problem of high lexical variation in Twitter text and combined the two approaches to obtain the final results. Our system is robust and achieves good performance on the Twitter test data as well as the SMS test data.

1 Introduction

The challenge of the SemEval-2013 Task 2 (Task B) is the "Message Polarity Classification" (Wilson et al., 2013). Specifically, the task was to classify whether a given message has positive, negative or neutral sentiment; for messages conveying both positive and negative sentiment, whichever is stronger should be chosen.

In recent years, text messaging and microblogging such as tweeting has gained its popularity. Since these short messages are often used not only to discuss facts but also to share opinions and sentiments, sentiment analysis on this type of data has lately become interesting. However, some features of this type of data make natural language processing challenging. For example, the messages are usually short and the language used can be very informal, with misspellings, creative spellings, slang, URLs and special abbreviations. Some research has already been done attempting to address these problems, to enable sentiment analysis on this type of data, in particular on Twitter data, and even to use the outcome of sentiment analysis to make predictions (Jansen et al., 2009; Barbosa and Feng, 2010; Bifet and Frank, 2010; Davidov et al., 2010; Jiang et al., 2011; Pak and Paroubek, 2010; Saif et al., 2012; Tumasjan et al., 2010).

As the research mentioned above, our system used a machine learning based approach for sentiment analysis. Our system combines results from an SVM classifier using a wide range of features as well as votes derived from character n-gram language models to do the final prediction.

The rest of this paper is organized as follows. Section 2 describes the features used for the SVM classifier. Section 3 describes how the votes from character n-gram language models were derived. Section 4 describes the details of our method. And finally section 5 presents the results.

2 Features

We pre-processed the tweets as follows: i) tokenized the tweets using a tokenizer suitable for Twitter data, which, for example, recognize emoticons and hashtags; ii) replaced all URLs with the token *twitterurl*; iii) replaced all Twitter usernames with the token *@twitterusername*; iv) converted all tokens into lower case; v) replaced all sequences of repeated characters by three characters, for example, convert *gooooood* to *goood*, this way we recognize

*Second Joint Conference on Lexical and Computational Semantics (*SEM), Volume 2: Seventh International Workshop on Semantic Evaluation (SemEval 2013)*, pages 520–524, Atlanta, Georgia, June 14-15, 2013. ©2013 Association for Computational Linguistics

the emphasized usage of the word; vi) expanded abbreviations with a dictionary,[1] which we will refer to as *noslang* dictionary; vii) appended *_neg* to all words from one position before a negation word to the next punctuation mark.

We represented each given tweet using 6 feature families:

- **Lexical features** (UG, BG): Number of times each unigram appears in the tweet (*UG*); number of times each bigram appears in the tweet (*BG*).
- **POS features** (POS_U, POS_B): Number of times each POS appears in the tweet divided by number of tokens of that tweet (*POS_U*); number of times each POS bigram appears in the tweet (*POS_B*). To tag the tweet we used the *ark-twitter-nlp tagger*.[2]
- **Statistical features** (STAT): Various readability scores (ARI, Flesch Reading Ease, RIX, LIX, Coleman Liau Index, SMOG Index, Gunning Fog Index, Flesch-Kincaid Grade Level) of the tweet; some simple statistics of the tweet (average count of words per sentence, complex word count, syllable count, sentence count, word count, char count). We calculated the statistics and scores after pre-processing step vi). We then normalized these scores so that they had mean 0 and standard deviation 1.
- **Stylistic features** (STY): Number of times an emoticon appears in the tweet, number of words which are written in all capital letters, number of words containing characters repeated consecutively more than three times, number of words containing characters repeated consecutively more than four times. We calculated these features after pre-processing step i). We used the binarized and the logarithmically scaled version of these features.
- **Abbreviation features** (ABB): For every term in the *noslang* dictionary, we checked whether it was present in the tweet or not and used this as a feature.
- **URL features** (URL): We expanded the URLs in the Twitter text and collected all the domain names which the URLs in the training set point to, and used them as binary features.

Feature sets *UG*, *BG*, *POS_U*, *POS_B* are common features for sentiment analysis (Pang et al., 2002). Remus (2011) showed that incorporating readability measures as features can improve sentence-level subjectivity classification. Stylistic features have also been used in sentiment analysis on Twitter data (Go et al., 2010). Some abbreviations express sentiment which is not apparent from word level. For example *lolwtime*, which means *laughing out loud with tears in my eyes*, expresses positive sentiment overall, but this does not follow directly at the sentiment of individual words, so the feature set *ABB* might be helpful. Finally, we conjecture that a tweet including an URL pointing to `youtube.com` is more likely to be subjective than a tweet including an URL pointing to a news website.

3 Integrating votes from language models based on character n-grams

Language Models can be used for text classification tasks. Since the goal of the SemEval-2013 Task 2 (Task B) is to classify each tweet into one of the three classes: *positive*, *negative* or *neutral*, a language model approach can be used.

Emoticon-smoothed language models have been used to do Twitter sentiment analysis (Liu et al., 2012). The language models used there were based on words. However, there is evidence (Aisopos et al., 2012; Raaijmakers and Kraaij, 2008) showing that super-word character n-gram features can be quite effective for sentiment analysis on short informal data. This is because noise and mis-spellings tend to have smaller impact on substring patterns than on word patterns. Our system used language models based on character n-grams to improve the performance of sentiment analysis on tweets.

For every tweet we constructed 3 sequences of character-trigrams and 4 sequences of character-four-grams. For instance, the tweet `"Hello World!"` would have 7 corresponding substring representations:

`<s><s>H ell o_W orl d!</s>,`
`<s>He llo _Wo rld !</s></s>,`

[1] `http://www.noslang.com`

[2] `http://www.ark.cs.cmu.edu/TweetNLP/`

```
Hel lo␣ Wor ld!,
<s><s><s>H ello ␣Wor ld!</s>
<s><s>He llo␣ Worl d!</s></s>,
<s>Hel lo␣W orld !</s></s></s>,
Hell o␣Wo rld!
```

where <s> means start of a sentence, </s> means end of a sentence, ␣ means whitespace. Using the corresponding sequences of character-trigrams from all positive tweets in training set we trained a language model LM_3^+. To train the language model we used Chen and Goodman's modified Kneser-Ney discounting for N-grams from the SRILM toolkit (Stolcke, 2002). Given a new sequence of character-trigrams derived from a positive tweet, it should give a lower perplexity value than a language model trained on sequences of character-trigrams from negative tweets.

In this way we obtained 6 language models: LM_3^- from character-trigram sequences of negative tweets, LM_3^N from character-trigram sequences of neutral tweets, LM_3^+ from character-trigram sequences of positive tweets, LM_4^- from character-four-grams sequences of negative tweets, LM_4^N from character-four-gram sequences of neutral tweets, LM_4^+ from character-four-gram sequences of positive tweets.

For every new tweet, we first obtain the 7 corresponding substring representations. Then for each substring representation, we calculate 3 votes from the language models. For instance, for a sequence of character-trigrams, we first calculate three perplexity valuesP_3^-, P_3^N, P_3^+ using language models LM_3^-, LM_3^N, LM_3^+ then produce votes according to the following discretization function:

$$vote(LM_n^x, LM_n^y) = \begin{cases} 1 & \text{if } P_n^x \geq P_n^y; \\ -1 & \text{else.} \end{cases}$$

where $n \in \{3, 4\}$ is the length of the character n-gram, $x, y \in \{-, +, N\}$ are class labels and P_n^x, P_n^y are the corresponding perplexity values. In this way we obtain 21 votes for every tweet. However, in the final classification, every sentence got 42 votes, of which 21 were derived from bigram language models of the substrings and 21 were from trigram language models of these substrings.

Feature Sets	Accuracy
UG,BG,POS_U,POS_B,STAT,STY,ABB,URL	0.692
BG,POS_U,POS_B,STAT,STY,ABB,URL	0.641
POS_U,POS_B,STAT,STY,ABB,URL	0.579
POS_U,STAT,STY,ABB,URL	0.564
STAT,STY,ABB,URL	0.524
STY,ABB,URL	0.474
STY,URL	0.454
URL	0.441

Table 1: Cross validation average accuracy with different feature sets. we started with all 8 feature sets and removed feature sets one by one, where we always first removed the feature set that resulted in the biggest drop in accuracy.

4 Methods

In this section we describe the methods used by our system.

Firstly, we did feature selection on all the features described in Section 2. Using *Mutual Information* (Shannon and Weaver, 1949) and 10-fold cross validation we chose the top 13,500 features. Using these features we trained an SVM classifier with the training data. As the implementation of the SVM classifier we used *liblinear* (Fan et al., 2008). The SVM classifier was then used to produce initial predictions for messages in the development set, the Twitter test set and the SMS test set.

Then, we represented every message in the development set, the Twitter test set and the SMS test set using the 42 votes we described in Section 3 together with the predictions of the SVM classifier we described above. Using the Bagging algorithm from the WEKA machine learning toolkit (Hall et al., 2009) and the development set data, we trained a new classifier and used this classifier for the final prediction on Twitter test data and SMS test data.

5 Results

5.1 Feature analysis

To study the effectiveness of different features, we started with all 8 feature sets and removed feature sets one by one, where we always first removed the feature set that resulted in the biggest drop in accuracy. We did 10 fold cross validation on training set

Feature Sets	Accuracy
POS_U, POS_B, STAT, STY, ABB, URL	0.579
POS_B, STY, ABB, URL	0.571
POS_U, STY, ABB, URL	0.557
STAT, STY, ABB, URL	0.524
STY, ABB, URL	0.474

Table 2: Cross validation average accuracy with further combination of feature sets.

	Accuracy	F1 (pos, neg)
Majority Baseline	0.4123	0.2919
SVM Classifier	0.6612	0.5414
SVM + LM Votes	0.6457	0.5384

Table 3: Overall accuracy and average F1 score for positive and negative classes on Twitter test data.

and used average accuracy as a metric.

As we can see from Table 1, lexical features were the most important features – they counted for more than 0.11 loss of accuracy when removed from the features. POS features and statistical features were also important, POS bigrams more so than POS unigrams. Stylistic, abbreviation and URL features, on the contrary, seem to be only of moderate usefulness.

To further investigate the relationship between the feature sets POS_U, POS_B and STAT, we did additional experiments. From Table 2, we can see that removing all three feature sets caused a decrease in accuracy to 0.47, including just one feature set POS_B, POS_U or STAT resulted in accuracy above 0.57, 0.55 and 0.52 respectively. This shows that all three feature sets were quite effective and POS_B was most useful. However, adding all of the three feature sets only caused an increase in accuracy to 0.579, which suggests that they were highly correlated.

	Accuracy	F1 (pos, neg)
Majority Baseline	0.2350	0.1902
SVM Classifier	0.6504	0.5811
SVM + LM Votes	0.6418	0.5670

Table 4: Overall accuracy and average F1 score for positive and negative classes on SMS test data.

5.2 Effectiveness of language model features

To evaluate the effectiveness of features derived from language models of character n-grams, we compared the performance of our SVM classifier and that of the classifier combining the SVM classifier results and language model features.[3] We performed our experiments on both of the Twitter test data and the SMS test data. The results in Table 3 and Table 4 suggested that in our current setup, language model features were not very helpful.

Table 3 and Table 4 also show that our system improved the performance greatly compared to Majority baseline system,[4]. Compared with other participants in the SemEval-2013 Task 2, our system achieved average performance on Twitter test data. However, it has been the ninth best out of all 48 systems for the performance on SMS test data. This shows that our system can be easily adapted to different contexts without a big drop in performance. One reason for that might be that we did not use any sentiment lexicon developed specifically for Twitter data and we used high level features like the statistical features and POS features for our classification.

6 Conclusion

This paper briefly reports our system designed for the SemEval-2013 Task 2: sentiment analysis in Twitter. We first used an SVM classifier with a wide range of features. We found that simple statistics of the tweets, for example word count or readability scores, can help in sentiment analysis on Twitter text.

We then used character n-gram language models to address the problem of high lexical variation in Twitter text and combined the two approaches to obtain the final results. Although in our current setup, features derived from character n-gram language models do not perform very well, they may benefit from a larger training data set.

Acknowledgments

This work was funded by DFG projects SFB 732. We would like to thank our colleagues at IMS.

[3] We accidentally used feature set POS_B two times in our representation, but it didn't change the results significantly.

[4] To be consistent with the evaluation metric, we chose the majority class of positive and negative classes.

References

Fotis Aisopos, George Papadakis, Konstantinos Tserpes, and Theodora Varvarigou. 2012. Content vs. context for sentiment analysis: a comparative analysis over microblogs. In *Proceedings of the 23rd ACM conference on Hypertext and social media*, HT '12, pages 187–96, New York, NY, USA. ACM.

Luciano Barbosa and Junlan Feng. 2010. Robust sentiment detection on twitter from biased and noisy data. In *Proceedings of the 23rd International Conference on Computational Linguistics: Posters*, COLING '10, pages 36–44, Stroudsburg, PA, USA. Association for Computational Linguistics.

Albert Bifet and Eibe Frank. 2010. Sentiment knowledge discovery in twitter streaming data. In *Proceedings of the 13th international conference on Discovery science*, DS'10, pages 1–15, Berlin, Heidelberg. Springer-Verlag.

Dmitry Davidov, Oren Tsur, and Ari Rappoport. 2010. Enhanced sentiment learning using twitter hashtags and smileys. In *Proceedings of the 23rd International Conference on Computational Linguistics: Posters*, COLING '10, pages 241–249, Stroudsburg, PA, USA. Association for Computational Linguistics.

Rong-En Fan, Kai-Wei Chang, Cho-Jui Hsieh, Xiang-Rui Wang, and Chih-Jen Lin. 2008. LIBLINEAR: a library for large linear classification. *J. Mach. Learn. Res.*, 9:1871–1874, June.

Alec Go, Richa Bhayani, and L. Huang. 2010. Exploiting the unique characteristics of tweets for sentiment analysis. Technical report, Technical Report, Stanford University.

Mark Hall, Eibe Frank, Geoffrey Holmes, Bernhard Pfahringer, Peter Reutemann, and Ian H. Witten. 2009. The WEKA data mining software: an update. *SIGKDD Explor. Newsl.*, 11(1):10–18, November.

Bernard J. Jansen, Mimi Zhang, Kate Sobel, and Abdur Chowdury. 2009. Twitter power: Tweets as electronic word of mouth. *J. Am. Soc. Inf. Sci. Technol.*, 60(11):2169–2188, November.

Long Jiang, Mo Yu, Ming Zhou, Xiaohua Liu, and Tiejun Zhao. 2011. Target-dependent twitter sentiment classification. In *Proceedings of the 49th Annual Meeting of the Association for Computational Linguistics: Human Language Technologies - Volume 1*, HLT '11, pages 151–160, Stroudsburg, PA, USA. Association for Computational Linguistics.

Kun-Lin Liu, Wu-Jun Li, and Minyi Guo. 2012. Emoticon smoothed language models for twitter sentiment analysis. In *Twenty-Sixth AAAI Conference on Artificial Intelligence*.

A. Pak and P. Paroubek. 2010. Twitter as a corpus for sentiment analysis and opinion mining. *LREC*.

Bo Pang, Lillian Lee, and Shivakumar Vaithyanathan. 2002. Thumbs up? sentiment classification using machine learning techniques. In *Proceedings of EMNLP*, pages 79–86.

Stephan Raaijmakers and Wessel Kraaij. 2008. A shallow approach to subjectivity classification. *Proceedings of ICWSM*, pages 216–217.

Robert Remus. 2011. Improving sentence-level subjectivity classification through readability measurement. May. Proceedings of the 18th Nordic Conference of Computational Linguistics NODALIDA 2011.

Hassan Saif, Yulan He, and Harith Alani. 2012. Semantic sentiment analysis of twitter. In Philippe Cudr-Mauroux, Jeff Heflin, Evren Sirin, Tania Tudorache, Jrme Euzenat, Manfred Hauswirth, Josiane Xavier Parreira, Jim Hendler, Guus Schreiber, Abraham Bernstein, and Eva Blomqvist, editors, *The Semantic Web ISWC 2012*, number 7649 in Lecture Notes in Computer Science, pages 508–524. Springer Berlin Heidelberg, January.

Claude E. Shannon and Warren Weaver. 1949. *Mathematical Theory of Communication*. University of Illinois Press.

Andreas Stolcke. 2002. SRILMAn extensible language modeling toolkit. In *In Proceedings of the 7th International Conference on Spoken Language Processing (ICSLP 2002*, page 901904.

Andranik Tumasjan, Timm O. Sprenger, Philipp G. Sandner, and Isabell M. Welpe. 2010. Predicting elections with twitter: What 140 characters reveal about political sentiment. *Proceedings of the Fourth International AAAI Conference on Weblogs and Social Media*.

Theresa Wilson, Zornitsa Kozareva, Preslav Nakov, Sara Rosenthal, Veselin Stoyanov, and Alan Ritter. 2013. SemEval-2013 task 2: Sentiment analysis in twitter. In *Proceedings of the International Workshop on Semantic Evaluation*, SemEval '13, June.

sielers : Feature Analysis and Polarity Classification of Expressions from Twitter and SMS Data

Harshit Jain, Aditya Mogadala and Vasudeva Varma
Search and Information Extraction Lab, IIIT-H
Hyderabad
India
harshit.jain@research.iiit.ac.in, aditya.m@research.iiit.ac.in,
vv@iiit.ac.in

Abstract

In this paper, we describe our system for the SemEval-2013 Task 2, Sentiment Analysis in Twitter. We formed features that take into account the context of the expression and take a supervised approach towards subjectivity and polarity classification. Experiments were performed on the features to find out whether they were more suited for subjectivity or polarity Classification. We tested our model for sentiment polarity classification on Twitter as well as SMS chat expressions, analyzed their F-measure scores and drew some interesting conclusions from them.

1 Introduction

In recent years there has been a huge growth in popularity of vaious social media microblogging platforms like Twitter. Users freely share their personal opinions on various events and entities on these platforms. However, while character constraints make sure the opinions are short and to the point, they also contribute to the noisy nature of Twitter data.

The contextual polarity of the phrase in which a particular instance of a word appears may be quite different from the word's prior polarity. Positive words are used in phrases expressing negative sentiments, or vice versa. Also, quite often words that are positive or negative out of context are neutral in context, meaning they are not even being used to express a sentiment. This is evident from the example of underlined phrase in the following tweet:

> *Lana Del Rey at Hammersmith Apollo in May... Very badly want tickets*

In a technique with large lexicon of words marked with their prior polarity, *badly* would have a negative score making the whole sentence with negative sentiment. Even if we perform phrase-level analysis for the phrase "*Very badly*", *Very* only acts as an intensifier for *badly* and the whole sentence is still marked negative. It's only when we look further from the underlined phrase that we realize that "*Very badly*" in the context of wanting something shows positive sentiment.

Early work on sentiment analysis is based on document-level analysis of reviews (Pang, B., and Lee, L., 2004). This approach isn't feasible for microblogging data due to the extremely small size of individual documents. The results on the effectiveness of part-of-speech features are mixed. While most regard POS features helpful in subjectivity classification (Barbosa, L. and Feng, J., 2010), some report very insignificant improvement on using them (Kouloumpis, E., Wilson, T. and Moore, J., 2011). However, most phrase-level approaches began with a large lexicon of words marked with their prior polarity (Kim, S. M., and Hovy, E., 2004; Hu, M., and Liu, B, 2004). Wilson, Wiebe and Hoffman (2005) sought to include contextual polarity in the foray by using various dependency relation based features for subjectivity and polarity classification. Our goal is to perform contextual sentiment polarity classification in the domain of noisy expressions from tweets and SMS messages.

2 Data

We use the annotated Twitter expressions provided by SemEval-2013 Task 2 (Wilson et al., 2013) or-

*Second Joint Conference on Lexical and Computational Semantics (*SEM), Volume 2: Seventh International Workshop on Semantic Evaluation (SemEval 2013)*, pages 525–529, Atlanta, Georgia, June 14-15, 2013.

ganizers for training our model. Each instance of the data contains an expression and its parent tweet. There are a total of 24939 tweet expressions in the training dataset and they are annotated into four classes:

- **Objective**: Expressions carrying no opinion by themselves or even in the context of their parent tweet.
- **Positive**: Expressions carrying positive sentiment in the context of the parent tweet.
- **Negative**: Expressions carrying negative sentiment in the context of the parent tweet.
- **Neutral**: Expressions carrying prior subjectivity but are rendered objective in the context of their parent tweet.

Two separate lexicons for emoticons and interjections having non-zero prior polarities were created. 47 Subjective emoticons were extracted from training data as well as from various popular chat services. 212 Subjective interjections were extracted from training data as well from Wiktionary[1].

We test our trained model on two separate test datasets provided by SemEval-2013 Task 2 organizers, 1) Twitter expressions and 2) SMS expressions.

2.1 Preprocessing

Data preprocessing consists of three steps: 1) Tokenization, 2) Part-of-Speech (POS) tagging, and 3) Normalization. For the first two steps we use Twitter NLP and Part-of-Speech Tagging system (Gimpel, K., et al., 2011). It is a Tokenizer and POS Tagger made for Twitter dataset and thus contains separate POS tags for hash-tags(*#*), at-mention(*@*), URLs and E-Mail addresses(*U*) and emoticons(*E*). The POS Tagger identifies common abbreviations and tags them accordingly. We use Twitter NLP and Part-of-Speech Tagging system for the SMS expressions too due to similar noisy nature of SMS data. For the normalization process, all upper case letters are converted to lower case, and instances of repeated characters are replaced by a repetition of two characters. This is done so that existing legal words having characters repeating two times aren't harmed. #hash-tags are stripped of the # character and then treated as a normal word/phrase, at-mention(@) denote the name of a person/organization and thus they are treated as proper noun and since URLs don't carry any sentiment, they are ignored in the expression. We expect the normalization process to aid in forming better features and in turn improving the performance of the system as a whole.

3 Features

We use three types of features for our classification experiments,

- Phrase Prior Polarity Features
- POS Tag Pattern Features
- Noisy data specific Features

Both Phrase Prior Polarity and POS Tag features are computed for the expression to be analyzed as well as, if available, two words [2] before and after the expression.

3.1 Phrase Prior Polarity Feature

Every expression in the dataset is represented by its aggregate positive and negative polarity score. Senti-Wordnet (Baccianella, S., Esuli, A., and Sebastiani, F., 2010), Emoticon Lexicon and an Interjection Lexicon are used to calculate these prior polarities. Bigrams and trigrams are identified by their presence in Senti-Wordnet. For each identified unigram, bigram or trigram, we compute the mean of all its subjective wordnet sense scores under the POS tag assigned to it. If a unigram word isn't present in Senti-Wordnet, its stemmed[3] form is searched keeping the original POS Tag. We perform negation detection by enabling a flag whenever a word occurring in negation list appears. The negation list consists of words like *no*, *not*, *never*, etc, as well all words ending with *-n't*. Negation words act as polarity reversers, for e.g., consider the following expression: *"not so sure"*. In a simple bag of words approach, *"not so sure"* wouldn't be classified as negative due to the presence of *sure*. To overcome this,

[1] http://en.wiktionary.org/wiki/Category:English_interjections

[2] The figure of two words was reached empirically upon trying various lengths.

[3] The stemmer used is Snowball Stemmer for English.

prior polarities of all words are reversed on the occurrence of a negation word. Some negation words such as *no*, *not*, *never*, also carry their own negative score (-1), in case no subjective word is found in the expression, their individual negative score is added to the aggregate prior polarity of the expression. Adjectives and adverbs are treated as polarity shifters. They either shift the prior polarities of nouns and verbs, or in case of objective nouns and verbs, contribute their own prior polarities to the expression, e.g., *"exceedingly slow"*, *"little truth"*, *"amazing car"*, etc.

On encountering any emoticon or interjection in the expression that is present in our lexicon, its corresponding score is added to the aggregate prior polarity of the expression.

Finally, both positive and negative prior polarities of the expression are normalized by the number of words in the expression after tokenization.

3.2 POS Tag Pattern Feature

Both Tweets and SMS messages are extremely short. Twitter is a social microblogging platform having just 140 character space for a tweet while SMS messages have little word length due to typing constraints on a mobile device. All the above factors contribute to the noisiness of data. Hence, it isn't enough to find prior polarities of n-grams occurring in the expression. We thus formed a heuristic technique of using POS tag patterns as features. POS tag patterns carry information regarding POS tags combined with the location of their occurrence in the expression as a feature. For e.g., the POS tag pattern for the expression *"not so sure"* in the tweet

> *@thehuwdavies you think the Boro will beat Swansea? I'm not so sure, December/January is when we implode*

will be *RRA*, where R = Adverb and A = Adjective.

3.3 Noisy data specific Features

Interjections and emoticons are useful indicators of subjectivity in a sentence. Even if many interjections or emoticons don't carry a defininte sentiment polarity, they do indicate that some sort of opinion from the user is available in the tweet or sms. Some examples of interjections and emoticons with no fixed prior polarity are, *"wow"*, *"oh my god"*, *":-o"*, etc.

4 Experiments and Results

Our goal for these experiments is two-fold. First, we want to evaluate the effectiveness of our features when using them for subjectivity classification as compared to sentiment polarity classification. Second, we want to evaluate and compare the performance of our learnt model when tested upon Twitter and SMS expression data. We use Naive Bayes classifier in Weka (Hall, M., et al., 2009) as the learning algorithm.

Feature Analysis between Subjectivity and Polarity Classification For our first set of experiments, we re-label all positive, negative and neutral expressions as subjective for subjectivity classification in the training dataset. For polarity classification we remove all objective expressions from the training dataset and perform 3-way classification between positive, negative and neutral expressions. In both cases we perform 10-fold cross validation on the training dataset. For subjectivity classification we have 24939 tweet expressions with 15565 objective and 9374 subjective expressions. Subjective expressions contain 5787 positive, 3131 negative and 456 neutral expressions. Table 1 shows the accuracy of subjectivity and sentiment polarity classification results and improvement due to each feature.

It is fairly evident from Table 1 that phrase prior polarity features are equally important for both subjectivity and sentiment polarity classification. The same however, doesn't completely hold true for the other two feature types. While POS Tag pattern features provide an improvement of 1.89% in subjectivity classification accuracy, they only provide a 0.64% increase in accuracy in polarity classification. Many inferences can be drawn from this result and a deeper analysis is required on POS tag patterns to prove that this wasn't a mere aberration. Emoticon and interjection feature too give lower improvement in accuracies during sentiment polarity classification (0.44%) as compared to subjectivity classification (0.83%). This, however, is expected since most common emoticons and interjections with prior polarities are already covered in the total score of the expression. Thus, the noisy data based binary features have significant contribution only when the emoticons and interjections aren't present in the lexicon. This implies that these binary features only

Features	Subjectivity	Polarity
f1	86.58	72.93
f1 + f2	88.47	73.57
f1 + f2 + f3	89.3	74.01
f1 + f2 + f3 - context	84.38	72.25

f1	:	Phrase Prior Polarity Features
f2	:	POS Tag Pattern Features
f3	:	Noisy Data Specific Features
context	:	Phrase Prior Polarity and POS Tag pattern features defined for 2 words before and after the expression

Table 1: Accuracies for all three features used for Subjectivity and Sentiment Polarity Classification.

Class	Precision	Recall	F-measure
positive	0.8120	0.8120	0.8120
negative	0.6477	0.7073	0.6762
neutral	0.3333	0.0375	0.0674

(a) Twitter expression data

Class	Precision	Recall	F-measure
positive	0.6823	0.8263	0.7475
negative	0.7520	0.6947	0.7222
neutral	0.0588	0.0063	0.0114

(b) SMS expression data

Table 2: Precision, Recall and F-measure scores for positive, negative and neutral classes computed on Twitter and SMS expressions data.

hint towards the expression being subjective. The *context* features, i.e., phrase prior polarity and POS tag pattern features defined for 2 words before and after the expression also carry more significance during subjectivity classification than in sentiment polarity classification.

Polarity Classification comparison for Twitter and SMS expression data For the second set of experiments comparing the performance of polarity classification in Twitter expressions and SMS expressions, we use the polarity classification model learnt in the above experiment. Tables 2(a) and 2(b) shows the precision, recall and F-measure scores for both Twitter and SMS expressions.

The polarity classification accuracies for Twitter and SMS expressions are 74.76% and 70.82%, respectively. Closer inspection of test data shows that SMS expressions exhibit more aggressive usage of abbreviations and slangs and are in general noisier than Twitter expressions. This is probably due to the fact that typing on a cellphone is more cumbersome than on a keyboard. The quantitative distribution of positive, negative and neutral classes in both datasets affects the F-measure scores of individual classes. This is evident from the difference in positive and negative F-measures of Twitter and SMS expressions data. In both datasets, neutral class F-measure is extremely low. This is partially expected due to the low quantity of neutral class expressions in Twitter (160/4435) and SMS (159/2334) data. Still, it seems that more fine-grained analysis of neutral expressions is required for better polarity classification accuracy.

Our method ranks 16th (F-measure: 0.7441) out of 28 participating systems for Twitter data and 12th (F-measure: 0.7348) out of 26 participating systems for SMS data. The best performing system have 0.8893(NRC-Canada) and 0.8837(GUMLTLT) averaged(positive, negative) F-measure score for Twitter and SMS data, respectively.

5 Conclusions

Our experiments on features show that phrase prior polarity features give good results for both subjectivity and polarity classification. POS tag pattern features, emoticon and interjection features, on the other hand, are better suited for subjectivity classification. A deeper analysis is required and various relational and dependency features should be identified and used to improve the performance of polarity classification. SMS expressions are noisier in general than Twitter expressions and thus the polarity classifier gives less accurate results for it. However, both of these datasets face problems common to the polarity classifier. More research is needed with a balanced dataset to understand various underlying relational causes for an expression to become neutral and to further confirm the conclusions of this paper.

References

Baccianella, Stefano, Andrea Esuli, and Fabrizio Sebastiani. 2010. Sentiwordnet 3.0: An enhanced lexical resource for sentiment analysis and opinion mining. *Proceedings of LREC*. Malta.

Barbosa, Luciano, and Junlan Feng. 2010. Robust sentiment detection on twitter from biased and noisy data. *Proceedings of Coling*. Beijing.

Gimpel, Kevin, Nathan Schneider, Brendan O'Connor, Dipanjan Das, Daniel Mills, Jacob Eisenstein, Michael Heilman, Dani Yogatama, Jeffrey Flanigan, and Noah A. Smith. 2011. Part-of-Speech Tagging for Twitter: Annotation, Features, and Experiments. *Proceedings of ACL 2011*.

Hall, Mark, Eibe Frank, Geoffrey Holmes, Bernhard Pfahringer, Peter Reutemann, and Ian H. Witten. 2009. The WEKA data mining software: an update. *ACM SIGKDD Explorations Newsletter*, 11(1), 10–18.

Hu, Minqing, and Bing Liu. 2004. Mining and summarizing customer reviews. *KDD-2004*.

Kim, Soo-Min, and Eduard Hovy. 2004. Determining the sentiment of opinions. *Coling-2004*.

Kouloumpis, Efthymios, Theresa Wilson, and Johanna Moore. 2011. Twitter Sentiment Analysis: The Good the Bad and the OMG!. *Proceedings of ICWSM*. Barcelona.

Pak, Alexander, and Patrick Paroubek. 2010. Twitter as a corpus for sentiment analysis and opinion mining. *Proceedings of LREC*. Malta.

Pang, Bo, and Lillian Lee. 2004. A sentimental education: Sentiment analysis using subjectivity summarization based on minimum cuts. *Proceedings of the ACL*.

Theresa Wilson and Zornitsa Kozareva and Preslav Nakov and Sara Rosenthal and Veselin Stoyanov and Alan Ritter. *SemEval-2013 Task 2: Sentiment Analysis in Twitter*. Proceedings of the International Workshop on Semantic Evaluation. SemEval '13. June 2013. Atlanta, Georgia.

Theresa Wilson, Janyce Wiebe, and Paul Hoffmann. 2005. Recognizing contextual polarity in phrase-level sentiment analysis. *Proceedings of Human Language Technology Conference and Conference on Empirical Methods in Natural Language Processing (HLT/EMNLP)*. Vancouver.

Kea: Expression-level Sentiment Analysis from Twitter Data

Ameeta Agrawal
Computer Science and Engineering
York University
Toronto, Canada
ameeta@cse.yorku.ca

Aijun An
Computer Science and Engineering
York University
Toronto, Canada
aan@cse.yorku.ca

Abstract

This paper describes an expression-level sentiment detection system that participated in the subtask A of SemEval-2013 Task 2: Sentiment Analysis in Twitter. Our system uses a supervised approach to learn the features from the training data to classify expressions in new tweets as positive, negative or neutral. The proposed approach helps to understand the relevant features that contribute most in this classification task.

1 Introduction

In recent years, Twitter has emerged as an ubiquitous and an opportune platform for social activity. Analyzing the sentiments of the tweets expressed by an international user-base can provide an approximate view of how people feel. One of the biggest challenges of working with tweets is their short length. Additionally, the language used in tweets is very informal, with creative spellings and punctuation, misspellings, slang, new words, URLs, and genre-specific terminology and abbreviations, such as, RT for "re-tweet" and #hashtags, which are a type of tagging for tweets. Although several systems tackle the task of analyzing sentiments from tweets, the task of analyzing sentiments at term or phrase-level within a tweet has remained largely unexplored.

This paper describes the details of our expression-level sentiment detection system that participated in the subtask A of SemEval-2013 Task 2: Sentiment Analysis in Twitter (Wilson et al., 2013). The goal is to mark expressions (a term or short phrases) in a tweet with their contextual polarity. This is challenging given the fact that the entire length of a tweet is restricted to just 140 characters. We describe the creation of an SVM classifier that is used to classify the contextual polarity of expressions within tweets. A feature set derived from various linguistic features, parts-of-speech tagging and prior sentiment lexicons was used to train the classifier.

2 Related Work

Sentiment detection from Twitter data has attracted much attention from the research community in recent times (Go et al., 2009; Pang et al., 2002; Pang and Lee, 2004; Wilson et al., 2005; T. et al., 2012). However, most of these approaches classify entire tweets by their overall sentiment (positive, negative or neutral).

The task at hand is to classify expressions with their *contextual* sentiment. Most of these expressions can be found in sentiment lexicons already annotated with their general polarity, but the focus of this task is to detect the polarity of that expression within the context of the tweet it appears in, and therefore, given the context, the polarity of the expression might differ from that found in any lexicon. One of the primary goals of this task is to facilitate the creation of a corpus of tweets with sentiment expressions marked with their contextual sentiments.

Wilson, Wiebe and Hoffman (Wilson et al., 2005) explored the challenges of contextual polarity of sentiment expressions by first determining whether an expression is neutral or polar and then disambiguating the polarity of the polar expressions. Nasukawa and Yi (Nasukawa and Yi, 2003) classified

*Second Joint Conference on Lexical and Computational Semantics (*SEM), Volume 2: Seventh International Workshop on Semantic Evaluation (SemEval 2013)*, pages 530–534, Atlanta, Georgia, June 14-15, 2013.

the polarity of target expressions using manually developed patterns. Both these approaches, however, experimented with general webpages and online reviews but not Twitter data.

3 Task Setup

This paper describes the task of recognizing contextual sentiments of expressions within a tweet. Formally, given a message containing a marked instance of a word or a phrase, the task is to determine whether that instance is positive, negative or neutral in that context.

A corpus of roughly 8343 twitter messages was made available by the task organizers, where each tweet included an expression marked as positive, negative or neutral. Also available was a development data set containing 1011 tweets with similarly marked expressions. The data sets included messages on a broad range of topics such as a mixture of entities (e.g., Gadafi, Steve Jobs), products (e.g., kindle, android phone), and events (e.g., Japan earthquake, NHL playoffs). Keywords and hashtags were used to identify and collect messages relevant to the selected topic, which were then annotated using Mechanical Turk. Further details regarding the task setup may be found in the task description paper (Wilson et al., 2013).

The evaluation consisted of classifying 4435 expressions in a Twitter data set. Furthermore, to test the generalizability of the systems, the task organizers provided a test data set consisting of 2334 SMS messages, each containing a marked expression, for which no prior training data set was made available.

4 System Description

Our aim by participating in the SemEval-2013 Sentiment Analysis in Twitter task was to investigate what features are most useful in distinguishing the different polarities. The various steps of building our system are described in detail as follows.

4.1 Tokenization

Tweets are known for being notoriously noisy due to their length restricted to just 140 characters which forces users to be creative in order to get their messages across. This poses an inherent challenge when analyzing tweets which need to undergo some significant preprocessing. The first step includes tokenizing the words in the tweet. Punctuation is identified during the tokenization process and marked for inclusion as one of the features in the feature set. This includes Twitter-specific punctuation such as "#" hashtags, specific emoticons such as ":)" and any URL links are replaced by a "URL" placeholder.

4.2 *n*-gram features

Each expression consists of one or more words, with the average number of words in an expression in the training data set found to be 2. We derive lower-case unigram and bigram as well as the full string features from the expressions which are represented by their frequency counts in the feature set. The *n*-grams were cleaned (stripped of any punctuation) before being included in the feature set as they were observed to provide better results than noisy *n*-grams. Note that the presence of punctuation did become a part of the feature set as described in 4.3. We also experimented with word-splitting, especially found in hashtags (e.g., #iamsohappy); however, contrary to our initial supposition, this step resulted in poorer results overall due to word-splitting error propagation and was therefore avoided.

4.3 POS tagging

For tagging the various parts-of-speech of a tweet, we use the POS tagger (Gimpel et al., 2011) that is especially designed to work with English data from Twitter. The tagging scheme encompasses 25 tags (please see (Gimpel et al., 2011) for the full listing), including some Twitter-specific tags (which could make up as much as 13% of all tags as shown in their annotated data set) such as "#" hashtag (indicates topic/category for tweet), "@" at-mention (indicates another user as a recipient of a tweet), "RT" re-tweets and URL or email addresses. The punctuation (such as ":-)", ":b", "(:", amongst others) from the *n*-grams is captured using the "emoticon" and "punctuation" tags that are explicitly identified by this POS tagger trained especially for tweets.

Table 1 shows an example using a subset of two POS tags for an expression (# Adj. and # Emoticon denotes the number of adjectives and emoticons respectively). Other POS tags include nouns (NN), verbs (VB) and so on. Features incorporating the information about the parts-of-speech of the expres-

Esperance will be **without star player** Youssef Msakni for the first leg of the Champions League final against Al Ahly on Saturday. #AFRICA											
Prior Polarity		Length		POS in Expression		POS in Tweet		n-grams			
Pos.	Neg.	Exp.	Tweet	#Adj.	#Emoticon	#Adj.	#NN	"without"	"star"	"without star"	...
0	0	3	23	0	0	1	13	1	1	1	...

Table 1: Sample feature set for an expression (denoted in bold)

sion as well as the tweet denoted by their frequencies produced better results than using a binary notation. Hence frequency counts were used in the feature set.

4.4 Prior sentiment lexicon

A prior sentiment lexicon was generated by combining four already existing polarity lexicons including the Opinion Lexicon (Hu and Liu, 2004), the SentiWordNet (Esuli and Sebastiani, 2006), the Subjectivity Clues database (Wilson et al., 2005) and the General Inquirer (Stone and Hunt, 1963). If any of the words in the expression are also found in the prior sentiment lexicon, then the frequencies of such prior positive and negative words are included as features in the feature set.

4.5 Other features

Other features found to be useful in the classification process include the length of the expression as well as the length of the tweet. A sample of the feature set is shown in Table 1.

4.6 Classifier

During development time, we experimented with different classifiers but in the end, the Support Vector Machines (SVM), using the polynomial kernel, trained over tweets from the provided train and development data outperformed all the other classifiers. The final feature set included four main features plus the n-grams as well as the features depicting the presence or absence of a POS in the expression and the tweet.

5 Experiments and Discussion

The task organizers made available a test data set composed of 4435 tweets where each tweet contained an instance of an expression whose sentiment was to be detected. Another test corpus of 2334 SMS messages was also used in the evaluation to test how well a system trained on tweets generalizes on other data types.

The metric for evaluating the systems is F-measure. We participated in the "constrained" version of the task which meant working with only the provided training data and no additional tweets/SMS messages or sentences with sentiment annotations were used. However, other resources such as sentiment lexicons can be incorporated into the system.

Table 2, which presents the results of our submission in this task, lists the F-score of the positive, negative and neutral classes on the Twitter test data, whereas Table 3 lists the results of the SMS message data. As it can be observed from the results, the negative sentiments are classified better than the positive ones. We reckon this may be due to the comparatively fewer ways of expressing a positive emotion, while the negative sentiment seems to have a much wider vocabulary (our sentiment lexicon has 25% less positive words than negative). Whereas the positive class has a higher precision, the negative class seems to have a more notable recall. The most striking observation, however, is the extremely low F-score for the neutral class. This may be due to the highly skewed proportion (less than 5%) of neutral instances in the training data. In future work, it will be interesting to see how balancing out the proportions of the three classes affects the classification accuracy.

We also ran some ablation experiments on the provided Twitter and SMS test data sets after the submission. Table 4 reports the findings of experiments where, for example, "- prior polarities" indicates a feature set excluding the prior polarities. The metric used here is the macro-averaged F-score of the positive and the negative class. The baseline measure implements a simple SVM classifier using only the words as unigram features in the expression. Interestingly, contrary to our hypothesis during development time, using the POS of the entire tweet was the least helpful feature. Since this was an expression level classification task, it seems that using the POS features of the entire tweet may misguide the classifier. Unsurprisingly, the prior polarities turned out to be the most important part of the feature set for this classification task as it seems that many of the expressions' contextual polarities remained same as their prior polarities.

Class	Precision	Recall	F-score
Positive	0.93	0.47	0.62
Negative	0.50	0.95	0.65
Neutral	0.15	0.12	0.13
Macro-average			**0.6394**

Table 2: Submitted results: Twitter test data

Class	Precision	Recall	F-score
Positive	0.85	0.39	0.53
Negative	0.59	0.96	0.73
Neutral	0.18	0.06	0.09
Macro-average			**0.6327**

Table 3: Submitted results: SMS test data

	Twitter	SMS
Baseline	0.821	0.824
Full feature set (submitted)	*0.639*	*0.632*
- Prior polarities	0.487	0.494
- Lengths	0.612	0.576
- POS expressions	0.646	0.615
- POS tweets	**0.855**	**0.856**

Table 4: Macro-averaged F-score results using different feature sets

6 Conclusion

This paper presented the details of our system which participated in the subtask A of SemEval-2013 Task 2: Sentiment Analysis in Twitter. An SVM classifier was trained on a feature set consiting of prior polarities, various POS and other Twitter-specific features. Our experiments indicate that prior polarities from sentiment lexicons are significant features in this expression level classification task. Furthermore, a classifier trained on just tweets can generalize considerably well on SMS message data as well. As part of our future work, we would like to explore what features are more helpful in not only classifying the positive class better, but also distinguishing neutrality from polarity.

Acknowledgments

We would like to thank the organizers of this task and the reviewers for their useful feedback. This research is funded in part by the Centre for Information Visualization and Data Driven Design (CIV/DDD) established by the Ontario Research Fund.

References

Andrea Esuli and Fabrizio Sebastiani. 2006. Sentiwordnet: A publicly available lexical resource for opinion mining. In *In Proceedings of the 5th Conference on Language Resources and Evaluation (LRECâ06*, pages 417–422.

Kevin Gimpel, Nathan Schneider, Brendan O'Connor, Dipanjan Das, Daniel Mills, Jacob Eisenstein, Michael Heilman, Dani Yogatama, Jeffrey Flanigan, and Noah A. Smith. 2011. Part-of-speech tagging for twitter: annotation, features, and experiments. In *Proceedings of the 49th Annual Meeting of the Association for Computational Linguistics: Human Language Technologies: short papers - Volume 2*, HLT '11, pages 42–47, Stroudsburg, PA, USA. Association for Computational Linguistics.

Alec Go, Richa Bhayani, and Lei Huang. 2009. Twitter sentiment classification using distant supervision. *Processing*, pages 1–6.

Minqing Hu and Bing Liu. 2004. Mining and summarizing customer reviews. In *Proceedings of the tenth ACM SIGKDD international conference on Knowledge discovery and data mining*, KDD '04, pages 168–177, New York, NY, USA. ACM.

Tetsuya Nasukawa and Jeonghee Yi. 2003. Sentiment analysis: capturing favorability using natural language processing. In *Proceedings of the 2nd international conference on Knowledge capture*, K-CAP '03, pages 70–77, New York, NY, USA. ACM.

Bo Pang and Lillian Lee. 2004. A sentimental education: sentiment analysis using subjectivity summarization based on minimum cuts. In *Proceedings of the 42nd Annual Meeting on Association for Computational Linguistics*, ACL '04, Stroudsburg, PA, USA. Association for Computational Linguistics.

Bo Pang, Lillian Lee, and Shivakumar Vaithyanathan. 2002. Thumbs up?: sentiment classification using machine learning techniques. In *Proceedings of the ACL-02 conference on Empirical methods in natural language processing - Volume 10*, EMNLP '02, pages 79–86, Stroudsburg, PA, USA. Association for Computational Linguistics.

Philip J. Stone and Earl B. Hunt. 1963. A computer approach to content analysis: studies using the general inquirer system. In *Proceedings of the May 21-23, 1963, spring joint computer conference*, AFIPS '63 (Spring), pages 241–256, New York, NY, USA. ACM.

Amir Asiaee T., Mariano Tepper, Arindam Banerjee, and Guillermo Sapiro. 2012. If you are happy and you know it... tweet. In *Proceedings of the 21st ACM international conference on Information and knowledge management*, CIKM '12, pages 1602–1606, New York, NY, USA. ACM.

Theresa Wilson, Janyce Wiebe, and Paul Hoffmann. 2005. Recognizing contextual polarity in phrase-level sentiment analysis. In *Proceedings of the conference on Human Language Technology and Empirical Methods in Natural Language Processing*, HLT '05, pages 347–354, Stroudsburg, PA, USA. Association for Computational Linguistics.

Theresa Wilson, Zornitsa Kozareva, Preslav Nakov, Sara Rosenthal, Veselin Stoyanov, and Alan Ritter. 2013. Semeval-2013 task 2: Sentiment analysis in twitter. In *Proceedings of the International Workshop on Semantic Evaluation*, SemEval '13, June.

UoM: Using Explicit Semantic Analysis for Classifying Sentiments

Sapna Negi
University of Malta
Msida, MSD2080, MALTA
sapna.negi13@gmail.com

Mike Rosner
University of Malta
Msida, MSD2080, MALTA
mike.rosner@um.edu.mt

Abstract

In this paper, we describe our system submitted for the Sentiment Analysis task at SemEval 2013 (Task 2). We implemented a combination of Explicit Semantic Analysis (ESA) with Naive Bayes classifier. ESA represents text as a high dimensional vector of explicitly defined topics, following the distributional semantic model. This approach is novel in the sense that ESA has not been used for Sentiment Analysis in the literature, to the best of our knowledge.

1 Introduction

Semantic relatedness measure gives the comparison of different terms or texts on the basis of their meaning or the content. For instance, it can be said that the word "computer" is semantically more related to "laptop" than "flute". Sentiment analysis refers to the task of determining the overall contextual polarity of the written text. In this paper, we propose the use of semantic relatedness models, specifically Explicit Semantic Analysis (ESA), to identify textual polarity. There are different approaches to model semantic relatedness like WordNet based models (Banerjee and Banerjee, 2002), distributional semantic models (DSMs) etc. DSMs follow the distributional hypothesis, which says that words occurring in the same contexts tend to have similar meanings (Harris, 1954). Therefore, considering sentiment classification problem, distributional hypothesis suggests that the words or phrases referring to positive polarity would tend to co-occur, and similar assumptions can be made for the negative terms.

DSMs generally utilize large textual corpora to extract the distributional information relying on the co-occurrence information and distribution of the terms. These models represent the text in the form of high-dimensional vectors highlighting the co-occurrence information. Semantic relatedness between two given texts is calculated by using these vectors, thus, following that the the semantic meaning of a text can be inferred from its usage in different contexts. There are several different computational models following distributional semantics hypothesis. Latent Semantic Analysis (LSA), Latent Dirichlet Allocation (LDA) (Blei et. al., 2003), Explicit Semantic Analysis (ESA) are some examples of such models. However, in this work, we investigated the use of ESA for the given task of sentiment analysis (SA).

There are two sub-tasks defined in Task 2 at SemEval 2013 (SemEval, 2013). We participated in *Message Polarity Classification* sub-task, where we are required to automatically classify the sentiment of a given message into positive, negative, or neutral. The task deals with the short texts coming from Twitter and SMS (Short Message Service). We are provided with 8,000 - 12,000 twitter messages annotated with their sentiment label for the purpose of training the models. In this work, we present our approach for sentiment classification which uses a combination of ESA and Naive Bayes classifier. The rest of the paper is structured as follows : Section 2 discusses some related work in this context. Section

*Second Joint Conference on Lexical and Computational Semantics (*SEM), Volume 2: Seventh International Workshop on Semantic Evaluation (SemEval 2013)*, pages 535–538, Atlanta, Georgia, June 14-15, 2013.

3 briefly explains ESA. Section 4 describes our approaches while Section 5 explains the submitted runs for our system to the task. Section 6 reports the results, and we conclude in section 7.

2 Related Work

The research in SA initiated with the classical machine learning algorithms like Naive Bayes, Maximum Entropy etc. using intuitive features like unigrams, bigrams, parts of speech information, position of words, adjectives etc. (Pang et. al., 2002). However, such approaches are heavily dependent upon the given training data, and therefore can be very limited for SA due to out of vocabulary words and phrases, and different meanings of words in different contexts (Pang and Lee, 2008). Due to these problems, several methods have been investigated to use some seed words for extracting more positive and negative terms with the help of lexical resources like WordNet etc., for instance, SentiWordNet, which defines the polarity of the word along with the intensity. In this paper, we model the sentiment classification using DSMs based on explicit topic models (Cimiano et. al., 2009), which incorporate correlation information from a corpus like Wikipedia, to generalize from a few known positive or negative terms. There have been some other attempts to utilize topic models in this regards, but they mainly focussed on latent topic models (Lin and He, 2009) (Maas et. al., 2011). Joint sentiment topic model introduced LDA based unsupervised topic models in sentiment analysis by pointing out that sentiments are often topic dependent because same word/phrase could represent different sentiments for different topics (Lin and He, 2009). The recent work by Maas et. al. (Maas et. al., 2011) on using latent concept models presented a mixture model of unsupervised and supervised techniques to learn word vectors capturing semantic term-document information along with the sentiment content.

3 Explicit Semantic Analysis

Explicit Semantic Analysis (ESA) is a technique for computing semantic relatedness between texts using distributional information (Gabrilovich and Markovitch, 2007). ESA represents text as vectors of concepts explicitly defined by humans, like Wikipedia articles. This provides an intuitive and easily understandable topic space for humans, in contrast to the latent topic space in latent models.Input texts are represented as multidimensional vectors of weighted concepts. The procedure of computing semantic relatedness involves comparing the vectors corresponding to the given texts e.g. using cosine product. The magnitude of each dimension in the vector is the associativity weight of the text to that explicit concept/dimension. To quantify this associativity, the textual content related to the explicit concept/dimension is utilized. This weight can be calculated by considering different methods, for instance, tf-idf score. ESA has been proved to be a generalized vector space model (Gottron et. al., 2011).

4 Methodology

We implemented a combination of traditional machine learning based approach for SA using Naive Bayes algorithm, and ESA based sentiment identification. To perform sentiment classification solely using ESA, we asses the similarity of a new text against the text whose sentiment is already known, using ESA. More similar is a text to a particular sentiment annotated text, better are its chances to belong to the same sentiment class. On the other hand, we followed a standard classification approach by learning Naive Bayes over the given training data. Finally, we consult both ESA and Naive Bayes for classifying the text. The overall probability of a text belonging to a particular sentiment class was determined by weighted sum of ESA similarity score, and the scores given by Naive Bayes classifier. The sentiment class with the highest total score was accepted as the sentiment of the input text. The individual weights of ESA and Naive Bayes were determined by linear regression for our experiments.

5 System Description

We created three bags of words (BOW) corresponding to the different sentiment classes (positive, negative, and neutral) annotated in the training data. These BOWs were used as the definition of the particular sentiment class for making the ESA comparisons, and for learning Naive Bayes. We used unigrams and bigrams as features for the Naive

Task	Approach	F score	Highest F score	Rank
Twitter, with constrained data	ESA with Naive Bayes	.5182	.6902	24/35
SMS, with constrained data	ESA with Naive Bayes	.422	.6846	24/28
Twitter, with unconstrained data	ESA with Naive Bayes	.4507	.6486	16/16
SMS, with unconstrained data	ESA with Naive Bayes	.3522	.4947	15/15
Twitter, with constrained data	ESA	.35	.6902	NA

Table 1: Results

Bayes algorithm. The ESA implementation was replicated from the version available on Github[1], replacing the Wikipedia dump by the version released in February 2013.

We submitted two runs each for Twitter and SMS test data. The first run (constrained) used only the provided training data for learning while the second run (unconstrained) used a combination of external training data coming from the popular movie review dataset (Pang et. al., 2002), and the data provided with the task.

6 Results and discussion

The first four entries provided in the table 1 correspond to the four runs submitted in SemEval-2013 Task 2. The fifth entry corresponds to the results of a separate experiment performed by us, to estimate the influence of ESA on SA. According to the F-scores, ESA is unable to identify the sentiment in the texts following the mentioned approach. The results suggest that combining Naive Bayes to the system improved the overall scores. However, even the combined system could not perform well. Also, the mixing of external data lowered the scores indicating incompatibility of the external training data with the provided data.

7 Conclusion

We presented an approach of using ESA for sentiment classification. The submitted system follow a combination of standard Naive Bayes model and ESA based classification. The results of the task suggests that the approach we used for ESA based classification is unable to identify the sentiment accurately. As a future step, we plan to investigate more on the usability of ESA for sentiment classification, for instance, by using suitable features in the concept definitions, and weighing them according to the different sentiment classes.

[1]https://github.com/kasooja/clesa

References

Maas, A.L., Daly, R.E., Pham, P.T., Huang, D., Ng, A.Y., Potts, C.: Learning word vectors for sentiment analysis. In: Proceedings of the 49th Annual Meeting of the Association for Computational Linguistics: Human Language Technologies - Volume 1. pp. 142–150. HLT '11, Association for Computational Linguistics, Stroudsburg, PA, USA (2011), http://dl.acm.org/citation.cfm?id=2002472.2002491

Lin, C., He, Y.: Joint sentiment/topic model for sentiment analysis. In: Proceedings of the 18th ACM conference on Information and knowledge management. pp. 375–384. CIKM '09, ACM, New York, NY, USA (2009), http://doi.acm.org/10.1145/1645953.1646003

Cimiano, P., Schultz, A., Sizov, S., Sorg, P., Staab, S.: Explicit versus latent concept models for cross-language information retrieval. In: Proceedings of the 21st international jont conference on Artifical intelligence. pp. 1513–1518. IJCAI'09, Morgan Kaufmann Publishers Inc., San Francisco, CA, USA (2009), http://dl.acm.org/citation.cfm?id=1661445.1661688

Pang, B., Lee, L.: Opinion mining and sentiment analysis. Found. Trends Inf. Retr. 2(1-2), 1–135 (Jan 2008), http://dx.doi.org/10.1561/1500000011

Pang, B., Lee, L., Vaithyanathan, S.: Thumbs up?: sentiment classification using machine learning techniques. In: Proceedings of the ACL-02 conference on Empirical methods in natural language processing - Volume 10. pp. 79–86. EMNLP '02, Association for Computational Linguistics, Stroudsburg, PA, USA (2002), http://dx.doi.org/10.3115/1118693.1118704

Wilson, T., Kozareva, Z., Nakov, P., Rosenthal, S., Stoyanov, V., Ritter, A.: SemEval-2013 task 2: Sentiment analysis in twitter. In: Proceedings of the International Workshop on Semantic Evaluation. SemEval '13 (June 2013)

Banerjee, S., Banerjee, S.: An adapted lesk algorithm for word sense disambiguation using wordnet. In: In Proceedings of the Third International Conference on Intelligent Text Processing and Computational Linguistics. pp. 136–145 (2002)

David M. Blei, Andrew Y. Ng, and Michael I. Jordan. Latent dirichlet allocation. *J. Mach. Learn. Res.*, 3:993–1022, March 2003.

P. W. Foltz, W. Kintsch, and T. K. Landauer. The measurement of textual coherence with latent semantic analysis. *Discourse Processes*, 25:285–307, 1998.

Evgeniy Gabrilovich and Shaul Markovitch. Computing semantic relatedness using wikipedia-based explicit semantic analysis. In *In Proceedings of the 20th International Joint Conference on Artificial Intelligence*, pages 1606–1611, 2007.

Thomas Gottron, Maik Anderka, and Benno Stein. Insights into explicit semantic analysis. In *Proceedings of the 20th ACM international conference on Information and knowledge management*, CIKM '11, pages 1961–1964, New York, NY, USA, 2011. ACM.

Zellig Harris. Distributional structure. *Word*, 10(23):146–162, 1954.

bwbaugh : Hierarchical sentiment analysis with partial self-training

Wesley Baugh
Department of Computer Science
University of North Texas
brianbaugh@my.unt.edu

Abstract

Using labeled Twitter training data from SemEval-2013, we train both a subjectivity classifier and a polarity classifier separately, and then combine the two into a single hierarchical classifier. Using additional unlabeled data that is believed to contain sentiment, we allow the polarity classifier to continue learning using self-training. The resulting system is capable of classifying a document as *neutral*, *positive*, or *negative* with an overall accuracy of 61.2% using our hierarchical Naive Bayes classifier.[1]

1 Introduction

Many people use social networks, such as Twitter, to connect and communicate with others. Users of social networks often share their experiences, such as watching a recent movie or tv show, reading a book, or a newly tried product or service. In addition, social networks provide an avenue for discussion of current events, such as politics. Many people and companies are often concerned with how others perceive their product—which is sometimes themselves, as is the case for politicians—or their service. By understanding and reacting to what the consumer is thinking, they can attempt to maximize their good press as well as to help minimize the bad. It would therefore be useful to use the information users of social networks share to perform sentiment analysis in order to understand how people perceive targets of interest.

In general, sentiment analysis often involves the use of machine learning, especially Naive Bayes, SVM, and MaxEnt classifiers [Jose]. Features general include n-grams and POS tags [Go et al., 2009; Pak and Paroubek, 2010; Jose], as well as sentiment lexicons [Jose]. Go et al. [2009] achieved around 82.5% accuracy for positive-negative polarity detection, Jose achieved around 76% accuracy for subjective-objective classification, and Pak and Paroubek [2010] achieved around 70% accuracy for a combined subjectivity-polarity classifier.

While determining whether a document known to be subjective is positive or negative (polarity detection) is relatively easy, a currently more difficult task in sentiment analysis is identifying whether a document is subjective or objective (subjectivity analysis). Many approaches simply ignore the objective class [Go et al., 2009], which does not work for real world problems as there are a substantial amount of documents that are either partially or wholly objective [Koppel and Schler, 2006].

Many previous methods focus on either subjectivity analysis or polarity detection. Our method incorporates both subtasks into a single overall system in order to perform sentiment analysis.

2 Background

The sentiment analysis in Twitter task of SemEval-2013 [Wilson et al., 2013] provides 9,864 labeled tweets from Twitter to be used as a training dataset. Each instance is labeled as either `positive`, `negative`, or `neutral`, and was annotated through Amazon's Mechanical Turk. The terms of service for Twitter puts restrictions on the

[1] A working demo of the system will be available for a short time at: `http://infertweet.bwbaugh.com`

*Second Joint Conference on Lexical and Computational Semantics (*SEM), Volume 2: Seventh International Workshop on Semantic Evaluation (SemEval 2013)*, pages 539–542, Atlanta, Georgia, June 14-15, 2013.

type of data that may be re-released, therefore participants SemEval-2013 Task 2 participants were required to download tweets directly from Twitter. Due to deleted or otherwise unavailable tweets, this system was only able to download approximately 8,750 training instances. Additionally, a development dataset was provided with 1,654 labeled tweets, of which 340 are `negative`, 739 are `neutral`, and 575 are `positive`. The provided test set consisted of 3,813 instances, of which 601 are `negative`, 1640 are `neutral`, and 1572 are `positive`.

In related work, Go et al. [2009] generated an automatically labeled noisy gold standard by searching for tweets that contained one of several emoticons[2] (e.g. :) or :() that were mapped to either the `positive` or `negative` class depending on the type of emoticon in the text. This system also collected approximately one million tweets using emoticons as a keyword search for matching, however the data remained unlabeled. Though these tweets are unlabeled, they are presumed to be subjective—either `positive` or `negative` but not `neutral`—because of the intuitive association of emoticons with sentiment.

3 Approach

The system uses a custom implementation of Multinomial Naive Bayes as the classifier.[3] We create a hierarchical classifier, which in this case consists of two binary classifiers. The first-level is the subjectivity classifier, which can output `objective` (neutral) or `subjective`. If the output of the first level is `subjective`, then the second-level polarity classifier decides if the instance is `positive` or `negative`.

Both classifiers (subjective and polarity) are trained on approximately 8,750 training instances, which come from the released SemEval-2013 training dataset. The subjective classifier is not given any

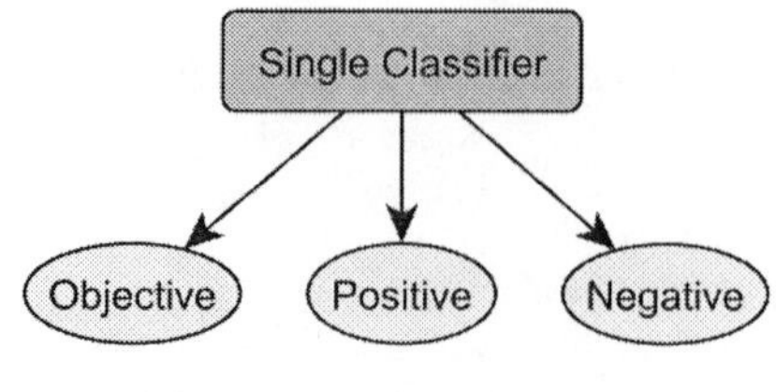

Figure 1: A single multinomial classifier, which can output any class label.

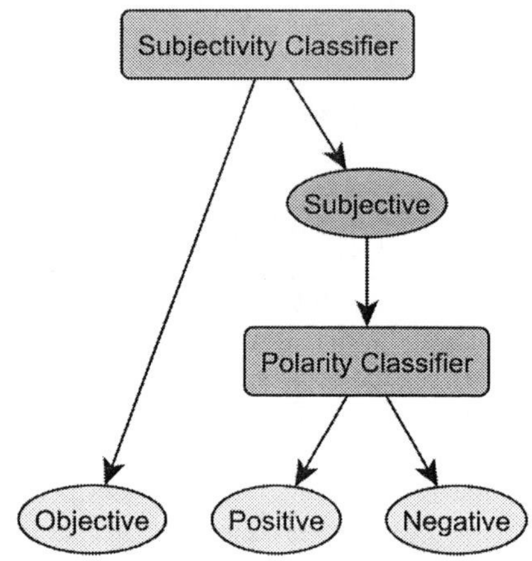

Figure 2: A hierarchical classifier, which in this case consists of two binary classifiers. The first level is a subjectivity classifier, with an output of either *subjective* or *neutral*. The second level is a sentiment polarity classifier, with an output of either *positive* or *negative*.

additional training data. The system then uses its current model to classify approximately one million *unlabeled* tweets that are believed to be subjective. The unlabeled tweets were classified one at a time. If the system classified the tweet as subjective, it was used to train the polarity classifier only if the confidence in the predicted label was greater than `0.8`. We stopped the system after approximately 910k total training instances were used.

The core features extracted are unigrams and bigrams. Bigrams had an additional `__start__` and `__end__` token at the beginning and end of the full text of the training instance.

As part of a preprocessing step, we attempted to find URLs in the text and replace them with a special `__URL__` token. We shortened characters repeated more than twice, such that "haaaaaaate" would become "haate". We attempted to find dates in the text and replace them with a special `__DATE__` token.

[2]The term *emoticon* comes from a blending of the words "emotion" and "icon".

[3] The machine learning components (Multinomial Naive Bayes) were written for this system as a Python library, and will be available on GitHub: `https://github.com/bwbaugh/infer`. That toolkit was then used as a foundation for writing the code for the system, which will also be available on GitHub: `https://github.com/bwbaugh/infertweet`.

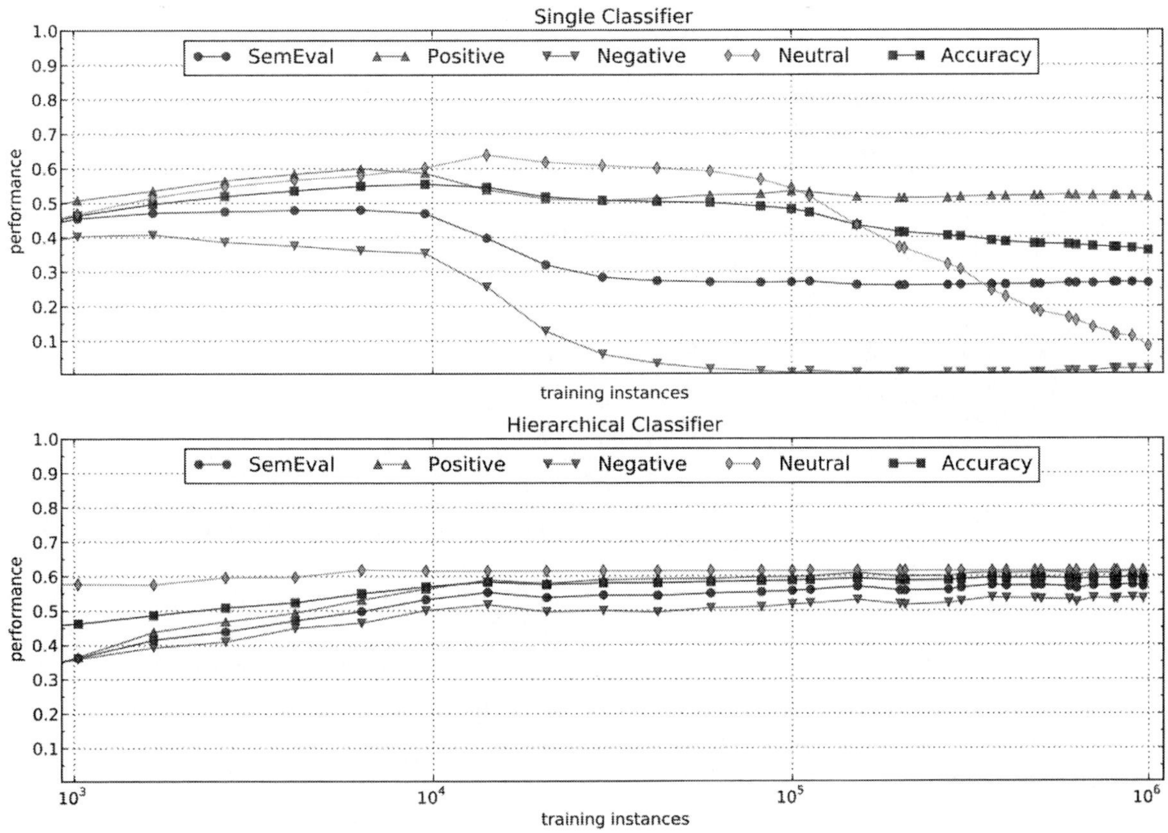

Figure 3: Performance of the single (non-hierarchical) and hierarchical classifiers on the development set vs. the number of training instances. The performance metric for *positive*, *negative* and *neutral* is F-measure, *SemEval* is the simple average of the positive and negative performance, and *accuracy* is the overall number of correct instances. The first 8,750 instances are labeled, while the rest are unlabeled instances that were added using self-training.

4 Experiments

4.1 Design

The system was incrementally trained one tweet at a time, with the performance checked every so often by using the current model to classify the development set instances. Once all of the labeled training data had been used, the subjectivity classifier was given no additional training instances, and the remainder of the subjectively charged unlabeled data was used to train the polarity classifier.

Variables experimented on included: extracting n-grams up to size 4 and trying all combinations; mapping Twitter usernames to a special token; mapping substrings recognized as a date to a special token; combining a negation token such as "not" to the following token; deleting characters repeated more than twice; mapping numbers to a special token; counting exclamation points; the confidence threshold above which the predicted label for an unlabeled instance would be used for training.

In addition to collecting unlabeled data using emoticon keywords, we also experimented with using sentences from Wikipedia as neutrally labeled text, as well as using a random subsample of all English-language tweets from the Twitter public stream as a source of unlabeled data for any class.

We also tried using a single non-hierarchical classifier using each source of unlabeled data.

4.2 Results

4.2.1 SemEval-2013 development set

Using additional unlabeled data with the single multinomial classifier always resulted in overall degraded performance.

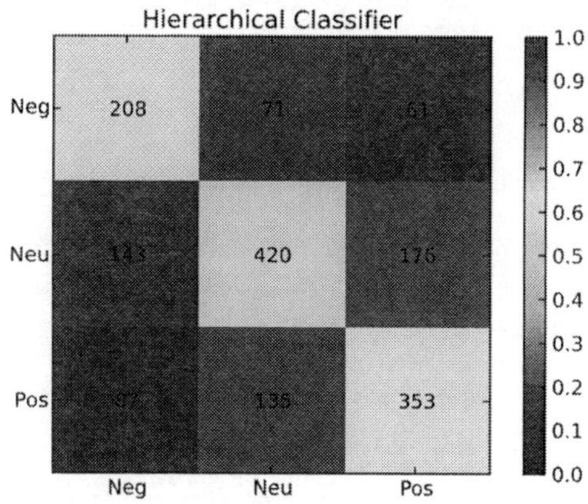

Figure 4: The confusion matrix on the development set produced after training on a total of approximately 970k training instances. Rows are the true labels while columns are the predicted labels.

4.2.2 SemEval-2013 test set

gs \ pred	negative	neutral	positive
negative	324	203	74
neutral	196	1168	276
positive	233	498	841

Table 1: Confusion matrix (hierarchical)

class	prec	recall	fscore
negative	0.4303	0.5391	0.4786
neutral	0.6249	0.7122	0.6657
positive	0.7061	0.5350	0.6088

Table 2: Performance (hierarchical)

The average F-score of the `positive` and `negative` classes is 0.5437, which is the main evaluation metric used by SemEval-2013 Task 2. The overall accuracy is 61.2%.

4.2.3 Discussion

By using a hierarchical classifier, we are able to prevent degradation of the performance of the classifier on neutrally labeled instances by only applying additional training data to the polarity classifier.

The use of additional unlabeled data results in an increase in performance for the hierarchical classifier as seen in Figure 3. However, the increase in performance comes with an exponential increase in the number of unlabeled instances. Using appropriate feature selection for online algorithms, such as feature hashing, a system like this could train indefinitely on additional data from a Twitter stream without running out of memory.

The system's lack of high-quality sources for additional `objective-OR-neutral` data—either labeled or unlabeled—appears to be our biggest obstacle to increasing performance at this time. The poor performance of the single multinomial classifier when given additional unlabeled data can also likely be attributed to this reason. Identifying additional high-quality sources of neutral data would likely go a long way towards improving the overall system performance. Active learning approaches could also be applied with the goal of improving the subjectivity classifier.

5 Conclusion

Using a hierarchical classifier comprised of two Naive Bayes classifiers, we are able to improve the performance of polarity detection with the addition of unlabeled data in an online setting by isolating the subjectivity classifier.

References

Alec Go, Richa Bhayani, and Lei Huang. Twitter sentiment classification using distant supervision. *CS224N Project Report, Stanford*, pages 1–12, 2009.

Anthony K Jose. Twitter sentiment analysis.

Moshe Koppel and Jonathan Schler. The importance of neutral examples for learning sentiment. *Computational Intelligence*, 22(2):100–109, 2006.

Alexander Pak and Patrick Paroubek. Twitter as a corpus for sentiment analysis and opinion mining. In *Proceedings of LREC*, volume 2010, 2010.

Theresa Wilson, Zornitsa Kozareva, Preslav Nakov, Alan Ritter, Sara Rosenthal, and Veselin Stoyanov. Semeval-2013 task 2: Sentiment analysis in twitter. In *Proceedings of the 7th International Workshop on Semantic Evaluation*, 2013.

Serendio: Simple and Practical lexicon based approach to Sentiment Analysis

Prabu Palanisamy, Vineet Yadav and Harsha Elchuri
Serendio Software Pvt Ltd
Guindy, Chennai 600032, India
{prabu, vineet, harsha}@serendio.com

Abstract

This paper describes the system developed by the Serendio team for the SemEval-2013 Task 2 competition (Task A). We use a lexicon based approach for discovering sentiments. Our lexicon is built from the Serendio taxonomy. The Serendio taxonomy consists of positive, negative, negation, stop words and phrases. A typical tweet contains word variations, emoticons, hashtags etc. We use preprocessing steps such as stemming, emoticon detection and normalization, exaggerated word shortening and hashtag detection. After the preprocessing, the lexicon-based system classifies the tweets as positive or negative based on the contextual sentiment orientation of the words. Our system yields an F-score of 0.8004 on the test dataset.

1 Introduction

Social media websites like Twitter, Facebook etc. are a major hub for users to express their opinions online. On these social media sites, users post comments and opinions on various topics. Hence these sites become rich sources of information to mine for opinions and analyze user behavior and provide insights for:

- User behavior
- Product feedback
- User intentions
- Lead generation

Businesses spend an enormous amount of time and money to understand their customer opinions about their products and services. Thus Sentiment Analysis has become a hot research area since 2002. Sentiment Analysis is used to determine sentiments, emotions and attitudes of the user. The text used for analysis can range from big document (e.g. Product reviews from Amazon, blogs) to small status message (e.g. Tweets, Facebook comments). In this paper, we confine to Twitter data i.e classify a tweet to have a positive, negative or neutral sentiment.

The rest of the paper is organized as follows. In Section 2, we study relevant previous work on Sentiment Analysis on Twitter data. In Section 3, we describe each processing step of our approach in detail. In Section 4, we experiment with the training and the lexicon. In Section 5, we report and evaluate the final result obtained from the test data published by the SemEval team. In Section 6, we present our conclusions and outline our future work.

2 Related Work

Sentiment Analysis on raw text is a well known problem. The Liu (2012) book covers the entire field of Sentiment Analysis. Sentiment Analysis can be done using Machine learning or a Lexicon-based approach. We use our lexicon based approach in our study. The rest of the paper is confined to Lexicon based approach

2.1 Lexicon based approach

The lexicon based approach is based on the assumption that the contextual sentiment orientation is the

*Second Joint Conference on Lexical and Computational Semantics (*SEM), Volume 2: Seventh International Workshop on Semantic Evaluation (SemEval 2013)*, pages 543–548, Atlanta, Georgia, June 14-15, 2013.

sum of the sentiment orientation of each word or phrase. Turney (2002) identifies sentiments based on the semantic orientation of reviews. (Taboada et al., 2011; Melville et al., 2011; Ding et al., 2008) use lexicon based approach to extract sentiments.

Sentiment Analysis on microblogs is more challenging compared to longer discourses like reviews. Major challenges for microblog sentiment analysis are short length status message, informal words, word shortening, spelling variation and emoticons. Sentiment Analysis on Twitter data have been researched by (Bifet and Frank, 2010; Bermingham and Smeaton, 2010; Pak and Paroubek, 2010). We use our lexicon based approach to extract sentiments. The open lexicon such as Sentiwordnet (Esuli and Sebastiani, 2006; Baccianella et al., 2010), Q-wordnet (Agerri and García-Serrano, 2010), WordNet-Affect (Strapparava and Valitutti, 2004) are developed for supporting Sentiment Analysis. Studies have been made on preprocessing tweets. Han and Baldwin (2011) used a classifier to detect word variation and match the related word. Kaufmann and Kalita (2010) gives the full preprocessing approach to convert a tweet to normal text. Sentiment Analysis on Twitter data is not confined to raw text. Analyzing Emoticons have been an interesting study. Go et al. (2009) used emoticons to classify the tweets as positive or negative and train standard classifiers such as Naive Bayes, Maximum Entropy, and Support Vector Machines. Hashtag may have some sentiment in it. Davidov et al. (2010) used 50 hashtags and 15 emoticons as sentiment labels for classification to allow diverse sentiment types for the tweet. Negation and intensifier play an important role in Sentiment Analysis. Negation word can reverse the polarity, where as intensifier increases sentiment strength. Taboada et al. (2011) studied role of the intensifier and negation in the lexicon based Sentiment Analysis. Wiegand et al. (2010) survey the role of negation in Sentiment Analysis.

3 Serendio Approach

Serendio sentiment engine extracts and analyzes sentiments for a given product and feature set. Serendio sentiment engine currently works for eight different domains such as banking, tablets, smartphones, televisions, apparel, gaming, automobiles and e-readers. In this section, we will introduce Serendio's Sentiment engine and the enhancements that were made to handle the SemEval Task 2, Task A - Contextual Polarity Disambiguation (Wilson et al., 2013). The main steps of our approach are explained in detail in the subsections.

3.1 Creation of lexicon

The lexicon can be created either manually (Taboada et al., 2011; Tong et al., 2001) or expanding automatically from a seed of words (Kanayama et al., 2006; Kaji and Kitsuregawa, 2007; Turney, 2002; Turney and Littman, 2003). In our study, the lexicon is manually created. It is a one time process. Two types of lexicons are created.

Common lexicon: This contains data that would have the same semantic meaning or sense across different domains and categories.

- **Common or default sentiment words**. Positive and Negative sentiment words that have the same sentiment value or sense across different domains. For e.g. sentiment word "good" always represents a positive sentiment and it is independent of any category. Positive or Negative sentiment words have a sentiment score of +1 or -1 to indicate the respective polarity.

- **Negation Words**. Negation words are the words which reverse the polarity of sentiment. For example, "The battery life is not good" has negative sentiment

- **Blind Negation Words**. In the sentence, "The T.V needs a better remote", "needs" is a blind negation word. Blind negation words operate at a sentence level and points out the absence or presence of some sense that is not desired in a product feature.

- **Split words**. Split words are the words used for splitting sentences into clauses. The split words list consists of conjunctions and punctuation marks. For example the complex sentence, "Camera is good but the battery is bad" is split into two clauses "Camera is good" and "Battery is bad".

Category specific lexicon: Category specific lexicon contains the (1) Product Catalog which identifies all the products that we are interested in. (2) Feature Catalog which is a list of attributes that the product has. This enables the Serendio engine to do analysis at the feature level. (3) Sentiment words (positive and negative) that are specific to the category. For example, for a category such as Televisions, a product would be Samsung TV. The feature would be LCD screen and the word "glare" would be the category specific negative sentiment word.

The semeval task 2 contains Twitter data that cannot be pinned to any specific category. So for this task, only the common lexicon was used.

3.2 Preprocessing

A typical tweet contains word variations, emoticons, hashtags etc. The objective of the preprocessing step is to normalize the text into an appropriate form to extract the sentiments. Below are the preprocessing steps used.

- **POS Tagging.** POS Tagger gives part of speech tag associated with words. POS tagging is done using NLTK (Bird, 2006).

- **Stemming.** Stemmer gives the stem word. Serendio lexicon contains stem words only. So non stem words are stemmed and replaced with stem words. For example, words like 'loved', 'loves', 'loving', 'love' are replaced with 'lov'. This would aid the engine to do the word match from the text to the lexicon. Stemming is done using NLTK

- **Exaggerated word shortening.** Words which have same letter more than two times and not present in the lexicon are reduced to the word with the repeating letter occurring just once (Kouloumpis et al., 2011). For example, the exaggerated word "NOOOOOO" is reduced to "NO".

- **Emoticon detection.** Emoticon has some sentiment associated with it. Twitter NLP (Ritter et. al , 2011; Ritter et. al , 2012) is used to extract emoticons along with the sentiments in the Twitter data.

- **Hashtag detection.** The hashtag is a topic or a keyword that is marked with a tweet. Hashtag is a phrase starting with # with no space between them. Hashtags are identified and sentiments are extracted from them.

3.3 Sentiment calculation

Sentiment calculation is the aggregation of the sum of the sentiment bearing entities of the tweet. Entities can be text, emoticons and hashtags. The sentiment calculation algorithm is shown in Algorithm 1. The sentiment calculation is based on a set of heuristics built on the sentiment orientation of the words. Blind negation words are extracted from the sentence. The presence of the blind negation words indicate negative sentiment. If the sentence contains a blind negation word then other steps are skipped and sentiment is blindly assigned as negative. Next, sentiment words are extracted. The sentiment polarity of the word can be changed due to negation words that occur in proximity (2 word distance). If a sentiment word is not present, then the sentiment negation word becomes additive to the negative sentiment list. The sentence "I can not deal it" has the negation word "not" and it does not contain a sentiment word. So the negation word just gets added to the negative sentiment word. Sentiments from emoticons are extracted with the help of Twitter NLP. Sentiment words within the hashtag are extracted by python regex functions. For example, from the hashtag "#ihateu", the word "hate" is extracted as a sentiment word. The sentiment of the tweet is aggregated as the sum of the sentiments from all the entities.

4 Experimental Data

The training data consist of real time tweets. 9451 subjective expressions are marked from all the tweets and are labeled as positive or negative or neutral. The average number of words of the marked subjective expression is around 2 to 3 words. The common dictionary that is constructed is shown in Table 2. The Serendio sentiment engine is run on the training data set. We identify the correct sentiment of the the phrases which are misclassified as neutral, we include the phrases in our lexicon with their appropriate sentiments.

Algorithm 1: Sentiment Calculation

Data: Preprocessed Twitter data
Result: Output: Positive, Negative, Neutral
Find the list of sentiment words $SentiList$, its position in the sentence;
Find the list of sentiment negation words $SentiNegat$, its position in the sentence;
Find the list of blind negation words $BlindNegat$, its position in the sentence;
if $BlindNegat$ **then**
    return negativity;
else
    if *SentiList and SentiNegat* **then**
        foreach *word in the SentiList* **do**
            if *word is atmost the distance of 2 from SentiNegat* **then**
                Revert the polarity of the word;
            end
        end
    else
        if $SentiNegat$ **then**
            Add the $SentiNegat$ to the negative $SentiList$;
        end
    end
end
$SentiSum$=0;
foreach *word in the SentiList* **do**
    $SentiSum$=$SentiSum$+sentiment of *word*;
end
if *Hashtag is present* **then**
    Find all the sentiment words in hash tag using regex matching and add them to $SentiList$
end
if *Emoticon is present* **then**
    Find sentiment of the emoticon and add emoticon,it's sentiment to $SentiList$
end
$SentiType$="neutral";
if $SentiSum > 0$ **then**
    $SentiType$="positive";
end
if $SentiSum < 0$ **then**
    $SentiType$="negative";
end
return $SentiType$;

Table 1: Training Data

Sentiment type	Expression count
Positive	5865
Negative	3120
Neutral	466

Table 2: Lexicon Details

Data type	Count
Blind Negation word	7
Negation	13
Positive sentiment word	1260
Negative sentiment word	1703
Split word	16

5 Result and Discussion

Our sentiment engine performed reasonably well. Please see Table 3 for Precision and Recall measurements. The recall rates are lower because of our lexicons lack of coverage of all the sentiment words. Informal language of tweets posed another challenge for identifying negative sentiments. For example, swear words such as "sh*t" and "f**k" are generally considered as negative sentiment words. Phrases such as "This sh*t is good" and "F**king awesome" were identified as negative sentiments when in fact they were expressing positive sentiments.

Table 3: Results

	POSITIVE	NEGATIVE
PRECISION	0.9361	0.8884
RECALL	0.7132	0.7912

The Serendio lexicon that we used has sentiment words with a sentiment attached to it. By integrating with a lexical source such as Sentiwordnet, we feel we could get a more nuanced word sense disambiguation. For example, the word "good" is considered to have positive polarity. According to Sentiwordnet 3.0, good as an adjective has 21 different senses with different sentiments. For example, the sentiment word "good" in the phrase "A good mile from here" gives an objective sense, not in a positive sense.

6 Conclusion

In this paper we presented our system that we used for the SemEval-2013 Task 2 for doing Sentiment Analysis for Twitter data. We got an F-score of 0.8004 on the test data set.

We presented a lexicon based method for Sentiment Analysis with Twitter data. We provided practical approaches to identifying and extracting sentiments from emoticons and hashtags. We also provided a method to convert non-grammatical words to grammatical words and normalize non-root to root words to extract sentiments.

A lexicon based approach is a simple, viable and practical approach to Sentiment Analysis of Twitter data without a need for training. A Lexicon based approach is as good as the lexicon it uses. To achieve better results, word sense disambiguation should be combined with the existing lexicon approach.

7 Acknowledgments

We would like to thank the organizers of SemEval 2013. We also would like to express our gratitude to the various reviewers for their encouragement and positive feedback.

References

Rodrigo Agerri and Ana García-Serrano. 2010. Q-WordNet: Extracting polarity from WordNet senses. *Seventh Conference on International Language Resources and Evaluation, Malta.*

Stefano Baccianella, Andrea Esuli and Fabrizio Sebastiani. 2010. Sentiwordnet 3.0: An enhanced lexical resource for sentiment analysis and opinion mining. *Proceedings of the 7th conference on International Language Resources and Evaluation (LREC10), Valletta, Malta, May.*

Adam Bermingham and Alan F Smeaton. 2010. Classifying sentiment in microblogs: is brevity an advantage? *Proceedings of the 19th ACM international conference on Information and knowledge management* 1833–1836, ACM.

Albert Bifet and Eibe Frank. 2010. Sentiment knowledge discovery in twitter streaming data. *Discovery Science* 1–14, Springer.

Steven Bird. 2006. NLTK: the natural language toolkit. *Proceedings of the COLING/ACL on Interactive presentation sessions* 69–72, Association for Computational Linguistics.

Kushal Dave, Steve Lawrence and David M Pennock. 2003. Mining the peanut gallery: Opinion extraction and semantic classification of product reviews. *Proceedings of the 12th international conference on World Wide Web* 519–528, ACM.

Dmitry Davidov, Oren Tsur and Ari Rappoport. 2010. Enhanced sentiment learning using twitter hashtags and smileys. *Proceedings of the 23rd International Conference on Computational Linguistics* 241 –249, Association for Computational Linguistics.

Xiaowen Ding, Bing Liu and Philip S Yu. 2008. A holistic lexicon-based approach to opinion mining. *Proceedings of the international conference on Web search and web data mining* 231–240, ACM.

Andrea Esuli and Fabrizio Sebastiani. 2006. Sentiwordnet: A publicly available lexical resource for opinion mining. *Proceedings of LREC Volume 6*, 417–422.

Alec Go, Richa Bhayani and Lei Huang. 2009. Twitter sentiment classification using distant supervision. *CS224N Project Report, Stanford* 1–12.

Bo Han and Timothy Baldwin. 2011. Lexical normalisation of short text messages: Makn sens a# twitter. *Proceedings of the 49th Annual Meeting of the Association for Computational Linguistics: Human Language Technologies Volume 1* , 368–378.

Nobuhiro Kaji and Masaru Kitsuregawa. 2007. Building lexicon for sentiment analysis from massive collection of HTML documents. *Proceedings of the joint conference on empirical methods in natural language processing and computational natural language learning (EMNLP-CoNLL)* 1075–1083, Association for Computational Linguistics.

Hiroshi Kanayama and Tetsuya Nasukawa. 2006. Fully automatic lexicon expansion for domain-oriented sentiment analysis. *Proceedings of the 2006 Conference on Empirical Methods in Natural Language Processing* 355–363,Association for Computational Linguistics.

Max Kaufmann and Jugal Kalita. 2010. Syntactic normalization of Twitter messages. *International Conference on Natural Language Processing* Kharagpur, India.

Efthymios Kouloumpis, Theresa Wilson and Johanna Moore. 2011. Twitter sentiment analysis: The good the bad and the omg. *Proceedings of the Fifth International AAAI Conference on Weblogs and Social Media* 538–541.

Bing Liu. 2008 Sentiment analysis and opinion mining. *Synthesis Lectures on Human Language Technologies*, 1–167,Morgan & Claypool Publishers.

Prem Melville, Wojciech Gryc and Richard D Lawrence. 2011. Sentiment analysis of blogs by combining lexical knowledge with text classification. *Proceedings of the 15th ACM SIGKDD international conference on Knowledge discovery and data mining*, 1275–1284, ACM.

Alexander Pak and Patrick Paroubek. 2010. Twitter as a corpus for sentiment analysis and opinion mining. *Proceedings of LREC*, Volume 2010.

Bo Pang and Lillian Lee. 2008. Opinion mining and sentiment analysis. *Foundations and trends in information retrieval Volume 2 number 1-2*, 1–135, Now Publishers Inc.

Bo Pang, Lillian Lee and Shivakumar Vaithyanathan. 2002. Thumbs up?: sentiment classification using machine learning techniques. *Proceedings of the ACL-02 conference on Empirical methods in natural language processing Volume 10*, 79–86, Association for Computational Linguistics.

Ellen Riloff, Janyce Wiebe and Theresa Wilson. 2003. Learning subjective nouns using extraction pattern bootstrapping. *Proceedings of the seventh conference on Natural language learning at HLT-NAACL 2003-Volume 4* 25–32, Association for Computational Linguistics.

Alan Ritter, Sam Clark, Mausam and Oren Etzioni. 2011. Named Entity Recognition in Tweets: An Experimental Study. *EMNLP*.

Alan Ritter, Mausam, Oren Etzioni, Sam Clark. 2012. Open Domain Event Extraction from Twitter. *KDD*.

Carlo Strapparava and Alessandro Valitutti. 2004. WordNet-Affect: an affective extension of WordNet. *Proceedings of LREC* 1083–1086.

Maite Taboada, Julian Brooke, Milan Tofiloski, Kimberly Voll and Manfred Stede. 2011. Lexicon-based methods for sentiment analysis. *Computational linguistics*, volume 37, number2, 267–307, MIT Press.

Richard M Tong 2001. An operational system for detecting and tracking opinions in on-line discussions. *In Working Notes of the ACM SIGIR 2001 Workshop on Operational Text Classification* 1–6,New York, NY.

Peter Turney and Michael Littman. 2003. Measuring praise and criticism: Inference of semantic orientation from association. *ACM Transactions on Information Systems* 21(4):315–346.

Peter Turney. 2002. Thumbs up or thumbs down?: semantic orientation applied to unsupervised classification of reviews. *Proceedings of the 40th annual meeting on association for computational linguistics*, 417–424, Association for Computational Linguistics.

Michael Wiegand, Alexandra Balahur, Benjamin Roth, Dietrich Klakow, Andrés Montoyo. 2010. A survey on the role of negation in sentiment analysis. *Proceedings of the workshop on negation and speculation in natural language processing* 60–68, Association for Computational Linguistics.

Theresa Wilson, Zornitsa Kozareva, Preslav Nakov, Alan Ritter, Sara Rosenthal and Veselin Stoyonov. 2013. SemEval-2013 Task 2: Sentiment Analysis in Twitter. *Proceedings of the 7th International Workshop on Semantic Evaluation* Association for Computation Linguistics.

SZTE-NLP: Sentiment Detection on Twitter Messages

Viktor Hangya, Gábor Berend, Richárd Farkas
University of Szeged
Department of Informatics
hangyav@gmail.com, {berendg,rfarkas}@inf.u-szeged.hu

Abstract

In this paper we introduce our contribution to the SemEval-2013 Task 2 on "Sentiment Analysis in Twitter". We participated in "task B", where the objective was to build models which classify tweets into three classes (positive, negative or neutral) by their contents. To solve this problem we basically followed the supervised learning approach and proposed several domain (i.e. microblog) specific improvements including text preprocessing and feature engineering. Beyond the supervised setting we also introduce some early results employing a huge, automatically annotated tweet dataset.

1 Introduction

In the past few years, the popularity of social media has increased. Many studies have been made in the area (Jansen et al., 2009; O'Connor et al., 2010; Bifet and Frank, 2010; Sang and Bos, 2012). People post messages on a variety of topics, for example products, political issues, etc. Thus a big amount of user generated data is created day-by-day. The manual processing of this data is impossible, therefore automatic procedures are needed.

In this paper we introduce an approach which is able to assign sentiment labels to Twitter messages. More precisely, it classifies tweets into positive, negative or neutral polarity classes. The system participated in the *SemEval-2013 Task 2: Sentiment Analysis in Twitter, Task–B Message Polarity Classification* (Wilson et al., 2013). In our approach we used a unigram based supervised model because it has been shown that it works well on short messages like tweets (Jiang et al., 2011; Barbosa and Feng, 2010; Agarwal et al., 2011; Liu, 2010). We reduced the size of the dictionary by normalizing the messages and by stop word filtering. We also explored novel features which gave us information on the polarity of a tweet, for example we made use of the acronyms in messages.

In the "constrained" track of *Task–B* we used the given training and development data only. For the "unconstrained" track we downloaded tweets using the Twitter Streaming API[1] and automatically annotated them. We present some preliminary results on exploiting this huge dataset for training our classifier.

2 Approach

At the beginning of our experiments we used a unigram-based supervised model. Later on, we realized that the size of our dictionary is huge, so in the normalization phase we tried to reduce the number of words in it. We investigated novel features which contain information on the polarity of the messages. Using these features we were able to improve the precision of our classifier. For implementation we used the MALLET toolkit, which is a Java-based package for natural language processing (McCallum, 2002).

2.1 Normalization

One reason for the unusually big dictionary size is that it contains one word in many forms, for exam-

[1] https://dev.twitter.com/docs/streaming-apis/streams/public

*Second Joint Conference on Lexical and Computational Semantics (*SEM), Volume 2: Seventh International Workshop on Semantic Evaluation (SemEval 2013)*, pages 549–553, Atlanta, Georgia, June 14-15, 2013.

ple in upper and lower case, in a misspelled form, with character repetition, etc. On the other hand, it contained numerous special annotations which are typical for blogging, such as Twitter-specific annotations, URL's, smileys, etc. Keeping these in mind we made the following normalization steps:

- First, in order to get rid of the multiple forms of a single word we converted them into lower case form then we stemmed them. For this purpose we used the Porter Stemming Algorithm.
- We replaced the @ and # Twitter-specific tags with the *[USER]* and *[TAG]* notations, respectively. Besides we converted every URL in the messages to the *[URL]* notation.
- Smileys in messages play an important role in polarity classification. For this reason we grouped them into positive and negative smiley classes. We considered *:), :-),:), :D, =), ;), ;), (:* and *:(, :-(, : (,):,) :* smileys as positive and negative, respectively.
- Since numbers do not contain information regarding a message polarity, we converted them as well to the *[NUMBER]* form. In addition, we replaced the question and exclamation marks with the *[QUESTION_MARK]* and *[EXCLAMATION_MARK]* notations. After this we removed the unnecessary characters `'"#$%&()*+,./:;<=>\^{}~`, with the exception that we removed the `'` character only if a word started or ended with it.
- In the case of words which contained character repetitions – more precisely those which contained the same character at least three times in a row –, we reduced the length of this sequence to three. For instance, in the case of the word *yeeeeahhhhhhh* we got the form *yeeeahhh*. This way we unified these character repetitions, but we did not loose this extra information.
- Finally we made a stop word filtering in order to get rid of the undesired words. To identify these words we did not use a stop word dictionary, rather we filtered out those words which appeared too frequently in the training corpus. We have chosen this method because we would like to automatically detect those words which are not relevant in the classification.

Before the normalization step, the dictionary contained approximately $41,000$ words. After the above introduced steps we managed to reduce the size of the dictionary to $15,000$ words.

2.2 Features

After normalizing Twitter messages, we searched for special features which characterize the polarity of the tweets. One such feature is the polarity of each word in a message. To determine the polarity of a word, we used the SentiWordNet sentiment lexicon (Baccianella et al., 2010). In this lexicon, a positive, negative and an objective real value belong to each word, which describes the polarity of the given word. We consider a word as positive if the related positive value is greater than 0.3, we consider it as negative if the related negative value is greater than 0.2 and we consider it as objective if the related objective value is greater than 0.8. The threshold of the objective value is high because most words are objective in this lexicon. After calculating the polarity of each word we created three new features for each tweet which are the number of positive, negative and objective words, respectively. We also checked if a negation word precedes a positive or negative word and if so we inverted its polarity.

We also tried to group acronyms by their polarity. For this purpose we used an acronym lexicon which can be found on the `www.internetslang.com` website. For each acronym we used the polarity of each word in the acronym's description and we determined the polarity of the acronym by calculating the rate of positive and negative words in the description. This way we created two new features which are the number of positive and negative acronyms in a given message.

Our intuition was that people like to use character repetitions in their words for expressing their happiness or sadness. Besides normalizing these tokens (see Section 2.1), we created a new feature as well, which represents the number of this kind of words in a tweet.

Beyond character repetitions people like to write words or a part of the text in upper case in order to call the reader's attention. Because of this we created another feature which is the number of upper case words in the given text.

3 Collected Data

In order to achieve an appropriate precision with supervised methods we need a big amount of training data. Creating this database manually is a hard and time-consuming task. In many cases it is hard even for humans to determine the polarity of a message, for instance:

> After a whole 5 hours away from work, I get to go back again, I'm so lucky!

In the above tweet we cannot decide precisely the polarity because the writer can be serious or just sarcastic.

In order to increase the size of the training data we acquired additional tweets, which we used in the unconstrained run for *Task–B*. We created an application which downloads tweets using the Twitter Streaming API. The API supports language filtering, which was used to get rid of non-English messages. Our manual investigations of the downloaded tweets revealed, however, that this filter allows a big amount of non-English tweets, which is probably due to the fact that some Twitter users did not set their language. We used Twitter4J[2] API (which is a Java library for the Twitter API) for downloading these tweets. We automatically annotated the downloaded tweets using the *Twitter Sentiment*[3] web application, similar to Barbosa and Feng (2010) but we used only one annotator. This web application also supports language detection, but after this extra filtration, our dataset still contained a considerable amount of non-English messages. After 16 hours of data collection we got 350,000 annotated tweets, where the distribution of neutral, positive and negative classes was approximately 60%, 20%, 20%, respectively. For further testing purposes we have chosen 10,000 tweets from each class.

4 Results

We report results on the two official test sets of the shared task. The "twitter" test set consists of 3,813 tweets while the "sms" set consists of 2,094 sms messages. We evaluated both test databases in two ways, in the so-called constrained run we only used the official training database, while in the unconstrained run we also used a part of the additional data, which was mentioned in the 3 section. The official training database contained 4,028 positive, 1,655 negative and 3,821 neutral tweets while for the unconstrained run we used an additional 10,000 tweets from each class. This way in each phase we got four kinds of runs, which were evaluated with the Naïve Bayes and Maximum Entropy classifiers.

In Table 1 the evaluation of the unigram-based model with the Naïve Bayes learner can be seen. The table contains the F-scores for the positive, negative and neutral labels for each of the four runs. The *avg* column contains the average F-score for the positive and negative labels, which was the official evaluation metric for *SemEval-2013 Task 2*. We got the best scores for the neutral label whilst the worst scores are obtained for the negative label, which is due to the fact that there were much less negative instances in the training database. It can be seen that the F-scores for the unconstrained run are better both for the tweet and sms test databases. For the unigram-based model the F-scores are higher when we used the Maximum Entropy model (see Table 2).

	pos	neg	neut	avg
twitter-constrained	0.59	0.09	0.65	0.34
twitter-unconstrained	0.60	0.17	0.65	0.38
sms-constrained	0.46	0.16	0.63	0.31
sms-unconstrained	0.47	0.38	0.53	0.42

Table 1: Unigram-based model, Naïve Bayes learner

	pos	neg	neut	avg
twitter-constrained	0.60	0.33	0.67	0.46
twitter-unconstrained	0.60	0.40	0.66	0.50
sms-constrained	0.47	0.31	0.69	0.39
sms-unconstrained	0.52	0.47	0.66	0.49

Table 2: Unigram-based model, Maximum Entropy learner

In Tables 3 and 4 the evaluation results can be seen for the normalized model. The normalization

[2]http://twitter4j.org
[3]http://www.sentiment140.com

step increased the precision for both learning algorithms and the Maximum Entropy learner is still better than Naïve Bayes. Besides this we noticed that for both learners in the case of the tweet test database, the unconstrained run had lower scores than the constrained whilst in the case of the sms test database this phenomenon did not appear.

	pos	neg	neut	avg
twitter-constrained	0.65	0.32	0.67	0.48
twitter-unconstrained	0.62	0.21	0.63	0.41
sms-constrained	0.56	0.27	0.72	0.41
sms-unconstrained	0.52	0.35	0.66	0.43

Table 3: Normalized model, Naïve Bayes learner

	pos	neg	neut	avg
twitter-constrained	0.66	0.40	0.68	0.53
twitter-unconstrained	0.61	0.42	0.64	0.51
sms-constrained	0.61	0.38	0.77	0.49
sms-unconstrained	0.57	0.47	0.72	0.52

Table 4: Normalized model, Maximum Entropy learner

The evaluation results of the feature-based model can be seen in Tables 5 and 6. In the case of the Naïve Bayes learner, the features did not increase the F-scores, only for the sms-unconstrained run. For the other runs the achieved scores decreased. In the case of the Maximum Entropy learner the features increased the F-scores, slightly for the constrained runs and a bit more for the unconstrained runs.

From this analysis we can conclude that the normalization of the messages yielded a considerable increase in the F-scores. We discussed above that this step also significantly reduced the size of the dictionary. The features increased the precision too, especially for the unconstrained run. This means that these features represent properties which are useful for those training data which are not from the same corpus as the test messages. We compared two machine learning algorithms and from the results we concluded that the Maximum Entropy learner performs better than the Naïve Bayes on this task. Our experiments also showed that the external, automatically labeled training database helped only in the classification of sms messages. This is due to the fact that the smses and our external database are from a different distribution than the official tweet database.

	pos	neg	neut	avg
twitter-constrained	0.65	0.32	0.67	0.48
twitter-unconstrained	0.62	0.17	0.79	0.39
sms-constrained	0.56	0.38	0.74	0.47
sms-unconstrained	0.54	0.29	0.70	0.41

Table 5: Feature-based model, Naïve Bayes learner

	pos	neg	neut	avg
twitter-constrained	0.66	0.41	0.69	0.54
twitter-unconstrained	0.63	0.43	0.65	0.53
sms-constrained	0.62	0.39	0.79	0.50
sms-unconstrained	0.61	0.49	0.75	0.55

Table 6: Feature-based model, Maximum Entropy learner

5 Conclusions and Future Work

Recently, sentiment analysis on Twitter messages has gained a lot of attention due to the huge amount of Twitter users and their tweets. In this paper we examined different methods for classifying Twitter and sms messages. We proposed special features which characterize the polarity of the messages and we concluded that due to the informality (slang, spelling mistakes, etc.) of the messages it is crucial to normalize them properly.

In the future, we plan to investigate the utility of relations between Twitter users and between their tweets and we are interested in topic-dependent sentiment analysis.

Acknowledgments

This work was supported in part by the European Union and the European Social Fund through project FuturICT.hu (grant no.: TÁMOP-4.2.2.C-11/1/KONV-2012-0013).

References

Apoorv Agarwal, Boyi Xie, Ilia Vovsha, Owen Rambow, and Rebecca Passonneau. 2011. Sentiment Analysis of Twitter Data. In *Proceedings of the Workshop on Language in Social Media (LSM 2011)*, pages 30–38, June.

Stefano Baccianella, Andrea Esuli, and Fabrizio Sebastiani. 2010. SentiWordNet 3.0: An Enhanced Lexical Resource for Sentiment Analysis and Opinion Mining. In Nicoletta Calzolari (Conference Chair), Khalid Choukri, Bente Maegaard, Joseph Mariani, Jan Odijk, Stelios Piperidis, Mike Rosner, and Daniel Tapias, editors, *Proceedings of the Seventh International Conference on Language Resources and Evaluation (LREC'10)*, Valletta, Malta, May. European Language Resources Association (ELRA).

Luciano Barbosa and Junlan Feng. 2010. Robust Sentiment Detection on Twitter from Biased and Noisy Data. In *Poster volume*, Coling 2010, pages 36–44, August.

Albert Bifet and Eibe Frank. 2010. Sentiment Knowledge Discovery in Twitter Streaming Data.

Bernard J. Jansen, Mimi Zhang, Kate Sobel, and Abdur Chowdury. 2009. Twitter Power: Tweets as Electronic Word of Mouth. In *Journal of the American society for information science and technology*, pages 2169–2188.

Long Jiang, Mo Yu, Ming Zhou, Xiaohua Liu, and Tiejun Zhao. 2011. Target-dependent Twitter Sentiment Classification. In *Proceedings of the 49th Annual Meeting of the Association for Computational Linguistics*, pages 151–160, June.

Bing Liu. 2010. Sentiment Analysis and Subjectivity. In N. Indurkhya and F. J. Damerau, editors, *Handbook of Natural Language Processing*.

Andrew Kachites McCallum. 2002. Mallet: A machine learning for language toolkit. http://mallet.cs.umass.edu.

Brendan O'Connor, Ramnath Balasubramanyan, Bryan R. Routledge, and Noah A. Smith. 2010. From Tweets to Polls: Linking Text Sentiment to Public Opinion Time Series. In *Proceedings of the International AAAI Conference on Weblogs and Social Media*, May.

Erik Tjong Kim Sang and Johan Bos. 2012. Predicting the 2011 Dutch Senate Election Results with Twitter. In *Proceedings of the 13th Conference of the European Chapter of the Association for Computational Linguistics*, pages 53–60, April.

Theresa Wilson, Zornitsa Kozareva, Preslav Nakov, Sara Rosenthal, Veselin Stoyanov, and Alan Ritter. 2013. SemEval-2013 Task 2: Sentiment Analysis in Twitter. In *Proceedings of the International Workshop on Semantic Evaluation*, SemEval '13, June.

BOUNCE: Sentiment Classification in Twitter using Rich Feature Sets

Nadin Kökciyan†, Arda Çelebi†, Arzucan Özgür, Suzan Üsküdarlı

Department of Computer Engineering
Bogazici University
Istanbul, Turkey
{nadin.kokciyan,arda.celebi,arzucan.ozgur,suzan.uskudarli}@boun.edu.tr

Abstract

The widespread use of Twitter makes it very interesting to determine the opinions and the sentiments expressed by its users. The shortness of the length and the highly informal nature of tweets render it very difficult to automatically detect such information. This paper reports the results to a challenge, set forth by SemEval-2013 Task 2, to determine the positive, neutral, or negative sentiments of tweets. Two systems are explained: System A for determining the sentiment of a phrase within a tweet and System B for determining the sentiment of a tweet. Both approaches rely on rich feature sets, which are explained in detail.

1 Introduction

Twitter consists of a massive number of posts on a wide range of subjects, making it very interesting to extract information and sentiments from them. For example, answering questions like 'What do Twitter users feel about the brand X?' are quite interesting. The constrained length and highly informal nature of tweets presents a serious challenge for the automated extraction of such sentiments.

Twitter supports special tokens (i.e. mentions and hashtags), which have been utilized to determine the sentiment of tweets. In (Go et al., 2009), emoticons are used to label tweets. In (Davidov et al., 2010), Twitter emoticons as well as hashtags are used to label tweets. O'Connor et al. (2010) demonstrated a correlation between sentiments identified in public opinion polls and those in tweets. A subjectivity lexicon was used to identify the positive and negative words in a tweet. In (Barbosa and Feng, 2010), subjective tweets are used for sentiment classification. They propose the use of word specific (e.g. POS tags) and tweet specific (e.g. presence of a link) features. Most of these studies use their own annotated data sets for evaluation, which makes it difficult to compare the performances of their proposed approaches.

Sentiment Analysis in Twitter 2013 (SemEval 2013 Task 2) (Wilson et al., 2013) presented a challenge for exploring different approaches examining sentiments conveyed in tweets: interval-level (phrase-level) sentiment classification (TaskA) and message-level sentiment classification (TaskB). Sentiment are considered as *positive, negative,* or *neutral*. For TaskA, the goal is to determine the sentiment of an interval (consecutive word sequence) within a tweet. For TaskB, the goal is to determine sentiment of an entire tweet. For example, let's consider a tweet like '*Can't wait* until the DLC for ME3 comes out tomorrow. *:-)*'. For TaskA, the interval 0-1 (*Can't wait*) is 'positive' and the interval 10-10 (*:-)*) is 'positive'. For TaskB, this tweet is 'positive'.

In this paper, we present two systems, one for TaskA and one for TaskB. In both cases machine learning methods were utilized with rich feature sets based on the characteristics of tweets. Our results suggest that our approach is promising for sentiment classification in Twitter.

2 Approach

The task of detecting the sentiments of a tweet or an interval therein, is treated as a classification of

† These authors contributed equally to this work

*Second Joint Conference on Lexical and Computational Semantics (*SEM), Volume 2: Seventh International Workshop on Semantic Evaluation (SemEval 2013)*, pages 554–561, Atlanta, Georgia, June 14-15, 2013.

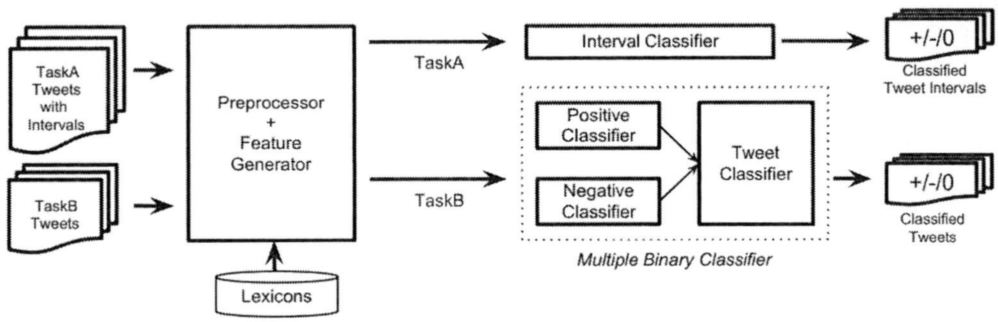

Figure 1: The Overview of BOUNCE System

tweets into positive, negative, or neutral sets. Figure 1 gives the overview of our approach. The Preprocessor module tokenizes the tweets that are used by the Feature Generator. At this stage, the tweets are represented as feature vectors. For TaskA, the feature vectors are used by the Interval Classifier that predicts the labels of the tweet intervals. For TaskB, the feature vectors are used by the Positive Classifier and the Negative Classifier which report on the positivity and negativity of the tweets. The Tweet Classifier determines the tweet labels using a rule-based method. Each step is described in detail in the following subsections.

2.1 Lexicons

The core of our approach to sentiment analysis relies on word lists that are used to determine the positive and negative words or phrases. Several acquired lists are used in addition to one that we curated. AFINN (Nielsen, 2011) is the main sentiment word list including 2477 words rated between -5 to 5 for valence. SentiWordNet (Baccianella et al., 2010), derived from the Princeton English WordNet (Miller, 1995), assigns positive, negative, or objective scores to each synset in WordNet. We considered the average of a word's synsets as its SentiWordNet score. Thus, synsets are disregarded and no disambiguation of the sense of a word in a given context is done. The SentiWordNet score of a word is not used if it has objective synsets, since it indicates that the word might have been used in an objective sense. We use a list of emotion words and categories that is created by DeRose[1]. Furthermore, a slang dictionary downloaded from the Urban Dictionary[2] containing over 16,000 phrases (with no sentiment) is used. Finally, we curated a sentiment word list initiated with a list of positive and negative words obtained from General Inquirer (Stone et al., 1966), and refined by sentiment emitting words from a frequency-based ordered word list generated from the training data set of SemEval-2013 Task A. Naturally, this list is more specialized to the Twitter domain.

2.2 Preprocessing

Prior to feature generation, tweets were preprocessed to yield text with more common wording. For this, CMU's Ark Tokenizer and Part-of-Speech (POS) Tagger (Gimpel et al., 2011), which has been specifically trained for tweets, was used. Tweets are tokenized and POS tagged.

2.3 Feature Sets

In addition to the lexical or syntactic characteristics, the manner in which tweets are written may reveal sentiment. Orthogonal shapes of words (esp. fully or partially capitalized words), expressions of a single word or a phrase in the form of a hashtag, positions of certain tokens in a tweet are prominent characteristics of tweets. In addition to these, tweets may convey multiple sentiments. This leads to sequence-based features, where we append features for each sentiment emitted by a word or a phrase in a tweet. Moreover, since TaskA asks for sentiment of intervals in a tweet, we also engineer features to catch clues from the surrounding context of the interval,

[1] http://derose.net/steve/resources/emotionwords/ewords.html

[2] http://www.urbandictionary.com

such as the sentiments and lengths of the neighboring intervals. For TaskB, the usage of hashtags and last words in tweets were occasionally sentimental, thus we considered them as features as well. We explain all features in detail in Section 3.

2.4 Classification

Maximum entropy models (Berger et al., 1996) have been used in sentiment analysis (Fei et al., 2010). They model all given data and treat the remainder as uniform as possible making no assumptions about what is not provided. For this, TaskA system uses the MaxEnt tool (Zhang, 2011).

Naive Bayes is a simple probabilistic model based on *Bayes' Theorem* that assumes independence between features. It has performed well in sentiment classification of Twitter data (Go et al., 2009; Bifet and Frank, 2010). TaskB data was not evenly distributed. There were very few negative tweets compared to positive tweets. Using a single classifier to distinguish the classes from each other resulted in poor performance in identifying negative tweets. Therefore, TaskB system utilizes multiple binary classifiers that use the one-vs-all strategy. Maximum Entropy and Naive Bayes models were considered and the model that performed best on the development set was chosen for each classifier. As a result, the positive classifier (B_{pos}) is based on the Maximum Entropy model, whereas the negative classifier (B_{neg}) is based on Naive Bayes. TaskB system uses the Natural Language Toolkit (Loper and Bird, 2002).

3 Systems

In this section, TaskA and TaskB systems are explained in detail. All features used in the final experiments for both tasks are shown in Table 1.

3.1 TaskA System

TaskA is a classification task where we classify a given interval as having positive, negative or neutral sentiment. TaskA feature sets are shown in Table 1.

lexical features: These features use directly words (or tokens) from tweets as features. *single-word* feature uses the word of the single-word intervals, whereas *slang* features are created for matching uni-grams and bi-grams from our slang dictionary. We also use emoticons as features, as well as the words or phrases that emit emotion according to the lexicons described in Section 2.1.

score-based features: These features use the scores obtained from the AFINN and SentiWordNet (SWN) lexicons. We use separate scores for the positive and negative sentiments, since one interval may contain multiple words with opposite sentiment. In case of multiple positive or negative occurances, we take the arithmetic mean of those.

shape-based features: These features capture the length of an interval, whether it contains a capitalized word or all words are capitalized, whether it contains a URL, or ends with an exclamation mark.

tag-based features: In addition to numeric values of sentiments, we use the tokens 'positive' and 'negative' to express the type of sentiment. When multiple words emit a sentiment in a given interval, their corresponding tokens are appended to create a single feature out of it, *sequences*. Moreover, we have another set of features which also contains the POS tags of these sentiment words.

indicator features: These features are used in order to expose how many sentiment emitting words from our currated large lexicon exist in a given interval. *hasNegation* indicates the presence of a negation word like *not* or *can't* in the interval, whereas *numOfPosIndicators* and *numOfNegIndicators* gives the number of tokens that convey positive and negative sentiment, respectively.

context features: In addition to the features generated from the given interval, these features capture the context information from the neighboring intervals. Feature *surroundings* combines the length of the interval along with the lengths of the intervals on both sides, whereas *surrounding-shape* and *extra-surrounding-shape* features use number of positive and negative sentiment indicators for the intervals. We also use their normalized forms (those starting with *norm-*) where we divide the number of indicators by the length of the interval. Features with *-extra-* use two adjacent intervals from both sides. Intervals that are not available are represented with *NA*.

3.2 TaskB System

TaskB is a classification task where we determine the sentiment (positive, negative, or neutral) of a tweet. TaskB system uses a rule-based method to

<table>
<tr><th>Feature Set</th><th>Feature</th><th>Example Feature Instance</th><th>used by</th></tr>
<tr><td rowspan="4">lexical-based</td><td>single-word-*</td><td>*single-word-worst*</td><td>A, B</td></tr>
<tr><td>slang-*</td><td>*slang-shit*</td><td>A, B_{pos}</td></tr>
<tr><td>emoticons-*</td><td>*emoticons-:)*</td><td>A</td></tr>
<tr><td>emitted-emotions-*</td><td>*emitted-emotions-angry*</td><td>A, B</td></tr>
<tr><td rowspan="2">score-based</td><td>afinn-positive:#, afinn-negative:#</td><td>*afinn-positive:4, afinn-negative:-2*</td><td>A, B</td></tr>
<tr><td>swn-positive:#, swn-negative:#</td><td>*swn-positive:2, swn-negative:-3*</td><td>A</td></tr>
<tr><td rowspan="5">shape-based</td><td>length-#</td><td>*length-10*</td><td>A</td></tr>
<tr><td>hasAllCap-T/F</td><td>*hasAllCap-T*</td><td>A</td></tr>
<tr><td>fullCap-T/F</td><td>*fullCap-T*</td><td>A</td></tr>
<tr><td>hasURL-T/F</td><td>*hasURL-F*</td><td>A, B</td></tr>
<tr><td>endsWExlamation-T/F</td><td>*endsWExlamation-T*</td><td>A, B_{neg}</td></tr>
<tr><td rowspan="3">tag-based</td><td>our-seq-*</td><td>*our-seq-positive-positive*</td><td>A, B</td></tr>
<tr><td>our-tag-seq-*, swn-seq-*, swn-tag-seq-*</td><td>*afinn-seq-positive-a-positive-n*</td><td>A</td></tr>
<tr><td>afinn-seq-*, afinn-tag-seq-*</td><td>*afinn-seq-positive-a-negative-n*</td><td>A</td></tr>
<tr><td rowspan="3">indicators</td><td>hasNegation-T/F</td><td>*hasNegation-F*</td><td>A</td></tr>
<tr><td>numOfPosIndicators-#</td><td>*numOfPosIndicators-2*</td><td>A</td></tr>
<tr><td>numOfNegIndicators-#</td><td>*numOfNegIndicators-0*</td><td>A</td></tr>
<tr><td rowspan="6">context</td><td>surroundings-#-#-#</td><td>*surroundings-1-2-NA*</td><td>A</td></tr>
<tr><td>surr-shape-#-#-#</td><td>*surrounding-shape-NA-2-1*</td><td>A</td></tr>
<tr><td>extra-surr-shape-#-#-#-#-#</td><td>*extra-surr-shape-NA-2-1-0-1*</td><td>A</td></tr>
<tr><td>norm-surr-shape-#-#-#</td><td>*norm-surr-shape-0.5-0.2-0.0*</td><td>A</td></tr>
<tr><td>norm-extra-surr-shape-#-#-#-#-#</td><td>*norm-extra-surr-shape-NA-0.5-0.2-0.0-0.2*</td><td>A</td></tr>
<tr><td>left-sentiment-*, right-sentiment-*</td><td>*left-sentiment-positive*</td><td>A</td></tr>
<tr><td rowspan="4">twitter-tags</td><td>hasEmoticon-T/F</td><td>*hasEmoticon-T*</td><td>B</td></tr>
<tr><td>hasMention-T/F</td><td>*hasMention-T*</td><td>B</td></tr>
<tr><td>hasHashtag-T/F</td><td>*hasHashtag-F*</td><td>B</td></tr>
<tr><td>[emoticon|mention|hash]-count-#</td><td>*mention-count-3*</td><td>B</td></tr>
<tr><td rowspan="2">repetition</td><td>unigram-$*_n$</td><td>*unigram-[no+]*</td><td>B</td></tr>
<tr><td>*$character*-count-#</td><td>*o-count-7*</td><td>B</td></tr>
<tr><td rowspan="2">lastword</td><td>lastword-$*_n$</td><td>*lastword-[OMG+]*</td><td>B</td></tr>
<tr><td>lastwordshape-*</td><td>*lastwordshape-XXXX*</td><td>B</td></tr>
<tr><td>chat</td><td>chatword-*</td><td>for word 'gz': *chatword-congratulations*</td><td>B</td></tr>
<tr><td>interjection</td><td>interjection-$*_n$</td><td>*interjection-[lo+l]*</td><td>B</td></tr>
<tr><td rowspan="3">negation</td><td>negword-$*_n$</td><td>*negword-never*</td><td>B_{neg}</td></tr>
<tr><td>negword-count-#</td><td>*negword-count-3*</td><td>B_{neg}</td></tr>
<tr><td>negcapword-count-#</td><td>*negcapword-count-1*</td><td>B_{neg}</td></tr>
<tr><td rowspan="3">hash</td><td>hashword-*</td><td>*hashword-good*</td><td>B</td></tr>
<tr><td>hashtag-#*</td><td>*hashtag-#good*</td><td>B</td></tr>
<tr><td>hash-sentiment-[positive|negative]</td><td>*hash-sentiment-positive*</td><td>B</td></tr>
<tr><td>lingemotion</td><td>[noun|verb|adverb|adjective]-*$emotion*</td><td>*noun-fear*</td><td>B</td></tr>
<tr><td rowspan="5">oursent</td><td></td><td>for tweet: a *nice* morning.. I *hate* work.. *damn*!</td><td></td></tr>
<tr><td>oursent-*</td><td>*oursent-nice, oursent-hate, oursent-damn*</td><td>B</td></tr>
<tr><td>oursent-longseq-*</td><td>*oursent-longseq-pnn*</td><td>B</td></tr>
<tr><td>oursent-shortseq-*</td><td>*oursent-shortseq-pn*</td><td>B</td></tr>
<tr><td>oursent-first-last-*</td><td>*oursent-first-last-pn*</td><td>B</td></tr>
<tr><td rowspan="5">afinn-phrases</td><td>phrase-firstsense-[positive|negative]</td><td>*phrase-firstsense-positive*</td><td>B</td></tr>
<tr><td>phrase-lastsense-[positive|negative]</td><td>*phrase-lastsense-negative*</td><td>B</td></tr>
<tr><td>afinnword-*</td><td>*afinnword-nice, afinnword-hate, afinnword-damn*</td><td>B</td></tr>
<tr><td>afinn-firstsense-[positive|negative]</td><td>*afinn-firstsense-positive*</td><td>B</td></tr>
<tr><td>afinn-lastsense-[positive|negative]</td><td>*afinn-lastsense-positive*</td><td>B</td></tr>
<tr><td>emo</td><td>emo-pattern-*</td><td>for =) : *emo-pattern-HAPPY*</td><td>B</td></tr>
</table>

Table 1: Feature sets used in TaskA and TaskB

Dataset	Type	Positive	Negative	Neutral+Objective	Tot. No. of Instances
TaskA	Training	5290 (5865)	2771(3120)	16118 (17943)	24179 (26928)
	Development	589 (648)	392 (430)	1993 (2202)	2974 (3280)
	Test	2734	1541	160	4435
TaskB	Training	3274 (3640)	1291 (1458)	4155 (4586)	8720 (9684)
	Development	523 (575)	309 (340)	674 (739)	1506 (1654)
	Test	1572	601	1640	3813

Table 2: Number of instances used in TaskA and TaskB

decide on the sentiment label of a tweet. For each tweet, the probabilities of belonging to the positive class ($Prob_{pos}$) and negative class ($Prob_{neg}$) are computed by the B_{pos} and B_{neg} classifiers, respectively. If $Prob_{pos}$ is greater than $Prob_{neg}$, and greater than a predefined threshold, then the tweet is classified as 'positive', otherwise it is classified as 'neutral'. On the other hand, if $Prob_{neg}$ is greater than $Prob_{pos}$, and greater than the predefined threshold, then the tweet is classified as 'negative', otherwise it is classified as 'neutral'. The threshold is set to 0.45, since it gives the optimal F-score on the development set. TaskB features along with examples are shown in Table 1.

twitter-tags: *hasEmoticon*, *hasMention*, *hasURL*, and *hasHashtag* indicate whether the corresponding term (e.g. mention) exists in the tweet.

repetition: Words with repeating letters are added as a feature $*_n$. $*_n$ represents the normalized version (i.e., no repeating letters) of a word. For example, 'nooooooo' is shortened to *[no+]*. We also keep the count of the repeated character.

wordshape: Shape of each word in a tweet is considered. For example, the shape of 'NOoOo!!' is 'XXxXx!!'.

lastword: The normalized form and the shape of the last word are used as features. For example, if the lastword is 'OMGG', then *lastword* '[OMG+]' and *lastwordshape* 'XXXX' are used as features.

chat: A list of chat abbreviations that express sentiment is manually created. Each abbreviation is replaced by its corresponding word.

interjection: An interjection is a word that expresses an emotion or sentiment (e.g. hurraah, loool). Interjection $word_n$ is used as a feature.

negation: We manually created a negation list extended by word clusters from (Owoputi et al., 2013). A negation word is represented by spellings such as not, n0t, and naht. Each negation $word_n$ (e.g neve[r+]) is considered. We keep the count of negation words and all capitalized negation words.

hash: If the hashtag is '#good' then *#good* and *good* become hash features. If the hashtag is a sentiment expressing word according to our sentiment word list, then we keep the sentiment information.

lingemotion: Nodebox Linguistics[3] package gives emotional values of words for expressions of emotions such as fear and sadness. POS augmented expression information is used as a feature.

oursent: Each word in a tweet that exists in our sentiment word list is considered. When multiple sentiment expressing words are found, a sentiment sequence feature is used. *oursent-longseq* keeps the long sequence, whereas *oursent-shortseq* keeps same sequence without repetitive sentiments. We also consider the first and last sentiments emitted by a tweet.

afinn: We consider each word that exists in AFINN. If a negation exists before this word, the opposite sentiment is considered. For example, if a tweet contains the bigram 'not good', then the sentiment of the bigram is set to 'negative'. The AFINN scores of the positive and negative words, as well as the first and last sentiments emitted by the tweet are considered.

phrases: Each n-gram ($n > 1$) of a tweet that exists in our sentiment phrase list is considered.

afinn-phrases: Phrases are retrieved using the *phrases* feature. Each sentiment that appears in a phrase is kept, hence we obtain a sentiment sequence. The first and last sentiments of this sequence are also considered. Then, the phrases are removed from the tweet text and the *afinn* feature is applied.

emo: We manually created an emoticon list where

[3]http://nodebox.net/code/index.php/Linguistics

each term is associated with an emotion pattern such as HAPPY. These emotion patterns are used as a feature.

others: B_{pos} uses the *slang* feature from the lexical feature set, and B_{neg} uses *endsWExlamation* feature from the indicators feature set.

4 Experiments and Results

4.1 Data

The data set provided by the task organizers was annotated by using Amazon Mechanical Turk[4]. The annotations of the tweets in the training and development sets were provided to the task participants. However, the tweets had to be downloaded from Twitter by using the script made available by the organizers. We were unable to download all the tweets in the training and development sets, since some tweets were deleted and others were not publicly accessible due to their updated authorization status. The number of actual tweets (numbers in parentheses) and the number of collected tweets are shown in Table 2. Almost 10% of the data for both tasks are missing. For the test data, however, the tweets were directly provided to the participants.

4.2 Results on TaskA

We start our experiments with features generated from lexicons and emoticons. Called our baseline, it achieved an f-score of 47.8 on the devset in Table 3. As we add other features at each step, we reach an average f-score of 81.6 on the devset at the end. Among those features, the most contributing ones are lexical feature *single-word*, indicator feature *hasNegation*, and especially shape feature *length*. The success of the *length* feature is mostly due to the nature of intervals, where the long ones tend to be neutral, and the rest are mostly positive or negative. Another noteworthy result is that our curated word list contributed more compared to the others. When the final model is used on the test set, we get the results in Table 5. Having low neutral f-score might be due to the fact that there were only a few neutral intervals in the test set, which might indicate that their characteristics may not be the same as the ones in the devset.

[4]https://www.mturk.com/mturk/

Added Features	Avg. F-Score
afinn-positive, afinn-negetive swn-positive, swn-negative, emoticons, emitted-emotions	47.8
+ hasAllCap, fullCap, hasURL, endsWExclamation	50.1
+ slang	51.5
+ single-word	56.8
+ afinn-seq, swn-seq, afinn-tag-seq, swn-tag-seq	57.7
+ our-seq, our-tag-seq	60.2
+ hasNegation	64.8
+ numOfPosIndicators, numOfNegIndicators	65.3
+ length	75.2
+ left-sentiment, right-sentiment	76.5
+ surroundings, surrounding-shape	78.9
+ extra-surrounding-shape	80.6
+ norm-surrounding-shape, norm-extra-surrounding-shape	**81.6**

Table 3: Macro-averaged F-Score on the TaskA dev. set

Added Features	Average F-Score
oursent (baseline)	58.59
+ afinn-phrases	64.64
+ tags + hash	65.43
+ interjection + chat	65.53
+ emo + lingemotion	65.92
+ repetition + lastword	66.01
+ negation + others	**66.32**

Table 4: Macro-averaged F-Score on the TaskB dev. set

4.3 Results on TaskB

The baseline model is considered to include *oursent* feature that gives an average f-score of 58.59. Next, we added the *afinn phrases* feature which increased the average f-score to 64.64. This increase can be explained by the sentiment scores and sequence patterns that *afinn-phrases* is based on. Following that model, the other added features slightly increased the average f-score to 66.32 as shown in Table 4. The final model is used over the test set of TaskB, where we obtained an f-score of 63.53 as shown in Table 5.

	Class	Precision	Recall	F-Score
	positive	89.7	88.3	89.0
TestA	negative	86.6	82.7	84.6
	neutral	10.7	18.1	13.4
average(pos+neg)		88.15	85.5	**86.8**
	positive	82.3	55.6	66.4
TestB	negative	48.7	80.2	60.6
	neutral	68.2	73.3	70.7
average(pos+neg)		65.56	67.93	**63.53**

Table 5: Results on the test sets for both tasks

5 Conclusion

We presented two systems one for TaskA (a Maximum Entropy model) and one for TaskB (Maximum Entropy + Naive Bayes models) based on using rich feature sets. For Task A, we started with a baseline system that just uses ordinary features like sentiment scores of words. As we added new features, we observed that lexical features and shape-based features are the ones that contribute most to the performance of the system. Including the context features and the indicator feature for negations led to considerable improvement in performance as well. For TaskB, we first created a baseline model that uses sentiment words and phrases from the AFINN lexicon as features. Each feature that we added to the system resulted in improvement in performance. The *negation* and *endsWExclamation* features only improved the performance of the negative classifier, whereas the *slang* feature only improved the performance of the positive classifier.

Our results show that using rich feature sets with machine learning algorithms is a promising approach for sentiment classification in Twitter. Our TaskA system ranked 3rd among 23 systems and TaskB system ranked 4th among 35 systems participating in SemEval 2013 Task 2.

References

Stefano Baccianella, Andrea Esuli, and Fabrizio Sebastiani. 2010. SentiWordNet 3.0: An Enhanced Lexical Resource for Sentiment Analysis and Opinion Mining. In *Proceedings of the Seventh Conference on International Language Resources and Evaluation (LREC'10)*, Valletta, Malta, May. European Language Resources Association (ELRA).

Luciano Barbosa and Junlan Feng. 2010. Robust sentiment detection on twitter from biased and noisy data. In *Proceedings of the 23rd International Conference on Computational Linguistics: Posters*, COLING '10, pages 36–44, Stroudsburg, PA, USA. Association for Computational Linguistics.

Adam L. Berger, Stephen A. Della Pietra, and Vincent J. Della Pietra. 1996. A maximum entropy approach to natural language processing. *Computational Linguistics*, 22:39–71.

Albert Bifet and Eibe Frank. 2010. Sentiment knowledge discovery in twitter streaming data. In *Proceedings of the 13th international conference on Discovery science*, DS'10, pages 1–15, Berlin, Heidelberg. Springer-Verlag.

Dmitry Davidov, Oren Tsur, and Ari Rappoport. 2010. Enhanced sentiment learning using twitter hashtags and smileys. In *Proceedings of the 23rd International Conference on Computational Linguistics: Posters*, COLING '10, pages 241–249, Stroudsburg, PA, USA. Association for Computational Linguistics.

Xiaoxu Fei, Huizhen Wang, and Jingbo Zhu. 2010. Sentiment word identification using the maximum entropy model. In *International Conference on Natural Language Processing and Knowledge Engineering (NLP-KE)*, pages 1–4.

Kevin Gimpel, Nathan Schneider, Brendan O'Connor, Dipanjan Das, Daniel Mills, Jacob Eisenstein, Michael Heilman, Dani Yogatama, Jeffrey Flanigan, and Noah A. Smith. 2011. Part-of-speech tagging for twitter: annotation, features, and experiments. In *Proceedings of the 49th Annual Meeting of the Association for Computational Linguistics: Human Language Technologies: short papers - Volume 2*, HLT '11, pages 42–47. Association for Computational Linguistics.

Alec Go, Richa Bhayani, and Lei Huang. 2009. Twitter sentiment classification using distant supervision. Technical report, Stanford University.

Edward Loper and Steven Bird. 2002. Nltk: the natural language toolkit. In *Proceedings of the ACL-02 Workshop on Effective tools and methodologies for teaching natural language processing and computational linguistics - Volume 1*, ETMTNLP '02, pages 63–70, Stroudsburg, PA, USA. Association for Computational Linguistics.

George A. Miller. 1995. Wordnet: A lexical database for english. *Communications of the ACM*, 38:39–41.

Finn Å. Nielsen. 2011. A new ANEW: Evaluation of a word list for sentiment analysis in microblogs. In *Proceedings of the ESWC2011 Workshop on 'Making Sense of Microposts': Big things come in small packages.*

Brendan O'Connor, Ramnath Balasubramanyan, Bryan R. Routledge, and Noah A. Smith. 2010. From Tweets to Polls: Linking Text Sentiment to Public Opinion Time Series. In *Proceedings of the International AAAI Conference on Weblogs and Social Media*.

Olutobi Owoputi, Brendan O'Connor, Chris Dyer, Kevin Gimpel, Nathan Schneider, and Noah A. Smith. 2013. Improved part-of-speech tagging for online conversational text with word clusters. In *Proceedings of NAACL*.

Philip J. Stone, Dexter C. Dunphy, Marshall S. Smith, and Daniel M. Ogilvie. 1966. *The General Inquirer: A Computer Approach to Content Analysis*. MIT Press.

Theresa Wilson, Zornitsa Kozareva, Preslav Nakov, Sara Rosenthal, Veselin Stoyanov, and Alan Ritter. 2013. SemEval-2013 task 2: Sentiment analysis in twitter. In *Proceedings of the International Workshop on Semantic Evaluation*, SemEval '13, June.

Le Zhang. 2011. Maximum entropy modeling toolkit for python and c++. `http://homepages.inf.ed.ac.uk/lzhang10/maxent_toolkit.html`. Accessed: 2013-04-13.

nlp.cs.aueb.gr: Two Stage Sentiment Analysis

Prodromos Malakasiotis, Rafael Michael Karampatsis
Konstantina Makrynioti and **John Pavlopoulos**
Department of Informatics
Athens University of Economics and Business
Patission 76, GR-104 34 Athens, Greece

Abstract

This paper describes the systems with which we participated in the task Sentiment Analysis in Twitter of SEMEVAL 2013 and specifically the Message Polarity Classification. We used a 2-stage pipeline approach employing a linear SVM classifier at each stage and several features including BOW features, POS based features and lexicon based features. We have also experimented with Naive Bayes classifiers trained with BOW features.

1 Introduction

During the last years, Twitter has become a very popular microblogging service. Millions of users publish messages every day, often expressing their feelings or opinion about a variety of events, topics, products, etc. Analysing this kind of content has drawn the attention of many companies and researchers, as it can lead to useful information for fields, such as personalized marketing or social profiling. The informal language, the spelling mistakes, the slang and special abbreviations that are frequently used in tweets differentiate them from traditional texts, such as articles or reviews, and present new challenges for the task of sentiment analysis.

The Message Polarity Classification is defined as the task of deciding whether a message M conveys a positive, negative or neutral sentiment. For instance M_1 below expresses a positive sentiment, M_2 a negative one, while M_3 has no sentiment at all.

M_1: GREAT GAME GIRLS!! On to districts Monday at Fox!! Thanks to the fans for coming out :)

M_2: Firework just came on my tv and I just broke down and sat and cried, I need help okay

M_3: Going to a bulls game with Aaliyah & hope next Thursday

As sentiment analysis in Twitter is a very recent subject, it is certain that more research and improvements are needed. This paper presents our approach for the subtask of Message Polarity Classification (Wilson et al., 2013) of SEMEVAL 2013. We used a 2-stage pipeline approach employing a linear SVM classifier at each stage and several features including bag of words (BOW) features, part-of-speech (POS) based features and lexicon based features. We have also experimented with Naive Bayes classifiers trained with BOW features.

The rest of the paper is organised as follows. Section 2 provides a short analysis of the data used while section 3 describes our approach. Section 4 describes the experiments we performed and the corresponding results and section 5 concludes and gives hints for future work.

2 Data

Before we proceed with our system description we briefly describe the data released by the organisers. The training set consists of a set of IDs corresponding to tweet messages, along with their annotations. A message can be annotated as positive, negative or neutral. In order to address privacy concerns, rather than releasing the original Tweets, the organisers chose to provide a python script for downloading the data. This resulted to different training sets for the participants since tweets may often become

*Second Joint Conference on Lexical and Computational Semantics (*SEM), Volume 2: Seventh International Workshop on Semantic Evaluation (SemEval 2013)*, pages 562–567, Atlanta, Georgia, June 14-15, 2013.

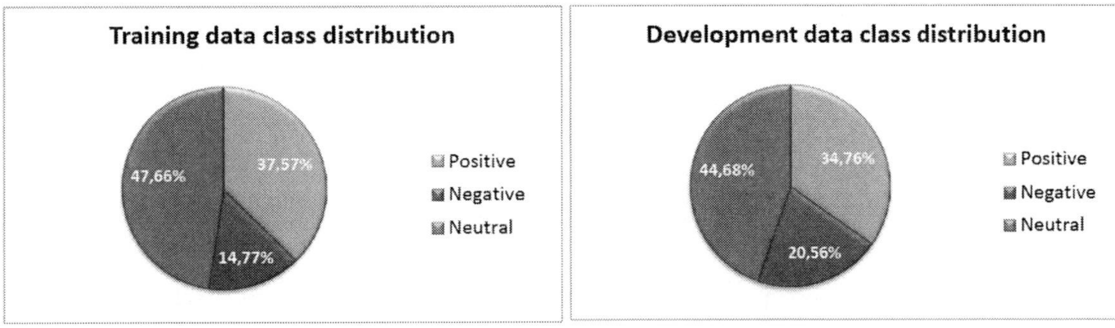

(a) (b)

Figure 1: Train and Development data class distribution.

unavailable due to a number of reasons. Concerning the development and test sets the organisers downloaded and provided the tweets. [1] A first analysis of the data indicates that they suffer from a class imbalance problem. Specifically the training data we have downloaded contain 8730 tweets (3280 positive, 1289 negative, 4161 neutral), while the development set contains 1654 tweets (575 positive, 340 negative, 739 neutral). Figure 1 illustrates the problem on train and development sets.

3 System Overview

The system we propose is a 2–stage pipeline procedure employing SVM classifiers (Vapnik, 1998) to detect whether each message M expresses positive, negative or no sentiment (figure 2). Specifically, during the first stage we attempt to detect if M expresses a sentiment (positive or negative) or not. If so, M is called "subjective", otherwise it is called "objective" or "neutral".[2] Each subjective message is then classified in a second stage as "positive" or "negative". Such a 2–stage approach has also been suggested in (Pang and Lee, 2004) to improve sentiment classification of reviews by discarding objective sentences, in (Wilson et al., 2005a) for phrase-level sentiment analysis, and in (Barbosa and Feng, 2010) for sentiment analysis on Twitter messages.

[1]A separate test set with SMS messages was also provided by the organisers to measure performance of systems over other types of message data. No training and development data were provided for this set.

[2]Hereafter we will use the terms "objective" and "neutral" interchangeably.

3.1 Data Preprocessing

Before we could proceed with feature engineering, we performed several preprocessing steps. To be more precise, a twitter specific tokeniser and part-of-speech (POS) tagger (Ritter et al., 2011) were used to obtain the tokens and the corresponding POS tags which are necessary for a particular set of features to be described later. In addition to these, six lexicons, originating from Wilson's (2005b) lexicon, were created. This lexicon contains expressions that given a context (i.e., surrounding words) indicate subjectivity. The expression that in most context expresses sentiment is considered to be "strong" subjective, otherwise it is considered weak subjective (i.e., it has specific subjective usages). So, we first split the lexicon in two smaller, one containing strong and one containing weak subjective expressions. Moreover, Wilson also reports the polarity of each expression out of context (prior polarity) which can be positive, negative or neutral. As a consequence, we further split each of the two lexicons into three smaller according to the prior polarity of the expression, resulting to the following six lexicons:

S_+ : Contains strong subjective expressions with positive prior polarity.

S_- : Contains strong subjective expressions with negative prior polarity.

S_0 : Contains strong subjective expressions with neutral prior polarity.

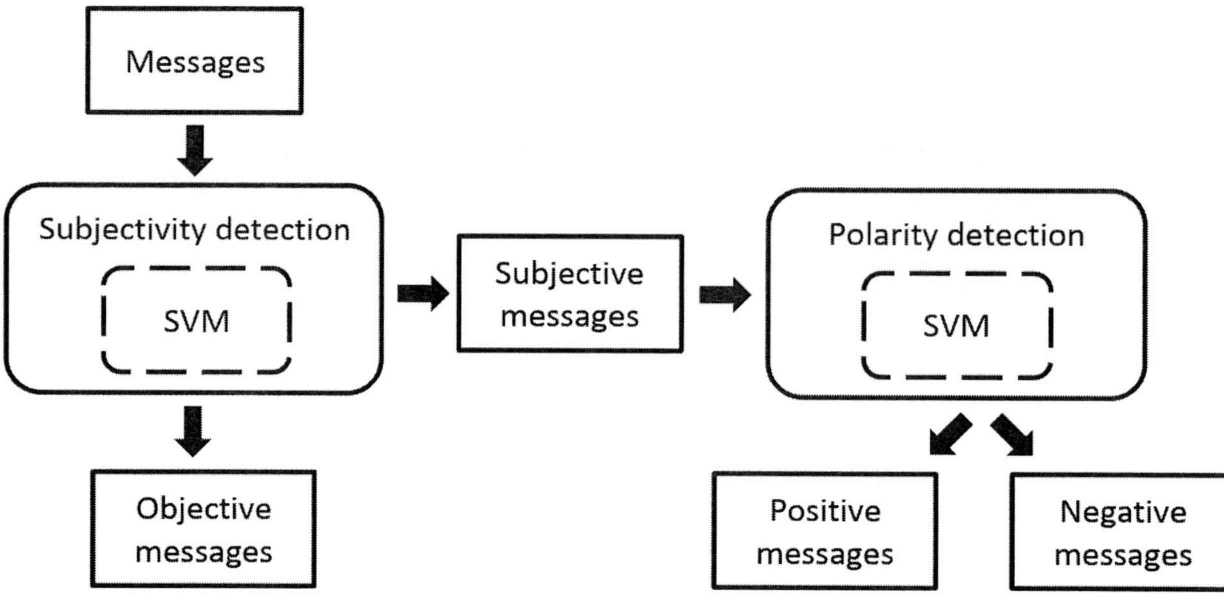

Figure 2: Our 2–stage pipeline procedure.

W_+ : Contains weak subjective expressions with positive prior polarity.

W_- : Contains weak subjective expressions with negative prior polarity.

W_0 : Contains weak subjective expressions with neutral prior polarity.

Adding to these, three more lexicons were created, one for each class (positive, negative, neutral). In particular, we employed Chi Squared feature selection (Liu and Setiono, 1995) to obtain the 100 most important tokens per class from the training set. Very few tokens were manually erased to result to the following three lexicons.

T_+ : Contains the top-94 tokens appearing in positive tweets of the training set.

T_- : Contains the top-96 tokens appearing in negative tweets of the training set.

T_0 : Contains the top-94 tokens appearing in neutral tweets of the training set.

The nine lexicons described above are used to calculate precision ($P(t,c)$), recall ($R(t,c)$) and $F-measure$ ($F_1(t,c)$) of tokens appearing in a message with respect to each class. Equations 1, 2 and 3 below provide the definitions of these metrics.

$$P(t,c) = \frac{\#\text{tweets that contain token } t \text{ and belong to class } c}{\#\text{tweets that contain token } t} \quad (1)$$

$$R(t,c) = \frac{\#\text{tweets that contain token } t \text{ and belong to class } c}{\#\text{tweets that belong to class } c} \quad (2)$$

$$F_1(t,c) = \frac{2 \cdot P(t,c) \cdot R(t,c)}{P(t,c) + R(t,c)} \quad (3)$$

3.2 Feature engineering

We employed three types of features, namely boolean features, POS based features and lexicon based features. Our goal is to build a system that is not explicitly based on the vocabulary of the training set, having therefore better generalisation capability.

3.2.1 Boolean features

Bag of words (BOW): These features indicate the existence of specific tokens in a message. We used feature selection with Info Gain to obtain the 600 most informative tokens of the training set and we then manually removed 19 of them to result in 581 tokens. As a consequence we get 581 features that can take a value of 1 if a message contains the corresponding token and 0 otherwise.

Time and date: We observed that time and date often indicated events in the train data and such messages tend to be objective. Therefore, we added two more features to indicate if a message contains time and/or date expressions.

Character repetition: Repetitive characters are often added to words by users, in order to give emphasis or to express themselves more intensely. As a consequence they indicate subjectivity. So we added one more feature having a value of 1 if a message contains words with repeating characters and 0 otherwise.

Negation: Negation not only is a good subjectivity indicator but it also may change the polarity of a message. We therefore add 5 more features, one indicating the existence of negation, and the remaining four indicating the existence of negation that precedes (in a distance of at most 5 tokens) words from lexicons S_+, S_-, W_+ and W_-.

Hash-tags with sentiment: These features are implemented by getting all the possible substrings of the string after the symbol # and checking if any of them match with any word from S_+, S_-, W_+ and W_- (4 features). A value of 1 means that a hash-tag containing a word from the corresponding lexicon exists in a message.

3.2.2 POS based features

Specific POS tags might be good indicators of subjectivity or objectivity. For instance adjectives often express sentiment (e.g., beautiful, frustrating) while proper nouns are often reported in objective messaged. We, therefore, added 10 more features based on the following POS tags:

1. adjectives,
2. adverbs,
3. verbs,
4. nouns,
5. proper nouns,
6. urls,
7. interjections,
8. hash-tags,
9. happy emoticons, and
10. sad emoticons.

We then constructed our features as follows. For each message we counted the occurrences of tokens with these POS tags and we divided this number with the number of tokens having any of these POS tags. For instance if a message contains 2 adjectives, 1 adverb and 1 url then the features corresponding to adjectives, adverbs and urls will have a value of $\frac{2}{4}$, $\frac{1}{4}$ and $\frac{1}{4}$ respectively while all the remaining features will be 0. These features can be thought of as a way to express how much specific POS tags affect the sentiment of a message.

Going a step further we calculate precision ($P(b,c)$), recall ($R(b,c)$) and $F - measure$ ($F_1(b,c)$) of POS tags bigrams with respect to each class (equations 4, 5 and 6 respectively).

$$P(b,c) = \frac{\#\text{tweets that contain bigram } b \text{ and belong to class } c}{\#\text{tweets that contain bigram } b} \quad (4)$$

$$R(b,c) = \frac{\#\text{tweets that contain bigram } b \text{ and belong to class } c}{\#\text{tweets that belong to class } c} \quad (5)$$

$$F_1(b,c) = \frac{2 \cdot P(b,c) \cdot R(b,c)}{P(b,c) + R(b,c)} \quad (6)$$

For each bigram (e.g., adjective-noun) in a message we calculate $F_1(b,c)$ and then we use the average, the maximum and the minimum of these values to create 9 additional features. We did not experiment over measures that weight differently Precision and Recall (e.g., F_b for $b = 0.5$) or with different combinations (e.g., F_1 and P).

3.2.3 Lexicon based features

This set of features associates the words of the lexicons described earlier with the three classes. Given a message M, similarly to the equations 4 and

6 above, we calculate $P(t, c)$ and $F_1(t, c)$ for every token $t \in M$ with respect to a lexicon. We then obtain the maximum, minimum and average values of $P(t, c)$ and $F_1(t, c)$ in M. We note that the combination of P and F_1 appeared to be the best in our experiments while $R(t, c)$ was not helpful and thus was not used. Also, similarly to section 3.2.2 we did not experiment over measures that weight differently Precision and Recall (e.g., F_b for $b = 0.5$). The former metrics are calculated with three variations:

(a) **Using words:** The values of the metrics consider only the words of the message.

(b) **Using words and priors:** The same as (a) but adding to the calculated metrics a prior value. This value is calculated on the entire lexicon, and roughly speaking it is an indicator of how much we can trust L to predict class c. In cases that a token t of a message M does not appear in a lexicon L the corresponding scores of the metrics will be 0.

(c) **Using words and their POS tags:** The values of the metrics consider the words of the message along with their POS tags.

(d) **Using words, their POS tags and priors**: The same as (c) but adding to the calculated metrics an apriori value. The apriori value is calculated in a similar manner as in (b) with the difference that we consider the POS tags of the words as well.

For case (a) we calculated minimum, maximum and average values of $P(t, c)$ and $F_1(t, c)$ with respect to S_+, S_-, S_0, W_+, W_- and W_0 considering only the words of the message resulting to 108 features. Concerning case (b) we calculated average $P(t, c)$ and $F_1(t, c)$ with respect to S_+, S_-, S_0, W_+, W_- and W_0, and average $P(t, c)$ with respect to T_+, T_- and T_0 adding 45 more features. For case (c) we calculated minimum, maximum and average $P(t, c)$ with respect to S_+, S_-, S_0, W_+, W_- and W_0 (54 features), and, finally, for case (d) we calculated average $P(t, c)$ and $F_1(t, c)$ with respect to S_+, S_-, S_0, W_+, W_- and W_0 to add 36 features.

Class	F_1
Positive	0.6496
Negative	0.4429
Neutral	0.7022
Average	0.5462

Table 1: F_1 for development set.

4 Experiments

As stated earlier we use a 2–stage pipeline approach to identify the sentiment of a message. Preliminary experiments on the development data showed that this approach is better than attempting to address the problem in one stage during which a classifier must classify a message as positive, negative or neutral. To be more precise we used a Naive Bayes classifier and BOW features using both 1–stage and 2–stage approaches. Although we considered the 2–stage approach with a Naive Bayes classifier as a baseline system we used it to submit results for both twitter and sms test sets.

Having concluded to the 2–stage approach we employed for each stage an SVM classifier, fed with the 855 features described in section 3.2.[3] Both SVMs use linear kernel and are tuned in order to find the optimum C parameter. Observe that we use the same set of features in both stages and let the classifier learn the appropriate weights for each feature. During the first stage, the classifier is trained on the entire training set after merging positive and negative classes to one superclass, namely subjective. In the second stage, the classifier is trained only on positive and negative tweets of the training and is asked to determine whether the messages classified as subjective during the first stage are positive or negative.

4.1 Results

In order to obtain the best set of features we trained our system on the downloaded training data and measured its performance on the provided development data. Table 1 illustrates the F_1 results on the development set. A first observation is that there is a considerable difference between the F_1 of the negative class and the other two, with the former be-

[3]We used the LIBLINEAR distribution (Fan et al., 2008)

Class	F1
Positive	0.6854
Negative	0.4929
Neutral	0.7117
Average	0.5891

Table 2: F_1 for twitter test set.

Class	F1
Positive	0.6349
Negative	0.5131
Neutral	0.7785
Average	0.5740

Table 3: F_1 for sms test set.

ing significantly decreased. This might be due to the quite low number of negative tweets of the initial training set in comparison with the rest of the classes. Therefore, the addition of 340 negative examples from the development set emerged from this imbalance and proved to be effective as shown in table 2 illustrating our results on the test set regarding tweets. Unfortunately we were not able to submit results with this system for the sms test set. However, we performed post-experiments after the gold sms test set was released. The results shown on table 3 are similar to the ones obtained for the twitter test set which means that our model has a good generalisation ability.

5 Conclusion and future work

In this paper we presented our approach for the Message Polarity Classification task of SEMEVAL 2013. We proposed a pipeline approach to detect sentiment in two stages; first we discard objective messages and then we classify subjective (i.e., carrying sentiment) ones as positive or negative. We used SVMs with various extracted features for both stages and although the system performed reasonably well, there is still much room for improvement. A first problem that should be addressed is the difficulty in identifying negative messages. This was mainly due to small number of tweets in the training data. This was somewhat alleviated by adding the negative instances of the development data but still our system reports lower results for this class as compared to positive and neutral classes. More data or better features is a possible improvement. Another issue that has not an obvious answer is how to proceed in order to improve the 2–stage pipeline approach. Should we try and optimise each stage separately or should we optimise the second stage taking into consideration the results of the first stage?

References

Luciano Barbosa and Junlan Feng. 2010. Robust sentiment detection on twitter from biased and noisy data. In *Proceedings of the 23rd International Conference on Computational Linguistics: Posters*, COLING '10, pages 36–44, Beijing, China. Association for Computational Linguistics.

Rong-En Fan, Kai-Wei Chang, Cho-Jui Hsieh, Xiang-Rui Wang, and Chih-Jen Lin. 2008. Liblinear: A library for large linear classification. *The Journal of Machine Learning Research*, 9:1871–1874.

Huan Liu and Rudy Setiono. 1995. Chi2: Feature selection and discretization of numeric attributes. In *Tools with Artificial Intelligence, 1995. Proceedings., Seventh International Conference on*, pages 388–391. IEEE.

Bo Pang and Lillian Lee. 2004. A sentimental education: sentiment analysis using subjectivity summarization based on minimum cuts. In *Proceedings of the 42nd Annual Meeting on Association for Computational Linguistics*, ACL '04, Barcelona, Spain. Association for Computational Linguistics.

Alan Ritter, Sam Clark, Mausam, and Oren Etzioni. 2011. Named entity recognition in tweets: An experimental study. In *EMNLP*, pages 1524–1534.

V. Vapnik. 1998. *Statistical learning theory*. John Wiley.

Theresa Wilson, Janyce Wiebe, and Paul Hoffmann. 2005a. Recognizing contextual polarity in phrase-level sentiment analysis. In *Proceedings of the conference on Human Language Technology and Empirical Methods in Natural Language Processing*, HLT '05, pages 347–354, Vancouver, British Columbia, Canada. Association for Computational Linguistics.

Theresa Wilson, Janyce Wiebe, and Paul Hoffmann. 2005b. Recognizing contextual polarity in phrase-level sentiment analysis. In *Proceedings of the conference on Human Language Technology and Empirical Methods in Natural Language Processing*, pages 347–354. Association for Computational Linguistics.

Theresa Wilson, Zornitsa Kozareva, Preslav Nakov, Sara Rosenthal, Veselin Stoyanov, and Alan Ritter. 2013. SemEval-2013 task 2: Sentiment analysis in twitter. In *Proceedings of the International Workshop on Semantic Evaluation*, SemEval '13, June.

NILC_USP: A Hybrid System for Sentiment Analysis in Twitter Messages

Pedro P. Balage Filho and Thiago A. S. Pardo
Interinstitutional Center for Computational Linguistics (NILC)
Institute of Mathematical and Computer Science, University of São Paulo
São Carlos - SP, Brazil
{balage, taspardo}@icmc.usp.br

Abstract

This paper describes the NILC_USP system that participated in *SemEval-2013 Task 2: Sentiment Analysis in Twitter*. Our system adopts a hybrid classification process that uses three classification approaches: rule-based, lexicon-based and machine learning approaches. We suggest a pipeline architecture that extracts the best characteristics from each classifier. Our system achieved an F-score of 56.31% in the Twitter message-level subtask.

1 Introduction

Twitter and Twitter messages (tweets) are a modern way to express sentiment and feelings about aspects of the world. In this scenario, understanding the sentiment contained in a message is of vital importance in order to understand users behavior and for market analysis (Java et al., 2007; Kwak et al., 2010). The research area that deals with the computational treatment of opinion, sentiment and subjectivity in texts is called sentiment analysis (Pang et al., 2002).

Sentiment analysis is usually associated with a text classification task. Sentiment classifiers are commonly categorized in two basic approaches: lexicon-based and machine learning (Taboada et al., 2011). A lexicon-based classifier uses a lexicon to provide the polarity, or semantic orientation, of each word or phrase in the text. A machine learning classifier learns features (usually the vocabulary) from annotated corpus or labeled examples.

In this paper, we present a hybrid system for sentiment classification in Twitter messages. Our system combines three different approaches: rule-based, lexicon-based and machine learning. The purpose of our system is to better understand the use of a hybrid system in Twitter text and to verify the performance of this approach in an open evaluation contest.

Our system participated in *SemEval-2013 Task 2: Sentiment Analysis in Twitter* (Wilson et al., 2013). The task objective was to determine the sentiment contained in Twitter messages. The task included two sub-tasks: a expression-level classification (Task A) and a message-level classification (Task B). Our system participated in Task B. In this task, for a given message, our system should classify it as positive, negative, or neutral.

Our system was coded using Python and the CLiPS Pattern library (De Smedt and Daelemans, 2012). This last library provides the part-of-speech tagger and the SVM algorithm used in this work[1].

2 Related work

Despite the significant number of works in sentiment analysis, few works have approached Twitter messages. Agarwal et al. (2011) explored new features for sentiment classification of twitter messages. Davidov et al. (2010) studied the use of hashtags and emoticons in sentiment classification. Diakopoulos and Shamma (2010) analyzed the people's sentiment on Twitter for first U.S. presidential debate in 2008.

The majority of works in sentiment analysis uses either machine learning techniques or lexicon-based

[1] Our system code is freely available at http://github.com/pedrobalage/SemevalTwitterHybridClassifier

*Second Joint Conference on Lexical and Computational Semantics (*SEM), Volume 2: Seventh International Workshop on Semantic Evaluation (SemEval 2013)*, pages 568–572, Atlanta, Georgia, June 14-15, 2013.

techniques. However, some few works have presented hybrid approaches. König and Brill (2006) propose a hybrid classifier that utilizes human reasoning over automatically discovered text patterns to complement machine learning. Prabowo and Thelwall (2009) evaluates the effectiveness of different classifiers. This study showed that the use of multiple classifiers in a hybrid manner could improve the effectiveness of sentiment analysis.

3 System architecture

Our system is organized in four main components: normalization, rule-based classifier, lexicon-based classifier and machine learning classifier. These components are connected in a pipeline architecture that extracts the best characteristics from each component. The Figure 1 shows the system architecture.

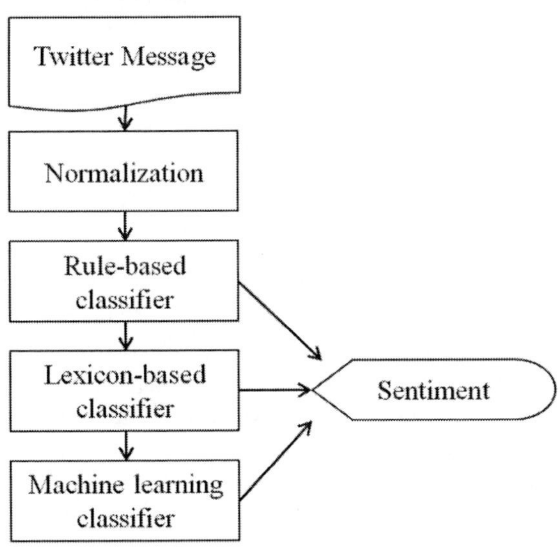

Figure 1: System architecture

In this pipeline architecture, each classifier, in a sequential order, evaluates the Twitter message. In each step, the classifier may determine the polarity class of the message if a certain degree of confidence is achieved. If the classifier may not achieve this confidence threshold, the classifier in the next step is called. The machine learning classifier is the last step in the process. It is responsible to determine the polarity if the previous classifiers failed to achieve the confidence level required to classification. The normalization component is responsible to correct and normalize the text before the classifiers use it.

This architecture improves the classification process because it takes advantage of the multiple approaches. For example, the rule-based classifier is the most reliable classifier. It achieves good results when the text is matched by a high-confidence rule. However, due the freedom of language, rules may not match 100% of the unseen examples, consequently it has a low recall rate.

Lexicon-based classifiers, for example, are very confident in the process to determine if a text is polar or neutral. Using sentiment lexicons, we can determine that sentences containing sentiment words are polar and sentences that do not contain such words are neutral. Moreover, the presence of a high number of positive or negative words in the text may be a strong indicative of the polarity.

Finally, machine learning is known to be highly domain adaptive and to be able to find deep correlations (Taboada et al., 2011). This last classifier might provide the final decision when the previous methods failed. In the following sub-sections, we describe in more details the components in which our system is based on. In the next section, we explain how the confidence level was determined.

3.1 Normalization and rule-based classifier

The normalization module is in charge of correcting and normalizing the texts. This module performs the following operations:

- Elements such as hashtags, urls and mentions are transformed into a consistent set of codes;
- Emoticons are grouped into representative categories (such as happy, sad, laugh) and converted to particular codes;
- Signals of exaltation (such as repetitive exclamation marks) are recognized;
- A simple misspelling correction is performed;
- Part-of-speech tagging is performed.

The rule-based classifier is very simple. The only rules applied here are concerned to the emoticons found in the text. Empirically, we evidenced that positive emoticons are an important indicative of positiveness in texts. Likewise, negative emoticons indicate negativeness tendency. This module returns the number of positive and negative emoticons matched in the text.

3.2 Lexicon-based classifier

The lexicon-based classifier is based on the idea that the polarity of a text can be summarized by the sum of the individual polarity values of each word or phrase present in the text. In this assumption, a sentiment lexicon identifies polar words and assigns polarity values to them (known as semantic orientations).

In our system, we used the sentiment lexicon provided by SentiStrength (Thelwall et al., 2010). This lexicon provides an emotion vocabulary, an emoticons list, a negation list and a booster word list.

In our algorithm, we sum the semantic orientations of each individual word in the text. If the word is negated, the polarity is inverted. If the word is intensified (boosted), we increase its polarity by a factor determined in the sentiment lexicon. A lexicon-based classifier usually assumes the signal of the final score as the sentiment class: positive, negative or neutral (score zero).

3.3 Machine learning classifier

The machine learning classifier uses labeled examples to learn how to classify new instances. The algorithm learns by using features extracted from these examples. In our classifier, we used the SVM algorithm provided by CLiPS Pattern. The features used by the classifier are bag-of-words, the part-of-speech set, and the existence of negation in the sentence.

4 Hybrid approach and tuning

The organization from *SemEval-2013 Task 2: Sentiment Analysis in Twitter* provided three datasets for the task (Wilson et al., 2013). A training dataset (TrainSet), with 6,686 messages[2], a development dataset (DevSet), with 1,654 messages, and two testing datasets (TestSets), with 3,813 (Twitter TestSet) and 2,094 (SMS TestSet) messages each.

As we said in the previous section, our system is a pipeline of classifiers where each classifier may assign a sentiment class if it achieves a particular confidence threshold. This confidence threshold is a fixed value we set for each system in order to have a decision boundary. This decision was made by inspecting the results table obtained with the development set, as shown below.

Table 1 shows how the rule-based classifier performed in the development dataset. The classifier score consists in the difference between the number of positive emoticons and the number of negative emoticons found in the message. For example, for score of -1 we had 22 negative, 4 neutral and 2 positive messages.

Table 1: Correlation between the rule-based classifier scores and the gold standard classes in the DevSet

Rule-based	Gold Standard Class		
classifier score	Negative	Neutral	Positive
-1	22	4	2
0	311	708	496
1	7	24	71
2		2	4
3 to 6		1	2

Inspecting the Table 1 we adjusted the rule-based classifier boundary to decide when the score is different from zero. For values greater than zero, the classifier will assign the positive class and, for values below zero, the classifier will assign the negative class. For values equal zero, the classifier will call the lexicon-based classifier.

Table 2 is similar to the Table 1, but it now shows the scores obtained by the lexicon-based classifier for the development set. This score is the message semantic orientation computed by the sum of the semantic orientation for each individual word.

Inspecting Table 2, we adjusted the lexicon-based classifier to assign the positive class when the total score is greater than 3 and negative class when the total score is below -3. Moreover, we evidenced that, compared to the other classifiers, the lexicon-based classifier had better performance to determine the neutral class. Therefore, we adjusted the lexicon-based classifier to assign the neutral class when the total score is zero. For any other values, the machine learning classifier is called.

Finally, Table 3 shows the confusion matrix for the machine learning classifier in the development

[2]The number of messages may differ from other participants because the data was collected by crawling

Table 2: Correlation between the lexicon-based classifier score and the gold standard classes in the DevSet

Lexicon-based classifier scores	Gold Standard Class Negative	Neutral	Positive
-11 to -6	26	8	4
-5	15	6	4
-4	31	20	9
-3	32	24	5
-2	57	86	22
-1	25	31	20
0	74	354	115
1	26	70	42
2	28	87	103
3	12	29	81
4	8	9	56
5	2	6	42
6 to 13	4	9	72

dataset. The machine learning classifier does not operate with a confidence threshold, so no decisions were made for this classifier. We see that machine learning classifier does not have a good accuracy in general. Our hybrid approach proposed aims to overcome this problem. Next section shows the results achieved for the Semeval test dataset.

Table 3: Confusion matrix for the machine learning classifier in the DevSet

Machine learning classifier class	Gold Standard Class Negative	Neutral	Positive
negative	35	6	11
neutral	232	595	262
positive	73	138	302

5 Results

Table 4 shows the results obtained by each individual classifier and the hybrid classifier for the test dataset. In the task, the systems were evaluated with the average F-Score obtained for positive and negative classes[3]. We see that the Hybrid approach could improve in relation to each classifier score, confirming our hypothesis.

[3] *Semeval-2013 Task 2: Sentiment Analysis in Twitter* compares the systems by the average F-score for positive and negative classes. For more information see Wilson et al. (2013)

Table 4: Average F-score (positive and negative) obtained by each classifier and the hybrid approach

Classifier	Twitter TestSet	SMS TestSet
Rule-based	0.1437	0.0665
Lexicon-Based	0.4487	0.4282
Machine Learning	0.4999	0.4029
Hybrid Approach	**0.5631**	**0.5012**

Table 5 shows the results in terms of precision, recall and F-score for each class by the hybrid classifier in the Twitter dataset. Inspecting our algorithm for the Twitter dataset, we had 277 examples classified by the rule-based classifier, 2,312 by the lexicon-based classifier and 1,224 the by machine learning classifier. The results for the SMS dataset had similar values.

Table 5: Results for Twitter TestSet

Class	Precision	Recall	F-Score
positive	0.6935	0.6145	0.6516
negative	0.5614	0.4110	0.4745
neutral	0.6152	0.7427	0.6729

6 Conclusion

We described a hybrid classification system used for *Semeval-2013 Task 2: Sentiment Analysis in Twitter*. This paper showed how a hybrid classifier might take advantage of multiple sentiment analysis approaches and how these approaches perform in a Twitter dataset.

A future direction of this work would be improving each individual classifier. In our system, we used simple methods for each employed classifier. Thus, we believe the hybrid classification technique applied might achieve even better results. This strengthens our theory that hybrid techniques might outperform the current state-of-art in sentiment analysis.

Acknowledgments

We would like to thank the organizers for their work constructing the dataset and overseeing the task. We also would like to thank FAPESP and CNPq for financial support.

References

Apoorv Agarwal, Boyi Xie, Ilia Vovsha, Owen Rambow, and Rebecca Passonneau. 2011. Sentiment analysis of twitter data. In *Proceedings of the Workshop on Languages in Social Media*, LSM '11, pages 30–38, Stroudsburg, PA, USA. Association for Computational Linguistics.

Dmitry Davidov, Oren Tsur, and Ari Rappoport. 2010. Enhanced sentiment learning using twitter hashtags and smileys. In *Proceedings of the 23rd International Conference on Computational Linguistics: Posters*, COLING '10, pages 241–249, Stroudsburg, PA, USA. Association for Computational Linguistics.

Tom De Smedt and Walter Daelemans. 2012. Pattern for python. *The Journal of Machine Learning Research*, 13:2063–2067.

Nicholas A. Diakopoulos and David A. Shamma. 2010. Characterizing debate performance via aggregated twitter sentiment. In *Proceedings of the SIGCHI Conference on Human Factors in Computing Systems*, CHI '10, pages 1195–1198, New York, NY, USA. ACM.

Akshay Java, Xiaodan Song, Tim Finin, and Belle Tseng. 2007. Why we twitter: understanding microblogging usage and communities. In *Proceedings of the 9th WebKDD and 1st SNA-KDD 2007 workshop on Web mining and social network analysis*, WebKDD/SNA-KDD '07, pages 56–65, New York, NY, USA. ACM.

Arnd Christian König and Eric Brill. 2006. Reducing the human overhead in text categorization. In *Proceedings of the 12th ACM SIGKDD international conference on Knowledge discovery and data mining*, KDD '06, pages 598–603, New York, NY, USA. ACM.

Haewoon Kwak, Changhyun Lee, Hosung Park, and Sue Moon. 2010. What is twitter, a social network or a news media? In *Proceedings of the 19th international conference on World wide web*, WWW '10, pages 591–600, New York, NY, USA. ACM.

Bo Pang, Lillian Lee, and Shivakumar Vaithyanathan. 2002. Thumbs up? Sentiment Classification using Machine Learning Techniques. In *Proceedings of the ACL-02 conference on Empirical methods in natural language processing - EMNLP '02*, pages 79–86, Morristown, NJ, USA, July. Association for Computational Linguistics.

Rudy Prabowo and Mike Thelwall. 2009. Sentiment analysis: A combined approach. *Journal of Informetrics*, 3(2):143–157.

Maite Taboada, Julian Brooke, Milan Tofiloski, Kimberly Voll, and Manfred Stede. 2011. Lexicon-Based Methods for Sentiment Analysis. *Computational Linguistics*, 37(2):267–307, June.

Mike Thelwall, Kevan Buckley, Georgios Paltoglou, Di Cai, and Arvid Kappas. 2010. Sentiment in short strength detection informal text. *Journal of the American Society for Information Science and Technology*, 61(12):2544–2558, December.

Theresa Wilson, Zornitsa Kozareva, Preslav Nakov, Sara Rosenthal, Veselin Stoyanov, and Alan Ritter. 2013. SemEval-2013 task 2: Sentiment analysis in twitter. In *Proceedings of the International Workshop on Semantic Evaluation*, SemEval '13, June.

UNITOR-HMM-TK: Structured Kernel-based Learning for Spatial Role Labeling

Emanuele Bastianelli[(†)(⋆)], **Danilo Croce**[(‡)], **Daniele Nardi**[(⋆)], **Roberto Basili**[(‡)]

(†) DICII
University of Roma Tor Vergata
Rome, Italy
{bastianelli}@ing.uniroma2.it

(‡) DII
University of Roma Tor Vergata
Rome, Italy
{croce,basili}@info.uniroma2.it

(⋆) DIAG
University of Roma La Sapienza
Rome, Italy
{nardi}@dis.uniroma1.it

Abstract

In this paper the UNITOR-HMM-TK system participating in the Spatial Role Labeling task at SemEval 2013 is presented. The spatial roles classification is addressed as a sequence-based word classification problem: the SVM^{hmm} learning algorithm is applied, based on a simple feature modeling and a robust lexical generalization achieved through a Distributional Model of Lexical Semantics. In the identification of spatial relations, roles are combined to generate candidate relations, later verified by a SVM classifier. The Smoothed Partial Tree Kernel is applied, i.e. a convolution kernel that enhances both syntactic and lexical properties of the examples, avoiding the need of a manual feature engineering phase. Finally, results on three of the five tasks of the challenge are reported.

1 Introduction

Referring to objects or entities in the space, as well as to relations holding among them, is one of the most important functionalities in natural language understanding. The detection of spatial utterances thus finds many applications, such as in GPS navigation systems, or Human-Robot Interaction (HRI).

In Computational Linguistics, the task of recognizing spatial information is known as Spatial Role Labeling (SpRL), as discussed in (KordJamshidi et al., 2010). Let us consider the sentence:

$$[A\ man]_{\text{TRAJECTOR}}\ is\ sitting\ [on]_{\text{SPATIAL\_INDICATOR}}\ [a\ chair]_{\text{LANDMARK}}\ and\ talking\ on\ the\ phone. \quad (1)$$

where three roles are labeled: the phrase "*A man*" refers to a TRAJECTOR, "*a chair*" to a LANDMARK and they are related by the spatial expression "*on*" denoted as SPATIAL INDICATOR. The last role establishes the type of the spatial relation, e.g. `Regional`. The ambiguity of natural language makes this task very challenging. For example, in the same Example 1, another preposition "*on*" can be considered, but the phrase "*the phone*" is not a spatial role, as it refers to a communication mean. This mainly depends on the semantics of the grammatical head words, i.e. *chair* and *phone*. Such phenomena are crucial in many learning frameworks, as in kernel-based learning (Shawe-Taylor and Cristianini, 2004), where the decision is based on the similarity between training and testing data.

This paper describes the UNITOR-HMM-TK system participating in the Semeval 2013 Spatial Role Labeling Task (Kolomiyets et al., 2013), addressing three of the five defined sub-tasks:

- **Task A: Spatial Role Classification**. It consists in labeling short sentences with spatial roles among SPATIAL INDICATOR, TRAJECTOR and LANDMARK.
- **Task B: Relation Identification**. It consists in the identification of relations among roles identified in Task A. This task does not involve the semantic relation classification.
- **Task C: Spatial Role Classification**. It consists in labeling short documents with spatial roles among the extended role set: TRAJECTOR, LANDMARK, SPATIAL INDICATOR, MOTION_INDICATOR, PATH, DIRECTION and DISTANCE.

The UNITOR-HMM-TK system addresses both the problems of identifying spatial roles and relations as a sequence of two main classification steps.

*Second Joint Conference on Lexical and Computational Semantics (*SEM), Volume 2: Seventh International Workshop on Semantic Evaluation (SemEval 2013)*, pages 573–579, Atlanta, Georgia, June 14-15, 2013.

In the first step, each word in the sentence is classified by a sequence-based classifier with respect to the possible spatial roles. It is in line with other methods based on sequence-based classifier for SpRL (Kordjamshidi et al., 2011; Kordjamshidi et al., 2012b). Our labeling has been inspired by the work in (Croce et al., 2012), where the SVM^{hmm} learning algorithm, formulated in (Altun et al., 2003), has been applied to the classical FrameNet-based Semantic Role Labeling. The main contribution in (Croce et al., 2012) is the adoption of shallow grammatical features (e.g. POS-tag sequences) instead of the full syntax of the sentence, in order to avoid over-fitting over training data. Moreover, lexical information has been generalized through the use of a Word Space, in line with (Schutze, 1998; Sahlgren, 2006): it consists in a Distributional Model of Lexical Semantics derived from the unsupervised analysis of an unlabeled large-scale corpus. The result is a geometrical space where words with similar meaning, e.g. involved in a paradigmatic or almost-synonymic relations, will be projected in similar vectors. As an example, we expect that a word like "*table*", maybe a LANDMARK in a training example, is more similar to "*chair*" as compared with "*phone*".

In the second step, all roles found in a sentence are combined to generate candidate relations, which are then verified by a Support Vector Machine (SVM) classifier. As the entire sentence is informative to determine the proper conjunction of all roles, we apply a kernel function within the classifier, that enhances both syntactic and lexical information of the examples. We adopted the *Smoothed Partial Tree Kernel* (SPTK), defined in (Croce et al., 2011): it is convolution kernel that allows to measure the similarity between syntactic structures, which are partially similar and whose nodes can differ, but are semantically related. Each example is represented as a tree structure directly derived from the sentence dependency parse, thus avoiding the manual definition of features. Similarity between lexical nodes is measured in the same Word Space mentioned above.

In the rest of the paper, Section 2 discusses the SVM^{hmm} based approach. The SPTK-based learning algorithm will be presented in Section 3. Finally, results obtained in the competition are discussed in Section 4.

2 Sequential Tagging for Spatial Role Classification

The system proposed for the *Spatial Role Classification* task is based on the SVM^{hmm} formulation discussed in (Altun et al., 2003). It extends classical SVMs by learning a discriminative model isomorphic to a k-order Hidden Markov Model through the Structural SVM formulation (Tsochantaridis et al., 2005). In the discriminative view of SVM^{hmm}, given an observed input word sequence $\mathbf{x} = (x_1 \ldots x_l) \in \mathcal{X}$ of feature vectors $x_1 \ldots x_l$, the model predicts a sequence of labels $\mathbf{y} = (y_1 \ldots y_l) \in \mathcal{Y}$ after learning a linear discriminant function $F : \mathcal{X} \times \mathcal{Y} \rightarrow \mathbb{R}$ over input/output pairs. Each word is then modeled as a set of linear features that express lexical information as well as syntactic information surrogated by POS n-grams. With respect to other works using SVM^{hmm} for SpRL, such as (Kordjamshidi et al., 2012b), we investigate another set of possible features, as the ones proposed in (Croce et al., 2012): the aim is to provide an agile system that takes advantages in adopting only shallow grammatical features, thus ignoring the full syntactic information of a sentence. The syntactic features derived from a dependency parse process are surrogated by POS n-grams. According to this, our feature modeling adopts the `IOB` notation discussed in (Croce et al., 2012). It provides a class label for each token, mapping them into artificial classes representing the beginning (`B`), the inside (`I`) or ending (`O`) of a spatial role, plus the label of the classified role (i.e. B_{SPIND} for the starting token of a SPATIAL INDICATOR); words external to every role are labeled with the special class (_). According to this notation, the labeling of Example 1 can be expressed as follows: "*A*/B_{TRAJ} *man*/O_{TRAJ} *is*/_ *sitting*/_ *on*/B_{SPIND} *a*/B_{LAND} *chair*/O_{LAND} *and*/_ . . . ".

In order to reduce the complexity of the entire classification task, two phases are applied. In Task A, as in (Kordjamshidi et al., 2011), the first phase aims at labeling only SPATIAL INDICATOR, as they should relate remaining spatial expressions. For the same reason, in Task C we first label only SPATIAL INDICATOR and MOTION INDICATOR. Roles classified in this step are considered *pivot* and they can be used as features for the classification of the other roles: TRAJECTORS and LANDMARKS for

Task A while TRAJECTORS, LANDMARKS, PATHS, DISTANCES and DIRECTIONS for Task C.

For the classification of SPATIAL and MOTION INDICATOR, each word, such as the first "*on*" occurrence in the Example 1, is modeled through the following features: its lemma (*on*) and POS tag (IN); the left and right lexical contexts, represented by the n words before (*man*::NN *is*::VBZ *sitting*::VBG) and after (*a*::DT *chair*::NN *and*::CC); the left and right syntactic contexts as the POS n-grams occurring *before* (i.e. NN_VBZ VBZ_VBG NN_VBZ_VBG) and *after* (i.e. DT_NN NN_CC DT_NN_CC) the word.

For the TRAJECTOR and LANDMARK classification in Task A, each word is represented by the same features described above, plus the following ones (with respect to Example 1, the token relative to the word *man*): lemma of the SPATIAL INDICATOR (*on*); *Positional Feature*: distance from the SPATIAL INDICATOR in terms of number of tokens (-3); relative position with respect to the SPATIAL INDICATOR, that is *before* or *after* (*before*); a boolean feature that indicates whether or not the current token is a SPATIAL INDICATOR; the number of words composing the SPATIAL INDICATOR (here 1).

In Task C, for the classification with respect to the complete set of roles, each word is modeled by the previous features together with the following: distance from the MOTION INDICATOR in terms of number of tokens; relative position with respect to the MOTION INDICATOR (before and after); a boolean feature that indicates whether or not the current token is a MOTION INDICATOR; the number of words that composes the MOTION INDICATOR. In both Tasks A and C the symbols SI and MI to represent a SPATIAL INDICATOR or a MOTION INDICATOR are used respectively to represent the target pivot role within any n-gram.

In order to increase the robustness of our modeling, we extended the lexical information with features derived from a distributional analysis over large texts. In essence, we represent the lexical semantic similarity between different words with similar meaning. We extend a supervised approach through the adoption of vector based models of lexical meaning: a large-scale corpus is statistically analyzed and a Word Space, (Sahlgren, 2006), is acquired as follows. A word-by-context matrix M is obtained through a large scale corpus analysis. Then the *Latent Semantic Analysis* (Landauer and Dumais, 1997) technique is applied to reduce the space dimensionality. Moreover it provides a way to project a generic word w_i into a k-dimensional space where each row corresponds to the representation vector $\vec{w_i}$. In such a space, the distance between vectors reflects the similarity between corresponding words. The resulting feature vector representing w_i is then augmented with $\vec{w_i}$, as in (Croce et al., 2010), where the benefits of such information have been reported in the FrameNet-based Semantic Role Labeling task.

3 Relation identification

The UNITOR-HMM-TK system tackles *Relation Identification* task by determining which spatial roles, discovered in the previous classification phase, can be combined to determine valid spatial relations. Our method is inspired by the work of (Roberts and Harabagiu, 2012), where all possible spatial roles are first generated through heuristics and then combinatorially combined to acquire candidate relations; valid spatial relations are finally determined using a SVM classifier. We aim at reducing the potentially huge search space, by considering only spatial roles proposed by our sequential tagging approach, described in Section 2. Most importantly, we avoid the manual feature engineering phase of (Roberts and Harabagiu, 2012). Candidate relations are not represented as vectors, whose dimensions are manually defined features useful for the target classification. We directly apply the Smoothed Partial Tree-Kernel (SPTK), proposed in (Croce et al., 2011), to estimate the similarity among a specific tree representation.

Tree kernels exploit syntactic similarity through the idea of convolutions among substructures. Any tree kernel computes the number of common substructures between two trees T_1 and T_2 without explicitly considering the whole fragment space. Its general equation is reported hereafter:

$$TK(T_1, T_2) = \sum_{n_1 \in N_{T_1}} \sum_{n_2 \in N_{T_2}} \Delta(n_1, n_2)$$

where N_{T_1} and N_{T_2} are the sets of the T_1's and T_2's nodes respectively, and $\Delta(n_1, n_2)$ is equal to the number of common fragments rooted in the n_1 and n_2 nodes[1]. The SVM classifier is thus trained in

[1]To have a similarity score between 0 and 1, a normalization

a implicit very high-dimensional space, where each dimension reflects a possible tree sub-structure, thus avoiding the need of an explicit feature definition. The function Δ determines the nature of such space. For example, Syntactic Tree Kernel (STK) are used to model complete context free rules as in (Collins and Duffy, 2001).

The algorithm for SPTK (Croce et al., 2011) pushes for more emphasis on lexical nodes. The Δ function allows to recursively matches tree structures and lexical nodes: this allows to match fragments having same structure but different lexical nodes, by assigning a score proportional to the product of the lexical similarities, thus generalizing grammatical and lexical information in training data. While similarity can be modeled directly over lexical resources, e.g. WordNet as discussed in (Pedersen et al., 2004), their development can be very expensive, thus limiting the coverage of the resulting convolution kernel, especially in specific application domains. Again, a Word Space model is adopted: given two words, the term similarity function σ is estimated as the cosine similarity between the corresponding projections.

As proposed in (Croce et al., 2011), the SPTK is applied to examples modeled according the *Grammatical Relation Centered Tree* (GRCT) representation, which is derived from the original dependency parse structure. Figure 1 shows the GRCT for Example 1: non-terminal nodes reflect syntactic relations, such as subject (NSUBJ); pre-terminals are the POS, such as nouns (NN), and leaves are lexemes, such as *man::n*[2]. Non-terminal nodes associated with a role are enriched with the role name, e.g. $\text{NSUBJ}_{\text{TRAJ}}$. All nodes not covering any role are pruned out, so that all information not concerning spatial aspects that would introduce noise is ignored.

In this setting, positive examples are provided by considering sentences labeled by roles involved in a valid relation. The definition of negative examples is more difficult. We considered all roles labelled by the SVM^{hmm} based system, discussed in Section 2. For each incorrect labeling over the annotated material, a set of negative examples is acquired by combining all proposed roles. In order to avoid over-fitting, a n-fold schema has been applied: it is needed to avoid the SVM^{hmm} labeling the same sentences used for training. Moreover, constraints over the relation are imposed to avoid violations of the Spatial Role theory: in Task B each relation must be composed at least by a SPATIAL_INDICATOR, LANDMARK and a TRAJECTOR or by a SPATIAL_INDICATOR, implicit LANDMARK and a TRAJECTOR. Let us consider a possible labeling of Example 1: "$[A\ man]_{\text{TRAJ}}$ *is sitting* $[on]_{\text{SPIND}}$ $[a\ chair]_{\text{LAND}}$ *and talking* $[on]_{\text{SPIND}}[the\ phone]_{\text{LAND}}$"; here, the second SPATIAL_INDICATOR "*on*" and the LANDMARK "*the phone*" are incorrectly labeled. A negative example is thus obtained by considering these roles togheter with the TRAJECTOR "*the phone*", as shown in Figure 2. Other two negative examples can be generated by combining the remaining two roles.

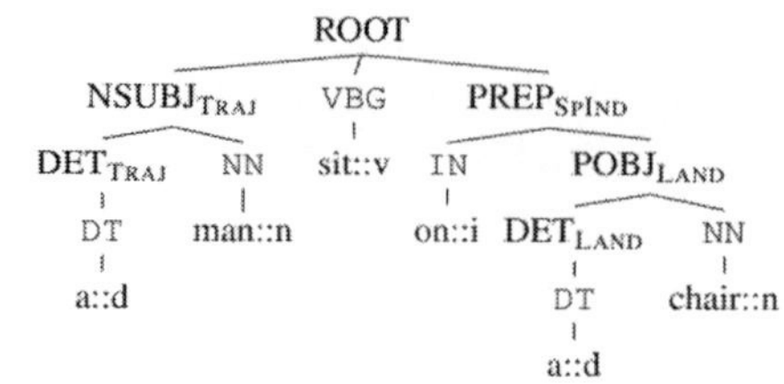

Figure 1: GRCT representation of a *positive* example derived from a correct labeling from Example 1

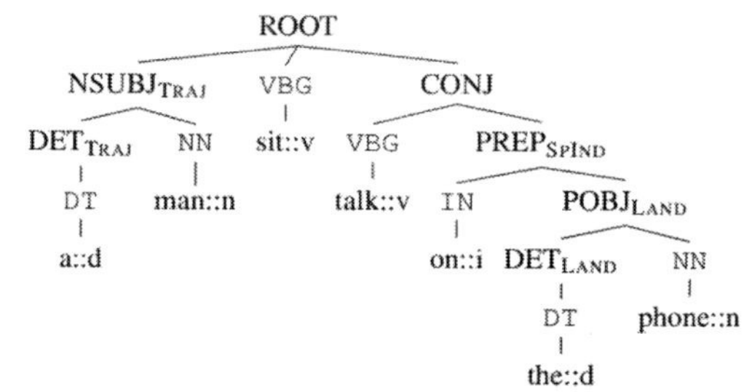

Figure 2: GRCT representation of a *negative* example derived from a wrong labeling from Example 1

4 Results

In this section experimental results of the UNITOR-HMM-TK system in the Spatial Role Labeling task at SemEval 2013 are reported. In Tasks A and B, the dataset is a corrected version

in the kernel space, i.e. $\frac{TK(T_1,T_2)}{\sqrt{TK(T_1,T_1)\times TK(T_2,T_2)}}$ is applied.

[2]Each word is lemmatized to reduce data sparseness, but they are enriched with POS tags to avoid confusing words from different grammatical categories.

of the same training dataset employed in (Kordjamshidi et al., 2012a)[3]. The dataset for Task C was part of the Confluence corpus[4]. More details about the dataset are provided in (Kolomiyets et al., 2013). In all experiments, sentences are processed with the Stanford CoreNLP[5], for Part-of-Speech tagging, lemmatization (Task A and C) and dependency parsing (Task B).

The sequential labeling system described in Section 2 has been made available by the SVM^{hmm} software[6]. The estimation of the semantically Smoothed Partial Tree Kernel (SPTK), described in Section 3 is made available by an extended version of SVM-LightTK software[7] (Moschitti, 2006), implementing the smooth matching between tree nodes. Similarity between lexical nodes is estimated as the cosine similarity in the co-occurrence Word Space described above, as in (Croce et al., 2011).

The co-occurrence Word Space is acquired through the distributional analysis of the UkWaC corpus (Baroni et al., 2009). First, all words occurring more than 100 times (i.e. the *targets*) are represented through vectors. The original space dimensions are generated from the set of the 20,000 most frequent words (i.e. *features*) in the UkWaC corpus. One dimension describes the Pointwise Mutual Information score between one feature, as it occurs on a left or right window of 3 tokens around a target. Left contexts of targets are treated differently from the right ones, in order to capture asymmetric syntactic behaviors (e.g., useful for verbs): 40,000 dimensional vectors are thus derived for each target. The Singular Value Decomposition is applied and the space dimensionality is reduced to $k = 100$.

4.1 Results in Task A

Two different runs were submitted for Task A. The first takes into account all roles labeled accordingly to the approach described in Section 2. Results, in term of precision, recall and F-measure for each spatial role are shown in Table 1. The second run considers only those roles composing the relations that are positively classified in Task B and it will be discussed in Section 4.2.

A tuning phase has been carried out through a 10-fold cross validation: it allowed to find the best classifier parameters. The evaluation of the system performances is measured using a character based measure, i.e. considering the number of characters in the span that overlap a role in the gold-standard test.

Spatial Role	*Precision*	*Recall*	*F-Measure*
SPATIAL INDICATOR	0.967	0.889	0.926
TRAJECTOR	0.684	0.681	0.682
LANDMARK	0.741	0.835	0.785

Table 1: Task A results (first run)

The overall performances of the first run are very promising in terms of both precision and recall. In particular, the SPATIAL INDICATOR labeling achieves a significant F-Measure of 0.926 with a precision of 0.967. The sequence labeling approach provides good results for the LANDMARK and the TRAJECTOR roles too. Unfortunately, these results are not comparable with the performances obtained the last year edition of the SpRL task, where a grammatical head word-based measure has been applied.

The main difficulty in the SPATIAL INDICATOR classification concerns the tagging of a larger or smaller span for the roles, as for *"at the back"* that is tagged as *"at the back of"*. On the contrary, for roles like *"to the left and the right"* the system produces a tag covering just the first three words, *"to the left"*, because this shortest sequence was far more represented within the training set. Some roles corresponding to unknown word sequences, such as *"on the very right"*, were not labeled, leading to the little drop in terms of recall for the SPATIAL INDICATOR.

Another issue in the TRAJECTOR and LANDMARK labeling is due to the absence of specific role sequences in the training set, such as LANDMARK-TRAJECTOR-SPATIAL INDICATOR labeled in the test sentence "*there is a [coffee table]$_{\text{LANDMARK}}$ with a [sofa]$_{\text{TRAJECTOR}}$ [around]$_{\text{SP.IND}}$*": the SVM^{hmm} classifier in fact tends to discard any sequence unseen during training. Another issue concerns the difficulty in assigning the TRAJECTOR role to the proper SPATIAL INDICATOR: in the sentence *"a bench with a person lying on it"* where both *"a bench"* and *"a person"* are tagged as TRAJECTOR.

[3]The initial number of sentences was of 600, but it decreased after the elimination of 21 duplicated sentences.

[4]Three of the original 95 files were ignored because of some issues with their format. See http://confluence.org

[5]http://nlp.stanford.edu/software/corenlp.shtml

[6]http://www.cs.cornell.edu/People/tj/svm_light/svm_hmm.html

[7]http://disi.unitn.it/moschitti/Tree-Kernel.htm

4.2 Results in Task B

Task B has been tackled using the SPTK-based Relation Identification approach, described in Section 3. In particular, the SVM classifier is fed with 741 positive examples, corresponding to the number of gold relations, while the negative examples generation process, described in Section 3, yielded 2,256 examples. The same Word Space described in the previous section has been used to compute the semantic similarity within the SPTK. For the tuning phase, a 80-20 fixed split has been applied.

For this task, two different measures are presented. The *Relaxed* measure considers a relation correct if each role composing it has at least one character overlapping the corresponding gold role. The *Strict* measure considers a relation correct only if each role in it has all the characters overlapping with the gold role. The first measure is more comparable with the one used in (Kordjamshidi et al., 2012a), where a relation is considered correct only if each grammatical head word of the involved roles were correctly labeled. The results achieved in this task by our system are reported in Table 2.

Spatial Role	*Precision*	*Recall*	*F-Measure*
RELAXED	0.551	0.391	0.458
STRICT	0.431	0.306	0.358

Table 2: Task B results

The problem for this task is more challenging. In fact, the overall task is strictly biased by the quality of the SVM^{hmm} based classifier and inherits all the limitations underlined in Section 4.2. This mostly affects the recall, because every error generated during the role classification is cumulative and losing only one role in Task A implies a misclassification of the whole relation. However, it is important to notice that these results have been achieved without any manual feature engineering nor any heuristics or hand coded lexical resource.

Spatial Role	*Precision*	*Recall*	*F-Measure*
SPATIAL INDICATOR	0.968	0.585	0.729
TRAJECTOR	0.682	0.493	0.572
LANDMARK	0.801	0.560	0.659

Table 3: Task A results (second run)

In the second run of Task A, we evaluate the contribution of this syntactic information to filter out roles. In Table 3 results of the second run for Task A are reported (see previous Section). As expected, the recall measure shows a performance drop with respect to results shown in Table 1: the results proposed in the first run represents an upperbound to the recall as any novel role is added here. However, the precision measure for the LANDMARK role classification is improved of about 10%.

Spatial Role	*Precision*	*Recall*	*F-Measure*
SPATIAL INDICATOR	0.609	0.479	0.536
MOTION INDICATOR	0.892	0.294	0.443
TRAJECTOR	0.565	0.317	0.406
LANDMARK	0.662	0.476	0.554
PATH	0.775	0.295	0.427
DIRECTION	0.312	0.229	0.264
DISTANCE	0.946	0.331	0.490

Table 4: Task C results

4.3 Results in Task C

In Task C the extended set of roles is considered. According to this, the number of possible labels to be learnt by the system increases, thus making the problem more challenging. As for Task A, here the SVM^{hmm} has been trained over the whole training set, using a 10-fold cross validation in the tuning phase. Moreover, the sentences of the Confluence corpus are far more complex than the ones from the CLEF corpus. Confluence sentences have a more narrative nature with respect to the CLEF sentences, that are simple description of images. The combination of these two factors resulted in a large drop in the performance, especially for the recall.

As shown by the results in Table 4, DIRECTION is the most difficult role to be classified, probably because it is represented by many different word sequences. Other roles are found in few instances, but almost all correct, as for DISTANCE and MOTION INDICATOR. The high value of *Precision* for the DISTANCE role is justified by the fact that when this role is composed by a number, (i.e. *"530 meters"*), the system identified and classified it well, while for a representation with only words (i.e. *"very close"*) the system did not retrieved it at all.

Acknowledgements This work has been partially funded by European Union VII Framework Programme under the project Speaky for Robot within the framework of the ECHORD Project.

References

Y. Altun, I. Tsochantaridis, and T. Hofmann. 2003. Hidden Markov support vector machines. In *Proceedings of the International Conference on Machine Learning*.

Marco Baroni, Silvia Bernardini, Adriano Ferraresi, and Eros Zanchetta. 2009. The wacky wide web: a collection of very large linguistically processed web-crawled corpora. *Language Resources and Evaluation*, 43(3):209–226.

Michael Collins and Nigel Duffy. 2001. Convolution kernels for natural language. In *Proceedings of Neural Information Processing Systems (NIPS'2001)*, pages 625–632.

Danilo Croce, Cristina Giannone, Paolo Annesi, and Roberto Basili. 2010. Towards open-domain semantic role labeling. In *ACL*, pages 237–246.

Danilo Croce, Alessandro Moschitti, and Roberto Basili. 2011. Structured lexical similarity via convolution kernels on dependency trees. In *Proceedings of EMNLP*, Edinburgh, Scotland, UK.

Danilo Croce, Giuseppe Castellucci, and Emanuele Bastianelli. 2012. Structured learning for semantic role labeling. *In Intelligenza Artificiale*, 6(2):163–176, January.

Oleksandr Kolomiyets, Parisa Kordjamshidi, Steven Bethard, and Marie-Francine Moens. 2013. Semeval-2013 task 2: Spatial role labeling. In *Proceedings of the 7th International Workshop on Semantic Evaluation*. Association for Computational Linguistics.

Parisa KordJamshidi, Martijn van Otterlo, and Marie-Francine Moens. 2010. Spatial role labeling: Task definition and annotation scheme. In *LREC*.

Parisa Kordjamshidi, Martijn Van Otterlo, and Marie-Francine Moens. 2011. Spatial role labeling: Towards extraction of spatial relations from natural language. *ACM Trans. Speech Lang. Process.*, 8(3):4:1–4:36, December.

Parisa Kordjamshidi, Steven Bethard, and Marie-Francine Moens. 2012a. Semeval-2012 task 3: Spatial role labeling. In *SemEval 2012*, pages 365–373, Montréal, Canada, 7-8 June. Association for Computational Linguistics.

Parisa Kordjamshidi, Paolo Frasconi, Martijn Van Otterlo, Marie-Francine Moens, and Luc De Raedt. 2012b. Relational learning for spatial relation extraction from natural language. In *Proceedings of the 21st international conference on Inductive Logic Programming*, ILP'11, pages 204–220, Berlin, Heidelberg. Springer-Verlag.

T. Landauer and S. Dumais. 1997. A solution to plato's problem: The latent semantic analysis theory of acquisition, induction and representation of knowledge. *Psychological Review*, 104(2):211–240.

Alessandro Moschitti. 2006. Efficient convolution kernels for dependency and constituent syntactic trees. In *ECML*, pages 318–329, Berlin, Germany, September.

Ted Pedersen, Siddharth Patwardhan, and Jason Michelizzi. 2004. WordNet::Similarity - Measuring the Relatedness of Concept. In *Proc. of 5th NAACL*, Boston, MA.

Kirk Roberts and Sanda Harabagiu. 2012. Utd-sprl: A joint approach to spatial role labeling. In *SemEval 2012)*, pages 419–424, Montréal, Canada, 7-8 June. Association for Computational Linguistics.

Magnus Sahlgren. 2006. *The Word-Space Model*. Ph.D. thesis, Stockholm University.

Hinrich Schutze. 1998. Automatic word sense discrimination. *Journal of Computational Linguistics*, 24:97–123.

John Shawe-Taylor and Nello Cristianini. 2004. *Kernel Methods for Pattern Analysis*. Cambridge University Press.

Ioannis Tsochantaridis, Thorsten Joachims, Thomas Hofmann, and Yasemin Altun. 2005. Large margin methods for structured and interdependent output variables. *J. Machine Learning Reserach.*, 6, December.

EHU-ALM: Similarity-Feature Based Approach for Student Response Analysis

Itziar Aldabe, Montse Maritxalar
IXA NLP Group
University of Basque Country (UPV-EHU)
itziar.aldabe@ehu.es
montse.maritxalar@ehu.es

Oier Lopez de Lacalle
University of Edinburgh
IKERBASQUE,
Basque Foundation for Science
oier.lopezdelacalle@gmail.com

Abstract

We present a 5-way supervised system based on syntactic-semantic similarity features. The model deploys: Text overlap measures, WordNet-based lexical similarities, graph-based similarities, corpus-based similarities, syntactic structure overlap and predicate-argument overlap measures. These measures are applied to question, reference answer and student answer triplets. We take into account the negation in the syntactic and predicate-argument overlap measures. Our system uses the domain-specific data as one dataset to build a robust system. The results show that our system is above the median and mean on all the evaluation scenarios of the SemEval-2013 task #7.

1 Introduction

In this paper we describe our participation with a feature-based supervised system to the SemEval-2013 task #7: The Joint Student Response Analysis and 8th Recognizing Textual Entailment Challenge (Dzikovska et al., 2013). The goal of our participation is to build a generic system that is robust enough across domains and scenarios. A domain-specific system requires new training examples when shifting to a new domain. However, domain-specific data is difficult to obtain and creating new resources is expensive.

We seek robustness by mixing the instances from BEETLE and SCIENTSBANK. We show our strategy is suitable to build a generic system that performs competitively on any domain in the 5-way task.

The paper proceeds as follows. Section 2 describes the system presenting the learning features and the runs. In Section 3 we show the optimization details, followed by the results (Section 4) and a preliminary error analysis (Section 5).

2 System description

Our system aims for robustness using the domain-specific training data as one dataset. Therefore, we do not differentiate between examples from the given domains (BEETLE and SCIENTSBANK) when training the system. In contrast, our approach dintinguishes between new questions (*unseen answer* vs. *unseen question*) as well as question types (*how*, *what* and *why*) by means of simple heuristics.

The runs are organized according to different system designs. Although all the runs use the same feature set, we split the training set to build more specialized classifiers. Training examples are grouped depending on: i) the answer is unseen; ii) the question is unseen; and iii) the question type (i.e. *what*, *how*, *why*). Each run defines a framework to explore the different ways to approach the problem. While the first run is the simplest and is the most generic in nature, the third tries to split the task into simpler problems and creates more specialized classifiers.

2.1 Similarity learning features

Our model is based on various text similarity features. Almost all of the measures are computed between question, reference answer and student answer triplets. The measures based on syntactic structure and predicate-argument overlaps are only applied to the student and reference answer pairs. In

*Second Joint Conference on Lexical and Computational Semantics (*SEM), Volume 2: Seventh International Workshop on Semantic Evaluation (SemEval 2013)*, pages 580–584, Atlanta, Georgia, June 14-15, 2013. ©2013 Association for Computational Linguistics

total, we defined 30 features which can be grouped as follows:

Text overlap measures The similarity of two texts is computed based on the number of overlapping words. We obtain the similarity of two texts based on the F-Measure, the Dice Coefficient, The Cosine, and the Lesk measures. For that, we use the implementation available in the Text::Similarity package[1].

WordNet-based lexical similarities All the similarity metrics based on WordNet (Miller, 1995) follow the methodology proposed in (Mihalcea et al., 2006). For each open-class word in one of the input texts, we obtain the maximun semantic similarity or relatedness value matching the same open-class words in the other input text. The values of each matching are summed up and normalized by the length of the two input texts as explained in (Mihalcea et al., 2006). We compute the measures of Resnik, Lin, Jiang-Conrath, Leacock-Chodorow, Wu-Palmer, Banerjee-Pedersen, and Patwardhan-Pedersen provided in the WordNet::Similarity package (Patwardhan et al., 2003).

Graph-based similarities The similarity of two texts is based on a graph-based representation (Agirre and Soroa, 2009) of WordNet. The method is a two-step process: first the personalized PageRank over WordNet is computed for each text. This produces a probability distribution over WordNet. Then, the probability distributions are encoded as vectors and the cosine similarity between those vectors is calculated.

Corpus-based similarities We compute two corpus-based similarity measures: Latent Semantic Analysis (Deerwester et al., 1990) and Latent Dirichlet Allocation (Blei et al., 2003). We estimate 100 dimensions for LSA and 50 topics for LDA. Both models are obtained from a subset of the English Wikipedia following the hierarchy of science categories. We started with a small set of categories and recovered the articles below the sub-hierarchy. We only went 3 levels down to avoid noisy articles as the category system is rather flat. The similarity of two texts is the cosine similarity between the resulting vectors associated with each text in the latent space.

[1] http://www.d.umn.edu/ tpederse/text-similarity.html

Syntactic structure overlap The role of syntax is studied by the use of graph subsumption based on the approach proposed in (McCarthy et al., 2008). The text is mapped into a graph with nodes representing words and links indicating syntactic dependencies between them. The similarity of two texts is computed based on the overlap of the syntactic structures. Negation is handled explicitly in the graph.

Predicate-argument overlap The similarity of two texts is computed by analyzing the overlap of the predicates and their associated semantic arguments. The system looks for verbal and nominal predicates. The similarity is also based on the approach proposed in (McCarthy et al., 2008). The graph is represented with words as nodes and the semantic role of arguments as links. First, the verbal propositions and their arguments are automatically obtained (Björkelund et al., 2009) as represented in PropBank (Palmer et al., 2005). Second, a generalization of the predicates is obtained based on VerbNet (Kipper, 2005) and NomBank (Meyers et al., 2004). Finally, the similarity of two texts is computed based on the overlap of the predicate-argument relations.

2.2 Architecture of the runs

Generic Framework RUN1 This is the simplest framework for the assessment of student answers. The system relies on a single classifier, which has been optimized on the unseen question scenario. The scenario is simulated by splitting the training set so that each question and its answers are in the same fold.

Unseen Framework RUN2 This framework relies on two classifiers. The first is tuned on an unseen answer scenario and the second is prepared for the question scenario (cf. RUN1). In order to build the unseen answer classifier, we split the training set so that answers to the same question can occur in different folders. In test time, the instance is classified depending on whether it is an unseen answer or an

	BEETLE			SCIENTSBANK				OVERALL
	Uns-answ	Uns-qst	All	Uns-answ	Uns-qst	Uns-dom	All	All
RUN1	0.499 (6)	0.352 (7)	0.404	0.396 (7)	0.283 (4)	0.345 (3)	0.348	0.406
RUN2	0.526 (4)	0.352 (7)	0.413	0.418 (6)	0.283 (4)	0.345 (3)	0.350	0.414
RUN3	0.502 (5)	0.370 (6)	0.415	0.424 (5)	0.260 (8)	0.337 (5)	0.340	0.403
LOWEST	0.170	0.173	-	0.089	0.095	0.121	-	-
BEST	0.619	0.552	-	0.478	0.307	0.380	-	-
MEAN	0.435	0.343	-	0.341	0.240	0.267	-	-
MEDIAN	0.437	0.326	-	0.376	0.259	0.268	-	-

Table 1: 5-way results of the runs in F1 macro-average on BEETLE and SCIENTSBANK domains across different scenarios. Along with the runs, the LOWEST and the BEST system in each scenario are shown. The MEAN and MEDIAN of the dataset are also presented. Finally, the OVERALL results are showed summing up both domains. Uns-answ refers to unseen answers scenario, Uns-qst stands for unseen question, Uns-dom unseen domain and All refers to the sum of all scenarios. The run results are presented together with the ranked position in the task.

unseen question[2].

Question-type Framework RUN3 The run consists of a set of question-type expert classifiers. We divided the training set based on whether an instance reflected a *what*, *how* or *why* question. We then partitioned each question type into unseen answer and unseen question scenarios. In total, the framework deploys 6 classifiers, i.e. a test instance is classified according to the question type and scenario. We set heuristics to automatically distinguish the instance type.

3 Optimization on training set

We set a heuristic to create the training instances. For each student answer, if the matching reference answer is indicated in it, we create a triplet with the question, the student answer, and the matching reference answer. If there is no matching answer, the reference answer is randomly selected giving preference to the *best* reference answers.

Once we have a training set, we split it into different ways to simulate the scenarios described in Section 2.2. All the models are optimized using 10-fold cross-validation of the pertaining training set. For the classifiers in RUN1 and RUN2 we used 8910 training instances. For RUN3 the instances were divided as follows: 1235 instances for *how* questions, 3089 for *what* questions and 4589 for *why* questions. In total, we obtained 8 models which were distributed through the runs.

[2]We treat unseen-domain instances as unseen-question instances.

Our approach uses Support Vector Machine (Chang and Lin, 2011) to build the classifiers. As the number of features is not high, we used the gaussian kernel in order to solve the non-linear problem. The main parameters of the kernel (γ and C) were tuned using grid search over the parameter in the cross-validation setting. We focused on optimizing the F1 macro average of the classifier in order to avoid a bias towards the major classes. Each of the 8 classifiers were tuned independently.

The triplets of question, student answer and reference answer of the test instances were always created selecting the first reference answer of the given set of answers.

4 Results

A total of 8 teams participated in the 5-way task, submitting a total of 16 system runs (Dzikovska et al., 2013). Table 1 shows the performance obtained by our systems across domains and different scenarios. Our three runs ranked differently based on the evaluation scenario: beetle-uns-answ (6,4,5 rank for RUN1, RUN2, RUN3, respectively); beetle-uns-qst (7,7,6); scientsbank-uns-answ (7,6,5); scientsbank-uns-qst (4,4,8) and scientsbank-uns-dom (3,3,5). We also evaluated our runs on the entire domain (All columns) and on the whole test set (OVERALL).

The results show we built robust systems. Despite being below the best system of each evaluation scenario, the results show that the runs are competitive. All our runs are above the median and outperform the average results on each evaluation. Overall, the results attained in SCIENTSBANK are lower than in

BEETLE. This might be due to the questions and answers being longer in SCIENTSBANK, making it difficult to obtain good patterns.

As regards our runs, there is no significant overall difference. While RUN3 performs better in BEETLE unseen question and SCIENTSBANK unseen answer, in the rest of scenarios RUN2 outperforms the rest of the runs. As expected, RUN2 outperforms RUN1 in the unseen answer scenario since the former has a module specializing in unseen answers. However, although RUN3 is an ensemble of six classifiers, it is not the best run. This is probably because the training sets are not big enough.

Unseen framework (RUN2)			
	Prec	Rec	F1
correct	0.552	0.677	0.608
partially correct	0.324	0.323	0.323
contradictory	0.239	0.121	0.160
irrelevant	0.472	0.377	0.419
non domain	0.415	0.849	0.557
Macro average	0.400	0.469	0.414
Micro average	0.443	0.464	0.446

Table 2: results of the RUN2 system on a entire test set.

Table 2 shows the detailed results of the RUN2 system on the entire test set. It is noticeable the low results obtained on the *contradictory* class. This might be because the defined features are not able to model negation properly and do not deal with antonymy. Surprisingly, the *non domain* class is not the most problematic, even if the system was trained on a low number of instances.

5 Preliminary Error Analysis

We conducted a preliminary error analysis and studied some of the misclassified test instances to detect some problematic issues and to define improvements to our approach.

Example 5.1 *Sam and Jasmine were sitting on a park bench eating their lunches. A mosquito landed on Sam's arm and Sam began slapping at it. When he did that, he knocked Jasmine's soda into her lap, causing her to jump up. What was Sam's response?*

R: Sam's response was to slap the mosquito.

S1: Sam's response was to say sorry

S2: To smack the bee.

Some of the detected errors suggest that our use of syntax and lexical overlap is not sufficient to identify the correct class. Our system marks the student answer S1 from Example 5.1[3] as correct. The reference answer and the student answer share a great number of words and the dependency trees are almost identical, but not the meanings. In addition, the question contains additional information that may require other types of features to correctly classify the instance.

The predicate-argument overlap feature tries to generalize the predicate information to find similarities between verbs with the same meaning. However, our system does not always work in a correct way. The verb *smack* in the student answer S2 and the verb *slap* in the reference answer mean the same. Our system classifies the answer incorrectly. If we look at PropBank and VerbNet, we find that there is not mapping between PropBank and VerbNet for these particular verbs.

Example 5.2 *Why do you think the other terminals are being held in a different electrical state than that of the negative terminal?*

R: Terminals 4, 5 and 6 are not connected to the negative battery terminal

S1: They are connected to the positive battery terminal

We consider the negation as part of the syntactic and predicate-argument overlap measures. However, our system does not characterize the similarity between *not connected to the negative* and *connected to the positive* (Example 5.2). This type of examples suggest that the system needs to model the negation and antonyms with additional features.

In the future, further error analysis will be carried out to design features to better model the problem. We also anticipate creating a specialized feature space for each question type.

Acknowledgments

This research was partially funded by the Ber2Tek project (IE12-333), the SKaTeR project (TIN2012-38584-C06-02) and the NewsReader project (FP7-ICT-2011-8-316404).

[3]R refers to the reference answer and S1 and S2 to student answers.

References

Eneko Agirre and Aitor Soroa. 2009. Personalizing pagerank for word sense disambiguation. In *Proceedings of the 12th conference of the European chapter of the Association for Computational Linguistics (EACL-2009)*, Athens, Greece.

Anders Björkelund, Love Hafdell, and Pierre Nugues. 2009. Multilingual semantic role labeling. In *Proceedings of The Thirteenth Conference on Computational Natural Language Learning (CoNLL-2009)*, pages 43–48.

David M. Blei, Andrew Y. Ng, and Michael I. Jordan. 2003. Latent Dirichlet allocation. *Journal of Machine Learning Research*, 3:993–1022.

Chih-Chung Chang and Chih-Jen Lin. 2011. Libsvm: A library for support vector machines. *ACM Trans. Intell. Syst. Technol.*, 2(3):27:1–27:27, May.

Scott Deerwester, Susan Dumais, Goerge Furnas, Thomas Landauer, and Richard Harshman. 1990. Indexing by Latent Semantic Analysis. *Journal of the American Society for Information Science*, 41(6):391–407.

Myroslava O. Dzikovska, Rodney Nielsen, Chris Brew, Claudia Leacock, Danilo Giampiccolo, Luisa Bentivogli, Peter Clark, Ido Dagan, and Hoa Trang Dang. 2013. Semeval-2013 task 7: The joint student response analysis and 8th recognizing textual entailment challenge. In **SEM 2013: The First Joint Conference on Lexical and Computational Semantics*, Atlanta, Georgia, USA, 13-14 June. Association for Computational Linguistics.

Karin Kipper. 2005. *VerbNet: A broad-coverage, comprehensive verb lexicon*. Ph.D. thesis, University of Pennsylvania.

Philip M. McCarthy, Vasile Rus, Scott A. Crossley, Arthur C. Graesser, and Danielle S. McNamara. 2008. Assessing forward-, reverse-, and average-entailment indices on natural language input from the intelligent tutoring system, iSTART. In D. Wilson and G. Sutcliffe, editors, *Proceedings of the 21st International Florida Artificial Intelligence Research Society Conference*, pages 201–206, Menlo Park, CA: The AAAI Press.

Adam Meyers, Ruth Reeves, Catherine Macleod, Rachel Szekely, Veronika Zielinska, Brian Young, and Ralph Grishman. 2004. The nombank project: An interim report. In A. Meyers, editor, *HLT-NAACL 2004 Workshop: Frontiers in Corpus Annotation*, pages 24–31, Boston, Massachusetts, USA, May 2 - May 7. Association for Computational Linguistics.

Rada Mihalcea, Courtney Corley, and Carlo Strapparava. 2006. Corpus-based and knowledge-based measures of text semantic similarity. In *Proceedings the American Association for Artificial Intelligence (AAAI 2006)*, Boston.

George A. Miller. 1995. Wordnet: A lexical database for english. *Communications of the ACM*, 38(11):39–41.

Martha Palmer, Dan Gildea, and Paul Kingsbury. 2005. The proposition bank: A corpus annotated with semantic role. *Computational Linguistics*, 31(1):71–106.

Siddharth Patwardhan, Satanjeev Banerjee, and Ted Pedersen. 2003. Using measures of semantic relatedness for word sense disambiguation. In *Proceedings of the Fourth International Conference on Intelligent Text Processing and Computational Linguistics*.

CNGL: Grading Student Answers by Acts of Translation

Ergun Biçici
Centre for Next Generation Localisation,
Dublin City University, Dublin, Ireland.
ebicici@computing.dcu.ie

Josef van Genabith
Centre for Next Generation Localisation,
Dublin City University, Dublin, Ireland.
josef@computing.dcu.ie

Abstract

We invent referential translation machines (RTMs), a computational model for identifying the translation acts between any two data sets with respect to a reference corpus selected in the same domain, which can be used for automatically grading student answers. RTMs make quality and semantic similarity judgments possible by using retrieved relevant training data as interpretants for reaching shared semantics. An MTPP (machine translation performance predictor) model derives features measuring the closeness of the test sentences to the training data, the difficulty of translating them, and the presence of acts of translation involved. We view question answering as translation from the question to the answer, from the question to the reference answer, from the answer to the reference answer, or from the question and the answer to the reference answer. Each view is modeled by an RTM model, giving us a new perspective on the ternary relationship between the question, the answer, and the reference answer. We show that all RTM models contribute and a prediction model based on all four perspectives performs the best. Our prediction model is the 2nd best system on some tasks according to the official results of the Student Response Analysis (SRA 2013) challenge.

1 Automatically Grading Student Answers

We introduce a fully automated student answer grader that performs well in the student response analysis (SRA) task (Dzikovska et al., 2013) and especially well in tasks with unseen answers. Automatic grading can be used for assessing the level of competency for students and estimating the required tutoring effort in e-learning platforms. It can also be used to adapt questions according to the average student performance. Low scored topics can be discussed further in classrooms, enhancing the overall coverage of the course material.

The quality estimation task (QET) (Callison-Burch et al., 2012) aims to develop quality indicators for translations at the sentence-level and predictors without access to the reference. Bicici et al. (2013) develop a top performing machine translation performance predictor (MTPP), which uses machine learning models over features measuring how well the test set matches the training set relying on extrinsic and language independent features.

The student response analysis (SRA) task (Dzikovska et al., 2013) addresses the following problem. Given a question, a known correct reference answer, and a student answer, assess the correctness of the student's answer. The student answers are categorized as correct, partially correct incomplete, contradictory, irrelevant, or non domain, in the 5-way task; as correct, contradictory, or incorrect in the 3-way task; and as correct or incorrect in the 2-way task.

The *student answer correctness prediction problem* involves finding a function f approximating the student answer correctness given the question (Q), the answer (A), and the reference answer (R):

$$f(Q, A, R) \approx q(A, R). \quad (1)$$

We approach f as a supervised learning problem with (Q, A, R, $q(A, R)$) tuples being the training

*Second Joint Conference on Lexical and Computational Semantics (*SEM), Volume 2: Seventh International Workshop on Semantic Evaluation (SemEval 2013)*, pages 585–591, Atlanta, Georgia, June 14-15, 2013. ©2013 Association for Computational Linguistics

data and $q(A, R)$ being the target correctness score.

We model the problem as a translation task where one possible interpretation is translating Q (source to translate, S) to R (target translation, T) and evaluating with A (as reference target, RT) (QRA). Since the information appearing in the question may be repeated in the reference answer or may be omitted in the student answer, it also makes sense to concatenate Q and A when translating to R (QARQA). We obtain 4 different perspectives on the ternary relationship between Q, A, and R depending on how we model their relationship as an instance of translation:

$$\begin{aligned} QAR &: S = Q, & T = A,\ RT = R. \\ QRA &: S = Q, & T = R,\ RT = A. \\ ARA &: S = A, & T = R,\ RT = A. \\ QARQA &: S = Q + A, & T = R,\ RT = Q + A. \end{aligned}$$

2 The Machine Translation Performance Predictor (MTPP)

In machine translation (MT), pairs of source and target sentences are used for training statistical MT (SMT) models. SMT system performance is affected by the amount of training data used as well as the *closeness* of the test set to the training set. MTPP (Biçici et al., 2013) is a top performing machine translation performance predictor, which uses machine learning models over features measuring how well the test set matches the training set to predict the quality of a translation without using a reference translation. MTPP measures the coverage of individual test sentence features and syntactic structures found in the training set and derives feature functions measuring the closeness of test sentences to the available training data, the difficulty of translating the sentence, and the presence of acts of translation involved.

Features for Translation Acts

MTPP uses n-gram features defined over text or common cover link (CCL) (Seginer, 2007) structures as the basic units of information over which similarity calculations are made. Unsupervised parsing with CCL extracts links from base words to head words, which allow us to obtain structures representing the grammatical information instantiated in the training and test data. Feature functions use statistics involving the training set and the test sentences to determine their closeness. Since they are language independent, MTPP allows quality estimation to be performed extrinsically. Categories for the 283 features used are listed below and their detailed descriptions are presented in (Biçici et al., 2013) where the number of features are given in $\{\#\}$.

- *Coverage* $\{110\}$*:* Measures the degree to which the test features are found in the training set for both S ($\{56\}$) and T ($\{54\}$).
- *Synthetic Translation Performance* $\{6\}$*:* Calculates translation scores achievable according to the n-gram coverage.
- *Length* $\{4\}$*:* Calculates the number of words and characters for S and T and their ratios.
- *Feature Vector Similarity* $\{16\}$*:* Calculates the similarities between vector representations.
- *Perplexity* $\{90\}$*:* Measures the fluency of the sentences according to language models (LM). We use both forward ($\{30\}$) and backward ($\{15\}$) LM based features for S and T.
- *Entropy* $\{4\}$*:* Calculates the distributional similarity of test sentences to the training set.
- *Retrieval Closeness* $\{24\}$*:* Measures the degree to which sentences close to the test set are found in the training set.
- *Diversity* $\{6\}$*:* Measures the diversity of co-occurring features in the training set.
- *IBM1 Translation Probability* $\{16\}$*:* Calculates the translation probability of test sentences using the training set (Brown et al., 1993).
- *Minimum Bayes Retrieval Risk* $\{4\}$*:* Calculates the translation probability for the translation having the minimum Bayes risk among the retrieved training instances.
- *Sentence Translation Performance* $\{3\}$*:* Calculates translation scores obtained according to $q(T, R)$ using BLEU (Papineni et al., 2002), NIST (Doddington, 2002), or F_1 (Biçici and Yuret, 2011b) for q.

3 Referential Translation Machine (RTM)

Referential translation machines (RTMs) we develop provide a computational model for quality and semantic similarity judgments using retrieval of relevant training data (Biçici and Yuret, 2011a; Biçici, 2011) as interpretants for reaching shared semantics (Biçici, 2008). We show that RTM achieves very good performance in judging the semantic similarity of sentences (Biçici and van Genabith, 2013) and we can also use RTM to automatically assess the correctness of student answers to obtain better results than the baselines proposed by (Dzikovska et al., 2012), which achieve the best performance on some tasks (Dzikovska et al., 2013).

RTM is a computational model for identifying the acts of translation for translating between any given two data sets with respect to a reference corpus selected in the same domain. RTM can be used for automatically grading student answers. An RTM model is based on the selection of common training data relevant and close to both the training set and the test set where the selected relevant set of instances are called the interpretants. Interpretants allow shared semantics to be possible by behaving as a reference point for similarity judgments and providing the context. In semiotics, an interpretant I interprets the signs used to refer to the real objects (Biçici, 2008). RTMs provide a model for computational semantics using interpretants as a reference according to which semantic judgments with translation acts are made. Each RTM model is a data translation model between the instances in the training set and the test set. We use the FDA (Feature Decay Algorithms) instance selection model for selecting the interpretants (Biçici and Yuret, 2011a) from a given corpus, which can be monolingual when modeling paraphrasing acts, in which case the MTPP model is built using the interpretants themselves as both the source and the target side of the parallel corpus. RTMs map the training and test data to a space where translation acts can be identified. We view that acts of translation are ubiquitously used during communication:

Every act of communication is an act of translation (Bliss, 2012).

Translation need not be between different languages and paraphrasing or communication also contain acts of translation. When creating sentences, we use our background knowledge and translate information content according to the current context.

Given a training set `train`, a test set `test`, and some monolingual corpus $\mathcal{C}$, preferably in the same domain as the training and test sets, the RTM steps are:

1. $T = \texttt{train} \cup \texttt{test}$.
2. select$(T, \mathcal{C}) \rightarrow \mathcal{I}$
3. MTPP$(\mathcal{I}, \texttt{train}) \rightarrow \mathcal{F}_{\texttt{train}}$
4. MTPP$(\mathcal{I}, \texttt{test}) \rightarrow \mathcal{F}_{\texttt{test}}$

Step 2 selects the interpretants, $\mathcal{I}$, relevant to the instances in the combined training and test data. Steps 3 and 4 use $\mathcal{I}$ to map `train` and `test` to a new space where similarities between the translation acts can be derived more easily. RTM relies on the representativeness of $\mathcal{I}$ as a medium for building translation models for translating between `train` and `test`.

Our encouraging results in the SRA task provides a greater understanding of the acts of translation we ubiquitously use when communicating and how they can be used to predict the performance of translation, judging the semantic similarity of text, and evaluating the quality of student answers. RTM and MTPP models are not data or language specific and their modeling power and good performance are applicable across different domains and tasks. RTM expands the applicability of MTPP by making it feasible when making monolingual quality and similarity judgments and it enhances the computational scalability by building models over smaller but more relevant training data as interpretants.

4 Experiments

SRA involves the prediction on Beetle (student interactions when learning conceptual knowledge in the basic electricity and electronics domain) and SciEntsBank (science assessment questions) datasets. SciEntsBank is harder due to containing questions from multiple domains (Dzikovska et al., 2012). SRA challenge results are evaluated with the weighted average F_1, $F_1^w = \frac{1}{N}\sum_{c \in C} N_c F_1(c)$ and the macro average F_1, $F_1^m = \frac{1}{|C|}\sum_{c \in C} F_1(c)$ (Dzikovska et al., 2012).

The lexical baseline system is based on measures of lexical overlap using 4 features: the number of overlapping words, F_1, Lesk (Lesk, 1986), and cosine scores over the words when comparing A and R ({4}) and Q and R ({4}). Lesk score is calculated as: $L(A, R) = \sum_{p \in M} |p|^2 / (|A||R|)$, where M contains the maximal overlapping phrases that match in

A and R and $|p|$ is the length of a phrase [1]. This lexical baseline is highly competitive: no submission performed better in the 2-way Beetle unseen questions task.

4.1 RTM Models

We obtain CNGL results for the SRA task as follows. For each perspective described in Section 1, we build an RTM model. Each RTM model views the SRA task from a different perspective using the 283 features extracted dependent on the interpretants using MTPP. We extract the features both on the training set of 4155 and the test set of 1258 (Q, A, R) sentence triples for the Beetle task and the training set of 5251 and the test set of 5835 (Q, A, R) sentence triples for the SciEntsBank task. The addition of lexical overlap baseline features slightly helps. We use the best reference answer if the reference answer is not identified in the training set.

The training corpus used is the English side of an out-of-domain corpus on European parliamentary discussions, Europarl (Callison-Burch et al., 2012) [2], to which we also add the unique sentences from R. In-domain corpora are likely to improve the performance. We do not perform any linguistic processing or use other external resources. We use only extrinsic features, or features that are ignorant of any information intrinsic to, and dependent on, a given language or domain. We use the training corpus to build a 5-gram target LM. We use ridge regression (RR) and support vector regression (SVR) with RBF kernel (Smola and Schölkopf, 2004). Both of these models learn a regression function using the features to estimate a numerical target value. The parameters that govern the behavior of RR and SVR are the regularization λ for RR and the C, ϵ, and γ parameters for SVR. At testing time, the predictions are bound so as to have scores in the range $[0, 1]$, $[0, 2]$, or $[0, 4]$ and rounded for finding the predicted category.

4.2 Training Results

Table 1 lists the 10-fold cross-validation (CV) results on the training set for RR and SVR for different RTM systems without the parameter optimization. As we combine different perspectives, the performance improves and we use the QAR+QRA+ARA+QARQA system for our submissions using RR for run 1, SVR for run 2. ARA performs the best among individual perspectives. Each additional perspective adds another 283 features to the representation.

F_1^m / F_1^w	Beetle		SciEntsBank	
Model	RR	SVR	RR	SVR
QAR	.38/.49	.45/.57	.21/.30	.28/.36
QRA	.33/.50	.33/.53	.22/.31	.29/.42
ARA	.45/.54	.50/.60	.21/.30	.30/.38
QARQA	.35/.50	.40/.58	.20/.27	.27/.40
QAR+ARA	.47/.55	.49/.61	.26/.36	.32/.39
QAR+ARA+QARQA	.48/.57	.49/.62	.31/.38	.29/.40
QAR+QRA+ARA+QARQA	.48/.56	.48/.61	.31/.38	.29/.40

Table 1: Performance on the training set without tuning.

We perform tuning on a subset of the Beetle and SciEntsBank datasets separately after including the baseline lexical overlap features and optimize against the performance evaluated with R^2, the coefficient of determination. SVR performance is given in Table 2. The CNGL system significantly outperforms the lexical overlap baseline in all tasks for Beetle and in the 2-way task for SciEntsBank. For 3-way and 5-way, CNGL performs slightly better.

F_1^m / F_1^w	Beetle			SciEntsBank		
System	2	3	5	2	3	5
Lexical	.74/.75	.53/.56	.46/.53	.61/.64	.43/.55	.29/.41
CNGL	.84/.84	.61/.63	.55/.63	.74/.75	.47/.56	.30/.41

Table 2: Optimized SVR results vs. lexical overlap baseline on the training set for 2-way, 3-way, or 5-way tasks.

4.3 SRA Challenge Results

The SRA task test set also contains instances that belong to unseen questions (uQ) and unseen domains (uD), which make it harder to predict. The training data provided for the task correspond to learning with unseen answers (uA). Table 3 presents the SRA challenge results containing the lexical overlap, our CNGL SVR submission (RR is slightly worse), and the maximum and mean results [3].

According to the official results, CNGL SVR is the 2nd best system based on 5-way evaluation (4th

[1] http://search.cpan.org/dist/Text-Similarity/

[2] We use WMT'13 corpora from www.statmt.org/wmt13/.

[3] Max is not the performance of the best performing system but the maximum result obtained for each metric and subtask.

	F_1^m / F_1^w	Beetle		SciEntsBank		
	System	uA	uQ	uA	uQ	uD
2	Lexical	.80/.79	.74/.72	.64/.62	.65/.63	.66/.65
	CNGL	.80/.81	.67/.68	.55/.57	.56/.58	.56/.57
	Mean	.71/.72	.61/.62	.64/.66	.60/.62	.61/.63
	Max	.84/.84	.72/.73	.77/.77	.74/.74	.70/.71
3	Lexical	.55/.58	.48/.50	.40/.52	.39/.52	.42/.55
	CNGL	.57/.59	.45/.47	.33/.38	.31/.37	.31/.36
	Mean	.54/.55	.41/.42	.48/.56	.39/.51	.39/.51
	Max	.72/.73	.58/.60	.65/.71	.47/.63	.49/.62
5	Lexical	.42/.48	.41/.46	.30/.44	.26/.40	.25/.40
	CNGL	.43/.55	.38/.47	.20/.27	.21/.30	.22/.29
	Mean	.44/.51	.34/.40	.34/.46	.24/.38	.26/.37
	Max	.62/.70	.55/.61	.48/.64	.31/.49	.38/.47

Table 3: SRA challenge results: CNGL SVR submission, the lexical overlap baseline, and the maximum and mean results for 2-way, 3-way, or 5-way tasks. uA, uQ, and uD correspond to unseen answers, questions, and domains.

result overall) and the 3rd best system based on 2-way and 3-way evaluation (5th result overall) on the uQ Beetle task. The SVR model performs better than the lexical baseline and the mean result in the Beetle task but performs worse in the SciEntsBank. The lower performance is likely to be due to using an out-of-domain training corpus for building the RTM models and on the uQ and uD tasks, it may also be due to optimizing on the uA task only. The lower performance in SciEntsBank is also due to multiple question domains (Dzikovska et al., 2012).

SVR	Beetle			SciEntsBank		
F_1^w	2	3	5	2	3	5
(a) QAR+ARA	.86	.66	.64	.77	.56	.42
(b) QAR+ARA+QARQA	.86	.66	.65	.77	.57	.45
(c) QAR+QRA+ARA+QARQA	.85	.64	.63	.77	.58	.45
F_1^m	2	3	5	2	3	5
(a) QAR+ARA	.86	.64	.55	.76	.47	.34
(b) QAR+ARA+QARQA	.85	.64	.55	.76	.48	.36
(c) QAR+QRA+ARA+QARQA	.85	.62	.54	.76	.49	.35

Table 4: Improved SVR performance on the training set with tuning for 2-way, 3-way, or 5-way tasks.

4.4 Improved RTM Models

We improve the RTM model with the expansion of our representation by adding the following features:

- *Character n-grams* $\{4\}$: Calculates the cosine between the character n-grams (for n=2,3,4,5) obtained for S and T (Bär et al., 2012).
- *LIX* $\{2\}$: Calculates the LIX readability score (Wikipedia, 2013; Björnsson, 1968) for S and T. [4]

Table 4 lists the improved results on the training set after tuning, which shows about 0.04 increase in all scores when compared with Table 1 and Table 2.

	F_1^m/F_1^w	Beetle		SciEntsBank		
	Model	uA	uQ	uA	uQ	uD
2	(a)	.81/.82	.70/.71	.55/.57	.58/.58	.56/.57
	(b)	.80/.81	.71/.72	.69/.70	.54/.56	.56/.58
	(c)	.79/.79	.70/.71	.60/.59	.57/.58	.55/.57
3	(a)	.59/.61	.48/.49	.26/.34	.34/.40	.26/.32
	(b)	.60/.62	.47/.48	.36/.43	.31/.38	.29/.34
	(c)	.58/.60	.46/.48	.41/.48	.30/.39	.29/.34
5	(a)	.47/.56	.37/.45	.19/.22	.22/.33	.22/.29
	(b)	.43/.56	.36/.45	.26/.37	.23/.33	.21/.30
	(c)	.42/.52	.40/.48	.27/.39	.24/.33	.20/.30

Table 5: Improved SVR results on the SRA task test set.

	F_1^m/F_1^w	SciEntsBank		
	Model	uA	uQ	uD
2	(a)	.56/.57	.54/.55	.53/.55
	(b)	.57/.58	.53/.54	.56/.57
	(c)	.57/.58	.55/.57	.57/.59
3	(a)	.36/.45	.33/.44	.39/.49
	(b)	.35/.40	.36/.44	.39/.48
	(c)	.37/.46	.36/.48	.40/.50
5	(a)	.24/.34	.23/.33	.26/.39
	(b)	.24/.36	.25/.38	.26/.38
	(c)	.24/.36	.21/.32	.28/.39

Table 6: Improved TREE results on the SRA task test set.

Table 5 presents the improved SVR results on the SRA task test set, which shows about 0.03 increase in all scores when compared with Table 3. SVR becomes the 2nd best system and 2nd best result in 2-way evaluation and the 3rd best system from the top based on 2-way and 3-way evaluation (5th result overall) on the uQ Beetle task.

[4] LIX=$\frac{A}{B} + C\frac{100}{A}$, where A is the number of words, C is words longer than 6 characters, B is words that start or end with any of ".", ":", "!", "?" similar to (Hagström, 2012).

We observe that decision tree regression (Hastie et al., 2009) (TREE) generalizes to uQ and uD domains better than the RR or SVR models especially in the SciEntsBank corpus. Table 6 presents TREE results on the SRA SciEntsBank test set, which shows significant increase in uQ and uD tasks when compared with Table 5.

5 Conclusion

Referential translation machines provide a clean and intuitive computational model for automatically grading student answers by measuring the acts of translation involved and achieve to be the 2nd best system on some tasks in the SRA challenge. RTMs make quality and semantic similarity judgments possible based on the retrieval of relevant training data as interpretants for reaching shared semantics.

Acknowledgments

This work is supported in part by SFI (07/CE/I1142) as part of the Centre for Next Generation Localisation (www.cngl.ie) at Dublin City University and in part by the European Commission through the QTLaunchPad FP7 project (No: 296347). We also thank the SFI/HEA Irish Centre for High-End Computing (ICHEC) for the provision of computational facilities and support.

References

Daniel Bär, Chris Biemann, Iryna Gurevych, and Torsten Zesch. 2012. Ukp: Computing semantic textual similarity by combining multiple content similarity measures. In **SEM 2012: The First Joint Conference on Lexical and Computational Semantics – Volume 1: Proceedings of the main conference and the shared task, and Volume 2: Proceedings of the Sixth International Workshop on Semantic Evaluation (SemEval 2012)*, pages 435–440, Montréal, Canada, 7-8 June. Association for Computational Linguistics.

Ergun Biçici and Josef van Genabith. 2013. CNGL-CORE: Referential translation machines for measuring semantic similarity. In **SEM 2013: The First Joint Conference on Lexical and Computational Semantics*, Atlanta, Georgia, USA, 13-14 June. Association for Computational Linguistics.

Ergun Biçici and Deniz Yuret. 2011a. Instance selection for machine translation using feature decay algorithms. In *Proceedings of the Sixth Workshop on Statistical Machine Translation*, pages 272–283, Edinburgh, Scotland, July. Association for Computational Linguistics.

Ergun Biçici and Deniz Yuret. 2011b. RegMT system for machine translation, system combination, and evaluation. In *Proceedings of the Sixth Workshop on Statistical Machine Translation*, pages 323–329, Edinburgh, Scotland, July. Association for Computational Linguistics.

Ergun Biçici, Declan Groves, and Josef van Genabith. 2013. Predicting sentence translation quality using extrinsic and language independent features. *Machine Translation*.

Ergun Biçici. 2011. *The Regression Model of Machine Translation*. Ph.D. thesis, Koç University. Supervisor: Deniz Yuret.

Ergun Biçici. 2008. Consensus ontologies in socially interacting multiagent systems. *Journal of Multiagent and Grid Systems*.

Carl Hugo Björnsson. 1968. *Läsbarhet*. Liber.

Chris Bliss. 2012. Comedy is translation, February. http://www.ted.com/talks/chris_bliss_comedy_is_translation.html.

Peter F. Brown, Stephen A. Della Pietra, Vincent J. Della Pietra, and Robert L. Mercer. 1993. The mathematics of statistical machine translation: Parameter estimation. *Computational Linguistics*, 19(2):263–311, June.

Chris Callison-Burch, Philipp Koehn, Christof Monz, Matt Post, Radu Soricut, and Lucia Specia. 2012. Findings of the 2012 workshop on statistical machine translation. In *Proceedings of the Seventh Workshop on Statistical Machine Translation*, pages 10–51, Montréal, Canada, June. Association for Computational Linguistics.

George Doddington. 2002. Automatic evaluation of machine translation quality using n-gram co-occurrence statistics. In *Proceedings of the second international conference on Human Language Technology Research*, pages 138–145, San Francisco, CA, USA. Morgan Kaufmann Publishers Inc.

Myroslava O. Dzikovska, Rodney D. Nielsen, and Chris Brew. 2012. Towards effective tutorial feedback for explanation questions: A dataset and baselines. In *Proceedings of the 2012 Conference of the North American Chapter of the Association for Computational Linguistics: Human Language Technologies*, pages 200–210, Montréal, Canada, June. Association for Computational Linguistics.

Myroslava O. Dzikovska, Rodney Nielsen, Chris Brew, Claudia Leacock, Danilo Giampiccolo, Luisa Bentivogli, Peter Clark, Ido Dagan, and Hoa Trang Dang. 2013. Semeval-2013 task 7: The joint student response analysis and 8th recognizing textual entailment challenge. In **SEM 2013: The First Joint Conference on Lexical and Computational Semantics*, Atlanta, Georgia, USA, 13-14 June. Association for Computational Linguistics.

Kenth Hagström. 2012. Swedish readability calculator. https://github.com/keha76/Swedish-Readability-Calculator.

Trevor Hastie, Robert Tibshirani, and Jerome Friedman. 2009. *The Elements of Statistical Learning: Data Mining, Inference and Prediction*. Springer-Verlag, 2nd edition.

Michael Lesk. 1986. Automatic sense disambiguation using machine readable dictionaries: how to tell a pine cone from an ice cream cone. In *Proceedings of the 5th annual international conference on Systems documentation*, SIGDOC '86, pages 24–26, New York, NY, USA. ACM.

Kishore Papineni, Salim Roukos, Todd Ward, and Wei-Jing Zhu. 2002. BLEU: a method for automatic evaluation of machine translation. In *Proceedings of 40th Annual Meeting of the Association for Computational Linguistics*, pages 311–318, Philadelphia, Pennsylvania, USA, July. Association for Computational Linguistics.

Yoav Seginer. 2007. *Learning Syntactic Structure*. Ph.D. thesis, Universiteit van Amsterdam.

Alex J. Smola and Bernhard Schölkopf. 2004. A tutorial on support vector regression. *Statistics and Computing*, 14(3):199–222, August.

Wikipedia. 2013. Lix. http://en.wikipedia.org/wiki/LIX.

Celi: EDITS and Generic Text Pair Classification

Milen Kouylekov
Celi S.R.L.
via San Quintino 31
Torino,10121, Italy
kouylekov@celi.it

Luca Dini
Celi S.R.L.
via San Quintino 31
Torino,10121, Italy
dini@celi.it

Alessio Bosca
Celi S.R.L.
via San Quintino 31
Torino,10121, Italy
alessio.bosca@celi.it

Marco Trevisan
Celi S.R.L.
via San Quintino 31
Torino, Italy
trevisan@celi.it

Abstract

This paper presents CELI's participation in the SemEval The Joint Student Response Analysis and 8th Recognizing Textual Entailment Challenge (Task7) and Cross-lingual Textual Entailment for Content Synchronization task (Task 8).

1 Introduction

Recognizing an existing relation between two text fragments received a significant interest as NLP task in the recent years. A lot of the approaches were focused in the filed of Textual Entailment(TE). TE has been proposed as as a comprehensive framework for applied semantics (Dagan and Glickman, 2004), where the need for an explicit mapping between linguistic objects can be, at least partially, bypassed through the definition of semantic inferences at the textual level. In the TE framework, a text (T) is said to entail the hypothesis (H) if the meaning of H can be derived from the meaning of T. Initially defined as binary relation between texts (**YES/NO** there is an entailment or there is not) the TE evolved in the third RTE3 (Giampiccolo et al., 2007) challenge into a set of three relations between texts: **ENTAILMENT**, **CONTRADICTION** and **UNKNOWN**. These relations are interpreted as follows:

- ENTAILMENT - The T entails the H.
- CONTRADICTION - The H contradicts the T
- UNKNOWN - There is no semantic connection between T and H.

With more and more applications available for recognizing textual entailment the researches focused their efforts in finding practical applications for the developed systems. Thus the Cross-Lingual Textual Entailment task (CLTE) was created using textual entailment (TE) to define cross-lingual content synchronization scenario proposed in (Mehdad et. al., 2011), (Negri et. al., 2011) (Negri et. al., 2012). The task is defined by the organizers as follows: Given a pair of topically related text fragments (T1 and T2) in different languages, the CLTE task consists of automatically annotating it with one of the following entailment judgments:

- Bidirectional: the two fragments entail each other (semantic equivalence)
- Forward: unidirectional entailment from T1 to T2
- Backward: unidirectional entailment from T2 to T1
- No Entailment: there is no entailment between T1 and T2

The textual entailment competition also evolved. In this year SEMEVAL The Joint Student Response Analysis and 8th Recognizing Textual Entailment Challenge - JRSA-RTE8 (Task7) the textual entailment was defined in three subtasks:

5-way task , where the system is required to classify the student answer according to one of the following judgments:

- Correct, if the student answer is a complete and correct paraphrase of the reference answer;

*Second Joint Conference on Lexical and Computational Semantics (*SEM), Volume 2: Seventh International Workshop on Semantic Evaluation (SemEval 2013)*, pages 592–597, Atlanta, Georgia, June 14-15, 2013. ©2013 Association for Computational Linguistics

- Partially_correct_incomplete, if the student answer is a partially correct answer containing some but not all information from the reference answer;

- Contradictory, if the student answer explicitly contradicts the reference answer;

- Irrelevant, if the student answer is "irrelevant", talking about domain content but not providing the necessary information;

- Non_domain, if the student answer expresses a request for help, frustration or lack of domain knowledge - e.g., "I don't know", "as the book says", "you are stupid".

3-way task , where the system is required to classify the student answer according to one of the following judgments:

- correct

- contradictory

- incorrect, conflating the categories of partially_correct_incomplete, irrelevant or non_domain in the 5-way classification

2-way task , where the system is required to classify the student answer according to one of the following judgments:

- correct

- incorrect, conflating the categories of contradictory and incorrect in the 3-way classification.

Following the overall trend, we have decided to convert our system for recognizing textual entailment EDITS from a simple YES/NO recognition system into a generic system capable of recognizing multiple semantic relationships between two texts.

EDITS (Kouylekov and Negri, 2010) and (Kouylekov et. al., 2011) is an open source package for recognizing textual entailment, which offers a modular, flexible, and adaptable working environment to experiment with the RTE task over different datasets. The package allows to: *i)* create an entailment engine by defining its basic components *ii)* train such entailment engine over an annotated RTE corpus to learn a model; and *iii)* use the entailment engine and the model to assign an entailment judgments and a confidence score to each pair of an unannotated test corpus.

We define the recognition of semantic relations between two texts as a classification task. In this task the system takes as an input two texts and classifies them in one of a set of predefined relations. We have modified EDITS in order to handle the so defined task.

Having this in mind we have participated in JRSA-RTE8 (task 7) and CLTE2 (task 8) with the same approach. We have merged EDITS with some features from the TLike system described in our last participation in CLTE (Kouylekov et. al., 2011). For each of the tasks we have created a specialized components that are integrated in EDITS as one of the system's modules.

2 EDITS and Generic Text Pair Classification

As in the previous versions, the core of EDITS implements a distance-based framework. Within this framework the system implements and harmonizes different approaches to distance computation between texts, providing both *edit distance* algorithms, and *similarity* algorithms. Each algorithm returns a normalized distance score (a number between 0 and 1). Each algorithm algorithm depends on two generic modules defined by the system's user:

- Matcher - a module that is used to align text fragments. This module uses semantic techniques and entailment rules to find equivalent textfragments.

- Weight Calculator - a module that is used to give weight to text fragments. The weights are used to determine the importance of a text portion to the overall meaning of the text.

In the previous versions of the system at the training stage, distance scores calculated over annotated T-H pairs are used to estimate a threshold that best separates positive (YES) from negative (NO) examples. The calculated threshold was used at a test stage to assign an entailment judgment and a confidence score to each test pair. In the new version of the system we used a machine learning classifier to classify the T-H pairs in the appropriate category. The overall architecture of the system is shown in Figure 1.

The new architecture is divided in two sets of modules: Machine Learning and Edit Distance. In the Edit Distance set various distance algorithms are used to calculate the distance between the two texts. Each of these algorithms have a custom matcher and weight calculator. The distances calculated by each of these algorithms are used as features for the classifiers of the Machine Leaning modules. The machine learning modules are structured in two levels:

- Binary Classifiers - for each semantic relation we create a binary classifier that distinguishes between the members of the relation and the members of the other relations. For example: For 3way task (Task 7) the system created 3 binary classifiers one for each relation.
- Classifier - a module that makes final decision for the text pair taking the output (decision and confidence) of the binary classifiers as an input.

We have experimented with other configurations of the machine leaning modules and selected this one as the best performing on the available datasets of the previous RTE competitions. In the version of EDITS avalble online other configurations of the machine leaning modules will be available using the flexibility of the system configuration.

We have used the algorithms implemented in WEKA (Hall et al., 2009) for the classification modules. The binary modules use SMO algorithm. The top classifier uses NaiveBayes.

The input to the system is a corpus of text pairs each classified with one semantic relation. We have used the format of the previous RTE competitions in order to be compliant. The goal of the system is to create classifier that is capable of recognizing the correct relation for an un-annotated pair of texts.

The new version of EDITS package allows to:

- Create an *Classifier* by defining its basic components (*i.e.* algorithms, matchers, and weight calculators);
- Train such *Classifier* over an annotated corpus (containing T-H pairs annotated in terms of entailment) to learn a *Model*;
- Use the *Classifier* and the *Model* to assign an entailment judgment and a confidence score to each pair of an un-annotated test corpus.

3 Resources

Like our participation in the 2012 SemEval Crosslingual Textual Entailment for Content Synchronization task (Kouylekov et. al., 2011), our approach is based on four main resources:

- A system for Natural Language Processing able to perform for each relevant language basic tasks such as part of speech disambiguation, lemmatization and named entity recognition.
- A set of word based bilingual translation modules.(Employed only for Task 8)
- A semantic component able to associate a semantic vectorial representation to words.
- We use Wikipedia as multilingual corpus.

NLP modules are described in (Bosca and Dini, 2008), and will be no further detailed here.

Word-based translation modules are composed by a bilingual lexicon look-up component coupled with a vector based translation filter, such as the one described in (Curtoni and Dini, 2008). In the context of the present experiments, such a filters has been deactivated, which means that for any input word the component will return the set of all possible translations. For unavailable pairs, we make use of triangular translation (Kraaij, 2003).

As for the semantic component we experimented with a corpus-based distributional approach capable of detecting the interrelation between different terms in a corpus; the strategy we adopted is similar to Latent Semantic Analysis (Deerwester et. al., 1990) although it uses a less expensive computational solution based on the Random Projection algorithm (Lin et. al., 2003) and (Bingham et. al., 2001). Different works debate on similar issues: (Turney, 2001) uses LSA in order to solve synonymy detection questions from the well-known TOEFL test while the method presented by (Inkpen, 2001) or by (Baroni and Bisi, 2001) proposes the use of the Web as a corpus to

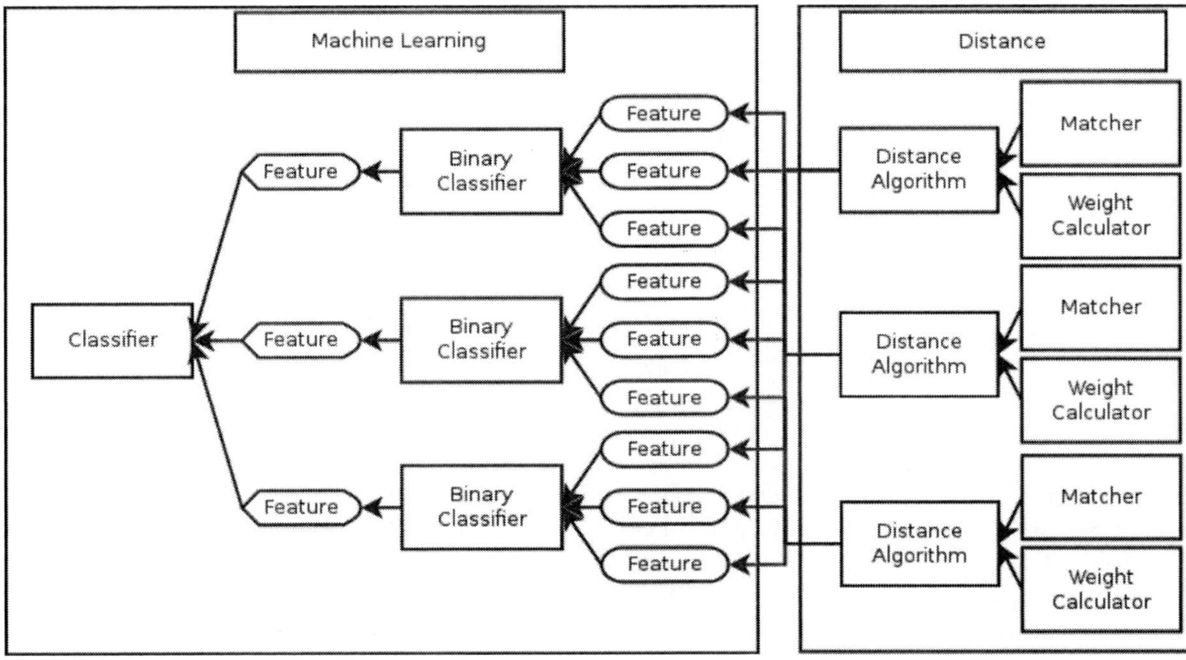

Figure 1: EDITS Architecture

compute mutual information scores between candidate terms.

We use Wikipedia as a corpus for calculating word statistics in different languages. We have indexed using Lucene[1] the English, Italian, French, German, Spanish distributions of the resource.

The semantic component and the translation[2] modules are used as core components in the matcher module. IDF calculated on Wikipedia is used as weight for the words by the weight calculator model.

4 JRSA-RTE8

In the JRSA-RTE8 we consider the reference answers as T (text) and the student answer as H (hypothesis). As the reference answers are often more than one, we considered as input to the machine learning algorithms the distance between the student answer and the **closest** reference answer. We define the closest reference answer as the reference answer with minimum distance according to the distance algorithm.

[1] *http://lucene.apache.org*

[2] Translation module is used only for Task 8.

4.1 Systems

We have submitted **two** runs in the SemEval JRSA-RTE8 challenge (Task 7). The systems were executed on each of the sub tasks of the main task.

System 1 The distance algorithm used in the first system is Word Overlap. The algorithm tries to find the words of a source text between the words of the target text. We have created two features for each binary classifier: 1) Feature 1 - word overlap of H into T (words of H are matched by the words in T; 2) Feature 2 - word overlap T into H (Words of T are matched by the words in H).

System 2 In the second system the we have used only Feature 1.

We have created separate models for the Beatle dataset and the sciEntsBank dataset. The results obtained are shown in Table 1.

4.2 Analysis

The results obtained are in line with our previous participations in the RTE challenges (Kouylekov et. al., 2011). Of course as we described before in our papers (Kouylekov et. al., 2011) the potential of the edit distance algorithm is limited. Still it provides a

Task	Beatle Q	Beatle A	sciEntsBank Q	sciEntsBank A	sciEntsBank D
2way					
run 1	0.6400	0.6570	0.5930	0.6280	0.6160
run 2	0.4620	0.4480	0.5560	0.5930	0.5710
3way					
run 1	0.5510	0.4950	0.5240	0.5780	0.5490
run 2	0.4150	0.4400	0.4390	0.5030	0.4770
5way					
run 1	0.4830	0.4470	0.4130	0.4340	0.4170
run 2	0.3850	0.4320	0.2330	0.2370	0.2540

Table 1: Task 7 Results obtained. (Accuracy)

good performance and provides a solid potential for some close domain tasks as described in (Negri and Kouylekov, 2009). We were quite content with the new machine learning based core. The selected configuration performed in an acceptable manner. The results obtained were in line with the cross accuracy obtained by our system on the training set which shows that it is not susceptible to over-training.

5 CLTE

5.1 Systems

We have submitted **two** runs in the CLTE task (Task 8).

System 1 The distance algorithm used in the first system is Word Overlap as we did for task 7. We have created two features for each binary classifier: 1) Feature 1 - word overlap of H into T (words of H are matched by the words in T; 2) Feature 2 - word overlap T into H (Words of T are matched by the words in H).

System 2 In the second system we have made a slight modification of the matcher that handled numbers.

The matcher module for this task used the translation modules defined in Section 3. We have created a model for each language pair.

The results obtained are shown in Table 2.

5.2 Analysis

The results obtained are quite disappointing. Our system obtained on the test set of the last CLTE competition (CLTE1) quite satisfactory results (clte1-test). All the results obtained for this competition are near or above the medium of the best systems. Our algorithm did not show signs of over-training (the accuracy of the system on the test and on the training of CLTE1 were almost equal). Having this in mind we expected to obtain scores at least in the margins of 0.45 to 0.5. This does not happen according us due to the fact that this year dataset has characteristics quite different than the last year. To test this hypothesis we have trained our system on half of the dataset (clte2-half-training) ,given for test this year, and test it on the rest (clte-half-test). The results obtained demonstrate that the dataset given is more difficult for our system than the last years one. The results also prove that our system is probably too conservative when learning from examples. If the test set is similar to the training it performs in consistent manner on both, otherwise it demonstrates severe over-training problems.

6 Conclusions

In this paper we have presented a generic system for text pair classification. This system was evaluated on task 7 and task 8 of Semeval 2013 and obtained satisfactory results. The new machine learning module of the system needs improvement and we plan to focus our future efforts in it.

We plan to release the newly developed system as version 4 of the open source package EDITS available at *http://edits.sf.net*.

Acknowledgments

This work has been partially supported by the ECfunded project Galateas (CIP-ICT PSP-2009-3-250430).

Run	Spanish	Italian	French	German
run1	0.34	0.324	0.346	0.349
run2	0.342	0.324	0.34	0.349
clte2-half-training	0.41	0.43	0.40	0.44
clte2-half-test	0.43	0.44	0.41	0.43
clte1-test	0.52	0.51	0.54	0.55

Table 2: Task 8. Results obtained. (Accuracy)

References

Baroni M., Bisi S. 2004. Using cooccurrence statistics and the web to discover synonyms in technical language In Proceedings of LREC 2004

Bentivogli L., Clark P., Dagan I., Dang H, Giampiccolo D. 2011. The Seventh PASCAL Recognizing Textual Entailment Challenge In Proceedings of TAC 2011

Bingham E., Mannila H. 2001. Random projection in dimensionality reduction: Applications to image and text data. In Knowledge Discovery and Data Mining, ACM Press pages 245250

Bosca A., Dini L. 2008. Query expansion via library classification system. In CLEF 2008. Springer Verlag, LNCS

Curtoni P., Dini L. 2006. Celi participation at clef 2006 Cross language delegated search. In CLEF2006 Working notes.

Dagan I. and Glickman O. 2004. Probabilistic Textual Entailment: Generic Applied Modeling of Language Variability. Learning Methods for Text Understanding and Mining Workshop.

Deerwester S., Dumais S.T., Furnas G.W., Landauer T.K., Harshman R. 1990. Indexing by latent semantic analysis. Journal of the American Society for Information Science 41 391407

Giampiccolo; Bernardo Magnini; Ido Dagan; Bill Dolan. 2007. The Third PASCAL Recognizing Textual Entailment Challenge. Proceedings of the ACL-PASCAL Workshop on Textual Entailment and Paraphrasing. June 2007, Prague, Czech Republic

Hall M., Frank E., Holmes G., Pfahringer B., Reutemann P., Witten I. 2009 The WEKA Data Mining Software: An Update; SIGKDD Explorations, Volume 11, Issue 1.

Inkpen D. 2007. A statistical model for near-synonym choice. ACM Trans. Speech Language Processing 4(1)

Kouylekov M., Negri M. An Open-Source Package for Recognizing Textual Entailment. 48th Annual Meeting of the Association for Computational Linguistics (ACL 2010) ,Uppsala, Sweden. July 11-16, 2010

Kouylekov M., Bosca A., Dini L. 2011. EDITS 3.0 at RTE-7. Proceedings of the Seventh Recognizing Textual Entailment Challenge (2011).

Kouylekov M., Bosca A., Dini L., Trevisan M. 2012. CELI: An Experiment with Cross Language Textual Entailment. In Proceedings of the 6th International Workshop on Semantic Evaluation (SemEval 2012).

Kouylekov M., Mehdad Y. and Negri M. 2011 Is it Worth Submitting this Run? Assess your RTE System with a Good Sparring Partner Proceedings of the TextInfer 2011 Workshop on Textual Entailment

Kraaij W. 2003. Exploring transitive translation methods. In Vries, A.P.D., ed.: Proceedings of DIR 2003.

Lin J., Gunopulos D. 2003. Dimensionality reduction by random projection and latent semantic indexing. In proceedings of the Text Mining Workshop, at the 3rd SIAM International Conference on Data Mining.

Mehdad Y.,Negri M., Federico M.. 2011. Using Parallel Corpora for Cross-lingual Textual Entailment. In Proceedings of ACL-HLT 2011.

Negri M., Bentivogli L., Mehdad Y., Giampiccolo D., Marchetti A. 2011. Divide and Conquer: Crowdsourcing the Creation of Cross-Lingual Textual Entailment Corpora. In Proceedings of EMNLP 2011.

Negri M., Kouylekov M., 2009 Question Answering over Structured Data: an Entailment-Based Approach to Question Analysis. RANLP 2009 - Recent Advances in Natural Language Processing, 2009 Borovets, Bulgaria

Negri M., Marchetti A., Mehdad Y., Bentivogli L., Giampiccolo D. Semeval-2012 Task 8: Cross-lingual Textual Entailment for Content Synchronization. In Proceedings of the 6th International Workshop on Semantic Evaluation (SemEval 2012). 2012.

Turney P.D. 2001. Mining the web for synonyms: Pmi-ir versus lsa on toefl. In EMCL 01: Proceedings of the 12th European Conference on Machine Learning, London, UK, Springer-Verlag pages 491502

LIMSIILES: Basic English Substitution for Student Answer Assessment at SemEval 2013

Martin Gleize
LIMSI-CNRS & ENS
B.P. 133 91403 ORSAY CEDEX, France
gleize@limsi.fr

Brigitte Grau
LIMSI-CNRS & ENSIIE
B.P. 133 91403 ORSAY CEDEX, France
bg@limsi.fr

Abstract

In this paper, we describe a method for assessing student answers, modeled as a paraphrase identification problem, based on substitution by Basic English variants. Basic English paraphrases are acquired from the Simple English Wiktionary. Substitutions are applied both on reference answers and student answers in order to reduce the diversity of their vocabulary and map them to a common vocabulary. The evaluation of our approach on the SemEval 2013 Joint Student Response Analysis and 8th Recognizing Textual Entailment Challenge data shows promising results, and this work is a first step toward an open-domain system able to exhibit deep text understanding capabilities.

1 Introduction

Automatically assessing student answers is a challenging natural language processing task (NLP). It is a way to make test grading easier and improve adaptive tutoring (Dzikovska et al., 2010), and is the goal of the SemEval 2013's task 7, titled *Joint Student Response Analysis*. More specifically, given a question, a known correct "reference answer" and a 1- or 2-sentence student answer, the goal is to determine the student's answer accuracy (Dzikovska et al., 2013). This can be seen as a paraphrase identification problem between student answers and reference answers.

Paraphrase identification searches whether two sentences have essentially the same meaning (Culicover, 1968). Automatically generating or extracting semantic equivalences for the various units of language – words, phrases, and sentences – is an important problem in NLP and is being increasingly employed to improve the performance of several NLP applications (Madnani and Dorr, 2010), like question-answering and machine translation.

Paraphrase identification would benefit from a precise and broad-coverage semantic language model. This is unfortunately difficult to obtain to its full extent for any natural language, due to the size of a typical lexicon and the complexity of grammatical constructions. Our hypothesis is that the simpler the language lexicon is, the easier it will be to access and compare meaning of sentences. This assumption is justified by the multiple attempts at controlled natural languages (Schwitter, 2010) and especially simplified forms of English. One of them, Basic English (Ogden, 1930), has been adopted by the Wikipedia Project as the preferred language of the Simple English Wikipedia[1] and its sister project the Simple English Wiktionary[2].

Our method starts with acquiring paraphrases from the Simple English Wiktionary's definitions. Using those, we generate variants of both sentences whose meanings are to be compared. Finally, we compute traditional lexical and semantic similarity measures on those two sets of variants to produce features to train a classifier on the SemEval 2013 datasets in order to take the final decision.

2 Acquiring simplifying paraphrases

Simple Wiktionary word definitions are different from usual dictionary definitions. Aside from the

[1] http://simple.wikipedia.org
[2] http://simple.wiktionary.org

*Second Joint Conference on Lexical and Computational Semantics (*SEM), Volume 2: Seventh International Workshop on Semantic Evaluation (SemEval 2013)*, pages 598–602, Atlanta, Georgia, June 14-15, 2013.

simplified language, they often prefer to give a complete sentence where the word – e.g. a verb – is used in context, along with an explanation of what it means. To define the verb *link*, Simple Wiktionary states that *If you link two or more things, you make a connection between them* (1), whereas the standard Wiktionary uses the shorter and more cryptic *To connect two or more things*.

We notice in this example that the definition from Simple Wiktionary consists of two clauses, linked by a subordination relation. It's actually the case for a lot of verb definitions: a quick statistical study shows that 70% of these definitions are composed of two clauses, an independent clause, and a subordinate clause (often an adverbial clause). One clause illustrates how the verb is used, the other gives the explanation and the actual dictionary definition, as in example (1). These definitions are the basis of our method for acquiring paraphrases.

2.1 Pre-processing

We use the Stanford Parser to parse the definitions and get a dependency graph (De Marneffe and Manning, 2008). Using a few hand-written rules, we then retrieve both parts of the definition, which we call the *word part* and the *defining part* (see table 1 page 3 for examples). We can do this for definitions of verbs, but also for nouns, like *the giraffe is the tallest land animal in the world* to define *giraffe*, or adjectives, like *if something is bright it gives out or fills with much light* to define *bright*. We only provide the details of our method for processing verb definitions, as they correspond to the most complex cases, but we proceed similarly for noun, adjective and adverb definitions.

2.2 Argument matching

Word and defining parts alone are not paraphrases, but we can obtain phrasal paraphrases from them. If we see word part and defining part as two semantically equivalent predications, we have to identify the two predicates with their arguments, then match arguments with corresponding meaning, i.e. match arguments which designate the same entity or assume the same semantic function in both parts, as showed in Table 2.

For verb definitions, we identify the predicates as

you	$\rightarrow$	you
link	$\rightarrow$	make
$\emptyset$	$\rightarrow$	a connection
$\emptyset$	$\rightarrow$	between
two or more things	$\rightarrow$	them

Table 2: Complete matching for the definition of verb *link*

the main verbs in both clauses (hence *link* matching with *make* in table 2) and their arguments as a POS-filtered list of their syntactic descendants. Then, our assumption is that every argument of the word part predicate is present in the defining part, and the defining part predicate can have extra arguments (like *a connection*).

We define $s(A, B)$, the *score* of the pair of arguments (A, B), with argument A in the word part and argument B in the defining part. We then define a *matching* M as a set of such pairs, such that every element of every possible pair of arguments is found at most one time in M. A *complete matching* is a matching M that matches every argument in the word part, i.e., for each word part argument A, there exists a pair of arguments in M which contains A. Finally, we compute the *matching score* of M, $S(M)$, as the sum of scores of all pairs of M.

The *score* function $s(A, B)$ is a hand-crafted linear combination of several features computed on a pair of arguments (A, B) including:

- Raw string similarity. Sometimes the same word is reused in the defining part.
- Having an equal/compatible dependency relation with their respective main verb.
- Relative position in clause.
- Relative depth in parsing tree. These last 3 features assess if the two arguments play the same syntactic role.
- Same gender and number. If different, it's unlikely that the two arguments designate the same entity.
- If (A, B) is a pair (noun phrase, pronoun). We hope to capture an anaphoric expression and its antecedent.

Word (POS-tag)	Word part	Defining part
link (V)	you link two or more things	you make a connection between them
giraffe (N)	the giraffe	the tallest land animal in the world
bright (Adj)	something is bright	it gives out or fills with much light

Table 1: Word part and defining part of some Simple Wiktionary definitions

- WordNet similarity (Pedersen et al., 2004). If words belong to close synsets, they're more likely to identify the same entity.

2.3 Phrasal paraphrases

We compute the complete matching M which maximizes the matching score $S(M)$. Although it is possible to enumerate all matchings, it is intractable; therefore when predicates have more than 4 arguments, we prefer constructing a best matching with a beam search algorithm. After replacing each pair of arguments with linked variables, and attaching unmatched arguments to the predicates, we finally obtain phrasal paraphrases of this form:

$\langle$ X link Y, X make a connection between Y $\rangle$

3 Paraphrasing exercise answers

3.1 Paraphrase generation and pre-ranking

Given a sentence, and our Simple Wiktionary paraphrases (about 20,650 extracted paraphrases), we can generate sentential paraphrases by simple syntactic pattern matching –and do so recursively by taking previous outputs as input–, with the intent that these new sentences use increasingly more Basic English. We generate as many variants starting from both reference answers and student answers as we can in a fixed amount of time, as an anytime algorithm would do. We prioritize substituting verbs and adjectives over nouns, and non Basic English words over Basic English words.

Given a student answer and reference answers, we then use a simple Jaccard distance (on lowercased lemmatized non-stopwords) to score the closeness of student answer variants to reference answer variants: we measure how close the vocabulary used in the two statements has become. More specifically, for each reference answer A, we compute the n closest variants of the student answer to A's variant set. In our experiments, $n = 10$. We finally rank the reference answers according to the average distance from their n closest variants to A's variant set and keep the top-ranked one for our classification experiment. Figure 1 illustrates the whole process.

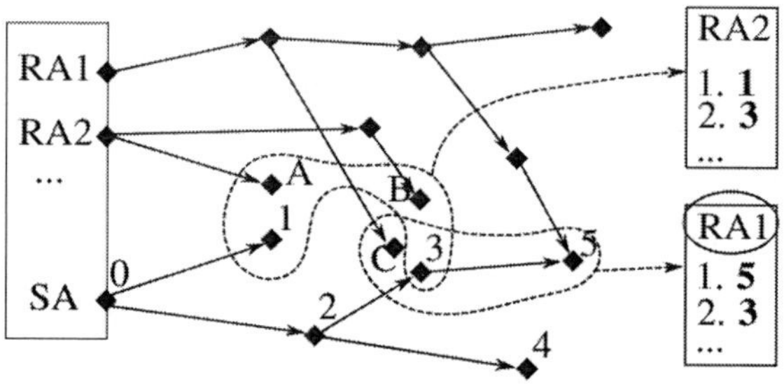

Figure 1: Variants are generated from all reference answers (RA) and the student answer (SA). For each reference answer RA, student answer variants are ranked based on their lexical distance from the variants of RA. The reference with the n closer variants to the student variants is kept (here: RA1).

3.2 Classifying student answers

SemEval 2013 task 7 offers 3 problems: a 5-way task, with 5 different answer judgements, and 3-way and 2-way tasks, conflating more judgement categories each time. Two different corpora, Beetle and SciEntsBank, were labeled with the 5 following labels: Correct, Partially_correct_incomplete, Contradictory, Irrelevant and Non_Domain, as described in (Dzikovska et al., 2012). We see the n-way task as a n-way classification problem. The instances of this problem are the pairs (student answer, reference answer).

We compute for each instance the following features: For each of the n closest variants of the student answer to some variant of the reference answer computed in the pre-ranking phase:

- Jaccard similarity coefficient on non-stopwords.
- A boolean representing if the two statements have the same polarity or not, where polarity

is defined as the number of *neg* dependencies in the Stanford Parser dependency graph.

- Number of "paraphrasing steps" necessary to obtain the variant from a raw student answer.
- Highest WordNet similarity of their respective nouns.
- WordNet similarity of the main verbs.

General features:

- Answer count (how many students typed this answer), provided in the datasets.
- Length ratio between the student answer and the closest reference answer.
- Number of (non-stop)words which appear neither in the question nor the reference answers.

We train an SVM classifier (with a one-against-one approach to multiclass classification) on both Beetle and SciEntsBank, for each n-way task.

3.3 Evaluation

Table 3 presents our system's overall accuracy on the 5-way task, along with the top scores at SemEval 2013, mean scores, and baselines –majority class and lexical overlap– described in (Dzikovska et al., 2012).

System	Beetle unseen answers	SciEntsBank unseen questions
Majority	0.4010	0.4110
Lexical overlap	0.5190	0.4130
Mean	0.5326	0.4078
ETS-run-1	0.5740	**0.5320**
ETS-run-2	**0.7150**	0.4010
Simple Wiktio	0.5330	**0.4820**

Table 3: SemEval 2013 evaluation results.

Our system performs slightly better in overall accuracy on Beetle unseen answers and SciEntsBank unseen questions than both baselines and the mean scores. While results are clearly below the best system trained on the Beetle corpus questions, we hold the third best score for the 5-way task on SciEntsBank unseen questions, while not fine-tuning our system specifically for this corpus. This is rather encouraging as to how suitable Simple Wiktionary is as a resource to extract open-domain knowledge from.

4 Discussion

The system we present in this paper is the first step towards an open-domain machine reading system capable of understanding and reasoning. Direct modeling of the semantics of a full natural language appears too difficult. We therefore decide to first project the English language onto a simpler English, so that it is easier to model and draw inferences from.

One complementary approach to a minimalistic language model, is to accept that texts are replete with gaps: missing information that cannot be inferred by reasoning on the text alone, but require a certain amount of background knowledge. Penas and Hovy (2010) show that these gaps can be filled by maintaining a background knowledge base built from a large corpus.

Although Simple Wiktionary is not a large corpus by any means, it can serve our purpose of acquiring basic knowledge for assessing exercise answers, and has the advantage to be in constant evolution and expansion, as well as interfacing very easily with the richer Wiktionary and Wikipedia.

Our future work will be focused on enriching and improving the robustness of our knowledge acquisition step from Simple Wiktionary, as well as introducing a true normalization of English to Basic English.

Acknowledgments

We acknowledge the Wikimedia Foundation for their willingness to provide easily usable versions of their online collaborative resources.

References

P.W. Culicover. 1968. *Paraphrase generation and information retrieval from stored text.* In Mechanical Translation and Computational Linguistics, 11(12), 7888.

Marie-Catherine de Marneffe and Christopher D. Manning. 2008. *Stanford typed dependencies manual.* Technical report, Stanford University.

Myroslava O. Dzikovska, Diana Bental, Johanna D. Moore, Natalie Steinhauser, Gwendolyn Campbell, Elaine Farrow, and Charles B. Callaway. 2010. *Intelligent tutoring with natural language support in the BEETLE II system.* In Proceedings of Fifth European Conference on Technology Enhanced Learning (EC-TEL 2010), Barcelona.

Myroslava O. Dzikovska, Rodney D. Nielsen and Chris Brew. 2012. *Towards Effective Tutorial Feedback for Explanation Questions: A Dataset and Baselines.* In Proceedings of the 2012 Conference of the North American Chapter of the Association for Computational Linguistics: Human Language Technologies (NAACL-HLT 2012), Montreal.

Myroslava O. Dzikovska, Rodney Nielsen, Chris Brew, Claudia Leacock, Danilo Giampiccolo, Luisa Bentivogli, Peter Clark, Ido Dagan and Hoa Trang Dang. 2013. *SemEval-2013 Task 7: The Joint Student Response Analysis and 8th Recognizing Textual Entailment Challenge.* In Proceedings of the 7th International Workshop on Semantic Evaluation (SemEval 2013), in conjunction with the Second Joint Conference on Lexical and Computational Semantics (*SEM 2013). Atlanta, Georgia, USA. 13-14 June.

Nitin Madnani and Bonnie J. Dorr. 2010. *Generating phrasal and sentential paraphrases: A survey of data-driven methods.* In Computational Linguistics 36 (3), 341-387.

Charles Kay Ogden. 1930. *Basic English: A General Introduction with Rules and Grammar.* Paul Treber, London.

Ted Pedersen, Siddharth Patwardhan, and Jason Michelizzi. 2004. *WordNet::similarity–measuring the relatedness of concepts.* In Proceedings of the Nineteenth National Conference on Artificial Intelligence(AAAI-04), pages 10241025.

Anselmo Penas and Eduard H. Hovy. 2010. *Filling Knowledge Gaps in Text for Machine Reading.* COLING (Posters) 2010: 979-987, Beijing.

Rolf Schwitter. 2010. *Controlled Natural Languages for Knowledge Representation.* COLING (Posters) 2010, Beijing.

CU : Computational Assessment of Short Free Text Answers - A Tool for Evaluating Students' Understanding

Ifeyinwa Okoye
Institute of Cognitive Science
Dept. of Computer Science
University of Colorado
Boulder, CO 80309, USA
okoye@colorado.edu

Steven Bethard
Institute of Cognitive Science
Dept. of Computer Science
University of Colorado
Boulder, CO 80309, USA
bethard@colorado.edu

Tamara Sumner
Institute of Cognitive Science
Dept. of Computer Science
University of Colorado
Boulder, CO 80309, USA
sumner@colorado.edu

Abstract

Assessing student understanding by evaluating their free text answers to posed questions is a very important task. However, manually, it is time-consuming and computationally, it is difficult. This paper details our shallow NLP approach to computationally assessing student free text answers when a reference answer is provided. For four out of the five test sets, our system achieved an overall accuracy above the median and mean.

1 Introduction

Assessing student understanding is one of the holy grails of education (Redecker et al., 2012). If we (teachers, tutors, intelligent tutors, potential employers, parents and school administrators) know what and how much a student knows, then we know what the student still needs to learn. And then, can efficiently and effectively educate the student. However, the task of assessing what exactly a student understands about a particular topic can be expensive, difficult and subjective.

Using multiple choice questionnaires is one of the most prevalent forms of assessing student understanding because it is easy and fast, both manually and computationally. However there has been a lot of pushback from educators about the validity of results gotten from multiple choice questionnaires.

Assessing student understanding by evaluating student free text answers either written or spoken is one of the preferred alternatives to multiple choice questionnaires. As an assessment tool, free text answers can illuminate what and how much a student knows since the student is forced to recall terms and make connections between those terms rather than just picking one out of several options. However, assessing free text answers manually is tedious, expensive and time-consuming, hence the search for a computational option.

There are three main issues that can limit the computational approach and corresponding performance when assessing free text answers: (1) the unit of assessment, (2) the reference and (3) the level of assessment. The unit of assessment can be words, facets, phrases, sentences, short answers or essays. The reference is the correct answer and what is being compared to the student answer. Most researchers generate the reference manually (Noorbehbahani and Kardan, 2011; Graesser et al., 2004) but some have focused on automatically generating the reference (Ahmad, 2009). The level of assessment can be coarse with 2 categories such as correct and incorrect or more finer-grained with up to 19 categories as in (Ahmad, 2009). In general, the finer-grained assessments are more difficult to assess.

2 The Student Response Analysis Task

The student response analysis task was posed as follows: Given a question, a known correct/reference answer and a 1 or 2 sentence student answer, classify the student answer into two, three or five categories. The two categories were *correct* and *incorrect*; the three categories were *correct*, *contradictory* and *incorrect*; while the five categories were *correct*, *partially correct but incomplete*, *contradictory*, *irrelevant* and *not in the domain* (Dzikovska et al., 2013).

We chose to work on the 2-way response task only

*Second Joint Conference on Lexical and Computational Semantics (*SEM), Volume 2: Seventh International Workshop on Semantic Evaluation (SemEval 2013)*, pages 603–607, Atlanta, Georgia, June 14-15, 2013.

because for our application, we need to simply know if a student answer is correct or incorrect. Our application is an interactive essay-based personalized learning environment (Bethard et al., 2012).

The overarching goal of our application is to create a scalable online service that recommends resources to users based on the their conceptual understanding expressed in an essay or short answer form. Our application automatically constructs a domain knowledge base from digital library resources and identifies the core concepts in the domain knowledge base.It detects flaws and gaps in users' science knowledge and recommends digital library resources to address users' misconceptions and knowledge gaps. The gaps are detected by identifying the core concepts which the user has not discussed. The flaws (incorrect understanding/misconceptions) are currently being identified by a process of (1) segmenting a student essay into sentences, (2) aligning the student sentence to a sentence in the domain knowledge base and (3) using the system we developed for the student response analysis task to determine if the student sentence is correct or incorrect.

The development of our misconception detection algorithm has been limited by the alignment task. However, with the data set from the student response analysis task containing correct alignments, we hope to be able to use it to make improvements to our misconception detection algorithm. We discuss our current misconception detection system below.

3 System Description

Our system mainly exploits shallow NLP techniques, in particular text overlap, to see how much we can gain from using a simple system and how much more some more semantic features could add to the simple system. Although we have access to the question which a 1-2 sentence student answer corresponds to, we chose not to use that in our system because in our application we do not have access to that information. We were trying to build a system that would work in our current essay-based application.

Some of the student answers in the dataset have a particular reference answer which they match. However, we do not make use of this information in our system either. We assume that for a particular question, all the corresponding reference answers can be used to determine the correctness of any of the student answers.

3.1 Features

The features we use are:

1. **CosineSimilarity** : This is the average cosine similarity (Jurafsky and James, 2000) between a student answer vector and all the corresponding reference answer vectors. The vectors are based on word counts. The words were lowercased and included stopwords and punctuations.

2. **CosineSimilarityNormalized** : This is the average cosine similarity between a student answer vector and all the corresponding reference answer vectors, with the word counts within the vectors divided by the word counts in Gigaword, a background corpus. We divided the raw counts by the counts in Gigaword to ensure that punctuations, stopwords and other non-discriminatory words do not artificially increase the cosine similarity.

3. **UnigramRefStudent** : This is the average unigram coverage of the reference answers by a student answer. To calculate this, the student answer and all the corresponding reference answers are tokenized into unigrams. Next, for each reference answer, we count the number of unigrams in the reference answer that are contained in the student answer and divide it by the number of unigrams in the reference answer. The value we get for this feature, is the average over all the reference answers.

4. **UnigramStudentRef** : This is the average unigram coverage of the student answer by the reference answers. To calculate this, the student answer and all the corresponding reference answers are tokenized into unigrams. Next, for each reference answer, we count the number of unigrams in the student answer that are contained in the reference answer and divide it by the number of unigrams in the student answer. The value we get for this feature, is the average over all the reference answers.

5. **BigramRefStudent** : This is similar to the UnigramRefStudent feature, but using bigrams.

6. **BigramStudentRef** : This is similar to the UnigramStudentRef feature, but using bigrams.

7. **LemmaRefStudent** : This is similar to the UnigramRefStudent feature, but in this case, the lemmas are used in place of words.

8. **LemmaStudentRef** : This is similar to the UnigramStudentRef feature, but in this case, the lemmas are used in place of words.

9. **UnigramPosRefStudent** : This is similar to the UnigramRefStudent feature, but we use part-of-speech unigrams for this feature in place of word unigrams.

10. **UnigramPosStudentRef** : This is similar to the UnigramStudentRef feature, but we use part-of-speech unigrams for this feature in place of word unigrams.

11. **BigramPosRefStudent** : This is similar to the BigramRefStudent feature, but we use part-of-speech bigrams for this feature in place of word unigrams.

12. **BigramPosStudentRef** : This is similar to the BigramStudentRef feature, but we use part-of-speech bigrams for this feature in place of word unigrams.

3.2 Implementation

We used the ClearTK (Ogren et al., 2008) toolkit within Eclipse to extract features from the student and reference sentences. We trained a LibSVM (Chang and Lin, 2011) binary classifier to classify a feature vector into two classes, correct or incorrect. We used the default parameters for LibSVM except for the cost parameter, for which we tried different values. However, the default value of 1 gave us the best result on the training set. Our two runs/systems are essentially the same system but with a cost parameter of 1 and 10.

4 Results

The Student Response Analysis Task overall result can be found in the Task description paper (Dzikovska et al., 2013). The CU system achieved a ranking of above the mean and median for four of the five different test sets. We perfomed below the mean and median on the sciEntsBank unseen answers. The accuracy result for the test data is shown in Table 4. The results on our training data and a breakdown of the contribution of each feature is shown in Table 5. In Table 5 ALL refers to all the features while ALL-CosineSimilarity is all the features excluding the CosineSimilarity feature.

System	**beetle unseen answers**	**beetle unseen questions**	**sciEnts Bank unseen answers**	**sciEnts Bank unseen questions**	**sciEnts Bank unseen domains**
CU run 1	0.786	0.718	0.656	0.674	0.693
CU run 2	0.784	0.717	0.654	0.671	0.691

Table 1: Overall Accuracy results for CU system on the test Data

5 Discussion

As can be seen from Table 4 and further elaborated on in (Dzikovska et al., 2013), there were two main datasets, Beetle and SciEntsBank. The Beetle data set has multiple reference answer per question while the SciEntsBank has one reference answer per question. Our system did better on the beetle data set than the SciEntsBank data set, both during development and on the final test sets. This leads us to believe that our system will do well when there are multiple reference answers rather than just one.

We analyzed the training data to understand where our system was failing and what we could do to make it better. We tried removing stopwords before constructing the feature vectors but that made the results worse. Here are two examples where removing the stopwords will make it impossible to ascertain the validity of the student answer:

- *It was connected.* becomes *connected*

- *It will work because that is closing the switch.* becomes *work closing switch*

Because the student answers are free text and use pronouns in place of the nouns that were in the question, the stop words are important to provide context.

	Feature Type	Beetle & sciEnts Bank
1	ALL	0.703
2	ALL - CosineSimilarity	0.702
3	ALL - CosineSimilarityNormalized	0.700
4	ALL - UnigramRefStudent	0.702
5	ALL - UnigramStudentRef	0.701
6	ALL - BigramRefStudent	0.702
7	ALL - BigramStudentRef	0.699
8	ALL - LemmaRefStudent	0.701
9	ALL - LemmaStudentRef	0.700
10	ALL - UnigramPosRefStudent	0.703
11	ALL - UnigramPosStudentRef	0.703
12	ALL - BigramPosRefStudent	0.702
13	ALL - BigramPosStudentRef	0.702

Table 2: Accuracy results for 5X cross validation on the training data

Currently, we are working on extracting and adding several features that we did not use for the task due to time constraints, to see if they improve our result. Some of the things we are working on are:

1. **Resolving Coreference**
   We will use the current state-of-art coreference system and assume that the question precedes the student answer in a paragraph when resolving coreference.

2. **Compare main predicates**
   The question is how to assign a value to the semantic similarity between the main predicates. If the predicates are *separate* and *connect*, then there should be a way to indicate that the mention of one of them in the reference, precludes the validity of the student answer being correct if it mentions the other. However, we also have to take negation into account here. *not separated* and *connected* should be marked as very similar if not equal. We plan to include the algorithm from the best system in the semantic similarity task to our current system.

3. **Compare main subject and object from a syntactic parse or the numbered arguments in semantic role label arguments**
   We have to resolve coreference for this to work well. And again, we run into the problem of how to assign a semantic similarity value to two words that might not share the same synset in ontologies such as Wordnet.

4. **Optimize parameters and explore other classifiers** Throughout developing and testing our system, we used only the LibSVM classifier and only optimized the cost parameter. However, there might be a different classifier or set of options that can model the data better. We hope to run through most of the classifiers available and see if using a different one, with different options improves our accuracy.

6 Conclusion

We have shown that there is value in using shallow NLP features to judge the validity of free answer text when the reference answers are given. However, looking at the sentences that our system labeled as correct and the gold standard incorrect or vice versa, it is clear that we have to delve into more semantic features if we want our system to be more accurate. We hope to keep working on this task in subsequent years to ensure continuous improvements in systems that can assess student knowledge by evaluating free answer texts. Such systems will be able to give students the formative feedback they need to help them learn better. In addition, such systems will provide teachers, intelligent tutors and administrators with feedback about student knowledge, so as to help them adapt their curriculum, teaching and tutoring methods to better serve students' knowledge needs.

References

Faisal Ahmad. 2009. *Generating conceptually personalized interactions for educational digital libraries using concept maps*. Ph.D. thesis, University of Colorado at Boulder.

Steven Bethard, Haojie Hang, Ifeyinwa Okoye, James H Martin, Md Arafat Sultan, and Tamara Sumner. 2012. Identifying science concepts and student misconceptions in an interactive essay writing tutor. In *Proceedings of the Seventh Workshop on Building Educational Applications Using NLP*, pages 12–21. Association for Computational Linguistics.

Chih-Chung Chang and Chih-Jen Lin. 2011. Libsvm: a library for support vector machines. *ACM Transactions on Intelligent Systems and Technology (TIST)*, 2(3):27.

Myroslava O. Dzikovska, Rodney Nielsen, Chris Brew, Claudia Leacock, Danilo Giampiccolo, Luisa Bentivogli, Peter Clark, Ido Dagan, and Hoa Trang Dang. 2013. Semeval-2013 task 7: The joint student response analysis and 8th recognizing textual entailment challenge. In **SEM 2013: The First Joint Conference on Lexical and Computational Semantics*, Atlanta, Georgia, USA, 13-14 June. Association for Computational Linguistics.

Arthur Graesser, Shulan Lu, George Jackson, Heather Mitchell, Mathew Ventura, Andrew Olney, and Max Louwerse. 2004. AutoTutor: A tutor with dialogue in natural language. *Behavior Research Methods*, 36:180–192.

Daniel Jurafsky and H James. 2000. Speech and language processing an introduction to natural language processing, computational linguistics, and speech.

F Noorbehbahani and AA Kardan. 2011. The automatic assessment of free text answers using a modified bleu algorithm. *Computers & Education*, 56(2):337–345.

Philip V Ogren, Philipp G Wetzler, and Steven J Bethard. 2008. Cleartk: A uima toolkit for statistical natural language processing. *Towards Enhanced Interoperability for Large HLT Systems: UIMA for NLP*, page 32.

Christine Redecker, Yves Punie, and Anusca Ferrari. 2012. eassessment for 21st century learning and skills. In *21st Century Learning for 21st Century Skills*, pages 292–305. Springer.

CoMeT: Integrating different levels of linguistic modeling for meaning assessment

Niels Ott   Ramon Ziai   Michael Hahn   Detmar Meurers
Sonderforschungsbereich 833
Eberhard Karls Universität Tübingen
{nott,rziai,mhahn,dm}@sfs.uni-tuebingen.de

Abstract

This paper describes the CoMeT system, our contribution to the SemEval 2013 Task 7 challenge, focusing on the task of automatically assessing student answers to factual questions. CoMeT is based on a meta-classifier that uses the outputs of the sub-systems we developed: CoMiC, CoSeC, and three shallower bag approaches. We sketch the functionality of all sub-systems and evaluate their performance against the official test set of the challenge. CoMeT obtained the best result (73.1% accuracy) for the 3-way unseen answers in Beetle among all challenge participants. We also discuss possible improvements and directions for future research.

1 Introduction

Our contribution to the SemEval 2013 Task 7 challenge (Dzikovska et al., 2013) presented here is based on our research in the A4 project[1] of the SFB 833, which is dedicated to the question how meaning can be computationally compared in realistic situations. In realistic situations, utterances are not necessarily well-formed or complete, there may be individual differences in situative and world knowledge among the speakers. This can complicate or even preclude a complete linguistic analysis, leading us to the following research question: Which linguistic representations can be used effectively and robustly for comparing the meaning of sentences and text fragments computationally?

[1] http://purl.org/dm/projects/sfb833-a4

In order to work on effective and robust processing, we base our work on reading comprehension exercises for foreign language learners, of which we are also collecting a large corpus (Ott et al., 2012). Our first system, CoMiC, is an alignment-based approach which exists in English and German variants (Meurers et al., 2011a; Meurers et al., 2011b). CoMiC uses various levels of linguistic abstraction from surface tokens to dependency parses. Further work that we are starting to tackle includes the utilization of Information Structure (Krifka, 2007) in the system.

The second approach emerging from the research project is CoSeC (Hahn and Meurers, 2011; Hahn and Meurers, 2012), a semantics-based system for meaning comparison that was developed for German from the start and was ported to operate on English for this shared task. As a novel contribution in this paper, we present CoMeT (Comparing Meaning in Tübingen), a system that employs a meta-classifier for combining the output of CoMiC and CoSeC and three shallower bag approaches.

In terms of the general context of our work, short answer assessment essentially comes in the two flavors of meaning comparison and grading, the first trying to determine whether or not two utterances convey the same meaning, the latter aimed at grading the abilities of students (cf. Ziai et al., 2012). Short answer assessment is also closely related to the field of Recognizing Textual Entailment (RTE, Dagan et al., 2009), which this year is directly reflected by the fact that SemEval 2013 Task 7 is the Joint Student Response Analysis and 8th Recognizing Textual Entailment Challenge.

*Second Joint Conference on Lexical and Computational Semantics (*SEM), Volume 2: Seventh International Workshop on Semantic Evaluation (SemEval 2013)*, pages 608–616, Atlanta, Georgia, June 14-15, 2013.

Turning to the organization of this paper, section 2 introduces the three types of sub-systems and the meta-classifier. In section 3, we report on the evaluation results of each sub-system both for our development set as well as for the official test set of the shared task. We then discuss possible causes and implications of the findings we made by participating in the shared task.

2 Systems

The CoMeT system that we describe in this paper is a combination of three types of sub-systems in one meta-classifier. CoSeC and CoMiC are systems that align linguistic units in the student answer to those in the reference answer. In contrast, the bag-based approaches employ a vocabulary of words, lemmas, and Soundex hashes constructed from all of the student answers in the training data. In the meta-classifier, we tried to combine the benefits of the named sub-systems into one large system that eventually computed our submission to the SemEval 2013 Task 7 challenge.

2.1 CoMiC

CoMiC (Comparing Meaning in Context) is an alignment-based system, i.e., it operates on a mapping of linguistic units found in a student answer to those given in a reference answer. CoMiC started off as a re-implementation of the Content Assessment Module (CAM) of Bailey and Meurers (2008). It exists in two flavors: CoMiC-DE for German, described in Meurers et al. (2011b), and CoMiC-EN for English, described in Meurers et al. (2011a). Both systems are positioned in the landscape of the short answer assessment field in Ziai et al. (2012). In this paper, we refer to CoMiC-EN simply as CoMiC.

Sketched briefly, CoMiC operates in three stages:

1. *Annotation* uses various NLP modules to equip student answers and reference answers with linguistic abstractions of several types.

2. *Alignment* creates links between these linguistic abstractions from the reference answer to the student answer.

3. *Classification* uses summary statistics of these alignment links in machine learning in order to assign labels to each student answer.

Automatic *annotation* and *alignment* are implemented in the Unstructured Information Management Architecture (UIMA, Ferrucci and Lally, 2004). Our UIMA modules mainly wrap around standard NLP tools of which we provide an overview in Table 1. We used the standard statistical models which are provided with the NLP tools.

Annotation Task	NLP Component
Sentence Detection	OpenNLP[2]
Tokenization	OpenNLP
Lemmatization	morpha (Minnen et al., 2001)
Spell Checking	Edit distance (Levenshtein, 1966), SCOWL word list[3]
Part-of-speech Tagging	TreeTagger (Schmid, 1994)
Noun Phrase Chunking	OpenNLP
Synonyms and Semantic Types	WordNet (Fellbaum, 1998)
Similarity Scores	PMI-IR (Turney, 2001) on UkWaC (Baroni et al., 2009)
Dependency Relations	MaltParser (Nivre et al., 2007)
Keyword extraction	Heads from dependency parse

Table 1: NLP tools used for CoMiC and Bag Approaches

Annotation ranges from very basic linguistic units such as sentences and tokens with POS and lemmas, over NP chunks, up to full dependency parses of the input. For distributional semantic similarity via PMI-IR (Turney, 2001), a local search engine based on Lucene (Gospodnetić and Hatcher, 2005) querying the UkWaC corpus (Baroni et al., 2009) was used, since all major search engines meanwhile have shut down their APIs.

After the annotation of linguistic units has taken place, *candidate alignment links* are created within UIMA. In a simple example case, a candidate alignment link is a pair of tokens that is token identical in the student answer and in the reference answer. The same token in the student answer may also be part of a candidate alignment link that maps to another token in the reference answer that, e.g., has the same lemma, or is a possible synonym, or again is token identical. Other possible links are based on spelling-corrected tokens, semantic types, or high values of the PMI-IR similarity measure.

Words that are present in the reading comprehension question and that are also found in the student answer are excluded from alignment, resulting in a very

[2] http://incubator.apache.org/opennlp
[3] http://wordlist.sourceforge.net

basic implementation of an approach to *givenness* (cf. Halliday, 1967, p. 204 and many others since).

Subsequently, a *globally optimal alignment* of linguistic units in the reference answer and student answer is determined using the Traditional Marriage Algorithm (Gale and Shapley, 1962).

At this point, processing within UIMA comes to an end with an output module that generates the files containing the features for machine learning. These features basically are summary statistics of the types of alignment links. An overview of these numeric features used is given in Table 2.

Feature	Description
1. Keyword Overlap	Percent of keywords aligned (relative to target)
2./3. Token Overlap	Percent of aligned target/learner tokens
4./5. Chunk Overlap	Percent of aligned target/learner chunks
6./7. Triple Overlap	Percent of aligned target/learner triples
8. Token Match	Percent of token alignments that were token-identical
9. Similarity Match	Percent of token alignments that were similarity-resolved
10. Type Match	Percent of token alignments that were type-resolved
11. Lemma Match	Percent of token alignments that were lemma-resolved
12. Synonym Match	Percent of token alignments that were synonym-resolved
13. Variety of Match (0-5)	Number of kinds of token-level alignments

Table 2: Features used in CoMiC's classification phase

Current versions of CoMiC use the WEKA toolkit (Hall et al., 2009), allowing us to experiment with different machine learning strategies. In general, any type of classification can be trained in this machine learning phase, a binary *correct* vs. *incorrect* decision as in the 2-way task being the simplest case. The best results with CoMiC on our held-out development set were achieved using WEKA's J48 classifier, which is an implementation of decision tree based on Quinlan (1993).

In terms of linguistic abstractions, CoMiC leaves the choice of representations used to its alignment step. However, in the final machine learning step, no concrete information about linguistic units is present any more. The machine learning component only sees alignment configurations which are independent of concrete words, phrases, or any other linguistic information. This high level of abstraction suggests that CoMiC should perform better than other approaches on unseen topics and unseen questions, since it does not rely on concrete units as, e.g., a bag-of-words approach does.

2.2 CoSeC

CoSeC (Comparing Semantics in Context) performs meaning comparison on the basis of an underspecified semantic representation robustly derived from the learner and the reference answers. The system was developed for German (Hahn and Meurers, 2012), on the basis of which we created the English CoSeC-EN for the SemEval 2013 Task 7 challenge.

Using an explicit semantic formalism in principle makes it possible to precisely represent meaning differences. It also supports a direct representation of Information Structure as a structuring of semantics representations (Krifka, 2007).

CoSeC is based on Lexical Resource Semantics (LRS, Richter and Sailer, 2004). Being an underspecified semantic formalism, LRS avoids the costly computation of all readings and provides access to the building blocks of the semantic representation, while additional constraints provide the information about their composition.

As described in Hahn and Meurers (2011), LRS representations can be derived automatically using a two-step approach based on part-of-speech tags assigned by TreeTagger (Schmid, 1994) and dependency parses by MaltParser (Nivre et al., 2007). First, the dependency structure is transformed into a completely lexicalized syntax-semantics interface representation, which abstracts away from some form variation at the surface. These representations are then mapped to LRS representations. The approach is robust in that it always results in an LRS structure, even for ill-formed sentences.

CoSeC then aligns the LRS representations of the reference answer and the student answer to each other and also to the representation of the question. The alignment approach takes into account local criteria, namely the semantic similarity of pairs of elements that are linked by the alignment, as well as global criteria measuring the extent to which the alignment preserves structure at the levels of variables and the subterm structure of the semantic formulas.

Local similarity of semantic expressions is estimated using WordNet (Fellbaum, 1998), FrameNet (Baker et al., 1998), PMI-IR (Turney, 2001) on the UkWaC (Baroni et al., 2009) as used in CoMiC, the Minimum Edit Distance (Levenshtein, 1966), and special parameters for comparing functional elements such as quantifiers and grammatical function labels.

Based on the alignments, the system marks elements which are not linked to elements in the question or which are linked to the semantic contribution of an alternative in an alternative question as "focused". This is intended as a first approximation of the concept of *focus* in the sense of Information Structure (von Heusinger, 1999; Kruijff-Korbayová and Steedman, 2003; Krifka, 2007), an active field of research in linguistics addressing the question how the information in sentences is packaged and integrated into discourse. Focus elements are expected to be particularly relevant for determining the correctness of an answer (Meurers et al., 2011b).

Overall meaning comparison is then done based on a set of numerical scores computed from the alignments and their quality. For each of these scores, a threshold is empirically determined, over which the student answer is considered to be correct. Among the scores discussed by Hahn and Meurers (2011), *weighted*-target *focus*, consistently scored best in the development set. This score measures the percentage of terms in the semantic representation of the reference answer which are linked to elements of the student answer in relation to the number of all elements in the representation of the reference answer. Only terms that were marked as focused in the preceding step are counted. Functional elements, i.e., quantifiers, predicates representing grammatical function labels, or the lambda operator, are weighted differently from other elements.

This threshold method can only be used to perform 2-way classification. Unlike the machine learning step in CoMiC, it does not generalize to 3-way or 5-way classification.

The alignment algorithm uses several numerical parameters, such as weights for the different components measuring semantic similarities, weights for the different overall local and global criteria, and the weight of the *weighted*-target *focus* score. These parameters are optimized using Powells algorithm combined with grid-based line optimization (Press et al., 2002). To avoid overfitting, the parameters and the threshold are determined on disjoint partitions of the training set.

In terms of linguistic abstractions, meaning assessment in CoSeC is based entirely on underspecified semantic representations. Surface forms are indirectly encoded by the structure of the representation and the predicate names, which are usually derived from the lemmas. As with CoMiC, parameter optimization and the determination of the thresholds for the numerical scores do not involve concrete information about linguistic objects. Again, the high level of abstraction suggests that CoSeC should perform better than other approaches on unseen topics and unseen questions.

2.3 The Bag Approaches

Inspired by the bag-of-words concept that emerged from information retrieval (Salton and McGill, 1983), we designed a system that uses bag representations of student answers. For each student answer, there are three bags, each containing one of the following representations: words, lemmas and Soundex hashes of that answer. The question ID corresponding to the answer is added to each bag as a pseudo-word, allowing the machine learner to adjust to question-specific properties. Based on the bag representations, the approach compares a given student answer to a model trained on all other known student answers. On the one hand, this method ignores the presence of reference answers (although they could be added to the training set as additional correct answers), on the other hand it makes use of information not taken into account by alignment-based systems such as CoMiC or CoSeC.

Concerning pre-processing, the linguistic analyses such as tokenization and lemmatization are identical to those of CoMiC, since the bag generator technically is just another output module of the UIMA-based pipeline used there. No stop-word list is used. The bags are fed into a support vector-based machine learner. We used WEKA's Sequential Minimal Optimization (SMO, Platt, 1998) implementation with the radial basis function (RBF) kernel, since it yielded good results on our development set and since it supports output of the estimated probabilities for each class. The optimal gamma parameter and complexity constant were estimated via 10-fold grid search.

In terms of abstractions, all bag-based approaches simply disregard word order and in case of binary bags even word frequency. Still, a bit of the relation between words is essentially encoded in their morphology. This piece of information is discarded in the bags of lemmas, eventually, e.g., putting words like "bulb" and "bulbs" in the same vector slot. Further away from the surface are the Soundex hashes, a phonetic representation of English words patented by Russell (1918). The well-known algorithm transforms similar-sounding English words into the same representation of characters and numbers, thereby ironing out many spelling mistakes and common confusion cases of homophones such as "there" vs. "their". The MorphAdorner[4] implementation we used returns empty Soundex hashes for input tokens that do not start with a letter of the alphabet. However, we found in our experiments, that the presence of these empty hashes in the bags has a positive impact on performance. This is most likely due to the fact that it discriminates answers containing punctuation (not a letter of the alphabet) from those which do not.

Since the bag approaches use Soundex as phonetic equivalence classes, but no semantic equivalence classes, they should perform best on the unseen answers data in which most lexical material from the test set is likely to already be present in the training set.

2.4 CoMeT: A Meta-Classifier

As described in the previous sections, our subsystems perform short answer evaluation on different representations and at different levels of abstraction. The bag approaches are very surface-oriented, whereas CoSeC uses a semantic formalism to compare answers to each other. We expected each system to show its strengths in different test scenarios, so a way was needed to combine the predictions of different systems into the final result.

CoMeT (Comparing Meaning in Tübingen) is a meta-classifier which builds on the predictions of our individual systems (feature stacking, see Wolpert, 1992). The rationale is that if systems are complementary, their combination will perform better (or at least as good) than any individual system on its own. The design is as follows:

Each system produces predictions on the training set, using 10-fold cross-validation, and on the test set. In addition to the predicted class, each system was also made to output probabilities for each possible class (cf., e.g., Tetreault et al., 2012a). The class probabilities were then used as features in the meta classifier to train a model for the test data. In addition to the probabilities, we also used the question ID and module ID in the meta-classifier, in the hope that they would allow differentiation between scenarios. For example, an unseen question ID means that we are not testing on unseen answers and thus predictions from systems with more abstraction from the surface may be preferred.

The class probabilities come from different sources, depending on the system. In the case of CoMiC, they are extracted directly from the decision trees. For the bag approaches, we used WEKA's option to fit logistic models to the SVM output after classification in order to estimate probabilities. Finally, the CoSeC probabilities are derived directly from its final score. As mentioned in section 2.2, CoSeC only does binary classification, so those probabilities are used in the meta-classifier for all tasks.

Based on the results on our internal development set (see section 3.1), we chose different system combinations for different scenarios. For unseen topics and unseen questions, we used only CoMiC in combination with CoSeC, since the inclusion of the bag approaches had a negative impact on results. For unseen answers, we additionally included the bag models. All meta-classification was done using WEKA's Logistic Regression implementation. The results are discussed in section 3.

3 Evaluation

In this section, we present the results for each of the sub-systems, both on the custom-made split of the training data we used in our development, as well as on the official test data of the SemEval 2013 Task 7 challenge. Subsequently, we discuss possible causes for issues raised by our evaluation results.

[4] http://morphadorner.northwestern.edu

3.1 Development Set

In order to be as close as possible to the final test setting, we replicated the official test scenarios on the training set, resulting in a *train/dev/test* split for each of the corpora. For Beetle, we held out all answers to two random questions for each module to form the unseen questions scenario, and five random answers from each remaining question to form the unseen answers scenario. For SciEntsBank, we held out module *LF* for *dev* and module *VB* for *test* to form the unseen topics scenario, because they have an average number of questions (11). The *LF* module turned out to be far more skewed towards incorrect answers (76.8%) than the training set on average (57.5%). While this skewedness needs to be taken into account for the interpretation of the development results, it did not have a negative effect on our final test results. Furthermore, analogous to Beetle, we held out all answers to one random question for each remaining module for unseen-questions, and two random answers from each remaining question for unseen answers.

The *dev* set was used for tuning and design decisions concerning which individual systems to combine in the stacked classifier, while we envisaged the *test* set to be used as a final checkpoint before submission.

The accuracy results for all sub-systems on the development set are reported in detail in Table 3. The majority baseline reflects the accuracy a system would achieve by always labelling any student answer as "incorrect", hence it is equivalent to the percentage of incorrect answers in the data. The lexical baseline is the performance of the system provided by the challenge organizers.

	Beetle		SciEntsBank		
System	d-uA	d-uQ	d-uA	d-uQ	d-uT
Maj. Baseline	57.14%	59.28%	54.30%	60.70%	76.84%
Lex. Baseline	75.43%	71.10%	63.44%	66.05%	59.54%
CoMiC	76.57%	71.52%	67.20%	70.23%	64.63%
Bag of Words	85.14%	62.03%	80.65%	54.65%	73.79%
~ of Lemmas	85.71%	58.02%	80.11%	52.33%	74.55%
~ of Soundex	86.86%	60.76%	81.18%	53.95%	72.77%
CoSeC	76.00%	74.89%	64.52%	73.49%	68.96%
CoMeT	88.00%	75.95%	81.18%	66.74%	68.45%

Table 3: Development set: accuracy for 2-way task (uA: unseen answers, uQ: unseen questions, uT: unseen topics)

The systems presented in section 2 performed as expected: The Bag-of-Soundex system achieved its best scores on the unseen answers where overlap of vocabulary was most likely, outperforming CoMiC and CoSeC with accuracy values as high as 86.86%. For Beetle unseen answers, the meta-classifier operated as expected and improved the overall results to 88.86%. For SciEntsBank unseen answers, it remained stable at 81.18%.

As expected, CoMiC and CoSeC with their alignment not depending on vocabulary outperformed the bag approaches in the other scenarios, in which the question or even the domain were not known during training. However, both alignment-based systems failed on SciEntsBank's unseen topics in comparison to the rather high majority baseline.

3.2 Official Test Set

For our submission to the SemEval 2013 Task 7 challenge, we trained our sub-systems on the entire official training set. The overall performance of the CoMeT system on all sub-tasks is shown in Table 4.

		Beetle		SciEntsBank		
		uA	uQ	uA	uQ	uT
Lexical	2-way	79.7%	74.0%	66.1%	67.4%	67.6%
Overlap	3-way	59.5%	51.2%	55.6%	54.0%	57.7%
Baseline	5-way	51.9%	48.0%	43.7%	41.3%	41.5%
Best	2-way	84.5%	74.1%	77.6%	74.5%	71.1%
System	3-way	73.1%	59.6%	72.0%	66.3%	63.7%
	5-way	71.5%	62.1%	64.3%	53.2%	51.2%
CoMeT	2-way	83.8%	70.2%	77.4%	60.3%	67.6%
	3-way	**73.1%**	51.8%	71.3%	54.6%	57.9%
	5-way	68.8%	48.8%	60.0%	43.7%	42.1%

Table 4: Official test set: overall accuracy of CoMeT (uA: unseen answers, uQ: unseen questions, uT: unseen topics)

While CoMeT won the Beetle 3-way task in unseen answers, our main focus is on the 2-way task. The results for the 2-way task of our sub-systems on the official test set are shown in Table 5.
The first row of the table reports the results of the winning system of the challenge; the two baselines are computed as before. In general, the accuracy values of CoMeT exhibit a drop of around 5% from our development set to the official test set. The meta-classifier was unable to benefit from the different sub-systems except for the unseen answers in SciEntsBank that slightly outperformed the best bag approach.

System	Beetle uA	Beetle uQ	SciEntsBank uA	SciEntsBank uQ	SciEntsBank uT
Best	84.50%	74.10%	77.60%	74.50%	71.10%
Maj. Baseline	59.91%	58.00%	56.85%	58.94%	57.98%
Lex. Baseline	79.70%	74.00%	66.10%	67.40%	67.60%
CoMiC	76.08%	70.57%	67.96%	66.30%	67.97%
Bag of Words	83.14%	67.52%	75.93%	57.84%	59.84%
~ of Lemmas	83.60%	67.16%	76.67%	58.25%	58.81%
~ of Soundex	84.05%	68.38%	75.93%	57.57%	58.02%
CoSeC	62.19%	63.61%	67.22%	58.94%	62.36%
CoMeT	83.83%	70.21%	77.41%	60.30%	67.62%
CoSeC*	75.40%	70.82%	72.04%	64.94%	70.60%
CoMeT*	84.51%	71.43%	79.26%	65.35%	69.53%

Table 5: Official test set: accuracy for 2-way task (uA: unseen answers, uQ: unseen questions, uT: unseen topics)

Even though it does not live up to the standards of the bag approaches in their area of expertise (unseen answers), the CoMiC systems outperforms the bags on the unseen question and unseen topic sub-sets as expected. Note that on unseen topics, CoMiC still scores 10% above the majority baseline on the official test set, in contrast to the drop of more than 10% below the baseline for the corresponding (skewed) development set.

However, the results for CoSeC are around 10% lower on the unseen questions, and almost 7% lower on the unseen topics of the test data than on the development set, a drop that the overall meta-classifier (CoMeT) was unable to catch. Investigating this drop in comparison to our development set, we checked the correctness of the training script and discovered a bug in the CoSeC setup that led to the parameters and the thresholds being computed on the same partition of the training set, i.e., the system overfitted to this partition, while the remainder of the training set was not used for training. Correcting the bug resulted in CoSeC accuracy values broadly comparable to those of CoMiC, as was the case on the development set. This confirms that the reason for the drop in the submission was not a flaw in the CoSeC system as such, but a programming bug in a peripheral component.

With this bug fixed, CoSeC performs 5%–13% better on the test set, and the meta-classifier would have been able to benefit from the regularly performing CoSeC, improving in performance up to 5%. These two amended systems are listed as CoSeC* and CoMeT* in Table 5. For the two unseen answers scenarios, CoMeT* would outperform the best scoring systems of the challenge in the 2-way task.

3.3 Discussion

In this section, we try to identify some general tendencies from studying the results. Firstly, we can observe that due to the strong performance of the bag models, unseen answers scores are generally higher than their counterparts. It seems that if questions have been seen before, surface-oriented methods outperform more abstract approaches. However, the picture is different for unseen domains and unseen questions. We are generally puzzled by the fact that many systems in the shared task scored worse on unseen questions, where in-domain training data is available, than on unseen domains, where this is not the case. The CoMeT classifier suffered especially in unseen questions of SciEntsBank, scoring lower than our best system would have on its own (see Table 5); even after the CoSeC bug was fixed, CoMeT* still scored worse there than CoMiC on its own.

In general, we likely would have benefited from domain adaptation, as described in, e.g., Daume III (2007). Consider that the input for the meta-classifier always consists of the same set of features produced via standard cross-validation, regardless of the test scenario. Instead, the trained model should have different feature weights depending on what the model will be tested on.

4 Conclusion and Outlook

We presented our approach to Task 7 of SemEval 2013, consisting of a combination of surface-oriented bag models and the increasingly abstract alignment-based systems CoMiC and CoSeC. Predictions of all systems were combined using a meta classifier in order to produce the final result for CoMeT.

The results presented show that our approach performs competitively, especially in the unseen answers test scenarios, where we obtained the best result of all participants in the 3-way task with the Beetle corpus (73.1% accuracy). As expected, the unseen topics scenario proved to be more challenging, with results at 67.6% accuracy in the 2-way task for CoMeT. Surprisingly, CoMeT performed consistently worse in the unseen questions scenarios, which we attribute to rather low CoSeC results there and to the way the meta classifier is trained, which currently does not take into account the test scenario it is trained for and instead uses the module and question IDs as features, which turned out not to be an effective domain adaptation approach.

In our future research, work on CoMiC will concentrate on integrating two aspects of the context: First, we are planning to develop an automatic approach to focus identification in order to pinpoint the essential parts of the student answers. Second, for data sets where a reading text is available, we will try to automatically determine the location of the relevant source information given the question, which can then be used as alternative or additional reference material for answer evaluation.

The CoMiC system currently also relies on the Traditional Marriage Algorithm to select the optimal global alignment between student answer and reference answer. We plan to replace this algorithm by a machine learning component that can handle this selection in a data-driven way.

For CoSeC, we plan to develop an extension that allows for *n-to-m* mappings, hence improving the alignment performance for multi-word units such as, e.g., phrasal verb constructions.

The bag approaches could be augmented by exploring additional levels of abstractions, e.g., semantic equivalence classes constructed via WordNet lookup.

In sum, while we will also plan to explore optimizations to the training setup of the meta-classifier (e.g., domain adaptation along the lines of Daume III, 2007), the main focus of our further research lies in improving the individual sub-systems, which then again are expected to push the overall performance of the CoMeT meta-classifier system.

Acknowledgements

We are thankful to Sowmya Vajjala and Serhiy Bykh for their valuable advice on meta-classifiers and other machine learning techniques. We also thank the reviewers for their comments; in consultation with the SemEval organizers we kept the length at 8 pages plus references, the page limit for papers describing multiple systems.

References

Stacey Bailey and Detmar Meurers. 2008. Diagnosing meaning errors in short answers to reading comprehension questions. In Joel Tetreault, Jill Burstein, and Rachele De Felice, editors, *Proceedings of the 3rd Workshop on Innovative Use of NLP for Building Educational Applications (BEA-3) at ACL'08*, pages 107–115, Columbus, Ohio. http://aclweb.org/anthology/W08-0913.pdf.

Collin F. Baker, Charles J. Fillmore, and John B. Lowe. 1998. The berkeley framenet project. In *Proceedings of the 36th Annual Meeting of the Association for Computational Linguistics and 17th International Conference on Computational Linguistics*, volume 1, pages 86–90, Montreal, Quebec, Canada.

Marco Baroni, Silvia Bernardini, Adriano Ferraresi, and Eros Zanchetta. 2009. The wacky wide web: A collection of very large linguistically processed web-crawled corpora. *Journal of Language Resources and Evaluation*, 3(43):209–226.

Walter Daelemans, Jakub Zavrel, Ko van der Sloot, and Antal van den Bosch, 2007. *TiMBL: Tilburg Memory-Based Learner Reference Guide, ILK Technical Report ILK 07-03*. Induction of Linguistic Knowledge Research Group Department of Communication and Information Sciences, Tilburg University, Tilburg, The Netherlands, July 11. Version 6.0.

Ido Dagan, Bill Dolan, Bernardo Magnini, and Dan Roth. 2009. Recognizing textual entailment: Rational, evaluation and approaches. *Natural Language Engineering*, 15(4):i–xvii, 10.

Hal Daume III. 2007. Frustratingly easy domain adaptation. In *Proceedings of the 45th Annual Meeting of the Association of Computational Linguistics*, pages 256–263, Prague, Czech Republic, June. Association for Computational Linguistics.

Myroslava O. Dzikovska, Rodney Nielsen, Chris Brew, Claudia Leacock, Danilo Giampiccolo, Luisa Bentivogli, Peter Clark, Ido Dagan, and Hoa Trang Dang. 2013. Semeval-2013 task 7: The joint student response analysis and 8th recognizing textual entailment challenge. In **SEM 2013: The First Joint Conference on Lexical and Computational Semantics*, Atlanta, Georgia, USA, 13-14 June.

Christiane Fellbaum, editor. 1998. *WordNet: An Electronic Lexical Database*. MIT Press, Cambridge, Massachusetts.

David Ferrucci and Adam Lally. 2004. UIMA: An architectural approach to unstructured information processing in the corporate research environment. *Natural Language Engineering*, 10(3–4):327–348.

David Gale and Lloyd S. Shapley. 1962. College admissions and the stability of marriage. *American Mathematical Monthly*, 69:9–15.

Otis Gospodnetić and Erik Hatcher. 2005. *Lucene in Action*. Manning, Greenwich, CT.

Michael Hahn and Detmar Meurers. 2011. On deriving semantic representations from dependencies: A practical approach for evaluating meaning in learner corpora. In *Proceedings of the Intern. Conference on Dependency Linguistics (DEPLING 2011)*, pages 94–103, Barcelona. http://purl.org/dm/papers/hahn-meurers-11.html.

Michael Hahn and Detmar Meurers. 2012. Evaluating the meaning of answers to reading comprehension questions: A semantics-based approach. In *Proceedings of the 7th Workshop on Innovative Use of NLP for Building Educational Applications (BEA-7) at NAACL-HLT 2012*, pages 94–103, Montreal. http://aclweb.org/anthology/W12-2039.pdf.

Mark Hall, Eibe Frank, Geoffrey Holmes, Bernhard Pfahringer, Peter Reutemann, and Ian H. Witten. 2009. The WEKA data mining software: An update. In *The SIGKDD Explorations*, volume 11, pages 10–18.

Michael Halliday. 1967. Notes on Transitivity and Theme in English. Part 1 and 2. *Journal of Linguistics*, 3:37–81, 199–244.

Manfred Krifka. 2007. Basic notions of information structure. In Caroline Fery, Gisbert Fanselow, and Manfred Krifka, editors, *The notions of information structure*, volume 6 of *Interdisciplinary Studies on Information Structure (ISIS)*. Universitätsverlag Potsdam, Potsdam.

Ivana Kruijff-Korbayová and Mark Steedman. 2003. Discourse and information structure. *Journal of Logic, Language and Information (Introduction to the Special Issue)*, 12(3):249–259.

Vladimir I. Levenshtein. 1966. Binary codes capable of correcting deletions, insertions, and reversals. *Soviet Physics Doklady*, 10(8):707–710.

Detmar Meurers, Ramon Ziai, Niels Ott, and Stacey Bailey. 2011a. Integrating parallel analysis modules to evaluate the meaning of answers to reading comprehension questions. *IJCEELL. Special Issue on Automatic Free-text Evaluation*, 21(4):355–369. http://purl.org/dm/papers/meurers-ea-11.html.

Detmar Meurers, Ramon Ziai, Niels Ott, and Janina Kopp. 2011b. Evaluating answers to reading comprehension questions in context: Results for German and the role of information structure. In *Proceedings of the TextInfer 2011 Workshop on Textual Entailment*, pages 1–9, Edinburgh, Scotland, UK, July. http://aclweb.org/anthology/W11-2401.pdf.

Guido Minnen, John Carroll, and Darren Pearce. 2001. Applied morphological processing of English. *Natural Language Engineering*, 7(3):207–233.

Joakim Nivre, Jens Nilsson, Johan Hall, Atanas Chanev, Gülsen Eryigit, Sandra Kübler, Svetoslav Marinov, and Erwin Marsi. 2007. MaltParser: A language-independent system for data-driven dependency parsing. *Natural Language Engineering*, 13(1):1–41.

Niels Ott, Ramon Ziai, and Detmar Meurers. 2012. Creation and analysis of a reading comprehension exercise corpus: Towards evaluating meaning in context. In Thomas Schmidt and Kai Wörner, editors, *Multilingual Corpora and Multilingual Corpus Analysis*, Hamburg Studies in Multilingualism (HSM), pages 47–69. Benjamins, Amsterdam. http://purl.org/dm/papers/ott-ziai-meurers-12.html.

John C. Platt. 1998. Sequential minimal optimization: A fast algorithm for training support vector machines. Technical Report MSR-TR-98-14, Microsoft Research.

William H. Press, Saul A. Teukolsky, William T. Vetterling, and Brian P. Flannery. 2002. *Numerical Recipes in C++*. Cambridge University Press, Cambridge, UK.

J.R. Quinlan. 1993. *C4.5: Programs for Machine Learning*. Morgan Kaufmann Publishers.

Frank Richter and Manfred Sailer. 2004. Basic concepts of lexical resource semantics. In Arnold Beckmann and Norbert Preining, editors, *European Summer School in Logic, Language and Information 2003. Course Material I*, volume 5 of *Collegium Logicum*, pages 87–143. Publication Series of the Kurt Gödel Society, Wien.

Robert C. Russell. 1918. US patent number 1.261.167, 4.

Gerard Salton and Michael J. McGill. 1983. *Introduction to modern information retrieval*. McGraw-Hill, New York.

Helmut Schmid. 1994. Probabilistic part-of-speech tagging using decision trees. In *Proceedings of the International Conference on New Methods in Language Processing*, pages 44–49, Manchester, UK.

Joel Tetreault, Daniel Blanchard, Aoife Cahill, and Martin Chodorow. 2012. Native tongues, lost and found: Resources and empirical evaluations in native language identification. In *Proceedings of the 24th International Conference on Computational Linguistics (COLING)*, pages 2585–2602, Mumbai, India.

Peter Turney. 2001. Mining the web for synonyms: PMI-IR versus LSA on TOEFL. In *Proceedings of the Twelfth European Conference on Machine Learning (ECML-2001)*, pages 491–502, Freiburg, Germany.

Klaus von Heusinger. 1999. *Intonation and Information Structure. The Representation of Focus in Phonology and Semantics*. Habilitationssschrift, Universität Konstanz, Konstanz, Germany.

David H. Wolpert. 1992. Stacked generalization. *Neural Networks*, 5(2):241–259.

Ramon Ziai, Niels Ott, and Detmar Meurers. 2012. Short answer assessment: Establishing links between research strands. In Joel Tetreault, Jill Burstein, and Claudial Leacock, editors, *Proceedings of the 7th Workshop on Innovative Use of NLP for Building Educational Applications (BEA-7) at NAACL-HLT 2012*, pages 190–200, Montreal, June. http://aclweb.org/anthology/W12-2022.pdf.

UC3M: A kernel-based approach to identify and classify DDIs in biomedical texts.

Daniel Sanchez-Cisneros
Universidad Carlos III de Madrid
Avda. de la Universidad, 30
28911 Leganés - Madrid - Spain
dscisner@inf.uc3m.es

Abstract

The domain of DDI identification is constantly showing a rise of interest from scientific community since it represents a decrease of time and healthcare cost. In this paper we purpose a new approach based on shallow linguistic kernel methods to identify DDIs in biomedical manuscripts. The approach outlines a first step in the usage of semantic information for DDI identification. The system obtained an F1 measure of 0.534.

1 Introduction

In recent years a new discipline appeared in the biomedical domain for processing pharmacological manuscripts related to drug substances. This discipline is the so called *Pharmacovigilance*, and takes care of the management and control of Drug-Drug interactions (DDI) among other faculties. A DDI occurs when one drug influences the effect level or activity of another drug.

Some events such as *BioCreative*[1] and *BioNLP*[2] establish a benchmark of comparison in the field of natural language processing applied to biomedical domain. This is the case of *Semeval 2013: Extraction of Drug-Drug Interactions from BioMedical Texts*[3], where our system has been evaluated.

The field of DDI extraction from biomedical text has been faced from different perspectives such as rule-based approaches, SVM approaches and kernel-methods approaches, among others.

Segura-Bedmar et al. (2010) proposed an approach to extract DDI from biomedical texts based on Shallow Linguistic (SL) Kernel (Giuliano et al., 2006) methods obtaining an F1 measure of 60,01%. The system was evaluated over a DrugDDI dataset created in 2010 that contains 579 biomedical documents collected from the pharmacological database *DrugBank*[4]. The dataset contains a total of 3,160 DDIs.

Recently, the DDIExtraction2011 task[5] compared the latest advances in Information Extraction techniques applied to the DDI identification. The event provided a benchmark forum of 10 different approaches. The evaluation of the systems was made over the DrugDDI dataset. We now describe the most relevant works.

Thomas et al. (2011) developed a system by combining a preprocessing phase based on Charniak-Lease (Lease, Charniak, 2005) and Stanford (Marneffe et al., 2006) parsers, with a classification phase based on SL kernel (Giuliano et al., 2006), k-Band Shortest Path Spectrum (kBSPS) kernel (Airola et al., 2008), All Path Graphic (APG) kernel (Tikk et al., 2010) and case-based reasoning (CBR) (Aamodt, Plaza, 1994) techniques. The system obtained a F1 measure of 65.7%.

Chowdhury et al. (2011) presented a system combining a preprocessing phase based on Stanford parser and SPECIALIST (Browne, 2000) lexicon tool, with a classification phase based on Featured-Based kernel such as SL kernel and Tree-Based kernel such as Dependency tree (DT) kernel (Culotta and Sorensen, 2004) and Phrase Structure Tree (PST) kernel (Moschitti, 2004). The system achieved an F1 of 63.7%.

[1] http://www.biocreative.org/
[2] http://2013.bionlp-st.org/
[3] http://www.cs.york.ac.uk/semeval-2013/task9/

[4] http://www.drugbank.ca/
[5] http://labda.inf.uc3m.es/DDIExtraction2011/

*Second Joint Conference on Lexical and Computational Semantics (*SEM), Volume 2: Seventh International Workshop on Semantic Evaluation (SemEval 2013)*, pages 617–621, Atlanta, Georgia, June 14-15, 2013.

Björne et al. (2011) proposed a different approach by combining a preprocessing phase based on a collection of features and n-grams; with a classification based on support vector machine (SVM) (Vapnik, 1995). The SVM methods perform classification tasks by building hyperplanes in a multidimensional space that divide cases of different classes (binary classification). The system yielded an F1 measure of 62.99%.

Kernel methods seem to be the best choice for extracting DDI since they obtained the highest results. Thus, we decided to use kernel methods to identify and classify DDI in our system. Furthermore, we hypothesize that using semantic features of pharmacological substances, can provide valuable knowledge in the classification phase. Therefore, we decide to integrate semantic information in the classification process of kernel methods.

In this paper we present a kernel-based approach to identify and classify DDIs in biomedical text by using SL kernels. In section 2 we describe the system used for identifying DDIs. Section 3 present the results obtained by the system and a little comparison with other approaches. In section 4 we expose some conclusions obtained and ideas for future work.

2 Description of the systems

The system (see figure 1) is divided in three phases: (i) in the first phase the system makes a preprocessing of the documents in order to extract grammatical and semantic information about each word of the text. (ii) The second phase makes the classification of whether a pair of drugs is a DDI or not by using SL kernel methods. (iii) In the third phase, the system classifies all DDIs into the purpose type (*advice, effect, mechanism, int*) using SL kernel methods.

The corpus is processed sentence by sentence, using the identification tag provided for each sentence.

2.1 Preprocessing

In this phase we make a preprocessing of the documents to obtain linguistic and semantic information about the words and entities contained in the text. Since linguistic and semantic

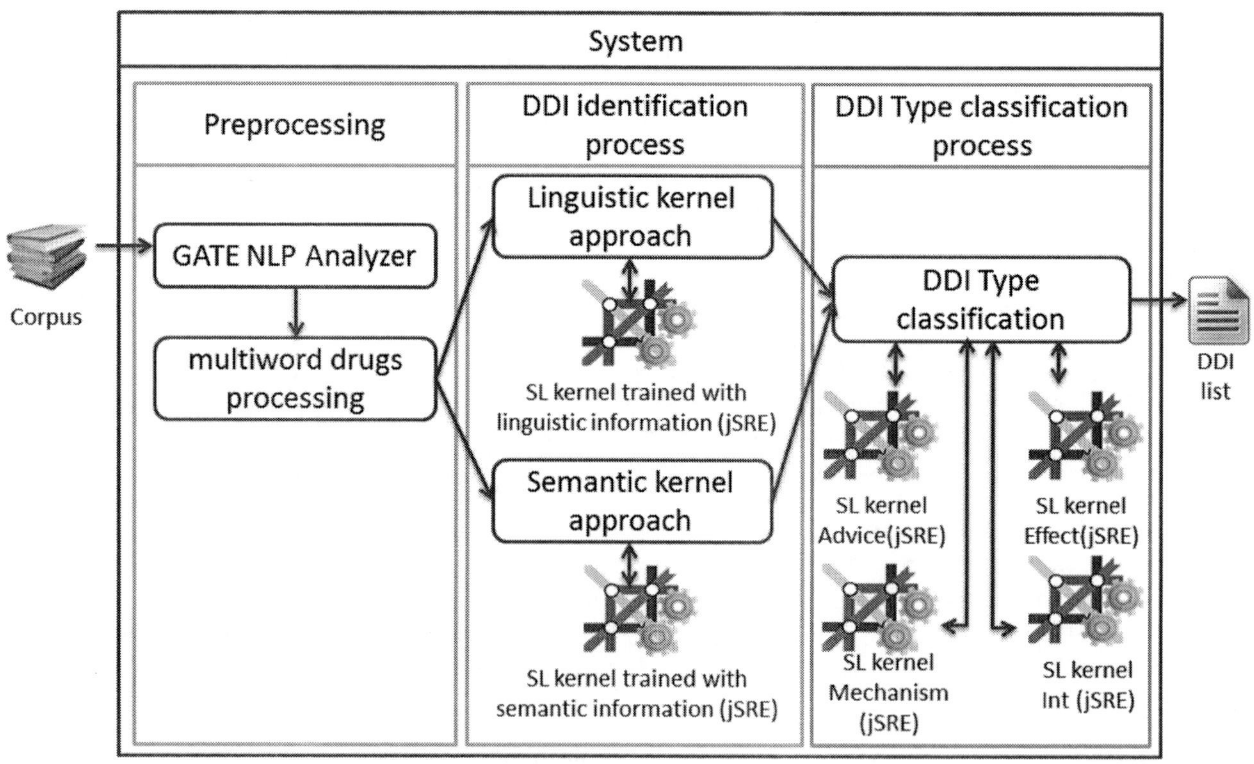

Figure 1: Architecture of the system.

approaches are based on different types of information, our participation in the task will be separated in two runs: first run will be based on linguistic information and second run will be based on semantic information.

Firstly, we process each sentence and obtain linguistic information about *part-of-speech* (PoS) tagging and lemmatization for each word contained in the text. To do so we use the Stanford parser[6] by using the GATE analyzer[7]. The result of this step is a list of words and PoS tags, but entity concepts are missing. Therefore, we make a multiword entities processing to keep the words related to the same concept together. For example, the entity *beta-adrenergic receptor blocker* is processed by Stanford parser as three different annotations nodes: *beta-adrenergic* as type JJ; *receptor* as type NN; and *blocker* as type NNS. Thus we unify the three words into an only one concept *beta-adrenergic_receptor_blocker* as type NNP. This information corresponds to the linguistic approach of our participation in the task (see figure 2b).

On the other hand, we process the text and collect semantic information about Anatomical Therapeutic Chemical (ATC) identification for each drug found in the text. The ATC code is a widely used classification system provided from WHO collaborating centre for Drug statistics methodology. The classification divides drugs in groups at five different levels according to the organ or system on which they act, and their therapeutic, pharmacological and chemical properties. The system obtains the ATC code of the drugs by searching the drug entities in the ATC Index resource[8]. Then, we associate the ATC code results with the drug entity. This information corresponds to the semantic approach of our participation in the task.

2.2 Identification of DDI

In this phase the system will predict whether a pair of drugs is a DDI or not by the use of Shallow linguistic Kernel methods. To do so we use the jSRE tool[9].

In one hand, the linguistic approach is based on shallow linguistic information such as PoS tagging and lemmatization. Therefore, the information introduced into the SL kernel model consists of: *token_identifier*, *ATC_code*, *token_lemmatization*, *POS_tag*, *entity_type* and *entity_label*; as show in figure 2b.

On the other hand, the semantic approach uses the semantic information of drugs (ATC codes) to increase the available knowledge in the kernel classification process. To do so, we trained a SL kernel model by replacing the token value with the ATC code value. In case of a non-drug token, we replace the token value with 0. This way the information introduced to the SL kernel model consists of: *token_identifier*, *ATC_code*, *token_lemmatization*, *POS_tag*, *entity_type* and *entity_label*; as show in figure 2c.

```
<Feature>
  <Name className="java.lang.String">string</Name><Value className="java.lang.String">beta-adrenergic</Value>
  <Name className="java.lang.String">category</Name><Value className="java.lang.String">JJ</Value>
</Feature>
<Feature>
  <Name className="java.lang.String">string</Name><Value className="java.lang.String">receptor</Value>
  <Name className="java.lang.String">category</Name><Value className="java.lang.String">NN</Value>
</Feature>
<Feature>
  <Name className="java.lang.String">string</Name><Value className="java.lang.String">blockers</Value>
  <Name className="java.lang.String">category</Name><Value className="java.lang.String">NNS</Value>
</Feature>
```

Figure 2a: Example of separated multiword entity.

```
8&&beta-adrenergic_receptor_blocker&&beta-adrenergic_receptor_blocker&&NNP&&group&&A
```

Figure 2b: Example of linguistic input token into the SL kernel.

```
0&&B01AB&&heparin&&NNP&&drug&&A
```

Figure 2c: Example of semantic input token into the SL kernel.

[6] http://nlp.stanford.edu/software/lex-parser.shtml.
[7] http://gate.ac.uk.
[8] http://www.whocc.no/atc_ddd_index/
[9] http://hlt.fbk.eu/en/technology/jSRE

2.3 Type classification of DDI

In the third phase, the system makes a classification of DDIs to determine the type of the interaction. To do so, the system face the classification task as a machine learning task, and use SL kernel methods. Hence, we train one SL kernel model for each possible values of DDI type: *advice, effect, mechanism, int*. To train the kernel models we separate by type each DDI of the training dataset. The result is four groups of training dataset, where the correspondent type class value are set to 1, and 0 otherwise. Once we trained the kernel models, each DDI go through four different prediction processes. The conflictive cases are solved by frequency of appearance. This step is the same for both linguistic and semantic approach. Finally, we collect the results and generate the task output format.

3 Results

The best result in DDI detection and classification (macro-average score) were obtained by the linguistic approach (run 2), achieving a F1 measure of 0.534.

Team	DDI Detection			DDI Detection and Classification (micro-average)			DDI Detection and Classification (macro-average)		
	P	R	F1	P	R	F1	P	R	F1
Run 1	0,632	0,725	**0,676**	0,495	0,568	**0,529**	0,527	0,541	**0,534**
Run 2	0,404	0,798	0,537	0,222	0,437	0,294	0,275	0,43	0,335

Table 1: Results obtained by the system.

Focusing on DDI detection results, we can see that linguistic approach also overcome the semantic approach, obtaining a F1 score of 0.676 and 0.537 respectively. This can be explained since the SL kernel optimizes linguistic information rather than semantic information. Therefore, ATC code format is not appropriate for SL kernel.

However, the score obtained by the linguistic approach using SL kernel with multiword entities processing seems to be higher than the average results obtained in DDIExtraction 2011 task. This may be due to the great improvement that DrugDDI corpus suffered since the last competition, by enriching the information of each entity.

Finally, we have a word to notice the decrease of the results from DDI detection evaluation to DDI detection and classification evaluation. This could be due to the complexity of the DDI type classification task. However, the final result of macro-average score shows huge margin of improvement.

4 Conclusion and future work

In this paper we present a kernel based approach to identify and classify DDIs by using SL kernel. The result obtained by the system achieves 0.534 F1 measure. From linguistic approach and semantic approach purposed for the participation in the task, the linguistic approach shows better results. However, we can not discard semantic information since we may have not used the appropriate semantic information for a shallow linguistic kernel.

Thus, a possible future work could be the research in semantic information processing to help in the classification process. Therefore, another future work could be the integration of pharmacological ontologies in the classification process since they increase the knowledge available for the classification task.

Acknowledgments

This work has been funded by MA2VICMR project (S2009/TIC-1542) and MULTIMEDICA project[10] (TIN 2010-20644-C03-01).

References

Aamodt A., Plaza E. 1994. *Case-Based Reasoning: Foundational Issues, Methodological Variations, and System Approaches*. AI Communications 7(1), P 39–59.

Airola, A., Pyysalo, S., Björne, J., Pahikkala, T., Ginter, F., Salakoski, T. 2008. *Allpaths graph kernel for protein-protein interaction extraction with evaluation of cross-corpus learning*. BMC Bioinformatics, 9 S11, S2.

Björne J., Airola A., Pahikkala T., Salakoski T. 2011. *Drug-Drug interaction extraction from biomedical*

[10] http://labda.inf.uc3m.es/multimedica/

texts with SVM and RLS classifiers. Proceedings of DDIExtraction2011, SEPLN 2011.

Browne A.C., McCray A.T., Srinivasan S. 2000. *The SPECIALIST Lexicon*. NLM, Bethesda.

Chowdhury MFM, Lavelli A. 2011. *Drug-drug Interaction Extraction Using Composite Kernels*. Proceedings of DDIExtraction2011, SEPLN 2011.

Giuliano C, Lavelli A, Romano L. 2006. *Exploiting shallow linguistic information for relation extraction from biomedical literature*. Proceedings of EACL 2006.

Culotta A., Sorensen J. 2004. *Dependency tree kernels for relation extraction*. Proceedings of the 42nd annual metting of the Association for Computational Linguistics.

Lease, M., Charniak, E. 2005. *Parsing biomedical literature*. Proceedings of IJCNLP'05.

Marneffe M.C., MacCartney B., Manning C.D. 2006. *Generating Typed Dependency Parses from Phrase Structure Parses*. Proceedings of LREC 2006.

Moschitti, A. 2004. *A study on convolution kernels for shallow semantic parsing*. Proceedings of the 42nd Annual Meeting of the Association for Computational Linguistics. ACL '04.

Segura-Bedmar, I., Martínez, P., Pablo-Sánchez, C.d. 2010. *Using a shallow linguistic kernel for drug-drug interaction extraction*. BMC BioInformatics.

Thomas P., Neves M., Solt I., Tikk D., Leser U. 2011. *Relation Extraction for Drug-Drug Interaction using Ensemble Learning*. Proceedings of DDIExtraction2011, SEPLN 2011.

Tikk, D., Thomas, P., Palaga, P., Hakenberg, J., Leser, U. 2010. *A comprehensive benchmark of kernel methods to extract protein-protein interactions from literature*. PLoS Comput Biol 6.

Vapnik, V.N. 1995. *The nature of statistical learning theory*. Springer-Verlag New York.

UEM-UC3M: An Ontology-based named entity recognition system for biomedical texts.

Daniel Sanchez-Cisneros
Universidad Carlos III de Madrid
Avda. de la Universidad, 30
28911 Leganés - Madrid - Spain
dscisner@inf.uc3m.es

Fernando Aparicio Gali
Universidad Europea de Madrid
C/ Tajo, s/n. Urb. El Bosque
28670-Villaviciosa de Odón- (Madrid)
fernando.aparicio@uem.es

Abstract

Drug name entity recognition focuses on identifying concepts appearing in the text that correspond to a chemical substance used in pharmacology for treatment, cure, prevention or diagnosis of diseases. This paper describes a system based on ontologies for identifying the chemical substances in biomedical text. The system achieves an F-1 measure of 0.529 in the task.

1 Introduction

Named entity recognition (NER) involves processing text and identifying certain occurrences of words belonging to particular categories of named entities. In recent years, much attention has been paid to the problem of recognizing gene and protein mentions in biomedical abstracts for different purposes such as information extraction, relation extraction or information retrieval. In this case we focus on the pharmacological domain. Furthermore, some initiatives have promoted the evaluation of different systems of named entity recognition and relation extraction in the pharmacological domain. This is the case of *Semeval 2013: Recognition and classification of drug names* task[1] (Segura-Bedmar et al., 2013), where the system presented in this communication has been evaluated.

Following the annotation guidelines of the task, a drug is a substance that is used in the treatment, cure, prevention or diagnosis of disease. Moreover, each drug name entity can be classified in four different types: *drug*, *brand*, *drug_n* and *group*. Our system uses biomedical ontologies and external resources (containing biomedical information) as input to determine whether we are treating a drug name entity or not.

The resource integration seems to represent an improvement since the knowledge available for identifying entities is higher. Some biomedical resources such as *Drugbank*[2], *Kegg*[3], *Pubchem*[4] or *Drugs.com*[5] focus on providing a compound of information collected from different sources.

Section 2 exposes some related work in the field of NER. In section 3 we describe the system used for identifying drug name entities. Section 4 presents the results obtained by the system and a little comparison with other approaches. In section 5 we outline some conclusions obtained and ideas for future work.

2 Related work

The field of NER has been very studied in recent years, and has been faced in many approaches. Since text structures are frequently used to characterize documents in text mining algorithms, there only stand out those based in terms and

[1] http://www.cs.york.ac.uk/semeval-2013/task9/data/uploads/task-9.1-drug-ner.pdf

[2] http://www.drugbank.ca/
[3] http://www.genome.jp/kegg/
[4] http://pubchem.ncbi.nlm.nih.gov/
[5] http://www.drugs.com/

*Second Joint Conference on Lexical and Computational Semantics (*SEM), Volume 2: Seventh International Workshop on Semantic Evaluation (SemEval 2013)*, pages 622–627, Atlanta, Georgia, June 14-15, 2013.

concepts. This is due to that concept-based systems represent the semantic content with a smaller number of characteristics, opposite to the term-based systems based on characters or words. Concept-based and term-based representations mainly differ in the implicit or explicit appearance, respectively, of the words identified in the document. This fact implies that concept-based extraction techniques are more complex, requiring the use of more advanced computational linguistics techniques and a greater dependence on knowledge domain.

One reference system that focuses on concept recognition in the biomedical domain is *MetaMap* (Aronson, 2001). MetaMap is a program developed by the National Library of Medicine (NLM) that uses the UMLS Metathesaurus for annotating the concepts in a given text. The program is designed to obtain the concept that best fits a particular phrase, finding its origin in an attempt to improve the retrieval of biomedical literature indexed in MEDLINE/PubMed. MetaMap is a program with many strengths, such as the power of linguistic analysis, the high performance setting possibilities and the variety of processing algorithms included. On the other hand, MetaMap shows some weaknesses such as the algorithms developing focused on English grammar texts, or high processing time lapse due to the complexity of the algorithms (not suitable for real-time systems). Metamap analysis time periods goes from less than a minute for short simple text to long hours for complex sentences.

Gimli (Campos et al., 2013) is an open source and high-performance solution for biomedical named entity recognition on scientific documents, supporting the automatic recognition of gene, proteins, DNA, RNA, and cell domain names. This tool implements a machine learning approach based on conditional random fields (CRF).

On the other hand, there exists a more recent concept extraction techniques based on ontologies. Ontologies link concept labels to their interpretations, ie specifications of their meanings including concept definitions and relations to other concepts. Apart from relations such as *isa* and *part-of*, generally present in almost any domain, ontologies also model domain-specific relations, eg *clinically-associated-with* and *has-manifestation* are specific associations for the biomedical domain. Therefore, ontologies reflect the structure of the domain and constrain the potential interpretations of terms. Thus, ontologies can provide rich concept knowledge of domain specific name entities. This is the case of *Open Biomedical Annotator* (*OBA*) (Jonquet et al., 2009), an impressive annotation system using ontologies, which provides online access for users and for other systems as a Web service. There are other examples of utilities for extracting concepts using ontologies (e.g. Terminizer (Hancock et al., 2009), Whatizit (Rebholz-Schuhmann et al., 2008) or Reflect (Pafilis et al., 2009)). However, the magnitude of ontologies and resources integrated under the OBA Web service is difficult to reach by other systems (Whetzel et al., 2011): in three years

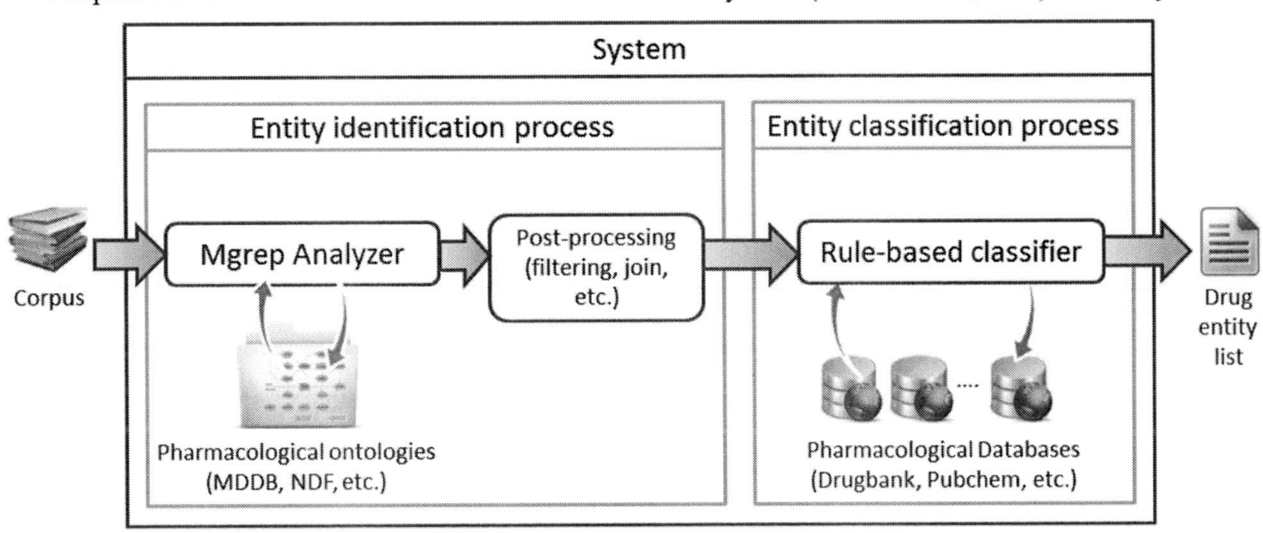

Figure 1: Architecture of the system.

(from 2008 to 2011), they have increased from 72 to 260 biomedical ontologies.

The concept recognition tool used by the OBA system -in order to find ontology concepts matching the terms extracted from texts- is called *Mgrep*. Although Mgrep is not a free tool, some results are presented in (Jonquet et al., 2008). A comparison between Mgrep and MetaMap can also be found in (Shah et al., 2009), where they make an evaluation over a biological and disease terms dictionaries with precision (0.87 to 0.71 respectively) and recall (1548 to 1730 recovered terms respectively) metrics. Thus, we decided to use Mgrep for identifying drug name entities in the system.

3 Description of the system

The system (see figure 1) is divided in two phases: (i) in one hand, the system must scan drug name entities without specifying any further information. This is the so-called entity identification process; (ii) on the other hand, the system classifies by using a rule-based process the type of the entities discovered previously. This is the so-called entity classification process.

The corpus is processed sentence by sentence, using the identification tag provided for each sentence.

3.1 Entity identification process

In this phase we analyze each sentence of the corpus with Mgrep analyzer. This tool allows us to set the ontologies we want to use in the analysis. All additional ontologies used in the analysis increases the computational complexity required.

The ontologies used in this first drug name identification phase belong to UMLS collection, and more specifically to the pharmacological domain:

- Master Drug Data Base[6] (MDDB): National Drug Data File ontology provides a codified drug dictionary, drug vocabulary, and drug pricing for prescription drugs and medication-based over-the-counter products in the United States. It supports the ever-changing world of drug information in healthcare.
- National Drug File[7] (NDF): this ontology contains information about a comprehensive set of drug database elements and clinical information approved by the U.S. Food and Drug Administration (FDA), and dietary supplements information.
- National Drug Data File (NDDF): this is an extension of the NDF ontology that includes chemical ingredients, clinical kinetics, diseases, dose forms, pharmaceutical preparations, physiological effects and

Annotations

TERM filter	ONTOLOGY filter	TYPE filter	CONTEXT
Pharmaceutical Preparations	National Drug File	ancestor	medicine containing kaolin or attapulgite - Ketoconazole - Central
Pharmaceutical Preparations	National Drug File	ancestor	affect the effect of Pirenzepine or whose effects may
Pharmaceutical Preparations	National Drug File	ancestor	Drug Interactions: Pirenzepine may interact with the

Figure 2a: Result of analysis with the Mgrep analyzer.

TERM filter	ONTOLOGY filter	TYPE filter	CONTEXT
Drug Products by Generic Ingredient Combinations	National Drug File	ancestor	Aventyl, Surmontil) - Potassium chloride (e.g., Kay Ciel)
Drug Products by Generic Ingredient Combinations	National Drug File	ancestor	Tofranil, Aventyl, Surmontil) - Potassium chloride (e.g., Kay Ciel)

Figure 2b: Example of multiword drug entity divided.

[6] http://www.medispan.com/medi-span-electronic-drug-file.aspx
[7] http://www.fdbhealth.com/fdb-medknowledge/

therapeutic categories.

- Ontology for Drug Discovery Investigations: this ontology contains information about description of drug discovery investigations from OBO[8] relation ontology.
- MESH Thesaurus[9]: this ontology contains sets of terms naming descriptors in a hierarchical structure. There exist 26,853 descriptors and over 213,000 entry terms in 2013 MeSH.

For each drug name entity identified the Mgrep analyzer provides information about the ontology concept recognized, term information, snippet of original text (see figure 2a). After identifying drug name entities we noticed some errors in the recognized concepts, thus we held a post-processing of the analysis results. Some entities are recognized by several ontologies at the same time, so it is necessary to filter repeated instances.

Biomedical complex name entities are not identified. To solve this, we join compound name entities by following the charoffset of the sentence. The system only links two or more drug entities that were next to each other, without punctuation between them. For example, *potassium chloride* (see figure 2b) is recognized separately in potassium and chloride, so we group it as *potassium chloride* concept.

As a result of this process we obtain a list of clear drug name entities that conforms our run 1 approach in the task. However, we elaborate a second filter based in a gazetteer containing terms with no useful meaning for our drug name entity identification purpose. This gazetteer contains terms such as *agent*, *compound* and *blocker*. The results of this second filter conforms our run 2 approach in the task. As a result of entity identification phase we obtain a list of drug name entities, but they are not identified as any type yet.

3.2 Entity classification process

In this phase we classify the list of pharmaceutical terms obtained from analysis phase. To do so, we elaborate a rule-based system following the annotation methods described in the task guidelines. This annotation method was based in biomedical resources, such as DrugBank, for determining aspects as if the drug entity is approved for human use, or if the drug entity is registered as a brand name. We can organize the general rules of the classification process by resources used:

- DrugBank: These rules search the drug entity in DrugBank resource and obtain several information:
  - Drug information: information about approval state of the drug (*approved*, *experimental*, *illicit*). A rule classifies a drug entity as *drug_n* when *experimental* or *illicit* state is found in a drug, otherwise the drug entity is catalogued as *drug* type.
  - Synonym list: list of possible registered names of the entity. A recursive process searches each synonym in DrugBank (obviating the synonym list this time), and applies the rules as if original drug entity were treated. The result of the recursive process affect to the original drug entity.
  - Brand name list: list of registered commercial brand names of the entity. If a drug name entity is found in the brand name list, then it is catalogued as a *brand* type.
  - Categories: information about general category of drug. If the drug is found as a category, then it is classified as *group* type.
- Pubchem: These rules search the drug entity and obtain information of drug identification and compound information and IUPAC name.
- ATC Index[10]: These rules look for the drug entity in ATC Index resource and determine whether the entity is *drug* or *group* depending on the level of ATC code found.
- Kegg: These rules search the drug entity in this resource and obtain information of drug categories. If the drug is found as a category, then it is classified as *group* type.
- MeSH[11]: These rules search information about MeSH tree categories classification of the drug entity. If the drug is found as a category, then it is classified as *group* type. Another rule makes a naïve processing of the MeSH

[8] http://www.obofoundry.org/ro/
[9] http://www.nlm.nih.gov/pubs/factsheets/mesh.html
[10] http://www.whocc.no/atc_ddd_index/
[11] http://www.ncbi.nlm.nih.gov/mesh/67055162

description text to evaluate if the drug entity were used in humans. If this information is found in the text, then the drug entity is classified as a *drug* type.

The described rules are representative examples of the complete rule-based system. There were assigned priorities to the rules, since some rules are more certain to describe a drug type than others. Thus, if a drug entity is found to be approved for using in humans after processing the MeSH text, but when looking the DrugBank state is found as illicit state, then the drug is classified as *drug_n* type since DrugBank offers a certain state of the drug, instead of a natural text description that may be classified as a false positive. Depending on the values collected on these biomedical resources the rule-based system determines whether the type of an entity is a *drug*, *group*, *brand* or *drug_n*.

4 Results

The best result in entity identification (exact matching) obtained by the system correspond to run 2, achieving a F1 measure of 0.609. On the other hand, the best results achieved in strict matching (boundary and type evaluation) correspond to run 2 again, with 0.529 F1 score.

Team	Partial matching			Exact matching			Strict matching		
	P	R	F1	P	R	F1	P	R	F1
Run 1	0.502	0.7	0.585	0.454	0.633	0.528	0.393	0.548	0.458
Run 2	0.653	0.685	**0.669**	0.594	0.624	**0.609**	0.517	0.542	**0.529**

Table 1: Results obtained by the system.

These results contrast with the result obtained by run 1, achieving a F1 measure of 0.528 and 0.458 in entity identification and strict matching evaluation respectively. Thus we can quantify the advantage of using a filter based on gazetteer in an average increment of 0.079 F1 measure.

We have noticed that the higher results are obtained in partial matching evaluation because of the relaxed conditions of the charoffset. This seems reasonable since complex multiword entity is hard to parse and define an exact charoffset.

On the other hand, we also noticed that evaluating the classification of the type decrement the best results obtained by the system from 0.609 to 0.529 of F1 score. This indicates that there is still a lot of improvement work in the rule-based system for type classification. A little error analysis was done in a set of 10 documents of the training dataset. The results show errors in conflictive entities that show multiples categories in DrugBank resource. Thus, for example *cocaine* drug entity contains tags of *illicit* and *approved* in DrugBank database, so the system classify this entity as *drug_n* instead of *drug*.

5 Conclusions and future work

In this paper we present a system for drug name entity recognition based on ontologies as participation for "Semeval 2013: Recognition and classification of drug names" task. The system is based on integration of biomedical resources for identification and classification of pharmacological entities. The best result of the system obtained an F1 measure of 0.529.

The usage of ontologies in named entity recognition task seems to be a good choice since we can select specific ontologies. A possible future work includes an improvement of rule-based system, including a bigger collection of biomedical resources. The entity classification could increase the results by creating an hybrid approach between rule-based methods and machine learning techniques. On the other hand, in the entities identification task, the system could include other biomedical text analyzers and establish a vote system. This would improve whether we consider an entity or not. Finally, in error analysis were noticed problems related to rule-based module. Therefore, an insightful improve could pass through making a context analysis in order to clear the ambiguity surrounding the drug entity.

Acknowledgments

This work has been funded by MA2VICMR project (S2009/TIC-1542) and MULTIMEDICA project[12] (TIN 2010-20644-C03-01).

References

[12] http://labda.inf.uc3m.es/multimedica/

Aronson, A.R. 2001. *Effective mapping of biomedical text to the UMLS Metathesaurus: the MetaMap program.*Proc AMIA Symp. 17–21.4.

Campos, D., Matos, S., Oliveira J.L.. 2013. *Gimli: open source and high-performance biomedical name recognition.* BMC Bioinformatics 14:54.

Hancock, D., Morrison N., Velarde G., Field D. 2009. *Terminizer - Assisting Mark-Up of Text Using Ontological Terms.* Nature Precedings.

Jonquet C., Musen M.A., Shah N. 2008. *A System for Ontology-Based Annotation of Biomedical Data.* Data Integration in the Life Sciences, Springer Berlin Heidelberg, Berlin, Heidelberg, pp. 144–152.

Jonquet, C., Shah N.H., Musen M.A. 2009. *The Open Biomedical Annotator,* Summit on Translat Bioinforma. 56–60.

Pafilis E., O'Donoghue S.I., Jensen L.J., Horn H., Kuhn M., Brown N.P., et al. 2009. *Reflect: augmented browsing for the life scientist.* Nature Biotechnology, 27, 508–510.

Rebholz-Schuhmann D., Arregui M., Gaudan S., Kirsch H., Jimeno A. 2008. *Text processing through Web services: calling Whatizit.* Bioinformatics. 24, 296–298.

Segura-Bedmar I., Martínez P., Herrero-Zazo M. 2013. *SemEval-2013 Task 9 : Extraction of Drug-Drug Interactions from Biomedical Texts (DDIExtraction 2013).* Proceedings of Semeval 2013.

Shah N.H., Bhatia N., Jonquet C., Rubin D., Chiang A.P., Musen M.A. 2009. *Comparison of concept recognizers for building the Open Biomedical Annotator.* BMC Bioinformatics.10, S14.

Whetzel P.L., Noy N.F., Shah N.H., Alexander P.R., Nyulas C., Tudorache T., et al. 2011. *BioPortal: enhanced functionality via new Web services from the National Center for Biomedical Ontology to access and use ontologies in software applications.* Nucleic Acids Research. 39, W541–W545.

WBI-DDI: Drug-Drug Interaction Extraction using Majority Voting

Philippe Thomas **Mariana Neves** **Tim Rocktäschel** **Ulf Leser**
Humboldt-Universität zu Berlin
Knowledge Management in Bioinformatics
Unter den Linden 6
Berlin, 10099, Germany
{thomas,neves,trocktae,leser}@informatik.hu-berlin.de

Abstract

This work describes the participation of the WBI-DDI team on the SemEval 2013 – Task 9.2 DDI extraction challenge. The task consisted of extracting interactions between pairs of drugs from two collections of documents (DrugBank and MEDLINE) and their classification into four subtypes: advise, effect, mechanism, and int. We developed a two-step approach in which pairs are initially extracted using ensembles of up to five different classifiers and then relabeled to one of the four categories. Our approach achieved the second rank in the DDI competition. For interaction detection we achieved F_1 measures ranging from 73 % to almost 76 % depending on the run. These results are on par or even higher than the performance estimation on the training dataset. When considering the four interaction subtypes we achieved an F_1 measure of 60.9 %.

1 Introduction

A drug-drug interaction (DDI) can be described as interplay between drugs taken during joint administration. DDIs usually lead to an increase or decrease in drug effects when compared to isolated treatment. For instance, sildenafil (Viagra) in combination with nitrates can cause a potentially live-threatening decrease in blood pressure (Cheitlin et al., 1999). It is therefore crucial to consider potential DDI effects when co-administering drugs to patients. As the level of medication generally is raising all over the world, the potential risk of unwanted side effects, such as DDIs, is constantly increasing (Haider et al., 2007).

Only a fraction of knowledge about DDIs is contained in specialized databases such as DrugBank (Knox et al., 2011). These structured knowledge bases are often the primary resource of information for researchers. However, the majority of new DDI findings are still initially reported in scientific publications, which results in the situation that structured knowledge bases lag behind recently published research results. Thus, there is an urgent need for researchers and database curators to cope with the fast growth of biomedical literature (Hunter and Cohen, 2006).

The SemEval 2013 – Task 9.2 (Extraction of Drug-Drug Interactions from BioMedical Texts) is a competitive evaluation of methods for extracting mentions of drug-drug interactions from texts (Segura-Bedmar et al., 2013). For training, the organizers provide a corpus annotated with drug-names and interactions between them. This corpus is composed of 572 articles collected from DrugBank and 142 PubMed abstracts. Interactions are binary (always between two drugs) and undirected, as target and agent roles are not annotated. Furthermore, the two interacting drugs are always mentioned within the same sentence. In contrast to the previous DDI-challenge 2011 (Segura-Bedmar et al., 2011), four different DDI-subtypes (advise, effect, mechanism, and int) have been introduced. Details about the four subclasses can be found in the task's annotation guideline.

*Second Joint Conference on Lexical and Computational Semantics (*SEM), Volume 2: Seventh International Workshop on Semantic Evaluation (SemEval 2013)*, pages 628–635, Atlanta, Georgia, June 14-15, 2013. ©2013 Association for Computational Linguistics

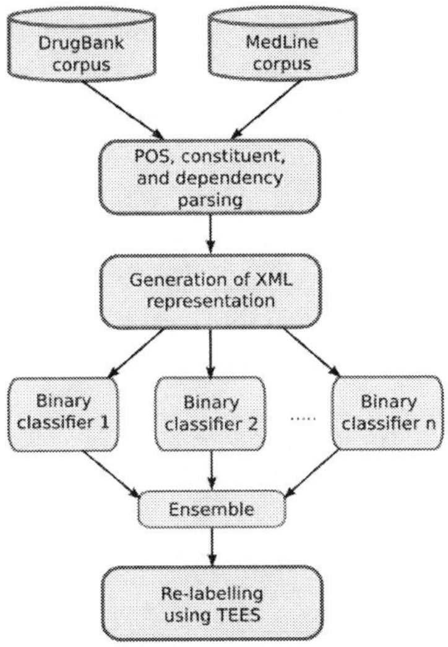

Figure 1: Workflow developed for the SemEval 2013 Task 9.2 challenge.

2 Methods

Binary relationship extraction is often tackled as a pair-wise classification problem, where all $\binom{n}{2}$ co-occurring entities in a sentence are classified as interacting or not. To account for the four different subtypes of DDIs, the problem definition could be translated into a multiclass classification problem between all co-occurring entities.

Contrary to that, we propose a two step strategy: First, we detect general drug-drug interactions regardless of subtype using a multitude of different machine-learning methods. The output of these methods is aggregated using a majority voting approach. Second, detected interactions are reclassified into one of the four possible DDI categories. The latter is referred to as DDI relabeling throughout this paper. A detailed view on the proposed workflow is depicted in Figure 1.

2.1 Preprocessing

Sentences have been parsed using Charniak-Johnson PCFG reranking-parser (Charniak and Johnson, 2005) with a self-trained re-ranking model augmented for biomedical texts (McClosky, 2010). Resulting constituent parse trees have been converted into dependency graphs using the Stanford converter (De Marneffe et al., 2006). In the last step, we created an augmented XML using the open source framework from Tikk et al. (2010). This XML file encompasses tokens with respective part-of-speech tags, constituent parse tree, and dependency parse tree information. This format has been subsequently transformed into a related XML format[1] used by two of the utilized classifiers. Properties of the training corpus are shown for DrugBank and MEDLINE in Table 1.

Corpus	Sentences	Pairs		
		Positive	Negative	Total
DrugBank	5,675	3,788	22,217	26,005
MEDLINE	1,301	232	1,555	1,787

Table 1: Basic statistics of the DDI training corpus shown for DrugBank and MEDLINE separately.

2.2 Machine Learning Methods

Tikk et al. (2010) systematically analyzed nine different machine learning approaches for the extraction of undirected binary protein-protein interactions. This framework has been successfully applied to other domains, such as the I2B2 relation extraction challenge (Solt et al., 2010), the previous DDI extraction challenge (Thomas et al., 2011), and to the extraction of neuroanatomical connectivity statements (French et al., 2012).

Drug entities are blinded by replacing the entity name with a generic string to ensure the generality of the approach. Without entity blinding drug names are incorporated as features, which clearly affects generalization capabilities of a classifier on unseen entity mentions (Pyysalo et al., 2008).

We decided to use the following methods provided by the framework: All-paths graph (APG) (Airola et al., 2008), shallow linguistic (SL) (Giuliano et al., 2006), subtree (ST) (Vishwanathan and Smola, 2002), subset tree (SST) (Collins and Duffy, 2001), and spectrum tree (SpT) (Kuboyama et al., 2007) method. The SL method uses only shallow linguistic features, *i.e.*, token, stem, part-of-speech tag and morphologic properties of the surrounding words. APG builds a classifier using surface features and a weighting

[1] `https://github.com/jbjorne/TEES/wiki/Interaction-XML`

scheme for dependency parse tree features. The remaining three classifier (ST, SST, and SpT) build kernel functions based on different subtree representations on the constituent parse tree. To calculate the constituent–tree kernels ST and SST we used the SVM-LIGHT-TK toolkit (Moschitti, 2006). Before applying these methods, constituent parse trees have been reduced to the shortest-enclosed parse following the recommendations from Zhang et al. (2006). For a more detailed description of the different methods we refer to the original publications.

In addition to the PPI framework, we also employed the general purpose relationship extraction tool "Turku Event Extraction System" (TEES) (Björne et al., 2011), a customized version of the case-based reasoning system Moara (Neves et al., 2009), and a self-developed feature based classifier which is referred to as SLW. Regarding TEES, we have used the edge extraction functionality for performing relationship extraction. TEES considers features related to the tokens (*e.g.*, part-of-speech tags), dependency chains, dependency path N-grams, entities (*e.g.*, entity types) and external resources, such as hypernyms in WordNet.

Moara is a case-based reasoning system for the extraction of relationships and events. During training, interaction pairs are converted into cases and saved into a HyperSQL database which are retrieved through case similarity during the classification. Cases are composed by the following features: the type of the entities (*e.g.* `Brand` and `Group`), the part-of-speech tag of the tokens between the two drugs (inclusive), the tags of the shortest dependency path between the two drugs, and the lemma of the non-entity tokens of the shortest dependency path using BioLemmatizer (Liu et al., 2012). We also consider the PHARE ontology (Coulet et al., 2011) in the lemma feature: When a lemma matches any of the synonyms contained in this ontology, the category of the respective term is considered instead. Case similarity is calculated by exact feature matching, except for the part-of-speech tags whose comparison is based on global alignment using insertion, deletion, and substitution costs as proposed by Spasic et al. (2005).

SLW is inspired by SL (Giuliano et al., 2006; Bunescu and Mooney, 2006) and uses the Breeze[2] library. We generate n-grams over sequences of arbitrary features (*e.g.* POS-tags, morphological and syntactical features) to describe the global context of an entity pair. Furthermore, we calculate features from the local context of entities, but in addition to SL, we include domain-specific features used for identifying and classifying pharmacological substances (see our paper for DDI Task 9.1 (Rocktäschel et al., 2013)). In addition, we take the name of the classes of a pair's two entities as feature to capture that entities of some class (*e.g.* `Brand` and `Group`) are more likely to interact than others (*e.g.* `Brand` and `Brand`).

2.3 Ensemble learning

Several community competitions previously noted that combinations of predictions from different tools help to achieve better results than one method alone (Kim et al., 2009; Leitner et al., 2010). More importantly, it is well known that ensembles increase robustness by decreasing the risk of selecting a bad classifier (Polikar, 2006). In this work we combined the output of several classifiers by using majority voting. The ensemble is used to predict DDIs regardless of the four different subtypes. This complies with the partial match evaluation criterion defined by the competition organizers.

2.4 Relabeling

To account for DDI subtypes, we compared two approaches: (a) using the subtype prediction of TEES; (b) training a multi-class classifier (SLW) on the available training data for DDI subtypes. We decided on using TEES, as it generated superior results over SLW (data not shown). Thus, previously identified DDIs are relabeled into one of the four possible subtypes using the most likely interaction subtype from TEES.

3 Results

3.1 Cross validation

In order to compare the different approaches, we performed document-wise 10-fold cross validation (CV) on the training set. It has been shown that such

[2] `http://www.scalanlp.org/`

Type	Pairs	Precision	Recall	F_1
total	3,119	78.6	78.6	78.6
effect	1,633	79.8	79.1	79.4
mechanism	1,319	79.8	79.2	79.4
advise	826	77.3	76.4	76.9
int	188	68.5	80.9	74.1

Table 4: Performance estimation for relabeling DDIs. Pairs denotes the number of instances of this type in the training corpus.

a setting provides more realistic performance estimates than instance-wise CV (Sætre et al., 2008). All approaches have been tested using the same splits to ensure comparability. For APG, ST, SST, and SpT we followed the parameter optimization strategy defined by Tikk et al. (2010). For TEES and Moara, we used the cost parameter C (50000) and best performing features, respectively, based on the CV results. For SL and SLW, we used the default parameters.

We performed several different CV experiments: First, we performed CV on the two corpora (DrugBank and MEDLINE) separately. Second, data from the other corpus has been additionally used during the training phase. This allows us to estimate the impact of additional, but potentially different text. CV results for DrugBank and MEDLINE are shown in Table 2 and 3 respectively.

3.2 Relabeling

Performance of relabeling is evaluated by performing 10-fold CV on the training set using the same splits as in previous analysis. Note that this experiment is solely performed on positive DDI instances to estimate separability of the four different DDI-subtypes. Results for relabeling are shown in Table 4.

3.3 Test dataset

For the test set we submitted results using the following three majority voting ensembles. For Run 1 we used Moara+SL+TEES, for Run 2 we used APG+Moara+SL+SLW+TEES and for Run 3 we used SL+SLW+TEES. Due to time constraints we did not use different ensembles for the two corpora. We rather decided to use ensembles which achieved generally good results for both training corpora. All classifiers, except APG, have been retrained on the combination of MEDLINE and DrugBank using the parameter setting yielding the highest F_1 in the training phase. For APG, we trained two different models: One model is trained on MEDLINE and DrugBank and one model is trained on DrugBank solely. The first model is applied on the MEDLINE test set and the latter on the DrugBank test set. Estimated results on the training corpus and official results on the test corpus are shown in Table 5.

4 Discussion

4.1 Training dataset

Document-wise CV results for the DrugBank corpus show no clear effect when using MEDLINE as additional training data. By using MEDLINE during the training phase we observe an average decrease of 0.3 percentage points (pp) in F_1 and an average increase of 0.7 pp in area under the receiver operating characteristic curve (AUC). The strongest impact can be observed for APG with a decrease of 2.3 pp in F_1. We therefore decided to train APG models for DrugBank without additional MEDLINE data. For almost all ensembles (with the exception of APG+SpT+SL) we observe superior results when using only DrugBank as training data. Interestingly, this effect can mostly be attributed to an average increase of 3.3 pp in recall, whereas precision remains fairly stable between ensembles using DrugBank solely and those with additional training data.

In contrast for MEDLINE, all methods largely benefit from additional training data with an average increase of 9.8 pp and 3.6 pp for F_1 and AUC respectively. For the ensemble based approaches, we observe an average increase of 13.8 pp for F_1 when using DrugBank data in addition.

When ranking the different methods by F_1 and calculating correlation between the two different corpora, we observe only a weak correlation (Kendall's $\tau = 0.286$, p$<$ 1). In other words, machine learning methods show varying performance-ranks between the two corpora. This difference is most pronounced for SL and SpT, with four ranks difference between DrugBank and MEDLINE. It is noteworthy that the two corpora are not directly

Method	Regular CV				Combined CV			
	P	R	F_1	AUC	P	R	F_1	AUC
SL	61.5	79.0	69.1	92.8	62.1	78.4	**69.2**	93.0
APG	77.2	62.6	**69.0**	91.5	75.9	59.8	66.7	91.6
TEES	77.2	62.0	**68.6**	87.3	75.5	60.9	67.3	86.9
SLW	73.7	60.0	65.9	91.3	73.4	61.2	**66.6**	91.3
Moara	72.1	55.2	**62.5**	—	72.0	54.7	62.1	—
SpT	51.4	73.4	60.3	87.3	52.7	71.4	**60.6**	87.7
SST	51.9	61.2	**56.0**	85.4	55.1	57.1	**56.0**	86.1
ST	47.3	64.2	54.2	82.3	48.3	64.3	**54.9**	82.7
SL+SLW+TEES	76.1	69.9	**72.7**	—	75.9	65.3	70.1	—
APG+SL+TEES	79.3	69.9	**74.2**	—	79.2	65.4	71.5	—
Moara+SL+TEES	79.9	69.6	**74.2**	—	79.6	65.1	71.6	—
Moara+SL+APG	81.4	70.6	**75.5**	—	81.3	70.3	75.3	—
APG+Moara+SL+SLW+TEES	84.0	68.1	**75.1**	—	83.7	64.2	72.6	—
APG+SpT+TEES	76.8	68.0	**72.1**	—	77.1	63.4	69.6	—
APG+SpT+SL	68.7	74.8	71.5	—	69.7	73.8	**71.6**	—

Table 2: Cross validation results on DrugBank corpus. Regular CV is training and evaluation on DrugBank only. Combined CV is training on DrugBank and MEDLINE and testing on DrugBank. Higher F_1 between these two settings are indicated in boldface for each method. Single methods are ranked by F_1.

Method	Regular CV				Combined CV			
	P	R	F_1	AUC	P	R	F_1	AUC
TEES	70.7	36.0	44.5	82.2	59.6	46.5	**51.4**	84.9
SpT	37.8	38.6	34.6	78.6	42.3	55.3	**47.1**	80.4
APG	46.5	44.3	42.4	82.3	38.1	62.2	**46.4**	82.8
SST	31.3	37.7	31.8	74.1	36.7	61.7	**44.9**	79.5
SL	43.7	40.1	38.7	78.9	34.7	67.1	**44.7**	81.1
SLW	58.0	14.3	20.4	73.4	50.1	38.0	**42.0**	82.4
Moara	49.8	31.9	37.6	—	45.6	43.2	**41.9**	—
ST	25.2	43.8	30.1	70.5	36.1	48.3	**39.8**	74.2
SL+SLW+TEES	73.6	29.0	37.6	—	55.2	52.7	**53.1**	—
APG+SL+TEES	60.7	37.9	43.4	—	49.9	62.4	**54.3**	—
Moara+SL+TEES	68.0	33.0	42.2	—	62.1	55.5	**57.4**	—
Moara+SL+APG	57.7	36.7	42.4	—	48.3	60.9	**52.8**	—
APG+Moara+SL+SLW+TEES	73.3	28.3	36.8	—	60.6	54.4	**56.5**	—
APG+SpT+TEES	58.5	37.4	41.7	—	57.5	59.2	**57.1**	—
APG+SpT+SL	48.3	39.9	40.0	—	43.6	64.3	**51.0**	—

Table 3: Cross validation results on MEDLINE corpus. Regular CV is training and evaluation on MEDLINE only. Combined CV is training on DrugBank and MEDLINE and testing on MEDLINE. Higher F_1 between these two settings are indicated in boldface for each method. Single methods are ranked by F_1.

Evaluation	Training									Test								
	Run 1			Run 2			Run 3			Run 1			Run 2			Run 3		
	P	R	F_1	P	R	F_1	P	R	F_1	P	R	F_1	P	R	F_1	P	R	F_1
Partial	78.7	67.3	72.6	82.9	66.4	73.7	75.2	67.6	71.2	84.1	65.4	73.6	86.1	65.7	74.5	80.1	72.2	75.9
Strict	65.7	56.1	60.5	70.0	56.0	62.2	63.0	56.7	59.7	68.5	53.2	59.9	69.5	53.0	60.1	64.2	57.9	60.9
-mechanism	61.8	49.7	55.1	68.1	50.0	57.7	59.2	50.3	54.4	72.2	51.7	60.2	74.9	52.3	61.6	65.3	58.6	61.8
-effect	68.8	57.9	62.9	71.8	57.6	63.9	66.1	57.4	61.5	63.7	57.5	60.4	63.6	55.8	59.5	60.7	61.4	61.0
-advise	64.6	60.5	62.5	68.2	59.7	63.6	61.1	61.5	61.3	73.3	53.4	61.8	74.5	55.7	63.7	69.0	58.4	63.2
-int	68.6	50.0	57.8	75.4	52.1	61.6	70.9	56.9	63.1	67.8	41.7	51.6	67.3	38.5	49.0	67.8	41.7	51.6

Table 5: Relation extraction results on the training and test set. Run 1 builds a majority voting on Moara+SL+TEES, Run 2 on APG+Moara+SL+SLW+TEES, and Run 3 on SL+SLW+TEES. Partial characterizes only DDI detection without classification of subtypes, whereas strict requires correct identification of subtypes as well.

comparable, as DrugBank is one order of magnitude larger in terms of instances than the MEDLINE corpus. Additionally, documents come from different sources and it is tempting to speculate that there might be a certain amount of domain specificity between DrugBank and MEDLINE sentences.

We tested for domain specificity by performing cross-corpus experiments, *i.e.*, we trained a classifier on DrugBank, applied it on MEDLINE and *vice versa*. When training on MEDLINE and testing on DrugBank, we observe an average decrease of about 15 pp in F_1 in comparison to DrugBank in-domain CV results. For the other setting, we observe a lower decrease of approximately 5 pp in comparison to MEDLINE in-domain CV results.

From the current results, it seems that the documents from DrugBank and MEDLINE have different syntactic properties. However, this requires a more detailed analysis of different aspects like distribution of sentence length, negations, or passives between the two corpora (Cohen et al., 2010; Tikk et al., 2013). We assume that transfer learning techniques could improve results on both corpora (Pan and Yang, 2010).

The DDI-relabeling capability of TEES is very balanced with F_1 measures ranging from 74.1 % to 79.4 % for all four DDI subclasses. This is unexpected since classes like "effect" occur almost ten times more often than classes like "int" and classifiers often have problems with predicting minority classes.

4.2 Test dataset

On the test set, our best run achieves an F_1 of 76 % using the partial evaluation schema. This is slightly better than the performance for DrugBank training data shown in Table 2 and substantially better than estimations for MEDLINE (see Table 3). With F_1 measures ranging between 74 % to 76 % only minor performance differences can be observed between the three different ensembles.

When switching from partial to strict evaluation scheme an average decrease of 15 pp in F_1 can be observed. As estimated on the training data, relabeling performance is indeed very similar for the different DDI-subtypes. Only for the class with the least instances (*int*), a larger decrease in comparison to the other three classes can be observed for the test set. In general, results for test set are on par or higher than results for the training set.

5 Conclusion

In this paper we presented our approach for the SemEval 2013 – Task 9.2 DDI extraction challenge. Our strategy builds on a cascaded (coarse to fine grained) classification strategy, where a majority voting ensemble of different methods is initially used to find generic DDIs. Predicted interactions are subsequently relabeled into four different subtypes. DDI extraction seems to be a more difficult task for MEDLINE abstracts than for DrugBank articles. In our opinion, this cannot be fully attributed to the slightly higher ratio of positive instances in DrugBank and points towards structural differences between the two corpora.

Acknowledgments

This work was supported by the German Research Foundation (DFG) [LE 1428/3-1] and the Federal

Ministry of Economics and Technology (BMWi) [KF 2205209MS2].

References

A. Airola, S. Pyysalo, J. Björne, T. Pahikkala, F. Ginter, and T. Salakoski. 2008. All-paths graph kernel for protein-protein interaction extraction with evaluation of cross-corpus learning. *BMC Bioinformatics*, 9 Suppl 11:S2.

J. Björne, J. Heimonen, F. Ginter, A. Airola, T. Pahikkala, and T. Salakoski. 2011. Extracting Contextualized Complex Biological Events with Rich Graph-Based Features Sets. *Computational Intelligence*, 27(4):541–557.

R. C. Bunescu and R. J. Mooney. 2006. Subsequence Kernels for Relation Extraction. *Advances in Neural Information Processing Systems*, 18:171.

E. Charniak and M. Johnson. 2005. Coarse-to-Fine n-Best Parsing and MaxEnt Discriminative Reranking. In *Proc. of ACL'05*, pages 173–180.

M. D. Cheitlin, A. M. Hutter, R. G. Brindis, P. Ganz, S. Kaul, R. O. Russell, and R. M. Zusman. 1999. Use of sildenafil (viagra) in patients with cardiovascular disease. *J Am Coll Cardiol*, 33(1):273–282.

K. Cohen, Helen L Johnson, Karin Verspoor, Christophe Roeder, and Lawrence E Hunter. 2010. The structural and content aspects of abstracts versus bodies of full text journal articles are different. *BMC Bioinformatics*, 11:492.

M. Collins and N. Duffy. 2001. Convolution Kernels for Natural Language. In *Proc. of NIPS'01*, pages 625–632.

A. Coulet, Y. Garten, M. Dumontier, R. Altman, M. Musen, and N. Shah. 2011. Integration and publication of heterogeneous text-mined relationships on the semantic web. *Journal of Biomedical Semantics*, 2(Suppl 2):S10.

M.C. De Marneffe, B. MacCartney, and C.D. Manning. 2006. Generating typed dependency parses from phrase structure parses. In *Proc. of LREC 2006*, pages 449–454.

L. French, S. Lane, L. Xu, C. Siu, C. Kwok, Y. Chen, C. Krebs, and P. Pavlidis. 2012. Application and evaluation of automated methods to extract neuroanatomical connectivity statements from free text. *Bioinformatics*, 28(22):2963–2970.

C. Giuliano, A. Lavelli, and L. Romano. 2006. Exploiting Shallow Linguistic Information for Relation Extraction from Biomedical Literature. In *Proc. of EACL'06*, pages 401–408.

S. I. Haider, K. Johnell, M. Thorslund, and J. Fastbom. 2007. Trends in polypharmacy and potential drug-drug interactions across educational groups in elderly patients in Sweden for the period 1992 - 2002. *Int J Clin Pharmacol Ther*, 45(12):643–653.

L. Hunter and K. Cohen. 2006. Biomedical language processing: what's beyond PubMed? *Mol Cell*, 21(5):589–594.

J.D. Kim, T. Ohta, S. Pyysalo, Y. Kano, and J. Tsujii. 2009. Overview of BioNLP'09 shared task on event extraction. In *Proc. of BioNLP'09*, pages 1–9.

C. Knox, V. Law, T. Jewison, P. Liu, S. Ly, A. Frolkis, A. Pon, K. Banco, C. Mak, V. Neveu, Y. Djoumbou, R. Eisner, A. Chi Guo, and D. S Wishart. 2011. Drugbank 3.0: a comprehensive resource for 'omics' research on drugs. *Nucleic Acids Res*, 39(Database issue):D1035–D1041.

T. Kuboyama, K. Hirata, H. Kashima, K. F. Aoki-Kinoshita, and H. Yasuda. 2007. A Spectrum Tree Kernel. *Information and Media Technologies*, 2(1):292–299.

F. Leitner, S.A. Mardis, M. Krallinger, G. Cesareni, L.A. Hirschman, and A. Valencia. 2010. An overview of BioCreative II. 5. *IEEE IEEE/ACM Transactions on Computational Biology and Bioinformatics*, pages 385–399.

H. Liu, T. Christiansen, W. Baumgartner, and K. Verspoor. 2012. Biolemmatizer: a lemmatization tool for morphological processing of biomedical text. *Journal of Biomedical Semantics*, 3(1):3.

D. McClosky. 2010. *Any Domain Parsing: Automatic Domain Adaptation for Natural Language Parsing*. Ph.D. thesis, Brown University.

A. Moschitti. 2006. Efficient Convolution Kernels for Dependency and Constituent Syntactic Trees. In *Proc. of ECML'06*, pages 318–329.

M. Neves, J.-M. Carazo, and A. Pascual-Montano. 2009. Extraction of biomedical events using case-based reasoning. In *Proc. of BioNLP'09*, pages 68–76.

S. J. Pan and Q. Yang. 2010. A Survey on Transfer

Learning. *IEEE Transactions on Knowledge and Data Engineering*, 22(10):1345–1359.

R. Polikar. 2006. Ensemble Based Systems in Decision Making. *IEEE Circuits and Systems Magazine*, 6(3):21–45.

S. Pyysalo, R. Sætre, J. Tsujii, and T. Salakoski. 2008. Why Biomedical Relation Extraction Results are Incomparable and What to do about it. In *Proc. of SMBM'08*, pages 149–152.

T. Rocktäschel, T. Huber, M. Weidlich, and U. Leser. 2013. WBI-NER: The impact of domain-specific features on the performance of identifying and classifying mentions of drugs. In *Proceedings of the 7th International Workshop on Semantic Evaluation (SemEval 2013)*.

R. Sætre, K. Sagae, and J. Tsujii. 2008. Syntactic features for protein-protein interaction extraction. In *Proc. of LBM'07*.

I. Segura-Bedmar, P. Martínez, and M. Herrero-Zazo. 2013. Semeval-2013 task 9: Extraction of drug-drug interactions from biomedical texts. In *Proc. of the 7th International Workshop on Semantic Evaluation (SemEval 2013)*.

I. Segura-Bedmar, P. Martínez, and D. Sanchez-Cisneros. 2011. The 1st ddiextraction-2011 challenge task: Extraction of drug-drug interactions from biomedical text. In *Proc. of the 1st Challenge Task on Drug-Drug Interaction Extraction 2011*, pages 1–9.

I. Solt, F. P. Szidarovszky, and D. Tikk. 2010. Concept, Assertion and Relation Extraction at the 2010 i2b2 Relation Extraction Challenge using parsing information and dictionaries. In *Proc. of i2b2/VA Shared-Task*.

I. Spasic, S. Ananiadou, and J. Tsujii. 2005. MaSTerClass: a case-based reasoning system for the classification of biomedical terms. *Bioinformatics*, 21(11):2748–2758.

P. Thomas, M. Neves, I. Solt, D. Tikk, and U. Leser. 2011. Relation extraction for drug-drug interactions using ensemble learning. In *Proc. of the 1st Challenge Task on Drug-Drug Interaction Extraction 2011*, pages 11–18.

D. Tikk, I. Solt, P. Thomas, and U. Leser. 2013. A detailed error analysis of 13 kernel methods for protein-protein interaction extraction. *BMC Bioinformatics*, 14(1):12.

D. Tikk, P. Thomas, P. Palaga, J. Hakenberg, and U. Leser. 2010. A comprehensive benchmark of kernel methods to extract protein-protein interactions from literature. *PLoS Comput Biol*, 6.

S. V. N. Vishwanathan and A. J. Smola. 2002. Fast Kernels for String and Tree Matching. In *Proc. of NIPS'02*, pages 569–576.

M. Zhang, J. Zhang, J. Su, and G. Zhou. 2006. A Composite Kernel to Extract Relations between Entities with Both Flat and Structured Features. In *Proc. of ICML'06*, pages 825–832.

UMCC_DLSI: Semantic and Lexical features for detection and classification Drugs in biomedical texts

Armando Collazo, Alberto Ceballo, Dennys D. Puig, Yoan Gutiérrez, José I. Abreu, Roger Pérez
DI, University of Matanzas
Autopista a Varadero km 3 ½
Matanzas, Cuba
{armando.collazo, dennys.puig, yoan.gutierrez, jose.abreu, roger.perez}@umcc.cu, alberto.ceballo@infonet.umcc.cu

Antonio Fernández Orquín, Andrés Montoyo, Rafael Muñoz
DLSI, University of Alicante
Carretera de San Vicente
S/N Alicante, Spain
antonybr@yahoo.com, {montoyo, rafael}@dlsi.ua.es

Franc Camara
Independent Consultant
USA
info@franccamara.com

Abstract

In this paper we describe UMCC_DLSI-(DDI) system which attempts to detect and classify drug entities in biomedical texts. We discuss the use of semantic class and words relevant domain, extracted with ISR-WN (Integration of Semantic Resources based on WordNet) resource to obtain our goal. Following this approach our system obtained an F-Measure of 27.5% in the DDIExtraction 2013 (SemEval 2013 task 9).

1. Introduction

To understand biological processes, we must clarify how some substances interact with our body and one to each other. One of these important relations is the drug-drug interactions (DDIs). They occur when one drug interacts with another or when it affects the level, or activity of another drug. DDIs can change the way medications act in the body, they can cause powerful, dangerous and unexpected side effects, and also they can make the medications less effective.

As suggested by (Segura-Bedmar *et al.*, 2011), *"...the detection of DDI is an important research area in patient safety since these interactions can become very dangerous and increase health care costs"*. More recent studies (Percha and Altman, 2013) reports that "*...Recent estimates indicate that DDIs cause nearly 74000 emergency room visits and 195000 hospitalizations each year in the USA*".

But, on the other hand, there is an expansion in the volume of published biomedical research, and therefore the underlying biomedical knowledge base (Cohen and Hersh, 2005). Unfortunately, as often happens, this information is unstructured or in the best case scenario semi-structured.

As we can see in (Tari *et al.*, 2010), "*Clinical support tools often provide comprehensive lists of DDIs, but they usually lack the supporting scientific evidences and different tools can return inconsistent results*".

Although, as mentioned (Segura-Bedmar *et al.*, 2011) "*there are different databases supporting healthcare professionals in the detection of DDI, these databases are rarely complete, since their update periods can reach up to three years*". In addition to these and other difficulties, the great amount of drug interactions are frequently reported in journals of clinical pharmacology and technical reports, due to this fact, medical literature becomes most effective source for detection of DDI. Thereby, the management of DDI is a critical issue due to the overwhelming amount of information available on them (Segura-Bedmar *et al.*, 2011).

*Second Joint Conference on Lexical and Computational Semantics (*SEM), Volume 2: Seventh International Workshop on Semantic Evaluation (SemEval 2013)*, pages 636–643, Atlanta, Georgia, June 14-15, 2013. ©2013 Association for Computational Linguistics

1.1. Task Description

With the aim of reducing the time the health care professionals invest on reviewing the literature, we present a feature-based system for drug detection and classification in biomedical texts.

The DDIExtraction2013 task was divided into two subtasks: Recognition and classification of drug names (Task 9.1) and Extraction of drug-drug interactions (Task 9.2). Our system was developed to be presented in the Task 9.1. In this case, participants were to detect and classify the drugs that were present in the test data set which was a set of sentences related to the biomedical domain obtained from a segmented corpus. The output consisted of a list mentioning all the detected drugs with information concerning the sentence it was detected from as well as its offset in that sentence (the position of the first and the last character of the drug in the sentence, 0 being the first character of a sentence). Also the type of the drug should have been provided.

As to the type, participants had to classify entities in one of these four groups[1]:

- Drug: any chemical agent used for treatment, cure, prevention or diagnose of diseases, which have been approved for human usage.
- Brand: any drug which firstly have been developed by a pharmaceutical company.
- Group: any term in the text designating a relation among pharmaceutical substances.
- No-Human: any chemical agent which affects the human organism. An active substance non-approved for human usage as medication.

In the next section of the paper, we present related works (Section 2). In Section 3, we discuss the feature-based system we propose. Evaluation results are discussed in Section 4. Finally, we conclude and propose future work (Section 5).

2. Related Work

One of the most important workshops on the domain of Bioinformatics has been BioCreAtIve (Critical Assessment of Information Extraction in Biology) (Hirschman *et al.*, 2005). This workshop has improved greatly the Information Extraction techniques applied to the biological domain. The goal of the first BioCreAtIvE challenge was to provide a set of common evaluation tasks to assess the state-of-the-art for text mining applied to biological problems. The workshop was held in Granada, Spain on March 28-31, 2004.

According to Hirschman, the first BioCreAtIvE assessment achieved a high level of international participation (27 groups from 10 countries). The best system results for a basic task (gene name finding and normalization), where a balanced 80% precision/recall or better, which potentially makes them suitable for real applications in biology. The results for the advanced task (functional annotation from free text) were significantly lower, demonstrating the current limitations of text-mining approaches.

The greatest contribution of BioCreAtIve was the creation and release of training and test data sets for both tasks (Hirschman *et al.*, 2005).

One of the seminal works where the issue of drug detection was mentioned was (Grönroos *et al.*, 1995). Authors argue the problem can be solved by using a computerized information system, which includes medication data of individual patients as well as information about non-therapeutic drug-effects. Also, they suggest a computerized information system to build decision support modules that, automatically give alarms or alerts of important drug effects other than therapeutic effects. If these warnings concern laboratory tests, they would be checked by a laboratory physician and only those with clinical significance would be sent to clinicians.

Here, it is important to note the appearance of the knowledgebase DrugBank[2]. Since its first release in 2006 (Wishart *et al.*, 2008) it has been widely used to facilitate in silico drug target discovery, drug design, drug docking or screening, drug metabolism prediction, drug interaction prediction and general pharmaceutical education. DrugBank has also significantly improved the power and simplicity of its structure query and text query searches.

[1] http://www.cs.york.ac.uk/semeval-2013/task9

[2] http://redpoll.pharmacy.ualberta.ca/drugbank/

Later on, in 2010 Tari propose an approach that integrates text mining and automated reasoning to derive DDIs (Tari *et al.*, 2010). Through the extraction of various facts of drug metabolism, they extract, not only the explicitly DDIs mentioned in text, but also the potential interactions that can be inferred by reasoning. This approach was able to find several potential DDIs that are not present in DrugBank. This analysis revealed that 81.3% of these interactions are determined to be correct.

On the DDIExtraction 2011 (Segura-Bedmar *et al.*, 2011) workshop (First Challenge Task on Drug-Drug Interaction Extraction) the best performance was achieved by the team WBI from Humboldt-Universitat, Berlin. This team combined several kernels and a case-based reasoning (CBR) system, using a voting approach.

In this workshop relation extraction was frequently and successfully addressed by machine learning methods. Some of the more common used features were co-occurrences, character n-grams, Maximal Frequent Sequences, bag-of-words, keywords, etc.

Another used technique is distant supervision. The first system evaluating distant supervision for drug-drug interaction was presented in (Bobić *et al.*, 2012), they have proposed a constraint to increase the quality of data used for training based on the assumption that no self-interaction of real-world objects are described in sentences. In addition, they merge information from IntAct and the University of Kansas Proteomics Service (KUPS) database in order to detect frequent exceptions from the distant supervision assumption and make use of more data sources.

Another important work related to Biomedical Natural Language Processing was BioNLP (Björne *et al.*, 2011) it is an application of natural language processing methods to analyze textual data on biology and medicine, often research articles. They argue that information extraction techniques can be used to mine large text datasets for relevant information, such as relations between specific types of entities.

Inspired in the previews works the system we propose makes use of machine learning methods too, using some of the common features described above, such as the n-grams and keywords and co-occurrences, but we also add some semantic information to enrich those features.

3. System Description

As it has been mentioned before, the system was developed to detect and classify drugs in biomedical texts, so the process is performed in two main phases:

- drug detection.
- drug classification.

Both phases are determined by the following stages, described in Figure 1:

I. Preprocessing
II. Feature extraction
III. Classification

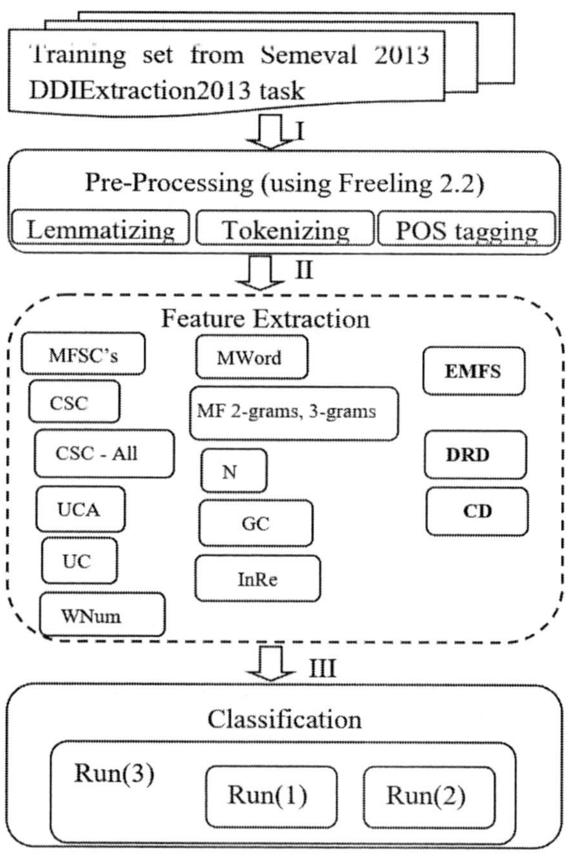

Figure 1. Walkthrough system process.

Given a biomedical sentence, the system obtains the lemmas and POS-tag of every token of the sentence, by means of Freeling tool[3]. After that, it is able to generate candidates according to certain parameters (see section 3.3).

Then, all the generated candidates are processed to extract the features needed for the learning methods, in order to determine which candidates are drugs.

After the drugs are detected, the system generates a tagged corpus, following the provided training corpus structure, containing the detected entities, and then it proceeds to classify each one of them. To do so, another supervised learning algorithm was used (see section 3.3).

3.1. Candidates generation

Drugs and drug groups, as every entity in Natural Language, follow certain grammatical patterns. For instance, a drug is usually a noun or a set of nouns, or even a combination of verbs and nouns, especially verbs in the past participle tense and gerunds. But, one thing we noticed is that both drugs and drug groups end with a noun and as to drug groups that noun is often in the plural.

Based on that idea, we decided to generate candidates starting from the end of each sentence and going forward.

Generation starts with the search of a pivot word, which in this case is a noun. When the pivot is found, it is added to the candidates list, and then the algorithm takes the word before the pivot to see if it complies with one of the patterns i.e. if the word is a noun, an adjective, a gerund or past participle verb. If it does, then it and the pivot form another candidate.

After that, the algorithm continues until it finds a word that does not comply with a pattern. In this case, it goes to the next pivot and stops when all the nouns in the sentence have been processed, or the first word of the sentence is reached.

3.2. Feature Description

For the DDIExtraction2013[4] task 9 three runs of the same system were performed with different features each time. The next sections describes the features we used.

3.2.1. Most Frequent Semantic Classes (MFSC)

Given a word, its semantic class label (Izquierdo *et al.*, 2007) is obtained from WordNet using the ISR-WN resource (Gutiérrez *et al.*, 2011; 2010). The semantic class is that associated to the most probable sense of the word. For each entity in the training set we take the words in the same sentence and for each word its semantic class is determined. This way, we identify the 400[5] most frequent semantic classes associated to words surrounding the entities in the training set.

For a candidate entity we use 400 features to encode information with regard to whether or not in its same sentence a word can be found belonging to one of the most frequent semantic classes.

Each one of these features takes a value representing the distance (measured in words) a candidate is from the nearest word with same semantic class which represents the attribute.

If the word is to the left of the candidate, the attribute takes a negative value, if it is to the right, the value is positive, and zero if no word with that semantic class is present in the sentence the candidate belongs to.

To better understand that, consider A1 is the attribute which indicates if in the sentence of the candidate a word can be found belonging to the semantic class 1. Thus, the value of A1 is the distance the candidate is from the closest word with semantic class 1 in the sentence that is being analyzed.

3.2.2. Candidate Semantic Class (CSC)

The semantic class of candidates is also included in the feature set, if the candidate is a multi-word, then the semantic class of the last word (the pivot word) is taken.

[3] http://nlp.lsi.upc.edu/freeling/

[4] http://www.cs.york.ac.uk/semeval-2013/task9/

[5] This value was extracted from our previous experiment.

3.2.3. Most Frequent Semantic Classes from Entities (EMFSC)

In order to add more semantic information, we decided to find the most frequent semantic classes among all the entities that were tagged in the training data set. We included, in the feature set, all the semantic classes with a frequency of eight or more, because all the classes we wanted to identify were represented in that threshold. In total, they make 29 more features. The values of every one of them, is the sum of the number of times it appears in the candidate.

3.2.4. Candidate Semantic Class All Words (CSC-All)

This feature is similar to CSC, but in this case the candidate is a multi-word, we not only look for the semantic class of the pivot, but also the whole candidate as one.

3.2.5. Drug-related domains (DRD)

Another group of eight attributes describes how many times each one of the candidates belongs to one of the following drug-related domains (DRD) (medicine, anatomy, biology, chemistry, physiology, pharmacy, biochemistry, genetics). These domains where extracted from WordNet Domains. In order to determine the domain that a word belongs to, the proposal of DRelevant (Vázquez *et al.*, 2007; Vázquez *et al.*, 2004) was used.

To illustrate how the DRD features take their values, consider the following sentence:

"…until the lipid response to Accutane is established."

One of the candidates the system generates would be "lipid response". It is a two-word candidate, so we take the first word and see if it belongs to one of the above domains. If it does, then we add one to that feature. If the word does not belong to any of the domains, then its value will be zero. We do the same with the other word. In the end, we have a collection where every value corresponds to each one of the domains. For the example in question the collection would be:

medicine	1
anatomy	0
biology	0
chemistry	0
physiology	1
pharmacy	0
biochemistry	0
genetics	0

Table 1. DRD value assignment example.

3.2.6. Candidate word number (WNum)

Because there are candidates that are a multi-word and others that are not, it may be the case that a candidate, which is a multi-word, has an EMFSC bigger than others which are not a multi-word, just because more than one of the words that conform it, have a frequent semantic class.

We decided to add a feature, called WNum, which would help us normalize the values of the EMFSC. The value of the feature would be the number of words the candidate has. Same thing happens with DRD.

3.2.7. Candidate Domain (CD)

The value of this nominal feature is the domain associated to the candidate. If the candidate is a multi-word; we get the domain of all the words as a whole. In both cases the domain for a single word as well as for a multi-word is determined using the relevant domains obtained by (Vázquez et al., 2007; Vázquez et al., 2004).

3.2.8. Maximum Frequent 2-grams, 3-grams

Drugs usually contain sequences of characters that are very frequent in biomedical domain texts. These character sequences are called *n*-grams, where *n* is the number of characters in the sequence. Because of that, we decided to add the ten most frequent *n*-grams with *n* between two and three. The selected *n*-grams are the following: "in" (frequency: 8170), "ne" (4789), "ine" (3485), "ti" (3234), "id" (2768), "an" (2704), "ro" (2688), "nt" (2593), "et" (2423), "en" (2414).

These features take a value of one if the candidate has the corresponding character sequence and zero if it does not. For instance: if we had the candidate "panobinostat" it will generate the following collection:

"in"	1
"ne"	0
"ine"	0
"ti"	0
"id"	0
"an"	1
"ro"	0
"nt"	0
"et"	0
"en"	0

Table 2. MF 2-gram, 3-gram.

3.2.9. Uppercase (UC), Uppercase All (UCA). Multi-word (MWord) and Number (N)

Other features say if the first letter of the candidate is an uppercase; if all of the letters are uppercase (UCA); if it is a multi-word (MWord) and also if it is in the singular or in the plural (N).

3.2.10. L1, L2, L3 and R1, R2, R3

The Part-of-Speech tags of the closest three surrounding words of the candidates are also included. We named those features L1, L2, and L3 for POS tags to the left of the candidate, and R1, R2, and R3 for those to the right.

3.2.11. POS-tagging combination (GC)

Different values are assigned to candidates, in order to identify its POS-tagging combination. For instance: to the following entity "combined oral contraceptives" taken from DDI13-train-TEES-analyses-130304.xml[6] training file, which was provided for task 9.1, corresponds 5120. This number is the result of combining the four grammatical categories that really matter to us: R for adverb, V for verb, J for adjective, N for noun.

A unique number was given to each combination of those four letters. We named this feature GC.

[6] http://www.cs.york.ac.uk/semeval-2013/task9

3.2.12. In resource feature (InRe)

A resource was created which contains all the drug entities that were annotated in the training corpus, so another attribute tells the system if the candidate is in the resource.

Since all of the entities in the training data set were in the resource this attribute could take a value of one for all instances. Thus the classifier could classify correctly all instances in the training data set just looking to this attribute, which is not desirable. To avoid that problem, we randomly set its value to zero every 9/10 of the training instances.

3.3. Classification

All the features extracted in the previous stages are used in this stage to obtain the two models, one for drug detection phase, and the other for drug classification phase.

We accomplished an extensive set of experiments in order to select the best classifier. All algorithms implemented in WEKA, except those that were designed specifically for a regression task, were tried. In each case we perform a 10-fold cross-validation. In all experiments the classifiers were settled with the default configuration. From those tests we select a decision tree, the C4.5 algorithm (Gutiérrez *et al.*, 2011; 2010) implemented as the J48 classifier in WEKA. This classifier yields the better results for both drug detection and drug classification.

The classifier was trained using a set of 463 features, extracted from the corpus provided by SemEval 2013, the task 9 in question.

As it was mentioned before, three runs were performed for the competition. Run (1) used the following features for drug detection: MFSC (only 200 frequent semantic classes), MF 2-grams, 3-grams, UC, UCA, MWord, N, L1, L2, L3, R1, R2, R3, CSC, CD, WNum, GC and InRe.

Drug classification in this run used the same features except for CD, WNum, and GC. Run (2) has all the above features, but we added the remaining 200 sematic classes that we left out in Run (1) to the detection and the classification models. In Run (3), we added EMFSC feature to the detection and the classification models.

4. Results

In the task, the results of the participants were compared to a gold-standard and evaluated according to various evaluation criteria:

- Exact evaluation, which demands not only boundary match, but also the type of the detected drug has to be the same as that of the gold-standard.
- Exact boundary matching (regardless of the type).
- Partial boundary matching (regardless of the type)
- Type matching.

Precision and recall were calculated using the scoring categories proposed by MUC [7]:

- COR: the output of the system and the gold-standard annotation agree.
- INC: the output of the system and the gold-standard annotation disagree.
- PAR: the output of the system and the gold-standard annotation are not identical but has some overlapping text.
- MIS: the number of gold-standard entities that were not identify by the system.
- SPU: the number of entities labeled by the system that are not in the gold-standard.

Table 3 , Table 4 and Table 5 show the system results in the DDIExtraction2013 competition for Run (1).

Run (2) and Run (3) results are almost the same as Run (1). It is an interesting result since in those runs 200 additional features were supplied to the classifier. In feature evaluation, using CfsSubsetEval and GeneticSearch with WEKA we found that all these new features were ranked as worthless for the classification. On the other hand, the following features were the ones that really influenced the classifiers: MFSC (215 features only), MF 2-grams, 3-grams ("ne", "ine", "ti", "ro", "et", "en"), WNum, UC, UCA, L1, R1, CSC, CSC-All, CD, DRD (anatomy, physiology, pharmacy, biochemistry), InRe, GC and EMFS, specifically music.n.01, substance.n.01, herb.n.01, artifact.n.01, nutriment.n.01, nonsteroidal_anti-inflammatory.n.01, causal_agent.n.01 have a frequency of 8, 19, 35, 575, 52, 80, 63 respectively.

Measure	Strict	Exact Matching	Partial Matching	Type
COR	319	354	354	388
INC	180	145	0	111
PAR	0	0	145	0
MIS	187	187	187	187
SPU	1137	1137	1137	1137
Precision	0.19	0.22	0.22	0.24
Recall	0.47	0.52	0.62	0.57

Table 3. Run (1), all scores.

Measure	Drug	Brand	Group	Drug_n
COR	197	20	93	9
INC	23	2	43	1
PAR	0	0	0	0
MIS	131	37	19	111
SPU	754	47	433	14
Precision	0.2	0.29	016	0.38
Recall	0.56	0.34	0.6	0.07
F1	0.3	0.31	0.26	0.12

Table 4. Scores for entity types, exact matching in Run (1).

	Precision	**Recall**	**F1**
Macro average	0.26	0.39	0.31
Strict matching	0.19	0.46	0.27

Table 5. Macro average and Strict matching measures in Run (1).

5. Conclusion and future works

In this paper we show the description of UMCC_DLSI-(DDI) system, which is able to detect and classify drugs in biomedical texts with acceptable efficacy. It introduces in this thematic the use of semantic information such as semantic classes and the relevant domain of the words, extracted with ISR-WN resource. With this approach we obtained an F-Measure of 27.5% in the Semeval DDI Extraction2013 task 9.

As further work we propose to eliminate some detected bugs (i.e. repeated instances, multiwords missed) and enrich our knowledge base (ISR-WN), using biomedical sources as UMLS[8], SNOMED[9] and OntoFis[10].

[7] http://www.itl.nist.gov/iaui/894.02/related_projects/muc/muc_sw/muc_sw_manual.html

[8] http://www.nlm.nih.gov/research/umls

[9] http://www.ihtsdo.org/snomed-ct/

[10] http://rua.ua.es/dspace/handle/10045/14216

Acknowledgments

This research work has been partially funded by the Spanish Government through the project TEXT-MESS 2.0 (TIN2009-13391-C04), "Análisis de Tendencias Mediante Técnicas de Opinión Semántica" (TIN2012-38536-C03-03) and "Técnicas de Deconstrucción en la Tecnologías del Lenguaje Humano" (TIN2012-31224); and by the Valencian Government through the project PROMETEO (PROMETEO/2009/199).

References

Björne, J.; A. Airola; T. Pahikkala and T. Salakoski Drug-Drug Interaction Extraction from Biomedical Texts with SVM and RLS Classifiers Proceedings of the 1st Challenge Task on Drug-Drug Interaction Extraction, 2011, 761: 35-42.

Bobić, T.; R. Klinger; P. Thomas and M. Hofmann-Apitius Improving Distantly Supervised Extraction of Drug-Drug and Protein-Protein Interactions EACL 2012, 2012: 35.

Cohen, A. M. and W. R. Hersh A survey of current work in biomedical text mining Briefings in bioinformatics, 2005, 6(1): 57-71.

Grönroos, P.; K. Irjala; J. Heiskanen; K. Torniainen and J. Forsström Using computerized individual medication data to detect drug effects on clinical laboratory tests Scandinavian Journal of Clinical & Laboratory Investigation, 1995, 55(S222): 31-36.

Gutiérrez, Y.; A. Fernández; A. Montoyo and S. Vázquez. Integration of semantic resources based on WordNet. XXVI Congreso de la Sociedad Española para el Procesamiento del Lenguaje Natural, Universidad Politécnica de Valencia, Valencia, SEPLN 2010, 2010. 161-168 p. 1135-5948

Gutiérrez, Y.; A. Fernández; A. Montoyo and S. Vázquez Enriching the Integration of Semantic Resources based on WordNet Procesamiento del Lenguaje Natural, 2011, 47: 249-257.

Hirschman, L.; A. Yeh; C. Blaschke and A. Valencia Overview of BioCreAtIvE: critical assessment of information extraction for biology BMC bioinformatics, 2005, 6(Suppl 1): S1.

Izquierdo, R.; A. Suárez and G. Rigau A Proposal of Automatic Selection of Coarse-grained Semantic Classes for WSD Procesamiento del Lenguaje Natural, 2007, 39: 189-196.

Percha, B. and R. B. Altman Informatics confronts drug–drug interactions Trends in pharmacological sciences, 2013.

Segura-Bedmar, I.; P. Martínez and D. Sánchez-Cisneros The 1st DDIExtraction-2011 challenge task: Extraction of Drug-Drug Interactions from biomedical texts Challenge Task on Drug-Drug Interaction Extraction, 2011, 2011: 1-9.

Tari, L.; S. Anwar; S. Liang; J. Cai and C. Baral Discovering drug–drug interactions: a text-mining and reasoning approach based on properties of drug metabolism Bioinformatics, 2010, 26(18): i547-i553.

Vázquez, S.; A. Montoyo and Z. Kozareva. Extending Relevant Domains for Word Sense Disambiguation. IC-AI'07. Proceedings of the International Conference on Artificial Intelligence USA, 2007.

Vázquez, S.; A. Montoyo and G. Rigau. Using Relevant Domains Resource for Word Sense Disambiguation. IC-AI'04. Proceedings of the International Conference on Artificial Intelligence, Ed: CSREA Press. Las Vegas, E.E.U.U., 2004.

Wishart, D. S.; C. Knox; A. C. Guo; D. Cheng; S. Shrivastava; D. Tzur; B. Gautam and M. Hassanali DrugBank: a knowledgebase for drugs, drug actions and drug targets Nucleic acids research, 2008, 36(suppl 1): D901-D906.

NIL_UCM: Extracting Drug-Drug interactions from text through combination of sequence and tree kernels

Behrouz Bokharaeian, Alberto Díaz
Natural Interaction Based on Language Group
Universidad Complutense de Madrid
Madrid 28011, Spain
{bokharaeian, albertodiaz}@fdi.ucm.es

Abstract

A drug-drug interaction (DDI) occurs when one drug affects the level or activity of another drug. Semeval 2013 DDI Extraction challenge is going to be held with the aim of identifying the state of the art relation extraction algorithms. In this paper we firstly review some of the existing approaches in relation extraction generally and biomedical relations especially. And secondly we will explain our SVM based approaches that use lexical, morphosyntactic and parse tree features. Our combination of sequence and tree kernels have shown promising performance with a best result of 0.54 F1 macroaverage on the test dataset.

1 Introduction

A drug-drug interaction occurs when one drug affects the level or activity of another drug, for instance, drug concentrations. This interaction can result on reducing its effectiveness or possibly increasing its side effects (Stockley, 2007). There are some helpful DDIs but most of them are dangerous (Aronson, 2007), for example, patients that take *clarithromycin* and *glibenclamide* concurrently may experiment *hypoglycaemia*.

There is a great amount of information about DDI described in papers that health experts have to consult in order to be updated. The development of tools for extracting this type of information from biomedical texts would produce a clear benefit for these professionals reducing the time necessary to review the literature. Semeval 2013 DDI Extraction challenge decided to being held with the aim of identifying the state of the art algorithms for automatically extracting DDI from biomedical articles. This challenge has two tasks: recognition and classification of drug names and extraction of drug-drug interactions. For the second task, the input corpus contains annotations with the drug names.

A previous Workshop on Drug-Drug Interaction Extraction (Segura-Bedmar et al., 2011) was held in 2011 in Huelva, Spain. The main difference is that the new challenge includes the classification of the drug-drug interactions in four types depending on the information that is described in the sentence making the task much more complicated than before. Additionally the current task involves DDIs from two different corpora with different characteristics (Segura-Bedmar et al., 2013).

We participated in the task of extracting drug-drug interactions with two approaches that exploit a rich set of tree and sequence features. Our implemented methods utilize a SVM classifier with a linear kernel and a rich set of lexical, morphosyntactic and semantic features (e.g. trigger words) extracted from texts. In addition some tree features such as shortest path and subtree features are used.

2 Related work

Due to the importance of detecting biological and medical relations several methods have been applied for extracting biological relation information from text. In (Song et al., 2010) is presented a method for extracting protein-protein interaction (PPI) through combination of an active learning technique and a semi-supervised SVM.

Another motivating work can be found in (Chen et

*Second Joint Conference on Lexical and Computational Semantics (*SEM), Volume 2: Seventh International Workshop on Semantic Evaluation (SemEval 2013)*, pages 644–650, Atlanta, Georgia, June 14-15, 2013.

al., 2011) in which a PPI Pair Extractor was developed that consists of a SVM for binary classification which exploits a linear kernel with a rich set of features based on linguistic analysis, contextual words, interaction words, interaction patterns and specific domain information.

Another PPI extraction method have been developed in (Li et al., 2010). They have applied an ensemble kernel composed of a feature-based kernel and a structure-based kernel. A more recent research on tree kernels has been carried out by (Guodong et al., 2010). They have introduced a context-sensitive convolution tree kernel, which specifies both context-free and context-sensitive sub-trees by taking into account the paths of their ancestor nodes as their contexts to capture structural information in the tree structure. A recent work (Simões et al., 2013) has introduced an approach for Relationship Extraction (RE) based on labeled graph kernels. The proposed kernel is a specification of a random walk kernel that exploits two properties: the words between the candidate entities and the combination of information from distinct sources. A comparative survey regarding different kernel based approaches and their performance can be found in (Frunza and Inkpen, 2008).

Using external knowledge and resources to the target sentence is another research direction in the relation extraction task that Chan and Roth have investigated in (Chan and Roth, 2010). They have reported some improvements by using external sources such as Wikipedia, comparing to basic supervised learning systems. Thomas and his colleagues in (Thomas et al., 2011) have developed a majority voting ensemble of contrasting machine learning methods using different linguistic feature spaces.

A more systematic and high quality investigation about feature selection in kernel based relation expression can be found in (Jiang and Zhai, 2011). They have explored a large space of features for relation extraction and assess the effectiveness of sequences, syntactic parse trees and dependency parse trees as feature subspaces and sentence representation. They conclude that, by means of a set of basic unit features from each subspace, a reasonably good performance can be achieved. But when the three subspaces are combined, the performance can slightly improve, which shows sequence, syntactic and dependency relations have much overlap for the task of relation extraction.

Although most of the previous researches in biomedical domain has been carried out with respect to protein-protein interaction extraction, and more recently on drug-drug interaction extraction, other types of biomedical relations are being studied: e.g. gene-disease (Airola et al., 2008), disease-treatment (Jung et al., 2012) and drug-disease.

3 Dataset

The dataset for the DDIExtraction 2013 task contains documents from two sources. It includes MedLine abstracts and documents from the DrugBank database describing drug-drug interactions (Segura-Bedmar et al., 2013). These documents are annotated with drug entities and with information about drug pair interactions: true or false.

In the training corpus the interaction type is also annotated. There are 4 types of interactions: *effect*, *mechanism*, *int*, *advice*.

The challenge corpus is divided into training and evaluation datasets (Table 1). The DrugBank training data consists of 572 documents with 5675 sentences. This subset contains 12929 entities and 26005 drug pair interactions. On the other hand, the MedLine training data consists of 142 abstracts with 1301 sentences, 1836 entities and 1787 pairs.

The distribution of positive and negative examples are similar in both subsets, 12.98% of positives instances on MedLine and 14.57% on DrugBank. With respect to the distribution of categories, the figures show that there is a small number of positive instances for categories *int* and *advice* on the MedLine subset. The *effect* type is the most frequent, outmatching itself on the MedLine subset.

The evaluation corpus contains 158 abstracts with 973 sentences and 5265 drug pair interactions from Drugbank, and 33 abstracts with 326 sentences and 451 drug pair interactions from Medline. It is worth to emphasize that the distribution of positive and negative examples is a bit greater (2.22%) in the DrugBank subset compared to the training data, but is almost doubled with respect to MedLine (12,98% to 21,06%). The categories *advice* and *int* have very few positive instances in the MedLine subset.

Training	pairs	negative DDIs	positive DDIs	effect	mechanism	advice	int
DrugBank	26005	22217	3788	1535	1257	818	178
MedLine	1787	1555	232	152	62	8	10
Test	pairs	negative DDIs	positive DDIs	effect	mechanism	advice	int
DrugBank	5265	4381	884	298	278	214	94
MedLine	451	356	95	62	24	7	2

Table 1: Basic statistics of the training and test datasets.

4 Method

Initially several experiments have been developed to explore the performance of shallow linguistic (SL) and parse tree based methods on a subset of the training corpus. Although the SL kernel achieved considerably good results we have found that the best option was the combination of different kernels using linguistic and tree features.

Our implemented kernel based approach consists of four different processes that have been applied sequentially: preprocessing, feature extraction, feature selection and classification (Figure 1). Our two submitted results were obtained by two different strategies. In the first outcome, all the DDIs and type of interactions were extracted in one step, as a 5-class categorization problem. The second run was carried out in two steps, initially the DDIs were detected and then the positively predicted DDIs were used to determine the type of the interaction. In the next subsection the four different processes are described.

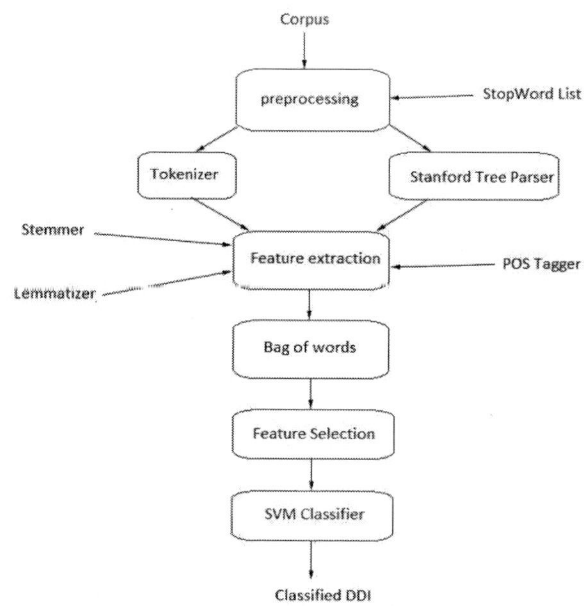

Figure 1: The different processes followed for our two submitted results.

4.1 Preprocessing

In this phase we have carried out two types of text preprocessing steps before training the classifier.

We have removed some stop words in special places in the sentences that clearly were a matter of concern and caused some inaccuracy, for example, removing question marks at the beginning of a sentence. We also carried out a normalization task for some tokens because of usage of different used encodings and processing methods, mainly html tags.

4.2 Feature extraction

Initially 49 feature classes were extracted for each instance that correspond to a drug pair interaction between Drug1 and Drug2:

- Word Features: Include Words of Drug1, words of Drug2, words between Drug1 and Drug2, three words before Drug1 and three words after Drug2. Lemmas and stems of all these words. We have used TreeTagger to obtain lemmas and Paice/Husk Stemmer (Paice, 1990) to obtain stems.
- Morphosyntactic Features: Include Part-of-speech (POS) tags of each drug words (Drug1 and Drug2), POS of the previous 3 and next 3 words. We have used TreeTagger.
- Constituency parse tree features: Include shortest path between Drug1 and Drug2 in the constituency parse tree, shortest path between first token in the sentence and Drug1, and shortest path between Drug2 and last token in the sentence in the parse tree, and all subtrees gener-

ated from the constituency parse tree. We have used Stanford parser [1] for producing tree features.

- Conjunction features: We have produced some new conjunction features by combination of different word features and morphosyntactic features such as POSLEMMA and POSSTEM for all the words before Drug1, words between Drug1 and Drug2 and words after Drug2.

- verbs features: Include verbs between Drug1 and Drug2, first verb before Drug1 and first verb after Drug2. Their stem, lemma and their conjunction features are also included.

- negation features: Only if the sentence contains negation statements. The features extracted include the left side tokens of the negation scope, the right side tokens of the negation scope and the tokens inside the negation scope. We have used NegEx[2] as negation detection algorithm.

Finally we have deployed a bag of words approach (BoW) for each feature class in order to obtain the final representation for each instance. We have limited the size of the vocabulary in the BoW representation with a different number depending on the data subset. We carried out several experiments to fix these numbers and at the end we have used 1000 words/feature class for MedLine and 6000 words/feature class for DrugBank.

4.3 Feature selection

We have conducted some feature selection experiments to select the best features for improving the results and reducing running time. We have finally used Information Gain ranker to eliminate the less effective features. We have computed the information gain for each feature class as the linear combination of the information gain of each corresponding word. Empirically we have selected the best 42 feature classes.

On the other hand, we have done a preliminary study of the effect of the negation related features. We have found more than 3000 sentences containing negation, most of them corresponds to sentences associated with negative examples of interactions. However, these features have been eliminated because we have not obtained a clear improvement when we combined them with the other features.

4.4 Classification

First we have performed several experiments with different supervised machine learning approaches such as SVM, Naivebayes, Randomtree, Random forest, Multilayer perceptron in addition to combination of methods. Finally we decided to use a SVM approach, the Weka Sequential Minimal Optimization (SMO) algorithm. We used the inner product of the BoW vectors as similarity function.

We have submitted two approaches:

- approach 1: SVM (Weka SMO) with 5 categories (effect, mechanism, int, advice and null).

- approach 2: We have extracted final results in two stages. In the first step we have used a SVM (Weka SMO) with 2 categories (positive and negative) and then we have used a second SVM classifier with 4 classes on positive extracted DDIs to train and extract the type of interaction in the test dataset.

The classifiers have been applied separately with each data subset, that is, a classifier per approach has been developed using the DrugBank training subset and has been evaluated using the DrugBank test subset, and the same process has been applied with the MedLine training and test subset.

5 Results

In this section we first show the evaluation results with our two approaches. Secondly an error analysis was carried out with a development set extracted from the training corpus.

5.1 Test data results

We have submitted two runs that corresponds with the approaches described in the previous section. Table 2 shows the results obtained with the first approach (one step) and Table 3 shows the results with the second approach (two steps).

It can be observed that the results on detection of DDI are better with the approach 2: 0.656 against 0.588 on F1. This result is a consequence that we

[1] http://nlp.stanford.edu/software/lex-parser.shtml
[2] http://code.google.com/p/negex/

Run	P	R	F1
NILUCM1 (All)	0.632	0.464	0.535
NILUCM2 (All)	0.547	0.507	0.526
NILUCM1 (Drugbank)	0.651	0.498	0.565
NILUCM2 (Drugbank)	0.558	0.542	0.550
NILUCM1 (Medline)	0.333	0.074	0.121
NILUCM2 (Medline)	0.221	0.073	0.110

Table 4: Macroaverage test set results.

have more information to obtain the detection of the interaction if we use the information from all the different types than if we obtain it joining the results obtained per each category. With respect to detection and classification the results are also better with approach 2 for a similar reason: 0.548 against 0.517 on F1.

With respect to the categories, in the more populated ones the general tendency of better results from approach 2 continues, especially in *effect* type: 0.556 against 0.489. With respect to *advice* and *int*, the recall is better in approach 2 but the improvement in precision is greater in approach1 giving a better result on F1 to approach 1, especially in *int* type: 0.427 against 0.393.

Table 4 shows the macroaverage results separated by subset data. The best results obtained for approach 1 are due to that this type of average gives equal weight to each category, favouring then the categories with less instances.

Other important insight that can be extracted from this table is that our results are much better for DrugBank dataset with both approaches. These results can be justified due to high similarity between sentences in Drugbank training and test corpus. In fact the Medline corpus commonly has more words unrelated to DDI subjects. In addition to this argument, the smaller number of training pairs in the Medline corpus can be other reason to obtain worst results.

5.2 Error analysis

We have extracted a stratified development corpus from the training corpus in order to perform an error analysis. We have used a 10% of the training corpus. It contains 2779 pairs, of which 397 are DDIs. Table 5 shows the results obtained with the two submitted approaches.

The results with our development corpus shows the same tendency, that is, approach 2 is better than approach 1 on detection of DDI and on microaverage classification. On the other hand, results are higher than those on test corpus because the information contained in the development corpus is more similar to the rest of training corpus than information on the test set.

We have performed an analysis of the errors produced for both approaches in the Detection and Classification of DDI subtask. The errors obtained are 112 false positives (Fp) and 116 false negatives (Fn) associated to approach 1, and 111 false positives (Fp) and 112 false negatives (Fn) to approach 2. Apart from the comments explained in the previous section about the small number of instances on the MedLine subset, we think the main problem is related with the management of long sentences with complex syntax. These sentences are more difficult for our approaches because the complexity of the sentence generates more errors in the tokenizing and parsing processes affecting the representation of the instances both in training and test phases. We show below some false positives and false negatives examples.

- The effects of **ERGOMAR** may be potentiated by **triacetyloleandomycin** which inhibits the metabolism of ergotamine. DrugBank. False negative.

- Prior administration of **4-methylpyrazole** (90 mg kg(-1) body weight) was shown to prevent the conversion of **1,3-difluoro-2-propanol** (100 mg kg(-1) body weight) to (-)-erythrofluorocitrate in vivo and to eliminate the fluoride and citrate elevations seen in 1,3-difluoro-2-propanol-intoxicated animals MedLine. False negative.

- Drug Interactions with Antacids Administration of 120 mg of **fexofenadine hydrochloride** (2 x 60 mg capsule) within 15 minutes of an aluminum and magnesium containing antacid (Maalox) decreased **fexofenadine** AUC by 41% and cmax by 43%. DrugBank. False positive.

- **Dexamethasone** at 10(-10) M or retinyl acetate

approach 1	Tp	Fp	Fn	total	P	R	F1
Detection of DDI	557	359	422	979	0.608	0.569	0.588
Detection and classification of DDI	490	426	489	979	0.535	0.501	0.517
Score for type mechanism	147	122	155	302	0.546	0.487	0.515
Score for type effect	200	258	160	360	0.437	0.556	0.489
Score for type advice	115	39	106	221	0.747	0.520	0.613
Score for type int	28	7	68	96	0.800	0.292	0.427

Table 2: Test corpus results (approach1).

approach 2	Tp	Fp	Fn	total	P	R	F1
Detection of DDI	631	315	348	979	0.667	0.645	0.656
Detection and classification of DDI	527	419	452	979	0.557	0.538	0.548
Score for type mechanism	146	102	156	302	0.589	0.483	0.531
Score for type effect	210	186	150	360	0.530	0.583	0.556
Score for type advice	139	96	82	221	0.591	0.629	0.610
Score for type int	32	35	64	96	0.478	0.333	0.393

Table 3: Test corpus results (approach2).

approach 1	Tp	Fp	Fn	total	P	R	F1
Detection of DDI:	292	101	105	397	0.743	0.736	0.739
Detection and Classification of DDI:	281	112	116	397	0.715	0.708	0.711
approach 2	Tp	Fp	Fn	total	P	R	F1
Detection of DDI:	296	102	101	397	0.744	0.746	0.745
Detection and Classification of DDI:	285	111	112	397	0.720	0.718	0.719

Table 5: Error analysis with a development corpus.

at about 3 X 10(-9) M inhibits **proliferation** stimulated by EGF. MedLine. False positive.

6 Conclusions

In this paper we have shown our approaches for the Semeval 2013 DDI Extraction challenge. We have explored different combinations of tree and sequence features using the Sequential Minimal Optimization algorithm.

The first approach uses a SVM with 5 categories, and the second one extracts the final results in two steps: detection with all the categories, and classification on the positive instances. The results are better for approach 2 mainly due to the improvement on the detection subtask because the information from all the categories is used.

We think some of our errors come from using a general tool (Stanford parser) to obtain the parse tree of the sentences. In the future we are going to explore other biomedical parsers and tokenizers.

With respect to the data used, we think the MedLine dataset needs to be greater in order to obtain more significant analysis and results. Our approaches are especially affected by this issue because the small number of positive instances on *advice* and *int* categories implies that the algorithm can not learn to classify new instances accurately. On the other hand, although n-fold cross validation is considered as the best model validation technique, it was time consuming for DDI and need powerful processors.

Another interesting future work is related with the application of simplification techniques in order to solve the problems in the processing of complex long sentences (Buyko et al., 2011).

References

A. Airola, S. Pyysalo, J. Bjorne, T. Pahikkala, F. Ginter, T. Salakoski. 2008. Allpaths graph kernel for protein-protein interaction extraction with evaluation of cross-corpus learning *BMC Bioinformatics*, 9(Suppl 11):S2.

JK. Aronson. 2007. Communicating information about drug interactions. *British Journal of Clinical Pharmacology*, 63(6):637–639.

E. Buyko, E. Faessler, J. Wermter, U. Hahn 2011. Syntactic Simplification and Semantic Enrichment - Trimming Dependency Graphs for Event Extraction. *Computational Intelligence*, 27(4):610–644.

Y. Chen, F. Liu, B. Manderick. 2011. Extract Protein-Protein Interactions from the Literature Using Support Vector Machines with Feature Selection. *Biomedical Engineering, Trends, Researchs and Technologies*, 2011.

YS. Chan and D. Roth. 2010. Exploiting Background Knowledge for Relation Extraction *COLING '10 Proceedings of the 23rd International Conference on Computational Linguistics*, pp:152–160.

O. Frunza and D. Inkpen. 2010. Extraction of disease-treatment semantic relations from biomedical sentences *Proceedings of the 2010 Workshop on Biomedical Natural Language Processing*, pp:91–98.

Z. Guodong, Q. Longhua, F. Jianxi. 2010. Tree kernel-based semantic relation extraction with rich syntactic and semantic information *International Journal on Information Sciences,*, 180(8):1313–1325.

J. Jiang and C. Zhai. 2011. A systematic exploration of the feature space for relation extraction *Proceedings of Human Language Technologies: The Conference of the North American Chapter of the Association for Computational Linguistics (NAACLHLT07)*, pp:113–120.

H. Jung, S. Choi, S. Lee, S. Song. 2012. Survey on Kernel-Based Relation Extraction.

L. Li, J. Ping, D. Huang. 2010. Protein-Protein Interaction Extraction from Biomedical Literatures Based on a Combined Kernel *Journal of Information & Computational Science*, 7(5):1065–1073.

Chris D. Paice 1990. Another stemmer. *ACM SIGIR Forum*, 24(3):56–61.

I. Segura-Bedmar, P. Martínez, D. Sánchez-Cisneros. 2011. *Proceedings of the 1st Challenge task on Drug-Drug Interaction Extraction (DDIExtraction 2011)* CEUR Workshop Proceedings, Vol. 761.

I. Segura-Bedmar, P. Martnez, M. Herrero-Zazo. 2013 SemEval-2013 Task 9: Extraction of Drug-Drug Interactions from Biomedical Texts. *In Proceedings of the 7th International Workshop on Semantic Evaluation (SemEval 2013).*

G. Simões, D. Matos, H. Galhardas. 2013. A Labeled Graph Kernel for Relationship Extraction. *CoRR*, abs/1302.4874.

M. Song, H. Yu, W. Han. 2010. Combining active learning and semi-supervised learning techniques to extract protein interaction sentences. *International Workshop on Data Mining in Bioinformatics* .

I H Stockley. 2007. *Stockley's Drug Interaction*. Pharmaceutical Press.

P. Thomas, M. Neves, I. Solt, D. Tikk, U. Leser. 2011. Relation extraction for drug- drug interactions using ensemble learning *Proceedings of the First Challenge task on Drug-Drug Interaction Extraction (DDIExtraction 2011)*, pp:11–17.

UTurku: Drug Named Entity Recognition and Drug-Drug Interaction Extraction Using SVM Classification and Domain Knowledge

Jari Björne, Suwisa Kaewphan and Tapio Salakoski
Turku Centre for Computer Science (TUCS)
Department of Information Technology
University of Turku
Joukahaisenkatu 3-5B, 20520 Turku, Finland
firstname.lastname@utu.fi

Abstract

The DDIExtraction 2013 task in the SemEval conference concerns the detection of drug names and statements of drug-drug interactions (DDI) from text. Extraction of DDIs is important for providing up-to-date knowledge on adverse interactions between co-administered drugs. We apply the machine learning based Turku Event Extraction System to both tasks. We evaluate three feature sets, syntactic features derived from deep parsing, enhanced optionally with features derived from DrugBank or from both DrugBank and MetaMap. TEES achieves F-scores of 60% for the drug name recognition task and 59% for the DDI extraction task.

1 Introduction

Drug-drug interactions (DDI) refer to one drug affecting the function of another when they are co-administered. These interactions are often adverse, frequently not well known and a source of potentially life-threatening unintended consequences for the patients. Databases such as DrugBank and Micromedex have been developed to store information about known DDIs, but at present their coverage remains limited and there can be inconsistencies in supplementary information (Knox et al., 2011; Wong et al., 2008). Text mining has been proposed as a solution for providing not only lists of DDIs but also a connection to the scientific evidence and supplementary information in the literature (Tari et al., 2010). Several groups of researchers are developing text-mining techniques to extract DDIs from literature and pharmaceutical documents (Tari et al., 2010; Segura-Bedmar et al., 2011a).

The DDIExtraction 2013 shared task concerns the detection of drug mentions and statements of DDIs from unannotated text (Segura-Bedmar et al., 2013). The first version of the DDIExtraction shared task was organized in 2011, with 10 teams participating from various universities (Segura-Bedmar et al., 2011b). The best result of 65.74% was achieved by team WBI of Humboldt University of Berlin (Thomas et al., 2011). University of Turku participated also in this task, placing 4th with an F-score of 62.99%, using the Turku Event Extraction System (Björne et al., 2011).

The Turku Event Extraction System (TEES)[1] is an open source program for extracting events and relations from biomedical texts. It was originally developed for extracting events in the BioNLP Shared Task scheme, and it models event extraction as a graph generation task, where keywords are nodes and the event arguments connecting them are edges. The system can be directly applied to pairwise relation extraction, representing relations as edges and the words they connect as nodes. The node detection system is somewhat similar to named entity recognition (NER) tools, and while quite flexible, can in many tasks exhibit lower performance and higher processing requirements than dedicated NER systems.

In the DDIExtraction 2013 task we apply the Turku Event Extraction system to detecting both drug name entities (task 9.1) as well as drug-drug interactions (task 9.2). We evaluate three different

[1] http://jbjorne.github.com/TEES/

*Second Joint Conference on Lexical and Computational Semantics (*SEM), Volume 2: Seventh International Workshop on Semantic Evaluation (SemEval 2013)*, pages 651–659, Atlanta, Georgia, June 14-15, 2013.

feature sets for both tasks. As a baseline system deep syntactic parsing is used to generate large graph-based feature sets. For additional features, we test the impact of labeling examples with information from external sources. We test both the DrugBank Open Data Drug & Drug Target database (Knox et al., 2011) as well as the MetaMap tool to enrich the features derived from the corpus text.

MetaMap is a publicly available program developed at NLM for automatic mapping of texts to UMLS Metathesaurus concepts (Aronson, 2001). The UMLS Metathesaurus is an extensive repository of biomedical vocabularies that is derived from NLM databases and other external sources that contain information about biomedical concepts, synonyms and the relationship among them (Bodenreider, 2004).

The version of TEES used in the 2011 DDIExtraction task had been publicly available as an open source project since July 2012, but as small modifications were required for compatibility with the 2013 task, we published an updated 2.1 version that task participants could use. To simplify utilization of the numerous analyses TEES produces we also provided our drug-drug interaction predictions freely available for all DDIExtraction 2013 task participants in the hope of encouraging further participation in this interesting shared task.

We demonstrate that TEES has good performance for both drug name detection as well as drug-drug interaction detection, achieving an F-score of 60% in the drug name detection task 9.1 and an F-score of 59% in the drug-drug interaction detection task 9.2. We show that external information from DrugBank and MetaMap can considerably improve extraction performance, but observe that the use of such information must always depend on the exact requirements of each text mining task.

2 Methods

We present a unified approach to drug name and DDI extraction, utilizing largely the same machine learning approaches in both tasks. We develop three variants for tasks 9.1 & 9.2 each, testing the baseline performance of TEES for these tasks, as well as the impact of using external databases as additional training data.

2.1 Turku Event Extraction System

The Turku Event Extraction System is described in detail in Björne et al. (2012). Here we give a general overview about applying the system for the current task. TEES processes text in a pipeline of components, starting from preprocessing tasks such as NER and parsing and proceeding to the multiple, consecutive steps of event extraction. As tasks 9.1 and 9.2 are independent of each other the entity and interaction detection components of TEES are used independently, and for preprocessing, only the parsing is done (See Figure 1).

2.2 Training data preparation

TEES is a machine learning system based on support vector machines (SVM) (Tsochantaridis et al., 2005). To train the system for a new task, two datasets are required: a *training* set on which the SVM model is trained, and a *development* set on which the newly trained model is tested to determine parameter settings for optimal performance (See Figure 2). The optimal model can then be used to detect what it was trained for on unannotated datasets, such as the hidden shared task *test* set.

The DDIExtraction 2013 corpus consists of two parts: A training corpus used for system development and a test corpus for evaluating the participating systems. The annotation of the test corpus is not revealed to task participants. To develop the system, we estimate performance on the training corpus using 10-fold cross validation. To provide the datasets TEES requires, the training corpus is randomly divided (on the document level) into ten parts. For predicting drug names or DDIs for each part, seven of the remaining nine parts are used as a training set and two as a development set for parameter optimization. When producing the final models for classifying the test corpus, five parts of the training corpus are used for training and the other five for parameter optimization. In both cases, the parameter optimization set is merged with the training set when producing the final model for classifying the test set.

The DDIExtraction 2013 corpus is provided in an XML format originally introduced as a unified format for several pairwise protein-protein interaction (PPI) corpora (Pyysalo et al., 2008). TEES uses a variant of this format as its internal data representa-

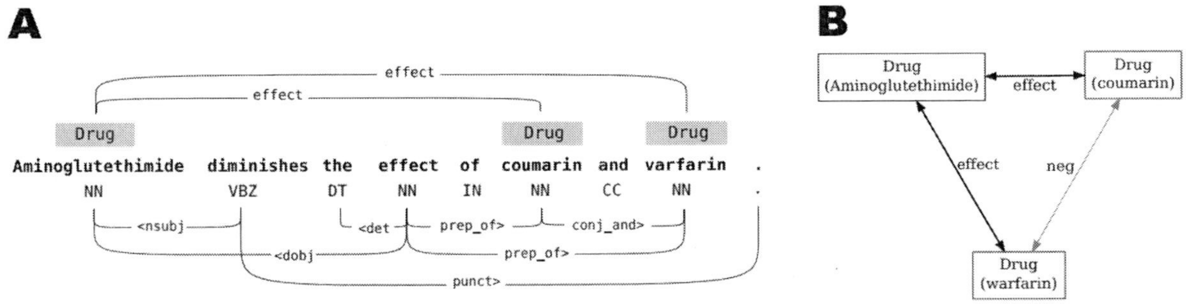

Figure 1: TEES graph representation for drug name and interaction extraction, with example sentence *DDI-DrugBank.d372.s2* from the DDIExtraction 2013 training corpus. A) Both the annotation (above the sentence) and the syntactic parse (below the sentence) are represented as graphs. Tokens form the nodes and dependencies the edges of the syntactic parse graph. Drug names form the nodes and DDIs the edges of the annotation graph. Drug name entities are linked to their syntactic head tokens, connecting the two graphs and allowing the parse to be used as a source of features. For DDI edges, most features are derived from the *shortest path of dependencies* connecting the two drug entities. B) For DDI extraction, one example is generated for each interaction type for each undirected pair of drug entities. The gray *neg* class edge is a negative example.

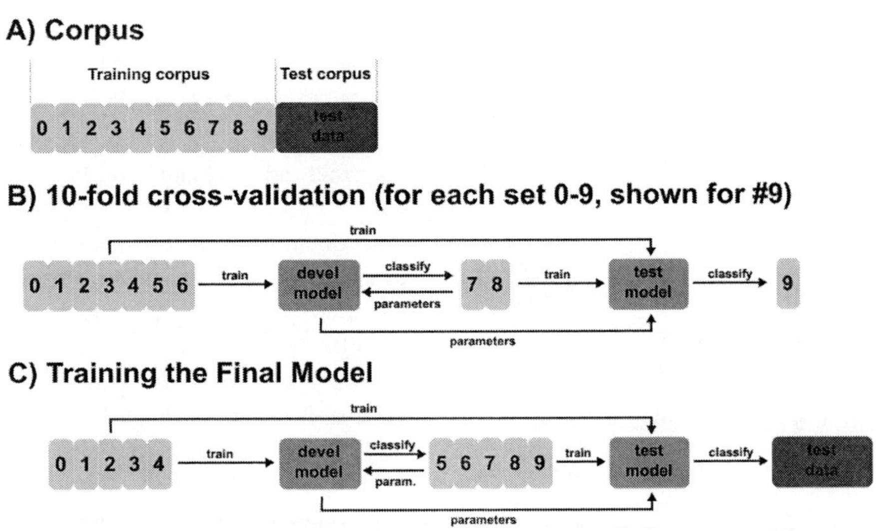

Figure 2: DDIExtraction 2013 corpus. A) To evaluate performance, and to provide analyses for the full training corpus, the training corpus is divided for 10-fold cross validation. B) Each of the ten parts is classified using seven of the remaining parts for training the model and the last two for optimizing parameters. After parameter optimization, all nine parts are used to train the model (with the optimal parameters) for classifying the test set. C) To classify the hidden DDIExtraction 2013 corpus half of the training corpus is used for training and the other half for determining optimal parameters. The test corpus is finally classified with a model trained using the full training corpus.

tion. While close to the DDIExtraction 2013 format, some differences exist, so we preprocess the corpora for compatibility with TEES. Namely, *ddi* elements are renamed as *interaction* elements, *entity* elements in task 9.2 are tagged with the *given* attribute to mark them as pre-annotated data for TEES and all character offsets are converted to the TEES format by increasing the end offset by one, resulting in spans denoted with the beginning character and end character plus one, a common convention in programming languages such as Java and Python.

Before use, all DDIExtraction 2013 corpora are parsed with the TEES preprocessing pipeline, using the BLLIP parser with David McClosky's biomodel to produce a Penn-tree style parse which is converted with the Stanford parser tools to the collapsed CC processed Stanford dependency scheme (Charniak and Johnson, 2005; McClosky, 2010; de Marneffe et al., 2006).

2.3 Drug name recognition with TEES

For drug name recognition the TEES entity detector module is used. Baseline syntactic features (model 1) are generated from the parse, using both information on the tokens and their linear context, as well as dependency chains starting from the entity head token. External data is added to the head token features, from where it is combined into more complex features. One example is generated for each token in the sentence, and these are classified into negatives or one of the positive classes.

As a new feature we generate all substrings starting from the first and last characters of the drug name, with the intention of detecting common prefixes and suffixes among the drug names.

2.4 Drug-drug interaction detection with TEES

For DDI extraction we use the TEES edge detector module. DDIs are typed, undirected edges, so one example is generated for each undirected pair of drug name entities present in the sentence (See Figure 1). The baseline syntactic features (model 1) are generated mostly from the *shortest path of dependencies* connecting the pair of drug name entities' head tokens. From this shortest path several feature groups are generated, including N-grams of various lengths, governor–dependent information for dependencies etc. External data is added into the two drug name entities, and combined into the path features.

We also use the TEES modification from DDIExtraction 2011 task where *conj_and* dependencies are ignored when calculating the shortest path, with the aim of including more of the relevant interaction words in the path.

2.5 Using DrugBank for Domain Knowledge

DrugBank[2] is a public database of information on drugs and drug targets. We use the downloadable XML version of the database.

For drug name recognition, for each candidate token, we add as features its presence as a known drug name in DrugBank and the *synonym*, *brand*, *group* and *category* annotations this drug may have. We also mark whether the candidate token exactly equals an annotation of one of these types, indicating cases where the token is e.g. a known brand name.

For DDI extraction, we mark as a feature whether the drug name pair is listed in DrugBank as having interactions or not. We also mark if one of the drug names is not listed in DrugBank.

2.6 Using MetaMap for Domain Knowledge

The MetaMap program has been used extensively for a wide array of BioNLP studies, such as automatic indexing of biomedical literature and concept-based text summarization (Reeve et al., 2007; Quanzhi and Yi-Fang Brook, 2006). For drug-related information extraction, two recent applications demonstrated that integrating the MetaMap program to their existing systems produces high overall performance in i.) identification and classification of the pharmaceutical substances and ii.) extraction of drug indication information (Segura-Bedmar et al., 2008; Fung et al., 2013).

MetaMap finds Metathesaurus concepts by performing a shallow syntactic analysis of the input text, producing a set of noun phrases. The noun phrases are then used to generate sets of variants which are consequently looked up from the Metathesaurus concepts. Matching concepts are evaluated against the original text and the strength of the mappings are calculated. The candidates are finally combined and the final scores are computed, where the highest score of a complete mapping represents

[2]`http://www.drugbank.ca/`

MetaMap's interpretation of the text.

The MetaMap program can be run both locally and remotely[3]. We ran the current version, MetaMap2012, remotely via the batch mode facility by converting the sentences of the DDIExtraction corpora into the MetaMap input format. Many of the applications that integrate MetaMap into their systems use the default settings that are claimed to be suitable for general purposes. However, we applied different options with the aim of increasing the coverage of Metathesaurus concepts found by MetaMap. The parameter set that influences the performance of MetaMap included; using a relaxed model, selecting the NLM2012AB Metathesaurus version, including all derivational variants, enabling unique acronym/abbreviation variants only, allowing candidates from one or two character words, preferring multiple concepts and using word sense disambiguation.

The Relaxed Model is provided by MetaMap in addition to the strict model which is offered as a default setting in which all types of filterings are applied. However, we chose the relaxed model in which only manual and lexical filterings are used. While the strict model is most appropriate for experiments that require the highest accuracy, it covers only 53% of the Metathesaurus strings. As we consider high coverage of concepts an important factor, we applied the relaxed model which consists of up to 83% of Metathesaurus strings.

The versions of Metathesaurus, Base, USAbase and NLM, provided with MetaMap are different in their Metathesaurus coverage and the license type required for using vocabulary sources. The NLM2012AB version which is offered at no cost for research purposes and covers all of the provided Metathesaurus was used in our work.

Variants, such as inflectional and derivational variants, are computed by MetaMap to account for the textual variation in the text. With this setting, many types of variants are generated recursively, and only acronyms and abbreviations are restricted to the unique ones. In addition, the candidates also include words that can be prepositions, conjunctions or determiners if they occur often enough in Metathesaurus.

[3]`http://metamap.nlm.nih.gov/`

Prefer multiple concepts causes MetaMap to score the mappings with more concepts higher than those with fewer concepts. This option is useful for discovering higher-order relationships among concepts found in the text and as such is assumed to be helpful for discovering the DDIs.

Word sense disambiguation attempts to solve lexical ambiguities by identifying the correct meaning of a word based on its context. By using this option in MetaMap, the program attempts to solve the ambiguities among equally scoring concepts by choosing the concept(s) based on semantic type.

We use the XML version of the MetaMap output which is post-processed by TEES to extract relevant features; candidate concepts, preferred concepts, CUI (Concepts Unique Identifier), score, semantic types and sources.

For drug name recognition, these are added as binary features for the candidate token, with the exception of the score, the value of which is normalized into the [0, 1] range. For DDI extraction, the binary features are added for the two drug names, and combined into the shortest path features.

2.7 Public analyses

The TEES 2.0 system used in DDIExtraction 2011 Shared Task has been public since summer 2012. While only small modifications are needed to make the DDIExtraction 2013 corpus usable with the TEES system, these can be complicated for new users. Therefore, to make sure our public DDIExtraction 2011 system is usable not only in theory, but easy enough to use in practice, we updated the system into the 2.1 version capable of automatically converting the DDIExtraction 2013 corpus and provided with precalculated models for DDI prediction.

To improve usability, we provided fully precalculated analysis files for the DDIExtraction 2013 corpus, produced using TEES 2.1. These analyses contain the TEES drug-drug interaction predictions, BLLIP Penn tree-bank style parses (using the McClosky biomodel), Stanford dependency parses (in the collapsed CC processed format) and syntactic head offsets for drug entities.

The analyses were calculated with the baseline TEES 2.1 system, without using the external datasets which were tested only later. The analyses were provided for task 9.2, which is the direct continuation of the 2011 task for which the public TEES system was already available.

The analyses for the DDIExtraction 2013 corpus were made available on February 25th 2013. Despite being published quite late in the training period there was interest in this supporting data, and before the task result submission deadline the analyses were downloaded 14 times. The test set analyses were provided for registered DDIExtraction 2013 participants during the test period.

3 Results and Discussion

Three feature sets were used to produce the results. The baseline set (model 1) consisted of the TEES entity and edge detectors which build a large feature set from syntactic parses. Model 2 adds DrugBank features to this baseline and model 3 further extends model 2 with MetaMap information.

Three runs using these models were submitted for both tasks 9.1 and 9.2. The results indicate the system was capable of detecting both drug names and drug-drug interactions with reasonable performance. The best F-scores were 60% for task 9.1 drug name detection and 59% for task 9.2 DDI extraction.

As task 9.1 is completely new, and task 9.2 was extended from the 2011 DDI extraction task with typed interactions and MEDLINE abstracts, the current results are not directly comparable with the 2011 ones. The evaluation metric closest to the 2011 task is task 9.2 DDI detection regardless of type, using only the DrugBank subset of the corpus. With this metric, our system achieved an F-score of 72% in 2013 vs. 62.99% in 2011, which may indicate higher baseline performance, potentially influenced by a larger training dataset.

3.1 Drug name recognition

The decision to not attempt detection of more than one token per drug entity proved to be not too detrimental to the final performance. In the training corpus, there are 14,765 drug name entities of which only 2,768 (18.7%) consist of more than one token, and of these only 38 are disjoint (not forming a continuous span). For our best performing drug name detection model (number 3) typed, partial span matching was at 78% F-score vs. typed, strict span matching at 65%. Therefore, detecting only a single token per entity resulted in a maximum loss of 13 percentage points (pp), but considering that a scheme designed to detect multi-token entities would be inherently more complex, potentially having lower performance, and that not all of the spans would be correctly detected, we feel this tradeoff in performance is worth it for the considerably more simple system design it allows.

Adding the external datasets to the classifier models proved to have a considerable impact on the task performance (See Table 1). The baseline system reached an F-score of 47% which was increased by 9 percentage points when including DrugBank information and a further 4 percentage points when also MetaMap information was included.

As seen from the type-specific F-scores (on the training corpus), *brand* class entity detection was improved by 30 pp when DrugBank information was added, and increased slightly further with MetaMap information (See Table 2). DrugBank lists brand names for many drugs, and when this information is added as a feature for each detected drug, determining the type of the drug is greatly improved.

The official primary metric in both tasks 9.1 and 9.2 is a macro-averaged F-score, which gives equal weight to performance in each class, emphasizing the importance of detecting also the difficult, small classes. In particular, the class *drug_n* (active substances not approved for use in humans for medical purposes) was very difficult to detect for our system. While performance remained low for all three models, including the MetaMap information gave a large relative increase in *drug_n* detection performance, increasing it from 2% F-score to 8% (See Table 2). With the macro-averaged overall performance, this resulted in model three with the MetaMap information having notably higher performance.

We hypothesized that the *drug_n* category might be hard to detect as it could contain entities similar to the *drug* category, which may differ only by approval for use in humans, information that is not likely present in the corpus. Analysis of classification errors (See Table 3) confirms this hypothesis, showing that *drug_n* entities are by far the most commonly misclassified ones. Addition of DrugBank and MetaMap information considerably reduces *drug_n* misclassifications into the *drug* category.

M	task	P	R	F
1	9.1	0.48 (0.70)	0.46 (0.51)	0.47 (0.59)
2	9.1	0.6 (0.77)	0.52 (0.59)	0.56 (0.67)
3	9.1	0.69 (0.76)	0.54 (0.59)	0.6 (0.66)
1	9.2	0.73 (0.69)	0.47 (0.44)	0.57 (0.54)
2	9.2	0.76 (0.69)	0.48 (0.45)	0.59 (0.55)
3	9.2	0.73 (0.68)	0.48 (0.44)	0.58 (0.53)

Table 1: Official results for TEES in the DDIExtraction 2013 task and in parentheses corresponding 10-fold cross-validation results on the training corpus. The three models (M) used are 1) baseline syntactic features, 2) baseline with DrugBank features and 3) baseline with both DrugBank and MetaMap features.

model	drug	brand	group	drug_n
1	0.72	0.6	0.48	0.02
2	0.78	0.9	0.49	0.02
3	0.78	0.91	0.48	0.08

Table 2: Per-class micro-average scores for the drug name recognition task 9.1.

Task rules allowed using the test corpus of task 9.2 (with annotated entities) as additional training data for task 9.1. Due to time constraints we did not use it for training, but it is likely that performance could be further enhanced by using it.

3.2 Drug-drug interaction extraction

Performance of the three feature sets in the 9.2 DDI extraction task are much closer than in the 9.1 drug name recognition task. Still, additional information from DrugBank and MetaMap slightly increase performance, but DrugBank alone outperforms using both MetaMap and DrugBank. With the performance difference range between the models being only 2 pp, we think the results remain inconclusive.

That external data did not provide a further increase might indicate that drug-drug interaction detection is mostly a matter of interpreting the syntactic parse, whereas drug-name recognition benefits more from dictionary matching methods.

As with task 9.1, we analyse the classification errors on the 10-fold classification performed on the training dataset for which annotations are publicly available (See Table 4). None of the DDI classes are as hard to detect as the drug name class *drug_n*, but the *int* class has much lower performance than the other classes, with most examples classified incorrectly as negatives.

4 Conclusions

We applied the Turku Event Extraction System 2.1 to detection of both drug names and drug-drug interactions in the DDIExtraction 2013 task. The system showed good performance for both tasks, but we must consider that name and interaction detection were evaluated in isolation. In real world text mining tasks, these steps will be consecutive and as such result in lower overall performance. TEES achieves good performance using deep syntactic parsing, but this is a computationally expensive processing step. When drug names are detected with TEES, all input sentences need to be parsed, but if some other method is used for drug name recognition, TEES can parse just the sentences with drug names, as only they can potentially contain DDIs, enabling much faster DDI extraction.

We showed that adding external data from the DrugBank database and from MetaMap preprocessing can considerably increase extraction performance. However, we assume this makes the system more dependent on such data being available for candidate drug names and DDIs in the text being processed, potentially making it harder to detect completely new names and interactions. Therefore, using external data is likely to introduce a tradeoff of higher performance vs. wider detection. Use of such data should be chosen according to the task, as in some cases the goal is to retrieve documents with known drugs and interactions, in others to maximize detection of information not yet in the databases.

As with previous TEES versions, we will provide our source code freely available under an open source license at the TEES project repository[4]. We will also include a wrapper for using the MetaMap tool via the TEES preprocessing pipeline, allowing it to be easily integrated into event and relation extraction tasks.

Acknowledgments

We thank CSC — IT Center for Science Ltd, Espoo, Finland for providing computational resources.

[4] `http://jbjorne.github.com/TEES/`

	neg	brand	drug_n	group	drug
neg	**99.57**	0.04	0.00	0.15	0.24
	99.60	0.03	0.00	0.14	0.22
	99.60	0.03	0.01	0.14	0.22
brand	21.43	**67.92**	0.07	0.63	9.95
	8.91	**89.70**	0.07	0.21	1.11
	8.63	**89.98**	0.07	0.28	1.04
drug_n	49.70	2.79	**12.18**	0.40	34.93
	63.27	0.00	**15.37**	1.00	20.36
	65.27	0.00	**15.37**	1.20	18.16
group	13.80	0.12	0.03	**85.15**	0.90
	14.13	0.00	0.03	**84.97**	0.87
	14.04	0.06	0.06	**85.00**	0.84
drug	6.71	0.69	0.10	0.75	**91.75**
	5.60	0.27	0.08	0.79	**93.27**
	6.20	0.32	0.08	0.69	**92.72**

Table 3: Task 9.1 drug name classification errors for the training corpus. Each cell in the table lists from top to bottom results for models one to three (baseline, baseline+DrugBank, baseline+DrugBank+MetaMap). The results are percentage of SVM examples of each class (vertical) classified into each potential class (horizontal).

	neg	int	advise	effect	mechanism
neg	**97.27**	0.02	0.52	1.09	1.09
	97.32	0.03	0.49	1.06	1.09
	97.40	0.03	0.47	1.04	1.05
int	61.70	**22.87**	0.53	9.57	5.32
	61.70	**23.40**	0.00	8.51	6.38
	70.74	**19.15**	0.00	7.45	2.66
advise	34.50	0.12	**60.17**	4.24	0.97
	34.02	0.24	**60.05**	4.36	1.33
	33.54	0.24	**60.77**	4.36	1.09
effect	38.59	0.41	3.85	**54.06**	3.08
	38.41	0.41	3.73	**54.30**	3.14
	39.18	0.41	3.68	**53.59**	3.14
mechanism	50.34	0.15	2.05	5.08	**42.38**
	48.75	0.15	1.82	5.08	**44.20**
	52.16	0.23	1.29	5.00	**41.32**

Table 4: Task 9.2 drug-drug interaction classification errors for the training corpus. Each cell in the table lists from top to bottom results for models one to three (baseline, baseline+DrugBank, baseline+DrugBank+MetaMap). The results are percentage of SVM examples of each class (vertical) classified into each potential class (horizontal).

References

Alan R Aronson. 2001. Effective mapping of biomedical text to the UMLS Metathesaurus: the MetaMap program. In *Proceedings of the AMIA Symposium*, page 17. American Medical Informatics Association.

Jari Björne, Antti Airola, Tapio Pahikkala, and Tapio Salakoski. 2011. Drug-drug interaction extraction from biomedical texts with SVM and RLS classifiers. In *Proc. of the 1st Challenge task on Drug-Drug Interaction Extraction (DDIExtraction 2011) at SEPLN 2011*, volume 761, pages 35–42, Sept 5.

Jari Björne, Filip Ginter, and Tapio Salakoski. 2012. University of Turku in the BioNLP'11 Shared Task. *BMC Bioinformatics*, 13(Suppl 11):S4.

Olivier Bodenreider. 2004. The unified medical language system (UMLS): integrating biomedical terminology. *Nucleic acids research*, 32(suppl 1):D267–D270.

Eugene Charniak and Mark Johnson. 2005. Coarse-to-fine n-best parsing and MaxEnt discriminative reranking. In *Proceedings of the 43rd Annual Meeting of the Association for Computational Linguistics (ACL'05)*, pages 173–180. Association for Computational Linguistics.

Marie-Catherine de Marneffe, Bill MacCartney, and Christopher Manning. 2006. Generating typed dependency parses from phrase structure parses. In *Proceedings of LREC-06*, pages 449–454.

Kin Wah Fung, Chiang S Jao, and Dina Demner-Fushman. 2013. Extracting drug indication information from structured product labels using natural language processing. *Journal of the American Medical Informatics Association*.

Craig Knox, Vivian Law, Timothy Jewison, Philip Liu, Son Ly, Alex Frolkis, Allison Pon, Kelly Banco, Christine Mak, Vanessa Neveu, Yannick Djoumbou, Roman Eisner, Anchi Guo, and David S. Wishart. 2011. Drugbank 3.0: a comprehensive resource for omics research on drugs. *Nucleic Acids Research*, 39(Database-Issue):1035–1041.

David McClosky. 2010. *Any domain parsing: automatic domain adaptation for natural language parsing*. Ph.D. thesis, Department of Computer Science, Brown University.

Sampo Pyysalo, Antti Airola, Juho Heimonen, Jari Björne, Filip Ginter, and Tapio Salakoski. 2008. Comparative analysis of five protein-protein interaction corpora. *BMC bioinformatics*, 9(Suppl 3):S6.

Li Quanzhi and Wu Yi-Fang Brook. 2006. Identifying important concepts from medical documents. *Journal of Biomedical Informatics*, 39(6):668 – 679.

Lawrence H Reeve, Hyoil Han, and Ari D Brooks. 2007. The use of domain-specific concepts in biomedical text summarization. *Information Processing & Management*, 43(6):1765–1776.

Isabel Segura-Bedmar, Paloma Martínez, and María Segura-Bedmar. 2008. Drug name recognition and classification in biomedical texts: a case study outlining approaches underpinning automated systems. *Drug discovery today*, 13(17):816–823.

Isabel Segura-Bedmar, Paloma Martínez, and César de Pablo-Sánchez. 2011a. A linguistic rule-based approach to extract drug-drug interactions from pharmacological documents. *BMC bioinformatics*, 12(Suppl 2):S1.

Isabel Segura-Bedmar, Paloma Martínez, and Daniel Sánchez-Cisneros. 2011b. The 1st DDIExtraction-2011 challenge task: extraction of drug-drug interactions from biomedical texts. In *Proceedings of the 1st Challenge Task on Drug-Drug Interaction Extraction 2011: 7 Sep 2011; Huelva, Spain*, pages 1–9.

Isabel Segura-Bedmar, Paloma Martínez, and Maria Herrero-Zazo. 2013. Semeval-2013 task 9: Extraction of drug-drug interactions from biomedical texts. In *Proceedings of the 7th International Workshop on Semantic Evaluation (SemEval 2013)*.

Luis Tari, Saadat Anwar, Shanshan Liang, James Cai, and Chitta Baral. 2010. Discovering drug–drug interactions: a text-mining and reasoning approach based on properties of drug metabolism. *Bioinformatics*, 26(18):i547–i553.

Philippe Thomas, Mariana Neves, Illés Solt, Domonkos Tikk, and Ulf Leser. 2011. Relation extraction for drug-drug interactions using ensemble learning. In *Proc. of the 1st Challenge task on Drug-Drug Interaction Extraction (DDIExtraction 2011) at SEPLN 2011*, page 11–18, Huelva, Spain, Sept 5.

Ioannis Tsochantaridis, Thorsten Joachims, Thomas Hofmann, and Yasemin Altun. 2005. Large margin methods for structured and interdependent output variables. *Journal of Machine Learning Research (JMLR)*, 6(Sep):1453–1484.

Chen-May Wong, Yu Ko, and Alexandre Chan. 2008. Clinically significant drug-drug interactions between oral anticancer agents and nonanticancer agents: profiling and comparison of two drug compendia. *The Annals of pharmacotherapy*, 42(12):1737–1748.

LASIGE: using Conditional Random Fields and ChEBI ontology

Tiago Grego
Dep. de Informática
Faculdade de Ciências
Universidade de Lisboa
Portugal
tgrego@fc.ul.pt

Francisco Pinto
Dep. de Química e Bioquímica
Faculdade de Ciências
Universidade de Lisboa
Portugal
frpinto@fc.ul.pt

Francisco M. Couto
Dep. de Informática
Faculdade de Ciências
Universidade de Lisboa
Portugal
fcouto@di.fc.ul.pt

Abstract

For participating in the SemEval 2013 challenge of recognition and classification of drug names, we adapted our chemical entity recognition approach consisting in Conditional Random Fields for recognizing chemical terms and lexical similarity for entity resolution to the ChEBI ontology. We obtained promising results, with a best F-measure of 0.81 for the partial matching task when using post-processing. Using only Conditional Random Fields the results are slightly lower, achieving still a good result in terms of F-measure. Using the ChEBI ontology allowed a significant improvement in precision (best precision of 0.93 in partial matching task), which indicates that taking advantage of an ontology can be extremely useful for enhancing chemical entity recognition.

1 Introduction

Most chemical named entity recognition systems can be classified in two approaches: dictionary based and machine learning based approaches. Dictionary based approaches are usually easier to implement and maintain, but require a reference chemical term dictionary and are dependent on its completeness and quality. The availability of public chemical databases has been an issue until recently, when several publicly available databases such as PubChem (Wang et al., 2009), DrugBank (Wishart et al., 2006) and ChEBI (Degtyarenko et al., 2007) were released. An example of a popular system that uses this approach is Whatizit (Rebholz-Schuhmann et al., 2008). Machine learning based approaches are not limited to a terminology and are thus better suited for finding novel chemical terms that are yet to be inserted in reference databases. However this approach requires training data for a classifier to be able to successfully learn and perform the chemical entity recognition task. Some methods combine both approaches and thus are hybrid systems that aim to take the best out of both approaches (Jessop et al., 2011; Rocktäschel et al., 2012).

An annotated corpus of patent documents was released by ChEBI, and using such corpus as training data we developed an chemical entity recognition system (Grego et al., 2009) that uses a machine learning approach based on Conditional Random Fields (CRF) (Lafferty et al., 2001). We furthermore expanded our method to allow resolution of recognized entities to the ChEBI ontology (Grego et al., 2012).

This paper describes how our system (Grego et al., 2012) was adapted to perform the task of recognition and classification of drug names, and presents the results obtained in the task 9.1 of the 7th International Workshop on Semantic Evaluation (SemEval 2013).

2 Task and Dataset

The Task 9 of SemEval 2013 involved two sub-tasks: (9.1) recognition and classification of drug names, and (9.2) extraction of drug-drug interactions from Biomedical Texts (SemEval, 2013). The recognition and classification of drug names (Task 9.1) comprises two steps. First is chemical named entity recognition, that consists in finding in a sentence the offsets for the start and end of a chemical entity.

*Second Joint Conference on Lexical and Computational Semantics (*SEM), Volume 2: Seventh International Workshop on Semantic Evaluation (SemEval 2013)*, pages 660–666, Atlanta, Georgia, June 14-15, 2013.

An exact match is achieved by correctly identifying both the start and end offset, as curators manually provided them. If there is a mismatch in the offsets but there is some overlap with a manual annotation, then it is considered a partial match, otherwise it is a recognition error.

The second step consists in classifying each recognized entity in one of four possible entity types: i) Drug is any pharmaceutical product approved for human use; ii) Brand is a drug that was first developed by a pharmaceutical company; iii) Group refers to a class or group of drugs; iv) Drug_n is an active substance that has not been approved for human use. Thus, the evaluation takes into account not only entity recognition, but also the assigned type. Type matching assessment considers the entity type evaluation from partial matching entity recognition, while strict matching considers the entity type evaluation from exact matching.

For training, the DDI corpus dataset was provided (Segura-Bedmar et al., 2006). This dataset contains two sub-datasets. One that consists of MedLine abstracts, and other that contains DrugBank abstracts. An unannotated test dataset was provided for testing and evaluating the systems.

3 CRF entity recognition

Our method uses CRFs for building probabilistic models based on training datasets. We used the MALLET (McCallum, 2002) implementation of CRFs. MALLET is a Java-based package for statistical natural language processing, document classification, clustering, topic modeling, information extraction, and other machine learning applications to text, which includes an implementation of linear chain CRFs.

A required first step in our method in the tokenization of the input text. For this task we have used a specifically adapted tokenizer for chemical text adapted from an open source project (Corbett et al., 2007).

Each token is then represented as a set of features. We kept using a set of features derived in our previous work (Grego et al., 2009), which includes for each token:

Stem: The stem of the token.

Prefix: The first three characters of the token.

Suffix: The last three characters of the token.

Number: Boolean that indicates if the token contains digits.

In addition to the set of features, each token is also given a label in accordance to the training data:

NO: A non-chemical token.

NE: A chemical entity represented by a single token.

S-NE: The first token of a multi-token chemical entity.

M-NE: A middle token of a multi-token chemical entity (only exists for entities composed by three or more tokens).

E-NE: The last token of a multi-token chemical entity.

The task of entity recognition will be the assignment of such labels to new, unannotated text, based on a model. The assigned label allows for named entities to be recognized and offsets provided.

For creating a model, it is required as input a set of annotated documents. Our method was initially developed using an annotated patent document corpus released to the public by the ChEBI team. This corpus can be found at [1], and we decided to keep using it as training data for a model. Together with this corpus, the DDI corpus training dataset provided for the task was used. The model produced by using this combination of training data, that we called All model, will be suited for general purpose chemical entity recognition.

We then prepared four datasets based on the DDI corpus dataset but containing only one type of annotated entities each. With that training data we prepared four more models, each trained only with one kind on entity type. Thus we have in total prepared five models:

All: A model trained with all entity types of the DDI corpus dataset, and the ChEBI released patent dataset.

[1] http://chebi.cvs.sourceforge.net/viewvc/chebi/chapati/patentsGoldStandard/

Drug: A model trained only with the entities of type drug in the DDI corpus dataset.

Brand: A model trained only with the entities of type brand in the DDI corpus dataset.

Group: A model trained only with the entities of type group in the DDI corpus dataset.

Drug_n: A model trained only with the entities of type drug_n in the DDI corpus dataset.

Using the type specific models it is possible to annotate text with only one entity type. Thus our method now has the capability of entity type classification in addition to named entity recognition, using these type specific models.

4 ChEBI resolution

After having recognized the named chemical entities, our method tries to perform their resolution to the ChEBI ontology. ChEBI (Chemical Entities of Biological Interest) is a freely available dictionary of small molecular entities. In addition to molecular entities, ChEBI contains groups (parts of molecular entities) and classes of entities, allowing for an ontological classification that specifies the relationships between molecular entities or classes of entities and their parents and/or children. The ontology structure provides an integrated overview of the relationships between chemical entities, both structural and functional.

The resolution method takes as input the string identified as being a chemical compound name and returns the most relevant ChEBI identifier along with a confidence score.

To perform the search for the most likely ChEBI term for a given entity an adaptation of FiGO, a lexical similarity method (Couto et al., 2005). Our adaptation compares the constituent words in the input string with the constituent words of each ChEBI term, to which different weights have been assigned according to its frequency in the ontology vocabulary (Grego et al., 2012). A resolution score between 0 and 1 is provided with the mapping, which corresponds to a maximum value in the case of a ChEBI term that has the exact name as the input string, and is lower otherwise.

5 Post-processing

To further improve the quality of the annotations provided by our method, some naïve rules were created and external resources used.

One of the rules implemented is derived from the resolution process, and corresponds in classifying an entity as type Group if its ChEBI name is plural. This is because ChEBI follows the convention of naming its terms always as a singular name, except for terms that represent classes of entities where a plural name can be used.

We have also used other resources in the post-processing besides ChEBI, namely a list of brand names extracted from DrugBank. This list of brand names was used to check if a given entity was part of that list, and if it was the entity should be of the type Brand.

A common English words list was also used as external resource in post-processing. If a recognized chemical entity was part of this list then it was a recognition error and should be filtered out and not be considered a chemical entity.

Some simple rules were also implemented in an effort to improve the quality of the annotations. For instance, if the recognized entity was found to be composed entirely by digits, then it should be filtered out because it is most certainly an annotation error. Also, if an entity starts or ends with a character such as "*", "–", ".", "," or "'", then those characters should be removed from the entity and the offsets corrected accordingly.

With such naïve but efficient rules it was expected that the performance of entity recognition would improve. An overview of the system architecture is provided in Figure 1.

6 Testing runs

Using different combinations of the described methods, three runs were submitted for evaluation and are now described.

Run 1: This run uses all of the described methods. Entity recognition is performed using all models, and the type classification is performed by using the type specific models in the following priority: if an entity was recognized using the Drug_n model, then type is Drug_n, else if it

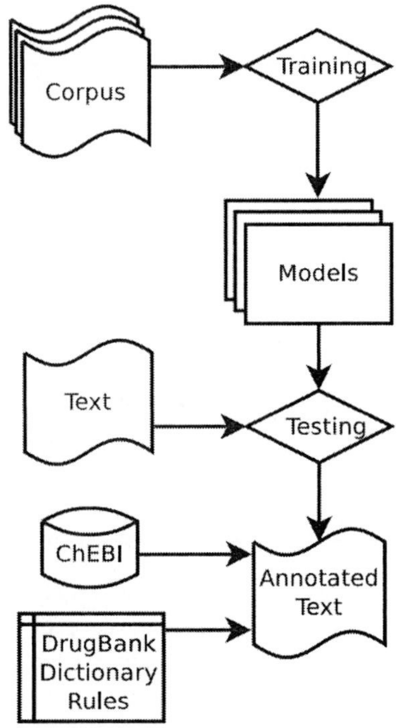

Figure 1: Overview of the system architecture. Based on annotated corpus, CRF models are created and used to annotate new documents.

was recognized using the Brand model, then type is Brand, else if it was recognized using the Group model, then type is Group, else and finally it is assigned the type Drug. Resolution to ChEBI is performed and all of the described post-processing rules applied.

Run 2: In this run only the classifiers are used. This means that the entity recognition is performed using all models, and the type classification is performed by using the type specific models as described in Run 1. However no extra processing is performed and the results are submitted as obtained directly from the classifiers.

Run 3: This run performs entity recognition in a similar way described in run 1, and performs entity recognition to the ChEBI ontology. However, only the entities successfully mapped to ChEBI, with a resolution score of at least 0.8, are considered. All the other entities are discarded in this phase. After resolution and the filtering of entities according to the resolution to ChEBI, all the described post-processing rules are applied in a similar way to Run 1.

7 Results and Discussion

The official evaluation results are presented in Table 1. We can observe that the obtained results are better for the DrugBank dataset than for the MedLine dataset. This may have happened because the DrugBank dataset is four times larger than the MedLine dataset, but also because while the DrugBank abstracts are quite focused in drug descriptions and use mostly systematic names, the MedLine ones are usually more generic and make more extensive use of trivial drug names. We obtained for the Run 1 a top F-measure of 0.81 in the full dataset for a partial matching assessment, and that value decreased to 0.78 when an exact matching assessment is considered. The values are very close, which means that our method is being able to efficiently find the correct offsets of the entities. However the F-measure decreases to 0.69 for partial matching and 0.66 for exact matching when the assignment of the entity type is considered. This means that there is room to improve in the task of classifying the chemical entities to the correct entity type.

Run 2 obtained results very similar to Run 1, only slightly less F-measure. The difference between those two runs was that Run 2 used only the classifiers, while Run 1 used rules and external resources in an effort to improve the results. We can thus conclude that the classifiers alone produce already good results and more sophisticated post-processing is required to obtain significant performance gains. Our post-processing was very simple as explained earlier, and can only slightly improve the results obtained with the CRF classifiers alone.

Run 3 obtained improved precision in all assessments. In this run only the entities that were successfully mapped to ChEBI were considered, and thus the precision of recognition was the best of our runs. This is because ChEBI contains high quality, manually validated chemical terms. If a recognized entity can be successfully mapped to this data source, then there is a good indication that it is, in fact, a valid chemical entity. However F-measure has decreased because of a loss in recall. ChEBI is still a young project containing slightly over 30,000 chem-

Assessment	Run	MedLine Dataset			DrugBank Dataset			Full Dataset		
		P	**R**	**F1**	**P**	**R**	**F1**	**P**	**R**	**F1**
Strict matching	1	0.6	0.54	**0.57**	0.82	0.72	**0.77**	0.7	0.62	**0.66**
	2	0.54	0.54	0.54	0.82	0.73	**0.77**	0.65	0.62	0.64
	3	**0.66**	0.48	0.56	**0.83**	0.58	0.68	**0.73**	0.52	0.61
Exact matching	1	0.78	0.7	**0.74**	0.89	0.78	**0.83**	0.83	0.74	**0.78**
	2	0.73	0.74	0.73	0.88	0.78	**0.83**	0.79	0.76	0.77
	3	**0.82**	0.6	0.69	**0.91**	0.63	0.74	**0.86**	0.61	0.72
Partial matching	1	0.81	0.73	**0.77**	0.91	0.8	**0.85**	0.86	0.76	**0.81**
	2	0.76	0.77	0.76	0.91	0.8	**0.85**	0.82	0.78	0.8
	3	**0.86**	0.63	0.72	**0.93**	0.65	0.76	**0.89**	0.64	0.74
Type matching	1	0.64	0.58	**0.61**	0.85	0.75	**0.8**	0.73	0.65	**0.69**
	2	0.57	0.58	0.58	0.85	0.75	**0.8**	0.69	0.66	0.67
	3	**0.71**	0.52	0.6	**0.87**	0.61	0.71	**0.78**	0.56	0.65

Table 1: Results obtained in Task 9.1 for the different assessments. Exact and Partial matching do not consider the entity type, while Strict and Type matching consider the entity type for Exact and Partial matching entity recognition respectively.

Entity Type	Run	MedLine Dataset			DrugBank Dataset			Full Dataset		
		P	**R**	**F1**	**P**	**R**	**F1**	**P**	**R**	**F1**
Drug	1	0.58	0.82	0.68	0.85	0.78	0.82	0.69	0.8	0.74
	2	0.51	0.82	0.63	0.83	0.81	0.82	0.64	0.82	0.72
	3	0.66	0.74	0.7	0.88	0.67	0.76	0.75	0.7	0.73
Brand	1	1	0.5	0.67	0.77	0.45	0.57	0.79	0.46	0.58
	2	0.67	0.33	0.44	0.91	0.4	0.55	0.88	0.39	0.54
	3	1	0.5	0.67	0.65	0.21	0.31	0.7	0.24	0.35
Group	1	0.7	0.54	0.61	0.82	0.85	0.83	0.76	0.67	0.71
	2	0.64	0.56	0.6	0.82	0.83	0.82	0.72	0.67	0.7
	3	0.7	0.47	0.56	0.83	0.69	0.76	0.76	0.56	0.65
Drug_n	1	0.48	0.11	0.18	0	0	0	0.42	0.11	0.17
	2	0.5	0.12	0.2	0	0	0	0.42	0.12	0.18
	3	0.48	0.1	0.17	0	0	0	0.41	0.1	0.16

Table 2: Results obtained in Task 9.1 for each entity type. In this evaluation only the entities of a specific type are considered at a time.

Run	MedLine Dataset			DrugBank Dataset			Full Dataset		
	P	**R**	**F1**	**P**	**R**	**F1**	**P**	**R**	**F1**
1	0.69	0.50	0.58	0.61	0.52	0.56	0.67	0.51	0.58
2	0.58	0.46	0.51	0.64	0.51	0.57	0.67	0.50	0.57
3	0.71	0.45	0.55	0.59	0.39	0.47	0.66	0.4	0.5

Table 3: Macro-average measures obtained for each run.

ical entities, which is still a low amount of entities when compared with other chemical databases (for example, PubChem contains more than 10 times that amount). However ChEBI is growing at a steady pace and we believe its coverage will keep increasing while maintaining the high quality that allows for an excellent precision. Thus, as ChEBI evolves, our approach will mantain the high levels of precision but with a lower reduction in recall.

ChEBI is not only a chemical dictionary, but an ontology. This allows for a comparison recognized entities through semantic similarity measures that can be used to further enhance chemical entity recognition (Ferreira and Couto , 2010; Couto and Silva , 2011). This comparison can also be extremely useful in other task such as drug-drug interaction extraction. Moreover, even if with a relatively small ChEBI, it can be possible to increase coverage by integrating other available resources using Ontology Matching techniques (Faria et al., 2012).

In Table 2 we have the official results obtained for each entity type, and we can observe that our method is efficient in correctly classifying the Drug and Group types, where it achieves an F-measure of 0.74 and 0.71 correspondingly. However our method has some difficulties in correctly classifying entities of the Brand type, where an F-measure of 0.58 was obtained. The Drug_n entity type has proven to be a very challenging type to be correctly classified, and our system failed the correct classification of this type in most situations. This is possibly because the percentage of entities of this type is very limited, and also because the difference between this type and the Drug type is the fact that the later has been approved for human use, while the former has not. The feature set used cannot efficiently discriminate this information and external information about drug approval for human usage must be used for efficient detection of this type.

Overall, Run 1 has obtained the best results. However, the results from Run 2 have been very similar, which shows that the classifiers have been successful and the post-processing of Run 1 has been minimal. Run 3 was designed for high precision, because only the entities successfully mapped to the ChEBI ontology were considered. It does improve the obtained precision, but suffers a drop in recall. Table 3 presents the macro-average measures obtained for each run.

8 Conclusions

This paper presents our participation in the 7th International Workshop on Semantic Evaluation (SemEval 2013) using a CRF-based chemical entity recognition method and a lexical similarity based resolution method. We prepared type-specific CRF models to allow both recognition and type classification of the chemical entities. Mapping of the entities to the ChEBI ontology was performed using a lexical similarity based method, and several post-processing rules using external resources where implemented.

We submitted different runs on annotated test data using different combination of such methods, and obtained a best precision of 0.89 and a best F-measure of 0.81 in the entity recognition task. For the task of entity recognitions and classification we have obtained a best precision of 0.78 and a best F-measure of 0.69. We concluded that the classifiers provide already good results by their own, that can be slightly improved by using some naïve external resources and rules.

However, using ChEBI allows for a significant increase of precision, which is encouraging. We believe this result is a good indication that as ChEBI matures, the methods that take advantage of its ontology structure for entity recognition and classification will benefit more from its usage, increasing the F-measure obtained in the task.

9 Acknowledgments

The authors want to thank the Portuguese Fundação para a Ciência e Tecnologia through the financial support of the SPNet project (PTDC/EBB-EBI/113824/2009), the SOMER project (PTDC/EIA-EIA/119119/2010) and the PhD grant SFRH/BD/36015/2007 and through the LASIGE multi-annual support. The authors also wish to thank the European Commission for the financial support of the EPIWORK project under the Seventh Framework Programme (Grant #231807).

References

P. Corbett, C. Batchelor and S. Teufel. 2007. Annotation of chemical named entities. *Proceedings of the Work-*

shop on BioNLP 2007: Biological, Translational, and Clinical Language Processing, 57–64.

F. M. Couto and M. J. Silva. 2011. Disjunctive shared information between ontology concepts: application to Gene Ontology. *Journal of Biomedical Semantics*, 2(5).

F. M. Couto, P. M. Coutinho and M. J. Silva. 2005. Finding genomic ontology terms in text using evidence content. *BMC Bioinformatics*, 6 (Suppl 1), S21.

K. Degtyarenko, P. Matos, M. Ennis, J. Hastings, M. Zbinden, A. McNaught, R. Alcantara, M. Darsow, M. Guedj and M. Ashburner. 2007. ChEBI: a database and ontology for chemical entities of biological interest. *Nucleic Acids Research*, 36, D344.

D. Faria, C. Pesquita, E. Santos, F. M. Couto, C. Stroe and I. F. Cruz 2012. Testing the AgreementMaker System in the Anatomy Task of OAEI 2012. *CoRR*, abs/1212.1625, `arXiv:1212.1625`.

J. D. Ferreira and F. M. Couto 2010. Semantic similarity for automatic classification of chemical compounds. *PLoS Computational Biology*, 6(9).

T. Grego, C. Pesquita, H. P. Bastos and F. M. Couto. 2012. Chemical Entity Recognition and Resolution to ChEBI. *ISRN Bioinformatics*, Article ID 619427.

T. Grego, P. Pezik, F. M. Couto and D. Rebholz-Schuhmann. 2009. Identification of Chemical Entities in Patent Documents. *Distributed Computing, Artificial Intelligence, Bioinformatics, Soft Computing, and Ambient Assisted Living*, volume 5518 of *Lecture Notes in Computer Science*, 934–941.

T. Grego, F. Pinto and F. M. Couto. 2012. Identifying Chemical Entities based on ChEBI. *Software Demonstration at the International Conference on Biomedical Ontologies (ICBO)*.

D. M. Jessop, S. E. Adams, E. L. Willighagen, L. Hawizy and P. Murray-Rust 2011. OSCAR4: a flexible architecture for chemical text-mining. *Journal of Cheminformatics*, 3(41).

J. Lafferty, A. McCallum and F. Pereira. 2001. Conditional random fields: Probabilistic models for segmenting and labeling sequence data. *Proceedings of the 18th International Conference on Machine Learning*, 282–289.

A. K. McCallum. 2002. Mallet: A machine learning for language toolkit. `http://mallet.cs.umass.edu`.

D. Rebholz-Schuhmann, M. Arregui, S. Gaudan, H. Kirsch and A. Jimeno. 2008. Text processing through Web services: calling Whatizit. *Bioinformatics*, 24(2):296–298.

T. Rocktäschel, M. Weidlich and U. Leser. 2012. ChemSpot: A Hybrid System for Chemical Named Entity Recognition. *Bioinformatics*, 28(12): 1633-1640.

I. Segura-Bedmar, P. Martínez and C. de Pablo-Sánchez 2006. Using a shallow linguistic kernel for drug-drug interaction extraction. *Journal of Biomedical Informatics*, 44(5): 789–804.

Y. Wang, J. Xiao, T. O. Suzek, J. Zhang, J. Wang and S. H. Bryant. 2009. PubChem: a public information system for analyzing bioactivities of small molecules. *Nucleic Acids Research*, 37, W623.

D. S. Wishart, C. Knox, A. C. Guo, S. Shrivastava, M. Hassanali, P. Stothard, Z. Chang and J. Woolsey. 2006. DrugBank: a comprehensive resource for in silico drug discovery and exploration. *Nucleic Acids Research*, 34, D668.

SemEval 2013. In Proceedings of the 7th International Workshop on Semantic Evaluation

UWM-TRIADS: Classifying Drug-Drug Interactions with Two-Stage SVM and Post-Processing

Majid Rastegar-Mojarad
University of Wisconsin-Milwaukee
Milwaukee, WI, USA
Rastega3@uwm.edu

Richard D. Boyce
University of Pittsburgh
Pittsburgh, PA, USA
rdb20@pitt.edu

Rashmi Prasad
University of Wisconsin-Milwaukee
Milwaukee, WI, USA
prasadr@uwm.edu

Abstract

We describe our system for the DDIExtraction-2013 shared task of classifying Drug-Drug interactions (DDIs) given labeled drug mentions. The challenge called for a five-way classification of all drug pairs in each sentence: a drug pair is either non-interacting, or interacting as one of four types. Our approach begins with the use of a two-stage weighted SVM classifier to handle the highly unbalanced class distribution: the first stage for a binary classification of drug pairs as interacting or non-interacting, and the second stage for further classification of interacting pairs from the first stage into one of the four interacting types. Our SVM features exploit stemmed words, lemmas, bigrams, part of speech tags, verb lists, and similarity measures, among others. For each stage, we also developed a set of post-processing rules based on observations in the training data. Our best system achieved 0.472 F-measure.

1 Introduction

Potential drug-drug interactions (DDIs), defined as the co-prescription of two drugs that are known to interact, are a significant source of preventable drug-related harm (i.e., adverse drug events, or ADEs) (Nebeker et al., 2004). Gurwitz et al, in their cohort study of ADEs among older Americans receiving ambulatory care, found that 13.3% of preventable errors leading to an ADE involved the co-prescription of drugs for which a "...well established, clinically important interaction" was known (Gurwitz et al., 2003). Nearly 7% (23/338) of the ADEs experienced by residents of two academic nursing homes over a nine-month period were attributable to DDIs (Gurwitz et al., 2005). Sixteen cohort and case-control studies reported an elevated risk of hospitalization in patients who were exposed to DDIs (Hines et al., 2011).

Failure to properly manage a DDI is a medical error, and the Institute of Medicine has noted that a lack of drug knowledge is one of the most frequent proximal causes of such errors (Committee on Identifying and Preventing Medication Errors, 2007). Indeed, health care providers often have inadequate knowledge of what drug interactions can occur, of patient specific factors that can increase the risk of harm from an interaction, and how to properly manage an interaction when patient exposure cannot be avoided (Chen et al., 2005; Hines et al., 2012).

Unfortunately, there is no single complete and authoritative source of DDI knowledge (Hines et al., 2012). Rather, there are multiple sources, each tasked with extracting, evaluating, and staying up-to-date with pertinent DDIs reported in the literature, and drug product labeling (Boyce et al., 2012). The dynamic nature of drug knowledge, combined with the enormity of the biomedical literature, makes this task extremely challenging. Hence, natural language processing methods for identifying and extracting DDIs are receiving increased attention.

In 2011, the first shared task challenge for DDI extraction, DDIExtraction-2011 (Segura-Bedmar et al., 2011), invited participants to develop automatic methods to extract DDIs. The task focused on the identification of all possible pairs of interacting drugs, without specifying anything further about the interactions. By contrast, the DDIExtraction-2013 (Segura-Bedmar et al., 2013) shared task emphasized the importance of recognizing *what is being asserted about the interaction*. Accordingly, the challenge called for a

*Second Joint Conference on Lexical and Computational Semantics (*SEM), Volume 2: Seventh International Workshop on Semantic Evaluation (SemEval 2013)*, pages 667–674, Atlanta, Georgia, June 14-15, 2013.

five-way classification of sentences for each drug-pair:

- *Advice*: the sentence notes a recommendation or advice related to the concomitant use of the two drugs (e.g., "... **UROXATRAL** should NOT be used in combination with other **alpha-blockers**.");
- *Effect*: the sentence states the effect of the drug interaction, including pharmacodynamic effect or mechanism of interaction (e.g., "**Quinolones** may enhance the effects of the oral anticoagulant, **warfarin**, ...");
- *Mechanism*: the sentence describes a pharmacokinetic mechanism (e.g., "**Grepafloxacin** is a competitive inhibitor of the metabolism of **theophylline**.").
- *Int:* the sentence mentions a drug interaction but doesn't provide any additional information (e.g., "The interaction of **omeprazole** and **ketoconazole** has been established.").
- *None:* the sentence does not show an interaction between the two drugs;

To focus on, and separately evaluate, different aspects of the problem, the 2013 shared task was divided into two subtasks. One task focused on the recognition and classification of drug names, while the other focused on the identification and classification of DDIs, with the drug names provided from the gold standard. In this paper, we describe our approach for handling the second task, namely, DDI identification and classification of all possible pairs of drugs in the provided corpus. Our approach combined machine-learning methods with the use of rules for post-processing. A key feature of our machine-learning approach is that it is specifically designed to handle the highly unbalanced class distribution via the use of a two-stage weighted SVM classifier. In addition to a variety of features exploited for the classifier, we also developed a set of post-processing rules, with a different set of rules applied after each stage of SVM classification. Finally, our approach is also aimed towards exploring the efficacy of methods that do not need to rely on syntactic-parse based features.

The paper is organized as follows. In the next section, we describe the training and test data set used in the challenge. In section 3, we describe our method, the classifiers used at each stage, their features, and post processing. In section 4, we present the evaluation and results. We conclude in Section 5 with discussion and future work.

2 Data

The DDIExtraction-2013 challenge provided a DDI corpus for development, containing 142 Medline abstracts on the subject of drug-drug interactions, and 572 documents describing drug-drug interactions from the DrugBank database. The corpus includes 6976 sentences that were annotated with four types of pharmacological entities and four types of DDIs. The DDIs types are: *advice, effect, mechanism, and int.*[1] Table 1 shows the number of instances for each type. Examples can be seen in Section 1. The test set includes 33 Medline abstracts and 158 DrugBank documents containing 1299 sentences and 5519 drug pairs.

Type		**Number**
Positive	Advice	827
	Effect	1700
	Mechanism	1322
	Int	188
Negative	None (non-interacting drugs)	23772
Total		**27809**

Table 1: Number of instances in each class

3 Methods

Classification of each drug pair in a sentence involved distinguishing between 5 classes, *advice, effect, mechanism, int and none*. As described in Section 2 (see Table 1), a major challenge in this task is posed by the unbalanced distribution of the classes. First, considering just the positive vs. negative classes, just 16.9% (4037/23772) of drug pairs are in the positive class, which include interacting drug pairs (labeled as *advice, effect, mechanism* and *int*). Furthermore, the four types

[1] http://www.cs.york.ac.uk/semeval-2013/task9/data/uploads/task-9.2-ddi-extraction.pdf

within the positive class are also unbalanced, with the *int* type constituting only 4.6% (188/4037) of the instances. A classifier trained on this data will, therefore, be biased towards the majority class(es). We employed a two-stage classification approach to cope with this problem, as described below.

3.1 Two-stage classification

Figure 1 shows the architecture of the system. In the first stage, we trained a binary classifier to classify drug pairs into *positive* and *negative* classes. Then, in the second stage, we considered only instances that were classified as positive by the first classifier, and classified them into *advice, effect, mechanism, and int* classes, using a multi-class classifier. A two-stage classifier offers a distinct advantage over a one-stage classifier for the DDI data set, which is highly skewed towards one class, but particularly because this majority class is also clearly semantically distinct from the other positive classes (see Table 1). By reframing part of this problem as a binary classification task, we can exploit binary classification techniques and allow the classifier to be particularly attentive to features distinguishing positive and negative drug pairs, while at the same time avoiding the bias against each of the non-majority classes. Our experiments with the training set confirm this idea.

Despite the above advantage of a two-stage SVM, however, the unbalanced class problem still remains, especially for training at the first stage, where we have 20854 negative instances and 4026 positives instances. In the second stage, the data is somewhat unbalanced as well, with 20.5% as *advice*, 42.2% as *effect*, 32.6% as *mechanism*, and only 4.7% as *int*. To handle this problem further, we explored different approaches and algorithms, including SMOTE (Chawla et al. 2002) and other resampling algorithms. Our best results over the training data were obtained with Support Vector Machine (SVM) with different class weights. We used LibSVM (Chang and Lin, 2011) and set class weights for each stage using results of cross-validation over the training data (see Table 3 for class weights).

As we wanted to pass the positively classified instances from the first stage to the second stage classifier, we favored the *positive* class in the first stage. This resulted in a relatively high number of false positives for the positive instances, which we attempted to reduce with a set of post-processing rules before sending them to the second stage classifier. A different set of post-processing rules were also developed to apply on the output of the second stage classifier.

3.2 Pre-processing

Before classification, all sentence instances in the training and test set were pre-processed for the following:

- All letters were changed to lower case.
- All drug names were normalized by replacing them with one of two strings; one used for drug mentions that were candidates for clas-

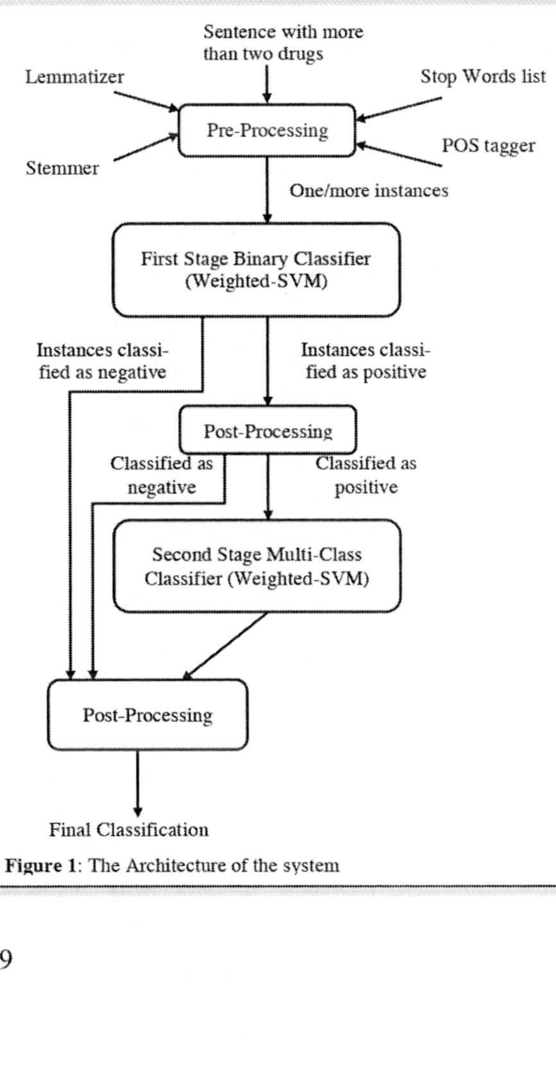

Figure 1: The Architecture of the system

sification in the instance, and the other used for all other drug mentions.

- All numbers were normalized by replacing them with the same string.
- Stop words and punctuation were removed. We used different stop word lists for different systems that were submitted to the challenge.
- Part of speech (POS) tags were obtained with the Stanford NLP tool (Toutanova et al, 2003).
- Words were stemmed with the Porter Stemmer (Porter, 1980).
- Words were lemmatized with the dragon tool (Zhou et al, 2007).
- Synsets for words were obtained using WordNet (Fellbaum, 1998).

3.3 Features

Since each sentence can have more than two drug mentions, we generated an instance of the sentence for each drug pair. We used different combinations of various features for the three different systems submitted to the challenge (Section 3.4.3). The following describes all the features separated into two categories: features per sentence and features per drug-pair instances.

Features per sentence: These are sentence-level features that have the same values across all instances of a sentence.

1- *Words*: This is a binary feature for all words that appeared more than once in the corpus, indicating the presence or absence of each such word in the sentence. We considered stemmed words as well as lemmatized words.

2- *Word bigrams*: This is a binary feature for all word bigrams that appeared more than once in the corpus, indicating the presence or absence of each such bigram in the sentence

3- *Number of words*: This feature represents the total number of words in the sentence

4- *Number of drug mentions*: This feature represents the total number of drug mentions in the sentence.

5- *Cosine similarity between centroid vector of each class and the instance*: Inspired by the vector space Information Retrieval approach, we added new features to represent the cosine similarity between a sentence and the centroid of normalized vectors for sentences assigned the class *X*. Cosine similarity is calculated based on modified tf*idf. We computed modified tf*idf for a word w in class *C*, based on the following formula:

$$(TF * IDF)_{w,C} = \log(count(w,C)+1) * \log(total\,\#\,Inst\,/\,(\#\,inst\_contains\_w+1))$$

TF is the logarithm of the number of times the word occurs in all sentences assigned to the class. IDF is 1.0 divided by the logarithm of number of instances in the class divided by the number of times the word occurs across all classes. To calculate the centroid vector for class C, a vector is created for each sentence in class C by giving each word in the sentence a modified TF*IDF weight. The centroid vector for class C is the mean of all vectors of sentences in class C. The Cosine similarity between a given instance and the centroid vector of each class is then used a feature.

Features per instance (for each drug-pair): In contrast to sentence-level features, these features may have different values across the different drug-pair instances. In each instance, we distinguished the two *main* drugs of interest for the instance from all other *additional* drugs mentioned in the instance.

1- *Number of words between two main drugs*: This represents the total number of words between the two main drugs.

2- *Number of drugs between two main drugs*: This represents the total number of additional drugs appearing between the two main drugs.

3- *Number of verbs*: We used the number of verbs in the instance as a feature, but relative to their sentential position. In particular, we split each instance into three sections: (i) before the first main drug, (ii) between the two main drugs, and (iii) after the second main drug. Then, we counted the number of verbs in each section, and used them as three different features.

4- *Number of verbs using class-specific verb lists*: For each class, we extracted two lists of verbs. The first list contains verbs that appeared in just that class but not in the others. Thus, the set of verbs extracted for each class are unique and different from the verbs associated with other classes. The second list includes all verbs that appeared in that class and their synonyms, extracted from WordNet. Then, for each of the three sentence sections, as described above, we created two features to represent the number of verbs from each of these lists that appeared in the section. (An alternative way to represent this feature would be to weight the verbs according to their relative frequencies in the different classes.)

5- *POS of words between two main drugs*: This is a binary feature for word POS tags obtained from POS tagging, and indicates the presence or absence of each POS between the two main drugs.

3.4 Post processing

As described in Section 3.1, we developed a set of post-processing rules for each stage of the classifier. Here, we describe these rules, developed on the basis of observations in the training data.

3.4.1 Post processing after the first stage

Post-processing rules for the first stage were designed to reduce the number of false positives for the positive class, since the weight assignment in this stage favors this class. We provide examples for each rule:

- The instance is classified as negative if both drug mentions have the same name, since a drug cannot interact with itself.

  "In controlled clinical trials of AUGMENTIN XR, 22 patients received concomitant allopurinol and AUGMENTIN XR."

- The instance is classified as negative if one of the drugs is a plural form of the other one, since, as above, they refer to the same drug.

  "Oral Anticoagulants: Interaction studies with warfarin failed to identify any clinically important effect on the serum concentrations of the anticoagulant or on its anticoagulant effect."

- The instance is classified as negative if one of the drug mentions refers to a drug class name of the other, since we don't expect a drug to interact with its class. Drug class names were obtained from a classification provided by the FDA.[2] In the example below, "MAOI" is the drug class name for "isocarboxazid".

  "You cannot take mazindol if you have taken a monoamine oxidase inhibitor (MAOI) such as isocarboxazid (Marplan), tranylcypromine (Parnate), or phenelzine (Nardil) in the last 14 days."

- The instance is classified as negative if "," or ", and" appears between the two main drug mentions, and is accompanied by an additional drug mention. This rules identifies contexts where drugs are mentioned as a set, in interaction with a different drug. The following sentences show "glyburide", "tolbutamide" and "glipzide" as part of a set of drugs in interaction with the additional drug "DIFLUCAN".

  "DIFLUCAN reduces the metabolism of tolbutamide, glyburide, and glipizide and increases the plasma concentration of these agents."

  *"DIFLUCAN reduces the metabolism of tolbutamide, glyburide, **and** glipizide and increases the plasma concentration of these agents."*

- The sentence is classified as negative if "," and additional drugs appear between the main drug mentions. Like the previous rule, this again recognizes drugs mentioned as a set but identifies non-adjacent mentions. For example, the following sentence doesn't express any interaction between "tolbutamide" and "glipizide", and the rule recognizes them as part of a set mention even though they are non-adjacent.

  "DIFLUCAN reduces the metabolism of tolbutamide, glyburide, and glipizide and increases the plasma concentration of these agents."

[2] http://www.fda.gov/ForIndustry/DataStandards/StructuredProductLabeling/ucm162549.htm

- The instance is classified as negative if "or" appears between the two main drug mentions and the sentence contains additional drug mentions. The presence of additional drug mentions in the sentence is required here since such conjoined pairs can interact with each other when they occur alone.

"Concurrent ingestion of antacid (20 mL of antacid containing aluminum hydroxide, magnesium hydroxide, and simethicone) did not significantly affect the exposure of oxybutynin ***or*** *desethyloxybutynin."*

3.4.2 Post processing after the second stage

Post-processing after the second classifier identifies sentences like the following:

"Coadministration of ***alosetron*** *and strong CYP3A4 inhibitors, such as* ***clarithromycin, teli thromycin, protease inhibitors, voriconazole,*** *and* ***itraconazole*** *has not been evaluated but should be undertaken with caution because of similar potential drug interactions."*

Examples like these illustrate that if drugs are mentioned as a set, then all drugs in the set must have the same interaction type with a drug mentioned outside the set. Thus, in the example, the interaction of each of "clarithromycin", "telithromycin", "protease inhibitors", "voriconazole", and "itraconazole" with "alosetron" should be classified in the same way. We used several syntactic and lexical cues to identify set mentions of drugs. Then, since the SVM classifier can make different decisions for each such pair (e.g., it may assign one label to the interaction of "clarithromycin" with "alosetron" and another label to the interaction of "telithromycin" with "alosetron"), we applied uniform labeling for the interaction of all such pairs. The majority label was used as the common label. Ties were not encountered in this data, although a solution would have to be devised otherwise.

An important consideration for this rule is that it uses both positively and negatively labeled instances. The former are taken from the result of the second stage classifier, and the latter from the negative instances of the first stage classifier and the negative instances of the first post-processor. These varied inputs to the rule are illustrated by the three ingoing arrows into the second post-processor in Figure 1.

3.4.3 Submitted Systems

We used the Weka (Hall et al. 2009) tool for all experiments and submitted three systems (System1, System 2, and System 3 in Table 2) to the challenge. All systems used the same two-stage approach and SVM classification (LibSVM), but differed in the use of some of the features (Section 3.3) and in the weights assignment (Table 3). We used linear kernel and the cost (C) was 1.2 and gamma was 0.5. In System 1, we used stemmed words (instead of lemmatized words) and a stop word list of 165 words. In System 2, we used stemmed words again, but a different

System	Metric	Drug-Bank	Medline	All
System 1	Prec	0.44	0.21	0.43
	Rec	0.49	0.23	0.47
	F	0.46	0.22	0.45
System 2	Prec	0.49	0.30	0.47
	Rec	0.49	0.41	0.47
	F	0.49	0.35	0.47
System 3	Prec	0.42	0.26	0.40
	Rec	0.51	0.47	0.50
	F	0.46	0.33	0.44

Table 2. Results of each system. The three systems are described in Section 3.4.3.

System	Stage	Class	Weight
System 1	First Stage	Positive	6.5
		Negative	1.0
	Second Stage	Advice	800.0
		Effect	600.0
		Int	3200.0
		Mechanism	500.0
System 2	First Stage	Positive	2.5
		Negative	1.0
	Second Stage	Advice	800.0
		Effect	600.0
		Int	3200.0
		Mechanism	500.0
System 3	First Stage	Positive	6.5
		Negative	1.0
	Second Stage	Advice	80.0
		Effect	60.0
		Int	320.0
		Mechanism	50.0

Table 3: Class weight assignments in different systems

stop word list of 263 words. Finally, in System 3, we used lemmatized words and the same stop word list of 263 words as in System 2. Weights assignment was different across all systems, as shown in Table 3.

4 Results

Table 2 shows the evaluation results of our system over the test set. Our best results are achieved with System 2, in which we used stemmed words and our 263 stop word list, in addition to the other features described in Section 3.3. Both the stop word list and the use of stemmed vs. lemmatized words can be seen to affect the performance. Clearly, a larger stop word list is more useful, since both System 2 and System 3 show an improvement over System 1. On the other hand, the use of lemmas (used in System 3) seems to be detrimental, compared with stemmed words.

5 Conclusion and future work

To the best of our knowledge, this is the first study to explore the value of a two-stage SVM classification process for performing the complex task of identifying sentences describing DDIs, and making the important distinction between statements providing advice, mechanism and effect, or declaring a pharmacokinetic and pharmacodynamic DDI: critical distinctions in the fields of pharmacology and pharmacy. We find that the use of a two-stage classifier to handle the problem of an unbalanced class distribution for the task of identifying and classifying DDIs is feasible but requires further development.

It's valuable to consider these results within the context of previous efforts for extracting DDIs. Ten research papers were presented at the 2011 SemEval Conference (Segura-Bedmar et al, 2011) which used a smaller DDI corpus (Medline abstracts were not included) and a simpler classification task (Segura-Bedmar et al, 2010). The best performing system in this challenge utilized an ensemble learning approach (Thomas et al, 2011) and produced an F-measure of 0.657. The second best performing method utilized composite kernels, a method that combines feature-based and kernel-based methods, and was found to perform with an F-measure of 0.64 (Chowdhury et al, 2011). Other NLP research has focused exclusively on extracting pharmacokinetic DDIs from either Medline (e.g., Airola et al, 2008) or drug product labeling (e.g., Boyce et al, 2012).

Due to time constraints, we couldn't test other classifiers such as Naïve Bayes, JRip and Randomforest in our approach. Future work will test if SVM is the best choice for the first stage binary classifier. It is possible that libShortText (Yu et al, 2013) works better than LibSVM because this task is for sentence classification. We also plan to explore if Naïve Bayes, JRip, or Randomforest could work better than SVM for the second stage multi-class classifier.

Since only three systems were permitted to the challenge, and since the labeled test data was not available until the time of writing, we did not have the opportunity to test the impact of all the features that we considered, or of the post-processing rules. This will be explored in future work.

We also plan to explore some variations to our approach. For example, we will try to incorporate some of the rules, especially those in the first post-processor, as features in our system. Finally, although we did utilize some semantic information from WordNet for this work, we would like to explore additional rich features, drawing on syntax, semantics and discourse.

References

Airola A., S. Pyysalo, J. Björne, T. Pahikkala, F. Ginter and T. Salakoski. 2008. All-paths graph kernel for protein-protein interaction extraction with evaluation of cross-corpus learning. *BMC Bioinformatics* 9. Suppl 11 (2008): S2

Boyce R. D., C. Collins, M. Clayton, J. Kloke and J. R. Horn. 2012. Inhibitory metabolic drug interactions with newer psychotropic drugs: inclusion in package inserts and influences of concurrence in drug interaction screening software. *The Annals of Pharmacotherapy* 46.10 (2012): 1287-1298

Boyce R. D., G. Gardner and H. Harkema. 2012. Using Natural Language Processing to Extract Drug-Drug Interaction Information from Package Inserts. *Proceedings of the 2012 Workshop on BioNLP*.

Chang C. and C. Lin. 2011. LIBSVM: a library for support vector machines. *ACM Transactions on Intelligent Systems and Technology*. 2(3): 27.

Chawla N. V., K. W. Boyer, L. O. Hall and W. P. Kegelmeyer. 2002. SMOTE: Synthetic Minority Over-sampling Technique. *Journal of Artificial Intelligence Research* 16: 321-357.

Chen Y. F., A. J. Avery, K. E. Neil, C. Johnson, M. E. Dewey and I. H. Stockley. 2005. Incidence and possible causes of prescribing potentially hazardous/contraindicated drug combinations in general practice. *Drug Safety*, 28(1): 67-80.

Chowdhury F. M., A. B. Abacha, A. Lavelli and P. Zweigenbaum. 2011. Two Different Machine Learning Techniques for Drug-Drug Interaction Extraction. *Proceedings of the 1st Challenge Task on Drug-Drug Interaction Extraction (DDIExtraction-2011)*, 19–26.

Committee on Identifying and Preventing Medication Errors, Aspden P, Wolcott J, Bootman JL, and Cronenwett LR. 2007. Preventing Medication Er rors: Quality Chasm Series. Washington, D.C. *The National Academies Press*.

Fellbaum C. 1998. *WordNet: An Electronic Lexical Database*. Cambridge, MA: MIT Press.

Gurwitz J. H., T. S. Field, L. R. Harrold, J. Rothschild, K. Debellis, A. C. Seger, C. Cadoret, L. S. Fish, L. Garber, M. Kelleher and D. W. Bates. 2003. Incidence and preventability of adverse drug events among older persons in the ambulatory setting. *Journal of the American Medical Association*, 289(9): 1107-1116.

Gurwitz J. H., T. S. Field, J. Judge, P. Rochon, L. R. Harrold, C. Cadoret, M. Lee, K. White, J. LaPrino, J. Erramuspe-Mainard, M. DeFlorio, L. Gavendo, J. Auger and D. W. Bates. 2005. The incidence of adverse drug events in two large academic long-term care facilities. *The American Journal of Medicine*, 118(3): 251-258.

Hall M., E. Frank, G. Holmes, B. Pfahringer, P. Reutemann and I. Witten. 2009. The WEKA Data Mining Software: An Update. *SIGKDD Explorations*, Volume 11, Issue 1.

Hines L. E., and J. E. Murphy. 2011. Potentially harmful drug-drug interactions in the elderly: a review. *The American Journal of Geriatric Pharmacotherapy*, 9(6): 364-377.

Hines L. E., D. C. Malone and J. E. Murphy. 2012. Recommendations for Generating, Evaluating, and Implementing Drug-Drug Interaction Evidence. *Pharmacotherapy: The Journal of Human Pharmacology and Drug Therapy*, 32(4): 304-313.

Nebeker J. R., P. Barach and M. H. Samore. 2004. Clarifying Adverse Drug Events: A Clinician's Guide to Terminology, Documentation, and Reporting. *Annals of Internal Medicine*, 140(10): 795-801.

Porter M. F. 1980. An algorithm for suffix stripping. *Program*, 14(3): 130-137.

Segura-Bedmar I., P. Martinez and C. Pablo-Sanchez. 2010. Extracting drug-drug interactions from biomedical texts. *BMC Bioinformatics* 11, Suppl 5, P9.

Segura-Bedmar I., P. Martinez and D. Sánchez-Cisneros. 2011. The 1st DDIExtraction-2011 challenge task: Extraction of Drug-Drug Interactions from biomedical texts. *Proceedings of the 1st Challenge Task on Drug-Drug Interaction Extraction (DDIExtraction-2011)*.

Segura-Bedmar I., P. Martínez and M. Herrero-Zazo. 2013. SemEval-2013 Task 9: Extraction of Drug-Drug Interactions from Biomedical Texts. *Proceedings of the 7th International Workshop on Semantic Evaluation (SemEval 2013)*.

Thomas P., M. Neves, I. Solt, D. Tikk and U. Leser. 2011. Relation Extraction for Drug-Drug Interactions using Ensemble Learning. *Proceedings of the 1st Challenge Task on Drug-Drug Interaction Extraction (DDIExtraction-2011)*.

Toutanova K., D. Klein, C. Manning and Y. Singer. 2003. Feature-Rich Part-of-Speech Tagging with a Cyclic Dependency Network. In *Proceedings of HLT-NAACL*, 173-180.

Yu H., C. Ho, Y. Juan and C. Lin. 2013. *LibShortText: A Library for Short-text Classification and Analysis*. Technical Report. http://www.csie.ntu.edu.tw/~cjlin/ papers/libshorttext.pdf.

Zhou X., X. Zhang and X. Hu. 2007. Dragon Toolkit: Incorporating Auto-learned Semantic Knowledge into Large-Scale Text Retrieval and Mining. In *Proceedings of the 19th IEEE International Conference on Tools with Artificial Intelligence (ICTAI)*, 197-201.

SCAI: Extracting drug-drug interactions using a rich feature vector

Tamara Bobić[1,2], Juliane Fluck[1], Martin Hofmann-Apitius[1,2]

[1]Fraunhofer SCAI
Schloss Birlinghoven
53754 Sankt Augustin
Germany

[2]B-IT, Bonn Universität
Dahlmannstraße 2
53113 Bonn
Germany

{tbobic, jfluck, hofmann-apitius}@scai.fraunhofer.de

Abstract

Automatic relation extraction provides great support for scientists and database curators in dealing with the extensive amount of biomedical textual data. The DDIExtraction 2013 challenge poses the task of detecting drug-drug interactions and further categorizing them into one of the four relation classes. We present our machine learning system which utilizes lexical, syntactical and semantic based feature sets. Resampling, balancing and ensemble learning experiments are performed to infer the best configuration. For general drug-drug relation extraction, the system achieves 70.4% in F_1 score.

1 Introduction

Drug-drug interactions (DDI) describe possible interference between pharmacological substances and are of critical importance in drug development and administration (August et al., 1997). A drug may alter the metabolism of another, thus causing an enhanced, reduced or even toxic effect in certain medical treatments. For example: *"Fluvoxamine inhibits the CYP2C9 catalyzed biotransformation of tolbutamide."* Automated extraction of DDI from biomedical literature allows for a more efficient maintenance of the drug knowledge databases and is beneficial for patients, health care professionals and the pharmaceutical industry.

Having in mind their biomedical importance, the objective of the first DDIExtraction challenge[1] in 2011 was to motivate the development and to evaluate the automatic relation extraction (RE) systems for DDI. Given annotated drug entities, the participants addressed the task of identifying undirected binary relations among them. The knowledge extraction was performed on the sentence level and the best system achieved 65.74% F_1 score (Thomas et al., 2011a).

The 2013 DDIExtraction challenge[2] (organized as Task 9 of SemEval 2013 (Segura-Bedmar et al., 2013)) is based on a similar task definition, but additionally includes the disambiguation between four types of interaction: *mechanism*, *effect*, *advise* and *int*. The evaluation of participating systems is two-fold, *i. e.* partial and strict. Partial evaluation considers that a prediction is correct when the pair label matches the gold annotation, while strict evaluation requires also a correct relation type to be assigned. The train and test corpora were generated from textual resources of DrugBank (Knox et al., 2011) database and MedLine[3] abstracts, dealing with the topic of DDI.

In the following sections we describe our supervised machine learning based approach for the extraction of DDI, using a rich feature vector (see Section 2.1). The base system employed LibLINEAR classifier, generating the first run submitted to the DDIExtraction challenge. Configurations coming from the two ensemble strategies (Section 2.2) produced the remaining prediction runs. Furthermore, we experimentally investigated the impact of train

[1]http://labda.inf.uc3m.es/DDIExtraction2011/

[2]http://www.cs.york.ac.uk/semeval-2013/task9/

[3]http://www.ncbi.nlm.nih.gov/pubmed/

*Second Joint Conference on Lexical and Computational Semantics (*SEM), Volume 2: Seventh International Workshop on Semantic Evaluation (SemEval 2013)*, pages 675–683, Atlanta, Georgia, June 14-15, 2013.

corpora imbalance on DDI detection through resampling strategies (Section 2.3). Finally, relation type disambiguation methodology is presented in Section 2.4.

2 Methods

We formulate the task of relation extraction as feature-based classification of co-occurring entities in a sentence. A sentence with n entities contains at most $\binom{n}{2}$ interacting pairs. For entity pairs that the classifier detects as "true", a post-processing step is performed where one of the four relation types is assigned, depending on the identified type-specific trigger words.

2.1 Features

To improve generalization of lexical information Porter stemming algorithm (Porter, 1980) was applied. All entities present in the sentence, which were not a part of the investigated pair, are renamed to a common neutral name (entity blinding).

For the generation of dependency-based features, sentences in the provided corpora were parsed using Charniak-Lease parser (Lease and Charniak, 2005; Thomas et al., 2011b). The resulting constituent parse trees were converted into Stanford dependency graphs (Marneffe et al., 2006). Following the idea of Thomas et al. (2011b), similar relations are treated equally by using their common parent type (unification of dependency types). An example is generalizing relations "subj", "nsubj" and "csubj" to a parent relation "subj".

In the following subsections the three groups of features (lexical, syntactical and semantic) with their corresponding members are described. Table 1 gives a more structured overview of the feature vector, organized by type. It should be noted that the listed features are used for the generation of all three prediction sets submitted to the DDI challenge.

2.1.1 Lexical features

Lexical features capture the token information around the inspected entity pair (EP). The sentence text is divided into three parts: text between the EP, text before the EP (left from the first entity) and text after the EP (right from the second entity). It has been observed that much of the relation information can be extracted by only considering these three contexts (Bunescu and Mooney, 2005b; Giuliano et al., 2006).

The majority of features are n-grams based, with $n \in \{1, 2, 3\}$. They encompass a narrow (window=3) and wide (window=10) surrounding context, along with the area between the entities. Additionally, combinations of the tokens from the three areas is considered, thus forming before-between, between-after and before-after conjunct features (narrow context).

2.1.2 Syntactic/Dependency features

Vertices (v) in the dependency graph are analyzed from a lexical (stemmed token text) and syntactical (POS tag) perspective, while the edges (e) are included using the grammatical relation they represent.

The majority of dependency-based features are constructed using the properties of edges and vertices along the shortest path (SP) of an entity pair. The shortest path subtree is conceived to encode grammatical relations with highest information content for a specific EP (Bunescu and Mooney, 2005a).

Similarly to lexical features, n-grams of vertices (edges) along the SP are captured. Furthermore, alternating sequences of vertices and edges (*v-walks* and *e-walks*) of length 3 are accounted for, following previous work (Kim et al., 2010; Miwa et al., 2010).

Apart from the SP-related features, incorporating information about the entities' parents and their common ancestor in the dependency graph is also beneficial. The lexical and syntactical properties of these vertices are encoded, along with the grammatical relations on the path from the entities to their common ancestor.

2.1.3 Semantic features

Semantic group of features deals with understanding and meaning of the context in which a particular entity pair appears.

A feature that accounts for hypothetical statements was introduced in order to reduce the number of false positives (phrases that indicate investigation in progress, but not actual facts). Negation (*e. g.* "not") detected close to the entity pair (narrow context) along with a check whether entities in the pair refer to the same real-word object (abbreviation or a repetition) represent features which also contribute to the reduction of false positive predictions.

Drug entities in the corpora were annotated with one of four classes (drug, drug_n, brand, group), which provided another layer of relation information for the classifier. Prior knowledge about true DDI coming from the train corpora is used as a feature, if a previously known EP is observed in the test data. Presence of other entities (which are not part of the inspected EP) in the sentence text is captured, together with their position relative to the EP.

Finally, mentions of general trigger (interaction) terms are checked in all three context areas. Moreover, interaction phrases specific to a certain DDI type (see Section 2.4) are accounted for.

2.2 Ensemble learning

Combining different machine learning algorithms was proposed as a direction for improvement of the classification accuracy (Bauer and Kohavi, 1999).

A synthesis of predictions using LibLINEAR, Naïve Bayes and Voting Perceptron classifiers is an attempt to approach and learn the relation information from different angles with a goal of increasing the system's performance. The three base models included in the ensemble are employed through their WEKA[4] (Hall et al., 2009) implementation with default parameter values and trained on the full feature vector described in Section 2.1.

LibLINEAR (Fan et al., 2008) is a linear support vector machine classifier, which has shown high performance (in runtime as well as model accuracy) on large and sparse data sets. Support vector machines (SVM, Cortes and Vapnik (1995)) have gained a lot of popularity in the past decade and very often are state-of-the-art approach for text mining challenges.

Naïve Bayes (Domingos and Pazzani, 1996) is a simple form of Bayesian networks which relies on the assumption that every feature is independent from all other features. Despite their naive design and apparently oversimplified assumptions, Naïve Bayes can often outperform more sophisticated classification methods and has worked quite well in many complex real-world situations. Furthermore, it can be robust to noise features and is quite insensitive to stratification (Provost, 2000), which is of high value in class imbalance scenarios.

[4] http://www.cs.waikato.ac.nz/ml/weka/

Corpus	Pos	Neg	Total
MedLine	232 (0.13)	1,555 (0.87)	1,787
DrugBank	3,788 (0.15)	22,217 (0.85)	26,005

Table 2: Ratio of positive and negative instances in the DrugBank and MedLine train corpora.

Voting Perceptron (Freund and Schapire, 1999) combines a series of perceptrons, which are linear classification algorithms that process elements in the train set one at a time ("online"). The system stores the number of iterations the perceptron "survives", *i. e.* when the training set instances are classified correctly. The obtained count represents a weight used for combining the prediction vectors by a weighted majority vote.

In the ensemble learning scenario we consider two strategies that aim at increasing the system's performance by either favoring precision or recall:

1. *"majority"* – a pair represents true relation only if majority of the classifiers support that claim
2. *"union"* – a pair represents true relation if at least one of the classifiers supports that claim

2.3 Train corpora imbalance

Analysis of the basic train corpora statistics reveals an unequal ratio of positive and negative instances, *i. e.* under-representation of true interacting pairs (see Table 2). Class distribution imbalance often causes machine learning algorithms to perform poorly on the minority class (Hulse et al., 2007), thus, in this case, affecting the recall of true relations.

In order to explore the sensitivity of our system to the positive/negative ratio, we performed random undersampling of the data, artificially obtaining a desirable ratio (50-50). All positive instances in the dataset were kept, while the same number of negative instances were randomly chosen. The reverse approach of oversampling was considered, but given the ample train data provided by the organizers, such strategy could pose run-time challenges.

The experimental setting is described as follows. MedLine and DrugBank train corpora were divided further into train (exp-train) and test (exp-test) sets,

	Feature
Lexical	1. n-grams of tokens between the EP
	2. n-grams of tokens before the EP (narrow context, window = 3)
	3. n-grams of tokens after the EP (narrow context, window = 3)
	4. n-grams of tokens before the EP (wide context, window = 10)
	5. n-grams of tokens after the EP (wide context, window = 10)
	6. conjucted positions: before-between, between-after and before-after
Syntactical / Dependency	7. dependency n-grams on the SP
	8. syntactical n-grams on the SP
	9. lexical n-grams on the SP
	10. lexical and syntactical *e-walks*
	11. lexical and syntactical *v-walks*
	12. SP length (number of edges)
	13. lexical and syntactical information of the entities' parents
	14. lexical and syntactical information of the entities' common ancestor
	15. dependency n-grams from both entities to their common ancestor
	16. common ancestor represents a verb or a noun
Semantic	17. hypothetical context
	18. negation close to the EP
	19. entities refer to the same object
	20. type of entities that form the EP
	21. prior knowledge (from the train data)
	22. other entities present close to the EP
	23. DDI trigger words (general)
	24. DDI types trigger words (specific)

Table 1: Overview of features used, stratified into groups. EP denotes an entity pair, SP represent the shortest path.

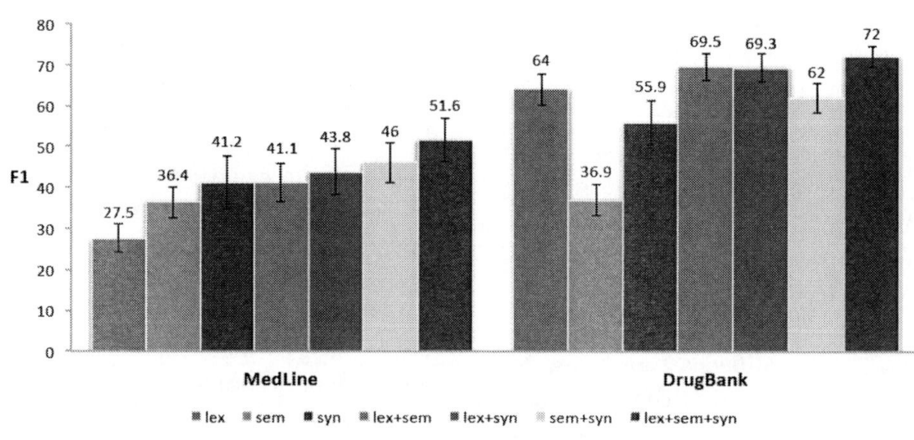

Figure 1: Contribution of individual feature sets and their combinations to the system's performance, evaluated by 10-fold cross-validation on the train corpora. *Lex* is an abbreviation for lexical, *sem* for semantic and *syn* for syntactical features.

Corpus	Exp-train pairs	Exp-test pairs
MedLine	1,259 (70.4%)	528 (29.6%)
DrugBank	18,148 (69.8%)	7,857 (30.2%)

Table 3: Experimental train and test subsets derived from the MedLine and DrugBank train corpora.

Relation	MedLine	DrugBank
mechanism	62 (0.27)	1257 (0.33)
effect	152 (0.66)	1535 (0.41)
advise	8 (0.03)	818 (0.21)
int	10 (0.04)	178 (0.05)

Table 4: The number of positive pairs for different DDI types in the train corpora. Ratios are given in brackets.

with an approximate ratio of 70-30. Instances from a particular document were always sampled to the same subset, in order to avoid information leakage. Table 3 gives an overview of the number of entity pairs each set comprises. The exp-train corpora were used for training the model in an original (full-size) and balanced (subsample) scenario, evaluated on the exp-test sets.

It should be noted that undersampling experiments were performed on the train corpora in order to inspect the impact of data imbalance on our system (results shown in Section 3.4). However, due to the challenge limitation of submitting only three runs, this configuration was ignored in favor of utilizing the complete train corpora.

2.4 Relation type assignment

The DDIExtraction challenge guidelines specify four classes of relations: *advise, mechanism, effect* and *int*. Table 4 illustrates the ratio of positive pairs assigned to each type in MedLine and DrugBank train corpora.

In Section 2.4.1, a brief outlook on the interaction type characteristics is given, along with some of the most common relation (trigger) phrases specific to them. Section 2.4.2 explains the methodology behind the process of relation type assignment.

2.4.1 Relations overview

Advise pertains to recommendations regarding co-administration of two or more drugs. Sentences describing these relations usually contain words such as: should, recommended, advisable, caution, avoid etc., as seen in the following examples:

- ***Barbiturates*** *and* ***glutethimide*** *should not be administered to patients receiving* ***coumarin*** *drugs.*
- *Concurrent therapy with* ***ORENCIA*** *and* ***TNF antagonists*** *is not recommended.*
- *The co-administration of* ***Fluvoxamine*** *Tablets and* ***diazepam*** *is generally not advisable.*

Effect is a relation type describing the signs or symptoms linked to the DDI, including the pharmacodynamic effect, *i. e.* mechanism of interaction. Some of the phrases often found to denote this type of relation are: effect, cause, decrease, increase, inhibit, activate, modulate etc. The following examples present expressions of an *effect* relation:

- *Pretreatment of megakaryocytes with extracellular* ***RR*** *(50 microM) also inhibited* ***InsP(3)****-induced responses.*
- *It is concluded that* ***neurotensin*** *modulates in an opposite way the function of the enkephalinergic neurons and the central action of* ***tuftsin****.*
- ***Diazepam*** *at doses of 0.25 mg/kg and 2.5 mg/kg injected with* ***morphine*** *was found to decrease the antinociceptive effect of* ***morphine****.*

Mechanism illustrates a more detailed description of the observed pharmacokinetic changes that includes biochemical information about metabolism, absorption, biotransformation, excretion etc. *Mechanism* relations often include mentions of *effect*-related interaction phrases, but provide an additional knowledge layer by addressing more complex biological concepts:

- ***Cholestyramine****, an anionic-binding resin, has a considerable effect in lowering the rate and extent of* ***fluvastatin*** *bioavailability.*
- *Additional* ***iron*** *significantly inhibited the absorption of* ***cobalt*** *in both dietary* ***cobalt*** *treatments.*
- ***Macrolide antibiotics*** *inhibit the metabolism of* ***HMG-CoA reductase inhibitors*** *that are metabolized by CYP3A4.*

Int relation implies sentences which only state that an interaction occurs, without providing much additional information about it. Trigger phrases that can be found in such sentences are usually limited to different lexical forms of "interaction":

- ***Rifampin** and **warfarin**: a drug interaction.*
- *In vitro interaction of **prostaglandin F2alpha** and **oxytocin** in placental vessels.*
- *Treatment with **antidepressant drugs** can directly interfere with blood glucose levels or may interact with **hypoglycemic agents**.*

2.4.2 Type disambiguation methodology

We approach the problem of relation type disambiguation as a post-processing step, utilizing identified (sentence level) trigger words as classification determinants. Precompiled relation trigger lists are generated by manual inspection of the train corpora, largely focusing on MedLine. The lists are specific to the four interaction types and non-overlapping.

Cases when a sentence contains trigger phrases from different relation classes are resolved by following a priority list:

1. *advise*
2. *mechanism*
3. *effect*
4. *int*

The rationale behind such priority assignment are the following observed patterns in the train corpora. Regardless of *effect* or *mechanism* connotation, if the sentence contains recommendation-like phrases (*e. g.* "should", "advisable"), it is almost always classified as an *advise*. Likewise, even though a relation might be describing an *effect*, if it contains a more detailed biochemical description, it is most likely representing *mechanism*. Finally, *effect* has advantage over *int* due to the simplicity of the *int* relation, along with the lowest observed frequency.

3 Results and Discussion

3.1 Baseline relation extraction performance

Performances of the submitted prediction runs are shown in Table 5, where the first row (run1) represents a system trained on the original (unbalanced) train corpora, using LibLINEAR classifier and a rich feature vector (see Section 2.1). The table offers results overview on MedLine, DrugBank and joined test corpora ("All"), using partial evaluation (general DDI detection).

The difference in performance on MedLine and Drugbank is apparent, measuring up to almost 25 percentage points (pp) in F_1 score (46.2% for MedLine and 71.1% for DrugBank). Due to a considerably larger size of the DrugBank corpus, overall results are greatly influenced by this corpus (F_1 = 69.0%).

The results imply system's sensitivity towards class imbalance, which manifests in favored precision over recall. However, this discrepancy is much less observed on DrugBank test corpus. Despite the similarity in class ratio, DrugBank is a more compact and homogenous corpus, with a relatively unified writing style. Coming from a manually curated database, it has a rather standardized way of describing interactions, resulting in higher performance of the relation extraction system. MedLine corpora, however, are derived from different journals and research groups which gives rise to extremely diverse writing styles and a more challenging task for information extraction.

3.2 Features contribution

Figure 1 illustrates the performance of the LibLINEAR classifier, when all combinations of the three different feature sets are explored.

It can be observed that the highest performance is always achieved when all the features are included during training (*lex+syn+sem*), resulting in 51.6% and 72.0% F_1 score for 10-fold cross-validation on MedLine and DrugBank train corpora respectively.

Lexical features appear to be most useful for the DrugBank corpus, achieving 88.9% of the maximum performance when used solely. MedLine, on the other hand, benefits the most from syntactic features that reach 79.8% of the best result, compared to 53.3% with lexical features. Semantic group of features exhibits a uniform performance for both corpora, achieving 36.4% and 36.9% of F_1 score. Finally, grouping of two or all three feature sets is always beneficial and results in higher performance than the constituting base configurations.

Classifier	MedLine			DrugBank			All		
	P	R	F_1	P	R	F_1	P	R	F_1
run1: LibLINEAR	**68.8**	34.7	46.2	83.6	61.9	71.1	82.6	59.2	69.0
run2: Majority	68.6	25.3	36.9	**83.7**	61.7	71.0	**82.9**	58.1	68.3
run3: Union	43.1	**52.6**	**47.4**	79.6	**68.1**	**73.4**	74.8	**66.6**	**70.4**

Table 5: Results of the three submitted runs on the test corpora.

Classifier	DrugBank	MedLine
LibLinear	654	48
Naïve Bayes	854	88
V. Perceptron	608	30
Majority	693	35
Union	980	116

Table 6: Number of positive predictions on MedLine and DrugBank test corpora, using different configurations.

3.3 Ensemble experiments

Performance of the majority and union ensemble configurations on the test corpora is presented in Table 5. Table 6 gives an overview of the number of predicted positive pairs by the ensemble, as well as those by the individual base classifiers.

Voting Perceptron behaves similarly to LibLinear, while Naïve Bayes demonstrates insensitivity in terms of class imbalance, predicting the highest number of positive pairs for both MedLine and DrugBank test corpora.

Union voting strategy tends to overcome the limitations of poor recall, resulting in highest performance on all test corpora (47.4% for MedLine, 73.4% for DrugBank and 70.4% for All) among the three runs. The superior result is obtained by diminishing precision in favor or recall, which was shown as beneficial in these use-cases. However, the F_1 score difference is slight (1.2 pp, 2.3 pp and 1.4 pp), as compared to the baseline system (run1).

Predictions using the union ensemble ranked 3rd in the general DDI extraction evaluation, achieving 5.5 pp and 9.6 pp of F_1 score less than the top two participating teams.

Train set	MedLine			DrugBank		
	P	R	F_1	P	R	F_1
original	48.4	39.6	43.6	75.1	62.4	68.2
balanced	37.2	70.4	48.7	60.8	72.7	66.2

Table 7: Comparison of results on the full train set and a balanced subsample, as evaluated on the MedLine and DrugBank train corpora.

3.4 Balanced training corpora

Table 7 presents relation extraction performance for training on a balanced subset, compared to the original unbalanced corpus.

In case of MedLine, an increase of around 5 pp in F_1 score can be observed for the balanced subsample. However, given a relatively high initial performance on DrugBank and the characteristics of that corpus, training on a subsample results in 2 pp reduced F_1 score. The raise of 30.8 pp in recall contributes greatly to the increased performance on MedLine, even though 11.2 pp of precision are lost. However, in case of DrugBank, a 10.3 pp increase in recall is not enough to compensate for the 14.3 pp loss in precision.

It can be observed that although undersampling approach removes information from the model training stage, the class balance plays a more significant role for the final performance.

3.5 Relation type disambiguation

Correct classification of interacting pairs into four defined classes was evaluated using macro and micro average measures.

While micro-averaged F_1 score is calculated by constructing a global contingency table and then calculating precision and recall, macro-averaged F_1 score is obtained by first calculating precision and recall for each relation type and then taking their

	MedLine			DrugBank			All		
	P	R	F_1	P	R	F_1	P	R	F_1
micro avg.	62.5	31.6	42.0	51.3	43.9	47.3	55.1	39.5	46.0
macro avg.	42.0	19.7	26.9	66.5	35.3	46.1	66.6	33.8	44.8
mechanism	70.0	29.2	41.2	58.0	39.2	46.8	53.2	39.1	45.0
effect	64.7	35.5	45.8	52.4	44.6	48.2	48.8	43.9	46.2
advise	18.2	28.6	22.2	50.7	65.0	57.0	50.5	63.3	56.2
int	0	0	0	100	1.1	2.1	100	1.0	2.1

Table 8: Results of DDI extraction when relation class detection is evaluated.

average (Segura-Bedmar et al., 2013). Therefore, macro average takes into consideration the relative frequency of each interaction class, while micro average treats all classes equally.

Table 8 shows an overview of performances for DDI extraction with relation class disambiguation, evaluated for each type separately, as well as cumulatively using micro and macro scores. For MedLine test corpus, the micro average F_1 score of 42% ranked 1st among all participating systems. However, the macro average score is much lower, due to poor performance on *advise* and *int* relation classes and occupies 5th position. Considering that our methodology gives advantage to relations which are observed more frequently, it is more adapted towards the micro measure.

The process of manually generating type-specific trigger lists was largely based on the MedLine train corpus due to its size, with the assumption that the relations in DrugBank are similarly expressed. However, both micro and macro scores for DrugBank ranked 7th, showing that adaptation of trigger word lists needs to be done, depending on the target corpus.

In general, lower performance for relation class assignment is partially due to incompleteness of the trigger lists, but also coming intrinsically from the relation priority hierarchy. Most of classification errors occur when a trigger word belonging to a "higher" priority class is identified in the sentence. In the following example the word "should" implies *advise* relation, although *guanfacine* and *CNS-depressant drug* express an *effect* relation:

*The potential for increased sedation when **guanfacine** is given with other **CNS-depressant drug** should be appreciated.*

Another example is a sentence mentioning "effect", but actually describing a simple *int* relation:

***Chloral hydrate** and **methaqualone** interact pharmacologically with orally administered anticoagulant agents, but the effect is not clinically significant.*

Furthermore, a lot of missclassifications occur in sentences which contain pairs and triggers from different types, resulting in all relations being assigned to the highest identified type.

4 Conclusion

We present a machine learning based system for extraction of drug-drug interactions, using lexical, syntactic and semantic properties of the sentence text. The system achieves competitive performance for the general DDI extraction, albeit demonstrating sensitivity to the train corpora class imbalance. We show that, depending on the use case, resampling, balancing and ensemble strategies are successful in tuning the system to favor recall over precision. The post-processing step of relation type assignment achieves top ranked results for the MedLine corpus, however, needs more adaption in case of DrugBank. Future work includes a comparison with a multi-classifier approach, which circumvents the manual task of trigger list generation, supporting the fully automated scenario of relation extraction.

Acknowledgments

The authors would like to thank Roman Klinger for fruitful discussions. T. Bobić was funded by the Bonn-Aachen International Center for Information Technology (B-IT) Research School.

References

J.T. August, F. Murad, W. Anders, J.T. Coyle, and A.P. Li. 1997. *Drug-Drug Interactions: Scientific and Regulatory Perspectives: Scientific and Regulatory Perspectives*. Advances in pharmacology. Elsevier Science.

E. Bauer and R. Kohavi. 1999. An empirical comparison of voting classification algorithms: Bagging, boosting, and variants. *Machine Learning*, 36(1-2).

R. C. Bunescu and R. J. Mooney. 2005a. A shortest path dependency kernel for relation extraction. In *HLT and EMNLP*.

R. C. Bunescu and R. J. Mooney. 2005b. Subsequence Kernels for Relation Extraction. *NIPS*.

C. Cortes and V. Vapnik. 1995. Support vector networks. In *Machine Learning*.

P. Domingos and M. Pazzani. 1996. Beyond independence: Conditions for the optimality of the simple bayesian classifier. In *ICML*.

E. Fan, K. Chang, C. Hsieh, X. Wang, and C. Lin. 2008. LIBLINEAR: A Library for Large Linear Classification. *Machine Learning Research*, 9.

Y. Freund and R. E. Schapire. 1999. Large margin classification using the perceptron algorithm. *Machine Learning*, 37(3).

C. Giuliano, A. Lavelli, and L. Romano. 2006. Exploiting shallow linguistic information for relation extraction from biomedical literature. In *Proc. of the 11st Conf. of the European Chapter of the Association for Computational Linguistics (EACL'06)*.

M. Hall, E. Frank, G. Holmes, B. Pfahringer, P. Reutemann, and I. H. Witten. 2009. The weka data mining software: An update. *SIGKDD Explorations*, 11.

J. V. Hulse, T. M. Khoshgoftaar, and A. Napolitano. 2007. Experimental perspectives on learning from imbalanced data. In *ICML*.

S. Kim, J. Yoon, J. Yang, and S. Park. 2010. Walk-weighted subsequence kernels for protein-protein interaction extraction. *BMC Bioinformatics*, 11.

C. Knox, V. Law, T. Jewison, P. Liu, S. Ly, A. Frolkis, A. Pon, K. Banco, C. Mak, V. Neveu, Y. Djoumbou, R. Eisner, A. Chi Guo, and D.S Wishart. 2011. Drugbank 3.0: a comprehensive resource for 'omics' research on drugs. *Nucleic Acids Res*, 39.

M. Lease and E. Charniak. 2005. Parsing biomedical literature. In *Proc. of IJCNLP'05*.

M. C. De Marneffe, B. Maccartney, and C. D. Manning. 2006. Generating typed dependency parses from phrase structure parses. In *LREC*.

M. Miwa, R. Saetre, J. D. Kim, and J. Tsujii. 2010. Event extraction with complex event classification using rich features. *Journal of bioinformatics and computational biology*, 8.

M. Porter. 1980. An algorithm for suffix stripping. *Program*, 14.

F. Provost. 2000. Machine learning from imbalanced data sets 101 (extended abstract).

I. Segura-Bedmar, P. Martnez, and M. Herrero-Zazo. 2013. Semeval-2013 task 9: Extraction of drug-drug interactions from biomedical texts. In *Proceedings of the 7th International Workshop on Semantic Evaluation (SemEval 2013)*.

P. Thomas, M. Neves, I. Solt, D. Tikk, and U. Leser. 2011a. Relation extraction for drug-drug interactions using ensemble learning. In *Proceedings of the 1st Challenge Task on Drug-Drug Interaction Extraction 2011*.

P. Thomas, S. Pietschmann, I. Solt, D. Tikk, and U. Leser. 2011b. Not all links are equal: Exploiting dependency types for the extraction of protein-protein interactions from text. In *Proceedings of BioNLP 2011 Workshop*.

UColorado_SOM: Extraction of Drug-Drug Interactions from BioMedical Text using Knowledge-rich and Knowledge-poor Features

Negacy D. Hailu negacy.hailu@ucdenver.edu
Lawrence E. Hunter larry.hunter@ucdenver.edu
K. Bretonnel Cohen kevin.cohen@gmail.com

University of Colorado, Anschutz Medical Campus

Abstract

In this paper, we present our approach to SemEval-2013 Task 9.2. It is a feature rich classification using LIBSVM for Drug-Drug Interactions detection in the BioMedical domain. The features are extracted considering morphosyntactic, lexical and semantic concepts. Tools like openDMAP and TEES are used to extract semantic concepts from the corpus. The best F-score that we got for Drug-Drug Interaction (DDI) detection is 50% and 61% and the best F-score for DDI detection and classification is 34% and 48% for test and development data respectively.

Keywords: text mining, event extraction, machine learning, feature extraction.

1 Introduction

Our approach to the Semeval 2013 drug-drug interaction task explored the potential for integrating knowledge-based approaches with supervised machine learning. In practice, most supervised machine learning systems are actually hybrids of machine learning and some knowledge-based approach. However, the integration between the two is typically quite loose, with the knowledge-based approach being realized either as heuristic preprocessing or post-processing of the results. The work reported here is an attempt to make a tighter coupling between knowledge-based methods and machine learning. In particular, we took the approach of using knowledge-based methods for feature extraction.

2 Methodology

In this challenge we approach the Drug-Drug interaction task 9.2 as a binary classification problem. A pair of drugs is interacting if there is some kind of influence between the two. Our approach for Drug-Drug interaction extraction 2013 mainly makes use of domain specific morphosyntactic, lexical and semantic features between paired drugs.

We applied Machine Learning classification techniques in order to determine whether a pair of drugs within a biomedical text is interacting or not. For a training set of labeled instances $(\mathbf{X}_i, y_i) = 1, 2, ..., l$ where $\mathbf{X}_i \in R^n$ and $\mathbf{y} \in \{1, -1\}^l$, the support vector machines (SVMs) optimization problem is defined as(Boser et al., 1992) (Cortes and Vapnik , 1995):

$$\hat{\alpha} = \arg\max_{\alpha,w,b} \left(\frac{1}{2}W^T W + C\sum_{i=1}^{l} \alpha_i\right) \quad (1)$$

$$\text{such that } y_i\left(W^T\phi(X_i) + b\right) > 1 - \alpha_i, \quad \alpha_i \geq 0.$$

2.1 Materials

The corpus is provided from two data sources. There are 572 documents describing drug-drug interactions from the DrugBank database and 142 abstracts on the subject of drug-drug interactions from MedLine (Isabel et.al., 2011). We prepared datasets for the entire corpus. Each instance in the dataset is a set of paired drugs. In our dataset, there are 27787 instances. 93.57% of them are from Drugbank database and the remaining are from MedLine abstracts. DDI shared task 2013 is not only interaction detection but the challenge also includes detec-

*Second Joint Conference on Lexical and Computational Semantics (*SEM), Volume 2: Seventh International Workshop on Semantic Evaluation (SemEval 2013)*, pages 684–688, Atlanta, Georgia, June 14-15, 2013.

tion of the type of interaction. In our approach, we treated each interaction type as one class.

2.2 Methods

LIBSVM is a library for support vector machines (LIBSVM, 2011). We used this tool for classifying the dataset. Basically, the problem is a multi-class classification problem. We applied the concept of one-vs-all multi-class classification technique to handle the multiple classes.

2.3 Feature Extraction

The features that we extracted for this challenge can be categorized into three types:

2.3.1 Morphosyntactic Features

- **Distance feature:** this is distance between paired drugs in number of words. The intuition here is that the closer two drugs are, the more chance that they might be interacting. Since this feature takes word count as its value, the text is split within white space when counting number of words. Punctuation marks are not considered when counting words.

- **Part-Of-Speech tags:** we chose the GENIA dependency parser for parsing the corpus for two reasons.

- **Dependency parser related features:** we construct the dependency tree using the GENIA dependency parser. Two features are extracted from the tree:
  - Presence of interaction word in the path from the target drug node to the root of the tree.
  - Distance from one target drug name to another one in the tree.

2.3.2 Lexical Features

- **Bigrams:** a sequence of bigrams is extracted for input text.

2.3.3 Semantic Features

- **Interaction words:** we collected the top 100 words that indicate drug-drug interaction. The presence of these words is one feature for our system. The words are checked before and after each target drug. Such words include: increase, decrease, inhibit, interaction, reduce, affect.
- **Presence of preposition within target drugs:** the text within the target drugs is tested to see if it has preposition or not. If the text has a preposition, the value is 1 otherwise it will have zero value.
- **Presence of other drugs within target drugs:** firstly, we collect all drug names into a list. The text within the target drugs is searched for the drug names and the value for this feature will have the number of hits.
- **Concept from OpenDMAP:** OpenDMAP is an ontology-driven, rule-based concept analysis and information extraction system (Hunter et.al., 2008). We used openDMAP to extract drug-drug interaction concepts from the DDI2013 corpus. We extracted pattern based features using OpenDMAP only if OpenDMAP recognizes target drugs.

3 Dataset Preparation

The challenge provided datasets from Drug-Bank database and MedLine abstracts. We split the dataset into 20% development data and 80% training data. Table1 shows the percentage of positive instances in the dataset.

DDI interaction	14.47%
Interaction type effect	6.07%
Interaction type advise	2.97%
Interaction type mechanism	4.75%
Interaction type int	0.68%

Table 1: positive instances for the different class types

The data is not balanced, as shown in table 1. We penalized the negative classes during training in order to balance the data.

In section 4 we present results for three runs. Run1 includes the basic features which are described in section 2.3. In Run2 we included feature values made available by TEES (Björne et.al., 2011). In addition to the features in the first two runs, in Run3 the list of interaction words were considered individually as features. In this run, weight penalty and different optimized LIBSVM parameters were considered.

4 Results

Table 2 shows the results for DDI detection only, for both development and test data. The best F1 score is 50% for test data and 61% for development data.

		Runs		
		1	2	3
test data	precision	0.37	0.38	0.4
	recall	0.73	0.75	0.64
	F1	0.49	0.5	0.49
development data	precision	0.28	0.82	0.62
	recall	0.78	0.46	0.59
	F1	0.41	0.59	0.61

Table 2: Partial Evaluation: only detection of DDI

Table 3 shows results for DDI detection and classification. The best F1 score is 34% for test data and 48% for development data.

		Runs		
		1	2	3
test data	precision	0.16	0.25	0.27
	recall	0.32	0.5	0.44
	F1	0.21	0.33	0.34
development data	precision	0.13	0.59	0.49
	recall	0.37	0.33	0.46
	F1	0.2	0.42	0.48

Table 3: Detection and classification of DDI

And finally, the scores for the individual DDI type for the best run are shown in table 4. Apparently, Run3 outperforms in all the scores as can be seen in tables 2 through 4.

		Run3		
		precision	recall	F1
test data	mechanism	0.39	0.29	0.33
	effect	0.21	0.63	0.31
	advise	0.45	0.39	0.42
	int	0.4	0.28	0.334
development data	mechanism	0.5	0.29	0.37
	effect	0.44	0.61	0.51
	advise	0.72	0.46	0.56
	int	0.08	0.1	0.09

Table 4: Best scores for DDI type, Run3

5 Discussion

Generally speaking, the performance of our system is better for DDI detection regardless of their types compared to classifying what kind of DDI they are.

Among the three runs that we submitted for the challenge, Run3 outperforms in all the scores as can be seen in tables 2 through 4 for the following reasons:

- weight penalty techniques are applied in Run3
- optimal cost and gamma parameters are selected while training for Run3
- Bag of interaction words are considered as individual features. This specially increases scores for detecting the individual DDI types.

The best F-score that we got for DDI detection is 61% for development data and 50% for test data as shown in Table 2. The reason why scores are better for DDI detection is that our approach is feature rich DDI detection and we believe that our features mainly target detecting DDIs. A further addition of features that distinguishes the DDI types will hopefully improve the scores for DDI classification. On the other hand, it has been observed that scores are lower for test data compared to development data. And the reason for this is due to optimization parameters that we heuristically chose during training are possibly favoring to development data than to test data. Another possible reason could be overfitting.

As shown in section 4, the knowledge-based lexical features produced our best run. The semantic parser made a smaller contribution to performance, almost certainly because of low coverage- - -historically, in past shared tasks on information extraction, its behavior has been characterized by very high precision but low recall.

5.1 Error Analysis

Table 5 shows false positive predictions collected from the results for Run3. In FP-1, the system predicts detecting the first pair (etanercept and anakinra) correctly and then classifying as type *effect* but it failed to determine whether **etanercept** is interacting with

interleukin-1 antagonist. A close examination of this sentence shows that the last two drugs are separated by parentheses and in fact the last drug is a further explanation of the second one. The system couldn't distinguish this concept — rather it is treating all the three drugs separately and both pairs i.e. (etanercept, anakinra) and (etanercept, interleukin-1 antagonist) are predicted the same. This is happening due the syntactic nature of the text. One possible way to avoid such confusion is to expand the sentence. In other words, we believe initial data clean up might improve the performance of the system. Avoiding punctuation marks such as parenthesis for this case and other delimiters and representing them in words if possible might improve the performance of the classifier.

It is also observed that there is poor prediction for pairs of drugs that have negation. The two examples, i.e. FP-2 and FP-3 in table 5 are wrongly predicted because there is no feature that handles negation in the system.

FP-1	Concurrent administration of **etanercept** (another TNF -blocking agent) and anakinra (an **interleukin-1 antagonist**) has been associated with an increased risk of serious infections, and increased risk of neutropenia and no additional benefit compared to these m edicinal products alone.
FP-2	When used in external subcutaneous infusion pumps for insulin, **NovoLog** should not be mixed with any other **insulins** or diluent.
FP-3	With the exception of **albuterol**, there are no formal studies fully evaluating the interaction effects of **ATROVENT** Inhalation Aerosol and these drugs with respect to effectiveness.

Table 5: False positive samples. In this table false positive DDIs are in bold font.

False negative predictions have a negative effect on the recall evaluation parameter. In table 6 we show false negative predictions and their possible analysis for the development data. A close analysis of FN-1 and FN-2 shows that both sentences have a comma between the paired drugs. From a linguistic point of view, the punctuation mark comma can be used to separate interdependent clauses. Representing this dependency as a feature might help to avoid false negatives. FN-3 are a bit different and it apprears that there is much knowledge that can be extracted from the given text which is in number format. Currently, the features that we have don't extract information written in numbers. Also, the list of interaction words doesn't include words like **administered, administration** though words like **co-administration, coadministered** are included. A further development of the list of interaction words will avoid such false predictions.

FN-1	Anticholinergic agents: Although **ipratropium bromide** is minimally absorbed into the systemic circulation, there is some potential for an additive interaction with concomitantly used **anticholinergic medications**.
FN-2	Lymphocytopenia has been reported in patients receiving **CAMPTOSAR**, and it is possible that the administration of **dexamethasone** as antiemetic prophylaxis may have enhanced the likelihood of this effect.
FN-3	**Betaseron** administration to three cancer patients over a dose range of 0.025 mg to 2.2 mg led to a dose-dependent inhibition of **antipyrine** elimination.14 The effect of alternate-day administration of 0.25 mg of Betaseron on drug metabolism in MS patients is unknown.

Table 6: False negative samples. In this table false negative DDIs are in bold format.

6 Conclusion

Our approach to Extraction of Drug-Drug Interactions from BioMedical Texts task 9.2 is a feature rich SVM classification. The performance on detecting Drug-Drug interactions is encouraging but it is a bit lower when it comes to further classfying the type of the interaction. As described in section 5.1, addition of features such as negation will reduce false positive prediction and this will increase precision score. Further development of the list of interaction words is also a important task to handle the different forms of words that could indicate an interaction type. We have also observed that pattern-based semantic features are not well extracted in our system.

References

Segura-Bedmar, I., Martínez, P, Herrero-Zazo, M. SemEval-2013 Task 9: Extraction of Drug-Drug Interactions from Biomedical Texts. *In Proceedings of the 7th International Workshop on Semantic Evaluation (SemEval 2013)*

Chang, Chih-Chung and Lin, Chih-Jen 2011. *LIBSVM: A library for support vector machines*, volume 2. Software available at `http://www.csie.ntu.edu.tw/~cjlin/libsvm`

Hunter, L, Z Lu, J Firby, WA Baumgartner, Jr., HL Johnson, PV Ogren, KB Cohen. . OpenDMAP: An open-source, ontology-driven concept analysis engine, with applications to capturing knowledge regarding protein transport, protein interactions and cell-type-specific gene expression. *BMC Bioinformatics 2008, 9:78.*

Jari Björne, Filip Ginter, Juho Heimonen, Antti Airola, Tapio Pahikkala and Tapio Salakoski. 2011. *TEES: Event Extraction Software.* Software available at `http://jbjorne.github.com/TEES/`

Isabel Segura-Bedmar, Paloma Martínez, Cesar de Pablo-sachnez Using a shallow linguistic kernel for drug-drug interaction Extraction. 2011. *Journal of Biomedical Informatics*, 44(5):789-804..

Boser, Bernhard E. and Guyon, Isabelle M. and Vapnik, Vladimir N. A training algorithm for optimal margin classifiers. *Proceedings of the fifth annual workshop on Computational learning theory.*

C. Cortes and V. Vapnik. *Support-vector network.* Machine Learning, 20:273-297

Isabel Segura-Bedmar, Paloma Martínez, and Daniel Sánchez-Cisneros The 1st DDIExtraction-2011 challenge task: Extraction of Drug-Drug Interactions from biomedical texts *Proceedings of the 1st Challenge task on Drug-Drug Interaction Extraction*

Philippe Thomas, Mariana Neves, Illes Solt, Domonkos Tikk, and Ulf Leser. Relation Extraction for Drug-Drug Interactions using Ensemble Learning *Proceedings of the 1st Challenge task on Drug-Drug Interaction Extraction*

Md. Faisal Mahbub Chowdhury, Asma Ben Abacha, Alberto Lavelli, and Pierre Zweigenbau. Two Different Machine Learning Techniques for Drug-drug Interaction Extraction *Proceedings of the 1st Challenge task on Drug-Drug Interaction Extraction*

Md. Faisal Mahbub Chowdhury, and Alberto Lavelli. Drug-drug Interaction Extraction Using Composite Kernels *Proceedings of the 1st Challenge task on Drug-Drug Interaction Extraction*

Jari Björne, Antti Airola, Tapio Pahikkala, and Tapio Salakoski Drug-Drug Interaction Extraction with RLS and SVM Classiffers *Proceedings of the 1st Challenge task on Drug-Drug Interaction Extraction*

JAnne-Lyse Minard, Anne-Laure Ligozat, Brigitte Grau, and Lamia Makour Feature selection for Drug-Drug Interaction detection using machine-learning based approaches *Proceedings of the 1st Challenge task on Drug-Drug Interaction Extraction*

Sandra Garcia-Blasco, Santiago M. Mola-Velasco, Roxana Danger, and Paolo Rosso Automatic Drug-Drug Interaction Detection: A Machine Learning Approach With Maximal Frequent Sequence Extraction *Proceedings of the 1st Challenge task on Drug-Drug Interaction Extraction*

Jacinto Mata Vázquez, Ramón Santano, Daniel Blanco, Marcos Lucero, and Manuel J. Maña López A machine learning approach to extract drugdrug interactions in an unbalanced cataset *Proceedings of the 1st Challenge task on Drug-Drug Interaction Extraction*

Stefania Rubrichi, Matteo Gabetta, Riccardo Bellazzi, Cristiana Larizza, and Silvana Quaglini Drug-Drug Interactions Discovery Based on CRFs SVMs and Rule-Based Methods *Proceedings of the 1st Challenge task on Drug-Drug Interaction Extraction*

Man Lan, Jiang Zhao, Kezun Zhang, Honglei Shi, and Jingli Cai An experimental exploration of drug-drug interaction extraction from biomedical texts *Proceedings of the 1st Challenge task on Drug-Drug Interaction Extraction*

Shreyas Karnik, Abhinita Subhadarshini, Zhiping Wang, Luis Rocha and Lang Li Extraction of drug-drug interactions using all paths graph kernel *Proceedings of the 1st Challenge task on Drug-Drug Interaction Extraction*

UoS: A Graph-Based System for Graded Word Sense Induction

David Hope, Bill Keller
University of Sussex
Cognitive and Language Processing Systems Group
Brighton, Sussex, UK
davehope@gmail.com, billk@sussex.ac.uk

Abstract

This paper presents UoS, a graph-based Word Sense Induction system which attempts to find all applicable senses of a target word given its context, grading each sense according to its suitability to the context. Senses of a target word are induced through use of a non-parameterised, linear-time clustering algorithm that returns maximal quasi-strongly connected components of a target word graph in which vertex pairs are assigned to the same cluster if either vertex has the highest edge weight to the other. UoS participated in SemEval-2013 Task 13: Word Sense Induction for Graded and Non-Graded Senses. Two system were submitted; both systems returned results comparable with those of the best performing systems.

1 Introduction

Word Sense Induction (WSI) is the task of automatically discovering word senses from text. In principle, WSI avoids reliance on a pre-defined sense inventory.[1] Whereas the related task of Word Sense Disambiguation (WSD) can only assign pre-defined senses to words on the basis of context, WSI follows the dictum that "*The meaning of a word is its use in the language.*" (Wittgenstein, 1953) to discover senses through examination of context of use in large text corpora. WSI, therefore, may be applied to discover new, rare, or domain specific senses; senses undefined in existing sense inventories.[2]

Previous WSI evaluations (Agirre and Soroa, 2007; Manandhar et al., 2010) have approached sense induction in terms of finding the single most salient sense of a target word given its context. However, as shown in Erk and McCarthy (2009), a graded notion of sense may be more applicable, as multiple senses of the target word may be perceived by readers. The SemEval-2013 WSI evaluation described in this paper is designed to explore the possibility of finding all perceived senses of a target word in a single contextual instance. The aim for participants in the task is therefore to design a system that will induce a set of graded (weighted) senses of a target word in a particular context.

The paper is organised as follows: Section 2 introduces SemEval-2013 Task 13: Word Sense Induction for Graded and Non-Graded Senses; Section 3 presents UoS, the system that participated in the task; Section 4 reports evaluation results, showing that UoS returns scores comparable with those of the best performing systems.

2 SemEval-2013 Task 13

2.1 Aim

The aim for participants in SemEval-2013 Task 13: Word Sense Induction for Graded and Non-Graded Senses is to construct a system that will: (1) induce the senses of a given set of target words and (2), label each test set context (instance) of a target word with

[1] In practice, evaluation of a WSI system requires the use of a gold standard sense inventory such as WordNet (Miller et al., 1990) or OntoNotes (Hovy et al., 2006).

[2] Surveys of WSI and WSD approaches are found in Navigli (2009) and Navigli (2012).

*Second Joint Conference on Lexical and Computational Semantics (*SEM), Volume 2: Seventh International Workshop on Semantic Evaluation (SemEval 2013)*, pages 689–694, Atlanta, Georgia, June 14-15, 2013.

all applicable target word senses. Candidate senses are drawn from the WordNet 3.1 sense inventory. Systems must therefore return a set of graded senses for each target word in a particular context, where a numeric weight signifies (grades) each sense's applicability to the context. A non-graded sense is simply the highest graded (weighted) sense out of all graded senses.

2.2 Test Set

The test set consists of 4806 instances of 50 target words: 20 verbs (1901 instances), 20 nouns (1908), and 10 adjectives (997).[3] Instances are extracted from the Open American National Corpus, being a mix of both written and spoken contexts of target words.[4] Only 542 instances are assigned more than one sense by annotators, thus have graded senses. This figure somewhat detracts from the task's aim as just 11.62% of the test set can be assigned graded senses.

2.3 Evaluation Measures

Systems are evaluated in two ways: (1) in a WSD task and (2), a clustering task. In the first evaluation, systems are assessed by their ability to correctly identify which WordNet 3.1 senses of the target word are applicable in a given instance, and to quantify, and so, rank, senses according to their level of applicability. The supervised evaluation method of previous SemEval WSI tasks (Agirre and Soroa, 2007; Manandhar et al., 2010) is applied to map induced senses to WordNet 3.1 senses, with the mapping function of Jurgens (2012) used to account for the applicability weights. Three evaluation metrics are used -

- *Jaccard Index*: measures the overlap between gold standard senses and those returned by a WSI system.
- *Positionally-Weighted Kendall's Tau*: measures the ability of a system to rank senses by their applicability.
- *Weighted Normalized Discounted Cumulative Gain (NDCG)*: measures the agreement in applicability ratings, accounting for both the ranking and difference in weights assigned to senses.

In the second evaluation, similarity between a participant's clustering solution and that of the gold standard set of senses is measured using two metrics -

- *Fuzzy Normalised Mutual Information* (NMI): extends the method of Lancichinetti et al. (2009) to compute NMI between overlapping (fuzzy) clusters. Fuzzy NMI measures the alignment of system and gold standard senses independently of the cluster sizes, so returns a measure of how well a WSI system would perform regardless of the sense distribution in a corpus.
- *Fuzzy B-Cubed*: adapts the overlapping B-Cubed measure defined in Amigó et al. (2009) to the fuzzy clustering setting. As an item-based, rather than cluster-based, measure, Fuzzy B-Cubed is sensitive to cluster size skew, thus captures the expected performance of a WSI system on a new corpus where the sense distribution is the same.

3 The UoS System

The UoS system uses a graph-based model of word co-occurrence to induce target word senses as follows:

3.1 Constructing a Target Word Graph

A graph $G = (V, E)$ is constructed for each target word. V is a set of vertices and $E \subseteq V \times V$ a set of edges. Each vertex $v \in V$ represents a word found in a dependency relation with the target word. Words are extracted from the dependency-parsed version of ukWaC (Ferraresi et al., 2008). In this evaluation V consists of the 300 highest ranked dependency relation words.[5] Words are ranked using the Normalised Pointwise Mutual Information

[3] Stated as 4664 instances on the task website. Note that the figure of 4806 is for the revised test set.

[4] `http://www.americannationalcorpus.org/OANC/index.html`.

[5] $|V| = 300$ was found to return the best results on the trial set over the range $|V| = [100, 200, 300, ..., 1000]$.

(NPMI) measure (Bouma, 2009)[6], defined for two words w_1, w_2 as:

$$NPMI(w_1, w_2) = \frac{\left(\log \frac{p(w_1, w_2)}{p(w_1)\, p(w_2)}\right)}{-\log p(w_1, w_2)}. \quad (1)$$

An edge $(v_i, v_j) \in E$ is a pair of vertices. An edge represents a symmetrical relationship between vertices v_i and v_j; here, that words w_i and w_j co-occur in ukWaC contexts. Each edge (v_i, v_j) is assigned a weight $w(v_i, v_j)$ to quantify the significance of w_i, w_j co-occurrence, the weight being the value returned by $NPMI(w_i, w_j)$.

3.2 Clustering the Target Word Graph

A clustering algorithm is applied to the target word graph, partitioning it to a set of clusters. Each set of words in a cluster is taken to represent a sense of the target word. The clustering algorithm applied is MaxMax, a non-parameterised, linear-time algorithm shown to return good results in previous WSI evaluations (Hope and Keller, 2013). MaxMax transforms the weighted, undirected target word graph G into an unweighted, directed graph G', where edge direction in G' indicates a *maximal affinity* relationship between two vertices. A vertex v_i is said to have maximal affinity to a vertex v_j if the edge weight $w(v_i, v_j)$ is maximal amongst the weights of all edges incident on v_i. Clusters are identified by finding root vertices of quasi-strongly connected (QSC) subgraphs in G' (Thulasiraman and Swamy, 1992). A directed subgraph is said to be QSC if, for any vertices v_i and v_j, there is a root vertex v_k (not necessarily distinct from v_i and v_j) with a directed path from v_k to v_i and a directed path from v_k to v_j.[7]

3.3 Merging Clusters

MaxMax tends to generate many fine-grained sense clusters. Clusters are therefore merged using two measures: *cohesion* and *separation* (Tan et al., 2006). The cohesion of a cluster C_i is defined as:

$$cohesion(C_i) = \frac{\sum_{\substack{x \in C_i, \\ y \in C_i}} w(x, y)}{|C_i|}. \quad (2)$$

Separation between two clusters C_i, C_j is defined as:

$$separation(C_i, C_j) = 1 - \left(\frac{\sum_{\substack{x \in C_i, \\ y \in C_j}} w(x, y)}{|C_i| \times |C_j|}\right). \quad (3)$$

Cluster pairs with high cohesion and low separation are merged, the intuition being that words in such pairs will retain a relatively high degree of semantic similarity. High cohesion is defined as greater than average cohesion. Low separation is defined as a reciprocal relationship between two clusters: if a cluster C_i has the lowest separation to a cluster C_j (out of all clusters) and C_j the lowest separation to C_i, then the two (high cohesion) clusters are merged.[8]

3.4 Assigning Graded Word Senses to Target Words

Each test instance is labelled with graded senses of the target word. A score is computed for the test instance and each target word cluster as the reciprocal of the separation measure, where C_i is the set of content words in the instance (nouns, verbs, adjectives, and adverbs, minus the target word itself) and C_j, the words in the cluster. The cluster with the lowest separation score is taken to be the most salient sense of the target word, with all other positive separation scores taken to be perceived, graded senses of the target word in that particular instance.

4 Evaluation Results

Two sets of results were submitted. The first, UoS (top 3), returns the three highest scoring senses for each instance; the second, UoS (# WN senses), returns the n = number of target word senses in WordNet 3.1 most cohesive clusters, as defined by Equation (2).

Results for the seven participating WSI systems are reported in Tables 1 and 2. The ten baselines, provided by the organisers of the task, are -

[6] Application of the Log Likelihood Ratio measure (Dunning, 1993) returned the same set of words. Though not required here, *NPMI* has the useful properties that: if w_1 and w_2 always co-occur $NPMI = 1$; if w_1 and w_2 are distributed as expected under independence $NPMI = 0$, and if w_1 and w_2 never occur together, $NPMI = -1$.

[7] MaxMax is described in detail in Hope and Keller (2013).

[8] The average number of WordNet 3.1 senses for target words is 8.58. MaxMax returns an average of 59.54 clusters for target words; merging results in an average of 21.86 clusters.

System/*Baseline*	Jaccard Index F-Score	Positionally Weighted Tau F-Score	Weighted NDCG F-Score
UoS (top 3)	0.232	0.625	0.374
AI-KU (r5-a1000)	0.244	0.642	0.332
AI-KU	0.197	0.620	0.387
Unimelb (50k)	0.213	0.620	0.371
Unimelb (5p)	0.218	0.614	0.365
UoS (# WN senses)	0.192	0.596	0.315
AI-KU (a1000)	0.197	0.606	0.215
Most Frequent Sense	**0.552**	0.560	**0.718**
Senses Eq. Weighted	0.149	**0.787**	0.436
Senses, Avg. Weight	0.187	0.613	0.499
One sense	0.192	0.609	0.288
1 of 2 random senses	0.220	0.627	0.287
1 of 3 random senses	0.244	0.633	0.287
1 of n random senses	0.290	0.638	0.286
1 sense per instance	0.000	0.945	0.000
SemCor, MFS	0.455	0.465	0.339
SemCor, All Senses	0.149	0.559	0.489

Table 1: Results for the WSD evaluation: all instances.

- *SemCor, Most Frequent Sense (MFS)*: labels each instance with the MFS in SemCor.[9]

- *SemCor, All Senses*: labels each instance with all SemCor senses, weighting each according to its frequency in SemCor.

- *1 sense per instance*: labels each instance with a unique induced sense, equivalent to the *1 cluster per instance* baseline of the SemEval-2010 WSI task (Manandhar et al., 2010).

- *One sense*: labels each instance with the same induced sense, equivalent to the *MFS* baseline of the SemEval-2010 WSI task.

- *Most Frequent Sense*: labels each instance with the sense that is most frequently selected by annotators for all target word instances.

- *Senses Avg. Weighted*: labels each instance with all senses. Each sense is scored according to its average applicability rating from the gold standard labelling.

- *Senses Eq. Weighted*: labels each instance with all senses, equally weighted.

- *1 of 2 random senses*: labels each instance with one of two randomly selected induced senses.

- *1 of 3 random senses*: labels each instance with one of three randomly selected induced senses.

- *1 of n random senses*: labels each instance with one of *n* randomly selected induced senses, where *n* is the number of senses for the target word in WordNet 3.1.[10]

As noted by the task's organisers[11], the *SemCor* scores are the fairest baselines for participating systems to compare against as they have no knowledge of the test set sense distribution; the other baselines are more challenging as they have knowledge of the test set sense distribution and annotator grading.

4.1 Summary Analysis of Evaluation Results

Given the number of evaluation metrics (16 in total on the task website), individual analysis of system results per metric is beyond the scope of this paper. However, a ranking of systems may be obtained by taking a summed ranked score; that is, by adding

[9] http://www.cse.unt.edu/~rada/downloads.html#semcor.

[10] For the random senses baselines, induced senses are mapped to WordNet 3.1 senses using the mapping procedure described in Agirre and Soroa (2007). The mapping is provided by the task organisers.

[11] http://www.cs.york.ac.uk/semeval-2013/task13/index.php?id=results

System/*Baseline*	Fuzzy NMI	Fuzzy B-Cubed Precision	Fuzzy B-Cubed Recall	Fuzzy B-Cubed F-Score
Unimelb (50k)	0.060	0.524	0.447	0.483
Unimelb (5p)	0.056	0.470	0.449	0.459
AI-KU	0.065	0.838	0.254	0.390
AI-KU (r5-a1000)	0.039	0.502	0.409	0.451
UoS (top 3)	0.045	0.479	0.420	0.448
UoS (# WN senses)	0.047	0.988	0.112	0.201
AI-KU (a1000)	0.035	0.905	0.194	0.320
One sense	0.000	**0.989**	0.455	**0.623**
1 of 2 random senses	0.028	0.495	**0.456**	0.474
1 of 3 random senses	0.018	0.329	0.455	0.382
1 of n random senses	0.016	0.168	0.451	0.245
1 sense per instance	**0.071**	0.000	0.000	0.000

Table 2: Results for the cluster-based evaluation: all instances.

up each system's rankings over all evaluation metrics. The summed ranking finds that UoS (top 3) is placed first. If the WSD and cluster-based evaluations are considered separately, then UoS (top 3) is ranked, respectively, first and fourth. However, this result is countered by the relatively poor performance of UoS (# WN senses), being ranked fifth overall. Considering baselines, UoS (top 3) equals or surpasses the SemCor baseline scores 67% of the time, and 54% for the more challenging baselines; UoS (# WN senses) scores, respectively, 50% and 44%.

All instances results were supplemented with single-sense (non-graded) and multi-sense (graded) splits at a later date.[12] These results show (again, using a ranked score) that for single-sense instances, AI-KU is the best performing system, with UoS (top 3) placed fifth, and UoS (# WN senses) last. Both UoS (top 3) and UoS (# WN senses) surpass the *SemCor MFS* baseline, with UoS (top 3) surpassing or equalling the harder baselines 79% of the time, and UoS (# WN senses) 68% of the time. For multi-sense instances, AI-KU is, again, the best performing system, with UoS (# WN senses) placed second and UoS (top 3) sixth. UoS (top 3) surpasses or equals the *SemCor* baseline scores 67% of the time; UoS (# WN senses) 83% of the time. UoS (top3) passes/equals, the harder baselines 63% of the time, with UoS (# WN senses) doing so 67% of the time. These results are somewhat confounding as one would expect a system that performs well in the main set of results (all instances), as UoS (top 3) does, to do so in at least one of the single-sense / multi-sense splits: this is clearly not the case. Indeed, the results suggest that UoS (# WN senses), found to perform poorly over all instances, is better suited to the task's aim of finding graded senses.

[12] `http://www.cs.york.ac.uk/semeval-2013/task13/index.php?id=results` (4/4/2013)

5 Conclusion

This paper presented UoS, a graph-based WSI system that participated in SemEval-2013 Task 13: Word Sense Induction for Graded and Non-Graded Senses. UoS applied the MaxMax clustering algorithm to find a set of sense clusters in a target word graph. The number of clusters was found automatically through identification of root vertices of maximal quasi-strongly connected subgraphs. Evaluation results showed the UoS (top 3) system to be the best performing system (all instances), if a simple ranking over all evaluation measures is applied. The second system, UoS (# WN senses), performed poorly, being ranked fifth out of the seven participating WSI systems. Note, however, that the number of evaluation metrics applied, and the wide variability in each system's performances over different metrics and different splits of instance types, make it difficult to judge exactly which system is the best performing. Future research therefore aims to carry out a detailed analysis of the results and to assess whether the measures applied in the evaluation adequately reflect the performance of WSI systems.

References

Eneko Agirre and Aitor Soroa. 2007. SemEval-2007 Task 02: Evaluating Word Sense Induction and Discrimination Systems. In *Proceedings of the 4th International Workshop on Semantic Evaluations*, pages 7–12. Association for Computational Linguistics. Prague, Czech Republic.

Enrique Amigó, Julio Gonzalo, Javier Artiles, and Felisa Verdejo. 2009. A Comparison of Extrinsic Clustering Evaluation Metrics Based on Formal Constraints. *Information Retrieval*, 12(4):461–486.

Gerlof Bouma. 2009. Normalized (Pointwise) Mutual Information in Collocation Extraction. *Proceedings of GSCL*, pages 31–40.

T. Dunning. 1993. Accurate Methods for the Statistics of Surprise and Coincidence. *Computational Linguistics*, 19(1):61–74.

Katrin Erk and Diana McCarthy. 2009. Graded Word Sense Assignment. In *Proceedings of the 2009 Conference on Empirical Methods in Natural Language Processing: Volume 1*, pages 440–449, Singapore. Association for Computational Linguistics.

Adriano Ferraresi, Eros Zanchetta, Marco Baroni, and Silvia Bernardini. 2008. Introducing and evaluating ukWaC, a very large web-derived corpus of english. In *Proceedings of the 4th Web as Corpus Workshop (WAC-4) Can we beat Google*, pages 47–54. Marrakech, Morocco.

David Hope and Bill Keller. 2013. MaxMax: A Graph-Based Soft Clustering Algorithm Applied to Word Sense Induction. In A. Gelbukh, editor, *CICLing 2013, Part I, LNCS 7816*, pages 368–381. Springer-Verlag Berlin Heidelberg. to appear.

Eduard Hovy, Mitchell Marcus, Martha Palmer, Lance Ramshaw, and Ralph Weischedel. 2006. OntoNotes: the 90% Solution. In *Proceedings of the Human Language Technology Conference of the NAACL*, pages 57–60. Association for Computational Linguistics.

David Jurgens. 2012. An Evaluation of Graded Sense Disambiguation Using Word Sense Induction. *Proceedings of *SEM First Joint Conference on Lexical and Computational Semantics, 2012. Association for Computational Linguistics*, pages 189–198. Montreal,Canada.

Andrea Lancichinetti, Santo Fortunato, and János Kertész. 2009. Detecting the Overlapping and Hierarchical Community Structure in Complex Networks. *New Journal of Physics*, 11(3):033015.

Suresh Manandhar, Ioannis P. Klapaftis, Dmitriy Dligach, and Sameer S. Pradhan. 2010. SemEval-2010 Task 14: Word Sense Induction and Disambiguation. In *Proceedings of the 5th International Workshop on Semantic Evaluation*, pages 63–68. Association for Computational Linguistics. Uppsala, Sweden.

George A. Miller, Richard Beckwith, Christiane Fellbaum, Derek Gross, and Katherine J. Miller. 1990. Introduction to WordNet: An On-line Lexical Database. *International Journal of Lexicography*, 3(4):235.

Roberto Navigli. 2009. Word Sense Disambiguation: A Survey. *ACM Computing Surveys (CSUR)*, 41(2):10.

Roberto Navigli. 2012. A Quick Tour of Word Sense Disambiguation, Induction and Related Approaches. In *SOFSEM 2012: Theory and Practice of Computer Science*, volume 7147 of *Lecture Notes in Computer Science*, pages 115–129. Springer Berlin / Heidelberg.

Pang-Ning Tan, Michael Steinbach, and Vipin Kumar. 2006. *Introduction to Data Mining*. Pearson Addison Wesley.

K. Thulasiraman and N.S. Swamy. 1992. *Graphs: Theory and Algorithms*. Wiley.

Ludwig Wittgenstein. 1953. *Philosophical Investigations*. Blackwell.

Author Index